BARBARA ROSSMAN
475 MAIN ST.

Understanding and Using English

Understanding and Using English

REVISED AND ENLARGED

Newman B. Birk   *Genevieve B. Birk*

TUFTS COLLEGE

THE ODYSSEY PRESS   *New York*

FOURTH PRINTING OF THE REVISED AND ENLARGED EDITION

To the Teacher

COLLEGE FRESHMEN often feel aggrieved when they learn that they are required to take "another English course," particularly a course in composition. They have "had" English, they say, for the past twelve years, and during those years they have gone over the same material (punctuation, grammar, spelling) again and again. Perhaps they haven't mastered that material, but at any rate it is familiar and stale, and why shouldn't they study something more advanced, something practical, or at least something new and interesting?

Teachers of freshman composition have different ways of dealing with the attitudes of boredom, complacency, resignation, and even indignation which they find in many of their students. Some instructors clench themselves and push their students once more along the dusty road. Other instructors prefer to appeal to the student's reason and to his intellectual curiosity. They concentrate on putting him in a receptive frame of mind by demonstrating to him (1) that he does not already know all that he really needs to know about English, and (2) that English can be a stimulating subject, at least as "advanced" and "practical" and "new and interesting" as any of his other college subjects. We hope that this book will be helpful to instructors who belong to the second group.

The new *Understanding and Using English* is an enlargement and revision of the earlier *Understanding and Using English*. Its general purposes are the same: to introduce the student to the study of English on a college level; to give him an informed awareness of the nature and power of language; to demonstrate the live relationship between classroom study and the language that he hears and reads, speaks and writes; and finally to supply him with concrete guidance that will help him to use English appropriately and effectively and to interpret it intelligently. We have tried to present all the material in the book as concretely as possible. We believe that many truths about language and about effective English can be made self-evident.

v

This revised edition of *Understanding and Using English* has been expanded in two major ways. First, we have added the materials (full introductions and readings) for a detailed study of the various types of prose. Second, we have substantially enlarged the Handbook in order to include all the information about grammar and mechanics that even the ill-prepared student will need for study or for reference. With these and other additions and revisions, the new *Understanding and Using English* probably contains sufficient material for a year's course in English. We think, however, that some teachers may wish to supplement it with other readings. Since this text provides instruction for the analysis of types of prose ranging from the news report to the short story, teachers who must consider economy can round out the course with inexpensive books which have not been edited for study.

Understanding and Using English has been carefully planned to lead the student, by means of an orderly series of steps, to an integrated knowledge of his language and its uses. Our experience in teaching the earlier edition, and the experience of other teachers and of students who have used the book, have convinced us that this integrated knowledge is best achieved by following, for the first seven chapters, the present arrangement of material.

Chapters One and Two present a general non-technical study of language, with a discussion of the emotional as well as the plain-sense meanings of words, of the differences between fact and opinion, of the dangers of abstract words, and of the effects of charged language. This discussion seems to us essential for the student's realistic understanding of the working of language and for his critical judgment of the language he uses. Some instructors have told us that they have assigned Chapters One and Two later in the term, with satisfactory results. We feel, however, that beginning the course with a study of these first two chapters has the very important persuasive value of making the student receptive to the study of English by showing him areas he has not been aware of and relationships he has never seen before. The dusty road does not seem so dusty when it leads to something new.

In Chapter Three we deal with the conventions of correct expression—punctuation, agreement, reference of pronouns, use of modifiers, etc. These and other matters are, of course, treated fully in the Handbook. In this chapter we have selected for emphasis the basic conventions and the common trouble-spots in college writing. Errors and blunders in expression are, we believe, most readily eliminated when the student understands how violations of accepted conventions may confuse his reader and defeat the purpose of his communication. What he has learned about communication in the first two chapters will enable him to see more easily the necessity of avoiding the blunders explained and illustrated in Chapter Three.

The next two chapters are concerned with levels of usage, appropriate expression, the value of concrete expression, and the methods by which skillful writers achieve economy and conciseness, originality, variety in sentences, and emphasis. The discussion of these matters of choice and style is also integrated with the material in the first chapters; we have made every effort to explain and to demonstrate how different styles produce different effects and so alter the total meaning of the communication. Chapter Six is focused on the paragraph, the basic unit of composition.

Chapters Seven, Eight, and Nine have the common purpose of showing language in action and of simultaneously demonstrating to the student the techniques of reading and the techniques of writing different kinds of prose. In Chapter Seven we analyze an essay by Stuart Chase to show how the principles of good expression actually work in a longer context; this chapter is intended to pull together the material in the first six chapters and to serve as a bridge between theory and practice—the practice of the student and the practice of professional writers. Chapter Eight discusses—under the headings Informative Writing, Persuasive Writing, and Communication of Experience—the techniques of reading and of writing different types of prose, and gives examples of these types with accompanying comments and questions. Chapter Nine is a collection of readings, offered without editorial apparatus, for the student's independent analysis and application of what he has learned. Many instructors will wish to change the order of readings in Chapters Eight and Nine, and to work out the order best suited to their interests and to the organization of their particular courses. These readings have been selected not only for illustrative purposes, but also for their reflective, provocative, and not always unanimous assertions about central human values.

The last five chapters of the book are concerned directly with the student's own practice; they may be assigned at any time, in any order, or may be read independently by the student. Chapter Ten gives detailed guidance in writing short informal themes, Chapter Eleven in writing longer research papers. In Chapter Twelve we have assembled instructions and advice about such practical matters as writing examinations, writing business letters, writing social notes and personal letters, public speaking, and conversation. Chapter Thirteen deals with reading—reading for study, reading rapidly, and reading critically. The book ends with a chapter on vocabulary and the importance of the right word in communicating full and exact meaning.

We have already said of the Handbook that it is intended to supply all the information about grammar and mechanics that even an ill-prepared student will need for study or reference. The substance of Sections Two, Three, Four, and Five is made clear by the Table of Contents. Two other sections of the Handbook, however, call for further comment. Section Six, Writing Assignments, attempts to go beyond the conventional "topics for themes" by giving in some detail thirty-two writing assignments that grow out of the material in the text. For convenience in reference, these assignments follow the arrangement of material in the book; they are intended to supply a variety of suggestions but not to establish a particular sequence for themes. In Section One, Understanding Grammar, we have tried to provide an approach to grammar which will enable a poor student to see for himself where his knowledge of grammatical terminology and relationships is deficient, and to advance, step by step, to an adequate knowledge. At the same time, we have tried to organize this material in such a way that the well-trained student can gain the additional information he may need without being obliged to suffer once more a review of the grammar he already knows. In this section of the Handbook we are particularly indebted to R. W. Pence's *A Grammar of Present Day English,* an exceptionally lucid treatment of the subject.

Many authors and publishers have contributed to this book by giving us permission to use copyrighted material. Our specific indebtedness to them is acknowledged elsewhere.

Equally great, and impossible to acknowledge specifically, is our indebtedness to such students of language and modern usage as I. A. Richards, C. K. Ogden, S. I. Hayakawa, Charles C. Fries, George O. Curme, H. W. Fowler, H. L. Mencken, Albert H. Marckwardt, Porter G. Perrin, and Robert C. Pooley, and to the National Council of Teachers of English and the American Council on Education. Their work, forming as it does a body of ideas and information about current English, has influenced and guided us in preparing this book. Finally we are indebted and grateful to the members of the freshman English staff and the students of Tufts College whose criticism has aided us in writing the book, and whose comments have encouraged us to believe that teachers and students will like it, and that it will help college students in understanding and using English.

Medford, Massachusetts   N.B.B.
March, 1951   G.B.B.

Acknowledgments

THE AUTHORS are grateful to the following writers, publishers, and literary agents for permission to use the materials listed below.

Beverly F. Ames: pages from her research paper, "A Study of the Effects of the Atomic Bombings of Hiroshima and Nagasaki."

Appleton-Century-Crofts: "Agnosticism and Christianity" from *Science and the Christian Tradition* by Thomas Henry Huxley; passages from *Why Men Fight* by Bertrand Russell and *An Approach to Literature* by C. Brooks, J. T. Purser, and R. P. Warren.

Robert M. Bear: passage from "Speed While You Read," published in the *American Magazine*, September, 1941.

Adolf A. Berle, Jr.: "Roosevelt's Rendezvous with History."

The Bobbs-Merrill Company: passage from *Scarlet Sister Mary* by Julia Peterkin.

The Boston *Globe:* "Slow Motion."

Brandt & Brandt: selection from *Nineteen Eighty-Four* by George Orwell.

Columbia University Press: "Skunk" from *The Columbia Encyclopedia*, Second Edition.

Coward-McCann: "The Life and Death of a Worm" and a passage from "Mephitis, the Skunk," both from *Down to Earth* by Alan Devoe.

Thomas Y. Crowell Company: "Epic" and "Free Verse" from *The Reader's Encyclopedia* edited by William Rose Benét.

Crowell-Collier Publishing Company: passage from "Speed While You Read" by Robert M. Baer, in the *American Magazine*, September, 1941.

Current History: "A Trip to Czardis" by Edwin Granberry, published in the *Forum*, April, 1932.

Carter Davidson: passage from "What I Expect of English Teachers," published in the College English Association *News Letter*.

Doubleday & Company: passage from "Little White Girl" from *The Southern Album* by Sara Haardt.

Encyclopaedia Britannica, Inc.: passage from "Socialism" by G. D. H. Cole, *Encyclopaedia Britannica*, 14th Edition.

Henry Pratt Fairchild: passage from *Economics for the Millions*.

Funk & Wagnalls Company: passage by Charles Earle Funk from *The College Standard Dictionary*, Emphatype Edition.

Harcourt, Brace and Company: "Babbitt before Breakfast" from *Babbitt* by Sinclair Lewis, "Mrs. Miniver Comes Home" from *Mrs. Miniver* by Jan Struther, "I Get a Colt to Break In" from *The Autobiography of Lincoln Steffens*, "Lincoln Speaks at Gettysburg" from *Abraham Lincoln: the War Years* by Carl Sandburg, selection from *Nineteen Eighty-Four* by George Orwell; passages from *Orlando* by Virginia Woolf, *The Autobiography of Lincoln Steffens*, *Boston Adventure* by Jean Stafford, *Hollywood: the Movie Colony—the Movie Makers* by Leo C. Rosten, *Microbe Hunters* by Paul de Kruif, *Idle Money, Idle Men* by Stuart Chase, and *Language in Action* by S. I. Hayakawa.

Harper & Brothers: "Four Kinds of Thinking" from *The Mind in the Making* by James Harvey Robinson, "Present and Future" by William Maxwell Aitkin, Lord Beaverbrook, in *Roosevelt and Hopkins* by Robert E. Sherwood, synonyms for *difference* from *The American College Dictionary;* passages from *Devils, Drugs and Doctors* by Howard W. Haggard, *Only Yesterday* by Frederick L. Allen, *Proper Studies* by Aldous Huxley, and "Usage Levels and Dialect Distribution" by Charles C. Fries in *The American College Dictionary.*

Granville Hicks: passage from *I Like America.*

Henry Holt and Company: passages from *Proposed Roads to Freedom* by Bertrand Russell and *Psychology* by William James.

Houghton Mifflin Company: passages from *Kit Carson* by Stanley Vestal, *Looking Backward* by Edward Bellamy, *Patterns of Culture* by Ruth Benedict, *Mein Kampf* by Adolf Hitler (trans. Ralph Manheim), and *Mont Saint Michel and Chartres* by Henry Adams.

Alfred A. Knopf: "The Gentleman from San Francisco" by Ivan Bunin (trans. A. Yarmolinsky), "Father Opens My Mail" from *Life with Father* by Clarence Day, "Marriage à la Mode" from *The Garden Party* by Katherine Mansfield; passages from *Serenade* and *The Postman Always Rings Twice* by James M. Cain, *Buddenbrooks* by Thomas Mann, *Lady Chatterley's Lover* by D. H. Lawrence, *How New Will the Better World Be?* by Carl Becker, and "A Cup of Tea" and "Widowed" from *The Short Stories of Katherine Mansfield.*

J. B. Lippincott Company: passage from *Thunder on the Left* by Christopher Morley.

Longmans, Green & Co.: "Religious Faith" from *The Will to Believe* by William James.

Andrew Nelson Lytle: passage from "Mister McGregor."

The Macmillan Company: "The Luxury of Integrity" from *The Nemesis of American Business* by Stuart Chase; passages from *The Renaissance* by Walter Pater and *Public Opinion* by Walter Lippmann.

Elsie McKeogh: "Prelude to Reunion" by Oliver La Farge.

Ellen Masters: passage from *Anne Rutledge* from *Spoon River Anthology* by Edgar Lee Masters.

G. & C. Merriam Company: definition of *finish* from *Webster's New Collegiate Dictionary.*

The Nation: "The Riddles of Franklin Roosevelt" by Raymond Swing.

The New American Library of World Literature: passage from *Heredity, Race and Society* by L. C. Dunn and T. Dobzhansky.

The New Yorker: "Another Go at F. D. R." by Hamilton Basso.

The *New York Times Book Review:* "Roosevelt's Rendezvous with History" by Adolf A. Berle, Jr.

W. W. Norton & Company: passage from *Mysticism and Logic* by Bertrand Russell.

Harold Ober Associates: "The Bear" by William Faulkner.

Oxford University Press: passages from *Dictionary of Modern English Usage* by H. W. Fowler.

Penguin Books Limited: passage from *Thinking to Some Purpose* by L. Susan Stebbing.

The Philosophical Library: "Science and Religion" from *Out of My Later Years* by Albert Einstein and "Does Human Nature Change?" from *Problems of Men* by John Dewey.

PM: passage from "Who are the Real Liberals?" by Albert Deutsch.

Popular Science Monthly: "Be Your Own Weatherman" by Carl Warden.

Public Affairs Committee: passage from *Know Your Heart* by Howard Blakeslee.

G. P. Putnam's Sons: passage from *The Art of Writing* by Sir Arthur Quiller-Couch.

Rinehart & Company: passages from *The Naked and the Dead* by Norman Mailer and *The Fall of the City* by Archibald MacLeish.

The Rotarian: "Does Human Nature Change?" by John Dewey.

Charles Scribner's Sons: "The Lantern-Bearers" by Robert Louis Stevenson, "In Another Country" from *Men without Women* by Ernest Hemingway; passages from "Pulvis et Umbra" and *Essays on Literature* by Robert Louis Stevenson, *The Enjoyment of Poetry* by Max Eastman, *Of Time and the River* by Thomas Wolfe, and *The Fortunes of Oliver Horn* by F. H. Smith.

Simon and Schuster: "The Monster" from *Of Men and Music* by Deems Taylor; passages from *Color Blind* by Margaret Halsey, *How to Read a Book* by Mortimer J. Adler, and *Peace of Mind* by Joshua Loth Liebman.

The Technology Review: "The Builders" by Vannevar Bush.

James Thurber: "Which" from *Ladies' and Gentlemen's Guide to Modern English Usage;* passage from *Let Your Mind Alone!*

Time: "Let's Wait" by the Editors of *Time.*

U. S. News & World Report: "Flying Saucers—the Real Story."

The Viking Press: "Arrangement in Black and White" from *The Portable Dorothy Parker,* "Breakfast" from *The Long Valley* by John Steinbeck, "Former Teachers" from *Philosopher's Holiday* by Irwin Edman; passages from "The Harness" from *The Long Valley, The Grapes of Wrath,* and *Cannery Row* by John Steinbeck, *Candle in the Dark* by Irwin Edman, *Sons and Lovers* by D. H. Lawrence, and "The Philosopher" from *Winesburg, Ohio* by Sherwood Anderson.

Yale University Press: "The Ideal Democracy" from *Modern Democracy* by Carl Becker; passages from *New Liberties for Old* by Carl Becker and *On Understanding Science* by James B. Conant.

Contents

READINGS IN DESCRIPTIVE WRITING

READINGS IN THE PERSONAL ESSAY

READINGS IN THE SIMPLE NARRATIVE

READINGS IN THE SHORT STORY

HANDBOOK

Understanding and Using English

Chapter One
Language and Meaning

ONE OF THE PLEASURES of the first year of college is studying new subjects—psychology, economics, sociology, geology, for example—which open up areas of thought and information previously not known. Equally pleasurable and stimulating is the experience of finding new meaning in subjects already "taken"; of integrating and expanding old knowledge; of seeing new horizons beyond familiar doors. The study of English on a college level can offer this experience, particularly to the student who realizes that his native language is not merely a subject studied in school, but is a shaping force in his society, an instrument which he must use, and which he needs to understand.

Modern man lives in a world of words, and the kind of world he lives in depends to a surprisingly large extent on the words he uses and hears. Words can make or prevent wars, solemnize marriages or invalidate them, form constitutions or destroy them, sell shoddy or superior products or ideas, justify man's worst actions or express his highest ideals. Because of the immense power of language, of even a few words, advertisers pay large sums for the best slogan or jingle, and responsible statesmen weigh each phrase of their carefully prepared speeches. Lawyers may spend hours in court trying to fix the meaning of a single word, and one of the principal functions of our Supreme Court is interpreting the words of the law of the land.

Since language is so important, it is strange that in our society more people have a reasonably accurate idea of how an automobile works and how to handle it than of how their language works and how to handle it. Even poor drivers know what the accelerator and the steering wheel and even the brake are for, and have some knowledge of the relationship between the cylinders and the gasoline and the spark. They can use road maps to drive a car from New York to San Francisco and can arrive at San Francisco without difficulty.

But despite twelve years of required English before college, most

3

college freshmen have little or no knowledge of how their language actually works. Language for them is often a baffling vehicle to operate; the road maps that they have been given during twelve years sometimes confuse and frustrate them instead of providing guidance. For one thing, they have often been led to accept and to follow uncritically a large number of rules for the writing of "correct" English. Suppose we look at some of these "rules."

1. "Never end a sentence with a preposition." Must we *always* say, "On which chair do you wish me to sit?" and never, "Which chair do you want me to sit on?" Of course not.

2. "Don't use contractions." Many English teachers have written this as a comment on themes. Are the teachers using incorrect English?

3. "Avoid slang." Does this mean that a sports writer or a person writing on jazz must avoid all use of slang?

4. "Never begin a sentence with *but* or *and*." Never? But we are doing it at this very moment.

5. "Always use a comma between two independent clauses joined by *and, but, for, or, nor*." In "I was there and he wasn't," what good would a comma after "there" do? Probably none at all.

6. "Every sentence must have a subject and a predicate." If this is *always* true, why do so many able writers—Steinbeck, Dos Passos, Thomas Wolfe, to name just a few—frequently write sentences that are incomplete, and why do such sentences get into English texts as models of style?

The truth is that dogmatic rules for writing are valuable in training young people to write acceptably, but are not, by themselves, adequate guides for mature students. In order to use language freely and effectively the college student needs to start with a general consideration of the nature of language and of the principles which underlie the rules. He will then be in a position to exercise judgment in following conventional rules or in departing from them.

The preceding paragraph states the central thesis of this book: the best use of English involves sound general **understanding of language,** adequate **knowledge of the accepted conventions** (of punctuation, grammar, capitalization, spelling), sometimes stated as "rules," and **informed judgment** in using this knowledge of language and language conventions to achieve appropriate and effective expression. Uncritical and slavish following of rules may produce what some teachers of English call "correct" English, but such English often is not appropriate to the occasion and to the intention of the writer.

Language has been called "the dress of thought"; like dress it needs to be *appropriate*. Formality and a certain type of correctness are sometimes necessary and desirable, but for everyday expression (written and spoken) a less formal language is usually appropriate, and a different and less formal standard of correctness applies.

If Charles Meade, a student, receives a formal invitation, conventions of etiquette and language demand that he write his reply in very formal language, as follows: "Mr. Charles Meade accepts with pleasure [or regrets that he is unable to accept] the kind invitation of President Lawrence Carmason to a dinner for the Senior Class at the Statler Hotel on Tuesday, April the tenth, at eight o'clock." In replying to the formal invitation Charles must use the prescribed formal language; any variation from it would be inappropriate and would not achieve his intention of making the proper polite response. Another college student, James Mangle, who receives the same invitation and writes in reply, "Dear Prexy, Thanks for your invitation. I'm sorry that I can't make it. I have a dinner date with my roommate's beautiful sister. . . ." is obviously using language inappropriately and is violating his intention: instead of making a fitting response he is making himself absurd. On the other hand, if James Mangle had received, not the formal invitation, but a hastily written card from a close friend, who was inviting him to a victrola party on Friday night, James could *appropriately* have sent to his friend the same informal note that he blunderingly sent to the college president. Furthermore, a formal reply of the sort properly used in answering the formal invitation would here be inappropriate and ludicrous.

If we say that "good English" is "correct" English, we are likely to confuse ourselves and others. It is better to define good English as English which is **appropriate** (1) to the **occasion** (i.e., the **audience**, the **subject**, the **time** and **place**), and (2) to the **intention** of the writer or speaker.

More will be said in a later chapter on the subject of appropriateness. At present we need to consider other generalizations that are necessary for a sound understanding of language.

I. COMMUNICATING MEANING: THE PARTS OF MEANING

The most important function of language is to communicate meaning. However, language does have certain secondary uses, the most important of which is thinking in words to solve problems. Since we are primarily concerned here with communication, we shall only suggest in passing that the words one thinks in may have a great deal to do with the way one solves particular problems and reaches crucial decisions. In what words, for example, did President Truman and his advisers think when they decided to use the atomic bomb in the war against Japan? They could have thought, "Shall we bring the war to a quick end and save the lives of thousands of American soldiers?" They could also have thought, "What will be the effect on the men, women, and children of the bombed city, and what will be the effect on other nations when they see the use the United States has made of atomic power?" This example is over-simplified, of course, but it may suggest how the words we think in can affect our decisions and our actions.

Other noncommunicative uses of language can be mentioned and passed over rapidly. When one writes lists or notes for himself, or very personal diaries, when he sings to himself, talks to himself, or swears at a chair that he has run into in the dark, he uses words not for communication but simply for his own convenience and satisfaction. About such use of language little helpful or enlightening comment can be made—except perhaps that of the moralist on the language addressed to the chair.

We are concerned, however, with the major function of language —the *communicative* function; for our purposes, therefore, we can define language as a verbal means of **communicating something** to **someone** for some **purpose.** An analysis of this definition makes it evident that each time language is used for communication there are three things involved: (1) the "something" to be communicated, (2) the speaker or writer and his purpose or "intention," and (3) the hearer or reader. Strangely enough, there is no one word in the English language which refers to speaker-or-writer and no one word which refers to hearer-or-reader. In these circumstances it becomes necessary to fix on suitable terminology. When occasion arises we shall use the term "communicator" to refer to the speaker-or-writer and the term "receiver" to refer to the hearer-or-reader.

Now that our terms, "language" "communicator," "receiver," are established, we are ready to look at the process of verbal communication and to see how language works. First, something takes place in the mind of Communicator C. Perhaps he has a toothache and wants sympathy from Receiver R, or perhaps he sees a car coming and wants to get R out of the way. In any case there are at the moment two things of importance in C's mind—something he wants to say and some reason he has for saying it, some purpose. The function of language is to convey this something from the mind of C to the mind of R, and words are the medium by which it is conveyed. (It is perhaps worth saying here that the communication is never complete, is always approximate.) *C*'s mind directs his vocal cords to produce certain sounds. The sound waves thus produced strike the ear of *R*, and *R*'s mind responds in such a way that something goes on in *R*'s mind very like what is going on in *C*'s. If *C* writes to *R*, the process is similar except that visual symbols take the place of sound symbols.

This process of conveying something from the mind of *C* to the mind of *R* we call **verbal communication,** and the something that is communicated we call **meaning.** Since primitive man made his first blundering efforts to speak, language has come to be an extraordinarily complex, subtle, and effective instrument for conveying meaning. It enables us to know a great deal about what was going on in the mind of Plato twenty-three hundred years ago, and it would enable an American scientist, if he wished, to communicate by words alone to a Russian scientist five thousand miles away all the knowledge we now have about the hydrogen bomb.

As these two examples indicate, the something conveyed, the meaning, which language communicates can be infinitely various. Although *meaning* is a very useful word, it may stand in the way of our thinking intelligently about language because it appears to give to language a simplicity that language really does not have. We need to go beneath the word *meaning,* to break it up into its components. For convenience we can say that there are three parts or aspects of meaning, and we can label these parts of meaning **plain sense, intention,** and **attitude.** It is important to fix in mind the definitions of these three terms.

The **plain-sense** part of meaning may be briefly defined as the **fact or idea** to be communicated, the statement or statements that are made.

Intention means the same thing as *purpose* as we have been using that word. It may be defined as the effect which the communicator wishes to produce on his hearer or reader. For example, the intention of *C* is to get *R* to move out of the path of the car, or to sympathize with him because of his toothache; the intention of a politician may be to persuade the citizens to vote for him; the intention behind the weather report or behind a mathematics text is to inform the reader about coming weather or about mathematics. Although in some communication intention may be complex and changing, we can say that in general a communicator has one of three primary intentions: (1) he wants simply to communicate plain sense as clearly as he can (i.e., *to inform*); (2) he wants to communicate plain sense *and* to influence the feelings of the receiver (i.e., *to persuade or convince*); or (3) he wants to communicate experience—to enable others to share his feelings, attitudes, states of mind, or at any rate to cause them to experience certain feelings, attitudes, states of mind. Poets, novelists, short-story writers—all artists who use the medium of language—usually have the primary intention of communicating experience rather than informing or persuading. And language used primarily to entertain or amuse or supply escape from daily routine can also be said to have communication of experience as its chief aim, for escaping, or being amused or entertained is a kind of experience.

At times—in very casual conversation, for example—a communicator may hardly know what his intention is and may have trouble stating it if he is asked to do so. Thus he may communicate without conscious awareness of his intention. At other times, however, one may be very conscious of his intention and may select his language very carefully to realize that intention—for example in a letter applying for a position that the applicant is eager to get.

The **attitude** part of meaning also needs to be examined in some detail. It may be defined as the **feeling** of the communicator (1) toward **himself,** (2) toward his **receiver,** and (3) toward his **subject.** If an acquaintance were to say to the present readers, "My paper was easily the best in the class. I just dashed it off, of course. It's too bad you are so slow and stupid that you can't write as well as I do," the readers might well object to the speaker's "attitude." And in objecting they might say that the speaker was conceited (attitude toward himself), was too proud of his paper (attitude toward subject), and was condescending toward his hearers (attitude toward receiver). If the speaker had said, "When the professor told me that my paper was the best in the class, I was ashamed because I had just dashed it off and I knew you had worked hard and long on yours," he would be expressing a different attitude toward himself, his hearers, and his subject. The two examples that we have just used are supposedly bits of conversation, and here attitude is usually an important part of meaning. In certain other types of communication, attitude may be much less important. In an encyclopedia article, for example, the writer concentrates on the plain sense and appropriately keeps in the background his feelings about himself, his subject, and his reader. In communication of this sort the style is **impersonal;** in communication which conveys and emphasizes the personality and feelings of the author the style is said to be **personal.** Both personal and impersonal style are aspects of attitude.

In informative writing, plain sense is the most important part of meaning, though intention and attitude are still present. In a chemistry text, for example, plain sense is clearly primary, and the wise reader spends his time attending to the facts and formulas presented.

Here the general intention is obvious; the writer wishes to inform. The attitude may be described as impersonal and unemotional; the writer takes his subject seriously, or he wouldn't be writing a book about it, but he is not primarily concerned with using language to convey his feelings about himself, or his subject, or his reader. He has used language successfully if he has presented the facts clearly to the particular type of reader he is writing for.

But in many kinds of communication, intention and attitude are more important than plain sense. A common fallacy is the idea that communicating plain sense is *always* the main function of language. Actually there are many uses of language, literary, social, and political, in which plain sense is secondary, and in which intention and attitude are of primary importance. If the reader will examine his own use of language for one day he will see that a good part of the time he is not concerned primarily with communicating facts and ideas. He gets up on a cold rainy day and says "Good morning" to everyone he meets; he says "Good-by" (originally a kind of blessing meaning "God be with you") to people whom he has no desire to bless. When he is introduced to someone, he may say, "How do you do," even though he does not care how the person does; or he may say, less properly, "Pleased to meet you," though he would have chosen to avoid the introduction. When he writes an angry letter to a laundry that has lost three of his shirts, he begins it "Dear Sir" and ends with "Very truly yours." A good deal of his light conversation deals with the weather, in which perhaps neither he nor his companion is interested. All these polite or conventional uses of language are primarily intention or attitude, and people unconsciously accept them as such. To a casual "How are you?" a man with a toothache may well say, "Fine, thanks."

Language is also used to establish or to maintain friendly relations. When we joke, or tell stories, or chat in a friendly way about trivial matters, we are frequently more interested in letting people know that we like them and in causing them to like us than we are in exchanging information. People sometimes talk merely because they find silence embarrassing or because they feel that they will be considered unfriendly if they are silent.

Another common use of language in which plain sense is not of primary importance is the expressing and sharing of our feelings and beliefs, our response to experience. Bacon wrote that communicating with friends doubles joys and cuts griefs in half; language is the main medium through which this communication and sharing occur. We may enjoy talking to people who have the same political or social or philosophical ideas as ours, not because we are gaining new facts or ideas but because we enjoy agreeing with someone— or, better, having someone agree with us.

That language is frequently, perhaps most commonly, used for purposes other than communicating plain sense seems hard to deny, yet many "practical" people take a severe view when they read literature, and insist that plain sense should be most important there. Such people think that when they have a synopsis of a story they have the "meaning of the story" and believe that a sentence summary of a poem is the essence of the poem. Actually, of course, the short-story writer, novelist, essayist, dramatist, or poet, although he is dealing with facts and ideas, is not primarily concerned with them; they are frequently only a small part of the whole meaning he wishes to convey, just as they are likely to be a small part of a love letter or an intimate conversation. Men don't live by facts and ideas (plain sense) alone. They think and know, and much of their language deals with thought and knowledge, but they also feel and respond. Even mathematicians and engineers fall in love and have friends and quarrel among themselves, and they use language to express their emotions and attitudes. "Practical" people would be more practical if they recognized these facts about language. Practical politicians and advertisers and propagandists already know them and profit from them; they may even use the word *practical* to move the emotions and so influence the actions of unsuspecting practical people.

What has been said thus far about the importance of intention and attitude should not, however, lead us to underestimate the very great significance of plain sense in language. Men have to inform one another, to educate one another, to convince one another by facts and by logic; and when language is used for these purposes, plain sense is the most important part of the meaning. The point to bear in mind is not that plain sense is unimportant, but that intention and attitude are much more important than most people realize when they use the word *meaning*.

II. THE MEANING OF WORDS AND THE IMPORTANCE OF CONTEXT

In the previous section we analyzed the term *meaning* in its relationship to language; now we need to look closely at **words**, the particles which are fitted together to produce meaning. A consideration of how words come to have meaning for us will throw some light on their nature and will help us to use them more wisely. Here, as often, it is best to start with an example and to work through it toward a generalization.

In the sentence, "The horse won the race," the word *horse* has a reasonably definite meaning for all of us. We all know that it refers to a quadruped about five feet high at the shoulder and that the animal has a mane and a tail, and hooves instead of feet. The question of interest here is: how does the word *horse* come to have this meaning? One answer, of course, is that we have been brought up among English-speaking people. If we were German we should call the animal *das Pferd;* if we were French we should call it *le cheval.* It just happens that people in our society have applied the word *horse* to the animal. How and why that happened is beyond our present inquiry; we are concerned with the question: how did the English word *horse* come to have its meaning *for us?* We will find our answer in our past experiences with the word and with the animal it refers to. Since *horse* is a common word and horses are common things, we probably had our first experience with the word early. Perhaps we saw the animal, and our parents told us it was called a horse; perhaps we saw or heard the word, and someone used other words to explain its meaning. Later on we read or heard the word frequently, and perhaps we saw animals, horses, and applied the word to them. At any rate we established a relationship between the word *horse* and the actual animal, so that the word came to call to mind the animal, and the animal came to call to mind the word: the word *horse* had come to have meaning for us.

To use technical language, we can say that we learned the meaning of the word from hearing it in various **contexts.** Since *context* is a very important word in the discussion of language, it requires careful definition. **Context** may be generally defined as **the setting in which the locution** [1] **is used.** When we came across the word *horse* in our primer, the context was the other words with which the word *horse* was used. If there was a picture of a horse in the primer, that too was a part of the context, for it helped us to understand what *horse* means. When we saw an actual animal horse by the roadside and someone told us that the animal was called horse, the whole experience of seeing the horse and hearing the word was the context for us. The **context,** then, is **anything, surrounding words** or **surrounding circumstances,** which helps to make clear to us just what a word (locution) refers to. After we have met the word in a number of contexts we get a *general* idea of what the word "means." It was

---

[1] *Locution* is a convenient term used to refer to a word or to a group of related words. A locution therefore may be a single word, a phrase, a clause, or an entire sentence.

because of this general idea we had developed of the meaning of the word *horse* that we were able on seeing the word in the sentence, "The horse won the race," to assume that in that context it referred to a quadruped about five feet high at the shoulder and that such an animal has a mane and a tail, and hooves instead of feet.

Before going further with the discussion of context and meaning, we need to introduce another technical term, the word *referent*. The referent may be defined as the thing or idea to which the word refers. In the sentence "The horse won the race," the referent of *horse* is the actual living, breathing horse that won the race. The communicator, then, was using the word *horse* to refer to a particular horse at a particular moment. To receive the full and exact meaning of the word as he used it we would need to perceive the actual horse as he perceived it; we would then know its color and height and the like, and we would see it running. Actually, of course, language seldom if ever communicates this full and exact meaning: it simply approximates it, and this approximation is usually enough for every-day purposes.

It is worth noting here that the referent, the thing to which the word refers, is different every time the word is used; hence the word, although it has certain conventional general meanings, never means *exactly* the same thing twice. After the general conventional meaning of a word has become established, the function of the context is to make clearer to us the meaning of the word on the particular occasion when it is used. In our illustrative sentence, for example, the words *won the race* give us a more particular idea of what *horse* means here. We assume that the horse is a race horse, and we have a more definite mental picture of race horses than we have of horses in general. If we read on and find out what kind of race it was and perhaps what color the horse was, the context will then give us a still more definite idea of the animal itself, the *referent*.

The meaning of the word *horse* may seem complicated enough already, but we have in fact simplified it by assuming that *horse* always refers to animal horse. When we stop to think, we realize that this is not true. What, for example, does the word *horse* refer to in the following sentences?

> On the merry-go-round the children preferred to ride on the *horses* and the lions. [Here *horse* means imitation horse.]
> The carpenter sawed the board on the *horse*. [Here *horse* means a wooden frame.]
> That woman is a *horse*. [Here the word probably means large-boned and awkward.]

These examples show that the word *horse* is used to refer not only to various particular animal horses but also to non-animate things and even to ideas ("awkward," "large-boned"). They show also what complicated symbols words are and how context helps us in identifying their referents in a particular situation.

Let us take a still more complicated example of the way meaning is determined by context: the sentence, "Put out the light, and then put out the light." Although grammatically this is a well-constructed sentence, standing by itself it does not "make sense," does not convey any clear and definite meaning. The reader knows the generally accepted, "dictionary" meanings of each word in the sentence, but he does not have enough of the context to understand the significance of the sentence. Since the individual words have a good many different dictionary meanings, he cannot tell which one is appropriate here. *Put out* and *light* are particularly puzzling just because each expression does have so many different general meanings. Notice some of the meanings that these words have in different contexts:

To *put out* the cat [place him outside]
To *put out* effort [expend effort]
To *put out* a baseball player [cause an "out" in baseball]
To be *put out* by what someone does to you [inconvenienced or exasperated]
To *put out* the light [extinguish it]
A *light* burden [not heavy]
A *light* shade [not dark]
To see the *light* [the truth]
To see the *light* [the illumination]
To be in a *light* mood [gay, carefree]
To *light* a fire [cause the fuel to blaze]
The speed of *light* [light rays]
*Light*headed [dizzy, unstable, fickle]

These are only a few of the many meanings that *put out* and *light* may have in different contexts.

It seems evident that the sentence, "Put out the light, and then put out the light," like the single word *horse*, cannot be clear and exact in its meaning until we place it in a larger context. The larger context for this particular sentence is Shakespeare's play, *Othello*. To get the *full* meaning of the quoted sentence, it would be necessary to read the whole play. A brief summary of the immediately relevant material, however, will suffice here; that is, it will provide sufficient context to transform what at first seems a kind of nonsense sentence into a poignantly meaningful expression. Othello, a just and admirable man, is played upon by his subordinate, Iago, with the result that he believes his innocent wife guilty of infidelity. Although Othello loves his wife Desdemona so deeply that she is the "light" of his life, of his happiness, he convinces himself that the "cause" of justice, virtue, honor, demands that "she must die, else she'll betray more men." The following lines from the play, which contain the sentence we have been considering, are spoken by Othello as he is about to extinguish the light, a candle or lamp, and then to smother the woman he loves. He extinguishes the candle because he fears that his resolution will fail if the light enables him to see Desdemona:

> It is the cause, it is the cause, my soul:
> Let me not name it to you, you chaste stars!
> It is the cause. Yet I'll not shed her blood,
> Nor scar that whiter skin of hers than snow
> And smooth as monumental alabaster.
> Yet she must die, else she'll betray more men.
> Put out the light, and then put out the light:
> If I quench thee, thou flaming minister,
> I can again thy former light restore,
> Should I repent me: but once put out thy light,
> Thou cunning'st pattern of excelling nature,
> I know not where is that Promethean heat
> That can thy light relume. When I have pluck'd the rose,
> I cannot give it vital growth again;
> It needs must wither . . .

After this soliloquy Othello accuses Desdemona, refuses to believe her protestations of innocence, and smothers her, only to find out soon afterward that he has been tricked by Iago and that Desdemona was entirely innocent. Othello kills himself because he has in truth "put out the light, and then put out the light."

On page 11 we defined context as the setting (surrounding words or surrounding circumstances) which helps us to interpret the meaning of a locution. The line spoken by Othello illustrates the force and significance of surrounding words in making clear the meaning of words and even of sentences. In fact, not only words and sentences, but also paragraphs and even larger units of expression often depend upon context for their full meaning.

Quite evidently the context supplied by surrounding words is important. Equally important is the context supplied by surrounding circumstances. George Washington's *Farewell Address* will serve as an illustration. Because this address is a kind of sacred national document, any quotation from it or reference to it is sure to engage respectful attention and to have considerable persuasive force. For this reason writers and speakers frequently quote from it to emphasize and support some point which they wish to establish. Such quotation is often perfectly appropriate and justifiable. Sometimes, however, communicators distort the original meaning because they disregard the surrounding circumstances, the context, of the famous address. After World War I, for example, some people opposed our joining the League of Nations because Washington said to "avoid entangling alliances"; again, after World War II, there were those who argued in the same way against our participation in the United Nations. Although Washington did not use the phrase "avoid entangling alliances" in his *Farewell Address,* we can assume for the purposes of our illustration that that is a fair statement of what his language meant. We need to remember, however, that the date of the *Farewell Address* was 1796; when it was written the United States was different, and the alternatives to "entangling alliances" were also different. The United States was then a weak nation obliged to deal with stronger powers; advances in transportation had not produced the closely related "One World" that we live in today; oceans were still effective barriers, and the airplane and the atomic bomb had not been invented. In its context—here the whole period of history in which Washington lived and thought—the policy of avoiding entangling alliances was a sound one. But to apply Washington's words to a situation in a strikingly different period of history is to take them out of context, to give them a meaning different from that which they had when they were spoken.

If we choose an example from everyday life the point is still clearer: the mother of Charles, a child of eight, might say with perfect truth, "A size-one play sandal is large enough for my son," but anyone who insisted that Charles at the age of forty should follow his mother's wishes and wear a size-one play sandal would be taking the statement out of context in much the same way that the "entangling alliances" phrase is sometimes taken out of context.

One of the first rules for understanding language is: see what the expression means *in its context.* When context changes, meaning changes.

III. REFERENTIAL MEANING AND ATTITUDINAL MEANING

In the last section, we were placing most emphasis on the **referential** meaning of words. The function of the **referential** meaning of words is **to refer to** (in the sense of pointing to or calling to mind) **certain things or ideas.** If we are driving along in a car and our companion says, "Look at that old tire there under the tree," he is *verbally pointing* to the object by naming it and by telling us where to look. If he says that his brother is studying, he *calls to mind* our idea of study. In brief we can say that referential meaning is the plain sense part of meaning.

Attitudinal meaning, on the other hand, is that part of meaning which conveys **attitudes;** i.e., emotions, states of mind, feelings toward subject, self, and receiver. In the sentence, "Put out the light, and then put out the light," the *referential* meaning might be approximated by "I'll extinguish the light and then smother Desdemona," for this paraphrase contains the facts and ideas that Othello is expressing. In the same sentence the *attitudinal* meaning is much more complex and elusive. It tells us not only what Othello is going to do but how he *feels* about it, and a large part of this attitudinal meaning is concentrated in the metaphorical and richly suggestive second use of the word *light.* A comparison of the original line with our effort at referential paraphrase will give some idea of how significant the attitudinal meaning here is.

Attitudinal meaning is determined by context in much the same way that referential meaning is. In the preceding section we saw that our whole past experience with a word (*horse,* for instance) in different contexts tends to fix for us a certain set of general referential meanings for the word (animal horse, carpenter's horse, merry-go-round horse). If someone uses the word *horse* and we want to determine its referential meaning, the immediate context enables us to tell which of its general meanings is intended. In the context, "The *horse* won a race," we can tell that animal horse is referred to. Since words usually have *attitudinal* as well as *referential* meanings, when the referential meaning of a word varies in different contexts, the attitudinal meaning varies with it. Because we respond differently to a word as it is used to *refer* to different things, our feeling varies to fit the thing referred to (referent). In the phrases, *race horse, horse meat, horse sense, horse play,* for example, the actual *referent* of the word *horse* changes, and as the referent (the thing-referred-to) changes, our response (attitude) also changes: we may feel admiration for the beauty and speed of a race horse, feel a distaste for horse meat, feel respectful toward horse sense, feel impatience with horse play. Other words work the same way: *machine* and *grafter* for example, produce different feelings in us as they refer in different contexts to sewing machine or political machine, to grafter of trees or dishonest receiver of money:

She sewed the shirt on the *machine*.
Votes were bought by the political *machine*.

He is a skillful *grafter* of trees.
He is a politician and a *grafter*.

As we think about the examples given, it becomes evident that the attitudinal meaning of a word, like the referential meaning, is usually dependent upon (1) the general conventional meanings of the word and (2) the context in which the word is used. As we listen or read, our minds select the particular meaning indicated by the context, and respond to that meaning. In this process we find what things or ideas words refer to, and we also feel a series of emotional charges (attractions or repulsions), as we think of the referents of the words. These charges are the **attitudinal meaning** of the passage. Language which gives us a number of strong charges can be called **charged language**, and words that give strong charges can be called **charged words.**

IV. CHARGED WORDS

Words differ in the amount of charge and in the way they get the charge that they carry. Some words, because of the way we have generally used them and because of our emotions about the things they generally refer to, seem to carry an unusual amount of emotional meaning *independent* of context and of referent. The word *as word* is already charged, "precharged" by our previous associations with it. Consequently the strong emotional meaning in the word often blocks any discriminating thought about what the word refers to in a particular context and makes us respond only to the charge that the word itself carries for us. Precharged words cause us to prejudge referents. During World War I some people objected to the playing of Beethoven's symphonies because Beethoven was a "German." These people supply us with an example of a precharged word in action. They were reacting to the word *German,* and it blocked their thinking about the referent, the actual music of a great composer who deserves the respect of all civilized men.

Other charged words are much more lightly charged by the way they have generally been used. They carry with them a cluster of suggestions or *connotations,* favorable or unfavorable, which are not strong enough to block all consideration of the referent, but which are likely to color our feeling about the referent. In the statements "She is a thin girl" and "She is a slender girl," *thin* and *slender* differ in their connotations. Most people will respond less favorably to the idea of a "thin" girl; the response will be still less favorable if she is described as "skinny." These lightly charged words are, of course, common in everyday speech and writing. To refer to an automobile as a *jalopy*, or to a very industrious student as a *grind*, or to one's college as *alma mater* is to use lightly charged, connotative words.

Still other charged words get their charge, light or heavy, not simply from our store of past associations and our feeling about the word, but from the feeling aroused in us by the word's referent as we think of it in a particular context. The same word may have strong emotional meaning in one context and little emotional meaning in another; or it may carry a positive charge in one context and a negative charge when another context calls to mind a different referent. In the sentences "A fire crackled cheerfully on the hearth" and "A fire is raging through the South End," the word *fire* is very differently charged by the image of the referent which the surrounding words bring to mind. The charge carried by the second *light* in the line from *Othello* comes from the feeling aroused by a referent which has been established by context; *light* is, therefore, a "context-charged" word.

With the understanding that charged words vary a great deal in the origin and the intensity of the emotional meaning they carry, we can proceed to consider some of the common types of charged words. Most of the words we shall discuss are precharged rather than context-charged; and, though people differ in their responses to these words, most of them are quite heavily charged for many people.

Home, mother, God, father, love, bride, sea, and *sky* are some of the **charged words of everyday living.** For nearly everyone, the words themselves seem to be loaded with a power to produce an immediate emotional response of some sort; the word *God* produces an emotional response even in atheists, and the word *father* produces a response in orphans. These charged words of everyday living get their particular power from the fact that we hear and see them frequently in contexts that involve our feelings; consequently we build up strong emotional associations for them. Such words are of course powerful conductors of attitudinal meaning and are important in all communication which has even the secondary aim of expressing or evoking emotion. (Why, for example, do undertakers call their establishments funeral *homes?*)

Another type of charged words is **taboo words**—for example, profanity and all of the "four-letter" words which refer to bodily functions and which small boys write on walls and sidewalks. Most people have built up inhibitions about these taboo words even though they may use them occasionally; and, as everyone knows, such words have great shocking power.

A good many **proper names** also belong in the category of charged words. A few pages back we considered the persuasive power of statements made by George Washington. Much of this persuasive power can be attributed to the name, George Washington, and to the favorable emotional associations that Americans have with that name. Proper names that are charged with meaning, like charged words dealing with everyday living, may be charged positively or negatively. For Americans, for example, the names Washington, Jefferson, Lincoln, have a strong positive charge, and the names Hitler, Mussolini, Tojo, Quisling, since they are the names of recent national foes, have a negative charge. We are likely to feel a favorable response to anything associated with the first group and an unfavorable response to anything associated with the second group. Such responses are perfectly natural, and they often serve good ends, as they did when they helped to unite the people of this country in the immense task of winning World War II. Sometimes, however, they may be harmful, for our emotions may be so moved as to prevent our analyzing and absorbing the referential meaning that is over-shadowed by the emotive meaning.

Most of the charged words that we have dealt with thus far are relatively *concrete* words (i.e., words with specific, easily grasped referents). Such words, used even in short contexts, usually have a comparatively clear and definite referential meaning for different receivers. In conversation, for example, it is seldom if ever necessary for us to stop and explain what particular meaning we are giving to such concrete words and names as *father, mother, bride, Abraham Lincoln, Thomas Jefferson,* because the context of the situation helps to establish a definite referent. We usually know what mother is being talked about and whether the Washington referred to is George Washington-a-boy-of-ten, or George Washington-President-of-his-country.

Abstract words may also be charged. They differ from the concrete words we have been discussing in that they very frequently do not have the same clear and definite referential meaning for different receivers. Since the term *abstract word* is itself abstract, we need to establish its meaning by use of examples before we consider abstract words that are charged. We have seen that *concrete* words when used even in brief contexts generally communicate a definite enough referential meaning to enable us to understand one another. When a farmer tells his son to "water the horses," the meaning of these concrete words is certainly clear enough for everyday purposes; if the son is obedient, the horses get watered and the farmer's plain-sense communication has been successful.

But *abstract words* sometimes cause trouble. If the same farmer tells his son that "the American way of life is being threatened by communism," or that "socialized medicine would destroy liberty," the referential meaning (plain sense) is much less clear and definite. If the son is intelligent and also inconsiderate—if, for example, he is a college student—he may ask his father what he means by such abstract words as *American way of life* and *communism* or by *socialized medicine* and *liberty*. It would have been easy for the farmer to make completely clear what horses were to receive what water (i.e., to define his words *horses* and *water*), but when he tries to define the abstract words his son has asked about, he has a different and difficult problem. Quite possibly the son will challenge his definition, "But what you call communism isn't communism; communism means . . ." Then he will give his own definition of the term. An hour or so later each may still be insisting that communism "means" this or that, and still later the father and son may go to bed, each sure that his definition was "the correct" definition, and each puzzled and depressed by the "wrongheadedness" of the other.

This unhappy farmer and his unhappy son have been dealing with abstract words, and, what makes it worse, with abstract words which are emotionally charged. **Abstract words** may be defined as words which name **qualities** (intelligence, honor), **concepts** (evolution, scientific method, value), and **conditions** (poverty, insanity). The very words in our definition—*qualities, concepts, conditions*—are themselves abstract words.

Assuming that the term *abstract word* now has a clear enough meaning for our purposes, we are in a position to explore the significance of **charged abstract words.** Such words, like precharged concrete words, appear to have the power to evoke a strong emotional response, positive or negative, whenever they are used. The following list of abstract words that are emotionally precharged for many people will supply examples and will also give the reflective reader a chance to consider which are most charged for him and why.

Communist, fascist, socialistic, progressive, liberal, totalitarian, undemocratic, Republican, Democrat, capitalist, labor, reactionary, un-American, radical, freedom, liberty, free enterprise, regimentation, collectivism, foreigners, religion, science, virtue, decency, Protestant, Catholic, moral, sin, immorality, faith, atheist, morality, truth, beauty, success, happiness, Christian, sex, justice, peace, war, loyalty, sportsmanship

It is hard to overestimate the almost magical influence that these words and others like them have on the private and public concerns of men. A glance at the haphazard and incomplete list above will demonstrate that such words are woven into the fabric of human living; when men talk or write or read or think about such subjects as government, economics, sociology, history, philosophy, religion, ethics, law, literature, art, current events—even language itself— they cannot escape abstract words, for abstract words must be used in dealing with such subjects; and it is, or at least seems to be, inevitable that some of these words will (1) have a different referential meaning for different people, and (2) become charged positively or negatively with emotion—will, in short, be *charged abstract words*.

Because such words have great emotional power it is a delicate matter to write about them. Each reader of this book, for example, probably feels that *some* of the words in the list above do have a clear and definite meaning. People who feel very strongly against "fascists" are often quite sure that they know, and that every intelligent person ought to know, just what a fascist is, just what the term properly means. On the other hand the people to whom the "anti-fascists" apply the label "fascist" very often indignantly deny the label; they may say they are not fascists, they are "patriots." In such circumstances we must conclude either that the term *fascist* means different things to the two groups concerned or that one of them is deliberately making a false statement. Before we jump to conclusions we need to examine other words from our list. Suppose now we try the word *communist*. Those who dislike communists are quite sure that they know, and that every intelligent person should know, just what a communist is. But again some of those who are labeled "communists" indignantly deny the label. They may say they are not communists, they are "progressives" or "liberals."

Other words on the list produce similar results. Some people say that the success of America is founded on "free enterprise"; others reply that what is called free enterprise is not really free enterprise, it is "special privilege" and "monopoly." Some opponents of Plan E (a city-manager plan of government) say the plan is "communistic"; proponents say it is not, it is most "democratic." Some Republicans charge the Democratic party with being dominated by "labor unions"; Democrats deny this and assert that the Republican party is run by "big business." Liberal Protestants may say that Catholics are not truly "religious"; Catholics may reply that these liberal Protestants are not truly "religious." John Dewey advocates the application of "science" to social matters; Monsignor Sheen says that John Dewey is really advocating "scientism" and not science. Some people who did not like Franklin D. Roosevelt called him a "dictator"; those who did like him were angered, and disagreed with some feeling. To one user of the word, a "capitalist" is a "bloated exploiter"; to another he is instead a man of energy, foresight, and intelligence who provides employment for less able people. Because Einstein does not believe in a "personal God" and defines "religion" as devotion to some suprapersonal cause, many people would say that he is an "atheist" and has no "religion." Russians say that they have "freedom" (meaning freedom from want, assured employment) and that we don't; Americans reply that Russians don't have freedom (meaning free choice of occupation, civil liberties, etc.) but we do.

In all the illustrations given, one person or group is asserting something about an abstract term which is denied by another group. Each feels that the other is not telling the "truth." In each case we can say either that the term means different things to different people (i.e., that the referential meaning is different), or that one-half of the people mentioned are actually engaging in deliberate falsehood. Since many differences of this sort occur every day between people who seem honest, intelligent, and well intentioned, it seems that it often is the unfixed referential meaning of the abstractions used, and not deliberate falsehood, that produces the contradiction. In fact it often happens that each person in a disagreement feels so sure he is telling the "truth" that he accuses the other person of "distorting the truth"; and the accused person is frequently stung by the "injustice" of the accusation and the "dishonesty" of his accuser.

It is perhaps clear by now that these charged abstract words really do have different referential meanings for different people. Further examples will show that they also have different emotional associations (charges), positive and negative, for different people. Those who choose to call themselves "progressives" do so because the word stands to them for their set of beliefs; and since the word serves as a symbol or label for what they believe, it naturally has a positive charge for them. People who call themselves "conservatives" have a similar favorable feeling toward the word *conservative* for similar reasons. But since "progressives" and "conservatives" are in frequent conflict, it is equally natural that for the progressive, *conservative* is a negatively charged term and that for the conservative, *progressive* is a negatively charged term.

Since charged abstract words deal with matters that are of utmost importance to men, and since, as we have seen, they may mean different things, both referentially and emotively, when different men use them or hear them, it naturally follows that they produce confusion and exasperation, and cause misunderstanding and ill-feeling. It is clear too that they can produce such results even when they are used by intelligent and well-intentioned people.

We have by no means exhausted the types of charged words, but enough has been said to give some meaning to the word *charged* and to label certain common and influential types of charged words: *charged words of everyday living, charged taboo words, charged proper names,* and *charged abstract words.* We need to consider now two special types of charged abstract words: *charged words of personal attitude,* and *charged words of race or nationality.*

Charged words of personal attitude serve to express our tastes or distastes, our approval or disapproval; they convey not facts but attitudes and opinions. Examples are: *interesting, dull, pretty, ugly, disgusting, attractive, sound, absurd.* Such words deserve attention because they usually seem to have much more referential meaning than they actually have. When two students read the same book and one calls it interesting and the other calls it dull, each is likely to think that he has made a referential statement, that he has communicated a fact about the book. Actually neither has given any information about the book itself. The "fact" communicated is a fact about what is going on in the student's mind, a fact about how he feels toward the book, what his attitude is. Similarly, if we say that the Republican party or the Democratic party is the "best" party, we have expressed an opinion and revealed something about ourselves, but we have not stated a fact. Unless we distinguish clearly between fact and opinion, it is easy to deceive ourselves or to be deceived by others.

Charged words of race and nationality work in the same deceptive way, but more subtly, and with more serious consequences.[2] Sometimes they give a certain amount of accurate, referential information; sometimes they give little or none. When we are told that a man is an Italian, for example, we have little or no sure information about him, for the only statement that we can make with certainty about all Italians is that they live in Italy or that some of their ancestors lived in Italy. There are no physical traits which all Italians have in common—some are blond and others are dark, some are short and others are tall; and there are no traits of personality or intellect which all Italians share—some are educated and some are not, some are quick to anger and others are slow, some speak Italian and others do not. The word *Italian* is applied to people (Dante, Marconi, Al Capone, Mussolini, Garibaldi, Michelangelo) who have

[2] A full explanation of why such words affect us as they do would require an excursion into the special fields of biology, psychology, anthropology, and perhaps sociology. Students who are particularly interested in race will find much information in *Heredity, Race, and Society,* written by L. C. Dunn and Theodosius Dobzhansky, biologists, and published by The New American Library of World Literature, Inc.

nothing in common except the fact that they or their ancestors were born in Italy.

What has been said of the word *Italian* is also true of *German, Irishman, American, Frenchman,* and numerous other words of nationality. In every case the word tells us nothing certain about the man except that he or his ancestors were or are natives of a particular country. The word *Jew* actually tells us less than any of the words mentioned above, for there is nothing that is common to all people called Jews, neither nationality nor, as was originally the case, a common religion.

Some words of race and nationality do convey a certain amount of referential meaning. *Negro, Japanese, Chinese, American Indian* are likely to give some information about the physical appearance of the human being to whom they are applied. To say, for example, that Ralph Johnson Bunche, United Nations diplomat, is a Negro is to make a statement with some referential meaning; from that statement we gain a general idea of his skin color, head shape, and hair. But even when words of race or nationality do have some referential meaning, they often focus interest on what is least significant about a human being. Certainly skin color, head shape, and hair are not the most important considerations if one is trying to evaluate Mr. Bunche as a person. To do that it is necessary to consider such things as his doctoral degree from Harvard, his post-doctoral fellowship from the Social Science Research Council, and his widely acclaimed mediation of the Jewish-Arab warfare in Palestine, for which he was awarded the 1950 Nobel Peace Prize.

Charged words of race and nationality are deceptive because to many people they seem to have more referential meaning, to give more information, than they actually do. Often they are precharged words which cause us to prejudge the referent. Words like *Negro* and *Japanese* which give a limited amount of referential meaning about physical characteristics frequently misguide because they lead people to jump from physical characteristics to judgments of character and personality. To argue from physical traits to character traits is to use the kind of poor logic found in such generalizations as "All blondes are unreliable," or "All red-haired people are hot tempered." A particular fair-haired person may be a model of reliability and a particular red-haired person may be a model of calm.

Because labels of race and nationality are misleading, we use language well if whenever possible we tear off the precharged label and look directly at the referent, the individual to whom the label refers. If we fail to look behind the label we are likely to become victims of words and to respond undiscriminatingly to the emotional charges of words that have little or no referential meaning. Jews, Negroes, Italians, Germans, Russians, Americans, English, Japanese —all races and all nationalities are made up of individuals, each with a multitude of individual traits, good and bad. We know what extraordinarily complicated creatures we and our friends and the members of our group are; we should realize that all human beings, as biologists and psychologists tell us, are strikingly like us. Like us they should be judged as individuals on the basis of what they are and what they do, not prejudged on the basis of the precharged words of race and nationality.

CHAPTER REVIEW

If your reading of this chapter has been adequate you should

1. be able to define accurately and explain clearly the meaning of the following terms:

good English	locution
plain sense	referential meaning
intention	attitudinal meaning
attitude	charged words
context	precharged words
referent	connotative words

2. be able to distinguish between and give examples of the following terms:

plain sense, intention, attitude
personal and impersonal style
word and referent
referential and attitudinal meaning
concrete and abstract words

3. be able to state the important things that one should be aware of concerning:

✓context and meaning
charged abstract words
charged words of personal attitude
charged words of race and nationality

EXERCISES

I. Make a list of the first ten words that come into your mind. How many of them have more than one general meaning? How many are often used figuratively (i.e., in metaphors and similes)?

Can you think of any word which always has exactly the same meaning?

II. The analogy between dress and language has been mentioned on page 4. What further analogy can you see between the two?

III. *A*, making an important long-distance call, is interrupted by *B*. *A* thinks of three ways of conveying to *B* that he does not want to be disturbed: (1) "Excuse me, please; this is a very important long-distance call"; (2) "Hello, be with you in a minute"; (3) "Shut the door and be quiet." Consider the difference in plain sense, attitude, and intention of these three communications. If you were the speaker, which expression would you use, and why? Is one of the expressions "better English" than the other two?

IV. "The board is on the fence." What different meanings can this sentence have, and what determines its meaning?

V. In the following passage find examples of precharged words, lightly charged words, and context-charged words:

The Mayor spoke forthrightly. He stated the facts without attempting to conceal his honest indignation: "These political obstructionists who are willing to sacrifice the health and safety of children to achieve selfish ends and to discredit my administration have endeavored to stop my program of reconstruction. The blame for the delay in opening the schools must be placed squarely on the shoulders of a group of hungry political office-seekers who practiced false economy in the past and are making a serious attempt to discredit good government."

VI. In the sentences below, substitute for each italicized locution an expression with a similar referential meaning but a less favorable connotation.

Examples:
She *placed a moist cloth* on his forehead. [slapped a wet rag]
He *talked steadily* for half an hour. [droned on]

   1. He *strode* onto the platform and *smiled* at the audience.
   2. The woman *reproved* her *carefree* daughter for the *untidiness* of the girl's room.
   3. The *policeman* had a *large, strong* neck.
   4. He *left college* because he *had difficulty with* English, mathematics, and biology.
   5. The army *withdrew to a strategic position*.
   6. He read the *description on the jacket* of the book.
   7. He is a *high-ranking officer* in the Navy and a *strict disciplinarian*.
   8. He *closed* the door, *tossed* the book on the table, and *called to* his wife.
   9. He is *an affectionate* parent who *treats his children with indulgence*.
   10. She is an *unmarried woman* of fifty who is always ready *to give in-*

formation about her neighbors and who *takes an interest in everything they do.*

11. He *frankly admitted* that he had *misrepresented the facts,* and he *asked* for *considerate treatment.*

12. The Mayor spoke *forthrightly.* He *stated the facts* without *attempting to conceal* his *honest indignation.*

VII. In the light of what you have learned about language, comment on the use of language in the following statements.

1. I'm telling you the truth. He's the meanest man in the world.

2. I don't care if he was born in this country and has a good reputation in town. You can't trust a Jap.

3. Tests show that clothes wash 60% whiter with Bubblo, the Magic Soap.

4. He must be a communist. He has a lot of radical literature around his house.

5. How do I know his parents are ignorant Polacks? Why, I've met them, and they can't even speak good English.

6. I don't believe in socialized medicine because it's undemocratic.

7. The book was so dull, I went to sleep before I was half through it.

8.

Promote Alderman

JOHN E. JONES

to

REPRESENTATIVE

Lifelong resident of Greentown
Educated in Greentown schools
Father of six children
Alderman 1946–1947–1948
Familiar with problems of the veteran,
taxpayer, and workingman

ELECT JOHN E. JONES   REPRESENTATIVE

Chapter Two

Charged Meaning

IN CHAPTER ONE we have examined the parts of meaning, the importance of context in determining the meanings of words, the difference between referential and attitudinal meaning, and certain influential types of charged words. Chapter Two continues this discussion of language and meaning. Here we shall consider in more detail the effects of charged words, and analyze the characteristics, techniques, and uses of charged language. This chapter, like Chapter One, is designed to give the student a sounder general understanding of how his language works, and how language affects thinking and action.

I. CHARGED WORDS IN ACTION

As we watch the effect of charged words, we see that in addition to causing arguments and misunderstandings, they influence the thoughts, opinions, and actions of men. Many people who hear the word *communist* associated with the city-manager form of government known as "Plan E" will feel unfavorably inclined toward the plan, and perhaps will vote against it without stopping to consider just what the word *communist* means in this context, and in just what ways, if any, this term applies to the complex many-sided *actuality:* Plan E *functioning* in particular communities. People who hear that cooperatives are "socialistic" may be similarly influenced, may associate the word *socialism* with the word *cooperative,* and so feel favorably or unfavorably disposed (depending on what emotion the word *socialistic* arouses in them) toward the actual cooperatives. If, on the other hand, people hear or read that Plan E is a "truly democratic" form of city government and that cooperatives fit well into the "American way of life," they are likely to carry over the favorable associations, charges, that these phrases have, and to be favorably disposed toward Plan E and toward cooperatives. People feel differently toward the same referent ("thing" or "idea") as different words are used to refer to it. This kind of transferred emotional meaning is so common that we are all victims of it. It may be worth noting here, by the way, that those who are intimately informed about the thing itself, Plan-E-in-operation or cooperatives-in-operation, are much less likely to have their opinion changed by the charged words which others apply to that thing, even though they are pleased or annoyed by the use of the words, than those who are less well informed.

Charged words, abstract or concrete, may be used for different purposes and with different intentions. Much of the time the user is innocent of any concealed intention; he thinks he is giving information, is stating a "fact." For him the words have, or seem to have, clear referential meaning, and he is simply trying to convey that meaning. The farmer and his college-student son, for example, belong in this category, and their whole frustrating discussion grew out of their honest intentions and their ignorance of the characteristics of charged abstract words. A good many misunderstandings in daily life are produced in the same way. The college student who in good faith describes a girl as a "beauty" and even more concretely as a "good dancer" and arranges for an acquaintance to take the girl dancing may be trusting too much in the referential meaning that these charged words have *for him*.[1] The acquaintance may have a disappointing evening because the girl is "too thin to be beautiful" and "too tall to be a good dancer." *Beauty* and *good dancer* mean different things to different people.

Between people who know each other and each other's opinions and attitudes well, however, expressions that are usually charged and abstract often convey a kind of referential meaning that is adequate for some purposes of communication. One reason we find it easy to talk to our friends is that over a period of time the whole context of our association has enabled us to fix on a somewhat similar referential meaning for some of the abstract words we use frequently. We can say to these friends that such and such a bill before Congress will "hurt business" or is "anti-labor," and the friends will have a fairly clear idea of the referential meaning of the expressions as we use them. On the other hand, a stranger present at the same conversation would be likely to carry away from it little meaning or at least little of *our* meaning.

Charged words may also be used intentionally for emotive effect. Some newspapers and periodicals frequently use such words in their

---

[1] These two expressions illustrate the fact that it is hard to place words in definite categories. Here, for example, *beauty* can be called a charged abstract word and also a charged word of personal attitude. In the phrase "good dancer," *dancer* is a fairly concrete word, but *good*, like *beauty*, is a charged abstract word which conveys personal attitude.

editorial columns and cartoons, in captions under photographs, and even in their headlines and titles. (Words in cartoons, by the way, have a particularly forceful charge, for along with the word—*labor* or *management,* for example—the cartoonist gives the pictorial representation that he would like us to associate with the word or to accept as the meaning of the word. Illustrated advertisements work in a similar way.) Many syndicated columnists, editorial writers, and radio commentators are artists in using charged abstract words and other techniques of "charged language." Largely by the use of charged expressions, they exert tremendous persuasive power over their audiences, and cause many uninformed people to approve, almost mechanically, what such communicators approve, and to condemn what they condemn. Thus their audiences may come to believe on the basis of a few facts and much charged language that "labor leaders are all racketeers" or that "labor is the only bulwark against fascism." When one tries to think of the names of those who are skilled in using charged words to influence, subtly or obviously, for "good causes" or "bad," the emotions of their audience, a strangely assorted list comes to mind—William Randolph Hearst, Gabriel Heatter, Walter Winchell, Dorothy Thompson, Westbrook Pegler, Fulton Lewis, Jr. Students are invited to examine objectively the use of charged words by their own favorite columnist, editorial writer, or news commentator. Most students will not need to be invited to "tear to pieces" the speeches and writings of those writers and radio commentators with whom they strongly disagree.

It is worth noting here that we need to be slow in judging the intentions and character of people who use heavily charged words. (This applies, of course, to those whose names have just been mentioned.) If Thomas Paine had not so powerfully used charged language in *The Crisis* we might not now be citizens of the United States of America; and it seems clear that the heavily charged speeches of Winston Churchill did much to hearten the English people during the darkest days of World War II. *Some* of the most unrestrained users of heavily charged words are not the "subversive" or "mercenary" or "hypocritical" villains that we take them to be. They may be people who are well intentioned and who are simply trying to give forceful expression to their own deep convictions, to "truth" as they see it. Charity is a virtue we practice too seldom in judging the character and intentions of those who attack our cherished beliefs. We are too ready to call those with whom we agree "impassioned defenders of the truth" and those with whom we disagree "dishonest propagandists" who have "ulterior motives." Socrates thought that all men seek the good, and most men fail, through ignorance, to find it. A knowledge of how language works should promote judicious tolerance at the same time that it decreases our gullibility.

In this charitable frame of mind we can approach the political use of language, one of the richest fields for the student of charged words. Those who phrase party platforms, *all* party platforms, are not using words just to state what the party stands for and what it will do if it is in power. They are using words also to get votes, and they can't help knowing that charged words often supply the current necessary to carry voters to the polls. People seeking political office naturally use words for the same purpose. Why is it that candidates for political office deal with the issues only in very general language, paint such lurid pictures of one another during campaigns, and then after the election reconcile themselves so easily to that public calamity, the election of their opponent? It is because of accepted political folkways, and also because of certain facts about language. For one thing, the use of charged language arouses people and makes them want to vote; many citizens take the charged language of politicians much more seriously than do the politicians themselves. For another thing, abstract and charged language is much safer politically than definite, referential statement. It is generally safer for a candidate to say that he will "eliminate abuses and give honest and economical government" than to name the abuses he will eliminate (thereby losing the votes of those closely associated with the abuses), and the particular economies he will practice (thereby losing the votes of those whom the economies will affect adversely).

Still another reason for the use of charged political language is that the candidate has to gain the attention of the voters, to interest them, or they won't listen to him. Modern government is not an easy subject to make interesting or clear to a general audience; this is true even of local government, and national government is much more complicated and abstract. If a candidate really resolved that he would try, by means of referential language and reason, to convince his audiences that they should vote for him, he would then be obliged to give his stand on various issues and his reasons for his stand. Since most of the public is unaware of the facts on complex issues—for example, foreign policy—our candidate would find it necessary, in explaining his reasons, to present complex subjects in reasonably concrete referential language, in short to educate the voters, instead of following the usual procedure of appealing primarily to their emotions and fixed ideas. But it is notorious that many people, even some college students, regard being educated as a strenuous, and frequently a "dull" and "uninteresting" experience. It looks, then, as though our "really informative" candidate might lose his audience to his more stimulating, dramatic, name-calling opponent. When one examines the problems that even a well-intentioned, widely informed candidate is obliged to face, it is not surprising that most office-seekers use the charged words and vague generalities of "political language." Such language interests voters and attracts votes; at the same time, it conceals the candidate's ignorance on some issues (candidates can't know all the facts about all the issues) and allows him to avoid making particular statements which might cause some voters not to vote for him. As long as political language produces enough votes, politicians are likely to continue to employ it.

This discussion of the political use of language is not intended to encourage cynicism. When we say that the intention of the politician is to get votes, we refer only to immediate intention. Certainly there are many admirable candidates for political office who have the long-run intention of contributing their part to good government. The fact is that the *kind of language* one uses is to a considerable degree dictated by the *kind of activity* that one engages in. Scientists *as* scientists must use referential language; because they are dealing with the facts of the physical world, they must use words that refer to such facts. Politicians and others who address the general public must speak in language that is meaningful emotionally as well as referentially. It is noticeable that when scientists want to convince the public of the dangers or the possibilities that lie in atomic power, they too use language that is colored with emotion.

It is true that many politicians carry the use of political language to extremes that are hard to justify, but before we condemn all politicians for the way they use language, we need to consider what, in the very nature of language, may make them speak as they do; and also just what we should do and say if we were candidates. As voters we can do our part in making candidates more informative by not being so gullible as to vote the "straight party ticket," and by insisting that those for whom we cast our votes must, at least part of the time, talk informatively about the issues. When presumably informed or educated people are unaware of the character of political language, they are likely to be deceived by it or to be disgusted with politics in general. Either gullibility or disgusted indifference contributes to the election of self-seeking and verbally clever candidates instead of the informed, competent leaders that we need. Good citizens are not those who parrot the slogans of political language, nor are they ostriches who bury their heads in the sand to stop up their ears. This last comparison is unfair to ostriches: *they* do not really bury their heads, and they have no obligations as citizens.

II. CHARGED WORDS AND SLANTING: CHARGED LANGUAGE

Thus far our examples of charged words have been given with just enough context to make our point clear. Now we can consider the effect produced by charged words and other emotive devices in a longer context where they **work together** to produce **charged language**. From this point on we shall use the term *charged language* to describe language which uses to a marked degree any or all of the devices for conveying a favorable or unfavorable impression. Language may be intentionally or unintentionally charged, and it may, of course, be charged favorably or unfavorably, positively or negatively. Much of the language we use in daily life is unintentionally charged; we frequently are communicating feelings, "attitudes," even when we stoutly believe that we are conveying nothing but "plain sense." For the present we can stop with this very general description of charged language. As we go on, examples and further discussion will make the meaning of the term clearer.

Below are passages which show how charged words work together in a context of some length to produce charged language, and to influence our judgments and attitudes as we read or listen. These passages, not intended to be models of style, were written by a clever student who was told to choose as his subject a person in action, and to write two descriptions, each using the "same facts." The instructions required that one description be charged positively and the other negatively, so that the first would make the reader favorably inclined toward the person and the action, and the second would make the reader unfavorably inclined.

Here is the favorably charged description. Read it carefully and form your opinion of the person before you go on to read the second description.

CORLYN

Corlyn paused at the entrance to the room and glanced about. A well-cut black dress draped subtly about her slender form. Her long blonde hair gave her chiseled features the simple frame they required. She smiled an engaging smile as she accepted a cigarette from her escort. As he lit it for her she looked over the flame and into his eyes. Corlyn had that rare talent of making every male feel that he was the one man in the world.

She took his arm and they descended the steps into the room. She walked with an effortless grace and spoke with equal ease. They each took a cup of coffee and joined a group of friends near the fire. The flickering light danced across her face and lent an ethereal quality to her beauty. The good conversation, the crackling logs, and the stimulating coffee gave her a feeling of internal warmth. Her eyes danced with each leap of the flames.

Taken by itself this passage might seem just a description of an attractive girl. The favorable charging has been done so skillfully that it is inconspicuous. Now we can turn to the unfavorably charged description of the "same" girl engaged in the "same" actions.

CORLYN

Corlyn halted at the entrance to the room and looked around. A plain black dress hung on her thin frame. Her stringy bleached hair accentuated her harsh features. She smiled an inane smile as she took a cigarette from her escort. As he lit it for her she stared over the lighter and into his eyes. Corlyn had a habit of making every male feel that he was the last man on earth.

She grasped his arm and they walked down the steps and into the room. Her pace was fast and ungainly, as was her speech. They each reached for some coffee and broke into a group of acquaintances near the fire. The flickering light played across her face and revealed every flaw. The loud talk, the fire, and the coffee she had gulped down made her feel hot. Her eyes grew more red with each leap of the flames.

When the reader compares these two charged descriptions, he can see how charged words work in the context of charged language. One needs to read the two versions several times to appreciate all the subtle differences between them. Charged language, it is clear, is something more than a group of obviously charged words strung together. In the descriptions of Corlyn, innocent-looking words work together to carry to the reader a judgment of a person and a situation. If the reader had seen only the first description of Corlyn, he might well have thought that he had formed his "own judgment on the basis of the facts." And the examples just given only begin to suggest the techniques that may be used in charged language. For one thing, the two descriptions contain no really good example of the use of charged abstractions; for another, because of the instructions given, the writer could not make use of *slanting*.

Since *slanting* plays an important part in producing the impression we get from what we read or hear, we need a definition of the term and some illustrations. We can define **slanting** as the **selecting** of material (facts, figures—all the details that combine to produce the substance of the communication) and the **emphasizing** of that material to produce in the receiver a favorable or unfavorable impression.

Perhaps the best way to illustrate slanting is to show the different impressions that one may get of a subject, in this case a dog, as a result of different ways of selecting and emphasizing facts.

A. Balanced presentation

Our dog, Toddy, sold to us as a cocker, produces various reactions in various people. Those who come to the back door she usually growls and barks at (a milkman has said that he is afraid of her); those who come to the front door, she whines at and paws, and she tries to lick their faces unless we have forestalled her by putting a newspaper in her mouth. (Some of our friends encourage these displays of affection; Mrs. Firmly, another friend, calmly slaps the dog with a newspaper and says, "I know how hard dogs are to train.")Toddy knows and responds to a number of words and phrases, and polite guests sometimes remark that she is a "very intelligent dog." She has fleas in the spring, and she sheds, at times copiously, the year round. Her blonde hairs are conspicuous when they are on people's clothing or on rugs or furniture. Her color and her large brown eyes frequently produce favorable comment. An expert on cockers would say that her ears are too short and set too high and that she is at least six pounds too heavy.

The passage above is made up of facts, verifiable facts,[2] deliberately selected and emphasized to produce a *balanced* impression. Both favorable and unfavorable facts are used, and an effort has been made to alternate favorable and unfavorable details so that neither will receive greater emphasis by position, proportion, or subordination. We shall use the term *balanced presentation* to refer to this impartial selection and emphasis, and reserve the word *slanting* for selecting and emphasizing to produce a favorable or unfavorable impression.

B. Slanted *against*

That dog! She put her paws on my white dress as soon as I came in the door, and she made so much noise that it was two minutes before she had quieted down and we could talk. Then the gas man came and she did a great deal of barking. And her hairs! They are on the rug and on the furniture. If you wear a dark dress they stick to it like lint. When Mrs. Firmly came in she actually hit the dog with a newspaper to make it stay down, and she made some remark about training dogs. I wish the Birks would take the hint or get rid of that noisy, short-eared, overweight "cocker" of theirs.

This unfavorably slanted version is based on the same facts, but now these facts have been selected and given a new emphasis. The

[2] Verifiable facts are facts that can be checked and agreed upon and proved to be true by people who wish to verify them. That a particular theme received a failing grade is a verifiable fact; one needs merely to see the theme with the grade on it. That the instructor should have failed the theme is not, strictly speaking, a verifiable fact but a matter of opinion. Possibly student and teacher will not agree on this matter of opinion. That women on the average live longer than men is a verifiable fact; that they live better is a matter of opinion, a "value judgment."

speaker, using her selected facts to give her impression of the dog, is quite possibly unaware of her negative "slanting."

Now for a favorably slanted version:

C. Slanted *for*

What a friendly dog! When I walked in the door, there she was with a newspaper in her mouth, whining and standing on her hind legs and wagging her tail all at the same time. And what an intelligent dog. If you suggest going for a walk, she will get her collar from the kitchen and hand it to you, and she brings Mrs. Birk's slippers whenever Mrs. Birk says she is "tired" or mentions slippers. At a command she catches balls, rolls over, "speaks," or stands on her hind feet and twirls around. She sits up and balances a piece of bread on her nose until she is told to take it; then she tosses it up and catches it. If you are eating something, she sits up in front of you and "begs" with those big dark brown eyes set in that light, buff-colored face of hers. When I got up to go and told her I was leaving, she rolled her eyes at me and looked sad. She certainly is an affectionate and an intelligent dog.

Speaker *C*, like Speaker *B*, is selecting from the "facts" of balanced version A, and is emphasizing his facts to communicate his impression. Both version C and version B, however, contain expressions which are not facts but which instead serve to convey personal judgments. Examples of such attitudinal expressions in C are: "What a friendly dog!" . . . "an intelligent dog" . . . "looked sad" . . . "She certainly is an affectionate dog"; similar attitudinal expressions in B are: "That dog!" . . . "and her hairs!" . . . "hint," and perhaps "noisy." All these expressions, even "that dog" and "and her hairs," are used in their context to convey subjective judgments, interpretations of fact, about which different people—Speaker *B* and Speaker *C*, for example—will not agree. Except for these attitudinal expressions, versions B and C, like balanced version A, are examples of "pure reporting" (i.e., consist only of verifiable facts).

If one now reads versions A, B, and C, discounting the attitudinal expressions, he will be reading three examples of pure "reporting," and yet he will see that *selection* and *emphasis* (slanting) of facts, can give three very different impressions of the same dog, and that the different meanings of the three passages are a result of the different ways the speakers slanted the facts. Some people say that figures don't lie, and many people believe that if they have "facts" they have the "truth." When we carefully examine language in action, we see that unless *all relevant* figures and facts are presented, figures and facts may be so selected and so emphasized that one version will make us take a very unfavorable attitude and another a very favorable attitude. Since it is usually impossible to give all the relevant figures

and facts, fair-minded people generally at least try to give a representative sampling of favorable and unfavorable details.

The vast importance of slanting in our daily lives becomes evident
when we realize that nearly all our knowledge has been sifted for us
by the deliberate or unintentional slanting (selection and emphasis)
of those who gave us our information. All that we know, all that
anyone knows, about many important subjects has passed through
the minds (often biased) of others and has been subjected to the
process of selection and emphasis. Russians who have not been to
America, Americans who have not been to Russia, must rely entirely
on what others tell them; and such information is, it seems, inevitably,
though very often unintentionally, slanted for or against. Anyone
who reads the five or ten most recent books on Russia will see deliberate or unintentional, favorable or unfavorable, slanting, and will
find that the books give very different impressions of that country. It
doesn't solve the problem either, though it may help, to "know someone who has been to Russia." This someone cannot know all the
facts, and probably he, like the rest of us, has certain preconceived
opinions which cause him to see clearly what he wants to see and to
see dimly or not at all what he does not want to see. The Russians,
since their sources are more controlled than ours, would seem to
have an even more difficult problem in knowing about this country.
Perhaps enough has been said to make it apparent that awareness
of slanting is important and that the "truth" about Russia or the
"truth" about this country is not simple and is not easy to arrive
at.

What applies to our knowledge of other countries also applies in
varying degrees to our knowledge of such subjects as labor laws, tax
legislation, poll-tax laws, and to our judgments of such nationally
known figures as Dean Acheson, Harold Stassen, Eleanor Roosevelt,
George C. Marshall, Dwight D. Eisenhower, Douglas MacArthur,
Thomas E. Dewey, Joseph Martin, Henry Wallace, John Foster
Dulles, Joseph McCarthy, Robert A. Taft, Estes Kefauver, Walter
Reuther, John L. Lewis, etc. (This is so true that it is hard even to
list such subjects without unintentionally slanting by the very selection of examples and the order in which they appear.) We can't help
having opinions on issues and on important individuals—indeed we
are in all conscience obliged to have them—but we need to realize
that many of our most cherished opinions are at best based on facts
and interpretations of facts supplied by others and slanted by their
conscious or unconscious selection and emphasis; at worst our opinions may be based mainly on the feelings that interested people have
excited in us by deliberate slanting and by use of the other devices

of charged language. If we want to be fair-minded and intelligent, we must be willing to subject our opinions to continual testing, and must realize that after all they *are opinions,* personal judgments more or less trustworthy, and are *not* the "truth." The truth includes all the facts. In complex matters we can't know *all* the facts, and we could not state them if we did. Opinions are simply our approximations of truth.

Looking back for a moment to the three descriptions of the dog, Toddy, we can see that merely by the slanting of verifiable facts, three different attitudes can be produced toward such a relatively concrete and uncomplex subject as a single dog. (This confining of information to verifiable facts is the same limitation, by the way, that our newspaper reporters, radio news reporters, and foreign correspondents are supposed to observe.) Often, though, people who use charged language—and all of us do—may slant by introducing not only relevant, verifiable facts but also irrelevant facts, and relevant or irrelevant impression, opinion, inference, innuendo, irony and the like. All of these additions to verifiable fact may also be used in the process of slanting, because they are all products of selection or techniques of emphasis. In heavily charged language the effect is usually produced by a combination of slanting (in this broad sense of the term) and charged words; and these two aspects of charged language work so closely together that it is often difficult to say whether a particular effect is produced by slanting or by the charged words that clothe the slanted fact or idea.

In the following examples, passages B and C will illustrate how slanting and charged words work together in context to produce heavily charged language. Passage B is charged and slanted in favor of Senator Patwell and the poll tax; passage C is charged and slanted against them. Passage A is intended to be a specimen of balanced reporting, and to supply the verifiable facts on which B and C are based. A is as near as we can come to a brief objective account, and, therefore, is *not* a specimen of charged language.

A. Verifiable facts: balanced version

The poll tax is again being discussed in the Senate. Senator Borgam Patwell (Democrat, Mississippi), who opposes the antipoll-tax measure now under consideration, held the Senate floor for eight hours today. In the course of his speech Senator Patwell read from letters of Washington and Robert E. Lee and quoted passages from the Bible. Senator Angelo Patriarca (Democrat, New York), after he had charged that Senator Patwell was "filibustering," frequently raised points of order and called for the floor. Senatorial discussion of the bill will continue again tomorrow.

B. Charged language: charged and slanted for a certain type of Southern reader

The poll tax is again being attacked by a group of Northern politicians who stay in office by following the line of left-wing pressure groups and by weeping crocodile tears over the "rights" of Negroes. People with common sense, whether or not they have much book learning, know that there are good reasons for the poll-tax laws or they wouldn't have been put on the statute books by our forefathers and left there by our fathers. The laws that were good enough for our fathers are still good enough for us. We believe in equal rights for equals, and we can't help it if God made the Negro inferior to the white man. If the Negro isn't different, why did the Lord make his skin black? George Washington, who had slaves, knew that the way to deal with Negroes is to keep them in their place. Robert E. Lee, who led our forefathers in their fight against Yankee oppression and Yankee dictatorship, knew it. The fact is that our good Negroes know it too, and old Uncle Charlie and old Aunt Mandy don't want to vote; they leave that to the "white folks." Mississippi's distinguished Senator, Borgam Patwell, descendant of General "Light Horse" Patwell, takes our common-sense point of view. Yesterday in the hushed Senate chamber our Senator delivered an eloquent and moving address in which he defended our Southern way of life against meddling Northerners and denounced the meddlers in the words of the Scripture itself. Angelo Patriarca, who got into office through the votes of Communists and other Negro-lovers and foreign riff-raff, was a typical example of the opposition and of the tactics they used in trying to impose this dangerous legislation on the South. Angelo (Italian for Angel!) Patriarca used shyster parliamentary tricks to interrupt Mississippi's Senator. On one occasion he broke in when Senator Patwell was repeating a passage from the Bible. Tomorrow Senator Patwell will again spearhead the fight to preserve States' rights and white men's rights.

C. Charged language: charged and slanted for a "liberal" or "progressive" New York audience

Senator Borgam "Molasses" Patwell is at it again. This Old Deal Southern Democrat from the black belt today spewed super-race and fascist propaganda on disgusted or half-awake Senators for eight long hours. In the course of his windy tirade he libeled George Washington by associating with that respected name his own antidemocratic and anti-American prejudices. He exalted the kind of sectionalism that should have died with the Civil War, and he expressed race attitudes that would have pleased Hitler. He even distorted the words of the Bible to preach the un-Christian hate-mongering of Gerald L. K. Smith and the Ku Klux Klan, that group of "one-hundred-per-cent Americans" who hide Nazi swastika beliefs under their KKK nightshirts. Angelo Patriarca, New York's crusading liberal Senator, tried by skillful use of parliamentary rules to dam the muddy flow of "Molasses" Patwell. (Patwell got his nickname from his cynical remark to his close—very close—friend, the president of the reactionary NAM, that

"It takes molasses to catch votes.") We know what we would like Patwell to catch—and it isn't votes. Today democracy suffered another setback at the hands of the gentlemanly Senator from the very old South. Tomorrow is another day. May the dead past bury its dead.

Passages B and C are written in heavily charged language, in which words in context gain additional force from surrounding words, and themselves add force to those words. Thus a kind of counter-action takes place in which words act on, and react to, one another to produce the strong current of charged language. A full analysis of these intricate interactions is not desirable here, but perhaps a list of some of the common devices of charged language that appear in these passages will give a clearer idea of how charged language works. (In actual use, of course, these devices frequently overlap. Hence one should not feel surprised at seeing the same expression listed more than once.) In the charged passages B and C we find:

1. *Irrelevant facts.* These are an aspect of slanting frequently seen in B and C.

In B	In C
Patwell's ancestry	Patwell's reactionary NAM friend.

2. *Charged words of personal attitude.*

In B	In C
our *good* Negroes	eight *long* hours
Mississippi's *distinguished* Senator	*windy tirade*
dangerous legislation	

3. *Charged proper names.* ·

In B	In C
God	libeled *George Washington*
Washington	*Hitler*
Robert E. Lee	*Ku Klux Klan*
Mississippi's Senator	*New York's* Senator
the *Bible*	reactionary *NAM*

4. *Charged words of race and nationality.*

In B	In C
Negroes	*race* attitude
Negro-lovers	*"one-hundred-per-cent*
foreign riff-raff	*Americans"*
	Nazi

5. *Other charged words and expressions.* Various types of charged words are numerous here. We call attention to just a few.

In B	In C
Northern politicians	*Molasses*
stay in office	*black belt*
following the line	*propaganda*
left-wing pressure groups	*antidemocratic*
common sense	
our forefathers	

6. *Name-calling.* This category of course is included under charged words, but the device is so frequently used that it deserves particular mention. Only a few of the more striking examples are listed here.

In B	In C
Yankee	*Molasses*
Communists	*Old Deal Southern Democrat*
Negro-lovers	*Nazi swastika* beliefs
riff-raff	

7. *Inferences* (the communicator's interpretation of what goes on in the minds of others), and *personal opinions* and *impressions stated as fact.* These three devices are put together because they so often shade into one another.

In B	In C
people with common sense	*disgusted* . . . Senators
know	
God made the Negro inferior	

8. *Innuendo* (indirect aspersion, unfavorable implication). There is a good deal of innuendo in these passages, some of it impossible to make clear without fuller discussion.

In B	In C
stay in office	*attitudes that would have*
weeping crocodile tears	*pleased Hitler*
Italian for angel!	*nightshirts*
	close—very close—friend
	May the *dead past* bury its *dead.*

9. *Irony and ridicule.*

In B	In C
Angelo (*Italian for angel!*)	*gentlemanly*
	their *KKK nightshirts*

10. *The false appearance of logical reasoning.*[3] In B the passage beginning with *"People with common sense . . ."* and ending with *"make his skin black?"*

11. *Charged questions.* In B: *"If the Negro isn't different, why did the Lord make his skin black?"*

12. *The use of quotation marks in writing* (or of "so-called" in speech) to imply false meaning of words and therefore a dishonest use of the quoted expression.

In B	In C
the *"rights"* of Negroes	*"one-hundred-per-cent Americans"*

13. *Charged metaphors and personification.* Such figures of speech can be very powerful. When they work in charged language, they are always worth particular attention. We have listed some inconspicuous, mild expressions and also some heavily charged ones.

In B	In C
attacked	*spewed propaganda*
pressure groups	*windy tirade*
spearhead the fight	*hide Nazi swastika beliefs under*
crocodile tears	*their KKK nightshirts*
	to dam the muddy flow
	Democracy suffered another setback
	dead past bury its dead

Charged language used to persuade or convince gains some of its most telling effects not so much from particular words and phrases as from the whole positive or negative drift or slant of the passage. Such drift is often produced by the **"right-on-our-side"** technique. The communicator is trying to lead receivers to share, and to identify themselves with, the attitude he takes or appears to take. He does this by presenting two opposing sides. On one side (the communicator's, which he slants favorably as "our side") are admirable people motivated by high principles and striving to do good; on the other side are undesirable and even hateful people bent on doing harm. The receiver is intended to be sympathetic with "our side" and to identify himself emotionally with "our" cause. In version B, for example, the people on "our side" or associated with it are "Mississippi's distinguished Senator," "George Washington," "Robert E. Lee," and even God; those on the other side are the self-seeking officeholder, Patriarca, and his supporters—"Negroes," "foreign riffraff," "Communists," and other "Negro-lovers." Those on our side

---

[3] Logical reasoning is discussed on pp. 270–283.

seek to preserve all that is best in the "Southern way of life," and those on the other side are determined to "impose" "Yankee" laws and to destroy the wise and traditional Southern civilization. Passage C uses the same techniques, but now those who are intended to engage the reader's admiration are "liberal" Senator Patriarca and other believers in "democracy" who are opposing "Molasses" Patwell and the "antidemocratic and un-American prejudices" held by "reactionaries and fascists." The "right-on-our-side" technique is a common method of slanting and is to be found very often in persuasive writing or speaking.

The following excerpts from two reviews [4] of the same book are less highly charged than the passages we have been considering; but they are charged, nevertheless, to persuade the reader to accept opinions which the reviewers honestly hold.

A. THE RIDDLES OF FRANKLIN ROOSEVELT

John Gunther calls his new Roosevelt book both a "profile" and a "summary." It also is a compilation to about a third of its length, composed in the now established Gunther technique, of an impressive assortment of details, some of facts important and trivial, some of ideas deliberately artless and penetrating. Thus the Roosevelt story has been accorded the treatment of the notable "Inside" works that have given Mr. Gunther a unique place in political journalism. It need not be debated whether this treatment assures a satisfactory biography; it does not. Mr. Roosevelt was both too complex and too paradoxical to be illuminated by a catalogue of his contradictions and questions about his qualities. He needs the synthesis of a great interpretative biography, operating like a shaft of light that reveals unity formed out of disunity and harmony underlying discord. Mr. Gunther has not undertaken to write this biography. It is not his method or his art. He is a compiler, as was Mr. Sandburg writing about Lincoln. He does not go in for the portraiture that grows out of selection, that is, the suppression of detail. He must note everything, stop and conjecture about everything, delight in everything, and both marvel and cavil.

All this makes a book that is informative, entertaining, and in this case also important, and because Mr. Gunther is an indefatigable gatherer of detail, a book that is fresh even in the familiar field of Rooseveltiana. But Mr. Gunther has not departed from his established formula. He writes about F. D. R. as he writes about a continent. But since F. D. R. was not a continent, it is clear that Mr. Gunther does not write about him *because* he understands him and feels compelled to share his understanding. He is searching, and we share his search.

[4] Raymond Swing, "The Riddles of Franklin Roosevelt," *The Nation,* June 3, 1950; the editors of *Time,* "Let's Wait," *Time,* June 5, 1950. The complete reviews, with two other reviews of the same book, are printed on pp. 319–329.

B. LET'S WAIT

Journalist John Gunther has made a career of breezing through countries, even whole continents, and persuading his readers that he is giving them inside stuff. His "Inside" (Europe, Latin America, Asia, U.S.A.) books have considerable popular virtues: they can be read in a hammock, they seldom induce thought, and they almost never leave a deep residue of conviction or concern. Writing with ebullience and wide-eyed surprise, he projects men and events just far enough beyond the daily-news level to satisfy those who dislike being serious but are plagued by the need to seem informed.

In *Roosevelt in Retrospect,* Gunther has brought these talents to bear on the complex personality of Franklin Delano Roosevelt. In spite of his avowed aim of getting at his subject's "root qualities and basic sources of power," Gunther has conspicuously failed to "pin something of his great substance against the wall of time." Getting inside a man is something quite different from getting into a continent or a country; it takes more than visas. What Gunther has achieved is a lively journalistic profile pieced together with materials largely lifted from the mushrooming literature on F. D. R. and loosely held together by Gunther's own surface researches.

Writing "as objectively as possible," Gunther is obviously too dazzled by the Roosevelt glitter to do a balanced job.

A comparison of statements made about particular topics will highlight some of the techniques of charged language used in the reviews. For example, on the subject of Mr. Gunther's "Inside" books:

In A	In B
the notable "Inside" works that have given Mr. Gunther a unique place in political journalism	His "Inside" . . . books have considerable popular virtues: they can be read in a hammock, they seldom induce thought, . . .

On the parallel between this book and the "Inside" books:

In A	In B
He writes about F. D. R. as he writes about a continent. He is searching and we share his search.	Getting inside a man is something quite different from getting into a continent or a country; it takes more than visas.

On Mr. Gunther's method:

In A	In B
the now established Gunther technique	breezing through countries, even whole continents, and

In A (continued)	In B (continued)
an impressive assortment of details	persuading his readers that he is giving them inside stuff
He is a compiler, as was Mr. Sandburg writing about Lincoln.	pieced together with materials largely lifted from the mushrooming literature on F. D. R.
an indefatigable gatherer of detail	and loosely held together by Gunther's own surface researches

On the value of the book:

In A	In B
Mr. Gunther has not undertaken to write this [great interpretative] biography. It is not his method or his art.	Gunther has conspicuously failed to "pin something of his great substance against the wall of time."
a book that is informative, entertaining, and in this case also important, . . . a book that is fresh even in the familiar field of Rooseveltiana	a lively journalistic profile pieced together with materials largely lifted from the mushrooming literature on F.D.R.

On Mr. Gunther's attitude toward his subjects:

In A	In B
deliberately artless and penetrating	wide-eyed surprise
delight in everything, and both marvel and cavil	obviously too dazzled

Passage B, with its conspicuous use of irony and ridicule, is much more heavily charged and slanted than passage A. Passage A illustrates the inconspicuously charged language which many readers do not think of as charged at all.

III. SUMMARY AND CONCLUSION

Let us now take a general view of the ground that we have covered in the first two chapters. Such a view can best be given in a series of summary statements:

1. Mere formal rules are not adequate guides for the mature student of English. *Good English* is not just "correct" English; it is expression that is *appropriate* to the *occasion* and to the *intention* of the communicator.

2. Since the main function of language is communication, we may define *language* as a verbal means of *communicating something* to

someone for some *purpose*. Hence it involves (*a*) the *meaning*, (*b*) the *communicator,* and (*c*) the *receiver*.

3. For the purpose of analysis we can break up meaning into three parts: *plain sense, intention,* and *attitude*.

4. Depending on the intention of the communicator, language may be used (*a*) *to inform* (*b*) *to persuade or convince,* or (*c*) *to communicate experience*.

5. Though isolated words may have certain *general* meanings, the *particular meaning* (*referential* or *attitudinal*) of a word is usually determined by its *context*.

6. Words may have two kinds of meaning: (*a*) they may refer to *things or ideas* (*referential meaning*) or (*b*) they may convey *feeling* (*attitudinal meaning*).

7. The ideas, attitudes, and actions of men may be profoundly influenced by the use of *charged words* and by the *slanting* of material. *Slanting* is the *selecting* and *emphasizing* of material, and a *charged word* is an *emotion-arousing word* used to clothe the raw material selected in slanting. Language which uses to a marked degree *charged words* or the techniques of *slanting,* or both, is called *charged language*.

8. The most common devices and techniques of charged language are: (*a*) the false appearance of logical reasoning; (*b*) slanting by including irrelevant material for purposes of persuasion; (*c*) use of charged words of personal attitude; charged words of race and nationality; name-calling; charged proper names; charged questions; inference, innuendo, irony, ridicule; charged metaphors, similes, personifications; and other charged words and expressions; (*d*) the "right-on-our-side" technique, another aspect of slanting.

As the reader looks over this brief summary and considers the facts about language given in these two chapters, he needs to be reminded that any general treatment of a large subject is likely to misrepresent by oversimplifying, or by emphasizing some points and omitting or touching very lightly on others.

It has been difficult in this short view—perhaps we should call it a glimpse—to draw fine distinctions and to make the qualifying statements that prevent oversimplification. For example, we have dealt with the parts of meaning as if these parts could be separated and examined individually. Actually, of course, meaning is not just a mixture of plain sense, intention, and attitude; it is a fused unit more like a chemical compound. In it the parts unite to produce a new and different unity much as the elements hydrogen and oxygen and sulphur unite to produce sulphuric acid. Inserting the word *not* into a verbal compound is like changing an acid into a salt, and any slight change in phrasing produces a change in meaning. Because it is similar to a variable compound and because a different compound is produced each time the elements are united in different proportions, language is extremely complex and difficult to describe. Our simplified picture is intended to give a general understanding, not a precise description.

The emphasis that we have given to parts of the material is also likely to be misleading unless the reader realizes that our chief aim has been to deal with the trouble-spots in language, those aspects or uses of language about which one cannot afford to be ignorant. The emphasis that we have placed on highly charged words, for example, could cause a reader to overlook the fact that some very slightly charged, "connotative" words may be equally important; they communicate subtle overtones and shades of feeling. When we want to let others know exactly what our attitudes are or when we want to know exactly what the attitudes of others are, connotative words carry an important part of meaning.

Our emphasis on the language of persuasion (often heavily charged) also is likely to mislead the reader. It may seem to make the persuasive use of language much more important than the other uses. The fact is, of course, that language is very frequently used for purposes other than persuasion. But an examination of the primarily informative use of language would lead into the realm of science and exact knowledge, and an examination of the artistic or creative use of language would lead into the realm of literature. There are good reasons why we should not, in the present chapter, trespass on either realm: the literary use of language is best understood by reading literature and cannot be given adequate treatment without the accompaniment of such reading; the informative or scientific use of language, though very important, does not offer the same problems in communication that the other two, persuasive and literary, do, for it is little complicated by the use of attitudinal language. When men use language primarily to inform—as they do in instructions, directions, reports, and in dealing with the facts of the physical sciences—they communicate with some difficulty, it is true, but with amazing accuracy and with comparatively little misunderstanding. It is when *feeling* is an important part of meaning that men have really serious and crucial misunderstandings.

Charged language deserves further comment here, for we have said much about the harm it may do and little about its equally great power for good. It is true that charged language may be used to spread prejudice and hate and discord, but it can also promote fairness and tolerance and understanding. Through it human beings can communicate their most subtle feelings and experiences and can give vital, compelling expression to the highest, most civilized ideals of human conduct. Wise and kindly men—Socrates, Jesus, Shakespeare, Franklin, Lincoln—have used language in this way and have left for all mankind a heritage at least as rich as the vast store of factual information which language also preserves for us and enables us to add to and to pass on. Men have to know facts, but they cannot live by facts and logic alone. John Stuart Mill, although he had been trained from infancy to be one of the most factual and logical of men, came to recognize what he called the motive power of emotion and turned to Wordsworth's poetry for the *attitude* of peace and joy and serenity that he found there. Like Mill, we must have beliefs and values, and only by attitudinal language, the language of feeling, can beliefs and values be given meaningful expression.

More than we realize, our lives are shaped by the language that we use and that others use. If we do not gain some understanding, some mastery, of language, other people's language will gain mastery over us. If we respond automatically to positively and negatively charged words as steel filings do to an electro-magnet, we are not free, intelligent human beings but puppets moved by the strings of language in the hands of a skillful manipulator. Having a mastery of language does not, however, mean that we should never use charged language and never respond to it.[5] It means that we should not respond thoughtlessly to charged language used for subhuman ends, and that we should try not to use ignorantly or carelessly the sometimes irresistible force of emotional language.

For mastery over language one needs skill in communication and skill in interpretation. These skills can be gained most rapidly by first taking a broad general view of language; then by studying the necessary particulars about the conventions and use of English; and finally by putting this general and particular knowledge into actual practice in one's own reading, listening, speaking, writing, and thinking.

CHAPTER REVIEW

If your reading of this chapter has been adequate you should

1. be able to define accurately and explain clearly the meaning of the following terms:

---

[5] The student who is alert to the devices of charged language should have realized as he read this chapter that there are in it passages in which charged language is aimed at the reader (see Exercise IV, p. 52).

slanting
charged language
the "right-on-our-side" technique

2. be able to distinguish between and give examples of the following terms:

verifiable fact and opinion
charged words and slanting

3. be able to state the important things that one should be aware
of concerning:

political language
the use and abuse of charged language

If your reading of the first two chapters has been adequate, you
should understand all statements and be able to define all terms in
the summary, pages 45–46.

EXERCISES

I. On August 29, 1950, President Harry S. Truman wrote a letter
which caused nation-wide comment—and some political embarrassment to him. The letter, dictated to a secretary and addressed to
Representative McDonough of California, was a response to Mc-
Donough's suggestion that the President appoint a Marine to the
Joint Chiefs of Staff, along with representatives of the Army, Navy,
and Air Corps. The President's letter said:

My dear Congressman McDonough:
I read with a lot of interest your letter in regard to the Marine Corps.
For your information the Marine Corps is the Navy's police force, and as
long as I am President that is what it will remain. They have a propaganda
machine that is almost equal to Stalin's.
Nobody desires to belittle the efforts of the Marine Corps, but when
the Marine Corps goes into the Army it works with and for the Army, and
that is the way it should be.
I am more than happy to have your expression of interest in this naval
military organization. The Chief of Naval Operations is the chief of staff
of the Navy of which the Marines are a part.

Sincerely yours,
Harry S. Truman

The President apparently thought that he was writing a private
letter; but it was placed in *The Congressional Record* of September 1,
1950, was reprinted on September 3 and 4 in New York and Washington newspapers, and aroused a storm of comment and protest. On

September 6, President Truman apologized to the Marine Corps, expressing his "sincere regret" at "the unfortunate choice of the language which I used." "What I had in mind at the time the letter was written," he explained to General Gates, the Marine Corps commandant, "was the specific question raised by Mr. McDonough. I have been disturbed by the number of communications which have been brought to my attention proposing that the Marines have such representation. I feel that inasmuch as the Marine Corps is by law an integral part of the Department of the Navy it is already represented on the Joint Chiefs of Staff by the Chief of Naval Operations."

Below are some of the comments on the President's first letter, reported in newspapers and magazines and over the radio in early September, 1950. Study the use of language in these comments. What is the attitude and what is the intention of the author of each comment? Point out evidence.

"Shocking."

"Indiscreet, incorrect, and uncalled for."

"It is an insult to the Marine Corps."

"It must have been a monumental misunderstanding on Mr. Truman's part."

"It is inconceivable how the Marines could be mentioned along with Russia's propaganda machine. The most corrupt, dishonest, dishonorable propaganda machine the world has ever known is that of Joe Stalin's."

"Every Marine feels bitter resentment that the blood of the Marines shed from 1775 to today in Korea should be characterized as propaganda."

"Most unfortunate."

"A very unthoughtful letter."

"President Truman has lowered himself unbelievably and immeasurably, and quite despicably, in the esteem of the American people by his gratuitous and insulting libel against the United States Marine Corps."

"We think it is up to him [Truman] to come to our convention and not for us to go to him asking for any explanation. After all we're not in the position of a suppliant. He's the one who has made the break."

"This won't lose him many votes. The Marines are too busy fighting to vote."

"I am loyal to the President of the United States. I am loyal, also, to the Marine Corps."

"The most incredible statement I've ever heard of."

"This is one of the most, if not the most, astoundingly insulting letters about a glorious American institution that any President of the United States has ever written so far as I know. I presume that ghosts from the Halls of Montezuma, from Chateau Thierry and Tarawa will be aroused today over this insult to this glorious and sacrificial body of Americans who have done so much on the beachheads over the world and who have colored those beachheads with their blood."

"Everyone makes a boner now and then."

"The fundamental tragedy of this ill-timed statement of the President is that it is quite obvious that there is no one available in high places to advise the President as to the mission and functions of the Marine Corps."

"The criticism should fall on Mr. McDonough who was overzealous or politically-minded enough to release the letter at this time. I have always been partial to the Republicans but I cannot see political mud-slinging of this nature at a time like this."

"It is possible that the President inadvertently signed a letter authored by someone else."

II. The following passage is a collection of verifiable facts about a college professor. Read the passage, and then see the questions below.

Professor Bestworst, a man of sixty, teaches a course in English. The twenty-five students in the course average two and a half hours of study a day, and three of the students who received a grade of C spent an average of four hours a day. The two A students spent respectively an hour and a half and three hours. Professor Bestworst starts the class exactly at the beginning of the hour. Usually he also stops exactly on the hour, but four times he talked over, once for ten minutes. He announced at the beginning of the term that students could expect ten-minute unannounced quizzes at the beginning of the hour on the assignment for that day, and he gave eight such quizzes, one on the day before Christmas vacation. He graded all the quizzes, wrote detailed comments on a number of them, and returned them. Students never complain that they cannot hear Professor Bestworst, and the secretary whose office is next to his classroom says that she overhears him quite clearly. She says also that she hears frequent laughter from the students. Miss Languish, a C student in the class, says that the course is dull and is unreasonably hard, and Miss Beaver, a B student, says that it is the best course in the college and that she would like to take it again. One student in the class estimated that Professor Bestworst said "I think" or "I believe" or "it seems to me" an average of thirty times each class hour; another student said that the professor was undogmatic and did not require students to agree with him. Girls in the class who scrutinize Professor Bestworst's dress comment favorably on his ties but notice that he often wears the same suit for two weeks and that on winter days he sometimes lectures with his galoshes on.

1. What general conclusions about the professor and his course do you think it would be fair to draw?

2. What might be said by a student who liked the professor very much? By one who was hostile toward the professor?

3. With the facts as a basis, write two passages of charged language, one favorable and the other unfavorable, about Professor Bestworst.

III. Write three descriptions (each about 150 words) of a person or place that you know. Selecting from the same basic facts, but using any devices of charging and slanting you wish to use, try in the first account to create a favorable impression of the subject and in the second an unfavorable impression. In the third account, write an impartial or balanced report of the same person or place. This third account should consist entirely of verifiable facts. Make it at least as long as the other two, and try, by means of verifiable detail, to make it as interesting to the reader as the charged and slanted versions.

IV. On pages 40–43 two passages have been analyzed to illustrate the techniques of charging and slanting. Jot down notes for a similar analysis of the five passages quoted below. In your analysis consider the use of the following:

> the "right-on-our-side" technique
> irrelevant facts
> charged words of personal attitude
> charged words of race and nationality
> name-calling and charged proper names
> other charged words and expressions
> inferences
> innuendo
> irony and ridicule
> the false appearance of logical reasoning
> charged metaphors, similes, and personifications
> any other devices for influencing the emotions of the reader

1. The following paragraph was taken from page 32 of this book. It represents the honest opinion of the writer, but it was deliberately written in charged language. (Students who read it and did not notice the charging evidently are not sufficiently alert to the techniques of charging and slanting. Other passages in Chapters One and Two also have been deliberately written in language that is somewhat charged; discovering these passages might be an interesting exercise for curious readers.)

It is true that many politicians carry the use of political language to extremes that are hard to justify, but before we condemn all politicians for the way they use language, we need to consider what, in the very nature of language, may make them speak as they do; and also just what we should do and say if we were candidates. As voters we can do our part in making candidates more informative by not being so gullible as to vote the "straight party ticket," and by insisting that those for whom we cast our votes must, at least part of the time, talk informatively about the issues. When presumably informed or educated people are unaware of the character of political language, they are likely to be deceived by it or to be disgusted with politics in general. Either gullibility or disgusted indifference contributes to the election of self-seeking and verbally clever candidates instead of the informed, competent leaders that we need. Good citizens are not those who parrot the slogans of political language, nor are they ostriches who bury their heads in the sand to stop up their ears. This last comparison is unfair to ostriches: *they* do not really bury their heads, and they have no obligations as citizens.

2. This paragraph was taken from *Color Blind,* by Margaret Halsey, a very popular nonfiction book published in 1946.

"There will always be prejudice, and there is nothing anyone can do about it, so why try?" This pronouncement, made with an air of hearty and complacent cynicism, is usually regarded by its owners as an example of fine Olympian detachment. And so it is, although fine Olympian detachment about things which are not personally inconvenient is a state easily attained by babies on leading strings and puppies in a basket. The assertion that nothing can be done about prejudice is suspicious in character, but it is certainly true that prejudice will always exist. So will sickness and disease, but that scarcely seems sufficient reason for telling our medical scientists to put on their hats, close up their laboratories, and give the spirochetes, bacilli and viruses a free hand.[6]

3. This passage is the first paragraph in *The Crisis,* a history-making book written by Thomas Paine in 1776.

These are the times that try men's souls. The summer soldier and the sunshine patriot will in this crisis shrink from the service of his country; but he that stands it NOW deserves the love and thanks of man and woman. Tyranny, like hell, is not easily conquered; yet we have this consolation with us, that the harder the conflict, the more glorious the triumph. What we obtain too cheap, we esteem too lightly: 'tis dearness only that gives everything its value. Heaven knows how to put a proper price upon its goods; and it would be strange indeed if so celestial an article as FREEDOM should not be highly rated. Britain, with an army

[6] Reprinted from *Color Blind* by permission of Simon and Schuster, Inc. Copyright, 1946, by Margaret Halsey.

to enforce her tyranny, has declared that she has a right (*not only to*) TAX but "to BIND *us in* ALL CASES WHATSOEVER," and if being *bound in that manner* is not slavery, then is there not such a thing as slavery upon earth. Even the expression is impious, for so unlimited a power can belong only to GOD.

4. The following paragraphs are taken from pages 101 and 104 of *Heredity, Race and Society* (1946) written by L. C. Dunn and Theodosius Dobzhansky. (The material omitted between paragraph 1 and paragraph 2 is an analysis of the relationship between blood type and race.) Although these passages are primarily informative, the writers are also interested in persuading and convincing. Contrast paragraph 1 with paragraph 3.

People differ in the color of skin, eyes, hair, in stature, bodily proportions, and in many other traits. Each trait is determined by several, often by many genes. How many variable genes there are in man is unknown; certainly hundreds, possibly thousands. Because of this, some of us have blue and others brown eyes, some have prominent and others flat noses, some are tall and others short. Such differences are, of course, common among people of the same country, state, town, members of a family, and even brothers and sisters. We do not suppose that every person with blue eyes belongs to a different race from everybody with brown eyes. It would be absurd to do so because blue- and brown-eyed children are frequently born to the same parents. It happens, however, that certain genes are more frequent among the inhabitants of some countries than of others. Thus, blue eyes are very common in most parts of the United States but rather rare in most parts of Mexico. It is this and similar differences which make it possible to say that the inhabitants of the United States are in general racially distinct from the inhabitants of Mexico. Races can be defined as populations which differ in the frequencies of some gene or genes.

.   .   .   .

The most important lesson we can learn from this is that the races differ in blood group type only in a relative way. There are no absolute differences in which one race is all of one blood type and another all of another type. Consider what this means. Suppose your blood is group O, that you are wounded and need a blood transfusion and that many persons have offered to donate their blood, whom should you choose as a blood donor? The old and obsolete theory of heredity, and the ideas about race based upon it, would counsel you that a blood most similar to yours would be found in a person of the same race, and particularly in your close relatives, brothers or sisters. You may also hear that you should choose as blood donor a person of upright character and good disposition, otherwise you may be contaminated by bad blood.

But you had better disregard such advice. If your brother has A, B or AB blood the transfusion would probably be fatal to you because his corpuscles would clump in your blood and clog the small blood vessels. On the other hand, a native of any land who possesses blood of group O will be a better donor regardless of his race or moral qualities. It is wiser to choose your donor according to his blood type which is determined by his individual heredity than according to the race from which he sprang. It is this property of his blood that matters, not his skin color, intelligence, or morals. By analogy, if you wish to hear good music it is wise to choose an artist who is a good musician; his blood group does not matter, nor is his skin color relevant. When you vote in a political election, the intelligence and honesty of the candidate, not his blood group or musical abilities, are relevant.

5. The following paragraph is taken from Volume II, Chapter 2, of Hitler's *Mein Kampf,* published in 1926.

Since nationality or rather race does not happen to lie in language but in the blood, we would only be justified in speaking of a Germanization if by such a process we succeeded in transforming the blood of the subjected people. But this is impossible. Unless a blood mixture brings about a change, which, however, means the lowering of the level of the higher race. The final result of such a process would consequently be the destruction of precisely those qualities which had formerly made the conquering people capable of victory. Especially the cultural force would vanish through a mating with the lesser race, even if the resulting mongrels spoke the language of the earlier, higher race a thousand times over. For a time, a certain struggle will take place between the different mentalities, and it may be that the steadily sinking people, in a last quiver of life, so to speak, will bring to light surprising cultural values. But these are only individual elements belonging to the higher race, or perhaps bastards in whom, after the first crossing, the better blood still predominates and tries to struggle through; but never final products of a mixture. In them a culturally backward movement will always manifest itself.

V. Bring to class three examples of charged language which you have read in newspapers or magazines or have heard on the radio. Be prepared to discuss the intention of the writer or speaker in each case, and to analyze the particular techniques he has used to accomplish his intention.

Chapter Three

Conventions and Meaning

IN ORDER TO USE LANGUAGE appropriately and effectively, the college student needs not only a general sense of how language works, but a more particular knowledge of how he can produce particular effects with his own use of language. His use of English will determine, in many important situations in his life, the way he impresses people, and the extent, therefore, to which he can communicate his ideas and put those ideas into effect in the limited sphere in which he moves or in the world. Writing college papers and examinations, writing letters, communicating with clients or patients or employers or employees, addressing clubs and church groups and community organizations, talking with friends and acquaintances and with business or professional associates, writing for experts in a particular field—these are only a few of the activities for which the college student needs or will probably need skill in the use of English. People may fail, in personal and professional life, because they express themselves and their potentialities poorly. Their ideas may be ignored or undervalued because they do not communicate them clearly and impressively.

The skillful use of language comes partially from understanding certain facts about language which we have discussed briefly in the first two chapters; it comes also from a knowledge of methods—of special techniques by which intended results are obtained. The purpose of most of the rest of this book is to analyze and to give advice about the techniques which the skillful and intelligent user of English should know. The purpose of this chapter is to discuss certain basic techniques which are established by convention.

In all our activities we are guided, or at least strongly influenced, by the practices which are considered right, or correct, or polite by the society into which we happen to be born. We dress, eat, dance, furnish our houses, conduct ourselves at weddings and funerals, in churches and in classrooms, in at least rough conformity to a set of unwritten laws, knowing that if we deviate too far from standard practice we shall be condemned as queer, or ill-mannered, or ignorant. The conventions of language are simply part of this whole body of convention which is woven into our lives.

Some of the conventions of language, like many social conventions, are relatively unimportant matters of form, the observance of which depends on circumstances: a conventional rule for the use of the comma, for example, may be comparable to the conventional rule of speaking to strangers only after a formal introduction; neither the comma nor the introduction may in all circumstances be necessary. Other conventions, both of manners and of language, have a greater practical usefulness because they establish procedures which it is convenient to have established. For example, good manners require a man to allow a woman to precede him through the door he has opened; having this practice established by convention is useful: it saves confusion and indecision at doors. Similarly, in language, certain uniform practices in capitalization, punctuation, and spelling are convenient for writers and readers: the writer is saved the trouble of working out his own system, and the reader is spared the greater trouble of adjusting to the personal eccentricities of each author. A writer may have good reason to take liberties with some of these conventional practices, just as a man may with good reason precede a woman through a door; but unless the reason is clear, he may appear to be discourteous and uninformed.

Still other conventions of manners and of language are so deeply rooted in custom or principle that one who violates them is certain to be judged ignorant or stupid or boorish or inexcusably careless by people trained in the conventions. The host who invites a guest to dinner and fails to provide a chair for him at the table violates a basic principle of hospitality; the writer who, through a comparable confusion of numbers, uses singular verbs with plural subjects violates a similarly basic principle of grammar. The person invited to eat the dinner or to read the book is justifiably annoyed; his impression of the host or of the writer is an unfavorable one.

Consideration of this unfavorable impression brings one to the heart of the relationship between conventions and meaning. Ordinarily, the failure to observe the conventions of language does not interfere seriously with the *plain sense* part of meaning. The person who talks with his mouth full of food usually can be understood; but his listeners are unlikely to be favorably impressed by what he is saying or to hope that he will continue his communication. In much the same way, though a reader may be temporarily confused by a lack of punctuation, by misplaced modifiers, or by faulty parallelism, he can usually grasp the *plain sense* of the passage in spite of these obstacles. He will, however, feel an irritated disrespect for the writer who makes his communication needlessly difficult, and will be offended by the writer's apparent *attitude* of discourtesy and disregard for his reader. Under these circumstances, the writer's *intention* will almost certainly be defeated: a reader is not easily persuaded or convinced by one with whom he is irritated, nor is he likely to trust the information of a writer who seems imprecise or incompetent.

In this chapter we shall consider the conventions of usage most important for college students to know.[1] Many of these conventions embody basic principles of grammar and construction; they must not be violated by a writer who expects the attention of educated readers. Other conventions discussed here are largely matters of accepted form; the writer who has a good sense of style and is working for a particular effect has some freedom in following or departing from them. The average college student, however, is unwise to take liberties with standard practice. He should remember that the conventional usage is safe, and that departures from it may produce an unfavorable response and a consequent loss of the full meaning he intended.

I. CAPITALIZATION

Our system of capitalization is an example of a practically useful convention; it saves trouble by establishing a uniform method of marking sentence beginnings and titles, and of distinguishing between common nouns and proper nouns and the adjectives derived from them. Capitalization is not completely standardized; capitals are sometimes used for emphasis or as a token of respect. Most capitalization is, however, conveniently prescribed by convention.

A capital is used as the initial letter of:

1. A sentence, and usually each line of poetry.

2. A sentence directly quoted within another sentence. (He said, "You are right.")

3. All proper nouns—proper nouns name particular persons, places, races, and things—and adjectives derived from proper nouns. (Mary, Germany, Wilson Avenue, Bunker Hill Monument, Indian, Negro, Wednesday, Good Friday, the Bell Telephone Company, Spanish, Dickensian, Parisian, Roman candle.)

4. Names of deity and pronouns referring to deity. (God, His will, the Holy Spirit.)

5. Names of sacred books or the equivalents of the names. (Bible, Koran, Old Testament, the Scripture.)

[1] Conventions of usage not discussed in this chapter can be found in the Handbook.

6. Important words in the titles of books and articles. (*Under the Greenwood Tree.*)

7. Titles of honor preceding a particular name. (Major Jackson, President Brown, Professor Smith, Senator Jones, Chairman Humphrey.)

8. Academic degrees and their abbreviations. (Doctor of Laws, Master of Arts, B.A., Ph.D.)

College students ordinarily have little trouble with capitalization. Their only common difficulty comes from failing to distinguish between words used to name a *particular* person, place, or thing (used, that is, as proper nouns), and the same words used in a general way, and therefore not conventionally capitalized. Some illustrations will clarify this distinction.

> I told the whole story to Mother. [*Mother* here takes the place of a proper name, and so is capitalized.]
> I told the whole story to my mother.

> He had an audience with the King. [*King* refers to a particular person.]
> He had seen enough of kings and queens. [The words *kings* and *queens* are used generally.]

> He went to Elliot High School and then to Oberlin College. [Names of particular institutions]
> Since he barely got through high school, he is sure to fail in college.

> I used to live on Quincy Street, but now I live on Ashland Boulevard. [Proper names]
> They are planning to make this street into a boulevard.

> He intends to vote for Mayor Dawson.
> Dawson hopes to be elected mayor.

> I am taking Mathematics 2 and History 2. [Names of particular courses]
> I am taking mathematics and history. [*But*] I am taking French and English. [Names derived from proper nouns]

> He comes from the South and does not like the Middle West. [Proper names of sections of the country]
> He lives two miles south of town.

II. CONVENTIONAL USES OF COMMAS

Students whose punctuation is uncertain should make a careful study of the section in the Handbook which describes (under the heading **Punctuation**) the common marks of punctuation and lists their conventional uses. We are concerned here only with the comma, the mark of punctuation most frequently used, and the one, therefore, responsible for most errors in punctuation marked in student themes. Nearly all these errors come, first, from an unsure, haphazard use of superfluous commas; and, second, from inattention to certain principles of clear communication embodied in three basic "rules" for the use of the comma:

1. Use a comma between independent clauses joined by *and, but, for, or,* or *nor.*

2. Use a comma to set off an adverbial clause or a long phrase preceding the main part of the sentence.

3. Use commas to set off nonrestrictive modifiers; do not use commas to set off restrictive modifiers.

Before we examine these rules, the reasons underlying them, and the liberties one may take with them, it is wise to consider the function of the comma as a mark of punctuation. The conventional rules are valuable as safe guides in determining its use; but good sense, based on an understanding of how punctuation works, may be even more valuable. The comma is a light mark of punctuation, lighter than the semicolon, much lighter than the period. It separates words within a sentence which, though very closely related, need, for clarity or emphasis, to be divided by a slight pause. The purpose of the comma is to indicate the slight pause. For this reason, commas should *not* be used to separate words which form an organic unit in the sentence; they should *not* separate a subject from its verb in a simple sentence, a verb from its object, an adjective from its noun, or a conjunction from the clause it introduces. The following examples illustrate a haphazard misuse of commas: the commas clutter the sentences, creating pauses where no pauses should occur; they interrupt the reading of the sentences.

Gay streamers and floating balloons, decorated the gymnasium.
The way to success, is often, a long and difficult road.
Mother said, she disapproved of the plan.
I refuse to go unless, you go with me.
The angry, members of the committee, protested loudly, but, the chairman was firm.

The organic and therefore proper use of commas can often, as in these sentences, be determined by reading the sentence aloud. Unless a comma is demanded by some well-established convention, it should be used only when a slight pause is natural, or is needed for clarity or emphasis.

Let us consider now the three rules for the use of the comma listed above. What are the reasons for them? Can they be violated?

1. *Use a comma between independent clauses joined by "and," "but," "for," "or," or "nor":*

He promised to be here at six, but I don't expect him until seven.

Some handbooks on writing state this rule without qualification. Actually, the comma between independent clauses is often omitted in informal writing, particularly if the clauses are not long. The comma after *six* is unnecessary in the sentence just cited; the sentence is perfectly clear without it. There is, however, a reason for this convention of using the comma between independent clauses joined by a conjunction: [2] frequently the subject of the second clause can momentarily be misread as the object of the first clause or the object of the preposition *for*. The following sentences will illustrate; commas are needed between clauses to prevent temporary misreading:

> I did not have time to buy the gift for Father hurried me away. [One naturally reads *gift for Father.*]
> I went to the railroad station to meet Mary and Frances went to the bus depot. [One reads *to meet Mary and Frances.*]
> I must call for the doctor said to let him know. [One reads *call for the doctor.*]

Because such temporary confusion can easily occur, many teachers insist that their students follow the rule and always use a comma between independent clauses joined by *and, but, for, or,* or *nor.* Certainly that conventional usage is safe. The student who takes liberties with it should be sure that he is not causing his reader the annoyance of stumbling over an unclearly punctuated sentence.

2. *Use a comma to set off an adverbial clause or a long phrase preceding the main part of the sentence:*

> Since I gave you my promise, I will be there.

Here, and in many other sentences of similar construction, the comma after the introductory clause or phrase is not really necessary. But it is generally advisable to follow this rule of punctuation, or at least to be aware of it, for two reasons: first, there is a natural pause for emphasis before a main clause which begins in the middle of a sentence, and the comma marks that emphatic pause; second, the omission of the comma, like the omission of the comma between main clauses, frequently produces misreading. Commas are confusingly omitted in the following sentences, even though some of the introductory clauses and phrases are short:

> While he was riding his horse lost a shoe.
> After all I had done my best to help him.
> By testing emotional reactions are determined.
> To one who is interested in farming land has beauty and character.

[2] Note the fact that the comma *precedes* the conjunction.

On the whole, it is easier to follow the convention of using the comma to set off the introductory clause or phrase than it is to examine each sentence to be sure that it is immediately clear. The use of the comma in this situation is never "wrong." The omission of it may be, because it may cause the reader to go back and to supply for himself the pause for clarity which should have been indicated by the writer.

3. *Use commas to set off nonrestrictive modifiers; do not use commas to set off restrictive modifiers:*

> Charles Smith, who is ten years old, should know better than to throw stones.
> People who live in glass houses shouldn't throw stones.

This conventional rule of punctuation is deeply rooted in common sense and logic. A restrictive modifier *identifies* or *restricts* the meaning of the word it modifies. It is not set off by commas because it is an essential part of the context and is necessary to fix or limit the meaning of the word:

> Students who are failing any course are requested to see the Dean. [*Who are failing any course* is a restrictive clause; it identifies the students requested to see the Dean.]

A nonrestrictive modifier merely gives *additional* information about an *already identified* subject. It is set off by commas because it is simply an appositive or a conveyor of fact which is supplementary, not essential, to the main point of the sentence:

> My oldest sister, who married a British sailor, is visiting us. [*Oldest* clearly identifies the sister; hence *who married a British sailor* is clearly a nonrestrictive modifier.]

Confusion or distortion of meaning may result from the illogical punctuation of restrictive and nonrestrictive modifiers. Consider the difference in meaning in the following sentences:

> All our money, which we had left on the beach, was taken by the thief.
> All our money which we had left on the beach was taken by the thief.
> [In the first sentence the loss is apparently more serious: all our money was taken. In the second sentence, only the money which we had left on the beach was taken. The writer who has had three dollars stolen while he was swimming is probably giving misinformation if he records his loss in the form of the first sentence.]
>
> The members of the football team, who ate at the hotel, have ptomaine poisoning.
> The members of the football team who ate at the hotel have ptomaine poisoning.

[The coach would be more distressed by the situation represented in the first sentence.]

The logical punctuation of restrictive and nonrestrictive modifiers can usually be determined by reading the sentence aloud. If the modifier is naturally set off with pauses when one reads, it should be set off by commas in the written sentence.

III. CONVENTIONAL PUNCTUATION OF SENTENCES

According to the broadest definition, a sentence is any locution spoken or punctuated as an independent unit of discourse. For practical purposes, however, the following more limited and more exact definition should be memorized and used: A sentence is an *independent assertion* which contains a *subject* and a *predicate*.[3] The conventional marks of the sentence are, of course, the capital letter at the beginning and the period at the end. A writer violates conventional practice if he uses these marks of a sentence to enclose a group of words which is not a sentence, or if he joins separate sentences with only a comma (or with no punctuation) between them. *Fragmentary sentences* and *run-together sentences* are the results of thoughtless violations of sentence conventions. They are generally considered very serious errors in writing.

A. Fragmentary Sentences

Any "sentence" which lacks a subject or a predicate or fails to make an independent assertion is, according to our definition, an incomplete sentence. Some incomplete sentences, as we shall see later, are entirely acceptable. They occur frequently in speech, particularly in conversation, and sometimes in writing. Acceptable incomplete sentences convey clearly and appropriately the meaning the communicator wishes to convey. A fragmentary sentence, on the other hand, is an unsatisfactory incomplete sentence; it is a subordinate part of a sentence confusingly written as a sentence (i.e., begun with a capital letter and followed by a period). It forces the reader, who has learned to expect the completion of an idea within the conventional signs of the sentence, to stop and mentally correct the writer's careless or ignorant punctuation. Sometimes a fragment needs simply to be attached to the preceding or following sentence, of which it

---

[3] Statements in the imperative mood (*Shut the door. Be ready at six.*) are classified as complete sentences even though the subject is not expressed. In such sentences the subject *you* is said to be understood. For a full discussion of the sentence see page 713.

may be a dependent part; sometimes it needs to be rewritten so that it becomes an independent statement.

UNSATISFACTORY: He arrived late. *Having been detained at the office.* [A participial phrase written as a sentence]
REVISED: Having been detained at the office, he arrived late.

UNSATISFACTORY: I enjoy realistic writers. *Like Erskine Caldwell and John O'Hara.* [A prepositional phrase written as a sentence]
REVISED: I enjoy realistic writers like Erskine Caldwell and John O'Hara.

UNSATISFACTORY: I am taking three sciences. *Biology and chemistry and geology.* [Appositives written as a sentence]
REVISED: I am taking three sciences: [or a dash] biology, chemistry, and geology.

UNSATISFACTORY: At three o'clock he was ready to leave. *When suddenly he saw her hurrying through the crowd.* [A dependent clause written as a sentence]
REVISED: At three o'clock he was ready to leave. Suddenly he saw her hurrying through the crowd.

Fragmentary sentences like those above are considered serious errors because they indicate incompetence. They suggest that the writer does not know the difference between a complete sentence and a part of a sentence. There are, however, as we have said, certain types of grammatically incomplete sentences which are common and acceptable, particularly in informal writing. Exclamations, questions, answers to questions, certain transitional expressions, and bits of dialogue, though they may lack a subject or a verb or may fail to make independent assertions, are often quite properly written as sentences:

What an examination!

Questions? Of course I had questions. What I needed was answers, and I sought those answers in my reading.

Is our policy the correct one? *Perhaps so.* We need, though, to be aware of certain obstacles.

To return now to the causes of this act of aggression. [A transitional phrase leading into a new paragraph]

"Going to the play tonight?"
"No. Have to study. Exam tomorrow."

Also, in modern narrative writing one sometimes finds an impressionistic setting down of detail in incomplete sentences:

It was a beautiful calm day. *Not a ripple on the water. Not a cloud in the sky.*

Deciding what can properly be punctuated as a sentence involves, then, like many other matters of English usage, the application of good judgment rather than rigid rules about what is and what is not an acceptable sentence. Since the careless or illiterate fragmentary sentence is so jarring to an educated reader, many English instructors require students to mark with an asterisk any incomplete sentences that they use, and to indicate in a note at the bottom of the page that the incomplete construction is intentional. Average students, whose sense of style is unsure, will be wise to avoid incomplete sentences except in exclamations and in the writing of dialogue.

B. Run-together Sentences

The error of using a comma or no punctuation at all between two independent clauses where a semicolon is required produces a run-together sentence. In order to recognize and to avoid run-together sentences, one must know what an independent clause is,[4] and how a sequence of two independent clauses is conventionally written and punctuated. Independent statements which are not felt to be closely joined in meaning cause no difficulty; they are, of course, punctuated as separate sentences. When two independent statements are felt to be closely related, the relationship may be expressed in the following ways:

1. The two independent clauses, even though closely related, may be written as separate sentences if the writer wants an emphatic break between them.

2. The two independent clauses may be written in a single sentence and joined by a pure conjunction.[5] For independent clauses so joined the general rule is to place a comma before the conjunction, but often the comma is not essential. (See the discussion of this use of the comma, pages 60–61.)

3. The two clauses may be placed in the same sentence without a pure conjunction to join them, in which case they are separated by a semicolon. Use of a comma or of no punctuation would produce a run-together sentence.

The following sentences illustrate these three conventional ways

---

[4] An independent clause is a group of words containing a subject and a predicate and capable of making an independent assertion.

[5] Pure conjunctions are easier to name than to define explicitly. The most common pure conjunctions are *and, but, for, or, nor. So, yet,* and *then* may sometimes be used as pure conjunctions (i.e. as pure connectives) but they may also be used as conjunctive adverbs. Conjunctive adverbs are preceded by a semicolon when they are used to join independent clauses in the same sentence. For a discussion of conjunctive adverbs see page 738.

of joining independent clauses which are felt to be closely related in meaning:

> I wanted to go to the movie. He wanted to stay at home. [Separate sentences are used to emphasize each of the two closely related ideas.]
>
> I wanted to go to the movie, and he wanted to stay at home. [Two closely related independent clauses are joined by a pure conjunction. Here the comma is conventional but not essential.]
>
> I wanted to go to the movie; he wanted to stay at home. [The two independent clauses are not joined by a pure conjunction. The semicolon is essential. A comma or no punctuation after *movie* would make this a run-together sentence.]

A general rule which will help students avoid run-together sentences is: Between two independent clauses in the same sentence *not* joined by *and, but, for, or,* or *nor,* use a semicolon. The following sentences, taken from student papers, violate this rule and are run-together sentences:

> I am taking five courses, three of them are interesting. [The comma before *three* should be a semicolon.]
>
> He was tired after his winter of work he decided to take a vacation. [There should be a semicolon or a period before *he*.]
>
> Chillingworth's chief joy was in making Dimmesdale suffer, therefore his life was empty when he could no longer torture Dimmesdale. [A comma is not a heavy enough mark of punctuation here; the two independent clauses are not joined by *and, but, for, or,* or *nor*.]

Although run-together sentences can sometimes be made satisfactory simply by putting a semicolon or a period between the independent clauses, often this change in punctuation is only a superficial technical improvement. For an effective sentence, the essentially weak structure needs to be revised:

> UNSATISFACTORY: I make many mistakes in writing, most of them are in spelling and punctuation.
> TECHNICALLY IMPROVED: I make many mistakes in writing; most of them are in spelling and punctuation.
> REVISED: I make many mistakes in writing, most of them in spelling and punctuation.
> UNSATISFACTORY: Next Tuesday is April 14, this is my sister's birthday.
> TECHNICALLY IMPROVED: Next Tuesday is April 14; this is my sister's birthday.
> REVISED: Next Tuesday, April 14, is my sister's birthday.

Careless run-together sentences are, like fragmentary sentences, considered one of the most serious errors in writing, and for much the same reasons: they suggest incompetence, and they are an annoyance to the reader; he is forced to make the separation of ideas which the writer should have made for him. And yet it is by no means correct to say dogmatically that independent clauses should never be joined merely by a comma. In modern narrative writing, one not infrequently finds closely related main clauses deliberately run together to give an effect of rapid movement or breathless action. The following informal passages, each written by a careful modern craftsman, will illustrate:

They strictly minded their business. Just the same, there would be a pair of eyes behind a newspaper that weren't on the newspaper, or maybe a waitress would stop by somebody, and say something, and there'd be a laugh just a little louder than a waitress's gag is generally worth. He sat there, with a kind of a foolish look on his face, snapping his fingernail against his glass, and then I felt a prickle go up my spine. He was getting up, he was coming over.—JAMES M. CAIN, *Serenade*

A few frogs lost their heads and floundered among the feet and got through and these were saved. But the majority decided to leave this pool forever, to find a new home in a new country where this kind of thing didn't happen. A wave of frantic, frustrated frogs, big ones, little ones, brown ones, green ones, men frogs and women frogs, a wave of them broke over the bank, crawled, leaped, scrambled. They clambered up the grass, they clutched at each other, little ones rode on big ones. And then—horror on horror—the flashlights found them.—JOHN STEINBECK, *Cannery Row*

The inexperienced writer should remember, however, that run-together sentences have no place in formal writing, and that they are still widely regarded as evidence of illiteracy even in informal writing. If the student wishes to use run-together sentences in informal, fast-moving narrative, he should probably, as with incomplete sentences, star the passage and indicate to his instructor in a footnote that his punctuation is deliberate. Most students should avoid this experimental punctuation.

IV. AGREEMENT OF SUBJECT AND VERB

The subject and verb of a sentence must agree in person and number. College students are not ignorant of this basic principle, but they sometimes slip into careless mistakes in grammar and logic when intervening words blur the subject-verb relationship. The following sentences are examples of careless nonagreement:

Each sentence of these essays *were* filled with both obvious and subtle meanings.

My *understanding* of many problems *have* been clarified.

The *teacher,* as well as the students, *were* exasperated with the schedule.
Economy of expression and coherence is characteristic of a good theme.
Neither Mary nor John *have* arrived.
My *list* of reasons *are* long.

Correct agreement is simply a matter of attention—of seeing clearly what the subject of the verb is.

Collective nouns (*crowd, audience, jury, congregation,* etc.) may present a choice between a singular and a plural verb. The singular verb is used when the group is considered a unit, the plural verb when members of the group are thought of separately:

A majority is needed before a vote can be taken.
The majority were on their feet before the vote was called for.

The committee is appointed by the president.
The committee were loud in their expressions of disapproval.

The number of errors accounts for the grade.
A number of students are leaving early.

V. REFERENCE OF PRONOUNS

Another basic principle of grammar is that a pronoun should refer clearly to its antecedent, and should agree with that antecedent in number, person, and gender. Writing becomes inexact and confusing when a pronoun may refer to more than one antecedent, when it is too far from its antecedent for clarity, or when it seems, because of its position, to refer to the wrong antecedent. Students who frequently make errors in reference of pronouns can eliminate such errors by asking themselves two questions: (1) Does the pronoun refer clearly and indisputably to its antecedent? (2) Does the pronoun agree with the antecedent in number, person, and gender? (See "Pronouns: Reference" page 755.)

The following sentences illustrate types of faulty reference:

My father is a doctor, and I want to study *it* too. [Inexact; no antecedent for *it* in the sentence]
Each student must bring *their* dictionaries to class. [Ungrammatical reference; change in number]
She refused to return the ring, *which* was what he wanted. [Ambiguous; does *which* refer to the ring or to her refusal to return it?]
John gave him five dollars when *he* was a freshman in college. [Unclear; is *he* John or the recipient of the five dollars?]
The furniture van had not arrived, the telephone was still disconnected, and there was no food in the house. The dog was sick, too. *This* was very depressing. [Vague; the whole situation, or the sickness of the dog?]

His book gives a detailed account of what went on in Germany before the war, and of the mobilization of the home front by Hitler. *He* was impressed with the passiveness of the German people. [Misleading; *he* seems to refer to Hitler rather than to the author of the book.]

Inexact thinking as well as inexact expression is often responsible for obscure or ambiguous reference. Frequently the only way to correct an error or weakness in reference is to rewrite the sentence or even the entire passage.

VI. SPELLING

Spelling is important because it is so often the first basis on which a writer is judged. Of all the conventions we are discussing in this chapter, conventional spelling is probably the clearest example of an established procedure to which one must conform not because the procedure is logical, and not because nonconformity destroys the plain sense of the communication (a word is seldom so badly misspelled as to be unrecognizable), but simply because many readers respond unfavorably, with irritation, disrespect, and mistrust, to the writer who cannot spell.

An occasional misspelling, particularly of an uncommon word, is not a serious error. Conspicuously poor spelling is serious, however, because it suggests that the writer is unfamiliar with printed material, or unable to learn what most educated people learn without great difficulty, or both. Such errors as confusing *there* and *their, too* and *to, its* and *it's, quite* and *quiet,* and misspelling words like *receive, believe, tries, beginning,* which are spelled according to established rules, create an impression of illiteracy. To many people, spelling is an index to the writer's education and intelligence. Actually it is not a reliable index; but the fact remains that one is judged by the way he spells.

The student who is genuinely a "bad speller" can improve enormously as soon as he realizes the importance of reasonably correct spelling, and as soon as he is willing to work to achieve it. He should, first, keep a list of words which he misspells, and practice writing and rewriting them until the correct spelling is fixed. Second, he should learn basic rules for spelling, and memorize at least one good list of words commonly misspelled. (See **Spelling,** in the Handbook, for spelling rules and a list of the words most commonly misspelled by college freshmen.) Third, in revising his papers he should look up in the dictionary any words about which he is at all uncertain; if he has misspelled a word in the first draft of his theme, he should write it correctly several times, absorbing its new appearance, erasing the old impression. And fourth, particularly if he omits syllables or letters in his misspellings, he should check his pronunciation. Faulty pronunciation is often the reason for misspelling: one who says "idear" for idea, "goverment" for government, "draw" for drawer, "quanity" for quantity, "athaletic" for athletic, "accidently" for accidentally, "wether" for whether, "libary" for library, "labratory" for laboratory, "Febuary" for February, "morden" for modern, will almost inevitably spell these words incorrectly.

Above all, the student whose spelling is weak should not take the attitude that poor spelling is an incurable affliction to which he should be stoically—or, even worse, cheerfully—resigned. If he is in earnest, he can become a competent speller.

VII. MODIFIERS

The nature of English grammar, the fact that we have a relatively uninflected language, requires that modifiers, for clarity, be close to the locution which they modify. A modifier is called *misplaced* when its position is such that it appears to modify the wrong word, and *dangling* when the word it should modify has been omitted.

At the age of ten, my grandfather gave me a gold watch. [Misplaced; seems to modify *my grandfather*.]

To work efficiently, the room must be warm enough. [Dangling; appears to say the room may work efficiently; the actual worker has been left out of the sentence.]

Running down the street, the house came into view.

She wore a chain around her neck *of hammered gold.*

I *almost* read all of my history assignment last night.

I heard his sad story *before dying.*

Sentences containing misplaced modifiers can usually be made satisfactory simply by changing the word order so that the modifier stands as close as possible to the word it modifies:

She wore a chain *of hammered gold* around her neck.

Sentences with dangling modifiers need to be recast so that the dangling modifier is changed to a subordinate clause containing the subject of the action:

As we ran down the street, the house came into view.

Or, the modifier may be kept and the rest of the sentence changed to include the word properly modified, in a position as close as possible to the modifier:

Running down the street, we saw the house.

Dangling and misplaced modifiers are usually merely absurd, as the above sentences demonstrate; they seldom distort the plain-sense meaning intended, but they do cast doubt on the good sense as well as the grammatical competence of the writer. Very occasionally they are misleading:

Being an only child, my mother gave me everything I wanted. [The sentence says the mother was an only child; probably another meaning is intended.]

Patrolling fifty miles to the north, the enemy has a secret air base. [If the writer means that he, not the enemy, was patrolling, he has given misinformation.]

Hopeless about her condition, the doctor cheered her by describing the new drug. [Is the doctor hopeless, as the sentence says?]

VIII. CONSISTENCY IN STRUCTURE AND STYLE

Consistency is harmony or congruity within a sentence, or between closely related sentences. More specifically, consistency means avoiding sudden, unnecessary shifts in subject; in voice, mood, or tense of verbs; in style; or in levels of usage.[6] Such undesirable shifts force the reader to adjust, often in mid-sentence, to an unnecessary change from past to present tense, from indicative to imperative mood, from impersonal to personal style, from formal to vulgate English. The shifts are rarely confusing, as far as plain sense is concerned, but they are distracting and awkward, and, like dangling modifiers, they cause the reader to question the writer's competence.

The following sentences show inconsistencies of the sort which may easily occur in hasty writing. They should be removed in revision.

INCONSISTENT: You fill the tube with air; next the tube is put in the casing. [Active to passive; shift in subject]

REVISED: You fill the tube with air; next you put the tube in the casing.

INCONSISTENT: He left for the office as soon as his breakfast had been eaten. [Active to conspicuously weak passive]

REVISED: He left for the office as soon as he had eaten his breakfast.

INCONSISTENT: When the mother died, the men in Roaring Camp decide to care for the baby. [Shift in tense]

REVISED: When the mother died, the men in Roaring Camp decided to care for the baby.

[6] Levels of usage are discussed fully in Chapter Four. Briefly, they are: formal English (the English used by educated people on formal occasions), informal English (the English used by educated people in familiar or informal speech and writing), and vulgate English (the English used by people of little or no education).

INCONSISTENT: If you are diligent you will do well. One must remember that college is primarily for study. [Personal to impersonal]
REVISED: If you are diligent you will do well. You must remember that college is primarily for study.

INCONSISTENT: Mrs. Grantham sought revenge by fouling up her rival's debut. [Shift in level]
REVISED: Mrs. Grantham sought revenge by ruining her rival's debut.

INCONSISTENT: First sandpaper the surface carefully; then the varnish should be put on. [Imperative to indicative; active to passive]
REVISED: First sandpaper the surface carefully; then put the varnish on.

Since many inconsistencies are unnecessary shifts from active to passive voice, it is appropriate here to say a word about the weakness, in general, of passive verbs. It is sometimes necessary to use passive verbs, but, as their name suggests, they are less emphatic than active verbs. They are likely, too, to produce involved, wordily indirect, or vague sentences:

POOR: A good movie was seen last night by Jack and me. [Involved and indirect]
IMPROVED: Jack and I saw a good movie last night.

POOR: The grating of wheels on the driveway was heard. [Vague; uninformative. Heard by whom?]
IMPROVED: I heard the grating of wheels on the driveway. [Or] The wheels grated on the driveway.

One should avoid the passive voice, then, not only when using it would cause inconsistency, but also when a passive statement would be more involved and less effective than an active statement.

IX. SUBORDINATION

Subordination may be defined as expressing in dependent clauses, or phrases, or single words, ideas which are not significant enough to be expressed in a main clause or an independent sentence. Children, as everyone knows, express themselves in a sentence structure which gives equal weight to all ideas, and does not establish an exact relationship between those ideas: "We went into town on the streetcar, and there were a lot of people, and Daddy asked me if I wanted a balloon, and I said yes, and so he bought me one." Or, perhaps: "I have a cat. The cat is yellow. Jimmie has a dog. His dog is big. It is brown. I like cats better." Adults, the educated reader assumes, will see more clearly the connections between their ideas, and will not need to communicate them in sprawling "and-and" sentences, or in choppy "primer" sentences. When adults write like children, their communications naturally do not hold the interest of the mature reader.

By means of subordination, mature writers achieve emphasis, economy, and clarity in writing: emphasis because the important idea is expressed in a main clause, and less important ideas are subordinated to it; economy, because whole sentences can often be reduced to single words; and clarity, because subordination and subordinating conjunctions work together to show exact relationships between unequal parts of the sentence. Subordination is, then, an element of style, not simply a matter of convention. In later chapters we shall discuss subordination as a tool of effective, emphatic expression. At present we are concerned chiefly with the basic principles of subordination, and with the failures in communication produced by failures to subordinate intelligently. The degree of subordination a writer uses is determined by context, or by the total effect he wants his writing to produce. It is possible to oversubordinate—to pile too many ideas into dependent clauses or phrases in a single sentence. More common in student writing, though, is undersubordination— giving too much emphasis to minor ideas which do not deserve that emphasis.

The following passages illustrate the process of subordination and some of the principles of skillful subordination:

LACK OF SUBORDINATION: The house was white. It stood on a hill. The hill was north of town. [Choppy "primer" sentences; three ideas are given equal weight in separate short sentences.]

SUBORDINATION: The white house stood on the hill north of town. [The two less important sentences are reduced to a word and a phrase.]

LACK OF SUBORDINATION: He came at eight o'clock, and Helen was sitting by the fireplace, and she was gazing moodily at the burning coals. [Sprawling "and-and" sentence; again three ideas are given equal emphasis.]

METHODS OF SUBORDINATION: (The method chosen will depend on the idea the writer wishes to emphasize; the most important idea will, of course, be in the main clause.) When he came at eight o'clock, *Helen was sitting by the fireplace,* gazing moodily at the burning coals. At eight o'clock *he found Helen* gazing moodily at the burning coals as she sat by the fireplace. Sitting by the fireplace, *Helen was moodily gazing* at the burning coals when he came at eight o'clock. At eight o'clock, when Helen was sitting by the fireplace, moodily gazing at the burning coals, *he came.*

LACK OF SUBORDINATION: He went away. I have been unhappy.

SUBORDINATION FOR CLOSER AND CLEARER RELATIONSHIP: I have been unhappy since he went away.

LACK OF SUBORDINATION: I was afraid to see him and I didn't go to the party.

SUBORDINATION: Because I was afraid to see him, I didn't go to the party.

LACK OF SUBORDINATION: I received the notice and I went to the Dean's office.

SUBORDINATION: As soon as I received the notice I went to the Dean's office.

LACK OF SUBORDINATION: My parents wanted me to study but I wasn't interested in studying. I enjoyed going around with the crowd too much. My high-school marks were not very good. Now I have come to college and I intend to work harder. I want to get better grades. [Here the writer appears incapable of thinking through the relationship between ideas which are obviously related and are not of the equal importance he gives them in his immature sentences.]

SUBORDINATION AND CONDENSATION: Although my parents wanted me to study, I was more interested in going around with the crowd; as a result, my marks in high school were not very good. In college I intend to work harder and to get better grades.

The elementary failure in subordination, as these passages demonstrate, is a complete lack of subordination—the writing of "primer" sentences, or loose "and-and" sentences, in which the sentence structure gives equal weight to unequal ideas, fails to establish the exact relationship between those ideas, and creates the impression that the writer is not able to think through a complex idea.

A second, more subtle, failure in subordination occurs when the major idea, which should be given emphasis by being put in a main clause, is ineffectively expressed in a subordinate clause. The following sentences illustrate this "upside-down subordination":

POOR: I read in today's New York *Times* about a position with your company for which I am applying.

MORE EFFECTIVE: I am applying for the position with your company which I read about in today's New York *Times*.

POOR: When he suddenly picked up a rock and threw it at me, I was talking to him.

MORE EFFECTIVE: While I was talking to him, he suddenly picked up a rock and threw it at me.

Failure in subordination is a mark of immature writing and immature thinking. Since it indicates that the writer has not been able to see the relationship between the parts of a complex idea, and to grasp the relative value of those parts, lack of subordination or faulty subordination provokes irritation and skepticism in a thoughtful reader. Skillful subordination, on the other hand, clarifies and emphasizes important ideas, and gives the reader the impression of an able mind at work.

X. PARALLELISM

When elements in a sentence have the same function or the same relationship within the sentence, they are conventionally, and logically, expressed in the same grammatical form. The parallel form serves to bind together these equal or similar parts of the sentence, and to show clearly that they have a similar relationship to the whole:

I like | | | to swim,
to dance, and
to play cards.

[*Or*]

I like | | swimming,
dancing, and
playing cards.

[*Not*]

I like | | swimming,
to dance, and
play cards.

When the parallel locutions are similar in length and rhythm as well as in grammatical construction, they are said to be *balanced*. The following passages are examples of parallelism and balance:

To err is *human, to forgive divine.*—ALEXANDER POPE, *Essay on Criticism*

But, in a larger sense, *we cannot dedicate, we cannot consecrate, we cannot hallow,* this ground. The brave men, *living and dead,* who struggled here, have consecrated it, far above our poor power to *add* or *detract.* The world *will little note nor long remember what we say here;* but it *can never forget what they did here.*—ABRAHAM LINCOLN, *Gettysburg Address*

Those whose lives are fruitful *to themselves, to their friends* or *to the world* are *inspired by hope* and *sustained by joy:* they see in imagination *the things that might be* and *the way in which they are to be brought into existence.*—BERTRAND RUSSELL, *Proposed Roads to Freedom*

Faulty parallelism occurs when the same grammatical form is not used for logically parallel locutions, or when locutions which are not logically parallel are put into parallel constructions. The following sentences illustrate deviations from the principle of parallelism:

FAULTY: The student was told to report to the registrar and that his bill should be paid at once. [He was told two things; they should be expressed in the same construction.]

REVISED: The student was told to report to the registrar and to pay his bill at once.

FAULTY: He was tall, handsome, and working hard to earn money for his tuition. [The ideas are not logically parallel, and should not be thrown into the same construction.]
REVISED: He was a tall, handsome boy who was working hard to earn money for his tuition.

FAULTY: His work was writing letters and to answer the telephone.
REVISED: His work was writing letters and answering the telephone.

FAULTY: From college he hoped to gain a knowledge of physics, valuable connections, and how to get along with people.
REVISED: From college he hoped to gain a knowledge of physics, valuable connections, and an ability to get along with people.

In the faulty sentences above, the meaning is clear; the revisions simply improve the form without affecting the sense. Often, though, in more complex passages, faulty parallelism may throw the reader into hopeless confusion. To return to our analogy of language and manners, let us suppose that a man introduces three women to his hostess, by saying, "This is Dorothy, and this is my sister Mildred, and this is Mrs. Watkins." If all three women are his sisters, he has, by his nonparallel expression, failed seriously to clarify their relationship to him and to one another. In much the same way, faulty parallelism in a complicated sentence may seriously confuse the reader about the relationship of ideas, and therefore about the meaning of the sentence.

The following passages show how parallelism, well used, is a means of packing a number of closely related ideas and details into a single sentence, and keeping their relationship perfectly clear by means of the parallel forms. The first, from a modern novel, is a picture of the color and sound and sensation of an autumn day; the second, from a nineteenth-century essay, is an explanation of the aims of education. As you read the passages, consider how difficult it would be to follow the writers' ideas through their long sentences without the help of the parallel structures; note, too, the rhythm and power, as well as the complex clarity, produced by skillful parallelism.

Around them, above them, below them—from the living and shining air of autumn, from the embrowned autumnal earth, from the great shapes of the hills behind them with their molten mass of color—dull browns, rich bitter reds, dark bronze, and mellow yellow—from the raw crude clay of the piedmont earth and the great brown stubble of the cotton fields—from a thousand impalpable and unutterable things, there came this glorious breath of triumph and delight. It was late October, there was a smell of smoke upon the air, an odor of burning leaves, the barking of a dog, a misty red, a pollenated gold in the rich, fading, sorrowful, and exultant light of the day,—and far off, a sound of great wheels pounding on a rail, the wailing whistle, and the tolling bell of a departing train.—THOMAS WOLFE, *Of Time and the River*

But a University training is the great ordinary means to a great but ordinary end; it aims at raising the intellectual tone of society, at cultivating the public mind, at purifying the national taste, at supplying true principles to popular enthusiasm and fixed aims to popular aspiration, at giving enlargement and sobriety to the ideas of the age, at facilitating the exercise of political power, and refining the intercourse of private life. It is the education which gives a man a clear conscious view of his own opinions and judgments, a truth in developing them, an eloquence in expressing them, and a force in urging them. It teaches him to see things as they are, to go right to the point, to disentangle a skein of thought, to detect what is sophistical, and to discard what is irrelevant. It prepares him to fill any post with credit, and to master any subject with facility. It shows him how to accommodate himself to others, how to throw himself into their state of mind, how to bring before them his own, how to influence them, how to come to an understanding with them, how to bear with them. He is at home in any society, he has common ground with every class; he knows when to speak and when to be silent; he is able to converse, he is able to listen; he can ask a question pertinently, and gain a lesson seasonably, when he has nothing to impart himself; he is ever ready, yet never in the way; he is a pleasant companion, and a comrade you can depend upon; he knows when to be serious and when to trifle, and he has a sure tact which enables him to trifle with gracefulness and to be serious with effect. He has the repose of mind which lives in itself, while it lives in the world, and which has resources for its happiness at home when it cannot go abroad. He has a gift which serves him in public, and supports him in retirement, without which good fortune is but vulgar, and with which failure and disappointment have a charm. The art which tends to make a man all this, is in the object which it pursues as useful as the art of wealth or the art of health, though it is less susceptible of method, and less tangible, less certain, less complete in its result.—JOHN HENRY NEWMAN, *The Idea of a University*

A thorough understanding of the conventions of usage discussed in this chapter is essential for successful communication. Nonstandard capitalization, the confusing use or omission of commas, sentence fragments, careless run-together sentences, nonagreement of subject and verb, unclear reference of pronouns, poor spelling, dangling and misplaced modifiers, inconsistencies, failures in subordination, faulty parallelism—these are, to the educated reader, signs of the writer's deficiency in judgment or in knowledge.

Understanding the conventions and scrutinizing one's writing to be sure that no careless violations have crept in will not, in itself, produce positively successful writing. It will, however, free the writer from awkward and misleading expression, and from the adverse criticism of his readers. When he has mastered the conventions, he is in the position of a person who, attending a social function, need not worry about the way to eat his cake, the proper formula for an introduction, or the appropriateness of his clothes. Free from the danger of making mistakes which would cause people to disrespect him, he is ready to concentrate on really effective communication.

CHAPTER REVIEW

Undesirable violations of the conventions discussed in this chapter are marked in student themes, with the nature of the fault indicated by a marginal word or symbol. These are the symbols which many instructors use:

Cap	Unconventional capitalization
Comma	Misuse or omission of a comma
P	Faulty punctuation
Rest	Mispunctuation of a restrictive or nonrestrictive modifier
Frag	Fragmentary sentence
Run	Careless run-together sentence
Agr	Nonagreement of subject and verb
Ref	Faulty reference of pronouns
Sp	Error in spelling
Mod	Dangling or misplaced modifier
Shift	Inconsistency in structure or style
Sub	Lack of subordination or poor subordination
Par, or ‖	Faulty parallelism

If your reading of the chapter has been adequate, you should be able to explain and to illustrate each of the faults listed above, and also to answer the following questions:

1. Which of the conventions discussed in this chapter can never be violated?

2. With which ones may a writer take liberties? Under what circumstances?

3. Which of the violations listed above are likely to interfere most seriously with the reader's grasp of the plain sense of the passage?

4. Which ones will obscure the plain sense very little, if at all, but may, nevertheless, cause the reader to feel irritation or contempt for the writer?

EXERCISES [7]

I. Most of the following passages are poorly punctuated, although in some of them the punctuation is a matter of judgment. Correct or revise all sentences in which commas are confusingly omitted or misused, and all unsatisfactory fragmentary and run-together sentences.

1. The play lasted for three hours, however the audience liked it.
2. I hope to be elected to Phi Beta Kappa, Chiefly to please my parents.
3. Jane is a good friend when she makes a promise she always keeps it.
4. I have swallowed too much salt water and sand is in my hair. A miserable day.
5. Members of the Medical Corps were always busy. Caring for the wounded, driving ambulances, examining flyers, and doing many other important tasks.
6. Our house is small for entertaining therefore we must limit the party. To twelve or fourteen people.
7. I waited forty minutes for Betty is always late.
8. The Dean took no action, indeed there was no action he could take.
9. As I expected the invitation came this morning.
10. Some columnists should be jailed for libel. Charles B. Muddle, for example.
11. I spend most of my time studying. Being the studious type.
12. He was happily married, he enjoyed his work, he had high hopes for the future. Then the sudden disaster.
13. Children, who are public nuisances, should be kept at home.
14. Though reading the material several times, still not comprehending it as well as I should.
15. Some people may consider him competent, I do not agree.

II. Revise the sentences below to eliminate errors in agreement, faulty reference of pronouns, and dangling or misplaced modifiers. (Not all the sentences need revision.)

1. Never beat a dog with your hand. Use a newspaper. This will make him afraid of you.
2. Walking along the road, the sun came up over my right shoulder.
3. As the woman and her daughter watched the oncoming car, she gave a terrified cry.
4. Using the boy's idiom and characteristic speech give the story its atmosphere.
5. The days are long when doing unpleasant work.
6. To be productive, you should set out tomato plants before the first of June.

[7] Further exercises on the conventions of punctuation and grammatical usage will be found in the Handbook.

7. This collection of essays have been carefully chosen.

8. I received the message just as I was ready to leave, thus ruining my plans.

9. If you think that John needs money, you should do it in a diplomatic way.

10. Driving furiously down the street, he barely missed the group of children playing near the curb.

11. Since puppyhood I had not seen my sister's dog, but she greeted me enthusiastically.

12. At the time of the explosion the girl said she was in the outer office.

13. She was angry when he tried to give her advice, which was very interesting.

14. Falling over the goal line, the touchdown was made.

15. The sun greeted me as I came out of the house with a golden glow.

16. Neither he nor his partner are entirely blameless.

17. The boy asked his father to take his temperature.

18. The housemother found the girls who had disobeyed rules in the vestibule with their dates.

19. My uncle is in dentistry, and I plan to be one too.

20. He carried the kitten in his car that was only three weeks old.

III. Revise any of the passages below which need revision, improving parallelism and subordination, and eliminating inconsistencies.

1. This book is interesting, lively, and also an informative piece of writing.

2. By nine o'clock the book was read, the cat was put out, and he had gone to bed.

3. Jane was alone in the house. The wind banged a shutter and she was frightened.

4. We never tired of exploring the old house; happy hours were spent there.

5. Friendships I will make here and how to be tolerant of others will be valuable all my life.

6. After his history assignment had been prepared, he went to a movie.

7. He told her she was selfish, demanding, and to leave him alone.

8. My employer is a kind man; he often lets you go home early.

9. If your work improves, so will your marks. One should realize that most teachers are fair.

10. Shelley expresses movingly the feeling of beauty, but when you get down to the idea, he doesn't put it across very well.

11. I was waiting for the bus. I was going to Chicago. I started a conversation with a girl who was in the station too.

12. She said he was old and a poor dancer and didn't want to see him.

13. Because he was a scholar, deeply learned in ancient civilization, I thought that when he talked about the Greeks he would know his stuff.

14. The more you know about language, the more convinced one becomes of the importance of context.

15. Tom took his seat in the classroom, looked at the examination, and,
with a reproachful glance at the professor, begins to write.

16. Tom received the examination paper, looked at it hopefully, sighed
audibly, and walked disconsolately away.

17. The driver puts the car in neutral and pushes the starter. Turn on
the ignition first.

18. Being too early, even if it wastes valuable time, is better than to get
there late.

19. The Taft-Hartley bill is highly controversial: labor groups have denounced it; employers have defended it; and it has been passed by Congress
over the President's veto.

20. My first date was with a medical student. He was in his second year
at medical school. He was tall. He was handsome. He was the one all the
girls in the dormitory wanted to meet. He was supposed to come at nine
o'clock and he was late. He came at nine-thirty. I met him at the door. I
was afraid he hadn't wanted to come at all and that was the reason he was
a half hour late. I was very nervous. I wanted to make a good impression.

IV. All the following passages, taken from freshman themes,
contain errors or violations of conventional usage. Give the exact
name, whenever you can, of the fault or faults in each passage, and
indicate how the passage could be made satisfactory.

1. As an inexperienced writer I tend to expend too much energy and
flow of speech upon the first few points and then telescoping the rest as
the task begins to wear upon me.

2. After complying with all the rules I have fulfilled my obligation in
writing this theme except for one thing that is, that this theme should be
five hundred words it will be found that I am lacking approximately one
hundred words, but quality not quantity is asked for.

3. A great deal depends upon the commander in charge of a division
to be able to read quickly with full understanding a message from his
superiors, since the lives of thousands of men might hang in the balance
of this commander's quick wit in reading knowledge.

4. I learned long ago that such forms of oral work teaches more than
any other method.

5. The people I did write these letters to were my friends with whom
I had much in common and know me as I am.

6. Because my reading capacity is so limited, I am resigned to make such
a deficiency my excuse, although being inexcusable.

7. The derivation of these facts are most extraordinary.

8. I hope to hear from you soon, I remain respectively yours.

9. In reply to your advertisement for an assistant to one of your account
executives in the Sunday Transcript, I would like to submit my qualifications.

10. I have worked in the administrative offices of the Edison Power company for two years; thus, I believe, giving me a reasonable background for personnel work.

11. We who recognize the word leprosy have come across it at some time or other in our reading and know that it is a horrible sort of skin disease.

12. Leprosy is mentioned quite often in the bible where it was regarded in the biblical stories as a manifestation of evil and outcasts made of those persons suspected of having contracted the disease.

13. He made the seemingly insignificant discovery that when a beam of white light, passing through a prism, it is broken down into varied bands of color.

14. In making up an advertisement, one must be skillful, have a complete knowledge of the product, well trained and experienced.

15. The twenties were a time of prosperity and prohibition made it a daring epoch.

16. As a boy Franklin had always longed to go to sea and many a day was spent by his sitting on the shore and watching the ships go in and out.

17. The most important discovery was Irving's grave, a lieutenant under Franklin.

18. He was admitted to knighthood by a formal ceremony, dressed in the hauberk and donned the helmet.

19. He knew he had to pay the coal bill which he remembered the correct amount.

20. He admired her courage above all the rest of her good qualities seeming secondary to this one.

V. Supply the punctuation marks and capital letters needed in the following passage. If you are uncertain about the use of any mark of punctuation, or about the position of quotation marks used with other marks, consult the section on punctuation in the Handbook.

he walked restlessly to the window stared for the twentieth time at the deserted bus stop in front of the high school then turned to look at the clock again it was nearly six she had called an hour and ten minutes ago

darling she had said ill be home early just as soon as i can get a bus and i have the most marvelous news

what is it he had asked

its a surprise you be guessing and ill see you soon oh i almost forgot what i called for will you put some potatoes in the oven we have to eat early you know because we have to leave for the waldens party about seven

an hour and ten minutes ago now it was six oclock the potatoes were done he had taken them out of the oven wondering helplessly if you could rewarm a baked potato

a bus ground to a stop across the street and he rushed to the window again a woman loaded with bundles got off then two small boys and an old man with a cane the bus pulled away there wouldnt be another one for at least ten minutes theres no point in worrying he thought she probably stopped to do some shopping she said she was coming right home but she probably remembered that she hadnt bought any food for dinner he went to the kitchen to see

the potatoes which he had put on the side of the stove were getting cold opening the door of the frigidaire he checked over the supplies everything was there lamb chops frozen peas lettuce tomatoes and margarine the can of maxwell house coffee was full and there was a half loaf of swedish rye bread in the bread box he knew that she couldnt be shopping theres no point in worrying though he told himself again

back in the living room he picked up the penguin book portrait of jennie that he had bought in the station on the way home sat down in the chair opposite the clock and stared at the first page he could see molly coming out of her office building hurrying to get home to tell him her good news maybe it was a raise maybe an extra weeks vacation she hurried across the street not watching not seeing the third avenue bus bearing down on her there was a screech of brakes a womans high scream a crowd gathered he could see their horrified faces he could see the blood spattering the blue dress she had worn this morning

he jumped to his feet the clock which was if anything slow said six fifteen he would call the police he would

suddenly he heard her running up the stairs and he jerked open the door

oh john she said breathlessly i got a ride home with janet but she had a few errands to do and it took forever were you worried

of course i wasnt worried he shouted but this is a fine way to treat your husband the potatoes are stone cold

VI. The following passage is a corruption of a paragraph from an essay by Stuart Chase. The original sentences have been cut into monotonous, choppy sentences which give equal stress to important and unimportant ideas. Revise and combine the sentences, subordinating the less important ideas, and adding transitional words when they are needed for clarity.

There are ten million factory employees in America today. There are two million in the building trades. There are two hundred thousand engineers. Few of them can take pride in what they make. How many of them can hold up their hands and say that they take pride in it? Many of them are operating specialized processes. They don't know what they are helping to produce. The majority are probably still aware of it. The show of hands is not impressive. Consider the weighted silks. Consider the bulk of the patent-medicine traffic. Consider the jerry-built bungalows. I have talked to the carpenters working on them. Consider shoes that dissolve into their essential paper. Consider rickety furniture. It is brave in varnish. Consider commodity after commodity. Consider process after process. One will see why the show of hands is not impressive. The reason is sufficiently clear.

Chapter Four

Exercising Intelligent Choice

WE HAVE SEEN, in Chapter Three, that some of the techniques for using English well are determined by convention. One cannot, for example, spell words phonetically or impressionistically with no regard for the dictionary spelling, or violate established forms of English grammar and sentence structure, or take liberties with some of the accepted uses of punctuation marks, without incurring the disapproval of academically and socially educated people who expect other educated people to know and conform to these basic conventions. The intelligent user of English, therefore, must know the conventions. He may take liberties with some of them; but before he does, he should consciously weigh the positive gain in violating accepted usage against the probable displeasure of receivers who have definite standards in mind.

Many important uses of English, however, do not involve established conventions, but are matters of choice and judgment. The communicator needs to choose, among a number of possible, and equally correct, ways of expressing an idea, the way best suited to the circumstances and to his intention. He needs to select not simply an acceptable word, but the word exactly right in its connotation—that is, in its suggestion, its emotional charge as well as its referential meaning—for the purpose of his communication. He needs to use, not simply a correctly constructed sentence, but the sentence which, by its phrasing and emphasis, will drive its idea into the receiver's mind. His ability to choose wisely will depend first, of course, on his awareness of alternatives.

The ignorant speaker or writer uses the first expression that occurs to him because he is not aware of alternatives. The lazy speaker or writer accepts the first phrasing of his idea because thinking of other possible expressions of the idea would involve undesired effort. The intelligent speaker or writer considers the alternatives and exercises intelligent choice. In time, he develops habits and patterns of judgment; his choice, in some matters, becomes automatic.

In this chapter we shall consider three of the many aspects of English which involve choice. The intelligent communicator will choose an appropriate level of usage; he will choose words suited to the time and place; and he will, for clear and exact communication, choose concrete rather than abstract expressions.

I. THE APPROPRIATE LEVEL OF USAGE

During the past twenty years, students of language, observing and describing current English, have been pointing out that different degrees of education and different social situations produce different levels of English usage, that is, differences in construction, pronunciation, and vocabulary. The purpose of these studies of language is not to establish any level as "good English" or any as "bad English," but to establish the fact that the different levels exist, and that their existence should be recognized in a realistic approach to the study or teaching of current English. Three main levels of usage are the result of differences in education and social status. We shall call these levels formal English, informal English, and vulgate [1] English.

The lines between the levels of usage are not distinct: thousands of words, as well as the conventional sentence structure of English, are common to all three, and many sentences could be properly classified either as formal or as informal English. Furthermore, the levels are not static: since good usage at a particular time is determined by the practice of educated people of that time, expressions once considered vulgate have, through general usage by educated people, been accepted as part of informal English; and numerous expressions once in good standing are now regarded as vulgarisms because they are no longer used by educated people. The levels, then, are not settled and not mutually exclusive; but, in spite of their shifting and overlapping, it is possible to point out certain characteristics of vocabulary and construction which distinguish these three kinds of usage.

[1] This level of usage is variously called "vulgar" English, "illiterate" English, "popular" English, and "vulgate" English. The word *vulgar,* because of the way it is commonly used, is likely to give a wrong impression of this level of language; *illiterate,* since one of its meanings is "unable to read and write," may be misleading; and *popular* may make this use of uncultivated English seem more desirable than it actually is. We have, therefore, chosen the term *vulgate,* first popularized by H. L. Mencken in *The American Language.*

A. Formal English

Formal English is the English, more often written than spoken, used by highly educated people addressing an audience of their peers. One finds examples of formal English in scholarly articles and theses, in formal lectures to specialized audiences, in technical and scientific writing, in many textbooks, in most sermons, and in some essays, novels, and poetry intended for well-educated and cultivated readers. Characteristic of formal English are long sentences, often in parallel and balanced construction, often with modifiers interrupting the normal sentence order; periodic sentences—sentences with the meaning suspended until the end; triads—three parallel phrases or clauses; and allusions—brief references—to literature or history which only a well-educated audience would understand. Formal English is likely to be impersonal rather than personal in its style; the writer usually is concerned with communicating his subject rather than his feeling toward it. Contractions (*can't, won't, shouldn't,* etc.) are avoided in formal usage. An important characteristic of formal English is a wide and exact vocabulary, frequently specialized or technical.

Some examples will clarify these generalizations. The following passage of formal English was written by a twentieth-century historian:

To have faith in the dignity and worth of the individual man as an end in himself, to believe that it is better to be governed by persuasion than by coercion, to believe that fraternal good will is more worthy than a selfish and contentious spirit, to believe that in the long run all values are inseparable from the love of truth and the disinterested search for it, to believe that knowledge and the power it confers should be used to promote the welfare and happiness of all men rather than to serve the interests of those individuals and classes whom fortune and intelligence endow with temporary advantage—these are the values which are affirmed by the traditional democratic ideology. . . . The case for democracy is that it accepts the rational and humane values as ends, and proposes as the means of realizing them the minimum of coercion and the maximum of voluntary assent. We may well abandon the cosmological temple in which the democratic ideology originally enshrined these values without renouncing the faith it was designed to celebrate. The essence of that faith is belief in the capacity of man, as a rational and humane creature, to achieve the good life by rational and humane means. The chief virtue of democracy, and the sole reason for cherishing it, is that with all its faults it still provides the most favorable conditions for achieving that end by those means.—CARL L. BECKER, *New Liberties for Old*

This passage, with its formal vocabulary and sentence structure, illustrates many of the traits of formal English. The most conspicuously formal construction is the periodic first sentence; the main idea, suspended until the end, is preceded by five parallel phrases: *To have faith . . . to believe . . . to believe . . . to believe . . . to believe . . . these are the values. . . .* Conspicuously formal words are *coercion, contentious, ideology, cosmological, enshrined.*

Another example of formal English, the conclusion of Henry Adams' *Mont-Saint-Michel and Chartres,* also begins with a periodic sentence, and employs a consistently formal and exact vocabulary which is appropriate to the discussion of the significance of the Gothic cathedral:

Of all the elaborate symbolism which has been suggested for the Gothic cathedral, the most vital and most perfect may be that the slender nervure, the springing motion of the broken arch, the leap downwards of the flying buttress,—the visible effort to throw off a visible strain,—never let us forget that Faith alone supports it, and that, if Faith fails, Heaven is lost. The equilibrium is visibly delicate beyond the line of safety; danger lurks in every stone. The peril of the heavy tower, of the restless vault, of the vagrant buttress; the uncertainty of logic, the inequalities of the syllogism, the irregularities of the mental mirror,—all these haunting nightmares of the Church are expressed as strongly by the Gothic cathedral as though it had been the cry of human suffering, and as no emotion had ever been expressed before or is likely to find expression again. The delight of its aspiration is flung up to the sky. The pathos of its self-distrust and anguish of doubt is buried in the earth as its last secret. You can read out of it whatever else pleases your youth and confidence; to me, this is all.—HENRY ADAMS, *Mont-Saint-Michel and Chartres*

In this passage, *nervure, vagrant,* and *syllogism* are probably the most conspicuously formal words. The formality of the writing lies, however, less in particular words than in the general level of language and the structure of sentences. The passage contains, in addition to the periodic sentence already noted, a number of balanced sentences, and some good examples of the triads, or triple constructions, which occur frequently in formal English: "The peril *of the heavy tower, of the restless vault, of the vagrant buttress; the uncertainty of logic, the inequalities of the syllogism, the irregularities of the mental mirror, . . .*"

The following paragraph, written by a contemporary philosopher, is another example of formal English. It is less formal in vocabulary and sentence structure than the two passages just quoted. The reader should note, though, the exact vocabulary, the balanced sentences, and the numerous triads.

But if men forget that the future will some day be a present, they forget, too, that the present is already here, and that even in a dark time some of the brightness for which they long is open to the responsive senses, the welcoming heart, and the liberated mind. The moments as they pass even now have their tang and character. They may yield even now the contagious joy of feeling and perception. Here are the familiar flowers, the music we love, the poetry by which we are moved. Here are the books and companions, the ideas and the relaxations, the gaieties and the co-operative tasks of our familiar world. These things may be threatened, they may be precarious, they may be ours only by the grace of God, or of geographical or economic accident. But undeniably, beckoningly, along with the portents and alarms, here they are. Here, in all tragic times, they always have been, affording challenge and delight to the senses, solace and nourishment for the affections, and friendly stimulus to the understanding.—IRWIN EDMAN, *Candle in the Dark*

College students, in most of their communication, will not be using formal English. They will, however, hear formal English in lectures, and read it in texts, critical articles, and literature. They will also, in their formal papers and reports, and in their later communication with professional groups, need to use as well as understand this level of English.

B. Vulgate English

At the other end of the scale, vulgate English—nearly always spoken, seldom written except in fiction which reproduces this type of speech—is the English used by people with little or no education. As we have said before, vulgate English has in common with higher levels of usage hundreds of nouns, verbs, adjectives, adverbs, and prepositions. One of the chief characteristics of vulgate English, however, is its limited vocabulary; people of little education seldom use, seldom know, words which express subtle or complex meanings. It is possible to express almost any idea in the language of vulgate, but many words may be needed to define or clarify the idea, because the definitive, more formal word is not known: "He's plastered all the time; what I mean is he can't help himself. Doc says it's a disease-like. He can't seem to get along without liquor." Speaking more formally, one could say, "He's an alcoholic," or, perhaps, "He is a dipsomaniac."

Other characteristics of vulgate English are the misuse of words, the use of nonexistent words, and the corruption of what is now considered correct or conventional grammatical form. The following sentences illustrate these traits of vulgate English:

I wanted to tell you something, but I *disremember.*
He said he was going *irregardless* of what she *suspicioned.*

He said he *didn't have no* interest in *this here* election.
He *taken* his sister to a movie.
He *run over* and *laid* down on the grass.

Slang is an important part of vulgate English, and, indeed, of language in general. In the area of slang and shoptalk, vulgate and informal English overlap. *Shoptalk* is the talk, often consisting of verbal short cuts, which is used by people in the same occupation. (*Prexy, math, ec, soc, dorm, cat lab,* for instance, have been used by generation after generation of college students.) This type of slang, particularly when it names something new in a trade or profession, may eventually take its place as an accepted part of informal usage; *close-up* and *fade-out* from the movie industry, and *squeeze play* from baseball and bridge are examples. Most slang is, however, by its very nature faddish and ephemeral. It aims at an ever-changing novelty and liveliness, chiefly through incongruous figures of speech. The virtue of slang as a part of language is this novelty and freshness—when it is new. Its weaknesses are that it so quickly becomes unoriginal; that it is often unintelligible to a general audience; and that it conveys a poor impression of the user, who appears to lack the power of individual expression, since he relies heavily on stereotyped expressions which have been provided for him. Slang is used in the informal conversation of educated people, and in very informal writing. It becomes objectionable when it is overused, or used inappropriately in those situations which require more formal language.

Since college students will be speaking to and writing for educated groups, they will, of course, need a command of English well above the vulgate level in order to express complex ideas in a manner which merits attention and respect.

The following passages illustrate some of the differences between vulgate English and a third level of usage, informal English. The first excerpt, from a short story, reproduces a certain type of vulgate speech; the second presents a similar idea, expressed in high informal English, from the translation of a novel by Thomas Mann:

I can smell death. It's a gift, I reckon, one of them no-count gifts like good conversation that don't do you no good no more. Once Cousin John Mebane come to see us, and as he leaned over to pat me on the head— he was polite and hog-friendly to everybody, chillun and poverty-wropped kin especial—I said, "Cousin John, what makes you smell so funny?" Ma all but took the hide off'n me; but four days later they was dressen him in his shroud. Then I didn't know what it was I'd smelled, but by this time I'd got better acquainted with the meanen.—ANDREW NELSON LYTLE, "Mister McGregor"

She wept bitterly when the hour came to bid little Johann farewell. He put his arms about her and embraced her. Then, with his hands behind his back, resting his weight on one leg while the other poised on the tip of the toes, he watched her out of sight; his face wore the same brooding, introspective look with which he had stood at his father's death-bed, and his grandmother's bier, witnessed the breaking-up of the great household, and shared in so many events of the same kind, though of lesser outward significance. The departure of old Ida belonged to the same category as other events with which he was already familiar: breakings-up, closings, endings, disintegrations—he had seen them all. Such events did not disturb him— they had never disturbed him. But he would lift his head, with the curling light-brown hair, inflate one delicate nostril, and it was as if he cautiously sniffed the air about him, expecting to perceive that odour, that strange and yet familiar odour which, at his grandmother's bier, not all the scent of the flowers had been able to disguise.—THOMAS MANN, *Buddenbrooks*

C. Informal English

Informal English, the English most commonly spoken and written by educated people, lies between vulgate and formal English and overlaps both of these levels. It ranges from the very informal usage in the everyday conversation of educated people, which, as we have said, may include some slang and shoptalk, to the rather formal informality of newspaper editorials, lectures for unspecialized audiences, and informal essays. It employs, characteristically, a wider and more exact vocabulary than is typical of vulgate English, and a less formal and specialized vocabulary than that of formal English. Informal English is, in its sentence structure, less elaborate than formal English. Its sentences are likely to be shorter, and to have the directness and rhythm of speech. It is more often personal than impersonal; that is, the communicator includes himself and his feelings and attitudes in his communication. Allusions in informal English are usually to widely understood current events rather than to the historical and literary events of which formal English assumes understanding. This book, designed primarily for college freshmen, is written in a rather high level of informal English, as are most current magazine articles, novels, short stories, and plays. Informal English is, in short, the level of English which most educated people will be using in most of their activities in life. College students should, therefore, aim at a high informal level in most of their writing.

The diagram on page 91 shows the overlapping of the levels of usage we have been describing, and may clarify for the reader the meaning and relationship of the three levels.

The intelligent user of English should develop an awareness of levels so that he can exercise judgment in choosing the level best

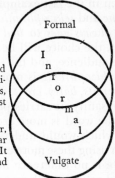

Formal

English which is used by highly educated people addressing an audience of their peers. Found often in poetry, formal essays, scholarly articles, lectures, and sermons.

High informal English, used in many newspaper editorials, personal essays, stories, novels, lectures, and in most business correspondence.

Informal

English words and constructions common to all levels.

Low informal, or familiar, English, used in familiar conversation and letters. It may include some slang and shoptalk.

Vulgate

English below the level of cultivated speech and writing.

suited to his intention, his audience, and the circumstances in which he is speaking or writing. Formal English is not always the "best" level; it may, in fact, be extremely inappropriate and ineffective if the subject is simple or personal, or if the audience expects an easy, informal discussion. Nor is vulgate English necessarily "bad"; talking the language of the audience, even if that language is vulgate, may, in exceptional circumstances, accomplish the speaker's purpose; some political speakers know this well. The best level is the one which will be most effective in the whole context of the communication. Choosing it wisely requires an awareness of the different levels of expression which are possible, and of the different effects they are likely to produce.

Consider the choice involved in the following expressions of the same idea:

He's nuts.
He's insane.
He's schizophrenic.

He pounded it out on the keys.
He played some lively music.
He played a gavotte.

We put on the feed bag at six.
We eat at six.
We dine at six.

He always lays down for his beauty sleep at ten.
He always hits the sack at ten.
He always goes to bed at ten.
He habitually retires at ten.

In most cases, particularly if the communication is written, the slang expressions will be rejected as inappropriate; certainly the ungrammatical vulgate expression in the last example will be. But how will one choose between *insane* and *schizophrenic, some lively music* and *a gavotte, eat* and *dine, always goes to bed* and *habitually retires?* To a considerable extent, the choice will be determined by the formality of the subject, the audience, and the circumstances. It should be noted, though, that *schizophrenic* is more exact than *insane* (as *insane* is more exact than *nuts, batty, crazy,* etc.); for one who knows the word, it defines the insanity; it carries precise information. The same is true of *gavotte;* the word is more accurate than *some lively music.* For an audience which would understand them, then, there would be an advantage in using these more exact, more formal words. On the other hand, there is no difference in exactness between *eat* and *dine, goes to bed* and *retires;* furthermore, the simple informal expressions seem more appropriate than the formal ones for simple statements about habits of eating and going to bed; in most circumstances, therefore, they would be the right expressions to choose.

Some college students err in trying to write too formally; they strive for elegance and impressiveness by substituting formal locutions for informal ones which have the same referential meaning and which are more appropriate for the material under discussion. Formal words used unnecessarily in an informal context are "heavy words"; they have too much bulk or weight for the situation; the result of using them is strained, pretentious, "heavy" writing. The following sentences are examples of this undesirable heaviness in the expression of comparatively slight ideas:

I endeavored to peruse the volume. [I tried to read the book.]
I anticipate the termination of the current seméster. [I anticipate, or look forward to, the end of this semester.]
I requested her permission to view the kittens. [I asked her to let me see the kittens.]
I decided to wend my way to my place of residence. [I decided to go home.]

Writers of such pompous absurdities need to be told to say what they have to say as simply and directly as possible. Usually they are happy to learn that they can relax and write more naturally.

Many college students, on the other hand, relax too much. They need to raise the level of usage in their writing, not by straining for elegance, and not by trying to ornament their prose with long or heavy words, but by using accurately words which have precise meanings and which are appropriate to the subjects they are discussing. Such words often, though not always, belong to a high informal or formal level. Lack of adequate vocabulary, as well as an unsure sense of the levels of usage, probably accounts for the lapses into incongruous informality in the following sentences:

I admired the clear, concise way Einstein *put across* the thought. [expressed or conveyed]

He gave *a bunch of figures on the amount of the soil washing away.* [statistics on soil erosion]

We become familiar with many modern ideas and the trends *in back of them.* [which produced them]

Primitive tribes believed in *a God that had the shape and looked like a man.* [an anthropomorphic God]

The essays were all stimulating, though the one by John Dewey was *rough.* [difficult, or complex, or abstract—something which says more exactly what the writer means]

When I came to college I *was all set to be* a premedical student. [intended to be]

Every statement was *well covered with proof* by his own experiments and those of other authorities. [substantiated]

After an analysis of immigrations to the United States, the author *got going on the bad ideas of race.* [discussed the misconceptions about race]

Hamlet was disturbed and unbalanced when he found that his father had been *bumped off.* [murdered]

The reader will note that one objection to these sentences is that their level is not consistent; a more serious objection is that the extreme informality is not appropriate to an academic discussion of such subjects as Dewey, Einstein, Hamlet, and anthropology.

In general, then, the college student should develop an awareness of the levels of usage which will enable him to choose the level best suited to the occasion and to his intention. The level will not always be the same. Students preparing for the professions will, perhaps more than others, realize that a competent doctor, lawyer, teacher, sociologist, or psychologist must be effective, linguistically, on more than one level, since he must address his colleagues in a way which engenders respect, and must also communicate clearly and effectively with people who lack his training and vocabulary. The best preparation for this multiple communication is practicing good informal usage, and, at the same time, developing an ability to use words on the higher level when those words convey meaning accurately to an audience which understands and expects them.

II. CONSIDERATION OF PLACE AND TIME

Localisms or provincialisms are expressions peculiar to a particular place or section of the country. In that area they are inconspicuous, an accepted part of informal speech. Examples of localisms are *I reckon* (think), *you all, I'll go a piece* (part of the way), *she wants out* (wants to go out). Outside the locality in which they are common, such expressions are conspicuous, sometimes unclear, often considered "bad English." They are used in narrative writing to give local color and flavor, but they are out of place in formal English, and usually in informal writing. Even in informal speech to an audience unfamiliar with the expressions they should be used with caution, since they may create a poor impression, or may be imperfectly understood.

The different names for common things used in different sections of the United States (*woodchuck—groundhog; poke—sack; spider—skillet; pit—seed; stoop—porch; tonic—soft drink*) are sometimes a hazard to communication. It is wise, therefore, to adopt the term familiar to the audience addressed. One will be misunderstood if he persists in offering *tonic* to a person who considers it a medicine; and he will be unrealistic if he maintains that *tonic* is the "right" term and *soft drink* the "wrong" one. Both are right—in their place.

Consideration of time means, chiefly, writing modern English; that is, avoiding obsolete words (words no longer in use) and archaic words (out-of-date words very seldom used). Inexperienced writers sometimes strive for a "literary" effect by using such expressions as *wot, mayhap, peradventure, in sooth, e'en so, quoth he, methinks.* These archaisms, and others, are out of place in modern writing. They are sometimes used for humor, but the result is usually less humorous than the writer hoped.

In the use of very new words, too, some discrimination should be practiced. Hundreds of newly coined words appear in print each year. Some of them are widely accepted and understood, and are eventually included in dictionaries. Examples of comparatively new and very new words, many of them necessary names for new things, are *draftee, Wave, blitz, jeep, iron curtain, genocide, quisling, existentialism, radar, plutonium, decontrol, cortisone, Dixiecrat, canasta, cold war, Titoism, H-bomb, bloodmobile, airlift.* One should feel no hesitation about using such commonly accepted new words, even though, when the words are very new, they are not in the dictionaries.

It is, however, wise to avoid, in writing, new linguistic inventions which have not been widely used, which may not be widely understood, and which belong, thus far, in the realm of novelty-language. Current examples of such innovations, often involving an extension, or a new grammatical form, of an accepted word, are: *DAR-ism, me-tooism, brass-hattism, smug-busting, telethought, rubbleized,*

Veep and *Veepess, to religify, disadmire.* One may defeat the purpose
of language—clear and effective communication—if he uses expressions which, like some of these, are obscure or which may offend the
reader or listener by their unconventional, unfamiliar form.

Dictionaries are, in general, conservative about attaching the labels
obsolete (*Obs.*) and archaic to words which, in fact, have long been
out of current usage. They are also, because they cannot be revised
every year, slow in admitting new words. The modern writer must,
consequently, employ common sense and personal experience, as
well as the dictionary, in making his choice of words.

III. CONCRETE EXPRESSION

Students who have had training in writing themes have usually
been told repeatedly to use concrete words and to develop their
material with concrete detail. Frequently, though, the reason for
the advice is obscure; the instructions are regarded as the whim of
a particular teacher who "wanted us to use examples."

In Chapter One we have discussed part of the principle which
underlies this insistence on concreteness: abstract terms like *truth,
justice, freedom, honor, rights of individuals, liberty, socialism,
American way,* do not have clear and definite referential meaning
for different receivers unless their meaning is established by the context. They are necessary in language for expressing general ideas,
pronouncing judgments, and stating conclusions; and they are
powerful, carrying as they so often do a heavy emotional charge. But
because of their multiple meanings and emotional associations, they
often confuse rather than clarify; at best, unless they are defined by
concrete illustration, they leave only a vague impression of what
the communicator had in mind when he used them.

Concrete words, on the other hand, point to things which have
existence in the physical world, on the nature and meaning of which,
therefore, people can agree. Concrete words like *cat, desk, chair, typewriter, piano, tree,* call up an image of the object named. It is true,
of course, that there are different kinds of cats, chairs, typewriters;
still, in a context, the label carries a reasonably definite meaning.
Concrete words, therefore, communicate more exactly the image or
idea which the writer has in mind.

The conventional terms *abstract* and *concrete* are actually relative
terms; that is, there are degrees of abstractness and concreteness. A
word which gives more particulars about its referent is said to be
"more concrete" or "less abstract" than a word which gives fewer
particulars. *Collie,* for example, is more concrete than *dog* because

the word *collie* tells more about its referent (pointed nose, long hair, bushy tail, etc.) than *dog* does. The following list illustrates an ascending scale from concrete to abstract: *Prince* (name of a particular collie), *collie, dog, animal, living creature.*

The writer trying to express himself definitely often needs to choose, then, not simply between abstract and concrete words, but between concrete and more concrete words. Notice the degrees of definite meaning in the following sets of expressions:

I bought
- a piece of furniture.
- a chair.
- a Morris chair.

She went out to get
- some food.
- some vegetables.
- some carrots.

From his window he can see
- a masterpiece of nature.
- a tree.
- a red maple.

The speaker discussed
- world problems.
- our foreign policy.
- our relations with Germany.
- the question of arming Western Germany.

He is happy about
- his academic success.
- his high grades.
- his *A*'s in chemistry and biology.

She
- is in an awkward situation.
- is in trouble with the bank.
- has overdrawn her account.

The most concrete expressions, *Morris chair, carrots, red maple,* etc., communicate most exactly the writer's meaning. Writing becomes clearer, and also more interesting, when, as often as possible, such concrete expressions are substituted for more general words.

Concreteness is often achieved, not simply by substituting a specific word for a general one, but by concrete *expansion* of a general statement. The expansion consists of specific examples and details which enable the reader to visualize more clearly or understand more exactly what the writer means. The following sentences illustrate both of these methods of achieving concreteness—*substitution* of concrete terms and *expansion* by concrete detail:

Our dog attacked someone today.
Our Irish setter came around the corner of the house this morning with

part of the grocery boy's black-and-white jacket in his mouth. [Substitution and expansion]

He engages in un-American activities.
He is a member of the Ku Klux Klan. [Substitution]

The house was disorderly.
In Jean's house there were papers on the floor, glasses and beer bottles on the mantel, and egg-smeared plates in the sink. [Substitution and expansion]

A dangling modifier often produces a ridiculous sentence.
A dangling modifier often produces a ridiculous sentence—for example, "Walking up the road, the moon shone brightly." [Expansion]

He seemed embarrassed.
He shuffled his feet and stammered; his cheeks and ears glowed. [Substitution and expansion]

He objected to the college requirements.
He objected to having to take two years of French or German and a year of mathematics. [Substitution and expansion]

Having a wonderful time.
Having a wonderful time swimming and surf-boarding and dating the beautiful redhead you introduced me to last summer. [Expansion]

A third way of attaining concreteness is the use of *figures of speech,* particularly similes and metaphors, which make or imply comparisons. In similes the comparison is stated, and is usually introduced by *like* or *as:* He had a laugh *like* thunder; she was as changeable *as* New England weather. In metaphors the comparison is implied: her *kittenish* ways; the *merry-go-round* of modern living. Although figurative language is sometimes considered purely literary and rare in everyday usage, actually figures of speech are a very important part of common language. Slang is largely figurative: *out in left field with snowshoes on, tight as a drum, mad as a wet hen, wet blanket, slick chick.* And current idiom is full of such figures of speech as *cauliflower ears, red-baiting, witch hunt, on the horns of a dilemma, bury the hatchet, fish story, tall tale, red tape, sandwiched, skeleton in the closet, hand-to-mouth, break the ice, cold shoulder, family tree.* Figures of speech are, in fact, the very lifeblood of language; and one of their principal values is that they make a general and abstract idea specific by associating it with something concrete and familiar.

Figurative language should be used with discretion, for it presents two pitfalls: strained or inappropriate comparisons (*her eyes glowed like a lighthouse light*); and trite expressions (*tired as a dog, white as a sheet, sober as a judge, like a rat in a trap*). But good, fresh comparisons are one of the most valuable tools of the writer interested in communicating his ideas clearly and vividly. Some examples will show this vivifying, clarifying power of figurative language.

Lord Chesterfield, writing in the eighteenth century when watches were rare possessions, used a simile to advise his son how to "wear" learning:

Wear your learning like your watch, in a private pocket; and do not pull it out and strike it, merely to show that you have one. If you are asked what o'clock it is, tell it, but do not proclaim it hourly and unasked, like the watchman.

Mortimer J. Adler, writing for a contemporary audience, uses this figure of speech to clarify the complex subject of intelligent reading:

Every book has a skeleton hidden between its boards. Your job is to find it. A book comes to you with flesh on its bare bones and clothes over its flesh. It is all dressed up. I am not asking you to be impolite or cruel. You do not have to undress it or tear the flesh off its limbs to get at the firm structure that underlies the soft. But you must read the book with X-ray eyes, for it is an essential part of your first apprehension of any book to grasp its structure.[2]

Albert Deutsch, in the newspaper *PM,* packed his writing with figurative language to make concrete and immediately clear his point about the varied meanings attached to the abstract word *liberal:*

What is a liberal? Is he, as some cynics suggest, a man with both feet planted firmly in midair? Or one with his mind open—at both ends? Or, as one hard-bitten critic defined him, "a radical with a wife and two kids?" . . . Where, in this suicidal panic [of so-called liberals deserting liberal causes] are the liberals who traditionally have looked beyond the label to evaluate the substance, who wouldn't be panicked by the mad cries of the smear hounds.

The plain truth is that the house of liberalism looks too much like Noah's Ark these days, filled with a strange assortment of creatures. Some of the old tenants find it too crowded for comfort.—ALBERT DEUTSCH, "Who Are the Real Liberals?"—*PM,* February 28, 1947

Thus far in this discussion we have been concerned chiefly with the power of concrete words to convey clear referential meaning. But concrete words and concrete figures of speech have another, equally important, power—the power to evoke strong and definite feeling. Charged abstract words, as we have seen, often produce a strong emotional response; but that response is likely to be a confused cloud

[2] Reprinted from *How to Read a Book* by permission of Simon and Schuster, Inc. Copyright, 1940, by Mortimer J. Adler.

of feeling, aroused by the word, unfocused on any particular referent, and possibly far removed from the idea in the communicator's mind. With concrete words the feeling is different. Since concrete words refer to more definite things, the emotion they evoke will be a more definite and relevant emotion; it will spring, not from an habitual reaction to a multiple-meaninged *word,* but from a fresh reaction to the *image of a particular thing* called up by the word. When communication is concrete, the reader has the sense of being present in the situation or experience; of seeing what the writer saw, touching and smelling and hearing as the writer did. He comes closer, therefore, to sharing the writer's feeling. A more exact emotional meaning is communicated.

Here is a simple example of the difference in emotional meaning between abstract and concrete expression:

> He treated his daughter cruelly.
> He beat his little seven-year-old daughter Eleanor with his belt until red welts stood out on her thin shoulders and arms.

The second sentence illustrates concrete expansion of a general idea: the situation is clarified because the daughter is given a name and an age, and the type of cruelty is specified. But we are concerned here not simply with the difference in plain-sense clarity or definiteness, but with the difference in the emotions which the two statements produce. Since treating a daughter cruelly may mean anything from beating her to speaking to her sharply, the general statement is unlikely to produce anything more than a vague emotion. Or, if a reader does respond definitely because of some personal association he has with a father's cruelty to a daughter, he is reading into this general statement and responding emotionally to something the writer may not have intended; his response is, then, a response to an idea in his own mind which may be remote from what the communicator is trying to say. When, however, as in the second sentence, the meaning is made concrete and explicit, when one is told the age of the daughter and is given an image of red welts on thin shoulders and arms, the emotional reaction is more specifically what the writer intended.

The purpose of a great deal of writing is to convey to the reader the writer's sense of a whole experience. When the reader can grasp the facts, observations, and sensations which are the bases of the whole experience, he can more nearly grasp the total meaning, referential and emotional, which the writer is trying to convey.

Modern writing is increasingly concrete, but concreteness is by no means a characteristic only of modern style. If we consider the great pieces of literature, those writings which, generation after generation, have been most appealing to men, we see that a large part of their human appeal lies in the power they have, not only to clarify ideas, but also to stir the senses and to clarify emotion by calling to mind vivid images which produce definite feelings. Much of the power of Biblical prose lies in its concrete imagery. The language of the Bible represents such abstract ideas as death, grief, God, wisdom, love, in terms of concrete actions and concrete, familiar experience. It is language which makes pictures in the mind:

He shall come down *like rain upon the mown grass.*

Thou makest us *a byword* among the heathen, *a shaking of the head* among the people.

Yet a little sleep, a little slumber, *a little folding of the hands to sleep.*

As the crackling of thorns under a pot, so is the laughter of a fool.

I shall light a candle of understanding in thine heart, which shall not be put out.

The *grasshopper* shall be *a burden,* and desire shall fail; because man goeth to *his long home,* and *the mourners go about the streets.*

Set me as a seal upon thine heart, as a seal upon thine arm; for love is strong as death; jealousy is *cruel as the grave; the coals thereof are coals of fire,* which *hath a most vehement flame.*

Homer's *Iliad* has this same picture-creating quality which makes the experience, and the reader's feeling for it, immediate and real. Hector, the Trojan hero, speaks to his wife before going into battle:

"So [if Troy is defeated] shalt thou abide in Argos and *ply the loom at another woman's bidding,* and *bear water* from fount Messeis or Hypereia, being grievously entreated, and sore constraint shall be laid upon thee. And then shall one say that *beholdeth thee weep:* 'This is the wife of Hector, that was foremost in battle of the *horse-taming Trojans* when men fought about Ilios.' Thus shall one say hereafter, and fresh grief will be thine for lack of such an husband as thou hadst to ward off the day of thraldom. But me in death *may the heaped-up earth be covering,* ere I *hear thy crying* and *thy carrying into captivity.*"

The language of Shakespeare is packed with image-evoking expressions by which the general idea is made particular and graphic:

> 'Tis better to be lowly born
> And range with humble livers in content
> Than to be *perked up in a glistening grief*
> And *wear a golden sorrow.*

> Though yet of Hamlet our dear brother's death
> *The memory be green;* and that it us befitted
> To *bear our hearts in grief,* and our whole kingdom
> *To be contracted in one brow of woe.* . . .

> Leave her to heaven
> And *to those thorns that in her bosom lodge*
> *To prick and sting her.*

> Have *stooped my neck* under your injuries,
> And *sigh'd my English breath in foreign clouds,*
> *Eating the bitter bread of banishment.*

> *Pluck* from the memory *a rooted sorrow,*
> *Raze out the written troubles of the brain.*

The appeal of this famous passage from John Donne lies in the vivid figurative phrasing of the idea:

No man is an island, entire of itself; every man is a piece of the continent, a part of the main: if a clod be washed away by the sea, Europe is the less, as well as if a promontory were, as well as if a manor of thy friends or of thine own were; any man's death diminishes me, because I am involved in mankind. And therefore never send to know for whom the bell tolls; it tolls for thee.

Some excerpts from modern writing, closer to the writing students will be able to do, will further illustrate the value of concrete words in giving the reader an immediate and accurate perception of the writer's meaning. In a passage from a novel, Julia Peterkin, by a collection of concrete details, gives a picture, which no general statement could convey, of a house decorated for a wedding:

"Fire couldn' catch me today, Auntie. Not me," Mary said, but she stood farther back and ate her potato slowly while she looked around at all the things she had done to make the room attractive. Every board in the floor had been scrubbed white with lye and sand, her hands were still sore with lye cuts. The walls were fresh covered with newspapers bought from Grab-All with eggs; circles of fringed papers sewed to barrel hoops and tied to the rafters looked like big lanterns as they swung gently overhead in the cold drafts of morning air which fell through the broken shingles in the roof. The wide rock hearth was newly reddened with clay, and the mantel-shelf had a newspaper cover which she had carefully scalloped and cut with holes to make blossoms and stars. That was lovely. She tried hard to get one more paper to fix a cover like it for the water-shelf where the cake and wine stood, but not another paper was to be had for eggs or peanuts or anything else. June whitewashed the shelf with the white clay that fell in lumps out of the side of the duck dam gully and it matched the whitened front door and window-blinds, and looked clean and nice enough.[3]

Paul de Kruif, writing about an early "microbe hunter," expands the first general sentence of his paragraph with details about what

[3] From *Scarlet Sister Mary* by Julia Peterkin, copyright 1928. Used by special permission of the publishers, The Bobbs-Merrill Company.

Leeuwenhoek did, specifically, with his microscope. The detail is not only informative; it conveys the interest and excitement of the activity:

Now this self-satisfied dry-goods dealer began to turn his lenses onto everything he could get hold of. He looked through them at the muscle fibers of a whale and the scales of his own skin. He went to the butcher shop and begged or bought ox-eyes and was amazed at how prettily the crystalline lens of the eye of the ox is put together. He peered for hours at the build of the hairs of a sheep, of a beaver, of an elk, that were transformed from their fineness into great rough logs under his bit of glass. He delicately dissected the head of a fly; he stuck his brain on the fine needle of his microscope—how he admired the clear details of the marvelous big brain of that fly! He examined the cross-sections of the wood of a dozen different trees and squinted at the seeds of plants. He grunted "Impossible!" when he first spied the outlandish large perfection of the sting of a flea and the legs of a louse. That man Leeuwenhoek was like a puppy who sniffs—with a totally impolite disregard of discrimination—at every object of the world around him!—Paul de Kruif, *Microbe Hunters*

The following paragraphs by Thomas Wolfe are part of a long passage in which, by calling up particular sights, smells, and sounds, he communicates the meaning of the word and the idea "October." Notice also, in the second paragraph, his use of figurative language.

The corn is shocked: it sticks out in hard yellow rows upon dried ears, fit now for great red barns in Pennsylvania, and the big stained teeth of crunching horses. The indolent hooves kick swiftly at the boards, the barn is sweet with hay and leather, wood and apples—this, and the clean dry crunching of the teeth is all: the sweat, the labor, and the plow is over. The late pears mellow on a sunny shelf; smoked hams hang to the warped barn rafters; the pantry shelves are loaded with 300 jars of fruit. Meanwhile the leaves are turning, turning, up in Maine, the chestnut burrs plop thickly to the earth in gusts of wind, and in Virginia the chinkapins are falling.

There is a smell of burning in small towns in afternoon, and men with buckles on their arms are raking leaves in yards as boys come by with straps slung back across their shoulders. The oak leaves, big and brown, are bedded deep in yard and gutter: they make deep wadings to the knee for children in the streets. The fire will snap and crackle like a whip, sharp acrid smoke will sting the eyes, in mown fields the little vipers of the flame eat past the black coarse edges of burned stubble like a line of locusts. Fire drives a thorn of memory in the heart.—Thomas Wolfe, *Of Time and the River*

The inexperienced writer, unlike the writers we have just quoted, frequently assumes that his readers know intuitively, and therefore do not need to be told, the contents of his mind. He believes that when he has written "She wore a strange hat," he has described the hat, because the image of green feathers and yellow veil is completely clear in his own mind. Or, thinking of a gray farmhouse, beaten by rain, set in an expanse of treeless, plowed acres, he feels that he has conveyed that picture when he writes, "The countryside was dreary."

The following very poor freshman theme illustrates the appalling vagueness which may come from the assumption that the reader of the paper can also read the writer's mind. The assignment was to write a well-organized paragraph on the student's reason for coming to college.

One good reason why I came to college is to acquire a higher education. I believe that a college education is the only way in which a young man may equip himself to cope with the many difficult tasks and obstacles which he will encounter in life. During college life, the student has to carry on a great many responsibilities which will indeed prove themselves to be a tremendous factor in future life. Another of the beneficial factors of college life are the activities which will be a true asset in the near future. A college education is a necessity for my chosen profession. Whether I am successful in my ambition or not, I will still have a priceless education which I may be dependent upon, a priceless education which will prove beneficial in both society and livelihood. In this day of scientific triumphs, no man can be successful in a profession without attending a school of higher learning. The acquisition of knowledge is not only essential for the enjoyment of higher standards of living and the finer things of life, but also is a source of self-satisfaction and pleasure. Knowledge provides an individual with a broad perspective, thereby giving an opportunity to enjoy a fuller and better life.

This paper has many weaknesses, but its chief weakness is that it says nothing. Among the marginal comments made on it were: "Be specific," "Give examples," "Too general," "What profession?" "Vague, trite, and meaningless," "What do you mean?" The writer of the theme, faced with the comments and a grade of F, was at first bewildered by both. Knowing what he meant by "responsibilities," "activities," and "my chosen profession," and having, perhaps, a hazy idea of what he meant by "finer things of life," etc., he failed to realize how incomplete his communication had been.

Compare the following paragraph, written on the same assignment, by a student who had chosen the same profession as the writer of the first theme:

My plans were forcibly interrupted immediately after my graduation from high school by induction into the United States Army. Even so, I was more fortunate than others with my ambitions, because I was at least assigned to the branch of service which would test my hope and make my decision final. From the time I entered high school I had intended to study medicine. After being assigned to the Medical Department of the Army and attending a three months' course to become a Surgical Technician, I

realized that my desire for a medical education was a true one and not like
a small boy's fancy to be an Indian or a fireman. Overseas, assigned to a
general hospital, I had an opportunity to see not only the glorious side
of medicine, but also the long tedious hours of physical and mental labor
which make up the life of the physician today. Our medical officers and
nurses were often busy from early morning until late at night, only to be
awakened again after an hour's sleep to cope with some new emergency.
They were always ready and willing to work. I attempted to gain as much
knowledge of medical science as possible from these men. Necessarily the
things I learned were of the practical sort as my education was inadequate
for diagnosis and therapy. Now three school years have been lost to me,
and I want to learn medical science as soon as I can in the best way that
I can. Therefore, college is a means to an end and a beginning of my life
work.

Here, though the writing is not excellent—it could well be more
concrete toward the end—the writer has, by his specific statements,
communicated his meaning clearly.

The following passage is an example of thin, generally vague
writing:

When I hear the word "Maine" I think of the winters I spent there
when I was a boy. Winter in Maine was so different from summer. It was
hard in many ways, for we had frequent blizzards, and we lived in an
isolated farmhouse. But I remember many things that were pleasant, like
playing in the snow and the coziness of the house inside when there was
a storm outside.

Now read this passage from another student theme. The writer
here, by recording specific details, recollections, and sensations,
brings to life for the reader the experience and the pleasure of the
boy during the Maine winter:

For all its force and fury, winter was mainly memorable to the boy for
little things; sights and sounds that hit his sharpened senses like a silver
hammer: the soft glow of early lamplight; the ticktack of sleet on frosted
windowpanes; the song of the wind in the chimney; the gray blur of the
sheep snuggled in their pen at nightfall; the look of the cows chewing their
cuds; the morning crackle of birch bark in the kitchen stove; the stirring
jangle of sleigh bells; the stillness of winter woods. Winter's ways were so
different from those of the slow, sweet scroll of summer, on which buds
swelled into blossoms, sunshine melted into rain, day drifted into night.
But winter had many enchantments. The boy felt their quick tug as he
trudged home from school, bent low to the gale, and suddenly saw through
the swirling snow the smoke of his own chimney; as he jumped shivering
into bed and felt the warm, flannel-wrapped soapstone which his mother
had tucked between the blankets; as he raced downhill on his sled with
the ends of red scarf streaming out behind him.

He felt the enchantment most of all at night when a blizzard was beating in baffled fury against the stout walls of the farmhouse. How good was the snugness of that sanctuary! Never did the kitchen seem so warm and cheerful, the lamplight quite so bright. By the time his mother had brought her sewing close to the lamp and his father's stockinged feet were propped up on the open oven, the boy would have the corn popper waiting. First he tried the top of the stove with a spit-wet finger. The sizzle mustn't be too sharp or too soft—only a trained ear could catch the proper pitch.

Another example of porous, thin, abstract writing:

I remember the little boy I was many years ago. There was nothing distinctive about him. Like other children of that age, he amused himself with his own toys and his own games. He was, I'm afraid, often into mischief. Then he grew older, and one day he was ready to go to school.

And now, this excellent paragraph from another freshman theme:

The little boy's exact age was that of children still able to create their own toys—the challenge of a ball to be caught; the enchanting beckon of an unwatched ladder to make one tall; the swift decisiveness of a scissors, teaching that lines cut away leave empty spaces. And music, too. His music was in the midnight-creak of stairs leading down from his room, or the patter of rain, or the clatter of horses' hoofs on a tar road. His days were for testing, touching, stretching, and trying. He learned that wood was hard, and solid for its weight; that swinging was not all fun, that someone had to push; that Pussy scratched sometimes. He heard a church bell, he saw a rainbow, he felt velvet, he tasted dirt, he smelled wet grass, he poked at a worm. It was the age of the boundless world, when marbles are soldiers. But, as he grew older, each one turned into a marble again, and one day they were forgotten somewhere, where children's toys are always forgotten.

Abstract words, with their power to summarize, to generalize, to relate, and to arouse feeling, are indispensable. But the writer who is interested in making clear exactly what he means, or in sharing his experience with others, will write as concretely as possible, and will define his abstractions with concrete examples, figures of speech, and concrete details. Concreteness is not hard to achieve; it comes, though, from a habit of mind which many inexperienced writers have not developed—the habit of remembering and setting down the actual observations, facts, and thoughts which are the basis of a general statement, and which make that general statement understandable and real to the reader.

CHAPTER REVIEW

If your reading of the chapter has been adequate, you should be able to define, illustrate, and supply any other important information about each of the following terms, and to give clear, full answers to the questions below.

formal English	localisms
vulgate English	concrete words
informal English	abstract words
slang	concrete substitution
shoptalk	concrete expansion
"heavy words"	figurative language

1. What are the characteristics of each of the three main levels of usage?

2. What are the advantages of formal English? Of informal English?

3. Why is extensive use of slang undesirable?

4. How can one determine the appropriate level of usage?

5. What are the values of concrete expression?

6. By what specific methods can one achieve concreteness in expression?

EXERCISES

I. The three passages below present similar ideas in formal, informal, and vulgate English. Point out in each passage the specific traits of style and language which establish its level and which are characteristic of that level of usage.

What a monstrous specter is this man, the disease of the agglutinated dust, lifting alternate feet or lying drugged with slumber; killing, feeding, growing, bringing forth small copies of himself; grown upon with hair like grass, fitted with eyes that move and glitter in his face; a thing to set children screaming;—and yet looked at nearlier, known as his fellows know him, how surprising are his attributes! Poor soul, here for so little, cast among so many hardships, filled with desires so incommensurate and so inconsistent, savagely surrounded, savagely descended, irremediably condemned to prey upon his fellow lives: who should have blamed him had he been of a piece with his destiny and a being merely barbarous? And we look and behold him instead filled with imperfect virtues: infinitely childish, often admirably valiant, often touchingly kind; sitting down, amidst his momentary life, to debate of right and wrong and the attributes of the deity; rising up to do battle for an egg or die for an idea; singling out his friends and his mate with cordial affection; bringing forth in pain, rearing with long-suffering solicitude, his young. To touch the heart of his mystery, we find in him one thought, strange to the point of lunacy: the thought of duty; the thought of something owing to himself, to his neighbor, to his God; an ideal of decency, to which he would rise if it were possible; a limit of shame, below which, if it be possible, he will not stoop.—ROBERT LOUIS STEVENSON, *Pulvis et Umbra*

In fact, I'm amazed at how much goodness there is in people even in a system that puts a premium on badness. It's striking to see how generous we can be when our imaginations are touched by a great emergency, a flood, say, or a fire. It's encouraging to see how much sheer heroism there is, how people will forget their own skins and risk their lives for others. I know plenty of dishonest people, but I know few who seem to enjoy their dishonesty, and even they might have been all right if they'd been caught young enough.

If people are as good as this when it pays to be bad, what mightn't we expect of them if the incentive to disloyalty and dishonesty could be taken away? I have known a man to go out of his way to help me when I was in trouble, and then try to cheat me out of three cents on an order of groceries. I'd trust that man in a cooperative society, and I'd trust myself, though I've done my share of dishonest things.—GRANVILLE HICKS, *I Like America*

"This here ol' man jus' lived a life an' jus' died out of it. I don't know whether he was good or bad, but that don't matter much. He was alive, an' that's what matters. An' now he's dead, an' that don't matter. Heard a fella tell a poem one time, an' he says, 'All that lives is holy.' Got to thinkin', an' purty soon it means more than the words says."—JOHN STEINBECK, *The Grapes of Wrath*

II. Criticize the levels of usage in the following sentences, suggesting revisions when the usage seems inappropriate. In judging appropriateness, you will need to consider the probable context of each sentence.

1. I deem it advantageous to take math along with chem.
2. "I tell ya, Gertie, men are all alike; they's none of them won't hand ya that line."
3. When we penetrate to the final entities, the startling fact of spatial existence discloses itself.
4. Upon his admission to the institution of his choice, he entertained hopes of affiliating himself with a fraternal organization.
5. However, because of his misdemeanors, he was, before initiation, kicked out.
6. The President announced the plan of building a new dormitory as soon as funds are available.
7. Prexy says they're going to build a new dorm when they get the money.
8. Prexy announced the plan of erecting a new dorm as soon as the cash is available.
9. The night closed down, black, cavernous, deep in palpable loneliness. I've got the jitters, he thought.
10. "Listen, Prof, maybe I messed up the English exam; O.K., but I knew it cold. I think I rate another try."

III. Rewrite the following sentences, making them more interesting and more exact by using concrete words and details. The rewritten version may consist of more than one sentence.

1. He bought several articles of clothing for which he had to pay a large sum.

2. I read a book until late last night.

3. She put the utensils into a large container.

4. We had a conversation about a controversial question.

5. He had been indulging in a certain amount of entertainment during his stay in the city.

6. As he stepped onto the porch, the bundle he was carrying broke open and the contents spilled.

7. She wore a brightly colored costume.

8. He belongs to some radical organizations.

9. His business is selling machinery.

10. She was worried about losing an important paper.

11. This sentence is poorly constructed.

12. He spoke on matters of local interest, denouncing communist infiltration into education.

13. The committee decided to raise funds for local improvements.

14. I am busy today with a number of social engagements.

15. He performed a good deed.

16. When the teacher wasn't looking, we were likely to misbehave.

17. The vehicle moved along the road at a rapid rate.

18. I hid in the far corner of the yard, among the trees and flowers.

19. She was the picture of health.

20. My little brother is always asking me absurd questions.

21. Because of his misdemeanors, he came within the grip of the law.

22. A member of the faculty influenced me in choosing my vocation.

23. I voted for Brown for Congress because he has a good record.

24. He does well in games that require physical endurance.

25. She constantly irritates me in little ways.

IV. Write a paragraph of at least 200 words in which, by means of accurate concrete statement and detail, you expand one of the general statements below.

1. It was a dismal rainy night.

2. I was impressed with his efficiency.

3. The world looks different in the very early morning.

4. The house belonged to another age.

5. People on the subway are interesting.

6. So late at night, the dormitory seemed strange.

7. This neighborhood is restful (or depressing).

8. I like the view from my window.

9. At this time of year the campus is attractive.

10. Already one sees signs of approaching winter.

11. College has changed a few of my ideas.

12. I am learning some interesting things in college.

13. My college teachers are not what I expected.

14. The Chapel audience was inattentive.
15. He gave a dull (or effective) speech.
16. The room expressed the personality of its owner.
17. He (she) tried to appear sophisticated.
18. His dress and actions led me to believe he was a senior.

Chapter Five

Developing an Effective Style

STYLE IS A HARD-TO-DEFINE QUALITY of excellence and distinction in expression. Let us assume that a writer has something to say, some idea or experience that is worth communicating; let us further assume that his writing is free from careless or ignorant violations of the conventions. Still his writing may be so colorless, boring, and ineffectual that his readers will stop reading after the first few paragraphs, or, if they continue, will be unimpressed or unconvinced by what he says. Such a writer has failed in communication, not because he lacks material and not because he makes blunders, but because his writing has no characteristic flavor, no distinctive quality to interest the reader. His style is poor; or, as we sometimes say, he has no style.

There is not, of course, a single "good style" or "right style," for style is highly individual. It is compounded of many elements, including the writer's personality, his way of thinking, his choice of words, his arrangement of words, the length and rhythm of his sentences. A particular style cannot, then, be imposed on a writer; in a sense, style cannot be taught, because it is the result of the writer's accurate and effective expression of himself—an individual unlike any other. But in developing his own style, the student can learn much about how to express himself accurately and effectively by analyzing and practicing the techniques that are used in successful writing.

Nearly all interesting and effective writing has these characteristics: it is economical and concise in language; it is original in expression; its sentences are varied to avoid monotony and to produce the exact effect the writer wants; it gives precise emphasis to important words and ideas. In this chapter we shall discuss some of the techniques by which these elements of style are achieved.

110

I. ECONOMY AND CONCISENESS

The briefest expression is not always the best. Writing stripped to bare statements of facts, without supporting and elaborating detail, will lack both clarity and interest; great literature loses its quality of greatness if it is reduced to a plain-sense paraphrase. At the same time, in all effective prose every word counts. No words occupy space without contributing positively, either referentially or emotively, to the meaning of the passage. Economical and concise expression comes, then, not simply from using fewer words, but from choosing words which work, and so warrant the space they take in the sentence.

We shall give examples in this section of various types of wordiness, and show how one or two working words can often effectively replace five or six weak words. The reader should bear in mind, however, as he reads the examples given here, what has been said earlier about the importance of context. In brief examples, phrases and sentences are necessarily presented without context. It is possible to imagine certain contexts in which the wordy expressions which we condemn would be acceptable, or even desirable: a wordy phrasing of an idea may, for instance, establish an informality or an attitude of modesty which the communicator wants to establish; there are occasions on which one wishes to speak generally, even vaguely, rather than concisely; in conversation, if one does not immediately think of the exact word, a roundabout phrasing is usually preferable to a long, awkward pause in which one gropes for the right word. Context can never be disregarded, and brief examples, taken out of context, are subject to modification by particular contexts.

With these necessary qualifications, we can proceed to a discussion of various ways of achieving economy and conciseness in writing.

A. Avoiding Padding and Jargon

The first step in economical expression is recognizing and eliminating useless words. *Padding* is a term for words and phrases which add nothing except unnecessary length to a sentence, which clutter it and obscure its meaning. Usually padding can simply be struck out, leaving the sentence cleaner and clearer without the dead weight of this meaningless verbiage; sometimes, when the padding is removed, some rephrasing or substitution is required. Common types of padding are illustrated in the phrases and sentences which follow:

1. Awkward and meaningless repetition of the idea:

six *in number*	*first* beginning
round *in shape*	*resultant* effect
red *in color*	*so* consequently *as a result*
large *in size*	*most* paramount
repeat *again*	*absolutely* parallel
continue *on*	*entirely* unique
endorse *on the back*	*complete* absence
recur *again*	*habitual* custom
each *and every*	received free *gratis*
true fact	sunset *in the west*
necessary requisite	*of a* useful *character*
important essential	biography *of his life*
exchanged cards *with each other*	my *own* autobiography
at the age of ten *years old*	modern house *of today*
always invariably arrived late	I thought *in my own mind*
came punctually *on time*	six A.M. *in the morning*

2. Wordy delaying of the subject:

There are many students *who* should not be in college. [Many students should not be in college.]

It happens that I have known him for twelve years.

There is one circumstance *which* is in his favor.

There are two reasons *that* I have for not going: *the first is that* I have an exam to study for; *the second is that* I have no money. [I have two reasons for not going: I have an exam to study for, and I have no money.]

3. Wordy phrasing:

He spoke to me *concerning the matter* of my future. [about my future]

He *put in an appearance*. [appeared]

I am interested in work *along the line of* radio. [work in radio]

He went to the theater *on the occasion of* his birthday. [on his birthday]

A large percentage of people are gullible. [Many people]

In the case of most people, *they* believe what they read. [Most people believe]

I consulted a lawyer *with regard to* the accident. [about]

During the time that she was in college she worked in the cafeteria. *This was due to the fact that* she needed money. [While she was in college she worked at the cafeteria because she needed money]

She *came in contact with* many interesting people. [met, if this is what *came in contact with* really means]

I wish to ask your advice *in respect to the matter of* raising funds for the organization. [about raising funds]

My *field of* work is *that of* teaching. [My work is teaching.]

I shall go *despite the fact that* I am ill. [although I am ill]

More than two hundred years ago, Alexander Pope wrote of such wordiness:

> Words are like leaves; and where they most abound
> Much fruit of sense beneath is rarely found.

Padding is not always as deliberate as its name may indicate; very frequently, though, it springs from the lazy hope (conscious or only half-conscious) of meeting a writing assignment by filling space with words. Padding is not an acceptable substitute for the "fruit of sense."

A kind of wordiness closely akin to padding is *jargon.* Jargon is verbose, puffed-up, pretentious language, full of unnecessarily long and formal expressions, and inappropriate borrowings of semi-technical terms from such fields as sociology, psychology, education, and economics. The writer of jargon hopes to achieve dignity and impressiveness by his learned polysyllabic words. He achieves, instead, pomposity and obscurity. As the following examples show, jargon often consists of the "heavy words" discussed in Chapter Four:

higher institution of learning [school, or college, or university]
extensive conflagration [big fire]
He was in the $10,000 income bracket. [He earned $10,000.]
discharge his financial liabilities [pay his debts]
The individual rejoined in the negative. [He said no.]
She rendered a vocal selection. [She sang.]
He was the recipient of the munificent presentation. [He received the costly gift.]
He had an inferiority complex [or a phobia] about the Germanic tongue. [He did poorly in German.]
in the initial instance [in the first place]
Terminate the illumination. [Turn off the lights.]
a substantial segment of the population [many people]
an over-all report [a report]

Sir Arthur Quiller-Couch has ridiculed jargon (he includes in the term what we have called "padding") by jargonizing the famous "to be or not to be" soliloquy in *Hamlet*. These are Shakespeare's lines:

> To be, or not to be—that is the question:
> Whether 'tis nobler in the mind to suffer
> The slings and arrows of outrageous fortune
> Or to take arms against a sea of troubles,
> And by opposing end them. To die—to sleep—
> No more; and by a sleep to say we end
> The heartache, and the thousand natural shocks
> That flesh is heir to. 'Tis a consummation
> Devoutly to be wish'd.

The translation into jargon:

To be, or the contrary? Whether the former or the latter be preferable would seem to admit of some difference of opinion; the answer in the present case being of an affirmative or of a negative character according as to whether one elects on the one hand to mentally suffer the disfavor of fortune, albeit in an extreme degree, or on the other to boldly envisage adverse conditions in the prospect of eventually bringing them to a conclusion. The condition of sleep is similar to, if not indistinguishable from that of death; and with the addition of finality the former might be considered identical with the latter: so that in this connection it might be argued with regard to sleep that, could the addition be effected, a termination would be put to the endurance of a multiplicity of inconveniences, not to mention a number of downright evils incidental to our fallen humanity, and thus a consummation achieved of a most gratifying nature.—SIR ARTHUR QUILLER-COUCH, *On the Art of Writing*

Padding and jargon are the worst enemies of concise expression, but they are also easy to recognize and eliminate. The way to avoid them is to keep one's writing as simple and direct as possible.

B. Cutting Clauses

Cutting clauses is a method of subordination. It means reducing clauses, either independent or dependent, to concise phrases or even single words which do the work of the whole clause. The following sentences will illustrate this reduction. The reader should note that the revised sentences are better not only because they say the same thing in fewer words, but also because they are free of weak clauses and are therefore more emphatic.

The wind which blew through the cracks made a whistling sound. [two clauses, one independent, one dependent]

REVISED: The wind whistled through the cracks. [one clause; an exact verb cuts out five words]

He walked down the street as if he had a purpose. [two clauses, one independent, one dependent]

REVISED: He walked purposefully down the street. [one clause; an adverb takes the place of six words]

The student who is conscientious prepares every day for each of the courses he is taking. [three clauses]

REVISED: The conscientious student prepares for his courses every day. [one clause; an adjective (conscientious) and a pronominal adjective (his) cut out two weak clauses]

Mr. Brown, who is a devoted husband, bought his wife a mink coat which cost $6000.

REVISED: Mr. Brown, a devoted husband, bought his wife a six-thousand-dollar mink coat.

She made a slip of the tongue which revealed her fear, but she did not know it.
REVISED: Unconsciously, by a slip of the tongue, she revealed her fear.

As he walked through the crowd he bumped with his shoulders people who were in the way.
REVISED: He shouldered his way through the crowd.

Skillful parallel expression often helps to cut clauses and produce clearer and more concise expression:

It seemed to me, as I told her, that she should take the noon train. I advised her to make her reservations early. I also thought she should wire Aunt Mary that she was coming.
CUT AND IMPROVED BY PARALLELISM: I advised her to take the noon train, to make her reservations early, and to wire Aunt Mary that she was coming.

In the following example, parallelism provides more polished as well as more economical expression:

He asked just a few simple things of life. He wanted one or two small luxuries, like wine with his dinner. It was important to him to be absorbed in whatever work he did. And he yearned for romantic love.
IMPROVED BY PARALLELISM: He asked of life, quite simply, wine with his dinner, absorption in his work, and romance in his love.

C. Choosing Exact Words

Economy and conciseness come, above all, from using exact words which convey immediately and accurately a complex idea. Colorless and general verbs like *walk, go, said, look,* can often be replaced by concrete verbs which convey the action more vividly and exactly. We have seen examples of the value of strong verbs in cutting clauses (He *shouldered* his way through the crowd. The wind *whistled* through the cracks). In the following examples, an accurate verb can do in one stroke the work of a weak verb and a qualifying phrase:

He *walked* down the street *in an unsteady way.* [tottered or lurched or staggered—whatever he actually did]
The dishes *fell* to the floor *with a loud noise.* [crashed or clattered]
He *sat* in the chair *looking idle and lazy.* [lolled]
He *walked* along *slowly.* [sauntered, ambled]
He *looked* at her *in an angry way.* [glowered, glared]
He *went through* the blocks, *separating them* according to color. [sorted]
The dog *gave a high, excited bark.* [yelped or yipped]
He *looked* at her *with his mouth open.* [gaped]
They were trying to *get* money from him *by dishonest means.* [extort]
He *took* the bank funds *and ran away with them.* [absconded with]

He *had funny expressions on his face* as he talked. [grimaced]
He *looked* at her *with a self-satisfied and affected smile.* [smirked]

Loose, wordy expression is frequently the result of the writer's not knowing, or not being careful enough to use, the exact name for a thing or a process. The following sentences illustrate the economy of accurate naming:

The teacher leaned on the *little stand that held his notes.* [lectern]
The conductor lifted *the stick that he uses to direct the orchestra.* [his baton]
We read a *fourteen-line poem* by Shakespeare. [sonnet]
She has *a big red dog with long ears.* [an Irish setter]
The way he stood when he was ready to hit the golf ball was not good. [His stance]
He *hit a drive that curved to the right and went* into the woods. [sliced his drive]
He made the touchdown by *starting in one direction, then turning and going in the other.* [reversing his field]
She *led the queen from her hand, hoping that if the person on her left had the king he would play it and she could take the trick with the ace on the board.* [finessed her queen to the ace on the board]

As we pointed out earlier, in the discussion of levels of usage, formal words are often more precise than their informal equivalents. Sometimes, therefore, semiformal or formal words are necessary for economical and concise expression. The following sentences are taken from freshman themes written in class, with little time for revision. The sentences would have been improved if the wordy informal locutions, most of them clauses, had been replaced by accurate, more formal words:

It seemed it just had to happen the way it did. [It seemed inevitable.]
Once the words were said, they couldn't be taken back. [The words were irrevocable.]
She told a story that no one could believe. [She told an incredible story.]
He had no weak point where he could be attacked. [He was invulnerable.]
The exercises were such that we couldn't do without them. [The exercises were indispensable.]
She faced two courses of action and didn't know which one to choose. [She was in a dilemma.]

The use of exact words offers endless possibilities for improvement. Inaccurate expression is often the result of carelessness—of not bothering to think of the accurate word or to discriminate between roughly synonymous terms. Often, though, inaccurate expression is the result of inadequate vocabulary—of not knowing well, and therefore not being able to use naturally and confidently, the exact word which does the work of five or six words. Most college students need to extend their active vocabularies in order to achieve concise and economical expression.

It is very important for the reader, as he considers this discussion of economy and conciseness, to understand that elaboration of a general statement for clarity and vividness, and repetition for desired emphasis are *not* wordiness. On the contrary, additional concrete detail often makes a meaningless statement rich and meaningful by enabling the reader to feel and see the particular things the writer felt and saw. Repetition of words or phrases may drive home an idea, or may create an atmosphere or arouse an emotion which is an important part of the writer's communication. The longer expression of an idea is sometimes preferable to the short one, for sometimes the very length and rhythm of a longer sentence establish a tone or a feeling which is part of the full meaning intended. The long locutions below are examples; their length as well as their phrasing carries the desired tone of solemnity and dignity:

> Fourscore and seven years ago, our fathers brought forth on this continent . . .
> SHORTER, BUT LESS EFFECTIVE: Eighty-seven years ago our fathers made here . . .

> The President of the United States gave an address.
> SHORTER, BUT LESS EFFECTIVE if one wishes to emphasize the dignity of the occasion: Eisenhower spoke.

Economical and concise expression is probably the most striking trait of really good English. But, when an inexperienced writer understands this and begins to prune his writing, there is some danger that he will cut out the vital as well as the useless parts. Economy and precision, properly understood, are not achieved simply by brevity, and never by sacrificing words or details which contribute positively either to the development of sense or to the communication of atmosphere or emotion. True economy and conciseness come from removing the lazy clutter of padding, jargon, weak clauses, and purposeless circumlocution, and replacing it with clear, strong, working words.

II. ORIGINALITY

Effective writing is original because it communicates accurately the thought, observation, knowledge, experience, and, except in very impersonal writing, the personality of a human being who is not exactly like any other human being in the world. Originality should not be confused with eccentricity or straining for the unconventional. It is simply the direct expression of an individual alive in the world, seeing with his own eyes and hearing with his own ears, absorbing experience, and using language to relate the things he sees and hears and believes.

One of the obstacles to individual writing is the *trite expression* or *cliché*. Clichés are phrases which have become stale through overuse. Too-familiar combinations of words (*tired but happy, icy chill, last but not least, pure and simple, conspicuous by its absence*); worn-out quotations ("to be, or not to be," "kill the fatted calf," "home sweet home") ; and worn-out figures of speech (*like a rat in a trap, sober as a judge, busy as a bee*)—these are the principal categories of trite expressions. At one time such expressions were new and vivid; now they have lost their force and have become mere words, incapable of carrying fresh meaning.

No one can entirely avoid overused phrases, in speech or in writing; and indeed it is sometimes difficult to distinguish between clichés and expressions which, though used for years, have never become outworn but are an accepted and ageless part of our language. For example, is "damn with faint praise" a frayed quotation or simply familiar idiom? Is "freedom from fear" a relatively new cliché or simply a well-known phrasing of an idea? Furthermore (and this makes it particularly difficult to be dogmatic about avoiding triteness), a cliché in an unusual context, or a cliché spoken ironically, or a cliché twisted to have a different meaning in context, may be witty and effective. It is impossible to say, therefore, that worn-out phrases, quotations, and figures of speech should never be used. It is possible, however, to say that they should not be used unconsciously. The intelligent communicator, realizing that these once striking expressions have been dulled by continuous and lazy use, will avoid them unless he can give them a fresh twist, or unless some unusual element in the situation or in his intention makes it advisable for him to express himself tritely.

Students who have not read widely are often insensitive to triteness. There is no easy cure for this insensitivity; but, as an aid in recognizing clichés, we are listing here a number of too well-worn expressions, figures of speech, and quotations:

bright and shining faces	darkness overtook us
few and far between	dull thud
at one fell swoop	ominous silence
history tells us	doting parents [or] fond parents
after all is said and done	blushing bride
it stands to reason	the time of my life

proud possessor
humble origin
shadow of a doubt
tale of woe
fast and furious
breathe a sigh of relief
peace reigned supreme
finer things of life
with bated breath
pangs of remorse
depths of despair
wreathed in smiles
Mother Nature
Father Time
watery grave
irony of fate
crack of dawn
budding genius
soul of honor
trees like sentinels
tide of battle
bolt from the blue
rears its ugly head
diamond in the rough
in the arms of Morpheus
bright as a pin
smart as a whip
sly as a fox
brave as a lion
pretty as a picture
clear as a bell

tired as a dog
sick as a dog
dead as a doornail
brown as a berry
cool as a cucumber
pale as death
slow as molasses
green with envy
snake in the grass
work like a Trojan
calm before the storm
hit the nail on the head
chip off the old block
burn the midnight oil
get down to brass tacks
acid test
run like a flash
better late than never
age before beauty
method in his madness
all the world's a stage
people who live in glass houses
in the spring a young man's fancy
sadder but wiser
all that glitters is not gold
all work and no play
eat, drink, and be merry
wine, women, and song
lean and hungry look
improve each shining hour
cradle of the deep

Some use of trite expressions is, as we have said, unavoidable; the writer, and especially the speaker, cannot consider every phrase and reject it if it has been used before; and he may have some particular reason for using a cliché. But he should familiarize himself with common clichés and be sure that, in his writing at least, they do not occur frequently as serious substitutes for more individual and more exact expression. Some students have the idea that trite expressions are humorous. They are not, unless they are given some new and clever turn. Nor does putting them in quotation marks justify their use. The quotation marks simply indicate that the writer knows the expression is a poor one, and that, despite his knowledge, he is too lazy to find a better way of phrasing his idea.

Habitual triteness is evidence that the writer is not really think-ing about his subject or making a serious effort to communicate it accurately. He is, instead, taking refuge in ready-made phrases which hazily approximate his meaning. Consider, for example, the following passage:

> Her fond parents thought her a budding genius; but although she was as smart as a whip and was always burning the midnight oil, she had no sense of the finer things of life. All work and no play makes Jill a dull girl.

What is the person described actually like? What, if he were forced to emerge from his smoke screen of clichés, would the writer have to communicate?

Eliminating triteness does not automatically produce distinctively original expression, but it clears the way for the originality which is well within the power of any college student—the accurate and interesting expression of his own fresh observation and thought.

III. VARIETY IN SENTENCES

Although the inexperienced writer is not always aware of it, sound and rhythm are very important parts of effective style. An undesirable repetition of the same sound, the same sentence length, and the same sentence structure will be irritating to a trained reader, or will lull him into utter disinterest. Sometimes an unwisely repeated sentence structure produces an effect like that of the recitation of poetry by third-grade pupils: the real meaning is lost in the monotonously repeated rhythm.

Variety in sentences is very closely related to effective emphasis, which we shall discuss in the next section. Indeed, it is difficult to separate the two qualities, even for purposes of discussion. We shall, however, point out in this section certain types of monotony which the skillful writer avoids, and outline some of the techniques by which he varies his sentence pattern. In applying these techniques, he must also apply the principles of emphasis.

Careless repetition of words, illustrated in the sentences below, is a kind of monotony easily recognized and easily avoided:

> *Time* has proved that Ibsen was a writer ahead of his *time*. Most of his plays are *timely* today.

> We admired the *location* where his new house was to be *located*.

> I *noted* in my *notes* all the important facts about this *noted* general.

> All of the members of the *community gathered* at these *community gatherings*.

> I am *attracted* by the *current attraction* at the *current* burlesque show.

Monotony in sentence length and repetition of sentence pattern are perhaps less conspicuous than repeated words; but, unless patterned sentences are used judiciously, for deliberate emphasis, they are even more ineffective and boring than thoughtlessly repeated words. The following passages illustrate some of the common types of monotonous sentence patterns:

> He walked down the street. He scanned the numbers on the houses. He found the one he wanted. He went up the steps. He hesitated a moment. Then he rang the bell. [Repeated choppy sentences, with the same subject-verb order: *he walked, he scanned, he found,* etc.]
> He walked down the street and scanned the numbers on the houses. He found the one he wanted and went up the steps. He hesitated a moment and then rang the bell. [Simple sentences with compound predicates]
> Walking down the street, he scanned the numbers on the houses. Finding the one he wanted, he went up the steps. Hesitating only a moment, he rang the bell. [Repeated introductory phrases]
> As he walked down the street, he scanned the numbers on the houses. When he found the one he wanted, he went up the steps. After he had hesitated for a moment, he rang the bell. [Repeated introductory clauses before the main clause]
> He scanned the numbers on the houses as he walked down the street. He went up the steps when he found the one he wanted. He rang the bell after he had hesitated for a moment. [Dependent clauses trailing the main clause]

The first step in achieving variety in sentence movement is, of course, recognizing such monotonous sentence patterns. Reading the passage aloud and actually hearing it is probably the surest way of detecting the repeated rhythm. The monotony should then be remedied by the following techniques:

1. Varying the length of sentences; using occasional short sentences among longer ones, or occasional long sentences if the prevailing style is terse.

2. Using parallel and balanced constructions, not continuously, but as a change from simpler constructions. Robert Louis Stevenson, writing on style, simultaneously described and demonstrated the value of varied parallelism:

> Nor should the balance be too striking and exact, for the one rule is to be infinitely various; to interest, to disappoint, to surprise, and yet still to gratify; to be ever changing, as it were, the stitch, and yet still to give the effect of an ingenious neatness.

3. Intermingling loose and periodic sentences. In loose sentences, the sentence continues after the main thought has been expressed:

We know that the young prince died, although we know little more.

In periodic sentences, the meaning is suspended until the end of the sentence:

About the subsequent events, the terrified repledging of loyalty, the whispered conspiracies, the promises exchanged behind locked doors, *we know but little.*

Frequent and elaborate periodic sentences are more characteristic of formal than of informal style. Occasional periodic sentences, however, are excellent for varied movement as well as for the heightened suspense and emphasis of the sentences themselves.

4. Changing the position of modifiers and parenthetic elements for variety in movement and for better emphasis:

He met a most attractive girl at the party.
At the party he met a most attractive girl.
He met, at the party, a most attractive girl.

Consequently, he is no longer interested in Marie.
He is, consequently, no longer interested in Marie.
He is no longer interested, consequently, in Marie.

5. Changing the usual subject-verb-object order of some sentences:

He could never forgive this. [subject-verb-object]
This he could never forgive. [object-subject-verb]

At the last minute Sally rushed in. [subject-verb]
At the last minute in rushed Sally. [verb-subject]

By means of some of these devices, the walking-down-the-street passages cited on page 121 could be revised and varied as follows:

He walked down the street, scanning the numbers on the houses. When he found the one he wanted, he walked up the steps, hesitated a moment, and then rang the bell.

[*Or*]

He scanned the numbers on the houses as he walked down the street. Finding the one he wanted, he went up the steps and hesitated a moment. Then he rang the bell.

Sentence variety is closely related to emphasis because as the writer begins to vary his sentence length and structure and to change the position of modifying elements, he must consider what ideas he wants to emphasize by structure and position. Variety in sentences is not merely a matter of form and style. It is organic expression, in which sound and structure and rhythm all contribute to the full meaning the writer wishes to communicate. The following passage from *The Autobiography of Lincoln Steffens* illustrates well the relationship between variety and emphasis. Below the passage is a partial analysis of the methods Steffens uses to achieve both variety and emphasis.

[1] It was conversation I was hearing, the free, passionate, witty exchanges of studied minds as polished as fine tools. [2] They were always courteous; no two ever spoke together; there were no asides; they all talked to the question before the house, and while they were on the job of exposition anyone, regardless of his side, would contribute his quota of facts, or his remembrance of some philosopher's opinion or some poet's perfect phrase for the elucidation or the beautification of the theme. [3] When the differences rose the urbanity persisted. [4] They drank their California wine with a relish, they smoked the room thick, and they pressed their views with vigor and sincerity and eloquence; but their good temper never failed them. [5] It was conversation. [6] I had heard conversation before; I have heard conversation sometimes since, but rarely, and never like my remembrance of those wonderful Saturday nights in San Francisco —which were my preparation for college.

[7] For those conversations, so brilliant, so scholarly, and so consciously unknowing, seemed to me, silent in the background, to reveal the truth that even college graduates did not know anything, really. [8] Evidences they had, all the testimony of all the wise men in the historical world on everything, but no decisions. [9] None. [10] I must go to college to find out more, and I wanted to. [11] It seemed as if I had to go soon. [12] My head, busy with questions before, was filled with holes that were aching voids as hungry, as painful, as an empty stomach. [13] And my questions were explicit; it was as if I were not only hungry; I was hungry for certain foods. [14] My curiosity was no longer vague.

[1] Loose sentence, medium length, with the complex appositive following the main clause.

[2] Long sentence; a series of short statements followed by a long, complex one, with parallel phrasing.

[3] Short sentence; a subordinate clause preceding the main clause which contains the main idea.

[4] Long sentence; parallel clauses.

[5] Short emphatic restatement of the topic idea of the paragraph.

[6] Long sentence with parallel phrasing, mounting rhythmically to a climax. "Conversation" repeated for emphasis.

[7] Long periodic sentence, with parallel phrasing and skillful placing of modifiers. "Conversation" repeated at the beginning for emphasis and transition.

[8] Object-subject-verb order to emphasize "evidences" and contrast "decisions" at the end of the sentence; long appositive.

[9] One word sentence for emphasis, after three rather long sentences.

[10] Compound sentence.

[11] Shorter complex sentence.

[12] Longer complex sentence with interrupting modifiers.
[13] Three clauses, the closely related ideas separated for emphasis.
[14] Short emphatic statement of the topic idea.

An even more striking example of organic expression, that is, of fitting the expression to the whole purpose, is the following passage from Virginia Woolf, an artist in modern prose. In the first paragraph, long complicated sentences are used to describe the complexity of darkness and sound and light; short sentences are used for dramatic action and realization: "Orlando leapt to his feet"; "The Queen had come." The short-sentence pattern of the second paragraph might seem, in a hasty eye-reading, to violate all principles of sentence variety. More careful reading will show that those short sentences are functional; they are used deliberately to communicate Orlando's distraught state of mind and at the same time his frantic, separate actions. The reader should note, too, how skillfully the short-sentence pattern is broken, just before it would become monotonous.

After an hour or so—the sun was rapidly sinking, the white clouds had turned red, the hills were violet, the woods purple, the valleys black— a trumpet sounded. Orlando leapt to his feet. The shrill sound came from the valley. It came from a dark spot down there; a spot compact and mapped out; a maze; a town, yet girt about with walls; it came from the heart of his own great house in the valley, which, dark before, even as he looked and the single trumpet duplicated and reduplicated itself with other shriller sounds, lost its darkness and became pierced with lights. Some were small hurrying lights, as if servants dashed along corridors to answer summonses; others were high and lustrous lights, as if they burnt in empty banqueting halls made ready to receive guests who had not come; and others dipped and waved and sank and rose, as if held in the hands of troops of serving men, bending, kneeling, rising, receiving, guarding, and escorting with all dignity indoors a great Princess alighting from her chariot. Coaches turned and wheeled in the courtyard. Horses tossed their plumes. The Queen had come.
Orlando looked no more. He dashed down the hill. He let himself in at a wicket gate. He tore up the winding staircase. He reached his room. He tossed his stockings to one side of the room, his jerkin to the other. He dipped his head. He scoured his hands. He pared his fingernails. With no more than six inches of looking glass and a pair of old candles to help him, he had thrust on crimson breeches, lace collar, waistcoat of taffeta, and shoes with rosettes on them as big as double dahlias in less than ten minutes by the stable clock. He was ready. He was flushed. He was excited. But he was terribly late.—VIRGINIA WOOLF, *Orlando*

Because monotony is a common weakness in college writing, most students will profit by reading their themes aloud and listening carefully for monotonously repeated patterns. At first the process of breaking the pattern by changing the wording, structure, or length of some sentences may be purely mechanical. But as the writer deliberately—even laboriously—practices putting a verb before its subject now and then, interrupting a conventional sentence with modifiers and appositives, using some periodic sentences, tying related ideas together in parallel constructions, changing his pace with long and short sentences, he begins to develop a sense of the organic relationship between the pattern of sentences and the pattern of thought. From telling himself, "I ought to have a short sentence among all these long ones," he progresses to "This idea should hit hard; I'll put it by itself in a short sentence." Instead of thinking, "I have four subject-verb-object constructions in a row; better change one or two," he thinks, "The object here is the most important word in the sentence; I'll pull it out of its normal position to give it emphasis." At this point he is no longer merely avoiding monotony; he is beginning to achieve that functional and organic variety which is an important part of effective expression.

IV. EMPHASIS

Emphasis in writing is more of a problem than emphasis in speaking. In speech, we depend a great deal on gestures, facial expressions, long pauses, and particularly on tone of voice to stress important words and ideas. The amateur in writing often attempts to reproduce the accents of speech by underlining and capitalizing, by frequent use of exclamation points, and by intensives like *very, so, most, frightfully, perfectly:*

> I was so very tired at the end of the day, but I felt that I had never had such a perfectly wonderful time. It was simply marvelous!! I wouldn't have missed it for anything! And I met the most wonderful Man!

Such devices for emphasis may be appropriate in informal correspondence, where they suggest to the reader the vocal stress the writer would have given the words; but they are not effective in more impersonal writing, where the writer's vocal tone is irrelevant. Skillful writers seldom rely on mechanical devices or many intensives for emphasis; they get emphasis by their choice of words, sentence form, and arrangement of sentences in the paragraph and paragraphs in the whole piece of writing.

Here and there in the preceding sections of this book we have discussed a number of weaknesses which make writing unemphatic. It will be well to review them briefly before we discuss further ways of achieving effective emphasis:

1. *A thoughtlessly repeated sentence pattern is unemphatic.* It gives the same weight and the same rhythm to ideas which are actually varied and therefore should be distinguished by varied expression.

2. *Improper subordination destroys emphasis.* In the examples below, lack of subordination gives equal stress to unequal ideas; the most important idea, therefore, is not emphasized:

> I was walking around Walden Pond. It was a cool day last September. I saw a child fall in the water.
>
> We reached the top of the hill and Mary wanted to rest and so we stopped.

Upside-down subordination, that is, putting the main idea in a subordinate clause or phrase, robs that idea of its proper emphasis:

> He made his third proposal, which she accepted.
> He eluded his opponent, crossing the goal line.

3. *Overuse of the passive voice is unemphatic* because the passive is often weak, wordy, and indirect. Weak passives like the ones in the following sentences should be avoided in favor of more emphatic active statements:

> Your communication of August 26 was received by me today.
> This paper is late because difficulties were run into by the writer.
> As we opened the gate, a snarling dog was seen on the steps.
> Many hours are spent by students in talking about their work instead of doing it.

4. *Clichés are unemphatic* because they are forceless and dull, and because they suggest laziness or disinterest on the part of the writer.

5. *Padding, jargon, weak clauses, and circumlocutions are destroyers of emphasis.* Their wordiness waters the meaning of the sentence and sometimes actually submerges it.

6. *Euphemism, a kind of circumlocution which we have not discussed before, is another enemy of emphasis.* Our word *euphemism* is derived from the Greek *eu* meaning "well" and *phanai,* "to speak"; the Greek word *euphēmizein* meant "to use fair words, or words of good omen." Now, however, *euphemism* is a term applied to a mild, soothing, usually vague expression which is substituted for a precise, or blunt, or less agreeable term. It is a linguistic device by which people avoid talking about, and often thinking about, unpleasant realities. Common examples of euphemisms are:

> *passed away* or *departed from this world,* for "died"
> *perspire,* for "sweat"
> *expectorate,* for "spit"
> *social disease,* for "syphilis"

lung affliction, for "tuberculosis"
indisposed, for "sick"
visually handicapped, for "blind"
mortician, for "undertaker"
paying guest, for "boarder"
sanitation engineer, for "garbage collector"
deferred payment, for "installment buying"
defensive maneuver, for "retreat"
plant food, for "manure"

There are, of course, certain social and conversational situations in which euphemisms may be desirable. For example, good judgment would suggest saying "plant food" if the person to whom one is talking considers "manure" a shocking word; and tact and kindness might recommend "he passed away" or some other euphemism for "death" in conversation with one recently bereaved. But increasingly in modern writing euphemisms are rejected, because they are roundabout, inexact, hesitant, and weak. Like other vague terms and circumlocutions, they carry the reader away from, instead of bringing him close to the real meaning. They should be used only when a situation involving personal feelings demands a delicate avoidance of fact. Normally the blunt factual term should be used because it is more precise and more emphatic.

The writer who has learned to choose exact words, to subordinate skillfully, and to avoid wordiness, triteness, monotony, weak passive constructions, and euphemisms, has gone far toward emphatic expression. His writing will become more effective as he also learns to use *pause, position,* and *repetition* for emphasis.

A. Emphasis by Pause

In speech, the pause is a common and effective device for emphasis. A pause before a word or statement arouses interest in what is to come; a pause after a word or statement stresses its importance by giving the audience time to absorb it. In writing, commas, dashes, semicolons, periods, paragraph breaks, and chapter divisions all create pauses which emphasize the material immediately preceding and following the pause. The degree of emphasis depends on the length of the stop indicated by the punctuation. Beginnings and ends of sentences and beginnings and ends of paragraphs derive much of their emphasis from the fact that the beginnings follow and the ends are followed by full stops. We have discussed earlier the emphatic quality of the occasional very short sentence. It is emphatic not only because it differs from the sentences around it, but because its few words stand between, and are emphasized by, two stops.

Advertising commonly uses short sentences and even one-sentence paragraphs, so that each idea will make its impact separately and emphatically on the mind of the reader.

A writer who is addressing an intelligent audience will, of course, take care that the ideas emphasized by his pauses are worthy of stress. He will use pauses to throw emphasis exactly where he wants it in the sentence or the paragraph, and in the exact degree. The following examples show how different kinds of pause work to create different emphases:

He was flushed, he was excited, but he was terribly late.
STRONGER EMPHASIS BY MEANS OF HEAVIER PAUSES: He was flushed. He was excited. But he was terribly late.

First Mrs. Brown arrived, then Mrs. Jones, and last of all Mrs. Fitzpatrick.
STRONGER EMPHASIS, BY MEANS OF ADDITIONAL PAUSES, to Mrs. Fitzpatrick and the fact that she arrived late: First Mrs. Brown arrived, then Mrs. Jones, and, last of all—Mrs. Fitzpatrick.

I swear that this is not at all unusual.
STRONGER EMPHASIS ON "NOT" AND "AT ALL" because they precede and follow the pause of a sentence interrupter: This is not, I swear, at all unusual.

SHIFT IN EMPHASIS (AND IN MEANING) BY A SHIFT IN PAUSE; (context would determine the best emphasis): However, Malcolm refused to give serious consideration to this important question.
Malcolm refused to give serious consideration, however, to this important question.
Malcolm refused, however, to give serious consideration to this important question.
Malcolm, however, refused to give serious consideration to this important question.

GREATER EMPHASIS ON THE LAST TWO SENTENCES BY MEANS OF A PARAGRAPH PAUSE: He crept along, on his hands and knees again. The seconds passed like individual units, almost as if he heard a clock ticking. He could have sobbed every time he heard a man mutter in his sleep. They were all around him! He seemed to exist in several parts now; there was the sore remote protest of his palms and kneecap, the choking swollen torment of his throat, and the unbearable awareness of his brain. He was very close to the final swooning relaxation a man feels when he is being beaten unconscious and no longer cares whether he can get up. Very far away he could hear the murmuring of the jungle in the night.

At a curve in the trail he halted, peered around, and almost screamed. A man was sitting at a machine gun about three feet away.—NORMAN MAILER, *The Naked and the Dead*

B. Emphasis by Position

Position is closely related to pause because, as we have just seen, pauses create positions of emphasis. Since the beginning and, particularly, the end of a sentence naturally receive the greatest emphasis, those positions should be occupied by words which the writer wishes to stress.

The delayed beginning, which we have mentioned as a type of padding, wastes the emphatic first place in the sentence on non-contributing words:

> There are many men who enjoy beating their wives.
> MORE EMPHATIC: Many men enjoy beating their wives.

> It was on Christmas Eve that I finally made up my mind.
> MORE EMPHATIC: On Christmas Eve I finally made up my mind.

> There is some hope on his part of getting home Friday.
> MORE EMPHATIC: He has some hope of getting home Friday.

Avoiding such wasted emphasis is not, however, enough. One should use sentence beginnings to emphasize important elements which, in a conventionally arranged sentence, would be buried in the middle of the sentence. The following examples show the emphasis given words and phrases when they are taken out of their normal position and put in place of the subject at the beginning of the sentence:

> *Sorrowfully* she turned and walked down the road. [The adverb *sorrowfully* is emphasized by being taken out of its normal position after *turned.*]
> *Evidences* they had . . . but no decisions. [The object is emphasized by being put before the subject and verb.]
> *Desperately* he struggled to untie the last knot.
> *Across the field* he fled in terror.
> *John* I admire; *his brother* I detest.

Such inversion, or changing of the normal sentence order, should, of course, be practiced with discretion. The force of the unusual order is lost, and the writing becomes stilted and strained, if an unconventional pattern is used repeatedly.

The end of the sentence is a position even more emphatic than the beginning, partly because it is followed by the period stop, and partly because there is a well-established general expectation that important things come last. In informal speech, sentences frequently trail off in weak modifiers and afterthoughts. In writing, such sentences should be revised to end strongly with words and ideas that merit a prominent position and receive an added emphasis from it.

UNEMPHATIC: Julia made a vehement protest, however.
MORE EMPHATIC: Julia, however, made a vehement protest.

UNEMPHATIC: We loudly denounced him as soon as he came.
MORE EMPHATIC: As soon as he came we loudly denounced him.

UNEMPHATIC: The divorce rate is now decreasing—at least I read that in the *Herald*.
MORE EMPHATIC: According to the *Herald*, the divorce rate is now decreasing.

UNEMPHATIC: We were surprised at his daring, not at his knowledge.
MORE EMPHATIC: We were surprised, not at his knowledge, but at his daring.

UNEMPHATIC: He was patient with their conversation in the next room, but he slammed the door when they turned on the radio.
MORE EMPHATIC: He was patient with their conversation in the next room, but when they turned on the radio he slammed the door.[1]

Here are two sentences about Leonardo da Vinci's *Last Supper:*

Leonardo painted the Last Supper on the damp wall of the refectory, oozing with mineral salts. The effort to see the Eucharist as one taking leave of his friends, not as the pale Host of the altar, was strange after all the mystic developments of the middle age.

Walter Pater, in *The Renaissance,* wrote them this way:

On the damp wall of the refectory, oozing with mineral salts, Leonardo painted the Last Supper. . . . Strange, after all the mystic developments of the middle age, was the effort to see the Eucharist, not as the pale Host of the altar, but as one taking leave of his friends.

In Pater's first sentence, the main clause is emphasized by its position at the end; in the second, the two important ideas, "strange" and "as one taking leave of his friends," are given emphasis by a sentence arrangement which puts them at beginning and end.

The strongest sentences build to a climax. The elaborate periodic sentence, with its thought suspended until the end of the sentence, is a striking example of climactic arrangement:

To those among us, however, who have lived long enough to form some just estimate of the rate of the changes which are, hour by hour in accelerating catastrophe, manifesting themselves in the laws, the arts, and the creeds of men, it seems to me, that now at least, if never at any former

[1] The reader should be reminded that particular contexts might well justify some of the sentences we have marked "unemphatic." If, for example, the last sentence (about the radio and the slamming of the door) occurred in a discussion of this man's aversion to radio, the clause "when they turned on the radio," even though it is subordinate, might be important enough to deserve the end position.

time, the thoughts of the true nature of our life, and of its powers and responsibilities, should present themselves with absolute sadness and sternness.—JOHN RUSKIN, *Sesame and Lilies*

But in less elaborate sentences, too, parallel elements should be arranged in an order of increasing importance.

And now abideth faith, hope, charity, these three; but the greatest of these is charity. [The final clause states what the position of *charity*, last in the series, has already suggested.]

> The lark's on the wing;
> The snail's on the thorn:
> God's in his heaven—
> All's right with the world!

> A jug of wine, a loaf of bread, and thou
> Beside me singing in the wilderness.

> Not for just an hour, not for just a day,
> Not for just a year, but always.

And so, when their day is over, when their good and their evil have become eternal by the immortality of the past, be it ours to feel that, where they suffered, where they failed, no deed of ours was the cause; but wherever a spark of the divine fire kindled in their hearts, we were ready with encouragement, with sympathy, with brave words in which high courage glowed.[2]—BERTRAND RUSSELL, "A Free Man's Worship"

Violation of the natural order of climax robs a sentence of its force, unless the anticlimax is used deliberately for humor. The two sentences below illustrate intentional anticlimax; the writer wishes to emphasize the items which by most standards are the least important:

At the end of nine holes, the minister had lost his temper, his religion, and his golf ball.
Colonel McGunthrie has survived World War I, World War II, and twenty years of marriage to Mrs. McGunthrie.

The following sentences are examples of thoughtless anticlimax:

It was a stupendous performance, and very good.
She had no illusions. She distrusted her husband, herself, and her friends.
We find these psychological reactions in frogs, in guinea pigs, in men, and in rats.

In paragraphs, as in sentences, the position of elements is important. The principles of emphasis are much the same: the first and last

---

[2] Reprinted from *Mysticism and Logic* by Bertrand Russell, by permission of W. W. Norton and Company, Inc. Copyright, 1929, by the publishers.

sentences of the paragraph hold the positions of greatest emphasis; good paragraphs, like good sentences, begin strongly and build to a strong ending.

C. Emphasis by Repetition

We have said a good deal about wordy and ineffective repetition: the needless repetition of ideas ("punctually on time"), the careless repetition of words ("gathered at the gathering"), and the thoughtless repetition of the same sentence pattern. Repetition can be, however, one of the most effective means of emphasis. Skillfully used, it impresses key words and phrases on the reader's mind, creates emotional effects, and binds together sentences in a paragraph.

Specific illustration will show, more clearly than any amount of general exposition, the force of effective repetition. By repetition, Coleridge in *The Ancient Mariner* produces an effect not carried by the simple statement, "I was alone on a wide sea with no one to pity me." Read the stanza several times, letting the repetitions sink in— *alone, all, wide,* and the *s* sounds in *sea, saint, soul:*

> Alone, alone, all, all alone,
> Alone on a wide, wide sea!
> And never a saint took pity on
> My soul in agony.

James Harvey Robinson, in the following paragraph, emphatically repeats the pronoun *my,* which is the crux of his idea:

The little word *my* is the most important one in all human affairs, and properly to reckon with it is the beginning of wisdom. It has the same force whether it is *my* dinner, *my* dog, and *my* house, or *my* faith, *my* country, and *my* God. We not only resent the imputation that our watch is wrong, or our car shabby, but that our conception of the canals of Mars, of the pronunciation of "Epictetus," of the medicinal value of salicine, or the date of Sargon I, are subject to revision.—JAMES HARVEY ROBINSON, *The Mind in the Making*

Count and *counting* are repeated by William James to emphasize the idea that separate actions do count in the formation of habits and of character:

Every smallest stroke of virtue or of vice leaves its never so little scar. The drunken Rip Van Winkle, in Jefferson's play, excuses himself for every fresh dereliction by saying, "I won't count this time!" Well! he may not count it, and a kind Heaven may not count it; but it is being counted none the less. Down among his nerve-cells and fibres the molecules are counting it, registering and storing it up to be used against him when the next temptation comes. Nothing we ever do is, in strict scientific literalness, wiped out.—WILLIAM JAMES, *Psychology*

Thomas Wolfe often uses repetition to create atmosphere and emotion. In the following passage, the phrase *in the night, in the dark* is repeated for lyric emphasis and power; it integrates the separate details in the paragraph:

Father, in the night time, in the dark, I have heard the thunder of the fast express. In the night, in the dark, I have heard the howling of the winds among great trees, and the sharp and windy raining of the acorns. In the night, in the dark, I have heard the feet of rain upon the roofs, the glut and gurgle of the gutter spouts, and the soaking gulping throat of all the mighty earth, drinking its thirst out in the month of May—and heard the sorrowful silence of the river in October. The hill-streams foam and welter in a steady plunge, the mined clay drops and melts and eddies in the night, the snake coils cool and glistening under dripping ferns, the water roars down past the mill in one sheer sheet-like plunge, making a steady noise like wind, and in the night, in the dark, the river flows by us to the sea.—THOMAS WOLFE, *Of Time and the River*

Archibald MacLeish, in the foreword to his radio play, *The Fall of the City,* is concerned with stressing the importance, in the untelevised radio play, of the spoken word. Repetition of *word* and some repetition of sentence pattern emphasize his idea and bind his sentences to the central theme of the paragraph:

The first fact which everyone knows is that radio is a mechanism which carries to an audience sounds and nothing but sounds. A radio play consists of words and word equivalents and nothing else. There is no visible actor disguised to assume a part. There is no stage-set contrived to resemble a place. There is only the spoken word—an implement which poets have always claimed to use with a special authority. There is only the word-excited imagination—a theater in which poets have always claimed peculiar rights to play. Nothing exists save as the word creates it. The word dresses the stage. The word brings on the actors. The word supplies their look, their clothes, their gestures. The more packed and allusive the word, the more illuminating its rhythms, the more perfectly is the scene prepared, the more convincingly is the play enacted.

Effective emphasis, involving as it does so many of the principles and techniques of good expression, might well be the subject of a whole book on writing. Effective emphasis occurs when the writer knows surely what he wants to say, when he says it in strong concise words, and when he uses sentence form and rhythm, order and position, pause, and controlled repetition to produce the exact stress he desires.

CHAPTER REVIEW

If your reading of the chapter has been adequate, you should be able to explain and to illustrate each topic in the following outline of the chapter:

I. Economy and conciseness
   A. Avoiding padding and jargon
      1. Padding
         a. Awkward and meaningless repetition of the idea
         b. Wordy delaying of the subject
         c. Wordy phrasing
      2. Jargon
   B. Cutting clauses
      1. Techniques of cutting clauses
      2. Use of parallelism
   C. Choosing exact words
      1. Accurate verbs
      2. Accurate names
      3. Accurate formal words
II. Originality: avoiding clichés
III. Variety in sentences
   A. Kinds of monotony to avoid
      1. Careless repetition of words
      2. Monotony in sentence pattern
   B. Ways of varying sentence patterns
      1. Varying length
      2. Using some parallel and balanced constructions
      3. Intermingling loose and periodic sentences
      4. Changing the position of modifiers and parenthetic elements
      5. Varying the subject-verb-object order
IV. Emphasis
   A. Destroyers of emphasis
      1. Repeated sentence patterns
      2. Improper subordination
      3. Overuse of the passive voice
      4. Clichés
      5. Padding, jargon, weak clauses, and circumlocution
      6. Euphemism
   B. Emphasis by pause
   C. Emphasis by position
      1. Sentence beginnings
      2. Sentence endings
   D. Emphasis by repetition

EXERCISES

I. The following varied passages, most of them famous or familiar, represent different kinds of effective expression. Analyze the style of each passage to see what makes the expression of the idea distinctive and memorable. Consider the elements of style discussed in this chapter: economy and conciseness; originality of phrasing; variety in sentences; emphasis by pause, position, and repetition. Consider, too, concreteness in expression, use of figurative language, parallelism and balance, alliteration, sentence rhythm, charged words, and, whenever you know the context, the communicator's intention and attitude, and the appropriateness of the language used.

Veni, vidi, vici. (I came, I saw, I conquered.)

Liberté, égalité, fraternité.

Life, liberty, and the pursuit of happiness.

United we stand, divided we fall.

Sighted sub sank same.

Blood, sweat, and tears.

The land of the free and the home of the brave.

In the beginning was the Word, and the Word was with God, and the Word was God.
The same was in the beginning with God.
All things were made by Him; and without Him was not any thing made that was made.
In Him was life; and the life was the light of men.
And the light shineth in darkness; and the darkness comprehended it not.—The Gospel According to St. John

Read not to contradict and confute; nor to believe and take for granted; nor to find talk and discourse; but to weigh and consider. Some books are to be tasted, others to be swallowed, and some few to be chewed and digested; that is, some books are to be read only in parts; others to be read, but not curiously; and some few to be read wholly, and with diligence and attention.—Francis Bacon, "Of Studies"

Man is born free; and everywhere he is in chains. One thinks himself the master of others, and still remains a greater slave than they. How did this change come about? I do not know. What can make it legitimate? That question I think I can answer.—Jean Jacques Rousseau, *The Social Contract*

Sir, a woman's preaching is like a dog's walking on his hinder legs. It is not done well; but you are surprised to find it done at all.—Samuel Johnson

Is life so dear or peace so sweet as to be purchased at the price of chains and slavery? Forbid it, Almighty God! I know not what course others may take, but as for me, give me liberty, or give me death!—Patrick Henry, Speech in the Virginia Convention, 1775

When my eyes shall be turned to behold for the last time the sun in heaven, may I not see him shining on the broken and dishonored fragments of a once glorious Union; on States dissevered, discordant, belligerent; on a land rent with civil feuds, or drenched, it may be, in fraternal blood! Let their last feeble and lingering glance rather behold the gorgeous ensign of the republic, now known and honored throughout the earth, still full high advanced, its arms and trophies streaming in their original lustre, not a stripe erased or polluted, nor a single star obscured, bearing for its motto, no such miserable interrogatory as "What is all this worth?" nor those other words of delusion and folly, "Liberty first and Union afterwards"; but everywhere, spread all over in characters of living light, blazing on all its ample folds, as they float over the sea and over the land, and in every wind under the whole heavens, that other sentiment, dear to every true American heart,—Liberty *and* Union, now and for ever, one and inseparable!— Daniel Webster, Speech on Foot's Resolution, 1830

With malice toward none; with charity for all; with firmness in the right, as God gives us to see the right, let us strive on to finish the work we are in; to bind up the nation's wounds; to care for him who shall have borne the battle, and for his widow, and his orphan—to do all which may achieve and cherish a just and lasting peace among ourselves, and with all nations.— Abraham Lincoln, Second Inaugural Address, 1865

I wish to preach not the doctrine of ignoble ease but the doctrine of the strenuous life.—Theodore Roosevelt, 1899

We are accepting this challenge of hostile purpose because we know that in such a Government, following such methods, we can never have a friend; and that in the presence of its organized power, always lying in wait to accomplish we know not what purpose, there can be no assured security for the democratic Governments of the World. We are now about to accept gauge of battle with this natural foe of liberty and shall, if necessary, spend the whole force of the nation to check and nullify its pretensions and its power. We are glad, now that we see the facts with no veil of false pretense about them, to fight thus for the ultimate peace of the world and for the liberation of its peoples, the German peoples in-cluded: for the rights of nations great and small and the privilege of men everywhere to choose their way of life and of obedience. The world must be made safe for democracy.—Woodrow Wilson, Address for Declaration of War Against Germany, 1917

I am certain that my fellow Americans expect that on my induction into the Presidency I will address them with a candor and a decision which the present situation of our Nation impels. This is preeminently the time to speak the truth, the whole truth, frankly and boldly. Nor need we shrink from honestly facing conditions in our country today. This great Nation will endure as it has endured, will revive and will prosper. So, first of all, let me assert my firm belief that the only thing we have to fear is fear itself —nameless, unreasoning, unjustified terror which paralyzes needed efforts to convert retreat into advance.—FRANKLIN D. ROOSEVELT, First Inaugural Address, 1933

If it had not been for these thing I might have live out my life talking at street corners to scorning men. I might have die, unmarked, unknown, a failure. Now we are not a failure. This is our career and our triumph. Never in our full life could we hope to do such work for tolerance, for justice, for man's understanding of man, as now we do by accident. Our words, our lives, our pains—nothing! The taking of our lives—lives of a good shoemaker and a poor fishpeddler—all! That last moment belongs to us—that agony is our triumph.—BARTOLOMEO VANZETTI, Last Speech to the Court, 1927

You all know the reasons which have impelled me to renounce the Throne. But I want you to understand that in making up my mind I did not forget the country or the Empire which as Prince of Wales, and lately as King, I have for twenty-five years tried to serve. But you must believe me when I tell you that I have found it impossible to carry the heavy burden of responsibility and to discharge my duties as King as I would wish to do without the help and support of the woman I love.

And I want you to know that the decision I have made has been mine and mine alone. This was a thing I had to judge entirely for myself. The other person most nearly concerned has tried up to the last to persuade me to take a different course. I have made this, the most serious decision of my life, only upon the single thought of what would in the end be best for all.—PRINCE EDWARD, Broadcast after his Abdication, 1936

We shall go on to the end, we shall fight in France, we shall fight on the seas and oceans, we shall fight with growing confidence and growing strength in the air, we shall defend our Island, whatever the cost may be, we shall fight on the beaches, we shall fight on the landing grounds, we shall fight in the fields and in the streets, we shall fight in the hills; we shall never surrender, and even if, which I do not for a moment believe, this Island or a large part of it were subjugated and starving, then our Empire beyond the seas, armed and guarded by the British Fleet, would carry on the struggle, until, in God's good time, the New World, with all its power and might, steps forth to the rescue and the liberation of the old.—WINSTON CHURCHILL, Speech after Dunkirk, 1940

II. Keeping in mind the passages of excellent prose in Exercise I, read the following passages and feel the difference. The sentences below contain many of the enemies of effective expression: padding, jargon, weak clauses, thoughtless repetition, clichés, undesirable euphemisms, inexact phrasing. Revise the sentences, expressing the ideas in concise and emphatic English.

1. One bad trait which he has is that he is of a selfish nature.

2. He announced himself to be in favor of terminating the employment of three sales representatives.

3. Because of the fact that I think that exercise is a necessary requisite to health, it is my habitual custom to take a walk every day.

4. It was over Labor Day that we made a trip in the car, driving to Lake Madison for the Labor Day week end.

5. There are two ways in which our opinions differ in respect to this institution of higher learning; they are, namely, that John feels that the pursuit of knowledge is made secondary to social activities and I do not; furthermore, he also thinks that teachers of outstanding quality are few and far between whereas I, on the other hand, think that by and large my professors are literally excellent.

6. She went to bed in the wee small hours, tired but happy after her day of honest toil.

7. Dr. Black is one of the most outstanding lecturers I have ever heard lecture, I believe.

8. It was during the time that I was in the Army that I became a sadder and wiser man in regard to the less desirable attributes of human nature.

9. As a matter of fact, she anticipates participating in the next dramatic production which will be given by the Dramatic Club.

10. The trouble in regard to most voters is due to the fact that at present, under conditions existing today, they cannot get accurate information in relation to the respective candidates for office.

11. He shuffled off this mortal coil on Tuesday and will be laid to rest at three o'clock this afternoon.

12. I recall the time in my past when the schoolhouse where I went to school was annihilated by fire.

13. The difficulty appeared to my simple mind to be of a magnitude so enormous that only with the utmost difficulty could I refrain from being in the depths of despair.

14. I am sure that I voice the sentiments of the entire class when I extend our heartfelt thanks to Mr. Wilson in connection with his generous financial contribution to the deficit in the class treasury.

15. My roommate has the power and ability to work with concentration on his work in spite of various and sundry influences which are in the nature of things distracting.

16. In the case of the game next Saturday, I am doubtful as to whether we will win it or lose it.

17. Wordsworth's "Michael" is highly indicative of the author's characteristics of literary production, namely in the fact that its subject matter deals with that of nature; it is a definitely pastoral poem in which Wordsworth has given us a visual picture of his complete love and enjoyment held in the simplicity of nature herself.

18. My counselor told me in a tone of warning that I must improve my grades soon, before the next marking period, which comes next month.

III. All the following passages, taken from freshman themes, are weak in expression. Some of them are conspicuously faulty; others have rather subtle deficiencies in style. Name the weakness or weaknesses of each as exactly as you can, then suggest improvements.

1. My main difficulty in writing a theme is the fact that there is a definite barrier between myself and the gateway to a large vocabulary.

2. Although I always enjoyed reading, the more literary type of work was avoided.

3. The interfraternity council should stress the visitation of each fraternity house by the freshman before he decides to pledge.

4. A good vocabulary is useless if one cannot use his knowledge of words in grammatically good sentences.

5. The teachers there didn't seem to consider a knowledge of many words as being essential, or at any rate, they didn't bother to concentrate on word study to any great extent.

6. Starting with her school days in Poland, up through the discovery of radium and to her death, the book was put in a beautiful array of incidents which she encountered.

7. However, once having gained enough confidence to write in my own style and express my ideas in my own way and not to have a fear of what the reaction might be to what are my own ideas I think that I will have achieved in great measure the clear, concise, good informal use of English which is likely to be so essential in theme writing.

8. I did not have the correct beginning in grammar school. I did as little studying as possible in grammar school but still make the grade. I never thoroughly learned grammar in grammar school and therefore I have found it hard.

9. The American newspaper serves as a disintegrator of every form of knowledge as well as the guiding light of great masses of the populace.

10. By means of the aerial tramway, the trip, which is about three-fourths of a mile, is completed in ten minutes. The tramway car, which is about fifteen feet long and five feet wide, is supported and pulled by a cable which is only an inch and a half in diameter. This cable, however, can easily withstand a strain of over 100,000 pounds, which is several times more weight than the small car and its passenger capacity of twenty-two people will put on it. The cars have elaborate braking systems which rarely see use because trouble is so infrequent. Furthermore, around both ends of the cable there are huge springs which ease the car to a gradual halt.

11. In recent years there has been a tremendous increase in the relative importance placed upon the role played by athletics in the over-all college picture by the majority of the more outstanding colleges and universities throughout the country.

12. I have never done much reading and I have not developed a reading background and this is a disadvantage and an obstacle to me.

13. St. Simon Zelotes was surnamed the Canaanite. He is believed to be a relative of Jesus. Nothing is recorded in the Scriptures of his life.

14. He was enrolled in the school of ancient and modern languages and devoted himself to Latin, Greek, French, Spanish and Italian and by the end of the term he had received first honors in Latin and French. He led a normal student's life and delighted in drinking and gambling, and by December of the same year had acquired very heavy gambling debts. He returned home at the close of the session and Mr. Allan paid part of the debt but refused to pay all of it and therefore would not allow Edgar to return to the university.

15. By writing this theme on the subject of being allowed greater freedom in choosing theme topics I do not seek to promulgate a decree calling for the revamping of the English teaching system, for I know that there are other matters which enter into the choice of subject topics. I also know that a great number of abuses incurred in secondary school training have been corrected in the English teaching systems of college but what I actually do seek is a means by which the student is allowed liberties to show his God-given talent and not a talent that is superimposed upon his nature and therefore discourages whatever literary genius may have been hidden deep within his inner self.

16. I had supposed college would be like service schools, a frantic effort merely to keep up. Surprisingly, it isn't that at all. Instead it's rather enjoyable. Unexpectedly, I found myself familiar with some subjects. Moreover, I discovered that a good instructor, and most of them are good, is sincerely fond of teaching his subject. Most thankfully, I found that I have a real desire to learn and to know. Consequently, I am becoming a more serious student than I once thought possible.

17. Having failed to apply my efforts sufficiently to matters primarily academic, I found myself at mid-years in some discomfort in regard to my courses. It is my present intention in the situation which now confronts me to turn over a new leaf.

18. The cost of constructing ads during these days of high cost of living is very expensive.

IV. Improve the following sentences by substituting an exact word or phrase for each of the italicized locutions.

1. The cabinet was pine with *a thin layer of walnut on top of the pine.*
2. The car *slid* over the ice *and then it went* into the fence.
3. His hair was *uncombed and standing up in various directions.*
4. He was teasing the dog by *stretching the rubber band and releasing it in the dog's face.*
5. He has to *make a list of the contents of his book in alphabetical order.*
6. She was not skillful in her drawing *in showing the relationship of things in regard to distance.*
7. He *penned a communication in which he gave his support to* the committee's action.
8. He had been a member of the club *ever since it was founded.*
9. He was a *man who was running* for *the office of* mayor.
10. His conversation was *full of witty thoughts tersely expressed.*

Chapter Six

Good Paragraphs

A PARAGRAPH IS A UNIT OF COMPOSITION. It indicates to the reader that between its indented beginning and its end, one stage of the writer's thinking, or one phase of the action he is describing is presented. A good paragraph is clearly related to the material that precedes it and the material that follows it. It has unity, coherence, and emphasis; and it usually attains these by developing a topic sentence or idea, by transitional devices to show relationships between sentences, and by skillful selection and arrangement of material in the paragraph.

To most high-school graduates the statements just made about paragraphs are familiar enough; yet good paragraphing in freshman compositions is so rare that the experienced instructor is surprised—and delighted—when he finds it. To write good paragraphs, one needs more than an ability to recite abstract statements about paragraphing, even though those statements are perfectly sound. One needs to understand the function of the paragraph; he needs a knowledge of methods of development; and he needs to analyze the work of skillful writers to see how they apply these methods. Also, of course, he needs to have something to say, and he needs to write and revise so that his knowledge of paragraphing will translate itself into skill in expression.

Perhaps the best way to understand the function of the paragraph is to consider the origin of the convention of organizing written matter into paragraphs. Although the fact is seldom mentioned, the indentation for a paragraph serves as a mark of punctuation, and paragraphing, like other devices for indicating pause, emphasis, or separation, became a convention of writing because it serves a purpose. Early manuscripts consisted of one unbroken page after another without punctuation, capitalization, or separation of words, and with no marking off of paragraphs. Such manuscripts put too much tax on the reader, for he was obliged to blunder along, trying to find where words ended, where the pauses were, which words were proper names, and where one block of thought or detail ended and another began.

During the early Middle Ages a series of devices was introduced to enable a writer to convey his meaning more efficiently, and to make reading less arduous. Division into paragraphs was one of these devices. At first such divisions were indicated not by indentation, as at present, but by the use of a mark much like our present symbol, ¶. Our word *paragraph* (*para,* beside and *grapho,* to write) grew out of this practice, although we now indent for new paragraphs instead of placing the symbol in the left-hand margin. Indentation for paragraphs in writing is paralleled in public speaking by a pause longer than the usual pause after a sentence, or by a gesture or movement indicating that the speaker has completed one small phase of his subject and is going on to another.

Anyone who understands how language works knows that communication is usually most effective when the receiver is given a general idea of the subject and then is supplied with organized small blocks of expression, each dealing with a phase of the subject and each clearly related to the preceding and succeeding blocks. In writing, paragraphs constitute such blocks. For good writing, therefore, good paragraphing is essential. If the paragraphs are poorly made or unsuccessfully cemented together, the whole structure of the communication is unsound.

This chapter gives information about ways of forming good paragraphs, and examples of good paragraphs which illustrate the generalizations of the text. The student should examine these illustrative paragraphs carefully, observing how the techniques described in this chapter are applied by skillful writers.

I. UNITY IN PARAGRAPHS

For convenience in discussion, paragraphs are often divided into three types: expository paragraphs, which give information or explain a problem or a process; narrative paragraphs, which tell a story or part of a story; and descriptive paragraphs, which describe people, places, or experiences. Most unified expository paragraphs have a *topic sentence,* that is, a sentence which expresses the central idea of this block of the composition. The topic sentence usually stands at the beginning of the paragraph, as a clear introductory statement of the new phase of the subject about to be discussed; but sometimes it comes in the middle of the paragraph, and sometimes at the end. In narrative and descriptive paragraphs, the topic sentence is frequently implied rather than stated; for example, a writer may set down a number of details about wind, cold, bare trees, etc., which give a single impression of bleakness, without the explicit statement "It was a bleak day." Such paragraphs have a *topic idea* rather than a topic sentence. A paragraph of any type has unity when it develops only one topic sentence or topic idea, and when every statement in the paragraph contributes to the development of that topic sentence or idea.

The following paragraph illustrates failure in unity:

Many veterans have difficulty for a while in their courses in college. Having been out of school for three or four years, they have lost the habit of study and the power to concentrate. Formulas in chemistry and mathematics, which are recited readily by students fresh from high school, are only dim memories to them. Their age and the greater sense of responsibility most veterans have is an advantage to them. Many of them held responsible positions in the Service, and now many of them have families dependent on them. Consequently, they are serious about getting an education.

[This paragraph has two topic ideas: (1) veterans have difficulty in their courses; (2) they have the advantage of age and a sense of responsibility. There are two possible remedies for this paragraph disunity: one is to introduce the paragraph with a topic sentence which covers both ideas— "Many veterans have both disadvantages and advantages in college"; a second, and better, remedy is to split the paragraph into two paragraphs, developing more fully each of the two ideas. The second is better because the ideas are underdeveloped as they stand.]

Another failure in unity is illustrated in the first paragraph of a theme on the X-ray:

Mass X-raying is the only method of stamping out tuberculosis. This method is a practical one: everyone in the armed forces was X-rayed, and on the civilian front the state has sent out mobile units which have covered many war plants. [The X-ray machine consists of a tube, a light-proof hood, a camera, a transformer, and a control panel.] Good X-ray technicians can check as many as four persons per minute for tuberculosis.

[The bracketed sentence is irrelevant here. It should be the topic sentence of a later paragraph describing the machine.]

Achieving unity in paragraphs is not difficult, but it does require effort and attention. Students should consciously build their paragraphs around topic sentences, and learn to examine the organization of the paragraphs as they revise their papers. Unity can be tested very simply by these two questions:

1. What is the topic sentence or topic idea?
2. Is every statement in the paragraph clearly relevant to this topic sentence or topic idea?

II. COHERENCE IN PARAGRAPHS

The sentences in a paragraph, in addition to being relevant to a single topic sentence or idea, must be clearly related to each other. One sentence should lead into the next, one idea coherently follow another, so that the reader is carried forward without confusion.

A. Arrangement of Material

A logical connection between statements comes, first of all, from a logical arrangement of a sequence of ideas. The basis of this arrangement may be the *time-relationship* between the statements in the paragraph: actions are set down in the chronological order in which they occurred. Descriptive paragraphs are often built on the *space-relationship* of the parts of the scene described: a writer may, for example, record his observations as he looks from left to right, or from near to far, or from far to near; if he jumps about, he is likely to create an impression of mental agitation on the part of the observer rather than a clear picture of the scene. Statements in the paragraph may also be arranged in a pattern of *cause to effect; general statement to particular example; the whole problem or process to its separate parts; problem to solution; question to answer.* The kind of arrangement will depend, of course, on the nature of the material; but a paragraph, to be coherent, must have a basic arrangement which is logical and clear.

The following paragraph is ineffective because the writer, describing the process of firing a 240-millimeter howitzer, has failed to present separate actions in their proper time-sequence:

Fire Direction Control receives the signal "Number One ready," and checks with the forward observer to see whether the round is still called for. The signal has been given by the gun-crew chief after he has checked to see that no one is in the way of the recoil mechanism. The operator at the gun position is instructed to "fire when ready." Of course, this is true only if conditions still call for artillery fire. The chief of the gun section gives the order "Fire," and the round is on the way. Before this, the breech-block man has released the safety mechanism, and the lanyard man has yanked the cord.

[The coherent, logical order of events is:

1. The gun-crew chief checks to see that no one is in the way.

2. He then gives the signal "Number One ready."

3. This signal is received by Fire Direction Control, which checks with the forward observer.

4. If the round is still called for, the operator is instructed to "fire when ready."

5. The chief of the gun crew then gives the order "Fire."

6. The breechblock man releases the safety mechanism; the lanyard man yanks the cord. The round is on its way.]

B. Transitions within Paragraphs

A second way of achieving coherence is the use of effective transitions. In addition to arranging his ideas in logical order, the writer must take care that the connections between his statements are made entirely clear to the reader. Transitions within paragraphs are words, phrases, or structures which supply the reader with a smooth and orderly passage from one idea to the next. The most common ways of establishing transitions between sentences in a paragraph are:

1. Using sentence connectives such as *therefore, however, on the other hand, at the same time, meanwhile, afterward, then.*

2. Repeating a key word that has occurred in the preceding sentence.

3. Using a clear pronoun reference to a word or idea in the preceding sentence.

4. Putting parallel thoughts in parallel constructions to show the relationship between them.

Closely related to transitions is intelligent subordination—that is, using subordination and subordinating conjunctions to show the relationship between important and less important ideas, and to help the reader grasp the main ideas of the paragraph.

The writer of the following confusing paragraph probably had arranged his ideas in logical sequence, but, in writing, he omitted so many connectives and subordinated so poorly that it is difficult to follow his thought:

I have decided one thing. The principal reason for enrolling in an educational institution is to obtain an education from books. Extracurricular activities teach much. I am eager to participate while in college. The problem of my poor high-school preparation is too large to be solved in a short time. My grades are low. I will not participate in extracurricular activities until I have found an answer.

IMPROVED IN COHERENCE: I have decided one thing: the principal reason for enrolling in an educational institution is to obtain an education from books. Although extracurricular activities teach much and I am eager to participate in them before I finish college, I have an immediate problem of low grades because of my poor high-school preparation. Until I have solved this problem I will not participate in extracurricular activities.

The paragraphs below illustrate clear connections between statements. In the first, an excerpt from a student theme, the writer shows the simple time-relationship between his statements by the expressions *in the weeks and months, at first, gradually, finally:*

In the weeks and months that followed I tried to understand and accept Dad's death. At first I had a thousand daydreams of his return. Always he was tired from a long, long trip, but alive and well. Gradually, though, my fantasies and hopes died away. I stopped listening for his voice; I stopped searching for his face in crowds. Finally I knew in my heart that he never would return. The god of my childhood was gone, and there was nothing.

The following paragraph, an eminent scientist's definition of science, shows a more complex relating of ideas. The paragraph is related to the preceding paragraph by an introductory transitional phrase, and its sentences are bound together by the repetition of key words (*concepts, fruitful, experiments and observations, quality*), and by clear pronoun references. We have italicized the principal connective devices:

> *As a first approximation,* we may say that science emerges from the other progressive activities of man to the extent that *new concepts* arise from *experiments and observations,* and the *new concepts in turn* lead to further *experiments and observations.* The case histories drawn from the last three hundred years show examples of *fruitful* and *fruitless concepts.* The texture of modern science is the result of the interweaving of the *fruitful concepts.* The test of a *new* idea is *therefore not only* its success in correlating the then-known facts *but much more* its success or failure in stimulating further *experimentation or observation* which *in turn* is *fruitful. This dynamic quality* of science viewed not as a practical undertaking but as development of *conceptual* schemes seems to me to be close to the heart of the best definition. It is *this quality* which can be demonstrated only by the historical approach, or else learned by direct professional experience.—JAMES B. CONANT, *On Understanding Science*

III. EMPHASIS IN PARAGRAPHS

We have said earlier, in the discussion of emphasis, that good paragraphs, like good sentences, should begin and end strongly. If a paragraph has unity, if it is a necessary block in the paper, and if its sentences are arranged in coherent order, the matter of emphasis usually takes care of itself. A paragraph which builds logically to a climax, with its topic sentence at the end, is naturally emphatic. A paragraph which begins with its topic sentence may, however, be in some danger of tapering off at the end unless the writer has clearly in mind the importance of the end position. A paragraph beginning with its topic sentence may end emphatically with a restatement or enlargement of the topic idea, or it may invite the reader to go on to the next paragraph.

The following paragraph, from the student theme previously

quoted, enlarges, in its last sentence, the topic idea stated in its first sentence:

There was nothing that Dad couldn't do. He could put a squirming brown worm on a hook, dive from the highest tower into the deep water below, or take our automobile apart and fix it. Once, when our old Hudson was back together again, there was a small square part left over; but the car ran just the same. I knew it would, because Father was an engineer. He built bridges, big buildings, a tunnel for my electric train, and a pen for the quivering gray rabbit that he brought home in his coat pocket. Dad could even play the piano and sing "Columbia the Gem of the Ocean." Sometimes I felt sorry for all the other boys in the world whose fathers were such ordinary men.

The paragraph below, from another student theme, develops one phase of the experience related in the paper, and leads the reader, in its last sentence, into the next phase:

Today, as I gaze over a gauze mask, my body wrapped in white and my hands in rubber, the operating room seems strangly unreal. Yesterday it was a room full of excitement and things to learn. Now its white walls seem to hold something far different. I can hardly convince myself that I am here not as an observer but as an instrument nurse. Suddenly I feel that I have no right to hold this position. Many doctors have told me of my responsibility. Mine is almost as great as theirs, they maintain, for if I mix the wrong drugs, have the wrong instruments ready, or have improperly sterilized equipment, the operation will be as much a failure as if the surgeon's scalpel slipped. The patient's life is in my hands, and I can't be too careful. I have checked everything twice, suction apparatus, sterile gauze, sterile sheets, sutures, needles. . . . Now the doctor is coming; the operation will begin.

IV. TRANSITIONS BETWEEN PARAGRAPHS

Much of what has been said about making clear connections between sentences within the paragraph applies to connections between paragraphs in a well-organized paper. Paragraphs, like the sentences which compose them, must have an arrangement which is basically logical and effective; they must also be linked in such a way that the reader is led easily from one of these units of composition into the next. Each paragraph, developing its single topic idea, at the same time is, and must clearly be, a part of an unbroken chain. In long papers, short transitional paragraphs which summarize briefly the preceding ideas and relate them to the idea following are often used to join long paragraphs or sections of the paper. In short papers, the common transitional devices are these:

1. Concluding a paragraph with a sentence which introduces the next phase of the action. The last paragraph quoted in the previous section is an example, with its concluding sentence, "Now the doctor is coming; the operation will begin."

2. Using in the first sentence of a paragraph a connective or a transitional word or phrase: *furthermore, therefore, as a result, in addition, on the contrary.*

3. Beginning a paragraph with a sentence which refers clearly to a statement at the end of the preceding paragraph or to its topic idea.

The following paragraph beginnings illustrate some of the common ways of linking paragraphs:

The *second* difficulty is overcrowded classrooms. [The first difficulty has been discussed in the paragraph before.]

Such objections can be answered easily. [*Such objections* refers clearly to the material in the preceding paragraph.]

Many high schools, then, are not giving the preparation the student needs. Should this fact be ignored by the colleges, or accepted as a real problem? [The first sentence summarizes the ideas of the preceding paragraph. The question introduces the topic idea of this paragraph.]

A week later, the merchants of the town decided to take action.

The increased cost of living, *however,* has invalidated *these gains.*

Besides using these questionable methods, salesmen are expected to make actual misrepresentations about the superior quality of expensive goods.

Pedestrians, *as well as drivers,* would benefit by *this change* in traffic regulations.

Obvious connections like *Now let us look at the other side of the question* should be avoided as much as possible; they are preferable to no connections at all, but they are mechanical and labored.

Good transitions between paragraphs are an inconspicuous but essential part of a good composition. They keep the organization of the paper clear; they prevent the reader's falling into a gulf between paragraphs, or having to leap from one thought to another; they give him a sense of continuity and progress, from the beginning of the paper to the end.

V. THE LENGTH OF PARAGRAPHS

It is impossible to lay down hard-and-fast rules about the length of paragraphs, because paragraph development and length differ widely with the importance of the idea being discussed, the nature of the composition, and the intention of the writer. Convention demands the use of a new paragraph for each new speech in written dialogue, however brief or fragmentary that speech is. In advertising, as we have noted earlier, short paragraphs are used to facilitate reading and to give separate emphasis to each idea. For the same reasons, paragraphs in newspapers and in business letters are usually short. Even in formal writing, one occasionally finds a one-sentence paragraph which is used for sharp emphasis, or which makes a transition between long paragraphs. In narrative writing, where a new paragraph is used for each new phase of the action of the story, some paragraphs may be long because certain phases of the action need full presentation; others may be very short because the action is minor or brief. The proper length of paragraphs cannot, then, be established dogmatically, but must be determined by the complexity of the material and the purpose of the author. We can only suggest here a general method of deciding how long paragraphs should be.

In the next section, on the development of paragraphs, we are quoting as examples seventeen paragraphs, nearly all of them from contemporary writing, and most of them expository—intended primarily to inform or to explain rather than to tell part of a story or to communicate experience. The shortest of these paragraphs is 105 words, the longest 336 words; the average length of the seventeen paragraphs is about 185 words. The average paragraph in this fairly typical selection, then, would occupy something like two-thirds of a double-spaced typed page. We offer this calculation, obviously not as a rule, but as a rough guide to the student in judging the length of his own paragraphs: in expository writing, his paragraphs should rarely exceed 300 words, and rarely fall below 100. Three or more paragraphs on a single page should, therefore, be a signal to him to re-examine his paragraphs; the length may be suitable to his subject, but the short paragraphs suggest that his material is not adequately developed. Also, the writer should look again at paragraphs which are longer than a manuscript page; they may be justified, but their unusual length suggests that two phases of the idea or the action have been thoughtlessly run toether.

VI. THE FULL DEVELOPMENT OF PARAGRAPHS

Although short paragraphs are not necessarily faulty, inadequately developed paragraphs are. A common weakness in student writing is the sketchy paragraph which, though it deals with an important phase of the subject, consists only of a topic sentence with a qualifying statement or two. Such skeleton paragraphs, lacking flesh, thought, vitality and color, convey little or no meaning to the reader. They give the impression of mental malnutrition—usually a correct impression. They are likely, too, to lead to another failure: the writer, seeing, as he looks at his manuscript, that his paragraphing is choppy, often tries to improve the appearance of his paper by combining paragraphs, with the result that he throws into one disunified paragraph two or more underdeveloped topic ideas. His realization that undeveloped paragraphs are a weakness in writing is, of course, commendable. The treatment for these starved paragraphs, however, is not to swell them by the addition of inappropriate bones, but to develop the flesh and substance which they should have.

If a topic sentence or topic idea is worth including in a paper, it is worth sufficient development to make it meaningful and interesting to the reader. In the following pages we shall discuss and illustrate four of the most useful methods of developing paragraphs. These methods are closely related; they are all ways of making material more concrete; and they are often used in combination. For convenience we shall discuss them separately under the headings *particularization, illustration, contrast and comparison,* and *definition.*

A. Particularization

Particularization means making a general statement or a general idea concrete and clear by listing the particular facts, instances, reasons, causes, statistics, and the like, which support or expand the general statement. In a paragraph developed by particularization, the topic sentence usually stands at the beginning, followed by substantiating or elaborating details.

The following paragraph on sports in the 1920's begins with a general topic sentence and is developed by particular facts and statistics:

The Post-war Decade was a great sporting era. More men were playing golf than ever before—playing it in baggy plus-fours, with tassels at the knee and checked stockings. There were five thousand golf-courses in the United States, there were said to be two million players, and it was estimated that half a billion dollars was spent annually on the game. The ability to play it had become a part of the almost essential equipment of the aspiring business executive. The country club had become the focus of social life in hundreds of communities. But it was an even greater era for watching sports than for taking part in them. Promoters, chambers of commerce, newspaper-owners, sports writers, press agents, radio broadcasters, all found profit in exploiting the public's mania for sporting shows and its willingness to be persuaded that the great athletes of the day were supermen. Never before had such a blinding light of publicity been turned upon the gridiron, the diamond, and the prize ring.—FREDERICK LEWIS ALLEN, *Only Yesterday*

The topic sentence of the paragraph below, "Kit liked it all," is followed by six incomplete sentences which particularize *all;* that is, they give a series of concrete pictures of what Kit liked. The last sentence of the paragraph pulls the details together and restates the topic idea:

Kit liked it all. The whitewashed, crumbling, flat-roofed, one-story *adobe* houses, with their mica windows guarded by iron bars or painted wooden shutters. The narrow, unpaved, winding lanes and alleys leading to the plaza and its naked cottonwoods. The long, shadowy, echoing *portales,* the rigid *vigas* thrusting their ends out through the walls, the heavy sagging gates of the hidden *patios.* The irrigated gardens, the fields, and the twin red-brown communal houses of the Indian pueblo up the stream. The soft gloom of the quiet interiors with their queer modeled fireplaces, their strings of red peppers, their gay Indian rugs, stacked along the walls for seats by day and beds by night, their Pueblo pottery and baskets, their silver-mounted saddles hung on pegs, their *santos* and grotesque holy pictures. Outside, their chimneys made of broken pots, their beehive ovens, and the white, white bread that was baked in them. Mountain, and meadow, and *'dobe* wall, Kit liked them all.—STANLEY VESTAL, *Kit Carson*

B. Illustration

Closely related to particularization, illustration means just what the word says—giving specific illustrations or examples to show the reader the exact meaning or application of a general statement. The examples may be brief, or they may be rather long illustrative anecdotes or experiences. Sometimes they are introduced by an expression like *for example* or *let us look at the case of Mr. X.;* usually their position, immediately following the general statement they illustrate, makes the mechanical introduction unnecessary. Illustration is one of the best methods of paragraph development because well-chosen examples are concrete, easy to understand, and always interesting.

Walter Lippmann, in the paragraph below, uses a long illustration to clarify his topic idea that people react, not to objective events, but to their often distorted mental images of those events:

The only feeling that anyone can have about an event he does not experience is the feeling aroused by his mental image of that event. That is why until we know what others think they know, we cannot truly understand their acts. I have seen a young girl, brought up in a Pennsylvania mining town, plunged suddenly from entire cheerfulness into a paroxysm of grief when a gust of wind cracked the kitchen window-pane. For hours she was inconsolable, and to me incomprehensible. But when she was able to talk, it transpired that if a window-pane broke it meant that a close relative had died. She was, therefore, mourning for her father, who had frightened her into running away from home. The father was, of course, quite thoroughly alive as a telegraphic inquiry soon proved. But until the telegram came, the cracked glass was an authentic message to that girl. Why it was authentic only a prolonged investigation by a skilled psychiatrist could show. But even the most casual observer could see that the girl, enormously upset by her family troubles, had hallucinated a complete fiction out of one external fact, a remembered superstition, and a turmoil of remorse, and fear and love for her father.—WALTER LIPPMANN, *Public Opinion*

Dr. Liebman uses two brief illustrations in the paragraph below to clarify the nature of neurotic fear:

The best illustration of the difference between normal and neurotic fear was given by Sigmund Freud himself. A person in an African jungle, he said, may quite properly be afraid of snakes. That is normal and self-protective. But if a friend of ours suddenly begins to fear that snakes are under the carpet of his city apartment, then we know that his fear is neurotic, abnormal. In attempting to estimate our own fears we may profitably apply Freud's serviceable yardstick. It would be quite normal for a Polish mother to fear that her children might die of starvation, but when a wealthy American mother comes into my study and tells me that her children are dying of slow malnutrition, I suspect that her fear is a morbid and neurotic shadow, based on her own feelings of guilt, fear, and hatred.[1]

Aldous Huxley combines several methods of development in the following paragraph. At the beginning he gives brief concrete examples to show that ordinarily we do not consider men equal; in the middle of the paragraph he restates the point his examples have made clear, and relates it to his topic idea; toward the end of the paragraph he uses a comparison to emphasize the topic idea, the inconsistency in our thinking about equality. (Worth noting in this paragraph, too, is the way the sentences and ideas are related: by parallel sentences; by repetition of key words; by the sentence connectives *and; at ordinary times, then; but when; or at any rate; similarly.*)

That all men are created equal is a proposition to which, at ordinary times, no sane human being has ever given his assent. A man who has to undergo a dangerous operation does not act on the assumption that one doctor is just as good as another. Editors do not print every contribution that reaches them. And when they require civil servants, even the most democratic governments make a careful selection among their theoretically equal subjects. At ordinary times, then, we are perfectly certain that men are not equal. But when, in a democratic country, we think or act politically, we are no less certain that men are equal. Or at any rate—which comes to the same thing in practice—we behave as though we were certain of men's equality. Similarly, the pious medieval nobleman who, in church, believed in forgiving enemies and turning the other cheek was ready, as soon as he had emerged again into the light of day, to draw his sword at the slightest provocation. The human mind has an almost infinite capacity for being inconsistent.—ALDOUS HUXLEY, "The Idea of Equality," *Proper Studies*

C. Contrast and Comparison

The paragraph just above illustrates a use of brief comparison for clarity and emphasis. In a paragraph developed entirely by contrast or comparison or by both, the writer sets side by side two people, things, or situations, and demonstrates in detail the similarities, or differences, or similarities and differences between them. Like particularization and illustration, contrast and comparison develop a general idea by making it detailed and concrete.

Frederick Lewis Allen, in the paragraph preceding the one quoted below, has made the point that the Republican "bosses" in 1920 had decided to choose a Presidential nominee who was a complete contrast to Woodrow Wilson. In this paragraph he explains the choice of Harding by a detailed contrasting of the two men:

Consider how perfectly Harding met the requirements. Wilson was a visionary who liked to identify himself with "forward-looking men"; Harding, as Mr. Lowry put it, was as old-fashioned as those wooden Indians which used to stand in front of cigar stores, "a flower of the period before safety razors." Harding believed that statesmanship had come to its apogee in the days of McKinley and Foraker. Wilson was cold; Harding was an affable small-town man, at ease with "folks"; an ideal companion, as one of his friends expressed it, "to play poker with all Saturday night." Wilson had always been difficult of access; Harding was accessible to the last degree. Wilson favored labor, distrusted business men as a class, and talked of "industrial democracy"; Harding looked back with longing eyes to the good old days when the government didn't bother business men with unnecessary regulations, but provided them with fat tariffs and instructed the Department of Justice not to have them on its mind. Wilson was at loggerheads with Congress, and particularly with the Senate; Harding was not only a Senator, but a highly amenable Senator. Wilson had been adept at making enemies; Harding hadn't an enemy in the world. He was genuinely genial. "He had no knobs, he was the same size and smoothness all the way round," wrote Charles Willis Thompson. Wilson thought in terms of the whole world; Harding was for America first. And finally, whereas Wilson wanted America to exert itself nobly, Harding wanted to give it a rest. At Boston, a few weeks before the Convention, he had correctly expressed the growing desire of the people of the country and at the same time had unwittingly added a new word to the language, when he said, "America's present need is not for heroics but healing; not nostrums but normalcy; not revolution but restoration; . . . not surgery but serenity." Here was a man whom a country wearied of moral obligations and the hope of the world could take to its heart.——FREDERICK LEWIS ALLEN, *Only Yesterday*

Comparison is particularly effective if something complex or unfamiliar can be clarified by comparing it with something simple or familiar. Edward Bellamy, in *Looking Backward*, writes from the point of view of one who has awakened in the year 2000 and is looking back at the undesirable social structure of his own day; in the following paragraph he explains this complex social and economic structure of the 1880's by comparing it to a simple thing—a stagecoach. A comparison like this of two ideas or situations is called an *analogy*.

By way of attempting to give the reader some general impression of the way people lived together in those days, and especially of the relations of the rich and poor to one another, perhaps I cannot do better than to compare society as it then was to a prodigious coach which the masses of humanity were harnessed to and dragged toilsomely along a very hilly and sandy road. The driver was hunger, and permitted no lagging, though the pace was necessarily very slow. Despite the difficulty of drawing the coach at all along so hard a road, the top was covered with passengers who never got down, even at the steepest ascents. These seats on top were very breezy and comfortable. Well up out of the dust, their occupants could enjoy the scenery at their leisure, or critically discuss the merits of the straining team. Naturally such places were in great demand and the competition for them was keen, every one seeking as the first end in life to secure a seat on the coach for himself and to leave it to his child after him. By the rule of the coach a man could leave his seat to whom he wished, but on the other hand there were many accidents by which it might at any time be wholly lost. For all that they were so easy, the seats were very insecure, and at every sudden jolt of the coach persons were slipping out of them and falling to the ground, where they were instantly compelled to take hold of the rope and help drag the coach on which they had before ridden so pleasantly. It was naturally regarded as a terrible misfortune to lose one's seat, and the apprehension that this might happen to them or their friends was a constant cloud upon the happiness of those who rode.

Stuart Chase, describing the Grand Coulee Dam, sees in it an achievement comparable to, and greater than, the construction of the Great Pyramid six thousand years ago. In the following paragraph he uses both comparison and contrast to convey his ideas about the dam, and to build to his topic sentence at the end of the paragraph:

One of these masses is built of cut stone, the other of poured concrete. One took 50,000 men twenty years to build, the other will take 5,000 men six years, in a task not only three times greater but vastly more complex and dangerous. Both structures relied on the labor of those who would otherwise have been unemployed. Egyptian peasants in the off season built Cheops; American workingmen and engineers shelved by a great depression are building Grand Coulee. Pyramids were houses for the dead. Dams are centers of energy for the living. It is better, I think, to live in the age of the Great Dams than in the age of the Great Pyramids.—STUART CHASE, *Idle Money Idle Men*

The two paragraphs below, from a modern novel, characterize and contrast two women through a description of their rooms. (Within the paragraphs, particularization is used to give a detailed picture of the rooms, and to set up the total contrast.)

As I watched her [Miss Pride], taking in with admiration each detail of her immaculate attire and her proud carriage, I heard, from the adjoining room, embedded in a yawn, the waking squeal of Mrs. McKenzie, a garrulous and motherly old woman whom I had always disliked. Her room was no pleasure to clean: her bed was strewn with corsets and short-sleeved night-dresses, and on her bedside table, I often found drying apple cores which I removed gingerly, having in my mind an image of her with her sparse hair unpinned sitting up in bed cropping with her large false teeth. Upon the bureau, amongst sticky bottles of vile black syrups and tonics and jars of fetid salve, there lay her bunion plasters and her ropes of brown hair which she sometimes arranged in a lofty cone on top of her head. Usually she was in the room when I entered and she saluted me with disgusting moonshine as "mother's little helper" or asked me if my "beauteous mamma" was sick.

Now in Miss Pride's room, there was never anything amiss. Perhaps once or twice a summer, I found a bottle of imported wine or whiskey on her writing desk; this was the only medicine she took and she took it regularly in small quantities. On the bureau, the china hair receiver did not receive a wisp of hair, and there were neither spots nor foreign objects upon the white linen runner. A hat-pin holder, sprouting long, knobbed needles, two cut-glass cologne bottles, and a black glove box, shaped like a small casket, were reflected in the clear swinging mirror. Though I should have loved to dearly, I had not the courage to investigate the drawers which were always neatly shut, but I was sure that they were in scrupulous order. The other old ladies, almost without exception, allowed the feet of stockings and the straps of camisoles to stream from each gaping tier like so many dispirited banners.—JEAN STAFFORD, *Boston Adventure*

D. Definition

Definition as a method of paragraph development means, not quoting a dictionary definition, but discussing fully and specifically the meaning of a word or a term so that the reader understands exactly what it stands for in the context of this piece of writing. Definition of this sort is particularly necessary when the author is using abstract terms which have different meanings for different people, when he is limiting his subject more than it usually is limited, or when he is writing on a topic likely to be unfamiliar to his readers. Full and exact definition paragraphs are often the most important part of a paper; without them the composition may be obscure or misleading.

Clear definition may be accomplished by one or more of these methods: by *analysis* (breaking a complex term or concept into its various parts); by *negation* or *exclusion* (showing what the term does *not* mean); by *restatement* (repetition in different words of the core of the definition); and by the methods of paragraph development already discussed, especially illustration and contrast and comparison. The paragraphs below will illustrate these methods.

Bertrand Russell, to make clear what he means by the abstract word *patriotism,* defines it by analysis; that is, he breaks the complex idea of patriotism into its component parts: love of home, liking for compatriots, pride, etc. The paragraph illustrates climactic arrangement of ideas as well as full definition.

Patriotism is a very complex feeling, built up out of primitive instincts and highly intellectual convictions. There is love of home and family and friends, making us peculiarly anxious to preserve our own country from invasion. There is the mild instinctive liking for compatriots as against foreigners. There is pride, which is bound up with the success of the community to which we feel that we belong. There is a belief, suggested by pride but reinforced by history, that one's own nation represents a great tradition and stands for ideals that are important to the human race. But besides all these, there is another element, at once nobler and more open to attack, an element of worship, of willing sacrifice, of joyful merging of the individual life in the life of the nation. This religious element in patriotism is essential to the strength of the State, since it enlists the best that is in most men on the side of national sacrifice.[2]

The following paragraph illustrates definition by negation or exclusion. In this transitional paragraph, James Harvey Robinson defines "creative thought" by first telling his readers that it is not like the three types of thinking he has discussed before:

This brings us to another kind of thought which can fairly easily be distinguished from the three kinds described above. It has not the usual qualities of the reverie, for it does not hover about our personal com-

[2] From *Why Men Fight* by Bertrand Russell, Appleton-Century-Crofts, Inc. Copyright, 1917. Used by permission of the publishers.

placencies and humiliations. It is not made up of the homely decisions forced on us by everyday needs, when we review our little stock of existing information, consult our conventional preferences and obligations, and make a choice of action. It is not the defense of our own cherished beliefs and prejudices just because they are our own—mere plausible excuses for remaining of the same mind. On the contrary, it is that peculiar species of thought which leads us to *change* our mind.—JAMES HARVEY ROBINSON, *The Mind in the Making*

The writer of the article on socialism in the *Encyclopædia Britannica* begins his discussion by defining the term and by indicating, as part of his definition, what the term does *not* mean in this discussion:

Socialism is the name given both to a widespread body of doctrines and to a world-wide movement taking many different forms. It has a long history behind it; and the word has been used in shifting senses as the ideas behind it have developed and the situations facing it changed. A short and comprehensive definition is therefore impossible. We can only say that Socialism is essentially a doctrine and a movement aiming at the collective organization of the community in the interests of the mass of the people by means of the common ownership and collective control of the means of production and exchange.

It is well to begin by ruling altogether out from the scope of this article certain popular uses of the term "Socialism" which were current, especially during the past generation. The well-known phrase "We are all Socialists now," and the constant references to "socialistic legislation," only serve to obscure the real meaning of the word. "We are all Socialists now" only means that everybody in these days, whatever his politics, is ready to agree to a greater amount of Government intervention both in industry and in the affairs of society generally than most people even conceived as possible a generation ago. And "socialistic legislation" is, as a rule, only a phrase indicating disapproval of any measure which increases this collective intervention or seeks in any way to promote a more equal distribution of income among the members of the community.—G. D. H. COLE, "Socialism," *Encyclopædia Britannica,* 14th edition

Definition by restatement is shown in the following paragraph. The author defines the field of anthropology by repeating, in different terms, the idea that anthropology is concerned with all cultures and not solely with our own:

The distinguishing mark of anthropology among the social sciences is that it includes for serious study other societies than our own. For its purposes any social regulation of mating and reproduction is as significant as our own, though it may be that of the Sea Dyaks, and have no possible historical relation to that of our civilization. To the anthropologist, our customs and those of a New Guinea tribe are two possible social schemes for dealing with a common problem, and in so far as he remains an anthropologist he is bound to avoid any weighing of one in favor of the other. He is interested in human behavior, not as it is shaped by one tradition, our own, but as it has been shaped by any tradition whatsoever. He is interested in the great gamut of custom that is found in various cultures, and his object is to understand the way in which these cultures change and differentiate, the different forms through which they express themselves, and the manner in which the customs of any peoples function in the lives of the individuals who compose them.—RUTH BENEDICT, *Patterns of Culture*

The term *loaded words* (the words we have called *charged*) is defined by a series of examples in this paragraph from S. I. Hayakawa's *Language in Action:*

In short, the process of reporting is the process of keeping one's personal feelings out. In order to do this, one must be constantly on guard against "loaded" words that reveal or arouse feelings. Instead of "sneaked in," one should say "entered quietly"; instead of "politicians," "congressmen" or "aldermen"; instead of "officeholder," "public official"; instead of "tramp," "homeless unemployed"; instead of "Chinaman," "Chinese"; instead of "dictatorial set-up," "centralized authority"; instead of "crack pots," "holders of uncommon views." A newspaper reporter, for example, is not permitted to write, "A bunch of fools who are suckers enough to fall for Senator Smith's ideas met last evening in the rickety firetrap that disfigures the south edge of town." Instead he says, "Between seventy-five and a hundred people were present last evening to hear an address by Senator Smith at the Evergreen Gardens near the South Side city limits."

A combination of analogy and contrast is used by Max Eastman in the first paragraph of *Enjoyment of Poetry* to define the term *poetic people:*

A simple experiment will distinguish two types of human nature. Gather a throng of people and pour them into a ferry-boat. By the time the boat has swung into the river you will find that a certain proportion have taken the trouble to climb upstairs, in order to be out on deck and see what is to be seen as they cross over. The rest have settled indoors, to think what they will do upon reaching the other side, or perhaps lose themselves in apathy or tobacco smoke. But leaving out those apathetic, or addicted to a single enjoyment, we may divide all the alert passengers on the boat into two classes—those who are interested in crossing the river, and those who are merely interested in getting across. And we may divide all the people on the earth, or all the moods of people, in the same way. Some of them are chiefly occupied with attaining ends, and some with receiving experiences. The distinction of the two will be more marked when we name the first kind practical, and the second poetic, for common knowledge recognizes that a person poetic or in a poetic mood is impractical, and a practical person is intolerant of poetry.

Many paragraphs, as we have said, are developed by a combination of these methods of particularization, illustration, contrast and comparison, and definition. The method or methods used will depend on the nature of the writer's material. How fully he develops particular paragraphs will depend, too, on his material and on the importance of these paragraphs in the whole paper.

What we have said about paragraph development is chiefly applicable to expository paragraphs. Descriptive and narrative paragraphs are so varied in their purposes that meaningful comment on them is almost impossible. Descriptive paragraphs are usually developed by a form of particularization: the writer, by means of a number of well-selected details, makes a person or a scene real to the reader. (The paragraphs above from *Kit Carson* and *Boston Adventure* are examples.) Descriptive paragraphs, as we have said earlier, often have instead of a topic sentence a topic idea which lies in the total impression the reader receives from all the details he is given. Narrative paragraphs are even harder to generalize about. Since they present one phase in the action of the story, their length and composition depend entirely on the emphasis the writer wishes to give that part of his narrative.

The division of paragraphs into three types—expository, descriptive, narrative—is convenient, because paragraphs with different purposes are developed differently. But this division should not mislead the student into thinking that writing falls into separate and exclusive categories, with exposition using only expository paragraphs, description made up of descriptive paragraphs, and narration of a chain of narrative paragraphs. Any sharp distinction of this sort between types of writing is, in fact, an artificial one; at best it is merely a convenient device for describing the primary intention of different pieces of writing. Actually, writing mainly concerned with informing or convincing often contains narrative and descriptive paragraphs; the writer, realizing that he will be most successful in his exposition if he makes his reader see and feel as well as know, may vividly describe scenes or situations, or may tell a story to make a point concrete and clear. Short stories and novels, of course, are likely to have numerous descriptive paragraphs. Frequently, too, they contain expository paragraphs, in which the writer informs the reader (either directly or through the speech of a character) about something the reader needs to know in order to understand the story. The three types of paragraphs are not uncommonly used in the same piece of writing.

A paragraph of any type is well developed when the topic idea is sufficiently expanded to be clear, concrete, and interesting to the reader, and when the length of development accords with the weight that this phase of the subject, or the action, should have in the balanced development of the whole composition.

VII. FIRST AND LAST PARAGRAPHS

Because beginning and concluding paragraphs occupy the positions of greatest emphasis in a composition, they deserve special attention.

The primary purpose of a beginning paragraph is to launch the subject and to interest the reader in it. Too often college writers have the idea that a first paragraph should "lead up to the subject." As a result, they often waste the important beginning of a paper in dull, laborious introductory remarks like "I intend to discuss three reasons . . ." or "In this paper I hope to prove . . ." Instead of wasting words, they should start at once to discuss or to prove, with a directness and vigor that immediately attract the reader. These tedious leading-up-to-the-subject paragraphs can often simply be struck out in the process of revision; the second paragraph, which actually gets into the subject, is likely to be a more effective beginning. Even worse than a merely dull and wasted beginning paragraph is the apologetic introduction: "Interior decorating is a very complicated business which I don't know much about, but I did work for a month last summer . . ." The reader, unless he is unhappily obliged to grade the paper, is at once discouraged from reading further. Good beginning paragraphs are direct and sure and interesting. An episode or a snatch of conversation focused on the subject, a vivid presentation of a situation or scene, an emphatic statement of an opinion, a clear definition of the topic to be discussed—these make effective beginnings because they awaken curiosity or interest.

The last paragraph of a paper should emphasize the idea the writer wishes to leave with the reader, and should give the reader a sense of finality and completion. The concluding paragraph is particularly important because, since it is last, it is likely to fix the reader's impression of the whole paper. That impression will be poor if the writer ends apologetically: "Of course I haven't been able to do justice to this subject." And the impression will be clouded if the writer concludes his paper with a collection of afterthoughts and incidental details which he feels should be mentioned, but for which he has not found room in the body of the composition. Such details should be either omitted or incorporated earlier, for placed at the end they scatter the reader's thoughts, and divert his attention from the main ideas. A final paragraph must be sharply focused.

A common type of conclusion is the summary, which briefly reviews the principal points covered in the paper. In a long paper, which has dealt with complex material, the summary ending is often desirable, even necessary. In a short informal paper, however, it is usually not desirable, because it seems mechanical and completely unnecessary; a reader of any intelligence does not need, and does not care, to be told what he has read within the last two minutes.

A thoughtful arrangement of the material in a paper in climactic order often automatically solves the problem of achieving an emphatic ending. If the writer is presenting four reasons for a belief he holds, or three or four arguments in favor of a course of action, and if he puts his most important point last, the development of that paramount reason or that particularly telling argument will serve as an emphatic conclusion.

Good closing paragraphs sometimes suggest a solution for a problem described in the paper. They may call on the reader to take some definite action. They may stimulate action or thought by posing a question: "The citizens of America have the power to demand better radio programs. When will they exercise that power?" They may give an illustration of how the advocated plan or idea has operated. They may restate, emphatically and in different terms, the topic idea of the paper. These last paragraphs should be carefully constructed, and carefully phrased, to give the exact emphasis and impression which the writer hopes the reader will carry away.

CHAPTER REVIEW

If your reading of the chapter has been adequate, you should be able to answer the following questions:

1. What is the function of the paragraph?
2. How can paragraph unity be tested?
3. What is meant by coherence? By what two methods is it attained?
4. What are the common ways of making transitions or connections between sentences within a paragraph? Between paragraphs?
5. Why is it impossible to lay down hard-and-fast rules about the length of paragraphs?
6. What advice is given to the student as a guide in determining the proper length of his paragraphs?
7. Explain clearly how paragraphs are developed by

particularization
illustration
contrast and comparison
definition

8. What are the important things to keep in mind about first paragraphs? About last paragraphs?

EXERCISES

I. The following paragraphs, all from modern writing, illustrate various kinds of paragraph development. Students may find it useful to apply these questions to each paragraph:

1. What is the topic sentence or topic idea?
2. By what method or methods is the paragraph developed?
3. Does the paragraph end strongly? If so, how has the writer accomplished the emphatic ending?
4. If two successive paragraphs from the same source are printed, why has the writer broken the passage into two paragraphs?
5. By what means does the writer tie together the sentences of his paragraphs?

We carry, then, the burden of our childhood expectations into maturity. No wonder that we grow afraid, become anxious, feel inferior. No wonder that we develop ulcers, hypertension, and heart conditions out of our restless and haunted compulsion to achieve the absolute. Yet, we will obtain inner peace only when we have declared a truce and made an armistice with the army of our childhood expectations. No one of us escapes limitations. We sometimes are angry, petty, lazy, callous, but we also are kindly, generous, creative. Some people are gifted with their hands, some people are gifted in the realm of art or music, some people are gifted in the realm of abstract ideas. Almost no one is gifted in all three realms. We are all limited, and we must accept ourselves with our limitations, recognizing that we can do what others cannot do, that we can contribute where others cannot contribute.[3]

Leeuwenhoek's day of days had come. Alexander had gone to India and discovered huge elephants that no Greek had ever seen before—but those elephants were as commonplace to Hindus as horses were to Alexander. Caesar had gone to England and come upon savages that opened his eyes with wonder—but these Britons were as ordinary to each other as Roman centurions were to Caesar. Balboa? What were his proud feelings as he looked for the first time at the Pacific? Just the same, that Ocean was as ordinary to a Central American Indian as the Mediterranean was to Balboa. But Leeuwenhoek? This janitor of Delft had stolen upon and peeped into

[3] Reprinted from *Peace of Mind* by permission of Simon and Schuster, Inc. Copyright, 1946, by Joshua Loth Liebman.

a fantastic sub-visible world of little things, creatures that had lived, had bred, had battled, had died, completely hidden from and unknown to all men from the beginning of time. Beasts these were of a kind that ravaged and annihilated whole races of men ten million times larger than they were themselves. Beings these were, more terrible than fire-spitting dragons or hydra-headed monsters. They were silent assassins that murdered babes in warm cradles and kings in sheltered palaces. It was this invisible, insignificant, but implacable—and sometimes friendly—world that Leeuwenhoek had looked into for the first time of all men of all countries.

This was Leeuwenhoek's day of days. . . .—PAUL DE KRUIF, *Microbe Hunters*

The warm kitchen air was like a stupor. This was the steady heart of the house. Ghostly moonlight might wash up to the sill, fragile fancies pervade other rooms: here strong central life went calmly on. In the range red coals slept deep, covered and nourished for the long night. The tall boiler, its silvery paint flaked and dulled, gave off drowsy heat. Under the table the cat Virginia, who was not to be shocked, lay solidly upright with her paws tucked in, sated with scraps and vibrating a strong stupid purr. The high grimed ceiling was speckled with motionless flies, roosting there after a hard day. Packages of groceries, series of yellow bowls and platters, were ranged on the shelves in comfortable order. This was not a modern kitchen, shiny, white and sterile, like a hospital. It was old, ugly, inconvenient, strong with the memory of meals arduously prepared; meals of long ago, for people now vanished.[4]

There are two philosophies of medicine: the primitive or superstitious, and the modern or rational. They are in complete opposition to one another. The former involves the belief that disease is caused by supernatural forces. Such a doctrine associates disease with sin; it is an aspect of religion which conceives diseases as due to certain forms of evil and attempts to control them by ceremonial and superstitious measures or to drive them away by wishful thinking. On the other hand, rational medicine is based on the conception that disease arises from natural causes; it associates sickness with ignorance. Civilized man tries to control the forces causing disease by material, not spiritualistic, means; he does not view disease as supernatural or the outcome of sin against moral laws, but rather as resulting from the violation of sanitary laws. He recognizes that knowledge is the sole means of preventing it. The measures he relies upon both to prevent and cure disease are those which have resulted from scientific investigation and which have been proved to be effective by experience.—HOWARD HAGGARD, *Devils, Drugs and Doctors*

I (to quit hiding behind the generalization of "the male") hate women because they almost never get anything exactly right. They say, "I have

---

[4] From *Thunder on the Left.* Copyright, 1925, by Christopher Morley. Published by J. B. Lippincott Company.

been faithful to thee, Cynara, after my fashion" instead of "in my fashion." They will bet you that Alfred Smith's middle name is Aloysius, instead of Emanuel. They will tell you to take the 2:57 train, on a day that the 2:57 does not run, or, if it does run, does not stop at the station where you are supposed to get off. Many men, separated from a woman by this particular form of imprecision, have never showed up in her life again. Nothing so embitters a man as to end up in Bridgeport, when he was supposed to get off at Westport.—JAMES THURBER, *Let Your Mind Alone*

When we use a word (or combination of words) either in speaking or in writing, our most obvious purpose is to indicate some thing, or some relation, or some property. What the word is used to indicate is sometimes called its "meaning." For example, suppose that you and I are standing on the shore of Sligo Bay and suddenly we see a large white bird flying overhead. I say to you, "That's a swan." I thereby indicate to you that the object we are looking at is a member of the class of birds called swans. The word "swan" as I used it has a plain, straightforward meaning. This meaning is non-personal, or, as it will be more convenient to say, "objective." Since the primary purpose of the usage of language in any scientific inquiry necessitates that the words used should be non-personal or objective, we may call such a use of language scientific. Sometimes we use words with the deliberate intention of evoking emotional attitudes in our hearers; we want them to respond in a certain way to what is said. Language thus used may be said to be emotive. A word used in this emotive manner can be said to be emotionally toned. If we speak for the sake of arousing emotional attitudes, then the use of emotionally toned words is good for the purpose. When, however, our purpose is to give a straightforward account of what we believe to be the case, emotionally toned language is bad language. In poetry and in oratory the use of emotionally toned language may be essential for the purpose the speaker wishes to achieve. It is, then, good language, for it is fitted to its purpose. If, however, we want to think something out, then we are hindered in our purpose by using emotionally toned language. Such language may be an insuperable obstacle to thinking effectively. This is a point of such importance that it is worth while to spend some trouble over it.—L. SUSAN STEBBING, *Thinking to Some Purpose*

A speaker uses irony when he deliberately says something he doesn't mean, but indicates at the same time by tone or gesture what he does mean. When a person says, "Oh, yeah," in a certain tone, we know that he means quite the contrary of what he says. In a poem on the Jubilee celebration of Queen Victoria the poet Housman addresses the soldiers who have fought all over the world for the British Empire. He tells them that God will save the Queen:

> Oh, God will save her, fear you not;
>   Be you the men you've been,
> Get you the sons your fathers got,
>   And God will save the Queen.

But the stanza is ironical, because he is saying more than the usual patriotic statement that God will save the Queen. He is really saying that God will save the Queen only if English manhood remains as strong as before and is as freely sacrificed. Understatement has an ironical quality. . . . But there are other types of irony. Irony always implies a kind of contrast. In Hardy's poem, "The Convergence of the Twain," the contrast between the hopes and intentions of the men who built the *Titanic* and the fate that destroyed the ship is treated ironically by the poet.—C. BROOKS, J. T. PURSER, R. P. WARREN, *An Approach to Literature*

Every student who attends an American college needs three types of education: general education, liberal education, and specialized education. By general education I mean that education which is required to become an effective member of the human race; it provides us with the means of communication with one another, with an understanding of the relationships between human beings and the institutions which they establish, with an analytical approach toward the physical universe of which we are all a part, and with a concept of the position which we hold in the stream of time and history. By liberal education I mean the education that frees us from the confines of the group, the patterns, and conventions, and enables us to become truly an individual; it is therefore the education which discovers our greatest abilities and interests and then develops them to the highest capacities which we can achieve. By specialized education I mean the education which will enable us to make a living in a competitive economic world; especially in America there is very little leisure class, and every educated person is expected to have some place in which he can render a valuable service to his fellow men.—CARTER DAVIDSON, "What I Expect of English Teachers"

"There will always be prejudice, and there is nothing anyone can do about it, so why try?" This pronouncement, made with an air of hearty and complacent cynicism, is usually regarded by its owners as an example of fine Olympian detachment. And so it is, although fine Olympian detachment about things which are not personally inconvenient is a state easily attained by babies on leading strings and puppies in a basket. The assertion that nothing can be done about prejudice is suspicious in character, but it is certainly true that prejudice will always exist. So will sickness and disease, but that scarcely seems sufficient reason for telling our medical scientists to put on their hats, close up their laboratories, and give the spirochetes, bacilli and viruses a free hand.[5]

The long arm of Hollywood can be seen in any home or department store, or by glancing into the nearest mirror. Indirect lighting, modern furniture, and resplendent bathrooms, those landmarks of man's ascent from barbarism, owe much to the silver screen. The off-the-face hat, invented to keep shadows off the faces of movie Lorelei who are paid for

[5] Reprinted from *Color Blind* by permission of Simon and Schuster, Inc. Copyright, 1946, by Margaret Halsey.

their unshadowed features, swept the feminine world in the past decade and reestablished a style which is two thousand years old. The movies helped to undermine the taboos which fought off a cosmeticized world. The short-vamp shoe, the decline of the American custom of eating peas with a knife, elegant feminine underthings, the popularity of Scotch and soda, and smoking by adolescents and women—all may be traced in some measure to Hollywood's persuasive power.—Leo C. Rosten, *Hollywood: The Movie Colony—the Movie Makers*

There are five ways to get wealth—to make it, to buy it, to find it, to have it given to you, and to steal it. Finding and giving are matters of chance or personal whim, and do not occur in any regular way. Stealing is frequently similar, and even when carefully organized on a large scale it is not recognized by society as a proper activity. Consequently, the science which deals with wealth limits itself to making and buying. This science is called economics.

The word "wealth" is used in the preceding paragraph, and all through this book, in a definite, scientific sense. In its broadest sense it may be considered to mean all material things that are, or by any possibility may be, useful to human beings, except their own bodies. It is customary, however, among students of economics to limit the definition of wealth to things that are owned by human beings, and this is logical because only things that are owned create economic problems. Let us, therefore, for the purposes of this book associate our definition of wealth invariably with the idea of ownership.—Henry Pratt Fairchild, *Economics for the Millions*

The tractors came over the roads and into the fields, great crawlers moving like insects, having the incredible strength of insects. They crawled over the ground, laying the track and rolling on it and picking it up. Diesel tractors, puttering while they stood idle; they thundered when they moved, and then settled down to a droning roar. Snub-nosed monsters, raising the dust and sticking their snouts into it, straight down the country, across the country, through fences, through dooryards, in and out of gullies in straight lines. They did not run on the ground, but on their own roadbeds. They ignored hills and gulches, water courses, fences, houses.

The man sitting in the iron seat did not look like a man; gloved, goggled, rubber dust mask over nose and mouth, he was a part of the monster, a robot in the seat. The thunder of the cylinders sounded through the country, became one with the air and the earth, so that earth and air muttered in sympathetic vibration. The driver could not control it— straight across country it went, cutting through a dozen farms and straight back. A twitch at the controls could swerve the cat', but the driver's hands could not twitch because the monster that built the tractor, the monster that sent the tractor out, had somehow got into the driver's hands, into his brain and muscle, had goggled him and muzzled him—goggled his mind, muzzled his speech, goggled his perception, muzzled his protest. He could not see the land as it was, he could not smell the land as it smelled; his feet did not stamp the clods or feel the warmth and power of the earth.

He sat in an iron seat and stepped on iron pedals. He could not cheer or beat or curse or encourage the extension of his power, and because of this he could not cheer or whip or curse or encourage himself. He did not know or own or trust or beseech the land. If a seed dropped did not germinate, it was nothing. If the young thrusting plant withered in drought or drowned in a flood of rain, it was no more to the driver than to the tractor. —JOHN STEINBECK, *The Grapes of Wrath*

II. Read again the paragraphs used for illustration in the text of this chapter, and pick out the topic sentence in each paragraph.

Chapter Seven

Language in Action

"The Luxury of Integrity"
Stuart Chase

THUS FAR IN THIS BOOK we have been concerned first with a broad general view of language, second with an examination of details about the conventions and use of English. Both the broad panoramic view and the detailed microscopic views are necessary preliminaries to a study of the motion picture of language, the complex drama in which choice of words, choice of detail, concrete or abstract expression, sentence structure, sentence length, organization, paragraph development, plain sense, and attitude work together to achieve the writer's intention. This chapter, and the next two chapters, present examples of the whole play—of language in action.

On the left-hand pages in this chapter we are printing "The Luxury of Integrity," an essay by Stuart Chase. The student should read the essay straight through, seeing the plan of development, responding to the effect that the whole essay produces, and ignoring the comments printed on the opposite pages. After his first reading, when he is ready to analyze the essay, he should examine it again, paragraph by paragraph, this time considering the comments and questions on the right-hand pages.

Mr. Chase is a well-known writer on social and economic subjects who has also written *The Tyranny of Words*, a popular book on language. "The Luxury of Integrity" appeared in *The Nemesis of American Business*, published in 1931. The student needs to keep in mind, as he reads the essay, its historical context; a number of brief allusions to events and situations current in 1931 are no longer timely. The essay is not dated, however, in its basic theme or its style.

Perhaps the most distinctive quality of Mr. Chase as a writer is his ability to present a complicated and abstract subject in a clear and interesting way to a general audience. Such writing calls for a lively style and skill in the use of informal English. "The Luxury of Integrity" is not intended to serve as a model for all kinds of writing; but it is a good example of lively, vigorous, concrete language aimed at a general audience, and it illustrates a number of the principles of effective expression.

THE LUXURY OF INTEGRITY *

STUART CHASE

[1] Once upon a time I worked for the United States Government. In the course of my official duties I was directed to make a rather particular and painstaking analysis of the profits of certain mammoth corporations. The welcome of the mammoth corporations, needless to say, was not warm.

[2] One of my subordinates in the investigation was continually getting into trouble. He was a likeable fellow, a good routine worker, always ready to do odd jobs after hours. I took a personal interest in his troubles; I loaned him money, patched up a quarrel between himself and his wife, gave him books to read, tried to help him slide a little more easily along his white-collar groove. That he was grateful, that he really respected and liked me, I do not doubt to this day. Yet here is what he did after two years of friendly association:

[3] He ransacked my private files and turned over any evidence showing liberal political tendencies on my part to the aforesaid mammoth corporations. He came into my office late one evening—fortified by a drink or two—and said, "Chase, I'm a Bolshevik. I'm fed up with the whole damned capitalist system. I'd like to help kick it over. I'd like to join something. You know about these so-cialists and I.W.W.'s. I see you reading pieces about them. Tell me all about it, shoot the works, tell me what I ought to join. I'll pay the dues."

[4] At first I thought the poor boy had really come to the end of his rope; that this was a last desperate gesture before the white-collar routine doomed him altogether. Then I began to realize that he was lying; that he was hoping to pick up some information from me which could be twisted in such a way as to discredit my work in the investigation. (Not that I had much to offer.) I went on with my columns of figures, and gradually his receptive attitude waned. "Aren't you going to tell me anything?" he whined. "No," I said. "And I guess you had better go."

[5] He took his hat and went and, as the door closed behind him, I knew that the man I had befriended could not afford the luxury of integrity. Someone was paying him to act as a spy. His government

---

* From Stuart Chase, *The Nemesis of American Business*. Copyright, 1931, by the Macmillan Company and used with their permission.

[1]   This is not a particularly good beginning, but it does supply facts that the reader will need later. The last sentence is an example of understatement.

[2]   In this paragraph Mr. Chase begins to give an example of the luxury of integrity. He gives the reader enough concrete information to show that his subordinate had good reason to consider Mr. Chase his friend. The last sentence leads into the next paragraph. The next-to-last sentence shows parallel structure in the two *that* clauses. By making the sentence periodic, Mr. Chase gives the main clause greater emphasis and also changes from the subject-predicate movement of the earlier sentences.

[3]   The dialogue adds concreteness and interest. It gives the reader the sense of being present.

[4]   Note the transitions—*at first, then*. The word *No* is given emphasis because *I said* follows it instead of coming at the beginning or the end of the speech.

[5]   Now Mr. Chase introduces a phrase that contains his title, and he goes on to state the point of his example: that his subordinate, like many other Americans, was unable to afford the luxury of integrity. The short sentences, *Someone had been paying him to act as a spy* and *He had been bought,* break up the pattern set by the longer sentences to provide variety and emphasis. The paragraph is given coherence from sentence to sentence by

salary was little enough, while his wife had definite ideas about her proper position in the world. He had been bought. (I doubt if the vendee got his money's worth.) I was bitter at the time, but today that bitterness is tinged with pity. He is only one among many Americans who increasingly cannot afford the luxury of integrity. His case is more dramatic perhaps, but essentially on all fours with the plight of nearly every man you meet upon the street. They, like him, have betrayed their personal sense of decency and honor because forces are loose, too powerful for ordinary clay to oppose.

[6]   In the custody and handling of transferable property Americans grow ever more dependable; but in that more subtle definition of integrity which bids a man play fair with his own soul, never, it seems to me, has the Republic sunk to lower levels. As the machine breeds increased specialization, increased technological unemployment, as mergers spread their threat to white-collar jobs, the case grows worse. The greater one's economic insecurity, the greater the tendency to sacrifice spiritual independence and to chant in dreary unison the simple credo of the yes man. It is my contention that for uncounted millions of Americans the price of integrity is more than they can afford. Nor should I be surprised if the ratio of growth in the process bore more than a casual relationship to the growth in urban as against rural population.

[7]   Even as the interlocking technical structure of industry makes for an increasing tenuousness in the condition of the live nerves of transport, power, and communication which provide city dwellers with physical necessities, so the psychological condition of the inhabitants of Megalopolis grows more precarious. Living in a crowd, it has become highly important to *fit in.* There are fewer square holes for square pegs; to make the close-locked wheels of industry turn, an employee must be as round as a ballbearing. This smooth and oily quality that eases the friction of the highly organized machine is in a way more vital than professional training, ability, or energy. One man may be genial and tactful by nature, while nine have to achieve tact and geniality by effort. For the milk of human kindness the most obvious substitute is soft soap.

II

[8]   The yes man had no place in the pioneer tradition. The pioneer had his faults and virtues. The faults included a prodigal wastefulness, a disposition to befoul one nest and move on to the next, a certain laxity in respect to the social amenities. The virtues included

the pronouns *he, his, him*. The last sentence emphatically expresses the topic idea of the paragraph. Notice how Mr. Chase has cut clauses in this last sentence; the sentence could have read: "They are like him; they have betrayed their personal sense of decency and honor because forces are loose which are too powerful for ordinary clay to oppose."

[6]   The first sentence is related to the previous paragraph by the repetition of key words—*American, integrity;* and it helps to define the abstract word *integrity* by distinguishing between it and dependability in handling transferable property. In both sentence 1 and sentence 2, Mr. Chase places subordinate ideas first and saves the emphatic final position for the most important ideas. The expressions *play fair with his own soul* and *never* receive special emphasis because each is followed by a pause. The whole paragraph repeats and elaborates the idea stated in paragraph 5. The last sentence leads the reader into paragraph 7.

[7]   This paragraph develops more fully the idea mentioned in the last sentence of paragraph 6; it explains why integrity decreases as the proportion of people living in cities increases. In this paragraph Mr. Chase has used expressions which could be trite, but has given them an original twist that makes them effective for his purpose. The figurative last sentence ends the paragraph emphatically with the witty play on *milk* and *soft soap*. In the first section of the essay Mr. Chase has aroused the reader's interest by a striking concrete example and has stated his thesis that in modern society a decreasing number of men can afford the luxury of integrity.

[8]   The first sentence serves as the topic sentence for paragraph 8 and also states the topic idea for the whole of Section II. The locution *yes man* echoes back to the *credo of the yes man* in paragraph 6. Paragraph 8 contains a particularly interesting combination of levels of language. Which

a sturdy independence, and the compulsion, if need arose, to look every man level in the eye and tell him to go to hell. Reasonably secure in the fruits of his own labor and thus economically independent, he could express in any company his honest opinions as forcibly as he pleased, and, subject to the local *mores*—the base line from which all human behavior must stem—he could translate his beliefs into tangible performance. He could vote for candidates he respected, agitate for reforms he believed in, refuse to do jobs which galled his sense of decency or craftsmanship, come and go as the seasons dictated, but not at the bidding of any overlord. His opinions may have been frequently deplorable, his acts often crude and peremptory, but he was free to be true to the best that he knew—and so, by the Eternal! a man, and not a rubber stamp.

[9]   His was not the gentleman's code of honor, but one less punctilious, more democratic, more human, and probably in the long run superior. The gentleman had a divided responsibility; he must not only seek to be true to himself, but he must maintain a wide margin between himself and the herd. The pioneer was of the herd and proud of it, and could thus devote himself single-mindedly to the one responsibility. Compare, let us say, a thousand assorted pioneers of the Berkshire Hills in Massachusetts in 1800, with a thousand assorted New York bank clerks in 1930, and, unless the monumental history of the Berkshires which I have lately ingested is a tissue of falsehoods, you will find about as many no men in the former area, as you will find yes men in the latter. The ratios, I should guess, have reversed themselves in one hundred and thirty years. With the no men will lie character, courage, individuality, saltiness. With the yes men will lie radios, automobiles, bath-tubs, and a complete paralysis of the will to act in accordance with their fundamental inclinations. That Berkshire babies were compounded of better stuff than bank-clerk babies, I absolutely deny. Opinion for opinion and belief for belief, it is probable that the New York thousand have a more civilized outlook, a better stock of human values in their heads, than had the Pittsfield thousand. But for the latter integrity was cheap and abundant, while for the former it is very dear. Like all luxuries, it can be bought, but few dare to pay the price. For the price may be the job, and the job means life or death.

[10]   If you object that most men and women are without a sense of honor, then call it early conditioning. From the cultural mulch in which we are reared—compounded of the influence of parents, school, church, folkways, literature—our personalities are formed. We take and we reject; we give lip service to much that our hearts do not subscribe to. But certain principles we make our own. Integrity

expressions in it are slang or at least clearly informal? Which are formal? Do you think that the variety of levels is intentional and serves some purpose? Also noteworthy are the ways of achieving variety in sentence structure. Sentence 5, *Reasonably secure in the fruits* . . . , is a good example of subordination, and sentence 6 of parallelism. The last sentence is a good example of emphasis. Why, and how is the emphasis obtained?

[9]   The first sentence, the topic sentence, linked to the preceding paragraph by the pronoun *his*, serves to introduce a paragraph developed by contrast and comparison. Variety in sentence length and sentence structure are outstanding characteristics of this paragraph. In the table below are given the *number* of words in each sentence and also the *opening words* of each sentence. A glance at the table will show the variety in sentence length and sentence beginning and will also make more conspicuous some of the transitional devices. The transitional devices are italicized.

23	*His* was not the gentleman's code . . .
28	*The gentleman* had a divided responsibility . . .
21	*The pioneer* was of the herd . . .
65	*Compare,* let us say, a thousand assorted *pioneers* . . .
14	*The ratios,* I should guess, have reversed . . .
10	*With the no men* will lie character . . .
26	*With the yes men* will lie radios . . .
15	That the *Berkshire babies* were compounded . . .
34	Opinion for opinion and belief for belief . . .
16	*But for the latter integrity* was cheap . . .
14	Like all luxuries, *it* can be bought . . .
14	*For the price* may be the job . . .

[10]   Sentence 2 illustrates the effective use of parallelism and of periodic structure. In most of this paragraph, Mr. Chase is still defining integrity. What means of definition does he use? What is the relationship between the second sentence and the last sentence in this paragraph?

consists in living up to them. I am not here concerned with those broad principles of morality which now as in the days of David and Solomon move more or less *in vacuo,* but rather with a far more concrete and personal standard. I ask only if your behavior squares with your conception of what honest behavior should be, and care not twopence how lofty or low the original conception. A stream can rise no higher than its source.

[11] The point is not that we traduce our honor to climb up—such behavior has affected a fixed fraction of the race since the Cro-Magnon man—but that most of us today are forced to traduce our honor to cling to what we've got; aye, to exist at all. It would be easier if life were simpler, but the perspiring super-salesmen take excellent care that life shall never simplify. No more have we won to a standard of living held respectable by our fellows, than presto! a new and higher standard confronts us—two-cars-per-family, college-for-all-the-children, annual models in furniture, country club memberships—and this we must attain on pain of social disapprobation. There is no level, but a steadily ascending curve which tolerates little margin of saving, no dependable economic security. While jobs grow more uncertain, desires, built in by the high-pressure fraternity, grow more clamorous. In this compound-pressure pump, the wayfaring man finds it almost impossible to be true to his innermost nature.

III

[12] Consider initially the simple and widespread practice of yesing the boss—to use the current phrase. The man with the strong jaw sits at the head of the conference table, his confreres gathered around him, each with pad and sharpened pencil. From the strong jaw comes the announcement of a certain policy—perhaps a wage reduction, perhaps a wage increase, perhaps a universal system of time clocks. He looks about him. The policy may be utterly repugnant to his staff but, "I check with you, chief," "check," "check," "check,"—the little threadbare word runs round the table. Not always, to be sure, but frequently enough to make our case. On any given business day, the number of such checks and yeses must be astronomical in magnitude. It would be interesting to chart their yearly curve superimposed upon a curve exhibiting the growth of mergers.

[13] The psychological effect of continually pretending to agree with that with which one does not agree is disastrous. An internal conflict is set up which tends to polarize work into neutrality. Initiative, concentration, straight thinking evaporate, leaving only pur-

[11] Notice that the topic idea of the paragraph is stated in the first sentence and in the last, and that each statement gains effectiveness from the use of figures of speech—*climb up . . . cling to what we've got* in the first sentence, and *compound-pressure pump* in the last sentence. Throughout the paragraph Mr. Chase uses figures of speech and concrete details to make a large and abstract idea concrete and interesting. The last sentence of paragraph 11 leads directly into paragraph 12; it states the generalization for which Mr. Chase is now going on to supply a number of particulars.

[12] The first sentence (also the topic sentence) of paragraph 12 makes it clear that Mr. Chase is giving an example, and the word *initially* in that sentence leads the reader to expect other examples to follow. A transition has been effected not only from paragraph 11 to paragraph 12, but from Section II to Section III. By now the larger organization of the essay begins to emerge. In Section I Mr. Chase gives a concrete example of the luxury of integrity and comments on his example; in Section II he is dealing more generally with the luxury of integrity, defining it and explaining how it has come about that integrity is less easy to practice than it was in the day of the pioneer. Now in Section III he begins by examples to *show* that today many people cannot, or do not, live up to their own standards of honesty.

[13] This paragraph comments on the practice of *yesing the boss* which was described in paragraph 12. The two paragraphs could have been combined and the topic sentence of paragraph 12 would then have served for both. Has Mr. Chase gained anything by the two separate paragraphs?

poseless activity. Probably less damage is suffered by the individual who knows in advance the fire he must pass through and deliberately makes up his mind to prostitute his talents. He is tragic enough, but a less unhappy exhibit on the whole than the hordes who fool themselves into thinking that they are doing honest work, unaware of the conflict beneath the surface. In business offices there is usually one of the former to ten of the latter.

[14] Next let us consider that very considerable fraction of the population engaged in making commodities which the maker knows to be evil, shoddy, adulterated, and a rank imposition upon the public. He may whistle cheerfully enough, say, "What the hell?" and believe that the plight of the public troubles him hardly at all. But deep down inside the continued outrage to his instinct of workmanship troubles him considerably. It is contrary to the whole history of mankind to waste good hours of labor on worthless or evil products.

[15] Not long ago I delivered an address on the Russian economic experiment. I told of the method whereby an oil pool was developed as a single geological unit without competitive drilling and its appalling waste. After the lecture an engineer came up to me. He seemed deeply stirred. "My God," he said, "do you suppose I could get a job in Russia? I'm sick of drilling wells in competitive fields, watching most of my work run to waste. I know how a pool ought to be organized, but with all this offset drilling we aren't allowed to organize it." In his excitement, it was only too plain that there was a tragic breach between his standard of workmanship and the work that he had to do.

[16] Of the ten million factory employees in America today, the two million in the building trades, and the two hundred thousand engineers, how many can hold up their hands and say that they take pride in what they make? Many of them, of course, are operating processes so specialized that they have no idea of what they are helping to produce, but the majority are probably still aware of it. The show of hands is not impressive. When one considers the weighted silks, the bulk of the patent-medicine traffic, jerry-built bungalows on Garden Crest developments (I have talked to the carpenters working on them), shoes that dissolve into their essential paper, rickety furniture brave in varnish—commodity after commodity, process after process, the reason is sufficiently clear.

[17] Leaving the factory, we come out upon the marketplace. Here we find a group almost as numerous as the producers, pushing goods which they know to be inferior or useless. A salesman has no canons

[14, 15, 16] In paragraph 14, *Next let us consider* serves to introduce another type of violation of integrity and to bring to an end the discussion of yesing the boss. Paragraphs 15 and 16 continue the discussion introduced in 14. More specifically, paragraph 14 introduces the subject of those who make shoddy or evil products, paragraph 15 illustrates how men feel who thus consciously violate their own standards of workmanship, and paragraph 16 suggests concretely how widespread such violation is. Again Mr. Chase has cut into several paragraphs material that is closely enough related to be combined into one. Has he gained or lost by so doing?

[16] Compare the following version with the paragraph of Mr. Chase, and observe his use of subordination: There are ten million factory employees in America today. There are two million in the building trades. There are two hundred thousand engineers. Few of them can take pride in what they make. How many of them can hold up their hands and say that they take pride in it? Many of them are operating specialized processes. They don't know what they are helping to produce. The majority are probably still aware of it. The show of hands is not impressive. Consider the weighted silks. Consider the bulk of patent-medicine traffic. Consider the jerry-built bungalows. I have talked to the carpenters working on them. Consider shoes that dissolve into their essential paper. Consider rickety furniture. It is brave in varnish. Consider commodity after commodity. Consider process after process. One will see why the show of hands is not impressive. The reason is sufficiently clear.

[17] Like paragraph 14 this paragraph begins with a topic sentence introduced by a transitional phrase. Also like 14, this paragraph introduces a series of closely related paragraphs (17, 18, 19, 20, 21), in this case a unified

of workmanship to be outraged, but if he has to sell an inferior product, and knows it, his case is not much happier than that of his fellow in the shop. He has to lie blatantly, loudly and continually. He has to tell the world that bad products are good. He becomes used to it, of course; he may even take a little pride in his sales charts. But that does not mean that somewhere behind the table-pounding, door-bell ringing, and copy-writing there is not a *man,* who, in the darkness of the night after an ill-advised dinner, does not sometimes wish to God he could earn his living doing something he believed in.

[18]   We now come to one of the saddest exhibits on the list. There may be more deplorable human behavior than the violation of hospitality practiced daily by uncounted thousands of house-to-house canvassers, but I am at a loss to know what it is. Since time out of mind it has been the kindly human custom to welcome the stranger at the gate. The reaction is doubtless tied up with a dim fear that, some day, you too may be a-wandering and need rest and welcome. On this ancient custom the up-and-coming canvasser is forced to trade. In company schools he is deliberately coached in ways and means for capitalizing the instant of hospitality, for gaining admission, a chair, a respectful audience—only to outrage it in the end.

[19]   Here, to quote an actual case, is a woman canvasser who announces herself as a member of the local school committee—only she is not a member of the school committee but recites a name which induces the lady of the house to think that she is. The "committee," it appears, recommends a certain book to aid the children's education. The visitor mentions the children by name, their ages, their bright looks. The lady of the house is pleased. The cost of the book is five dollars. Her face falls. She cannot afford five dollars. Haltingly, ashamedly, she confesses it. The canvasser turns on her with the sure-fire line, "Mrs. Green, don't you care enough about the future of your children to pay five dollars?" What mother can resist such an accusation? Company statistics coldly demonstrate that seven times out of ten it consummates a sale. Yet what troubles me is not the plight of Mrs. Green with a worthless volume on the parlor table, but the utter abandonment of self-respect on the part of the lady canvasser. Had she hit Mrs. Green with a blackjack as she stood defenseless and welcoming on her own doorstep, the loss of personal integrity could hardly have been greater. Hospitality is a particularly precious custom in a civilization which drifts so rapidly to cities and apartment houses. By ruthless violation the canvassers have all but killed it.

block of thought that deals with violations of integrity in salesmanship. By now it is evident that Mr. Chase, like most skillful writers, is presenting his thought according to a logical plan. His sections mark off the major divisions. Within these sections there are sometimes subdivisions that consist of more than a single paragraph, and each paragraph is then a small but unified part of the subdivision to which it belongs. Also worthy of attention is the emphatic way Mr. Chase ends his paragraphs. See the last sentence of each of the paragraphs in the present subdivision (paragraphs 17–21).

[18] *We now come* is a transitional phrase introducing one subdivision in the block of paragraphs on salesmanship. Note in this paragraph Mr. Chase's use of charged words to convey his feelings about the ideal of hospitality and about the canvassers who presume upon hospitality to sell their wares. Which words or expressions carry a particularly heavy charge?

[19] This paragraph, like paragraph 9, supplies an example of variety of sentence length and of skillful adaptation of sentence length to the impression that the writer wishes to produce. Notice particularly the effectiveness of the short sentences. That Mr. Chase varies sentence length to suit different subject matters is made evident when we compare the length of sentences in the present paragraph with the length of sentences in paragraph 9.

Length of sentences in paragraph 9 (average, twenty-five words): 23, 28, 21, 65, 14, 10, 26, 15, 34, 16, 14, 14.

Length of sentences in paragraph 19 (average, fifteen words): 48, 13, 12, 7, 9, 3, 5, 5, 20, 7, 14, 33, 28, 18, 10.

This paragraph gives information about an actual case of house-to-house canvassing and statistics on the results of this kind of canvassing; but Mr. Chase is not letting the facts speak for themselves. By what charged words does he promote sympathy for Mrs. Green and distaste for the canvasser's methods?

[20]   Not content with the assault in person, enterprising vendors of commodities, particularly of certain types of securities, are lately using the telephone to effect a sale. In one day at my office I was called to the telephone five times by total strangers giving a Wall Street address, succulently outlining the profit to be made by an immediate purchase of American Consolidated International Class B. To the first man I tried to be polite, to the second I was curt, for the other three I simply hung up the receiver. But the day was ruined by a feeling of baffled rage, partly at my assailants, and partly at myself for having to crush the habit of years of being courteous to those who had taken the trouble to call me on the telephone.

[21]   Yet canvassers, like the rest of us, must eat. I remember when I lived in Chicago a neighbor in the woolen business dropped in upon us one evening. We welcomed him into the living room and were somewhat surprised to find that he had a large box under his arm. His face was set. He opened the box and disclosed some excellent woolen sweaters and hose, male and female. We admired everything—the admiration of friends. Would we buy some? We were thunderstruck, but kept our faces straight, and bought. Obviously, our guest had struck a vein of bad luck and been reduced to capitalizing his acquaintanceships. Always afterwards he avoided us. Our friendship had come to an end. How many friends did that hard winter cost him?

IV

[22]   This brings us to that growing army of "publicity men" and women who sometimes do not—but frequently do—give the best of their years and their vitality to pushing causes in which they have no faith, and to booming personalities whom privately they designate as stuffed shirts. There are people among them whose shingle is out for any propaganda however worthless, and for any publicity seeker however shameless. As in the textile industry, there is overproduction in the publicity game, and a client is a client. How many nationalists at heart are writing purple copy for peace societies; how many socialists at heart lauding the benign activities of the power companies; how many intelligent judges of human character stirring the tom-toms for men they despise?

[23]   In this connection, the testimonial writer demands a note. If he—or she—really likes the product, well and good. In many cases he or she has never tried it. A thumping lie is exchanged for a bag of gold. The flight of Lindbergh from America to France was a fine

[20]   The phrase, *Not content with the assault in person,* refers, of course, to house-to-house canvassing. By using it Mr. Chase is able to lead the reader without break to another kind of *assault,* the use of the telephone to effect a sale.

[21]   What is the attitude of Mr. Chase toward the man and toward the man's actions, and what expressions convey attitude? Does Mr. Chase appear to blame the man? If not, where would he place the blame? How is suspense produced in this paragraph? Does Mr. Chase present his example abstractly or concretely?

[22]   The transition between Section III and Section IV is one of Mr. Chase's least effective transitions. The reference of *this,* the first word in paragraph 22, is not very clear, and there is no evident reason for beginning another section here except that to continue Section III would make that section seem disproportionately long. It looks as though Section IV is merely a continuation of Section III and as if Mr. Chase just thought that III was getting too long. The section heading does break up the page and it does emphasize the final question of Section III, *How many friends did that hard winter cost him?* It seems unwise, however, to give such emphasis to the idea of loss of friends when Mr. Chase's main concern still seems to be the loss of integrity. Paragraph 22, though, is well written. What examples do you find in it of parallelism? Of balance? Of effective repetition?

[23]   *In this connection*—does *this* have a clear antecedent? Is this short paragraph all right as it stands, or should it, rather, be expanded or joined to another paragraph? In the last two sentences Mr. Chase repeats the sound *fine* (*fine, finer*). Is this good or bad repetition?

and stirring achievement. But even finer to my mind is the fact that he has never sold his honor to a manufacturer.

[24]   Consider the activities of the ghost writer. According to the rules of this flourishing new profession, he writes the speech for somebody else to deliver or the article or book for somebody else to sign. In certain cases he endeavors to put into words the somebody else's general thoughts, but in other cases the somebody else has no general thoughts, and it is his function to supply them. Thus he foists on the public an entirely false picture of his client; he puts brains—his brains—into a man of straw; and far worse, he abuses the craft of letters which the Lord has given him by writing words in which he places no credence while neatly dodging responsibility by placing his client's name above them. As a writer I have frequently been invited to "ghost" under such circumstances and once or twice have been sorely tempted by the size of the fee. Fortunately my economic circumstances at the time were such that I could afford to refuse. Heaven knows when, unfortunately, they will be such that I cannot afford to refuse. But when I fall, I shall know that my position as a responsible professional man—voicing his own thoughts and signing his own stuff—has come to an end.

[25]   I know a writer of newspaper editorials. Himself a liberal, he has to grind out a thousand words daily which reflect the ultraconservative policy of the paper for which he works. He keeps a record like a batting average chart, noting the editorials to which he can subscribe against those to which he cannot. When he last showed it to me he was scoring about .150—say one out of seven.

[26]   Pot boiling is no new phenomenon. Many of the Humanists' greatest heroes were known to stoop to the practice from time to time. It may be defined as doing, for a cash consideration, work markedly below the level of the artist's best. In the past, stark necessity was its chief inspiration. Today as I go about among novelists, poets, playwrights, painters, I find a new motive widely voiced. We will, they say, "ghost-write" success stories, produce canned editorials and advertising copy, concoct synthetic drama (a new type of laboratory research), illustrate magnificent brochures, or what you will, in order that we may lay aside a cash reserve, and *then* watch us burn up Olympus. I am still watching. The formula in most cases is spurious. A continued and calculated flow of second-rate work is more than liable to poison the original spring. One can cite names—a number of very promising names—but it would be too painful. Enough that American art and literature have lost some distinguished ornaments because integrity comes too high.

[27]   Lastly we shall consider a usage almost as widespread as yesing

[24] The relationship between this paragraph and the material that precedes it is certainly clear. Is it made clear by logical order or by transitions or by both? In short, why is it easy for the reader to follow Mr. Chase's thought here? Why is *somebody else* repeated in sentences 2 and 3? Characterize the "attitude" of Mr. Chase in his remarks about his own refusal to do ghost-writing. Does he seem complacent and superior, for example? Is his tone appropriate to his general purpose here and elsewhere when he draws examples from his own experience? What expressions here communicate his attitude?

[25] What would the essay gain or lose if this paragraph were omitted? How is this paragraph related to the preceding paragraph? To the whole essay of which it is a part? Is a more explicit transition needed or would it be superfluous?

[26] What use has Mr. Chase made of the first sentence and the last sentence of the paragraph? What is the topic sentence or topic idea? The last sentence is incomplete. Is it a justifiable incomplete sentence? In the next-to-last sentence Mr. Chase shifts to the use of *One,* though he has written the rest of the paragraph in the first person. Is this an undesirable shift, or is there some justification for it?

[27] The first sentence is worth examination. What is the effect of *lastly?*

the boss, one indeed that may be said to be an integral part of the folkways of a pecuniary civilization. I refer to the art of backslapping in the interest of a profitable sale. Under the canons of this culture complex it is incumbent upon the vendor to welcome the prospective vendee with all the warmth and sympathy hitherto reserved for dear and chosen friends. He must be dined and wined (Mr. Jesse R. Sprague has admirably described the latter ceremony in a recent article in *Harper's*), his most infantile pronouncements must be received with the highest respect, one's home must be thrown open to him, his lightest fancy instantly satisfied. The fact that the company pays the bills is entirely beside the point. The point is that the whole procedure, like the canvasser's behavior, makes a mockery of natural human intercourse. Friendship is one of the few compensations for a complex life. To shower upon strangers and upon people who never could be one's friends, all the earnests of comradeship is to debase rare metal. The dismal panorama passes before us: Manufacturers' agents departing with suitcases of gin to dentists' conventions. . . . Rotary club luncheons with members roaring songs, embracing one another. . . . "Jim" calling to "Joe" (and Jim hates Joe)—all in the hope of more business. . . . The hearty dinner at home to the chief buyer for the National Widget Corporation with one's wife in a new and alluring frock, and carefully coached in the art of drawing out Mr. Blatterfein on his favorite topic—the postage stamps of the Hawaiian Islands. . . . The high and costly strategy employed by publisher B in weaning an author away from publisher A—the agent preferably to be an old college friend. . . . "Contact men" in dinner coats at weekend parties.

[28] Backslapping may not always be for business reasons, but it is usually for pecuniary reasons. I recall participating in a dinner to a man who was as stupid as he was rich. The basic idea of the dinner was to obtain money from him in order that a certain charity might make up its deficit. At the close of the banquet our guest arose and delivered himself of as monumental a series of banalities as it has ever been my ill fortune to hear. When he seated himself, amid vast applause, we, the hosts, arose one by one, and respectfully asked questions and were grateful for answers that we knew to be absurd. Finally we gave our guest a rousing vote of thanks for a most instructive evening. Later, because his publicity man had used my name, I wrote him a letter—a slimy, unctuous letter—recalling his brilliant address and the needs of the charity in question. I was never so pleased in my life as when he kicked us all downstairs, and never

Of the reference to *yesing the boss?* Neither *Webster's New Collegiate Dictionary* nor the *American College Dictionary* lists *backslapping.* Is Mr. Chase justified in using the word (sentence 2)?

(The passage from *The dismal panorama* to the end of the paragraph is grammatically a single sentence, though Mr. Chase has chosen to set off the parallel elements by capitalizing each and by placing ellipses after each. In this long sentence Mr. Chase is illustrating the principle of concreteness-by-expansion; each of the parallel elements is a concrete part of the "dismal panorama" mentioned at the beginning of the sentence.)

[28]   The first sentence is a good example of transition by repetition of a key word. In what levels of language do the following locutions belong: *backslapping, banalities, unctuous, kicked us all down stairs, abasement?* What difference do you see between the way Mr. Chase mixes levels of language and the undesirable mixture in the following sentence: "The King, after dining and interviewing ambassadors, decided to take a short snooze, but the Queen remonstrated and he knew she wasn't kidding." Why, in your opinion, did Mr. Chase place the paragraph on backslapping for charity in its present position? In the first sentence Mr. Chase uses the word *pecuniary.* Could a person unfamiliar with the word grasp its meaning by studying it in its present context? If so, how? What is the difference between *business reasons* and *pecuniary reasons?*

gave a penny. In some dim way it restored my self-respect. Charities
are worthy—some of them—but are they worth such abasement?

V

[29] We have but touched the surface of the phenomenon, but
already most of us are in it up to the waist, if not indeed completely
mired. Certain groups are less involved than others, and a rough
appraisal of relative saturation might prove instructive.

[30] The independent farmer, standing closest to the pioneer tradition, *leads the list*.[1] Despite the steady encroachments of business
motives upon his way of life—for agriculture is far more a way of
life than a pecuniary pursuit—he still has the best chance among all
classes of Americans to call his soul his own. Perhaps the independent storekeeper, surviving in those few remote neighborhoods where
chain stores and full-line forcing have not rendered his life a burden,
takes second place. I know a few still functioning in the White
Mountains of New Hampshire. They are the sort of men who will
not send a bill when the neighbor who owes it is ill or out of luck.

[31] *Next in line* we might place the housewife. More remote from
the commercial front than her spouse, she still frequently reserves
the right to speak her mind freely, "to stand right up in meeting,"
as we New Englanders say. I recall the case of a brilliant young
accountant who, shortly after winning his C.P.A., was given an opportunity to make a million dollars, more or less, in a few months'
time. All he had to do was to approach certain corporations with an
offer to split whatever rebates he might earn for them in their filed
income tax returns. His share in turn was to be split with a government examiner who supplied the names of such corporations as had
legitimate claims for rebates in past tax payments. He told his mother
of the glittering opportunity: "Jim," she said, "you know when I
come to wake you in the morning I shake you hard, and you don't
stir?" "Yes," he said. "And then I shake you even harder, and you
give a little moan?" "Yes." "And finally I shake as hard as I can
and you open one sleepy eye?" "Yes." "I'd hate to come in morning
after morning and find you awake." He turned down the job and has
been sleeping soundly ever since.

[32] *Reasonably high in the comparative scale* would come the
skilled manual worker affiliated with a strong trade union. One does
not find an unduly grave percentage of yes men among locomotive
engineers, machinists, or building trades workers. In the main they

---

[1] The italics in Section V are not Mr. Chase's but ours. Their purpose will be
made clear by the accompanying comment.

[29, 30]   Paragraph 29 is an example of a transitional paragraph. It serves to show the relationship between what has gone before and the whole section it introduces; also it sets up a figure of speech—*mired . . . saturation*—which Mr. Chase will use effectively later. Notice that in Section V he is using logical order in that he goes from those groups which have most integrity to those which have least and that he is using numerous transitions to keep clear the relationship between groups. We have italicized the chief transitional expressions in this section. A study of these italicized expressions will help the reader to see how to use transitions effectively. What would paragraph 30 lose if the last sentence were omitted?

[31]   This paragraph gains concreteness from the use of anecdote or example. Does it seem that Mr. Chase is departing from his topic idea of the housewife when he begins to talk about the young accountant? If so, when does the connection become clear? Is there justification for this apparent lack of coherence?

(How would this dialogue be paragraphed if Mr. Chase had followed convention? Has he gained anything by going contrary to convention? Is the last sentence of the paragraph to be considered literally true? What is its purpose?)

[32]   Which expression is more abstract, *skilled manual worker affiliated with a strong trade union* (sentence 1) or *locomotive engineers* (sentence 2)? What would be lost if sentences 1 and 2 were transposed? What does the word *objective* (sentence 3) mean in its present context?

are utterly dependent on their jobs, but their jobs are objective and technical, while the backing of the union—sometimes with its benefit clause—stiffens their independence and self-respect.

[33] *Next we might place* independent manufacturers and entrepreneurs. The great corporations are fast undermining them, financially and spiritually; but many sturdily maintain the Forsyte tradition, refuse to grow maudlin about Service, honestly admit they are in business for profit and not for public welfare, and take pride in producing a sound article, honestly sold. *Below them would stand* professional men and women, with physicians at the head of the group and lawyers at the bottom. There was a time when this class topped the whole list, but that was before competition became so keen; before the days of split fees, ambulance chasing, and yesing the president of the University. Professors, like canvassers, must eat. If the gentle reader is of a professional persuasion, he is doubtless an exception, but as a journeyman member of his class, I know that all too frequently I am not an exception.

[34] *On a level with professional people* would come the unskilled manual workers, with farm laborers at their head. They are largely a beaten lot, but many of them lose their jobs so often they get used to it, and accumulate, if not independence, at least a certain stoicism, a bitter crust against a bitter world. *Not far below them* we find the servant class—some two millions of them in America. Here we note a peculiar phenomenon. Servants are protected to a degree by their time-honored professional status. Nobody expects their work-a-day manners to reflect their real personalities, and thus they are enabled to preserve some semblance of integrity behind and remote from the frozen smiles and conventional obsequiousness of their trade.

[35] *From servants it is a long drop downward* to the salesman, though here again we note, or are beginning to note, a loss of human dignity which is freezing into a convention. It is the salesman's business to be hypocritical if necessary, just as it is the servant's business to be servile. We do not expect much from a salesman or a blurb-writer save words, and presently he may be able to save his soul by taking, in his business hours, some such conventionalized and definite status as the butler or the waiter takes.

[36] Salesmen are low in the scale of integrity, but at least they are alive. They have even been known to tell the boss what they thought of him and throw the job in his face. Clerks and office workers, being all but dead, must *stand still lower*. They are the saddest group of yes men on the whole list.

[37] *As we feel for the bottom,* we encounter in the murky gloom a large round object. Dragging it with some reluctance toward the

[33] The reference to the Forsyte tradition (second sentence) is an example of literary allusion. Mr. Chase is referring to the practices of the Forsyte family, particularly of old Jolyon, in the novels of John Galsworthy. Has Mr. Chase taken into account that some of his readers may not have read the novels? Would such readers still see his point? In paragraph 39 there is another reference to old Jolyon and the Forsyte tradition. What is the value of these two allusions in creating the total effect that Mr. Chase is seeking?

[34] In what sense are unskilled manual workers *on a level with* professional people (sentence 1)? Would this sentence have a different meaning if it were taken out of context? How is the meaning made clear by the present context?

[35] Mr. Chase has already written in detail about violations of integrity in salesmanship (paragraphs 17-21) and in writing publicity (paragraphs 22-23). Why then does he mention salesmen or "blurb-writers" again in this section of the essay?

[36] What does *alive* (sentence 1) mean in its present context?

[37, 38] These paragraphs gain force from their place in the climactic order of Section V and also from the use of the figure of speech (*mired*

light, we discover it to be a politician. To expect integrity from an elected public servant is almost to expect a miracle. When Mr. Dwight Morrow, running for senator in New Jersey, actually and honestly spoke his mind about prohibition the shock was almost too great for the country to bear. Editorial writers lost their heads completely at the wonder of it. The politician leads a harrowing economic life, granted; there are often sound reasons for his debasement, but this incident would seem to make it plain that it is not always good business, or good publicity, to flounder so persistently in the lower depths. Once and again the poor fellow might come up for air.

[38] *We would seem to have touched the bottom. Not quite. We have yet to deal* with certain types of corporation executives. As a class executives may be arranged up and down the scale, but enough of them at least to be identified as a subspecies are the least enviable exhibit in the whole national category, firmly anchored to the ocean floor. Their case is the more deplorable in that they have less excuse than most of us for being untrue to themselves. They have more economic security than all the rest of us combined. Instead of quaking for their jobs, they need quake only for their balance sheets. They have sold themselves, not to inexorable terms of livelihood, but to a legal abstraction, an almost mythical monster, in whose bowels is nothing more than a certificate of incorporation. (Some anthropologist should do a sound monograph on the totem worship and animism involved in the modern conception of a corporation.) They dare not open their mouths in public, put pen to paper, pronounce judgment on any social question, attend a banquet—almost take a bath—without first securing the received policy of the company for which they work. They move in a world of juggernauts and spooks which pass under the name of unfavorable publicity. They cower before the dire warnings of counsels on public relations. Instead of honestly admitting they are in business for profit, they squirt atomizers filled with the rank perfumes of "service," "good will," "public duty" in all directions, until the atmosphere of the nation bids fair to be choked with alien gases. They wriggle, this subspecies, into schools, universities, women's clubs, churches. They teach the teacher to teach the little children to wash their little hands with their little cakes of Banana Oil Soap. It is difficult to walk a block in Washington without bumping into one of their legislative agents. Even as the Russians substitute Communism for God, these gentlemen substitute their Corporation. It can do no wrong. Once I was walking the streets of Boston with the vice-president of a great financial institution. We came to a little decayed brick building near

. . . *saturation*) which was introduced in paragraph 29. The transitional expressions, *As we feel for the bottom* (paragraph 37) and *We would seem to have touched the bottom* (paragraph 38), keep the figure in the mind of the reader and also contribute much to the attitudinal meaning. It is worth noting that Mr. Chase is writing with particularly strong feeling in these two paragraphs and that he is using strongly charged language. Analyze the techniques of charged language used. Can you justify Mr. Chase's use of it? Is Mr. Chase prejudiced against all corporation executives? Does he offer satisfying reasons for the disapproval that he states?

[38] This paragraph is a good example of transition and coherence by means of parallelism and repetition of a pronoun (in this case *they*). Read the paragraph aloud to see how it moves.

(The sentence beginning *Some anthropologist* contains several words likely to be unfamiliar to most readers. Was the meaning of the sentence clear to you as you read the essay for the first time? If it was not, see the definitions below and then try to restate Chase's idea in your own words.

    anthropologist—one who studies the science of man and his works
    monograph—a treatise on a particular subject
    totem—an object that stands as an emblem of a class, family, or related
       group
    animism—a belief that all natural objects possess a soul)

(If, instead of the sentence in the text beginning *They teach* Mr. Chase had written "They cause the teachers to train children to wash their hands with soap," what different plain-sense meaning would the sentence have? What different attitudinal meaning?)

the docks. He stopped, with reverence in his every gesture, and all but took off his hat. "This," he said, "is where our Company first began to do business." We might have been visiting the birthplace of a saint.

[39]   I should like to see old Jolyon Forsyte at a few American directors' tables; I should like to hear him express his mind freely at a conference of Junior Executives. Here was a man who ransacked the world for tea, sold you only the finest, and took a good round profit on the transaction. He did not cower before sticks of type, cared not a damn about "unfavorable publicity," had no animistic corporate god to serve, and could call his soul his own.

[40]   I have been perhaps unduly harsh with that fraction of corporation executives who have forsworn all canons of personal integrity to serve a paper monster. But I should like them to know how their activities impress the outside public; and I would point out, furthermore, that the lesson taught the politicians by Mr. Morrow is equally applicable in their case. They could afford to substitute facts for propaganda far more frequently than they do. The type of publicity put out by the Baltimore and Ohio Railroad may serve as an example of winning real good will by honest methods as against the tricky and spurious variety.

[41]   If you think that I have been passing moral judgments, I have completely failed in writing this article. Questionable morals as reflected in graft, peculation, and legal crime lie quite outside the discussion. Such behavior is to be found in every civilization since Mesopotamia; whether the ratio is worse in modern America I do not know, and for the moment do not care. Owing to the colossal temptations for graft inspired by prohibition, it may well be worse at the present writing; but this, we trust, is a temporary phenomenon. All I have tried to say is that you and I, and Americans generally, have each a personal standard of honorable conduct. Under prevailing conditions, largely economic, it is frequently impossible to live within striking distance of that standard. Dr. Paul S. Achilles of Columbia, professor of vocational psychology, estimates that over fifty per cent of Americans are not happy in their work. (The suicide rate per thousand has jumped fivefold in seventy years.) I am but pointing out a major reason for that unhappiness. There is better stuff in us than we are permitted to express, and callous as routine may have made us, the failure of self-expression still hurts. In the end nothing but a greater margin of economic security—the rock which stiffened the backbone of the pioneer—can bring release.

[39] Has Mr. Chase violated unity in including this paragraph about Jolyon Forsyte? If not, how is the paragraph relevant and how has Mr. Chase made its relevance obvious? Consider especially the last sentence.

[40] What obvious and less obvious reasons can you give for Mr. Chase's praise of the Baltimore and Ohio Railroad?

[41] Students sometimes misread the last paragraph of this essay. It is generally said that the last paragraph is the place of greatest emphasis. Has Mr. Chase used it to emphasize the idea that is most important to him? If so, what is the idea and how has he emphasized it?

EXERCISES

I. Make a detailed topic outline of "The Luxury of Integrity." [2]

II. In 300 to 500 words, write a concise summary of "The Luxury of Integrity," which follows the organization of the essay and includes all of its main points.

III. The following list of words, taken from the Chase essay, should be part of the college student's vocabulary. Turn to the paragraph in the essay in which each word occurs (the paragraph number follows the word) and try to determine what the word means in its context. If the word is unfamiliar to you, look it up in the dictionary,[3] and then look again at the word in context to see which dictionary meaning is the appropriate one.

credo [6]	benign [22]
tenuousness [7]	credence [24]
precarious [7]	spurious [26]
prodigal [8]	pecuniary [27]
amenities [8]	incumbent [27]
compulsion [8]	banalities [28]
mores [8]	unctuous [28]
tangible [8]	abasement [28]
peremptory [8]	affiliated [32]
punctilious [9]	unduly [32]
disapprobation [11]	maudlin [33]
repugnant [12]	stoicism [34]
blatantly [17]	inexorable [38]
consummates [19]	anthropologist [38]
ruthless [19]	totem [38]
succulently [20]	animism [38]

[2] For information about outline form, see p. 827.

[3] It may be desirable to read pp. 834–837. Using the Dictionary.

Chapter Eight

Language in Action: Types of Prose

IN EFFECTIVE COMMUNICATION, a speaker or writer selects the style and organization which will best achieve his primary purpose. We have said earlier that language is generally used for one of three primary purposes: (1) to inform (to communicate plain sense alone); (2) to persuade or convince (to communicate plain sense and to influence the reader's opinions and feelings); (3) to communicate feeling, attitude, and experience. These purposes produce different types of communication, which we shall discuss under the headings Informative Writing, Persuasive Writing, and Communication of Experience.

That these categories are not rigid and exclusive is demonstrated by Stuart Chase's essay in Chapter Seven, and also by some of the readings in this chapter. A writer's intention is frequently complex; he may persuade in order to make his information more palatable, may inform in order to persuade, may inform or persuade in the process of communicating experience, may communicate experience for the purpose of informing or persuading. He may also wish to entertain as he conveys fact, opinion, or feeling. Although intention is often complex, the skillful writer knows exactly what he wants to do; his purpose—simple or complex—determines selection, arrangement, and presentation of material.

In the following pages, under the three headings Informative Writing, Persuasive Writing, and Communication of Experience, we shall discuss the special problems involved and the special techniques used in each type of prose. The readings after each discussion show these techniques in action.

I. INFORMATIVE WRITING

Informative writing presents, explains, and interprets facts. It answers one or more of the following questions: *What is it? Who is*

197

*it? How is it done? How does it operate? How did it develop? What
are the facts? What do the facts mean?* Encyclopedia articles, texts,
and newspaper and magazine articles which explain scientific discoveries, proposed legislation, international developments, etc. are
examples of writing focused on *What is it?* Biographical articles in
dictionaries and encyclopedias, profiles, and feature articles about
people answer *Who is it?* Cookbooks, manuals of instruction, and
the numerous how-to-do-it books and articles (how to swim, how
to prune shrubs, how to learn to dance in four easy lessons) give the
reader informative directions. Analyses ranging from a technical
analysis of a mechanism to a study of the Marshall Plan at work are
concerned with *How does it operate?* Histories, law books, medical
and sociological case histories, and articles on current problems show
how a concept or movement or condition developed. Facts about a
subject are presented in different ways by news stories, reports, sur-
veys, informal factual essays and articles, and scholarly articles. News
commentaries, and most reports, texts, and research articles deal not
only with facts but also with their relationship and interpretation:
What do the facts mean?

A great deal of our daily communication is, of course, noninforma-
tive. But for much of what we know, we are dependent upon factual
writing; furthermore we need, every day of our lives, the ability to
communicate informatively. We must be able to give directions, to
support our opinions with factual evidence, to clarify old thoughts
and new ideas, and to communicate facts which we have gleaned
from lectures, from conversation, from observation or research, and
from reading.

The basic requirements of good informative prose are these:

1. The writer must know his subject thoroughly.
2. He must present it clearly to an audience which does not have
his knowledge.
3. He must adjust his method of presentation and his style to the
particular audience he is addressing and must make his material
interesting to that audience.

A. Knowing the Subject

This first requirement of good informative writing hardly needs
elaboration. But it may be worth pointing out that a writer does
not know his subject, in the sense of being prepared to write about
it, until he knows it in some organized way. He may have worked
for years in an apple orchard, and yet he is not ready to write a paper
on the work behind the harvest until he has thought through the
successive stages of the familiar routine, sifted the major from the

minor tasks, and decided which of a hundred remembered details will be most informative to a reader. A student may have spent several weeks reading about penal institutions in preparation for the writing of a research paper; but he does not know that subject, even though his mind and his note cards are full of it, until he has limited the broad topic to something he can handle, has correlated his data, has weighed conflicting evidence, and has thought about a plan of presentation.

B. Presenting Material Clearly

An organized knowledge of the subject is one guarantee of clear presentation. However, the very thoroughness of a writer's knowledge may produce weaknesses in his communication unless he remembers constantly that his readers—some of them, at least—know less than he does. An able scholar is not always a good teacher of college freshmen; sometimes he takes too much for granted, and mistakenly assumes that his students understand terms and ideas which are familiar and elementary to him. So it may be with the writer. He needs to remember (1) to define any terms which might be strange to the reader; (2) to include, in directions, all important warnings and instructions about what *not* to do; (3) to cover every step in a process, and to supply necessary background which an uninformed reader cannot supply for himself.

This sentence from a paper on how to play tennis would be obscure to many readers: "A let ball is served again." The term needs to be defined in some such manner as this: "A ball is called *let* when it goes over the net and into the correct court, but touches the net on the way over. The server is permitted to serve another ball in place of the *let* ball."

The following paragraph from a paper on taking care of a lawn gives inadequate advice about killing crabgrass. It fails to describe crabgrass for the inexperienced lawn-grower, and it omits some important precautions:

By midsummer the home owner has another problem with his lawn. One of the greatest lawn pests, crabgrass, may be ruining the sunny areas of his yard. He should buy one of the many crabgrass killers now on the market, and apply it to the affected areas. Several applications may be needed before the crabgrass disappears.

This revision is more informative:

By midsummer the home owner has another problem with his lawn. One of the greatest lawn pests, crabgrass, may be ruining the sunny areas of his yard. Young crabgrass shoots can be distinguished from desirable grass by their broad, curved leaves, and their light yellow-green color. Mature crabgrass has heavy branches which spread out, crab-like and close to the ground, from a center shoot. The home gardener should spray one of the many commercial crabgrass killers on the affected areas, carefully following the directions which come with the exterminator. Four or five applications, about a week apart, may be needed to kill the crabgrass. The lawn should not be sprinkled for twenty-four hours after the spraying. A rain a few hours after application of the exterminator will necessitate applying it again.

Although the directions for their use do not say so, many crabgrass killers also kill clover. The owner who values the clover in his lawn should not use a crabgrass killer unless it is specifically guaranteed not to injure clover plants.

This excerpt from a recipe in a cookbook omits steps in the process as well as definitions of terms:

Add the eggs, flour, and baking powder. Pour the mixture into a shallow pan and bake in a moderate oven till done.

An inexperienced cook might not know that the eggs should be beaten, the flour sifted, and the pan oiled; "moderate oven" is vague, and "till done" unhelpful. The following directions are clearer:

Add the eggs, well-beaten. Sift the flour and baking powder together, and add them to the mixture. Transfer the mixture to a shallow oiled pan, and bake it in a moderately hot oven, 350 degrees, for twenty minutes.

Defining terms, giving warnings, and including all steps in a process simply require awareness of the reader's needs. The major problem in presenting material clearly is working out the best possible organization.

Because organization depends so much on the nature of the material, general comment on it is of little value. We are, therefore, listing below, and discussing separately, six organizational patterns or systems most commonly used in informative writing; they are: chronological arrangement, definition, analysis, cause-and-effect arrangement, general-to-particular or particular-to-general arrangement, and contrast and comparison. These patterns are sometimes used alone, sometimes in combination. Many of them are extensions to a longer composition of the methods of paragraph development discussed in Chapter Six.

1. Chronological Arrangement

Chronological arrangement means setting down events in the time order in which they occur. It is the arrangement naturally used in the writing of history, in biography, and in articles which trace the development of a movement, institution, or situation. It is also used in giving instructions or following a process from beginning to end. The writer needs to keep the time relationship of events clear to the reader by means of transitional expressions like *immediately after, while these events were taking place, the next day, for twenty years there were no further advances; then . . . , as soon as this step is completed.*

2. Definition

We have said that brief definition of terms which a reader may not know is vital to clear communication. The extended definition, in which the writer devotes several pages or an entire article or book to clarifying a term is also common in informative writing. Long articles and even books have been written to define such terms as *corporation, democracy, social security, socialized medicine, aggression, neurosis, race, existentialism.*

Definition, both brief and extended, is so important in informative writing that it is well to spend some time on the techniques of defining. A good definition—of any kind, of any length—nearly always does two things: (1) it puts the subject into the genus, or class, to which it belongs; (2) it differentiates the subject from other members of that class. Some sentence-definitions will illustrate the principle:

A verb is a part of speech [classification] which states the occurrence of an action or expresses a state or condition. [Differentiation from other parts of speech.]

Hydrogen is a gas [classification] which is odorless, colorless, and tasteless [differentiation] and which burns but does not support combustion. [Further differentiation.]

Hockey is a game [classification] in which opposing teams, using sticks curved at one end, try to drive a disk or ball into the opposing team's goal. [Complex differentiation, from other games, other team games, and other games which use sticks.]

The following attempts at defining, taken from examination papers, illustrate typical failures in definition:

Context determines the meaning of a passage. [Not a definition, because it tells what context does without telling what it is: that is, the first step in definition, classifying *context* as surrounding material, has been omitted. One unfamiliar with context could conclude from this attempt at definition that context means a skillful reader.]

An independent clause is a group of related words containing a subject and verb. [All right as far as it goes; the term is classified and differentiated from phrases and single words. But an independent clause is not distinguished from a subordinate clause; *and is capable of standing alone as a sentence* should be added for complete differentiation.]

A euphemism does not cause shock or unpleasantness. [A correct, though negative, statement about euphemism, but not a definition because the word is not classified. A good day, a peaceful sleep, an enjoyable party—hundreds of things—do not cause shock or unpleasantness.]

Context is where the surrounding material sheds light. [Meaningless definition because of faulty expression. In a good definition, the genus is given as a noun, and not as a *where, when,* or *if* clause: *context* is the *surrounding material; golf* is a *game;* a *robin* is a *bird.*]

A euphemism is when you say he passed away for he died. [One restricted example; no definition. Both basic steps, classification and differentiation, are omitted. This statement defines *funeral* as well as it does *euphemism.* Here too the definition form is incorrect; a euphemism is a mild soothing term; it is not "when you say."]

Extended definitions expand the two basic steps in definition, especially differentiation of the subject from other members of its class with which it might be confused. Extended definitions also clarify the subject in one or more of these ways: (1) by giving examples; (2) by comparing the subject with something familiar to the reader; (3) by comparing and contrasting it with related subjects; (4) by tracing its history or development; (5) by negating or excluding—showing what it does not mean or does not include as the author is using it; (6) by restating in different words the essentials of the definition; (7) by analyzing—breaking the subject into its components, and examining each part.

The following definitions, though not long, illustrate some of these techniques of clarification. The first defines *free verse* by a form of negation (telling what it does not do), then traces its history and development, restates some of its characteristics, indicates where examples of it can be found, and finally gives an example:

FREE VERSE (Fr. VERS LIBRE): Poetry that does not follow a conventional pattern of meter and rhyme but depends upon other devices, such as assonance, alliteration, and cadence, for its rhythmic effects. It was first officially employed by the French poets of the Symbolist movement, but unofficially it is as ancient as Anglo-Saxon verse and that of other early European languages. Walt Whitman was a prominent user of free verse in the 19th century, his work serving to influence later poets. Under the influence of Whitman and the Symbolists, free verse became the prevailing poetic form of the period of the 1920's and 1930's, especially in the U.S., although during the 1930's it began to be replaced by more formal verse making use of a modified system of rhyme, meter, and stanza, appropriate to the new subject matter of intellectual rather than wholly sensuous appeal.

Poets whose work outstandingly makes use of free verse and is most representative of the form at its height of popularity are: Amy Lowell and the other Imagists, Carl Sandburg, and Edgar Lee Masters. The following is a typical free-verse poem:

> Out of me unworthy and unknown
> The vibrations of deathless music
> "With malice toward none, with charity for all."
> Out of me the forgiveness of millions toward millions
> And the beneficent face of a nation
> Shining with justice and truth.
> I am Anne Rutledge who sleep beneath these weeds,
> Beloved in life of Abraham Lincoln,
> Wedded to him, not through union,
> But through separation.
> Bloom forever, O Republic,
> From the dust of my bosom.
>
> EDGAR LEE MASTERS, *Anne Rutledge,* from *The Spoon River Anthology.*[1]

The following paragraph defines *feature article* by contrasting it to the related news story, and using a concrete example to clarify the difference. (This passage shows, incidentally, that even definition need not be devoid of the writer's personality.)

FEATURE ARTICLE: A journalistic essay on some matter of timely interest. Distinct from a news "story" which chronicles an event of the day, the feature article is both more human in interest and somewhat less hurried in preparation. A news dispatch might, for instance, tell of an earthquake in Timbuktu. The enterprising newspaper will print the news details and then for several days fill many columns with feature articles on such subjects as *Life in Timbuktu* (illustrated with photographs—genuine or spurious); *Quaint Folklore of Timbuktu* (after some feature writer has perhaps found his way to the library); *Early Recollections of Timbuktu* by some octogenarian once a resident of the town, etc. These timely essays indirectly related to the day's news are feature articles, though, by extension, the term is also used to signify any human-interest story whether of timely moment or not.—THRALL AND HIBBARD, *A Handbook to Literature*

The following definition of *epic* illustrates partial analysis: it breaks a large subject into its two main divisions and cites examples in each division:

EPIC: A poem of dramatic character dealing by means of narration with the history, real or fictitious, of some notable action or series of actions

---

[1] The entire definition is from *The Reader's Encyclopedia,* by William Rose Benét. Copyright, 1948, Thomas Y. Crowell Company.

carried out under heroic or supernatural guidance. Epic poetry may be divided into two main classes: (*a*) the popular or national epic, including such works as the Greek *Iliad* and *Odyssey*, the *Sanscrit Mahabharata*, and the Teutonic *Nibelungenlied;* and (*b*) the literary or artificial epic, of which the *Aeneid*, Ariosto's *Orlando Furioso*, Tasso's *Jerusalem Delivered*, and Milton's *Paradise Lost* are examples.[2]

3. Analysis

Analysis, though related to definition, is not merely a method of definition. It is a major technique in informative writing, and requires separate discussion.

Analysis is a method of dividing a complex subject into its main parts, examining each of those parts, and showing their relationship to one another and to the whole. In a complete or formal analysis, used in scientific research, each of those parts is in turn divided, then each of the subdivisions is further divided, and so on down to the last possible unit. In nontechnical informative writing, partial or informal analysis is one of the two most important methods of making material clear; definition, with which it is often used, is the other. When a writer says near the beginning of his paper, "There are three main elements in the Philippine situation," or "Six different kinds of bird calls can be distinguished," or "The problem created by fraternities is fourfold," he is introducing an analysis of a subject too complex to be treated as a whole.

It may be useful to examine a few specific plans of analysis. The principle in each case is the same—breaking the whole into its parts —but the detailed pattern of analysis varies with the material.

The analysis of a mechanism (an electric razor, a gasoline engine, a carburetor, a kerosene stove, an electric door chime, etc.) usually falls into three large divisions: (1) the description of the whole mechanism; (2) the analysis of its main functional parts; (3) the operation of the mechanism. This is a typical outline:

ANALYSIS OF A MECHANISM

I. Description of the mechanism
    A. Definition
    B. Function
    C. Principle on which it works (gravity, friction, etc.)
    D. Main functional parts
II. Construction of the mechanism
    A. First main part
        1. Definition or description

---

[2] From *The Reader's Encyclopedia*, by William Rose Benét. Copyright, 1948, Thomas Y. Crowell Company.

2. Function
3. List of its subordinate parts (if the writer wants to carry the analysis further)
   B. Second main part ⎱
   C. Third main part ⎰ (developed like A)
   D., E., etc. (if there are more main parts)
III. Operation of the mechanism

The analysis of a process (changing a tire, playing badminton, baking sponge cake, cleaning upholstered furniture, setting up a darkroom, training a bird dog, laying asphalt tile, etc.) is likely to have four large divisions, because a process not only has main parts or steps, but also, nearly always, requires equipment or supplies. Unless the equipment is very simple, it is better described in a separate section of the paper than brought in suddenly when it is needed in the process.

ANALYSIS OF A PROCESS

I. Definition of the process
   A. Description of it as a whole
   B. Purpose (or value)
II. Requirements for carrying out the process
   A. Materials necessary
      1. Tools
      2. Other supplies
   B. Conditions necessary
III. Main steps in the process
   A. First main step
      1. Description
      2. Materials
   B. Second main step ⎱
   C. Third main step ⎰ (developed like A)
   D., E., etc. (if there are more steps)
IV. Results of the process

The analysis of an idea or of a problem cannot be cast into a standard form as can the analysis of a mechanism or a process, because the form will vary greatly with the material. For example, an analysis of the Schuman plan for the merging of Western European coal and steel production would involve an elaborate breakdown of the special problems of the six member nations, of the position of Great Britain, and of the economic and political aspects of the plan. An analysis of the idea of having college students grade or evaluate their teachers, on the other hand, would probably fall fairly simply into three divisions: (1) description of the proposed plan; (2) disadvantages or dangers; (3) advantages. In general, the analysis of an idea or a problem starts with a clear statement of the idea or problem, indicates the logical divisions into which it falls, discusses each division, and concludes with a summary of the material or a suggested solution for the problem. The following outline of a paper on the attitudes toward war reflected in a group of novels of World War I illustrates one type of analysis of an idea:

I. Introduction
  A. Statement of the topic idea: The novels of World War I reflect a common attitude toward war.
  B. Novels on which this study is based
II. Analysis of the novels
  A. Hemingway, *Farewell to Arms*
    1. Synopsis
    2. Attitudes toward war
  B. Hemingway, *The Sun also Rises*
    1. Synopsis
    2. Attitudes toward war
  C. Dos Passos, *Three Soldiers*
    1. Synopsis
    2. Attitudes toward war
  D. Remarque, *All Quiet on the Western Front*
    1. Synopsis
    2. Attitudes toward war
III. Summary and comparison of attitudes in the four novels.

4. Cause-and-Effect Arrangement

Cause-and-effect arrangement is the pattern of organization in which a writer discusses the causes of an event or situation, and then the effects—for example, the reasons (causes) for the failure of the League of Nations and the effects of that failure on international relations and world history. Many current articles, both popular and scholarly, are based on this plan of organization. A few recent examples are: the causes of the increased employment of women outside the home, and the effects of that employment; the causes of our position in Indo-China, and the effects of that position on our foreign policy and on world opinion; the causes of large college enrollments, and the present effects and probable future effects of the large number of college graduates. Within the cause-effect pattern, the writer often uses analysis; that is, he divides "cause" into three or four main causes, and "effect" into three or four main effects.

Sometimes a writer reverses the order, starting with the effects of a development or event, and then discussing its causes. This is particularly true when the effects (or possible effects) are dramatic, and when the writer wants to attract the interest of a large audience.

5. General-to-Particular or Particular-to-General Arrangement

General-to-particular arrangement means starting with a general, comprehensive statement, and then giving particular or specific facts and examples to support it. This method in the long informative article is analogous to the method of paragraph development which we have called *Particularization*—placing the topic sentence at the beginning and then supplying particular details to make it clear. Particular-to-general arrangement means starting with a series of facts and examples, and, on the basis of them, arriving at a conclusion.

To illustrate, let us suppose that you have, by means of interviews and questionnaires, made a study of the newspaper-reading habits of students in your college. Your returns show that 10 per cent of the students do not read a daily newspaper; 10 per cent read a paper thoroughly; 15 per cent scan the front page; 20 per cent read only the comics; 15 per cent read only the sports section; 15 per cent read only the comics and the sports section; 15 per cent read the front page, the comics, and the sports section. Given this data, you can organize an informative article in one of two ways. You can begin with a general statement like "Most of the students of X College do not read newspapers for the news," or "The Students of X College appear to be more interested in comics and sports than in current affairs"—and then proceed to give the evidence on which this initial statement is founded. This is general-to-particular arrangement. Or, you can present and analyze the evidence, and, on the basis of it, conclude with general statements about the newspaper-reading habits of students in your college. This is particular-to-general arrangement.

In writing which aims to give the reader the gist of the information as quickly and economically as possible, the general-to-particular organization is more common than the particular-to-general. News stories, summaries of news, and other reports usually state first (and frequently headline) a generalization, and supply particulars later in the story. Feature articles and informative essays, especially those which aim to persuade as well as to inform, are likely to start with particulars and lead the reader gradually to share the writer's conclusion. For example, in recent years many articles have been written about the conditions existing in hospitals for the insane. The straight news report starts with the investigator's conclusions: that the conditions are deplorable, that something must be done. The feature story, on the other hand, often starts with particular examples—the harmless inmate who has been confined in a strait jacket for five years, the ward with twice as many patients as beds, the cell in which four women have died of cold and starvation—and moves, from such particulars, to the conclusion that these conditions should and can be rectified. The examples are persuasive as well as informative in their effect.

A word of warning about generalizations is appropriate here. Any collection of data, however impressive it may appear, is unreliable if it represents only a segment, or an untypical sampling, of all the facts. The public-opinion polls, though often quite accurate in their sampling, demonstrated prior to the presidential election of 1948 the weakness of conclusions based on unrepresentative facts. A conclusion drawn from insufficient or questionable data is called, in logic, a "hasty generalization." We shall discuss hasty generalization more fully in connection with persuasive writing.

6. Contrast and Comparison

We have illustrated earlier the use of brief contrast and comparison to clarify material. Contrast, or comparison, or a combination of the two may also be the basic pattern on which a long article is organized. A writer may, for example, compare and contrast the earlier and later novels of Sinclair Lewis; or the novels of World War I and the novels of World War II; or the programs of the New Deal and the Fair Deal; or the military strength of two powers; or the political records of two candidates for office. If the subjects being compared are complex, they are broken by analysis into their main parts and compared part by part.

Analogy, the extended comparison in which something unfamiliar is compared to something familiar, is a useful device for clarification. The following analysis of a mechanism, written in very simple language for a general audience, clarifies by analogy the structure of the human heart:

To get an idea of what a heart does, imagine a four-room house, two downstairs, two upstairs. This house is the human heart. It is a duplex. This house is divided by a wall down the center, from roof to ground, making two separate, two-room apartments.

Out of the roof rise two broad chimneys, one on each side of the central dividing line. Each chimney serves only its own side of the duplex. Each one has no connection with the upper-floor room, but extends down to open, like a chute, into the ceiling of the lower room.

The chimneys are the two great arteries leading out of the heart. The one on the right goes to the lungs. The one on the left is the aorta, carrying blood to the rest of the body.

These two apartments with their two separated chimneys are the essentials of the human heart. The rooms all have names. The upper ones are auricles, left and right. The lower are ventricles, left and right.

This living house expands and contracts. Blue blood from the body's veins is piped into the upper right room. That room has a trap door in its floor—a valve which opens downward only. It lets the blue blood run down from the upper room to fill the ground-floor below.

While that filling job is happening on the right side of the duplex, red blood is doing the same thing on the upper left side. This red blood is piped in from the lungs, filling the upper left room and pouring through the trap door into the lower room.

When both lower rooms are filled, this duplex house contracts like an accordion. The contraction is stronger in the two lower rooms. They squeeze the blood up through the chimneys: the blue into the lungs, the red out to the body.

The machinery for this powerhouse is the heart muscle and four valves. The valves are the two trap doors between upper and lower rooms, and two more trap doors that open upward to let the blood flow through the two great arteries.

The powerhouse walls are the heart muscle with its inner and outer lining. The inner lining is called the *endocardium,* and this lining includes the four curious and foolproof valves, or trap doors. The heart muscle is called the *myocardium.* It is thicker around the lower left room, the pump to the aorta, than elsewhere. There it is about half an inch thick. The outer wall is a sack, completely enclosing the heart, and is called the *pericardium.*

If you recall these three names you will find one or another of them used by physicians as part of the names of a number of different types of heart disease.

The enlire living, duplex powerhouse is about the size of a large fist.[3]

We have omitted a diagram which accompanied the preceding analysis and which further clarified the structure of the heart. Diagrams, charts, maps, and graphs can be very useful in informative writing.

These six organizational patterns—chronological arrangement, definition, analysis, cause-and-effect, general-to-particular or particular-to-general, and contrast and comparison—are, as we have said, sometimes used singly, sometimes in combination. Having the patterns clearly in mind is helpful in reading as well as in writing informative prose, for an informative writer nearly always indicates in his opening paragraphs what his basic organization is going to be. If he says "We now have a new concept of democracy," the reader

[3] Quoted from *Know Your Heart,* by Howard Blakeslee, published by the Public Affairs Committee, Inc., New York City.

can expect extended definition of this new concept with, perhaps, some contrast to the old; if he says "Four problems confront the Security Council," the reader can expect a four-part analysis; if he says "The duck farmer's day begins at five o'clock," the reader can expect to be taken chronologically through the day. Being alert to such indications of pattern helps the reader to see the development as he goes along, and to emerge from his reading with an organized knowledge of the material.

In good informative writing the organization, in addition to being fundamentally clear and logical, must be pointed out so that the reader can follow it easily. Indicating at the beginning of the paper its pattern of organization is one way to aid the reader. Another is emphasizing the steps in the development or the relationship of points by means of expressions like *the third problem is, the next step is, in addition to this equipment the player needs, an hour later, in the second place, this instrument serves two purposes.*

The whole problem of making material clear involves one important question which we have not adequately considered: *Clear to whom?* This brings us, after a long excursion, to the third requirement of good informative writing: the writer must adjust his material and his style to the needs and interests of his audience.

C. Adjusting Material and Style to a Particular Audience

The passage analyzing the human heart, printed on page 208, was obviously written to explain the mechanism of the heart to an audience with no special knowledge of anatomy. A young doctor to whom we showed the passage read it and commented, "I guess it's all right, but I can't quite visualize the heart as a duplex." The device for simplification, very helpful to lay readers, was merely confusing to him with his first-hand and specialized knowledge. This same doctor gave us a paper which he had written on the brain operation called prefrontal lobotomy, and which we thought of including in this section of informative readings; we decided not to include it because the paper, though excellent for the audience at which it was aimed, was too technical for the average college freshman to understand. The writer, planning the presentation of his material, must first of all ask himself: How much do my readers know?

The answer to this question is not easy for the student writer, who often has the feeling of aiming at no audience at all. And yet he must make some assumptions about his readers before he can decide how to handle his material. He may (with the instructor's approval), state the kind of reader he would like to write for, and consistently aim his paper at that reader. The best general assumption to make, though, is that he is writing for an intelligent audience which does not have specialized knowledge in any field.[4] Particularly in analyzing processes and mechanisms, it is wise to assume that the intended readers must have any uncommon term and any step in the process clearly explained. There is a practical reason for this: much of the informative writing done by the college freshman is essentially training for later informative writing; at present he may necessarily write about simple subjects of which nearly every reader has some knowledge—how to drive a car, how to paddle a canoe, how an orange juicer operates; but the techniques of organizing this material and presenting it as if the reader knew nothing about it are the techniques he may sometime use in writing articles and reports and interoffice memos about more complex subjects which his readers will not already understand.

In addition to deciding how much his readers (or hypothetical readers) know, the informative writer needs to consider carefully his *attitude toward his subject:* Shall he let his feelings about the subject enter into his information? If so, how much? He needs to consider with equal care the *tone* of his writing. *Tone* may be defined as the attitude of the writer toward his audience and himself. It establishes the writer-reader relationship, which is an important, though often subtle, element in any communication. What kind of relationship does the writer want to establish with his readers: formal and impersonal? informal and personal? very informal, chatty and intimate?

Examples will clarify some of these differences in attitude and tone. The passage below is the article on *skunk* in *The Columbia Encyclopedia:*

skunk, carnivorous, nocturnal mammal of the weasel family. The common or striped skunk of the United States, Mexico, and Canada has thick black fur with two white stripes on the back. It is usually a little over 2 ft. long including the long, bushy tail. Because it destroys many insect pests it is protected in many states. Its ability to spray from the vents under the tail an oily liquid with an offensive, persistent odor protects it against most enemies. In the North the animals sleep through the winter. The small, slender spotted skunk (*Spilogale*) has several white stripes or lines of spots. It inhabits part of the SE and central United States, Mexico, and Central America. In the fur trade it is of less value than the striped skunk. The hognosed skunk (*Conepatus*) ranges from the SW United States through most of South America.[5]

---

[4] This question of the audience for student themes is discussed more fully in Chapter Ten.

[5] Reprinted from *The Columbia Encyclopedia*, Second Edition. Copyright 1950 by Columbia University Press.

The following passage (the first four paragraphs of an article called "Mephitis, the Skunk," which was originally published in *The American Mercury*) is another treatment of the same subject:

Cree Indians call him *Sikak;* mammalogists label him *Mephitis mephitis;* and his pelt, which this year is enjoying a great vogue among the ladies, is apt to be camouflaged beguilingly as *Alaska Sable* or *Black Marten.* Plainest and commonest name of all, certainly the most richly fraught with disparaging implication, is plain *skunk.*

Seldom, however, do we make any effort to know Mephitis better, or to understand him and his skunkly way of life. We are content to believe (as a writer uncharitably alleged three hundred years ago) that this glossy, plume-tailed cousin of the weasels is only an "evil-smelling child of the devil," and a rapacious poultry-thief. It is too bad that we subject little Sikak to such unrelenting ostracism, for we miss becoming acquainted with one of the most amiable of all our wood-folk.

It is usually late in April or in May that the baby skunk is ushered into life. He is one of a litter that may contain almost a dozen, and the place of his birth is most often a vault-chambered burrow in the frozen earth. This root-smelling underground cavity has been patiently lined with dry leaves and matted grasses against the chill of spring nights. The baby skunk's universe is a warm and pungent darkness, its silence broken only by tiny whimperings and the soft pad-pad of his mother's sharp-clawed paws as she goes and comes on periodic foragings for May-beetles and crickets.

It is necessary that the baby's life should be sequestered in this careful fashion, for newborn Mephitis is a helpless mite no larger than a meadow mouse. His little eyes, which will be black and bright as berries, are sealed tight shut as a kitten's. For two weeks and more he remains unseeing and defenseless. His father retires to a distant earth-tunnel of his own. It is the mother skunk who must lick and pat and smooth his soft new fur, must procure unaided a sufficiency of food to insure that she shall have an adequate milk supply for her prodigious brood.[6]

The expression of attitude toward the subject is very different in these two pieces. In the first, the attitude is impersonal; the author is merely reporting facts, both favorable (the skunk destroys insect pests) and unfavorable (the offensive, persistent odor of its spray); he is not concerned with arousing feeling about the animal. In the longer article, the author sets out, by means of two stylistic devices, to make his subject appealing and attractive: first, he humanizes the skunk by naming it and referring to it in the kind of terms usually associated with a human baby (*Mephitis, cousin, little Sikak, baby's life, new-born Mephitis*); second, he uses a number of other favorably charged locutions (*most amiable, helpless mite, little eyes, defense-*

---

[6] From *Down to Earth* by Alan Devoe. Copyright, 1940, by Alan Devoe. Reprinted by permission of Coward-McCann, Inc.

less, soft new fur). The writer is working hard, perhaps too hard, to personalize the skunk and so to make his writing interesting.

The writer-reader relationship is also different in the two selections. In the first it is impersonal; the writer keeps himself out of the communication. In the second it is personal; the biographer of Mephitis does not use "I" or address his readers directly as "you," but he identifies himself with his readers (*we are content, we miss*, etc.) even though he does not actually belong to the group which fails to understand skunks, and he writes conversationally (*it is too bad, all our wood-folk*). This personal writer-reader relationship is consistent, of course, with his personalizing of the skunk, and is another interest-arousing technique.

Many readers would say that the second passage, with its personal touch and human appeal, is more interesting than the first. Not everyone, however, would agree. It is certainly true that the passage uses devices for interest, as the encyclopedia article does not; but some readers might object that it is sentimental in its handling of the subject and that it labors the devices of *little Sikak, helpless mite, little eyes*, etc. until they are not really interesting. Readers sensitive to style might point out, also, a certain overelegance and straining for effect in the numerous adjective-noun and verb-adverb combinations, and in other heavy and wordy expressions: *camouflaged beguilingly, richly fraught, disparaging implication, rapacious poultry-thief, unrelenting ostracism, vault-chambered burrow, root-smelling underground cavity, ushered into life, it is necessary that the baby's life be sequestered in this careful fashion, procure unaided a sufficiency of food to insure that she shall have an adequate milk supply for her prodigious brood.* Furthermore, a reader who wanted to learn quickly the main facts about skunks would prefer the brief factual account. Informative writing, like other writing, should be interesting; but *Interesting to whom?* is a question as difficult as *Clear to whom?*

The professional writer can, by studying the publication at which he is aiming, estimate reasonably well both the amount of information his readers have and the kind of style and tone they are likely to expect. The student writer, lacking this advantage, can only consider thoughtfully three things—his assignment, his material, his hypothetical audience—and exercise his best judgment about the most appropriate style, approach to the material, and attitude toward the reader.

One of the first steps in this exercise of judgment is deciding exactly what his general intention is: whether it is simply to inform, or whether it is to inform and also to persuade or entertain. Some-

times the instructor has made the decision; the student has been told
to write a strictly informative paper. Sometimes the material itself—
the analysis of a mechanism, for example—demands or strongly suggests purely informative treatment. If the paper is to be strictly informative, the writer is usually not concerned with establishing a
personal relationship with his reader, and he usually avoids expressions of attitude and obvious interest-arousing devices. He assumes
that anyone who reads his article will be interested in straight information, not in being diverted or cajoled. The following introduction to a formal analysis of a vacuum cleaner is inappropriate:

> Few objects are so fascinating as the vacuum cleaner! What would the
> modern housewife do without it? Let us look more closely at this indis-
> pensable little household-helper.

It must be admitted, however, that such obvious devices for getting
attention are used in writing for a popular audience. This fact makes
sound generalization about them difficult, as does the fact that any
reader is happy to be interested while he is being informed. Probably the best practical procedure for the writer is to ask himself these
questions about any device for interesting the reader: Is it consistent
with the rest of my paper? Is it insultingly simple to an intelligent
reader? Does it clutter or obscure rather than clarify my information? If the answer to any of these questions is "Yes," or even "Perhaps," the device is better abandoned in favor of plain-sense communication.[7]

If, on the other hand, some persuasion or entertainment is appropriate to the material and is a secondary part of the informative
writer's intention, a personal, informal writer-reader relationship is
often (though not always) desirable. A paper which is partly persuasive may well begin not with a statement of principle or fact, but
with an example, a series of examples, an anecdote, or a personal
experience which will have persuasive as well as informative value.

Whether or not to use the first person ("I" or "we") in informative
writing, and whether or not to use direct address to the reader ("You
should first understand the principle") are questions related both

---

[7] In offering this criticism of obvious and inappropriate devices for interest, we
are by no means recommending that writing be dull. Most types of writing must
be interesting if they are to be read. It is true that teachers of composition develop
a remarkable power to struggle through dull, lifeless, mechanical writing; but they
are abnormal readers. Most students do not give enough thought to their practical
and humane obligation to make their papers interesting and readable. Interest,
though, should come from concrete detail and from lively or skillful expression
which is appropriate to the material and to the writer's personality; it should not
be a lace collar pinned on a tailored suit.

to the material and to the writer-reader relationship. These matters of mechanics produce a surprising number of problems; anyone who has struggled with the problems in his own writing is both amused and sympathetic when, in his reading, he finds evidences of the similar struggles of other writers. "I" is often too personal in semi-formal or formal writing; also it may focus attention on the writer rather than on the information. The editorial "we" is less personal, but it may create confusion because "we" may at one point in the writing mean the author or authors and, at another point, mean all-of-us—author and audience. Writers sometimes resort to "the writer of this article has found it advisable" as a desperate way out of the difficulty. Direct address to the reader is the clearest form for directions or advice which the reader is expected to follow: "you will need" is simpler and better than "the amateur carpenter needs," or "the would-be fisherman needs." But "you" can cause trouble too. Writers of English texts, for example, sometimes involve themselves in sentences like "It is imperative that the college student learn to punctuate correctly," because the simple "You must learn to punctuate correctly" would be poor in tone for a reader who felt that he had already learned to punctuate correctly. The indefinite "you," unless it is used with discretion, can also produce such startling statements as "You should be buried in an oak coffin," or "The fact that you are an illegitimate child need not wreck your life."

In view of these hazards, it is generally best to avoid direct address except in one of two situations. The first is in giving advice or directions to an audience expected to profit personally from such instructions; here, as we have said, the "you" technique works simply and well. The second situation occurs when the writer, giving information about something remote from the reader's knowledge, feels that he can make his information more vivid and meaningful if he carries the reader directly into an experience. For example, an article about life in London in the eighteenth century might begin, "If you had lived in London in 1750, you would have seen . . ."; or an article on deep-sea diving might begin, "When you, wearing your two-hundred-pound diving dress, are standing on the bottom of the ocean . . ." The reader has certainly not lived in 1750, and he may think it just as unlikely that he will ever be standing on the bottom of the ocean. These articles, in other words, are not directive; but association with the experience sometimes makes information more immediate and real to the reader.

When the informative writer has thought through the complex relationships of his material, his general intention, his attitude toward the reader, and his style, he should formulate a concise statement of his whole purpose in the paper he is going to write. Such a statement will crystallize his thinking, and will give focus and consistency to the paper. These are examples of clear and useful statements of purpose:

My purpose is to present an impersonal analysis of the style of Ernest Hemingway's short stories to a reader who does not know Hemingway's work.

My purpose is to give information about the origin of bebop to a reader with only an average knowledge of music, and to interest him in this type of music.

My purpose is to give directions which will enable the reader with little knowledge of gardening to have a successful rose garden.

My purpose is to present the facts about the political situation in South Korea at the beginning of the Korean war; this paper is written for a reader who knows something about Korea from newspaper accounts, but who has made no special study of the situation.

My purpose is to give an informal and (I hope) entertaining report on baby sitting to a reader inexperienced in this work.

My purpose is to give the beginning fisherman information about trout fishing, and, by using some of my personal experience, to persuade him to try this exciting sport.

Such a statement of purpose, somewhat modified, may be used at the beginning of the paper itself, particularly if the paper is long enough to require an introductory section or a preface. Whether or not it is used in the final paper, the clearly formulated statement of purpose supplies the writer with a yardstick. He may not be able to judge the total merit of his work, but he can at least measure it by what he intended to do for the reader he had in mind.

The following summary statements will provide a partial review of this introduction to informative writing:

1. Informative writing presents, explains, and interprets facts.

2. The informative writer must have an *organized* knowledge of his subject.

3. In presenting his material for a reader less informed than he, the writer should remember to define terms, to give necessary warnings, and to include and explain every step in a process.

4. The major problem in clear presentation is organization. The six organizational patterns most commonly used in informative writing are: chronological arrangement, definition, analysis, cause-and-effect arrangement, general-to-particular or particular-to-general arrangement, and contrast and comparison.

5. In adjusting material and style to a particular audience, the writer needs to consider (*a*) how much his readers know, (*b*) what attitude toward his subject is appropriate for his communication, and (*c*) what tone (writer-reader relationship) is appropriate and desirable.

6. If the writer's intention is purely to inform, he usually presents his material impersonally. If his intention is to persuade or entertain as well as to inform, he often establishes a personal, informal writer-reader relationship.

7. It is generally advisable to avoid direct address to the reader except in giving directions and advice which he is expected to follow.

8. A concise statement of purpose, formulated before an informative paper is written, will produce focus and consistency in the paper.

The readings in the following pages illustrate different styles and writer-reader relationships, and many of the techniques and organizational patterns of informative prose.

FLYING SAUCERS—THE REAL STORY *
U. S. News & World Report

The following article is an example of the informative report. Printed April 7, 1950, in the weekly news magazine *U. S. News and World Report*, it is an effort to assemble and interpret information about the flying saucers which had been a subject of rumor and conjecture for several years. Whether or not this is "the real story" of the saucers, time will tell. The article is, at any rate, a competent piece of informative writing. Like many reports, it has a general-to-particular organization: the conclusions are stated first; the supporting and clarifying details follow. Also like most well-written reports, the article uses unmistakably clear transitions and summary statements to aid the reader.

FLYING SAUCERS—THE REAL STORY:
U.S. BUILT FIRST ONE IN 1942
Jet-Propelled Disks Can Outfly Other Planes

Observers of "flying saucers" aren't just seeing things. They're real—aircraft that conform to accepted laws.

* Reprinted from *U. S. News & World Report*, "an independent weekly magazine on national and international affairs." Copyright 1950.

Sky disks, manned by regular pilots, can hover aloft, spurt ahead at tremendous speed, outmaneuver conventional craft.

No official announcements are being made yet. But about the only big secret left is who makes them. Evidence points to Navy experiments.

[1] The real story on "flying saucers" is finally coming to light. What the saucers are, how they operate, and how they have been tested in U.S., all can be told in detail at this time.

[2] That story, without violating present security regulations, points to these basic conclusions by engineers competent to appraise reports of reliable observers:

[3] Flying saucers, seen by hundreds of competent observers over most parts of U.S., are accepted as real. Evidence is that they are aircraft of a revolutionary type, a combination of helicopter and fast jet plane. They conform to well-known principles of aerodynamics. An early model of these saucers was built by U. S. engineers in 1942, achieved more than 100 successful test flights. That project was taken over by the Navy in wartime. Much more advanced models now are being built. Just where present saucers are being built also is indicated by evidence now available.

[4] In more detail, the story pieced together from nonsecret testimony of responsible U. S. scientists, private observers and military officials, is this:

[5] **Early models** of the flying saucer . . . were built by U. S. Government engineers of the National Advisory Committee for Aeronautics. Similar flying-saucer projects were begun in Germany and Italy at the same time, in 1942.

[6] The first U. S. model, designed by Charles H. Zimmerman, of NACA, was elliptical in shape, powered by two piston engines and driven by twin propellers. It had a maximum speed between 400 and 500 miles an hour. More important, it could rise almost vertically and its minimum speed for landing was only about 35 miles an hour, a great advantage in military and naval aircraft. And it was far more maneuverable than conventional military planes.

[7] Idea behind those original flying-saucer projects, both in U.S. and abroad in Germany and Italy, was to overcome basic drawbacks of conventional aircraft by new techniques. A plane that could rise almost straight would not need long airfields, could be used from any cleared area just behind front-line troops or from the deck of any Navy combat ship. If that plane, in addition, had great speed and more maneuverability, it could probably outfly any conventional aircraft. In the United States, the first model seemed to fulfill these

requirements, but the lessened stability of the wingless craft required more research.

[8] **Present flying saucers** apparently have overcome this problem of stability by use of very advanced design. An analysis of reports submitted by competent observers shows this:

[9] *What they look like,* first, is described in well-documented accounts. Those accounts show saucers to be exactly 105 feet in diameter, circular in shape. They have what appear to be jet nozzles arranged all around the outer rim, just below the center of gravity. They are made of a metal alloy, with a dull whitish color. There are no rudders, ailerons, or other protruding surfaces. From the side the saucers appear about 10 feet thick—there are no exact measurements from this angle in publicly available accounts. They are built in three layers, with the center layer slightly larger in diameter than the other two.

[10] That is the picture agreed on by qualified observers of saucers in flight—commercial aircraft pilots, fighter pilots who have chased these aircraft, trained airplane spotters, high-ranking Army and Air Force officers. It is backed by exact measurement made by a group of scientists last April near White Sands Proving Ground base, with instruments set up to observe high-altitude balloons, who suddenly observed a saucer and tracked it for several minutes, thereby getting reliable data on its size, speed, altitude and maneuverability.

[11] *How they operate* now can be told in some detail, too. Based on this description, the probable technique used by current saucers is explained by a top-level Government aeronautical engineer in this manner:

[12] Power for these aircraft, at their present stage of development, obviously is supplied by jet engines. Each saucer appears to have a series of variable-direction jet nozzles around its rim, with a complicated central control system. Fuel used is unknown—the exhaust flame has been observed to be red-orange in some cases, blue in others, missing in still others. The saucers appear to have the power to "coast" long distances, thus saving on fuel consumption.

[13] Direction of the aircraft and its velocity, in turn, evidently are controlled by the angle at which the jet nozzles are tilted, the numbering operating, the power applied. By choosing which nozzles to turn on or off and the angle of tilt, the pilot could make the saucer rise or descend vertically, hover, fly straight ahead, or make sharp turns. A right-angle turn, for example, could be made by turning off the rear jets, turning on the side and front nozzles. Great speed can be obtained by focusing to the rear all nozzles in the after half of the aircraft. With all nozzles pointed downward, the saucer

could rise straight off the ground, and, with less power, could descend the same way.

[14]   That is the explanation, based on accepted principles of aerodynamics, given by an authoritative engineer as the likely answer to how these saucer aircraft operate. As evidence that this explanation is correct, there are these actual cases of publicly observed saucer behavior:

[15]   Rows of window-like openings around the rims of saucers traveling at more than 500 miles an hour are mentioned in several documented reports. In all cases, these "windows" glowed as if they were jet-nozzle openings. The most recent of these reports was made last month by two experienced pilots of the Chicago and Southern Air Lines, who passed within 1,000 feet of a saucer traveling over Arkansas. Another similar report was made by two Eastern Air Lines pilots who narrowly missed colliding with a saucer in July, 1948, while flying a DC-3 over Georgia.

[16]   Saucers' ability to hover in mid-air, accelerate at tremendous speed, and then rise almost vertically is described in several reports, one documented by Air Force officers at Fort Knox, Ky. That saucer, seen by dozens of officers at the post, was chased by three military pilots flying fast F-51s. The saucer quickly outmaneuvered the planes.

[17]   Speed of one saucer was measured by ground instruments in the White Sands case as well over the speed of sound, indicating the use of a number of jet engines. Cruising speed has been estimated in other cases at 200 to 600 miles an hour.

[18]   What it all adds up to is this: Flying saucers being observed in many parts of the U.S. are not mysterious visitors from Mars. They are actual planes, soundly engineered on principles developed by U.S. in wartime. By using this new design, they can do things that no conventional aircraft can be expected to approach.

[19]   **Who's building the saucers** now being observed in test flights over U.S. is not yet publicly disclosed. It cannot be proved until a public announcement is made or until a saucer crashes away from its home base—which is highly unlikely because of its jet helicopter action that makes take-offs and landings almost completely safe. But there are these factors that point to an answer:

[20]   Official inquiry by the Air Force, in the face of overwhelming evidence that the saucers were real, was called off last December. This indicates clearly that top Air Force officials know where the saucers originate and are not concerned about them, as they would be if these aircraft were from Russia or Mars. These officials, at the same time, denied emphatically that a secret Air Force project is responsible.

[21] Best use of fully developed saucer aircraft, however, could be made in wartime not by the Air Force, but by the Navy. All fleet operations now require an air cover, even in antisubmarine warfare, and a plane that can rise like a helicopter could be used from any Navy combat ship, not only from big, expensive aircraft carriers. It was for that reason that the first U. S. flying saucer was purchased by the Navy after the original model was tested in 1942. The first full-size aircraft, built by Chance-Vought, was thoroughly tested by Navy engineers. Then a statement was released that this project had been dropped. Early experimenting with saucers, thus, centered in the Navy.

[22] Big spending on missile aircraft centers in the Navy now, too. More than twice as many dollars were spent by the Navy last year as by the Air Force on secret guided-missile research. There is no public accounting for these millions, the only Government funds aside from atomic-energy dollars that still are being spent with great secrecy.

[23] Surface indications, then, point to research centers of the U. S. Navy's vast guided-missile project as the scene of present flying-saucer development. That project has the scientists, the engineers, the dollars, the motive, and the background of early Navy development of saucer-type aircraft. This likelihood will remain, despite any future denials by the Navy front office, until secrecy is lifted on the big missile program.

[24] But, regardless of just where these saucers are being built now, the evidence points to a U. S. development that will mean a radical change in aircraft design in coming decades. In war, this combination of helicopter and fast jet plane will easily outfly any present types of military aircraft. In peacetime, the safety of a nearly crash-proof aircraft may be expected to revolutionize civil air transport. It all points to a big advance in the science of flying.

COMMENT AND QUESTIONS

"Flying Saucers—The Real Story" gives the reader all possible assistance in grasping the information and following the organization. The introductory material in boldface states the three main points of the article: (1) the reality of the saucers, (2) their general characteristics, (3) the likelihood that the Navy is making them; paragraph 3 repeats and expands the initial summary; the rest of the article supplies details, and the development is kept clear by the phrases in boldface which serve as an outline.

I. The following questions will check the efficiency of your reading. A good reader will not find it necessary to refer to the article.

1. In what particular ways, according to the article, were flying saucers designed to be superior to conventional aircraft?

2. What weakness did the first model have?

3. What, according to reports, do current saucers look like?

4. How is their power supplied?

5. How are they directed?

6. What specific evidence supports the probability that saucers are being developed by the Navy?

II. Within the large general-to-particular organization, smaller general-to-particular patterns are also used. Paragraphs 12 and 13, for example, explain the probable technique of the saucers; subsequent paragraphs describe particular observations which support the explanation. What other examples can you find of subordinate general-to-particular patterns?

III. The handling of transitions in the article is worth noting. Paragraph 2 is a transitional sentence which links paragraphs 1 and 3: "That story [a reference to paragraph 1] . . . points to these basic conclusions" [a lead into paragraph 3]. Point out other transitional paragraphs, and other methods of transition used in the article.

IV. Brief summary of one block of the material before another block is introduced also keeps the organization clear. Point out examples of this use of summary.

V. The writing in the article is very competent. A great deal of material is packed into a small space. As a result, however, grammatical precision and nicety of expression are occasionally sacrificed to brevity. What sentences can you find in which the expression suffers from the condensation of the material?

SLOW MOTION
Editors of the Boston *Globe*

The following editorial from the Boston *Globe* of June 19, 1950, illustrates definition and analysis of a problem.

[1] The United Nations convention outlawing genocide is hung up in a Senate committee and prospects of its ratification before Congress goes home are, according to those who know, rather doubtful.

This is an amazing situation, for nobody in America—in the Senate or out of it—condones the procedures which the convention would outlaw and punish—the gas-chamber executions of minority peoples, for example, or the kidnaping of thousands of children, as happened in Greece.

[2]   All the trouble is caused by certain technical questions of law, some of a specific nature and some general. Critics of the convention have discovered three phrases of its text to which they object. One they believe to be dangerous is that which says, "Genocide means any of the following acts, committed with intent to destroy in whole, or in part, a national, ethnical, racial or religious group, as such . . ."; they fear that the words "or in part" might imply that the killing of one or several persons would be considered genocide, bringing such crimes as murder and lynching under the convention.

[3]   Again they object to the words "mental harm" in the article of the convention which lists as a genocidal act "causing serious bodily or mental harm to members of the group"; they believe this might include emotional disturbances of members of any minority. And again, they dislike the word "complicity" in the inclusion among punishable acts that of "complicity in genocide." The word "complicity," they point out, is not used in American criminal law and has no exact meaning to Americans.

[4]   Their general objection is to the possibility that, by ratifying the convention, the Senate would be transferring to Federal jurisdiction an area of criminal jurisprudence belonging to the states, and would even be superseding state laws.

[5]   Experts have voiced opinions that all these fears are groundless. "In whole or in part," in the first case, "means substantially all the members of the group," according to an American Bar Association authority on international law; he is backed up by the State Department's legal adviser. "Mental harm," says ex-Secretary of War Robert P. Patterson, is used here to mean serious mental harm to a group; the U. N. committee which drafted the document had in mind the breaking down of a population with torture or drugs, an experiment the Japanese tried in China during the war. As for "complicity," this is the equivalent of "aiding and abetting," a term no American lawyer has to look up.

[6]   The general objection, the experts contend, is wholly invalid. Congress has the power under the Constitution to deal with offenses under the law of nations; the states have no statutes against genocide. In fact, as Senator McMahon has noted, "We have never had an act of genocide in the United States, and as far as I can see, we will never have one."

[7]   Meanwhile, to satisfy some of the criticisms, a subcommittee of the Foreign Relations Committee has attached three "understandings" to the document. An "understanding" is a diplomatic device for stating exactly what a signatory power understands a treaty to mean; the Senate has the right, under its ratifying power, to use it if it wishes. The three understandings declare the meaning of "in part" to be "a substantial portion of the group concerned"; the meaning of "mental harm" to be "permanent physical injury to mental faculties," and the meaning of "complicity" to be "aiding and abetting in the commission of the crime."

[8]   These understandings, if hair-splitting were felt to be necessary, would seem to have been sufficient to clear the deck for action in the whole Senate committee. But none has been taken and the slow process of getting the convention to the Senate floor for debate and a vote has not been begun.

[9]   Other nations must view this delay with astonishment. The draft of this new international law was one of the few measures that the General Assembly of the U.N. adopted without a dissenting vote. The whole world, or all of it that is truly civilized, abhors the crimes that it would stamp out. The United States should be leading the procession of ratifiers, not lagging behind.

COMMENT AND QUESTIONS

The first paragraph of this editorial supplies an example of polite definition. Not wishing to insult, by obvious defining, the newspaper readers who already understand *genocide,* but assuming that some readers will not know the meaning of the word, the writer defines it indirectly by giving two examples. The whole editorial, of course, attempts to clarify the meaning of the term as it is used in the convention outlawing genocide. Polite or indirect definition is a useful technique for the writer addressing a general audience.

I. Paragraph 2 of the editorial introduces the pattern of analysis: sentence 1 states that there are some specific and some general objections to the convention; sentence 2 divides the specific objections into criticisms of three phrases in the text. Trace the pattern of analysis, step by step, through the editorial.

II. This article, like most editorials, is persuasive as well as informative. At what point in the editorial does the persuasion begin?

III. How would you describe the tone of the writing?

BE YOUR OWN WEATHERMAN

CARL WARDEN

In the following selection, definition, analysis, and cause-and-effect arrangement are used in combination to explain a complex process—learning to forecast the weather. As its title suggests, the article also illustrates a personal, informal writer-reader relationship. "Be Your Own Weatherman" was published in *Popular Science Monthly* in March, 1940.

[1] Rainbow at night is the shepherd's delight. . . . Red sky at morning is a sailor's sure warning. . . . The higher the clouds, the finer the weather. . . .

[2] For centuries, sayings such as these have been part of the folklore of the sky. Modern science has proved the truth of many of these beliefs concerning clouds and winds as weather prophets. By understanding a few simple facts about the whys and wherefores of changes that take place over your head, you can foresee, with reasonable accuracy, the coming of storms and rapid shifts in temperature. You don't have to know anything about aneroid barometers or wind gauges. It doesn't make any difference if you can't tell an isobar from an iceberg. With two eyes as your only equipment, you can read the weather from the sky.

[3] Take the clouds, for instance. Divided into four general types—nimbus, cirrus, stratus, and cumulus—they form one of the most important sources of clews to weather. Nimbus clouds are the thick banks, sometimes with ragged edges, from which rain or snow is falling. Cirrus clouds, consisting of ice crystals, are the thin, feathery wisps that glide across the sky at high altitudes. Stratus clouds, as the name implies, collect in layers and often thicken into an unbroken, leaden mass without form or structure, while the fluffy, cottonlike billows that appear during clear weather are the familiar cumulus variety.

[4] Other important clouds are either variations or combinations of these four basic types. Cirro-cumulus, for example, the sailor's "mackerel sky," a good-weather cloud, is a combination of cirrus and cumulus. Cumulo-nimbus, combining cumulus and nimbus, is the awesome "thunderhead" that occurs in spring and summer. Rising like huge mounds of white smoke from the dark base of a gigantic fire, they tower up to tremendous heights and often hold millions of

gallons of rain. When the prefix "alto" or "fracto" is included in the name of a cloud, remember that the former merely means high, and the latter broken. Alto-stratus clouds are, therefore, high stratus, and fracto-cumulus are wind-broken cumulus.

[5]   In general, the cumulus and cirrus clouds are classified as fair-weather types, while the stratus and nimbus are associated with rain or snow. Rain generally falls from the gray nimbus clouds, but it may also occur with cumulo-nimbus and sometimes with strato-cumulus. In winter, alto-stratus clouds may produce snow, but only on rare occasions will rain fall from them.

[6]   However, a better guide to weather changes is found in the sequence of the clouds—since, as bad weather approaches your locality, the clouds normally form in a definite order. First to appear after a period of good weather are the cirrus clouds. Blown along at speeds that sometimes exceed 200 miles an hour, and at heights as great as 50,000 feet, they often precede the center of an approaching storm by several days. If the wind is blowing thin cirrus wisps from the northwest or the west and the sky is a bright blue, look for fair weather to continue for twenty-four hours or more; but if the cirrus clouds are developing into a translucent blanket, rain or snow generally follows.

[7]   Trailing cirrus in this parade of the clouds is the stratus variety, the commonest of all. When these clouds form their gray cover over the sky, it is usually a sure indication that a storm is on its way toward you. Eventually, unless the wind shifts into the west, they normally thicken to form nimbus or rain clouds.

[8]   As the storm center progresses and passes over you, the nimbus formation will break up and the skies will clear. The next morning will be cloudless. Soon, however, the fourth basic type, cumulus clouds, will begin to form against the bright blue sky to complete one cycle of the clouds from fair weather through rain or snow and back to fair weather again.

[9]   Cirrus, stratus, nimbus, cumulus—knowing this normal sequence of the clouds gives you a good start in learning to predict the weather. For if you see stratus clouds forming, you know that nimbus or rain clouds are generally next in line. And when nimbus clouds begin to break up, and you sight cumulus puffs through the holes the wind has torn, it's a good bet that clear weather is on the way. However, there are exceptions to every rule, and if you see huge mounds of cumulus clouds lying close to the horizon in the direction from which the wind is blowing, expect a storm within a comparatively short time.

[10]   But clouds can serve the amateur weather forecaster in other

ways. They may give you tips about what the temperature will be. For example, if clouds disappear from the sky at nightfall, the temperature probably will drop during the night. And if thin cirrus clouds, nicknamed "mare's-tails," are blowing across the sky from the north, fair and warmer weather is on the way.

[11] The clouds can also serve as a weather vane to tell you the direction of the winds, which form another important factor in weather prediction. To use them for this purpose, always look at them in relation to some object on the ground—a church steeple, a tall tree, or the corner of a building. Observe those flying directly overhead, for perspective may fool you if you concentrate on the clouds near the horizon. And if cloud movements are very slow, support your head firmly against a solid object to make sure that it is the *clouds* that are moving in a certain direction, and not your own eyes.

[12] In general, north and west winds are associated with fair weather, and south and east winds with rain and squalls. An enduring southeast wind, particularly on the east coast, is a sure sign of rain. But the shifting of the wind from one direction to another is the important point for a weather forecaster. For when gentle westerly winds begin to swing around into the south and east, it is a fairly reliable indication that a storm center is on the way. Conversely, a shift in the opposite direction is a good sign, for if the wind is blowing from almost any direction and then shifts into the west, the approach of a period of good weather is practically an assured fact.

[13] But why does the shifting of the wind have a bearing on weather changes? To understand that, first glance at the weather map . . . issued daily by the U. S. Weather Bureau and . . . mailed to anyone for a nominal sum. You will notice certain areas marked "high" and others marked "low." As the Bureau points out in its weather-map explanation pamphlet, "lows" indicate areas where the atmospheric pressure, or weight of the air, is low because of warm, rising currents of air. These "lows" mark the centers of general storms, which may cover an area as wide as 1,000 miles. "Highs," on the other hand, indicate areas of high atmospheric pressure and are generally the centers of fair weather. The arrows on the map, which fly *with* the wind—not into it—and show its direction at various observation stations, demonstrate the shifting of the wind.

[14] In the northern hemisphere, winds blow in a general counterclockwise direction toward and around the center of a "low," and clockwise around a "high." Moreover, these pressure centers move across the United States roughly from west to east, traveling at an average rate of about 500 miles a day in summer and over 700 miles

a day in winter, the "lows" normally preceded by warmer temperatures and the "highs" by colder, though not invariably.

[15] Therefore, the wind in your locality is likely to shift into the
south or east as a "low," or storm center, approaches you from the
west. And when the storm has passed, and a period of good weather
is on its way, the wind will tend to shift into the west or northwest.

[16] Generally, rain is most prevalent in the southeast section of
these circular storm centers. A daily weather map will tell you pretty
accurately whether your locality lies in this southeast sector, but you
can establish the fact roughly without this printed aid by applying
a law worked out by Buys Ballot, a famous Dutch meteorologist:
When you stand with your back to the prevailing wind, atmospheric
pressure will generally be lower toward your left and higher toward
your right. That means that if a "low" is approaching and you are
standing with your back to a southwest wind, the center of the "low,"
or storm area, will be toward your left, and you will therefore be
in the "low's" southeast sector where rain is more prevalent.

[17] Numberless variations on this sequence of clouds, winds, and
temperatures are possible, of course, but figuring them out forms
part of the duties of the professional and much of the fun of the
amateur weather forecaster. The official weather experts have the
advantage of long years of scientific training, plus a host of valuable
meteorological instruments, such as barometers, wet- and dry-bulb
thermometers, automatic weather balloons, and theodolites. But
from accurate observations of the clouds, in addition to wind directions and temperature changes, you can sometimes make a better
prediction for your immediate locality than the U. S. Weather Bureau, although their batting average over a long period and over
wider areas is bound to be better.

[18] As you become more and more proficient in your forecasting,
buy a small pocket notebook and keep an accurate day-to-day log of
your observations. Make notes on the cloud formations, the temperature, the direction of the wind, and the amount of rain, snow, and
hail. After a period of a year or so, your log will provide you with
a complete history of the weather in your locality and, by allowing
you to compare present conditions with past performances, will help
you to read weather clews more accurately.

[19] Don't expect to gain fame as a weather prophet the first week
you make predictions. For, in addition to good working knowledge
of the whys and wherefores of weather, you must learn to make
accurate observations and then draw the correct conclusions from
this evidence you find in the sky. That takes practice—but so does
everything else. Good luck to you as a weather forecaster!

COMMENT AND QUESTIONS

The title "Be Your Own Weatherman," the first paragraph of familiar sayings about weather, and the second paragraph of informal direct address to the reader ("You don't have to know anything . . .") set the tone of a popular, informal article on a subject which could be given more formal or even technical treatment.

I. Does the tone, including the direct address to the reader, contribute to or detract from the effectiveness of the article?

II. Besides direct address, what techniques does the writer use to appeal to the interests and experience of the reader?

III. If you have absorbed the writer's information, you will be able to answer the following questions:

1. What are the four types of clouds? What are the characteristics of each?

2. Which two are fair-weather clouds? Which two are associated with rain or snow?

3. What is the normal sequence of clouds, and how does knowing the sequence help in predicting weather?

4. What is the relationship of shifting winds to the weather?

IV. The transitions in this article between paragraphs and between the larger divisions of the material are worth studying. Note especially the transitional statements at the beginning of paragraphs 3, 6, 10, 11, and 13.

V. What are the main parts or divisions of the article? Why do they appear in their present order?

VI. What is the function of paragraph 11 in the whole organization?

THE LIFE AND DEATH OF A WORM *

ALAN DEVOE

Chronological arrangement and analysis of a mechanism are used together in the following selection to give information about a life process. Particularly worth noting as you read the essay are the techniques used to interest the reader in what could well be a dull subject—a worm. Alan Devoe is an American author, editor, and naturalist who has contributed essays and nature studies to many magazines. "The Life and Death of a Worm" is taken from *Down to Earth*, published in 1940.

[1]   In a damp earth tunnel under the subsoil a minute cocoon stirs gently with emergent life. Out of it, presently, there issues a tiny ribbon of pink crawling flesh. An earthworm, commonest of all the annelids, has been born.

[2]   The human infant, emerging out of foetal unawareness, comes into a world bright with colors and clamorous with sound. So does a guinea-pig baby or a new-hatched loon. The earthworm's birth is no such transition. Out of the darkness of the egg, this wriggling fragment of flesh and muscle emerges into a world that is hardly more fraught with awareness, hardly more informed by mind, than was the egg mass from which it came. The earthworm is unseeing, for it has no eyes. It is unhearing for it has no ears. The world into which it has been born is only a darkness and a silence.

[3]   But this eyeless and earless morsel of blood and skin is sensible of inner urgings, responsive from the moment of its birth to dim behests. It is stirred by vague restlessness, such as never infected a mushroom or a sumac root, and which is token of its membership in animal creation. It is blood brother, this blind, unhearing worm, to the high hawk and the running deer, and it is equipped with compulsions even as these are. It is not exempted from the twin necessities which are visited upon every creature of earth: the necessity to eat and the necessity to beget. These things being so, the earthworm stirs and wriggles in its dark earth-chamber, and sets forth presently on the great adventure of existence.

[4]   In obedience to an inner bidding it directs its body upward, toward the topsoil and the outer air. The way of its going is very slow, and it is this: just under the body skin runs a layer of circular muscles, and just under these a layer of muscles that lie longitudinally; alternately the earthworm contracts the circular muscles at its anterior end, rendering the body extended and thin, and contracts the longitudinal muscles, rendering the body short again. It is a slow, laborious way of locomotion, and effects a movement at all only because of a curious device. On each segment of the earthworm's body are arranged four pairs of tiny, spiny hairs, called setae, under the direct control of muscles. They extend obliquely backward from the sides and underparts of the earthworm's body, and the earthworm moves them as though they were little legs. As the worm thrusts upward now, boring blindly toward the outer otherworld which it cannot know exists, the setae press and grip the burrow wall and translate the worm's muscular churnings into a slow but steady movement.

[5]   Unhaltingly the earthworm struggles upward through the soil. Its infinitesimal brain, in an anterior segment above the pharynx, is incapable of harboring the thing that men call mind; a subtler

and stranger species of impulsion informs the nerve cords and directs the muscles in their work. Mindless, the earthworm is yet gifted with perceptions and recognitions. The pressures and stresses of the soil against its flesh are intelligible to it; the sensations of dryness or of moisture are somehow meaningful. When now, on its upward voyage, the earthworm reaches a stratum of hard dry soil through which it cannot penetrate by muscular effort alone, there comes to it—perhaps out of the misty realm called instinct, perhaps out of an otherwhere never to be plumbed—the knowledge of what must be done. The earthworm begins to eat.

[6]   Grain by grain it sucks the hard-packed soil into its muscular pharynx, grain by grain it reduces the barrier impeding its progress. Millimeter by millimeter, as the obstructing earth is nibbled away, the worm ascends toward outer air. It reaches the surface at last, thrusting its wriggling way through grass roots and the final crust, and when ultimately its tunneling is completed it deposits on the surface, in the form of castings, the swallowed earth which has passed through its alimentary canal. No man wholly understands the worm's earth-eating, or comprehends the chemistry whereby its body extracts from the eaten soil the bits of humus and vegetable matter which will give it nourishment. The feeding process of earthworms is a curious thing, and this much is known of it: from the pharynx the food goes to an oesophagus, and is there mixed with gland secretions which neutralize the acids. Thence it enters a thin-walled crop, and thence a gizzard, where it is ground to bits by spasmodic muscular contractions—and by the sharp grains of sand that have been swallowed—and is rendered ready for entrance into the worm's intestine. The network of tiny veins and arteries by which the earthworm's blood is circulated carries likewise waste products of the digested food, and on every segment of the body is a pair of organs, called nephridia, for the excretion of these wastes. Such is the manner of the earthworm's nourishment, and such the processes which have attended its upward voyage through the earth.

[7]   The earthworm has attained the outer world now, although no sight or sound can apprise it of that fact. In the damp darkness (for the ascension has been made at night) the earthworm fastens its tail by the setae to the top of the burrow, and, stretching its soft elastic body to full length, explores the neighborhood in which it finds itself. It is in quest of fallen leaves, of minute fragments of weed stalks and roots and decayed bark. Having no organs of sight, the earthworm is nevertheless able, perhaps by a dim awareness akin to scent, to detect the presence of these morsels and to seize on them; and it is able, further, to single out those foods for which it has

a special preference—such foods, for instance, as cabbage leaves and carrots.

[8]   Slowly the earthworm investigates the night, thrusting its blind naked head this way and that. Its recognition of the universe is hardly more complete than the recognition possessed by a burdock leaf or a floating water weed. The texture of its awareness is scarcely more complex. From time to time, now, as it forages blindly and deafly in the damp night air, it wriggles suddenly in response to the glinting of light or the vibrance of a tread upon the nearby earth. These are the things to which its delicate flesh responds—these the limits of the universe it can perceive. Presently, when it has taken in a sufficiency of food, it terminates its explorations for the night and withdraws once more to inner earth.

[9]   There is small variegation in the pattern of the earthworm's succeeding days. During the sunlit hours the worm stays buried in the cool darkness beneath the surface of the soil, for the thin slime of mucus that covers its skin would be dried up by the sun. But when the nights come—or when the sun is hidden and rain falls— the earthworm grows obscurely aware that it is time for seeking the outer world again, and once more the pink flesh thrusts upward. After this fashion does day follow day, unmarked by any incident but the worm's feeding and breathing. Even the breathing is almost as simple as a plant's. Blind and deaf and unequipped with mind, the earthworm also lacks lungs. It absorbs the oxygen directly through its body walls into the sluggish blood, and similarly, imperceptibly, the carbon dioxide is expelled.

[10]   Some time before it dies, the worm must beget young. The individual earthworm is both male and female, having the reproductive organs of each sex, and when the time for egg-laying comes it secretes from a thickened place in its body—the clitellum—a cocoon in which the eggs are secured. This done, the eggs are then fertilized by the spermatozoa of another worm, and the most vital of all animal rites has been accomplished. A few days or a few weeks longer the earthworm feeds and forages and pursues its eyeless way, and then the life goes out of it as unknowledgeably as it came, and the briefly animated morsel of blood and sinew reverts to parent earth.

[11]   An earthworm, I suppose, will hardly attract the contemplation of the kind of man who can be stirred by no less gaudy natural marvel than a Grand Canyon or a shooting star. Charles Darwin, though, thought earthworms were worth studying for forty years, and Darwin made some curious discoveries. He found, for instance, that in a single acre of ground there may be 50,000 worms, and he

found that they carry to the surface, in a single year, some eighteen tons of earth castings. The earthworms in an acre, Darwin learned, would in twenty years carry from the subsoil to the surface a layer of soil three inches thick; and it became evident to him that the honeycombing of the earth by its earthworms was what aerated the soil and made it porous and rendered it fit for man's agriculture.

[12] It is good sometimes to be reminded that the ephemeral shifts of politics and ideologies are not the things on which our human welfare actually depends. The ultimate welfare of our tribe depends on things like worms.

COMMENT AND QUESTIONS

I. What factual information about earthworms do you have as a result of reading "The Life and Death of a Worm"?

II. Six closely related techniques for interesting the reader are commonly used in informative writing aimed at a popular audience. These techniques, some of which we have mentioned before, are: (1) beginning with an attention-arousing device (a question, an exclamation, an anecdote); (2) associating the subject with the personal experience and interests of the reader; (3) translating abstract terms into concrete terms which the reader can more easily understand and relate to his own experience; (4) focusing on an individual instead of dealing generally with a large group; (5) using examples or comparisons which appeal to the reader; (6) arousing emotion about the subject in order to keep the reader sufficiently interested to read on and get the information. These devices are, of course, persuasive, although the primary intention of the writing may be informative. How many of these six techniques for interest are used in "The Life and Death of a Worm"? Point out specific examples.

III. In addition to certain other techniques, the writer of this article uses a dramatic, highly colored style. Notice, for example, the sentence structures and choice of words in paragraph 5. One of his stylistic devices is repetition: the fact that the worm is unseeing and unhearing is repeated in such phrases as "this blind unhearing worm," "boring blindly," "having no organs of sight," "its blind naked head," "forages blindly and deafly," "blind and deaf and unequipped with mind," "its eyeless way." Point out other examples in the article of dramatic style and repetition. Are these techniques appropriate to the material? Are they, in your opinion, effectively used, or overused?

IV. Paragraphs 4, 6, and 10 contain examples of inconspicuous definition of technical terms (setae, nephridia, clitellum). Also very skillful is the double pattern in the first seven paragraphs, by which the reader, following chronologically the life of the worm, also follows it in its physical progress up through the soil. By what technical means is the reader kept aware of this progress?

V. What do the last two paragraphs contribute to the article?

THE BUILDERS *

VANNEVAR BUSH

In the following selection, a contemporary scientist uses an extended analogy to analyze the process by which the structure of human knowledge is built. Vannevar Bush has had a distinguished career as Professor of Electrical Engineering at the Massachusetts Institute of Technology, inventor of electronic calculating machines, director of the government's wartime National Defense Research Committee and Office of Scientific Research and Development, and administrator of the atomic bomb project in its early stages. He is President of the Carnegie Institution of Washington, Chairman of the Research and Development Board, and the author of *Modern Arms and Free Men,* published in 1949. "The Builders" appeared in the January, 1945, issue of *The Technology Review.*

––––––––––

[1] The process by which the boundaries of knowledge are advanced, and the structure of organized science is built, is a complex process indeed. It corresponds fairly well with the exploitation of a difficult quarry for its building materials and the fitting of these into an edifice; but there are very significant differences. First, the material itself is exceedingly varied, hidden and overlaid with relatively worthless rubble, and the process of uncovering new facts and relationships has some of the attributes of prospecting and exploration rather than of mining or quarrying. Second, the whole effort is highly unorganized. There are no direct orders from architect or quarrymaster. Individuals and small bands proceed about their businesses unimpeded and uncontrolled, digging where they will, working over their material, and tucking it into place in the edifice.

[2] Finally, the edifice itself has a remarkable property, for its form is predestined by the laws of logic and the nature of human reasoning. It is almost as though it had once existed, and its building blocks

* Reprinted from *The Technology Review,* January, 1945, edited at the Massachusetts Institute of Technology.

had then been scattered, hidden, and buried, each with its unique form retained so that it would fit only in its own peculiar position, and with the concomitant limitation that the blocks cannot be found or recognized until the building of the structure has progressed to the point where their position and form reveal themselves to the discerning eye of the talented worker in the quarry. Parts of the edifice are being used while construction proceeds, by reason of the applications of science, but other parts are merely admired for their beauty and symmetry, and their possible utility is not in question.

[3] In these circumstances it is not at all strange that the workers sometimes proceed in erratic ways. There are those who are quite content, given a few tools, to dig away unearthing odd blocks, piling them up in the view of fellow workers, and apparently not caring whether they fit anywhere or not. Unfortunately there are also those who watch carefully until some industrious group digs out a particularly ornamental block; whereupon they fit it in place with much gusto, and bow to the crowd. Some groups do not dig at all, but spend all their time arguing as to the exact arrangement of a cornice or an abutment. Some spend all their days trying to pull down a block or two that a rival has put in place. Some, indeed, neither dig nor argue, but go along with the crowd, scratch here and there, and enjoy the scenery. Some sit by and give advice, and some just sit.

[4] On the other hand there are those men of rare vision who can grasp well in advance just the block that is needed for rapid advance on a section of the edifice to be possible, who can tell by some subtle sense where it will be found, and who have an uncanny skill in cleaning away dross and bringing it surely into the light. These are the master workmen. For each of them there can well be many of lesser stature who chip and delve, industriously, but with little grasp of what it is all about, and who nevertheless make the great steps possible.

[5] There are those who can give the structure meaning, who can trace its evolution from early times, and describe the glories that are to be, in ways that inspire those who work and those who enjoy. They bring the inspiration that not all is mere building of monotonous walls, and that there is architecture even though the architect is not seen to guide and order.

[6] There are those who labor to make the utility of the structure real, to cause it to give shelter to the multitude, that they may be better protected, and that they may derive health and well-being because of its presence.

[7] And the edifice is not built by the quarrymen and the masons alone. There are those who bring them food during their labors,

and cooling drink when the days are warm, who sing to them, and place flowers on the little walls that have grown with the years.

[8]   There are also the old men, whose days of vigorous building are done, whose eyes are too dim to see the details of the arch or the needed form of its keystone, who have built a wall here and there, and lived long in the edifice; who have learned to love it and who have even grasped a suggestion of its ultimate meaning; and who sit in the shade and encourage the young men.

COMMENT AND QUESTIONS

Analogy is used in informative writing, as we have said earlier, to make a complex or abstract idea more understandable and concrete. In some analogies, the writer compares abstract idea or situation *A* with familiar idea or situation *F*, and then explains, point by point, the likenesses between them. In other analogies the writer, having established his comparison, expands or analyzes situation *F*, and expects his readers to see its application to *A*. The reader of such analogy, of which "The Builders" is an example, must make this application. If his reading is successful, he receives simultaneously the literal meaning which the analogy is designed to clarify, and the force of the figurative language in which it is clothed.

I. What, stated in literal terms, are the three ways in which building knowledge differs from building an actual edifice?

II. What actual groups are referred to in the analysis of types of builders in paragraphs 3–8?

III. This analogy is persuasive as well as informative. Which groups of builders is the reader led, by Mr. Bush's treatment, to admire? Which groups is he led to condemn?

LINCOLN SPEAKS AT GETTYSBURG *

CARL SANDBURG

Chronological arrangement is the basic pattern used in the following chapter from a long biography of Lincoln. One of the distinctive features of this writing is the skillful weaving of a mass of fact and evidence into a highly readable historical narrative. Carl Sandburg, probably best known as a poet of the Midwest, is the author of *Chicago Poems; Cornhuskers;*

* Condensed from *Abraham Lincoln: The War Years* by Carl Sandburg, Copyright, 1939, by Harcourt, Brace and Company, Inc.

Smoke and Steel; The American Songbag; The People, Yes; and *Remembrance Rock,* a novel. His biography of Lincoln, *The Prairie Years* (two volumes) and *The War Years* (four volumes), won the 1940 Pulitzer Prize.

———〜———

[1] A printed invitation came to Lincoln's hands notifying him that on Thursday, November 19, 1863, exercises would be held for the dedication of a National Soldiers' Cemetery at Gettysburg. The same circular invitation had been mailed to Senators, Congressmen, the governors of Northern States, members of the Cabinet, by the commission of Pennsylvanians who had organized a corporation through which Maine, New Hampshire, Vermont, Massachusetts, Rhode Island, Maryland, Connecticut, New York, New Jersey, Pennsylvania, Delaware, West Virginia, Ohio, Indiana, Illinois, Michigan, Wisconsin, and Minnesota were to share the cost of a decent burying-ground for the dust and bones of the Union and Confederate dead.

[2] In the helpless onrush of the war, it was known, too many of the fallen had lain as neglected cadavers rotting in the open fields or thrust into so shallow a resting-place that a common farm plow caught in their bones. Now by order of Governor Curtin of Pennsylvania seventeen acres had been purchased on Cemetery Hill, where the Union center stood its colors on the second and third of July, and plots of soil had been alloted each State for its graves.

[3] The sacred and delicate duties of orator of the day had fallen on Edward Everett. An eminent cultural figure, perhaps foremost of all distinguished American classical orators, he was born in 1794, had been United States Senator, Governor of Massachusetts, member of Congress, Secretary of State under Fillmore, Minister to Great Britain, Phi Beta Kappa poet at Harvard, professor of Greek at Harvard, president of Harvard. His reputation as a public speaker began in the Brattle Street Unitarian Church of Boston. Two volumes of his orations published in 1850 held eighty-one addresses, two more volumes issued in 1859 collected one hundred and five speeches. His lecture on Washington, delivered a hundred and twenty-two times in three years, had in 1859 brought a fund of $58,000, which he gave to the purchase and maintenance of Mount Vernon as a permanent shrine. Other Everett lectures had realized more than $90,000 for charity causes. . . . No ordinary trafficker in politics, Everett had in 1860 run for Vice-President on the Bell-Everett ticket of the Constitutional Union party, receiving the electoral votes of Virginia, Kentucky, and Tennessee.

[4] The Union of States was a holy concept to Everett, and the slavery issue secondary, though when president of Harvard from 1846 to 1849 he refused to draw the color line, saying in the case of a Negro applicant, Beverly Williams, that admission to Harvard College depended on examinations. "If this boy passes the examinations, he will be admitted; and if the white students choose to withdraw, all the income of the College will be devoted to his education." Not often was he so provocative.

[5] On the basis of what Everett had heard about Lincoln he wrote in his journal shortly before the inauguration in '61 that the incoming President was "evidently a person of very inferior cast of character, wholly unequal to the crisis." Then on meeting the new President he recorded that he found him of better stuff than he had expected. As a strict worshiper of the Constitution and the Union he was drawn toward Lincoln's moderate slavery policy, writing to critics after the Administration had lost in the '62 fall elections, "It is my purpose to support the President to the best of my ability." Speaking publicly as a man of no party, and as the leading founder of the Mount Vernon memorial to George Washington, he trusted he would offend no candid opponent by saying that the main objection against Mr. Lincoln, "that personally he lacks fixedness of purpose," might on precisely the same grounds be brought against George Washington and his Administration. The President's "intellectual capacity" had been proved in his debates with Douglas. "He is one of the most laborious and indefatigable men in the country," said Everett, "and that he has been able to sustain himself under as great a load of care as was ever laid upon the head or the heart of a living man is in no small degree owing to the fact that the vindictive and angry passions form no part of his nature and that a kindly and playful spirit mingles its sweetness with the austere cup of public duty." . . .

[6] Serene, suave, handsomely venerable in his sixty-ninth year, a prominent specimen of Northern upper-class distinction, Everett was a natural choice of the Pennsylvania commissioners, who sought an orator for a solemn national occasion. When in September they notified him that the date of the occasion would be October 23, he replied that he would need more time for preparation, and the dedication was postponed till November 19.

[7] Lincoln meanwhile, in reply to the printed circular invitation, sent word to the commissioners that he would be present at the ceremonies. This made it necessary for the commissioners to consider whether the President should be asked to deliver an address when present. Clark E. Carr of Galesburg, Illinois, representing his

State on the Board of Commissioners, noted that the decision of the Board to invite Lincoln to speak was an afterthought. "The question was raised as to his ability to speak upon such a grave and solemn occasion. . . . Besides, it was said that, with his important duties and responsibilities, he could not possibly have the leisure to prepare an address. . . . In answer . . . it was urged that he himself, better than any one else, could determine as to these questions, and that, if he were invited to speak, he was sure to do what, under the circumstances, would be right and proper."

[8]   And so on November 2 David Wills of Gettysburg, as the special agent of Governor Curtin and also acting for the several States, by letter informed Lincoln that the several States having soldiers in the Army of the Potomac who were killed, or had since died at hospitals in the vicinity, had procured grounds for a cemetery and proper burial of their dead. "These grounds will be consecrated and set apart to this sacred purpose by appropriate ceremonies on Thursday, the 19th instant. I am authorized by the Governors of the various States to invite you to be present and participate in these ceremonies, which will doubtless be very imposing and solemnly impressive. It is the desire that after the oration, you, as Chief Executive of the nation, formally set apart these grounds to their sacred use by a few appropriate remarks."

[9]   Mr. Wills proceeded farther as to the solemnity of the occasion, and when Lincoln had finished reading the letter he understood definitely that the event called for no humor and that a long speech was not expected from him. "The invitation," wrote Clark E. Carr, "was not settled upon and sent to Mr. Lincoln until the second of November, more than six weeks after Mr. Everett had been invited to speak, and but little more than two weeks before the exercises were held."

[10]   On the second Sunday before the Gettysburg ceremonies were to take place Lincoln went to the studio of the photographer Gardner for a long-delayed sitting. Noah Brooks walked with him, and he carefully explained to Brooks that he could not go to the photographer on any other day without interfering with the public business and the photographer's business, to say nothing of his liability to be hindered en route by curiosity-seekers "and other seekers." On the White House stairs Lincoln had paused, turned, walked back to his office, and rejoined Brooks with a long envelope in his hand, an advance copy of Edward Everett's address to be delivered at the Gettysburg dedication. It was thoughtful of Everett to take care they should not cover the same ground in their speeches, he remarked to Brooks, who exclaimed over the length of the Everett address,

covering nearly two sides of a one-page supplement of a Boston news-paper. Lincoln quoted a line he said he had read somewhere from Daniel Webster: "Solid men of Boston, make no long orations." There was no danger that he should get upon the lines of Mr. Everett's oration, he told Brooks, for what he had ready to say was very short, or as Brooks recalled his emphasis, "Short, short, short." He had hoped to read the Everett address between sittings, but the photographer worked fast, Lincoln got interested in talk, and did not open the advance sheets while at Gardner's. In the photograph which Lincoln later gave to Brooks an envelope lay next to Lincoln's right arm resting on a table. In one other photograph made by Gardner that Sunday the envelope was still on the table. The chief difference between the two pictures was that in one Lincoln had his knees crossed and in the other the ankles.

[11]   Lamon noted that Lincoln wrote part of his intended Gettys-burg address at Washington, covered a sheet of foolscap paper with a memorandum of it, and before taking it out of his hat and reading it to Lamon he said that it was not at all satisfactory to him, that he was afraid he would not do himself credit nor come up to public expectation. He had been too busy to give it the time he would like to. . . .

[12]   Two men, in the weeks just before the Gettysburg ceremonies, had worked on Lincoln, doing their best to make him see himself as a world spokesman of democracy, popular government, the mass of people as opposed to aristocrats, classes, and special interests. John Murray Forbes, having read Lincoln's lively stump-speech letter to the Springfield, Illinois, mass meeting, wrote to Sumner on September 3, "I delight in the President's plain letter to plain people!" Forbes followed this five days later with a letter which Sumner carried to the White House and handed to Lincoln. It began with convincingly phrased praise of the Springfield letter, and proceeded into the unusual question: "Will you permit a suggestion from one who has nothing to ask for himself: one who would accept no office, and who seeks only to do his duty in the most private way possible?" With such an opening it could hardly be doubted that Lincoln read on into the next paragraphs—and read them more than once.

[13]   An aristocracy ruled the South and controlled it for war, be-lieved Forbes, pointing to "the aristocratic class who own twenty negroes and upwards" as numbering "about 28,000 persons, which is about the 178th part of 5,000,000" whites. So Forbes urged, "Let the people North and South see this line clearly defined between the people and the aristocrats, and the war will be over!" . . .

[14]   Thus while Lincoln shaped his speech to be made at Gettysburg

he did not lack specific advice that when the chance came he should stand up and be a world spokesman for those who called themselves democrats and liberals as opposed to what they termed "the aristocratic classes."

[15] Some newspapers now had it that the President was going to make a stump speech over the graves of the Gettysburg dead as a political play. Talk ran in Washington that by attending Governor Curtin's "show" the President would strengthen himself with the Curtin faction without alienating the opposing Cameron clique.

[16] Various definite motives besides vague intuitions may have guided Lincoln in his decision to attend and speak even though half his Cabinet had sent formal declinations in response to the printed circular invitations they had all received. Though the Gettysburg dedication was to be under interstate auspices, it had tremendous national significance for Lincoln because on the platform would be the State governors whose cooperation with him was of vast importance. Also a slander and a libel had been widely mouthed and printed that on his visit to the battlefield of Antietam nearly a year before he had laughed obscenely at his own funny stories and called on Lamon to sing a cheap comic song. Perhaps he might go to Gettysburg and let it be seen how he demeaned himself on a somber landscape of sacrifice.

[17] His personal touch with Gettysburg, by telegraph, mail, courier, and by a throng of associations, made it a place of great realities to him. Just after the battle there, a woman had come to his office, the doorman saying she had been "crying and taking on" for several days trying to see the President. Her husband and three sons were in the army. On part of her husband's pay she had lived for a time, till money from him stopped coming. She was hard put to scrape a living and needed one of her boys to help.

[18] The President listened to her, standing at a fireplace, hands behind him, head bowed, motionless. The woman finished her plea for one of her three sons in the army. He spoke. Slowly and almost as if talking to himself alone the words came and only those words:

[19] "I have two, and you have none."

[20] He crossed the room, wrote an order for the military discharge of one of her sons. On a special sheet of paper he wrote full and detailed instructions where to go and what to say in order to get her boy back.

[21] In a few days the doorman told the President that the same woman was again on hand crying and taking on. "Let her in," was the word. She had found doors opening to her and officials ready to help on seeing the President's written words she carried. She had

located her boy, camp, regiment, company. She had found him, yes, wounded at Gettysburg, dying in a hospital, and had followed him to the grave. And, she begged, would the President now give her the next one of her boys?

[22] As before he stood at the fireplace, hands behind him, head bent low, motionless. Slowly and almost as if talking to himself alone the words came and as before only those words:

[23] "I have two, and you have none."

[24] He crossed the room to his desk and began writing. As though nothing else was to do she followed, stood by his chair as he wrote, put her hand on the President's head, smoothed his thick and disorderly hair with motherly fingers. He signed an order giving her the next of her boys, stood up, put the priceless paper in her hand as he choked out the one word, "There!" and with long quick steps was gone from the room with her sobs and cries of thanks in his ears.

[25] Thus the Kentuckian, James Speed, gathered the incident and told it. By many strange ways Gettysburg was to Lincoln a fact in crimson mist. . . .

[26] Benjamin B. French, officer in charge of buildings in Washington, introduced the Honorable Edward Everett, orator of the day, who rose, bowed low to Lincoln, saying, "Mr. President." Lincoln responded, "Mr. Everett."

[27] The orator of the day then stood in silence before a crowd that stretched to limits that would test his voice. Beyond and around were the wheat fields, the meadows, the peach orchards, long slopes of land, and five and seven miles farther the contemplative blue ridge of a low mountain range. His eyes could sweep them as he faced the audience. He had taken note of it in his prepared and rehearsed address. "Overlooking these broad fields now reposing from the labors of the waning year, the mighty Alleghanies dimly towering before us, the graves of our brethren beneath our feet, it is with hesitation that I raise my poor voice to break the eloquent silence of God and Nature. But the duty to which you have called me must be performed;—grant me, I pray you, your indulgence and your sympathy." Everett proceeded, "It was appointed by law in Athens," and gave an extended sketch of the manner in which the Greeks cared for their dead who fell in battle. He spoke of the citizens assembled to consecrate the day. "As my eye ranges over the fields whose sods were so lately moistened by the blood of gallant and loyal men, I feel, as never before, how truly it was said of old that it is sweet and becoming to die for one's country."

[28] Northern cities would have been trampled in conquest but for

"those who sleep beneath our feet," said the orator. He gave an outline of how the war began, traversed decisive features of the three days' battles at Gettysburg, discussed the doctrine of State sovereignty and denounced it, drew parallels from European history, and came to his peroration quoting Pericles on dead patriots: "The whole earth is the sepulchre of illustrious men." The men of nineteen sister States had stood side by side on the perilous ridges. "Seminary Ridge, the Peach-Orchard, Cemetery, Culp, and Wolf Hill, Round Top, Little Round Top, humble names, henceforward dear and famous,—no lapse of time, no distance of space, shall cause you to be forgotten." He had spoken for an hour and fifty-seven minutes, some said a trifle over two hours, repeating almost word for word an address that occupied nearly two newspaper pages, as he had written it and as it had gone in advance sheets to many newspapers.

[29]   Everett came to his closing sentence without a faltering voice: "Down to the latest period of recorded time, in the glorious annals of our common country there will be no brighter page than that which relates THE BATTLE OF GETTYSBURG." It was the effort of his life and embodied the perfections of the school of oratory in which he had spent his career. His erect form and sturdy shoulders, his white hair and flung-back head at dramatic points, his voice, his poise, and chiefly some quality of inside goodheartedness, held most of his audience to him, though the people in the front rows had taken their seats three hours before his oration closed.

[30]   The Baltimore Glee Club sang an ode written for the occasion by Benjamin B. French, who had introduced Everett to the audience. The poets Longfellow, Bryant, Whittier, Lowell, George Boker, had been requested but none found time to respond with a piece to be set to music. The two closing verses of the ode by French immediately preceded the introduction of the President to the audience:

> Great God in Heaven!
> Shall all this sacred blood be shed?
> Shall we thus mourn our glorious dead?
> Oh, shall the end be wrath and woe,
> The knell of Freedom's overthrow,
>   A country riven?

> It will not be!
> We trust, O God! thy gracious power
> To aid us in our darkest hour.
> This be our prayer—"O Father! save
> A people's freedom from its grave.
>   All praise to Thee!"

[31]   Having read Everett's address, Lincoln knew when the moment drew near for him to speak. He took out his own manuscript from a coat pocket, put on his steel-bowed glasses, stirred in his chair, looked over the manuscript, and put it back in his pocket. The Baltimore Glee Club finished. The specially chosen Ward Hill Lamon rose and spoke the words "The President of the United States," who rose, and holding in one hand the two sheets of paper at which he occasion-ally glanced, delivered the address in his high-pitched and clear-carrying voice. The *Cincinnati Commercial* reporter wrote, "The President rises slowly, draws from his pocket a paper, and, when commotion subsides, in a sharp, unmusical treble voice, reads the brief and pithy remarks." Hay wrote in his diary, "The President, in a firm, free way, with more grace than is his wont, said his half dozen words of consecration." Charles Hale of the *Boston Advertiser,* also officially representing Governor Andrew of Massachusetts, had note-book and pencil in hand, took down the slow-spoken words of the President, as follows:

[31]   Fourscore and seven years ago, our fathers brought forth upon this continent a new nation, conceived in liberty and dedicated to the proposi-tion that all men are created equal.

Now we are engaged in a great civil war, testing whether that nation— or any nation, so conceived and so dedicated—can long endure.

We are met on a great battle-field of that war. We are met to dedicate a portion of it as the final resting place of those who have given their lives that that nation might live.

It is altogether fitting and proper that we should do this.

But, in a larger sense, we cannot dedicate, we cannot consecrate, we cannot hallow, this ground. The brave men, living and dead, who struggled here, have consecrated it, far above our power to add or to detract.

The world will very little note nor long remember what we say here; but it can never forget what they did here.

It is for us, the living, rather, to be dedicated, here, to the unfinished work that they have thus far so nobly carried on. It is rather for us to be here dedicated to the great task remaining before us; that from these honored dead we take increased devotion to that cause for which they here gave the last full measure of devotion; that we here highly resolve that these dead shall not have died in vain; that the nation shall, under God, have a new birth of freedom, and that government of the people, by the people, for the people, shall not perish from the earth.

[32]   In a speech to serenaders just after the battle of Gettysburg four and a half months before, Lincoln had referred to the founding of the republic as taking place "eighty-odd years since." Then he had hunted up the exact date, which was eighty-seven years since, and phrased it "Fourscore and seven years ago" instead of "Eighty-seven

years since." Also in the final copy Lincoln wrote "We have come" instead of the second "We are met" that Hale reported.

[33] In the written copy of his speech from which he read Lincoln used the phrase "our poor power." In other copies of the speech which he wrote out later he again used the phrase "our poor power." So it was evident that he meant to use the word "poor" when speaking to his audience, but he omitted it. Also in the copy held in his hands while facing the audience he had not written the words "under God," though he did include those words in later copies which he wrote. Therefore the words "under God" were decided upon after he wrote the text the night before at the Wills residence.

[34] The *New York Tribune* and many other newspapers indicated "[Applause.]" at five places in the address and "[Long continued applause.]" at the end. The applause, however, according to most of the responsible witnesses, was formal and perfunctory, a tribute to the occasion, to the high office, to the array of important men of the nation on the platform, by persons who had sat as an audience for three hours. Ten sentences had been spoken in five minutes, and some were surprised that it should end before the orator had really begun to get his outdoor voice.

[35] A photographer had made ready to record a great historic moment, had bustled about with his dry plates, his black box on a tripod, and before he had his head under the hood for an exposure, the President had said "by the people, for the people" and the nick of time was past for a photograph.

[36] The *New York Times* reporter gave his summary of the program by writing: "The opening prayer by Reverend Mr. Stockton was touching and beautiful, and produced quite as much effect upon the audience as the classic sentences of the orator of the day. President Lincoln's address was delivered in a clear loud tone of voice, which could be distinctly heard at the extreme limits of the large assemblage. It was delivered (or rather read from a sheet of paper which the speaker held in his hand) in a very deliberate manner, with strong emphasis, and with a most business-like air."

[37] The *Philadelphia Press* man, John Russell Young, privately felt that Everett's speech was the performance of a great actor whose art was too evident, that it was "beautiful but cold as ice." The *New York Times* man noted: "Even while Mr. Everett was delivering his splendid oration, there were as many people wandering about the fields, made memorable by the fierce struggles of July, as stood around the stand listening to his eloquent periods. They seem to have considered, with President Lincoln, that it was not what was *said* here, but what was *done* here, that deserved their attention. . . . In wan-

dering about these battlefields, one is astonished and indignant to find at almost every step of his progress the carcasses of dead horses which breed pestilence in the atmosphere. I am told that more than a score of deaths have resulted from this neglect in the village of Gettysburg the past summer; in the house in which I was compelled to seek lodgings, there are now two boys sick with typhoid fever attributed to this cause. Within a stone's throw of the whitewashed hut occupied as the headquarters of General Meade, I counted yesterday no less than ten carcasses of dead horses, lying on the ground where they were struck by the shells of the enemy."

[38]　The audience had expected, as the printed program stipulated, "Dedicatory Remarks, by the President of the United States." No eloquence was promised. Where eloquence is in flow the orator must have time to get tuned up, to expatiate and expand while building toward his climaxes, it was supposed. The *New York Tribune* man and other like observers merely reported the words of the address with the one preceding sentence: "The dedicatory remarks were then delivered by the President." These reporters felt no urge to inform their readers about how Lincoln stood, what he did with his hands, how he moved, vocalized, or whether he emphasized or subdued any parts of the address. Strictly, no address as such was on the program from him. He was down for just a few perfunctory "dedicatory remarks."

[39]　According to Lamon, Lincoln himself felt that about all he had given the audience was ordinary garden-variety dedicatory remarks, for Lamon wrote that Lincoln told him just after delivering the speech that he had regret over not having prepared it with greater care. "Lamon, that speech won't *scour*. It is a flat failure and the people are disappointed." On the farms where Lincoln grew up as a boy when wet soil stuck to the mold board of a plow they said it didn't "scour."

[40]　The near-by *Patriot and Union* of Harrisburg took its fling: "The President succeeded on this occasion because he acted without sense and without constraint in a panorama that was gotten up more for the benefit of his party than for the glory of the nation and the honor of the dead. . . . We pass over the silly remarks of the President; for the credit of the nation we are willing that the veil of oblivion shall be dropped over them and that they shall no more be repeated or thought of."

[41]　The *Chicago Times* held that "Mr. Lincoln did most foully traduce the motives of the men who were slain at Gettysburg" in his reference to "a new birth of freedom," the *Times* saying, "They gave their lives to maintain the old government, and the only Con-

stitution and Union." He had perverted history, misstated the cause for which they died, and with "ignorant rudeness" insulted the memory of the dead, the *Times* alleged: "Readers will not have failed to observe the exceeding bad taste which characterized the remarks of the President and Secretary of State at the dedication of the soldiers' cemetery at Gettysburg. The cheek of every American must tingle with shame as he reads the silly, flat, and dish-watery utterances of the man who has to be pointed out to intelligent foreigners as the President of the United States. And neither he nor Seward could refrain, even on that solemn occasion, from spouting their odious abolition doctrines. The readers of THE TIMES ought to know, too, that the valorous President did not dare to make this little journey to Gettysburg without being escorted by a bodyguard of soldiers. For the first time in the history of the country, the President of the United States, in traveling through a part of his dominions, on a peaceful, even a religious mission, had to be escorted by a bodyguard of soldiers . . . it was fear for his own personal safety which led the President to go escorted as any other military despot might go." In the pronouncement of a funeral sermon Mr. Lincoln had intruded an "offensive exhibition of boorishness and vulgarity," had alluded to tribal differences that an Indian orator eulogizing dead warriors would have omitted, "which he knew would excite unnecessarily the bitter prejudices of his hearers." Therefore the *Chicago Times* would inquire, "Is Mr. Lincoln less refined than a savage?"

[42]   A Confederate outburst of war propaganda related to Lincoln and the Gettysburg exercises was set forth in a *Richmond Examiner* editorial, and probably written by its editor, Edward A. Pollard, taking a day off from his merciless and occasionally wild-eyed criticism of President Jefferson Davis of the Confederacy. And the *Chicago Times,* which seldom let a day pass without curses on Lincoln for his alleged suppression of free speech and a free press, reprinted in full the long editorial from the *Examiner.* "The dramatic exhibition at Gettysburg is in thorough keeping with Yankee character, suited to the usual dignity of their chosen chief," ran part of the editorial scorn. "Stage play, studied attitudes, and effective points were carefully elaborated and presented to the world as the honest outpourings of a nation's heart. In spite of shoddy contracts, of universal corruption, and cruel thirst for southern blood, these people have ideas . . . have read of them in books . . . and determined accordingly to have a grand imitation of them. . . . Mr. Everett was equal to the occasion. He 'took down his Thucydides,' and fancied himself a Pericles commemorating the illustrious dead. The music, the eloquence, the bottled tears and hermetically sealed grief, pre-

pared for the occasion, were all properly brought out in honor of the heroes, whom they crimp in Ireland, inveigle in Germany, or hunt down in the streets of New York.

[43] "So far the play was strictly classic. To suit the general public, however, a little admixture of the more irregular romantic drama was allowed. A vein of comedy was permitted to mingle with the deep pathos of the piece. This singular novelty, and deviation from classic propriety, was heightened by assigning this part to the chief personage. Kings are usually made to speak in the magniloquent language supposed to be suited to their elevated position. On the present occasion Lincoln acted the clown."

[44] This was in the customary tone of the *Chicago Times* and relished by its supporting readers. Its rival, the *Chicago Tribune,* however, had a reporter who telegraphed (unless some editor who read the address added his own independent opinion) a sentence: "The dedicatory remarks of President Lincoln will live among the annals of man."

[45] The *Cincinnati Gazette* reporter added after the text of the address, "That this was the right thing in the right place, and a perfect thing in every respect, was the universal encomium."

[46] The American correspondent of the London *Times* wrote that "the ceremony was rendered ludicrous by some of the sallies of that poor President Lincoln. . . . Anything more dull and commonplace it would not be easy to produce."

[47] Count Gurowski, the only man ever mentioned by Lincoln to Lamon as his possible assassin, wrote in a diary, "Lincoln spoke, with one eye to a future platform and to re-election."

[48] The *Philadelphia Evening Bulletin* said thousands who would not read the elaborate oration of Mr. Everett would read the President's few words "and not many will do it without a moistening of the eye and a swelling of the heart." The *Detroit Advertiser and Tribune* said Mr. Everett had nobly told the story of the battle, "but he who wants to take in the very spirit of the day, catch the unstudied pathos that animates a sincere but simple-minded man, will turn from the stately periods of the professed orator to the brief speech of the President." The *Providence Journal* reminded readers of the saying that the hardest thing in the world is to make a good five-minute speech: "We know not where to look for a more admirable speech than the brief one which the President made at the close of Mr. Everett's oration. . . . Could the most elaborate and splendid oration be more beautiful, more touching, more inspiring, than those thrilling words of the President? They had in our humble judgment the charm and power of the very highest eloquence."

[49]   Later men were to find that Robert Toombs of Georgia had in 1850 opened a speech: "Sixty years ago our fathers joined together to form a more perfect Union and to establish justice. . . . We have now met to put that government on trial. . . . In my judgment the verdict is such as to give hope to the friends of liberty throughout the world."

[50]   Lincoln had spoken of an idea, a proposition, a concept, worth dying for, which brought from a Richmond newspaper a countering question and answer, "For what are we fighting? An abstraction."

[51]   The *Springfield Republican* had veered from its first opinion that Lincoln was honest but "a Simple Susan." Its comment ran: "Surpassingly fine as Mr. Everett's oration was in the Gettysburg consecration, the rhetorical honors of the occasion were won by President Lincoln. His little speech is a perfect gem; deep in feeling, compact in thought and expression, and tasteful and elegant in every word and comma. Then it has the merit of unexpectedness in its verbal perfection and beauty. We had grown so accustomed to homely and imperfect phrase in his productions that we had come to think it was the law of his utterance. But this shows he can talk handsomely as well as act sensibly. Turn back and read it over, it will repay study as a model speech. Strong feelings and a large brain were its parents—a little painstaking its *accoucheur*."

[52]   That scribbler of curious touch who signed himself "The Lounger" in *Harper's Weekly* inquired why the ceremony at Gettysburg was one of the most striking events of the war. "There are grave-yards enough in the land—what is Virginia but a cemetery?— and the brave who have died for us in this fierce war consecrate the soil from the ocean to the Mississippi. But there is peculiar significance in the field of Gettysburg, for there 'thus far' was thundered to the rebellion. . . . The President and the Cabinet were there, with famous soldiers and civilians. The oration by Mr. Everett was smooth and cold. . . . The few words of the President were from the heart to the heart. They can not be read, even, without kindling emotion. 'The world will little note nor long remember what we say here, but it can never forget what they did here.' It was as simple and felicitous and earnest a word as was ever spoken. . . . Among the Governors present was Horatio Seymour. He came to honor the dead of Gettysburg. But when they were dying he stood in New York sneeringly asking where was the victory promised for the Fourth of July? These men were winning that victory, and dying for us all; and now he mourns, *ex officio*, over their graves."

[53]   Everett's opinion of the speech he heard Lincoln deliver was written in a note to Lincoln the next day and was more than mere

courtesy: "I should be glad if I could flatter myself that I came as near to the central idea of the occasion in two hours as you did in two minutes." Lincoln's immediate reply was: "In our respective parts yesterday, you could not have been excused to make a short address, nor I a long one. I am pleased to know that, in your judgment, the little I did say was not entirely a failure."

[54] At Everett's request Lincoln wrote with pen and ink a copy of his Gettysburg Address, which manuscript was auctioned at a Sanitary Fair in New York for the benefit of soldiers. At the request of George Bancroft, the historian, he wrote another copy for a Soldiers' and Sailors' Fair at Baltimore. He wrote still another to be lithographed as a facsimile in a publication, *Autographed Leaves of Our Country's Authors*. For Mr. Wills, his host at Gettysburg, he wrote another. The first draft, written in Washington, and the second one, held while delivering it, went into John Hay's hands to be eventually presented to the Library of Congress.

[55] After the ceremonies at Gettysburg Lincoln lunched with Governor Curtin, Mr. Everett, and others at the Wills home, held a reception that had not been planned, handshaking nearly an hour, looking gloomy and listless but brightening sometimes as a small boy or girl came in line, and stopping one tall man for remarks as to just how high up he reached. At five o'clock he attended a patriotic meeting in the Presbyterian church, walking arm-in-arm with old John Burns, and listening to an address by Lieutenant Governor-elect Anderson of Ohio. At six-thirty he was on the departing Washington train. In the dining-car his secretary John Hay ate with Simon Cameron and Wayne MacVeagh. Hay had thought Cameron and MacVeagh hated each other, but he noted: "I was more than usually struck by the intimate, jovial relations that existed between men that hate and detest each other as cordially as do these Pennsylvania politicians."

[56] The ride to Washington took until midnight. Lincoln was weary, talked little, stretched out on one of the side seats in the drawing-room and had a wet towel laid across his eyes and forehead.

[57] He had stood that day, the world's foremost spokesman of popular government, saying that democracy was yet worth fighting for. He had spoken as one in mist who might head on deeper yet into mist. He incarnated the assurances and pretenses of popular government, implied that it could and might perish from the earth. What he meant by "a new birth of freedom" for the nation could have a thousand interpretations. The taller riddles of democracy stood up out of the address. It had the dream touch of vast and

furious events epitomized for any foreteller to read what was to come. He did not assume that the drafted soldiers, substitutes, and bounty-paid privates had died willingly under Lee's shot and shell, in deliberate consecration of themselves to the Union cause. His cadences sang the ancient song that where there is freedom men have fought and sacrificed for it, and that freedom is worth men's dying for. For the first time since he became President he had on a dramatic occasion declaimed, howsoever it might be read, Jefferson's proposition which had been a slogan of the Revolutionary War—"All men are created equal"—leaving no other inference than that he regarded the Negro slave as a man. His outwardly smooth sentences were inside of them gnarled and tough with the enigmas of the American experiment.

[58] Back at Gettysburg the blue haze of the Cumberland Mountains had dimmed till it was a blur in a nocturne. The moon was up and fell with a bland golden benevolence on the new-made graves of soldiers, on the sepulchers of old settlers, on the horse carcasses of which the onrush of war had not yet permitted removal. The *New York Herald* man walked amid them and ended the story he sent his paper: "The air, the trees, the graves are silent. Even the relic hunters are gone now. And the soldiers here never wake to the sound of reveille."

[59] In many a country cottage over the land, a tall old clock in a quiet corner told time in a tick-tock deliberation. Whether the orchard branches hung with pink-spray blossoms or icicles of sleet, whether the outside news was seedtime or harvest, rain or drouth, births or deaths, the swing of the pendulum was right and left and right and left in a tick-tock deliberation.

[60] The face and dial of the clock had known the eyes of a boy who listened to its tick-tock and learned to read its minute and hour hands. And the boy had seen years measured off by the swinging pendulum, and grown to man size, had gone away. And the people in the cottage knew that the clock would stand there and the boy never again come into the room and look at the clock with the query, "What is the time?"

[61] In a row of graves of the Unidentified the boy would sleep long in the dedicated final resting-place at Gettysburg. Why he had gone away and why he would never come back had roots in some mystery of flags and drums, of national fate in which individuals sink as in a deep sea, of men swallowed and vanished in a man-made storm of smoke and steel.

[62] The mystery deepened and moved with ancient music and inviolable consolation because a solemn Man of Authority had stood

at the graves of the Unidentified and spoken the words "We cannot consecrate—we cannot hallow—this ground. The brave men, living and dead, who struggled here, have consecrated it far above our poor power to add or detract. . . . From these honored dead we take increased devotion to that cause for which they gave the last full measure of devotion."

[63] To the backward and forward pendulum swing of a tall old clock in a quiet corner they might read those cadenced words while outside the windows the first flurry of snow blew across the orchard and down over the meadow, the beginnings of winter in a gun-metal gloaming to be later arched with a star-flung sky.

COMMENT AND QUESTIONS

I. Most of this selection is objective reporting of verifiable facts, with the verification or documentation of the facts incorporated into the writing. There are few obvious devices for interest, no diluting or popularizing of the material to make it more appealing. But most readers find the packed, informative account very absorbing. What is the basis of its interest?

II. Is the delineation of Edward Everett generally favorable or unfavorable? Explain.

III. What is the purpose of including in the account Lincoln's visit to the photographer (paragraph 10)?

IV. What purpose is served by including the visits of the woman to Lincoln's office (paragraphs 17–24)? By what means does Sandburg make these visits vivid and dramatic?

V. How does Sandburg give the reader a sense of the setting in which the ceremonies at Gettysburg took place?

VI. Study the conflicting reports and judgments of the ceremonies at Gettysburg (paragraphs 34–53) in the light of what you know about charged language. What techniques were used by the reporters? What forces were operating to influence their judgments? Do you think that some of those who disregarded or condemned Lincoln's speech were sincere?

VII. How do the last seven paragraphs (57–63) differ from the rest of the account in attitude toward the subject and in style? What do they contribute to the selection?

VIII. What does Sandburg mean by saying that Lincoln's smooth sentences were "gnarled and tough with the enigmas of the American experiment" (paragraph 57)?

THE IDEAL DEMOCRACY *

CARL L. BECKER

Extended definition, analysis of a concept, and cause-and-effect arrangement are illustrated by the following selection. The clear handling of complex material and the lucid, polished style, characteristic of all the writing
of Carl L. Becker, are worth careful study. Mr. Becker, who died in 1945,
was a distinguished American historian. He taught history at Pennsylvania
State College, Dartmouth, the Universities of Kansas and Minnesota, and
after 1917 at Cornell. Among his books are *The Heavenly City of the
Eighteenth Century Philosophers, Every Man His Own Historian, New
Liberties for Old, How New Will the Better World Be?* and *Modern
Democracy,* from which this selection is taken. "The Ideal Democracy"
was originally delivered as a lecture at the University of Virginia in 1940.
It therefore combines a generally formal style and tone with a personal
speaker-audience relationship.

———◡———

[1]   Democracy, like liberty or science or progress, is a word with
which we are all so familiar that we rarely take the trouble to ask
what we mean by it. It is a term, as the devotees of semantics say,
which has no "referent"—there is no precise or palpable thing or
object which we all think of when the word is pronounced. On the
contrary, it is a word which connotes different things to different
people, a kind of conceptual Gladstone bag which, with a little
manipulation, can be made to accommodate almost any collection
of social facts we may wish to carry about in it. In it we can as easily
pack a dictatorship as any other form of government. We have only
to stretch the concept to include any form of government supported
by a majority of the people, for whatever reasons and by whatever
means of expressing assent, and before we know it the empire of
Napoleon, the Soviet regime of Stalin, and the Fascist systems of
Mussolini and Hitler are all safely in the bag. But if this is what we
mean by democracy, then virtually all forms of government are
democratic, since virtually all governments, except in times of revolution, rest upon the explicit or implicit consent of the people. In
order to discuss democracy intelligently it will be necessary, therefore, to define it, to attach to the word a sufficiently precise meaning
to avoid the confusion which is not infrequently the chief result of
such discussions.

* From *Modern Democracy* by Carl Becker. Yale University Press.

[2]   All human institutions, we are told, have their ideal forms laid away in heaven, and we do not need to be told that the actual institutions conform but indifferently to these ideal counterparts. It would be possible then to define democracy either in terms of the ideal or in terms of the real form—to define it as government of the people, by the people, for the people; or to define it as government of the people, by the politicians, for whatever pressure groups can get their interests taken care of. But as a historian, I am naturally disposed to be satisfied with the meaning which, in the history of politics, men have commonly attributed to the word—a meaning, needless to say, which derives partly from the experience and partly from the aspirations of mankind. So regarded, the term democracy refers primarily to a form of government, and it has always meant government by the many as opposed to government by the one— government by the people as opposed to government by a tyrant, a dictator, or an absolute monarch. This is the most general meaning of the word as men have commonly understood it.

[3]   In this antithesis there are, however, certain implications, always tacitly understood, which give a more precise meaning to the term. Peisistratus, for example, was supported by a majority of the people, but his government was never regarded as a democracy for all that. Caesar's power derived from a popular mandate, conveyed through established republican forms, but that did not make his government any less a dictatorship. Napoleon called his government a democratic empire, but no one, least of all Napoleon himself, doubted that he had destroyed the last vestiges of the democratic republic. Since the Greeks first used the term, the essential test of democratic government has always been this: the source of political authority must be and remain in the people and not in the ruler. A democratic government has always meant one in which the citizens, or a sufficient number of them to represent more or less effectively the common will, freely act from time to time, and according to established forms, to appoint or recall the magistrates and to enact or revoke the laws by which the community is governed. This I take to be the meaning which history has impressed upon the term democracy as a form of government. It is, therefore, the meaning which I attach to it in these lectures.

[4]   The most obvious political fact of our time is that democracy as thus defined has suffered an astounding decline in prestige. Fifty years ago it was not impossible to regard democratic government, and the liberties that went with it, as a permanent conquest of the human spirit. In 1886 Andrew Carnegie published a book entitled *Triumphant Democracy*. Written without fear and without research,

the book was not an achievement of the highest intellectual distinction perhaps; but the title at least expressed well enough the prevailing conviction—the conviction that democracy had fought the good fight, had won the decisive battles, and would inevitably, through its inherent merits, presently banish from the world the most flagrant political and social evils which from time immemorial had afflicted mankind. This conviction could no doubt be most easily entertained in the United States, where even the tradition of other forms of government was too remote and alien to color our native optimism. But even in Europe the downright skeptics, such as Lecky, were thought to be perverse, and so hardheaded a historian as J. B. Bury could proclaim with confidence that the long struggle for freedom of thought had finally been won.

[5] I do not need to tell you that within a brief twenty years the prevailing optimism of that time has been quite dispelled. One European country after another has, willingly enough it seems, abandoned whatever democratic institutions it formerly enjoyed for some form of dictatorship. The spokesmen of Fascism and Communism announce with confidence that democracy, a sentimental aberration which the world has outgrown, is done for; and even the friends of democracy support it with declining conviction. They tell us that democracy, so far from being triumphant, is "at the crossroads" or "in retreat," and that its future is by no means assured. What are we to think of this sudden reversal in fortune and prestige? How explain it? What to do about it?

II

[6] One of the presuppositions of modern thought is that institutions, in order to be understood, must be seen in relation to the conditions of time and place in which they appear. It is a little difficult for us to look at democracy in this way. We are so immersed in its present fortunes that we commonly see it only as a "close-up," filling the screen to the exclusion of other things to which it is in fact related. In order to form an objective judgment of its nature and significance, we must therefore first of all get it in proper perspective. Let us then, in imagination, remove from the immediate present scene to some cool high place where we can survey at a glance five or six thousand years of history, and note the part which democracy has played in human civilization. The view, if we have been accustomed to take democratic institutions for granted, is a bit bleak and disheartening. For we see at once that in all this long time, over the habitable globe, the great majority of the human race

has neither known nor apparently much cared for our favorite institutions.

[7] Civilization was already old when democracy made its first notable appearance among the small city states of ancient Greece, where it flourished brilliantly for a brief century or two and then disappeared. At about the same time something that might be called democracy appeared in Rome and other Italian cities, but even in Rome it did not survive the conquest of the world by the Roman Republic, except as a form of local administration in the cities of the empire. In the twelfth and thirteenth centuries certain favorably placed medieval cities enjoyed a measure of self-government, but in most instances it was soon replaced by the dictatorship of military conquerors, the oligarchic control of a few families, or the encroaching power of autocratic kings. The oldest democracy of modern times is the Swiss Confederation, the next oldest is the Dutch Republic. Parliamentary government in England does not antedate the late seventeenth century, the great American experiment is scarcely older. Not until the nineteenth century did democratic government make its way in any considerable part of the world—in the great states of continental Europe, in South America, in Canada and Australia, in South Africa and Japan.

[8] From this brief survey it is obvious that, taking the experience of mankind as a test, democracy has as yet had but a limited and temporary success. There must be a reason for this significant fact. The reason is that democratic government is a species of social luxury, at best a delicate and precarious adventure which depends for success upon the validity of certain assumptions about the capacities and virtues of men, and upon the presence of certain material and intellectual conditions favorable to the exercise of these capacities and virtues. Let us take the material conditions first.

[9] It is a striking fact that until recently democracy never flourished except in very small states—for the most part in cities. It is true that in both the Persian and the Roman empires a measure of self-government was accorded to local communities, but only in respect to purely local affairs; in no large state as a whole was democratic government found to be practicable. One essential reason is that until recently the means of communication were too slow and uncertain to create the necessary solidarity of interest and similarity of information over large areas. The principle of representation was well enough known to the Greeks, but in practice it proved impracticable except in limited areas and for special occasions. As late as the eighteenth century it was still the common opinion that the republican form of government, although the best ideally, was un-

suited to large countries, even to a country no larger than France. This was the view of Montesquieu, and even of Rousseau. The view persisted into the nineteenth century, and English conservatives, who were opposed to the extension of the suffrage in England, consoled themselves with the notion that the American Civil War would confirm it—would demonstrate that government by and for the people would perish, if not from off the earth at least from large countries. If their hopes were confounded the reason is that the means of communication, figuratively speaking, were making large countries small. It is not altogether fanciful to suppose that, but for the railroad and the telegraph, the United States would today be divided into many small republics maneuvering for advantage and employing war and diplomacy for maintaining an unstable balance of power.

[10] If one of the conditions essential to the success of democratic government is mobility, ease of communication, another is a certain measure of economic security. Democracy does not flourish in communities on the verge of destitution. In ancient and medieval times democratic government appeared for the most part in cities, the centers of prosperity. Farmers in the early Roman Republic and in the Swiss Cantons were not wealthy to be sure, but equality of possessions and of opportunity gave them a certain economic security. In medieval cities political privilege was confined to the prosperous merchants and craftsmen, and in Athens and the later Roman Republic democratic government was found to be workable only on condition that the poor citizens were subsidized by the government or paid for attending the assemblies and the law courts.

[11] In modern times democratic institutions have, generally speaking, been most successful in new countries, such as the United States, Canada, and Australia, where the conditions of life have been easy for the people; and in European countries more or less in proportion to their industrial prosperity. In European countries, indeed, there has been a close correlation between the development of the industrial revolution and the emergence of democratic institutions. Holland and England, the first countries to experience the industrial revolution, were the first also (apart from Switzerland, where certain peculiar conditions obtained) to adopt democratic institutions; and as the industrial revolution spread to France, Belgium, Germany, and Italy, these countries in turn adopted at least a measure of democratic government. Democracy is in some sense an economic luxury, and it may be said that in modern times it has been a function of the development of new and potentially rich countries, or of the industrial revolution which suddenly dowered Europe with unaccus-

tomed wealth. Now that prosperity is disappearing round every next corner, democracy works less well than it did.

[12]　So much for the material conditions essential for the success of democratic government. Supposing these conditions to exist, democratic government implies in addition the presence of certain capacities and virtues in its citizens. These capacities and virtues are bound up with the assumptions on which democracy rests, and are available only in so far as the assumptions are valid. The primary assumption of democratic government is that its citizens are capable of managing their own affairs. But life in any community involves a conflict of individual and class interests, and a corresponding divergence of opinion as to the measures to be adopted for the common good. The divergent opinions must be somehow reconciled, the conflict of interests somehow compromised. It must then be an assumption of democratic government that its citizens are rational creatures, sufficiently so at least to understand the interests in conflict; and it must be an assumption that they are men of good will, sufficiently so toward each other at least to make those concessions of individual and class interest required for effecting workable compromises. The citizens of a democracy should be, as Pericles said the citizens of Athens were, if not all originators at least all sound judges of good policy.

[13]　These are what may be called the minimum assumptions and the necessary conditions of democratic government anywhere and at any time. They may be noted to best advantage, not in any state, but in small groups within the state—in clubs and similar private associations of congenial and like-minded people united for a specific purpose. In such associations the membership is limited and select. The members are, or may easily become, all acquainted with each other. Everyone knows, or may easily find out, what is being done and who is doing it. There will of course be differences of opinion, and there may be disintegrating squabbles and intrigues. But on the whole, ends and means being specific and well understood, the problems of government are few and superficial; there is plenty of time for discussion; and since intelligence and good will can generally be taken for granted there is the disposition to make reasonable concessions and compromises. The analogy must be taken for what it is worth. States may not be the mystical blind Molochs of German philosophy, but any state is far more complex and intangible than a private association, and there is little resemblance between such associations and the democracies of modern times. Other things equal, the resemblance is closest in very small states, and it is in

connection with the small city states of ancient Greece that the resemblance can best be noted.

[14] The Greek states were limited in size, not as is often thought solely or even chiefly by the physiography of the country, but by some instinctive feeling of the Greek mind that a state is necessarily a natural association of people bound together by ties of kinship and a common tradition of rights and obligations There must then, as Aristotle said, be a limit:

> For if the citizens of a state are to judge and distribute offices according to merit, they must know each other's characters; where they do not possess this knowledge, both the elections to offices and the decisions in the law courts will go wrong. Where the population is very large they are manifestly settled by haphazard, which clearly ought not to be. Besides, in over-populous states foreigners and metics will readily acquire citizenship, for who will find them out?

It obviously did not occur to Aristotle that metics and foreigners should be free to acquire citizenship. It did not occur to him, or to any Greek of his time, or to the merchants of the self-governing medieval city, that a state should be composed of all the people inhabiting a given territory. A state was rather an incorporated body of people within, but distinct from, the population of the community.

[15] Ancient and medieval democracies had thus something of the character of a private association. They were, so to speak, purely pragmatic phenomena, arising under very special conditions, and regarded as the most convenient way of managing the affairs of people bound together by community of interest and for the achievement of specific ends. There is no suggestion in Aristotle that democracy (polity) is intrinsically a superior form of government, no suggestion that it derives from a special ideology of its own. If it rests upon any superiority other than convenience, it is the superiority which it shares with any Greek state, that is to say, the superiority of Greek over barbarian civilization. In Aristotle's philosophy it is indeed difficult to find any clear-cut distinction between the democratic form of government and the state itself; the state, if it be worthy of the name, is always, whatever the form of government, "the government of freemen and equals," and in any state it is always necessary that "the freemen who compose the bulk of the people should have absolute power in some things." In Aristotle's philosophy the distinction between good and bad in politics is not between good and bad types of government, but between the good and the bad form of each type. Any type of government—monarchy, aristocracy,

polity—is good provided the rulers aim at the good of all rather than at the good of the class to which they belong. From Aristotle's point of view neither democracy nor dictatorship is good or bad in itself, but only in the measure that it achieves, or fails to achieve, the aim of every good state, which is that "the inhabitants of it should be happy." It did not occur to Aristotle that democracy (polity), being in some special sense in harmony with the nature of man, was everywhere applicable, and therefore destined by fate or the gods to carry throughout the world a superior form of civilization.

[16]   It is in this respect chiefly that modern democracy differs from earlier forms. It rests upon something more than the minimum assumptions. It is reinforced by a full-blown ideology which, by endowing the individual with natural and imprescriptible rights, sets the democratic form of government off from all others as the one which alone can achieve the good life. What then are the essential tenets of the modern democratic faith?

III

[17]   The liberal democratic faith, as expressed in the works of eighteenth- and early nineteenth-century writers, is one of the formulations of the modern doctrine of progress. It will be well, therefore, to note briefly the historical antecedents of that doctrine.

[18]   In the long history of man on earth there comes a time when he remembers something of what has been, anticipates something that will be, knows the country he has traversed, wonders what lies beyond—the moment when he becomes aware of himself as a lonely, differentiated item in the world. Sooner or later there emerges for him the most devastating of all facts, namely, that in an indifferent universe which alone endures, he alone aspires, endeavors to attain, and attains only to be defeated in the end. From that moment his immediate experience ceases to be adequate, and he endeavors to project himself beyond it by creating ideal worlds of semblance, Utopias of other time or place in which all has been, may be, or will be well.

[19]   In ancient times Utopia was most easily projected into the unknown past, pushed back to the beginning of things—to the time of P'an Ku and the celestial emperors, to the Garden of Eden, or the reign of King Chronos when men lived like gods free from toil and grief. From this happy state of first created things there had obviously been a decline and fall, occasioned by disobedience and human frailty, and decreed as punishment by fate or the angry gods. The mind of man was therefore afflicted with pessimism, a sense of guilt

for having betrayed the divine purpose, a feeling of inadequacy for bringing the world back to its original state of innocence and purity. To men who felt insecure in a changing world, and helpless in a world always changing for the worse, the future had little to offer. It could be regarded for the most part only with resignation, mitigated by individual penance or well-doing, or the hope of some miraculous intervention by the gods, or the return of the god-like kings, to set things right again, yet with little hope that from this setting right there would not be another falling away.

[20] This pervasive pessimism was gradually dispelled in the Western world, partly by the Christian religion, chiefly by the secular intellectual revolution occurring roughly between the fifteenth and the eighteenth centuries. The Christian religion gave assurance that the lost golden age of the past would be restored for the virtuous in the future, and by proclaiming the supreme worth of the individual in the eyes of God enabled men to look forward with hope to the good life after death in the Heavenly City. Meantime, the secular intellectual revolution, centering in the matter-of-fact study of history and science, gradually emancipated the minds of men from resignation to fate and the angry gods. Accumulated knowledge of history, filling in time past with a continuous succession of credible events, banished all lost golden ages to the realm of myth, and enabled men to live without distress in a changing world since it could be regarded as not necessarily changing for the worse. At the same time, a more competent observation and measurement of the action of material things disclosed an outer world of nature, indifferent to man indeed, yet behaving, not as the unpredictable sport of the gods, but in ways understandable to human reason and therefore ultimately subject to man's control.

[21] Thus the conditions were fulfilled which made it possible for men to conceive of Utopia, neither as a lost golden age of the past nor as a Heavenly City after death prepared by the gods for the virtuous, but as a future state on earth of man's own devising. In a world of nature that could be regarded as amenable to man's control, and in a world of changing social relations that need not be regarded as an inevitable decline and fall from original perfection, it was possible to formulate the modern doctrine of progress: the idea that, by deliberate intention and rational direction, men can set the terms and indefinitely improve the conditions of their mundane existence.

[22] The eighteenth century was the moment in history when men first fully realized the engaging implications of this resplendent idea, the moment when, not yet having been brought to the harsh appraisal of experience, it could be accepted with unclouded optimism.

Never had the universe seemed less mysterious, more open and visible, more eager to yield its secrets to common-sense questions. Never had the nature of man seemed less perverse, or the mind of man more pliable to the pressure of rational persuasion. The essential reason for this confident optimism is that the marvels of scientific discovery disclosed to the men of that time a God who still functioned but was no longer angry. God the Father could be conceived as a beneficent First Cause who, having performed his essential task of creation, had withdrawn from the affairs of men, leaving them competently prepared and fully instructed for the task of achieving their own salvation. In one tremendous sentence Rousseau expressed the eighteenth-century world view of the universe and man's place in it. "Is it simple," he exclaimed, "is it natural that God should have gone in search of Moses in order to speak to Jean Jacques Rousseau?" [23] God had indeed spoken to Rousseau, he had spoken to all men, but his revelation was contained, not in Holy Writ interpreted by Holy Church, but in the great Book of Nature which was open for all men to read. To this open book of nature men would go when they wanted to know what God had said to them. Here they would find recorded the laws of nature and of nature's God, disclosing a universe constructed according to a rational plan; and that men might read these laws aright they had been endowed with reason, a bit of the universal intelligence placed within the individual to make manifest to him the universal reason implicit in things and events. "Natural law," as Volney so clearly and confidently put it, "is the regular and constant order of facts by which God rules the universe; the order which his wisdom presents to the sense and reason of men, to serve them as an equal and common rule of conduct, and to guide them, without distinction of race or sect, toward perfection and happiness." Thus God had devised a planned economy, and had endowed men with the capacity for managing it: to bring his ideas, his conduct, and his institutions into harmony with the universal laws of nature was man's simple alloted task.

[24] At all times political theory must accommodate itself in some fashion to the prevailing world view, and liberal-democratic political theory was no exception to this rule. From time immemorial authority and obedience had been the cardinal concepts both of the prevailing world view and of political and social theory. From time immemorial men had been regarded as subject to overruling authority—the authority of the gods, and the authority of kings who were themselves gods, or descended from gods, or endowed with divine authority to rule in place of gods; and from time immemorial obedience to such divine authority was thought to be the primary

obligation of men. Even the Greeks, who were so little afraid of their gods that they could hob-nob with them in the most friendly and engaging way, regarded mortals as subject to them; and when they lost faith in the gods they deified the state as the highest good and subordinated the individual to it. But the eighteenth-century world view, making man the measure of all things, mitigated if it did not destroy this sharp contrast between authority and obedience. God still reigned but he did not govern. He had, so to speak, granted his subjects a constitution and authorized them to interpret it as they would in the supreme court of reason. Men were still subject to an overruling authority, but the subjection could be regarded as voluntary because self-imposed, and self-imposed because obedience was exacted by nothing more oppressive than their own rational intelligence.

[25] Liberal-democratic political theory readily accommodated itself to this change in the world view. The voice of the people was now identified with the voice of God, and all authority was derived from it. The individual instead of the state or the prince was now deified and endowed with imprescriptible rights; and since ignorance or neglect of the rights of man was the chief cause of social evils, the first task of political science was to define these rights, the second to devise a form of government suited to guarantee them. The imprescriptible rights of man were easily defined, since they were self-evident: "All men are created equal, [and] are endowed by their Creator with certain inalienable rights, among which are life, liberty, and the pursuit of happiness." From this it followed that all just governments would remove those artificial restraints which impaired these rights, thereby liberating those natural impulses with which God had endowed the individual as a guide to thought and conduct. In the intellectual realm, freedom of thought and the competition of diverse opinion would disclose the truth, which all men, being rational creatures, would progressively recognize and willingly follow. In the economic realm, freedom of enterprise would disclose the natural aptitudes of each individual, and the ensuing competition of interests would stimulate effort, and thereby result in the maximum of material advantage for all. Liberty of the individual from social constraint thus turned out to be not only an inherent natural right but also a preordained natural mechanism for bringing about the material and moral progress of mankind. Men had only to follow reason and self-interest: something not themselves, God and Nature, would do whatever else was necessary for righteousness.

[26] Thus modern liberal-democracy is associated with an ideology which rests upon something more than the minimum assumptions

essential to any democratic government. It rests upon a philosophy of universally valid ends and means. Its fundamental assumption is the worth and dignity and creative capacity of the individual, so that the chief aim of government is the maximum of individual self-direction, the chief means to that end the minimum of compulsion by the state. Ideally considered, means and ends are conjoined in the concept of freedom: freedom of thought, so that the truth may prevail; freedom of occupation, so that careers may be open to talent; freedom of self-government, so that no one may be compelled against his will.

[27]   In the possibility of realizing this ideal the prophets and protagonists of democracy exhibited an unquestioned faith. If their faith seems to us somewhat naïve, the reason is that they placed a far greater reliance upon the immediate influence of good will and rational discussion in shaping the conduct of men than it is possible for us to do. This difference can be conveniently noted in a passage from the *Autobiography* of John Stuart Mill, in which he describes his father's extraordinary faith in two things—representative government and complete freedom of discussion:

So complete was my father's reliance on the influence of reason over the minds of mankind, whenever it was allowed to reach them, that he felt as if all would be gained if the whole population were taught to read, if all sorts of opinions were allowed to be addressed to them by word and writing, and if by means of the suffrage they could nominate a legislature to give effect to the opinions they adopted. He thought that when the legislature no longer represented a class interest, it would aim at the general interest, honestly and with adequate wisdom; since the people would be sufficiently under the guidance of educated intelligence to make in general good choice of persons to represent them, and having done so to leave to those whom they had chosen a liberal discretion. Accordingly, aristocratic rule, the government of the few in any of its shapes, being in his eyes the only thing that stood between mankind and the administration of its affairs by the best wisdom to be found amongst them, was the object of his sternest disapprobation, and a democratic suffrage the principal article of his political creed.

[28]   The beliefs of James Mill were shared by the little group of Philosophical Radicals who gathered about him. They were, indeed, the beliefs of all those who in the great crusading days placed their hopes in democratic government as a panacea for injustice and oppression. The actual working of democratic government, as these devoted enthusiasts foresaw it, the motives that would inspire men and the objects they would pursue in that ideal democracy which so many honest men have cherished and fought for, have never been better described than by James Bryce in his *Modern Democracies*. In this ideal democracy, says Bryce,

the average citizen will give close and constant attention to public affairs, recognizing that this is his interest as well as his duty. He will try to comprehend the main issues of policy, bringing to them an independent and impartial mind, which thinks first not of its own but of the general interest. If, owing to inevitable differences of opinion as to what are the measures needed for the general welfare, parties become inevitable, he will join one, and attend its meetings, but will repress the impulses of party spirit. Never failing to come to the polls, he will vote for his party candidate only if satisfied by his capacity and honesty. He will be ready to . . . be put forward as a candidate for the legislature (if satisfied of his own competence), because public service is recognized as a duty. With such citizens as electors, the legislature will be composed of upright and capable men, single-minded in their wish to serve the nation. Bribery in constituencies, corruption among public servants, will have disappeared. Leaders may not always be single-minded, nor assemblies always wise, nor administrators efficient, but all will be at any rate honest and zealous, so that an atmosphere of confidence and goodwill will prevail. Most of the causes that make for strife will be absent, for there will be no privileges, no advantages to excite jealousy. Office will be sought only because it gives opportunity for useful public service. Power will be shared by all, and a career open to all alike. Even if the law does not—perhaps it cannot— prevent the accumulation of fortunes, these will be few and not inordinate, for public vigilance will close the illegitimate paths to wealth. All but the most depraved persons will obey and support the law, feeling it to be their own. There will be no excuse for violence, because the constitution will provide a remedy for every grievance. Equality will produce a sense of human solidarity, will refine manners, and increase brotherly kindness.

[29] Such is the ideal form of modern democracy laid away in heaven. I do not need to tell you that its earthly counterpart resembles it but slightly.

COMMENT AND QUESTIONS

Since "The Ideal Democracy" is the first of three lectures on democracy, it is somewhat inconclusive; Carl Becker does not answer all the questions he raises at the end of the first section, and he may leave in doubt his own opinion of democracy as a form of government. That opinion is stated in a passage from *New Liberties for Old* quoted on page 86 of this book.

One of the best ways to study the very skillful organization of this essay is to examine the first and last sentences of each paragraph, noticing how they state or emphasize topic ideas, and how they establish transitions between paragraphs and sections. The excellent use of examples and concrete statements to clarify abstract material is also worth noting.

I. What phase of the subject is treated in each of the three major divisions?

II. What methods of definition are used in section I?

III. Upon what material conditions does democracy depend for success?

IV. What minimum assumptions does democracy make about the capacities and virtues of its citizens?

V. What is the purpose of the analogy in paragraph 13?

VI. How does the modern democratic faith differ from early theories about democracy?

VII. How did the Christian religion change the idea that Utopia existed only in an unknown past?

VIII. How did the "secular intellectual revolution" between the fifteenth and eighteenth centuries change still further the concept of Utopia?

IX. What is the "modern doctrine of progress"?

X. Explain how the world view of the eighteenth century affected political theory and produced the modern democratic ideology.

XI. Why, according to Becker, were men of the eighteenth and early nineteenth centuries more optimistic than men today about the possibility of achieving ideal democracy?

XII. Does this essay explain the decline in the prestige of democracy in the world today?

XIII. Does Becker state or imply that democracy with all its faults is not the best system of government?

XIV. Outline the development of ideas in "The Ideal Democracy."

WHICH *

JAMES THURBER

Whether the following short selection primarily informs, or persuades, or communicates experience is a nice problem. We include it in this section of informative readings because we like it and want to put it somewhere. James Thurber's witty and satiric prose pieces and drawings are well known to readers of *The New Yorker*. His books include *My Life and Hard Times, The Middle-Aged Man on the Flying Trapeze, Let Your Mind Alone, Fables for Our Time,* and *My World—and Welcome to It.* "Which" is a section of "Ladies' and Gentlemen's Guide to English Usage," published

---

* From *Ladies' and Gentlemen's Guide to Modern English Usage* by James Thurber. Reprinted by permission.

in 1929 in *The New Yorker*. The reference to Fowler in the opening sentences is to H. W. Fowler, whose excellent and readable *Dictionary of Modern English Usage* Mr. Thurber is quoting.

[1] The relative pronoun "which" can cause more trouble than any other word, if recklessly used. Foolhardy persons sometimes get lost in which-clauses and are never heard of again. My distinguished contemporary, Fowler, cites several tragic cases, of which the following is one: "It was rumoured that Beaconsfield intended opening the Conference with a speech in French, his pronunciation of which language leaving everything to be desired . . ." That's as much as Mr. Fowler quotes because, at his age, he was afraid to go any farther. The young man who originally got into that sentence was never found. His fate, however, was not as terrible as that of another adventurer who became involved in a remarkable which-mire. Fowler has followed his devious course as far as he safely could on foot: "Surely what applies to games should also apply to racing, the leaders of which being the very people from whom an example might well be looked for . . ." Not even Henry James could have successfully emerged from a sentence with "which," "whom," and "being" in it. The safest way to avoid such things is to follow in the path of the American author, Ernest Hemingway. In his youth he was trapped in a which-clause one time and barely escaped with his mind. He was going along on solid ground until he got into this: "It was the one thing of which, being very much afraid—for whom has not been warned to fear such things—he . . ." Being a young and powerfully built man, Hemingway was able to fight his way back to where he had started, and begin again. This time he skirted the treacherous morass in this way: "He was afraid of one thing. This was the one thing. He had been warned to fear such things. Everybody has been warned to fear such things." Today Hemingway is alive and well, and many happy writers are following along the trail he blazed.

[2] What most people don't realize is that one "which" leads to another. Trying to cross a paragraph by leaping from "which" to "which" is like Eliza crossing the ice. The danger is in missing a "which" and falling in. A case in point is this: "He went up to a pew which was in the gallery, which brought him under a colored window which he loved and always quieted his spirit." The writer, worn out, missed the last "which"—the one that should come just before "always" in that sentence. But supposing he had got it in! We would have: "He went up to a pew which was in the gallery, which brought him under a colored window which he loved and which always

quieted his spirit." Your inveterate whicher in this way gives the effect of tweeting like a bird or walking with a crutch, and is not welcome in the best company.

[3]   It is well to remember that one "which" leads to two and that two "whiches" multiply like rabbits. You should never start out with the idea that you can get by with one "which." Suddenly they are all around you. Take a sentence like this: "It imposes a problem which we either solve, or perish." On a hot night, or after a hard day's work, a man often lets himself get by with a monstrosity like that, but suppose he dictates that sentence bright and early in the morning. It comes to him typed out by his stenographer and he instantly senses that something is the matter with it. He tries to reconstruct the sentence, still clinging to the "which," and gets something like this: "It imposes a problem which we either solve, or which, failing to solve, we must perish on account of." He goes to the watercooler, gets a drink, sharpens his pencil, and grimly tries again. "It imposes a problem which we either solve or which we don't solve and . . ." He begins once more: "It imposes a problem which we either solve, or which we do not solve, and from which . . ." The more times he does it the more "whiches" he gets. The way out is simple: "We must either solve this problem, or perish." Never monkey with "which." Nothing except getting tangled up in a typewriter ribbon is worse.

COMMENT AND QUESTIONS

I. Concrete figurative language is an important part of James Thurber's style. Point out the expressed and implied comparisons used in this selection. What does each one contribute to the total effect and meaning?

II. In paragraph 3 Mr. Thurber shifts to direct address and imperative mood. Is the shift disturbing to the reader? Can it be justified?

III. This essay might be called an analysis of the problem created by "which." What phase of the whole problem is treated in each of the three paragraphs?

IV. What informative advice have you received from this essay?

V. Would you have classified it as Informative Writing, Persuasive Writing, or Communication of Experience?

VI. Revise the following "which-mire":

This article, which comes from "Ladies' and Gentlemen's Guide to English Usage," which was published in 1929, was written by James Thurber, who is a contributor to *The New Yorker* in which magazine appear many of his stories and drawings which depict human beings who are caught in a society which is frustrating.

II. PERSUASIVE WRITING

Persuasive writing, as we are using the term, covers a range of material. It includes the formal logical argument used in debates, in courts of law, and in reflective writing; such argument appeals chiefly to reason. It also includes various kinds of formal and informal inducement which may appeal largely to feeling.

The line between informative writing and persuasive writing is indistinct, for the persuasive writer frequently presents and explains facts. He uses, too, all the informative techniques of organizing and clarifying material: chronological arrangement, definition, analysis, cause-and-effect arrangement, general-to-particular or particular-to-general arrangement, and contrast and comparison. He may use these techniques with a difference: instead of indicating his plan of organization as the informative writer usually does, he may partially conceal it, bringing his reader to a conclusion not by well-marked roads, but in more subtle and devious ways.

The division is indistinct, too, between persuasive writing and our third type of prose, communication of experience. Knowing that people respond to the problems and emotions of other human beings as they cannot respond to impersonal facts, figures, and percentages, the writer interested in persuading often uses individual human experience—real or fictitious—as a means to his end. In some short stories and novels, the author's fundamental purpose is persuasive; communication of experience is simply a method he employs to present ideas which would have less force if they were presented factually.

What distinguishes persuasive writing, in so far as it can be distinguished from other types of prose, is, then, not its content or its form, but its primary intention: it aims to influence opinions, attitudes, and actions; sometimes to change the reader's beliefs, sometimes to confirm or bolster with new data the beliefs he already holds.

The principal methods of persuasion are:

1. Persuasion by logical argument.
2. Persuasion by evaluation.
3. Persuasion by appeal to emotion.
4. Persuasion by irony and ridicule.

Though these methods overlap and are often used in combination, they are best clarified by division and separate discussion.

A. Persuasion by Logical Argument

The formal logical argument usually follows a basic plan of this kind: (1) The writer or speaker states the question clearly and fairly, defining any terms that might be ambiguous, and limiting the argument to the specific issues which he regards as important; he may in this preliminary step of his argument consider the history of the question and its present significance. (2) He states his position and supports that position by citing facts and authorities, and by reasoning from the evidence he presents. (3) He recognizes and refutes any outstanding arguments against his ideas. (4) He summarizes his argument and emphasizes the merits of his position or his proposal. The informal logical argument is likely to include these four steps too, but to follow a more personal, less orderly plan.

The writer of convincing argument must have studied his subject thoroughly. He must know exactly what the major issues are, so that he will not waste words in arguing trivial side issues or points on which there is general agreement. He must have not merely facts and authorities to support his position, but trustworthy, representative, up-to-date facts and reputable authorities. He must know his subject well enough to know more than one side of it. Argument, unlike some other kinds of persuasion, assumes opposition; understanding that opposition, being able to concede its strength on some points, but also to demonstrate its weakness on vital points, may be a large part of successful argumentation. In order to see weaknesses in the opposition, and in order to evaluate his own evidence and to arrive at sound conclusions, the writer needs, in addition to knowledge, skill in logical reasoning.

The reader of argument also needs this skill. If he is a critical reader, he will ask two questions about a piece of argumentative prose: Is the evidence good? Is the reasoning sound? In answering the first question he will be helped immeasurably, of course, if he has read and thought about the subject, if he himself has some command of the facts and some acquaintance with the recognized authorities in the field. But without this knowledge he still can make valid judgments about the evidence on which the writer's conclusions are based. He can see how well the writer's statements are substantiated. Some of them may be unsubstantiated, or practically so: "leading scientists agree," or "as psychologists tell us," or "the facts are well known," or "experiments have proved" is not equivalent to quoting scientists, psychologists, facts, or results of specific experiments. Some statements may have unreliable substantiation because the sources are unauthoritative or prejudiced: "the Podunk *Post-Examiner* of

April 10, 1951, says . . ."; "the last issue of *Popular Reading* contains an article which settles this issue for all time"; "John Smith's authoritative study [written in 1925] says the last word on college football"; "the *Daily Worker* gives an impartial account of the political situation." The reader can also recognize the citing of irrelevant authority—Thomas Jefferson, for example, quoted to support an argument against national health insurance; or a famous chemist quoted on old age pensions, or a prominent businessman on modern art. Persons competent in one field are not necessarily authorities in another. Finally, a reader can make some judgment of the evidence by asking himself how much of it there is, and whether the writer seems to have minimized or ignored evidence on the other side.

unimportant

In answering the second question—Is the reasoning sound?—the reader is aided by a knowledge of formal logic. Frequently, while reading or listening to argument, one has an elusive sense of illogic in the thinking, a feeling of something's-wrong-but-I-can't-put-my-finger-on-it. A knowledge of the two kinds of logical thought called *induction* and *deduction,* and of the common errors in logic, called *fallacies,* makes it easier to detect weaknesses in reasoning and also to recognize and to practice sound reasoning.

1. Induction

Induction is the process of examining a number of particulars or specific instances and on the basis of them arriving at a conclusion. The scientific method is largely inductive: the scientist observes a recurrent phenomenon and arrives at the conclusion or hypothesis that under certain conditions this phenomenon will always take place; if in the course of time further observation supports his hypothesis and if no exceptions are observed, his conclusion is generally accepted as truth and is sometimes called a law. In everyday living, too, we arrive at conclusions by induction. Every cat we encounter has claws; we conclude that all cats have claws. Every rose we smell is fragrant; we conclude that all roses are fragrant. An acquaintance has, on various occasions, paid back money he has borrowed; we conclude that he is frequently out of funds but that he pays his debts. Every Saturday morning for six weeks the new paper boy is late in delivering the paper; we conclude that he sleeps on Saturday mornings and we no longer look for the paper before nine o'clock.

In arriving at an inductive conclusion, it is usually impossible to examine every instance—the claws of every cat, for example, or the nervous system of every cockroach, or every case of diphtheria, or every ruptured appendix, or the opinion of every voter. Many inductions arrive, therefore, not at "truth" or "law" but at probability. The probability is very strong and the induction is sound if these three requirements have been met: (1) if a substantial number of instances have been examined; (2) if these instances are typical; (3) if the exceptions are infrequent and can be explained.

A conclusion based on too few instances or on untypical instances is called a *hasty generalization.* It is the most common fallacy in inductive reasoning, and is responsible for much misinformation and prejudice: "Negroes are lazy." "Why do you say that?" "Well we had a Negro cook who was the laziest mortal I ever saw, and look at Bob Jones—he doesn't even try to get a job." The speaker is, of course, generalizing on the basis of only two examples, assuming that these examples are typical, and ignoring the countless exceptions. The hasty generalization may also occur in scientific research; further research may reveal exceptions which modify or invalidate the earlier conclusion. Recent experimentation with the antihistamines suggests that the claims made in 1949 for these drugs as cold-cures were hasty generalization, the result of insufficient testing.[8]

The kind of induction we have described in the preceding paragraphs may be called *induction from instances,* to distinguish it from two somewhat different types of inductive thinking; these are *induction by analogy* and *cause-effect induction.*

Induction by analogy occurs when one observes that two things are similar in some ways, and then reasons, from the observed likenesses, that they are also similar in other ways. For example, Sir Isaac Newton observed that certain oily combustible substances—oils, turpentine, camphor, etc.—had refractive powers two or three times greater than might be expected from their densities. He reasoned by analogy that the diamond, with its very high refractive powers, was also combustible. This inference was correct.

Reasoning from analogy is dangerous, however, and argument by analogy alone is seldom convincing, because analogous situations or objects have differences as well as similarities and the differences may outweigh the similarities. Sir David Brewster, a nineteenth-century physicist and biographer of Sir Isaac Newton, pointed out that if Newton had reasoned from analogy the combustibility of greenockite and octahedrite, which also have high refractive powers, he would have been wrong. His reasoning about the diamond simply happened to be right. Long observation of Mars has given astronomers a body of data from which (by induction from instances) they have arrived at a number of conclusions about that planet. Some

---

[8] Studies made at Western Reserve, West Point, Cornell, and Minnesota, all indicating that the drugs are not effective remedies for colds, were summarized in *Consumer Reports,* July, 1950.

people have reasoned by analogy that since Mars has atmosphere, temperatures, and seasonal changes comparable to earth's, it must also have life comparable to ours. This conclusion stretches the analogy and disregards the observed differences between the two planets.

Analogy is not logical proof. In informative writing it is, as we have said earlier, a useful method of clarifying a difficult subject. Skillful analogy also has great persuasive power. But it should be used in conjunction with, not as a substitute for, more strictly logical reasoning; and it is effective only when the similarities are striking and the differences slight between the things being compared. The following induction by analogy is weak because the comparison is far-fetched and the differences are glaring:

Even the most durable machines break down if they are worked constantly for long periods of time. Their parts wear out; they become inefficient. Are students supposed to be stronger than machines? Do they deserve less attention and care? We should have shorter assignments and longer vacations.

The following famous passage illustrates effective analogy. The comparison is used not to prove, but to describe and to persuade:

In the field of world policy I would dedicate this Nation to the policy of the good neighbor—the neighbor who resolutely respects himself and because he does so, respects the rights of others—the neighbor who respects his obligations and respects the sanctity of his agreements in and with a world of neighbors.—FRANKLIN D. ROOSEVELT, *First Inaugural Address*

A third type of inductive thinking, *cause-effect induction,* is the process by which we observe effects and arrive at a conclusion about their cause; or we observe a set of circumstances (causes) and draw a conclusion about their effects; or we observe some effects and reason from them that there will be other effects. A doctor examines a patient, learns his symptoms, and from the data makes a diagnosis; he has started with the effects of the illness and reasoned to the cause of them. In cause-to-effect thinking the process is reversed because we can see the causes and, usually with the help of past inductions, can predict the effects. A student visits football practice two days before the opening game; he observes that two players are fighting on the field, that the captain and the coach are on bad terms, that the team's best passer is on the bench with a broken arm, and that the backfield is slow; seeing these causes, he predicts that this will not be a good team. Effect-to-effect thinking is chain reasoning which also usually relies on past inductions: "That little accident [cause] smashed the right front fender [observed effect]; Father will be angry and will make me pay for a new fender [further effect reasoned on the basis of past instances]; I won't be able to take Jane to the prom [ultimate effect]."

A great deal of scientific investigation deals with causal relationships; that is, with observing and describing those orderly connections between elements and events in the universe, on the basis of which causes can be assigned and effects predicted with accuracy. In our daily thinking, too, we make numerous cause-effect inductions, many of which, however, lack scientific exactitude; they need to be verified before they can be held as logical conclusions. The following effect-to-cause inductions are fairly typical of the kind of reasoning we hear and perhaps do every day. During a storm, the back door slams with such force that the glass breaks; we assume that the wind blew the door. A friend is obviously depressed on the day grades come out; we say that he is badly disappointed in his grades. An engagement is broken a month after the engaged girl's family loses its money; we conclude that the engagement was broken for that reason. . . . All these inductions need further verification, for the cause in each case may well be different from the one assigned: the door may have been slammed by a member of the family who is happy to have the storm blamed for it; the friend may be depressed and the engagement may have been broken for any number of reasons.

These examples illustrate two common fallacies in cause-effect induction. The first fallacy is oversimplifying, and attributing to a single cause effects which actually have complex causes. "I failed the course because the teacher was unreasonably hard" is sometimes an example of this oversimplification. Other familiar examples are: "The atomic bomb won World War II"; "The Hoover administration was responsible for the depression"; "The reason for the high cost of living is the high wages paid to labor."

Often closely related to oversimplification of the cause is the logical fallacy of seeing a cause-effect relationship between events which have only an accidental time relationship. This fallacy is called *post hoc ergo propter hoc,* Latin for "after that therefore because of that." A common instance of this reasoning is a statement like "I won't vote for the Democrats again. Six months after they got into office the city taxes went up two dollars." It is possible, of course, that the Democrats were responsible for the tax increase; but it is also possible that any administration would have found higher taxes necessary. Asserting without proof a cause-effect relationship simply because one event follows another is as illogical as asserting that breakfast causes lunch. Many superstitions are maintained by this *post hoc ergo propter hoc* thinking. A superstitious person walks under a ladder, and an hour later, for reasons entirely unrelated to that incident, has a quarrel with a good friend; he forgets or ignores the real causes of the quarrel, falls into the logical confusion of after-I-walked-under-the-ladder-therefore-because-I-walked-under-the-ladder, and is confirmed in his original faulty induction that walking under ladders brings bad luck.

2. Deduction

Deduction is the process of reasoning from a general principle to a particular case. The principle has been arrived at by induction, and the particular case is one which is covered by the principle. For example, human experience has established the universally accepted induction that all men must sometime die. We can, therefore, logically reason that a particular man will also die. This reasoning is deduction.

In formal logic, a deductive argument is expressed in a pattern called the *syllogism*. The syllogism has three parts: a major premise which states the principle; a minor premise which states the particular case covered by the principle; and a conclusion which follows logically from the two premises:

MAJOR PREMISE: All men must die
MINOR PREMISE: John is a man
CONCLUSION: Therefore John must die

Diagraming the syllogism often makes the relationship of statements clearer:

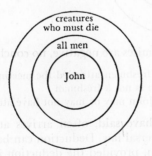

If all men are included in the larger circle of those who must die (major premise), and if John is included in the circle of all men (minor premise), then John is inevitably included in the circle of those who must die (conclusion).

A syllogism may also contain negative statements:

MAJOR PREMISE: No freshmen attended the meeting
MINOR PREMISE: John is a freshman
CONCLUSION: Therefore John did not attend the meeting

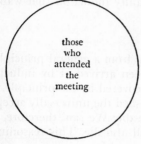 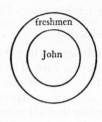

[*Or*]:

MAJOR PREMISE: Only freshmen attended the meeting
MINOR PREMISE: John is not a freshman
CONCLUSION: Therefore John did not attend the meeting

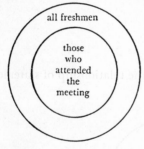

If, however, both premises are negative, no conclusion can be drawn:

MAJOR PREMISE: No freshmen attended the meeting
MINOR PREMISE: John is not a freshman
CONCLUSION: None (John may or may not have attended the meeting)

Induction, as we have said, often arrives at probability rather than at truth or universal law. Deduction can be certain; its conclusions can be relied on, provided the deduction is logical. Logicality here involves four factors: (1) the major premise must be accurate; (2) the minor premise must be accurate; (3) the relationship between the two premises must be logically correct; (4) the conclusion must follow inevitably from the premises. Faulty deduction occurs, therefore, (1) when the major premise is inaccurate; (2) when the minor premise is inaccurate; (3) when the relationship between the premises is ambiguous or illogical; (4) when the conclusion is a *non-sequitur* (Latin for "it does not follow").

a. Errors in the major premise

Although theoretically certain, deduction in practice often arrives at probable rather than at absolute truth because so many major premises express only probability. When the major premise is not even a statement of probable truth, the conclusion drawn from it is wholly untrustworthy. The conclusions of the following syllogisms are not reliable because the major premise in each case is a hasty, or unsound, generalization:

MAJOR PREMISE: All Irishmen have a sense of humor
MINOR PREMISE: He is Irish
CONCLUSION: Therefore he has a sense of humor

MAJOR PREMISE: College teachers are unsympathetic with students
MINOR PREMISE: He is a college teacher
CONCLUSION: Therefore he is unsympathetic with students

A form of hasty generalization frequently encountered in argument is the either-or major premise which fallaciously excludes all but two alternatives:

College students either get good grades or have a good time
Bill gets good grades
Therefore Bill does not have a good time

The conclusion may or may not be true; it is not logically valid because the major premise has excluded several possibilities, notably the possibility that one may get good grades and also have a good time.

b. Errors in the minor premise

Errors in the minor premise are usually the result of misinformation. The conclusions in the following syllogisms are invalid because the minor premise in each case is a misstatement of fact:

Poisonous snakes should be killed
Garter snakes are poisonous
Therefore garter snakes should be killed

Political parties which advocate the overthrow of our government by force should be suppressed
The Socialist Party advocates the overthrow of our government by force
Therefore it should be suppressed

c. Errors in relationship of the premises

Faulty relationship between the two premises is sometimes difficult to detect; for this reason it may produce a slippery illogic in
the reasoning. If the relationship between the premises is logically
correct, the subject of the major premise is the predicate of the minor
premise: *All X is Y; all Z is X; therefore Z is Y.* Also, there are three
terms (*X, Y, Z*) and only three used in the syllogism. The following
reasoning is faulty because the predicate of the minor premise is the
predicate (instead of the subject) of the major premise:

> All tigers are felines (*X is Y*)
> My cat is a feline (*Z is Y*)
> Therefore my cat is a tiger (∴ *Z is X*)

The illogic here is made apparent by the absurdity of the conclusion; but it may not be so apparent in a similarly constructed syllogism:

> All communists say Russia doesn't want war
> He says Russia doesn't want war
> Therefore he is a communist

Diagraming such arguments is a good way of seeing why the conclusion is invalid:

My cat and *he* are in the large circles of *felines* and *those who say
Russia doesn't want war,* but not necessarily in the smaller circles
of *tigers* and *communists.*

Another illogical relationship occurs when the meaning of terms
is shifted between the major premise and the minor premise. The
shifted meaning is equivalent to a fourth term in the syllogism. For
example:

Man is the only creature capable of reason
Mary is not a man
Therefore Mary is incapable of reason

The meaning of *man* has been shifted from *mankind* in the major premise to *male* in the minor premise. Other examples of shifted meanings are:

Men who have devoted themselves to the service of the community should hold public office
I have devoted myself to the service of the community by running a bakery for fifteen years
Therefore I should hold public office

Government employees who are sympathetic with Russian policy should be discharged
This government employee belonged in 1943 to an organization which was friendly toward Russia
Therefore he should be discharged

d. Errors in the conclusion

If the premises of a deduction are true and their relationship is correct, a valid conclusion is logically inescapable. A *non-sequitur* (it does not follow) is a leap to a conclusion not warranted by the premises. The *non-sequitur* is a common fallacy, especially in informal argument:

Anyone who works hard deserves a vacation now and then
I have worked hard
Therefore my parents should give me a trip to Bermuda

Men who have made sacrifices for their country should be honored
I have made sacrifices for my country
Therefore I should be President

We seldom encounter the complete syllogism except in discussions of logic and in very formal argument. More usual is a reduced form of the syllogism in which one or two of the three parts, though implied, are not stated. The reduced syllogism is called an *enthymeme*. Sometimes in the enthymeme the conclusion of the syllogism is omitted because it is obvious: *Students who are found cheating on examinations fail the course; Clarence has been found cheating on an examination;* [the obvious omitted conclusion: therefore Clarence will fail the course]. Sometimes the minor premise is omitted for the same reason: *I like candidates who speak their minds;* [omitted premise: you speak your mind]; *I'm going to vote for you.* Sometimes both the minor premise and the conclusion are omitted because the major premise adequately communicates them: *I don't have dates with men who don't have cars;* [omitted: you don't have a car; therefore I won't have a date with you]. Most frequently the major premise is omitted because the communicator assumes (often wrongly) that it is universally accepted and so does not require proof or even statement. One of the most useful skills of the receiver of argument, therefore, is the ability to supply the omitted major premise. By recognizing that premise and examining it critically, he can better judge the fallacy or the validity of the argument. The enthymemes below are familiar informal arguments; the major premise on which each one is based is put in brackets.

Jim must have been in a fight; he has a black eye. [Major premise: All black eyes are the result of fights.]

So he forgot he made the appointment. What can you expect? He's a college professor. [Major premise: College professors usually forget appointments. Or, College professors are absent-minded.]

He must be a grind! He got all A's last semester. [Students who get A records are grinds.]

He can't be a good doctor. He's in favor of socialized medicine. [No good doctor is in favor of socialized medicine.]

You're crazy, saying the meat tastes spoiled. I got it at the store just an hour ago. [Meat is always fresh when it is bought at stores.]

What a coward. He's a conscientious objector, you know. [All conscientious objectors are cowards.]

Naturally he's a delinquent. He reads ten comic books a week. [Reading comics always produces delinquency.]

Of course it's true; I read it in the paper. [Everything printed in the newspapers is true.]

They won't be happy together; he's two years younger than she. [Marriages are always unhappy if the man is younger than the woman.]

I think they'll be very nice neighbors. They have a new Cadillac. [People are nice neighbors if they have a new Cadillac.]

We're not talking about the same girl. The one I knew last summer had blond hair. [Once a blonde always a blonde.]

His mother has trained him to be neat around the house; he'll make a wonderful husband. [Any man who is neat around the house is a wonderful husband; also, a man trained by his mother to be neat around the house will continue to be neat when he is married.]

Although we have separated induction and deduction for purposes of discussion, the two mental processes work together in most acts of reasoning. A simple illustration of the interplay between them is this: A friend asks you one afternoon to go with him to a movie at the neighborhood theatre. You say, "No; it's Saturday." Behind your refusal lies an induction, based on instances in your own experience, that on Saturday afternoons many school children attend this theatre and are very noisy. You make a quick deduction: Every Saturday afternoon this theatre is full of noisy school children; this is Saturday; therefore the theatre will be full of noisy school children. Another inductive-deductive process also takes place. You have arrived at the generalization that you do not enjoy a movie if you cannot hear all of it. You reason: I do not want to go to a movie if I cannot hear all of it; I will not be able to hear all of it today (because of the noise of the children); therefore I do not want to go to this movie on this day. Still another reasoning process about your relationship with the friend who has asked you to go to the movie may occur. From your past experience with him you may have induced: Jack is not offended if for some good reason I refuse his invitations. Now you may deduce: I am refusing this invitation for a good reason; therefore Jack will not be offended. In this kind of thinking, the inductions and deductions are almost automatic. In more complex reasoning they are formulated only after conscious and disciplined thought.

We have discussed in the preceding pages a number of errors and weaknesses in reasoning: hasty generalization, faulty analogy, over-simplification of complex causes, *post hoc ergo propter hoc* argument, and fallacies in deduction, including shifting the meaning of terms and *non-sequitur*. Two other logical fallacies, not peculiar to induction or to deduction, but involving the quality of the whole argument, are _begging the question_ and _ignoring the question_.

Begging the question is assuming, without proof, the truth of a proposition which actually needs proof. If an arguer says, "This senseless language requirement should be abolished," he is, with the word *senseless*, begging the question; the question is whether or not the language requirement is senseless; if it is, it should of course be abolished; simply calling it senseless is not a logical argument in its disfavor. "This corrupt political machine should be replaced by good government" is another example of begging the question. No proof is offered that the government under attack is a "corrupt political machine," or that the government supported by the speaker will be "good." Both propositions are simply assumed. *Arguing in a circle* is one form of begging the question:

People who are poor lack ambition because if they didn't lack ambition they wouldn't be poor.

> The study of literature is worthwhile because literature is a worthwhile subject.

Such argument in a circle is sometimes baffling, particularly when the argument is long and the circular motion is therefore difficult to detect. What the arguer in a circle does, technically, is offer as proof of his first proposition a second proposition which can be proved only by proving the first.

Ignoring the question is diverting attention from the real issues, or shifting the argument to some other ground. It has many forms. Name-calling, introducing irrelevant facts, and using other devices of charged language may be means of ignoring the real question. Sometimes a new argument is introduced in an effort to obscure the original issue: "I told you, Dorothy, I can't afford to buy you a coat this winter." "I don't see why not. Susan Jones has a new coat. I should think you'd want me to be well dressed. It's a good thing someone in this family takes some pride in appearance. You haven't even shaved today." Arguing that an accused murderess should be acquitted because she is the mother of three children, and that a candidate should be mayor because he is the veteran of two wars are examples of ignoring the question by shifting from the central issues; the questions here are "Did she commit the murder?" and "Will he make a good mayor?" What is called argument *ad hominem* (to the man) is a way of ignoring the question by a shift from reasonable consideration of a measure to an attack on the character of the opponent; his ancestry, his religion, the fact that his first wife divorced him, that his son was arrested for speeding, etc. may be introduced to appeal to prejudice while the real question—the merits and defects of the measure itself—is ignored.

In summary, success in logical argument requires thorough knowledge of the subject and skill in logical reasoning. The critical reading of logical argument requires judgment, and some knowledge of logical processes and of the common logical fallacies. Being alert to hasty generalization, to faulty cause-effect reasoning, to conclusions which do not follow the premises, to question-begging, and to ignoring of the question will help the reader judge the soundness of the argument.

Tone—the attitude of the communicator toward himself and toward his audience—is very important in any kind of persuasion. In persuasion by logical argument, the writer may be formal or informal in his attitude toward his audience; but he is usually less concerned with getting their liking than with winning their respect. For this respect, he depends largely on the quality of the argument itself. If he presents the issues fairly; if he is reasonable in considering opposing points of view; if his evidence is good and his thinking clear and sound; if he respects the intelligence of his audience and assumes that they will not be convinced by slippery logic and devices like arguments *ad hominem,* he will almost certainly gain a respectful hearing for what he has to say.

As a rule, the most skillful argument is reasonable in tone as well as in thought; it gives the impression of trying to arrive at truth, not merely to win a case; it is good tempered, and free from dogmatism and conceit. Fighting-mad arguments and dogmatic statements do sometimes affect already-sympathetic or prejudiced audiences; but they are likely to alienate and offend an impartial audience. Benjamin Franklin, wise in argument and diplomacy, wrote in his autobiography:

I made it a rule to forbear all direct contradiction to the sentiments of others, and all positive assertion of my own. I even forbade myself . . . the use of every word or expression in the language that imported a fix'd opinion, such as *certainly, undoubtedly,* etc., and I adopted, instead of them, *I conceive, I apprehend,* or *I imagine* a thing to be so or so; or it *so appears to me at present.* When another asserted something that I thought an error, I deny'd myself the pleasure of contradicting him abruptly, and of showing immediately some absurdity in his proposition; and in answering I began by observing that in certain cases or circumstances his opinion would be right, but in the present case there *appear'd* or *seem'd* to me some difference, etc. I soon found the advantage of this change in my manner; the conversations I engag'd in went on more pleasantly. The modest way in which I propos'd my opinions procur'd them a readier reception and less contradiction; I had less mortification when I was found to be in the wrong, and I more easily prevail'd with others to give up their mistakes and join with me when I happened to be in the right.

And this mode, which I at first put on with some violence to natural inclination, became at length so easy, and so habitual to me, that perhaps for these fifty years past no one has ever heard a dogmatical expression escape me. And to this habit (after my character of integrity) I think it principally owing that I had early so much weight with my fellow-citizens when I proposed new institutions, or alterations in the old, and so much influence in public councils when I became a member; for I was but a bad speaker, never eloquent, subject to much hesitation in my choice of words, hardly correct in language, and yet I generally carried my points.

B. Persuasion by Evaluation

Persuasion by evaluation is found in reviews of books, movies, plays, etc.; in newspaper editorials; in commentaries on current affairs; and in critical books and articles of many kinds. The writer makes a judgment of a work or a situation, and asks his readers to accept that judgment. He may, in an evaluation of some length, supply a mass of evidence to support his opinion and may refer to or criticize the opinions of others; in such cases, persuasion by evaluation and persuasion by logical argument are the same thing. In short articles, however, the writer usually cites only a few instances to support or explain his evaluation; a book reviewer, for example, may quote a passage or two and refer to several specific instances of questionable fact or of careful scholarship in the book. Very short book reviews, because of limitations of space, may give no evidence to support the writer's evaluation. And certain newspaper columnists, sometimes for reasons other than limitations of space, fail to supply facts on which their judgment is presumably founded.

The reader, even though he is critical and not easily persuaded, has real problems in judging persuasive evaluation which gives little or no factual evidence to support the writer's conclusions. The best guide is probably the author's record and reputation: Is he a recognized authority? Have his training and experience equipped him to make sound judgments in this field? Does he have prejudices which influence his evaluations? Have his past evaluations been sound? The reputation of the newspaper or magazine in which an article appears may further help one judge the trustworthiness of the evaluation. Nearly every publication has a consistent slant on some matters and is, therefore, not completely impartial in selecting the material it prints.[9]

Familiarity with other opinions on the same subject is also useful to the reader. *The Book Review Digest* gives excerpts from various reviews of the same book. The reviews are often contradictory in their judgments; but the reader learns at least that one judgment is not necessarily the truth about the book, and the weight of critical opinion may support or may cause doubt about the opinion expressed in a particular review which he is trying to appraise. Reading several of the reviews quoted in the *Digest* (and preferably reading the book itself), and reading newspapers, magazines, and columnists with different slants will help one judge other people's evaluations.

Finally, the reader can ask himself whether or not the writer seems to be fair, and whether or not he is giving as much factual support of his judgment as space allows. If he is filling space with name-calling and appeals to emotion instead of with evidence, the reader is justified in questioning his integrity and therefore his evaluation.

The honest writer of evaluation does well to keep in mind the standards of the critical reader. In contemporary society, the writer has many unworthy models—victims of their own hysteria and prej-

[9] What is said here of columnists, newspapers, and magazines is equally true, of course, of radio and television programs.

udice, or hired propagators of the interests and prejudices of others —who are successful with prejudiced readers. Their disregard of fact, their emotional misstatements, their unfounded judgments are accepted, sometimes admired, and at least forgiven by their followers. By unbiased readers, such writers are condemned. The writer of evaluation has, however, good models too: those critics who, with a background of knowledge, give their considered judgment of a book, a play, an art exhibit, a concert; those columnists who study a situation, report the facts, weigh the evidence, and state their opinions; those statesmen who analyze a policy, and recommend or denounce it. The soundest evaluation is informative and logical. The honest writer should appeal to the reason, not merely the feeling, of his audience by giving as fully as possible the basis of his critical judgment.

C. Persuasion by Appeal to Emotion

We have discussed methods of persuasion by appeal to emotion so fully in the first two chapters of this book that it will be necessary here only to mention again the most commonly used techniques. They are: the introduction of irrelevant facts which arouse emotion; the use of charged words of personal attitude, charged words of race and nationality, name-calling, charged proper names, charged comparisons, charged questions, charged abstract words and other charged expressions; the statement of opinion as if it were fact; the use of innuendo, irony, and ridicule; the right-on-our-side technique.

In the earlier discussion of these persuasive devices we have emphasized, and perhaps overemphasized, their conscious, crafty, and even dishonest use. Some of the most moving human utterances, however, are not calculated appeals to emotion, but sincere expressions of feeling, from the heart to the heart. Such honest expression of emotion, accompanied by logical argument or solid evaluation, may be worthy of the highest respect.

Tone is particularly important in writing which persuades wholly or partly by appeal to emotion. The writer nearly always makes an effort to establish friendly relations with his readers, and to emphasize attitudes and loyalties which he shares with them. As a result, it is sometimes difficult to judge whether the writer is sincere or merely sounds sincere. The tireless interest of some radio announcers in the problems of the listener, and their enthusiasm for the products they advertise is, for example, convincing to many in their audience. Appraising the communicator's whole record, as well as the plain sense of the immediate communication, is useful in judging him. One may ask whether this feeling of enthusiasm, or admiration, or distaste is one which he has consistently expressed for his present subject, and whether he produces the same feeling for various subjects. If he does the latter, his sincerity is questionable.

Two elements of style, rhythm and repetition, are also of special importance in persuasion which appeals to emotion. The sound and rhythm of sentences and the movement of a whole piece of prose may in themselves convey and inspire feeling. Controlled repetition of key words and phrases often has cumulative emotional force. The reader, and particularly the writer of language which evokes feeling, should study these two elements of style. We have quoted earlier in this section Franklin D. Roosevelt's enunciation of the "good neighbor policy." Let us look at it again, not this time for its use of persuasive analogy, but for the added force the analogy gains from sentence rhythm and the repetition of significant words. The following passage strips the statement to its plain-sense meaning without regard for style:

In the field of world policy I would dedicate this Nation to the policy of the good neighbor. He resolutely respects himself and, therefore, the rights of others, his obligations in the world, and the sanctity of his agreements with other people.

Compare the original statement:

In the field of world policy I would dedicate this Nation to the policy of the good neighbor—the neighbor who resolutely respects himself and because he does so, respects the rights of others—the neighbor who respects his obligations and respects the sanctity of his agreements in and with a world of neighbors.

D. Persuasion by Irony and Ridicule

Irony and ridicule are methods of persuading by making attitudes opposed to those of the writer seem undesirable or absurd. They may be used, as we have pointed out earlier, to appeal to emotion. They may also be used to appeal, through wit, to intelligence. Irony and ridicule are not the same; it is possible to be ironical without ridiculing, and to ridicule without irony; but the two devices are often blended in persuasive writing.

Ridicule may be simply defined as mockery, intended to produce contemptuous laughter at the subject. *Irony,* however, is a complex term and idea. The word is derived from the Greek *eironeia,* meaning dissimulation or understatement. *Verbal irony* now is a figure of speech in which the real meaning is different from, sometimes the opposite of, the apparent or literal meaning. Examples of verbal irony are "A delightful examination, wasn't it?" and "We had a lovely time; it didn't matter a bit that he sent me pink roses for my orange dress and walked me six blocks to the dance in the rain." By an extension of meaning, *fictional irony* (sometimes called *dramatic irony* or *tragic irony*) occurs when a character in fiction or drama says, sees, or does something, the real significance of which is understood by the audience but not by the character himself. Another kind of fictional irony (the *irony of fate*) is produced by an unexpected turn of events or an outcome different from the one anticipated; for example, a woman labors for ten years to pay for a diamond necklace which she bought to replace one she borrowed and lost, only to find at the end of the story that the necklace she borrowed was paste.[10]

These different types of irony have in common the element of contrast—between what is said and what is meant, between what is not understood and what is realized, between what is expected and what occurs; contrast, in short, between what things seem to be and what they actually are. A reader must be able to perceive the contrast in order to appreciate or even understand irony. Irony therefore demands intellectual activity on the part of the reader.

Recognizing verbal irony in speech is usually easy, because the speaker's facial expression and tone of voice belie the literal meaning of his words. Verbal irony in writing is harder to recognize; the reader may take literally a passage written ironically unless he is alert to possible contrast between the writer's words and his intention. The reader of irony is likely to move, rapidly, through three mental steps: (1) it's strange that a serious and respectable writer should mean this; (2) this is too much; he can't possibly mean it; (3) of course he doesn't mean it; he's being ironical. For example, Jonathan Swift's *A Modest Proposal*, written in the eighteenth century to satirize the callous attitude of the English toward poverty-stricken Ireland, suggests with apparent seriousness that Irish children be sold for food to wealthy English families. The introduction of the proposal is misleading to an unsuspecting reader; Swift hopes to serve the nation, he says, by offering a "fair, cheap, and easy method" of making the numerous, ragged, burdensome Irish children "sound, useful members of the Commonwealth." As he goes on, the reader is quickly jolted from *this is strange* to *he can't possibly mean it* by the contrast between normal, humane attitudes and a statement like this:

I have been assured by a very knowing American of my acquaintance in London that a young healthy child, well nursed, is, at a year old, a most delicious, nourishing, and wholesome food, whether stewed, roasted, baked, or boiled; and I make no doubt that it will equally serve in a fricassee or a ragout.

[10] "The Necklace," by Guy de Maupassant.

The next paragraph, with its outrageous detail, can hardly leave in doubt the ironical intention of the treatise:

I do therefore humbly offer it to public consideration, that of the hundred and twenty thousand children already computed, twenty thousand may be reserved for breed; . . . that the remaining hundred thousand may, at a year old, be offered in sale to the persons of quality and fortune through the kingdom, always advising the mother to let them suck plentifully in the last month, so as to render them plump and fat for a good table. A child will make two dishes at an entertainment for friends, and when the family dines alone, the fore or hind quarter will make a reasonable dish, and seasoned with a little pepper or salt will be very good boiled on the fourth day, especially in winter.

Irony is sometimes, as in Swift's *A Modest Proposal,* harsh and biting; this heavy irony is very close to sarcasm, and frequently ridicules the situation or subject it is criticizing. Often, though, irony is light and good humored; such light irony, which may or may not be accompanied by ridicule, is a common form of wit. Ironical writing is, therefore, often humorous; and humor, skillfully and appropriately used, is itself a means of persuasion. The reader laughs with the communicator at something else.

In general, the distinction between irony and sarcasm is that sarcasm is personal and bitter. Irony, even heavy irony, is apparently less bitter because it is impersonal. The writer seems to be detached, self-possessed, judicious, not emotionally involved in the subject he is discussing. Because irony requires a perception of basic contrasts, and because it usually gives an impression of calm restraint, it is particularly effective with an intelligent audience. Such an audience is receptive to persuasion by a writer whose wit, intelligence, and apparent objectivity they enjoy and admire.

Successful persuasion by irony and ridicule is not easy to write. Nor is it easy to give instructions about writing a kind of prose which has so many forms and which requires a particular cast of mind: some people readily perceive the incongruous, the ridiculous, the contrasting elements in a situation, while others do not. It is possible, though, to point out three common weaknesses in the attempts at persuasive irony and ridicule of inexperienced writers. The first is the weakness of inappropriate or misdirected humor. Flippant comments thrown into a serious discussion, ridicule used to avoid the trouble of critical evaluation, and supposedly humorous gibes at an object worthy of understanding or sympathy are not persuasive; they raise questions about the writer's taste and judgment. A second weakness is produced by a lack of detachment and objectivity. When a writer shows a strong personal bias or an intrusive personal hatred toward a subject which he is trying to criticize by irony and ridicule, the reader is likely to shift in attention from the subject to the author, and to wonder what makes him so fanatical or bitter or vituperative; what, in short, is the matter with him. Such a shift is, of course, not persuasive in its effect. A third common weakness comes from the writer's fear that his readers will miss the point. He labors and verbally underlines his attempts at irony ("I love this course, the way I love spinach and cod-liver oil, if you know what I mean") to a point of distraction and irritation for an intelligent audience. The writer of persuasive irony and ridicule should have confidence in his readers; he should give them the pleasure of personal discovery and appreciation of the intended meaning.

The readings in the following pages have been arranged to illustrate, in order, persuasion by logical argument, persuasion by evaluation, persuasion by appeal to emotion, and persuasion by irony and ridicule. Most of them also illustrate a blending and combining of these four methods of persuasion.

PRESENT AND FUTURE *

WILLIAM MAXWELL AITKIN, LORD BEAVERBROOK

The following memorandum on the opening of a second front in World War II is an example of persuasion by logical argument. In June, 1943, Lord Beaverbrook handed this memorandum to Harry Hopkins, personal representative of President Franklin D. Roosevelt. Lord Beaverbrook—financier, member of Parliament, newspaper publisher; after 1940, Minister of Aircraft Production and member of Churchill's war cabinet; later, Minister of Supply and British lend-lease administrator in the United States—has played an active part in British public life in peace and in war. In "Present and Future" he is giving an analysis of a situation, is discussing certain alternative courses of action, and is forcefully presenting a case for establishing a second front by an attack through the Dardanelles or a landing in Northern France.

[1]   It was a year ago that the Prime Minister came to Washington to make the plans which have now culminated in the fall of all North Africa.

* From *Roosevelt and Hopkins* by Robert E. Sherwood. Copyright, 1948, Robert E. Sherwood. Published by Harper & Brothers.

[2]　The dominant question then was whether to launch a Second Front. The decision, taken against the sombre background of defeat in Libya and impending retreat in Russia, was that the project was too ambitious, and that a lesser objective should be chosen—the clearance of the southern shore of the Mediterranean. Such a plan involved gambling on Russia's ability to stand, *for one more campaign,* on her own. In the event, Russia did hold fast, and North Africa succeeded. These two achievements have meant, for the British and Americans, that the spectre of defeat has been almost entirely banished.

[3]　It is against a new background of established confidence that fresh decisions have now to be taken. The odds have moved heavily in favour of the Allies—the wasting assets of the Luftwaffe, the damage to German industry from the air, the strain on German manpower, the development of American strength, the Russian offensive successes, the opening of the Mediterranean—cumulatively these advantages are impressive.

[4]　But for all that, in the West and in the East, the game is still "all to play for." The Russians are only back where they were this time last year. The Anglo-Americans are nowhere on the mainland of Europe.

[5]　This year, as last, the dominant question is the Second Front. For this reason: that so long as it is unattempted, there remains for Germany not only the chance, albeit an outside one, to knock out or mortally wound the Russian armies, but also time to prepare the defences of "Festung Europa."

[6]　Can *we* afford more time for preparation? The Germans have a most powerful army in the East. The Russians used up men and resources at a heavy rate last winter in an offensive which stopped short of its fullest aims. There is always the risk that Japan will stab in the back. It cannot be said that Moscow, Baku or Leningrad are out of danger. It can still less be said that we and the Americans could in any measurable space of time win without Russian assistance.

[7]　Can the Germans ignore the threat of a Second Front? They can and certainly will. To do otherwise would be to allow the initiative to slip finally from their grasp. They are likely to go even further. They will ignore or treat lightly any blow from the West which is not delivered against a vital point. Knowing that the primary object of a Second Front would be to divert troops from the East they will go to almost any lengths to prevent that occurring.

[8]　Add to these factors the change in the Anglo-American situation in the last year. Then there were strong grounds for saying that a

Second Front would be nothing but a forlorn hope involving the risk of final disaster, and there was much truth in the contention that in a year we should be vastly stronger. Today, of the three major United Nations, we and the Russians are as strong as we shall ever be. Certainly American potential is still developing, and in a year's time the United States will be more powerfully armed. But can we afford the new delay? Even suppose that Germany leaves Russia alone, will she, given a "year of calm" in which to organize for defence, grow much weaker? Can bombing alone make all the difference? We have the weapons now, and the men, and the Germans are uncertain of themselves, their calculations seriously upset. None of these facts can guarantee success for the launching of a major Second Front. They do go far to insuring that its failure will not spell disaster.

[9]   Surely the inference is inescapable that the question today must be not whether but where to launch the Second Front. The preliminaries are over, brilliantly performed. If they do not prove to have been the curtain raiser, the conclusion will be hard to escape, in occupied Europe especially, that the main play is never destined for performance.

[10]   But the "where" of the Second Front is all-important. To be more than a diversion the attack must come at a spot where success will bring an immediate *mortal* threat to the enemy. The Second Front can, if it is a real one, apparently fail and yet succeed. It can, if it is only a diversion, apparently succeed and yet in reality fail.

[11]   The invasion of Italy? It might prove a major psychological blow at the enemy, but it could not guarantee decisive results. It could be parried by redrawing the southern boundary of the Fortress of Europe at the Alps and Dolomites, fighting a delaying action meanwhile.

[12]   The invasion of Northern Norway? It would mean a link-up with the Russians, but again the decisive threat to Europe would be lacking.

[13]   A landing in Southern Greece? The passes northwards to the Balkans and the Danube valley could be held by small forces.

[14]   When any of these objectives had been achieved, the game, so far as the core of German Europe was the goal (and there can be no other) would be still "all to play for."

[15]   But two places of attack promise immediate results. A descent, through the Dardanelles, with Turkish connivance or assistance, on the Eastern Balkans, would lay open the whole Danubian plain and jeopardize all the German forces in southern Russia. A landing in Northern France would point straight at Paris, at the Ruhr and at

the Rhine. If either plan succeeded the enemy would be exposed to an intolerable strain before he had time to conserve, perfect and organize his defences.

[16]   There are factors, such as the exact shipping position, relative to the Second Front, which may be unknown to the layman. There are two factors which the military will ignore at our peril. One is the danger to Russia, the other the danger of stalemate. There seems a real danger that we shall go on indefinitely sewing the last button on the last gaiter, and the risk is increased by the undoubted fact that a real Second Front will always entail big risks, always remain the most difficult operation in military warfare. But if we are not prepared to accept the risks, face the difficulties, suffer the casualties, then let us concentrate at once exclusively on the production of heavy bombers and think in terms of 1950.

COMMENT AND QUESTIONS

This memorandum is distinctive for its clarity, economy, and force of expression, and for its use of cold analysis in stating a problem, in considering and rejecting alternatives, and in proposing a course of action. Lord Beaverbrook's argument has four parts: (1) reasons for establishing a second front *now;* (2) reasons for rejecting Italy, Norway, and Greece as possible second fronts; (3) reasons for a descent through the Dardanelles or a landing in Northern France; and (4) restatement and emphatic conclusion.

I. Where does each of these parts end, and by what reasoning is each developed?

II. Although broken into a number of short paragraphs, this memorandum has an exceptionally coherent development. What devices of transition are most noticeable? Where is a summary statement used between main points?

III. What in general appears to be Lord Beaverbrook's attitude toward Russia, and what evidences of this attitude can you point to in the actual language of the memorandum?

IV. What is the relevance of paragraph 4 in the development of the whole argument?

V. Explain what Beaverbrook means in paragraph 10 when he makes the statement: "The Second Front can, if it is a real one, apparently fail and yet succeed." What does he mean by a *real* second front, and how do you know?

VI. Comment fully on the meaning and the implication of the last sentence of the memorandum, especially of the last few words: "and think in terms of 1950." (Remember that the memorandum was

written in 1943 and that Lord Beaverbrook had been Minister of
Aircraft Production.)

ON THE LIBERTY OF THOUGHT
AND DISCUSSION

JOHN STUART MILL

*The following selection is a sustained logical argument in favor of
freedom of thought and opinion. Although most students will need to spend
at least three hours on the essay in order to follow the close reasoning and
understand the clear but very complex structure of the argument, the time
will be well spent. John Stuart Mill (1806–1873) was an English writer,
economist, and logician who has been called "the saint of rationalism."
"On the Liberty of Thought and Discussion" is Chapter Two of his famous
essay* On Liberty, *published in 1859.*

[1]   The time, it is to be hoped, is gone by, when any defence would
be necessary of the "liberty of the press" as one of the securities against
corrupt or tyrannical government. No argument, we may suppose,
can now be needed, against permitting a legislature or an executive,
not identified in interest with the people, to prescribe opinions to
them, and determine what doctrines or what arguments they shall be
allowed to hear. This aspect of the question, besides, has been so
often and so triumphantly enforced by preceding writers, that it
needs not be specially insisted on in this place. Though the law of
England, on the subject of the press, is as servile to this day as it was
in the time of the Tudors, there is little danger of its being actually
put in force against political discussion, except during some temporary panic, when fear of insurrection drives ministers and judges
from their propriety; and, speaking generally, it is not, in constitutional countries, to be apprehended that the government, whether
completely responsible to the people or not, will often attempt to
control the expression of opinion, except when in doing so it makes
itself the organ of the general intolerance of the public. Let us suppose, therefore, that the government is entirely at one with the
people, and never thinks of exerting any power of coercion unless
in agreement with what it conceives to be their voice. But I deny
the right of the people to exercise such coercion, either by themselves or by their government. The power itself is illegitimate. The

best government has no more title to it than the worst. It is as noxious, or more noxious, when exerted in accordance with public opinion, than when in opposition to it. If all mankind minus one were of one opinion, and only one person were of the contrary opinion, mankind would be no more justified in silencing that one person, than he, if he had the power, would be justified in silencing mankind. Were an opinion a personal possession of no value except to the owner; if to be obstructed in the enjoyment of it were simply a private injury, it would make some difference whether the injury was inflicted only on a few persons or on many. But the peculiar evil of silencing the expression of an opinion is, that it is robbing the human race; posterity as well as the existing generation; those who dissent from the opinion, still more than those who hold it. If the opinion is right, they are deprived of the opportunity of exchanging error for truth: if wrong, they lose, what is almost as great a benefit, the clearer perception and livelier impression of truth, produced by its collision with error.

[2]   It is necessary to consider separately these two hypotheses, each of which has a distinct branch of the argument corresponding to it. We can never be sure that the opinion we are endeavouring to stifle is a false opinion; and if we were sure, stifling it would be an evil still.

[3]   First: the opinion which it is attempted to suppress by authority may possibly be true. Those who desire to suppress it, of course deny its truth; but they are not infallible. They have no authority to decide the question for all mankind, and exclude every other person from the means of judging. To refuse a hearing to an opinion, because they are sure that it is false, is to assume that *their* certainty is the same thing as *absolute* certainty. All silencing of discussion is an assumption of infallibility. Its condemnation may be allowed to rest on this common argument, not the worse for being common.

[4]   Unfortunately for the good sense of mankind, the fact of their fallibility is far from carrying the weight in their practical judgment which is always allowed to it in theory; for while every one well knows himself to be fallible, few think it necessary to take any precautions against their own fallibility, or admit the supposition that any opinion, of which they feel very certain, may be one of the examples of the error to which they acknowledge themselves to be liable. Absolute princes, or others who are accustomed to unlimited deference, usually feel this complete confidence in their own opinions on nearly all subjects. People more happily situated, who sometimes hear their opinions disputed, and are not wholly unused to be set

right when they are wrong, place the same unbounded reliance only on such of their opinions as are shared by all who surround them, or to whom they habitually defer; for in proportion to a man's want of confidence in his own solitary judgment, does he usually repose, with implicit trust, on the infallibility of "the world" in general. And the world, to each individual, means the part of it with which he comes in contact; his party, his sect, his church, his class of society; the man may be called, by comparison, almost liberal and large-minded to whom it means anything so comprehensive as his own country or his own age. Nor is his faith in this collective authority at all shaken by his being aware that other ages, countries, sects, churches, classes, and parties have thought, and even now think, the exact reverse. He devolves upon his own world the responsibility of being in the right against the dissentient worlds of other people; and it never troubles him that mere accident has decided which of these numerous worlds is the object of his reliance, and that the same causes which make him a Churchman in London, would have made him a Buddhist or a Confucian in Pekin. Yet it is as evident in itself, as any amount of argument can make it, that ages are no more infallible than individuals; every age having held many opinions which subsequent ages have deemed not only false but absurd; and it is as certain that many opinions now general will be rejected by future ages, as it is that many, once general, are rejected by the present.

[5]   The objection likely to be made to this argument would probably take some such form as the following. There is no greater assumption of infallibility in forbidding the propagation of error, than in any other thing which is done by public authority on its own judgment and responsibility. Judgment is given to men that they may use it. Because it may be used erroneously, are men to be told that they ought not to use it at all? To prohibit what they think pernicious, is not claiming exemption from error, but fulfilling the duty incumbent on them, although fallible, of acting on their conscientious conviction. If we were never to act on our opinions, because those opinions may be wrong, we should leave all our interests uncared for, and all our duties unperformed. An objection which applies to all conduct can be no valid objection to any conduct in particular. It is the duty of governments, and of individuals, to form the truest opinions they can; to form them carefully, and never impose them upon others unless they are quite sure of being right. But when they are sure (such reasoners may say), it is not conscientiousness but cowardice to shrink from acting on their opinions, and allow doctrines which they honestly think dangerous to the welfare of

mankind, either in this life or in another, to be scattered abroad without restraint, because other people, in less enlightened times, have persecuted opinions now believed to be true. Let us take care, it may be said, not to make the same mistake: but governments and nations have made mistakes in other things, which are not denied to be fit subjects for the exercise of authority: they have laid on bad taxes, made unjust wars. Ought we therefore to lay on no taxes, and, under whatever provocation, make no wars? Men, and governments, must act to the best of their ability. There is no such thing as absolute certainty, but there is assurance sufficient for the purposes of human life. We may, and must, assume our opinion to be true for the guidance of our own conduct: and it is assuming no more when we forbid bad men to pervert society by the propagation of opinions which we regard as false and pernicious.

[6]　I answer, that it is assuming very much more. There is the greatest difference between presuming an opinion to be true, because, with every opportunity for contesting it, it has not been refuted, and assuming its truth for the purpose of not permitting its refutation. Complete liberty of contradicting and disproving our opinion is the very condition which justifies us in assuming its truth for purposes of action; and on no other terms can a being with human faculties have any rational assurance of being right.

[7]　When we consider either the history of opinion, or the ordinary conduct of human life, to what is it to be ascribed that the one and the other are no worse than they are? Not certainly to the inherent force of the human understanding; for, on any matter not self-evident, there are ninety-nine persons totally incapable of judging of it for one who is capable; and the capacity of the hundredth person is only comparative; for the majority of the eminent men of every past generation held many opinions now known to be erroneous, and did or approved numerous things which no one will now justify. Why is it, then, that there is on the whole a preponderance among mankind of rational opinions and rational conduct? If there really is this preponderance—which there must be unless human affairs are, and have always been, in an almost desperate state—it is owing to a quality of the human mind, the source of everything respectable in man either as an intellectual or as a moral being, namely, that his errors are corrigible. He is capable of rectifying his mistakes, by discussion and experience. Not by experience alone. There must be discussion, to show how experience is to be interpreted. Wrong opinions and practices gradually yield to fact and argument; but facts and arguments, to produce any effect on the mind, must be brought before it. Very few facts are able to tell their own story,

without comments to bring out their meaning. The whole strength and value, then, of human judgment, depending on the one property, that it can be set right when it is wrong, reliance can be placed on it only when the means of setting it right are kept constantly at hand. In the case of any person whose judgment is really deserving of confidence, how has it become so? Because he has kept his mind open to criticism of his opinions and conduct. Because it has been his practice to listen to all that could be said against him; to profit by as much of it as was just, and expound to himself, and upon occasion to others, the fallacy of what was fallacious. Because he has felt, that the only way in which a human being can make some approach to knowing the whole of a subject, is by hearing what can be said about it by persons of every variety of opinion, and studying all modes in which it can be looked at by every character of mind. No wise man ever acquired his wisdom in any mode but this; nor is it in the nature of human intellect to become wise in any other manner. The steady habit of correcting and completing his own opinion by collating it with those of others, so far from causing doubt and hesitation in carrying it into practice, is the only stable foundation for a just reliance on it: for, being cognizant of all that can, at least obviously, be said against him, and having taken up his position against all gainsayers—knowing that he has sought for objections and difficulties, instead of avoiding them, and has shut out no light which can be thrown upon the subject from any quarter—he has a right to think his judgment better than that of any person, or any multitude, who have not gone through a similar process.

[8] It is not too much to require that what the wisest of mankind, those who are best entitled to trust their own judgment, find necessary to warrant their relying on it, should be submitted to by that miscellaneous collection of a few wise and many foolish individuals, called the public. The most intolerant of churches, the Roman Catholic Church, even at the canonisation of a saint, admits, and listens patiently to, a "devil's advocate." The holiest of men, it appears, cannot be admitted to posthumous honours, until all that the devil could say against him is known and weighed. If even the Newtonian philosophy were not permitted to be questioned, mankind could not feel as complete assurance of its truth as they now do. The beliefs which we have most warrant for have no safeguard to rest on, but a standing invitation to the whole world to prove them unfounded. If the challenge is not accepted, or is accepted and the attempt fails, we are far enough from certainty still; but we have done the best that the existing state of human reason admits of; we have neglected nothing that could give the truth a chance of reaching us:

if the lists are kept open, we may hope that if there be a better truth, it will be found when the human mind is capable of receiving it; and in the meantime we may rely on having attained such approach to truth as is possible in our own day. This is the amount of certainty attainable by a fallible being, and this the sole way of attaining it.

[9]   Strange it is, that men should admit the validity of the arguments for free discussion, but object to their being "pushed to an extreme"; not seeing that unless the reasons are good for an extreme case, they are not good for any case. Strange that they should imagine that they are not assuming infallibility, when they acknowledge that there should be free discussion on all subjects which can possibly be *doubtful,* but think that some particular principle or doctrine should be forbidden to be questioned because it is so *certain,* that is, because *they are certain* that it is certain. To call any proposition certain, while there is any one who would deny its certainty if permitted, but who is not permitted, is to assume that we ourselves, and those who agree with us, are the judges of certainty, and judges without hearing the other side.

[10]   In the present age—which has been described as "destitute of faith, but terrified at scepticism"—in which people feel sure, not so much that their opinions are true, as that they should not know what to do without them—the claims of an opinion to be protected from public attack are rested not so much on its truth, as on its importance to society. There are, it is alleged, certain beliefs so useful, not to say indispensable, to well-being that it is as much the duty of governments to uphold those beliefs, as to protect any other of the interests of society. In a case of such necessity, and so directly in the line of their duty, something less than infallibility may, it is maintained, warrant, and even bind, governments to act on their own opinion, confirmed by the general opinion of mankind. It is also often argued, and still oftener thought, that none but bad men would desire to weaken these salutary beliefs; and there can be nothing wrong, it is thought, in restraining bad men, and prohibiting what only such men would wish to practise. This mode of thinking makes the justification of restraints on discussion not a question of the truth of doctrines, but of their usefulness; and flatters itself by that means to escape the responsibility of claiming to be an infallible judge of opinions. But those who thus satisfy themselves, do not perceive that the assumption of infallibility is merely shifted from one point to another. The usefulness of an opinion is itself a matter of opinion: as disputable, as open to discussion, and requiring discussion as much as the opinion itself. There is the same need of an infallible judge of opinions to decide an opinion to be noxious, as to decide it to be false, unless

the opinion condemned has full opportunity of defending itself. And it will not do to say that the heretic may be allowed to maintain the utility or harmlessness of his opinion, though forbidden to maintain its truth. The truth of an opinion is part of its utility. If we would know whether or not it is desirable that a proposition should be believed, is it possible to exclude the consideration of whether or not it is true? In the opinion, not of bad men, but of the best men, no belief which is contrary to truth can be really useful: and can you prevent such men from urging that plea, when they are charged with culpability for denying some doctrine which they are told is useful, but which they believe to be false? Those who are on the side of received opinions never fail to take all possible advantage of this plea; you do not find *them* handling the question of utility as if it could be completely abstracted from that of truth: on the contrary, it is, above all, because their doctrine is "the truth," that the knowledge or the belief of it is held to be so indispensable. There can be no fair discussion of the question of usefulness when an argument so vital may be employed on one side, but not on the other. And in point of fact, when law or public feeling do not permit the truth of an opinion to be disputed, they are just as little tolerant of a denial of its usefulness. The utmost they allow is an extenuation of its absolute necessity, or of the positive guilt of rejecting it.

[11] In order more fully to illustrate the mischief of denying a hearing to opinions because we, in our own judgment, have condemned them, it will be desirable to fix down the discussion to a concrete case; and I choose, by preference, the cases which are least favourable to me—in which the argument against freedom of opinion, both on the score of truth and on that of utility, is considered the strongest. Let the opinions impugned be the belief in a God and in a future state, or any of the commonly received doctrines of morality. To fight the battle on such ground gives a great advantage to an unfair antagonist; since he will be sure to say (and many who have no desire to be unfair will say it internally), Are these the doctrines which you do not deem sufficiently certain to be taken under the protection of law? Is the belief in a God one of the opinions to feel sure of which you hold to be assuming infallibility? But I must be permitted to observe, that it is not the feeling sure of a doctrine (be it what it may) which I call an assumption of infallibility. It is the undertaking to decide that question *for others*, without allowing them to hear what can be said on the contrary side. And I denounce and reprobate this pretension not the less, if put forth on the side of my most solemn convictions. However positive any one's persuasion may be, not only of the falsity but of the

pernicious consequences—not only of the pernicious consequences, but (to adopt expressions which I altogether condemn) the immorality and impiety of an opinion; yet if, in pursuance of that private judgment, though backed by the public judgment of his country or his contemporaries, he prevents the opinion from being heard in its defence, he assumes infallibility. And so far from the assumption being less objectionable or less dangerous because the opinion is called immoral or impious, this is the case of all others in which it is most fatal. These are exactly the occasions on which the men of one generation commit those dreadful mistakes which excite the astonishment and horror of posterity. It is among such that we find the instances memorable in history, when the arm of the law has been employed to root out the best men and the noblest doctrines; with deplorable success as to the men, though some of the doctrines have survived to be (as if in mockery) invoked in defence of similar conduct towards those who dissent from *them,* or from their received interpretation.

[12] Mankind can hardly be too often reminded, that there was once a man named Socrates, between whom and the legal authorities and public opinion of his time there took place a memorable collision. Born in an age and country abounding in individual greatness, this man has been handed down to us by those who best knew both him and the age, as the most virtuous man in it; while *we* know him as the head and prototype of all subsequent teachers of virtue, the source equally of the lofty inspiration of Plato and the judicious utilitarianism of Aristotle, *"i maëstri di color che sanno,"* the two headsprings of ethical as of all other philosophy. This acknowledged master of all the eminent thinkers who have since lived—whose fame, still growing after more than two thousand years, all but outweighs the whole remainder of the names which make his native city illustrious—was put to death by his countrymen, after a judicial conviction, for impiety and immorality. Impiety, in denying the gods recognised by the State; indeed his accuser asserted (see the "Apologia") that he believed in no gods at all. Immorality, in being, by his doctrines and instructions, a "corrupter of youth." Of these charges the tribunal, there is every ground for believing, honestly found him guilty, and condemned the man who probably of all then born had deserved best of mankind to be put to death as a criminal.

[13] To pass from this to the only other instance of judicial iniquity, the mention of which, after the condemnation of Socrates, would not be an anti-climax: the event which took place on Calvary rather more than eighteen hundred years ago. The man who left on the memory of those who witnessed his life and conversation such an impression

of his moral grandeur that eighteen subsequent centuries have done homage to him as the Almighty in person, was ignominiously put to death, as what? As a blasphemer. Men did not merely mistake their benefactor; they mistook him for the exact contrary of what he was, and treated him as that prodigy of impiety which they themselves are now held to be for their treatment of him. The feelings with which mankind now regard these lamentable transactions, especially the latter of the two, render them extremely unjust in their judgment of the unhappy actors. These were, to all appearance, not bad men—not worse than men commonly are, but rather the contrary; men who possessed in a full, or somewhat more than a full measure, the religious, moral, and patriotic feelings of their time and people: the very kind of men who, in all times, our own included, have every chance of passing through life blameless and respected. The high-priest who rent his garments when the words were pronounced, which, according to all the ideas of his country, constituted the blackest guilt, was in all probability quite as sincere in his horror and indignation as the generality of respectable and pious men now are in the religious and moral sentiments they profess; and most of those who now shudder at his conduct, if they had lived in his time, and been born Jews, would have acted precisely as he did. Orthodox Christians who are tempted to think that those who stoned to death the first martyrs must have been worse men than they themselves are, ought to remember that one of those persecutors was Saint Paul.

[14] Let us add one more example, the most striking of all, if the impressiveness of an error is measured by the wisdom and virtue of him who falls into it. If ever any one, possessed of power, had grounds for thinking himself the best and most enlightened among his contemporaries, it was the Emperor Marcus Aurelius. Absolute monarch of the whole civilized world, he preserved through life not only the unblemished justice, but what was less to be expected from his Stoical breeding, the tenderest heart. The few failings which are attributed to him, were all on the side of indulgence: while his writings, the highest ethical product of the ancient mind, differ scarcely perceptibly, if they differ at all, from the most characteristic teachings of Christ. This man, a better Christian in all but the dogmatic sense of the word, than almost any of the ostensibly Christian sovereigns who have since reigned, persecuted Christianity. Placed at the summit of all the previous attainments of humanity, with an open, unfettered intellect, and a character which led him of himself to embody in his moral writings the Christian ideal, he yet failed to see that Christianity was to be a good and not an evil to the world, with his duties to which he was so deeply penetrated.

Existing society he knew to be in a deplorable state. But such as it was, he saw, or thought he saw, that it was held together, and prevented from being worse, by belief and reverence of the received divinities. As a ruler of mankind, he deemed it his duty not to suffer society to fall in pieces; and saw not how, if its existing ties were removed, any others could be formed which could again knit it together. The new religion openly aimed at dissolving these ties: unless, therefore, it was his duty to adopt that religion, it seemed to be his duty to put it down. Inasmuch then as the theology of Christianity did not appear to him true or of divine origin; inasmuch as this strange history of a crucified God was not credible to him, and a system which purported to rest entirely upon a foundation to him so wholly unbelievable, could not be foreseen by him to be that renovating agency which, after all abatements, it has in fact proved to be; the gentlest and most amiable of philosophers and rulers, under a solemn sense of duty, authorized the persecution of Christianity. To my mind this is one of the most tragical facts in all history. It is a bitter thought, how different a thing the Christianity of the world might have been, if the Christian faith had been adopted as the religion of the empire under the auspices of Marcus Aurelius instead of those of Constantine. But it would be equally unjust to him and false to truth, to deny, that no one plea which can be urged for punishing anti-Christian teaching, was wanting to Marcus Aurelius for punishing, as he did, the propagation of Christianity. No Christian more firmly believes that Atheism is false, and tends to the dissolution of society, than Marcus Aurelius believed the same things of Christianity; he who, of all men then living, might have been thought the most capable of appreciating it. Unless any one who approves of punishment for the promulgation of opinions, flatters himself that he is a wiser and better man than Marcus Aurelius—more deeply versed in the wisdom of his time, more elevated in his intellect above it—more earnest in his search for truth, or more singleminded in his devotion to it when found; let him abstain from that assumption of the joint infallibility of himself and the multitude, which the great Antoninus made with so unfortunate a result. . . .

[15] But, indeed, the dictum that truth always triumphs over persecution is one of those pleasant falsehoods which men repeat after one another till they pass into commonplaces, but which all experience refutes. History teems with instances of truth put down by persecution. If not suppressed for ever, it may be thrown back for centuries. To speak only of religious opinions: the Reformation broke out at least twenty times before Luther, and was put down.

Arnold of Brescia was put down. Fra Dolcino was put down. Savonarola was put down. The Albigeois were put down. The Vaudois were put down. The Lollards were put down. The Hussites were put down. Even after the era of Luther, whatever persecution was persisted in, it was successful. In Spain, Italy, Flanders, the Austrian empire, Protestantism was rooted out; and, most likely, would have been so in England, had Queen Mary lived, or Queen Elizabeth died. Persecution has always succeeded, save where the heretics were too strong a party to be effectually persecuted. No reasonable person can doubt that Christianity might have been extirpated in the Roman Empire. It spread, and became predominant, because the persecutions were only occasional, lasting but a short time, and separated by long intervals of almost undisturbed propagandism. It is a piece of idle sentimentality that truth, merely as truth, has any inherent power denied to error of prevailing against the dungeon and the stake. Men are not more zealous for truth than they often are for error, and a sufficient application of legal or even of social penalties will generally succeed in stopping the propagation of either. The real advantage which truth has consists in this, that when an opinion is true, it may be extinguished once, twice, or many times, but in the course of ages there will generally be found persons to rediscover it, until some one of its reappearances falls on a time when from favourable circumstances it escapes persecution until it has made such head as to withstand all subsequent attempts to suppress it. . . .

[16]   Let us now pass to the second division of the argument, and dismissing the supposition that any of the received opinions may be false, let us assume them to be true, and examine into the worth of the manner in which they are likely to be held, when their truth is not freely and openly canvassed. However unwillingly a person who has a strong opinion may admit the possibility that his opinion may be false, he ought to be moved by the consideration that, however true it may be, if it is not fully, frequently, and fearlessly discussed, it will be held as a dead dogma, not a living truth.

[17]   There is a class of persons (happily not quite so numerous as formerly) who think it enough if a person assents undoubtingly to what they think true, though he has no knowledge whatever of the grounds of the opinion, and could not make a tenable defence of it against the most superficial objections. Such persons, if they can once get their creed taught from authority, naturally think that no good, and some harm, comes of its being allowed to be questioned. Where their influence prevails, they make it nearly impossible for the re-

ceived opinion to be rejected wisely and considerately, though it
may still be rejected rashly and ignorantly; for to shut out discussion
entirely is seldom possible, and when it once gets in, beliefs not
grounded on conviction are apt to give way before the slightest semblance of an argument. Waiving, however, this possibility—assuming that the true opinion abides in the mind, but abides as a prejudice, a belief independent of, and proof against, argument—this
is not the way in which truth ought to be held by a rational being.
This is not knowing the truth. Truth, thus held, is but one superstition the more, accidentally clinging to the words which enunciate
a truth.

[18]   If the intellect and judgment of mankind ought to be cultivated, a thing which Protestants at least do not deny, on what can
these faculties be more appropriately exercised by any one, than on
the things which concern him so much that it is considered necessary
for him to hold opinions on them? If the cultivation of the understanding consists in one thing more than in another, it is surely in
learning the grounds of one's own opinions. Whatever people believe,
on subjects on which it is of the first importance to believe rightly,
they ought to be able to defend against at least the common objections. But, some one may say, "Let them be *taught* the grounds of
their opinions. It does not follow that opinions must be merely
parroted because they are never heard controverted. Persons who
learn geometry do not simply commit the theorems to memory, but
understand and learn likewise the demonstrations; and it would be
absurd to say that they remain ignorant of the grounds of geometrical
truths, because they never hear any one deny, and attempt to dis-
prove them." Undoubtedly: and such teaching suffices on a subject
like mathematics, where there is nothing at all to be said on the wrong
side of the question. The peculiarity of the evidence of mathematical
truths is that all the argument is on one side. There are no objections,
and no answers to objections. But on every subject on which difference of opinion is possible, the truth depends on a balance to be
struck between two sets of conflicting reasons. Even in natural philosophy, there is always some other explanation possible of the same
facts; some geocentric theory instead of heliocentric, some phlogiston
instead of oxygen; and it has to be shown why that other theory
cannot be the true one: and until this is shown, and until we know
how it is shown, we do not understand the grounds of our opinion.
But when we turn to subjects infinitely more complicated, to morals,
religion, politics, social relations, and the business of life, three-
fourths of the arguments for every disputed opinion consist in dis-
pelling the appearances which favour some opinion different from

it. The greatest orator, save one, of antiquity, has left it on record that he always studied his adversary's case with as great, if not still greater, intensity than even his own. What Cicero practised as the means of forensic success requires to be imitated by all who study any subject in order to arrive at the truth. He who knows only his own side of the case, knows little of that. His reasons may be good, and no one may have been able to refute them. But if he is equally unable to refute the reasons on the opposite side; if he does not so much as know what they are, he has no ground for preferring either opinion. The rational position for him would be suspension of judgment, and unless he contents himself with that, he is either led by authority, or adopts, like the generality of the world, the side to which he feels most inclination. Nor is it enough that he should hear the arguments of adversaries from his own teachers, presented as they state them, and accompanied by what they offer as refutations. That is not the way to do justice to the arguments, or bring them into real contact with his own mind. He must be able to hear them from persons who actually believe them; who defend them in earnest, and do their very utmost for them. He must know them in their most plausible and persuasive form; he must feel the whole force of the difficulty which the true view of the subject has to encounter and dispose of; else he will never really possess himself of the portion of truth which meets and removes that difficulty. Ninety-nine in a hundred of what are called educated men are in this condition; even of those who can argue fluently for their opinions. Their conclusion may be true, but it might be false for anything they know: they have never thrown themselves into the mental position of those who think differently from them, and considered what such persons may have to say; and consequently they do not, in any proper sense of the word, know the doctrine which they themselves profess. They do not know those parts of it which explain and justify the remainder; the considerations which show that a fact which seemingly conflicts with another is reconcilable with it, or that, of two apparently strong reasons, one and not the other ought to be preferred. All that part of the truth which turns the scale, and decides the judgment of a completely informed mind, they are strangers to; nor is it ever really known, but to those who have attended equally and impartially to both sides, and endeavoured to see the reasons of both in the strongest light. So essential is this discipline to a real understanding of moral and human subjects, that if opponents of all important truths do not exist, it is indispensable to imagine them, and supply them with the strongest arguments which the most skilful devil's advocate can conjure up.

[19]   To abate the force of these considerations, an enemy of free

discussion may be supposed to say, that there is no necessity for mankind in general to know and understand all that can be said against or for their opinions by philosophers and theologians. That it is not needful for common men to be able to expose all the mis-statements or fallacies of an ingenious opponent. That it is enough if there is always somebody capable of answering them, so that nothing likely to mislead uninstructed persons remains unrefuted. That simple minds, having been taught the obvious grounds of the truths inculcated on them, may trust to authority for the rest, and being aware that they have neither knowledge nor talent to resolve every difficulty which can be raised, may repose in the assurance that all those which have been raised have been or can be answered, by those who are specially trained to the task.

[20] Conceding to this view of the subject the utmost that can be claimed for it by those most easily satisfied with the amount of understanding of truth which ought to accompany the belief of it; even so, the argument for free discussion is no way weakened. For even this doctrine acknowledges that mankind ought to have a rational assurance that all objections have been satisfactorily answered; and how are they to be answered if that which requires to be answered is not spoken? or how can the answer be known to be satisfactory, if the objectors have no opportunity of showing that it is unsatisfactory? If not the public, at least the philosophers and theologians who are to resolve the difficulties, must make themselves familiar with those difficulties in their most puzzling form; and this cannot be accomplished unless they are freely stated, and placed in the most advantageous light which they admit of. The Catholic Church has its own way of dealing with this embarrassing problem. It makes a broad separation between those who can be permitted to receive its doctrines on conviction, and those who must accept them on trust. Neither, indeed, are allowed any choice as to what they will accept; but the clergy, such at least as can be fully confided in, may admissibly and meritoriously make themselves acquainted with the arguments of opponents, in order to answer them, and may, therefore, read heretical books; the laity, not unless by special permission, hard to be obtained. This discipline recognises a knowledge of the enemy's case as beneficial to the teachers, but finds means, consistent with this, of denying it to the rest of the world: thus giving to the *élite* more mental culture, though not more mental freedom, than it allows to the mass. By this device it succeeds in obtaining the kind of mental superiority which its purposes require; for though culture without freedom never made a large and liberal mind, it can make a clever *nisi prius* advocate of a cause. But in countries professing Protestant-

ism, this resource is denied; since Protestants hold, at least in theory, that the responsibility for the choice of a religion must be borne by each for himself, and cannot be thrown off upon teachers. Besides, in the present state of the world, it is practically impossible that writings which are read by the instructed can be kept from the uninstructed. If the teachers of mankind are to be cognizant of all that they ought to know, everything must be free to be written and published without restraint.

[21] If, however, the mischievous operation of the absence of free discussion, when the received opinions are true, were confined to leaving men ignorant of the grounds of those opinions, it might be thought that this, if an intellectual, is no moral evil, and does not affect the worth of the opinions, regarded in their influence on the character. The fact, however, is, that not only the grounds of the opinion are forgotten in the absence of discussion, but too often the meaning of the opinion itself. The words which convey it cease to suggest ideas, or suggest only a small portion of those they were originally employed to communicate. Instead of a vivid conception and a living belief, there remain only a few phrases retained by rote; or, if any part, the shell and husk only of the meaning is retained, the finer essence being lost. The great chapter in human history which this fact occupies and fills, cannot be too earnestly studied and meditated on.

[22] It is illustrated in the experience of almost all ethical doctrines and religious creeds. They are all full of meaning and vitality to those who originate them, and to the direct disciples of the originators. Their meaning continues to be felt in undiminished strength, and is perhaps brought out into even fuller consciousness, so long as the struggle lasts to give the doctrine or creed an ascendancy over other creeds. At last it either prevails, and becomes the general opinion, or its progress stops; it keeps possession of the ground it has gained, but ceases to spread further. When either of these results has become apparent, controversy on the subject flags, and gradually dies away. The doctrine has taken its place, if not as a received opinion, as one of the admitted sects or divisions of opinion: those who hold it have generally inherited, not adopted it; and conversion from one of these doctrines to another, being now an exceptional fact, occupies little place in the thoughts of their professors. Instead of being, as at first, constantly on the alert either to defend themselves against the world, or to bring the world over to them, they have subsided into acquiescence, and neither listen, when they can help it, to arguments against their creed, nor trouble dissentients (if there be such) with arguments in its favour. From this time may usually

be dated the decline in the living power of the doctrine. We often hear the teachers of all creeds lamenting the difficulty of keeping up in the minds of believers a lively apprehension of the truth which they nominally recognise, so that it may penetrate the feelings, and acquire a real mastery over the conduct. No such difficulty is complained of while the creed is still fighting for its existence: even the weaker combatants then know and feel what they are fighting for, and the difference between it and other doctrines; and in that period of every creed's existence, not a few persons may be found, who have realised its fundamental principles in all the forms of thought, have weighed and considered them in all their important bearings, and have experienced the full effect on the character which belief in that creed ought to produce in a mind thoroughly imbued with it. But when it has come to be an hereditary creed, and to be received passively, not actively—when the mind is no longer compelled, in the same degree as at first, to exercise its vital powers on the questions which its belief presents to it, there is a progressive tendency to forget all of the belief except the formularies, or to give it a dull and torpid assent, as if accepting it on trust dispensed with the necessity of realising it in consciousness, or testing it by personal experience, until it almost ceases to connect itself at all with the inner life of the human being. Then are seen the cases, so frequent in this age of the world as almost to form the majority, in which the creed remains as it were outside the mind, incrusting and petrifying it against all other influences addressed to the higher parts of our nature; manifesting its power by not suffering any fresh and living conviction to get in, but itself doing nothing for the mind or heart except standing sentinel over them to keep them vacant.

[23]   To what an extent doctrines intrinsically fitted to make the deepest impression upon the mind may remain in it as dead beliefs, without being ever realized in the imagination, the feelings, or the understanding, is exemplified by the manner in which the majority of believers hold the doctrines of Christianity. By Christianity I here mean what is accounted such by all churches and sects—the maxims and precepts contained in the New Testament. These are considered sacred, and accepted as laws, by all professing Christians. Yet it is scarcely too much to say that no one Christian in a thousand guides or tests his individual conduct by reference to those laws. The standard to which he does refer it, is the custom of his nation, his class, or his religious profession. He has thus, on the one hand, a collection of ethical maxims, which he believes to have been vouchsafed to him by infallible wisdom as rules for his government; and on the other, a set of everyday judgments and practices, which go a certain

length with some of those maxims, not so great a length with others, stand in direct opposition to some, and are, on the whole, a compromise between the Christian creed and the interests and suggestions of worldly life. To the first of these standards he gives his homage; to the other his real allegiance. All Christians believe that the blessed are the poor and humble, and those who are ill-used by the world; that it is easier for a camel to pass through the eye of a needle than for a rich man to enter the kingdom of heaven; that they should judge not, lest they be judged; that they should swear not at all; that they should love their neighbor as themselves; that if one take their cloak, they should give him their coat also; that they should take no thought for the morrow; that if they would be perfect, they should sell all that they have and give it to the poor. They are not insincere when they say that they believe these things. They do believe them, as people believe what they have always heard lauded and never discussed. But in the sense of that living belief which regulates conduct, they believe these doctrines just up to the point to which it is usual to act upon them. The doctrines in their integrity are serviceable to pelt adversaries with; and it is understood that they are to be put forward (when possible) as the reasons for whatever people do that they think laudable. But any one who reminded them that the maxims require an infinity of things which they never even think of doing, would gain nothing but to be classed among those very unpopular characters who affect to be better than other people. The doctrines have no hold on ordinary believers—are not a power in their minds. They have an habitual respect for the sound of them, but no feeling which spreads from the words of the things signified, and forces the mind to take *them* in, and make them conform to the formula. Whenever conduct is concerned, they look round for Mr. A and B to direct them how far to go in obeying Christ. . . .

[24]   It still remains to speak of one of the principal causes which make diversity of opinion advantageous, and will continue to do so until mankind shall have entered a stage of intellectual advancement which at present seems at an incalculable distance. We have hitherto considered only two possibilities: that the received opinion may be false, and some other opinion, consequently, true; or that, the received opinion being true, a conflict with the opposite error is essential to a clear apprehension and deep feeling of its truth. But there is a commoner case than either of these; when the conflicting doctrines, instead of being one true and the other false, share the truth between them; and the nonconforming opinion is needed to supply the remainder of the truth, of which the received doctrine embodies

only a part. Popular opinions, on subjects not palpable to sense, are often true, but seldom or never the whole truth. They are a part of the truth; sometimes a greater, sometimes a smaller part, but exaggerated, distorted, and disjointed from the truths by which they ought to be accompanied and limited. Heretical opinions, on the other hand, are generally some of these suppressed and neglected truths, bursting the bonds which kept them down, and either seeking reconciliation with the truth contained in the common opinion, or fronting it as enemies, and setting themselves up, with similar exclusiveness, as the whole truth. The latter case is hitherto the most frequent, as, in the human mind, one-sidedness has always been the rule, and many-sidedness the exception. Hence, even in revolutions of opinion, one part of the truth usually sets while another rises. Even progress, which ought to superadd, for the most part only substitutes, one partial and incomplete truth for another; improvement consisting chiefly in this, that the new fragment of truth is more wanted, more adapted to the needs of the time, than that which it displaces. Such being the partial character of prevailing opinions, even when resting on a true foundation, every opinion which embodies somewhat of the portion of truth which the common opinion omits, ought to be considered precious, with whatever amount of error and confusion that truth may be blended. No sober judge of human affairs will feel bound to be indignant because those who force on our notice truths which we should otherwise have overlooked, overlook some of those which we see. Rather, he will think that so long as popular truth is one-sided, it is more desirable than otherwise that unpopular truth should have one-sided assertors too; such being usually the most energetic, and the most likely to compel reluctant attention to the fragment of wisdom which they proclaim as if it were the whole.

[25] Thus, in the eighteenth century, when nearly all the instructed, and all those of the uninstructed who were led by them, were lost in admiration of what is called civilisation, and of the marvels of modern science, literature, and philosophy, and while greatly overrating the amount of unlikeness between the men of modern and those of ancient times, indulged the belief that the whole of the difference was in their own favour; with what a salutary shock did the paradoxes of Rousseau explode like bombshells in the midst, dislocating the compact mass of one-sided opinion, and forcing its elements to recombine in a better form and with additional ingredients. Not that the current opinions were on the whole farther from the truth than Rousseau's were; on the contrary, they were nearer to it; they contained more of positive truth, and very much less of error.

Nevertheless there lay in Rousseau's doctrine, and has floated down the stream of opinion along with it, a considerable amount of exactly those truths which the popular opinion wanted; and these are the deposit which was left behind when the flood subsided. The superior worth of simplicity of life, the enervating and demoralising effect of the trammels and hypocrisies of artificial society, are ideas which have never been entirely absent from cultivated minds since Rousseau wrote; and they will in time produce their due effect, though at present needing to be asserted as much as ever, and to be asserted by deeds, for words, on this subject, have nearly exhausted their power.

[26] In politics, again, it is almost a commonplace, that a party of order or stability, and a party of progress or reform, are both necessary elements of a healthy state of political life; until the one or the other shall have so enlarged its mental grasp as to be a party equally of order and of progress, knowing and distinguishing what is fit to be preserved from what ought to be swept away. Each of these modes of thinking derives its utility from the deficiencies of the other; but it is in a great measure the opposition of the other that keeps each within the limits of reason and sanity. Unless opinions favourable to democracy and to aristocracy, to property and to equality, to co-operation and to competition, to luxury and to abstinence, to sociality and individuality, to liberty and discipline, and all the other standing antagonisms of practical life, are expressed with equal freedom, and enforced and defended with equal talent and energy, there is no chance of both elements obtaining their due; one scale is sure to go up, and the other down. Truth, in the great practical concerns of life, is so much a question of the reconciling and combining of opposites, that very few have minds sufficiently capacious and impartial to make the adjustment with an approach to correctness, and it has to be made by the rough process of a struggle between combatants fighting under hostile banners. On any of the great open questions just enumerated, if either of the two opinions has a better claim than the other, not merely to be tolerated, but to be encouraged and countenanced, it is the one which happens at the particular time and place to be in a minority. That is the opinion which, for the time being, represents the neglected interests, the side of human well-being which is in danger of obtaining less than its share. I am aware that there is not, in this country, any intolerance of differences of opinion on most of these topics. They are adduced to show, by admitted and multiplied examples, the universality of the fact, that only through diversity of opinion is there, in the existing state of human intellect, a chance of fair play to all sides of

the truth. When there are persons to be found who form an exception to the apparent unanimity of the world on any subject, even if the world is in the right, it is always probable that dissentients have something worth hearing to say for themselves, and that truth would lose something by their silence.

[27] It may be objected, "But *some* received principles, especially on the highest and most vital subjects, are more than half-truths. The Christian morality, for instance, is the whole truth on that subject, and if any one teaches a morality which varies from it, he is wholly in error." As this is of all cases the most important in practice, none can be fitter to test the general maxim. But before pronouncing what Christian morality is or is not, it would be desirable to decide what is meant by Christian morality. If it means the morality of the New Testament, I wonder that any one who derives his knowledge of this from the book itself, can suppose that it was announced, or intended, as a complete doctrine of morals. The Gospel always refers to a pre-existing morality, and confines its precepts to the particulars in which that morality was to be corrected, or superseded by a wider and higher; expressing itself, moreover, in terms most general, often impossible to be interpreted literally, and possessing rather the impressiveness of poetry or eloquence than the precision of legislation. To extract from it a body of ethical doctrine, has never been possible without eking it out from the Old Testament, that is, from a system elaborate indeed, but in many respects barbarous, and intended only for a barbarous people. St. Paul, a declared enemy to this Judaical mode of interpreting the doctrine and filling up the scheme of his Master, equally assumes a pre-existing morality, namely that of the Greeks and Romans; and his advice to Christians is in a great measure a system of accommodation to that; even to the extent of giving an apparent sanction to slavery. What is called Christian, but should rather be termed theological, morality, was not the work of Christ or the Apostles, but is of much later origin, having been gradually built up by the Catholic Church of the first five centuries, and though not implicitly adopted by moderns and Protestants, has been much less modified by them than might have been expected. For the most part, indeed, they have contented themselves with cutting off the additions which had been made to it in the Middle Ages, each sect supplying the place by fresh additions, adapted to its own character and tendencies. That mankind owe a great debt to this morality, and to its early teachers, I should be the last person to deny; but I do not scruple to say of it that it is, in many important points, incomplete and one-sided, and that unless ideas and feelings, not sanctioned by it, had contributed

to the formation of European life and character, human affairs would have been in a worse condition than they now are. Christian morality (so called) has all the characters of a reaction; it is, in great part, a protest against Paganism. Its ideal is negative rather than positive; passive rather than active; Innocence rather than Nobleness; Abstinence from Evil, rather than energetic Pursuit of Good; in its precepts (as has been well said) "thou shalt not" predominates unduly over "thou shalt." In its horror of sensuality, it made an idol of asceticism, which has been gradually compromised away into one of legality. It holds out the hope of heaven and the threat of hell, as the appointed and appropriate motives to a virtuous life: in this falling far below the best of the ancients, and doing what lies in it to give to human morality an essentially selfish character, by disconnecting each man's feelings of duty from the interests of his fellow-creatures, except so far as a self-interested inducement is offered to him for consulting them. It is essentially a doctrine of passive obedience; it inculcates submission to all authorities found established; who indeed are not to be actively obeyed when they command what religion forbids, but who are not to be resisted, far less rebelled against, for any amount of wrong to ourselves. And while, in the morality of the best Pagan nations, duty to the State holds even a disproportionate place, infringing on the just liberty of the individual; in purely Christian ethics, that grand department of duty is scarcely noticed or acknowledged. It is in the Koran, not the New Testament, that we read the maxim—"A ruler who appoints any man to an office, when there is in his dominions another man better qualified for it, sins against God and against the State." What little recognition the idea of obligation to the public obtains in modern morality is derived from Greek and Roman sources, not from Christian; as, even in the morality of private life, whatever exists of magnanimity, highmindedness, personal dignity, even the sense of honour, is derived from the purely human, not the religious part of our education, and never could have grown out of a standard of ethics in which the only worth, professedly recognised, is that of obedience.

[28] I am as far as any one from pretending that these defects are necessarily inherent in the Christian ethics in every manner in which it can be conceived, or that the many requisites of a complete moral doctrine which it does not contain do not admit of being reconciled with it. Far less would I insinuate this of the doctrines and precepts of Christ himself. I believe that the sayings of Christ are all that I can see any evidence of their having been intended to be; that they are irreconcilable with nothing which a comprehensive morality requires; that everything which is excellent in ethics may

be brought within them, with no greater violence to their language than has been done to it by all who have attempted to deduce from them any practical system of conduct whatever. But it is quite consistent with this to believe that they contain, and were meant to contain, only a part of the truth; that many essential elements of the highest morality are among the things which are not provided for, nor intended to be provided for, in the recorded deliverances of the Founder of Christianity, and which have been entirely thrown aside in the system of ethics erected on the basis of those deliverances by the Christian Church. And this being so, I think it a great error to persist in attempting to find in the Christian doctrine that complete rule for our guidance which its author intended it to sanction and enforce, but only partially to provide. I believe, too, that this narrow theory is becoming a grave practical evil, detracting greatly from the moral training and instruction which so many well-meaning persons are now at length exerting themselves to promote. I much fear that by attempting to form the mind and feelings on an exclusively religious type, and discarding those secular standards (as for want of a better name they may be called) which heretofore coexisted with and supplemented the Christian ethics, receiving some of its spirit, and infusing into it some of theirs, there will result, and is even now resulting, a low, abject, servile type of character, which, submit itself as it may to what it deems the Supreme Will, is incapable of rising to or sympathising in the conception of Supreme Goodness. I believe that other ethics than any which can be evolved from exclusively Christian sources, must exist side by side with Christian ethics to produce the moral regeneration of mankind; and that the Christian system is no exception to the rule, that in an imperfect state of the human mind the interests of truth require a diversity of opinions. It is not necessary that in ceasing to ignore the moral truths not contained in Christianity men should ignore any of those which it does contain. Such prejudice, or oversight, when it occurs, is altogether an evil; but it is one from which we cannot hope to be always exempt, and must be regarded as the price paid for an inestimable good. The exclusive pretension made by a part of the truth to be the whole, must and ought to be protested against; and if a reactionary impulse should make the protestors unjust in their turn, this onesidedness, like the other, may be lamented, but must be tolerated. If Christians would teach infidels to be just to Christianity, they should themselves be just to infidelity. It can do truth no service to blink the fact, known to all who have the most ordinary acquaintance with literary history, that a large portion of the noblest and most valuable moral teaching has been the work, not only of men who did not know, but of men who knew and rejected, the Christian faith.

[29] I do not pretend that the most unlimited use of the freedom of enunciating all possible opinions would put an end to the evils of religious or philosophical sectarianism. Every truth which men of narrow capacity are in earnest about, is sure to be asserted, inculcated, and in many ways even acted on, as if no other truth existed in the world, or at all events none that could limit or qualify the first. I acknowledge that the tendency of all opinions to become sectarian is not cured by the freest discussion, but is often heightened and exacerbated thereby; the truth which ought to have been, but was not, seen, being rejected all the more violently because proclaimed by persons regarded as opponents. But it is not on the impassioned partisan, it is on the calmer and more disinterested bystander, that this collision of opinions works its salutary effect. Not the violent conflict between parts of the truth, but the quiet suppression of half of it, is the formidable evil; there is always hope when people are forced to listen to both sides; it is when they attend only to one that errors harden into prejudices, and truth itself ceases to have the effect of truth, by being exaggerated into falsehood. And since there are few mental attributes more rare than that judicial faculty which can sit in intelligent judgment between two sides of a question, of which only one is represented by an advocate before it, truth has no chance but in proportion as every side of it, every opinion which embodies any fraction of the truth, not only finds advocates, but is so advocated as to be listened to.

[30] We have now recognised the necessity to the mental well-being of mankind (on which all their other well-being depends) of freedom of opinion, and freedom of the expression of opinion, on four distinct grounds; which we will now briefly recapitulate.

[31] First, if any opinion is compelled to silence, that opinion may, for aught we can certainly know, be true. To deny this is to assume our own infallibility.

[32] Secondly, though the silenced opinion be an error, it may, and very commonly does, contain a portion of truth; and since the general or prevailing opinion on any subject is rarely or never the whole truth, it is only by the collision of adverse opinions that the remainder of the truth has any chance of being supplied.

[33] Thirdly, even if the received opinion be not only true, but the whole truth; unless it is suffered to be, and actually is, vigorously and earnestly contested, it will, by most of those who receive it, be

held in the manner of a prejudice, with little comprehension or feeling of its rational grounds. And not only this, but, fourthly, the meaning of the doctrine itself will be in danger of being lost, or enfeebled, and deprived of its vital effect on the character and conduct: the dogma becoming a mere formal profession, inefficacious for good, but cumbering the ground, and preventing the growth of any real and heartfelt conviction, from reason or personal experience. . . .

COMMENT AND QUESTIONS

In the first paragraph, which should be read very carefully, Mill limits the subject, states his point of view, and indicates the main divisions of the essay. Then he proceeds to support his opinion by presenting arguments in favor of it and by anticipating and refuting objections which might be raised. In the last paragraphs of this selection he summarizes his case.

I. The following rough outline was written by an able student. Not intended to be a model outline, it illustrates the kind of notes an intelligent reader may take as an aid to understanding the development and main ideas of a complex piece of writing. Such notes are of value, too, when one wishes to review material previously read. The outline is printed here to illustrate one type of note-taking, and to give a general view of the content of the essay. As you read it, recall the detailed development of each point, and read again parts of the essay that you remember only vaguely.

Evil of silencing opinion is that it robs the human race. If opinion is right, people are deprived of opportunity of exchanging error for truth. If opinion is wrong, they lose the clearer perception of truth produced by collision with error.

    I. Opinion to be suppressed may be true.
        A. People who want to suppress it say it is false, but people and ages are not infallible.
        B. Man is capable of rectifying his mistakes only through experience and discussion.
            1. Beliefs can be relied on only when there has been a standing invitation to prove them wrong.
            2. Even RC church has devil's advocate.
            3. The lists must be kept open, to give a chance of receiving a better truth.
        C. Poor argument that "useful" beliefs should be protected.
            1. Usefulness of an opinion is itself a matter of opinion.
            2. Truth of an opinion is part of its utility.

D. Illustrations of mischief of denying a hearing to opinions because we condemn them. When the opinion is called impious or immoral, men of one generation most often make dreadful mistakes which horrify posterity.
1. Socrates—impiety and immorality.
2. Jesus—blasphemy.
3. Christianity itself—dissolution of society.
E. Idea that truth triumphs over persecution is false. It can be put down. Truth has only this advantage—in the course of ages it will generally be rediscovered in more favorable circumstances.

II. Opinion to be suppressed may not be true; but consider how beliefs are held if discussion on them is not allowed.
A. If not fearlessly discussed, a belief becomes a dead dogma.
B. Blind belief, proof against argument, is prejudice, superstition; this is not the way truth should be held by a rational being.
C. He who knows only his side of the case knows little of that. One really knows a doctrine by knowing the arguments against it.
D. Not knowing grounds of opinion is a moral evil as well as an intellectual one: in the absence of discussion, not only the grounds of the belief but the meaning of it is forgotten. New creeds have meaning in the lives and characters of members; later, when hereditary and passively accepted, the belief is outside the mind, encrusting it against other perhaps more vital influences. Doctrines of Christianity used as an example here.

III. Conflicting doctrines often share the truth between them.
A. We should consider precious, dissenting doctrines which contain some portion of the truth.
B. Since popular truth is one-sided, unpopular truth should have one-sided assertors too.
C. Rousseau in 18th century emphasized a neglected side of truth.
D. Minority opinion needs to be heard; it represents neglected interests.
E. Argument that Christian morality is not the whole truth of morality.
1. What is it?
a. New Testament refers to pre-existent morality of Old Testament, in many respects barbarous.
b. St. Paul assumes pre-existing morality of Greece and Rome (slavery).
c. Morality actually built up by Catholic Church in first five centuries.
2. Christian morality is negative, passive, obedient, selfish—not social.
3. Sayings of Christ contain and were meant to contain only part of truth.
4. Ethics derived from other sources must exist with Christian ethics for moral regeneration of mankind.
F. There is always hope when people are forced to listen to both sides;

when they hear only one, error hardens into prejudice and truth is exaggerated into falsehood.
IV. Conclusion.
  A. Opinion compelled to silence may be true. To deny this is to assume infallibility.
  B. Though silenced opinion be error, it may contain a portion of the truth.
  C. Even if popular opinion is true, without discussion it will be held as prejudice, with no comprehension of rational grounds.
  D. The meaning of the uncontested doctrine will be lost or enfeebled, deprived of any vital effect on character or conduct.

II. In the last sentence of paragraph 4, Mill speaks of opinions once generally accepted and now thought false. What examples of such opinions can you give from your knowledge of history, science, and the like?

III. How is Mill's discussion of the canonization of a saint (paragraph 8) relevant to his argument?

IV. What distinction does Mill make between feeling sure of a doctrine and assuming infallibility? What is his attitude toward each?

V. What fact is Mill attempting to establish in his discussion of Socrates (paragraph 12) and of Jesus (paragraph 13)? Has Mill chosen effective examples to prove his point? Explain. Comment on the last sentence in paragraph 13.

VI. What further or different fact is he illustrating in his discussion (paragraph 14) of Marcus Aurelius? Has he shown skill in choosing an example? See the last sentence of the paragraph and comment on it as a specimen of argument. Can you reduce this sentence to a syllogism?

VII. In paragraph 15, how does Mill prove that truth does not always triumph over persecution? How does he explain the survival of persecuted truth?

VIII. In paragraph 16, what does Mill mean by "received opinions"? What are examples of received opinions in our own society?

IX. In paragraphs 22–23, Mill discusses the "decline in the living power of [an uncontested] doctrine." Just what does he mean? What example does he give? Can you suggest other examples?

X. In paragraph 25, Mill speaks favorably of Rousseau. Why? And how is Rousseau related to Mill's main argument?

XI. What, according to Mill (paragraph 26), is the value of the two-party system of government?

XII. What is the major premise for Mill's whole argument? (See Mill's summary, paragraphs 30–33.) Depending on how you phrase it, you may find one major premise, or more than one.

JOHN GUNTHER'S *ROOSEVELT IN RETROSPECT:* FOUR REVIEWS

The four reviews in the following pages are evaluations of the same book. "Roosevelt's Rendezvous With History," by Adolf A. Berle, Jr., appeared in the *New York Times Book Review,* June 4, 1950; "Another Go at F. D. R.," by Hamilton Basso, in *The New Yorker,* June 3, 1950; "Let's Wait," in *Time* magazine, June 5, 1950; and "The Riddles of Franklin Roosevelt," by Raymond Swing, in *The Nation,* June 3, 1950.

1. ROOSEVELT'S RENDEZVOUS WITH HISTORY

ADOLF A. BERLE, JR.

Men famous enough to be remembered have two careers. One is in life; the second, in history. Struggle begins at death for possession of the name, reputation and memory of a really great man; contesting factors push backward to sanctify, or to blacken, the facts of his actual life. Contest continues through generations, sometimes centuries.

So it is proving in the case of Franklin Roosevelt. He had unquestioned greatness. Undeniably his career in history has begun. Unblushingly, friend and foe seek to establish or diminish his stature.

It is fortunate, then, that John Gunther, perhaps the best-known reporter of our generation, has patiently collected and impartially chronicled a great body of intimate but fugitive fact material of Roosevelt's life which otherwise could easily have been lost. He has done an extensive, rich and authentic job. Of outstanding interest is the careful record of comment, anecdote, conversation and explanation from Roosevelt's own lips borne in the memory of living men; this, save for some such record, would have vanished in a few years.

Yet it is crucial; President Roosevelt's habit was to express his mind freely to his friends, his colleagues, even to casual contacts; the windows of his personality were always open. He kept no diary; and his day-to-day thoughts and impressions survive chiefly through diaries and recollections of his contemporaries. In giving these permanent lodging, Gunther has served history well—and written a thrilling book.

The collection of Lincolniana by Herndon was undertaken because Herndon wanted the fact to prevail over the mounting mythology; Lincoln, the man, he believed, was greater than any legend. Gunther apparently had the same idea about Roosevelt. In any case, as early as 1944 he found a rising tide of myths about Roosevelt, and then planned and now has performed, some part, at least, of the same service for Roosevelt. It was none too soon. Prehensile hands already are clutching at the great name. For a time the Communists strove to annex it; though they rapidly gave up. Conservative extremists seek to make him into the image of a would-be Fuehrer, struggling to become dictator. John T. Flynn contents himself by portraying Roosevelt as an egotist-weakling, justifying the worst suspicions of Roosevelt-haters, while Charles A. Beard saw a Machiavellian steering America into avoidable war under the false banner of peace. Little, if any, of this extremism will survive Gunther's report of fact. But then, Gunther's study will not altogether please those to whom Roosevelt had become as Gunther puts it, "anthropomorphic, a virtual god."

Those who knew and loved the man will welcome the volume. In storm and in sunshine, in weakness, in strength, in laughter and in anger, in times when he was everlastingly right, in times when he was clearly wrong, here is Franklin Roosevelt. As a human being he is incomparably greater than any myth.

And yet, not all the man is here—though this is hardly Gunther's fault. As he said, "the President is inexhaustible," and endless material is not yet in. Published autobiographies and diaries of his intimates (the list is already long and growing) are, as they should be, books primarily about their authors rather than about Roosevelt. He himself, no stranger to historical method, quite realized that he had a rendezvous with history—and enjoyed the idea thoroughly. For that reason he caused to be collected all his papers, running literally into millions, and had them placed in the Hyde Park library for anyone who wished to examine. No living human being has yet put this prodigious record together.

Even when it is distilled into biography, a central mystery will probably remain unsolved; the explanation of one crippled man's power to transmit unlimited hope, confidence and strength to millions upon millions of men and women in all parts of the earth who never saw his face, or to give comfort through a golden, radio-transmitted voice. A poet may solve that problem. A journalist can only record the fact.

In analysis of events, Gunther does as well as perhaps can be done, given the material he was using. Historical research may vary some of his conclusions, though I think the general results will stand up well. Gunther's review of Yalta—the most controversial episode in the Rooseveltian epic—may serve as illustration.

The Yalta Conference, judged in hindsight and by its fruits, was a failure, with tragic consequences. Gunther analyzes it as a Rooseveltian gamble for high stakes: for world peace, based on moral relationships, no less. (He believes that had Roosevelt lived to see the peace through, the gamble might well have been won instead of lost.) His conclusion is that Roosevelt's Yalta policy was largely dictated by the military and that failure was in considerable part attributable to mistaken military intelligence.

This judgment is convincingly supported, and is generally confirmed by serious students. So also is Gunther's demonstration that Roosevelt before his death clearly understood Russian double-dealing, though Gunther thinks Russia shifted to an anti-Western policy immediately after Yalta, which accounts partly for the ensuing misfortunes. This theory is not supported, and is probably not the fact: Russia did undoubtedly conceal her actual objectives which seem to have been determined on some months earlier, and only revealed the change later. Charges of "sell-out" and "betrayal" at Yalta are nevertheless effectively refuted.

The verdict is that Roosevelt, on the advice of his generals, underestimated the strength of the American position and, with Churchill, was out-traded. Gunther states fairly the huge risk run by the President in the light of the knowledge available to him had he alienated Stalin while Japan was still formidable. This is the reasoned analysis of a fair-minded journalist. It should clarify the whole controversy.

Reporting is an art most highly exercised when its skill is most concealed. A brilliant feature of this volume lies in the portraits, sketches on huge canvas, occasionally illuminated by a deft phrase or simile. In reviewing the intimate life of Franklin and Eleanor, the author describes the partnership of the man and his wife in history—noting that the pair are fairly comparable to Ferdinand and Isabella. The story, sometimes humorous, sometimes matter-of-fact, sometimes poignant, is drawn to scale. So also are the more earthy episodes of Roosevelt's strictly political career.

One fact, curiously, fails to find a place in the record. For while he played politics with gusto and skill, the President with one lobe of his brain regarded it as unpleasant, corrosive business. One reason for his constantly calling in new men, not engaged in political life, was a latent desire, occasionally expressed, to liberate his operations, if possible, from the limitations and implications of a game he knew too well. One of his conceptions of himself was as a political engineer, giving reality where possible to the academic thought of his time.

A man of Roosevelt's stature seldom bothers to attempt, and still more rarely succeeds in, conscious explanation of himself or analysis of his "mission." Certainly Roosevelt did not. With sure instinct, Gunther chooses for record the single conscious profession the President ever did make of his own function—that of educator. Evidence exists for this beyond that adduced in this volume. Repeatedly Roosevelt spoke of men who did not understand his social objectives as "illiterate," needing to be taught. The Four Freedoms, thrown out across the world and embodied in the Atlantic Charter, were designed to draw out men's minds in a brilliant combination of instruction and hope.

Again as a result of his teaching, any return to the conception of the Presidency held by, say, Calvin Coolidge, is an intellectual impossibility. His idea that diplomacy is a people's prerogative, not a mysterious rite carried on between sovereigns, has changed the whole conduct of foreign affairs. Roosevelt repeatedly thought of himself as a teacher who, like all great teachers, studied as well as taught.

Because the reporter is recording reality and fighting myth, the book soft-pedals the high emotional content of the material. The passionate love which the President inspired is merely suggested. Only dimly described is the hatred he engendered in certain groups.

Generation of these emotions was a part of the man. It is why some seek to defeat him in history as bitterly as some opposed him in life. It is also the reason why unending thousands file, day by day, in silence through a quiet garden, past a simple stone, on which is inscribed only,

FRANKLIN DELANO
ROOSEVELT

1882–1945

2. ANOTHER GO AT F.D.R.*

HAMILTON BASSO

In the foreword to *Roosevelt in Retrospect* (Harper), John Gunther declares that it was not his intention to write a full-dress history of the Roosevelt years or a biography in the orthodox manner. He describes his book as "an attempt at analysis as well as a mere narrative; a gathering of sources and an interpretation rather than a reminiscence or revelation." I am not altogether sure that I know what Mr. Gunther is trying to say (what is a "mere" narrative, how could it have been a reminiscence unless he has something to reminisce about, what does "revelation" mean in the context?), but I deduce that he wishes us to understand that his intention was (1) to accumulate all the material he could about Roosevelt, (2) to tell the story of his life, and (3) to investigate in some detail his character and personality.

Mr. Gunther, in his "Inside" books, has already demonstrated his ability to accumulate masses of material, and he has also shown that he knows how to put a story together, but he is weak in the area of analysis and interpretation. He is the only man alive who can take on a whole continent without losing his breath, yet though I have always admired his journalistic muscularity, I invariably get the impression, after a continent has been made to say uncle, that we are still just where we started. And so it is with this book about Franklin D. Roosevelt. As a fact finder, a gossip gatherer, and an anecdote collector, Mr. Gunther is excellent; as an interpreter, he leaves a great deal to be desired.

Another thing that works against Mr. Gunther is that he is traveling over well-trodden ground. In his bibliography, he lists a hundred and twenty books, the large majority of which are mainly concerned with F.D.R. It is true that Mr. Gunther has gone out and found a considerable amount of material on his own, but it is the same *kind* of material. We have already had enough anecdotes about Roosevelt's humor, his garrulity, his interest in stamps, his fondness for the sea, and his ability to go to sleep as soon as he went to bed. Nor do we need any further information about his reluctance to fire the people he liked, his dependence on Harry Hopkins, the way he and his staff of eminent ghostwriters constructed his speeches, and his opinion of such men as Willkie, Hoover, and Dewey. It has been put into the record over and over again. What is now required is a real attempt at biography. After all this cutting of bait—quite necessary, I might add—the time has come for somebody to start to fish.

Mr. Gunther, in explaining why he wrote the book he did, asserts that a full-length biography must await what he calls "the slow sifting of years of scholarship." The same assertion has been made by others. I doubt, however, whether the difficulties that admittedly exist are so big a hump as he implies. We don't need the complete Roosevelt, in as many volumes as are now being assembled to present the complete Jefferson, to know Roosevelt thoroughly. All of the really essential information is in hand. What we don't know, of course, is the final effect his influence and long administration will have upon the United States and the rest of the world. But that is not a matter of research; it is a matter of waiting for history.

Partisanship is the chief obstacle in the way of a good, judicious biography of Roosevelt. The emotions he stirred up, pro and con, have not yet died down. The Democratic Party is still riding his coat-tails, and the Republicans are still forcefully doing battle with him. Mr. Gunther, it turns out, is one of the more uncritical of Roosevelt's admirers. He is in there all the time getting in his licks for his hero. Here is a sample, and a necessarily long one, of what I mean:

> On another occasion Mr. Steinhardt got a remarkable insight on the way the President's subtle mind worked. Home on leave from Istanbul, he asked FDR for a decision on a critical difference then developing between our-selves and the British on Lend Lease in Turkey. . . . Roosevelt hardly appeared to be listening, and brushed him off with a ten-minute monologue on, of all unrelated things, three impending appointments to the Federal judiciary in New York. . . . He had made up his mind on the first two, but not the third. The Democratic National Committee was supporting one . . . candidate, the state chairman another, and a powerful senator still another. FDR himself favored a fourth man, and he asked Steinhardt, with his wide experience of the New York bar, if he knew anything against him. "No," the Ambassador replied. Roosevelt then waved him out cheer-fully, adding almost as an after-thought: "Oh—on that Lend Lease matter, see Hopkins." By this technique FDR had killed several birds. He avoided making a decision himself on the Lend Lease dispute, which was already the cause of a serious tussle between Hopkins and Sumner Welles. More-over, by sending Steinhardt to Hopkins rather than Welles, he implied that he favored the Hopkins view, while not actually taking sides. Finally, he had obtained Steinhardt's opinion on an entirely different matter; the Ambassador had said no more than the single word "No," but Roosevelt was quite capable of using this so that, if anybody did oppose the man he favored, he could claim that Steinhardt had supported him.

Now, this is surely a peculiar performance by Roosevelt. He pays no attention to his Ambassador, he ducks out of making an important decision, he takes sides in a devious manner, and he prepares to hide behind another man's innocent, unsuspecting word. But Mr. Gunther doesn't see it that way; to him, it's a remarkable example of the work-ings of a subtle mind. And so it goes throughout the book. Item: Al-though Roosevelt collected everything he could about himself, includ-ing a complete newsreel history running to hundreds of thousands of feet of film, he wasn't vainglorious; "perhaps the best analysis would be to say that he had a passionate adhesive interest in history of any kind, and was therefore naturally interested in his own." Item: Al-though there may be some truth in the charge that Roosevelt got along by sabotaging his friends and placating his enemies, and although some good men "were thrown to the dogs without any thanks at all," there was a sound reason—"A president cannot always give thanks, because the president is an institution, not just a man."

But Mr. Gunther's book fails not only because he writes as a partisan apologist. Much more important is that lack of analytical ability. "I once heard it said that Roosevelt's most effective quality was receptivity," he writes. "But also he transmitted. He was like a kind of universal joint, or rather a switchboard, a transformer. The whole energy of the country, the whole power of one hundred and forty million people, flowed into him and through him; he not only felt this power, but he utilized it, he transmitted it. Why does a country, if lucky, produce a great man when he is most needed? Because it really believes in something and focuses the entire energy of its national desires into a single human being; the supreme forces of the time converge into a single vessel. Roosevelt could manipulate this power, shooting it out at almost any angle, to provoke response, to irradiate ideas and men, to search out enormous issues. He was like a needle, always quivering, oscillating, responding to new impulses, throbbing at the slightest variation in current—a magnetic instrument measuring ceaselessly the tone and intensity of public impact. But no matter how much the needle quivered and oscillated, it seldom varied far from its own true north." This is a fair sample of Mr. Gunther's analytical method. But what does it mean? I don't know. Does Mr. Gunther?

3. LET'S WAIT *

Editors of *Time*

Journalist John Gunther has made a career of breezing through countries, even whole continents, and persuading his readers that he is giving them inside stuff. His "Inside" (Europe, Latin America, Asia, U.S.A.) books have considerable popular virtues: they can be read in a hammock, they seldom induce thought, and they almost never leave a deep residue of conviction or concern. Writing with ebullience and wide-eyed surprise, he projects men and events just far enough beyond the daily-news level to satisfy those who dislike being serious but are plagued by the need to seem informed.

In *Roosevelt in Retrospect,* Gunther has brought these talents to bear on the complex personality of Franklin Delano Roosevelt. In spite of his avowed aim of getting at his subject's "root qualities and basic sources of power," Gunther has conspicuously failed to "pin something of his great substance against the wall of time." Getting inside a man is something quite different from getting into a continent or a country; it takes more than visas. What Gunther has achieved is a lively journalistic profile pieced together with materials largely lifted from the mushrooming literature on F.D.R. and loosely held together by Gunther's own surface researches.

Shudders & Secrets. Writing "as objectively as possible," Gunther is obviously too dazzled by the Roosevelt glitter to do a balanced job. Even when he concedes F.D.R.'s political deviousness and lack of candor, he is much more interested in finding excuses for them than in showing their damaging consequences. They "arose not so much out of duplicity but from . . . agreeableness . . . and his marked distaste for hurting friends."

Gunther's mouth often seems as wide open as his eyes. Noting that F.D.R. and his mother both nearly died at his birth from an overdose of chloroform, he pontificates: "Of such hairbreadths is history made." A shudder passes over him when he recalls that Roosevelt was elected governor of New York in 1928 by only 25,000 votes: "His whole future career was made possible by less than 1 per cent of the electorate. What would have happened to America in the turbulent 1930's—and later—if this minuscule handful of voters had gone the other way?" Admirers of F.D.R. who have as much faith in the U.S. as Roosevelt had will feel that the nation would have survived. At times, Gunther's bald style fails him and his subject entirely: "Young Roosevelt was still at Harvard. Presently he found himself in love with Eleanor. He kept this passion a great secret, however; he did not even tell his roommate. . . . Late in 1903 he asked her to marry him, and she at once accepted." The Roosevelt romance will probably get more imaginative treatment one day.

Poodles & Poker. *Roosevelt in Retrospect* nonetheless has Gunther's reader-tested qualities of liveliness and high quota of anecdote. Example: F.D.R. was economical. As a young man he disliked paying more than $2 for a shirt, and in the White House he charged Mrs. Harry Hopkins 50¢ a day for the keep of her poodle. Gunther names the only man who ever called F.D.R. an s.o.b. to his face: Leon Henderson. Myrna Loy was the President's favorite actress, and he loved poker. He saved and filed Christmas cards and he kept the bullet fired at him by an assassin in Miami. When F.D.R. flew to Casablanca, a strong swimmer was brought along to keep him afloat should the plane crash.

For such tidbits and for its admiring enthusiasm, *Roosevelt in Retrospect* will be attractive reading for a ready-made audience. But it was F.D.R. himself who used to put off would-be biographers with the warning: "Let's wait a hundred years."

4. THE RIDDLES OF FRANKLIN ROOSEVELT

RAYMOND SWING

John Gunther calls his new Roosevelt book both a "profile" and a "summary." It also is a compilation to about a third of its length, composed in the now established Gunther technique, of an impressive assortment of details, some of facts important and trivial, some of ideas deliberately artless and penetrating. Thus the Roosevelt story has been accorded the treatment of the notable "Inside" works that have given Mr. Gunther a unique place in political journalism. It need not be debated whether this treatment assures a satisfactory biography; it does not. Mr. Roosevelt was both too complex and too paradoxical to be illuminated by a catalogue of his contradictions and questions about his qualities. He needs the synthesis of a great interpretative biography, operating like a shaft of light that reveals unity formed out of disunity and harmony underlying discord. Mr. Gunther has not undertaken to write this biography. It is not his method or his art. He is a compiler, as was Mr. Sandburg writing about Lincoln. He does not go in for the portraiture that grows out of selection, that is, the suppression of detail. He must note everything, stop and conjecture about everything, delight in everything, and both marvel and cavil.

All this makes a book that is informative, entertaining, and in this case also important, and because Mr. Gunther is an indefatigable gatherer of detail, a book that is fresh even in the familiar field of Rooseveltiana. But Mr. Gunther has not departed from his established formula. He writes about F.D.R. as he writes about a continent. But since F.D.R. was not a continent, it is clear that Mr. Gunther does not write about him *because* he understands him and feels compelled to share his understanding. He is searching, and we share his search. Mr. Roosevelt will remain one of the most difficult men of destiny to understand. But sooner or later someone will write *as though* he understood him, and a true biography will result.

What Mr. Gunther's book does suggest, though somewhat faintly, is that understanding Mr. Roosevelt is impossible without understanding first the greatness of the era in which he became the most notable world figure. We still are too close to that era to see its dimensions. The depression and America's rescue from it are only a minor part of the drama. The coming war is a larger part; and then the war itself, with its now forgotten dangers and its now unappreciated victory, forms the stupendous climax. What is mysterious about Mr. Roosevelt's career is that he went through each of these phases, not as an intellectual leader who had mastered in advance the requirements of each, but as a political leader who had to come to grips with the problems as they grew acute, and did so groping his way, and only in time became master of events. He conquered the depression not with mind but with spirit. He was slow and tardy in feeling the rising peril of Nazi and Japanese ambition. And once the war was on, he was to lead the country through two years of mortifying defeat and impotence. But in each phase he rallied the forces that came into dominance. Only when a future generation is able to appraise the full nature of the tragic conflict of the era will Mr. Roosevelt's title to historic rank be clear. Mr. Gunther has moments when he is caught up by the forces of the time and feels their overwhelming power both for success or failure. But he does not let himself go in for re-creating this time, and failing to do so he fails to assign Mr. Roosevelt to his final rank. He believes he knows what the rank is, and suggests it persistently by his device of compilation and questioning. But not being ready to write the history of the Roosevelt era in its titanic perspective, he is unable to make Mr. Roosevelt a Titan.

Whatever else can be said about Mr. Roosevelt, he will count in the end for a series of achievements in all of which he began as a novice and then, by his phenomenal political talents, ended as architect and builder—and one who finished what he built. The one exception appears to be in regard to the peace. This he did not complete, and no political heir has had the vision and the power to complete it. Now, because he did not live to build the peace, some of his contemporaries hold it against him, as though it was due to a shortcoming in his nature and genius. And in this view, because men have forgotten the dire perils they were in during World War II, and how near they came to defeat and how dramatic were the developments that staved it off, the victory passes as of minor moment and with it the leadership of Mr. Roosevelt. Mr. Gunther might have expended some of his indubitable gifts in drawing with greater attention the backdrop before which F.D.R. was to act, and thus have established his stature. But though he knows quite well what the stature was, he only affirms it, and does not measure it with the arts of creative writing.

It surely is somewhat unfair to a man who has written a really good book to chide him for not writing a better one. Mr. Gunther may simply have lacked the time—the years—to have tackled the better one. What he has given lies within his quite generous means. He has produced the best new work on Mr. Roosevelt I have seen (excepting Sherwood's, which is also about Hopkins). It is highly readable, arresting, sometimes annoyingly naïve, but always disarmingly honest and scrupulously fair.

A future writer who is to attempt true portraiture will find postulated in this book all the riddles of which Mr. Roosevelt's complicated nature was made. But unless F.D.R. is to remain for all time simply a beloved but bewildering paradox, Mr. Gunther has provided only a sourcebook, albeit one of warmth, candor, and devotion.

COMMENT AND QUESTIONS

I. If you have not read *Roosevelt in Retrospect,* what is your opinion, after reading these four reviews, of John Gunther's book?

II. If you have read the book, which review best accords with your own judgment, and why?

III. Do any of the four reviewers agree on any points about the book? If so, what? On what main points do they disagree?

IV. Do any of the reviewers seem to you to be influenced by their personal feeling about the subject of the book, Franklin D. Roosevelt?

V. What agreement and disagreement do you find in the reviews about the author, John Gunther?

VI. The slanting by means of emphasis in the reviews affords an interesting study. What points are emphasized, to the exclusion of other points, in each review? Does the order in which the reviews appear represent a kind of slanting? If so, is the slanting favorable or unfavorable to Gunther and to Roosevelt? Explain.

VII. Which reviews use irony and ridicule as part of the technique of persuasion? Where do you think these techniques are most effectively used? Explain.

VIII. Which reviews appeal to emotion? Comment on the validity and the effectiveness of this appeal.

IX. Which review seems to you to be the most fair and to give the most convincing evidence to support the reviewer's opinion? Which review seems the least fair and the least convincing?

X. Read *Roosevelt in Retrospect* and, with the approval of your instructor, write a critical evaluation of the book and of these four reviews.

THE MONSTER *

DEEMS TAYLOR

The following selection by an American composer and critic is an evaluation. Deems Taylor has composed two operas and many symphonic poems and songs, and is music commentator for the Columbia Broadcasting System. "The Monster" is taken from one of his books of criticism, *Of Men and Music,* published in 1937.

[1] He was an undersized little man, with a head too big for his body—a sickly little man. His nerves were bad. He had skin trouble. It was agony for him to wear anything next to his skin coarser than silk. And he had delusions of grandeur.

[2] He was a monster of conceit. Never for one minute did he look at the world or at people, except in relation to himself. He was not only the most important person in the world, to himself; in his own eyes he was the only person who existed. He believed himself to be one of the greatest dramatists in the world, one of the greatest thinkers, and one of the greatest composers. To hear him talk, he was Shakespeare, and Beethoven, and Plato, rolled into one. And you would have had no difficulty in hearing him talk. He was one of the most exhausting conversationalists that ever lived. An evening with him was an evening spent in listening to a monologue. Sometimes he was brilliant; sometimes he was maddeningly tiresome. But whether he was being brilliant or dull, he had one sole topic of conversation: himself. What *he* thought and what *he* did.

[3] He had a mania for being in the right. The slightest hint of disagreement, from anyone, on the most trivial point, was enough to set him off on a harangue that might last for hours, in which he proved himself right in so many ways, and with such exhausting volubility, that in the end his hearer, stunned and deafened, would agree with him, for the sake of peace.

[4] It never occurred to him that he and his doing were not of the most intense and fascinating interest to anyone with whom he came in contact. He had theories about almost any subject under the sun, including vegetarianism, the drama, politics, and music; and in support of these theories he wrote pamphlets, letters, books . . .

thousands upon thousands of words, hundreds and hundreds of pages. He not only wrote these things, and published them—usually at somebody else's expense—but he would sit and read them aloud, for hours, to his friends and his family.

[5] He wrote operas; and no sooner did he have the synopsis of a story, but he would invite—or rather summon—a crowd of his friends to his house and read it aloud to them. Not for criticism. For applause. When the complete poem was written, the friends had to come again, and hear *that* read aloud. Then he would publish the poem, sometimes years before the music that went with it was written. He played the piano like a composer, in the worst sense of what that implies, and he would sit down at the piano before parties that included some of the finest pianists of his time, and play for them, by the hour, his own music, needless to say. He had a composer's voice. And he would invite eminent vocalists to his house, and sing them his operas, taking all the parts.

[6] He had the emotional stability of a six-year-old child. When he felt out of sorts, he would rave and stamp, or sink into suicidal gloom and talk darkly of going to the East to end his days as a Buddhist monk. Ten minutes later, when something pleased him, he would rush out of doors and run around the garden, or jump up and down on the sofa, or stand on his head. He could be grief-stricken over the death of a pet dog, and he could be callous and heartless to a degree that would have made a Roman emperor shudder.

[7] He was almost innocent of any sense of responsibility. Not only did he seem incapable of supporting himself, but it never occurred to him that he was under any obligation to do so. He was convinced that the world owed him a living. In support of this belief, he borrowed money from everybody who was good for a loan—men, women, friends, or strangers. He wrote begging letters by the score, sometimes groveling without shame, at others loftily offering his intended benefactor the privilege of contributing to his support, and being mortally offended if the recipient declined the honor. I have found no record of his ever paying or repaying money to anyone who did not have a legal claim upon it.

[8] What money he could lay his hands on he spent like an Indian rajah. The mere prospect of a performance of one of his operas was enough to set him running up bills amounting to ten times the amount of his prospective royalties. On an income that would reduce a more scrupulous man to doing his own laundry, he would keep two servants. Without enough money in his pocket to pay his rent, he would have the walls and ceiling of his study lined with pink silk. No one will ever know—certainly he never knew—how much money he

owed. We do know that his greatest benefactor gave him $6,000 to pay the most pressing of his debts in one city, and a year later had to give him $16,000 to enable him to live in another city without being thrown into jail for debt.

[9]   He was equally unscrupulous in other ways. An endless procession of women marches through his life. His first wife spent twenty years enduring and forgiving his infidelities. His second wife had been the wife of his most devoted friend and admirer, from whom he stole her. And even while he was trying to persuade her to leave her first husband he was writing to a friend to inquire whether he could suggest some wealthy woman—*any* wealthy woman—whom he could marry for her money.

[10]   He was completely selfish in his other personal relationships. His liking for his friends was measured solely by the completeness of their devotion to him, or by their usefulness to him, whether financial or artistic. The minute they failed him—even by so much as refusing a dinner invitation—or began to lessen in usefulness, he cast them off without a second thought. At the end of his life he had exactly one friend left whom he had known even in middle age.

[11]   He had a genius for making enemies. He would insult a man who disagreed with him about the weather. He would pull endless wires in order to meet some man who admired his work, and was able and anxious to be of use to him—and would proceed to make a mortal enemy of him with some idiotic and wholly uncalled-for exhibition of arrogance and bad manners. A character in one of his operas was a caricature of one of the most powerful music critics of his day. Not content with burlesquing him, he invited the critic to his house and read him the libretto aloud in front of his friends.

[12]   The name of this monster was Richard Wagner. Everything that I have said about him you can find on record—in newspapers, in police reports, in the testimony of people who knew him, in his own letters, between the lines of his autobiography. And the curious thing about this record is that it doesn't matter in the least.

[13]   Because this undersized, sickly, disagreeable, fascinating little man was right all the time. The joke was on us. He *was* one of the world's great dramatists; he *was* a great thinker; he *was* one of the most stupendous musical geniuses that, up to now, the world has ever seen. The world did owe him a living. People couldn't know those things at the time, I suppose; and yet to us, who know his music, it does seem as though they should have known. What if he did talk about himself all the time? If he had talked about himself for twenty-four hours every day for the span of his life he would not have uttered

half the number of words that other men have spoken and written about him since his death.

[14]   When you consider what he wrote—thirteen operas and music dramas, eleven of them still holding the stage, eight of them unquestionably worth ranking among the world's great musico-dramatic masterpieces—when you listen to what he wrote, the debts and heartaches that people had to endure from him don't seem much of a price. Eduard Hanslick, the critic whom he caricatured in *Die Meistersinger* and who hated him ever after, now lives only because he was caricatured in *Die Meistersinger*. The women whose hearts he broke are long since dead; and the man who could never love anyone but himself has made them deathless atonement, I think, with *Tristan und Isolde*. Think of the luxury with which for a time, at least, fate rewarded Napoleon, the man who ruined France and looted Europe; and then perhaps you will agree that a few thousand dollars' worth of debts were not too heavy a price to pay for the *Ring* trilogy.

[15]   What if he was faithless to his friends and to his wives? He had one mistress to whom he was faithful to the day of his death: Music. Not for a single moment did he ever compromise with what he believed, with what he dreamed. There is not a line of his music that could have been conceived by a little mind. Even when he is dull, or downright bad, he is dull in the grand manner. There is a greatness about his worst mistakes. Listening to his music, one does not forgive him for what he may or may not have been. It is not a matter of forgiveness. It is a matter of being dumb with wonder that his poor brain and body didn't burst under the torment of the demon of creative energy that lived inside him, struggling, clawing, scratching to be released; tearing, shrieking at him to write the music that was in him. The miracle is that what he did in the little space of seventy years could have been done at all, even by a great genius. Is it any wonder that he had no time to be a man?

COMMENT AND QUESTIONS

I. This evaluation is built on a pattern of contrast, with the first eleven paragraphs devoted to Wagner's unpleasant qualities and the last three, introduced by the turn in paragraph 12, to his genius. For an analysis of the essay, list in order the topic ideas in the first eleven paragraphs.

II. What is the reason for the sequence of ideas in these eleven paragraphs? Could the order be changed without loss?

III. How many of the unpleasant qualities discussed in the first section are referred to and justified in the last three paragraphs?

IV. What does Mr. Taylor gain by withholding the "monster's" identity until paragraph 12?

V. How well are the two contrasting judgments of Wagner supported by factual evidence?

VI. Point out some of the techniques Mr. Taylor uses to appeal to emotion.

VII. State in the form of a syllogism Mr. Taylor's argument in the last three paragraphs. Do you agree with his major premise?

DUNKIRK

WINSTON CHURCHILL

The evacuation of Dunkirk, regarded by military experts as a miracle of World War II, has become a symbol of victory in defeat. Badly defeated in May, 1940, by the Germans in Belgium, the British and French armies fell back to Dunkirk, the only port on the French coast still in Allied hands. A fleet of rescue boats—destroyers, ferries, tugboats, fishing smacks—every boat available—set out from the British coast across the channel and, shuttling back and forth under heavy German attack, rescued 335,000 men from the beaches of Dunkirk. On June 4, 1940, Winston Churchill, prime minister of Great Britain, gave the following account of the evacuation to the House of Commons. His address is an informative report, an evaluation, and an appeal to emotion.

―――――――

[1] From the moment that the French defenses at Sedan and on the Meuse were broken at the end of the second week of May, only a rapid retreat to Amiens and the south could have saved the British and French Armies who had entered Belgium at the appeal of the Belgian King; but this strategic fact was not immediately realized. The French High Command hoped they would be able to close the gap, and the Armies of the north were under their orders. Moreover, a retirement of this kind would have involved almost certainly the destruction of the fine Belgian Army of over 20 divisions and the abandonment of the whole of Belgium. Therefore, when the force and scope of the German penetration were realized and when a new French Generalissimo, General Weygand, assumed command in place of General Gamelin, an effort was made by the French and British Armies in Belgium to keep on holding the right hand of the Belgians and to give their own right hand to a newly created French

Army which was to have advanced across the Somme in great strength to grasp it.

[2]   However, the German eruption swept like a sharp scythe around the right and rear of the Armies of the north. Eight or nine armored divisions, each of about four hundred armored vehicles of different kinds, but carefully assorted to be complementary and divisible into small self-contained units, cut off all communications between us and the main French Armies. It severed our own communications for food and ammunition, which ran first to Amiens and afterwards through Abbeville, and it shore its way up the coast to Boulogne and Calais, and almost to Dunkirk. Behind this armored and mechanized onslaught came a number of German divisions in lorries, and behind them again there plodded comparatively slowly the dull brute mass of the ordinary German Army and German people, always so ready to be led to the trampling down in other lands of liberties and comforts which they have never known in their own.

[3]   I have said this armored scythe-stroke almost reached Dunkirk— almost but not quite. Boulogne and Calais were the scenes of desperate fighting. The Guards defended Boulogne for a while and were then withdrawn by orders from this country. The Rifle Brigade, the 60th Rifles, and the Queen Victoria's Rifles, with a battalion of British tanks and a thousand Frenchmen, in all about four thousand strong, defended Calais to the last. The British Brigadier was given an hour to surrender. He spurned the offer, and four days of intense street fighting passed before silence reigned over Calais, which marked the end of a memorable resistance. Only thirty unwounded survivors were brought off by the Navy, and we do not know the fate of their comrades. Their sacrifice, however, was not in vain. At least two armored divisions, which otherwise would have been turned against the British Expeditionary Force, had to be sent to overcome them. They have added another page to the glories of the light divisions, and the time gained enabled the Graveline water lines to be flooded and to be held by the French troops.

[4]   Thus it was that the port of Dunkirk was kept open. When it was found impossible for the Armies of the north to reopen their communications to Amiens with the main French Armies, only one choice remained. It seemed, indeed, forlorn. The Belgian, British and French Armies were almost surrounded. Their sole line of retreat was to a single port and to its neighboring beaches. They were pressed on every side by heavy attacks and far outnumbered in the air.

[5]   When, a week ago today, I asked the House to fix this afternoon as the occasion for a statement, I feared it would be my hard lot to

announce the greatest military disaster in our long history. I thought
—and some good judges agreed with me—that perhaps 20,000 or
30,000 men might be re-embarked. But it certainly seemed that the
whole of the French First Army and the whole of the British Expeditionary Force north of the Amiens-Abbeville gap would be
broken up in the open field or else would have to capitulate for lack
of food and ammunition. These were the hard and heavy tidings for
which I called upon the House and the nation to prepare themselves a week ago. The whole root and core and brain of the British
Army, on which and around which we were later to build, and are
to build, the great British Armies in the later years of the war, seemed
about to perish upon the field or to be led into an ignominious and
starving captivity.

[6]   That was the prospect of a week ago. But another blow which
might well have proved final was yet to fall upon us. The King of the
Belgians had called upon us to come to his aid. Had not this Ruler
and his Government severed themselves from the Allies, who rescued
their country from extinction in the late war, and had they not
sought refuge in what has proved to be a fatal neutrality, the French
and British Armies might well at the outset have saved not only
Belgian but perhaps even Poland. Yet at the last moment, when
Belgium was already invaded, King Leopold called upon us to come
to his aid, and even at the last moment we came. He and his brave,
efficient Army, nearly half a million strong, guarded our left flank
and thus kept open our only line of retreat to the sea. Suddenly, without prior consultation, with the least possible notice, without the
advice of his Ministers and upon his own personal act, he sent a
plenipotentiary to the German Command, surrendered his Army,
and exposed our whole flank and means of retreat.

[7]   I asked the House a week ago to suspend its judgment because
the facts were not clear, but I do not feel that any reason now exists
why we should not form our own opinions upon this pitiful episode.
The surrender of the Belgian Army compelled the British at the
shortest notice to cover a flank to the sea more than 30 miles in length.
Otherwise all would have been cut off, and all would have shared the
fate to which King Leopold had condemned the finest Army his
country had ever formed. So in doing this and in exposing this flank,
as anyone who followed the operations on the map will see, contact
was lost between the British and two out of the three corps forming
the First French Army, who were still farther from the coast than we
were, and it seemed impossible that any large number of Allied troops
could reach the coast.

[8]   The enemy attacked on all sides with great strength and fierce-

ness, and their main power, the power of their far more numerous Air Force, was thrown into battle or else concentrated upon Dunkirk and the beaches. Pressing in upon the narrow exit, both from the east and from the west, the enemy began to fire with cannon upon the beaches by which alone the shipping could approach or depart. They sowed magnetic mines in the channels and seas; they set repeated waves of hostile aircraft, sometimes more than a hundred strong in one formation, to cast their bombs upon the single pier that remained, and upon the sand dunes upon which the troops had their eyes for shelter. Their U-boats, one of which was sunk, and their motor launches took their toll of the vast traffic which now began. For four or five days an intense struggle reigned. All their armored divisions—or what was left of them—together with great masses of infantry and artillery, hurled themselves in vain upon the ever-narrowing, ever-contracting appendix within which the British and French Armies fought.

[9] Meanwhile, the Royal Navy, with the willing help of countless merchant seamen, strained every nerve to embark the British and Allied troops; 220 light warships and 650 other vessels were engaged. They had to operate upon the difficult coast, often in adverse weather, under an almost ceaseless hail of bombs and an increasing concentration of artillery fire. Nor were the seas, as I have said, themselves free from mines and torpedoes. It was in conditions such as these that our men carried on, with little or no rest, for days and nights on end, making trip after trip across the dangerous waters, bringing with them always men whom they had rescued. The numbers they have brought back are the measure of their devotion and their courage. The hospital ships, which brought off many thousands of British and French wounded, being so plainly marked were a special target for Nazi bombs, but the men and women on board never faltered in their duty.

[10] Meanwhile, the Royal Air Force, which had already been intervening in the battle, so far as its range would allow, from home bases, now used part of its main metropolitan fighter strength, and struck at the German bombers and at the fighters which in large numbers protected them. This struggle was protracted and fierce. Suddenly the scene has cleared, the crash and thunder has for the moment—but only for the moment—died away. A miracle of deliverance, achieved by valor, by perseverance, by perfect discipline, by faultless service, by resource, by skill, by unconquerable fidelity, is manifest to us all. The enemy was hurled back by the retreating British and French troops. He was so roughly handled that he did not hurry their departure seriously. The Royal Air Force engaged the

main strength of the German Air Force, and inflicted upon them losses of at least four to one; and the Navy, using nearly a thousand ships of all kinds, carried over 335,000 men, French and British, out of the jaws of death and shame, to their native land and to the tasks which lie immediately ahead. We must be very careful not to assign to this deliverance the attributes of a victory. Wars are not won by evacuations. But there was a victory inside this deliverance, which should be noted. It was gained by the Air Force. Many of our soldiers coming back have not seen the Air Force at work; they saw only the bombers which escaped its protective attack. They underrate its achievements. I have heard much talk of this; that is why I go out of my way to say this. I will tell you about it.

[11] This was a great trial of strength between the British and German Air Forces. Can you conceive a greater objective for the Germans in the air than to make evacuation from these beaches impossible, and to sink all these ships which were displayed, almost to the extent of thousands? Could there have been an objective of greater military importance and significance for the whole purpose of the war than this? They tried hard, and they were beaten back; they were frustrated in their task. We got the Army away; and they have paid four-fold for any losses which they have inflicted. Very large formations of German aeroplanes—and we know that they are a very brave race—have turned on several occasions from the attack of one-quarter of their number of the Royal Air Force, and have dispersed in different directions. Twelve aeroplanes have been hunted by two. One aeroplane was driven into the water and cast away by the mere charge of a British aeroplane, which had no more ammunition. All of our types—the Hurricane, the Spitfire, and the new Defiant—and all our pilots have been vindicated as superior to what they have at present to face.

[12] When we consider how much greater would be our advantage in defending the air above this Island against an overseas attack, I must say that I find in these facts a sure basis upon which practical and reassuring thoughts may rest. I will pay my tribute to these young airmen. The great French Army was very largely, for the time being, cast back and disturbed by the onrush of a few thousands of armored vehicles. May it not also be that the cause of civilization itself will be defended by the skill and devotion of a few thousand airmen? There never has been, I suppose, in all the world, in all the history of war, such an opportunity for youth. The Knights of the Round Table, the Crusaders, all fall back into the past—not only distant but prosaic; these young men, going forth every morn to guard their native land and all that we stand for, holding in their hands

these instruments of colossal and shattering power, of whom it may be said that

> "Every morn brought forth a noble chance
> And every chance brought forth a noble knight,"

deserve our gratitude, as do all of the brave men who, in so many ways and on so many occasions, are ready, and continue ready, to give life and all for their native land.

[13] I return to the Army. In the long series of very fierce battles, now on this front, now on that, fighting on three fronts at once, battles fought by two or three divisions against an equal or somewhat larger number of the enemy, and fought fiercely on some of the old grounds that so many of us knew so well—in these battles our losses in men have exceeded 30,000 killed, wounded, and missing. I take occasion to express the sympathy of the House to all who have suffered bereavement or who are still anxious. The President of the Board of Trade is not here today. His son has been killed, and many in the House have felt the pangs of affliction in the sharpest form. But I will say this about the missing: We have had a large number of wounded come home safely to this country, but I would say about the missing that there may be very many reported missing who will come back home, some day, in one way or another. In the confusion of this fight it is inevitable that many have been left in positions where honor required no further resistance from them.

[14] Against this loss of over 30,000 men, we can set a far heavier loss certainly inflicted upon the enemy. But our losses in material are enormous. We have perhaps lost one-third of the men we lost in the opening days of the battle of 21st March, 1918, but we have lost nearly as many guns—nearly one thousand—and all our transport, all the armored vehicles that were with the Army in the north. This loss will impose a further delay on the expansion of our military strength. That expansion had not been proceeding as fast as we had hoped. The best of all we had to give had gone to the British Expeditionary Force, and although they had not the numbers of tanks and some articles of equipment which were desirable, they were a very well and finely equipped Army. They had the first-fruits of all that our industry had to give, and that is gone. And now here is this further delay. How long it will be, how long it will last, depends upon the exertions which we make in this Island. An effort the like of which has never been seen in our records is now being made. Work is proceeding everywhere, night and day, Sundays and week days. Capital and Labor have cast aside their interests, rights, and customs and put them into the common stock. Already the flow of munitions

has leaped forward. There is no reason why we should not in a few months overtake the sudden and serious loss that has come upon us, without retarding the development of our general program.

[15]   Nevertheless, our thankfulness at the escape of our Army and so many men, whose loved ones have passed through an agonizing week, must not blind us to the fact that what has happened in France and Belgium is a colossal military disaster. The French Army has been weakened, the Belgian Army has been lost, a large part of those fortified lines upon which so much faith had been reposed is gone, many valuable mining districts and factories have passed into the enemy's possession, the whole of the Channel ports are in his hands, with all the tragic consequences that follow from that, and we must expect another blow to be struck almost immediately at us or at France. We are told that Herr Hitler has a plan for invading the British Isles. This has often been thought of before. When Napoleon lay at Boulogne for a year with his flat-bottomed boats and his Grand Army, he was told by someone, "There are bitter weeds in England." There are certainly a great many more of them since the British Expeditionary Force returned.

[16]   The whole question of home defense against invasion is, of course, powerfully affected by the fact that we have for the time being in this Island incomparably more powerful military forces than we have ever had at any moment in this war or the last. But this will not continue. We shall not be content with a defensive war. We have our duty to our Ally. We have to reconstitute and build up the British Expeditionary Force, once again, under its gallant Commander-in-Chief, Lord Gort. All this is in train; but in the interval we must put our defenses in this Island into such a high state of organization that the fewest possible numbers will be required to give effective security and that the largest possible potential offensive effort may be realized. On this we are now engaged. It will be very convenient, if it be the desire of the House, to enter upon this subject in a secret Session. Not that the Government would necessarily be able to reveal in very great detail military secrets, but we like to have our discussions free, without the restraint imposed by the fact that they will be read the next day by the enemy; and the Government would benefit by views freely expressed in all parts of the House by Members with their knowledge of so many different parts of the country. I understand that some request is to be made upon this subject, which will be readily acceded to by His Majesty's Government.

[17]   We have found it necessary to take measures of increasing

stringency, not only against enemy aliens and suspicious characters of other nationalities, but also against British subjects who may become a danger or a nuisance should the war be transported to the United Kingdom. I know there are a great many people affected by the orders which we have made who are the passionate enemies of Nazi Germany. I am very sorry for them, but we cannot, at the present time and under the present stress, draw all the distinctions which we should like to do. If parachute landings were attempted and fierce fighting attendant upon them followed, these unfortunate people would be far better out of the way, for their own sakes as well as for ours. There is, however, another class, for which I feel not the slightest sympathy. Parliament has given us the powers to put down Fifth Column activities with a strong hand, and we shall use those powers, subject to the supervision and correction of the House, without the slightest hesitation until we are satisfied, and more than satisfied, that this malignancy in our midst has been effectively stamped out.

[18] Turning once again, and this time more generally, to the question of invasion, I would observe that there has never been a period in all these long centuries of which we boast when an absolute guarantee against invasion, still less against serious raids, could have been given to our people. In the days of Napoleon the same wind which would have carried his transports across the Channel might have driven away the blockading fleet. There was always the chance, and it is that chance which has excited and befooled the imaginations of many Continental tyrants. Many are the tales that are told. We are assured that novel methods will be adopted, and when we see the originality of malice, the ingenuity of aggression, which our enemy displays, we may certainly prepare ourselves for every kind of novel stratagem and every kind of brutal and treacherous maneuver. I think that no idea is so outlandish that it should not be considered and viewed with a searching, but at the same time, I hope, with a steady eye. We must never forget the solid assurances of sea power and those which belong to air power if it can be locally exercised.

[19] I have, myself, full confidence that if all do their duty, if nothing is neglected, and if the best arrangements are made, as they are being made, we shall prove ourselves once again able to defend our Island home, to ride out the storm of war, and to outlive the menace of tyranny, if necessary for years, if necessary alone. At any rate, that is what we are going to try to do. That is the resolve of His Majesty's Government—every man of them. That is the will of Parliament and

the nation. The British Empire and the French Republic, linked together in their cause and in their need, will defend to the death their native soil, aiding each other like good comrades to the utmost of their strength. Even though large tracts of Europe and many old and famous States have fallen or may fall into the grip of the Gestapo and all the odious apparatus of Nazi rule, we shall not flag or fail. We shall go on to the end, we shall fight in France, we shall fight on the seas and oceans, we shall fight with growing confidence and growing strength in the air, we shall defend our Island, whatever the cost may be, we shall fight on the beaches, we shall fight on the landing grounds, we shall fight in the fields and in the streets, we shall fight in the hills; we shall never surrender, and even if, which I do not for a moment believe, this Island or a large part of it were subjugated and starving, then our Empire beyond the seas, armed and guarded by the British Fleet, would carry on the struggle, until, in God's good time, the New World, with all its power and might, steps forth to the rescue and the liberation of the old.

COMMENT AND QUESTIONS

I. Winston Churchill's prose, though overformal and too oratorical for everyday use, is excellent of its kind, and worth study for the stylistic techniques Churchill uses to gain his effects. The last paragraph of "Dunkirk" is the passage most worth analysis. Notice the length, structure, and rhythm of sentences, and, particularly in the famous long last sentence, the variation within the pattern of parallelism and repetition.

II. Paragraphs 8–10 are interesting examples of dramatic narration. What techniques does Churchill use to make the reported action intense and vivid?

III. Summarize Churchill's evaluation of the events which he is reporting to the House of Commons.

IV. What is his attitude toward the possible invasion of England?

V. This speech, in addition to giving information and a reasonable appraisal of the situation after Dunkirk, was designed to inspire courage and determination for the hard days which lay ahead. To what emotions does Churchill appeal in an effort to inspire that determination? In what particular passages do you find his language most effective in serving his intention?

VI. Read the first four paragraphs to see where Churchill subtly places blame and to what parts of the Allied forces he awards praise. Would a French statesman give the account in the same way?

VII. Would it be to Churchill's advantage to place the King of the

Belgians in an unfavorable light? Consider in detail Churchill's treatment of him in paragraphs 6 and 7.

VIII. Churchill's account would still be clear if paragraph 5 were omitted. What purpose does this paragraph serve?

ARRANGEMENT IN BLACK AND WHITE *

DOROTHY PARKER

The following short story is an example of persuasion by irony and ridicule. Dorothy Parker, famous during the 1920's and 1930's for her caustic wit and sophisticated humor, is the author of numerous poems, sketches, and short stories. Some of her books are *Enough Rope, Sunset Gun, Not So Deep as a Well* (collected poems), *After Such Pleasures,* and *Here Lies* (collected prose pieces). "Arrangement in Black and White" was published in *Laments for the Living* in 1930, and is included in *The Portable Dorothy Parker* published in 1944.

~~~

The woman with the pink velvet poppies wreathed round the assisted gold of her hair traversed the crowded room at an interesting gait combining a skip with a sidle, and clutched the lean arm of her host.

"Now I got you!" she said. "Now you can't get away!"

"Why, hello," said her host. "Well. How are you?"

"Oh, I'm finely," she said. "Just simply finely. Listen. I want you to do me the most terrible favor. Will you? Will you please? Pretty please?"

"What is it?" said her host.

"Listen," she said. "I want to meet Walter Williams. Honestly, I'm just simply crazy about that man. Oh, when he sings! When he sings those spirituals! Well, I said to Burton, 'It's a good thing for you Walter Williams is colored,' I said, 'or you'd have lots of reason to be jealous.' I'd really love to meet him. I'd like to tell him I've heard him sing. Will you be an angel and introduce me to him?"

"Why, certainly," said her host. "I thought you'd met him. The party's for him. Where is he, anyway?"

"He's over there by the bookcase," she said. "Let's wait till those

* From *The Portable Dorothy Parker,* copyright, 1927, 1944, by Dorothy Parker. Reprinted by permission of The Viking Press, Inc., New York.

people get through talking to him. Well, I think you're simply marvelous, giving this perfectly marvelous party for him, and having him meet all these white people, and all. Isn't he terribly grateful?"

"I hope not," said her host.

"I think it's really terribly nice," she said. "I do. I don't see why on earth it isn't perfectly all right to meet colored people. I haven't any feeling at all about it—not one single bit. Burton—oh, he's just the other way. Well, you know, he comes from Virginia, and you know how they are."

"Did he come tonight?" said her host.

"No, he couldn't," she said. "I'm a regular grass widow tonight. I told him when I left, 'There's no telling what I'll do,' I said. He was just so tired out, he couldn't move. Isn't it a shame?"

"Ah," said her host.

"Wait till I tell him I met Walter Williams!" she said. "He'll just about die. Oh, we have more arguments about colored people. I talk to him like I don't know what, I get so excited. 'Oh, don't be so silly,' I say. But I must say for Burton, he's heaps broader-minded than lots of these Southerners. He's really awfully fond of colored people. Well, he says himself, he wouldn't have white servants. And you know, he had this old colored nurse, this regular old nigger mammy, and he just simply loves her. Why, every time he goes home, he goes out in the kitchen to see her. He does, really, to this day. All he says is, he says he hasn't got a word to say against colored people as long as they keep their place. He's always doing things for them—giving them clothes and I don't know what all. The only thing he says, he says he wouldn't sit down at the table with one for a million dollars. 'Oh,' I say to him, 'you make me sick, talking like that.' I'm just terrible to him. Aren't I terrible?"

"Oh, no, no, no," said her host. "No, no."

"I am," she said. "I know I am. Poor Burton! Now, me, I don't feel that way at all. I haven't the slightest feeling about colored people. Why, I'm just crazy about some of them. They're just like children— just as easy-going, and always singing and laughing and everything. Aren't they the happiest things you ever saw in your life? Honestly, it makes me laugh just to hear them. Oh, I like them. I really do. Well, now, listen, I have this colored laundress, I've had her for years, and I'm devoted to her. She's a real character. And I want to tell you, I think of her as my friend. That's the way I think of her. As I say to Burton, 'Well, for Heaven's sakes, we're all human beings!' Aren't we?"

"Yes," said her host. "Yes, indeed."

"Now this Walter Williams," she said. "I think a man like that's a real artist. I do. I think he deserves an awful lot of credit. Goodness, I'm so crazy about music or anything, I don't care what color he is. I honestly think if a person's an artist, nobody ought to have any feeling at all about meeting them. That's absolutely what I say to Burton. Don't you think I'm right?"

"Yes," said her host. "Oh, yes."

"That's the way I feel," she said. "I just can't understand people being narrow-minded. Why, I absolutely think it's a privilege to meet a man like Walter Williams. Now, I do. I haven't any feeling at all. Well, my goodness, the good Lord made him, just the same as He did any of us. Didn't He?"

"Surely," said her host. "Yes, indeed."

"That's what I say," she said. "Oh, I get so furious when people are narrow-minded about colored people. It's just all I can do not to say something. Of course, I do admit when you get a bad colored man, they're simply terrible. But as I say to Burton, there are some bad white people, too, in this world. Aren't there?"

"I guess there are," said her host.

"Why, I'd really be glad to have a man like Walter Williams come to my house and sing for us, some time," she said. "Of course, I couldn't ask him on account of Burton, but I wouldn't have any feeling about it at all. Oh, can't he sing! Isn't it marvelous, the way they all have music in them? It just seems to be right *in* them. Come on, let's us go on over and talk to him. Listen, what shall I do when I'm introduced? Ought I to shake hands? Or what?"

"Why, do whatever you want," said her host.

"I guess maybe I'd better," she said. "I wouldn't for the world have him think I had any feeling. I think I'd better shake hands, just the way I would with anybody else. That's just exactly what I'll do."

They reached the tall young Negro, standing by the bookcase. The host performed introductions; the Negro bowed.

"How do you do?" he said.

The woman with the pink velvet poppies extended her hand at the length of her arm and held it so for all the world to see, until the Negro took it, shook it, and gave it back to her.

"Oh, how do you do, Mr. Williams," she said. "Well, how do you do. I've just been saying, I've enjoyed your singing so awfully much. I've been to your concerts, and we have you on the phonograph and everything. Oh, I just enjoy it!"

She spoke with great distinctness, moving her lips meticulously, as if in parlance with the deaf.

"I'm so glad," he said.

"I'm just simply crazy about that 'Water Boy' thing you sing," she

said. "Honestly, I can't get it out of my head. I have my husband
nearly crazy, the way I go around humming it all the time. Oh, he
looks just as black as the ace of—Er. Well, tell me, where on earth do
you ever get all those songs of yours? How do you ever get hold of
them?"

"Why," he said, "there are so many different—"

"I should think you'd love singing them," she said. "It must be
more fun. All those darling old spirituals—oh, I just love them! Well,
what are you doing now? Are you still keeping up your singing? Why
don't you have another concert, some time?"

"I'm having one the sixteenth of this month," he said.

"Well, I'll be there," she said. "I'll be there, if I possibly can. You
can count on me. Goodness, here comes a whole raft of people to talk
to you. You're just a regular guest of honor! Oh, who's that girl in
white? I've seen her some place."

"That's Katherine Burke," said her host.

"Good Heavens," she said, "is that Katherine Burke? Why, she
looks entirely different off the stage. I thought she was much better
looking. I had no idea she was so terribly dark. Why, she looks almost
like—oh, I think she's a wonderful actress! Don't you think she's a
wonderful actress, Mr. Williams? Oh, I think she's marvelous. Don't
you?"

"Yes, I do," he said.

"Oh, I do, too," she said. "Just wonderful. Well, goodness, we must
give someone else a chance to talk to the guest of honor. Now, don't
forget, Mr. Williams, I'm going to be at that concert if I possibly can.
I'll be there applauding like everything. And if I can't come, I'm
going to tell everybody I know to go, anyway. Don't you forget!"

"I won't," he said. "Thank you so much."

The host took her arm and piloted her into the next room.

"Oh, my dear," she said. "I nearly died! Honestly, I give you my
word, I nearly passed away. Did you hear that terrible break I made?
I was just going to say Katherine Burke looked almost like a nigger.
I just caught myself in time. Oh, do you think he noticed?"

"I don't believe so," said her host.

"Well, thank goodness," she said, "because I wouldn't have embarrassed him for anything. Why, he's awfully nice. Just as nice as
he can be. Nice manners, and everything. You know, so many colored
people, you give them an inch, and they walk all over you. But he
doesn't try any of that. Well, he's got more sense, I suppose. He's
really nice. Don't you think so?"

"Yes," said her host.

"I liked him," she said. "I haven't any feeling at all because he's a colored man. I felt just as natural as I would with anybody. Talked to him just as naturally, and everything. But, honestly, I could hardly keep a straight face. I kept thinking of Burton. Oh, wait till I tell Burton I called him 'Mister'!"

COMMENT AND QUESTIONS

We shall have more to say in a later section about techniques of describing people. It is worth noting here, however, that the first paragraph of this story is a clever brief description. The woman's movement and gesture characterize her, and the details of "the pink velvet poppies wreathed round the assisted gold of her hair" create a picture and at the same time suggest the woman's artificiality. Except for this first paragraph, the story is almost completely objective: the author seldom passes judgment or directly ridicules the character; the author stays out of the story and lets the character make herself ridiculous. The irony lies, of course, in the contrast between the woman's idea of herself as a liberal, tolerant person, and the idea the reader receives of the kind of person she is.

I. Aside from the attitudes she expresses, what are the qualities of this woman's speech?

II. How would you characterize the host? How are his attitudes revealed to the reader?

III. What impression does one get of Walter Williams?

IV. The woman with the pink velvet poppies holds many stereotyped ideas about Negroes. What are these ideas? What questionable major premises does she take for granted?

V. This story may be an example of persuasion aimed at an audience which already accepts the author's views. Do you think that a reader with strong anti-Negro prejudice would condemn the woman with the velvet poppies, or would understand what Dorothy Parker is trying to do in the story? At what point in the story is it clear to an unprejudiced reader that this woman and her attitudes are not admirable?

III. COMMUNICATION OF EXPERIENCE

Communication of experience can best be distinguished from other types of writing by its intention, which is not primarily to inform or to persuade but to communicate vividly some kind of experience. In many popular stories and novels, it is true, the experience presented bears little resemblance to actuality; it offers the reader a romantic escape from life-as-it-is to life-as-it-might-be. The serious communicator, however, tries to carry the reader into, not away from, real situations and emotions. Using his knowledge, his observation, and his imagination, he creates a picture of life which he believes is true, and which he hopes will give the reader a deeper understanding of life itself.

We shall discuss in this section four forms of communication of experience: descriptive writing, the reflective personal essay, the simple narrative, and the short story. This division of types is, like other divisions we have made, largely a matter of convenience; it is designed to facilitate discussion of the somewhat different problems and techniques of somewhat different literary forms. Actually, in modern writing, description is nearly always a subordinate part of an essay or a narrative, rarely an independent whole; and the borderlines are indefinite between the simple narrative and the personal essay, and between the simple narrative and the complex narrative called the short story.

For effective writing and reading of prose which communicates experience, it is important to understand three aspects of technique and style. They are *point of view, symbolism,* and *suggestion.*

Point of view is the angle of narration used in descriptive and narrative writing. It is the answer to two closely related questions: Who observes the events recorded in this piece of writing? From what physical or psychological position are the events observed?

Angles of narration may be roughly classified as *third-person point of view* and *first-person point of view.* Each of these categories has subdivisions and variations which are best understood by seeing how they work in specific pieces of prose. The following summary merely outlines some possible variations within each of the two main points of view.

1. *Third-person point of view.* If the author is writing in the third person, he may use:

(a) *The omniscient point of view.* With this point of view, the omniscient (that is, all-knowing) author can read the minds of all his characters, can record their secret thoughts as well as their actions, can be in two places at the same time if he chooses. In short, the omniscient author has superhuman powers and knowledge. He is godlike. He usually comments on and interprets the events of the story for the reader. This point of view is probably the most common angle of narration.

(b) *The limited omniscient point of view.* The author, instead of roving freely in the minds of his characters, takes up residence in the mind of only one, and presents that character's view of and reaction to occurrences. This point of view is particularly good in the short story because its focus on one character produces a desirable unity and often an interesting slant on the action.

(*c*) *The objective point of view.* The author, deliberately staying out of the minds of his characters, reports their speech and action, and lets the reader draw his own conclusions about what they think and feel. This objective reporting is sometimes called the *fly-on-the-wall point of view;* the author, like a fly, is present and seeing, but unseen; he does not intrude in the story. The objective point of view, generally somewhat modified, is often used in modern fiction. It demands skill on the part of both writer and reader, for the writer must so present characters and events that they speak for themselves, without author-comment, and the reader must be able to interpret the reported events, and also the thoughts and feelings which are merely suggested by the action.

2. *First-person point of view.* If the author is writing in the first person, the "I" who observes events may be:

(*a*) *The author himself, or a passive observer or narrator.*

(*b*) *The major character,* telling his own story.

(*c*) *A minor character,* viewing and judging the happenings in which he has a minor role.

Any first-person point of view necessarily limits the material to what the narrator can know, what he is in a position to observe. The advantages of the first person are that it has a ring of authority and truth—it appears to be a first-hand account for which the "I" personally vouches; and it permits very informal narration and recollection of past events.

Besides the points of view summarized above, there are two interesting angles of narration which may be either third-person or first-person. They are the *innocent-eye point of view* and *stream of consciousness.* The *innocent-eye point of view* is used when a story is told by (in the first person) or through the mind of (in the third person) a character who does not fully understand the events which he witnesses. The innocent-eye observer is often a child; but he may, by an extension of the word *innocent*, be anyone whose perception is deficient, because of youth, or ignorance, or a distorted code of ethics, or mental limitations. For example, the first part of William Faulkner's novel *The Sound and the Fury* is told through the mind of an idiot, whose brain records, without comprehending, the sounds and images and action which are part of his daily experience. The effect of innocent-eye writing is ironical: the reader understands more than he is actually told, and sometimes the opposite of what he is told.

Stream-of-consciousness writing attempts to transfer to the printed page the content of a human mind—the complex, intermingled flow of conscious and subconscious thoughts, images, sensations, and recollections. In pure stream-of-consciousness prose, best exemplified in the writing of James Joyce, there is apparently no selection of material; the author tries to reproduce the mental processes in their entirety, and he usually omits conventional punctuation and capitalization in order to represent graphically the continuous, unbroken flow of thought. In modified stream-of-consciousness writing, the author selects from the whole flow of thought the material relevant to his purpose, and generally uses some conventional punctuation to make reading easier. The value of stream-of-consciousness writing is that it puts the reader into direct contact with the thoughts of another human being; it also takes him into a mental process in which, if the writing is successful, he recognizes the working of a mind much like his own.

Symbolism is a device for communicating meaning by the use of some material object which stands for an abstract relationship or idea. Symbolism is not merely literary; in everyday living, hundreds of symbols like wedding rings, fraternity pins, Phi Beta Kappa keys, trophies, flags, military decorations, and religious emblems derive meaning not from their own worth, but from the larger concept of which they are the concrete token. Similarly, in literature, a symbol is any concrete article or action which, though perhaps insignificant of itself, has become invested with value. Symbolism is particularly useful in the short story as a means of communicating a state of mind without author-comment and interpretation. A tree cut down, a picture hung, a letter destroyed, a door opened, may convey complex feeling or decision provided the tree, the picture, the letter, or the door stands for something, has been given a meaning beyond itself.

Suggestion in writing is the technique of supplying the reader with clear clues to the full meaning intended, but at the same time leaving something to his intelligence and imagination. Full and explicit statement of the meaning is desirable in informative writing; in communication of experience, however, full explanation, especially of feeling, is likely to produce slushy sentimentality, and to cheapen and weaken the emotion by overhandling. The following passage is a rather extreme, but not untypical example of the excessive emotionalizing found in some popular fiction:

She looked at the picture of her son, killed in Korea. Her boy. Her little boy. Her baby. Dead on the battlefield. Never to come home, to know her mother love again. A sob welled up from her anguished heart.

A writer with more restraint and more respect for his audience would probably write: "She looked at the picture of her youngest son, killed in Korea," and trust his readers to understand the mother's feelings. And readers of taste would be more moved by the simple suggestive statement than by the trite and clumsy playing on their heartstrings of the longer passage.

"Heard melodies are sweet," Keats wrote, "but those unheard are sweeter." For the same reason, understatement of emotion is nearly always more effective than overstatement: it enriches the experience by leaving the imagination of the reader free. Not hampered, or repelled, by obvious efforts to stir his emotions, he has the satisfaction of arriving at his own understanding of the experience. The skillful writer leads the reader to this understanding, but does not verbally insist that he respond in a particular way.

Several of the techniques we have already discussed in this chapter are useful in achieving rich suggestion rather than direct exposition of emotional experiences. Irony is one of these techniques. Since irony is understatement, or statement different from the meaning intended, or contrast between appearance and actuality, it leaves a great deal to the reader's intelligence. The objective point of view, with which the author reports action without interpreting the action for the reader, is another method of suggestion. Also, a symbol may be used to convey a state of mind or feeling without explicit comment. In grasping the full meaning of restrained statement, irony, objective presentation, and symbolism, the reader has that sense of personal discovery and realization which is one of the pleasures of reading.

A. DESCRIPTIVE WRITING

The basis of good description is close observation and vivid concrete details which enable the reader to visualize the person or scene described. A mere accumulation of details may, however, produce a blurred, conglomerate impression instead of a sharply drawn picture. The descriptive writer therefore selects details which produce a unified effect, and arranges those details according to some principle or pattern which makes visualization easy for the reader. *Dominant impression* is the technical term for the unified effect or central theme to which descriptive details contribute.

Since describing people and describing places involve somewhat different techniques, it is best to consider them separately.

1. Describing People

When, in actual experience, we meet a person we have not seen before, we usually get a quick first impression either of his general appearance or of some outstanding feature. Further observation shows us the particulars which produce that general impression and other features which make up this individual. Thus we may note immediately that a man looks shabby and worn, and then observe such details as his too-tight overcoat with only one button, his shapeless hat, and his bent shoulders. Or, we may be struck by a woman's extraordinary height before we consciously notice the color of her hair, the expression of her face, or her clothes.

A writer, in describing people, is likely to use this pattern of natural observation: some outstanding quality followed by more closely-observed details. He seldom describes the person systematically from head to toe, but instead chooses a few striking traits of appearance, manner, or dress. Also—and this is very important—he selects at least some details which *individualize the character;* which differentiate him from similar people; which make him not simply a type, but distinctly, uniquely himself.

The following passages are brief illustrations of individualizing detail:

Morel was then twenty-seven years old. He was well set-up, erect, and very smart. He had wavy black hair that shone again, and a vigorous black beard that had never been shaved. His cheeks were ruddy, and his red, moist mouth was noticeable because he laughed so often and so heartily. He had that rare thing, a rich, ringing laugh.—D. H. LAWRENCE, *Sons and Lovers*

Doctor Parcival was a large man with a drooping mouth covered by a yellow mustache. He always wore a dirty white waistcoat out of the pockets of which protruded a number of the kind of black cigars known as stogies. His teeth were black and irregular and there was something strange about his eyes. The lid of the left eye twitched; it fell down and snapped up; it was exactly as though the lid of the eye were a window shade and someone stood inside the doctor's head playing with the cord.—SHERWOOD ANDERSON, *Winesburg, Ohio*

Point of view, in writing about people, means the identity of the observer and his attitude toward the person described. The observer may be the author frankly slanting his material and shaping the reader's judgment of the person; or he may appear to be a completely objective reporter, even though he is, in fact, slanting by his selection of detail. The observer may, in a short story, be another character who likes or dislikes or does not understand the person he is describing.

In the following passage, the author is openly influencing the reader's judgment by including his own opinions clothed in charged expressions like *semi-rattlesnake, decidedly bad, uncouth and unpicturesque:*

He was a prim-faced, red-nosed man, with a long thin countenance and a semi-rattlesnake sort of eye—rather sharp, but decidedly bad. He wore very short trousers, and black cotton stockings: which, like the rest of his apparel, were particularly rusty. His looks were starched, but his white neckerchief was not; and its long limp ends straggled over his closely buttoned waistcoat in a very uncouth and unpicturesque fashion.—CHARLES DICKENS, *Pickwick Papers*

The paragraph below is an example of the objective point of view. The description consists of factual statements which appear to be verifiable. Note, too, how the various details contribute to the dominant idea of the respect this character inspires:

Peter Randall was one of the most highly respected farmers of Monterey County. Once, before he was to make a little speech at a Masonic convention, the brother who introduced him referred to him as a example for young Masons of California to emulate. He was nearing fifty; his manner was grave and restrained, and he wore a carefully tended beard. From every gathering he reaped the authority that belongs to the bearded man. Peter's eyes were grave, too; blue and grave almost to the point of sorrowfulness. People knew there was force in him, but force held caged. Sometimes, for no apparent reason, his eyes grew sullen and mean, like the eyes of a bad dog; but that look soon passed, and the restraint and probity came back into his face. He was tall and broad. He held his shoulders back as though they were braced, and he sucked in his stomach like a soldier. Inasmuch as farmers are usually slouchy men, Peter gained an added respect because of his posture.—JOHN STEINBECK, "The Harness," *The Long Valley*

In the following paragraph from a short story, the author uses the limited omniscient point of view to describe a little Negro girl as she appears to her white playmate. The reader sees Pinky through Susie's eyes:

There was a scurrying, as of a frantic little animal, along the path from Aunt Hester's cabin, and Pinky dropped on the ground beside her. She wasn't very black—her satiny yellow skin merely looked as if she had a good tan—and Aunt Hester had trained her stiff black hair to lie flat to her head. Susie loved the feel of Pinky's skin, and the smell of the magnolia balm Aunt Hester greased her hair with, and the fresh starchy smell of Pinky's calico dresses. She loved everything about Pinky with all her heart.—SARA HAARDT, "Little White Girl"

Real people are almost never entirely static or motionless. If they are, their immobility is so unusual that it is an individualizing characteristic. Movement, gestures, physical attitudes, and speech are inseparable parts of personality. Good description, therefore, *vitalizes a character;* that is, it shows him in some typical pose or action. In brief description, the pose or action may serve better than an enumeration of physical traits to give a sense of the whole person:

> The woman with the pink velvet poppies wreathed round the assisted gold of her hair traversed the crowded room at an interesting gait combining a skip with a sidle, and clutched the lean arm of her host.— DOROTHY PARKER, "Arrangement in Black and White"

Extended description—in novels, for example—often starts with a passive sketch of the character, and then shows him in revealing action:

> Mr. Chadband is a large yellow man, with a fat smile, and a general appearance of having a good deal of train oil in his system. Mrs. Chadband is a stern, severe-looking, silent woman. Mr. Chadband moves softly and cumbrously, not unlike a bear who has been taught to walk upright. He is very much embarrassed about the arms, as if they were inconvenient to him, and he wanted to grovel; is very much in a perspiration about the head; and never speaks without first putting up his great hand, as delivering a token to his friends that he is going to edify them.
>
> "My friends," says Mr. Chadband. "Peace be on this house! On the master thereof, on the mistress thereof, on the young maidens, and on the young men! My friends, why do I wish for peace? What is peace? Is it war? No. Is it strife? No. Is it lovely, and gentle, and beautiful, and pleasant, and serene, and joyful? O yes! Therefore my friends, I wish for peace, upon you and upon yours."—CHARLES DICKENS, *Bleak House*

Mr. Chadband's bear-like motion, his raised hand, and his habits of speech not only vitalize him, but also differentiate him from other large fat men.

2. Describing Places

In describing places, as in describing people, the writer follows the principle of selecting details which contribute sharply to a dominant impression, and which individualize the place so that it is not merely typical but has a quality of its own. The following description, from one of the stories printed in this chapter, gives a dominant impression of bareness and poverty; the room described is individualized by the possessions of its occupant. This passage also illustrates one of the close relationships between description of people and description of places. The boy who lives in this room is not presented, but he is indirectly described by his surroundings. The passage is an example of *suggestive description:* the reader understands more than he is explicitly told.

> The room was furnished with what the college issued: a desk, placed dead center under the overhead light, a table, three wooden chairs, a bed, a bureau, and an empty fireplace, the brick floor of which was free of ashes and cigarette butts. One shelf of the bookcase was almost filled with text-

books, a one-volume edition of Shakespeare, and a Bible. On the table were two notebooks and a dictionary, a cup and saucer, a plate, and a small electric stove with a saucepan on it. A calendar and two pine cones had been arranged on the mantelpiece in an effort at decoration. There was a framed photograph of a middle-aged woman on the bureau, and two neckties hung from a corner of the mirror. The room looked as if its occupant had moved in that afternoon and would leave tomorrow.—OLIVER LA FARGE, "Prelude to Reunion"

Point of view in describing places is more complicated than point of view in describing people. It involves, in addition to the attitude or psychological position of the observer, his physical position in relation to the scene he is presenting. Is he moving or stationary? If he is moving, by what means of locomotion, and how fast? If he is stationary, is he below, or above, or on the same level as what he observes? Is he standing, or sitting, or lying on his back? His physical position will make a great deal of difference in what he sees, and the reader must understand that position in order to visualize the scene.

Point of view in the sense of the psychological attitude of the observer also influences selection and arrangement of detail. If the feeling of the observer about what he sees is more important than the scene itself, the description is likely to follow an *impressionistic pattern,* in which details are set down in no order except the order in which they impress, or strike the attention of the observer. Such impressionistic description, with its focus on inward reactions, is sometimes called *subjective,* in contrast to *objective* writing which focuses on external objects. Impressionistic description is a useful method of communicating a state of mind and indirectly characterizing the observer; it is, therefore, another technique of suggestion. The dominant impression in this kind of writing is usually a consistent emotional tone, because all the recorded details are colored by the feelings of the person who sees them.

The following passage is an example of impressionistic description. No effort is made to describe the scene systematically; instead, details are set down as they impinge on the consciousness of a spoiled and wealthy woman who emerges from an exclusive shop on a winter afternoon and for a moment feels herself unsheltered in the world. The "little box" referred to in the passage is an extravagant trifle which she has considered buying.

The discreet door shut with a click. She was outside on the step, gazing at the winter afternoon. Rain was falling, and with the rain it seemed the dark came too, spinning down like ashes. There was a cold bitter taste in the air, and the new-lighted lamps looked sad. Sad were the lights in the houses opposite. Dimly they burned as if regretting something. And people hurried by, hidden under their hateful umbrellas. Rosemary felt a strange pang. She pressed her muff to her breast; she wished she had the little box, too, to cling to. Of course, the car was there. She'd only to cross the pavement. But still she waited. There are moments, horrible moments in life, when one emerges from shelter and looks out, and it's awful. One oughtn't to give way to them. One ought to go home and have an extra-special tea.[11]

When a writer is primarily interested in presenting the scene itself rather than the reactions of the observer, he follows an *orderly pattern* designed to give the reader an orderly objective picture of what the observer (either author or character) sees. The basis of this orderly pattern may be a logical relationship of details. For example, the passage about the college student's room on page 354 describes first what the college has provided, and then what the student has added to the room. Other orderly patterns of this kind are based on contrast: between the age of a house, for example, and the modernity of one room; or between a first impression and a modified second impression.

The most common orderly patterns in describing places are, however, based on space-relationships between elements in the scene. If the observer is moving, the reader follows him in his progress with the help of space-connectives like *at the top of the hill, around the corner, half way up the stairs.* If the observer is stationary, the reader can visualize the scene when details are set down in some consistent pattern such as left-to-right or right-to-left (in the description of a room or a landscape); near-to-far or far-to-near (in the description of a large or complex scene); up-to-down or down-to-up (in the description of a building, a hill, or a street). The following example of orderly description uses a near-to-far arrangement of detail:

Below him, bounding from rock to rock, ran the brook, laughing in the sunlight and tossing the spray high in the air in a mad frolic. Across this swirling line of silver lay a sparse meadow strewn with rock, plotted with squares of last year's crops—potatoes, string beans, and cabbages, and now combed into straight green lines of early buckwheat and turnips. Beyond this a ragged pasture, fenced with blackened stumps, from which came the tinkle of cow bells, and farther on the grim, silent forest—miles and miles of forest seamed by a single road leading to Moose Hillock and the Great Stone Face.—F. H. SMITH, *The Fortunes of Oliver Horn*

In practice, the impressionistic-subjective point of view and the orderly-objective point of view are frequently combined. A writer

[11] From Katherine Mansfield, "A Cup of Tea," *Short Stories of Katherine Mansfield*, Alfred A. Knopf, Inc.

often wishes to present simultaneously a picture of the scene and the mood of the person who observes it. The passage below contains an example of orderly near-to-far description and at the same time communicates the attitude of the observer:

> He was standing in the sunny window. Geraldine went up to him. She put her hand on his arm and gave it a gentle squeeze. How pleasant it was to feel that rough man's tweed again. Ah, how pleasant! She rubbed her hand against it, touched it with her cheek, sniffed the smell.
>
> The window looked out on to flower beds, a tangle of michaelmas daisies, late dahlias, hanging heavy, and shaggy little asters. Then there came a lawn strewn with yellow leaves with a broad path beyond and a row of gold-fluttering trees. An old gardener, in woollen mitts, was sweeping the path, brushing the leaves into a neat little heap. Now, the broom tucked in his arm, he fumbled in his coat pocket, brought out some matches, and scooping a hole in the leaves, he set fire to them.
>
> Such lovely blue smoke came breathing into the air through those dry leaves; there was something so calm and orderly in the way the pile burned that it was a pleasure to watch. The old gardener stumped away and came back with a handful of withered twigs. He flung them on and stood by, and little light flames began to flicker.[12]

The preceding quotation illustrates a final principle: effective description of places *vitalizes the scene and appeals to the reader's senses*. The most common fault of weak description is that it presents a dead black and white drawing, without movement, without color, with nothing but a bleak visual representation of the scene. It is like a map or a poor photograph in which objects are too remote and too still to seem real. Just as we know people in their complexity of appearance, expression, speech, and motion, so we know places in a complexity of sight and sound and smell, and sometimes the taste, and often the feel of things. The skillful writer brings a place to life, and communicates to the reader all the physical impressions and sensations which are part of experiencing that scene.

The brief examples in the preceding pages, taken out of context and used to illustrate specific principles of good descriptive writing, do not give an entirely accurate view of description at work. As we have said earlier, description in modern writing is nearly always a subordinate part of an essay or narrative; it may, however, be a highly important contributor to the total effect of a piece of prose. The longer readings in the following pages, and also the essays and narratives printed later in this chapter, show descriptive writing in

---

[12] From Katherine Mansfield, "Widowed," *Short Stories of Katherine Mansfield*, Alfred A. Knopf, Inc.

action. Combined with other techniques of communication, it is used to clarify ideas, to create integrated scenes in which both people and places come alive, and to make a story real.

MRS. MINIVER COMES HOME *

JAN STRUTHER

Description of a place and indirect description or characterization of the woman through whose mind it is seen are illustrated by the following selection. Particularly worth noting in the description is the appeal to various senses. Jan Struther is an English poet and novelist. "Mrs. Miniver Comes Home" is the first chapter of *Mrs. Miniver,* a series of sketches of family life published in 1940.

It was lovely, thought Mrs. Miniver, nodding good-bye to the flower-woman and carrying her big sheaf of chrysanthemums down the street with a kind of ceremonious joy, as though it were a cornucopia; it was lovely, this settling down again, this tidying away of the summer into its box, this taking up of the thread of one's life where the holidays (irrelevant interlude) had made one drop it. Not that she didn't enjoy the holidays: but she always felt—and it was, perhaps, the measure of her peculiar happiness—a little relieved when they were over. Her normal life pleased her so well that she was half afraid to step out of its frame in case one day she would find herself unable to get back. The spell might break, the atmosphere be impossible to recapture.

But this time, at any rate, she was safe. There was the house, as neat and friendly as ever, facing her as she turned the corner of the square; its small stucco face as indistinguishable from the others, to a stranger, as a single sheep in a flock, but to her apart, individual, a shade lighter than the house on the left, a shade darker than the house on the right, with one plaster rosette missing from the lintel of the front door and the first-floor balcony almost imperceptibly crooked. And there was the square itself, with the leaves still as thick on the trees as they had been when she left in August; but in August they had hung heavily, a uniform dull green, whereas now, crisped and brindled by the first few nights of frost, they had taken on a new, various beauty. Stepping lightly and quickly down the square, Mrs.

Miniver suddenly understood why she was enjoying the forties so much better than she had enjoyed the thirties; it was the difference between August and October, between the heaviness of late summer and the sparkle of early autumn, between the ending of an old phase and the beginning of a fresh one.

She reached her doorstep. The key turned sweetly in the lock. That was the kind of thing one remembered about a house: not the size of the rooms or the colour of the walls, but the feel of door-handles and light-switches, the shape and texture of the banister-rail under one's palm; minute tactual intimacies, whose resumption was the essence of coming home.

Upstairs in the drawing-room there was a small bright fire of logs, yet the sunshine that flooded in through the open windows had real warmth in it. It was perfect: she felt suspended between summer and winter, savouring the best of them both. She unwrapped the chrys-anthemums and arranged them in a square glass jar, between herself and the light, so that the sun shone through them. They were the big mop-headed kind, burgundy-coloured, with curled petals; their beauty was noble, architectural; and as for their scent, she thought as she buried her nose in the nearest of them, it was a pure distillation of her mood, a quintessence of all that she found gay and intoxicating and astringent about the weather, the circumstances, her own age and the season of the year. Oh, yes, October certainly suited her best. For the ancients, as she had inescapably learnt at school, it had been the eighth month; nowadays, officially, it was the tenth: but for her it was always the first, the real New Year. That laborious affair in January was nothing but a name.

She turned away from the window at last. On her writing-table lay the letters which had come for her that morning. A card for a dress-show; a shooting invitation for Clem; two dinner-parties; three sherry-parties; a highly aperitive notice of some chamber-music concerts; and a letter from Vin at school—would she please send on his umbrella, his camera, and his fountain-pen, which leaked rather? (But even that could not daunt her today.)

She rearranged the fire a little, mostly for the pleasure of handling the fluted steel poker, and then sat down by it. Tea was already laid: there were honey sandwiches, brandy-snaps, and small ratafia biscuits; and there would, she knew, be crumpets. Three new library books lay virginally on the fender-stool, their bright paper wrappers unsullied by subscriber's hand. The clock on the mantelpiece chimed, very softly and precisely, five times. A tug hooted from the river. A sudden breeze brought the sharp tang of a bonfire in at the window. The jigsaw was almost complete, but there was still one piece missing. And then, from the other end of the square, came the familiar sound of the Wednesday barrel-organ, playing, with a hundred apocryphal trills and arpeggios, the "Blue Danube" waltz. And Mrs. Miniver, with a little sigh of contentment, rang for tea.

COMMENT AND QUESTIONS

"Mrs. Miniver Comes Home" uses a limited omniscient point of view; the author takes up residence in the mind of her character, and the reader is given the elements in the scene not objectively but as they impress Mrs. Miniver. At the same time, the description has an orderly pattern: the reader moves with Mrs. Miniver along the street, down the square, into the house.

I. What is the dominant impression in this piece of writing?

II. What does one know about Mrs. Miniver?

III. Point out examples of individualizing detail in the description of the house.

IV. How is the scene vitalized?

V. How many colors are mentioned or suggested in the passage?

VI. What physical sensations are communicated to the reader? How many senses are appealed to, and by what particular details?

NINETEEN EIGHTY-FOUR *

GEORGE ORWELL

The following passage, the opening pages of the novel *Nineteen Eighty-four*, contains brief descriptions of people. Chiefly, though, it is a description of a place and a civilization. By means of vivid, realistic detail, it communicates the experience of living in another world. George Orwell, English author and critic whose real name was Eric Blair, died in 1950. *Nineteen Eighty-Four* was published in 1949.

It was a bright cold day in April, and the clocks were striking thirteen. Winston Smith, his chin nuzzled into his breast in an effort to escape the vile wind, slipped quickly through the glass doors of Victory Mansions, though not quickly enough to prevent a swirl of gritty dust from entering along with him.

The hallway smelt of boiled cabbage and old rag mats. At one end of it a colored poster, too large for indoor display, had been tacked to the wall. It depicted simply an enormous face, more than a meter wide: the face of a man of about forty-five, with a heavy black mustache and ruggedly handsome features. Winston made for the stairs. It was no use trying the lift. Even at the best of times it was seldom working, and at present the electric current was cut off during daylight hours. It was part of the economy drive in preparation for Hate Week. The flat was seven flights up, and Winston, who was thirty-nine, and had a varicose ulcer above his right ankle, went slowly, resting several times on the way. On each landing, opposite the lift shaft, the poster with the enormous face gazed from the wall. It was one of those pictures which are so contrived that the eyes follow you about when you move. BIG BROTHER IS WATCH-ING YOU, the caption beneath it ran.

Inside the flat a fruity voice was reading out a list of figures which had something to do with the production of pig iron. The voice came from an oblong metal plaque like a dulled mirror which formed part of the surface of the right-hand wall. Winston turned a switch and the voice sank somewhat, though the words were still distinguishable. The instrument (the telescreen, it was called) could be dimmed, but there was no way of shutting it off completely. He moved over to the window: a smallish, frail figure, the meagerness of his body merely emphasized by the blue overalls which were the uniform of the Party. His hair was very fair, his face naturally sanguine, his skin roughened by coarse soap and blunt razor blades and the cold of the winter that had just ended.

Outside, even through the shut window pane, the world looked cold. Down in the street little eddies of wind were whirling dust and torn paper into spirals, and though the sun was shining and the sky a harsh blue, there seemed to be no color in anything except the posters that were plastered everywhere. The black-mustachio'd face gazed down from every commanding corner. There was one on the house front immediately opposite. BIG BROTHER IS WATCH-ING YOU, the caption said, while the dark eyes looked deep into Winston's own. Down at street level another poster, torn at one corner, flapped fitfully in the wind, alternately covering and uncovering the single word INGSOC. In the far distance a helicopter skimmed down between the roofs, hovered for an instant like a blue-bottle, and darted away again with a curving flight. It was the Police Patrol, snooping into people's windows. The patrols did not matter, however. Only the Thought Police mattered.

Behind Winston's back the voice from the telescreen was still babbling away about pig iron and the overfulfillment of the Ninth

Three-Year Plan. The telescreen received and transmitted simultaneously. Any sound that Winston made, above the level of a very low whisper, would be picked up by it; moreover, so long as he remained within the field of vision which the metal plaque commanded, he could be seen as well as heard. There was of course no way of knowing whether you were being watched at any given moment. How often, or on what system, the Thought Police plugged in on any individual wire was guesswork. It was even conceivable that they watched everybody all the time. But at any rate they could plug in your wire whenever they wanted to. You had to live—did live, from habit that became instinct—in the assumption that every sound you made was overheard, and except in darkness, every movement scrutinized.

Winston kept his back turned to the telescreen. It was safer; though, as he well knew, even a back can be revealing. A kilometer away the Ministry of Truth, his place of work, towered vast and white above the grimy landscape. This, he thought with a sort of vague distaste—this was London, chief city of Airstrip One, itself the third most populous of the provinces of Oceania. He tried to squeeze out some childhood memory that should tell him whether London had always been quite like this. Were there always these vistas of rotting nineteenth-century houses, their sides shored up with balks of timber, their windows patched with cardboard and their roofs with corrugated iron, their crazy garden walls sagging in all directions? And the bombed sites where the plaster dust swirled in the air and the willow herb straggled over the heaps of rubble; and the places where bombs had cleared a larger patch and there had sprung up sordid colonies of wooden dwellings like chicken houses? But it was no use, he could not remember: nothing remained of his childhood except a series of bright-lit tableaux, occurring against no background and mostly unintelligible.

The Ministry of Truth—Minitrue, in *Newspeak*—was startlingly different from any other object in sight. It was an enormous pyramidal structure of glittering white concrete, soaring up, terrace after terrace, three hundred meters into the air. From where Winston stood it was just possible to read, picked out on its white face in elegant lettering, the three slogans of the Party:

WAR IS PEACE
FREEDOM IS SLAVERY
IGNORANCE IS STRENGTH

The Ministry of Truth contained, it was said, three thousand rooms above ground level, and corresponding ramifications below. Scattered about London there were just three other buildings of similar appearance and size. So completely did they dwarf the surrounding architecture that from the roof of Victory Mansions you could see all four of them simultaneously. They were the homes of the four Ministries between which the entire apparatus of government was divided: the Ministry of Truth, which concerned itself with news, entertainment, education, and the fine arts; the Ministry of Peace, which concerned itself with war; the Ministry of Love, which maintained law and order; and the Ministry of Plenty, which was responsible for economic affairs. Their names, in *Newspeak:* Minitrue, Minipax, Miniluv, and Miniplenty.

The Ministry of Love was the really frightening one. There were no windows in it at all. Winston had never been inside the Ministry of Love, nor within half a kilometer of it. It was a place impossible to enter except on official business, and then only by penetrating through a maze of hidden machine-gun nests. Even the streets leading up to its outer barriers were roamed by gorilla-faced guards in black uniforms, armed with jointed truncheons.

Winston turned round abruptly. He had set his features into the expression of quiet optimism which it was advisable to wear when facing the telescreen. He crossed the room into the tiny kitchen. By leaving the Ministry at this time of day he had sacrificed his lunch in the canteen, and he was aware that there was no food in the kitchen except a hunk of dark-colored bread which had got to be saved for tomorrow's breakfast. He took down from the shelf a bottle of colorless liquid with a plain white label marked VICTORY GIN. It gave off a sickly, oily smell, as of Chinese rice-spirit. Winston poured out nearly a teacupful, nerved himself for a shock, and gulped it down like a dose of medicine.

Instantly his face turned scarlet and the water ran out of his eyes. The stuff was like nitric acid, and moreover, in swallowing it, one had the sensation of being hit on the back of the head with a rubber club. The next moment, however, the burning in his belly died down and the world began to look more cheerful. He took a cigarette from a crumpled packet marked VICTORY CIGARETTES and incautiously held it upright, whereupon the tobacco fell out onto the floor. With the next he was more successful. He went back to the living room and sat down at a small table that stood to the left of the telescreen. From the table drawer he took out a penholder, a bottle of ink, and a thick, quarto-sized blank book with a red back and a marbled cover.

For some reason the telescreen in the living room was in an unusual position. Instead of being placed, as was normal, in the end wall, where it could command the whole room, it was in the longer wall, opposite the window. To one side of it there was a shallow alcove in which Winston was now sitting, and which, when the flats were built, had probably been intended to hold bookshelves. By sitting in the alcove, and keeping well back, Winston was able to remain outside the range of the telescreen, so far as sight went. He could be heard, of course, but so long as he stayed in his present position he could not be seen. It was partly the unusual geography of the room that had suggested to him the thing that he was now about to do.

But it had also been suggested by the book that he had just taken out of the drawer. It was a peculiarly beautiful book. Its smooth creamy paper, a little yellowed by age, was of a kind that had not been manufactured for at least forty years past. He could guess, however, that the book was much older than that. He had seen it lying in the window of a frowsy little junk shop in a slummy quarter of the town (just what quarter he did not now remember) and had been stricken immediately with an overwhelming desire to possess it. Party members were not supposed to go into ordinary shops ("dealing on the free market," it was called), but the rule was not strictly kept, because there were various things such as shoelaces and razor blades which it was impossible to get hold of in any other way. He had given a quick glance up and down the street and then had slipped inside and bought the book for two dollars fifty. At the time he was not conscious of wanting it for any particular purpose. He had carried it guiltily home in his brief case. Even with nothing written in it, it was a compromising possession.

The thing that he was about to do was to open a diary. This was not illegal (nothing was illegal, since there were no longer any laws), but if detected it was reasonably certain that it would be punished by death, or at least by twenty-five years in a forced-labor camp. Winston fitted a nib into the penholder and sucked it to get the grease off. The pen was an archaic instrument, seldom used even for signatures, and he had procured one, furtively and with some difficulty, simply because of a feeling that the beautiful creamy paper deserved to be written on with a real nib instead of being scratched with an ink pencil. Actually he was not used to writing by hand. Apart from very short notes, it was usual to dictate everything into the speak-write, which was of course impossible for his present purpose. He dipped the pen into the ink and then faltered for just a second. A tremor had gone through his bowels. To mark the paper was the decisive act. In small clumsy letters he wrote:

April 4th, 1984.

He sat back. A sense of complete helplessness had descended upon him. To begin with, he did not know with any certainty that this *was* 1984. It must be round about that date, since he was fairly sure that his age was thirty-nine, and he believed that he had been born in 1944 or 1945; but it was never possible nowadays to pin down any date within a year or two.

For whom, it suddenly occurred to him in wonder, was he writing this diary? For the future, for the unborn. His mind hovered for a moment round the doubtful date on the page, and then fetched up with a bump against the *Newspeak* word *doublethink.* For the first time the magnitude of what he had undertaken came home to him. How could you communicate with the future? It was of its nature impossible. Either the future would resemble the present, in which case it would not listen to him, or it would be different from it, and his predicament would be meaningless.

For some time he sat gazing stupidly at the paper. The telescreen had changed over to strident military music. It was curious that he seemed not merely to have lost the power of expressing himself, but even to have forgotten what it was that he had originally intended to say. For weeks past he had been making ready for this moment, and it had never crossed his mind that anything would be needed except courage. The actual writing would be easy. All he had to do was to transfer to paper the interminable restless monologue that had been running inside his head, literally for years. At this moment, however, even the monologue had dried up. Moreover, his varicose ulcer had begun itching unbearably. He dared not scratch it, because if he did so it always became inflamed. The seconds were ticking by. He was conscious of nothing except the blankness of the page in front of him, the itching of the skin above his ankle, the blaring of the music, and a slight booziness caused by the gin.

Suddenly he began writing in sheer panic, only imperfectly aware of what he was setting down. His small but childish handwriting straggled up and down the page, shedding first its capital letters and finally even its full stops:

April 4th, 1984. Last night to the flicks. All war films. One very good one of a ship full of refugees being bombed somewhere in the Mediterranean. Audience much amused by shots of a great huge fat man trying to swim away with a helicopter after him. first you saw him wallowing along in the water like a porpoise, then you saw him through the helicopters gunsights, then he was full of holes and the sea round him turned pink and he sank as suddenly as though the holes had let in the water. audience shouting with laughter when he sank. then you saw a lifeboat full of children with a helicopter hovering over it. there was a middleaged woman might have been a jewess sitting up in the bow with a little boy about three years old in her arms. little boy screaming with fright and hiding his head between her breasts as if he was trying to burrow right into her and the woman putting her arms around him and comforting him although she was blue with fright herself. all the time covering him up as much as possible as if she thought her arms could keep the bullets off him. then the helicopter planted a 20 kilo bomb in among them terrific flash and the boat went all to matchwood. then there was a wonderful shot of a childs arm going up up up right up into the air a helicopter with a camera in its nose must have followed it up and there was a lot of applause from the party seats but a woman down in the prole part of the house suddenly started kicking up a fuss and shouting they didnt oughter of showed it not in front of the kids they didnt it aint right not in front of kids it aint until the police turned her turned her out i don't suppose anything happened to her nobody cares what the proles say typical prole reaction they never—

Winston stopped writing, partly because he was suffering from cramp. He did not know what had made him pour out this stream of rubbish. But the curious thing was that while he was doing so a totally different memory had clarified itself in his mind, to the point where he almost felt equal to writing it down. It was, he now realized, because of this other incident that he had suddenly decided to come home and begin the diary today.

It had happened that morning at the Ministry, if anything so nebulous could be said to happen.

It was nearly eleven hundred, and in the Records Department, where Winston worked, they were dragging the chairs out of the cubicles and grouping them in the center of the hall, opposite the big telescreen, in preparation for the Two Minutes Hate. Winston was just taking his place in one of the middle rows when two people whom he knew by sight, but had never spoken to, came unexpectedly into the room. One of them was a girl whom he often passed in the corridors. He did not know her name, but he knew that she worked in the Fiction Department. Presumably—since he had sometimes seen her with oily hands and carrying a spanner—she had some mechanical job on one of the novel-writing machines. She was a bold-looking girl of about twenty-seven, with thick dark hair, a freckled face, and swift, athletic movements. A narrow scarlet sash, emblem of the Junior Anti-Sex League, was wound several times around the waist of her overalls, just tightly enough to bring out the shapeliness of her hips. Winston had disliked her from the very first moment of seeing her. He knew the reason. It was because of the atmosphere of hockey fields and cold baths and community hikes and general clean-mindedness which she managed to carry about with her. He disliked nearly all women, and especially the young and pretty ones. It was always the women, and above all the young ones, who were the most bigoted adherents of the Party, the swallowers of slogans, the amateur spies and nosers-out of unorthodoxy. But this particular girl gave him the impression of being more dangerous than most. Once when they passed in the corridor she had given him a quick sidelong glance which seemed to pierce right into him and for a moment had filled him with black terror. The idea had even crossed his mind that she might be an agent of the Thought Police. That, it was true, was very unlikely. Still, he continued to feel a peculiar uneasiness, which had fear mixed up in it as well as hostility, whenever she was anywhere near him.

The other person was a man named O'Brien, a member of the Inner Party and holder of some post so important and remote that Winston had only a dim idea of its nature. A momentary hush passed over the group of people round the chairs as they saw the black overalls of an Inner Party member approaching. O'Brien was a large, burly man with a thick neck and a coarse, humorous, brutal face. In spite of his formidable appearance he had a certain charm of manner. He had a trick of resettling his spectacles on his nose which was curiously disarming—in some indefinable way, curiously civilized. It was a gesture which, if anyone had still thought in such terms, might have recalled an eighteenth-century nobleman offering his snuff-box. Winston had seen O'Brien perhaps a dozen times in almost as many years. He felt deeply drawn to him, and not solely because he was intrigued by the contrast between O'Brien's urbane manner and his prizefighter's physique. Much more it was because of a secretly held belief—or perhaps not even a belief, merely a hope—that O'Brien's political orthodoxy was not perfect. Something in his face suggested it irresistibly. And again, perhaps it was not even unorthodoxy that was written in his face, but simply intelligence. But at any rate he had the appearance of being a person that you could talk to, if somehow you could cheat the telescreen and get him alone. Winston had never made the smallest effort to verify this guess; indeed, there was no way of doing so. At this moment O'Brien glanced at his wrist watch, saw that it was nearly eleven hundred, and evidently decided to stay in the Records Department until the Two Minutes Hate was over. He took a chair in the same row as Winston, a couple of places away. A small, sandy-haired woman who worked in the next cubicle to Winston was between them. The girl with dark hair was sitting immediately behind.

The next moment a hideous, grinding screech, as of some monstrous machine running without oil, burst from the big telescreen at the end of the room. It was a noise that set one's teeth on edge and bristled the hair at the back of one's neck. The Hate had started.

COMMENT AND QUESTIONS

In this selection, the omniscient author gives the reader some description of Winston, but for the most part he limits his omniscience to Winston's mind and through that mind views the nightmarish world of 1984. Had he limited his point of view entirely to his character's mind, he could not have described Winston except by some device like having him stand in front of a mirror and so see himself as others see him.

I. Does the description in the first three pages follow an orderly or an impressionistic pattern, or both? Explain.

II. How is the scene Winston observes from the window vitalized?

III. What details in the selection best convey the quality of the civilization in which Winston lives? What details best convey his personal misery? What things does he so take for granted that they cause him no personal misery?

IV. How is sound used in the passage to give the reader a sense of the scene?

V. The entry Winston pours out on the pages of his diary is a kind of stream-of-consciousness writing. What is its purpose in the selection?

VI. What individualizing details are included in the brief description of Winston, of the girl with dark hair, and of O'Brien?

BABBITT BEFORE BREAKFAST *

SINCLAIR LEWIS

In the following selection, the opening chapter of the novel *Babbitt*, description of people and description of places work together to depict a character. When Sinclair Lewis created George F. Babbitt in 1922, he added two words, *Babbitt* and *babbittry* to the English language. *The American College Dictionary* defines a Babbitt as "a self-satisfied person

* From *Babbitt* by Sinclair Lewis, copyright, 1922, by Harcourt, Brace and Company, Inc.

who conforms readily to middle-class ideas and ideals, especially of business success." Sinclair Lewis (1885–1951) was a well-known novelist who, in 1930, became the first American author to be awarded the Nobel Prize for distinction in world literature. His best novels, *Main Street, Babbitt, Arrowsmith,* and *Dodsworth,* were written in the 1920's.

I

The towers of Zenith aspired above the morning mist; austere towers of steel and cement and limestone, sturdy as cliffs and delicate as silver rods. They were neither citadels nor churches, but frankly and beautifully office-buildings.

The mist took pity on the fretted structures of earlier generations: the Post Office with its shingle-tortured mansard, the red brick minarets of hulking old houses, factories with stingy and sooted windows, wooden tenements colored like mud. The city was full of such grotesqueries, but the clean towers were thrusting them from the business center, and on the farther hills were shining new houses, homes—they seemed—for laughter and tranquillity.

Over a concrete bridge fled a limousine of long sleek hood and noiseless engine. These people in evening clothes were returning from an all-night rehearsal of a Little Theater play, an artistic adventure considerably illuminated by champagne. Below the bridge curved a railroad, a maze of green and crimson lights. The New York Flyer boomed past, and twenty lines of polished steel leaped into the glare.

In one of the skyscrapers the wires of the Associated Press were closing down. The telegraph operators wearily raised their celluloid eye-shades after a night of talking with Paris and Peking. Through the building crawled the scrubwomen, yawning, their old shoes slapping. The dawn mist spun away. Cues of men with lunch-boxes clumped toward the immensity of new factories, sheets of glass and hollow tile, glittering shops where five thousand men worked beneath one roof, pouring out the honest wares that would be sold up the Euphrates and across the veldt. The whistles rolled out in greeting a chorus cheerful as the April dawn; the song of labor in a city built—it seemed—for giants.

II

There was nothing of the giant in the aspect of the man who was beginning to awaken on the sleeping-porch of a Dutch Colonial house in that residential district of Zenith known as Floral Heights.

His name was George F. Babbitt. He was forty-six years old now, in April, 1920, and he made nothing in particular, neither butter nor shoes nor poetry, but he was nimble in the calling of selling houses for more than people could afford to pay.

His large head was pink, his brown hair thin and dry. His face was babyish in slumber, despite his wrinkles and the red spectacle-dents on the slopes of his nose. He was not fat but he was exceedingly well fed; his cheeks were pads, and the unroughened hand which lay helpless upon the khaki-colored blanket was slightly puffy. He seemed prosperous, extremely married and unromantic; and altogether unromantic appeared this sleeping-porch, which looked on one sizable elm, two respectable grass-plots, a cement driveway, and a corrugated iron garage. Yet Babbitt was again dreaming of the fairy child, a dream more romantic than scarlet pagodas by a silver sea.

For years the fairy child had come to him. Where others saw but Georgie Babbitt, she discerned gallant youth. She waited for him, in the darkness beyond mysterious groves. When at last he could slip away from the crowded house he darted to her. His wife, his clamoring friends, sought to follow, but he escaped, the girl fleet beside him, and they crouched together on a shadowy hillside. She was so slim, so white, so eager! She cried that he was gay and valiant, that she would wait for him, that they would sail—

Rumble and bang of the milk-truck.

Babbitt moaned, turned over, struggled back toward his dream. He could see only her face now, beyond misty waters. The furnace-man slammed the basement door. A dog barked in the next yard. As Babbitt sank blissfully into a dim warm tide, the paper-carrier went by whistling, and the rolled-up *Advocate* thumped the front door. Babbitt roused, his stomach constricted with alarm. As he relaxed, he was pierced by the familiar and irritating rattle of someone cranking a Ford: snap-ah-ah, snap-ah-ah, snap-ah-ah. Himself a pious motorist, Babbitt cranked with the unseen driver, with him waited through taut hours for the roar of the starting engine, with him agonized as the roar ceased and again began the infernal patient snap-ah-ah—a round, flat sound, a shivering cold-morning sound, a sound infuriating and inescapable. Not till the rising voice of the motor told him that the Ford was moving was he released from the panting tension. He glanced once at his favorite tree, elm twigs against the gold patina of sky, and fumbled for sleep as for a drug. He who had been a boy very credulous of life was no longer greatly interested in the possible and improbable adventures of each new day.

He escaped from reality till the alarm-clock rang, at seven-twenty.

III

It was the best of nationally advertised and quantitatively produced alarm-clocks, with all modern attachments, including cathedral chime, intermittent alarm, and a phosphorescent dial. Babbitt was proud of being awakened by such a rich device. Socially it was almost as creditable as buying expensive cord tires.

He sulkily admitted now that there was no more escape, but he lay and detested the grind of the real-estate business, and disliked his family, and disliked himself for disliking them. The evening before, he had played poker at Vergil Gunch's till midnight, and after such holidays he was irritable before breakfast. It may have been the tremendous home-brewed beer of the prohibition-era and the cigars to which that beer enticed him; it may have been resentment of return from this fine, bold man-world to a restricted region of wives and stenographers, and of suggestions not to smoke so much.

From the bedroom beside the sleeping-porch, his wife's detestably cheerful "Time to get up, Georgie boy," and the itchy sound, the brisk and scratchy sound, of combing hairs out of a stiff brush.

He grunted; he dragged his thick legs, in faded baby-blue pajamas, from under the khaki blanket; he sat on the edge of the cot, running his fingers through his wild hair, while his plump feet mechanically felt for his slippers. He looked regretfully at the blanket—forever a suggestion to him of freedom and heroism. He had bought it for a camping trip which had never come off. It symbolized gorgeous loafing, gorgeous cursing, virile flannel shirts.

He creaked to his feet, groaning at the waves of pain which passed behind his eyeballs. Though he waited for their scorching recurrence, he looked blurrily out at the yard. It delighted him, as always; it was the neat yard of a successful business man of Zenith, that is, it was perfection, and made him also perfect. He regarded the corrugated iron garage. For the three-hundred-and-sixty-fifth time in a year he reflected, "No class to that tin shack. Have to build me a frame garage. But by golly it's the only thing on the place that isn't up-to-date!" While he stared he thought of a community garage for his acreage development, Glen Oriole. He stopped puffing and jiggling. His arms were akimbo. His petulant, sleep-swollen face was set in harder lines. He suddenly seemed capable, an official, a man to contrive, to direct, to get things done.

On the vigor of his idea he was carried down the hard, clean, unused-looking hall into the bathroom.

Though the house was not large it had, like all houses on Floral

Heights, an altogether royal bathroom of porcelain and glazed tile and metal sleek as silver. The towel-rack was a rod of clear glass set in nickel. The tub was long enough for a Prussian Guard, and above the set bowl was a sensational exhibit of toothbrush holder, shaving-brush holder, soap-dish, sponge-dish, and medicine-cabinet, so glittering and so ingenious that they resembled an electrical instrument-board. But the Babbitt whose god was Modern Appliances was not pleased. The air of the bathroom was thick with the smell of a heathen toothpaste. "Verona been at it again! 'Stead of sticking to Lilidol, like I've re-peat-ed-ly asked her, she's gone and gotten some confounded stinkum stuff that makes you sick!"

The bath-mat was wrinkled and the floor was wet. (His daughter Verona eccentrically took baths in the morning, now and then.) He slipped on the mat, and slid against the tub. He said "Damn!" Furiously he snatched up his tube of shaving-cream, furiously he lathered, with a belligerent slapping of the unctuous brush, furiously he raked his plump cheeks with a safety-razor. It pulled. The blade was dull. He said, "Damn—oh—oh—damn it!"

He hunted through the medicine-cabinet for a packet of new razor-blades (reflecting, as invariably, "Be cheaper to buy one of these dinguses and strop your own blades,") and when he discovered the packet, behind the round box of bicarbonate of soda, he thought ill of his wife for putting it there and very well of himself for not saying "Damn." But he did say it, immediately afterward, when with wet and soap-slippery fingers he tried to remove the horrible little envelope and crisp clinging oiled paper from the new blade.

Then there was the problem, oft-pondered, never solved, of what to do with the old blade, which might imperil the fingers of his young. As usual, he tossed it on top of the medicine-cabinet, with a mental note that some day he must remove the fifty or sixty other blades that were also temporarily piled up there. He finished his shaving in a growing testiness increased by his spinning headache and by the emptiness in his stomach. When he was done, his round face smooth and streamy and his eyes stinging from soapy water, he reached for a towel. The family towels were wet, wet and clammy and vile, all of them wet, he found, as he blindly snatched them—his own face-towel, his wife's, Verona's, Ted's, Tinka's, and the lone bath-towel with the huge welt of initial. Then George F. Babbitt did a dismaying thing. He wiped his face on the guest-towel! It was a pansy-embroidered trifle which always hung there to indicate that the Babbitts were in the best Floral Heights society. No one had ever used it. No guest had ever dared to. Guests secretively took a corner of the nearest regular towel.

He was raging, "By golly, here they go and use up all the towels, every doggone one of 'em, and they use 'em and get 'em all wet and sopping, and never put out a dry one for me—of course, I'm the goat! —and then I want one and—I'm the only person in the doggone house that's got the slightest doggone bit of consideration for other people and thoughtfulness and consider there may be others that may want to use the doggone bathroom after me and consider—"

He was pitching the chill abominations into the bath-tub, pleased by the vindictiveness of that desolate flapping sound; and in the midst his wife serenely trotted in, observed serenely, "Why, Georgie dear, what are you doing? Are you going to wash out the towels? Why, you needn't wash out the towels. Oh, Georgie, you didn't go and use the guest-towel, did you?"

It is not recorded that he was able to answer.

For the first time in weeks he was sufficiently roused by his wife to look at her.

IV

Myra Babbitt—Mrs. George F. Babbitt—was definitely mature. She had creases from the corners of her mouth to the bottom of her chin, and her plump neck bagged. But the thing that marked her as having passed the line was that she no longer had reticences before her husband, and no longer worried about not having reticences. She was in a petticoat now, and corsets which bulged, and unaware of being seen in bulgy corsets. She had become so dully habituated to married life that in her full matronliness she was as sexless as an anemic nun. She was a good woman, a kind woman, a diligent woman, but no one, save perhaps Tinka her ten-year-old, was at all interested in her or entirely aware that she was alive.

After a rather thorough discussion of all the domestic and social aspects of towels she apologized to Babbitt for his having an alcoholic headache; and he recovered enough to endure the search for a B.V.D. undershirt which had, he pointed out, malevolently been concealed among his clean pajamas.

He was fairly amiable in the conference on the brown suit.

"What do you think, Myra?" He pawed at the clothes hunched on a chair in their bedroom, while she moved about mysteriously adjusting and patting her petticoat and, to his jaundiced eye, never seeming to get on with her dressing. "How about it? Shall I wear the brown suit another day?"

"Well, it looks awfully nice on you."

"I know, but gosh, it needs pressing."

"That's so. Perhaps it does."

"It certainly could stand being pressed, all right."

"Yes, perhaps it wouldn't hurt it to be pressed."

"But gee, the coat doesn't need pressing. No sense in having the whole darn suit pressed, when the coat doesn't need it."

"That's so."

"But the pants certainly need it, all right. Look at them—look at those wrinkles—the pants certainly do need pressing."

"That's so. Oh, Georgie, why couldn't you wear the brown coat with the blue trousers we were wondering what we'd do with them?"

"Good Lord! Did you ever in all my life know me to wear the coat of one suit and the pants of another? What do you think I am? A busted bookkeeper?"

"Well, why don't you put on the dark gray suit today, and stop in at the tailor and leave the brown trousers?"

"Well, they certainly need— Now where the devil is that gray suit? Oh, yes, here we are."

He was able to get through the other crises of dressing with comparative resoluteness and calm.

His first adornment was the sleeveless dimity B.V.D. undershirt, in which he resembled a small boy humorlessly wearing a cheesecloth tabard at a civic pageant. He never put on B.V.D.'s without thanking the God of Progress that he didn't wear tight, long, old-fashioned undergarments, like his father-in-law and partner, Henry Thompson. His second embellishment was combing and slicking back his hair. It gave him a tremendous forehead, arching up two inches beyond the former hair-line. But most wonder-working of all was the donning of his spectacles.

There is character in spectacles—the pretentious tortoise-shell, the meek pince-nez of the schoolteacher, the twisted silver-framed glasses of the old villager. Babbitt's spectacles had huge, circular, frameless lenses of the very best glass; the ear-pieces were thin bars of gold. In them he was the modern business man; one who gave orders to clerks and drove a car and played occasional golf and was scholarly in regard to Salesmanship. His head suddenly appeared not babyish but weighty, and you noted his heavy, blunt nose, his straight mouth and thick, long upper lip, his chin overfleshy but strong; with respect you beheld him put on the rest of his uniform as a Solid Citizen.

The gray suit was well cut, well made, and completely undistinguished. It was a standard suit. White piping on the V of the vest added a flavor of law and learning. His shoes were black laced boots, good boots, honest boots, standard boots, extraordinarily uninteresting boots. The only frivolity was in his purple knitted scarf. With considerable comment on the matter to Mrs. Babbitt (who, acrobatically fastening the back of her blouse to her skirt with a safety-pin, did not hear a word he said), he chose between the purple scarf and a tapestry effect with stringless brown harps among blown palms, and into it he thrust a snake-head pin with opal eyes.

A sensational event was changing from the brown suit to the gray the contents of his pockets. He was earnest about these objects. They were of eternal importance, like baseball or the Republican Party. They included a fountain pen and a silver pencil (always lacking a supply of new leads) which belonged in the right-hand upper vest pocket. Without them he would have felt naked. On his watch-chain were a gold penknife, silver cigar-cutter, seven keys (the use of two of which he had forgotten), and incidentally a good watch. Depending from the chain was a large, yellowish elk's-tooth—proclamation of his membership in the Benevolent and Protective Order of Elks. Most significant of all was his loose-leaf pocket note-book, that modern and efficient note-book which contained the addresses of people whom he had forgotten, prudent memoranda of postal money-orders which had reached their destinations months ago, stamps which had lost their mucilage, clippings of verses by T. Cholmondeley Frink and of the newspaper editorials from which Babbitt got his opinions and his polysyllables, notes to be sure and do things which he did not intend to do, and one curious inscription—D.S.S.D.M.Y. P.D.F.

But he had no cigarette-case. No one had ever happened to give him one, so he hadn't the habit, and people who carried cigarette-cases he regarded as effeminate.

Last, he stuck in his lapel the Boosters' Club button. With the conciseness of great art the button displayed two words: "Boosters—Pep!" It made Babbitt feel loyal and important. It associated him with Good Fellows, with men who were nice and human, and important in business circles. It was his V.C., his Legion of Honor ribbon, his Phi Beta Kappa key.

With the subtleties of dressing ran other complex worries. "I feel kind of punk this morning," he said. "I think I had too much dinner last evening. You oughtn't to serve those heavy banana fritters."

"But you asked me to have some."

"I know, but— I tell you, when a fellow gets past forty he has to look after his digestion. There's a lot of fellows that don't take proper care of themselves. I tell you at forty a man's a fool or his doctor—I mean, his own doctor. Folks don't give enough attention to this matter of dieting. Now I think— Course a man ought to have a good meal after the day's work, but it would be a good thing for both of us if we took lighter lunches."

"But, Georgie, here at home I always do have a light lunch."

"Mean to imply I make a hog of myself, eating down-town? Yes, sure! You'd have a swell time if you had to eat the truck that new steward hands out to us at the Athletic Club! But I certainly do feel out of sorts, this morning. Funny, got a pain down here on the left side—but no, that wouldn't be appendicitis, would it? Last night, when I was driving over to Verg Gunch's, I felt a pain in my stomach, too. Right here it was—kind of a sharp shooting pain. I— Where'd that dime go to? Why don't you serve more prunes at breakfast? Of course I eat an apple every evening—an apple a day keeps the doctor away—but still, you ought to have more prunes, and not all these fancy doodads."

"The last time I had prunes you didn't eat them."

"Well, I didn't feel like eating 'em, I suppose. Matter of fact, I think I did eat some of 'em. Anyway—I tell you it's mighty important to— I was saying to Verg Gunch, just last evening, most people don't take sufficient care of their diges—"

"Shall we have the Gunches for our dinner, next week?"

"Why, sure; you bet."

"Now see here, George: I want you to put on your nice dinner-jacket that evening."

"Rats! The rest of 'em won't want to dress."

"Of course they will. You remember when you didn't dress for the Littlefields' supper-party, and all the rest did, and how embarrassed you were."

"Embarrassed, hell! I wasn't embarrassed. Everybody knows I can put on as expensive a Tux. as anybody else, and I should worry if I don't happen to have it on sometimes. All a darn nuisance, anyway. All right for a woman, that stays around the house all the time, but when a fellow's worked like the dickens all day, he doesn't want to go and hustle his head off getting into the soup-and-fish for a lot of folks that he's seen in just reg'lar ordinary clothes that same day."

"You know you enjoy being seen in one. The other evening you admitted you were glad I'd insisted on your dressing. You said you felt a lot better for it. And oh, Georgie, I do wish you wouldn't say 'Tux.' It's 'dinner-jacket.' "

"Rats, what's the odds?"

"Well, it's what all the nice folks say. Suppose Lucile McKelvey heard you calling it a 'Tux.' "

"Well, that's all right now! Lucile McKelvey can't pull anything on me! Her folks are common as mud, even if her husband and her dad are millionaires! I suppose you're trying to rub in *your* exalted social position! Well, let me tell you that your revered paternal ancestor, Henry T., doesn't even call it a 'Tux.'! He calls it a 'bobtail jacket for a ringtail monkey,' and you couldn't get him into one unless you chloroformed him!"

"Now don't be horrid, George."

"Well, I don't want to be horrid, but Lord! you're getting as fussy as Verona. Ever since she got out of college she's been too rambunctious to live with—doesn't know what she wants—well, I know what she wants!—all she wants is to marry a millionaire, and live in Europe, and hold some preacher's hand, and simultaneously at the same time stay right here in Zenith and be some blooming kind of a socialist agitator or boss charity-worker or some damn thing! Lord, and Ted is just as bad! He wants to go to college, and he doesn't want to go to college. Only one of the three that knows her own mind is Tinka. Simply can't understand how I ever came to have a pair of shilly-shallying children like Rone and Ted. I may not be any Rockefeller or James J. Shakespeare, but I certainly do know my own mind, and I do keep right on plugging along in the office and— Do you know the latest? Far as I can figure out, Ted's new bee is he'd like to be a movie actor and— And here I've told him a hundred times, if he'll go to college and law-school and make good, I'll set him up in business and— Verona just exactly as bad. Doesn't know what she wants. Well, well, come on! Aren't you ready yet? The girl rang the bell three minutes ago."

V

Before he followed his wife, Babbitt stood at the westernmost window of their room. This residential settlement, Floral Heights, was on a rise; and though the center of the city was three miles away —Zenith had between three and four hundred thousand inhabitants now—he could see the top of the Second National Tower, an Indiana limestone building of thirty-five stories.

Its shining walls rose against April sky to a simple cornice like a streak of white fire. Integrity was in the tower, and decision. It bore its strength lightly as a tall soldier. As Babbitt stared, the nervousness was soothed from his face, his slack chin lifted in reverence. All he articulated was "That's one lovely sight!" but he was inspired by the rhythm of the city; his love of it renewed. He beheld the tower as a temple-spire of the religion of business, a faith passionate, exalted, surpassing common men; and as he clumped down to breakfast he whistled the ballad "Oh, by gee, by gosh, by jingo" as though it were a hymn melancholy and noble.

COMMENT AND QUESTIONS

I. Sinclair Lewis in this novel is the omniscient author, reading the minds of his characters, freely commenting on his material, and openly influencing the reader's judgment. Many of his comments are ironical or satirical. Point out some examples of such author-comments.

II. What dominant impression is given in the description of the city of Zenith in Section I?

III. Section II is complex description in which Babbitt's appearance, his surroundings, his dreams and sensations, and external sounds are skillfully interwoven. What do we learn about Babbitt from this section?

IV. What purpose is served by the alarm clock? By the iron garage? By the description of the bathroom in Section III?

V. What details seem to you particularly good in the scene of Babbitt-in-action with the razor blades and towels (Section III)? Why do you like them?

VI. What are the characteristics of Babbitt's speech? What purposes are served by the talk about his brown suit, about his digestion, about his dinner jacket, and about his children (Section IV)?

VII. What traits are revealed by the contents of his pockets? By his having no cigarette case? By his Boosters' Club button?

VIII. Notice that the chapter ends, as it begins, with a description of Zenith, this time as it looks to Babbitt. What is the difference between Babbitt's attitude toward the city and the author's attitude?

IX. In the course of the novel, Babbitt emerges as a character who, for all his faults, is in many ways likeable, and certainly human and understandable. In this first chapter, are any likeable qualities revealed? What is the dominant impression of him as a person?

BREAKFAST *

JOHN STEINBECK

Description of scene and description of people are woven complexly into the presentation of a total experience in the following story. John Steinbeck

* From *The Portable Steinbeck,* copyright, 1943, by John Steinbeck. Reprinted by permission of The Viking Press, Inc., New York.

is an outstanding contemporary American writer. *Tortilla Flat, In Dubious Battle, Of Mice and Men, The Grapes of Wrath* (winner of the 1940 Pulitzer Prize), and *Cannery Row* are some of his novels. Many critics think that the best of Steinbeck's writing is in his short stories in *The Long Valley* (1938), from which this selection is taken.

This thing fills me with pleasure. I don't know why, I can see it in the smallest detail. I find myself recalling it again and again, each time bringing more detail out of a sunken memory, remembering brings the curious warm pleasure.

It was very early in the morning. The eastern mountains were black-blue, but behind them the light stood up faintly colored at the mountain rims with a washed red, growing colder, greyer and darker as it went up and overhead until, at a place near the west, it merged with pure night.

And it was cold, not painfully so, but cold enough so that I rubbed my hands and shoved them deep into my pockets, and I hunched my shoulders up and scuffled my feet on the ground. Down in the valley where I was, the earth was that lavender grey of dawn. I walked along a country road and ahead of me I saw a tent that was only a little lighter grey than the ground. Beside the tent there was a flash of orange fire seeping out of the cracks of an old rusty iron stove. Grey smoke spurted up out of the stubby stovepipe, spurted up a long way before it spread out and dissipated.

I saw a young woman beside the stove, really a girl. She was dressed in a faded cotton skirt and waist. As I came close I saw that she carried a baby in a crooked arm and the baby was nursing, its head under her waist out of the cold. The mother moved about, poking the fire, shifting the rusty lids of the stove to make a greater draft, opening the oven door; and all the time the baby was nursing, but that didn't interfere with the mother's work, nor with the light quick gracefulness of her movements. There was something very precise and practiced in her movements. The orange fire flicked out of the cracks in the stove and threw dancing reflections on the tent.

I was close now, and I could smell frying bacon and baking bread, the warmest, pleasantest odors I know. From the east the light grew swiftly. I came near to the stove and stretched my hands out to it and shivered all over when the warmth struck me. Then the tent flap jerked up and a young man came out and an older man followed him. They were dressed in new blue dungarees and in new dungaree coats with the brass buttons shining. They were sharp-faced men, and they looked much alike.

The younger had a dark stubble beard and the older had a grey stubble beard. Their heads and faces were wet, their hair dripped with water, and water stood out on their stiff beards and their cheeks shone with water. Together they stood looking quietly at the lightening east; they yawned together and looked at the light on the hill rims. They turned and saw me.

"Morning," said the older man. His face was neither friendly nor unfriendly.

"Morning, sir," I said.

"Morning," said the young man.

The water was slowly drying on their faces. They came to the stove and warmed their hands at it.

The girl kept to her work, her face averted and her eyes on what she was doing. Her hair was tied back out of her eyes with a string and it hung down her back and swayed as she worked. She set tin cups on a big packing box, set tin plates and knives and forks out too. Then she scooped fried bacon out of the deep grease and laid it on a big tin platter, and the bacon cricked and rustled as it grew crisp. She opened the rusty oven door and took out a square pan full of high big biscuits.

When the smell of the hot bread came out, both of the men inhaled deeply. The young man said softly, "Keerist!"

The elder man turned to me, "Had your breakfast?"

"No."

"Well, sit down with us, then."

That was the signal. We went to the packing case and squatted on the ground about it. The young man asked, "Picking cotton?"

"No."

"We had twelve days' work so far," the young man said.

The girl spoke from the stove. "They even got new clothes."

The two men looked down at their new dungarees and they both smiled a little.

The girl set out the platter of bacon, the brown high biscuits, a bowl of bacon gravy and a pot of coffee, and then she squatted down by the box too. The baby was still nursing, its head up under her waist out of the cold. I could hear the sucking noises it made.

We filled our plates, poured bacon gravy over our biscuits and sugared our coffee. The older man filled his mouth full and he chewed and chewed and swallowed. Then he said, "God Almighty, it's good," and he filled his mouth again.

The young man said, "We been eating good for twelve days."

We all ate quickly, frantically, and refilled our plates and ate quickly again until we were full and warm. The hot bitter coffee scalded our throats. We threw the last little bit with the grounds in it on the earth and refilled our cups.

There was color in the light now, a reddish gleam that made the air seem colder. The two men faced the east and their faces were lighted by the dawn, and I looked up for a moment and saw the image of the mountain and the light coming over it reflected in the older man's eyes.

The two men threw the grounds from their cups on the earth and they stood up together. "Got to get going," the older man said.

The younger turned to me. "'Fyou want to pick cotton, we could maybe get you on."

"No. I got to go along. Thanks for breakfast."

The older man waved his hand in a negative. "O.K. Glad to have you." They walked away together. The air was blazing with light at the eastern skyline. And I walked away down the country road.

That's all. I know, of course, some of the reasons why it was pleasant. But there was some element of great beauty there that makes the rush of warmth when I think of it.

COMMENT AND QUESTIONS

Using a first-person point of view and an informal style to relate an experience that was meaningful to him, John Steinbeck has written a story rich in suggestion: only suggested are the relationships and the background of the three people he knew in this interval of breakfast; and suggested rather than explicitly stated—left to the reader to understand from what is set down—is the reason for the author's warm pleasure in remembering the experience.

I. What physical sensations are communicated, and what appeals to the senses are made in the story?

II. How does the fact that it was a cold morning contribute to the experience?

III. Particularly worth noting is the pattern of light that runs through the narrative. Trace this pattern in relation to the recorded events.

IV. Steinbeck's style here is very simple, with simple sentence structures and what might seem an unconsidered repetition of words; for example: "The younger had a dark stubble beard and the older had a grey stubble beard. Their heads and faces were wet, their hair dripped with water, and water stood out on their stiff beards and their cheeks shone with water." Is there a reason for this extremely simple style?

V. What can you deduce about the two men and the girl who gave the author breakfast?

VI. What purpose does the baby serve in the story?

VII. What are "some of the reasons why it was pleasant" that Steinbeck speaks of in the last paragraph?

VIII. What does he mean by "the element of great beauty there"?

B. THE REFLECTIVE PERSONAL ESSAY

The word *essay* is applied to such varied literary compositions that it can be defined only in general terms: an essay is a short prose-discussion of ideas relating to a particular subject. This name for a literary work was first used by the sixteenth century French philosopher Montaigne, who called his self-analytical prose pieces *essais* or "attempts," to distinguish them from complete formal dissertations. Since then, the term has become extremely elastic. Essays have been classified under such headings as critical essay, editorial essay, factual essay, research essay, historical essay, philosophical essay, reflective essay, biographical essay, character essay, narrative essay, nature essay, and familiar essay. These headings overlap and are of little practical value. They do show, though, the range of this literary form and its close relationship at several points to other types of prose. Factual, research, and historical essays, for example, are very close to informative articles; the difference is that the works called essays emphasize ideas and not simply facts. Character essays, which present a real or fictitious character who stands for an idea, and narrative essays, which present an idea by telling a story or anecdote, carry the essay into the realm of fiction. The familiar essay, which presents very informally and usually entertainingly the writer's personality, thoughts, and feelings, is similar to the good personal letter; indeed, familiar essays are sometimes written in letter form.

Another, and perhaps more useful, way of classifying essays is dividing them into two large groups: (1) formal essays; (2) personal or informal essays. This distinction is by no means an absolute one; but the formal essay is, in general, characterized by its serious treatment of serious ideas, problems, or beliefs; by formal style and organization; by a dignified and often (though not always) impersonal tone. Of the twelve categories of essays listed in the preceding paragraph, the first six (critical, editorial, factual, research, historical, and philosophical) are usually formal; the last six (reflective, biographical, character, narrative, nature, and familiar) are usually, in varying degrees, informal.

The personal essay is, as its name indicates, always informal and personal in style and tone. In content it may range from a discussion of values to humorous observations on getting up early in the morning or getting in late at night. Its organization is sometimes loose and informal, in the manner of the personal letter. Its purpose is to present in an interesting and lively way the thoughts, observations, and experiences of the writer.

Although we have not always used the term *essay*, a number of the selections in this chapter on types of prose can properly be classified as essays. Devoe's "The Life and Death of a Worm" can be called a nature essay; Sandburg's "Lincoln Speaks at Gettysburg" an historical essay; Thurber's "Which" a familiar essay; Mill's "On the Liberty of Thought and Discussion" a philosophical essay; Taylor's "The Monster" a critical essay. The simple narratives printed in the next section are examples, also, of biographical essays. It is apparent that essays differ in intention as well as in character: some aim primarily to inform, others to persuade, and still others to communicate experience.

In this section we are presenting a type of essay which lies on the shadowy boundary between the formal and the informal essay. The reflective personal essay communicates meaningful personal experience on which the writer has seriously reflected. Thus it has the style and tone of the informal essay, and, at the same time, some of the substance and essential seriousness of purpose of the formal essay. The writer, often using description and narrative as part of his method, re-creates his experiences for the reader, and leads the reader to share both the experiences and the set of values which they imply. Many reflective personal essays have, therefore, a dual intention: to communicate experience and to persuade the reader to accept an idea or a philosophy which clearly emerges from the experience.

The writer of the informal reflective essay is not obviously a preacher or a teacher; he usually maintains a tone of tolerant and friendly discussion; he is simply telling the reader what he has known and what he has felt and thought about it. The *point of view* in this kind of writing is, of course, first person; but most successful essayists try to give a reasonably objective report of their experience so that the reader has the sense of understanding that experience for himself, without undue pressure from the author.

The reflective personal essay offers the analytical reader a study of various techniques of language in action. It also has immediate value for the student writer. The best college compositions are (whether or not they are dignified by the name) reflective personal essays. They are papers in which the student vividly and thoughtfully recalls and evaluates his own experience, and sees that experience in relation to some serious idea.

FORMER TEACHERS *

IRWIN EDMAN

In the following selection, a philosopher and teacher looks back on his own student days and comments on the personalities, methods, and ideas of those who taught him. Professor of Philosophy at Columbia since 1935; author of *Four Ways of Philosophy, Candle in the Dark, Arts and the Man;* contributor to *The New Yorker* as well as to scholarly journals, Irwin Edman is one of the most readable and one of the most rewarding of modern philosophers. "Former Teachers" is Chapter Twelve of *Philosopher's Holiday* (1938), and is preceded by a chapter entitled "Former Students."

[1]   By an easy transition I am led from reflection about former students to meditation on former teachers. For I have had teachers as well as pupils, and in considering what effect one has had, or failed to have, on one's one-time students, I cannot help looking back on teachers who, though they might be embarrassed to acknowledge it, or insistent on denying it, had an influence over me. I shall leave out my early love for Miss Foley in 4A, or Miss Carpendale in 7B, whom I feared horribly, partly because she taught me the impossible subject of arithmetic, and partly because of her immense height and blazing red hair and unrelenting expression and deep mannish voice. I felt rather sorry for the trim little teacher of shopwork (another impossible subject) when I heard Miss Carpendale had married him. I was sure even then that that was the way it had happened.

[2]   I shall begin rather with high school, for I don't remember that in grade school anybody aroused my mind and imagination. That event came in my first term at Townsend Harris Hall, the preparatory school, called at the time the academic department, of the College of the City of New York. The man involved was named Michael J. Kelleher, an enthusiastic, curly-haired Irishman, who, at the top of his voice but with a winning cadence, dragooned us into liking *The Ancient Mariner* and *Ivanhoe.* He also dragooned

some of us into liking our own writing. He was the first one, save, perhaps, Miss Foley, to make me think I could write. Miss Foley's observation had been based on one sentence. I had written a self-portrait of a camel. The last sentence was: "I do not need water for days at a time; I have it with me." She said that was very good and very well informed. Mr. Michael Kelleher wrote in a large bold hand on a theme of mine: "This has the sweet breath of the country about it." It was an essay on Central Park.

[3] But I recall Mr. Michael Kelleher chiefly because he gave us the contagious impression of so liking poetry that he simply had to tell us about it. Since we were the fourth class he had each morning, it occurred to me even then that it was very remarkable that he should be able to care so deeply and vividly about Rebecca and Rowena still. But he did. It was, I found out, the first year he had taught. I have often thought since it might be well to have a big turn-over in the teaching profession. But that is not really necessary. For, years later, finding myself in the neighbourhood of my old school, I decided to hunt out my old teacher. It was not quite the end of the hour and I heard the powerful cadenced voice of Mr. Kelleher still making clear to fourteen-year-olds the wonder and mystery of *The Ancient Mariner*. I could hear him and even see his figure outlined through the transparent glass of the door:

> "Alone, alone, all, all alone,
> Alone on a wide, wide sea,
> And never a saint took pity on
> My soul in agony. . . ."

The remembered shiver went up my spine. Mr. Kelleher was a born teacher of poetry. He did not explain it; he communicated it by contagion.

[4] There were three other high school teachers I remember. One was the beautifully dressed, slim Mr. Knickerbocker who taught us French. His technique belied his debonair appearance. There was no languid elegance about his methods. He spent the first fifteen minutes of each hour rapidly going around the class making certain that we knew the new words in each lesson. It was a martinet method, but it worked. One did not twice come to class unprepared, to have Mr. Knickerbocker's clear blue eyes briefly stare one into humiliation if one guessed, or could not even guess, the meaning of a word. There was not much about appreciation of French literature, and I presume such methods now would be regarded as unimaginative drill. But one knew a great many words with precision before the term was over.

[5] My third debt to my high school teachers is to Bird W. Stair, now a professor in the College of the City of New York. He had just come to New York from Indiana; he used the English class as an introduction to ideas, and I suspect my feeling that literature was the vehicle, sensuous and imaginative, of ideas came from him. After three terms with him I had learned once and for all that books, even old ones, were distillations of life, and began to think less of literature with a capital L. As I look back on it now, I am quite sure that Mr. Stair found Burke's Speech on Conciliation and *Macbeth* the springboards for various ideas that had a rather tenuous connexion with them. "English" became at his hands an introduction to philosophy, manners, contemporary political ideas, journalism, and love. These ideas were not always directly germane to the text; but they were ideas, and though their accent and their origin were Middle-Western—Middle Western *revolte*—they were an introduction to the great world and to the realm of mind.

[6] The fourth teacher I recall in high school is one who, if he still lives, may possibly remember me. If he does, he recalls me as the worst student of mathematics he ever had. Rumour circulated in the school that Mr. Powell, an urbane, sad man who looked like a banker, was a very wealthy man who taught simply to occupy his time. I never believed it; no one would, I thought, teach solid geometry for amusement. If I were rich, I kept on thinking during the class, I should buy a yacht; I should go around the world. I should, if I must teach, teach English. Mr. Powell noticed my mind wandering; he also noticed when I came up to the blackboard for a demonstration that mathematics was not my *forte*. He called me to him once at the end of the hour. "You do not seem stupid," he said, "but mathematics seems a lot of hocus pocus to you." For the most part, it still does; and I regret it very much. For I am told on good authority that in the logistic symbols of the newer mathematics lies hid the secret of the universe. I recall also that Plato said a gift for mathematics was essential to a philosopher. But it is too late to do anything about it now; it was too late then. And when it came to trigonometry, I, too, was "alone on a wide, wide sea," and Mr. Powell I always remember as the only teacher of mathematics ever to take pity on my soul in agony.

[7] When one speaks of one's old teachers, it is generally to one's college teachers that one refers. For it is then, if one is lucky, that one comes in contact with men who communicate and articulate the things and ideas which become the seeds of one's later intellectual and imaginative life. Every college has five or six men who in essence

are its educational system. I was very lucky. For during my under-graduate days at Columbia, there was a galaxy of teachers available to the student who in their respective ways and as a group would be hard to duplicate at any college in any period. As a freshman straight from high school, I heard Charles A. Beard lecture on American Government; as a sophomore—and in 1914—I heard Carlton Hayes lecture on European History; as a junior I heard John Erskine talk on Shakespeare, and was in a small class where he taught us, really taught us, writing; and in my senior year I had the unique and irrecoverable experience of traversing the history of philosophy with Frederick J. E. Woodbridge. It was not until my graduate study that I came to know John Dewey.

[8]　Charles A. Beard illustrates something very remarkable about the art of teaching. Today everybody, even the literary youngsters, are interested in government. For even literature seems less in the Ivory Tower than it did in 1913. But the study of government, then officially known at Columbia as "Politics," did not, to most of us addicted to poetry and music, seem to be our meat, and there was nothing in the dark blue tome, Beard's *American Government and Politics,* that seemed arresting. There were endless details about the mechanisms and structure of State and Federal government. It was not the Beard of the *Economic Interpretation of the Constitution.*

[9]　But his lectures were another matter. The lanky figure leaning against the wall, drawling wittily with half-closed eyes, made the questions of government seem the most vital that anyone could broach, and touched matters that lay far deeper than the mere forms of constitutional government.

[10]　Every good teacher has his own special art; with some, it is a genius for a clarity that sometimes is more lucid than the complex-ities of the subject justify. Sometimes it is a talent for apophthegm or leading suggestion, a word that evokes a vista or an idea that opens a world. I cannot now quite remember what Professor Beard's special technique was. He was clear, he was suggestive, he was witty. But none of these things could quite account for the hold he had on the smug and the rebels alike, on both the pre-lawyers and pre-poets. I suspect it was a certain combination of poetry, philosophy, and honesty in the man himself, a sense he communicated that politics mattered far beyond the realm commonly called political, and an insight he conveyed into the life that forms of government furthered or betrayed. One morning he came into class as usual, stood against the wall, and, half-closing his eyes, said:

[11]　"Gentlemen, today we are to discuss the budget system in State government. I am sure that must seem to you a dull subject.

But if you will tell me, gentlemen, how much *per capita* a nation spends on its Army, on its Navy, on education, on public works, I shall be able to tell you, I think, as much about that nation as if you gave me the works of its poets and philosophers."

[12]   We listened with revised and revived attention to an exposition, full of figures and detail, of the State budget system. Charles A. Beard showed us what politics had to do with the life beyond it and which it made possible. And he taught us, too, the difference between the forms of government and the living substance of its operations. Under his easy, drawling manner, we sensed a passionate concern for an understanding of the realities of government, the economic forces and the interested persons involved in it, and the ideal of government: the liberation of the energies of men. Nobody who has ever listened to Beard can disdain the study of politics in favour of the study of "higher things." He has been too well taught, as tragic world events have since shown, how government may nourish or destroy "higher things."

[13]   Up to the autumn of 1914 Europe seemed to most American college students a solar system away. In the autumn of 1914, when the war had been going on two months, Europe came for the first time in the imagination of many Americans to be vivid and near. European history ceased to be the anthropology and the archaeology of distant peoples who spoke remote languages. It became as alive as yesterday's events: it was what explained today's news. It was, therefore, no wonder that at the beginning of the college year Carlton Hayes's course in "Europe since 1815" had become the most popular course in Columbia College. But it was not only the war that accounted for that. Carlton Hayes had for some time been one of the most popular professors in the college. His lectures were the most famous dramatic spectacle on the campus. Nor was it as a performance alone that they were famous. Everyone had heard that Hayes could actually make clear French political parties; I have never met anybody since who could or can.

[14]   The complicated history of Germany in the second half of the nineteenth century took shape as well as drama under his presentation of it. And in the midst of being taught and taught clearly, one had the incidental and additional pleasure of hearing a man to whom the great castastrophe of war had its roots in a past he knew, in the traditions of nations among whom he had lived familiarly, and in the desperate mythologies of nationalism, to which he had given special study and concern. One was treated, besides, to unforgettable vignettes of Disraeli dropping his morning walking stick as the cannons boomed noon at Gibraltar; of the Manchester school of econ-

omists, the "spiritual advisers" to the robber barons of early nine-teenth-century industrial England; of the black walnut furniture of the Victorian period; of the times and the manners of Louis Na-poleon; of the studies that produced the *Communist Manifesto.* One was shaken out of the smugness of the middle-class world in which most students were brought up and out of the provincial American-ism in which most of us had lived.

[15]   It did not matter, it served only as spice, that some of the barbs delivered in a dry voice by this baldish, sharp-featured man in his thirties were directed at us, at our very smugness, at our laziness, or at our fathers: when he was explaining the attitude of the manu-facturers of the early Industrial Revolution, he reminded us that we all knew manufacturers; "some of your fathers," he drawled, "are manufacturers." It did matter a little to some of us that he mocked poetry and philosophy (this *in re* Shelley and Godwin) . . . "phi-losophy is what is taught in Philosophy Hall . . ." But it did not matter much. For during a whole year, we sat through a whole cen-tury of European history, and Bismarck, Garibaldi, Social Legisla-tion in England. Benevolent Tories like Shaftesbury and reformers like Cobden and Bright, "nationalism"—what devastating force Carlton Hayes put and can still put into the word—democracy, the Third Republic, became familiar parts of our imagination. In the midst of cries of "pro-German" and "pro-Ally," "preparedness" and "pacifism," during the three years before America went into the war, we knew somewhat better than many of our older compatriots what had brought the tornado about. Carlton Hayes had brought European history, as Charles Beard had brought American govern-ment, from the abstraction of a textbook to an experience lived and a problem to be faced. And it always surprised some of us that, in the midst of the lectures—first-rate theatrical performances, words shot out for emphasis, silences sustained for a moment, gestures and movements deployed like those of a good actor—when we looked down at our notes, they were as ordered and clear as if we had listened to a scholastic metronome . . . I confess with shame that I achieved only a B.

[16]   You were allowed, if you had a fairly good academic record, to take in the senior year a graduate course that was at the time one of the famous academic enterprises of the period. It was James Harvey Robinson's course in the History of the Intellectual Classes in West-ern Europe. Everyone who had gone to high school knew the two volumes of Robinson and Beard's *Development of Modern Europe.* But the Robinson we came to know as a legend and a rumour by the

time we were sophomores was the Robinson who had invented the "new history"—the history of causes and consequences, the history that treated politics as the surface of more fundamental matters, economic and social and cultural, and that regarded the date of the invention of the steam engine as more important than the dates of a king, and the industrial use of steam as more significant than monarchies and dynasties. We had also heard of Robinson, along with Dewey and Beard, as among the intellectual-liberal forces that were making our university famous in some quarters, notorious in others. And, finally, we had heard of the remarkable brilliance of the lectures in History 72.

[17] The latter was a graduate course to which undergraduates, a handful of us, were admitted on sufferance. The majority of the class of over two hundred were graduate students of history, many of them women high school teachers from all over the country, particularly the West and South. Professor Robinson was a short man, with thin, greying hair and a deprecating, half-tired, half-amused, drawling voice. He seemed to be having a half-weary good time examining the origins of human stupidity, and those vestigial remains of our culture that blocked the free and hopeful functioning of human intelligence. It took us a few weeks in the course to get to the beginnings of *intellectual* history. For Robinson, with saturnine delight, liked to show us the mind of the child, the slave, and the animal still functioning in us. Once he brought in a leading editorial from the New York *Times* to illustrate the theme, and another time quoted from a batch of Sunday sermons reported in that journal the next day. The course was not a course in intellectual heroes, but a course in the changing fashions of adult follies taken seriously in various ages. It only gradually became clear what intellectual heroes were presiding over the whole story as he gave it. They were Freud and Marx and Dewey and the anthropologists, and H. G. Wells, the prophet, then, of intelligence reshaping the world. There were only two or three gods of the past left unbesmirched, or whose clay feet were not recognized. They were Lucretius, who saw the diabolism of religion; Francis Bacon, who saw the human possibilities of science; Voltaire, who exhibited the foolishness of superstition. Plato was a man who believed in Truth, Goodness, and Beauty because he saw the actual world as a chaos which, Robinson loved to remind us, he compared to "a man with a running nose. . . ." Aristotle's science was childish (Robinson did not know how soon again it was to be fashionable and how more fundamental than fashion it is); St. Augustine was a most amusingly and scandalously human saint. It was not until the enlightenment of the eighteenth century that any-

body, so most of us gathered from the course, was very enlightened.
[18]   Many of the graduate students were shocked, especially by the
treatment of religion. The undergraduates from Columbia College
had heard much of this before and had no faith (as did some of the
graduate students) to have taken away. One of the young women
complained to Professor Robinson: "You are taking away my faith."
He looked at her oddly. "But if I took away a headache," he said
simply, "you would not complain."
[19]   We undergraduates enjoyed the sallies, the freshness, the irrev-
erence, and enjoyed, too, the fundamental feeling that lay at the
basis of it all—that man, if he took his own intelligence into his
hands—could make the world less a shambles and an idiocy than it
had so often been. It was in the great days of the liberal faith when
trust in intelligence was in the ascendant. If Robinson made the
world appear a satire to intelligent observation, he made it seem a
lyric hope to generosity and understanding. Dixon Ryan Fox, now
President of Union College, was the young instructor who took the
third quiz hour with the undergraduates. He felt it his special obligation to let us see the other side. And after a week, when he knew
Robinson had been "exposing" modern Protestantism, he called in
the chaplain as a counterweight. He need not have bothered; we had
our own grains of salt. One of the reasons we had grains of salt was
that some of us had been studying with a man who will go down, I
am quite certain, as one of the great philosophical teachers of our
generation. His slender published writings will live, but they will
live for a small circle of students. But Frederick J. E. Woodbridge
has educated a whole generation of students in philosophy; and a
whole circle of them scattered over the country, including Morris
Cohen and Sidney Hook and J. H. Randall, Jr., and Herbert Schnei-
der (to mention only a few), are living testimonies to his influence
and his power. In my college days, the great thing was to have taken
his course in the History of Philosophy. Some of us were taking it
at the same time that we took Robinson's History of the Intellectual
Classes in Western Europe. It was rather a different story we were
told. It was not a story, but a succession of experiences of philosophers
whose importance lay "not in their truth but in their power." It was
a shock that turned into a liberation for those of us who had come
to philosophy looking for *the* Truth with a dogmatic capital letter.
There were other shocks, too. Much that was said in the textbooks
we never heard in class, or we heard the contrary. Professor Woodbridge, who looked like a bishop and would have made a very eloquent one, talked like a poet whose theme happened to be the human
mind. He talked most like a poet on the days when he was most

interested; one remembers what days those were: the early Greeks, Plato, Aristotle, Marcus Aurelius, Lucretius, Spinoza with his sovereign detachment, and Locke with his sovereign common sense. He was not an unprejudiced observer and we rather liked the frankness and the brevity with which he dismissed the Germans and Rousseau. But what one was most moved by was the things by which he himself was most moved: the Plato who was the son of Apollo, the poet and the dramatist of ideas; Marcus Aurelius, the disillusioned statesman whistling to keep up his comical courage; Lucretius looking out with dramatic sympathy and equable understanding on the eternal nature of things. We were impressed by a mind whose maturity had not dulled its enthusiasms, and an understanding uncorrupted by the technical controversies of the academy, by the routine of the classroom, by the burden of administration of an elder statesman, for Woodbridge was graduate Dean of the University. He taught a whole generation of students of philosophy to keep their eye on the object, to see a thinker in his own terms, to cease to raise foolish and irrelevant questions, and above all, to raise the central and relevant ones about a man's teaching. On Aristotle's metaphysics, he began by reminding us that Aristotle was asking the simple and the ultimate question: "What does it mean to be? . . ." We found ourselves astonished to be reminded that the Middle Ages were in their own time not the Middle Ages at all. We were made aware of Locke's simple English attempt to be sensible, tolerant, and direct, and learned to understand what Spinoza meant and why he saw it as a liberation to see all things under the form of eternity. For in that wonderful class, as Will Durant (sitting next to me in alphabetical order) remarked, we were listening not to a professor of philosophy but to philosophy itself. It was impossible to feel you were listening to a doctrine; Professor Woodbridge has never founded a school. You were hearing philosophy itself and came to understand it as an attempt to speak in the categories of mind of the categories of things. [20] I did not—I think not many of us did—understand it all. But we began to understand what understanding meant, in words that had eloquence without rhetoric. We heard great things nobly uttered. We learnt no doctrine but we grasped the significance of intellectual procedure; and to a whole generation of philosophers, though Professor Woodbridge has long since ceased to be their teacher, he remains their teacher still. He made us understand as none else had done, to use one of his own phrases, "the enterprise of learning."

[21] A figure more widely known outside purely academic circles was and is John Dewey. In 1915 his name was already, if not a household, certainly a schoolroom word. His *How We Think* was used in

all the normal schools of the country, and even fashionable ladies dipped into his far from easy books. I had read almost all of Dewey I could get hold of by the time I was a senior, but it was not until my first year as a graduate student that I heard, or, I believe, saw him. His familiar figure and speech, seeming at first that of a Vermont farmer, the casual gait, the keen but often absent eyes, seem so familiar now that I can scarcely believe I did not know them before.

[22] I admit the first lecture was quite a shock, a shock of dullness and confusion, if that can be said. It was at any rate a disappointment. I had not found Dewey's prose easy, but I had learned that its difficulty lay for the most part in its intellectual honesty, which led him to qualify an idea in one sentence half a page long. In part also it lay in the fact that this profoundly original philosopher was struggling to find a vocabulary to say what had never been said in philosophy before, to find a diction that would express with exactness the reality of change and novelty, philosophical words having been used for centuries to express the absolute and the fixed. Once one had got used to the long sentences, with their string of qualifying clauses, to the sobriety, to the lack of image and of colour, one sensed the liberating force of this philosophy. Here was not an answer but a quest for light in the living movement of human experience; in the very precariousness of experience there lay open to the perplexed human creature the possibilities that peril itself provocatively suggested. I had found here, as have so many of my generation, a philosophy that, instead of laying down a diagram of an ideal universe that had nothing to do with the one of actual human doings and sufferings, opened a vision of conscious control of life, of a democracy operating through creative intelligence in the liberation of human capacities and natural goods. In *How We Think* I had learned that thinking itself was simply a discipline of the animal habit of trial and error, and of the possible human habit of imagination and foresight. In *Democracy and Education* I had gathered that it was not in the forms of democratic government that true democracy lay, but in the substance of intelligent co-operation, largely dependent on education. Dewey was not easy, but once one had mastered his syntax, a vision of a liberal and liberated commonwealth was one's reward, and a philosophy that was not only a vision but a challenge.

[23] I was naturally prepared, therefore, to expect something of intellectual excitement from the lectures in "Psychological Ethics." Intellectual excitement was the last term to describe what I experienced that September afternoon. The course came, in the first place, directly after lunch. It was well attended; there were even some fashionably dressed society ladies, for Dewey had become a vogue.

But this famous philosopher who had written so much on "Interest in Education" as the essence of the educational process could not, save by a radical distortion of the term, be said at first hearing to sound interesting. He had none of the usual tricks or gifts of the effective lecturer. He sat at his desk, fumbling with a few crumpled yellow sheets and looking abstractedly out the window. He spoke very slowly in a Vermont drawl. He looked both very kindly and very abstracted. He hardly seemed aware of the presence of a class. He took little pains to underline a phrase, or emphasize a point, or, so at first it seemed to me, to make any. Occasionally he would apparently realise that people in the back of the room might not hear his quiet voice: he would then accent the next word, as likely as not a preposition or a conjunction. He seemed to be saying whatever came into his head next, and at one o'clock on an autumn afternoon to at least one undergraduate what came next did not always have or seem to have a very clear connexion with what had just gone before. The end of the hour finally came and he simply stopped; it seemed to me he might have stopped anywhere. But I soon found that it was my mind that had wandered, not John Dewey's. I began very soon to do what I had seldom done in college courses—to take notes. It was then a remarkable discovery to make on looking over my notes to find that what had seemed so casual, so rambling, so unexciting, was of an extraordinary coherence, texture, and brilliance. I had been listening to a man actually *thinking* in the presence of a class. As one became accustomed to Dewey's technique, it was this last aspect of his teaching that was most impressive—and educative. To attend a lecture of John Dewey was to participate in the actual business of thought. Those pauses were delays in creative thinking, when the next step was really being considered, and for the glib dramatics of the teacher-actor was substituted the enterprise, careful and candid, of the genuine thinker. Those hours came to seem the most arresting educational experiences, almost, I have ever had. One had to be scrupulously attentive and one learned to be so. Not every day or in every teacher does one overhear the palpable processes of thought. One came to enjoy and appreciate the homely metaphor, "the fork in the road," the child and his first attempts to speak, the New England town meeting, instead of the classical images one had been accustomed to from more obviously eloquent lips. Moreover, if one listened attentively one discovered apophthegm and epigram delivered as casually and sleepily as if they were clichés. I remember one instance. It had been rather a long lecture designed to show that the crucial tests of the morals of a group came in what that group regarded as violations of its conventions. The bell rang.

Professor Dewey began to crumple up his notes. "And so," he said, "I think sometimes one can tell more about the morals of our society from the inmates of its jails than from the inmates of its universities." The student next to me who had been semi-dozing stirred in half-alarmed surprise.

[24]   I learned later in a seminar to see Dewey's greatest gifts as a teacher, that of initiating inquiry rather than that of disseminating a doctrine. The subject matter of the seminar was innocent enough and removed from the immediacies of current controversy. It was a year's course, meeting every Tuesday afternoon, on "The Logic of John Stuart Mill." The seminar remains in my memory, it must be added, not simply for John Dewey or John Stuart Mill. It consisted, looking back on it and indeed as it appeared then, of a very remarkable group. It included two now well-known professors of philosophy, Brand Blanshard of Swarthmore College and Sterling Lamprecht of Amherst, Paul Blanshard, later to become Commissioner of Accounts under Mayor LaGuardia, and Albert C. Barnes, the inventor and manufacturer of Argyrol and collector of French paintings, even then a grey-haired man who used to come up from Philadelphia every week with his secretary expressly to study philosophy with his friend John Dewey.

[25]   I do not suppose Professor Dewey said more than five percent of the words actually uttered in that seminar. For the latter consisted largely of papers presented by various members of the group. But one remembered what he said. The subject matter was obviously close to him, for had not Mill been one of the great nineteenth century leaders of the empirical school of thought; had he not been, in his way, a pragmatist and, like Dewey himself, a liberal? But one noticed particularly Dewey's gift for pointing to the exact difficulty or the exact limitations of a man or a paper; his capacity for sympathetically seeing what a student was driving at, even when he did not quite succeed in saying it, and Dewey's candid expression of his own position or his own prejudices.

[26]   One instance of Dewey's frankness comes to my mind. There was among the group a young lady who had come from England where she had studied philosophy with Bertrand Russell at Cambridge. She listened patiently for weeks to Dewey's varied insistence that the truth of an idea was tested by its use. One day she burst out toward the close of the seminar in the sharp, clipped speech of the educated Englishwoman: "But, professor, I have been taught to believe that true means true; that false means false, that good means good and bad means bad; I don't understand all this talk about more or less true, more or less good. Could you explain more exactly?"

[27] Professor Dewey looked at her mildly for a moment and said: "Let me tell you a parable. Once upon a time in Philadelphia there was a paranoiac. He thought he was dead. Nobody could convince him he was alive. Finally, one of the doctors thought of an ingenious idea. He pricked the patient's finger. 'Now,' he said, 'are you dead?' 'Sure,' said the paranoiac, 'that proves that dead men bleed. . . .' Now I'll say true or false if you want me to, but I'll mean better or worse."

[28] There are all kinds of talents that go to make up a great teacher. Among those not commonly noted in the textbooks are simplicity and candour. These qualities in Dewey even an undergraduate could recognize and understand.

[29] I cannot say that John Erskine seemed to me a great man in the sense that Woodbridge and Dewey did and do, nor did *The Private Life of Helen of Troy,* for all its bright entertainment, lead me to think I had been obtuse on this point as an undergraduate. But I am convinced he was a very remarkable teacher and it has always seemed to me a pity that he gave up the profession of distinguished teaching for that of the popular novelist. Erskine's quality as a teacher was that of communication by contagion; you felt the quality of the authors he talked about and books seemed to have something to do with life rather than libraries.

[30] Literature was an exercise in imagination, not in archaeology and there must be thousands of students besides myself who learned to read authors in their own terms, to enjoy them for their own sakes, from John Erskine's famous course in Elizabethan Literature. It is true that one enjoyed Professor Erskine for other reasons. He had wit—often malicious—in his own right, and, when he was in the vein, poetry and philosophy, too. He obviously loved poetry and it seemed to him both to matter and a matter of course that we should love it, too. One felt about him something of the prima donna lecturer; it was evidenced by the pointed silence that would occur while some unfortunate late-comer found his way to his seat. It was clear, too, from the way in which, not infrequently, Shakespeare or Marlowe or Castiglione would be the springboards for little bravura lectures by our teacher on the importance of love or of being a cultivated gentleman, the latter one of his favourite themes. But if he was sometimes the prima donna, he always respected the materials he taught, and for many years no one at Columbia was a more devoted servant to the art and to the love of literature than he. And not the least of his services to that art were, first, the noble and musical way in which he read poetry itself; and secondly, the pains he took to encourage signs of that art among undergraduates. Other

teachers might make literature seem a set of documents to be investigated; no one quite knew why. Erskine made it an art to be lived and loved.

[31]   It is occasionally said that a good student needs no teachers and that all that he does need is a library and leisure. Neither the poor nor the good student needs bad teachers or bored ones; he is better off without them. But he is very fortunate indeed if he can look back on his college days and enumerate half a dozen men who, by their passion for ideas, their clarity about them, their love for the communication of them, their exemplification in their own being of intellectual discipline and candour, have given a meaning to facts that, even with leisure and libraries, he would not have been as likely to find by himself.

[32]   I feel my college generation at Columbia was very fortunate. Half a dozen good teachers in a college are enough to make it distinguished. We had more than half a dozen very exceptional ones. But then I think current undergraduates at Columbia, if they are discerning, will, looking back, be able to say the same.

COMMENT AND QUESTIONS

The kind of writing found in "Former Teachers" is not easy to imitate. It is a product of wide knowledge, sharp observation, deep and lively interest in people and ideas, and careful attention to style. Such writing is not produced by mechanical application of techniques. By examining it closely, however, you can learn much that can be applied in your own writing.

I. Edman's handling of the writer-reader relationship, particularly through subtle shifts in pronouns (sometimes "I," sometimes "we," sometimes "you"), is worth studying. See paragraph 15, which at first uses "we" and later "I," and paragraph 16, which starts with "you" and shifts back to "we." What reasons can you find for these changes? Glance through the essay to see other similar changes, and try to state the reasons for each.

II. Leaf through the essay looking only at the first sentence in each paragraph, and notice the unobtrusive but effective way in which the organization is made clear and the paragraphs are joined by transitions. Notice also how many of the paragraphs begin with topic sentences.

III. From your examination of topic sentences and your first reading, make a rough outline of the essay.

IV. Read paragraphs 9–11 and point out examples of Edman's way of vitalizing people by describing them, showing them in action,

and telling anecdotes about them. Where else in the essay do you find
him using these techniques with particular success?

V. For what reasons does Edman admire Frederick J. E. Woodbridge (paragraphs 19–20)? Has he communicated his reasons mean-
ingfully to the reader? If so, how? Notice also the style and sentence
structure in these paragraphs.

VI. Edman's treatment of John Dewey in paragraphs 21–23 produces a kind of suspense. What is the nature of this suspense, and
how is it achieved?

VII. For what kind of reader is Edman writing in this essay? Is
he, in your opinion, writing over the heads of college freshmen?

VIII. Has Edman enjoyed his courses more than most college
students do? If so, is it simply because he has had such good teachers?

IX. What characteristics do Edman's best teachers appear to have
in common?

X. If your instructor finds the topic acceptable, write an essay
similar to Edman's about two or three of your own former teachers.
Try to imitate Edman's techniques of vitalizing people. Your essay,
like Edman's, should contain reflective comment and evaluation.

THE LANTERN-BEARERS *

ROBERT LOUIS STEVENSON

The following reflective essay is built on a personal experience which
becomes the symbol of a larger idea. Robert Louis Stevenson (1850–1894),
Scottish novelist, essayist, and poet, was one of the distinguished stylists of
the late nineteenth century. He is probably best known today for his
stories of fantasy and romantic adventure, among them *Treasure Island,
Kidnapped, The Master of Ballantrae,* and *The Strange Case of Dr. Jekyll
and Mr. Hyde.* "The Lantern-Bearers" was published in 1888.

I

[1]   These boys congregated every autumn about a certain easterly
fisher-village, where they tasted in a high degree the glory of existence. The place was created seemingly on purpose for the diversion
of young gentlemen. A street or two of houses, mostly red and many
of them tiled; a number of fine trees clustered about the manse and

* Published by Charles Scribner's Sons.

the kirkyard, and turning the chief street into a shady alley; many
little gardens more than usually bright with flowers; nets a-drying,
and fisher-wives scolding in the backward parts; a smell of fish, a
genial smell of seaweed; whiffs of blowing sand at the street-corners;
shops with golf-balls and bottled lollipops; another shop with penny
pickwicks (that remarkable cigar) and the *London Journal*, dear to
me for its startling pictures, and a few novels, dear for their suggestive names: such, as well as memory serves me, were the ingredients of the town. These, you are to conceive posted on a spit
between two sandy bays, and sparsely flanked with villas—enough
for the boys to lodge in with their subsidiary parents, not enough
(not yet enough) to cocknify the scene: a haven in the rocks in front:
in front of that, a file of gray islets: to the left, endless links and
sandwreaths, a wilderness of hiding-holes, alive with popping rabbits
and soaring gulls: to the right, a range of seaward crags, one rugged
brow beyond another; the ruins of a mighty and ancient fortress on
the brink of one; coves between—now charmed into sunshine quiet,
now whistling with wind and clamorous with bursting surges; the
dens and sheltered hollows redolent of thyme and southernwood, the
air at the cliff's edge brisk and clean and pungent of the sea—in
front of all, the Bass Rock, tilted seaward like a doubtful bather, the
surf ringing it with white, the solan-geese hanging round its summit
like a great and glittering smoke. This choice piece of seaboard was
sacred, besides, to the wrecker; and the Bass, in the eye of fancy, still
flew the colors of King James; and in the ear of fancy the arches of
Tantallon still rang with horseshoe iron, and echoed to the commands of Bell-the-Cat.

[2]   There was nothing to mar your days, if you were a boy summer-
ing in that part, but the embarrassment of pleasure. You might golf
if you wanted; but I seem to have been better employed. You might
secrete yourself in the Lady's Walk, a certain sunless dingle of elders,
all mossed over by the damp as green as grass, and dotted here and
there by the stream-side with roofless walls, the cold homes of an-
chorites. To fit themselves for life, and with a special eye to acquire
the art of smoking, it was even common for the boys to harbor there;
and you might have seen a single penny pickwick, honestly shared
in lengths with a blunt knife, bestrew the glen with these appren-
tices. Again, you might join our fishing-parties, where we sat perched
as thick as solan-geese, a covey of little anglers, boy and girl, angling
over each other's heads, to the much entanglement of lines and loss
of podleys and consequent shrill recrimination—shrill as the geese
themselves. Indeed, had that been all, you might have done this
often; but though fishing be a fine pastime, the podley is scarce to

be regarded as a dainty for the table; and it was a point of honor that a boy should eat all that he had taken. Or again, you might climb the Law, where the whale's jawbone stood landmark in the buzzing wind, and behold the face of many counties, and the smokes and spires of many towns, and the sails of distant ships. You might bathe, now in the flaws of fine weather, that we pathetically call our summer, now in a gale of wind, with the sand scourging your bare hide, your clothes thrashing abroad from underneath their guardian stone, the froth of the great breakers casting you headlong ere it had drowned your knees. Or you might explore the tidal rocks, above all in the ebb of springs, when the very roots of the hills were for the nonce discovered; following my leader from one group to another, groping in slippery tangle for the wreck of ships, wading in pools after the abominable creatures of the sea, and ever with an eye cast backward on the march of the tide and the menaced line of your retreat. And then you might go Crusoeing, a word that covers all extempore eating in the open air; digging perhaps a house under the margin of the links, kindling a fire of the sea-ware, and cooking apples there—if they were truly apples, for I sometimes suppose the merchant must have played us off with some inferior and quite local fruit, capable of resolving, in the neighborhood of fire, into mere sand and smoke and iodine; or perhaps pushing to Tantallon, you might lunch on sandwiches and visions in the grassy court, while the wind hummed in the crumbling turrets; or clambering along the coast, eat geans * (the worst, I must suppose, in Christendom) from an adventurous gean-tree that had taken root under a cliff, where it was shaken with an ague of east wind, and silvered after gales with salt, and grew so foreign among its bleak surroundings that to eat of its produce was an adventure in itself.

[3] There are mingled some dismal memories with so many that were joyous. Of the fisher-wife, for instance, who had cut her throat at Canty Bay; and of how I ran with the other children to the top of the Quadrant, and beheld a posse of silent people escorting a cart, and on the cart, bound in a chair, her throat bandaged, and the bandage all bloody—horror!—the fisher-wife herself, who continued thenceforth to hag-ride my thoughts, and even to-day (as I recall the scene) darkens daylight. She was lodged in the little old jail in the chief street; but whether or no she died there, with a wise terror of the worst, I never inquired. She had been tippling; it was but a dingy tragedy; and it seems strange and hard that, after all these years, the poor crazy sinner should be still pilloried on her cart in the scrap-book of my memory. Nor shall I readily forget a certain

* Wild cherries.

house in the Quadrant where a visitor died, and a dark old woman continued to dwell alone with the dead body; nor how this old woman conceived a hatred to myself and one of my cousins, and in the dread hour of the dusk, as we were clambering on the garden-walls, opened a window in that house of mortality and cursed us in a shrill voice and with a marrowy choice of language. It was a pair of very colorless urchins that fled down the lane from this remarkable experience! But I recall with a more doubtful sentiment, compounded out of fear and exultation, the coil of equinoctial tempests; trumpeting squalls, scouring flaws of rain; the boats with their reefed lugsails scudding for the harbor mouth, where danger lay, for it was hard to make when the wind had any east in it; the wives clustered with blowing shawls at the pier-head, where (if fate was against them) they might see boat and husband and sons—their whole wealth and their whole family—engulfed under their eyes; and (what I saw but once) a troop of neighbors forcing such an unfortunate homeward, and she squalling and battling in their midst, a figure scarcely human, a tragic Maenad.

[4] These are things that I recall with interest; but what my memory dwells upon the most, I have been all this while withholding. It was a sport peculiar to the place, and indeed to a week or so of our two months' holiday there. Maybe it still flourishes in its native spot; for boys and their pastimes are swayed by periodic forces inscrutable to man; so that tops and marbles reappear in their due season, regular like the sun and moon; and the harmless art of knucklebones has seen the fall of the Roman empire and the rise of the United States. It may still flourish in its native spot, but nowhere else, I am persuaded; for I tried myself to introduce it on Tweedside, and was defeated lamentably; its charm being quite local, like a country wine that cannot be exported.

[5] The idle manner of it was this:—

[6] Toward the end of September, when school-time was drawing near and the nights were already black, we would begin to sally from our respective villas, each equipped with a tin bull's-eye lantern. The thing was so well known that it had worn a rut in the commerce of Great Britain; and the grocers, about the due time, began to garnish their windows with our particular brand of luminary. We wore them buckled to the waist upon a cricket belt, and over them, such was the rigor of the game, a buttoned top-coat. They smelled noisomely of blistered tin; they never burned aright, though they would always burn our fingers; their use was naught; the pleasure of them merely fanciful; and yet a boy with a bull's-eye under his top-coat asked for nothing more. The fishermen used lanterns about their boats, and

it was from them, I suppose, that we had got the hint; but theirs were not bull's-eyes, nor did we ever play at being fishermen. The police carried them at their belts, and we had plainly copied them in that; yet we did not pretend to be policemen. Burglars, indeed, we may have had some haunting thoughts of; and we had certainly an eye to past ages when lanterns were more common, and to certain story-books in which we had found them to figure very largely. But take it for all in all, the pleasure of the thing was substantive; and to be a boy with a bull's-eye under his top-coat was good enough for us.

[7]   When two of these asses met, there would be an anxious "Have you got your lantern?" and a gratified "Yes!" That was the shibboleth, and very needful too; for, as it was the rule to keep our glory contained, none could recognize a lantern-bearer, unless (like the polecat) by the smell. Four or five would sometimes climb into the belly of a ten-man lugger, with nothing but the thwarts above them—for the cabin was usually locked, or choose out some hollow of the links where the wind might whistle overhead. There the coats would be unbottoned and the bull's-eye discovered, and in the checkering glimmer, under the huge windy hall of the night, and cheered by a rich steam of toasting tinware, these fortunate young gentlemen would crouch together in the cold sand of the links or on the scaly bilges of the fishing-boat, and delight themselves with inappropriate talk. Woe is me that I may not give some specimens—some of their foresights of life, or deep inquiries into the rudiments of man and nature, these were so fiery and so innocent, they were so richly silly, so romantically young. But the talk, at any rate, was but a condiment; and these gatherings themselves only accidents in the career of the lantern-bearer. The essence of this bliss was to walk by yourself in the black night; the slide shut, the top-coat buttoned; not a ray escaping, whether to conduct your footsteps or to make your glory public: a mere pillar of darkness in the dark; and all the while, deep down in the privacy of your fool's heart, to know you had a bull's-eye at your belt, and to exult and sing over the knowledge.

II

[8]   It is said that a poet has died young in the breast of the most stolid. It may be contended, rather, that this (somewhat minor) bard in almost every case survives, and is the spice of life to his possessor. Justice is not done to the versatility and the unplumbed childishness of man's imagination. His life from without may seem but a rude mound of mud; there will be some golden chamber at the heart of it, in which he dwells delighted; and for as dark as his pathway seems to the observer, he will have some kind of bull's-eye at his belt.

[9] It would be hard to pick out a career more cheerless than that of Dancer, the miser, as he figures in the "Old Bailey Reports," a prey to the most sordid persecutions, the butt of his neighborhood, betrayed by his hired man, his house beleaguered by the impish schoolboy, and he himself grinding and fuming and impotently fleeing to the law against these pin-pricks. You marvel at first that any one should willingly prolong a life so destitute of charm and dignity; and then you call to memory that had he chosen, had he ceased to be a miser, he could have been freed at once from these trials, and might have built himself a castle and gone escorted by a squadron. For the love of more recondite joys, which we cannot estimate, which, it may be, we should envy, the man had willingly foregone both comfort and consideration. "His mind to him a kingdom was"; and sure enough, digging into that mind, which seems at first a dust-heap, we unearth some priceless jewels. For Dancer must have had the love of power and the disdain of using it, a noble character in itself; disdain of many pleasures, a chief part of what is commonly called wisdom; disdain of the inevitable end, that finest trait of mankind; scorn of men's opinions, another element of virtue; and at the back of all, a conscience just like yours and mine, whining like a cur, swindling like a thimble-rigger, but still pointing (there or thereabout) to some conventional standard. Here were a cabinet portrait to which Hawthorne perhaps had done justice; and yet not Hawthorne either, for he was mildly minded, and it lay not in him to create for us that throb of the miser's pulse, his fretful energy of gusto, his vast arms of ambition clutching in he knows not what: insatiable, insane, a god with a muck-rake. Thus, at least, looking in the bosom of the miser, consideration detects the poet in the full tide of life, with more, indeed, of the poetic fire than usually goes to epics; and tracing that mean man about his cold hearth, and to and fro in his discomfortable house, spies within him a blazing bonfire of delight. And so with others, who do not live by bread alone, but by some cherished and perhaps fantastic pleasure; who are meat salesmen to the external eye, and possibly to themselves are Shakespeares, Napoleons, or Beethovens; who have not one virtue to rub against another in the field of active life, and yet perhaps, in the life of contemplation, sit with the saints. We see them on the street, and we can count their buttons; but Heaven knows in what they pride themselves! Heaven knows where they have set their treasure!

[10] There is one fable that touches very near the quick of life: the fable of the monk who passed into the woods, heard a bird break into song, hearkened for a trill or two, and found himself on his return a stranger at his convent gates; for he had been absent fifty years,

and of all his comrades there survived but one to recognize him. It is not only in the woods that this enchanter carols, though perhaps he is native there. He sings in the most doleful places. The miser hears him and chuckles, and the days are moments. With no more apparatus than an ill-smelling lantern I have evoked him on the naked links. All life that is not merely mechanical is spun out of two strands: seeking for that bird and hearing him. And it is just this that makes life so hard to value, and the delight of each so incommunicable. And just a knowledge of this, and a remembrance of those fortunate hours in which the bird has sung to us, that fills us with such wonder when we turn the pages of the realist. There, to be sure, we find a picture of life in so far as it consists of mud and of old iron, cheap desires and cheap fears, that which we are ashamed to remember and that which we are careless whether we forget; but of the note of that time-devouring nightingale we hear no news.

[11] The case of these writers of romance is most obscure. They have been boys and youths; they have lingered outside the window of the beloved, who was then most probably writing to some one else; they have sat before a sheet of paper, and felt themselves mere continents of congested poetry, not one line of which would flow; they have walked alone in the woods, they have walked in cities under the countless lamps; they have been to sea, they have hated, they have feared, they have longed to knife a man and maybe done it; the wild taste of life has stung their palate. Or, if you deny them all the rest, one pleasure at least they have tasted to the full—their books are there to prove it—the keen pleasure of successful literary composition. And yet they fill the globe with volumes, whose cleverness inspires me with despairing admiration, and whose consistent falsity to all I care to call existence, with despairing wrath. If I had no better hope than to continue to revolve among the dreary and petty businesses, and to be moved by the paltry hopes and fears with which they surround and animate their heroes, I declare I would die now. But there has never an hour of mine gone quite so dully yet; if it were spent waiting at a railway junction, I would have some scattering thoughts, I could count some grains of memory, compared to which the whole of one of these romances seems but dross.

[12] These writers would retort (if I take them properly) that this was very true; that it was the same with themselves and other persons of (what they call) the artistic temperament; that in this we were exceptional, and should apparently be ashamed of ourselves; but that our works must deal exclusively with (what they call) the average man, who was a prodigious dull fellow, and quite dead to all but the paltriest considerations. I accept the issue. We can only know others

by ourselves. The artistic temperament (a plague on the expression!) does not make us different from our fellow-men, or it would make us incapable of writing novels; and the average man (a murrain on the word!) is just like you and me, or he would not be average. It was Whitman who stamped a kind of Birmingham sacredness upon the latter phrase; but Whitman knew very well, and showed very nobly, that the average man was full of joys and full of a poetry of his own. And this harping on life's dulness and man's meanness is a loud profession of incompetence; it is one of two things: the cry of the blind eye, *I cannot see,* or the complaint of the dumb tongue, *I cannot utter.* To draw a life without delights is to prove that I have not realized it. To picture a man without some sort of poetry—well, it goes near to prove my case, for it shows an author may have little enough. To see Dancer only as a dirty, old, small-minded, impotently fuming man, in a dirty house, besieged by Harrow boys, and probably beset by small attorneys, is to show myself as keen an observer as . . . the Harrow boys. But these young gentlemen (with a more becoming modesty) were content to pluck Dancer by the coat-tails; they did not suppose they had surprised his secret or could put him living in a book: and it is there my error would have lain. Or say that in the same romance—I continue to call these books romances, in the hope of giving pain—say that in the same romance which now begins really to take shape, I should leave to speak of Dancer, and follow instead the Harrow boys; and say that I came on some such business as that of my lantern-bearers on the links; and described the boys as very cold, spat upon by flurries of rain, and drearily surrounded, all of which they were; and their talk was silly and indecent, which it certainly was. I might upon these lines, and had I Zola's genius, turn out, in a page or so, a gem of literary art, render the lantern-light with the touches of a master, and lay on the indecency with the ungrudging hand of love; and when all was done, what a triumph would my picture be of shallowness and dulness! how it would have missed the point! how it would have belied the boys! To the ear of the stenographer, the talk is merely silly and indecent; but ask the boys themselves, and they are discussing (as it is highly proper they should) the possibilities of existence. To the eye of the observer they are wet and cold and drearily surrounded; but ask themselves, and they are in the heaven of a recondite pleasure, the ground of which is an ill-smelling lantern.

III

[13]   For, to repeat, the ground of a man's joy is often hard to hit. It may hinge at times upon a mere accessory, like the lantern, it may

reside, like Dancer's, in the mysterious inwards of psychology. It may consist with perpetual failure, and find exercise in the continued chase. It has so little bond with externals (such as the observer scribbles in his note-book) that it may even touch them not; and the man's true life, for which he consents to live, lie altogether in the field of fancy. The clergyman, in his spare hours, may be winning battles, the farmer sailing ships, the banker reaping triumph in the arts; all leading another life, plying another trade from that they choose; like the poet's housebuilder, who, after all is cased in stone,

"By his fireside, as impotent fancy prompts,
Rebuilds it to his liking."

In such a case the poetry runs underground. The observer (poor soul, with his documents!) is all abroad. For to look at the man is but to court deception. We shall see the trunk from which he draws his nourishment; but he himself is above and abroad in the green dome of foliage, hummed through by winds and nested in by nightingales. And the true realism were that of the poets, to climb up after him like a squirrel, and catch some glimpse of the heaven for which he lives. And the true realism, always and everywhere, is that of the poets: to find out where joy resides, and give it a voice far beyond singing.

[14]　For to miss the joy is to miss all. In the joy of the actors lies the sense of any action. That is the explanation, that the excuse. To one who has not the secret of the lanterns, the scene upon the links is meaningless. And hence the haunting and truly spectral unreality of realistic books. Hence, when we read the English realists, the incredulous wonder with which we observe the hero's constancy under the submerging tide of dulness, and how he bears up with his jibbing sweetheart, and endures the chatter of idiot girls, and stands by his whole unfeatured wilderness of an existence, instead of seeking relief in drink or foreign travel. Hence in the French, in that meat-market of middle-aged sensuality, the disgusted surprise with which we see the hero drift sidelong, and practically quite untempted, into every description of misconduct and dishonor. In each, we miss the personal poetry, the enchanted atmosphere, that rainbow work of fancy that clothes what is naked and seems to ennoble what is base; in each, life falls dead like dough, instead of soaring away like a balloon into the colors of the sunset; each is true, each inconceivable; for no man lives in the external truth, among salts and acids, but in the warm, phantasmagoric chamber of his brain, with the painted windows and the storied walls.

[15]　Of this falsity we have had a recent example from a man who

knows far better—Tolstoi's *Powers of Darkness*. Here is a piece full of force and truth, yet quite untrue. For before Mikita was led into so dire a situation he was tempted, and temptations are beautiful at least in part; and a work which dwells on the ugliness of crime and gives no hint of any loveliness in the temptation, sins against the modesty of life, and even when a Tolstoi writes it, sinks to melodrama. The peasants are not understood; they saw their life in fairer colors; even the deaf girl was clothed in poetry for Mikita, or he had never fallen. And so, once again, even an Old Bailey melodrama, without some brightness of poetry and lustre of existence, falls into the inconceivable and ranks with fairy tales.

IV

[16] In nobler books we are moved with something like the emotions of life; and this emotion is very variously provoked. We are so moved when Levine labors in the field, when Andre sinks beyond emotion, when Richard Feverel and Lucy Desborough meet beside the river, when Antony, "not cowardly, puts off his helmet," when Kent has infinite pity on the dying Lear, when, in Dostoieffsky's *Despised and Rejected,* the uncomplaining hero drains his cup of suffering and virtue. These are notes that please the great heart of man. Not only love, and the fields, and the bright face of danger, but sacrifice and death and unmerited suffering humbly supported, touch in us the vein of the poetic. We love to think of them, we long to try them, we are humbly hopeful that we may prove heroes also.

[17] We have heard, perhaps, too much of lesser matters. Here is the door, here is the open air. *Itur in antiquam silvam.**

COMMENT AND QUESTIONS

This reflective essay—rich (perhaps too rich) in concrete detail, in language, and in its picture of human life—requires careful reading. First you need to follow its general development. In paragraphs 1–3 Stevenson describes his boyhood experiences as he remembers them; the reasons for the fullness and variety of details become evident later. In paragraphs 4–7 he introduces the bull's-eye lantern, then tells what it is and how the boys feel about it. In Section II, paragraphs 8 and 9, he further clarifies the meaning or symbolism of the lantern and shows that the miser, Dancer, has his lantern too. In paragraph 10 he introduces another symbol, the bird's song, which you will need to interpret. In the same paragraph he begins his attack on writers of realistic fiction by saying that they portray only

* One goes into the ancient forest.

the mud and fears of life. In paragraphs 11 and 12 he continues to argue against what he considers the false picture of life that realists present. At the end of Section II he returns to his lantern figure to show what realists fail to include in their writings. In Section III he continues to discuss the mysterious inner life of man and the deceptive appearance of man's outer life. In Section IV he deals with the way life is presented in what he calls "noble books," and the spirit and the view of life that they contain.

Much of this essay may appear to be mere description, or mere argument, sometimes intemperately stated, against a type of literature which Stevenson, himself an avowed romanticist, did not like. A critical reader may question the amount of descriptive detail, and may disagree with Stevenson's opinions of the realistic novelists; but he will also see that Stevenson is dealing with things more significant than bull's-eye lanterns and literary differences.

I. State in a sentence what you take to be the central idea of the essay.

II. Explain just what use Stevenson has made of the lantern figure in order to make this idea clear. Is the figure a good one for his purposes?

III. Can you see any reason why Stevenson wrote three long paragraphs before he introduced the boys and the lanterns? What details in these paragraphs show not the pleasantness but the unpleasantness and even the sordidness of life? Why did Stevenson include these details?

IV. Comment on Stevenson's interpretation of Dancer's character (paragraph 9).

V. How does Stevenson interpret the fable of the monk and the bird song, and how is the fable related to the main idea of the essay? Do you think that the essay would have been equally clear and effective if Stevenson had omitted the fable and had been content to use only the lantern figure?

VI. From paragraph 10 to the end of the essay Stevenson is stating his own view of life and is attacking the view of "realistic" novelists. Do you find places where Stevenson's reasoning seems questionable? In what passages do you find the most heavily charged language? (Students who have read such writers as Zola and Flaubert will be in a position to judge for themselves Stevenson's indictment of what he calls "realism.")

VII. Consider Stevenson's choice of words, the movement and rhythm of his sentences, his use of details and of figures of speech, especially in paragraphs 3, 6, 10, 13, and 14. Do you see why he is regarded as one of the distinguished prose writers of the nineteenth century?

VIII. Study the description of a place in paragraph 1. What techniques of description are used?

IX. When you think of the essay as a whole, what is your judgment of it? Why?

X. If your instructor approves, write a paper on one of the following subjects:

An Evaluation of Stevenson's "The Lantern-Bearers." (See Evaluating What One Reads, pages 679–683, for suggestions.)

Stevenson's View of Life as It Is Expressed in "The Lantern-Bearers," "Pulvis et Umbra," "An Apology for Idlers," and "Aes Triplex."

XI. If your instructor approves, write a reflective personal essay based on one or more of your own childhood experiences.

C. THE SIMPLE NARRATIVE

The simple narrative is a short, uncomplicated story in which events are set down in natural time-order. Probably the best way to clarify the scope and purpose of this type of prose is to compare it with other closely related literary forms. It differs from the essay, even the so-called narrative essay, in that the latter emphasizes an idea and tells its story in order to demonstrate that idea; the simple narrative invites the reader to share the happenings—usually human experiences—which it presents. For example, a composition entitled "Moving Day" might be an essay if all the recorded events of the day were focused on a central idea that possessions are more trouble than they are worth; it would be a simple narrative if the writer presented in vivid detail the experience of moving, for the sake of the experience itself.

The simple narrative differs from the short story chiefly in its simplicity of structure. The complex short story often departs from natural time-order and begins in the middle or near the end for purposes of unity and concentration; it maintains suspense about how the plot will develop; it builds to a climax; and it frequently leaves the reader with a mind full of suggestions about what is going to happen after the story itself has ended. The simple narrative, in addition to following a simple chronological order, has little or no suspense, does not necessarily mount to a climax, and ends simply and completely with the final occurrence in a chain of events—with the end of a day, for example, or the close of school, or the parting with a friend.

One might conclude, from this comparison, that the simple narrative is a colorless and unexciting literary form. This is not true. It is often the best method of presenting genuine experience; of writing about real people and real events, just as they were, just as they happened, without the distortion which too often occurs when an inexperienced writer is called upon to produce an essay or a short story. Simple narrative is the natural form for writing about subjects like these: First Date; I Get My Driver's License; I Cook My First Meal; I Get (or Lose) My First Job; An Embarrassing Encounter; The New Neighbors; The New Teacher; My Brother and I.

As the topics above suggest, simple narrative often uses the first-person point of view. This is not a requirement, and there are impersonal simple narratives; but the writer is frequently recording his own experience, or, as an interested observer, is recording a sequence of events or actions about which he has close knowledge. The first-person point of view, which is direct and which gives a sense of immediate contact between writer and material and between writer and reader, usually fits the content of this kind of prose. Subtle angles of narration like the innocent-eye point of view, or the third-person limited omniscient point of view which sees events through the mind of one character, are likely to be overintricate for the simple narrative.

An interesting technical study for both the writer and the critical reader of any kind of narrative is the balance between *summary* and *presentation* of material. *Summary* is general statement which gives the net result of action. *Presentation* is the full and dramatic development of scenes of action. This is summary:

> Mary tried in vain to find out from Jim how much money they owed.

This is presentation:

> Mary leaned across the table. "Listen, Jim. I want you to talk to me."
> "What about?" He kept on eating. "Any more coffee?"
> "Yes. I'll get it. Listen, Jim. I want to know about the bills from Holden's, and about Davis coming about the mortgage. . . ."
> "That's my business. Haven't I always paid my bills? What have you got to complain about? You got those new Venetian blinds, didn't you? Where's the coffee?"

In general, presentation is more effective than summary because it takes the reader into the full scene; but full presentation of trivial or repetitious scenes can become boring to the reader. The narrative writer must decide what is important enough to be presented and what can profitably be summarized or partly summarized. The balance he works out will determine the movement or *pace* of his story.

Since the simple narrative is usually a running account of something that happens over a period of time (the events of a day, or several days, or even several years), the writer necessarily summarizes a good deal. He plans his narrative, though, not as a chain of equal parts, but as a chain which links key scenes. When he comes to an action which is important, or particularly entertaining or revealing, he expands his summary into a partial or fully developed scene. This balance of summary and presentation is one of the techniques illustrated by the two narratives in the following pages.

FATHER OPENS MY MAIL *

CLARENCE DAY

The following account of a father-son relationship has been classified as an essay and as autobiography. It is both. It is also a simple narrative in that it relates a sequence of events in time-order. Clarence Day (1874–1935) is best known for his humorous autobiographical works, *God and My Father*, *Life With Father*, *Life With Mother*, and *Father and I*. "Father Opens My Mail" is a chapter of *Life With Father*, which was published in 1935 and dramatized in 1939.

―――――――――

There was a time in my boyhood when I felt that Father had handicapped me severely in life by naming me after him, "Clarence." All literature, so far as I could see, was thronged with objectionable persons named Clarence. Percy was bad enough, but there had been some good fighters named Percy. The only Clarence in history was a duke who did something dirty at Tewkesbury, and who died a ridiculous death afterwards in a barrel of malmsey.

As for the Clarences in the fiction I read, they were horrible. In one story, for instance, there were two brothers, Clarence and Frank. Clarence was a "vain, disagreeable little fellow" who was proud of his curly hair and fine clothes, while Frank was a "rollicking boy who was ready to play games with anybody." Clarence didn't like to play games, of course. He just minced around looking on.

* Reprinted from *Life with Father* by Clarence Day by permission of Alfred A. Knopf, Inc. Copyright, 1934, 1935, by Clarence Day.

One day when the mother of these boys had gone out, this story went on, Clarence "tempted" Frank to disobey her and fly their kite on the roof. Frank didn't want to, but Clarence kept taunting him and daring him until Frank was stung into doing it. After the two boys went up to the roof, Frank got good and dirty, running up and down and stumbling over scuttles, while Clarence sat there, giving him orders, and kept his natty clothes tidy. To my horror, he even spread out his handkerchief on the trapdoor to sit on. And to crown it all, this sneak told on Frank as soon as their mother came in.

This wasn't an exceptionally mean Clarence, either. He was just run-of-the-mill. Some were worse.

So far as I could ever learn, however, Father had never heard of these stories, and had never dreamed of there being anything objectionable in his name. Quite the contrary. And yet as a boy he had lived a good rough-and-tumble boy's life. He had played and fought on the city streets, and kept a dog in Grandpa's stable, and stolen rides to Greenpoint Ferry on the high, lurching bus. In the summer he had gone to West Springfield and had run down Shad Lane through the trees to the house where Grandpa was born, and had gone barefoot and driven the cows home just as though he had been named Tom or Bill.

He had the same character as a boy, I suppose, that he had as a man, and he was too independent to care if people thought his name fancy. He paid no attention to the prejudices of others, except to disapprove of them. He had plenty of prejudices himself, of course, but they were his own. He was humorous and confident and level-headed, and I imagine that if any boy had tried to make fun of him for being named Clarence, Father would simply have laughed and told him he didn't know what he was talking about.

I asked Mother how this name had ever happened to spring up in our family. She explained that my great-great-grandfather was Benjamin Day, and my great-grandfather was Henry, and consequently my grandfather had been named Benjamin Henry. He in turn had named his eldest son Henry and his second son Benjamin. The result was that when Father was born there was no family name left. The privilege of choosing a name for Father had thereupon been given to Grandma, and unluckily for the Day family she had been reading a novel, the hero of which was named Clarence.

I knew that Grandma, though very like Grandpa in some respects, had a dreamy side which he hadn't, a side that she usually kept to herself, in her serene, quiet way. Her romantic choice of this name probably made Grandpa smile, but he was a detached sort of man who didn't take small matters seriously, and who drew a good deal of private amusement from the happenings of everyday life. Besides, he was partly to blame in this case, because that novel was one he had published himself in his magazine.

I asked Mother, when she had finished, why I had been named Clarence too.

It hadn't been her choice, Mother said. She had suggested all sorts of names to Father, but there seemed to be something wrong with each one. When she had at last spoken of naming me after him, however, he had said at once that that was the best suggestion yet—he said it sounded just right.

Father and I would have had plenty of friction in any case. This identity of names made things worse. Every time that I had been more of a fool than he liked, Father would try to impress on me my responsibilities as his eldest son, and above all as the son to whom he had given his name, as he put it. A great deal was expected, it seemed to me, of a boy who was named after his father. I used to envy my brothers, who didn't have anything expected of them on this score at all.

I envied them still more after I was old enough to begin getting letters. I then discovered that when Father "gave" me his name he had also, not unnaturally, I had to admit, retained it himself, and when anything came for Clarence S. Day he opened it, though it was sometimes for me.

He also opened everything that came addressed to Clarence S. Day, Jr. He didn't do this intentionally, but unless the "Jr." was clearly written, it looked like "Esq.," and anyhow Father was too accustomed to open all Clarence Day letters to remember about looking carefully every time for a "Jr." So far as mail and express went, I had no name at all of my own.

For the most part nobody wrote to me when I was a small boy except firms whose advertisements I had read in the *Youth's Companion* and to whom I had written requesting them to send me their circulars. These circulars described remarkable bargains in magicians' card outfits, stamps and coins, pocket knives, trick spiders, and imitation fried eggs, and they seemed interesting and valuable to me when I got them. The trouble was that Father usually got them and at once tore them up. I then had to write for such circulars again, and if Father got the second one too, he would sometimes explode with annoyance. He became particularly indignant one year, I remember, when he was repeatedly urged to take advantage of a special bargain sale of false whiskers. He said he couldn't understand why these offerings kept pouring in. I knew why, in this case, but at other times I was often surprised myself at the number he got, not realizing that as a result of my postcard requests my or our name had been automatically put on several large general mailing lists.

During this period I got more of my mail out of Father's waste-basket than I did from the postman.

At the age of twelve or thirteen, I stopped writing for these child-ish things and turned to a new field. Father and I, whichever of us got at the mail first, began then to receive not merely circulars but personal letters beginning:

DEAR FRIEND DAY:

In reply to your valued request for one of our Mammoth Agents' Outfits, kindly forward postoffice order for $1.49 to cover cost of postage and pack-ing, and we will put you in a position to earn a large income in your spare time with absolutely no labor on your part, by taking subscriptions for *The Secret Handbook of Mesmerism,* and our *Tales of Blood* series.

And one spring, I remember, as the result of what I had intended to be a secret application on my part, Father was assigned "the exclusive rights for Staten Island and Hoboken of selling the Gem Home Popper for Pop Corn. Housewives buy it at sight."

After Father had stormily endured these afflictions for a while, he and I began to get letters from girls. Fortunately for our feelings, these were rare, but they were ordeals for both of us. Father had forgotten, if he ever knew, how silly young girls sound, and I got my first lesson in how unsystematic they were. No matter how private and playful they meant their letters to be, they forgot to put "Jr." on the envelope every once in so often. When Father opened these letters, he read them all the way through, sometimes twice, muttering to himself over and over: "This is very peculiar. I don't understand this at all. Here's a letter to me from some person I never heard of. I can't see what it's all about." By the time it had occurred to him that possibly the letter might be for me, I was red and embarrassed and even angrier at the girl than at Father. And on days when he had read some of the phrases aloud to the family, it nearly killed me to claim it.

Lots of fellows whom I knew had been named after their fathers without having such troubles. But although Father couldn't have been kinder-hearted or had any better intentions, when he saw his name on a package or envelope it never dawned on him that it might not be for him. He was too active in his habits to wait until I had a chance to get at it. And as he was also single-minded and prompt to attend to unfinished business, he opened everything automatically and then did his best to dispose of it.

This went on even after I grew up until I had a home of my own. Father was always perfectly decent about it, but he never changed. When he saw I felt sulky, he was genuinely sorry and said so, but he couldn't see why all this should annoy me, and he was surprised and amused that it did. I used to get angry once in a while when something came for me which I particularly hadn't wished him to see and which I would find lying, opened, on the hall table marked "For Jr.?" when I came in; but nobody could stay angry with Father—he was too utterly guiltless of having meant to offend.

He often got angry himself, but it was mostly at things, not at persons, and he didn't mind a bit (as a rule) when persons got angry at him. He even declared, when I got back from college, feeling dignified, and told him I wished he'd be more careful, that he suffered from these mistakes more than I did. It wasn't *his* fault, he pointed out, if my stupid correspondents couldn't remember my name, and it wasn't any pleasure to him to be upset at his breakfast by finding that a damned lunatic company in Battle Creek had sent him a box of dry bread crumbs, with a letter asserting that this rubbish would be good for his stomach. "I admit I threw it into the fireplace, Clarence, but what else could I do? If you valued this preposterous concoction, my dear boy, I'm sorry. I'll buy another box for you today, if you'll tell me where I can get it. Don't feel badly! I'll buy you a barrel. Only I hope you won't eat it."

In the days when Mrs. Pankhurst and her friends were chaining themselves to lamp posts in London, in their campaign for the vote, a letter came from Frances Hand trustfully asking "Dear Clarence" to do something to help Woman Suffrage—speak at a meeting, I think. Father got red in the face. "Speak at one of their meetings!" he roared at Mother. "I'd like nothing better! You can tell Mrs. Hand that it would give me great pleasure to inform all those crackpots in petticoats exactly what I think of their antics."

"Now, Clare," Mother said, "you mustn't talk that way. I like that nice Mrs. Hand, and anyhow this letter must be for Clarence."

One time I asked Father for his opinion of a low-priced stock I'd been watching. His opinion was that it was not worth a damn. I thought this over, but still wished to buy it, so I placed a scale order with another firm instead of with Father's office, and said nothing about it. At the end of the month this other firm sent me a statement setting forth each of my little transactions in full, and of course they forgot to put the "Jr." at the end of my name. When Father opened the envelope, he thought at first in his excitement that this firm had actually opened an account for him without being asked. I found him telling Mother that he'd like to wring their damned necks.

"That must be for me, Father," I said, when I took in what had happened.

We looked at each other.

"You bought this stuff?" he said incredulously. "After all I said about it?"

"Yes, Father."

He handed over the statement and walked out of the room.

Both he and I felt offended and angry. We stayed so for several days, too, but then we made up.

Once in a while when I got a letter that I had no time to answer I used to address an envelope to the sender and then put anything in it that happened to be lying around on my desk—a circular about books, a piece of newspaper, an old laundry bill—anything at all, just to be amiable, and yet at the same time to save myself the trouble of writing. I happened to tell several people about this private habit of mine at a dinner one night—a dinner at which Alice Duer Miller and one or two other writers were present. A little later she wrote me a criticism of Henry James and ended by saying that I needn't send her any of my old laundry bills because she wouldn't stand it. And she forgot to put on the "Jr."

"In the name of God," Father said bleakly, "this is the worst yet. Here's a woman who says I'd better not read *The Golden Bowl,* which I have no intention whatever of doing, and she also warns me for some unknown reason not to send her my laundry bills."

The good part of all these experiences, as I realize now, was that in the end they drew Father and me closer together. My brothers had only chance battles with him. I had war. Neither he nor I relished its clashes, but they made us surprisingly intimate.

COMMENT AND QUESTIONS

I. "Father Opens My Mail" has at first a rambling organization, partly because it is one chapter of a book on the author's experiences with his father, and partly because an informal, conversational style is part of its tone. Does the discussion of the name "Clarence" and the author's feeling about it have any direct bearing on the narrative of Father's opening Clarence, Jr.'s mail? What is the purpose of this introductory discussion?

II. Into what main stages or periods does the struggle between Clarence Day and his father fall?

III. Point out in each stage of experience the use of *summary* and of *presentation* of material. What reasons can you see for Clarence

Day's use of each method? Could any of the presented material have been summarized without loss?

IV. What characteristics of Father are revealed in this selection? What characteristics of Clarence Day, Jr.? Does it seem natural—or at least believable—that they should have warred over the mail?

V. Select two or three parts of this narrative which seem to you particularly good, and analyze those parts. Are they good because of the basic material, or because of skill in expression or presentation?

VI. Why is this selection classified as a simple narrative (or essay or autobiography) rather than as a short story?

I GET A COLT TO BREAK IN *

LINCOLN STEFFENS

The following narrative presents a series of episodes in a single phase (probably a year) of a boy's life. Lincoln Steffens (1866–1936) was a prominent American journalist and editor, best known in the early twentieth century for his exposés of corruption in business and government. "I Get a Colt to Break In" is one of the early chapters of his well-written and interesting *Autobiography,* published in 1931.

———

Colonel Carter gave me a colt. I had my pony, and my father meanwhile had bought a pair of black carriage horses and a cow, all of which I had to attend to when we had no "man." And servants were hard to get and to keep in those days; the women married, and the men soon quit service to seize opportunities always opening. My hands were pretty full, and so was the stable. But Colonel Carter seemed to think that he had promised me a horse. He had not; I would have known it if he had. No matter. He thought he had, and maybe he did promise himself to give me one. That was enough. The kind of man that led immigrant trains across the continent and delivered them safe, sound, and together where he promised would keep his word. One day he drove over from Stockton, leading a two-year-old which he brought to our front door and turned over to me as mine. Such a horse!

* From *The Antobiography of Lincoln Steffens,* copyright, 1931, by Harcourt, Brace and Company, Inc.

She was a cream-colored mare with a black forelock, mane, and tail and a black stripe along the middle of her back. Tall, slender, high-spirited, I thought then—I think now—that she was the most beautiful of horses. Colonel Carter had bred and reared her with me and my uses in mind. She was a careful cross of a mustang mare and thoroughbred stallion, with the stamina of the wild horse and the speed and grace of the racer. And she had a sense of fun. As Colonel Carter got down out of his buggy and went up to her, she snorted, reared, flung her head high in the air, and, coming down beside him, tucked her nose affectionately under his arm.

"I have handled her a lot," he said. "She is as kind as a kitten, but she is as sensitive as a lady. You can spoil her by one mistake. If you ever lose your temper, if you ever abuse her, she will be ruined forever. And she is unbroken. I might have had her broken to ride for you, but I didn't want to. I want you to do it. I have taught her to lead, as you can see; had to, to get her over here. But here she is, an unbroken colt; yours. You take and you break her. You're only a boy, but if you break this colt right, you'll be a man—a young man, but a man. And I'll tell you how."

Now, out West, as everyone knows, they break in a horse by riding out to him in his wild state, lassoing, throwing, and saddling him; then they let him up, frightened and shocked, with a yelling broncho-buster astride of him. The wild beast bucks, the cowboy drives his spurs into him, and off they go, jumping, kicking, rearing, falling, till by the weight of the man, the lash, and the rowels, the horse is broken—in body and spirit. This was not the way I was to break my colt.

"You must break her to ride without her ever knowing it," Colonel Carter said. "You feed and you clean her—you; not the stable man. You lead her out to water and to walk. You put her on a long rope and let her play, calling her to you and gently pulling on the rope. Then you turn her loose in the grass lot there and, when she has romped till tired, call her. If she won't come, leave her. When she wants water or food, she will run to your call, and you will pet and feed and care for her." He went on for half an hour, advising me in great detail how to proceed. I wanted to begin right away. He laughed. He let me lead her around to the stable, water her, and put her in the stable and feed her.

There I saw my pony. My father, sisters, and Colonel Carter saw me stop and look at my pony.

"What'll you do with him?" one of my sisters asked. I was bewildered for a moment. What should I do with the little red horse? I decided at once.

"You can have him," I said to my sisters.

"No," said Colonel Carter, "not yet. You can give your sisters the pony by and by, but you'll need him till you have taught the colt to carry you and a saddle—months; and you must not hurry. You must learn patience, and you will if you give the colt time to learn it, too. Patience and control. You can't control a young horse unless you can control yourself. Can you shoot?" he asked suddenly.

I couldn't. I had a gun and I had used it some, but it was a rifle, and I could not bring down with it such game as there was around Sacramento—birds and hares. Colonel Carter looked at my father, and I caught the look. So did my father. I soon had a shotgun. But at the time Colonel Carter turned to me and said:

"Can't shoot straight, eh? Do you know what that means? That means that you can't control a gun, and that means you can't control yourself, your eye, your hands, your nerves. You are wriggling now. I tell you that a good shot is always a good man. He may be a 'bad man' too, but he is quiet, strong, steady in speech, gait, and mind. No matter, though. If you break in this colt right, if you teach her her paces, she will teach you to shoot and be quiet."

He went off downtown with my father, and I started away with my colt. I fed, I led, I cleaned her, gently, as if she were made of glass; she was playful and willing, a delight. When Colonel Carter came home with my father for supper, he questioned me.

"You should not have worked her today," he said. "She has come all the way from Stockton and must be tired. Yes, yes, she would not show her fatigue; too fine for that, and too young to be wise. You have got to think for her, consider her as you would your sisters."

Sisters! I thought; I had never considered my sisters. I did not say that, but Colonel Carter laughed and nodded to my sisters. It was just as if he had read my thought. But he went on to draw on my imagination a centaur; the colt as a horse's body—me, a boy, as the head and brains of one united creature. I liked that. I would be that. I and the colt: a centaur.

After Colonel Carter was gone home I went to work on my new horse. The old one, the pony, I used only for business: to go to fires, to see my friends, run errands, and go hunting with my new shotgun. But the game that had all my attention was the breaking in of the colt, the beautiful cream-colored mare, who soon knew me—and my pockets. I carried sugar to reward her when she did right, and she discovered where I carried it; so did the pony, and when I was busy they would push their noses into my pockets, both of which were torn down a good deal of the time. But the colt learned. I taught her to run around a circle, turn and go the other way at a signal. My sisters helped me. I held the long rope and the whip (for signaling), while one of the girls led the colt; it was hard work for them, but they took it in turns. One would lead the colt round and round till I snapped the whip; then she would turn, turning the colt, till the colt did it all by herself. And she was very quick. She shook hands with each of her four feet. She let us run under her, back and forth. She was slow only to carry me. Following Colonel Carter's instructions, I began by laying my arm or a surcingle over her back. If she trembled, I drew it slowly off. When she could abide it, I tried buckling it, tighter and tighter. I laid over her, too, a blanket, folded at first, then open, and, at last, I slipped up on her myself, sat there a second, and as she trembled, slid off. My sisters held her for me, and when I could get up and sit there a moment or two, I tied her at a block, and we, my sisters and I, made a procession of mounting and dismounting. She soon got used to this, and would let us slide off over her rump, but it was a long, long time before she would carry me.

That we practiced by leading her along a high curb where I could get on as she walked, ride a few steps, and then, as she felt me and crouched, slip off. She never did learn to carry a girl on her back; my sisters had to lead her while I rode. This was not purposeful. I don't know just how it happened, but I do remember the first time I rode on my colt all the way round the lot and how, when I put one of the girls up, she refused to repeat. She shuddered, shook and frightened them off.

While we were breaking in the colt a circus came to town. The ring was across the street from our house. Wonderful! I lived in that circus for a week. I saw the show but once, but I marked the horse-trainers, and in the mornings when they were not too busy I told them about my colt, showed her to them, and asked them how to train her to do circus tricks. With their hints I taught the colt to stand up on her hind legs, kneel, lie down, and balance on a small box. This last was easier than it looked. I put her first on a low big box and taught her to turn on it; then got a little smaller box upon which she repeated what she did on the big one. By and by we had her so that she would step up on a high box so small that her four feet were almost touching, and there also she would turn.

The circus man gave me one hint that was worth all the other tricks put together. "You catch her doing something of herself that looks good," he said, "and then you keep her at it." It was thus that I taught her to bow to people. The first day I rode her out on to the streets was a proud one for me and for the colt, too, apparently. She did not walk, she danced; perhaps she was excited, nervous; anyhow

I liked the way she threw up her head, champed at the bit, and went, dancing, prancing down the street. Everybody stopped to watch us, and so, when she began to sober down, I picked her up again with heel and rein, saying, "Here's people, Lady," and she would show off to my delight. By constant repetition I had her so trained that she would single-foot, head down, along a country road till we came to a house or a group of people. Then I'd say, "People, Lady," and up would go her head, and her feet would dance.

But the trick that set the town talking was her bowing to anyone I spoke to. "Lennie Steffens' horse bows to you," people said, and she did. I never told how it was done; by accident. Dogs used to run out at us and the colt enjoyed it; she kicked at them sometimes with both hind hoofs. I joined her in the game, and being able to look behind more conveniently than she could, I watched the dogs until they were in range, then gave the colt a signal to kick. "Kick, gal," I'd say, and tap her ribs with my heel. We used to get dogs together that way; the colt would kick them over and over and leave them yelping in the road. Well, one day when I met a girl I knew I lifted my hat, probably muttered a "Good day," and I must have touched the colt with my heel. Anyway, she dropped her head and kicked—not much; there was no dog near, so she had responded to my unexpected signal by what looked like a bow. I caught the idea and kept her at it. Whenever I wanted to bow to a girl or anyone else, instead of saying "Good day," I muttered "Kick, gal," spurred her lightly, and—the whole centaur bowed and was covered with glory and conceit.

Yes, conceit. I was full of it, and the colt was quite as bad. One day my chum Hjalmar came into town on his Black Bess, blanketed. She had had a great fistula cut out of her shoulder and had to be kept warm. I expected to see her weak and dull, but no, the good old mare was champing and dancing, like my colt.

"What is it makes her so?" I asked, and Hjalmar said he didn't know, but he thought she was proud of the blanket. A great idea. I had a gaudy horse blanket. I put it on the colt, and I could hardly hold her. We rode down the main street together, both horses, and both boys, so full of vanity that everybody stopped to smile. We thought they admired, and maybe they did. But some boys on the street gave us another angle. They, too, stopped and looked, and as we passed, one of them said, "Think you're hell, don't you?"

Spoilsport!

We did, as a matter of fact; we thought we were hell. The recognition of it dashed us for a moment; not for long, and the horses paid no heed. We pranced, the black and the yellow, all the way down J Street, up K Street, and agreed that we'd do it again, often. Only I said, we wouldn't use blankets. If the horses were proud of a blanket, they'd be proud of anything unusually conspicuous. We tried a flower next time. I fixed a big rose on my colt's bridle just under her ear and it was great—she pranced downtown with her head turned, literally, to show off her flower. We had to change the decorations from time to time, put on a ribbon, or a bell, or a feather, but, really, it was not necessary for my horse. Old Black Bess needed an incentive to act up, but all I had to do to my horse was to pick up the reins, touch her with my heel, and say, "People"; she would dance from one side of the street to the other, asking to be admired. As she was. As we were.

I would ride down to my father's store, jump off my prancing colt in the middle of the street, and run up into the shop. The colt, free, would stop short, turn, and follow me right up on the sidewalk, unless I bade her wait. If anyone approached her while I was gone, she would snort, rear, and strike. No stranger could get near her. She became a frightened, frightening animal, and yet when I came into sight, she would run up to me, put her head down, and as I straddled her neck, she would throw up her head and pitch me into my seat, facing backwards, of course. I whirled around right, and off we'd go, the vainest boy and the proudest horse in the State.

"Hey, give me a ride, will you?" some boy would ask.

"Sure," I'd say, and jump down and watch the boy try to catch and mount my colt. He couldn't. Once a cowboy wanted to try her, and he caught her; he dodged her forefeet, grabbed the reins, and in one spring was on her back. I never did that again. My colt reared, then bucked, and, as the cowboy kept his seat, she shuddered, sank to the ground, and rolled over. He slipped aside and would have risen with her, but I was alarmed and begged him not to. She got up at my touch and followed me so close that she stepped on my heel and hurt me. The cowboy saw the point.

"If I were you, kid," he said, "I'd never let anybody mount that colt. She's too good."

That, I think, was the only mistake I made in the rearing of Colonel Carter's gift-horse. My father differed from me. He discovered another error or sin, and thrashed me for it. My practice was to work hard on a trick, privately, and when it was perfect, let him see it. I would have the horse out in our vacant lot doing it as he came home to supper. One evening, as he approached the house, I was standing, whip in hand, while the colt, quite free, was stepping carefully over the bodies of a lot of girls, all my sisters and all their girl friends. (Grace Gallatin, later Mrs. Thompson-Seton, was among them.) My father did not express the admiration I expected; he was frightened and furious. "Stop that," he called, and he came running around into the lot, took the whip, and lashed me with it. I tried to explain; the girls tried to help me explain.

I had seen in the circus a horse that stepped thus over a row of prostrate clowns. It looked dangerous for the clowns, but the trainer had told me how to do it. You begin with logs, laid out a certain distance apart; the horse walks over them under your lead, and whenever he touches one you rebuke him. By and by he will learn to step with such care that he never trips. Then you substitute clowns. I had no clowns, but I did get logs, and with the girls helping, we taught the colt to step over the obstacles even at a trot. Walking, she touched nothing. All ready thus with the logs, I had my sisters lie down in the grass, and again and again the colt stepped over them. None was ever touched. My father would not listen to any of this; he just walloped me, and when he was tired or satisfied and I was in tears, I blubbered a short excuse: "They were only girls." And he whipped me some more.

My father was not given to whipping; he did it very seldom, but he did it hard when he did it at all. My mother was just the opposite. She did not whip me, but she often smacked me, and she had a most annoying habit of thumping me on the head with her thimbled finger. This I resented more than my father's thoroughgoing thrashings, and I can tell why now. I would be playing Napoleon and as I was reviewing my Old Guard, she would crack my skull with that thimble. No doubt I was in the way; it took a lot of furniture and sisters to represent properly a victorious army; and you might think as my mother did that a thimble is a small weapon. But imagine Napoleon at the height of his power, the ruler of the world on parade, getting a sharp rap on his crown from a woman's thimble. No. My father's way was more appropriate. It was hard. "I'll attend to you in the morning," he would say, and I lay awake wondering which of my crimes he had discovered. I know what it is to be sentenced to be shot at sunrise. And it hurt, in the morning, when he was not angry but very fresh and strong. But you see, he walloped me in my own person; he never humiliated Napoleon or my knighthood, as my mother did. And I learned something from his discipline, something useful.

I learned what tyranny is and the pain of being misunderstood and wronged, or, if you please, understood and set right; they are pretty much the same. He and most parents and teachers do not break in their boys as carefully as I broke in my colt. They haven't the time that I had, and they have not some other incentives I had. I saw this

that day when I rubbed my sore legs. He had to explain to my indignant mother what had happened. When he had told it his way, I
gave my version: how long and cautiously I had been teaching my
horse to walk over logs and girls. And having shown how sure I was
of myself and the colt, while my mother was boring into his silence
with one of her reproachful looks, I said something that hit my father
hard.

"I taught the colt that trick, I have taught her all that you see
she knows, without whipping her. I have never struck her; not once.
Colonel Carter said I mustn't, and I haven't."

And my mother, backing me up, gave him a rap: "There," she
said, "I told you so." He walked off, looking like a thimble-rapped
Napoleon.

COMMENT AND QUESTIONS

I. This selection may be called a narrative essay as well as a
simple narrative. What central idea emerges from the story of
Steffens and his colt?

II. In what ways does Steffens' experience with the colt widen his
perception?

III. What is the reason for presenting so fully Colonel Carter's
advice about handling the colt?

IV. How would you characterize Steffens' attitude toward himself
in the narrative?

V. How does he make clear, before the closing paragraphs, that
he has never whipped the colt?

VI. What is the meaning of "rap" in the last paragraph?

VII. Lincoln Steffens writes very well. The paragraph in which
Colonel Carter draws in his imagination the centaur (page 419) is
one example of effective expression. Analyze the structure and movement of sentences to determine what makes this passage effective.
Point out other examples of particularly good writing in the selection.

D. THE SHORT STORY

The modern short story has many forms. *Action story, psychological story, plotted story, unplotted story, episodic story, commercial story, artistic story* are a few of the names used—not to set up a
complete classification of stories; that is impossible—but to describe
certain common types. A brief examination of these descriptive

names and what they stand for will demonstrate concretely the multiformity in short stories, and provide some standards by which to evaluate them.

The *action story* is the story in which the plot, the "what-happens," is developed by external, visible, physical action. Detective and adventure stories, westerns, and science fiction are examples of action stories. Characters in such stories think and feel as well as act, of course, but the major interest of the story is not in how they feel or why they act, but in what they do.

In contrast, the plot of the *psychological story* is developed largely or wholly by the inward, nonvisible working of the mind. The psychological story reveals the changes of feeling, the motivations, the mental states, the internal crises, and the decisions of its characters. An example of the psychological story is Checkhov's "The Lottery Ticket," in which a husband and wife read in a newspaper the first part of a winning lottery number, and believe that they very possibly hold the ticket which will bring them wealth. Enjoying anticipation, they refrain from looking at the rest of the number, and sit dreaming about what they will do with the money. The husband imagines the estate he will buy; experiences his life there; thinks of going abroad; thinks with displeasure that his wife would go with him and ruin his trip with her worries and economies; sees suddenly that she is old while he is still young and attractive and might easily marry again; realizes that the ticket is hers, not his; decides that she will begrudge him every penny of the money; and looks at his wife with the hatred he has begun to feel. She returns his look; her thoughts have followed his. When they find that they do not hold the winning ticket, the flare of mutual hatred dies; but they are left restless and dissatisfied with the life which contented them before. The entire action of the story takes no longer than ten minutes, and nearly all of it occurs in the characters' minds.

Although the psychological story as a type is not new, it has been notably developed in the last thirty years, with aid and impetus from the findings of modern psychology. The stream-of-consciousness story is one of its forms. Many short stories effectively combine the techniques of action and psychological fiction: the thoroughly explored inward action is influenced by and expressed in overt physical action.

The *plotted story* is what most people have in mind when they think of the short story. It is a narrative which has a more or less traditional pattern (to be discussed later in this section) of a clearly defined conflict, steadily rising action, definite climax, and dénouement or unraveling of the complications. The term *plotted story* has come to have an unfavorable connotation for some people, because it has been associated with contrived popular stories which have a great deal of plot in the sense of fast external action, but little substance, logic, and reality. This unfavorable association tends to minimize the genuine importance of plot in any short story. Plot is the planned structure or organization of the external or inward action. It does not in itself make a good story, as one can see by reading a synopsis which strips a story to plot alone. It is, though, an essential ingredient of fiction. Since any piece of writing properly called a short story has organized action of some kind, *highly plotted* and *lightly plotted* are more accurate descriptive labels than *plotted* and *unplotted.*

The inexact term *unplotted story* refers to the story in which the structure is so loose or subtle that it is not immediately apparent. The unplotted story may seem little more than a character sketch, a descriptive piece, or a presentation of mood, and it is likely to leave a reader who is accustomed to highly plotted stories with a sense of incompletion and puzzlement; he feels that nothing has happened. Further consideration of such a story may show him that the nothingness is a carefully planned effect; the author's purpose may be to create frustration or to present a situation which has no solution. Or the reader may see, when he reads the story again, that in his expectation of a dramatic climax he overlooked a subtly-rising emotion or realization which provides a basic structure and theme; because he was bound by an inflexible notion of what short stories ought to be, he failed to understand what this particular story was attempting to do. John Steinbeck's "Breakfast" (page 378) is an example of an unplotted story.

The *episodic story,* common in modern fiction, presents a single revealing episode or incident. It is highly concentrated and usually rich in suggestion, for the context—the past and future surrounding this brightly illuminated scene—is implied rather than explained. The episodic story often presents a character, or characters, at a time of crisis or decision; sometimes, though, it uses an undramatic, everyday incident which is typical of many others in the character's life. Its purpose, in either case, is to penetrate deeply into a segment of human experience.

Most modern writers try, not necessarily to confine a story to a single scene, but to condense the time-span of the story. By starting it as close to the climax and conclusion as the material allows, they achieve unity and concentration. Some material demands, of course, that the story cover a long period. For this kind of story, which in its time-structure is the opposite of the episodic story, there is no commonly used technical name.

A different sort of distinction between types of stories, a value judgment, is made by the terms *commercial story* and *artistic story*. The *commercial story* is the popular story intended to be read quickly, simply for diversion, by a large and not necessarily intelligent audience. It is found in pulp magazines, and in other magazines and newspapers which have a wide circulation, although not all stories in such publications are "commercial" in the present sense of the word. The commercial story is often, though not always, an action story; it is usually highly plotted; and its plot is usually a stereotyped formula: boy wins girl, poor boy makes good, wife retrieves husband from the other woman, etc. Because this type of story is designed for quick and unthoughtful reading, it has little subtlety, suggestion, or restraint. It explains fully, sometimes several times, any situation or feeling which the reader might not grasp. It uses obvious devices for creating suspense: "I would not have gone had I known what was in store for me." And it expresses certain conventional and popular, if questionable, ideas about life; for instance, that virtue is always rewarded, that criminals are always caught and punished, that married couples always (except for slight disturbances, perhaps like the one presented in the story) live happily ever after. Many commercial stories are technically very skillful, and they provide good entertainment for thousands of readers.

The *artistic story*, sometimes called the "quality" story, or the "literary" story or the "serious" story, differs in its effect and its purpose. It does more than entertain; it presents, in artistic form, a view of life or an insight into human experience which the writer believes will have meaning and value to others. The characters in this kind of story have the reality of living people; their experiences and reactions illuminate for the reader experiences and reactions of other human beings and of his own. The discussion and the readings in this section are intended primarily to supply guidance in the critical and appreciative reading of artistic stories. Because of their subtlety and use of suggestion, and because they do not always have an obvious plot, artistic stories are often not easy to read; but they are very rewarding.

It is probably quite clear from this discussion of types of stories that exceptions can be found to almost any generalization about their form and parts. Nevertheless, some generalizations and some analysis of structural parts are useful to both writer and reader. Most short stories have these eight elements:

1. Character
2. Setting
3. ⎫ Situation in which there is conflict ⎫
4. ⎪ Activating circumstance ⎪
5. ⎬ Rising action   ⎬   Plot
6. ⎪ Climax ⎪
7. ⎭ Dénouement ⎭
8. Controlling and unifying theme

Character is the most important element in many stories. If the
characters are well drawn, if they seem like real people, the reader
is interested in the story because he wants to know what happens to
these people. Characters in fiction are presented and made real by
the following methods, generally used in combination: description
of the character, description of his surroundings, interpretive comment by the author or another character, analysis of the character's
thoughts and feelings, presentation of his speech and action. Technically, character is often the basis of plot. Because a character be-
haves as he must behave, because a character is hot-tempered or
aggressive or careless or afraid, because two characters love or dislike
or misunderstand each other, the action of the story may logically
occur.

Setting is, in many stories, less essential than character. In the
purely psychological story, the external setting is insignificant; the
real setting is the interior of the human mind. In some stories setting
is used simply to give the reader, by means of scattered descriptive
details, clear sense-impressions of the background of the action; such
impressions make the story seem more true. In other stories, however,
setting is very important. The term *setting* has both narrow and wide
meaning. Narrowly it means the particular place (house, office, city
street) and the particular time and condition (rainy February morning, June night, three o'clock on a blazing summer afternoon) in
which action takes place. More widely, it means the whole geographical area (town, section, and country), the time in history, and the
social and economic environment in which events occur. Setting is
therefore of great significance in historical fiction and local-color
stories, and also in persuasive stories which present or criticize existing social, political, and economic conditions. Richard Wright's
powerful stories about southern Negroes (*Uncle Tom's Children*)
contain only brief descriptions of the immediate setting; but setting,
in the sense of environment, is the mainspring of their action. Sometimes character and setting together produce the plot of a story: a
character rebels against the setting in which he finds himself, or he

is not accepted by the people who dominate the environment in which he lives.

The *situation in which there is conflict* is essential in any short story. *Conflict* is a technical term which needs definition, and, when applied to the modern short story, broad interpretation. Conflict means any opposition of forces, or ideas, or values. It may take the form of a struggle (physical or psychological) between two people; or it may be opposition or contrast between two views of life, between things as they are and things as they might be, or between what a character does and what he wants to do. Narrative conflict often has more than one level. For example, a story presents the struggle between a son who wants to be an artist and a father who expects him to go into the family business; the immediate conflict is the clash of personalities and desires, but a deeper conflict may be the lack of understanding between two generations, or the opposition of artistic and materialistic values, or both. In some stories, the conflict is definitely resolved at the end; one force wins over the other: the hero defeats the villain, the detective traps the criminal, the character who has to make a decision makes it. In other stories, the reader knows, by suggestion, how the conflict is going to be resolved. In still others, a character (and the reader) comes to a sharp realization that the conflict exists and that it cannot be resolved.

The *activating circumstance* is a happening which produces or heightens the conflict, or sets the story in motion. In "The Lottery Ticket," discussed earlier, the activating circumstance is seeing in the newspaper the winning lottery number; from it stem the husband's and wife's dreams of wealth. The activating circumstance may be a dramatic incident like a chance encounter or a discovery which occurs at the beginning of the story; or it may be something that has happened before the opening of the story, like a meeting arranged or a will written long ago.

Rising action means the course of the story from the activating circumstance to the climax. The action may be either physical or psychological, and it may be presented in several scenes, or may, as in the episodic story, be concentrated in a single scene. The rising action proceeds steadily toward the *climax,* which is the high point and turning point of the story. The climax indicates what is going to happen, and the *dénouement* (or unraveling) carries the story to its end and often shows the effect of the climactic action. These three stages in the plot—rising action, climax, and dénouement—are not always clearly distinguishable. It may be hard to say what the climax of a story is, for the structural turning point of the action is not always the point of greatest interest for the reader; and there may be major and minor climaxes. Furthermore, some stories end with the climax and have no formal dénouement; the reader does his own unraveling.

The *controlling and unifying theme* is the central idea, the view of life, or the truth about human experience which the writer is expressing by means of his story. One of the characteristics of the short story as a literary form is that it produces a *single effect*. Unlike many novels, the short story has no subplots, no characters who appear and disappear without a clear purpose, no incidents or descriptive passages which are not strictly relevant to the main action, and no multiplicity of ideas. Characters, setting, action, details, and style are carefully planned so that everything in the story contributes to a single effect which communicates a single idea. This idea, which controls the writer's planning and selection of material, is the theme. Occasionally, in confession stories, for example, the theme is stated explicitly as a kind of moral: "And so I learned the hard way that love is more important than money." The artistic story, however, never moralizes, and seldom states directly its unifying theme. The reader derives that theme from the total effect of the story. Since most serious stories present a particular experience which at the same time, as part of its single effect, has wide or even universal application, the theme of a story can often be phrased both in particular and in general terms. The particular theme of a war story may be a young soldier's first combat experience; the general theme may be the horrors of war. The particular theme of Dorothy Parker's "Arrangement in Black and White" (page 343) is the prejudice of a woman who prides herself on her tolerance; the general theme is race prejudice in operation.

A concrete illustration may help to clarify these eight elements of the story. One of the best short stories to grow out of the depression of the 1930's is "The Happiest Man on Earth" by Albert Maltz. The *characters* in the story are Jesse Fulton and his brother-in-law Tom Brackett. Not presented, but significant elements in the story, are Jesse's wife, Ella (Tom's sister), and Jesse's children. The immediate *setting* is Tom's office, in which all the action takes place. The larger and more meaningful setting is the depression: Tom has lost his hardware store and now works, for thirty-five dollars a week, as a dispatcher in an oil company; Jesse has lost his job as a linotype operator, has been unable to find work, and has been on relief for six years. Jesse has walked from Kansas City, Missouri, to Tulsa, Oklahoma, to ask his brother-in-law, whom he has not seen for five years, for a job.

The immediate *situation with conflict* is the situation between the

two men, for Tom refuses to hire Jesse for the only job in his department—driving trucks of highly explosive nitroglycerin. The
deeper conflict is the six-year struggle of a man who wants to work
and to take care of his family, against economic forces beyond his
control. The *activating circumstance* has occurred before the technical opening of the story; two weeks earlier Jesse has met one of
Tom's drivers who has told him that his brother-in-law is hiring
men; given new hope by this information, Jesse has started his long
trek to Tulsa.

The *rising action* is the talk between the two men, in which the
conflict is clarified and heightened as Jesse pleads desperately for
the job and Tom steadily and angrily refuses. One out of every five
drivers gets killed in a year, Tom tells him; sooner or later they all
get killed; the man who gave Jesse news about the job was blown up
the night before; every minute of the day and night Jesse would be
wondering if tomorrow he would be dead. That doesn't matter,
Jesse tells his brother-in-law; what matters is that he has to do something for his family; he has to take care of Ella who is starving and
has lost her prettiness, and of his boy who can't walk because rickets
have softened his legs; he has to be able to respect himself again.
With the high pay for this dangerous work, Jesse continues over
Tom's protests, even if he lived only three months he could leave
Ella a thousand dollars; and he might last longer; maybe as long as
two years.

The *climax* of the story occurs when, unwillingly, wearily, Tom
tells him that he can start to drive that night. In the *dénouement,*
Jesse tries to thank Tom, leaves the office blinded by tears of joy, and
whispers to himself, "I'm the happiest man in the world. I'm the
happiest man on the whole earth." The initial conflict has been resolved at the end of the story: Jesse has won his argument and his
fight for work and self-respect. But the reader understands that he
will be killed soon, and the irony of his genuine happiness points up
the *theme* of the story: the ironic irrationality of a society in which
a man can be happy to have a job like this.

In addition to handling these eight story elements, the short-story
writer has four problems of technique. They are *point of view, exposition, logical preparation, and style.*

Since **point of view,** or angle of narration, has been discussed
earlier (see pages 348–350), it will be necessary here only to emphasize
its great importance in the short story. Sometimes the material and
theme of a story make a certain point of view inevitable; for example,
if the writer is trying to show the dissimilar reactions of two or more
people to the same event, he will naturally use the omniscient point

of view which enables the godlike author to enter the minds of all his characters. More often, though, the writer has a choice of points of view in telling a story; he can be the omniscient author, or he can limit his omniscience to the mind of one character, or he can be an objective reporter of action, or he can have one of the characters tell the story in the first person. He must decide what angle of narration, what slant on the material, will most surely produce the effect he wants. A good exercise for students interested in writing short stories is writing the same episode three or four times, using a different point of view each time. The episode will not be "the same" when it is seen through different eyes, and the writer will have learned something about the use of point of view as a technique of fiction. The reader of short stories, once he is aware of point of view, will find it interesting to see what the angle of narration contributes to particular stories that he reads, or what would have been lost had another point of view been used.

"The Happiest Man on Earth" combines an omniscient point of view with objective presentation. Much of the story is objective re- cording of the conversation between the two men; but the author gets into the minds of the characters, particularly at the beginning, to show Jesse's feelings when his brother-in-law at first does not know him, and Tom's thoughts as he looks at the shabby, gaunt man in whom he can hardly recognize his sister's husband. Also, at the end, after Jesse leaves the office whispering that he is the happiest man in the world, the omniscient author returns to a picture of Tom sitting hunched at his desk, listening to the painful beating of his heart, and gripping his head in his hands. The reason for this shift in focus from Jesse to Tom is that the reader, though he understands Jesse's happiness, does not share it. The reader feels like Tom. The effect of the story is therefore emphasized by the final picture which is made possible by an omniscient point of view. This combination of objective method with author-omniscience is frequently used. The completely objective story, in which the author enters no mind, and supplies no interpretation of the action, is very difficult to write and consequently rather rare.

The technical problem of **exposition** is closely related to point of view. Exposition in the short story is the explanation, commentary, and information about past events which the reader needs in order to understand the present action. We have said that modern short stories tend to be concentrated in time; they start late, close to the climax, after some of the action has already occurred. The writer therefore has the problem of informing the reader, without inter- rupting the forward movement of the story, about the past events which are part of the story situation. "The Happiest Man on Earth" illustrates the late beginning: the story opens with Jesse in the office of his brother-in-law, after six years of unemployment and its effects, after the activating circumstance that has led him to walk for two weeks to see Tom, after that two weeks' journey, and after Tom has come into the office and has jolted Jesse from joyful anticipation to misery by failing to recognize him. All these past events must be made clear to the reader.

Direct exposition, indirect exposition, dialogue, and *reflection and flashback* in the mind of a character are the four methods of handling exposition. The methods are often used in combination, and they are dependent on the point of view of the story.

Direct exposition occurs when an omniscient author or a first-person narrator simply tells the reader the facts he needs to know. The following passage illustrates direct exposition by an omniscient author:

> No one noticed the thin man, dressed in sober grey and carrying a brief case, who got off the train at Rockland. His name was Elmer Strong; he was forty years old; and he was a salesman for an insurance company in Hartford. He had been born and brought up in Rockland, but he had left home twenty years before after a quarrel with his father about the girl he later married. He had come back now because his father had asked him to. And he was sorry he had come.

Such direct exposition is often the simplest and most economical way of giving the reader necessary information. It is not suitable, though, for all types of stories, and it may give the impression that the writer is mechanically getting the facts out of the way and then going on with the story.

Indirect exposition is a more subtle way of supplying information without making bald informative statements. It is akin to the "suggestive description" discussed earlier in this chapter. If a writer mentions incidentally, as part of a scene in a story, the Lincoln convertible in the driveway, a gardener rounding the corner with a basket of cut flowers, and a group of girls standing beside the swimming pool, the reader understands without being told directly that the people who live in this place are wealthy. If a character sitting on a park bench eats with apparently ravenous hunger two-thirds of a loaf of bread, the reader understands that he has not eaten for some time and that he probably has no money. Indirect exposition allows the reader to draw his own conclusions (they are not always so obvious as the ones in the preceding sentences) from facts which can be objectively observed. Because indirect exposition is usually woven through a story instead of being presented in a block, it is, like expository dialogue and expository reflection and flashback, difficult to illustrate in a short passage. All three methods are illustrated in the short stories at the end of this section.

Dialogue is the most common method of exposition in stories which have an objective point of view or are largely objective in presentation. Effective dialogue, in addition to supplying facts, characterizes the people who are talking and develops the present situation. The background needed by the reader emerges gradually as an integrated part of the rising action.

Reflection and flashback are also techniques which integrate past and present action after the story is under way. They are used when the omniscient author enters the minds of all his characters, or, using a limited omniscient point of view, takes up residence in the mind of one person. *Reflection* is the mental commentary of a character on the present situation. It is used in "The Happiest Man on Earth" to describe Tom as he looks to Jesse and Jesse as he looks to Tom; the reflection gives the reader a picture of the two men without comment from the author, and also gives information about how much Jesse has changed as a result of his experience in the past years. A *flashback* is a character's recollection of past events, usually a full recollection of a scene from the past. It is a valuable method of exposition, and, skillfully used, it does not interrupt the immediate action of the story, because the flashback is suggested by and related to the action in the present scene.

Logical preparation, the third technical problem of the story writer, consists of establishing facts, circumstances, and traits of character in such a way that the action and outcome of the story are believable. Suspense is part of the technique of most stories, and the reader may feel surprise at what happens; but he should not have the feeling of being tricked, or of being called upon to accept an incredible coincidence or an act which is out of character. To use "The Happiest Man on Earth" once more—Tom Brackett consistently refuses, during the rising action of the story, to hire Jesse to drive the trucks of nitroglycerin; and yet his final consent is logical and believable because it has been prepared for in three ways. First, both Tom and the reader understand more vividly, as the conversation goes on, Jesse's desperate situation. Second, against Jesse's logical arguments and his carefully thought-out plan to keep Ella from knowing what work he is doing and to save money for her, Tom's emotional arguments become weaker and weaker. Third, the fact has been established that Tom, too, has had financial difficulties; he has a hard time getting along on his thirty-five dollars a week;

he has no means of helping his sister and brother-in-law, therefore, except by giving Jesse the job. Tom's financial situation, made clear early in the story, is part of the depression setting; it is also logical preparation for his final, helpless surrender.

The term *foreshadowing* means giving the reader hints or suggestions about coming action. The obvious foreshadowing found in many commercial stories ("Three hours later I was to regret my decision") is not desirable. But more subtle foreshadowing is often part of logical preparation. An example is a war story, "England to America" by Margaret Prescott Montague, in which a young American lieutenant spends his leave visiting the family of his English Flight Commander. The father and mother, the war-blinded brother, and the fiancée of his friend are wonderfully kind to him, and he enjoys his leave. But he has a sense of strain; there are unexpected silences and withdrawals; he has a repeated feeling of saying the wrong thing, of offending them in some way. He is shocked when he learns, just before he goes back to the front, that the family received word, the day before he came, of the death of his friend, and decided to conceal the news that would ruin his leave. Most readers feel some shock, too, at the end of the story; and yet the atmosphere of tension and the bewildering silences have prepared for it; normal behavior on the part of the family would have made the story quite unconvincing.

Other forms of logical preparation are introducing early, and in a way which seems natural, any aspect of character or any material object which is to be important later. If the climax of a story is to hinge on the selfish action of one of the characters, that trait of selfishness must be revealed by earlier thought or action of the character. If a gun is to be taken out of a drawer, its presence in the drawer must be established and explained, before the dramatic moment. If an object is to be used as a symbol—if, for example, a book is going to be thrown into the wastebasket to indicate the feeling of a character toward the person who gave him the book—that object, with its associations, must figure in the setting and earlier action of the story. The reader has a jarring sense of illogic and untruth when essential traits and objects make rabbit-out-of-the-hat appearances.

Style in the short story includes language, sentence rhythms, use of descriptive detail, and the movement or pace of the narrative; and it is affected by the material, the theme, and the point of view. Symbolism and suggestion are also aspects of style. Sometimes the style of a short story is distinctively and unmistakably the writer's own; any story he writes will be written in this way. His expression is a product of his personality and of the kind of material to which he is drawn by his individual cast of mind: he is interested in fast-moving external action, and he habitually reports it in a terse, short-sentenced style; or he is interested in the complexities of human reactions, and he has developed a complex style which best communicates the intricacies of inward experience. Often, though, a writer adjusts his style to the material and theme, and especially to the point of view which seems right for a particular story. In first-person stories, the author frequently assumes a personality very unlike his own; he must abandon his characteristic style, and consistently use the vocabulary and sentence structure typical of the narrator. When the author, writing in the third person, views events through the mind of one person, he does not use that person's language; but his story will seem more real if he colors his own language with the idioms and the figures of speech which are natural to that character. A third-person story told from a child's point of view is usually written in a style more mature than that of the child himself; a fairly simple style, however, is better suited than a complex one to the atmosphere of the story. Style is the distinctive expression of the writer, but it is profoundly influenced, sometimes beyond recognition, by the demands of his story. This is right, of course. In the short story, the story itself, and not the writer, is important. The writer is important only in so far as he is able, with his talent and his hard work, to communicate to others a separate and significant experience.

The five short stories in the following pages illustrate many, though by no means all, of the techniques of the artistic story. The stories are varied in structure, setting, theme, and style. As a group, they illustrate symbolism and suggestion, different kinds of exposition and logical preparation, different methods of characterization, and the effects of different points of view. Careful, analytical study of a few stories like these gives one an experience in reading which makes other stories more meaningful and enjoyable. Such analytical study is also the best possible training for the writing of short stories.

PRELUDE TO REUNION *

OLIVER LA FARGE

Oliver La Farge is an American anthropologist and writer of scholarly studies and of fiction. His novel *Laughing Boy*, a story of the Navajo Indians, won the 1930 Pulitzer Prize. "Prelude to Reunion" was published in

* Copyright, 1939, The New Yorker Magazine, Inc.

The New Yorker and reprinted in *Short Stories from The New Yorker* in 1940.

The room was furnished with what the college issued: a desk, placed dead center under the overhead light, a table, three wooden chairs, a bed, a bureau, and an empty fireplace, the brick floor of which was free of ashes and cigarette butts. One shelf of the bookcase was almost filled with textbooks, a one-volume edition of Shakespeare, and a Bible. On the table were two notebooks and a dictionary, a cup and saucer, a plate, and a small electric stove with a saucepan on it. A calendar and two pine cones had been arranged on the mantelpiece in an effort at decoration. There was a framed photograph of a middle-aged woman on the bureau, and two neckties hung from a corner of the mirror. The room looked as if its occupant had moved in that afternoon and would leave tomorrow.

The boy paced slowly, methodically, between the fireplace and the bookcase. Passing the window, he caught the smell of the night— the new, disturbing mildness of spring—and he could hear voices below on the campus. He was tall, thin, fair-haired, with too much Adam's apple and too long a nose. He was not thinking, he was stringing out the time before he should decide to take a walk.

In a few moments he would put on a necktie and coat and go downstairs. As he stepped outside, he would feel a faint anticipation, a nameless, automatic stirring of hope, which he would quickly discount by a defensive reflex, a moment of pain never admitted. Then he would stroll. If he met fellows who sat in his classes, he would walk a little faster until he passed them, but sometimes even so they would remember him and nod, or say "Hello" or even "Hello, Matterson." He would say "Hello" and go on by, letting them continue their appointed ways. His own pace, too, would be a declaration that he was going somewhere.

By one route or another he would come to the Women's School. Here his walk would be a swinging, unhesitating stride. He would not turn his head, he would just go on through, but his eyes would take in a wide range, the groups of girls and the pairs of girls and fellows. Last week, the first night of the warm weather, a man who sat next to him in biochemistry passed him with a girl. He said, "Hi, Matterson. Sparking?" He'd answered, "Hello, Newman. Just scouting," and Newman and the girl had laughed.

They were all just kids, really—as old as he, but nothing had taught them seriousness. His brain could run rings around them. He wasn't interested in their eternal play.

Beyond the School he would come out into the town, buy a paper, and then return to his room, the room he was walking up and down now, not thinking anything much except that it was time, perhaps, to go out and get a paper.

A firm knock on his door brought him up sharp. He moved to open it, then stood back and called, "Come in!"

The visitor, who entered rather self-consciously, was a well-dressed boy of medium height, neither fair nor dark, with a scrubbed, healthy face.

"Matterson?" he said. "I'm Bill Farraday. May I come in?"

"Hello. Sit down." His anger at himself for being so tense added to his stiffness.

"I live in this entry, 2 B."

Matterson knew well enough, as he knew that Farraday had his letter in hockey and was a candidate for class marshal. He nodded, watchful.

Farraday arranged himself with an effect of relaxation for which the chair was not well adapted. He looked around the room, said "Nice," then broke off. The thin boy understood; it wasn't a nice joint. Seeing that his visitor was ill at ease, he felt a shade more comfortable.

"Looks like spring had really come, doesn't it?" Farraday said. He became more assured at the sound of his own voice. "Here the winter's over, and this is the first time I've been up here." Matterson listened, guarded, protecting himself. "This college is so damn big you can't hope to know everyone, but I'd promised myself to meet all the men in this entry. You know how it is. You get tied up in so many things and the first thing you know the ice has melted and the ball team's coming out of the cage."

Matterson said, "Yeah."

"Where do you come from? You're not from around here, are you?"

"Vermont."

"Well! Why did you pick to come here?"

"I'm going into analytical chemistry and I wanted to be under MacPherson."

"Oh. Oh, yeah, sure." Farraday paused again, then took off as if from a cue. "You had a scholarship?"

"Not to start with; the first two years I worked my way. Then I got the Bernstein." He was proud of that; it was the best there was in science for undergraduates. "Now I'm hoping for the Marlin Fellowship if I can get my *magna cum* all right."

Farraday looked vaguely uncomfortable. The look passed. "Good for you. I admire a guy like you and I'm glad I came up." Again his flow of talk became smooth. His voice had a flattering frankness. "Yeah, when I get out of here I'll go to Wall Street, and I guess that twenty years from now I'll just be another bond salesman living the old country-club life, and I'll be bragging about how I used to know you. I've had it easy and you've had it tough."

The Vermonter felt an unfamiliar warmth run through him. "It's been tough sometimes," he said. He hesitated, then added with an effort, "I saw you shoot that long goal against Colmouth."

"Oh, that was just luck." Farraday was visibly pleased. He pulled out a pack of cigarettes. "Smoke?"

"No, thanks."

"Oh. Do you mind—"

"Go ahead."

"Come down to my room sometime, won't you? Sling the bull, you know. I generally have a little beer on hand—or ginger ale."

"I like beer." Matterson considered explaining that he didn't smoke on account of the expense, then decided not to.

Farraday brightened. "That's fine. I mean it. Drop in."

"Thanks." He wanted to say more, but didn't know how.

"Say, a man like you, working your way along, and then getting fellowships and things—I'd like your slant on this endowment business."

Matterson had read the ballyhoo with a mounting sense of discomfort. The University was driving for extra endowment and the Senior Class Committee had voted a graduation gift of fifteen thousand dollars, which would mean a little over twenty dollars a member. The gift was getting a big play from the Endowment Fund's publicity bureau in going after the graduates.

"Well," he said, "I guess it's a good idea."

"Yeah, I think so, too. Our tuition fees don't cover the cost of our education. When you average it up—the men on scholarship and things—the University gives us nearly a thousand dollars." Farraday caught himself up. "Of course," he said hastily, "that's what you expect the old place to do—help the men like you who really have brains. It's part of a university's proper function." He looked around. "Got an ash tray?"

"Chuck it in the fireplace."

Farraday threw the butt, then pulled out the pack again. "I guess I'm smoking a lot right now. What with finals coming on and all the boning up to do and one thing and another, I get kind of nervous." He lit up. "This endowment business on top of the rest has me about daffy. You see, I'm in charge of this entry and we're short on our quota. I dunno how it is, some of the fellows don't seem to appreciate what the old school does for them. I guess I'm a rotten collector; it kind of burns me up to get after a man if he isn't willing." He gave a short, unreal laugh. "Yeah, I hate doing it. I've upped my share to fifty bucks, though God knows, I guess it means the sheriff will be after me, what with the old unpaid bills and all." He made the last statement with a smile, as one man speaking to another of a common problem.

Matterson just watched him, saying nothing.

"I've got you down for five bucks," Farraday said. "Of course, it's up to you. You know what you can afford, spreading it over the next two months."

Matterson continued staring at him. Out of a swirl inside himself he said quietly, without a shade of defiance in his tone, "You can put me down for ten."

"Why, say, that's great. Say, that's the real spirit, Matterson. Wait till I tell some of the other men that, the ones who've been holding out." He pulled at his cigarette, held it a moment, threw it in the fireplace. "Yeah, that's great. Well, look, I've got to get after some of the others now." He rose. "Don't forget to drop in on me some-time."

Matterson said, "Sure. Thanks."

Farraday answered heartily, "Thanks to you. Well, so long. Be seeing you."

"So long."

Matterson sat and stared at the long-awaited, casual disorder of the two cigarette stubs in the fireplace. Then he stood with his hands in his pockets. Ten dollars was catastrophic. Double what the rich boy thought him good for—pride stiffened in him, covering the pain of a warm moment betrayed. More slowly than usual, he tied his necktie, put on his coat, and went out.

COMMENT AND QUESTIONS

A major pleasure and value of reading some short stories is that the reader is taken into a strange environment and into an experience different from his own. In other stories a major pleasure is recognition—seeing in someone else's situation and feeling the things one has personally felt or observed. Much good fiction brings simultaneously to the reader the familiar and the strange, the two-fold experience of recognition and surprise. Most college students will have a sense of recognition in reading "Prelude to Reunion." It has a reality rather rare in stories of college life; and it shows simply and clearly a number of the techniques of the artistic story.

I. We have mentioned earlier the suggestive description in the first paragraph of this story. The whole first section, from the beginning to the knock on the door, is, in fact, suggestive indirect exposition. What do we know about Matterson from his room, and from his pattern of behavior on his walks to buy a paper?

II. The dialogue in this story is worth study. The best way to learn the mechanics of writing dialogue is to examine a page or so of it in a story, noting the paragraphing and punctuation, and the techniques of handling bits of attendant action and the reactions of the speakers while the talk goes on. Good dialogue is, of course, more than mechanically satisfactory. It sounds natural, it reveals the characters, and it advances the story. Notice how the dialogue here is used for all three purposes, and also to supply further exposition about Matterson's past experience.

III. Why is Matterson watchful and guarded at the beginning of Farraday's call?

IV. At what point does the reader suspect Farraday's motives?

V. Explain why Matterson pledges ten dollars to the endowment fund.

VI. Do you think that Farraday will make a successful bond salesman? Why?

VII. The story uses a good deal of objective presentation, but the omniscient author knows and relates Matterson's habits on his walks in the past, and from time to time he gets into Matterson's mind and records the boy's thoughts and feelings. Would it be possible to tell this story from a completely objective point of view? Does the author enter Farraday's mind at all?

VIII. The two cigarette butts in the fireplace are a symbol. What do they stand for to Matterson? In what sense are they ironical? Notice how the whole business of the clean fireplace, Farraday's smoking, and the absence of an ash tray is woven naturally and informatively into the story.

IX. What is implied in the story's closing sentence?

X. Why is "Prelude to Reunion" a better title than "Episode of College"? How is the title related to the theme of the story?

A TRIP TO CZARDIS *

EDWIN GRANBERRY

Edwin Granberry, who teaches creative writing at Rollins College, is the author of three novels and a number of short stories, many of them with a Florida setting. "A Trip to Czardis" won the O. Henry Memorial Award as the best short story of 1932.

———

It was still dark in the pine woods when the two brothers awoke. But it was plain that day had come, and in a little while there would be no more stars. Day itself would be in the sky, and they would be going along the road. Jim waked first, coming quickly out of sleep and sitting up in the bed to take fresh hold of the things in his head, starting them up again out of the corners of his mind where sleep had tucked them. Then he waked Daniel and they sat up together in the bed. Jim put his arm around his younger brother, for the night had been dewy and cool with the swamp wind. Daniel shivered a little and whimpered, it being dark in the room and his baby concerns still on him somewhat, making sleep heavy on his mind and slow to give understanding its way.

"Hit's the day, Dan'l. This day that's right here now, we are goen. You'll recollect it all in a minute."

"I recollect. We are goen in the wagon to see Papa—"

"Then hush and don't whine."

"I were dreamen, Jim."

"What dreamen did you have?"

"I can't tell. But it were fearful what I dreamt."

"All the way we are goen this time. We won't stop at any places, but we will go all the way to Czardis to see Papa. I never see such a place as Czardis."

"I recollect the water tower—"

"Not in your own right, Dan'l. Hit's by my tellen it you see it in your mind."

"And lemonade with ice in it I saw—"

"That too I seen and told to you."

"Then I never seen it at all?"

"Hit's me were there, Dan'l. I let you play like, but hit's me who

* From the *Forum*, April, 1932.

went to Czardis. Yet I never till this day told half how much I see. There's sights I never told."

They stopped talking, listening for their mother's stir in the kitchen. But the night stillness was unlifted. Daniel began to shiver again.

"Hit's dark," he said.

"Hit's your eyes stuck," Jim said. "Would you want me to drip a little water on your eyes?"

"Oh!" cried the young one, pressing his face into his brother's side, "don't douse me, Jim, no more. The cold aches me."

The other soothed him, holding him around the body.

"You won't have e're chill or malarie ache today, Dan'l. Hit's a fair day—"

"I won't be cold?"

"Hit's a bright day. I hear mournen doves starten a'ready. The sun will bake you warm. . . . Uncle Holly might buy us somethen new to eat in Czardis."

"What would it be?"

"Hit ain't decided yet. . . . He hasn't spoke. Hit might be somethen sweet. Maybe a candy ball fixed onto a rubber string."

"A candy ball!" Daniel showed a stir of happiness. "Oh, Jim!" But it was a deceit of the imagination, making his eyes shine wistfully; the grain of his flesh was against it. He settled into a stillness by himself.

"My stomach would retch it up, Jim. . . . I guess I couldn't eat it."

"You might keep a little down."

"No . . . I would bring it home and keep it."

Their mother when they went to bed had laid a clean pair of pants and a waist for each on the chair. Jim crept out of bed and put on his clothes, then aided his brother on with his. They could not hear any noise in the kitchen, but hickory firewood burning in the kitchen stove worked a smell through the house, and in the forest guinea fowls were sailing down from the trees and poking their way along the half-dark ground toward the kitchen steps, making it known the door was open and that within someone was stirring about at the getting of food.

Jim led his brother by the hand down the dark way of yellow-pine stairs that went narrowly and without banisters to the rooms below. The young brother went huddling in his clothes, aguelike, knowing that warmth was near, hungering for his place by the stove, to sit in peace on the bricks in the floor by the stove's side and watch the eating, it being his nature to have a sickness against food.

They came in silence to the kitchen, Jim leading and holding his brother by the hand. The floor was lately strewn with fresh bright sand, and that would sparkle when the daybreak got above the forest, though now it lay dull as hoarfrost and cold to the unshod feet of the brothers. The door to the firebox of the stove was open, and in front of it their mother sat in a chair, speaking low as they entered, muttering under her breath. The two boys went near and stood still, thinking she was blessing the food, their mush being dipped up and steaming in two bowls. And they stood cast down until she lifted her eyes to them and spoke.

"Your clothes on already," she said. "You look right neat." She did not rise, but kept her chair, looking cold and stiff, with the cloth of her black dress sagging between her knees. The sons stood in front of her, and she laid her hand on first one head and then the other and spoke a little about the day, charging them to be sober and of few words, as she had raised them.

Jim sat on the bench by the table and began to eat, mixing dark molasses sugar through his bowl of mush. But a nausea began in Daniel's stomach at sight of the sweet, and he lagged by the stove, gazing at the food as it passed into his brother's mouth.

Suddenly a shadow filled the back doorway and Holly, their uncle, stood there looking in. He was lean and big and dark from wind and weather, working in the timber as their father had done. He had no wife and children and would roam far off with the timber gangs in the Everglades. This latter year he did not go far, but stayed near them. Their mother stopped and looked at the man, and he looked at her in silence. Then he looked at Jim and Daniel.

"You goen to take them after all?"

She waited a minute, seeming to get the words straight in her mind before bringing them out, making them say what was set there.

"He asked to see them. Nobody but God Almighty ought to tell a soul hit can or can't have."

Having delivered her mind, she went out into the yard with the man, and they spoke more words in an undertone, pausing in their speech.

In the silence of the kitchen Daniel began to speak out and name what thing among his possessions he would take to Czardis to give his father. But the older boy belittled this and that and everything that was called up, saying one thing was of too little consequence for a man, and that another was of no account because it was food. But when the older boy had abolished the idea and silence had regained, he worked back to the thought, coming to it roundabout and making it new and as his own, letting it be decided that each of them would take their father a pomegranate from the tree in the yard.

They went to the kitchen door. The swamp fog had risen suddenly. They saw their mother standing in the lot while their uncle hitched the horse to the wagon. Leaving the steps, Jim climbed to the first crotch of the pomegranate tree. The reddest fruits were on the top branches. He worked his way up higher. The fog was now curling up out of the swamp, making gray mountains and rivers in the air and strange ghost shapes. Landmarks disappeared in the billows, or half seen, they bewildered the sight, and an eye could so little mark the known or strange that a befuddlement took hold of the mind, like the visitations sailors beheld in the fogs of Okeechobee. Jim could not find the ground. He seemed to have climbed into the mountains. The light was unnatural and dark, and the pines were blue and dark over the mountains.

A voice cried out of the fog:

"Are worms gnawen you that you skin up a pomegranate tree at this hour? Don't I feed you enough?"

The boy worked his way down. At the foot of the tree he met his mother. She squatted and put her arm around him, her voice tight and quivering, and he felt tears on her face.

"We ain't come to the shame yet of you and Dan'l hunten your food off trees and grass. People seein' you gnawen on the road will say Jim Cameron's sons are starved, foragen like cattle of the field."

"I were getten the pomegranates for Papa," said the boy, resigned to his mother's concern. She stood up when he said this, holding him in front of her skirts. In a while she said:

"I guess we won't take any, Jim. . . . But I'm proud it come to you to take your papa somethen."

And after a silence, the boy said:

"Hit were Dan'l it come to, Mamma."

Then she took his hand, not looking down, and in her throat, as if in her bosom, she repeated:

"Hit were a fine thought and I'm right proud . . . though today we won't take anything. . . ."

"I guess there's better pomegranates in Czardis where we are goen—"

"There's no better pomegranates in Czardis than right here over your head," she said grimly. "If pomegranates were needed, we would take him his own. . . . You are older'n Dan'l, Jim. When we get to the place we are goen, you won't know your papa after so long. He will be pale and he won't be as bright as you recollect. So don't labor him with questions . . . but speak when it behooves you and let him see you are upright."

When the horse was harnessed and all was ready for the departure, the sons were seated on a shallow bed of hay in the back of the wagon and the mother took the driver's seat alone. The uncle had argued for having the top up over the seat, but she refused the shelter, remarking that she had always driven under the sky and would do it still today. He gave in silently and got upon the seat of his own wagon, which took the road first, their wagon following. This was strange, and the sons asked:

"Why don't we all ride in Uncle Holly's wagon?"

But their mother made no reply.

For several miles they traveled in silence through their own part of the woods, meeting no one. The boys whispered a little to themselves, but their mother and their uncle sat without speaking, nor did they turn their heads to look back. At last the narrow road they were following left the woods and came out to the highway, and it was seen that other wagons besides their own were going to Czardis. And as they got farther along, they began to meet many other people going to town, and the boys asked their mother what day it was. It was Wednesday. And then they asked her why so many wagons were going along the road if it wasn't Saturday and a market day. When she told them to be quiet, they settled down to watching the people go by. Some of them were faces that were strange, and some were neighbors who lived in other parts of the woods. Some who passed them stared in silence, and some went by looking straight to the front. But there were none of them who spoke, for their mother turned her eyes neither right nor left, but drove the horse on like a woman in her sleep. All was silent as the wagons passed, except the squeaking of the wheels and the thud of the horses' hoofs on the dry, packed sand.

At the edge of the town the crowds increased, and their wagon got lost in the press of people. All were moving in one direction.

Finally they were going along by a high brick wall on top of which ran a barbed-wire fence. Farther along the way in the middle of the wall was a tall, stone building with many people in front. There were trees along the outside of the wall, and in the branches of one of the trees Daniel saw a man. He was looking over the brick wall down into the courtyard. All the wagons were stopping here and hitching through the grove in front of the building. But their Uncle Holly's wagon and their own drove on, making way slowly as through a crowd at a fair, for under the trees knots of men were gathered, talking in undertone. Daniel pulled at his mother's skirts and whispered:

"What made that man climb up that tree?"

Again she told him to be quiet.

"We're not to talk today," said Jim. "Papa is sick and we're not to make him worse." But his high, thin voice made his mother turn cold. She looked back and saw he had grown pale and still, staring at the iron-barred windows of the building. When he caught her gaze, his chin began to quiver, and she turned back front to dodge the knowledge of his eyes.

For the two wagons had stopped now and the uncle gotten down and left them sitting alone while he went to the door of the building and talked with a man standing there. The crowd fell silent, staring at their mother.

"See, Jim, all the men up the trees!" Daniel whispered once more, leaning close in to his brother's side.

"Hush, Dan'l. Be still."

The young boy obeyed this time, falling into a bewildered stare at all the things about him he did not understand, for in all the trees along the brick wall men began to appear perched high in the branches, and on the roof of a building across the way stood other men, all gaping at something in the yard back of the wall.

Their uncle returned and hitched his horse to a ring in one of the trees. Then he hitched their mother's horse, and all of them got out and stood on the ground in a huddle. The walls of the building rose before them. Strange faces at the barred windows laughed aloud and called down curses at the men below.

Now they were moving, with a wall of faces on either side of them, their uncle going first, followed by their mother who held to each of them by a hand. They went up the steps of the building. The door opened, and their uncle stepped inside. He came back in a moment, and all of them went in and followed a man down a corridor and into a bare room with two chairs and a wooden bench. A man in a black robe sat on one of the chairs, and in front of him on the bench, leaning forward, looking down between his arms, sat their father. His face was lean and gray, which made him look very tall. But his hair was black, and his eyes were blue and mild and strange as he stood up and held the two sons against his body while he stooped his head to kiss their mother. The man in black left the room and walked up and down outside the corridor. A second stranger stood in the doorway with his back to the room. The father picked up one of the sons and then the other in his arms and looked at them and leaned their faces on his own. Then he sat down on the bench and held them against him. Their mother sat down by them and they were all together.

A few low words were spoken, and then a silence fell over them all. And in a while the parents spoke a little more and touched one another. But the bare stone floor and the stone walls and the un-accustomed arms of their father hushed the sons with the new and strange. And when the time had passed, the father took his watch from his pocket.

"I'm goen to give you my watch, Jim. You are the oldest. I want you to keep it till you are a grown man. . . . And I want you to always do what your Mama tells you. . . . I'm goen to give you the chain, Dan'l. . . ."

The young brother took the chain, slipped out of his father's arms, and went to his mother with it. He spread it out on her knee and began to talk to her in a whisper. She bent over him, and again all of them in the room grew silent.

A sudden sound of marching was heard in the corridor. The man rose up and took his sons in his arms, holding them abruptly. But their uncle, who had been standing with the man in the doorway, came suddenly and took them and went out and down through the big doorway by which they had entered the building. As the doors opened to let them pass, the crowd gathered around the steps pressed forward to look inside. The older boy cringed in his uncle's arms. His uncle turned and stood with his back to the crowd. Their mother came through the doors. The crowd fell back. Again through a passageway of gazing eyes, they reached the wagons. This time they sat on the seat beside their mother. Leaving their uncle and his wagon behind, they started off on the road that led out of town.

"Is Papa coming with Uncle Holly?" Jim asked in a still voice.

His mother nodded her head.

Reaching the woods once more and the silence he knew, Daniel whispered to his brother:

"We got a watch and chain instead, Jim."

But Jim neither answered nor turned his eyes.

COMMENT AND QUESTIONS

The gradual revealing of a situation by suggestion and restrained understatement is illustrated in this powerful story. The point of view is omniscient; but the author controls his omniscience in such a way that he records events largely as they appear to the two young boys; the effect, therefore, is much like the effect of an innocent-eye point of view. The language of the story contributes a great deal to its atmosphere. The characters speak in a dialect which is represented by a few consistent spellings and constructions ("hit," "goen," "I seen," "it come"); the author's own prose, without sharing the dialect, is colored by its idiom. This style is a subtle element in the story, but very important in establishing the setting and the reality of the whole experience.

I. Trace carefully the foreshadowing and logical preparation in the story. At what point does the reader understand that there is something strange about this trip to Czardis? At what point does the reader understand what the situation is?

II. What purpose is served by the early-morning talk between the two brothers? By the details about Daniel's queasy stomach? By the episode of the pomegranates?

III. What descriptive details in the first two pages of the story best give a sense of the physical environment in which the brothers live? Which details give a sense of their moral or spiritual environment?

IV. How is the mother characterized? How is Uncle Holly characterized?

V. What does Daniel's final remark ("We got a watch and chain instead, Jim") mean to him, and what does it indicate to the reader?

VI. What is the significance of the final sentence: "But Jim neither answered nor turned his eyes"?

VII. The unity of effect in this story—the focus on the boys' experience on this day—demands that the author exclude certain tangential but still interesting matters. What questions does the story leave unanswered? Are any of the answers suggested? Explain.

VIII. How would you define the conflict in this story?

MARRIAGE À LA MODE *

KATHERINE MANSFIELD

Katherine Mansfield (1888–1923) is one of the most important short-story writers of the twentieth century. Her work is distinguished for its subtlety and suggestion, its artistic expression, and its psychological insight. "Marriage à la Mode" was published in *The Garden Party* in 1922. Other volumes of Katherine Mansfield's stories are *Bliss, The Doves' Nest, The Little Girl,* and *The Aloe.*

On his way to the station William remembered with a fresh pang of disappointment that he was taking nothing down to the kiddies.

* Reprinted from *The Garden Party* by Katherine Mansfield by permission of Alfred A. Knopf, Inc. Copyright, 1922, by Alfred A. Knopf, Inc.

Poor little chaps! It was hard lines on them. Their first words always were as they ran to greet him, "What have you got for me, daddy?" and he had nothing. He would have to buy them some sweets at the station. But that was what he had done for the past four Saturdays; their faces had fallen last time when they saw the same old boxes produced again.

And Paddy had said, "I had red ribbing on mine *bee-*fore!"

And Johnny had said, "It's always pink on mine. I hate pink."

But what was William to do? The affair wasn't so easily settled. In the old days, of course, he would have taken a taxi off to a decent toyshop and chosen them something in five minutes. But nowadays they had Russian toys, French toys, Serbian toys—toys from God knows where. It was over a year since Isabel had scrapped the old donkeys and engines and so on because they were so "dreadfully sentimental" and "so appallingly bad for the babies' sense of form."

"It's so important," the new Isabel had explained, "that they should like the right things from the very beginning. It saves so much time later on. Really, if the poor pets have to spend their infant years staring at these horrors, one can imagine them growing up and asking to be taken to the Royal Academy."

And she spoke as though a visit to the Royal Academy was certain immediate death to any one. . . .

"Well, I don't know," William said slowly. "When I was their age I used to go to bed hugging an old towel with a knot in it."

The new Isabel looked at him, her eyes narrowed, her lips apart.

"*Dear* William! I'm sure you did!" She laughed in the new way.

Sweets it would have to be, however, thought William gloomily, fishing in his pocket for change for the taxi-man. And he saw the kiddies handing the boxes around—they were awfully generous little chaps—while Isabel's precious friends didn't hesitate to help themselves. . . .

What about fruit? William hovered before a stall just inside the station. What about a melon each? Would they have to share that, too? Or a pineapple for Pad, and a melon for Johnny? Isabel's friends could hardly go sneaking up to the nursery at the children's mealtimes. All the same, as he bought the melon William had a horrible vision of one of Isabel's young poets lapping up a slice, for some reason, behind the nursery door.

With his two very awkward parcels he strode off to his train. The platform was crowded; the train was in. Doors banged open and shut. There came such a loud hissing from the engine that people looked dazed as they scurried to and fro. William made straight for a first-class smoker, stowed away his suitcase and parcels, and taking a huge wad of papers out of his inner pocket, he flung down in the corner and began to read.

"Our client moreover is positive. . . . We are inclined to reconsider . . . in the event of—" Ah, that was better. William pressed back his flattened hair and stretched his legs across the carriage floor. The familiar dull gnawing in his breast quieted down. "With regard to our decision—" He took out a blue pencil and scored a paragraph slowly.

Two men came in, stepped across him, and made for the farther corner. A young fellow swung his golf clubs into the rack and sat down opposite. The train gave a gentle lurch; they were off. William glanced up and saw the hot, bright station slipping away. A red-faced girl raced along by the carriages; there was something strained and almost desperate in the way she waved and called. "Hysterical!" thought William dully. Then a greasy, black-faced workman at the end of the platform grinned at the passing train. And William thought, "A filthy life!" and went back to his papers.

When he looked up again there were fields, and beasts standing for shelter under the dark trees. A wide river, with naked children splashing in the shallows, glided into sight and was gone again. The sky shone pale, and one bird drifted high like a dark fleck in a jewel.

"We have examined our client's correspondence files. . . ." The last sentence he had read echoed in his mind. "We have examined . . ." William hung on to that sentence, but it was no good; it snapped in the middle, and the fields, the sky, the sailing bird, the water, all said, "Isabel." The same thing happened every Saturday afternoon. When he was on his way to meet Isabel there began those countless imaginary meetings. She was at the station, standing a little apart from everybody else; she was sitting in the open taxi outside; she was at the garden gate; walking across the parched grass; at the door, or just inside the hall.

And her clear, light voice said, "It's William," or "Hillo, William!" or "So William has come!" He touched her cool hand, her cool cheek.

The exquisite freshness of Isabel! When he had been a little boy, it was his delight to run into the garden after a shower of rain and shake the rose-bush over him. Isabel was that rose-bush, petal-soft, sparkling and cool. And he was still that little boy. But there was no running into the garden now, no laughing and shaking. The dull, persistent gnawing in his breast started again. He drew up his legs, tossed the papers aside, and shut his eyes.

"What is it, Isabel? What is it?" he said tenderly. They were in their bedroom in their new house. Isabel sat on a painted stool before the dressing-table that was strewn with little black and green boxes.

"What is what, William?" And she bent forward, and her fine light hair fell over her cheeks.

"Ah, you know!" He stood in the middle of the strange room and he felt a stranger. At that Isabel wheeled round quickly and faced him.

"Oh, William!" she cried imploringly, and she held up the hairbrush: "Please! Please, don't be so dreadfully stuffy and—tragic. You're always saying or looking or hinting that I've changed. Just because I've got to know really congenial people, and go about more, and am frightfully keen on—on everything, you behave as though I'd—" Isabel tossed back her hair and laughed—"killed our love, or something. It's awfully absurd"—she bit her lip—"and it's so maddening, William. Even this new house and the servants you grudge me."

"Isabel!"

"Yes, yes, it's true in a way," said Isabel quickly. "You think they are another bad sign. Oh, I know you do. I feel it," she said softly, "every time you come up the stairs. But we couldn't have gone on living in that other poky little hole, William. Be practical, at least! Why, there wasn't enough room for the babies even."

No, it was true. Every morning when he came back from chambers it was to find the babies with Isabel in the back drawing-room. They were having rides on the leopard skin thrown over the sofa back, or they were playing shops with Isabel's desk for a counter, or Pad was sitting on the hearthrug rowing away for dear life with a little brass fire shovel, while Johnny shot at pirates with the tongs. Every evening they each had a pick-a-back up the narrow stairs to their fat old Nanny.

Yes, he supposed it was a poky little house. A little white house with blue curtains and a window-box of petunias. William met their friends at the door with "Seen our petunias? Pretty terrific for London, don't you think?"

But the imbecile thing, the absolutely extraordinary thing was that he hadn't the slightest idea that Isabel wasn't as happy as he. God, what blindness! He hadn't the remotest notion in those days that she really hated that inconvenient little house, that she thought the fat Nanny was ruining the babies, that she was desperately lonely, pining for new people, new music and pictures and so on. If they hadn't gone to that studio party at Moira Morrison's—if Moira Morrison hadn't said as they were leaving, "I'm going to rescue your wife, selfish man. She's like an exquisite little Titania"—if Isabel hadn't gone with Moira to Paris—if—if . . .

The train stopped at another station. Bettingford. Good heavens! They'd be there in ten minutes. William stuffed the papers back into his pockets; the young man opposite had long since disappeared. Now the other two got out. The late afternoon sun shone on women in cotton frocks and little sunburnt, barefoot children. It blazed on a silky yellow flower with coarse leaves which sprawled over a bank of rock. The air ruffling through the window smelled of the sea. Had Isabel the same crowd with her this week-end? wondered William.

And he remembered the holidays they used to have, the four of them, with a little farm girl, Rose, to look after the babies. Isabel wore a jersey and her hair in a plait; she looked about fourteen. Lord! how his nose used to peel! And the amount they ate, and the amount they slept in that immense feather bed with their feet locked together. . . . William couldn't help a grim smile as he thought of Isabel's horror if she knew the full extent of his sentimentality.

"Hillo, William!" She was at the station after all, standing just as he had imagined, apart from the others, and—William's heart leapt—she was alone.

"Hallo, Isabel!" William started. He thought she looked so beautiful that he had to say something. "You look very cool."

"Do I?" said Isabel. "I don't feel very cool. Come along; your horrid old train is late. The taxi's outside." She put her hand lightly on his arm as they passed the ticket collector. "We've all come to meet you," she said. "But we've left Bobby Kane at the sweetshop, to be called for."

"Oh!" said William. It was all he could say for the moment.

There in the glare waited the taxi, with Bill Hunt and Dennis Green sprawling on one side, their hats tilted over their faces, while on the other, Moira Morrison, in a bonnet like a huge strawberry, jumped up and down.

"No ice! No ice! No ice!" she shouted gaily.

And Dennis chimed in from under his hat: "*Only* to be had from the fishmonger's."

And Bill Hunt, emerging, added, "With *whole* fish in it."

"Oh, what a bore!" wailed Isabel. And she explained to William how they had been chasing round the town for ice while she waited for him. "Simply everything is running down the steep cliffs into the sea, beginning with the butter."

"We'll have to anoint ourselves with the butter," said Dennis. "May thy head, William, lack not ointment."

"Look here," said William, "how are we going to sit? I'd better get up by the driver."

"No, Bobby Kane's by the driver," said Isabel. "You're to sit between Moira and me." The taxi started. "What have you got in those mysterious parcels?"

"De-cap-i-tated heads!" said Bill Hunt, shuddering beneath his hat.

"Oh, fruit!" Isabel sounded very pleased. "Wise William! A melon and a pineapple. How too nice!"

"No, wait a bit," said William, smiling. But he really was anxious. "I brought them down for the kiddies."

"Oh, my dear!" Isabel laughed, and slipped her hand through his arm. "They'd be rolling in agonies if they were to eat them. No"— she patted his hand—"you must bring them something next time. I refuse to part with my pineapple."

"Cruel Isabel! Do let me smell it!" said Moira. She flung her arms across William appealingly. "Oh!" The strawberry bonnet fell forward: she sounded quite faint.

"Lady in Love with a Pineapple," said Dennis, as the taxi drew up before the little shop with a striped blind. Out came Bobby Kane, his arms full of little packets.

"I do hope they'll be good. I've chosen them because of the colors. There are some round things which look really too divine. And just look at this nougat," he cried ecstatically, "just look at it! It's a perfect little ballet."

But at that moment the shopman appeared. "Oh, I forgot. They're none of them paid for," said Bobby, looking frightened. Isabel gave the shopman a note, and Bobby was radiant again.

"Hallo, William! I'm sitting by the driver." And bare-headed, all in white, with his sleeves rolled up to the shoulders, he leapt into his place. "Avanti!" he cried. . . .

After tea the others went off to bathe, while William stayed and made his peace with the kiddies. But Johnny and Paddy were asleep; the rose-red glow had paled, bats were flying, and still the bathers had not returned. As William wandered downstairs, the maid crossed the hall carrying a lamp. He followed her into the sitting-room. It was a long room, colored yellow. On the wall opposite William some one had painted a young man, over life-size, with very wobbly legs, offering a wide-eyed daisy to a young woman who had one very short arm and one very long, thin one. Over the chairs and sofa there hung strips of black material, covered with big splashes like broken eggs, and everywhere one looked there seemed to be an ash-tray full of cigarette ends. William sat down in one of the arm-chairs. Nowadays,

when one felt with one hand down the sides, it wasn't to come upon
a sheep with three legs or a cow that had lost one horn, or a very fat
dove out of the Noah's Ark. One fished up yet another little paper-
covered book of smudged-looking poems. . . . He thought of the wad
of papers in his pocket, but he was too hungry and tired to read. The
door was open; sounds came from the kitchen. The servants were
talking as if they were alone in the house. Suddenly there came a loud
screech of laughter and an equally loud "Sh!" They had remembered
him. William got up and went through the French windows into the
garden, and as he stood there in the shadow he heard the bathers
coming up the sandy road; their voices rang through the quiet.

"I think it's up to Moira to use her little arts and wiles."

A tragic moan from Moira.

"We ought to have a gramophone for the week-ends that played
'The Maid of the Mountains.' "

"Oh no! Oh no!" cried Isabel's voice. "That's not fair to William.
Be nice to him, my children! He's only staying until to-morrow evening."

"Leave him to me," cried Bobby Kane. "I'm awfully good at looking after people."

The gate swung open and shut. William moved on the terrace;
they had seen him. "Hallo, William!" And Bobby Kane, flapping his
towel, began to leap and pirouette on the parched lawn. "Pity you
didn't come, William. The water was divine. And we all went to a
little pub afterwards and had sloe gin."

The others had reached the house. "I say, Isabel," called Bobby,
"would you like me to wear my Nijinsky dress to-night?"

"No," said Isabel, "nobody's going to dress. We're all starving.
William's starving, too. Come along, *mes amis,* let's begin with
sardines."

"I've found the sardines," said Moira, and she ran into the hall,
holding a box nigh in the air.

"A Lady with a Box of Sardines," said Dennis gravely.

"Well, William, and how's London?" asked Bill Hunt, drawing
the cork out of a bottle of whiskey.

"Oh, London's not much changed," answered William.

"Good old London," said Bobby, very hearty, spearing a sardine.

But a moment later William was forgotten. Moira Morrison began
wondering what color one's legs really were under water.

"Mine are the palest, palest mushroom color."

Bill and Dennis ate enormously. And Isabel filled glasses, and
changed plates, and found matches, smiling blissfully. At one moment she said, "I do wish, Bill, you'd paint it."

"Paint what?" said Bill loudly, stuffing his mouth with bread.

"Us," said Isabel, "round the table. It would be so fascinating in twenty years' time."

Bill screwed up his eyes and chewed. "Light's wrong," he said rudely, "far too much yellow"; and went on eating. And that seemed to charm Isabel, too.

But after supper they were all so tired they could do nothing but yawn until it was late enough to go to bed. . . .

It was not until William was waiting for his taxi the next afternoon that he found himself alone with Isabel. When he brought his suit-case down into the hall, Isabel left the others and went over to him. She stooped down and picked up the suit-case. "What a weight!" she said, and she gave a little awkward laugh. "Let me carry it! To the gate."

"No, why should you?" said William. "Of course not. Give it to me."

"Oh, please let me," said Isabel. "I want to, really." They walked together silently. William felt there was nothing to say now.

"There," said Isabel triumphantly, setting the suit-case down, and she looked anxiously along the sandy road. "I hardly seem to have seen you this time," she said breathlessly. "It's so short, isn't it? I feel you've only just come. Next time—" The taxi came into sight. "I hope they look after you properly in London. I'm so sorry the babies have been out all day, but Miss Neil had arranged it. They'll hate missing you. Poor William, going back to London." The taxi turned. "Good-bye!" She gave him a little hurried kiss; she was gone.

Fields, trees, hedges streamed by. They shook through the empty, blind-looking town, ground up the steep pull to the station.

The train was in. William made straight for a first-class smoker, flung back into the corner, but this time he let the papers alone. He folded his arms against the dull, persistent gnawing, and began in his mind to write a letter to Isabel.

The post was late as usual. They sat outside the house in long chairs under colored parasols. Only Bobby Kane lay on the turf at Isabel's feet. It was dull, stifling; the day drooped like a flag.

"Do you think there will be Mondays in Heaven?" asked Bobby childishly.

And Dennis murmured, "Heaven will be one long Monday."

But Isabel couldn't help wondering what had happened to the salmon they had for supper last night. She had meant to have fish mayonnaise for lunch and now . . .

Moira was asleep. Sleeping was her latest discovery. "It's *so* wonderful. One simply shuts one's eyes, that's all. It's *so* delicious."

When the old ruddy postman came beating along the sandy road on his tricycle one felt the handlebars ought to have been oars.

Bill Hunt put down his book. "Letters," he said complacently, and they all waited. But heartless postman—O malignant world! There was the only one, a fat one for Isabel. Not even a paper.

"And mine's only from William," said Isabel mournfully.

"From William—already?"

"He's sending you back your marriage lines as a gentle reminder."

"Does everybody have marriage lines? I thought they were only for servants."

"Pages and pages! Look at her! A Lady Reading a Letter," said Dennis.

My darling, precious Isabel. Pages and pages there were. As Isabel read on her feeling of astonishment changed to a stifled feeling. What on earth had induced William . . . ? How extraordinary it was. . . . What could have made him . . . ? She felt confused, more and more excited, even frightened. It was just like William. Was it? It was absurd, of course; it must be absurd, ridiculous. "Ha, ha, ha! Oh dear!" What was she to do? Isabel flung back in her chair and laughed till she couldn't stop laughing.

"Do, do tell us," said the others. "You must tell us."

"I'm longing to," gurgled Isabel. She sat up, gathered the letter, and waved it at them. "Gather round," she said. "Listen, it's too marvellous. A love-letter!"

"A love-letter! But how divine!" *Darling, precious Isabel.* But she had hardly begun before their laughter interrupted her.

"Go on, Isabel; it's perfect."

"It's the most marvellous find."

"Oh, do go on, Isabel!"

God forbid, my darling, that I should be a drag on your happiness.

"Oh, oh! oh!"

"Sh! sh! sh!"

And Isabel went on. When she reached the end they were hysterical; Bobby rolled on the turf and almost sobbed.

"You must let me have it just as it is, entire, for my new book," said Dennis firmly. "I shall give it a whole chapter."

"Oh, Isabel," moaned Moira, "that wonderful bit about holding you in his arms."

"I always thought those letters in divorce cases were made up. But they pale before this."

"Let me hold it. Let me read it, mine own self," said Bobby Kane.

But, to their surprise, Isabel crushed the letter in her hand. She was laughing no longer. She glanced quickly at them all; she looked exhausted. "No, not just now. Not just now," she stammered.

And before they could recover she had run into the house, through the hall, up the stairs into her bedroom. Down she sat on the side of the bed. "How vile, odious, abominable, vulgar," muttered Isabel. She pressed her eyes with her knuckles and rocked to and fro. And again she saw them, but not four, more like forty, laughing, sneering, jeering, stretching out their hands while she read them William's letter. Oh, what a loathesome thing to have done! How could she have done it? *God forbid, my darling, that I should be a drag on your happiness.* William! Isabel pressed her face into the pillow. But she felt that even the grave bedroom knew her for what she was, shallow, tinkling, vain. . . .

Presently from the garden below there came voices.

"Isabel, we're all going for a bathe. Do come!"

"Come, thou wife of William!"

"Call her once before you go, call once yet!"

Isabel sat up. Now was the moment, now she must decide. Would she go with them, or stay here and write to William? Which, which should it be? "I must make up my mind." Oh, but could there be any question? Of course she would stay here and write.

"Titania!" piped Moira.

"Isa-bel?"

No, it was too difficult. "I'll—I'll go with them, and write to William later. Some other time. Later. Not now. But I shall *certainly* write," thought Isabel hurriedly.

And laughing in the new way, she ran down the stairs.

COMMENT AND QUESTIONS

I. Like many of Katherine Mansfield's stories, this story uses a shifting point of view. In the first two sections, the reader views events through William's eyes and mind; the last section is told largely from Isabel's point of view. Why does the author take up residence in William's mind to give the necessary background for the story, instead of giving it through Isabel's mind or by means of omniscient-author statements?

II. The handling of exposition in the first section is admirable. Study the complex interweaving of present action, present scene, reflection, and flashback. What do we learn from this first section about (*a*) William's relationship with his children; (*b*) the origin of the dull gnawing in his breast; (*c*) his feeling about Isabel; (*d*) his recent relationship with her; (*e*) his attitude toward her friends; (*f*) his business, and his financial situation; (*g*) his own tastes and character?

III. How is Isabel's laughing "in the new way" used in the story?

IV. Note the skillful brief descriptions of what William sees from the train, and of the sitting-room in his new house. How do the descriptions communicate his state of mind as well as the external scenes?

V. What characteristics do Isabel's friends, collectively, reveal, and how do they reveal the characteristics? How are the four friends, especially the three men, individualized? What is the profession, or at least the avocation, of each?

VI. This is both a psychological and an action story: the chief interest is in what goes on inside the characters and in why they behave as they do, but their feelings and impulses are translated into overt action. William's buying the melon and the pineapple, Isabel's carrying the suitcase, William's writing the letter, and Isabel's reading the letter aloud are all actions which express states of mind and clarify those states of mind for the reader without author-explanation. What feeling or feelings are expressed by each of these four actions?

VII. What is the logical preparation in the story for Isabel's reading the letter aloud?

VIII. The author does not directly pass judgment on Isabel. By what means is the reader led to condemn her?

IX. This story is in one sense unfinished: the relationship of William and Isabel is left suspended at the end. In an artistic sense, the story is very deftly finished by suggestion of Isabel's future course of action. What is she going to do? How do you know?

IN ANOTHER COUNTRY *

ERNEST HEMINGWAY

Ernest Hemingway is a well-known American novelist and short-story writer whose deliberately simple style, understatement of emotion, and narrative technique have been widely imitated by twentieth-century writers of the "hard-boiled" school. Hemingway's best novels are *The Sun Also Rises, Farewell to Arms,* and *For Whom the Bell Tolls.* "In Another Coun-

* Reprinted from *Men without Women* by Ernest Hemingway; copyright, 1926, 1927, by Charles Scribner's Sons; used by permission of the publishers.

try," one of his stories of World War I, was published in *Men Without Women* in 1926.

———◇———

In the fall the war was always there, but we did not go to it any more. It was cold in the fall in Milan and the dark came very early. Then the electric lights came on, and it was pleasant along the streets looking in the windows. There was much game hanging outside the shops, and the snow powdered in the fur of the foxes and the wind blew their tails. The deer hung stiff and heavy and empty, and small birds blew in the wind and the wind turned their feathers. It was a cold fall and the wind came down from the mountains.

We were all at the hospital every afternoon, and there were different ways of walking across the town through the dusk to the hospital. Two of the ways were alongside canals, but they were long. Always, though, you crossed a bridge across a canal to enter the hospital. There was a choice of three bridges. On one of them a woman sold roasted chestnuts. It was warm, standing in front of her charcoal fire, and the chestnuts were warm afterward in your pocket. The hospital was very old and very beautiful, and you entered through a gate and walked across a courtyard and out a gate on the other side. There were usually funerals starting from the courtyard. Beyond the old hospital were the new brick pavilions, and there we met every afternoon and were all very polite and interested in what was the matter, and sat in the machines that were to make so much difference.

The doctor came up to the machine where I was sitting and said: "What did you like best to do before the war? Did you practise a sport?"

I said: "Yes, football."

"Good," he said. "You will be able to play football again better than ever."

My knee did not bend and the leg dropped straight from the knee to the ankle without a calf, and the machine was to bend the knee and make it move as in riding a tricycle. But it did not bend yet, and instead the machine lurched when it came to the bending part. The doctor said: "That will all pass. You are a fortunate young man. You will play football again like a champion."

In the next machine was a major who had a little hand like a baby's. He winked at me when the doctor examined his hand, which was between two leather straps that bounced up and down and flapped the stiff fingers, and said: "And will I too play football, captain-doctor?" He had been a very great fencer, and before the war the greatest fencer in Italy.

The doctor went to his office in a back room and brought a photograph which showed a hand that had been withered almost as small as the major's, before it had taken a machine course, and after was a little larger. The major held the photograph with his good hand and looked at it very carefully. "A wound?" he asked.

"An industrial accident," the doctor said.

"Very interesting, very interesting," the major said, and handed it back to the doctor.

"You have confidence?"

"No," said the major.

There were three boys who came each day who were about the same age I was. They were all three from Milan, and one of them was to be a lawyer, and one was to be a painter, and one had intended to be a soldier, and after we were finished with the machines, sometimes we walked back together to the Café Cova, which was next door to the Scala. We walked the short way through the communist quarter because we were four together. The people hated us because we were officers, and from a wine-shop some one called out, "A basso gli ufficiali!" as we passed. Another boy who walked with us sometimes and made us five wore a black silk handkerchief across his face because he had no nose then and his face was to be rebuilt. He had gone out to the front from the military academy and been wounded within an hour after he had gone into the front line for the first time. They rebuilt his face, but he came from a very old family and they could never get the nose exactly right. He went to South America and worked in a bank. But this was a long time ago, and then we did not any of us know how it was going to be afterward. We only knew then that there was always the war, but that we were not going to it any more.

We all had the same medals, except the boy with the black silk bandage across his face, and he had not been at the front long enough to get any medals. The tall boy with a very pale face who was to be a lawyer had been a lieutenant of Arditi and had three medals of the sort we each had only one of. He had lived a very long time with death and was a little detached. We were all a little detached, and there was nothing that held us together except that we met every afternoon at the hospital. Although, as we walked to the Cova through the tough part of town, walking in the dark, with light and singing coming out of the wine-shops, and sometimes having to walk into the street when the men and women would crowd together on the sidewalk so that we would have had to jostle them to get by, we felt held together by there being something that had happened that they, the people who disliked us, did not understand.

We ourselves all understood the Cova, where it was rich and warm and not too brightly lighted, and noisy and smoky at certain hours, and there were always girls at the tables and the illustrated papers on a rack on the wall. The girls at the Cova were very patriotic, and I found that the most patriotic people in Italy were the café girls— and I believe they are still patriotic.

The boys at first were very polite about my medals and asked me what I had done to get them. I showed them the papers, which were written in very beautiful language and full of *fratellanza* and *abnegazione,* but which really said, with the adjectives removed, that I had been given the medals because I was an American. After that their manner changed a little toward me, although I was their friend against outsiders. I was a friend, but I was never really one of them after they had read the citations, because it had been different with them and they had done very different things to get their medals. I had been wounded, it was true; but we all knew that being wounded, after all, was really an accident. I was never ashamed of the ribbons, though, and sometimes, after the cocktail hour, I would imagine myself having done all the things they had done to get their medals; but walking home at night through the empty streets with the cold wind and all the shops closed, trying to keep near the street lights, I knew that I would never have done such things, and I was very much afraid to die, and often lay in bed at night by myself, afraid to die and wondering how I would be when I went back to the front again.

The three with the medals were like hunting-hawks; and I was not a hawk, although I might seem a hawk to those who had never hunted; they, the three, knew better and so we drifted apart. But I stayed good friends with the boy who had been wounded his first day at the front, because he would never know now how he would have turned out; so he could never be accepted either, and I liked him because I thought perhaps he would not have turned out to be a hawk either.

The major, who had been the great fencer, did not believe in bravery, and spent much time while we sat in the machines correcting my grammar. He had complimented me on how I spoke Italian, and we talked together very easily. One day I had said that Italian seemed such an easy language to me that I could not take a great interest in it; everything was so easy to say. "Ah yes," the major said. "Why, then, do you not take up the use of grammar?" So we took up the use of grammar, and soon Italian was such a difficult language that I was afraid to talk to him until I had the grammar straight in my mind.

The major came very regularly to the hospital. I do not think he ever missed a day, although I am sure he did not believe in the machines. There was a time when none of us believed in the machines, and one day the major said it was all nonsense. The machines were new then and it was we who were to prove them. It was an idiotic idea, he said, "a theory, like another." I had not learned my grammar, and he said I was a stupid impossible disgrace, and he was a fool to have bothered with me. He was a small man and he sat straight up in his chair with his right hand thrust into the machine and looked straight ahead at the wall while the straps thumped up and down with his fingers in them.

"What will you do when the war is over if it is over?" he asked me. "Speak grammatically!"

"I will go to the States."

"Are you married?"

"No, but I hope to be."

"The more of a fool you are," he said. He seemed very angry. "A man must not marry."

"Why, Signor Maggiore?"

"Don't call me 'Signor Maggiore.' "

"Why must not a man marry?"

"He cannot marry. He cannot marry," he said angrily. "If he is to lose everything, he should not place himself in a position to lose that. He should not place himself in a position to lose. He should find things he cannot lose."

He spoke very angrily and bitterly, and looked straight ahead while he talked.

"But why should he necessarily lose it?"

"He'll lose it," the major said. He was looking at the wall. Then he looked down at the machine and jerked his little hand out from between the straps and slapped it hard against his thigh. "He'll lose it," he almost shouted. "Don't argue with me!" Then he called to the attendant who ran the machines. "Come and turn this damned thing off."

He went back into the other room for the light treatment and the massage. Then I heard him ask the doctor if he might use his telephone and he shut the door. When he came back into the room, I was sitting in another machine. He was wearing his cape and had his cap on, and he came directly toward my machine and put his arm on my shoulder.

"I am so sorry," he said, and patted me on the shoulder with his good hand. "I would not be rude. My wife has just died. You must forgive me."

"Oh—" I said, feeling sick for him. "I am *so* sorry."

He stood there biting his lower lip. "It is very difficult," he said. "I cannot resign myself."

He looked straight past me and out through the window. Then he began to cry. "I am utterly unable to resign myself," he said and choked. And then crying, his head up looking at nothing, carrying himself straight and soldierly, with tears on both his cheeks and biting his lips, he walked past the machines and out the door.

The doctor told me that the major's wife, who was very young and whom he had not married until he was definitely invalided out of the war, had died of pneumonia. She had been sick only a few days. No one expected her to die. The major did not come to the hospital for three days. Then he came at the usual hour, wearing a black band on the sleeve of his uniform. When he came back, there were large framed photographs around the wall, of all sorts of wounds before and after they had been cured by the machines. In front of the machine the major used were three photographs of hands like his that were completely restored. I do not know where the doctor got them. I always understood we were the first to use the machines. The photographs did not make much difference to the major because he only looked out of the window.

COMMENT AND QUESTIONS

I. This story is likely, on first reading, to seem rambling and un-unified. It introduces the major early, leaves him while the first-person narrator talks about himself and his four friends, and then returns sharply to the major for the climax of the story. The narrator, who seems at first to be the main character, is really a minor character; this is the major's story, told from a point of view which gives it a sudden and unexpected impact. Close study of the story reveals the purpose of the apparently rambling narrative: it builds a physical and psychological setting in which the major's personal tragedy becomes more vivid and tragic than the general background of accepted tragedy which is the result of war. The narrator and his friends are, as a result of their war experience and their wounds, detached from normal life—even from the war. They live and move along accustomed routes to the hospital and to the Café Cova, but they are almost as dead as the dead game hanging in the fall wind. The narrator is physically, and all of them are psychologically "in another country." Enumerate the ways in which they are set apart from normal human experience. How is the narrator further set apart from the three boys from Milan? The major, however, is not detached and isolated, in spite of his wound—a wound very significant to the best fencer in Italy. How is the major's interest in life and in keeping his connections with normal human experience revealed?

II. The calculated simplicity of Hemingway's style is produced, technically, by lack of subordination and apparently artless repetition. Re-read the first two paragraphs of this story, noticing the cumulative effect of the simple "and-and" sentences and the rhythmic repetition of phrases and words. Part of the effect comes from the contrast between the simple expression and the grim, dramatic content; for example, the first sentence of the story, "In the fall the war was always there, but we did not go to it any more," is an understatement of the ideas that the war was still going on and was always present in the men's minds, but that they had been wounded. Point out other examples in the story of this kind of understatement. The short, choppy sentences in the last paragraph are another device for simplicity which Hemingway often uses, especially in his early fiction. (It is not advisable to imitate this simplicity; even in the hands of Hemingway, the master, it sometimes becomes mechanical or childish.)

III. Hemingway's dialogue has been much admired. What can you tell, from the little dialogue there is in this story, about the techniques he uses?

IV. Do you understand the major's anger in the climactic scene? What universal human psychology does it reveal?

V. The phrase "feeling sick for him" (in the paragraph " 'Oh—' " I said, feeling sick for him. " 'I am *so* sorry.' ") is an explicit expression of emotion which Hemingway does not often allow himself. Is it necessary in the story? What would be the effect of its omission?

VI. What is the significance of the major's saying "I cannot resign myself"?

VII. What is the conflict in the story?

VIII. What is the theme?

THE BEAR *

WILLIAM FAULKNER

William Faulkner, winner of the 1949 Nobel Prize for Literature, is regarded by many critics as the most brilliant living American novelist and short-story writer. Among his powerful novels of the South are *The Sound and the Fury, As I Lay Dying, Light in August, Absalom, Absalom,* and *Intruder in the Dust.* "The Bear" was published in *The Saturday Evening Post* in 1942.

———&———

He was ten. But it had already begun, long before that day when at last he wrote his age in two figures and he saw for the first time the camp where his father and Major de Spain and old General Compson and the others spent two weeks each November and two weeks again each June. He had already inherited then, without ever having seen it, the tremendous bear with one trap-ruined foot which, in an area almost a hundred miles deep, had earned itself a name, a definite designation like a living man.

He had listened to it for years: the long legend of corncribs rifled, of shotes and grown pigs and even calves carried bodily into the woods and devoured, of traps and deadfalls overthrown and dogs mangled and slain, and shotgun and even rifle charges delivered at point-blank range and with no more effect than so many peas blown through a tube by a boy—a corridor of wreckage and destruction beginning back before he was born, through which sped, not fast but rather with the ruthless and irresistible deliberation of a locomotive, the shaggy tremendous shape.

It ran in his knowledge before he ever saw it. It looked and towered in his dreams before he even saw the unaxed woods where it left its crooked print, shaggy, huge, red-eyed, not malevolent but just big—too big for the dogs which tried to bay it, for the horses which tried to ride it down, for the men and the bullets they fired into it, too big for the very country which was its constricting scope. He seemed to see it entire with a child's complete divination before he ever laid eyes on either—the doomed wilderness whose edges were being constantly and punily gnawed at by men with axes and plows who feared it because it was wilderness, men myriad and nameless even to one another in the land where the old bear had earned a name, through which ran not even a mortal animal but an anachronism, indomitable and invincible, out of an old dead time, a phantom, epitome and apotheosis of the old wild life at which the puny humans swarmed and hacked in a fury of abhorrence and fear, like pygmies about the ankles of a drowsing elephant: the old bear solitary, indomitable and alone, widowered, childless, and absolved of mortality—old Priam reft of his old wife and having outlived all his sons.

Until he was ten, each November he would watch the wagon containing the dogs and the bedding and food and guns and his father and Tennie's Jim, the Negro, and Sam Fathers, the Indian, son of a slave woman and a Chickasaw chief, depart on the road to town, to Jefferson, where Major de Spain and the others would join them. To the boy, at seven, eight, and nine, they were not going into the Big Bottom to hunt bear and deer, but to keep yearly rendezvous with the bear which they did not even intend to kill. Two weeks later they would return, with no trophy, no head and skin. He had not expected it. He had not even been afraid it would be in the wagon. He believed that even after he was ten and his father would let him go too, for those two weeks in November, he would merely make another one, along with his father and Major de Spain and General Compson and the others, the dogs which feared to bay at it and the rifles and shotguns which failed even to bleed it, in the yearly pageant of the old bear's furious immortality.

Then he heard the dogs. It was in the second week of his first time in the camp. He stood with Sam Fathers against a big oak beside the faint crossing where they had stood each dawn for nine days now, hearing the dogs. He had heard them once before, one morning last week—a murmur, sourceless, echoing through the wet woods, swelling presently into separate voices which he could recognize and call by name. He had raised and cocked the gun as Sam told him and stood motionless again while the uproar, the invisible course, swept up and past and faded; it seemed to him that he could actually see the deer, the buck, blond, smoke-colored, elongated with speed, fleeing, vanishing, the woods, the gray solitude, still ringing even when the cries of the dogs had died away.

"Now let the hammers down," Sam said.

"You knew they were not coming here too," he said.

"Yes," Sam said. "I want you to learn how to do when you didn't shoot. It's after the chance for the bear or the deer has done already come and gone that men and dogs get killed."

"Anyway," he said, "it was just a deer."

Then on the tenth morning he heard the dogs again. And he

readied the too-long, too-heavy gun as Sam had taught him, before Sam even spoke. But this time it was no deer, no ringing chorus of dogs running strong on a free scent, but a moiling yapping an octave too high, with something more than indecision and even abjectness in it, not even moving very fast, taking a long time to pass completely out of hearing, leaving then somewhere in the air that echo, thin, slightly hysterical, abject, almost grieving, with no sense of a fleeing, unseen, smoke-colored, grass-eating shape ahead of it, and Sam, who had taught him first of all to cock the gun and take position where he could see everywhere and then never move again, had himself moved up beside him; he could hear Sam breathing at his shoulder, and he could see the arched curve of the old man's inhaling nostrils.

"Hah," Sam said. "Not even running. Walking."

"Old Ben!" the boy said. "But up here!" he cried. "Way up here!"

"He do it every year," Sam said. "Once. Maybe to see who in camp this time, if he can shoot or not. Whether we got the dog yet that can bay and hold him. He'll take them to the river, then he'll send them back home. We may as well go back too; see how they look when they come back to camp."

When they reached the camp the hounds were already there, ten of them crouching back under the kitchen, the boy and Sam squatting to peer back into the obscurity where they had huddled, quiet, the eyes luminous, glowing at them and vanishing, and no sound, only that effluvium of something more than dog, stronger than dog and not just animal, just beast, because still there had been nothing in front of that abject and almost painful yapping save the solitude, the wilderness, so that when the eleventh hound came in at noon and with all the others watching—even old Uncle Ash, who called himself first a cook—Sam daubed the tattered ear and the raked shoulder with turpentine and axle grease, to the boy it was still no living creature, but the wilderness which, leaning for the moment down, had patted lightly once the hound's temerity.

"Just like a man," Sam said. "Just like folks. Put off as long as she could having to be brave, knowing all the time that sooner or later she would have to be brave to keep on living with herself, and knowing all the time beforehand what was going to happen to her when she done it."

That afternoon, himself on the one-eyed wagon mule which did not mind the smell of blood nor, as they told him, of bear, and with Sam on the other one, they rode for more than three hours through the rapid, shortening winter day. They followed no path, no trail even that he could see; almost at once they were in a country which he had never seen before. Then he knew why Sam had made him ride the mule which would not spook. The sound one stopped short and tried to whirl and bolt even as Sam got down, blowing its breath, jerking and wrenching at the rein, while Sam held it, coaxing it forward with his voice, since he could not risk tying it, drawing it forward while the boy got down from the marred one.

Then, standing beside Sam in the gloom of the dying afternoon, he looked down at the rotted over-turned log, gutted and scored with claw marks and, in the wet earth beside it, the print of the enormous warped two-toed foot. He knew now what he had smelled when he peered under the kitchen where the dogs huddled. He realized for the first time that the bear which had run in his listening and loomed in his dreams since before he could remember to the contrary, and which, therefore, must have existed in the listening and dreams of his father and Major de Spain and even old General Compson, too, before they began to remember in their turn, was a mortal animal, and that if they had departed for the camp each November without any actual hope of bringing its trophy back, it was not because it could not be slain, but because so far they had had no actual hope to.

"Tomorrow," he said.

"We'll try tomorrow," Sam said. "We ain't got the dog yet."

"We've got eleven. They ran him this morning."

"It won't need but one," Sam said. "He ain't here. Maybe he ain't nowhere. The only other way will be for him to run by accident over somebody that has a gun."

"That wouldn't be me," the boy said. "It will be Walter or Major or—"

"It might," Sam said. "You watch close in the morning. Because he's smart. That's how come he has lived this long. If he gets hemmed up and has to pick out somebody to run over, he will pick out you."

"How?" the boy said. "How will he know—" He ceased. "You mean he already knows me, that I ain't never been here before, ain't had time to find out yet whether I—" He ceased again, looking at Sam, the old man whose face revealed nothing until it smiled. He said humbly, not even amazed, "It was me he was watching. I don't reckon he did need to come but once."

The next morning they left the camp three hours before daylight. They rode this time because it was too far to walk, even the dogs in the wagon; again the first gray light found him in a place which he had never seen before, where Sam had placed him and told him to stay and then departed. With the gun which was too big for him, which did not even belong to him, but to Major de Spain, and which he had fired only once—at a stump on the first day, to learn the recoil and how to reload it—he stood against a gum tree beside a little bayou whose black still water crept without movement out of a canebrake and crossed a small clearing and into cane again, where, invisible, a bird—the big woodpecker called Lord-to-God by Negroes —clattered at a dead limb.

It was a stand like any other, dissimilar only in incidentals to the one where he had stood each morning for ten days; a territory new to him, yet no less familiar than that other one which, after almost two weeks, he had come to believe he knew a little—the same solitude, the same loneliness through which human beings had merely passed without altering it, leaving no mark, no scar, which looked exactly as it must have looked when the first ancestor of Sam Fathers' Chickasaw predecessors crept into it and looked about, club or stone ax or bone arrow drawn and poised; different only because, squatting at the edge of the kitchen, he smelled the hounds huddled and cringing beneath it and saw the raked ear and shoulder of the one who, Sam said, had had to be brave once in order to live with herself, and saw yesterday in the earth beside the gutted log the print of the living foot.

He heard no dogs at all. He never did hear them. He only heard the drumming of the woodpecker stop short off and knew that the bear was looking at him. He never saw it. He did not know whether it was in front of him or behind him. He did not move, holding the useless gun, which he had not even had warning to cock and which even now he did not cock, tasting in his saliva that taint as of brass which he knew now because he had smelled it when he peered under the kitchen at the huddled dogs.

Then it was gone. As abruptly as it had ceased, the woodpecker's dry, monotonous clatter set up again, and after a while he even believed he could hear the dogs—a murmur, scarce a sound even, which he had probably been hearing for some time before he even remarked it, drifting into hearing and then out again, dying away. They came nowhere near him. If it was a bear they ran, it was another bear. It was Sam himself who came out of the cane and crossed the bayou, followed by the injured bitch of yesterday. She was almost at heel, like a bird dog, making no sound. She came and crouched against his leg, trembling, staring off into the cane.

"I didn't see him," he said. "I didn't, Sam!"

"I know it," Sam said. "He done the looking. You didn't hear him neither, did you?"

"No," the boy said. "I—"

"He's smart," Sam said. "Too smart." He looked down at the hound, trembling faintly and steadily against the boy's knee. From the raked shoulder a few drops of fresh blood oozed and clung.

"Too big. We ain't got the dog yet. But maybe someday. Maybe not next time. But someday."

So I must see him, he thought. *I must look at him.* Otherwise, it seemed to him that it would go on like this forever, as it had gone on with his father and Major de Spain, who was older than his father, and even with old General Compson, who had been old enough to be a brigade commander in 1865. Otherwise, it would go on so forever, next time and next time, after and after and after. It seemed to him that he could never see the two of them, himself and the bear, shadowy in the limbo from which time emerged, becoming time; the old bear absolved of mortality and himself partaking, sharing a little of it, enough of it. And he knew now what he had smelled in the huddled dogs and tasted in his saliva. He recognized fear. *So I will have to see him,* he thought, without dread or even hope. *I will have to look at him.*

It was in June of the next year. He was eleven. They were in camp again, celebrating Major de Spain's and General Compson's birthdays. Although the one had been born in September and the other in the depth of winter and in another decade, they had met for two weeks to fish and shoot squirrels and turkey and run coons and wildcats with the dogs at night. That is, he and Boon Hoggenback and the Negroes fished and shot squirrels and ran the coons and cats, because the proved hunters, not only Major de Spain and old General Compson, who spent those two weeks sitting in a rocking chair before a tremendous iron pot of Brunswick stew, stirring and tasting, with old Ash to quarrel with about how he was making it and Tennie's Jim to pour whiskey from the demijohn into the tin dipper from which he drank it, but even the boy's father and Walter Ewell, who were still young enough, scorned such, other than shooting the wild gobblers with pistols for wagers on their marksmanship.

Or, that is, his father and the others believed he was hunting squirrels. Until the third day, he thought that Sam Fathers believed that too. Each morning he would leave the camp right after breakfast. He had his own gun now, a Christmas present. He went back to the tree beside the bayou where he had stood that morning. Using the compass which old General Compson had given him, he ranged from that point; he was teaching himself to be a better-than-fair woodsman without knowing he was doing it. On the second day he even found the gutted log where he had first seen the crooked print. It was almost completely crumbled now, healing with unbelievable speed, a passionate and almost visible relinquishment, back into the earth from which the tree had grown.

He ranged the summer woods now, green with gloom; if anything, actually dimmer than in November's gray dissolution, where, even at noon, the sun fell only in intermittent dappling upon the earth, which never completely dried out and which crawled with snakes— moccasins and water snakes and rattlers, themselves the color of the dappling gloom, so that he would not always see them until they moved, returning later and later, first day, second day, passing in the twilight of the third evening the little log pen enclosing the log stable where Sam was putting up the horses for the night.

"You ain't looked right yet," Sam said.

He stopped. For a moment he didn't answer. Then he said peacefully, in a peaceful rushing burst as when a boy's miniature dam in a little brook gives way, "All right. But how? I went to the bayou. I even found that log again. I—"

"I reckon that was all right. Likely he's been watching you. You never saw his foot?"

"I," the boy said—"I didn't—I never thought—"

"It's the gun," Sam said. He stood beside the fence, motionless— the old man, the Indian, in the battered faded overalls and the five-cent straw hat which in the Negro's race had been the badge of his enslavement and was now the regalia of his freedom. The camp— the clearing, the house, the barn and its tiny lot with which Major de Spain in his turn had scratched punily and evanescently at the wilderness—faded in the dusk, back into the immemorial darkness of the woods. *The gun,* the boy thought. *The gun.*

"Be scared," Sam said. "You can't help that. But don't be afraid. Ain't nothing in the woods going to hurt you unless you corner it, or it smells that you are afraid. A bear or a deer, too, has got to be scared of a coward the same as a brave man has got to be."

The gun, the boy thought.

"You will have to choose," Sam said.

He left the camp before daylight, long before Uncle Ash would wake in his quilts on the kitchen floor and start the fire for breakfast. He had only the compass and a stick for snakes. He could go almost a mile before he would begin to need the compass. He sat on a log, the invisible compass in his invisible hand, while the secret night sounds, fallen still at his movements, scurried again and then ceased for good, and the owls ceased and gave over to the waking of day birds, and he could see the compass. Then he went fast yet still quietly; he was becoming better and better as a woodsman, still without having yet realized it.

He jumped a doe and a fawn at sunrise, walked them out of the bed, close enough to see them—the crash of undergrowth, the white scut, the fawn scudding behind her faster than he had believed it could run. He was hunting right, upwind, as Sam had taught him; not that it mattered now. He had left the gun; of his own will and relinquishment he had accepted not a gambit, not a choice, but a condition in which not only the bear's heretofore inviolable anonymity but all the old rules and balances of hunter and hunted had been abrogated. He would not even be afraid, not even in the moment when the fear would take him completely—blood, skin, bowels, bones, memory from the long time before it became his memory— all save that thin, clear, immortal lucidity which alone differed him from this bear and from all the other bear and deer he would ever kill in the humility and pride of his skill and endurance, to which Sam had spoken when he leaned in the twilight on the lot fence yesterday.

By noon he was far beyond the little bayou, farther into the new and alien country than he had ever been. He was traveling now not only by the compass but by the old, heavy, biscuit-thick silver watch which had belonged to his grandfather. When he stopped at last, it was for the first time since he had risen from the log at dawn when he could see the compass. It was far enough. He had left the camp nine hours ago; nine hours from now, dark would have already been an hour old. But he didn't think that. He thought, *All right. Yes. But what?* and stood for a moment, alien and small in the green and topless solitude, answering his own question before it had formed and ceased. It was the watch, the compass, the stick—the three lifeless mechanicals with which for nine hours he had fended the wilderness off; he hung the watch and compass carefully on a bush and leaned the stick beside them and relinquished completely to it.

He had not been going very fast for the last two or three hours. He went no faster now, since distance would not matter even if he could have gone fast. And he was trying to keep a bearing on the tree where he had left the compass, trying to complete a circle which would bring him back to it or at least intersect itself, since direction would not matter now either. But the tree was not there, and he did as Sam had schooled him—made the next circle in the opposite direction, so that the two patterns would bisect somewhere, but crossing no print of his own feet, finding the tree at last, but in the wrong place—no bush, no compass, no watch—and the tree not even the tree, because there was a down log beside it and he did what Sam Fathers had told him was the next thing and the last.

As he sat down on the log he saw the crooked print—the warped, tremendous, two-toed indentation which, even as he watched it, filled with water. As he looked up, the wilderness coalesced, solidified—

the glade, the tree he sought, the bush, the watch and the compass glinting where a ray of sunshine touched them. Then he saw the bear. It did not emerge, appear; it was just there, immobile, solid, fixed in the hot dappling of the green and windless noon, not as big as he had dreamed it, but as big as he had expected it, bigger, dimensionless, against the dappled obscurity, looking at him where he sat quietly on the log and looked back at it.

Then it moved. It made no sound. It did not hurry. It crossed the glade, walking for an instant into the full glare of the sun; when it reached the other side it stopped again and looked back at him across one shoulder while his quiet breathing inhaled and exhaled three times.

Then it was gone. It didn't walk into the woods, the undergrowth. It faded, sank back into the wilderness as he had watched a fish, a huge old bass, sink and vanish into the dark depths of its pool without even any movement of its fins.

He thought, *It will be next fall.* But it was not next fall, nor the next nor the next. He was fourteen then. He had killed his buck, and Sam Fathers had marked his face with the hot blood, and in the next year he killed a bear. But even before that accolade he had become as competent in the woods as many grown men with the same experience; by his fourteenth year he was a better woodsman than most grown men with more. There was no territory within thirty miles of the camp that he did not know—bayou, ridge, brake, landmark, tree and path. He could have led anyone to any point in it without deviation, and brought them out again. He knew the game trails that even Sam Fathers did not know; in his thirteenth year he found a buck's bedding place, and unbeknown to his father he borrowed Walter Ewell's rifle and lay in wait at dawn and killed the buck when it walked back to the bed, as Sam had told him how the old Chickasaw fathers did.

But not the old bear, although by now he knew its footprints better than he did his own, and not only the crooked one. He could see any one of the three sound ones and distinguish it from any other, and not only by its size. There were other bears within these thirty miles which left tracks almost as large, but this was more than that. If Sam Fathers had been his mentor and the back-yard rabbits and squirrels at home his kindergarten, then the wilderness the old bear ran was his college, the old male bear itself, so long unwifed and childless as to have become its own ungendered progenitor, was his alma mater. But he never saw it.

He could find the crooked print now almost whenever he liked, fifteen or ten or five miles, or sometimes nearer the camp than that. Twice while on stand during the three years he heard the dogs strike its trail by accident; on the second time they jumped it seemingly, the voices high, abject, almost human in hysteria, as on that first morning two years ago. But not the bear itself. He would remember that noon three years ago, the glade, himself and the bear fixed during that moment in the windless and dappled blaze, and it would seem to him that it had never happened, that he had dreamed that too. But it had happened. They had looked at each other, they had emerged from the wilderness old as earth, synchronized to the instant by something more than the blood that moved the flesh and bones which bore them, and touched, pledged something, affirmed, something more lasting than the frail web of bones and flesh which any accident could obliterate.

Then he saw it again. Because of the very fact that he thought of nothing else, he had forgotten to look for it. He was still hunting with Walter Ewell's rifle. He saw it cross the end of a long blowdown, a corridor where a tornado had swept, rushing through rather than over the tangle of trunks and branches as a locomotive would have, faster than he had ever believed it could move, almost as fast as a deer even, because a deer would have spent most of that time in the air, faster than he could bring the rifle sights up with it. And now he knew what had been wrong during all the three years. He sat on a log, shaking and trembling as if he had never seen the woods before nor anything that ran them, wondering with incredulous amazement how he could have forgotten the very thing which Sam Fathers had told him and which the bear itself had proved the next day and had now returned after three years to reaffirm.

And now he knew what Sam Fathers had meant about the right dog, a dog in which size would mean less than nothing. So when he returned alone in April—school was out then, so that the sons of farmers could help with the land's planting, and at last his father had granted him permission, on his promise to be back in four days —he had the dog. It was his own, a mongrel of the sort called by Negroes a fyce, a ratter, itself not much bigger than a rat and possessing that bravery which had long since stopped being courage and had become foolhardiness.

It did not take four days. Alone again, he found the trail on the first morning. It was not a stalk; it was an ambush. He timed the meeting almost as if it were an appointment with a human being. Himself holding the fyce muffled in a feed sack and Sam Fathers with two of the hounds on a piece of a plowline rope, they lay down wind of the trail at dawn of the second morning. They were so close that the bear turned without even running, as if in surprised amazement at the shrill and frantic uproar of the released fyce, turning at bay against the trunk of a tree, on its hind feet; it seemed to the boy that it would never stop rising, taller and taller, and even the two hounds seemed to take a desperate and despairing courage from the fyce, following it as it went in.

Then he realized that the fyce was actually not going to stop. He flung, threw the gun away, and ran; when he overtook and grasped the frantically pin-wheeling little dog, it seemed to him that he was directly under the bear.

He could smell it, strong and hot and rank. Sprawling, he looked up to where it loomed and towered over him like a cloudburst and colored like a thunderclap, quite familiar, peacefully and even lucidly familiar, until he remembered: This was the way he had used to dream about it. Then it was gone. He didn't see it go. He knelt, holding the frantic fyce with both hands, hearing the abashed wailing of the hounds drawing farther and farther away, until Sam came up. He carried the gun. He laid it down quietly beside the boy and stood looking down at him.

"You've done seed him twice now with a gun in your hands," he said. "This time you couldn't have missed him."

The boy rose. He still held the fyce. Even in his arms and clear of the ground, it yapped frantically, straining and surging after the fading uproar of the two hounds like a tangle of wire springs. He was panting a little, but he was neither shaking nor trembling now.

"Neither could you!" he said. "You had the gun! Neither did you!"

"And you didn't shoot," his father said. "How close were you?"

"I don't know, sir," he said. "There was a big wood tick inside his right hind leg. I saw that. But I didn't have the gun then."

"But you didn't shoot when you had the gun," his father said. "Why?"

But he didn't answer, and his father didn't wait for him to, rising and crossing the room, across the pelt of the bear which the boy had killed two years ago and the larger one which his father had killed before he was born, to the bookcase beneath the mounted head of the boy's first buck. It was the room which his father called the office, from which all the plantation business was transacted; in it for the fourteen years of his life he had heard the best of all talking. Major de Spain would be there and sometimes old General Compson, and Walter Ewell and Boon Hoggenback and Sam Fathers and Tennie's Jim, too, were hunters, knew the woods and what ran them.

He would hear it, not talking himself but listening—the wilderness, the big woods, bigger and older than any recorded document of white man fatuous enough to believe he had bought any fragment of it or Indian ruthless enough to pretend that any fragment of it had been his to convey. It was of the men, not white nor black nor red, but men, hunters with the will and hardihood to endure and the humility and skill to survive, and the dogs and the bear and deer juxtaposed and reliefed against it, ordered and compelled by and within the wilderness in the ancient and unremitting contest by the ancient and immitigable rules which voided all regrets and brooked no quarter, the voices quiet and weighty and deliberate for retrospection and recollection and exact remembering, while he squatted in the blazing firelight as Tennie's Jim squatted, who stirred only to put more wood on the fire and to pass the bottle from one glass to another. Because the bottle was always present, so that after a while it seemed to him that those fierce instants of heart and brain and courage and wiliness and speed were concentrated and distilled into that brown liquor which not women, not boys and children, but only hunters drank, drinking not of the blood they had spilled but some condensation of the wild immortal spirit, drinking it moderately, humbly even, not with the pagan's base hope of acquiring the virtues of cunning and strength and speed, but in salute to them.

His father returned with the book and sat down again and opened it. "Listen," he said. He read the five stanzas aloud, his voice quiet and deliberate in the room where there was no fire now because it was already spring. Then he looked up. The boy watched him. "All right," his father said. "Listen." He read again, but only the second stanza this time, to the end of it, the last two lines, and closed the book and put it on the table beside him. "She cannot fade, though thou hast not thy bliss, for ever wilt thou love, and she be fair," he said.

"He's talking about a girl," the boy said.

"He had to talk about something," his father said. Then he said, "He was talking about truth. Truth doesn't change. Truth is one thing. It covers all things which touch the heart—honor and pride and pity and justice and courage and love. Do you see now?"

He didn't know. Somehow it was simpler than that. There was an old bear, fierce and ruthless, not merely just to stay alive, but with the fierce pride of liberty and freedom, proud enough of the liberty and freedom to see it threatened without fear or even alarm; nay, who at times even seemed deliberately to put that freedom and liberty in jeopardy in order to savor them, to remind his old strong bones and flesh to keep supple and quick to defend and preserve them. There was an old man, son of a Negro slave and an Indian king, inheritor on the one side of the long chronicle of a people who had learned humility through suffering, and pride through the endurance which survived the suffering and injustice, and on the other side, the chronicle of a people even longer in the land than the first, yet who no longer existed in the land at all save in the solitary brotherhood of an old Negro's alien blood and the wild and invincible spirit of an old bear. There was a boy who wished to learn humility and pride in order to become skillful and worthy in the woods, who suddenly found himself becoming so skillful so rapidly that he feared he would never become worthy because he had not learned humility and pride, although he had tried to, until one day and as suddenly he discovered that an old man who could not have defined either had led him, as though by the hand, to that point where an old bear and a little mongrel of a dog showed him that, by possessing one thing other, he would possess them both.

And a little dog, nameless and mongrel and many-fathered, grown, yet weighing less than six pounds, saying as if to itself, "I can't be dangerous, because there's nothing much smaller than I am; I can't be fierce, because they would call it just a noise; I can't be humble, because I'm already too close to the ground to genuflect; I can't be proud, because I wouldn't be near enough to it for anyone to know who was casting the shadow, and I don't even know that I'm not going to heaven, because they have already decided that I don't possess an immortal soul. So all I can be is brave. But it's all right. I can be that, even if they still call it just noise."

That was all. It was simple, much simpler than somebody talking in a book about youth and a girl he would never need to grieve over, because he could never approach any nearer her and would never have to get any farther away. He had heard about a bear, and finally got big enough to trail it, and he trailed it four years and at last met it with a gun in his hands and he didn't shoot. Because a little dog— But he could have shot long before the little dog covered the twenty yards to where the bear waited, and Sam Fathers could have shot at any time during that interminable minute while Old Ben stood on his hind feet over them. He stopped. His father was watching him gravely across the spring-rife twilight of the room; when he spoke, his words were as quiet as the twilight, too, not loud, because they did not need to be because they would last, "Courage, and honor, and pride," his father said, "and pity, and love of justice and of liberty. They all touch the heart, and what the heart holds to becomes truth, as far as we know the truth. Do you see now?"

Sam, and Old Ben, and Nip, he thought. And himself too. He had been all right too. His father had said so. "Yes, sir," he said.

COMMENT AND QUESTIONS

On one level this is an action story, a hunting story with a clear physical conflict: boy versus bear. On a deeper level it is a psychological story of a boy's inner growth, in which the bear becomes even larger than itself—a symbol of something which the boy, given a chance to kill the bear, is unwilling to destroy. The end of the story will have more meaning if you know Keats' "Ode on a Grecian Urn," the poem the father reads. In a Grecian urn, with scenes and figures cut in marble, Keats sees universal, permanent truth and beauty; the experience represented on the urn is, unlike experience in life itself, unchanging: the leafy trees on the urn will never be bare, the singer of unheard melodies will continue for all time to sing sweet songs, the lover will always love, and the girl he pursues will always be fair. Only with difficulty does the boy in the story see the connection between a poem about permanent beauty and value, and his unwillingness to shoot an old bear. The reader of the story must understand this connection. In it lies the theme of the story. This is the poem:

ODE ON A GRECIAN URN

Thou still unravished bride of quietness,
   Thou foster-child of silence and slow time,
Sylvan historian, who canst thus express
   A flowery tale more sweetly than our rhyme:
What leaf-fringed legend haunts about thy shape
   Of deities or mortals, or of both,
      In Tempe or the dales of Arcady?
   What men or gods are these? What maidens loth?
What mad pursuit? What struggle to escape?
      What pipes and timbrels? What wild ecstasy?

Heard melodies are sweet, but those unheard
   Are sweeter; therefore, ye soft pipes, play on;
Not to the sensual ear, but, more endeared,
   Pipe to the spirit ditties of no tone:
Fair youth, beneath the trees, thou canst not leave
   Thy song, nor ever can those trees be bare;
      Bold Lover, never, never canst thou kiss,
Though winning near the goal—yet, do not grieve;
   She cannot fade, though thou hast not thy bliss,
   For ever wilt thou love, and she be fair!

Ah, happy, happy boughs! that cannot shed
   Your leaves, nor ever bid the Spring adieu;

And, happy melodist, unwearièd,
For ever piping songs for ever new;
More happy love! more happy, happy love!
For ever warm and still to be enjoyed,
For ever panting, and for ever young;
All breathing human passion far above,
That leaves a heart high-sorrowful and cloyed,
A burning forehead, and a parching tongue.

Who are these coming to the sacrifice?
To what green altar, O mysterious priest,
Lead'st thou that heifer lowing at the skies,
And all her silken flanks with garlands dressed?
What little town by river or sea shore,
Or mountain-built with peaceful citadel,
Is emptied of this folk, this pious morn?
And, little town, thy streets for evermore
Will silent be; and not a soul to tell
Why thou art desolate, can e'er return.

O Attic shape! Fair attitude! with brede
Of marble men and maidens overwrought,
With forest branches and the trodden weed;
Thou, silent form, dost tease us out of thought
As doth eternity: Cold Pastoral!
When old age shall this generation waste,
Thou shalt remain, in midst of other woe
Than ours, a friend to man, to whom thou say'st,
"Beauty is truth, truth beauty,"—that is all
Ye know on earth, and all ye need to know.

I. Even before he sees it, the bear is more than a bear to the boy. What does it mean to him?

II. What does the bear finally symbolize?

III. List the successive stages of the boy's experience with the bear. What does he learn from each stage of experience?

IV. Explain this sentence in the fourth-from-last paragraph in the story: "There was a boy who wished to learn humility and pride in order to become skillful and worthy in the woods, who suddenly found himself becoming so skillful so rapidly that he feared he would never become worthy because he had not learned humility and pride, although he had tried to, until one day and as suddenly he discovered that an old man who could not have defined either had led him, as though by the hand, to that point where an old bear and a little mongrel of a dog showed him that, by possessing one thing other, he would possess them both."

V. What is the author's attitude toward the wilderness which is the home of the bear and the setting of most of the story?

VI. By close analysis of the sentences in the first three paragraphs of the story, try to determine the distinctive qualities of William Faulkner's style.

Chapter Nine

Language in Action:

Readings for Independent

Analysis

THE MATURE READER is on his own. In the process of becoming a mature reader, he is aided, we believe, by directions, and comments, and leading questions. But finally he must see the direction for himself; must make his own comments on structure, logic, expression, and style; must raise and answer his own questions about the intention, the quality, and the value of what he reads.

The selections in the following pages are presented with no comments and with no aids to reading other than brief introductory notes which identify the author and give the date of publication. In reading, understanding, and appraising the selections, the student should have in mind the method of evaluation outlined in the section "Evaluating What One Reads" in Chapter Thirteen, as well as the discussions in Chapter Eight of the special problems involved and the special techniques used in different types of prose.

APOLOGY *

(*The Defense of Socrates at His Trial*)

PLATO

In 399 B.C., Socrates, Greek teacher and philosopher, was accused of impiety and of corrupting the youth of Athens with false doctrines, and was

* Translated by Benjamin Jowett.

tried and condemned to death by a court of 501 Athenian citizens. The *Apology* is Socrates' speech to the court, reported by his pupil Plato.

———〜———

How you, O Athenians, have been affected by my accusers, I cannot tell; but I know that they almost made me forget who I was—so persuasively did they speak; and yet they have hardly uttered a word of truth. But of the many falsehoods told by them, there was one which quite amazed me;—I mean when they said that you should be upon your guard and not allow yourselves to be deceived by the force of my eloquence. To say this, when they were certain to be detected as soon as I opened my lips and proved myself to be anything but a great speaker, did indeed appear to me most shameless—unless by the force of eloquence they mean the force of truth; for if such is their meaning, I admit that I am eloquent. But in how different a way from theirs! Well, as I was saying, they have scarcely spoken the truth at all; but from me you shall hear the whole truth; not, however, delivered after their manner in a set oration duly ornamented with words and phrases. No, by heaven! but I shall use the words and arguments which occur to me at the moment; for I am confident in the justice of my cause: at my time of life I ought not to be appearing before you, O men of Athens, in the character of a juvenile orator—let no one expect it of me. And I must beg of you to grant me a favour:—If I defend myself in my accustomed manner, and you hear me using the words which I have been in the habit of using in the agora, at the tables of the money-changers, or anywhere else, I would ask you not to be surprised, and not to interrupt me on this account. For I am more than seventy years of age, and appearing now for the first time in a court of law, I am quite a stranger to the language of the place; and therefore I would have you regard me as if I were really a stranger, whom you would excuse if he spoke in his native tongue, and after the fashion of his country:—Am I making an unfair request of you? Never mind the manner, which may or may not be good; but think only of the truth of my words, and give heed to that: let the speaker speak truly and the judge decide justly.

And first, I have to reply to the older charges and to my first accusers, and then I will go on to the later ones. For of old I have had many accusers, who have accused me falsely to you during many years; and I am more afraid of them than of Anytus and his associates, who are dangerous, too, in their own way. But far more dangerous are the others, who began when you were children, and took possession of your minds with their falsehoods, telling of one Socrates, a wise man, who speculated about the heaven above, and searched into the earth beneath, and made the worse appear the better cause. The disseminators of this tale are the accusers whom I dread; for their hearers are apt to fancy that such enquirers do not believe in the existence of the gods. And they are many, and their charges against me are of ancient date, and they were made by them in the days when you were more impressible than you are now—in childhood, or it may have been in youth—and the cause when heard went by default, for there was none to answer. And hardest of all, I do not know and cannot tell the names of my accusers; unless in the chance case of a comic poet. All who from envy and malice have persuaded you—some of them having first convinced themselves—all this class of men are most difficult to deal with; for I cannot have them up here, and cross-examine them, and therefore I must simply fight with shadows in my own defence, and argue when there is no one who answers. I will ask you then to assume with me, as I was saying, that my opponents are of two kinds; one recent, the other ancient: and I hope that you will see the propriety of my answering the latter first, for these accusations you heard long before the others, and much oftener.

Well, then, I must make my defence, and endeavor to clear away in a short time, a slander which has lasted a long time. May I succeed, if to succeed be for my good and yours, or likely to avail me in my cause! The task is not an easy one; I quite understand the nature of it. And so leaving the event with God, in obedience to the law I will now make my defence.

. I will begin at the beginning, and ask what is the accusation which has given rise to the slander of me, and in fact has encouraged Meletus to prefer this charge against me. Well, what do the slanderers say? They shall be my prosecutors, and I will sum up their words in an affidavit: "Socrates is an evildoer, and a curious person, who searches into things under the earth and in heaven, and he makes the worse appear the better cause; and he teaches the aforesaid doctrines to others." Such is the nature of the accusation: it is just what you have yourselves seen in the comedy of Aristophanes, who has introduced a man whom he calls Socrates, going about and saying that he walks in air, and talking a deal of nonsense concerning matters of which I do not pretend to know either much or little—not that I mean to speak disparagingly of any one who is a student of natural philosophy. I should be very sorry if Meletus could bring so grave a charge against me. But the simple truth is, O Athenians, that I have nothing to do with physical speculations. Very many of those here present are witnesses to the truth of this, and to them I appeal. Speak then, you who have heard me, and tell your neighbours whether any of you have ever known me hold forth in few words or in many upon such matters. . . . You hear their answer. And from what they say of this part of the charge you will be able to judge of the truth of the rest.

As little foundation is there for the report that I am a teacher, and take money; this accusation has no more truth in it than the other. Although, if a man were really able to instruct mankind, to receive money for giving instruction would, in my opinion, be an honour to him. There is Gorgias of Leontium, and Prodicus of Ceos, and Hippias of Elis, who go the round of the cities, and are able to persuade the young men to leave their own citizens by whom they might be taught for nothing, and come to them whom they not only pay, but are thankful if they may be allowed to pay them. There is at this time a Parian philosopher residing in Athens, of whom I have heard; and I came to hear of him in this way:—I came across a man who has spent a world of money on the Sophists, Callias, the son of Hipponicus, and knowing that he had sons, I asked him: "Callias," I said, "if your two sons were foals or calves, there would be no difficulty in finding some one to put over them; we should hire a trainer of horses, or a farmer, probably, who would improve and perfect them in their own proper virtue and excellence; but as they are human beings, whom are you thinking of placing over them? Is there any one who understands human and political virtue? You must have thought about the matter, for you have sons; is there any one?" "There is," he said. "Who is he?" said I; "and of what country? and what does he charge?" "Evenus the Parian," he replied; "he is the man, and his charge is five minae." Happy is Evenus, I said to myself, if he really has this wisdom, and teaches at such a moderate charge. Had I the same, I should have been very proud and conceited; but the truth is that I have no knowledge of the kind.

I dare say, Athenians, that some one among you will reply, "Yes, Socrates, but what is the origin of these accusations which are brought against you; there must have been something strange which you have been doing? All these rumours and this talk about you would never have arisen if you had been like other men: tell us, then, what is the cause of them, for we should be sorry to judge hastily of you." Now, I regard this as a fair challenge, and I will endeavor to explain to you the reason why I am called wise and have such an evil fame. Please to attend then. And although some of you may think that I am joking, I declare that I will tell you the entire truth. Men of Athens, this reputation of mine has come of a certain sort of wisdom which I possess. If you ask me what kind of wisdom, I reply, wisdom such as may perhaps be attained by man, for to that extent I am inclined to believe that I am wise; whereas the persons of whom I was speaking have a superhuman wisdom, which I may fail to describe, because I have it not myself; and he who says that I have, speaks falsely, and is taking away my character. And here, O men of Athens, I must beg you not to interrupt me, even if I seem to say something extravagant. For the word which I will speak is not mine. I will refer you to a witness who is worthy of credit; that witness shall be the God of Delphi—he will tell you about my wisdom, if I have any, and of what sort it is. You must have known Chaerephon; he was early a friend of mine, and also a friend of yours, for he shared in the recent exile of the people, and returned with you. Well, Chaerephon, as you know, was very impetuous in all his doings, and he went to Delphi and boldly asked the oracle to tell him whether—as I was saying, I must beg you not to interrupt—he asked the oracle to tell him whether any one was wiser than I was, and the Pythian prophetess answered, that there was no man wiser. Chaerephon is dead himself; but his brother, who is in court, will confirm the truth of what I am saying.

Why do I mention this? Because I am going to explain to you why I have such an evil name. When I heard the answer, I said to myself, What can the God mean? and what is the interpretation of his riddle? for I know that I have no wisdom, small or great. What then can he mean when he says that I am the wisest of men? And yet he is a god, and cannot lie; that would be against his nature. After long consideration, I thought of a method of trying the question. I reflected that if I could only find a man wiser than myself, then I might go to the god with a refutation in my hand. I should say to him, "Here is a man who is wiser than I am; but you said that I was the wisest." Accordingly I went to one who had the reputation of wisdom, and observed him—his name I need not mention; he was a politician whom I selected for examination—and the result was as follows: When I began to talk with him, I could not help thinking that he was not really wise, although he was thought wise by many, and still wiser by himself; and thereupon I tried to explain to him that he thought himself wise, but was not really wise; and the consequence was that he hated me, and his enmity was shared by several who were present and heard me. So I left him, saying to myself, as I went away: Well, although I do not suppose that either of us knows anything really beautiful and good, I am better off than he is,—for he knows nothing, and thinks that he knows; I neither know nor think that I know. In this latter particular, then, I seem to have slightly the advantage of him. Then I went to another who had still higher pretensions to wisdom, and my conclusion was exactly the same. Whereupon I made another enemy of him, and of many others besides him.

Then I went to one man after another, being not unconscious of the enmity which I provoked, and I lamented and feared this: but necessity was laid upon me,—the word of God, I thought, ought to be considered first. And I said to myself, Go I must to all who appear to know, and find out the meaning of the oracle. And I swear to you, Athenians, by the dog I swear!—for I must tell you the truth—the result of my mission was just this: I found that the men most in repute were all but the most foolish; and that others less esteemed were really wiser and better. I will tell you the tale of my wanderings and of the "Herculean" labours, as I may call them, which I endured only to find at last the oracle irrefutable. After the politicians, I went to the poets; tragic, dithyrambic, and all sorts. And there, I said to myself, you will be instantly detected; now you will find out that you are more ignorant than they are. Accordingly I took them some of the most elaborate passages in their own writings, and asked what was the meaning of them—thinking that they would teach me something. Will you believe me? I am almost ashamed to confess the truth, but I must say that there is hardly a person present who would not have talked better about their poetry than they did themselves. Then I knew that not by wisdom do poets write poetry, but by a sort of genius and inspiration; they are like diviners or soothsayers who also say many fine things, but do not understand the meaning of them. The poets appeared to me to be much in the same case; and I further observed that upon the strength of their poetry they believed themselves to be the wisest of men in other things in which they were not wise. So I departed, conceiving myself to be superior to them for the same reason that I was superior to the politicians.

At last I went to the artisans. I was conscious that I knew nothing at all, as I may say, and I was sure that they knew many fine things; and here I was not mistaken, for they did know many things of which I was ignorant, and in this they certainly were wiser than I was. But I observed that even the good artisans fell into the same error as the poets;—because they were good workmen they thought that they also knew all sorts of high matters, and this defect in them overshadowed their wisdom; and therefore I asked myself on behalf of the oracle, whether I would like to be as I was, neither having their knowledge nor their ignorance, or like them in both; and I made answer to myself and to the oracle that I was better off as I was.

This inquisition has led to my having many enemies of the worst and most dangerous kind, and has given occasion also to many calumnies. And I am called wise, for my hearers always imagine that I myself possess the wisdom which I find wanting in others: but the truth is, O men of Athens, that God only is wise; and by his answer he intends to show that the wisdom of men is worth little or nothing; he is not speaking of Socrates, he is only using my name by way of illustration, as if he said, He, O men, is the wisest, who, like Socrates, knows that his wisdom is in truth worth nothing. And so I go about the world obedient to the god, and search and make enquiry into the wisdom of any one, whether citizen or stranger, who appears to be wise; and if he is not wise, then in vindication of the oracle I show him that he is not wise; and my occupation quite absorbs me, and I have no time to give either to any public matter of interest or to any concern of my own, but I am in utter poverty by reason of my devotion to the god.

There is another thing:—young men of the richer classes, who have not much to do, come about me of their own accord; they like to hear the pretenders examined, and they often imitate me, and proceed to examine others; there are plenty of persons, as they quickly discover, who think that they know something, but really know little or nothing; and then those who are examined by them instead of being angry with themselves are angry with me: This confounded Socrates, they say; this villainous misleader of youth!—and then if somebody asks them, Why, what evil does he practise or teach? they do not know, and cannot tell; but in order that they may not appear to be at a loss, they repeat the ready-made charges which are used against all philosophers about teaching things up in the clouds and under the earth, and having no gods, and making the worse appear the better cause; for they do not like to confess that their pretence of knowledge has been detected—which is the truth; and as they are numerous and ambitious and energetic, and are drawn up in battle array and have persuasive tongues, they have filled your ears with their loud and inveterate calumnies. And this is the reason why my three accusers, Meletus and Anytus and Lycon, have set upon me; Meletus, who has a quarrel with me on behalf of the poets; Anytus, on behalf of the craftsmen and politicians; Lycon, on behalf of the rhetoricians: and, as I said at the beginning, I cannot expect to get rid of such a mass of calumny all in a moment. And this, O men of Athens, is the truth and the whole truth; I have concealed nothing, I have dissembled nothing. And yet, I know that my plainness of speech makes them hate me, and what is their hatred but a proof that I am speaking the truth? Hence has arisen the prejudice against me; and this is the reason of it, as you will find out either in this or in any future enquiry.

I have said enough in my defence against the first class of my accusers; I turn to the second class. They are headed by Meletus, that good man and true lover of his country, as he calls himself. Against these, too, I must try to make a defence:—Let their affidavit be read: it contains something of this kind: It says that Socrates is a doer of evil, who corrupts the youth; and who does not believe in the gods of the State, but has other new divinities of his own. Such is the charge; and now let us examine the particular counts. He says that I am a doer of evil, and corrupt the youth; but I say, O men of Athens, that Meletus is a doer of evil, in that he pretends to be in earnest when he is only in jest, and is so eager to bring men to trial from a pretended zeal and interest about matters in which he really never had the smallest interest. And the truth of this I will endeavor to prove to you.

Come hither, Meletus, and let me ask a question of you. You think a great deal about the improvement of youth?

Yes, I do.

Tell the judges, then, who is their improver; for you must know, as you have taken the pains to discover their corrupter, and are citing and accusing me before them. Speak, then, and tell the judges who their improver is.—Observe, Meletus, that you are silent, and have nothing to say. But is not this rather disgraceful, and a very considerable proof of what I was saying, that you have no interest in the matter? Speak up, friend, and tell us who their improver is.

The laws.

But that, my good sir, is not my meaning. I want to know who the person is, who, in the first place, knows the laws.

The judges, Socrates, who are present in court.

What, do you mean to say, Meletus, that they are able to instruct and improve youth?

Certainly they are.

What, all of them, or some only and not others?

All of them.

By the goddess Here, that is good news! There are plenty of improvers, then. And what do you say of the audience,—do they improve them?

Yes, they do.

And the senators?

Yes, the senators improve them.

But perhaps the members of the assembly corrupt them?—or do they improve them?

They improve them.

Then every Athenian improves and elevates them; all with the exception of myself; and I alone am their corrupter? Is that what you affirm?

That is what I stoutly affirm.

I am very unfortunate if you are right. But suppose I ask you a question: How about horses? Does one man do them harm and all the world good? Is not the exact opposite the truth? One man is able to do them good, or at least not many;—the trainer of horses, that is to say, does them good, and others who have to do with them rather injure them? Is not that true, Meletus, of horses, or of any other animal? Most assuredly it is; whether you and Anytus say yes or no. Happy indeed would be the condition of youth if they had one corrupter only, and all the rest of the world were their improvers. But you, Meletus, have sufficiently shown that you never had a thought about the young: your carelessness is seen in your not caring about the very things which you bring against me.

And now, Meletus, I will ask you another question—by Zeus I will: Which is better, to live among bad citizens, or among good ones? Answer, friend, I say; the question is one which may be easily answered. Do not the good do their neighbours good, and the bad do them evil?

Certainly.

And is there any one who would rather be injured than benefited by those who live with him? Answer, my good friend, the law requires you to answer—does any one like to be injured?

Certainly not.

And when you accuse me of corrupting and deteriorating the youth, do you allege that I corrupt them intentionally or unintentionally?

Intentionally, I say.

But you have just admitted that the good do their neighbours good, and the evil do them evil. Now, is that a truth which your superior wisdom has recognized thus early in life, and am I, at my age, in such darkness and ignorance as not to know that if a man with whom I have to live is corrupted by me, I am very likely to be harmed by him; and yet I corrupt him, and intentionally, too— so you say, although neither I nor any other human being is ever likely to be convinced by you. But either I do not corrupt them, or I corrupt them unintentionally; and on either view of the case you lie. If my offence is unintentional, the law has no cognizance of unintentional offences: you ought to have taken me privately, and warned and admonished me; for if I had been better advised, I should have left off doing what I only did unintentionally—no doubt I should; but you would have nothing to say to me and refused to teach me. And now you bring me up in this court, which is a place not of instruction, but of punishment.

It will be very clear to you, Athenians, as I was saying, that Meletus has no care at all, great or small, about the matter. But still I should like to know, Meletus, in what I am affirmed to corrupt the young. I suppose you mean, as I infer from your indictment, that I teach them not to acknowledge the gods which the State acknowledges, but some other new divinities or spiritual agencies in their stead. These are the lessons by which I corrupt the youth, as you say.

Yes, that I say emphatically.

Then, by the gods, Meletus, of whom we are speaking, tell me and the court, in somewhat plainer terms, what you mean! For I do not as yet understand whether you affirm that I teach other men to acknowledge some gods, and therefore that I do believe in gods, and am not an entire atheist—this you do not lay to my charge,—but only you say that they are not the same gods which the city recognizes—the charge is that they are different gods. Or, do you mean that I am an atheist simply, and a teacher of atheism?

I mean the latter—that you are a complete atheist.

What an extraordinary statement! Why do you think so, Meletus? Do you mean that I do not believe in the godhead of the sun or moon, like other men?

I assure you judges, that he does not: for he says that the sun is stone, and the moon earth.

Friend Meletus, you think that you are accusing Anaxagoras: and you have but a bad opinion of the judges, if you fancy them illiterate to such a degree as not to know that these doctrines are found in the books of Anaxagoras the Clazomenian, which are full of them. And so, forsooth, the youth are said to be taught them by Socrates, when there are not infrequently exhibitions of them at the theatre (price of admission one drachma at the most); and they might pay their money, and laugh at Socrates if he pretends to father these extraordinary views. And so, Meletus, you really think that I do not believe in any god?

I swear by Zeus that you believe absolutely in none at all.

Nobody will believe you, Meletus, and I am pretty sure that you do not believe yourself. I cannot help thinking, men of Athens, that Meletus is reckless and impudent, and that he has written this indictment in a spirit of mere wantonness and youthful bravado. Has he not compounded a riddle, thinking to try me? He said to himself:—I shall see whether the wise Socrates will discover my facetious contradiction, or whether I shall be able to deceive him and the rest of them. For he certainly does appear to me to contradict himself in the indictment as much as if he said that Socrates is guilty of not believing in the gods, and yet of believing in them—but this is not like a person who is in earnest.

I should like you, O men of Athens, to join me in examining what I conceive to be his inconsistency; and do you, Meletus, answer. And I must remind the audience of my request that they would not make a disturbance if I speak in my accustomed manner:

Did ever man, Meletus, believe in the existence of human things, and not of human beings? . . . I wish, men of Athens, that he would answer, and not be always trying to get up an interruption. Did ever any man believe in horsemanship, and not in horses? or in flute-playing, and not in flute-players? No, my friend; I will answer to you and to the court, as you refuse to answer for yourself. There is no man who ever did. But now please to answer the next question: Can a man believe in spiritual and divine agencies, and not in spirits or demigods?

He cannot.

How lucky I am to have extracted that answer, by the assistance of the court! But then you swear in the indictment that I teach and believe in divine or spiritual agencies (new or old, no matter for that); at any rate, I believe in spiritual agencies,—so you say and swear in the affidavit; and yet if I believe in divine beings, how can I help believing in spirits or demigods;—must I not? To be sure I must; and therefore I may assume that your silence gives consent. Now what are spirits or demigods? are they not either gods or the sons of gods?

Certainly they are.

But this is what I call the facetious riddle invented by you: the demigods or spirits are gods, and you say first that I do not believe in gods, and then again that I do believe in gods; that is, if I believe in demigods. For if the demigods are the illegitimate sons of gods, whether by the nymphs or by any other mothers, of whom they are said to be the sons—what human being will ever believe that there are no gods if they are the sons of Gods? You might as well affirm the existence of mules, and deny that of horses and asses. Such nonsense, Meletus, could only have been intended by you to make trial of me. You have put this into the indictment because you had nothing real of which to accuse me. But no one who has a particle of understanding will ever be convinced by you that the same men can believe in divine and superhuman things, and yet not believe that there are gods and demigods and heroes.

I have said enough in answer to the charge of Meletus: any elaborate defence is unnecessary; but I know only too well how many are the enmities which I have incurred, and this is what will be my destruction if I am destroyed;—not Meletus, nor yet Anytus, but the envy and detraction of the world, which has been the death of many good men, and will probably be the death of many more; there is no danger of my being the last of them.

Some one will say: And are you not ashamed, Socrates, of a course of life which is likely to bring you to an untimely end? To him I may fairly answer: There you are mistaken: a man who is good for anything ought not to calculate the chance of living or dying; he ought only to consider whether in doing anything he is doing right or wrong—acting the part of a good man or of a bad. Whereas, upon your view, the heroes who fell at Troy were not good for much, and the son of Thetis above all, who altogether despised danger in comparison with disgrace; and when he was so eager to slay Hector, his goddess mother said to him, that if he avenged his companion Patroclus, and slew Hector, he would die himself—"Fate," she said, in these or the like words, "waits for you next after Hector"; he, receiving this warning, utterly despised danger and death, and instead of fearing them, feared rather to live in dishonour, and not to avenge his friend. "Let me die forthwith," he replies, "and be avenged of my enemy, rather than abide here by the beaked ships, a laughingstock and a burden of the earth." Had Achilles any thought of death and danger? For wherever a man's place is, whether the place which he has chosen or that in which he has been placed by a commander, there he ought to remain in the hour of danger; he should not think of death or of anything but of disgrace. And this, O men of Athens, is a true saying.

Strange, indeed, would be my conduct, O men of Athens, if I, who, when I was ordered by the generals whom you chose to command me at Potidaea and Amphipolis and Delium, remained where they placed me, like any other man, facing death—if now, when, as I conceive and imagine, God orders me to fulfill the philosopher's mission of searching into myself and other men, I were to desert my post through fear of death, or any other fear; that would indeed be strange, and I might justly be arraigned in court for denying the existence of the gods, if I disobeyed the oracle because I was afraid of death, fancying that I was wise when I was not wise. For the fear of death is indeed the pretence of wisdom, and not real wisdom, being a pretence of knowing the unknown; and no one knows whether death, which men in their fear apprehend to be the greatest evil, may not be the greatest good. Is not this ignorance of a disgraceful sort, the ignorance which is the conceit that a man knows what he does not know? And in this respect only I believe myself to differ from men in general, and may perhaps claim to be wiser than they are:—that whereas I know but little of the world below, I do not suppose that I know: but I do know that injustice and disobedience to a better, whether God or man, is evil and dishonourable, and I will never fear or avoid a possible good rather than a certain evil. And therefore if you let me go now, and are not convinced by Anytus, who said that since I had been prosecuted I must be put to death; (or if not that I ought never to have been prosecuted at all); and that if I escape now, your sons will all be utterly ruined by listening to my words—if you say to me, Socrates, this time we will not mind Anytus, and you shall be let off, but upon one condition, that you are not to enquire and speculate in this way any more, and that if you are caught doing so again you shall die;—if this was the condition on which you let me go, I should reply: Men of Athens, I honour and love you; but I shall obey God rather than you, and while I have life and strength I shall never cease from the practice and teaching of philosophy, exhorting any one whom I meet and saying to him after my manner: You, my friend,—a citizen of the great and mighty and wise city of Athens,—are you not ashamed of heaping up the greatest amount of money and honour and reputation, and caring so little about wisdom and truth and the greatest improvement of the soul, which you never regard or heed at all? And if the person with whom I am arguing, says: Yes, but I do care; then I do not leave him or let him go at once; but I proceed to interrogate and examine and cross-examine him, and if I think that he has no virtue in him, but only says that he has, I reproach him with undervaluing the greater, and overvaluing the less. And I shall repeat the same words to every one whom I meet, young and old, citizen and alien, but especially to the citizens, inasmuch as they are my brethren. For know that this is the command of God; and I believe that no greater good has ever happened in the State than my service to the God. For I do nothing but go about persuading you all, old and young alike, not to take thought for your persons or your properties, but first and chiefly to care about the greatest improvement of the soul. I tell you that virtue is not given by money, but that from virtue comes money and every other good of man, public as well as private. This is my teaching, and if this is the doctrine which corrupts the youth, I am a mischievous person. But if any one says that this is not my teaching, he is speaking an untruth. Wherefore, O men of Athens, I say to you, do as Anytus bids or not as Anytus bids, and either acquit me or not;

but whichever you do, understand that I shall never alter my ways, not even if I have to die many times.

Men of Athens, do not interrupt, but hear me; there was an understanding between us that you should hear me to the end: I have something more to say, at which you may be inclined to cry out; but I believe that to hear me will be good for you, and therefore I beg that you will not cry out. I would have you know, that if you kill such an one as I am, you will injure yourselves more than you will injure me. Nothing will injure me, not Meletus nor yet Anytus—they cannot, for a bad man is not permitted to injure a better than himself. I do not deny that Anytus may, perhaps, kill him, or drive him into exile, or deprive him of civil rights; and he may imagine, and others may imagine, that he is inflicting a great injury upon him: but there I do not agree. For the evil of doing as he is doing—the evil of unjustly taking away the life of another—is greater far.

And now, Athenians, I am not going to argue for my own sake, as you may think, but for yours, that you may not sin against the God by condemning me, who am his gift to you. For if you kill me you will not easily find a successor to me, who, if I may use such a ludicrous figure of speech, am a sort of gadfly, given to the State by God; and the State is a great and noble steed who is tardy in his motions owing to his very size, and requires to be stirred into life. I am that gadfly which God has attached to the State, and all day long and in all places am always fastening upon you, arousing and persuading and reproaching you. You will not easily find another like me, and therefore I would advise you to spare me. I dare say that you may feel out of temper (like a person who is suddenly awakened from sleep), and you think that you might easily strike me dead as Anytus advises, and then you would sleep on for the remainder of your lives, unless God in his care of you sent you another gadfly. When I say that I am given to you by God, the proof of my mission is this:—if I had been like other men, I should not have neglected all my own concerns or patiently seen the neglect of them during all these years, and have been doing yours, coming to you individually like a father or elder brother, exhorting you to regard virtue; such conduct, I say, would be unlike human nature. If I had gained anything, or if my exhortations had been paid, there would have been some sense in my doing so; but now, as you will perceive, not even the impudence of my accusers dares to say that I have ever exacted or sought pay of any one; of that they have no witness. And I have a sufficient witness to the truth of what I say—my poverty.

Some one may wonder why I go about in private giving advice and busying myself with the concerns of others, but do not venture to come forward in public and advise the State. I will tell you why. You have heard me speak at sundry times and in divers places of an oracle or sign which comes to me, and is the divinity which Meletus ridicules in the indictment. This sign, which is a kind of voice, first began to come to me when I was a child; it always forbids but never commands me to do anything which I am going to do. This is what deters me from being a politician. And rightly, as I think. For I am certain, O men of Athens, that if I had engaged in politics, I should have perished long ago, and done no good either to you or to myself. And do not be offended at my telling you the truth: for the truth is, that no man who goes to war with you or any other multitude, honestly striving against the many lawless and unrighteous deeds which are done in a state, will save his life; he who will fight for the right, if he would live even for a brief space, must have a private station and not a public one.

I can give you convincing evidence of what I say, not words only, but what you value far more—actions. Let me relate to you a passage of my own life which will prove to you that I should never have yielded to injustice from any fear of death and that "as I should have refused to yield" I must have died at once. I will tell you a tale of the courts, not very interesting perhaps, but nevertheless true. The only office of State which I ever held, O men of Athens, was that of senator: the tribe Antiochis, which is my tribe, had the presidency at the trial of the generals who had not taken up the bodies of the slain after the battle of Arginusae; and you proposed to try them in a body, contrary to law, as you all thought afterwards; but at the time I was the only one of the Prytanes who was opposed to the illegality, and I gave my vote against you; and when the orators threatened to impeach and arrest me, and you called and shouted, I made up my mind that I would run the risk, having law and justice with me, rather than take part in your injustice because I feared imprisonment and death. This happened in the days of the democracy. But when the oligarchy of the Thirty was in power, they sent for me and four others into the rotunda, and bade us bring Leon the Salaminian from Salamis, as they wanted to put him to death. This was a specimen of the sort of commands which they were always giving with the view of implicating as many as possible in their crimes; and then I showed, not in word only but in deed, that, if I may be allowed to use such an expression, I cared not a straw for death, and that my great and only care was lest I should do an unrighteous or unholy thing. For the strong arm of that oppressive power did not frighten me into doing wrong; and when we came out of the rotunda the other four went to Salamis and fetched Leon, but I went quietly home. For which I might have lost my life, had not the power of the Thirty shortly afterwards come to an end. And many will witness to my words.

Now, do you really imagine that I could have survived all these years, if I had led a public life, supposing that like a good man I had always maintained the right and had made justice, as I ought, the first thing? No, indeed, men of Athens, neither I nor any other man. But I have been always the same in all my actions, public as well as private, and never have I yielded any base compliance to those who are slanderously termed my disciples, or to any other. Not that I have any regular disciples. But if any one likes to come and hear me while I am pursuing my mission, whether he be young or old, he is not excluded. Nor do I converse only with those who pay; but any one, whether he be rich or poor, may ask and answer me and listen to my words; and whether he turns out to be a bad man or a good one, neither result can be justly imputed to me; for I never taught or professed to teach him anything. And if any one says that he has ever learned or heard anything from me in private which all the world has not heard, let me tell you that he is lying.

But I shall be asked, Why do people delight in continually conversing with you? I have told you already, Athenians, the whole truth about this matter: they like to hear the cross-examination of the pretenders to wisdom; there is amusement in it. Now, this duty of cross-examining other men has been imposed upon me by God; and has been signified to me by oracles, visions, and in every way in which the will of divine power was ever intimated to any one. This is true, O Athenians; or, if not true, would be soon refuted. If I am or have been corrupting the youth, those of them who are now grown up and have become sensible that I gave them bad advice in the days of their youth should come forward as accusers, and take their revenge; or if they do not like to come themselves, some of their relatives, fathers, brothers, or other kinsmen, should say what evil their families have suffered at my hands. Now is their time. Many of them I see in the court. There is Crito, who is of the same age and of the same deme with myself, and there is Critobulus his son, whom I also see. Then again there is Lysanias of Sphettus, who is the father of Aeschines—he is present; and also there is Antiphon of Cephisus, who is the father of Epigenes; and there are the brothers of several who have associated with me. There is Nicostratus the son of Theosdotides, and the brother of Theodotus (now Theodotus himself is dead, and therefore he, at any rate, will not seek to stop him); and there is Paralus the son of Demodocus, who had a brother

Theages; and Adeimantus the son of Ariston, whose brother Plato is present; and Aeantodorus, who is the brother of Apollodorus, whom I also see. I might mention a great many others, some of whom Meletus should have produced as witnesses in the course of his speech; and let him still produce them, if he has forgotten—I will make way for him. And let him say, if he has any testimony of the sort which he can produce. Nay, Athenians, the very opposite is the truth. For all these are ready to witness on behalf of the corrupter, of the injurer of their kindred, as Meletus and Anytus call me; not the corrupted youth only—there might have been a motive for that—but their uncorrupted elder relatives. Why should they too support me with their testimony? Why, indeed, except for the sake of truth and justice, and because they know that I am speaking the truth, and that Meletus is a liar.

Well, Athenians, this and the like of this is all the defence which I have to offer. Yet a word more. Perhaps there may be some one who is offended at me, when he calls to mind how he himself on a similar, or even a less serious occasion, prayed and entreated the judges with many tears, and how he produced his children in court, which was a moving spectacle, together with a host of relations and friends; whereas I, who am probably in danger of my life, will do none of these things. The contrast may occur to his mind, and he may be set against me, and vote in anger because he is displeased at me on this account. Now, if there be such a person among you,— mind, I do not say that there is,—to him I may fairly reply: My friend, I am a man, and like other men, a creature of flesh and blood, and not "of wood or stone," as Homer says; and I have a family, yes, and sons, O Athenians, three in number, one almost a man, and two others who are still young; and yet I will not bring any of them hither in order to petition you for an acquittal. And why not? Not from any self-assertion or want of respect for you. Whether I am or am not afraid of death is another question, of which I will not now speak. But, having regard to public opinion, I feel that such conduct would be discreditable to myself, and to you, and to the whole State. One who has reached my years, and who has a name for wisdom, ought not to demean himself. Whether this opinion of me be deserved or not, at any rate the world has decided that Socrates is in some way superior to other men. And if those among you who are said to be superior in wisdom and courage, and any other virtue, demean themselves in this way, how shameful is their conduct! I have seen men of reputation, when they have been condemned, behaving in the strangest manner; they seem to fancy that they were going to suffer something dreadful if they died, and that they could be immortal if you only allowed them to live; and I think that such are a dishonour to the State, and that any stranger coming in would have said of them that the most eminent men of Athens, to whom the Athenians themselves give honour and command, are no better than women. And I say that these things ought not to be done by those of us who have a reputation; and if they are done, you ought not to permit them; you ought rather to show that you are far more disposed to condemn the man who gets up a doleful scene and makes the city ridiculous, than him who holds his peace.

But, setting aside the question of public opinion, there seems to be something wrong in asking a favour of a judge, and thus procuring an acquittal, instead of informing and convincing him. For his duty is, not to make a present of justice, but to give judgment; and he has sworn that he will judge according to the laws, and not according to his own good pleasure; and we ought not to encourage you, nor should you allow yourselves to be encouraged, in this habit of per-jury—there can be no piety in that. Do not then require me to do what I consider dishonourable and impious and wrong, especially now, when I am being tried for impiety on the indictment of Meletus. For if, O men of Athens, by force of persuasion and entreaty I could overpower your oaths, then I should be teaching you to believe that there are no gods, and in defending should simply convict myself of the charge of not believing in them. But that is not so—far other-wise. For I do believe that there are gods, and in a sense higher than that in which any of my accusers believe in them. And to you and to God I commit my cause, to be determined by you as is best for you and me.

[The vote is taken and Socrates is convicted.]

There are many reasons why I am not grieved, O men of Athens, at the vote of condemnation. I expected it, and am only surprised that the votes are so nearly equal; for I had thought that the majority against me would have been far larger; but now, had thirty votes gone over to the other side, I should have been acquitted. And I may say, I think, that I have escaped Meletus. I may say more; for without the assistance of Anytus and Lycon, any one may see that he would not have had a fifth part of the votes, as the law requires, in which case he would have incurred a fine of a thousand drachmae.

And so he proposes death as the penalty. And what shall I propose on my part, O men of Athens? Clearly that which is my due. And what is my due? What returns shall be made to the man who has never had the wit to be idle during his whole life; but has been care-less of what the many care for—wealth, and family interests, and military offices, and speaking in the assembly, and magistracies, and plots, and parties. Reflecting that I was really too honest a man to be a politician and live, I did not go where I could do no good to you or to myself; but where I could do the greatest good privately to every one of you, thither I went, and sought to persuade every man among you that he must look to himself, and seek virtue and wisdom before he looks to his private interests, and look to the State before he looks to the interests of the State; and that this should be the order which he observes in all his actions. What shall be done to such an one? Doubtless some good thing, O men of Athens, if he has his reward; and the good should be of a kind suitable to him. What would be a reward suitable to a poor man who is your benefactor, and who desires leisure that he may instruct you? There can be no reward so fitting as maintenance in the Prytaneum, O men of Athens, a reward which he deserves far more than the citizen who has won the prize at Olympia in the horse or chariot race, whether the chariots were drawn by two horses or by many. For I am in want, and he has enough; and he only gives you the appearance of happiness, and I give you the reality. And if I am to estimate the penalty fairly, I should say that maintenance in the Prytaneum is the just return.

Perhaps you think that I am braving you in what I am saying now, as in what I said before about the tears and prayers. But this is not só. I speak rather because I am convinced that I never intentionally wronged any one, although I cannot convince you—the time has been too short; if there were a law at Athens, as there is in other cities, that a capital cause should not be decided in one day, then I believe that I should have convinced you. But I cannot in a moment refute great slanders; and, as I am convinced that I never wronged another, I will assuredly not wrong myself. I will not say of myself that I deserve any evil, or propose any penalty. Why should I? Because I am afraid of the penalty of death which Meletus proposes? When I do not know whether death is a good or an evil, why should I propose a penalty which would certainly be an evil? Shall I say imprisonment? And why should I live in prison, and be the slave of the magistrate of the year—of the Eleven? Or shall the penalty be a fine, imprisonment until the fine is paid? There is the same objection. I should have to lie in prison, for money I have none, and cannot pay. And if I say exile (and this may possibly be the penalty which you will affix), I must indeed be blinded by the love of life, if I am so irrational as to expect that when you, who are my own citizens, cannot endure my discourses and words, and have found them so grievous and odious that you will have no more of them, others are likely to endure me. No, indeed, men of Athens, that is not very likely. And what a life should I lead, at my age, wandering from city to city, ever changing my place of exile, and always being driven out! For I am quite sure that wherever I go, there, as here, the young men will flock to me; and if I drive them away, their elders will drive me out at their request; and if I let them come, their fathers and friends will drive me out for their sakes.

Some one will say: Yes, Socrates, but cannot you hold your tongue, and then you may go into a foreign city, and no one will interfere with you? Now, I have great difficulty in making you understand my answer to this. For if I tell you that to do as you say would be a disobedience to the God, and therefore that I cannot hold my tongue, you will not believe that I am serious; and if I say again that daily to discourse about virtue, and of those other things about which you hear me examining myself and others is the greatest good of man, and that the unexamined life is not worth living, you are still less likely to believe me. Yet I say what is true, although a thing of which it is hard for me to persuade you. Also, I have never been accustomed to think that I deserve to suffer any harm. Had I money I might have estimated the offence at what I was able to pay, and not have been much the worse. But I have none, and therefore I must ask you to proportion the fine to my means. Well, perhaps I could afford a mina, and therefore I propose that penalty: Plato, Crito, Critobulus, and Apollodorus, my friends here, bid me say thirty minae, and they will be the sureties. Let thirty minae be the penalty; for which sum they will be ample security to you.

[Socrates is condemned to death.]

Not much time will be gained, O Athenians, in return for the evil name which you will get from the detractors of the city, who will say that you killed Socrates, a wise man; for they will call me wise, even although I am not wise, when they want to reproach you. If you had waited a little while, your desire would have been fulfilled in the course of nature. For I am far advanced in years, as you may perceive, and not far from death. I am speaking now not to all of you, but only to those who have condemned me to death. And I have another thing to say to them: You think that I was convicted because I had no words of the sort which would have procured my acquittal —I mean, if I had thought fit to leave nothing undone or unsaid. Not so; the deficiency which led to my conviction was not of words— certainly not. But I had not the boldness or impudence or inclination to address you as you would have liked me to do, weeping and wailing and lamenting, and saying and doing many things which you have been accustomed to hear from others, and which, as I maintain, are unworthy of me. I thought at the time that I ought not to do anything common or mean when in danger: nor do I now repent of the style of my defence; I would rather die having spoken after my manner, than speak in your manner and live. For neither in war nor yet at law ought I or any man to use every way of escaping death. Often in battle there can be no doubt that if a man will throw away his arms, and fall on his knees before his pursuers, he may escape death; and in other dangers there are other ways of escaping death, if a man is willing to say and do anything. The difficulty, my friends, is not to avoid death, but to avoid unrighteousness; for that runs faster than death. I am old and move slowly, and the slower runner has overtaken me, and my accusers are keen and quick, and the faster runner, who is unrighteousness, has overtaken them. And now I depart hence condemned by you to suffer the penalty of death,—they too go their ways condemned by the truth to suffer the penalty of villainy and wrong; and I must abide by my award—let them abide by theirs. I suppose that these things may be regarded as fated,—and I think that they are well.

And now, O men who have condemned me, I would fain prophesy to you; for I am about to die, and in the hour of death men are gifted with prophetic power. And I prophesy to you who are my murderers, that immediately after my departure punishment far heavier than you have inflicted on me will surely await you. Me you have killed because you wanted to escape the accuser, and not to give an account of your lives. But that will not be as you suppose: far otherwise. For I say that there will be more accusers of you than there are now; accusers whom hitherto I have restrained: and as they are younger they will be more inconsiderate with you, and you will be more offended at them. If you think that by killing men you can prevent some one from censuring your evil lives, you are mistaken; that is not a way of escape which is either possible or honourable; the easiest and the noblest way is not to be disabling others, but to be improving yourselves. This is the prophecy which I utter before my departure to the judges who have condemned me.

Friends, who would have acquitted me, I would like also to talk with you about the thing which has come to pass, while the magistrates are busy, and before I go to the place at which I must die. Stay then a little, for we may as well talk with one another while there is time. You are my friends, and I should like to show you the meaning of this event which has happened to me. O my judges—for you I may truly call judges—I should like to tell you of a wonderful circumstance. Hitherto the divine faculty of which the internal oracle is the source has constantly been in the habit of opposing me even about trifles, if I was going to make a slip or error in any matter; and now as you see there has come upon me that which may be thought, and is generally believed to be, the last and worst evil. But the oracle made no sign of opposition, either when I was leaving my house in the morning, or when I was on my way to the court, or while I was speaking, at anything which I was going to say; and yet I have often been stopped in the middle of a speech, but now in nothing I either said or did touching the matter in hand has the oracle opposed me. What do I take to be the explanation of this silence? I will tell you. It is an intimation that what has happened to me is a good, and that those of us who think that death is an evil are in error. For the customary sign would surely have opposed me had I been going to evil and not to good.

Let us reflect in another way, and we shall see that there is great reason to hope that death is a good; for one of two things—either death is a state of nothingness and utter unconsciousness, or, as men say, there is a change and migration of the soul from this world to another. Now, if you suppose that there is no consciousness, but a sleep like the sleep of him who is undisturbed even by dreams, death will be an unspeakable gain. For if a person were to select the night in which his sleep was undisturbed even by dreams, and were to compare with this the other days and nights of his life, and then were to tell us how many days and nights he had passed in the course of his life better and more pleasantly than this one, I think that any man, I will not say a private man, but even the great king will not find many such days or nights, when compared with the others. Now, if death be of such a nature, I say that to die is gain; for eternity is then only a single night. But if death is the journey to another place, and there, as men say, all the dead abide, what good, O my friends and judges, can be greater than this? If, indeed, when the pilgrim arrives in the world below, he is delivered from the professors of justice in this world, and finds the true judges who are said to give judgment there, Minos and Rhadamanthus and Aeacus and Triptolemus, and other sons of God who were righteous in their own life, that pilgrimage will be worth making. What would not a man give if he might converse with Orpheus and Musaeus and Hesiod and Homer? Nay, if this be true, let me die again and again. I myself, too, shall have a wonderful interest in there meeting and conversing with Palamedes, and Ajax the son of Telamon, and any other ancient hero who has suffered death through an unjust judgment; and there will be no small pleasure, as I think, in comparing my own sufferings with theirs. Above all, I shall then be able to continue my search into true and false knowledge; as in this world, so also in the next; and I shall find out who is wise, and who pretends to be wise, and is not. What would not a man give, O judges, to be able to examine the leader of the great Trojan expedition; or Odysseus or Sisyphus, or numberless others, men and women too! What infinite delight would there be in conversing with them and asking them questions! In another world they do not put a man to death for asking questions; assuredly not. For besides being happier than we are, they will be immortal, if what is said is true.

Wherefore, O judges, be of good cheer about death, and know of a certainty, that no evil can happen to a good man, either in life or after death. He and his are not neglected by the gods; nor has my own approaching end happened by mere chance. But I see clearly that the time had arrived when it was better for me to die and be released from trouble; wherefore the oracle gave no sign. For which reason, also, I am not angry with my condemners, or with my accusers; they have done me no harm, although they did not mean to do me any good; and for this I may gently blame them.

Still, I have a favour to ask of them. When my sons are grown up, I would ask you, O my friends, to punish them; and I would have you trouble them, as I have troubled you, if they seem to care about riches, or anything, more than about virtue; or if they pretend to be something when they are really nothing,—then reprove them, as I have reproved you, for not caring about that for which they ought to care, and thinking that they are something when they are really nothing. And if you do this, both I and my sons will have received justice at your hands.

The hour of departure has arrived, and we go our ways—I to die, and you to live. Which is better God only knows.

SELF-RELIANCE

RALPH WALDO EMERSON

Ralph Waldo Emerson (1803–1882) was an American essayist and poet, and a leader in the Transcendentalist movement of the nineteenth century. "Self-Reliance" was published in *Essays* in 1841.

I read the other day some verses written by an eminent painter which were original and not conventional. The soul always hears an

admonition in such lines, let the subject be what it may. The sentiment they instil is of more value than any thought they may contain.
To believe your own thought, to believe that what is true for you in
your private heart is true for all men,—that is genius. Speak your
latent conviction, and it shall be the universal sense; for the inmost
in due time becomes the outmost,—and our first thought is rendered
back to us by the trumpets of the Last Judgment. Familiar as the voice
of the mind is to each, the highest merit we ascribe to Moses, Plato,
and Milton is, that they set at naught books and traditions, and spoke
not what men, but what *they* thought. A man should learn to detect
and watch that gleam of light which flashes across his mind from
within, more than the lustre of the firmament of bards and sages.
Yet he dismisses without notice his thought, because it is his. In every
work of genius we recognize our own rejected thoughts: they come
back to us with a certain alienated majesty. Great works of art have
no more affecting lesson for us than this. They teach us to abide by
our spontaneous impression with good-humored inflexibility then
most when the whole cry of voices is on the other side. Else to-morrow
a stranger will say with masterly good sense precisely what we have
thought and felt all the time, and we shall be forced to take with
shame our own opinion from another.

There is a time in every man's education when he arrives at the
conviction that envy is ignorance; that imitation is suicide; that he
must take himself for better, for worse, as his portion; that though the
wide universe is full of good, no kernel of nourishing corn can come
to him but through his toil bestowed on that plot of ground which
is given to him to till. The power which resides in him is new in nature, and none but he knows what that is which he can do, nor does
he know until he has tried. Not for nothing one face, one character,
one fact, makes much impression on him, and another none. This
sculpture in the memory is not without pre-established harmony. The
eye was placed where one ray should fall, that it might testify of that
particular ray. We but half express ourselves, and are ashamed of
that divine idea which each of us represents. It may be safely trusted
as proportionate and of good issues, so it be faithfully imparted, but
God will not have his work made manifest by cowards. A man is
relieved and gay when he has put his heart into his work and done
his best; but what he has said or done otherwise, shall give him no
peace. It is a deliverance which does not deliver. In the attempt his
genius deserts him; no muse befriends; no invention, no hope.

Trust thyself: every heart vibrates to that iron string. Accept the
place the divine providence has found for you, the society of your
contemporaries, the connection of events. Great men have always

done so, and confided themselves childlike to the genius of their age, betraying their perception that the absolutely trustworthy was seated at their heart, working through their hands, predominating in all their being. And we are now men, and must accept in the highest mind the same transcendent destiny; and not minors and invalids in a protected corner, not cowards fleeing before a revolution, but guides, redeemers, and benefactors, obeying the Almighty effort, and advancing on Chaos and the Dark.

What pretty oracles nature yields us on this text, in the face and behavior of children, babes, and even brutes! That divided and rebel mind, that distrust of a sentiment because our arithmetic has computed the strength and means opposed to our purpose, these have not. Their mind being whole, their eye is as yet unconquered, and when we look in their faces, we are disconcerted. Infancy conforms to nobody: all conform to it, so that one babe commonly makes four or five out of the adults who prattle and play to it. So God has armed youth and puberty and manhood no less with its own piquancy and charm, and made it enviable and gracious and its claims not to be put by, if it will stand by itself. Do not think the youth has no force, because he cannot speak to you and me. Hark! in the next room his voice is sufficiently clear and emphatic. It seems he knows how to speak to his contemporaries. Bashful or bold, then, he will know how to make us seniors very unnecessary.

The nonchalance of boys who are sure of a dinner, and would disdain as much as a lord to do or say aught to conciliate one, is the healthy attitude of human nature. A boy is in the parlor what the pit is in the playhouse; independent, irresponsible, looking out from his corner on such people and facts as pass by, he tries and sentences them on their merits, in the swift, summary way of boys, as good, bad, interesting, silly, eloquent, troublesome. He cumbers himself never about consequences, about interests; he gives an independent, genuine verdict. You must court him: he does not court you. But the man is, as it were, clapped into jail by his consciousness. As soon as he has once acted or spoken with *éclat,* he is a committed person, watched by the sympathy or the hatred of hundreds, whose affections must now enter into his account. There is no Lethe for this. Ah, that he could pass again into his neutrality! Who can thus avoid all pledges, and having observed, observe again from the same unaffected, unbiassed, unbribable, unaffrighted innocence, must always be formidable. He would utter opinions on all passing affairs, which being seen to be not private, but necessary, would sink like darts into the ear of men, and put them in fear.

These are the voices which we hear in solitude, but they grow faint and inaudible as we enter into the world. Society everywhere is in conspiracy against the manhood of every one of its members. Society is a joint-stock company, in which the members agree, for the better securing of his bread to each shareholder, to surrender the liberty and culture of the eater. The virtue in most request is conformity. Self reliance is its aversion. It loves not realties and creators, but names and customs.

Whoso would be a man must be a nonconformist. He who would gather immortal palms must not be hindered by the name of goodness, but must explore if it be goodness. Nothing is at last sacred but the integrity of your own mind. Absolve you to yourself, and you shall have the suffrage of the world. I remember an answer which when quite young I was prompted to make to a valued adviser, who was wont to importune me with the dear old doctrines of the church. On my saying, "What have I to do with the sacredness of traditions, if I live wholly from within?" my friend suggested: "But these impulses may be from below, not from above." I replied: "They do not seem to me to be such; but if I am the Devil's child, I will live then from the Devil." No law can be sacred to me but that of my nature. Good and bad are but names very readily transferable to that or this; the only right is what is after my constitution, the only wrong what is against it. A man is to carry himself in the presence of all opposition, as if everything were titular and ephemeral but him. I am ashamed to think how easily we capitulate to badges and names, to large societies and dead institutions. Every decent and well-spoken individual affects and sways me more than is right. I ought to go upright and vital, and speak the rude truth in all ways. If malice and vanity wear the coat of philanthropy, shall that pass? If an angry bigot assumes this bountiful cause of Abolition, and comes to me with his last news from Barbadoes, why should I not say to him: "Go love thy infant; love thy wood-chopper: be good-natured and modest: have that grace; and never varnish your hard, uncharitable ambition with this incredible tenderness for black folk a thousand miles off. Thy love afar is spite at home." Rough and graceless would be such greeting, but truth is handsomer than the affectation of love. Your goodness must have some edge to it,—else it is none. The doctrine of hatred must be preached as the counteraction of the doctrine of love when that pules and whines. I shun father and mother and wife and brother, when my genius calls me. I would write on the lintels of the door-post, *Whim*. I hope it is somewhat better than whim at last, but we cannot spend the day in explanation. Expect me not to show cause why I seek or why I exclude company. Then, again, do not tell me, as a good man did to-day, of my obligation to put all poor men in good situations. Are they *my* poor? I tell thee, thou foolish philanthropist, that I grudge the dollar, the dime, the cent, I give to such men as do not belong to me and to whom I do not belong. There is a class of persons to whom by all spiritual affinity I am bought and sold; for them I will go to prison, if need be; but your miscellaneous popular charities; the education at college of fools; the building of meeting-houses to the vain end to which many now stand; alms to sots; and the thousand-fold Relief Societies; —though I confess with shame I sometimes succumb and give the dollar, it is a wicked dollar which by and by I shall have the manhood to withhold.

Virtues are, in the popular estimate, rather the exception than the rule. There is the man *and* his virtues. Men do what is called a good action, as some piece of courage or charity, much as they would pay a fine in expiation of daily non-appearance on parade. Their works are done as an apology or extenuation of their living in the world,— as invalids and the insane pay a high board. Their virtues are penances. I do not wish to expiate, but to live. My life is for itself and not for a spectacle. I much prefer that it should be of a lower strain, so it be genuine and equal, than that it should be glittering and unsteady. I wish it to be sound and sweet, and not to need diet and bleeding. I ask primary evidence that you are a man, and refuse this appeal from the man to his actions. I know that for myself it makes no difference whether I do or forbear those actions which are reckoned excellent. I cannot consent to pay for a privilege where I have intrinsic right. Few and mean as my gifts may be, I actually am, and do not need for my own assurance or the assurance of my fellows any secondary testimony.

What I must do is all that concerns me, not what the people think. This rule, equally arduous in actual and in intellectual life, may serve for the whole distinction between greatness and meanness. It is the harder, because you will always find those who think they know what is your duty better than you know it. It is easy in the world to live after the world's opinion; it is easy in solitude to live after our own; but the great man is he who in the midst of the crowd keeps with perfect sweetness the independence of solitude.

The objection to conforming to usages that have become dead to you is, that it scatters your force. It loses your time and blurs the impression of your character. If you maintain a dead church, contribute to a dead Bible society, vote with a great party either for the government or against it, spread your table like base housekeepers, —under all these screens I have difficulty to detect the precise man you are. And, of course, so much force is withdrawn from your proper life. But do your work, and I shall know you. Do your work, and you shall reinforce yourself. A man must consider what a blind-man's-buff is this game of conformity. If I know your sect, I anticipate your argument. I hear a preacher announce for his text and topic the expediency of one of the institutions of his church. Do I not know beforehand that not possibly can he say a new and spontaneous word? Do I not know that, with all this ostentation of examining the grounds of the institution, he will do no such thing? Do I not know that he is pledged to himself not to look but at one side,—the permitted side, not as a man, but as a parish minister? He is a retained attorney, and these airs of the bench are the emptiest affectation. Well, most men have bound their eyes with one or another handkerchief, and attached themselves to some one of these communities of opinion. This conformity makes them not false in a few particulars, authors of a few lies, but false in all particulars. Their every truth is not quite true. Their two is not the real two, their four is not the real four; so that every word they say chagrins us, and we know not where to begin to set them right. Meantime nature is not slow to equip us in the prison-uniform of the party to which we adhere. We come to wear one cut of face and figure, and acquire by degrees the gentlest asinine expression. There is a mortifying experience in particular, which does not fail to wreak itself also in the general history; I mean "the foolish face of praise," the forced smile which we put on in company where we do not feel at ease in answer to conversation which does not interest us. The muscles, not spontaneously moved, but moved by a low usurping wilfulness, grow tight about the outline of the face with the most disagreeable sensation.

For non-conformity the world whips you with its displeasure. And therefore a man must know how to estimate a sour face. The by-standers look askance on him in the public street or in the friend's parlor. If this aversion had its origin in contempt and resistance like his own, he might well go home with a sad countenance; but the sour faces of the multitude, like their sweet faces, have no deep cause, but are put on and off as the wind blows and a newspaper directs. Yet is the discontent of the multitude more formidable than that of the senate and the college. It is easy enough for a firm man who knows the world to brook the rage of the cultivated classes. Their rage is decorous and prudent, for they are timid as being very vulnerable themselves. But when to their feminine rage the indignation of the people is added, when the ignorant and the poor are aroused, when the unintelligent brute force that lies at the bottom of society is made to growl and mow, it needs the habit of magnanimity and religion to treat it godlike as a trifle of no concernment.

The other terror that scares us from self-trust is our consistency; a reverence for our past act or word, because the eyes of others have no other data for computing our orbit than our past acts, and we are loath to disappoint them.

But why should you keep your head over your shoulder? Why drag about this corpse of your memory, lest you contradict somewhat you have stated in this or that public place? Suppose you should contradict yourself; what then? It seems to be a rule of wisdom never to rely on your memory alone, scarcely even in acts of pure memory, but to bring the past for judgment into the thousand-eyed present, and live ever in a new day. In your metaphysics you have denied personality to the Deity: yet when the devout motions of the soul come, yield to them heart and life, though they should clothe God with shape and color. Leave your theory, as Joseph his coat in the hand of the harlot, and flee.

A foolish consistency is the hobgoblin of little minds, adored by little statesmen and philosophers and divines. With consistency a great soul has simply nothing to do. He may as well concern himself with his shadow on the wall. Speak what you think now in hard words and to-morrow speak what to-morrow thinks in hard words again, though it contradict everything you said to-day.—"Ah, so you shall be sure to be misunderstood?"—Is it so bad, then, to be misunderstood? Pythagoras was misunderstood, and Socrates, and Jesus, and Luther, and Copernicus, and Galileo, and Newton, and every pure and wise spirit that ever took flesh. To be great is to be misunderstood.

I suppose no man can violate his nature. All the sallies of his will are rounded in by the law of his being, as the inequalities of Andes and Himmaleh are insignificant in the curve of the sphere. Nor does it matter how you gauge and try him. A character is like an acrostic or Alexandrian stanza;—read it forward, backward, or across, it still spells the same thing. In this pleasing, contrite wood-life which God allows me, let me record day by day my honest thought without prospect or retrospect, and, I cannot doubt, it will be found symmetrical, though I mean it not and see it not. My book should smell of pines and resound with the hum of insects. The swallow over my window should interweave that thread or straw he carries in his bill into my web also. We pass for what we are. Character teaches above our wills. Men imagine that they communicate their virtue or vice only by overt actions, and do not see that virtue or vice emit a breath every moment.

There will be an agreement in whatever variety of actions, so they be each honest and natural in their hour. For of one will, the actions will be harmonious, however unlike they seem. These varieties are lost sight of at a little distance, at a little height of thought. One tendency unites them all. The voyage of the best ship is a zigzag line of a hundred tacks. See the line from a sufficient distance, and it straightens itself to the average tendency. Your genuine action will explain itself, and will explain your other genuine actions. Your conformity explains nothing. Act singly, and what you have already done singly will justify you now. Greatness appeals to the future. If I can be firm enough to-day to do right, and scorn eyes, I must have done so much right before as to defend me now. Be it how it will, do right now. Always scorn appearances, and you always may. The force of character is cumulative. All the foregone days of virtue work their health into this. What makes the majesty of the heroes of the senate and the field, which so fills the imagination? The consciousness of a train of great days and victories behind. They shed a united light on the advancing actor. He is attended as by a visible escort of angels. That is it which throws thunder into Chatham's voice, and dignity into Washington's port, and America into Adam's eye. Honor is venerable to us because it is no ephemeris. It is always ancient virtue. We worship it to-day because it is not of to-day. We love it and pay it homage, because it is not a trap for our love and homage, but is self-dependent, self-derived, and therefore of an old immaculate pedigree, even if shown in a young person.

I hope in these days we have heard the last of conformity and consistency. Let the words be gazetted and ridiculous henceforward. Instead of the gong for dinner, let us hear a whistle from the Spartan fife. Let us never bow and apologize more. A great man is coming to eat at my house. I do not wish to please him; I wish that he should wish to please me. I will stand here for humanity, and though I would make it kind, I would make it true. Let us affront and reprimand the smooth mediocrity and squalid contentment of the times, and hurl in the face of custom, and trade, and office, the fact which is the upshot of all history, that there is a great responsible Thinker and Actor working wherever a man works; that a true man belongs to no other time or place, but is the centre of things. Where he is, there is nature. He measures you, and all men, and all events. Ordinarily, everybody in society reminds us of somewhat else, or of some other person. Character, reality, reminds you of nothing else; it takes place of the whole creation. The man must be so much, that he must make all circumstances indifferent. Every true man is a cause, a country, and an age; requires infinite spaces and numbers and time fully to accomplish his design;—and posterity seems to follow his steps as a train of clients. A man Cæsar is born, and for ages after we have a Roman Empire. Christ is born, and millions of minds so grow and cleave to his genius, that he is confounded with virtue and the possible of man. An institution is the lengthened shadow of one man; as Monachism, of the Hermit Antony; the Reformation, of Luther; Quakerism, of Fox; Methodism, of Wesley; Abolition, of Clarkson. Scipio, Milton called "the height of Rome"; and all history resolves itself very easily into the biography of a few stout and earnest persons.

Let a man then know his worth, and keep things under his feet. Let him not peep or steal, or skulk up and down with the air of a charity-boy, a bastard, or an interloper, in the world which exists for him. But the man in the street, finding no worth in himself which corresponds to the force which built a tower or sculptured a marble god, feels poor when he looks on these. To him a palace, a statue, or a costly book have an alien and forbidding air, much like a gay equipage, and seem to say like that, "Who are you sir?" Yet they all are his suitors for his notice, petitioners to his faculties that they will come out and take possession. The picture waits for my verdict: it is not to command me, but I am to settle its claims to praise. That popular fable of the sot who was picked up dead drunk in the street, carried to the duke's house, washed and dressed and laid in the duke's bed, and, on his waking, treated with all obsequious ceremony like the duke, and assured that he had been insane, owes its popularity to the fact, that it symbolizes so well the state of man, who is in the world a sort of sot, but now and then wakes up, exercises his reason and finds himself a true prince.

Our reading is mendicant and sycophantic. In history, our imagination plays us false. Kingdom and lordship, power and estate, are a gaudier vocabulary than private John and Edward in a small house and common day's work; but the things of life are the same to both; the sum total of both are the same. Why all this deference to Alfred, and Scanderbeg, and Gustavus? Suppose they were virtuous; did they wear out virtue? As great a stake depends on your private act to-day, as followed their public and renowned steps. When private men shall act with original views, the lustre will be transferred from the actions of kings to those of gentlemen.

The world has been instructed by its kings, who have so magnetized the eyes of nations. It has been taught by this colossal symbol the mutual reverence that is due from man to man. The joyful loyalty with which men have everywhere suffered the king, the noble, or the great proprietor to walk among them by a law of his own, make his own scale of men and things and reverse theirs, pay for benefits not with money but with honor, and represent the law in his person, was the hieroglyphic by which they obscurely signified their consciousness of their own right and comeliness, the right of every man.

The magnetism which all original action exerts is explained when we inquire the reason of self-trust. Who is the Trustee? What is the aboriginal Self, on which a universal reliance may be grounded? What is the nature and power of that science-baffling star, without parallax, without calculable elements, which shoots a ray of beauty even into trivial and impure actions, if the least mark of independence appear? The inquiry leads us to that source, at once the essence of genius, of virtue, and of life, which we call Spontaneity or Instinct. We denote this primary wisdom as Intuition, whilst all later teachings are tuitions. In that deep force, the last fact behind which analysis cannot go, all things find their common origin. For, the sense of being which in calm hours rises, we know not how, in the soul, is not diverse from things, from space, from light, from time, from man, but one with them, and proceeds obviously from the same source whence their life and being also proceed. We first share the life by which things exist, and afterwards see them as appearances in nature, and forget that we have shared their cause. Here is the fountain of action and of thought. Here are the lungs of that inspiration which giveth man wisdom, and which cannot be denied without impiety and atheism. We lie in the lap of immense intelligence, which makes us receivers of its truth and organs of its activity. When we discern justice, when we discern truth, we do nothing of ourselves, but allow a passage to its beams. If we ask whence this comes, if we seek to pry into the soul that causes, all philosophy is at fault. Its presence or its absence is all we can affirm. Every man discriminates between the voluntary acts of his mind, and his involuntary perceptions, and knows that to his involuntary perceptions a perfect faith is due. He may err in the expression of them, but he knows that these things are so, like day and night, not to be disputed. My wilful actions and acquisitions are but roving;—the idlest revery, the faintest native emotion, command my curiosity and respect. Thoughtless people contradict as readily the statements of perceptions as of opinions, or rather much more readily; for, they do not distinguish between perception and notion. They fancy that I choose to see this or that thing. But perception is not whimsical, it is fatal. If I see a trait, my children will see it after me, and in course of time, all mankind,— although it may chance that no one has seen it before me. For my perception of it is as much a fact as the sun.

The relations of the soul to the divine spirit are so pure, that it is profane to seek to interpose helps. It must be that when God speaketh he should communicate, not one thing, but all things; should fill the world with his voice; should scatter forth light, nature, time, souls, from the centre of the present thought; and new date and new create the whole. Whenever a mind is simple, and receives a divine wisdom, old things pass away,—means, teachers, texts, temples, fall; it lives now, and absorbs past and future into the present hour. All things are made sacred by relation to it,—one as much as another. All things are dissolved to their centre by their cause, and, in the universal miracle, petty and particular miracles disappear. If, therefore, a man claims to know and speak of God, and carries you backward to the phraseology of some old mouldered nation in another country, in another world, believe him not. Is the acorn better than the oak which is its fulness and completion? Is the parent better than the child into whom he has cast his ripened being? Whence, then, this worship of the past? The centuries are conspirators against the sanity and authority of the soul. Time and space are but physiological colors which the eye makes, but the soul is light; where it is, is day; where it was, is night; and history is an impertinence and an injury, if it be anything more than a cheerful apologue or parable of my being and becoming.

Man is timid and apologetic; he is no longer upright; he dares not say, "I think," "I am," but quotes some saint or sage. He is ashamed before the blade of grass or the blowing rose. These roses under my window make no reference to former roses or to better ones; they are for what they are; they exist with God to-day. There is no time to them. There is simply the rose; it is perfect in every moment of its existence. Before a leaf-bud has burst, its whole life acts; in the full-blown flower there is no more; in the leafless root there is no less. Its nature is satisfied, and it satisfies nature, in all moments alike. But man postpones or remembers; he does not live in the present, but with reverted eye laments the past, or, heedless of the riches that surround him, stands on tiptoe to foresee the future. He cannot be happy and strong until he too lives with nature in the present, above time.

This should be plain enough. Yet see what strong intellects dare not yet hear God himself, unless he speak the phraseology of I know not what David, or Jeremiah, or Paul. We shall not always set so great a price on a few texts, on a few lives. We are like children who repeat by rote the sentences of grandames and tutors, and, as they grow older, of the men of talents and character they chance to see,—painfully recollecting the exact words they spoke; afterwards, when they come into the point of view which those had who uttered these sayings, they understand them, and are willing to let the words go; for, at any time, they can use words as good when occasion comes. If we live truly, we shall see truly. It is as easy for the strong man to be strong, as it is for the weak to be weak. When we have new perception, we shall gladly disburden the memory of its hoarded treasures as old rubbish. When a man lives with God, his voice shall be as sweet as the murmur of the brook and the rustle of the corn.

And now at last the highest truth on this subject remains unsaid; probably cannot be said; for all that we say is the far-off remembering of the intuition. That thought, by what I can now nearest approach to say it, is this. When good is near you, when you have life in yourself, it is not by any known or accustomed way; you shall not discern the footprints of any other; you shall not see the face of man; you shall not hear any name; the way, the thought, the good, shall be wholly strange and new. It shall exclude example and experience. You take the way from man, not to man. All persons that ever existed are its forgotten ministers. Fear and hope are alike beneath it. There is somewhat low even in hope. In the hour of vision, there is nothing that can be called gratitude, nor properly joy. The soul raised over passion beholds identity and eternal causation, perceives the self-existence of Truth and Right, and calms itself with knowing that all things go well. Vast spaces of nature, the Atlantic Ocean, the South Sea,—long intervals of time, years, centuries,—are of no account. This which I think and feel underlay every former state of life and circumstances, as it does underlie my present, and what is called life, and what is called death.

Life only avails, not the having lived. Power ceases in the instant of repose; it resides in the moment of transition from a past to a new state, in the shooting of the gulf, in the darting to an aim. This one fact the world hates, that the soul *becomes;* for that forever degrades the past, turns all riches to poverty, all reputation to a shame, confounds the saint with the rogue, shoves Jesus and Judas equally aside. Why, then, do we prate of self-reliance? Inasmuch as the soul is present, there will be power not confident but agent. To talk of reliance is a poor external way of speaking. Speak rather of that which relies, because it works and is. Who has more obedience than I masters me, though he should not raise his finger. Round him I must revolve by the gravitation of spirits. We fancy it rhetoric, when we speak of eminent virtue. We do not yet see that virtue is Height, and that a man or a company of men, plastic and permeable to principles, by the law of nature must overpower and ride all cities, nations, kings, rich men, poets, who are not.

This is the ultimate fact which we so quickly reach on this, as on every topic, the resolution of all into the ever-blessed ONE. Self-existence is the attribute of the Supreme Cause, and it constitutes the measure of good by the degree in which it enters into all lower forms. All things real are so by so much virtue as they contain. Commerce, husbandry, hunting, whaling, war, eloquence, personal weight, are somewhat, and engage my respect as examples of its presence and impure action. I see the same law working in nature for conservation and growth. Power is in nature the essential measure of right. Nature suffers nothing to remain in her kingdoms which cannot help itself. The genesis and maturation of a planet, its poise and orbit, the bended tree recovering itself from the strong wind, the vital resources of every animal and vegetable, are demonstrations of the self-sufficing, and, therefore, self-relying soul.

Thus all concentrates; let us not rove; let us sit at home with the cause. Let us stun and astonish the intruding rabble of men and books and institutions, by a simple declaration of the divine fact. Bid the invaders take the shoes from off their feet, for God is here within. Let our simplicity judge them, and our docility to our own law demonstrate the poverty of nature and fortune beside our native riches.

But now we are a mob. Man does not stand in awe of man, nor is his genius admonished to stay at home, to put itself in communication with the internal ocean, but it goes abroad to beg a cup of water of the urns of other men. We must go alone. I like the silent church before the service begins, better than any preaching. How far off, how cool, how chaste the persons look, begirt each one with a precinct or sanctuary! So let us always sit. Why should we assume the faults of our friend, or wife, or father, or child, because they sit around our hearth, or are said to have the same blood? All men have my blood, and I have all men's. Not for that will I adopt their petulance or folly, even to the extent of being ashamed of it. But the isolation must not be mechanical, but spiritual, that is, must be elevation. At times the whole world seems to be in conspiracy to importune you with emphatic trifles. Friend, client, child, sickness, fear, want, charity, all knock at once at thy closet door, and say, "Come out unto us." But keep thy state; come not into their confusion. The power men possess to annoy me, I give them by a weak curiosity. No man can come near me but through my act. "What we love that we have, but by desire we bereave ourselves of the love."

If we cannot at once rise to the sanctities of obedience and faith, let us at least resist our temptations; let us enter into the state of war, and wake Thor and Woden, courage and constancy, in our Saxon breasts. This is to be done in our smooth times by speaking the truth. Check this lying hospitality and lying affection. Live no longer to the expectation of these deceived and deceiving people with whom we converse. Say to them, "O father, O mother, O wife, O brother, O friend, I have lived with you after appearances hitherto. Henceforward I am the truth's. Be it known unto you that henceforward I obey no law less than the eternal law. I will have no covenants but proximities. I shall endeavor to nourish my parents, to support my family, to be the chaste husband of one wife,—but these relations I must fill after a new and unprecedented way. I appeal from your customs. I must be myself. I cannot break myself any longer for you, or you. If you can love me for what I am, we shall be the happier. If you cannot, I will still seek to deserve that you should. I will not hide my tastes or aversions. I will so trust that what is deep is holy, that I will do strongly before the sun and moon whatever inly rejoices me, and the heart appoints. If you are noble, I will love you; if you are not, I will not hurt you and myself by hypocritical attentions. If you are true, but not in the same truth with me, cleave to your companions; I will seek my own. I do this not selfishly, but humbly and truly. It is alike your interest, and mine, and all men's, however long we have dwelt in lies, to live in truth. Does this sound harsh to-day? You will soon love what is dictated by your nature as well as mine, and, if we follow the truth, it will bring us out safe at last." But so you may give these friends pain. Yes, but I cannot sell my liberty and my power, to save their sensibility. Besides, all persons have their moments of reason, when they look out into the region of absolute truth; then will they justify me, and do the same thing.

The populace think that your rejection of popular standards is a rejection of all standard, and mere antinomianism; and the bold sensualist will use the name of philosophy to gild his crimes. But the law of consciousness abides. There are two confessionals, in one or the other of which we must be shriven. You may fulfil your round of duties by clearing yourself in the *direct,* or in the *reflex* way. Consider whether you have satisfied your relations to father, mother, cousin, neighbor, town, cat, and dog; whether any of these can upbraid you. But I may also neglect this reflex standard, and absolve me to myself. I have my own stern claims and perfect circle. It denies the name of duty to many offices that are called duties. But if I can discharge its debts, it enables me to dispense with the popular code.

If any one imagines that this law is lax, let him keep its commandment one day.

And truly it demands something godlike in him who has cast off the common motives of humanity, and has ventured to trust himself for a taskmaster. High be his heart, faithful his will, clear his sight, that he may in good earnest be doctrine, society, law, to himself, that a simple purpose may be to him as strong as iron necessity is to others!

If any man consider the present aspects of what is called by distinction *society*, he will see the need of these ethics. The sinew and heart of man seem to be drawn out, and we are become timorous, desponding whimperers. We are afraid of truth, afraid of fortune, afraid of death, and afraid of each other. Our age yields no great and perfect persons. We want men and women who shall renovate life and our social state, but we see that most natures are insolvent, cannot satisfy their own wants, have an ambition out of all proportion to their practical force, and do lean and beg day and night continually. Our housekeeping is mendicant, our arts, our occupations, our marriages, our religion, we have not chosen, but society has chosen for us. We are parlor soldiers. We shun the rugged battle of fate, where strength is born.

If our young men miscarry in their first enterprises, they lose all heart. If the young merchant fails, men say he is *ruined*. If the finest genius studies at one of our colleges, and is not installed in an office within one year afterwards in the cities or suburbs of Boston or New York, it seems to his friends and to himself that he is right in being disheartened, and in complaining the rest of his life. A sturdy lad from New Hampshire or Vermont, who in turn tries all the professions, who *teams it, farms it, peddles,* keeps a school, preaches, edits a newspaper, goes to Congress, buys a township, and so forth, in successive years, and always, like a cat, falls on his feet, is worth a hundred of these city dolls. He walks abreast with his days, and feels no shame in not "studying a profession," for he does not postpone his life, but lives already. He has not one chance, but a hundred chances. Let a Stoic open the resources of man, and tell men they are not leaning willows, but can and must detach themselves; that with the exercise of self-trust, new powers shall appear; that a man is the word made flesh, born to shed healing to the nations, that he should be ashamed of our compassion, and that the moment he acts from himself, tossing the laws, the books, idolatries, and customs out of the window, we pity him no more, but thank and revere him,—and that teacher shall restore the life of man to splendor, and make his name dear to all history.

It is easy to see that a greater self-reliance must work a revolution in all the offices and relations of men; in their religion; in their education; in their pursuits; their modes of living; their association; in their property; in their speculative views.

1. In what prayers do men allow themselves! That which they call a holy office is not so much as brave and manly. Prayer looks abroad and asks for some foreign addition to come through some foreign virtue, and loses itself in endless mazes of natural and supernatural, and mediatorial and miraculous. Prayer that craves a particular commodity,—anything less than all good,—is vicious. Prayer is the contemplation of the facts of life from the highest point of view. It is the soliliquy of a beholding and jubilant soul. It is the spirit of God pronouncing his works good. But prayer as a means to effect a private end is meanness and theft. It supposes dualism and not unity in nature and consciousness. As soon as the man is at one with God, he will not beg. He will then see prayer in all action. The prayer of the farmer kneeling in his field to weed it, the prayer of the rower kneeling with the stroke of his oar, are true prayers heard throughout nature, though for cheap ends. Caratach, in Fletcher's *Bonduca,* when admonished to inquire the mind of the god Audate, replies,—

> "His hidden meaning lies in our endeavors;
> Our valors are our best gods."

Another sort of false prayers are our regrets. Discontent is the want of self-reliance: it is infirmity of will. Regret calamities, if you can thereby help the sufferer: if not, attend your own work, and already the evil begins to be repaired. Our sympathy is just as base. We come to them who weep foolishly, and sit down and cry for company, instead of imparting to them truth and health in rough electric shocks, putting them once more in communication with their own reason. The secret of fortune is joy in our hands. Welcome evermore to gods and men is the self-helping man. For him all doors are flung wide: him all tongues greet, all honors crown, all eyes follow with desire. Our love goes out to him and embraces him, because he did not need it. We solicitously and apologetically caress and celebrate him, because he held on his way and scorned our disapprobation. The gods love him because men hated him. "To the persevering mortal," said Zoroaster, "the blessed Immortals are swift."

As men's prayers are a disease of the will, so are their creeds a disease of the intellect. They say with those foolish Israelites, "Let not God speak to us lest we die. Speak thou, speak any man with us, and we will obey." Everywhere I am hindered of meeting God in my brother, because he has shut his own temple doors, and recites

fables merely of his brother's or his brother's brother's God. Every
new mind is a new classification. If it prove a mind of uncommon
activity and power, a Locke, a Lavoisier, a Hutton, a Bentham, a
Fourier, it imposes its classification on other men, and lo! a new
system. In proportion to the depth of the thought, and so to the
number of the objects it touches and brings within reach of the pupil,
is his complacency. But chiefly is this apparent in creeds and churches,
which are also classifications of some powerful mind acting on the
elemental thought of duty, and man's relation to the Highest. Such
is Calvinism, Quakerism, Swedenborgism. The pupil takes the same
delight in subordinating everything to the new terminology, as a
girl who has just learned botany in seeing a new earth and new
seasons thereby. It will happen for a time, that the pupil will find
his intellectual power has grown by the study of his master's mind.
But in all unbalanced minds, the classification is idolized, passes for
the end, and not for a speedily exhaustible means, so that the walls
of the system blend to their eye in the remote horizon with the walls
of the universe; the luminaries of heaven seem to them hung on the
arch their master built. They cannot imagine how you aliens have
any right to see,—how you can see; "it must be somehow that you
stole the light from us." They do not yet perceive, that light, unsystematic, indomitable, will break into any cabin, even into theirs.
Let them chirp awhile and call it their own. If they are honest and
do well, presently their neat new pinfold will be too strait and low,
will crack, will lean, will rot and vanish, and the immortal light, all
young and joyful, million-orbed, million-colored, will beam over the
universe as on the first morning.

2. It is for want of self-reliance that the superstition of Travelling,
whose idols are Italy, England, Egypt, retains its fascination for all
educated Americans. They who made England, Italy, or Greece
venerable in the imagination did so by sticking fast where they were,
like an axis of the earth. In manly hours, we feel that duty is our
place. The soul is no traveller; the wise man stays at home, and when
his necessities, his duties, on any occasion, call him from his house,
or into foreign lands, he is at home still, and shall make men sensible,
by the expression of his countenance, that he goes the missionary of
wisdom and virtue, and visits cities and men like a sovereign, and
not like an interloper or a valet.

I have no churlish objection to the circumnavigation of the globe,
for the purposes of art, of study, and benevolence, so that the man is
first domesticated, or does not go abroad with the hope of finding
somewhat greater than he knows. He who travels to be amused, or to
get somewhat which he does not carry, travels away from himself,

and grows old even in youth among old things. In Thebes, in Palmyra, his will and mind have become old and dilapidated as they. He carries ruins to ruins.

Travelling is a fool's paradise. Our first journeys discover to us the indifference of places. At home I dream that at Naples, at Rome, I can be intoxicated with beauty, and lose my sadness. I pack my trunk, embrace my friends, embark on the sea, and at last wake up in Naples, and there beside me is the stern fact, the sad self, unrelenting, identical, that I fled from. I seek the Vatican, and the palaces. I affect to be intoxicated with sights and suggestions, but I am not intoxicated. My giant goes with me wherever I go.

3. But the rage of travelling is a symptom of a deeper unsoundness affecting the whole intellectual action. The intellect is vagabond, and our system of education fosters restlessness. Our minds travel when our bodies are forced to stay at home. We imitate; and what is imitation but the travelling of the mind? Our houses are built with foreign taste; our shelves are garnished with foreign ornaments; our opinions, our tastes, our faculties, lean, and follow the Past and the Distant. The soul created the arts wherever they have flourished. It was in his own mind that the artist sought his model. It was an application of his own thought to the thing to be done and the conditions to be observed. And why need we copy the Doric or the Gothic model? Beauty, convenience, grandeur of thought, and quaint expression are as near to us as to any, and if the American artist will study with hope and love the precise thing to be done by him, considering the climate, the soil, the length of the day, the wants of the people, the habit and form of the government, he will create a house in which all these will find themselves fitted, and taste and sentiment will be satisfied also.

Insist on yourself; never imitate. Your own gift you can present every moment with the cumulative force of a whole life's cultivation; but of the adopted talent of another, you have only an extemporaneous, half possession. That which each can do best, none but his Maker can teach him. No man yet knows what it is, nor can, till that person has exhibited it. Where is the master who could have taught Shakespeare? Where is the master who could have instructed Franklin, or Washington, or Bacon, or Newton? Every great man is a unique. The Scipionism of Scipio is precisely that part he could not borrow. Shakespeare will never be made by the study of Shakespeare. Do that which is assigned you, and you cannot hope too much or dare too much. There is at this moment for you an utterance brave and grand as that of the colossal chisel of Phidias, or trowel of the Egyptians, or the pen of Moses, or Dante, but different from all these. Not possibly will the soul all rich, all eloquent, with thousand-cloven tongue, deign to repeat itself; but if you can hear what these patriarchs say, surely you can reply to them in the same pitch of voice; for the ear and the tongue are two organs of one nature. Abide in the simple and noble regions of thy life, obey thy heart, and thou shalt reproduce the Foreworld again.

4. As our Religion, our Education, our Art look abroad, so does our spirit of society. All men plume themselves on the improvement of society, and no man improves.

Society never advances. It recedes as fast on one side as it gains on the other. It undergoes continual changes; it is barbarous, it is civilized, it is Christianized, it is rich, it is scientific; but this change is not amelioration. For everything that is given, something is taken. Society acquires new arts, and loses old instincts. What a contrast between the well-clad, reading, writing, thinking American, with a watch, a pencil, and a bill of exchange in his pocket, and the naked New-Zealander, whose property is a club, a spear, a mat, and an undivided twentieth of a shed to sleep under! But compare the health of the two men, and you shall see that the white man has lost his aboriginal strength. If the traveller tell us truly, strike the savage with a broad axe, and in a day or two the flesh shall unite and heal as if you struck the blow into soft pitch, and the same blow shall send the white to his grave.

The civilized man has built a coach, but has lost the use of his feet. He is supported on crutches, but lacks so much support of muscle. He has a fine Geneva watch, but he fails of the skill to tell the hour by the sun. A Greenwich nautical almanac he has, and so being sure of the information when he wants it, the man in the street does not know a star in the sky. The solstice he does not observe, the equinox he knows as little; and the whole bright calendar of the year is without a dial in his mind. His note-books impair his memory; his libraries overload his wit; the insurance office increases the number of accidents; and it may be a question whether machinery does not encumber; whether we have not lost by refinement some energy, by a Christianity intrenched in establishments and forms, some vigor of wild virtue. For every Stoic was a Stoic; but in Christendom where is the Christian?

There is no more deviation in the moral standard than in the standard of height or bulk. No greater men are now than ever were. A singular equality may be oberved between the great men of the first and of the last ages; nor can all the science, art, religion, and philosophy of the nineteenth century avail to educate greater men than Plutarch's heroes, three or four and twenty centuries ago. Not in time is the race progressive. Phocion, Socrates, Anaxagoras, Diogenes, are great men, but they leave no class. He who is really of their class will not be called by their name, but will be his own man, and, in his turn, the founder of a sect. The arts and inventions of each period are only its costume, and do not invigorate men. The harm of the improved machinery may compensate its good. Hudson and Behring accomplished so much in their fishing-boats, as to astonish Parry and Franklin, whose equipment exhausted the resources of science and art. Galileo, with an opera-glass, discovered a more splendid series of celestial phenomena than any one since. Columbus found the New World in an undecked boat. It is curious to see the periodical disuse and perishing of means and machinery, which were introduced with loud laudation a few years or centuries before. The great genius returns to essential man. We reckoned the improvements of the art of war among the triumphs of science, and yet Napoleon conquered Europe by the bivouac, which consisted of falling back on naked valor, and disencumbering it of all aids. The Emperor held it impossible to make a perfect army, says Las Cases, "without abolishing our arms, magazines, commissaries, and carriages, until, in imitation of the Roman custom, the soldier should receive his supply of corn, grind it in his hand-mill, and bake his bread himself."

Society is a wave. The wave moves onward, but the water of which it is composed does not. The same particle does not rise from the valley to the ridge. Its unity is only phenomenal. The persons who make up a nation to-day, next year die, and their experience with them.

And so the reliance on Property, including the reliance on governments which protect it, is the want of self-reliance. Men have looked away from themselves and at things so long, that they have come to esteem the religious, learned, and civil institutions as guards of property, and they deprecate assaults on these, because they feel them to be assaults on property. They measure their esteem of each other by what each has, and not by what each is. But a cultivated man becomes ashamed of his property, out of new respect for his nature. Especially he hates what he has, if he see that it is accidental, —came to him by inheritance, or gift, or crime; then he feels that it is not having; it does not belong to him, has no root in him, and merely lies there, because no revolution or no robber takes it away. But that which a man is, does always by necessity acquire, and what the man acquires is living property, which does not wait the beck of rulers, or mobs, or revolutions, or fire, or storm, or bankruptcies, but perpetually renews itself wherever the man breathes. "Thy lot or portion of life," said the Caliph Ali, "is seeking after thee; therefore be at rest from seeking after it." Our dependence on these foreign goods leads us to our slavish respect for numbers. The political parties meet in numerous conventions; the greater the concourse, and with each new uproar of announcement,—The delegation from Essex! The Democrats from New Hampshire! The Whigs of Maine! —the young patriot feels himself stronger than before by a new thousand of eyes and arms. In like manner the reformers summon conventions, and vote and resolve in multitude. Not so, O friends, will the God deign to enter and inhabit you, but by a method precisely the reverse. It is only as a man puts off all foreign support, and stands alone, that I see him to be strong and to prevail. He is weaker by every recruit to his banner. Is not a man better than a town? Ask nothing of men, and in the endless mutation, thou only firm column must presently appear the upholder of all that surrounds thee. He who knows that power is inborn, that he is weak because he has looked for good out of him and elsewhere, and so perceiving, throws himself unhesitatingly on his thought, instantly rights himself, stands in the erect position, commands his limbs, works miracles; just as a man who stands on his feet is stronger than a man who stands on his head.

So use all that is called Fortune. Most men gamble with her, and gain all, and lose all, as her wheel rolls. But do thou leave as unlawful these winnings, and deal with Cause and Effect, the chancellors of God. In the Will work and acquire, and thou hast chained the wheel of Chance, and shalt sit hereafter out of fear from her rotations. A political victory, a rise of rents, the recovery of your sick, or the return of your absent friend, or some other favorable event, raises your spirits, and you think good days are preparing for you. Do not believe it. Nothing can bring you peace but yourself. Nothing can bring you peace but the triumph of principles.

AGNOSTICISM AND CHRISTIANITY *

THOMAS HENRY HUXLEY

Thomas Henry Huxley (1825–1895) was an English biologist and teacher, known particularly for his defense of Darwin's theory of evolution, and for his lectures and writings explaining science to general audiences. The fol-

* From *Science and Christian Tradition* by Thomas Henry Huxley. Published by Appleton-Century-Crofts, Inc.

lowing selection is part of the essay "Agnosticism and Christianity," first printed in 1889.

⁓

The present discussion has arisen out of the use, which has become general in the last few years, of the terms "Agnostic" and "Agnosticism."

The people who call themselves "Agnostics" have been charged with doing so because they have not the courage to declare themselves "Infidels." It has been insinuated that they have adopted a new name in order to escape the unpleasantness which attaches to their proper denomination. To this wholly erroneous imputation, I have replied by showing that the term "Agnostic" did, as a matter of fact, arise in a manner which negatives it; and my statement has not been, and cannot be, refuted. Moreover, speaking for myself, and without impugning the right of any other person to use the term in another sense, I further say that Agnosticism is not properly described as a "negative" creed, nor indeed as a creed of any kind, except in so far as it expresses absolute faith in the validity of a principle which is as much ethical as intellectual. This principle may be stated in various ways, but they all amount to this: that it is wrong for a man to say that he is certain of the objective truth of any proposition unless he can produce evidence which logically justifies that certainty. This is what Agnosticism asserts; and, in my opinion, it is all that is essential to Agnosticism. That which Agnostics deny and repudiate, as immoral, is the contrary doctrine, that there are propositions which men ought to believe, without logically satisfactory evidence; and that reprobation ought to attach to the profession of disbelief in such inadequately supported propositions. The justification of the Agnostic principle lies in the success which follows upon its application, whether in the field of natural, or in that of civil, history; and in the fact that, so far as these topics are concerned, no sane man thinks of denying its validity.

Still speaking for myself, I add, that though Agnosticism is not, and cannot be, a creed, except in so far as its general principle is concerned; yet that the application of that principle results in the denial of, or the suspension of judgment concerning, a number of propositions respecting which our contemporary ecclesiastical "gnostics" profess entire certainty. And, in so far as these ecclesiastical persons can be justified in their old-established custom (which many nowadays think more honoured in the breach than the observance) of using opprobrious names to those who differ from them, I fully ad-

mit their right to call me and those who think with me "Infidels";
all I have ventured to urge is that they must not expect us to speak
of ourselves by that title.

The extent of the region of the uncertain, the number of the problems the investigation of which ends in a verdict of not proven, will
vary according to the knowledge and the intellectual habits of the
individual Agnostic. I do not very much care to speak of anything
as "unknowable." What I am sure about is that there are many topics
about which I know nothing; and which, so far as I can see, are out
of reach of my faculties. But whether these things are knowable by
any one else is exactly one of those matters which is beyond my
knowledge, though I may have a tolerably strong opinion as to the
probabilities of the case. Relatively to myself, I am quite sure that
the region of uncertainty—the nebulous country in which words
play the part of realities—is far more extensive than I could wish.
Materialism and Idealism; Theism and Atheism; the doctrine of
the soul and its mortality or immortality—appear in the history of
philosophy like the shades of Scandinavian heroes, eternally slaying
one another and eternally coming to life again in a metaphysical
"Nifelheim." It is getting on for twenty-five centuries, at least, since
mankind began seriously to give their minds to these topics. Generation after generation, philosophy has been doomed to roll the stone
uphill; and, just as all the world swore it was at the top, down it
has rolled to the bottom again. All this is written in innumerable
books; and he who will toil through them will discover that the
stone is just where it was when the work began. Hume saw this;
Kant saw it; since their time, more and more eyes have been cleaned
of the films which prevented them from seeing it; until now the
weight and number of those who refuse to be the prey of verbal
mystifications has begun to tell in practical life.

It was inevitable that a conflict should arise between Agnosticism
and Theology; or rather, I ought to say, between Agnosticism and
Ecclesiasticism. For Theology, the science, is one thing; and Ecclesiasticism, the championship of a foregone conclusion as to the truth
of a particular form of Theology, is another. With scientific Theology, Agnosticism has no quarrel. On the contrary, the Agnostic,
knowing too well the influence of prejudice and idiosyncrasy, even
on those who desire most earnestly to be impartial, can wish for nothing more urgently than that the scientific theologian should not only
be at perfect liberty to thresh out the matter in his own fashion; but
that he should, if he can, find flaws in the Agnostic position; and, even
if demonstration is not to be had, that he should put, in their full
force, the grounds of the conclusions he thinks probable. The scien-

tific theologian admits the agnostic principle, however widely his results may differ from those reached by the majority of Agnostics.

But, as between Agnosticism and Ecclesiasticism, or, as our neighbours across the Channel call it, Clericalism, there can be neither peace nor truce. The Cleric asserts that it is morally wrong not to believe certain propositions, whatever the results of a strict scientific investigation of the evidence of these propositions. He tells us that "religious error is, in itself, of an immoral nature." He declares that he has prejudged certain conclusions, and looks upon those who show cause for arrest of judgment as emissaries of Satan. It necessarily follows that, for him, the attainment of faith, not the ascertainment of truth, is the highest aim of mental life. And, on careful analysis of the nature of this faith, it will too often be found to be, not the mystic process of unity with the Divine, understood by the religious enthusiast; but that which the candid simplicity of a Sunday scholar once defined it to be. "Faith," said this unconscious plagiarist of Tertullian, "is the power of saying you believe things which are incredible."

Now I, and many other Agnostics, believe that faith, in this sense, is an abomination; and though we do not indulge in the luxury of self-righteousness so far as to call those who are not of our way of thinking hard names, we do feel that the disagreement between ourselves and those who hold this doctrine is even more moral than intellectual. It is desirable there should be an end of any mistakes on this topic. If our clerical opponents were clearly aware of the real state of the case, there would be an end of the curious delusion, which often appears between the lines of their writings, that those whom they are so fond of calling "Infidels" are people who not only ought to be, but in their hearts are, ashamed of themselves. It would be discourteous to do more than hint the antipodal opposition of this pleasant dream of theirs to facts.

The clerics and their lay allies commonly tell us, that if we refuse to admit that there is good ground for expressing definite convictions about certain topics, the bonds of human society will dissolve and mankind lapse into savagery. There are several answers to this assertion. One is that the bonds of human society were formed without the aid of their theology; and, in the opinion of not a few competent judges, have been weakened rather than strengthened by a good deal of it. Greek science, Greek art, the ethics of old Israel, the social organisation of old Rome, contrived to come into being, without the help of any one who believed in a single distinctive article of the simplest of the Christian creeds. The science, the art, the jurisprudence, the chief political and social theories, of the modern world have grown out of those of Greece and Rome—not by favour of, but in the teeth of, the fundamental teachings of early Christianity, to which science, art, and any serious occupation with the things of this world, were alike despicable.

Again, all that is best in the ethics of the modern world, in so far as it has not grown out of Greek thought, or Barbarian manhood, is the direct development of the ethics of old Israel. There is no code of legislation, ancient or modern, at once so just and so merciful, so tender to the weak and poor, as the Jewish law; and, if the Gospels are to be trusted, Jesus of Nazareth himself declared that he taught nothing but that which lay implicitly, or explicitly, in the religious and ethical system of his people.

"And the scribe said unto him, Of a truth, Teacher, thou hast well said that he is one; and there is none other but he and to love him with all the heart, and with all the understanding, and with all the strength, and to love his neighbour as himself, is much more than all the whole burnt offerings and sacrifices." (Mark xii: 32, 33.)

Here is the briefest of summaries of the teaching of the prophets of Israel of the eighth century; does the Teacher, whose doctrine is thus set forth in his presence, repudiate the exposition? Nay; we are told, on the contrary, that Jesus saw that he "answered discreetly," and replied, "Thou are not far from the kingdom of God."

So that I think that even if the creeds, from the so-called "Apostles' " to the so-called "Athanasian," were swept into oblivion; and even if the human race should arrive at the conclusion that, whether a bishop washes a cup or leaves it unwashed, is not a matter of the least consequence, it will get on very well. The causes which have led to the development of morality in mankind, which have guided or impelled us all the way from the savage to the civilized state, will not cease to operate because a number of ecclesiastical hypotheses turn out to be baseless. And, even if the absurd notion that morality is more the child of speculation than of practical necessity and inherited instinct, had any foundation; if all the world is going to thieve, murder, and otherwise misconduct itself as soon as it discovers that certain portions of ancient history are mythical; what is the relevance of such arguments to any one who holds by the Agnostic principle?

Surely, the attempt to cast out Beelzebub by the aid of Beelzebub is a hopeful procedure as compared to that of preserving morality by the aid of immorality. For I suppose it is admitted that an Agnostic may be perfectly sincere, may be competent, and may have studied the question at issue with as much care as his clerical opponents. But, if the Agnostic really believes what he says, the "dreadful consequence" argufier (consistently, I admit, with his own principles) virtually asks him to abstain from telling the truth, or to say what he believes to be untrue, because of the supposed injurious consequences to morality. "Beloved brethren, that we may be spotlessly moral, before all things let us lie," is the sum total of many an exhortation addressed to the "Infidel." Now, as I have already pointed out, we cannot oblige our exhorters. We leave the practical application of the convenient doctrines of "Reserve" and "Non-natural interpretation" to those who invented them.

I trust that I have now made amends for any ambiguity, or want of fulness, in my previous exposition of that which I hold to be the essence of the Agnostic doctrine. Henceforward, I might hope to hear no more of the assertion that we are necessarily Materialists, Idealists, Atheists, Theists, or any other ists, if experience had led me to think that the proved falsity of a statement was any guarantee against its repetition. And those who appreciate the nature of our position will see, at once, that when Ecclesiasticism declares that we ought to believe this, that, and the other, and are very wicked if we don't, it is impossible for us to give any answer but this: We have not the slightest objection to believe anything you like, if you will give us good grounds for belief; but, if you cannot, we must respectfully refuse, even if that refusal should wreck morality and insure our own damnation several times over. We are quite content to leave that to the decision of the future. The course of the past has impressed us with the firm conviction that no good ever comes of falsehood, and we feel warranted in refusing even to experiment in that direction.

RELIGIOUS FAITH *

WILLIAM JAMES

William James (1842–1910) was an American psychologist, philosopher, and Harvard professor. "Religious Faith" is an excerpt from *The Will to Believe*, a collection of essays and lectures published in 1897.

And now, in turning to what religion may have to say to the question,† I come to what is the soul of my discourse. Religion has meant

* From *The Will to Believe* by William James. Published by Longmans, Green & Co., Inc.   † The question of the meaning of life.

many things in human history; but when from now onward I use the word I mean to use it in the supernaturalist sense, as declaring that the so-called order of nature, which constitutes this world's experience, is only one portion of the total universe, and that there stretches beyond this visible world an unseen world of which we now know nothing positive, but in its relation to which the true significance of our present mundane life consists. A man's religious faith (whatever more special items of doctrine it may involve) means for me essentially his faith in the existence of an unseen order of some kind in which the riddles of the natural order may be found explained. In the more developed religions the natural world has always been regarded as the mere scaffolding or vestibule of a truer, more eternal world, and affirmed to be a sphere of education, trial, or redemption. In these religions, one must in some fashion die to the natural life before one can enter into life eternal. The notion that this physical world of wind and water, where the sun rises and the moon sets, is absolutely and ultimately the divinely aimed-at and established thing, is one which we find only in very early religions, such as that of the most primitive Jews. It is this natural religion (primitive still, in spite of the fact that poets and men of science whose good-will exceeds their perspicacity keep publishing it in new editions tuned to our contemporary ears) that, as I said a while ago, has suffered definitive bankruptcy in the opinion of a circle of persons, among whom I must count myself, and who are growing more numerous every day. For such persons the physical order of nature, taken simply as science knows it, cannot be held to reveal any one harmonious spiritual intent. It is mere *weather,* as Chauncey Wright called it, doing and undoing without end.

Now, I wish to make you feel, if I can in the short remainder of this hour, that we have a right to believe the physical order to be only a partial order; that we have a right to supplement it by an unseen spiritual order which we assume on trust, if only thereby life may seem to us better worth living again. But as such a trust will seem to some of you sadly mystical and execrably unscientific, I must first say a word or two to weaken the veto which you may consider that science opposes to our act.

There is included in human nature an ingrained naturalism and materialism of mind which can only admit facts that are actually tangible. Of this sort of mind the entity called "science" is the idol. Fondness for the word "scientist" is one of the notes by which you may know its votaries; and its short way of killing any opinion that it disbelieves in is to call it "unscientific." It must be granted that there is no slight excuse for this. Science has made such glorious leaps in the last three hundred years, and extended our knowledge of nature so enormously both in general and in detail; men of science, moreover, have as a class displayed such admirable virtues,—that it is no wonder if the worshippers of science lose their head. In this very University, accordingly, I have heard more than one teacher say that all the fundamental conceptions of truth have already been found by science, and that the future has only the details of the picture to fill in. But the slightest reflection on the real conditions will suffice to show how barbaric such notions are. They show such a lack of scientific imagination, that it is hard to see how one who is actively advancing any part of science can make a mistake so crude. Think how many absolutely new scientific conceptions have arisen in our own generation, how many new problems have been formulated that were never thought of before, and then cast an eye upon the brevity of science's career. It began with Galileo, not three hundred years ago. Four thinkers since Galileo, each informing his successor of what discoveries his own lifetime had seen achieved, might have passed the torch of science into our hands as we sit here in this room. Indeed, for the matter of that, an audience much smaller than the present one, an audience of some five or six score people, if each person in it could speak for his own generation, would carry us away to the black unknown of the human species, to days without a document or monument to tell their tale. Is it credible that such a mushroom knowledge, such a growth overnight as this, *can* represent more than the minutest glimpse of what the universe will really prove to be when adequately understood? No! our science is a drop, our ignorance a sea. Whatever else be certain, this at least is certain,—that the world of our present natural knowledge *is* enveloped in a larger world of *some* sort of whose residual properties we at present can frame no positive idea.

Agnostic positivism, of course, admits this principle theoretically in the most cordial terms, but insists that we must not turn it to any practical use. We have no right, this doctrine tells us, to dream dreams, or suppose anything about the unseen part of the universe, merely because to do so may be for what we are pleased to call our highest interests. We must always wait for sensible evidence for our beliefs; and where such evidence is inaccessible we must frame no hypotheses whatever. Of course this is a safe enough position *in abstracto*. If a thinker had no stake in the unknown, no vital needs, to live or languish according to what the unseen world contained, a philosophic neutrality and refusal to believe either one way or the other would be his wisest cue. But, unfortunately, neutrality is not only inwardly difficult, it is also outwardly unrealizable, where our relations to an alternative are practical and vital. This is because, as the psychologists tell us, belief and doubt are living attitudes, and involve conduct on our part. Our only way, for example, of doubting or refusing to believe, that a certain thing *is*, is continuing to act as if it were *not*. If, for instance, I refuse to believe that the room is getting cold, I leave the windows open and light no fire just as if it still were warm. If I doubt that you are worthy of my confidence, I keep you uninformed of all my secrets just as if you were *un*worthy of the same. If I doubt the need of insuring my house, I leave it un-insured as much as if I believed there were no need. And so if I must not believe that the world is divine, I can only express that refusal by declining ever to act distinctively as if it were so, which can only mean acting on certain critical occasions as if it were *not* so, or in an irreligious way. There are, you see, inevitable occasions in life when inaction is a kind of action, and must count as action, and when not to be for is to be practically against; and in all such cases strict and consistent neutrality is an unattainable thing.

And, after all, is not this duty of neutrality, where only our inner interests would lead us to believe, the most ridiculous of commands? Is it not sheer dogmatic folly to say that our inner interests can have no real connection with the forces that the hidden world may con-tain? In other cases divinations based on inner interests have proved prophetic enough. Take science itself! Without an imperious inner demand on our part for ideal logical and mathematical harmonies, we should never have attained to proving that such harmonies lie hidden between all the chinks and interstices of the crude natural world. Hardly a law has been established in science, hardly a fact ascertained, which was not first sought after, often with sweat and blood, to gratify an inner need. Whence such needs come from we do not know: we find them in us, and biological psychology so far only classes them with Darwin's "accidental variations." But the inner need of believing that this world of nature is a sign of something more spiritual and eternal than itself is just as strong and authori-tative in those who feel it, as the inner need of uniform laws of causation ever can be in a professionally scientific head. The toil of many generations has proved the latter need prophetic. Why *may* not the former one be prophetic, too? And if needs of ours outrun the visible universe, why *may* not that be a sign that an invisible universe is there? What, in short, has authority to debar us from trusting our religious demands? Science as such assuredly has no authority, for she can only say what is, not what is not; and the agnostic "thou shalt not believe without coercive sensible evidence" is simply an expression (free to any one to make) of private personal appetite for evidence of a certain peculiar kind.

Now, when I speak of trusting our religious demands, just what do I mean by "trusting"? Is the word to carry with it license to define in detail an invisible world, and to anathematize and excommunicate those whose trust is different? Certainly not! Our faculties of belief were not primarily given us to make orthodoxies and heresies withal; they were given us to live by. And to trust our religious demands means first of all to live in the light of them, and to act as if the invisible world which they suggest were real. It is a fact of human nature, that men can live and die by the help of a sort of faith that goes without a single dogma of definition. The bare assurance that this natural order is not ultimate but a mere sign or vision, the eternal staging of a many-storied universe, in which spiritual forces have the last word and are eternal,—this bare assurance is to such men enough to make life seem worth living in spite of every contrary presumption suggested by its circumstances on the natural plane. Destroy this inner assurance, however, vague as it is, and all the light and radiance of existence is extinguished for these persons at a stroke. Often enough the wild-eyed look at life—the suicidal mood—will then set in.

And now the application comes directly home to you and me. Probably to almost everyone of us here the most adverse life would seem well worth living, if we only could be *certain* that our bravery and patience with it were terminating and eventuating and bearing fruit somewhere in an unseen spiritual world. By granting we are not certain, does it then follow that a bare trust in such a world is a fool's paradise and lubberland, or rather that it is a living attitude in which we are free to indulge? Well, we are free to trust at our own risks anything that is not impossible, and that can bring analogies to bear in its behalf. That the world of physics is probably not absolute, all the converging multitude of arguments that make in favor of idealism tend to prove; and that our whole physical life may lie soaking in a spiritual atmosphere, a dimension of being that we at present have no organ for apprehending, is vividly suggested to us by the analogy of our domestic animals. Our dogs, for example, are in our human life but not of it. They witness hourly the outward body of events whose inner meaning cannot, by any possible operation, be revealed to their intelligence,—events in which they themselves often play the cardinal part. My terrier bites a teasing boy, and the father demands damages. The dog may be present at every step of the negotiations, and see the money paid, without an inkling of what it all means, without a suspicion that it has anything to do with *him;*

and he never *can* know in his natural dog's life. Or take another case
which used greatly to impress me in my medical-student days. Consider a poor dog whom they are vivisecting in a laboratory. He lies
strapped on a board and shrieking at his executioners, and to his
own dark consciousness is literally in a sort of hell. He cannot see a
single redeeming ray in the whole business; and yet all these dia-
bolical-seeming events are often controlled by human intentions
with which, if his poor benighted mind could only be made to catch
a glimpse of them, all that is heroic in him would religiously acquiesce. Healing truth, relief to future sufferings of beast and man,
are to be bought by them. It may be genuinely a process of redemption. Lying on his back on the board there he may be performing
a function incalculably higher than any that prosperous canine life
admits of; and yet, of the whole performance, this function is the
one portion that must remain absolutely beyond his ken.

Now turn from this to the life of man. In the dog's life we see the
world invisible to him because we live in both worlds. In human
life, although we only see our world, and his within it, yet encom-
passing both these worlds a still wider world may be there, as unseen
by us as our world is by him; and to believe in that world *may* be the
most essential function that our lives in this world have to perform.
But *"may* be! *may* be!" one now hears the positivist contemptuously
exclaim; "what use can a scientific life have for maybes?" Well, I reply,
the "scientific" life itself has much to do with maybes, and human
life at large has everything to do with them. So far as man stands for
anything, and is productive or originative at all, his entire vital function may be said to have to deal with maybes. Not a victory is gained,
not a deed of faithfulness or courage is done, except upon a maybe;
not a service, not a sally of generosity, not a scientific exploration or
experiment or text-book, that may not be a mistake. It is only by
risking our persons from one hour to another that we live at all.
And often enough our faith beforehand in an uncertified result *is
the only thing that makes the result come true.* Suppose, for instance,
that you are climbing a mountain, and have worked yourself into
a position from which the only escape is by a terrible leap. Have faith
that you can successfully make it, and your feet are nerved to its
accomplishment. But mistrust yourself, and think of all the sweet
things you have heard the scientists say of *maybes,* and you will
hesitate so long that, at last, all unstrung and trembling, and launching yourself in a moment of despair, you roll in the abyss. In such a
case (and it belongs to an enormous class), the part of wisdom as
well as of courage is to *believe what is in the line of your needs,* for

only by such belief is the need fulfilled. Refuse to believe, and you shall indeed be right, for you shall irretrievably perish. But believe, and again you shall be right, for you shall save yourself. You make one or the other of two possible universes true by your trust or mistrust,—both universes having been only *maybes*, in this particular, before you contributed your act.

Now, it appears to me that the question whether life is worth living is subject to conditions logically much like these. It does, indeed, depend on you *the liver*. If you surrender to the nightmare view and crown the evil edifice by your own suicide, you have indeed made a picture totally black. Pessimism, completed by your act, is true beyond a doubt, so far as your world goes. Your mistrust of life has removed whatever worth your own enduring existence might have given to it; and now, throughout the whole sphere of possible influence of that existence, the mistrust has proved itself to have had divining power. But suppose, on the other hand, that instead of giving way to the nightmare view, you cling to it that this world is not the *ultimatum*. Suppose you find yourself a very wellspring, as Wordsworth says, of—

> "Zeal and the virtue to exist by faith
> As soldiers live by courage; as, by strength
> Of heart, the sailor fights with roaring seas."

Suppose, however thickly evils crowd upon you, that your unconquerable subjectivity proves to be their match, and that you find a more wonderful joy than any passive pleasure can bring in trusting ever in the larger whole. Have you not now made life worth living on these terms? What sort of a thing would life really be, with your qualities ready for a tussle with it, if it only brought fair weather and gave these higher faculties of yours no scope? Please remember that optimism and pessimism are definitions of the world, and that our own reactions on the world, small as they are in bulk, are integral parts of the whole thing, and necessarily help to determine the definition. They may even be the decisive elements in determining the definition. A large mass can have its unstable equilibrium overturned by the addition of a feather's weight; a long phrase may have its sense reversed by the addition of the three letters n-o-t. This life *is* worth living, we can say, *since it is what we make it, from the moral point of view;* and we are determined to make it from that point of view, so far as we have anything to do with it, a success.

Now, in this description of faiths that verify themselves I have assumed that our faith in an invisible order is what inspires those efforts and that patience which make this visible order good for moral men. Our faith in the seen world's goodness (goodness now meaning fitness for successful moral and religious life) has verified itself by leaning on our faith in the unseen world. But will our faith in the unseen world similarly verify itself? Who knows?

Once more it is a case of *maybe;* and once more *maybes* are the essence of the situation. I confess that I do not see why the very existence of an invisible world may not in part depend on the personal response which any one of us may make to the religious appeal. God himself, in short, may draw vital strength and increase of very being from our fidelity. For my own part, I do not know what the sweat and blood and tragedy of this life mean, if they mean anything short of this. If this life be not a real fight, in which something is eternally gained for the universe by success, it is no better than a game of private theatricals from which one may withdraw at will. But it *feels* like a real fight,—as if there were something really wild in the universe which we, with all our idealities and faithfulnesses, are needed to redeem; and first of all to redeem our own hearts from atheisms and fears. For such a half-wild, half-saved universe our nature is adapted. The deepest thing in our nature is this *Binnenleben* (as a German doctor lately has called it), this dumb region of the heart in which we dwell alone with our willingnesses and unwillingnesses, our faiths and fears. As through the cracks and crannies of caverns those waters exude from the earth's bosom which then form the fountain-heads of springs, so in these crepuscular depths of personality the sources of all our outer deeds and decisions take their rise. Here is our deepest organ of communication with the nature of things; and compared with all these concrete movements of our soul all abstract statements and scientific arguments—the veto, for example, which the strict positivist pronounces upon our faith— sound to us like mere chatterings of the teeth. For here possibilities, not finished facts, are the realities with which we have acutely to deal; and to quote my friend William Salter, of the Philadelphia Ethical Society, "as the essence of courage is to stake one's life on a possibility, so the essence of faith is to believe that the possibility exists."

These, then, are my last words to you: Be *not* afraid of life. Believe that life *is* worth living, and your belief will help create the fact. The "scientific proof" that you are right may not be clear before the day of judgment (or some stage of being which that expression may serve to symbolize) is reached. But the faithful fighters of this hour, or the beings that then and there will represent them, may turn to the faint-hearted, who here decline to go on, with words like those with which Henry IV greeted the tardy Crillon after a great victory had been gained: "Hang yourself, brave Crillon! we fought at Arques, and you were not there."

SCIENCE AND RELIGION *

ALBERT EINSTEIN

Albert Einstein (1879–   ), German-born, naturalized-American theoretical physicist, is well known for his theory of relativity and his more recent generalized theory of gravitation. The following selection, first printed in 1941, has been reprinted as Part II of a longer essay "Science and Religion" in *Out of My Later Years,* a collection of Dr. Einstein's essays and addresses published in 1950.

It would not be difficult to come to an agreement as to what we understand by science. Science is the century-old endeavor to bring together by means of systematic thought the perceptible phenomena of this world into as thoroughgoing an association as possible. To put it boldly, it is the attempt at the posterior reconstruction of existence by the process of conceptualization. But when asking myself what religion is, I cannot think of the answer so easily. And even after finding an answer which may satisfy me at this particular moment, I still remain convinced that I can never under any circumstances bring together, even to a slight extent, all those who have given this question serious consideration.

At first, then, instead of asking what religion is, I should prefer to ask what characterizes the aspirations of a person who gives me the impression of being religious: a person who is religiously enlightened appears to me to be one who has, to the best of his ability, liberated himself from the fetters of his selfish desires and is preoccupied with thoughts, feelings, and aspirations to which he clings because of their super-personal value. It seems to me that what is important is the force of this super-personal content and the depth of the conviction concerning its overpowering meaningfulness, regardless of whether any attempt is made to unite this content with a Divine Being, for otherwise it would not be possible to count Buddha and Spinoza as religious personalities. Accordingly, a religious person is devout in

* From *Out of My Later Years.* Reprinted by permission of The Philosophical Library, Inc.

the sense that he has no doubt of the significance and loftiness of those super-personal objects and goals which neither require nor are capable of rational foundation. They exist with the same necessity and matter-of-factness as he himself. In this sense religion is the age-old endeavor of mankind to become clearly and completely conscious of these values and goals and constantly to strengthen and extend their effects. If one conceives of religion and science according to these definitions then a conflict between them appears impossible. For science can only ascertain what *is,* but not what should be, and outside of its domain value judgments of all kinds remain necessary. Religion, on the other hand, deals only with evaluations of human thought and action; it cannot justifiably speak of facts and relationships between facts. According to this interpretation, the well-known conflicts between religion and science in the past must all be ascribed to a misapprehension of the situation which has been described.

For example, a conflict arises when a religious community insists on the absolute truthfulness of all statements recorded in the Bible. This means an intervention on the part of religion into the sphere of science; this is where the struggle of the Church against the doctrines of Galileo and Darwin belongs. On the other hand, representatives of science have often made an attempt to arrive at fundamental judgments with respect to values and ends on the basis of scientific method, and in this way have set themselves in opposition to religion. These conflicts have all sprung from fatal errors.

Now, even though the realms of religion and science in themselves are clearly marked off from each other, nevertheless there exist between the two, strong reciprocal relationships and dependencies. Though religion may be that which determines the goal, it has, nevertheless, learned from science, in the broadest sense, what means will contribute to the attainment of the goals it has set up. But science can only be created by those who are thoroughly imbued with the aspiration towards truth and understanding. This source of feeling, however, springs from the sphere of religion. To this there also belongs the faith in the possibility that the regulations valid for the world of existence are rational, that is comprehensible to reason. I cannot conceive of a genuine scientist without that profound faith. The situation may be expressed by an image: science without religion is lame, religion without science is blind.

Though I have asserted above, that in truth a legitimate conflict between religion and science cannot exist, I must nevertheless qualify this assertion once again on an essential point, with reference to the actual content of historical religions. This qualification has to do with the concept of God. During the youthful period of mankind's spiritual evolution, human fantasy created gods in man's own image, who, by the operations of their will were supposed to determine, or at any rate to influence, the phenomenal world. Man sought to alter the disposition of these gods in his own favor by means of magic and prayer. The idea of God in the religions taught at present is a sublimation of that old conception of the gods. Its anthropomorphic character is shown, for instance, by the fact that men appeal to the Divine Being in prayers and plead for the fulfilment of their wishes.

Nobody, certainly, will deny that the idea of the existence of an omnipotent, just and omnibeneficent personal God is able to accord man solace, help, and guidance; also, by virtue of its simplicity the concept is accessible to the most undeveloped mind. But, on the other hand, there are decisive weaknesses attached to this idea in itself, which have been painfully felt since the beginning of history. That is, if this Being is omnipotent, then every occurrence, including every human action, every human thought, and every human feeling and aspiration is also His work; how is it possible to think of holding men responsible for their deeds and thoughts before such an Almighty Being? In giving out punishment and rewards He would to a certain extent be passing judgment on himself. How can this be combined with the goodness and righteousness ascribed to Him?

The main source of the present-day conflicts between the spheres of religion and of science lies in this concept of a personal God. It is the aim of science to establish general rules which determine the reciprocal connection of objects and events in time and space. For these rules, or laws of nature, absolutely general validity is required —not proven. It is mainly a program, and faith in the possibility of its accomplishment in principle is only founded on partial success. But hardly anyone could be found who would deny these partial successes and ascribe them to human self-deception. The fact that on the basis of such laws we are able to predict the temporal behavior of phenomena in certain domains with great precision and certainty, is deeply embedded in the consciousness of the modern man, even though he may have grasped very little of the contents of those laws. He need only consider that planetary courses within the solar system may be calculated in advance with great exactitude on the basis of a limited number of simple laws. In a similar way, though not with the same precision, it is possible to calculate in advance the mode of operation of an electric motor, a transmission system, or of a wireless apparatus, even when dealing with a novel development.

To be sure, when the number of factors coming into play in a phenomenological complex is too large, scientific method in most cases fails us. One need only think of the weather, in which case prediction even for a few days ahead is impossible. Nevertheless no one doubts that we are confronted with a causal connection whose causal components are in the main known to us. Occurrences in this domain are beyond the reach of exact prediction because of the variety of factors in operation, not because of any lack of order in nature.

We have penetrated far less deeply into the regularities obtaining within the realm of living things, but deeply enough nevertheless to sense at least the rule of fixed necessity. One need only think of the systematic order in heredity, and in the effect of poisons, as for instance alcohol on the behavior of organic beings. What is still lacking here is a grasp of connections of profound generality, but not a knowledge of order in itself.

The more a man is imbued with the ordered regularity of all events, the firmer becomes his conviction that there is no room left by the side of this ordered regularity for causes of a different nature. For him neither the rule of human nor the rule of Divine Will exists as an independent cause of natural events. To be sure, the doctrine of a personal God interfering with natural events could never be *refuted*, in the real sense, by science, for this doctrine can always take refuge in those domains in which scientific knowledge has not yet been able to set foot.

But I am persuaded that such behavior on the part of the representatives of religion would not only be unworthy but also fatal. For a doctrine which is able to maintain itself not in clear light but only in the dark, will of necessity lose its effect on mankind, with incalculable harm to human progress. In their struggle for the ethical good, teachers of religion must have the stature to give up the doctrine of a personal God, that is, give up that source of fear and hope which in the past placed such vast power in the hands of priests. In their labors they will have to avail themselves of those forces which are capable of cultivating the Good, the True, and the Beautiful in humanity itself. This is, to be sure, a more difficult but an incomparably more worthy task. After religious teachers accomplish the refining process indicated, they will surely recognize with joy that true religion has been ennobled and made more profound by scientific knowledge.

If it is one of the goals of religion to liberate mankind as far as possible from the bondage of egocentric cravings, desires, and fears, scientific reasoning can aid religion in yet another sense. Although it is true that it is the goal of science to discover rules which permit the association and foretelling of facts, this is not its only aim. It also seeks to reduce the connections discovered to the smallest possible number of mutually independent conceptual elements. It is in this striving after the rational unification of the manifold that it encounters its greatest successes, even though it is precisely this attempt which causes it to run the greatest risk of falling a prey to illusions. But whoever has undergone the intense experience of successful advances made in this domain, is moved by profound reverence for the rationality made manifest in existence. By way of the understanding he achieves a far-reaching emancipation from the shackles of personal hopes and desires, and thereby attains that humble attitude of mind towards the grandeur of reason incarnate in existence, which, in its profoundest depths, is inaccessible to man. This attitude, however, appears to me to be religious, in the highest sense of the word. And so it seems to me that science not only purifies the religious impulse of the dross of its anthropomorphism, but also contributes to a religious spiritualization of our understanding of life.

The further the spiritual evolution of mankind advances, the more certain it seems to me that the path to genuine religiosity does not lie through the fear of life, and the fear of death, and blind faith, but through striving after rational knowledge. In this sense I believe that the priest must become a teacher if he wishes to do justice to his lofty educational mission.

FOUR KINDS OF THINKING *

JAMES HARVEY ROBINSON

James Harvey Robinson (1863–1936) was an American teacher and historian.[1] The following selection is the second chapter of *The Mind in the Making*, published in 1921.

The truest and most profound observations on Intelligence have in the past been made by the poets and, in recent times, by story-writers. They have been keen observers and recorders and reckoned freely with the emotions and sentiments. Most philosophers, on the other hand, have exhibited a grotesque ignorance of man's life and have built up systems that are elaborate and imposing, but quite

* From *The Mind in the Making* by James Harvey Robinson. Copyright, 1921, by James Harvey Robinson; copyright, 1949, by Bankers Trust Company. Published by Harper & Brothers.

[1] See the portrayal of Robinson in Irwin Edman's essay "Former Teachers," p. 389.

unrelated to actual human affairs. They have almost consistently neglected the actual process of thought and have set the mind off as something apart to be studied by itself. *But no such mind, exempt from bodily processes, animal impulses, savage traditions, infantile impressions, conventional reactions, and traditional knowledge, ever existed,* even in the case of the most abstract of metaphysicians. Kant entitled his great work *A Critique of Pure Reason.* But to the modern student of mind pure reason seems as mythical as the pure gold, transparent as glass, with which the celestial city is paved.

Formerly philosophers thought of mind as having to do exclusively with conscious thought. It was that within man which perceived, remembered, judged, reasoned, understood, believed, willed. But of late it has been shown that we are unaware of a great part of what we perceive, remember, will, and infer; and that a great part of the thinking of which we are aware is determined by that of which we are not conscious. It has indeed been demonstrated that our unconscious psychic life far outruns our conscious. This seems perfectly natural to anyone who considers the following facts:

The sharp distinction between the mind and the body is, as we shall find, a very ancient and spontaneous uncritical savage prepossession. What we think of as "mind" is so intimately associated with what we call "body" that we are coming to realize that the one cannot be understood without the other. Every thought reverberates through the body, and, on the other hand, alterations in our physical condition affect our whole attitude of mind. The insufficient elimination of the foul and decaying products of digestion may plunge us into deep melancholy, whereas a few whiffs of nitrous monoxide may exalt us to the seventh heaven of supernal knowledge and godlike complacency. And *vice versa* a sudden word or thought may cause our heart to jump, check our breathing, or make our knees as water. There is a whole new literature growing up which studies the effects of our bodily secretions and our muscular tensions and their relation to our emotions and our thinking.

Then there are hidden impulses and desires and secret longings of which we can only with the greatest difficulty take account. They influence our conscious thought in the most bewildering fashion. Many of these unconscious influences appear to originate in our very early years. The older philosophers seem to have forgotten that even they were infants and children at their most impressionable age and never could by any possibility get over it.

The term "unconscious," now so familiar to all readers of modern works on psychology, gives offense to some adherents of the past. There should, however, be no special mystery about it. It is not a new animistic abstraction, but simply a collective word to include all the physiological changes which escape our notice, all the forgotten experiences and impressions of the past which continue to influence our desires and reflections and conduct, even if we cannot remember them. What we can remember at any time is indeed an infinitesimal part of what has happened to us. We could not remember anything unless we forgot almost everything. As Bergson says, the brain is the organ of forgetfulness as well as of memory. Moreover, we tend, of course, to become oblivious to things to which we are thoroughly accustomed, for habit blinds us to their existence. So the forgotten and the habitual make up a great part of the so-called "unconscious."

If we are ever to understand man, his conduct and reasoning, and if we aspire to learn to guide his life and his relations with his fellows more happily than heretofore, we cannot neglect the great discoveries, briefly noted above. We must reconcile ourselves to novel and revolutionary conceptions of the mind, for it is clear that the older philosophers, whose works still determine our current views, had a very superficial notion of the subject with which they dealt. But for our purposes, with due regard to what has just been said and to much that has necessarily been left unsaid (and with the indulgence of those who will at first be inclined to dissent), *we shall consider mind chiefly as conscious knowledge and intelligence, as what we know and our attitude toward it—our disposition to increase our information, classify it, criticize it, and apply it.*

We do not think enough about thinking, and much of our confusion is the result of current illusions in regard to it. Let us forget for the moment any impressions we may have derived from the philosophers, and see what seems to happen in ourselves. The first thing that we notice is that our thought moves with such incredible rapidity that it is almost impossible to arrest any specimen of it long enough to have a look at it. When we are offered a penny for our thoughts we always find that we have recently had so many things in mind that we can easily make a selection which will not compromise us too nakedly. On inspection we shall find that even if we are not downright ashamed of a great part of our spontaneous thinking it is far too intimate, personal, ignoble or trivial to permit us to reveal more than a small part of it. I believe this must be true of everyone. We do not, of course, know what goes on in other people's heads. They tell us very little and we tell them very little. The spigot of speech, rarely fully opened, could never emit more than driblets of the ever renewed hogshead of thought—*noch grosser wie's Heidelberger Fass.* We find it hard to believe that other people's thoughts are as silly as our own, but they probably are.

We all appear to ourselves to be thinking all the time during our waking hours, and most of us are aware that we go on thinking while we are asleep, even more foolishly than when awake. When uninterrupted by some practical issue we are engaged in what is now known as *reverie.* This is our spontaneous and favorite kind of thinking. We allow our ideas to take their own course and this course is determined by our hopes and fears, our spontaneous desires, their fulfillment or frustration; by our likes and dislikes, our loves and hates and resentments. There is nothing else anything like so interesting to ourselves as ourselves. All thought that is not more or less laboriously controlled and directed will inevitably circle about the beloved Ego. It is amusing and pathetic to observe this tendency in ourselves and in others. We learn politely and generously to overlook this truth, but if we dare to think of it, it blazes forth like the noontide sun.

The reverie or "free association of ideas" has of late become the subject of scientific research. While investigators are not yet agreed on the results, or at least on the proper interpretation to be given to them, there can be no doubt that our reveries form the chief index to our fundamental character. They are a reflection of our nature as modified by often hidden and forgotten experiences. We need not go into the matter further here, for it is only necessary to observe that the reverie is at all times a potent and in many cases an omnipotent rival to every other kind of thinking. It doubtless influences all our speculations in its persistent tendency to self-magnification and self-justification, which are its chief preoccupations, but it is the last thing to make directly or indirectly for honest increase of knowledge. Philosophers usually talk as if such thinking did not exist or were in some way negligible. This is what makes their speculations so unreal and often worthless.

The reverie, as any of us can see for himself, is frequently broken and interrupted by the necessity of a second kind of thinking. We have to make practical decisions. Shall we write a letter or no? Shall we take the subway or a bus? Shall we have dinner at seven or half past? Shall we buy U. S. Rubber or a Liberty Bond? Decisions are easily distinguishable from the free flow of the reverie. Sometimes they demand a good deal of careful pondering and the recollection of pertinent facts; often, however, they are made impulsively. They are a more difficult and laborious thing than the reverie, and we resent having to "make up our mind" when we are tired, or absorbed in a congenial reverie. Weighing a decision, it should be noted, does not necessarily add anything to our knowledge, although we may, of course, seek further information before making it.

A third kind of thinking is stimulated when anyone questions our belief and opinions. We sometimes find ourselves changing our minds without any resistance or heavy emotion, but if we are told that we are wrong we resent the imputation and harden our hearts. We are incredibly heedless in the formation of our beliefs, but find ourselves filled with an illicit passion for them when anyone proposes to rob us of their companionship. It is obviously not the ideas themselves that are dear to us, but our self-esteem, which is threatened. We are by nature stubbornly pledged to defend our own from attack, whether it be our person, our family, our property, or our opinion. A United States Senator once remarked to a friend of mine that God Almighty could not make him change his mind on our Latin-America policy. We may surrender, but rarely confess ourselves vanquished. In the intellectual world at least peace is without victory.

Few of us take the pains to study the origin of our cherished convictions; indeed, we have a natural repugnance to so doing. We like to continue to believe what we have been accustomed to accept as true, and the resentment aroused when doubt is cast upon any of our assumptions leads us to seek every manner of excuse for clinging to them. *The result is that most of our so-called reasoning consists in finding arguments for going on believing as we already do.*

I remember years ago attending a public dinner to which the Governor of the state was bidden. The chairman explained that His Excellency could not be present for certain "good" reasons; what the "real" reasons were the presiding officer said he would leave us to conjecture. This distinction between "good" and "real" reasons is one of the most clarifying and essential in the whole realm of thought. We can readily give what seem to us "good" reasons for being a Catholic or a Mason, a Republican or a Democrat, an adherent or opponent of the League of Nations. But the "real" reasons are usually on quite a different plane. Of course the importance of this distinction is popularly, if somewhat obscurely, recognized. The Baptist missionary is ready enough to see that the Buddhist is not such because his doctrines would bear careful inspection, but because he happened to be born in a Buddhist family in Tokio. But it would be treason to his faith to acknowledge that his own partiality for certain doctrines is due to the fact that his mother was a member of the First Baptist Church of Oak Ridge. A savage can give all sorts of reasons for his belief that it is dangerous to step on a man's shadow, and a newspaper editor can advance plenty of argument against the Bolsheviki. But neither of them may realize why he happens to be defending his particular opinion.

The "real" reasons for our beliefs are concealed from ourselves as well as from others. As we grow up we simply adopt the ideas presented to us in regard to such matters as religion, family relations, property, business, our country, and the state. We unconsciously absorb them from our environment. They are persistently whispered in our ear by the group in which we happen to live. Moreover, as Mr. Trotter has pointed out, these judgments, being the product of suggestion and not of reasoning, have the quality of perfect obviousness, so that to question them

. . . is to the believer to carry skepticism to an insane degree, and will be met by contempt, disapproval, or condemnation, according to the nature of the belief in question. When, therefore, we find ourselves entertaining an opinion about the basis of which there is a quality of feeling which tells us that to inquire into it would be absurd, obviously unnecessary, unprofitable, undesirable, bad form, or wicked, we may know that that opinion is a nonrational one, and probably, therefore, founded upon inadequate evidence.*

Opinions, on the other hand, which are the result of experience or of honest reasoning do not have this quality of "primary certitude." I remember when as a youth I heard a group of business men discussing the question of the immortality of the soul, I was outraged by the sentiment of doubt expressed by one of the party. As I look back now I see that I had at the time no interest in the matter, and certainly no least argument to urge in favor of the belief in which I had been reared. But neither my personal indifference to the issue, nor the fact that I had previously given it no attention, served to prevent an angry resentment when I heard *my* ideas questioned.

This spontaneous and loyal support of our preconceptions—this process of finding "good" reasons to justify our routine beliefs—is known to modern psychologists as "rationalizing"—clearly only a new name for a very ancient thing. Our "good" reasons ordinarily have no value in promoting honest enlightenment, because, no matter how solemnly they may be marshaled, they are at bottom the result of personal preference or prejudice, and not of an honest desire to seek or accept new knowledge.

In our reveries we are frequently engaged in self-justification, for we cannot bear to think ourselves wrong, and yet have constant illustrations of our weaknesses and mistakes. So we spend much time finding fault with circumstances and the conduct of others, and shifting on to them with great ingenuity the onus of our own failures and disappointments. *Rationalizing is the self-exculpation which*

* *Instincts of the Herd in Peace and War*, p. 44.

occurs when we feel ourselves, or our group, accused of misapprehension or error.

The little word *my* is the most important one in all human affairs, and properly to reckon with it is the beginning of wisdom. It has the same force whether it is *my* dinner, *my* dog, and *my* house, or *my* faith, *my* country, and *my* God. We not only resent the imputation that our watch is wrong, or our car shabby, but that our conception of the canals of Mars, of the pronunciation of "Epictetus," of the medicinal value of salicine, or the date of Sargon I, are subject to revision.

Philosophers, scholars, and men of science exhibit a common sensitiveness in all decisions in which their *amour propre* is involved. Thousands of argumentative works have been written to vent a grudge. However stately their reasoning, it may be nothing but rationalizing, stimulated by the most commonplace of all motives. A history of philosophy and theology could be written in terms of grouches, wounded pride, and aversions, and it would be far more instructive than the usual treatments of these themes. Sometimes, under Providence, the lowly impulse of resentment leads to great achievements. Milton wrote his treatise on divorce as a result of his troubles with his seventeen-year-old wife, and when he was accused of being the leading spirit in a new sect, the Divorcers, he wrote his noble *Areopagitica* to prove his right to say what he thought fit, and incidentally to establish the advantage of a free press in the promotion of Truth.

All mankind, high and low, thinks in all the ways which have been described. The reverie goes on all the time not only in the mind of the mill hand and the Broadway flapper, but equally in weighty judges and godly bishops. It has gone on in all the philosophers, scientists, poets, and theologians that have ever lived. Aristotle's most abstruse speculations were doubtless tempered by highly irrelevant reflections. He is reported to have had very thin legs and small eyes, for which he doubtless had to find excuses, and he was wont to indulge in very conspicuous dress and rings and was accustomed to arrange his hair carefully. Diogenes the Cynic exhibited the impudence of a touchy soul. His tub was his distinction. Tennyson in beginning his "Maud" could not forget his chagrin over losing his patrimony years before as the result of an unhappy investment in the Patent Decorative Carving Company. These facts are not recalled here as a gratuitous disparagement of the truly great, but to insure a full realization of the tremendous competition which all really exacting thought has to face, even in the minds of the most highly endowed mortals.

And now the astonishing and perturbing suspicion emerges that perhaps almost all that has passed for social science, political economy, politics, and ethics in the past may be brushed aside by future generations as mainly rationalizing. John Dewey has already reached this conclusion in regard to philosophy. Veblen and other writers have revealed the various unperceived presuppositions of the traditional political economy, and now comes an Italian sociologist, Vilfredo Pareto, who, in his huge treatise on general sociology, devotes hundreds of pages to substantiating a similar thesis affecting all the social sciences. This conclusion may be ranked by students of a hundred years hence as one of the several great discoveries of our age. It is by no means fully worked out, and it is so opposed to nature that it will be very slowly accepted by the great mass of those who consider themselves thoughtful. As a historical student I am personally fully reconciled to this newer view. Indeed, it seems to me inevitable that just as the various sciences of nature were, before the opening of the seventeenth century, largely masses of rationalizations to suit the religious sentiments of the period, so the social sciences have continued even to our own day to be rationalizations of uncritically accepted beliefs and customs.

It will become apparent as we proceed that the fact that an idea is ancient and that it has been widely received is no argument in its favor, but should immediately suggest the necessity of carefully testing it as a probable instance of rationalization.

This brings us to another kind of thought which can fairly easily be distinguished from the three kinds described above. It has not the usual qualities of the reverie, for it does not hover about our personal complacencies and humiliations. It is not made up of the homely decisions forced upon us by everyday needs, when we review our little stock of existing information, consult our conventional preferences and obligations, and make a choice of action. It is not the defense of our own cherished beliefs and prejudices just because they are our own—mere plausible excuses for remaining of the same mind. On the contrary, it is that peculiar species of thought which leads us to *change* our mind.

It is this kind of thought that has raised man from his pristine, subsavage ignorance and squalor to the degree of knowledge and comfort which he now possesses. On his capacity to continue and greatly extend this kind of thinking depends his chance of groping his way out of the plight in which the most highly civilized peoples of the world now find themselves. In the past this type of thinking has been called Reason. But so many misapprehensions have grown up around the word that some of us have become very suspicious of it. I suggest, therefore, that we substitute a recent name and speak of "creative thought" rather than of Reason. *For this kind of meditation begets knowledge, and knowledge is really creative inasmuch as it makes things look different from what they seemed before and may indeed work for their reconstruction.*

In certain moods some of us realize that we are observing things or making reflections with a seeming disregard of our personal preoccupations. We are not preening or defending ourselves; we are not faced by the necessity of any practical decision, nor are we apologizing for believing this or that. We are just wondering and looking and mayhap seeing what we never perceived before.

Curiosity is as clear and definite as any of our urges. We wonder what is in a sealed telegram or in a letter in which some one else is absorbed, or what is being said in the telephone booth or in low conversation. This inquisitiveness is vastly stimulated by jealousy, suspicion, or any hint that we ourselves are directly or indirectly involved. But there appears to be a fair amount of personal interest in other people's affairs even when they do not concern us except as a mystery to be unraveled or a tale to be told. The reports of a divorce suit will have "news value" for many weeks. They constitute a story like a novel or play or moving picture. This is not an example of pure curiosity, however, since we readily identify ourselves with others, and their joys and despair then become our own.

We also take note of, or "observe," as Sherlock Holmes says, things which have nothing to do with our personal interest and make no personal appeal either direct or by way of sympathy. This is what Veblen so well calls "idle curiosity." And it is usually idle enough. Some of us when we face the line of people opposite us in a subway train impulsively consider them in detail and engage in rapid inferences and form theories in regard to them. On entering a room there are those who will perceive at a glance the degree of preciousness of the rugs, the character of the pictures, and the personality revealed by the books. But there are many, it would seem, who are so absorbed in their personal reverie or in some definite purpose that they have no bright-eyed energy for idle curiosity. The tendency to miscellaneous observation we come by honestly enough, for we note it in many of our animal relatives.

Veblen, however, uses the term "idle curiosity" somewhat ironically, as is his wont. It is idle only to those who fail to realize that it may be a very rare and indispensable thing from which almost all distinguished human achievement proceeds, since it may lead to systematic examination and seeking for things hitherto undiscovered.

For research is but diligent search which enjoys the high flavor of primitive hunting. Occasionally and fitfully idle curiosity thus leads to creative thought, which alters and broadens our own views and aspirations and may in turn, under highly favorable circumstances, affect the views and lives of others, even for generations to follow. An example or two will make this unique human process clear.

Galileo was a thoughtful youth and doubtless carried on a rich and varied reverie. He had artistic ability and might have turned out to be a musician or painter. When he had dwelt among the monks at Valambrosa he had been tempted to lead the life of a religious. As a boy he busied himself with toy machines and he inherited a fondness for mathematics. All these facts are of record. We may safely assume also that, along with many other subjects of contemplation, the Pisan maidens found a vivid place in his thoughts.

One day when seventeen years old he wandered into the cathedral of his native town. In the midst of his reverie he looked up at the lamps hanging by long chains from the high ceiling of the church. Then something very difficult to explain occurred. He found himself no longer thinking of the building, worshipers, or the services; of his artistic or religious interests; of his reluctance to become a physician as his father wished. He forgot the question of a career and even the *graziosissime donne.* As he watched the swinging lamps he was suddenly wondering if mayhap their oscillations, whether long or short, did not occupy the same time. Then he tested this hypothesis by counting his pulse, for that was the only timepiece he had with him.

This observation, however remarkable in itself, was not enough to produce a really creative thought. Others may have noticed the same thing and yet nothing came of it. Most of our observations have no assignable results. Galileo may have seen that the warts on a peasant's face formed a perfect isosceles triangle, or he may have noticed with boyish glee that just as the officiating priest was uttering the solemn words, *ecce agnus Dei,* a fly lit on the end of his nose. To be really creative, ideas have to be worked up and then "put over," so that they become a part of man's social heritage. The highly accurate pendulum clock was one of the later results of Galileo's discovery. He himself was led to reconsider and successfully to refute the old notions of falling bodies. It remained for Newton to prove that the moon was falling, and presumably all the heavenly bodies. This quite upset all the consecrated views of the heavens as managed by angelic engineers. The universality of the laws of gravitation stimulated the attempt to seek other and equally important natural laws and cast grave doubts on the miracles in which mankind had hitherto believed. In short, those who dared to include in their thought the discoveries of Galileo and his successors found themselves in a new earth surrounded by new heavens.

On the 28th day of October, 1831, three hundred and fifty years after Galileo had noticed the isochronous vibrations of the lamps, creative thought and its currency had so far increased that Faraday was wondering what would happen if he mounted a disk of copper between the poles of a horseshoe magnet. As the disk revolved an electric current was produced. This would doubtless have seemed the idlest kind of an experiment to the stanch business men of the time, who, it happened, were just then denouncing the child-labor bills in their anxiety to avail themselves to the full of the results of earlier idle curiosity. But should the dynamos and motors which have come into being as the outcome of Faraday's experiment be stopped this evening, the business man of to-day, agitated over labor troubles, might, as he trudged home past lines of "dead" cars, through dark streets to an unlighted house, engage in a little creative thought of his own and perceive that he and his laborers would have no modern factories and mines to quarrel about had it not been for the strange practical effects of the idle curiosity of scientists, inventors, and engineers.

The examples of creative intelligence given above belong to the realms of modern scientific achievement, which furnishes the most striking instances of the effects of scrupulous, objective thinking. But there are, of course, other great realms in which the recording and embodiment of acute observation and insight have wrought themselves into the higher life of man. The great poets and dramatists and our modern story-tellers have found themselves engaged in productive reveries, noting and artistically presenting their discoveries for the delight and instruction of those who have the ability to appreciate them.

The process by which a fresh and original poem or drama comes into being is doubtless analogous to that which originates and elaborates so-called scientific discoveries; but there is clearly a temperamental difference. The genesis and advance of painting, sculpture, and music offer still other problems. We really as yet know shockingly little about these matters, and indeed very few people have the least curiosity about them. Nevertheless, creative intelligence in its various forms and activities is what makes man. Were it not for its slow, painful, and constantly discouraged operations through the ages man would be no more than a species of primate living on seeds, fruit, roots, and uncooked flesh, and wandering naked through the woods and over the plains like a chimpanzee.

The origin and progress and future promotion of civilization are ill understood and misconceived. These should be made the chief theme of education, but much hard work is necessary before we can reconstruct our ideas of man and his capacities and free ourselves from innumerable persistent misapprehensions. There have been obstructionists in all times, not merely the lethargic masses, but the moralists, the rationalizing theologians, and most of the philosophers, all busily if unconsciously engaged in ratifying existing ignorance and mistakes and discouraging creative thought. Naturally, those who reassure us seem worthy of honor and respect. Equally naturally those who puzzle us with disturbing criticisms and invite us to change our ways are objects of suspicion and readily discredited. Our personal discontent does not ordinarily extend to any critical questioning of the general situation in which we find ourselves. In every age the prevailing conditions of civilization have appeared quite natural and inevitable to those who grew up in them. The cow asks no questions as to how it happens to have a dry stall and a supply of hay. The kitten laps its warm milk from a china saucer, without knowing anything about porcelain; the dog nestles in the corner of a divan with no sense of obligation to the inventors of upholstery and the manufacturers of down pillows. So we humans accept our breakfasts, our trains and telephones and orchestras and movies, our national Constitution, or moral code and standards of manners, with the simplicity and innocence of a pet rabbit. We have absolutely inexhaustible capacities for appropriating what others do for us with no thought of a "thank you." We do not feel called upon to make any least contribution to the merry game ourselves. Indeed, we are usually quite unaware that a game is being played at all.

We have now examined the various classes of thinking which we can readily observe in ourselves and which we have plenty of reasons to believe go on, and always have been going on, in our fellow-men. We can sometimes get quite pure and sparkling examples of all four kinds, but commonly they are so confused and intermingled in our reverie as not to be readily distinguishable. The reverie is a reflection of our longings, exultations, and complacencies, our fears, suspicions, and disappointments. We are chiefly engaged in struggling to maintain our self-respect and in asserting that supremacy which we all crave and which seems to us our natural prerogative. It is not strange, but rather quite inevitable, that our beliefs about what is true and false, good and bad, right and wrong, should be mixed up with the reverie and be influenced by the same considerations which determine its character and course. We resent criticisms of our views

exactly as we do of anything else connected with ourselves. Our notions of life and its ideals seem to us to be *our own* and as such necessarily true and right, to be defended at all costs.

*We very rarely consider, however, the process by which we gained
our convictions.* If we did so, we could hardly fail to see that there
was usually little ground for our confidence in them. Here and there,
in this department of knowledge or that, some one of us might make
a fair claim to have taken some trouble to get correct ideas of, let
us say, the situation in Russia, the sources of our food supply, the
origin of the Constitution, the revision of the tariff, the policy of the
Holy Roman Apostolic Church, modern business organization, trade
unions, birth control, socialism, the League of Nations, the excess-
profits tax, preparedness, advertising in its social bearings; but only
a very exceptional person would be entitled to opinions on all of
even these few matters. And yet most of us have opinions on all these,
and on many other questions of equal importance, of which we may
know even less. We feel compelled, as self-respecting persons, to take
sides when they come up for discussion. We even surprise ourselves
by our omniscience. Without taking thought we see in a flash that it
is most righteous and expedient to discourage birth control by legislative enactment, or that one who decries intervention in Mexico is
clearly wrong, or that big advertising is essential to big business and
that big business is the pride of the land. As godlike beings why
should we not rejoice in our omniscience?

It is clear, in any case, that our convictions on important matters
are not the result of knowledge or critical thought, nor, it may be
added, are they often dictated by supposed self-interest. Most of
them are *pure prejudices* in the proper sense of that word. We do not
form them ourselves. They are the whisperings of "the voice of the
herd." We have in the last analysis no responsibility for them and
need assume none. They are not really our own ideas, but those of
others no more well informed or inspired than ourselves, who have
got them in the same careless and humiliating manner as we. It
should be our pride to revise our ideas and not to adhere to what
passes for respectable opinion, for such opinion can frequently be
shown to be not respectable at all. We should, in view of the considerations that have been mentioned, resent our supine credulity.
As an English writer has remarked:

If we feared the entertaining of an unverifiable opinion with the warmth
with which we fear using the wrong implement at the dinner table, if the
thought of holding a prejudice disgusted us as does a foul disease, then the
dangers of man's suggestibility would be turned into advantages.

The purpose of this essay [2] is to set forth briefly the way in which the notions of the herd have been accumulated. This seems to me the best, easiest, and least invidious educational device for cultivating a proper distrust for the older notions on which we still continue to rely.

The "real" reasons, which explain how it is we happen to hold a particular belief, are chiefly historical. Our most important opinions —those, for example, having to do with traditional, religious, and moral convictions, property rights, patriotism, national honor, the state, and indeed all the assumed foundations of society—are, as I have already suggested, rarely the result of reasoned consideration, but of unthinking absorption from the social environment in which we live. Consequently, they have about them a quality of "elemental certitude," and we especially resent doubt or criticism cast upon them. So long, however, as we revere the whisperings of the herd, we are obviously unable to examine them dispassionately and to consider to what extent they are suited to the novel conditions and social exigencies in which we find ourselves today.

The "real" reasons for our beliefs, by making clear their origins and history, can do much to dissipate this emotional blockade and rid us of our prejudices and preconceptions. Once this is done and we come critically to examine our traditional beliefs, we may well find some of them sustained by experience and honest reasoning, while others must be revised to meet new conditions and our more extended knowledge. But only after we have undertaken such a critical examination in the light of experience and modern knowledge, freed from any feeling of "primary certitude," can we claim that the "good" are also the "real" reasons for our opinions.

I do not flatter myself that this general show-up of man's thought through the ages will cure myself or others of carelessness in adopting ideas, or of unseemly heat in defending them just because we have adopted them. But if the considerations which I propose to recall are really incorporated into our thinking and are permitted to establish our general outlook on human affairs, they will do much to relieve the imaginary obligation we feel in regard to traditional sentiments and ideals. Few of us are capable of engaging in creative thought, but some of us can at least come to distinguish it from other and inferior kinds of thought and accord to it the esteem that it merits as the greatest treasure of the past and the only hope of the future.

---

[2] Mr. Robinson is here referring to the whole of *The Mind in the Making*, not simply to this chapter.

DOES HUMAN NATURE CHANGE? *

John Dewey (1859–) is an American philosopher and educator,[3] follower of William James, and founder of the progressive-school movement.
"Does Human Nature Change?" is a selection from *Problems of Men*, published in 1946.

———————

I have come to the conclusion that those who give different answers to the question I have asked in the title of this article are talking about different things. This statement in itself, however, is too
easy a way out of the problem to be satisfactory. For there is a real
problem, and so far as the question is a practical one instead of an
academic one, I think the proper answer is that human nature *does*
change.

By the practical side of the question, I mean the question whether
or not important, almost fundamental, changes in the ways of human
belief and action have taken place and are capable of still taking
place. But to put this question in its proper perspective, we have
first to recognize the sense in which human nature does not change.
I do not think it can be shown that the innate needs of men have
changed since man became man or that there is any evidence that
they will change as long as man is on the earth.

By "needs" I mean the inherent demands that men make because
of their constitution. Needs for food and drink and for moving about,
for example, are so much a part of our being that we cannot imagine
any condition under which they would cease to be. There are other
things not so directly physical that seem to me equally engrained
in human nature. I would mention as examples the need for some
kind of companionship; the need for exhibiting energy, for bringing
one's powers to bear upon surrounding conditions; the need for both
coöperation with and emulation of one's fellows for mutual aid and
combat alike; the need for some sort of aesthetic expression and
satisfaction; the need to lead and to follow, etc.

Whether my particular examples are well chosen or not does not
matter so much as does recognition of the fact that there are some
tendencies so integral a part of human nature that the latter would

* First published in *The Rotarian*, February, 1938. Reprinted by permission.
3 See the portrayal of Dewey in Irwin Edman's essay "Former Teachers" p. 392.

not be human nature if they changed. These tendencies used to be called instincts. Psychologists are now more chary of using that word than they used to be. But the word by which the tendencies are called does not matter much in comparison to the fact that human nature has its own constitution.

Where we are likely to go wrong, after the fact is recognized that there is something unchangeable in the structure of human nature, is the inference we draw from it. We suppose that the manifestation of these needs is also unalterable. We suppose that the manifestations we have got used to are as natural and as unalterable as are the needs from which they spring.

The need for food is so imperative that we call the persons insane who persistently refuse to take nourishment. But what kinds of food are wanted and used are a matter of acquired habit influenced by both physical environment and social custom. To civilized people today, eating human flesh is an entirely unnatural thing. Yet there have been peoples to whom it seemed natural because it was socially authorized and even highly esteemed. There are well-accredited stories of persons needing support from others who have refused palatable and nourishing foods because they were not accustomed to them; the alien foods were so "unnatural" they preferred to starve rather than eat them.

Aristotle spoke for an entire social order as well as for himself when he said that slavery existed by nature. He would have regarded efforts to abolish slavery from society as an idle and utopian effort to change human nature where it was unchangeable. For according to him it was not simply the desire to be a master that was engrained in human nature. There were persons who were born with such an inherently slavish nature that it did violence to human nature to set them free.

The assertion that human nature cannot be changed is heard when social changes are urged as reforms and improvements of existing conditions. It is always heard when the proposed changes in institutions or conditions stand in sharp opposition to what exists. If the conservative were wiser, he would rest his objections in most cases, not upon the unchangeability of human nature, but upon the inertia of custom; upon the resistance that acquired habits offer to change after they are once acquired. It is hard to teach an old dog new tricks and it is harder yet to teach society to adopt customs which are contrary to those which have long prevailed. Conservatism of this type would be intelligent, and it would compel those wanting change not only to moderate their pace, but also to ask how the changes they desire could be introduced with a minimum of shock and dislocation.

Nevertheless, there are few social changes that can be opposed on the ground that they are contrary to human nature itself. A proposal to have a society get along without food and drink is one of the few that are of this kind. Proposals to form communities in which there is no cohabitation have been made and the communities have endured for a time. But they are so nearly contrary to human nature that they have not endured long. These cases are almost the only ones in which social change can be opposed simply on the ground that human nature cannot be changed.

Take the institution of war, one of the oldest, most socially reputable of all human institutions. Efforts for stable peace are often opposed on the ground that man is by nature a fighting animal and that this phase of his nature is unalterable. The failure of peace movements in the past can be cited in support of this view. In fact, however, war is as much a social pattern as is the domestic slavery which the ancients thought to be an immutable fact.

I have already said that, in my opinion, combativeness is a constituent part of human nature. But I have also said that the manifestations of these native elements are subject to change because they are affected by custom and tradition. War does not exist because man has combative instincts, but because social conditions and forces have led, almost forced, these "instincts" into this channel.

There are a large number of other channels in which the need for combat has been satisfied, and there are other channels not yet discovered or explored into which it could be led with equal satisfaction. There is war against disease, against poverty, against insecurity, against injustice, in which multitudes of persons have found full opportunity for the exercise of their combative tendencies.

The time may be far off when men will cease to fulfill their need for combat by destroying each other and when they will manifest it in common and combined efforts against the forces that are enemies of all men equally. But the difficulties in the way are found in the persistence of certain acquired social customs and not in the unchangeability of the demand for combat.

Pugnacity and fear are native elements of human nature. But so are pity and sympathy. We send nurses and physicians to the battle-field and provide hospital facilities as "naturally" as we charge bayonets and discharge machine guns. In early times there was a close connection between pugnacity and fighting, for the latter was done largely with the fists. Pugnacity plays a small part in generating wars today. Citizens of one country do not hate those of another nation by instinct. When they attack or are attacked, they do not use their fists in close combat, but throw shells from a great distance at persons whom they have never seen. In modern wars, anger and hatred come after the war has started; they are effects of war, not the cause of it.

It is a tough job sustaining a modern war; all the emotional reactions have to be excited. Propaganda and atrocity stories are enlisted. Aside from such extreme measures there has to be definite organization, as we saw in the two World Wars, to keep up the morale of even non-combatants. And morale is largely a matter of keeping emotions at a certain pitch; and unfortunately fear, hatred, suspicion, are among the emotions most easily aroused.

I shall not attempt to dogmatize about the causes of modern wars. But I do not think that anyone will deny that they are social rather than psychological, though psychological appeal is highly important in working up a people to the point where they want to fight and in keeping them at it. I do not think, moreover, that anyone will deny that economic conditions are powerful among the social causes of war. The main point, however, is that whatever the sociological causes, they are affairs of tradition, custom, and institutional organization, and these factors belong among the changeable manifestations of human nature, not among the unchangeable elements.

I have used the case of war as a typical instance of what is changeable and what is unchangeable in human nature, in their relation to schemes of social change. I have selected the case because it is an extremely difficult one in which to effect durable changes, not because it is an easy one. The point is that the obstacles in the way are put there by social forces which do change from time to time, not by fixed elements of human nature. This fact is also illustrated in the failures of pacifists to achieve their ends by appeal simply to sympathy and pity. For while, as I have said, the kindly emotions are also a fixed constituent of human nature, the channel they take is dependent upon social conditions.

There is always a great outburst of these kindly emotions in time of war. Fellow feeling and the desire to help those in need are intense during war, as they are at every period of great disaster that comes home to observation or imagination. But they are canalized in their expression; they are confined to those upon our side. They occur simultaneously with manifestation of rage and fear against the other side, if not always in the same person, at least in the community generally. Hence the ultimate failure of pacifist appeals to the kindly elements of native human nature when they are separated from intelligent consideration of the social and economic forces at work. William James made a great contribution in the title of one of his essays, *The Moral Equivalent of War*. The very title conveys the point I am making. Certain basic needs and emotions are permanent. But they are capable of finding expression in ways that are radically different from the ways in which they now currently operate.

An even more burning issue emerges when any fundamental change in economic institutions and relations is proposed. Proposals for such sweeping change are among the commonplaces of our time. On the other hand, the proposals are met by the statement that the changes are impossible because they involve an impossible change in human nature. To this statement, advocates of the desired changes are only too likely to reply that the present system or some phase of it is contrary to human nature. The argument *pro* and *con* then gets put on the wrong ground.

As a matter of fact, economic institutions and relations are among the manifestations of human nature that are most susceptible of change. History is living evidence of the scope of these changes. Aristotle, for example, held that paying interest is unnatural, and the Middle Ages reëchoed the doctrine. All interest was usury, and it was only after economic conditions had so changed that payment of interest was a customary and in that sense a "natural" thing, that usury got its present meaning.

There have been times and places in which land was held in common and in which private ownership of land would have been regarded as the most monstrous of unnatural things. There have been other times and places when all wealth was possessed by an overlord and his subjects held wealth, if any, subject to his pleasure. The entire system of credit so fundamental in contemporary financial and industrial life is a modern invention. The invention of the joint-stock company with limited liability of individuals has brought about a great change from earlier facts and conceptions of property. I think the need of owning something is one of the native elements of human nature. But it takes either ignorance or a very lively fancy to suppose that the system of ownership that exists in the United States in 1946, with all its complex relations and its interweaving with legal and political supports, is a necessary and unchangeable product of an inherent tendency to appropriate and possess.

Law is one of the most conservative of human institutions; yet through the cumulative effect of legislation and judicial decisions it changes, sometimes at a slow rate, sometimes rapidly. The changes in human relations that are brought about by changes in industrial and legal institutions then react to modify the ways in which human nature manifests itself, and this brings about still further changes in institutions, and so on indefinitely.

It is for these reasons that I say that those who hold that proposals for social change, even of rather a profound character, are impossible and utopian because of the fixity of human nature confuse the resistance to change that comes from acquired habits with that which comes from original human nature. The savage, living in a primitive society, comes nearer to being a purely "natural" human being than does civilized man. Civilization itself is the product of altered human nature. But even the savage is bound by a mass of tribal customs and transmitted beliefs that modify his orginal nature, and it is these acquired habits that make it so difficult to transform him into a civilized human being.

The revolutionary radical, on the other hand, overlooks the force of engrained habits. He is right, in my opinion, about the indefinite plasticity of human nature. But he is wrong in thinking that patterns of desire, belief, and purpose do not have a force comparable to the inertia, the resistance to movement, possessed by these same objects when they are at rest. Habit, not original human nature, keeps things moving most of the time, about as they have moved in the past.

If human nature is unchangeable, then there is no such thing as education and all our efforts to educate are doomed to failure. For the very meaning of education is modification of native human nature in formation of those new ways of thinking, of feeling, of desiring, and of believing that are foreign to raw human nature. If the latter were unalterable, we might have training but not education. For training, as distinct from education, means simply the acquisition of certain skills. Native gifts can be trained to a point of higher efficiency without that development of new attitudes and dispositions which is the goal of education. But the result is mechanical. It is like supposing that while a musician may acquire by practice greater technical ability, he cannot rise from one plane of musical appreciation and creation to another.

The theory that human nature is unchangeable is thus the most depressing and pessimistic of all possible doctrines. If it were carried out logically, it would mean a doctrine of predestination from birth that would outdo the most rigid of theological doctrines. For according to it, persons are what they are at birth and nothing can be done about it, beyond the kind of training that an acrobat might give to the muscular system with which he is originally endowed. If a person is born with criminal tendencies, a criminal he will become and remain. If a person is born with an excessive amount of greed, he will become a person living by predatory activities at the expense of others; and so on. I do not doubt at all the existence of differences in natural endowment. But what I am questioning is the notion that they doom individuals to a fixed channel of expression. It is difficult indeed to make a silk purse out of a sow's ear. But the particular form which, say, a natural musical endowment will take depends upon the social influences to which one is subjected. Beethoven in a savage tribe would doubtless have been outstanding as a musician, but he would not have been the Beethoven who composed symphonies.

The existence of almost every conceivable kind of social institution at some time and place in the history of the world is evidence of the plasticity of human nature. This fact does not prove that all these different social systems are of equal value, materially, morally, and culturally. The slightest observation shows that such is not the case. But the fact in proving the changeability of human nature indicates the attitude that should be taken toward proposals for social changes. The question is primarily whether they, in special cases, are desirable or not. And the way to answer that question is to try to discover what their consequences would be if they were adopted. Then if the conclusion is that they are desirable, the further question is how they can be accomplished with a minimum of waste, destruction, and needless dislocation.

In finding the answer to this question, we have to take into account the force of existing traditions and customs; of the patterns of action and belief that already exist. We have to find out what forces already at work can be reinforced so that they move toward the desired change and how the conditions that oppose change can be gradually weakened. Such questions as these can be considered on the basis of fact and reason.

The assertion that a proposed change is impossible because of the fixed constitution of human nature diverts attention from the question of whether or not a change is desirable and from the other question of how it shall be brought about. It throws the question into the arena of blind emotion and brute force. In the end, it encourages those who think that great changes can be produced offhand and by the use of sheer violence.

When our sciences of human nature and human relations are anything like as developed as are our sciences of physical nature, their chief concern will be with the problem of how human nature is most effectively modified. The question will not be whether it is capable of change, but of how it is to be changed under given conditions. This problem is ultimately that of education in its widest

sense. Consequently, whatever represses and distorts the processes
of education that might bring about a change in human dispositions
with the minimum of waste puts a premium upon the forces that
bring society to a state of deadlock, and thereby encourages the use
of violence as a means of social change.

THE GENTLEMAN FROM SAN FRANCISCO *

IVAN BUNIN

Ivan Bunin (1870–   ) is a Russian poet and novelist who won the Nobel
Prize for Literature in 1933. "The Gentleman from San Francisco" was
written in 1915.

———————

"Alas, Alas, that great city Babylon, that mighty city!"—Revelation of
St. John.

The Gentleman from San Francisco—neither at Naples nor on
Capri could any one recall his name—with his wife and daughter,
was on his way to Europe, where he intended to stay for two whole
years, solely for the pleasure of it.

He was firmly convinced that he had a full right to a rest, enjoyment, a long comfortable trip, and what not. This conviction had a
two-fold reason: first he was rich, and second, despite his fifty-eight
years, he was just about to enter the stream of life's pleasures. Until
now he had not really lived, but simply existed, to be sure—fairly
well, yet putting off his fondest hopes for the future. He toiled un-
weariedly—the Chinese, whom he imported by thousands for his
works, knew full well what it meant—and finally he saw that he
had made much, and that he had nearly come up to the level of
those whom he had once taken as a model, and he decided to catch
his breath. The class of people to which he belonged was in the
habit of beginning its enjoyment of life with a trip to Europe, India,
Egypt. He made up his mind to do the same. Of course, it was first
of all himself that he desired to reward for the years of toil, but he
was also glad for his wife and daughter's sake. His wife was never
distinguished by any extraordinary impressionability, but then, all
elderly American women are ardent travelers. As for his daughter, a

* Translated by A. Yarmolinsky. Reprinted by permission of Alfred A. Knopf,
Inc. Copyright, 1923, by Alfred A. Knopf, Inc.

girl of marriageable age, and somewhat sickly—travel was the very thing she needed. Not to speak of the benefit to her health, do not happy meetings occur during travels? Abroad, one may chance to sit at the same table with a prince, or examine frescoes side by side with a multi-millionaire.

The itinerary the Gentleman from San Francisco planned out was an extensive one. In December and January he expected to relish the sun of southern Italy, monuments of antiquity, the tarantella, serenades of wandering minstrels, and that which at his age is felt most keenly—the love, not entirely disinterested though, of young Neopolitan girls. The Carnival days he planned to spend at Nice and Monte Carlo, which at that time of the year is the meeting-place of the choicest society, the society upon which depend all the blessings of civilization: the cut of dress suits, the stability of thrones, the declaration of wars, the prosperity of hotels. Some of these people passionately give themselves over to automobile and boat races, others to roulette, others, again, busy themselves with what is called flirtation, and others shoot pigeons, which soar so beautifully from the dovecote, hover awhile over the emerald lawn, on the background of the forget-me-not colored sea, and then suddenly hit the ground, like little white lumps. Early March he wanted to devote to Florence, and at Easter, to hear the Miserere in Paris. His plans also included Venice, Paris, bull-baiting at Seville, bathing on the British Islands, also Athens, Constantinople, Palestine, Egypt, and even Japan, of course, on the way back. . . . And at first things went very well indeed.

It was the end of November, and all the way to Gibraltar the ship sailed across seas which were either clad by icy darkness or swept by storms carrying wet snow. But there were no accidents, and the vessel did not even roll. The passengers—all people of consequence—were numerous, and the steamer, the famous *Atlantis*, resembled the most expensive European hotel with all improvements: a night refreshment-bar, Oriental baths, even a newspaper of its own. The manner of living was a most aristocratic one; passengers rose early, awakened by the shrill voice of a bugle, filling the corridors at the gloomy hour when the day broke slowly and sulkily over the grayish-green watery desert, which rolled heavily in the fog. After putting on their flannel pajamas, they took coffee, chocolate, cocoa; they seated themselves in marble baths, went through their exercises, whetting their appetites and increasing their sense of well-being, dressed for the day, and had their breakfast. Till eleven o'clock they were supposed to stroll on the deck, breathing in the chill freshness of the ocean, or they played table-tennis, or other games which arouse the appetite. At eleven o'clock a collation was served consisting of sandwiches and bouillon, after which people read their newspapers, quietly waiting for luncheon, which was more nourishing and varied than the breakfast. The next two hours were given to rest; all the decks were crowded then with steamer chairs, on which the passengers, wrapped in plaids, lay stretched, dozing lazily, or watching the cloudy sky and the foamy-fringed water hillocks flashing beyond the sides of the vessel. At five o'clock, refreshed and gay, they drank strong, fragrant tea; at seven the sound of the bugle announced a dinner of nine courses. . . . Then the Gentleman from San Francisco, rubbing his hands in an onrush of vital energy, hastened to his luxurious stateroom to dress.

In the evening, all the decks of the *Atlantis* yawned in the darkness, shone with their innumerable fiery eyes, and a multitude of servants worked with increased feverishness in the kitchens, dishwashing compartments, and wine-cellars. The ocean, which heaved about the sides of the ship, was dreadful, but no one thought of it. All had faith in the controlling power of the captain, a red-headed giant, heavy and very sleepy, who, clad in a uniform with broad golden stripes, looked like a huge idol, and but rarely emerged, for the benefit of the public, from his mysterious retreat. On the forecastle, the siren gloomily roared or screeched in a fit of mad rage, but few of the diners heard the siren: its hellish voice was covered by the sounds of an excellent string orchestra, which played ceaselessly and exquisitely in a vast hall, decorated with marble and spread with velvety carpets. The hall was flooded with torrents of light, radiated by crystal lustres and gilt chandeliers; it was filled with a throng of bejeweled ladies in low-necked dresses, of men in dinner-coats, graceful waiters, and deferential maîtres-d'hôtel. One of these—who accepted wine orders exclusively—wore a chain on his neck like some lord mayor. The evening dress, and the ideal linen, made the Gentleman from San Francisco look very young. Dry-skinned, of average height, strongly, though irregularly built, glossy with thorough washing and cleaning, and moderately animated, he sat in the golden splendor of this palace. Near him stood a bottle of amber-colored Johannisberg, and goblets of most delicate glass and of varied sizes, surmounted by a frizzled bunch of fresh hyacinths. There was something Mongolian in his yellowish face with its trimmed silvery moustache; his large teeth glimmered with gold fillings, and his strong, bald head had a dull glow, like old ivory. His wife, a big, broad and placid woman, was dressed richly, but in keeping with her age. Complicated, but light, transparent, and innocently immodest was the dress of his daughter, tall and slender, with magnificent hair gracefully combed; her breath was sweet with violet-scented tablets, and she had a number of tiny and most delicate pink pimples near her lips and between her slightly-powdered shoulder blades. . . .

The dinner lasted two whole hours, and was followed by dances in the dancing hall, while the men—the Gentleman from San Francisco among them—made their way to the refreshment bar, where negroes in red jackets and with eye-balls like shelled hard-boiled eggs, waited on them. There, with their feet on tables, smoking Havana cigars, and drinking themselves purple in the face, they settled the destinies of nations on the basis of the latest political and stock exchange news. Outside, the ocean tossed up black mountains with a thud; and the snowstorm hissed furiously in the rigging grown heavy with slush; the ship trembled in every limb, struggling with the storm and ploughing with difficulty the shifting and seething mountainous masses that threw far and high their foaming tails; the siren groaned in agony, choked by storm and fog; the watchmen in their towers froze and almost went out of their minds under the superhuman stress of attention. Like the gloomy and sultry mass of the inferno, like its last, ninth circle, was the submersed womb of the steamer, where monstrous furnaces yawned with red-hot open jaws, and emitted deep, hooting sounds, and where the stokers, stripped to the waist, and purple with reflected flames, bathed in their own dirty, acid sweat. And here, in the refreshment bar, carefree men, with their feet, encased in dancing shoes, on the table, sipped cognac and liqueurs, swam in waves of spiced smoke, and exchanged subtle remarks, while in the dancing hall everything sparkled and radiated light, warmth and joy. The couples now turned around in a waltz, now swayed in the tango; and the music, sweetly shameless and sad, persisted in its ceaseless entreaties. . . . There were many persons of note in this magnificent crowd: an ambassador, a dry, modest old man; a great millionaire, shaved, tall, of an indefinite age, who, in his old-fashioned dress-coat, looked liked a prelate; also a famous Spanish writer, and an international belle, already slightly faded and of dubious morals. There was also among them a loving pair, exquisite and refined, whom everybody watched with curiosity and who did not conceal their bliss; he danced only with her, sang—with great skill—only to her accompaniment, and they were so charming, so graceful. The captain alone knew that they had been hired by the company at a good salary to play at love, and that they had been sailing now on one, now on another steamer, for quite a long time.

In Gibraltar everybody was gladdened by the sun, and by the weather which was like early spring. A new passenger appeared aboard the *Atlantis* and aroused everybody's interest. It was the crown-prince of an Asiatic state, who traveled incognito, a small man, very nimble, though looking as if made of wood, broad-faced, narrow-eyed, in gold-rimmed glasses, somewhat disagreeable because of his long black moustache, which was sparse like that of a corpse, but otherwise—charming, plain, modest. In the Mediterranean the breath of winter was again felt. The seas were heavy and motley like a peacock's tail and the waves stirred up by the gay gusts of the tramontane, tossed their white crests under a sparkling and perfectly clear sky. Next morning, the sky grew paler and the skyline misty. Land was near. Then Ischia and Capri came in sight, and one could descry, through an opera-glass, Naples, looking like pieces of sugar strewn at the foot of an indistinct dove-colored mass, and above them, a snow-covered chain of distant mountains. The decks were crowded, many ladies and gentlemen put on light fur-coats; Chinese servants, bandy-legged youths—with pitch black braids down to the heels and with girlish, thick eyelashes—always quiet and speaking in a whisper, were carrying to the foot of the staircases, plaid wraps, canes, and crocodile-leather valises and hand-bags. The daughter of the Gentleman from San Francisco stood near the prince, who, by a happy chance, had been introduced to her the evening before, and feigned to be looking steadily at something far-off, which he was pointing out to her, while he was, at the same time, explaining something, saying something rapidly and quietly. He was so small that he looked like a boy among other men, and he was not handsome at all. And then there was something strange about him; his glasses, derby and coat were most commonplace, but there was something horse-like in the hair of his sparse moustache, and the thin, tanned skin of his flat face looked as though it were somewhat stretched and varnished. But the girl listened to him, and so great was her excitement that she could hardly grasp the meaning of his words, her heart palpitated with incomprehensible rapture and with pride that he was standing and speaking with her and nobody else. Everything about him was different: his dry hands, his clean skin, under which flowed ancient kingly blood, even his light shoes and his European dress, plain, but singularly tidy—everything hid an inexplicable fascination and engendered thoughts of love. And the Gentleman from San Francisco, himself, in a silk-hat, gray leggings, patent leather shoes, kept eyeing the famous beauty who was standing near him, a tall, stately blonde, with eyes painted according to the latest Parisian fashion, and a tiny, bent peeled-off pet-dog, to whom she addressed herself. And the daughter, in a kind of vague perplexity, tried not to notice him.

Like all wealthy Americans he was very liberal when traveling, and believed in the complete sincerity and goodwill of those who so painstakingly fed him, served him day and night, anticipating his slightest desire, protected him from dirt and disturbance, hauled things for him, hailed carriers, and delivered his luggage to hotels. So it was everywhere, and it had to be so at Naples. Meanwhile, Naples grew and came nearer. The musicians, with their shining brass instruments had already formed a group on the deck, and all of a sudden deafened everybody with the triumphant sounds of a ragtime march. The giant captain, in his full uniform appeared on the bridge and like a gracious pagan idol, waved his hands to the passengers—and it seemed to the Gentleman from San Francisco, as it did to all the rest, that for him alone thundered the march, so greatly loved by proud America, and that him alone did the captain congratulate on the safe arrival. And when the *Atlantis* had finally entered the port and all its many-decked mass leaned against the quay, and the gang-plank began to rattle heavily,—what a crowd of porters, with their assistants, in caps with golden galloons, what a crowd of various boys and husky ragamuffins with pads of colored postal cards attacked the Gentleman from San Francisco, offering their services! With kindly contempt he grinned at these beggars, and, walking towards the automobile of the hotel where the prince might stop, muttered between his teeth, now in English, now in Italian—"Go away! *Via. . . .*"

Immediately, life at Naples began to follow a set routine. Early in the morning breakfast was served in the gloomy dining-room, swept by a wet draught from the open windows looking upon a stony garden, while outside the sky was cloudy and cheerless, and a crowd of guides swarmed at the door of the vestibule. Then came the first smiles of the warm roseate sun, and from the high suspended balcony, a broad vista unfolded itself: Vesuvius, wrapped to its base in radiant morning vapors; the pearly ripple, touched to silver, of the bay, the delicate outline of Capri on the skyline; tiny asses dragging two-wheeled buggies along the soft, sticky embankment, and detachments of little soldiers marching somewhere to the tune of cheerful and defiant music.

Next on the day's program was a slow automobile ride along crowded, narrow, and damp corridors of streets, between high, many-windowed buildings. It was followed by visits to museums, lifelessly clean and lighted evenly and pleasantly, but as though with the dull light cast by snow; then to churches, cold, smelling of wax, always alike: a majestic entrance, closed by a ponderous, leather curtain, and inside—a vast void, silence, quiet flames of seven-branched candlesticks, sending forth a red glow from where they stood at the farther end, on the bedecked altar—a lonely old woman lost among the dark wooden benches, slippery gravestones under the feet, and somebody's *Descent from the Cross,* infallibly famous. At one o'clock —luncheon, on the mountain of San-Martius, where at noon the choicest people gathered, and where the daughter of the Gentleman from San Francisco once almost fainted with joy, because it seemed to her that she saw the prince in the hall, although she had learned from the newspapers that he had temporarily left for Rome. At five o'clock it was customary to take tea at the hotel, in a smart salon, where it was far too warm because of the carpets and the blazing fireplaces; and then came dinner-time—and again did the mighty, commanding voice of the gong resound throughout the building, again did silk rustle and the mirrors reflect files of ladies in low-necked dresses ascending the staircases, and again the splendid palatial dining hall opened with broad hospitality, and again the musicians' jackets formed red patches on the estrade, and the black figures of the waiters swarmed around the maître-d'hôtel, who, with extraordinary skill, poured a thick pink soup into plates. . . . As everywhere, the dinner was the crown of the day. People dressed for it as for a wedding, and so abundant was it in food, wines, mineral waters, sweets and fruits, that about eleven o'clock in the evening chambermaids would carry to all the rooms hot-water bags.

That year, however, December did not happen to be a very propitious one. The doormen were abashed when people spoke to them about the weather, and shrugged their shoulders guiltily, mumbling that they could not recollect such a year, although, to tell the truth, it was not the first year that they mumbled those words, usually adding that "things are terrible everywhere"; that unprecedented showers and storms had broken out on the Riviera, that it was snowing in Athens, that Aetna, too, was all blocked up with snow, and glowed brightly at night, and that tourists were fleeing from Palermo to save themselves from the cold spell. . . .

That winter, the morning sun daily deceived Naples; toward noon the sky would invariably grow gray, and a light rain would begin to fall, growing thicker and duller. Then the palms at the hotel porch glistened disagreeably like wet tin, the town appeared exceptionally dirty and congested, the museums too monotonous, the cigars of the drivers in their rubber raincoats, which flattened in the wind like wings, intolerably stinking, and the energetic flapping of their whips over their thin-necked nags—obviously false. The shoes of the signors, who cleaned the street-car tracks, were in a frightful state; the women who splashed in the mud, with black hair unprotected from the rain, were ugly and short legged; and the humidity mingled with the foul smell of rotting fish, that came from the foaming sea, was simply disheartening. And so, early-morning quarrels began to break out between the Gentleman from San Francisco and his wife; and their daughter now grew pale and suffered from headaches, and now became animated, enthusiastic over everything, and at such times was lovely and beautiful. Beautiful were the tender, complex feelings which her meeting with the ungainly man aroused in her—the man in whose veins flowed unusual blood, for, after all, it does not matter what in particular stirs up a maiden's soul: money, or fame, or nobility of birth. . . . Everybody assured the tourists that it was quite different at Sorrento and on Capri, that lemon-trees were blossoming there, that it was warmer and sunnier there, the morals purer, and the wine less adulterated. And the family from San Francisco decided to set out with all their luggage for Capri. They planned to settle down at Sorrento, but first to visit the island, tread the stones where stood Tiberius's palaces, examine the fabulous wonders of the Blue Grotto, and listen to the bagpipes of Abruzzi, who roam about the island during the whole month preceding Christmas and sing the praises of the Madonna.

On the day of departure—a very memorable day for the family from San Francisco—the sun did not appear even in the morning. A heavy winter fog covered Vesuvius down to its very base and hung like a gray curtain low over the leaden surge of the sea, hiding it completely at a distance of half a mile. Capri was completely out of sight, as though it had never existed on this earth. And the little steamboat which was making for the island tossed and pitched so fiercely that the family lay prostrated on the sofas in the miserable cabin of the little steamer, with their feet wrapped in plaids and their eyes shut because of their nausea. The older lady suffered, as she thought, most; several times she was overcome with sea-sickness, and it seemed to her then she was dying, but the chambermaid, who repeatedly brought her the basin, and who for many years, in heat and in cold, had been tossing on these waves, ever on the alert, ever kindly to all— the chambermaid only laughed. The lady's daughter was frightfully pale and kept a slice of lemon between her teeth. Not even the hope of an unexpected meeting with the prince at Sorrento, where he planned to arrive on Christmas, served to cheer her. The Gentleman from San Francisco, who was lying on his back, dressed in a large overcoat and a big cap, did not loosen his jaws throughout the voyage. His face grew dark, his moustache white, and his head ached heavily; for the last few days, because of the bad weather, he had drunk far too much in the evenings.

And the rain kept on beating against the rattling window panes, and water dripped down from them on the sofas; the howling wind attacked the masts, and sometimes, aided by a heavy sea, it laid the little steamer on its side, and then something below rolled about with a rattle.

While the steamer was anchored at Castellamare and Sorrento, the situation was more cheerful; but even here the ship rolled terribly, and the coast with all its precipices, gardens and pines, with its pink and white hotels and hazy mountains clad in curling verdure, flew up and down as if it were on swings. The rowboats hit against the sides of the steamer, the sailors and the deck passengers shouted at the top of their voices, and somewhere a baby screamed as if it were being crushed to pieces. A wet wind blew through the door, and from a wavering barge flying the flag of the Hotel Royal, an urchin kept on unwearyingly shouting "Kgoyal-al! Hotel Kgoyal-al! . . ." inviting tourists. And the Gentleman from San Francisco felt like the old man that he was, and it was with weariness and animosity that he thought of all these "Royals," "Splendids," "Excelsiors," and of all those greedy bugs, reeking with garlic, who are called Italians. Once, during a stop, having opened his eyes and half-risen from the sofa, he noticed in the shadow of the rock beach a heap of stone huts, miserable, mildewed through and through, huddled close by the water, near boats, rags, tin-boxes, and brown fishing nets, and as he remembered that this was the very Italy he had come to enjoy, he felt a great despair. . . . Finally, in twilight, the black mass of the island began to grow nearer, as though burrowed through at the base by red fires, the wind grew softer, warmer, more fragrant; from the dock-lanterns huge golden serpents flowed down the tame waves which undulated like black oil. . . . Then, suddenly, the anchor rumbled and fell with a splash into the water, the fierce yells of the boatmen filled the air—and at once everyone's heart grew easy. The electric lights in the cabin grew more brilliant, and there came a desire to eat, drink, smoke, move. . . . Ten minutes later the family from San Francisco found themselves in a large ferry-boat; fifteen minutes later they trod the stones of the quay, and then seated themselves in a small lighted car, which, with a buzz, started to ascend the slope, while vineyard stakes, half-ruined stone fences, and wet, crooked lemon trees, in spots shielded by straw sheds, with their glimmering orange-colored fruit and thick glossy foliage, were sliding down past the open car windows. . . . After rain, the earth smells sweet in Italy, and each of her islands has a fragrance of its own.

The island of Capri was dark and damp on that evening. But for a while it grew animated and lit up, in spots, as always in the hour of the steamer's arrival. On the top of the hill, at the station of the *funiculaire,* there stood already the crowd of those whose duty it was to receive properly the Gentleman from San Francisco. The rest of the tourists hardly deserved any attention. There were a few Russians, who had settled on Capri, untidy, absent-minded people, absorbed in their bookish thoughts, spectacled, bearded, with the collars of their cloth overcoats raised. There was also a company of long-legged, long-necked, round-headed German youths in Tyrolean costume, and with linen bags on their backs, who need no one's services, are everywhere at home, and are by no means liberal in their expenses. The Gentleman from San Francisco, who kept quietly aloof from both the Russians and the Germans, was noticed at once. He and his ladies were hurriedly helped from the car, a man ran before them to show them the way, and they were again surrounded by boys and those thickset Caprean peasant women, who carry on their heads the trunks and valises of wealthy travelers. Their tiny, wooden, footstools rapped against the pavement of the small square, which looked almost like an opera square, and over which an electric lantern swung in the damp wind; the gang of urchins whistled like birds and turned somersaults, and as the Gentleman from San Francisco passed among them, it all looked like a stage scene; he went first under some kind of medieval archway, beneath houses huddled close together, and then along a steep echoing lane which led to the hotel entrance, flooded with light. At the left, a palm tree raised its tuft above the flat roofs, and higher up, blue stars burned in the black sky. And again things looked as though it was in honor of the guests from San Francisco that the stony damp little town had awakened on its rocky island in the Mediterranean, that it was they who had made the owner of the hotel so happy and beaming, and that the Chinese gong, which had sounded the call to dinner through all the floors as soon as they entered the lobby, had been waiting only for them.

The owner, an elegant young man, who met the guests with a polite and exquisite bow, for a moment startled the Gentleman from San Francisco. Having caught sight of him, the Gentleman from San Francisco suddenly recollected that on the previous night, among other confused images which disturbed his sleep, he had seen this very man. His vision resembled the hotel keeper to a dot, had the same head, the same hair, shining and scrupulously combed, and wore the same frock-coat with rounded skirts. Amazed, he almost stopped for a while. But as there was not a mustard seed of what is called mysticism in his heart, his surprise subsided at once; in passing the corridor of the hotel he jestingly told his wife and daughter about this strange coincidence of dream and reality. His daughter alone glanced at him with alarm; longing suddenly compressed her heart, and such a strong feeling of solitude on this strange, dark island seized her that she almost began to cry. But, as usual, she said nothing about her feelings to her father.

A person of high dignity, Rex XVII, who had spent three entire weeks on Capri, had just left the island, and the guests from San Francisco were given the apartments he had occupied. At their disposal was put the most handsome and skillful chambermaid, a Belgian, with a figure rendered slim and firm by her corset, and with a starched cap, shaped like a small, indented crown; and they had the privilege of being served by the most well-appearing and portly footman, a black, fiery-eyed Sicilian, and by the quickest waiter, the small, stout Luigi, who was a fiend at cracking jokes and had changed many places in his life. Then the maître-d'hôtel, a Frenchman, gently rapped at the door of the American gentleman's room. He came to ask whether the gentleman and the ladies would dine, and in case they would, which he did not doubt, to report that there was to be had that day lobsters, roast beef, asparagus, pheasants, etc, etc.

The floor was still rocking under the Gentleman from San Francisco—so sea-sick had the wretched Italian steamer made him—yet, he slowly, though awkwardly, shut the window which had banged when the maître-d'hôtel entered, and which let in the smell of the distant kitchen and wet flowers in the garden, and answered with slow distinctness, that they would dine, that their table must be placed farther away from the door, in the depth of the hall, that they would have local wine and champagne, moderately dry and but slightly cooled. The maître-d'hôtel approved the words of the guest in various intonations, which all meant, however, only one thing; there is and can be no doubt that the desires of the Gentleman from San Francisco are right, and that everything would be carried out, in exact conformity with his words. At last he inclined his head and asked delicately:

"Is that all, sir?"

And having received in reply a slow "Yes," he added that today they were going to have the tarantella danced in the vestibule by Carmella and Giuseppe, known to all Italy and to "the entire world of tourists."

"I saw her on post card pictures," said the Gentleman from San Francisco in a tone of voice which expressed nothing. "And this Giuseppe, is he her husband?"

"Her cousin, sir," answered the maître-d'hôtel.

The Gentleman from San Francisco tarried a little, evidently musing on something, but said nothing, then dismissed him with a nod of his head.

Then he started making preparations, as though for a wedding: he turned on all the electric lamps, and filled the mirrors with reflections of light and the sheen of furniture, and opened trunks; he began to shave and to wash himself, and the sound of his bell was heard every minute in the corridor, crossing with other impatient calls which came from the rooms of his wife and daughter. Luigi, in his red apron, with the ease characteristic of stout people, made funny faces at the chambermaids, who were dashing by with tile buckets in their hands, making them laugh until the tears came. He rolled head over heels to the door, and, tapping with his knuckles, asked with feigned timidity and with an obsequiousness which he knew how to render idiotic:

"Ha sonata, Signore?" (Did you ring, sir?)

And from behind the door a slow, grating, insultingly polite voice, answered:

"Yes, come in."

What did the Gentleman from San Francisco think and feel on that evening forever memorable to him? It must be said frankly: absolutely nothing exceptional. The trouble is that everything on this earth appears too simple. Even had he felt anything deep in his heart, a premonition that something was going to happen, he would have imagined that it was not going to happen so soon, at least not at once. Besides, as is usually the case just after sea-sickness is over, he was very hungry, and he anticipated with real delight the first spoonful of soup, and the first gulp of wine; therefore, he was performing the habitual process of dressing, in a state of excitement which left no time for reflection.

Having shaved and washed himself, and dexterously put in place a few false teeth, he then, standing before the mirror, moistened and vigorously plastered what was left of his thick pearly-colored hair, close to his tawny-yellow skull. Then he put on, with some effort, a tight-fitting undershirt of cream-colored silk, fitted tight to his strong, aged body with its waist swelling out because of an abundant diet; and he pulled black silk socks and patent leather dancing shoes on his dry feet with their fallen arches. Squatting down, he set right his black trousers, drawn high by means of silk suspenders, adjusted his snow-white shirt with its bulging front, put the buttons into the shining cuffs, and began the painful process of hunting up the front button under the hard collar. The floor was still swaying under him, the tips of his fingers hurt terribly, the button at times painfully pinched the flabby skin in the depression under his Adam's apple, but he persevered, and finally, with his eyes shining from the effort, his face blue because of the narrow collar which squeezed his neck, he triumphed over the difficulties—and all exhausted, he sat down before the pier glass, his reflected image repeating itself in all the mirrors.

"It's terrible!" he muttered, lowering his strong, bald head and making no effort to understand what was terrible; then, with a careful and habitual gesture, he examined his short fingers with gouty callosities in the joints, and their large, convex, almond-colored nails, and repeated with conviction, "It's terrible!"

But here the stentorian voice of the second gong sounded throughout the house, as in a heathen temple. And having risen hurriedly, the Gentleman from San Francisco drew his tie more taut and firm around his collar, and pulled together his abdomen by means of a tight waistcoat, put on a dinner-coat, set to rights the cuffs, and for the last time he examined himself in the mirror. . . . This Carmella, tawny as a mulatto, with fiery eyes, in a dazzling dress in which orange-color predominated, must be an extraordinary dancer—it occurred to him. And cheerfully leaving his room, he walked on the carpet, to his wife's chamber, and asked in a loud tone of voice if they would be long.

"In five minutes, papa!" answered cheerfully and gaily a girlish voice. "I am combing my hair."

"Very well," said the Gentleman from San Francisco.

And thinking of her wonderful hair, streaming on her shoulders, he slowly walked down along corridors and staircases, spread with red velvet carpets, looking for the library. The servants he met hugged the walls, and he walked by as if not noticing them. An old lady, late for dinner, already bowed with years, with milk-white hair, yet bare-necked, in a light-gray silk dress, hurried at top speed, but she walked in a mincing, funny, hen-like manner, and he easily overtook her. At the glass door of the dining hall where the guests had already gathered and started eating, he stopped before the table crowded with boxes of matches and Egyptian cigarettes, took a great Manila cigar, and threw three liras on the table. On the winter veranda he glanced into the open window; a stream of soft air came to him from the darkness, the top of the old palm loomed up before him afar-off, with its boughs spread among the stars and looking gigantic, and the distant even noise of the sea reached his ear. In the library-room, snug, quiet, a German in round silver-bowed glasses and with crazy, wondering eyes stood turning the rustling pages of a newspaper. Having coldly eyed him, the Gentleman from San Francisco seated himself in a deep leather arm-chair near a lamp under a green hood, put on his pince-nez and twitching his head because of the collar which choked him, hid himself from view behind a newspaper. He glanced at a few headlines, read a few lines about the interminable Balkan war, and turned over the page with an habitual gesture. Suddenly, the lines blazed up with a glassy sheen, the veins of his neck swelled, his eyes bulged out, the pince-nez fell from his nose. . . . He dashed forward, wanted to swallow air—and made a wild, rattling noise; his lower jaw dropped, dropped on his shoulder and began to shake, the shirt-front bulged out—and the whole body, writhing, the heels catching in the carpet, slowly fell to the floor in a desperate struggle with an invisible foe. . . .

Had not the German been in the library, this frightful accident would have been quickly and adroitly hushed up. The body of the Gentleman from San Francisco would have been rushed away to some far corner—and none of the guests would have known of the occurrence. But the German dashed out of the library with outcries and spread the alarm all over the house. And many rose from their meal, upsetting chairs, others growing pale, ran along the corridors to the library, and the question, asked in many languages, was heard: "What is it? What has happened?" And no one was able to answer it clearly, no one understood anything, for until this very day men still wonder most at death and most absolutely refuse to believe in it. The owner rushed from one guest to another, trying to keep back those who were running and soothe them with hasty assurances, that this was nothing, a mere trifle, a little fainting-spell by which a Gentleman from San Francisco had been overcome. But no one listened to him, many saw how the footmen and waiters tore from the gentleman his tie, collar, waistcoat, the rumpled evening coat, and even—for no visible reason—the dancing shoes from his black silk-covered feet. And he kept on writhing. He obstinately struggled with death, he did not want to yield to the foe that attacked him so unexpectedly and grossly. He shook his head, emitted rattling sounds like one throttled, and turned up his eye-balls like one drunk with wine. When he was hastily brought into Number Forty-three,—the smallest, worst, dampest, and coldest room at the end of the lower corridor—and stretched on the bed—his daughter came running, her hair falling over her shoulders, the skirts of her dressing-gown thrown open, with bare breasts raised by the corset. Then came his wife, big, heavy, almost completely dressed for dinner, her mouth round with terror.

In a quarter of an hour all was again in good trim at the hotel. But the evening was irreparably spoiled. Some tourists returned to the dining hall and finished their dinner, but they kept silent, and it was obvious that they took the accident as a personal insult, while the owner went from one guest to another, shrugging his shoulders in impotent and appropriate irritation, feeling like one innocently victimized, assuring everyone that he understood perfectly well "how disagreeable this is," and giving his word that he would take all "the measures that are within his power" to do away with the trouble. Yet it was found necessary to cancel the tarantella. The unnecessary electric lamps were put out, most of the guests left for the beer hall, and it grew so quiet in the hotel that one could distinctly hear the tick-tock of the clock in the lobby, where a lonely parrot babbled something in its expressionless manner, stirring in its cage, and trying to fall asleep with its paw clutching the upper perch in a most absurd manner. The Gentleman from San Francisco lay stretched in a cheap iron bed, under coarse woolen blankets, dimly lighted by a single gas-burner fastened in the ceiling. An ice bag slid down on his wet, cold forehead. His blue, already lifeless face grew gradually cold; the hoarse, rattling noise which came from his mouth, lighted by the glimmer of the golden fillings, gradually weakened. It was not the Gentleman from San Francisco that was emitting those weird sounds; he was no more—someone else did it. His wife and daughter, the doctor, the servants were standing and watching him apathetically. Suddenly, that which they expected and feared happened. The rattling sound ceased. And slowly, slowly, in everybody's sight a pallor stole over the face of the dead man, and his features began to grow thinner and more luminous, beautiful with the beauty that he had long shunned and that became him well. . . .

The proprietor entered. "Gia e morto," whispered the doctor to him. The proprietor shrugged his shoulders indifferently. The older lady, with tears slowly running down her cheeks, approached him and said timidly that now the deceased must be taken to his room.

"O no, madam," answered the proprietor politely, but without any amiability and not in English, but in French. He was no longer interested in the trifle which the guests from San Francisco could now leave at his cash-office. "This is absolutely impossible," he said, and added in the form of an explanation that he valued this apartment highly, and if he satisfied her desire, this would become known over Capri and the tourists would begin to avoid it.

The girl, who had looked at him strangely, sat down, and with her handkerchief to her mouth, began to cry. Her mother's tears dried up at once, and her face flared up. She raised her tone, began to demand, using her own language and still unable to realize that the respect for her was absolutely gone. The proprietor, with polite dignity, cut her short: "If madam does not like the ways of this hotel, he dare not detain her." And he firmly announced that the corpse must leave the hotel that very day, at dawn, that the police had been informed, that an agent would call immediately and attend to all the necessary formalities. . . . "Is it possible to get on Capri at least a plain coffin?" madam asks. . . . Unfortunately not; by no means, and as for making one, there will be no time. It will be necessary to arrange things some other way. . . . For instance, he gets English sodawater in big, oblong boxes. . . . The partitions could be taken out from such a box. . . .

By night, the whole hotel was asleep. A waiter opened the window in Number 43—it faced a corner of the garden where a consumptive banana-tree grew in the shadow of a high stone wall set with broken glass on the top—turned out the electric light, locked the door, and went away. The deceased remained alone in the darkness. Blue stars looked down at him from the black sky, the cricket in the wall started his melancholy, care-free song. In the dimly lighted corridor two chambermaids were sitting on the window-sill, mending something. Then Luigi came in, in slippered feet, with a heap of clothes on his arm.

"*Pronto?*"—he asked in a stage whisper, as if greatly concerned, directing his eyes toward the terrible door, at the end of the corridor. And waving his free hand in that direction, "*Partenza!*" he cried out in a whisper, as if seeing off a train—and the chambermaids, choking with noiseless laughter, put their heads on each other's shoulders.

Then, stepping softly, he ran to the door, slightly rapped at it, and inclining his ear, asked most obsequiously in a subdued tone of voice:

"*Ha sonata, Signore?*"

And, squeezing his throat and thrusting his lower jaw forward, he answered himself in a drawling, grating, sad voice, as if from behind the door:

"Yes, come in. . . ."

At dawn, when the window panes in Number Forty-three grew white, and a damp wind rustled in the leaves of the banana tree, when the pale-blue morning sky rose and stretched over Capri, and the sun, rising from behind the distant mountains of Italy, touched into gold the pure, clearly outlined summit of Monte Solaro, when the masons, who mended the paths for the tourists on the island, went out to their work—an oblong box was brought to room number forty-three. Soon it grew very heavy and painfully pressed against the knees of the assistant doorman who was conveying it in a one-horse carriage along the white highroad which winded on the slopes, among stone fences and vineyards, all the way down to the seacoast. The driver, a sickly man, with red eyes, in an old short-sleeved coat and in worn-out shoes, had a drunken headache; all night long he had played dice at the eatinghouse—and he kept on flogging his vigorous little horse. According to Sicilian custom, the animal was heavily burdened with decorations: all sorts of bells tinkled on the bridle, which was ornamented with colored woolen fringes; there were bells also on the edges of the high saddle; and a bird's feather, two feet long, stuck in the trimmed crest of the horse, nodded up and down. The driver kept silence: he was depressed by his wrongheadedness and vices, by the fact that last night he had lost in gambling all the copper coins with which his pockets had been full—neither more nor less than four liras and forty centesimi. But on such a morning, when the air is so fresh, and the sea stretches near by, and the sky is serene with a morning serenity, a headache passes rapidly and one becomes carefree again. Besides, the driver was also somewhat cheered by the unexpected earnings which the Gentleman from San Francisco, who bumped his dead head against the walls of the box behind his back, had brought him. The little steamer, shaped like a great bug, which lay far down on the tender and brilliant blue filling to the brim the Neapolitan bay, was blowing the signal of departure, and the sounds swiftly resounded all over Capri. Every bend of the island, every ridge and stone was seen as distinctly as if there were no air between heaven and earth. Near the quay the driver was overtaken by the head doorman who conducted in an auto the wife and daughter of the Gentleman from San Francisco. Their faces were pale and their eyes sunken with tears and a sleepless night. And in ten minutes the little steamer was again stirring up the water and picking its way toward Sorrento and Castellamare, carrying the American family away from Capri forever. . . . Meanwhile, peace and rest were restored on the island.

Two thousand years ago there had lived on that island a man who became utterly entangled in his own brutal and filthy actions. For some unknown reason he usurped the rule over millions of men and found himself bewildered by the absurdity of this power, while the fear that someone might kill him unawares, made him commit deeds inhuman beyond all measure. And mankind has forever retained his memory, and those who, taken together, now rule the world, as incomprehensibly and, essentially, as cruelly as he did—come from all the corners of the earth to look at the remnants of the stone house he inhabited, which stands on one of the steepest cliffs of the island. On that wonderful morning the tourists, who had come to Capri for precisely that purpose, were still asleep in the various hotels, but

tiny long-eared asses under red saddles were already being led to the
hotel entrances. Americans and Germans, men and women, old and
young, after having arisen and breakfasted heartily, were to scramble
on them, and the old beggar-women of Capri, with sticks in their
sinewy hands, were again to run after them along stony, mountainous
paths, all the way up to the summit of Monte Tiberia. The dead old
man from San Francisco, who had planned to keep the tourists company but who had, instead, only scared them by reminding them
of death, was already shipped to Naples, and soothed by this, the
travelers slept soundly, and silence reigned over the island. The stores
in the little town were still closed, with the exception of the fish
and greens market on the tiny square. Among the plain people who
filled it, going about their business, stood idly by, as usual, Lorenzo,
a tall old boatman, a carefree reveller and once a handsome man,
famous all over Italy, who had many times served as a model for
painters. He had brought and already sold—for a song—two big
sea-crawfish, which he had caught at night and which were rustling
in the apron of Don Cataldo, the cook of the hotel where the family
from San Francisco had been lodged, and now Lorenzo could stand
calmly until nightfall, wearing princely airs, showing off his rags, his
clay pipe with its long reed mouth-piece, and his red woolen cap,
tilted on one ear. Meanwhile, among the precipices of Monte Solare,
down the ancient Phoenician road, cut in the rocks in the form of a
gigantic staircase, two Abruzzi mountaineers were coming from Ana-
capri. One carried under his leather mantle a bagpipe, a large goat's
skin with two pipes; the other, something in the nature of a wooden
flute. They walked, and the entire country, joyous, beautiful, sunny,
stretched below them; the rocky shoulders of the island, which lay
at their feet, the fabulous blue in which it swam, the shining morning vapors over the sea westward, beneath the dazzling sun, and the
wavering masses of Italy's mountains, both near and distant, whose
beauty human word is powerless to render. . . . Midway they slowed
up. Overshadowing the road stood, in a grotto of the rock wall of
Monte Solare, the Holy Virgin, all radiant, bathed in the warmth
and the splendor of the sun. The rust of her snow-white plaster-of-
Paris vestures and queenly crown was touched into gold, and there
were meekness and mercy in her eyes raised toward the heavens,
toward the eternal and beatific abode of her thrice-blessed Son. They
bared their heads, applied the pipes to their lips, and praises flowed
on, candid and humbly-joyous, praises to the sun and the morning,
to Her, the Immaculate Intercessor for all who suffer in this evil and
beautiful world, and to Him who had been born of her womb in the
cavern of Bethlehem, in a hut of lowly shepherds in distant Judea.

As for the body of the dead Gentleman from San Francisco, it was on its way home, to the shores of the New World, where a grave awaited it. Having undergone many humiliations and suffered much human neglect, having wandered about a week from one port warehouse to another, it finally got on that same famous ship which had brought the family, such a short while ago and with such a pomp, to the Old World. But now he was concealed from the living: in a tar-coated coffin he was lowered deep into the black hold of the steamer. And again did the ship set out on its far sea journey. At night it sailed by the island of Capri, and, for those who watched it from the island, its lights slowly disappearing in the dark sea, it seemed infinitely sad. But there, on the vast steamer, in its lighted halls shining with brilliance and marble, a noisy dancing party was going on, as usual.

On the second and the third night there was again a ball—this time in mid-ocean, during the furious storm sweeping over the ocean, which roared like a funeral mass and rolled up mountainous seas fringed with mourning silvery foam. The Devil, who from the rocks of Gibraltar, the stony gateway of two worlds, watched the ship vanish into night and storm, could hardly distinguish from behind the snow the innumerable fiery eyes of the ship. The Devil was as huge as a cliff, but the ship was even bigger, a many-storied, many-stacked giant, created by the arrogance of the New Man with the old heart. The blizzard battered the ship's rigging and its broad-necked stacks, whitened with snow, but it remained firm, majestic—and terrible. On its uppermost deck, amidst a snowy whirlwind there loomed up in a loneliness the cozy, dimly lighted cabin, where, only half awake, the vessel's ponderous pilot reigned over its entire mass, bearing the semblance of a pagan idol. He heard the wailing moans and the furious screeching of the siren, choked by the storm, but the nearness of that which was behind the wall and which in the last account was incomprehensible to him, removed his fears. He was reassured by the thought of the large, armored cabin, which now and then was filled with mysterious rumbling sounds and with the dry creaking of blue fires, flaring up and exploding around a man with a metallic headpiece, who was eagerly catching the indistinct voices of the vessels that hailed him, hundreds of miles away. At the very bottom, in the under-water womb of the *Atlantis,* the huge masses of tanks and various other machines, their steel parts shining dully, wheezed with steam and oozed hot water and oil; here was the gigantic kitchen, heated by hellish furnaces, where the motion of the vessel was being generated; here seethed those forces terrible in their concentration which were transmitted to the keel of the vessel, and into that endless round tunnel, which was lighted by electricity, and looked like a

gigantic cannon barrel, where slowly, with a punctuality and certainty that crushes the human soul a colossal shaft was revolving
in its oily nest, like a living monster stretching in its lair. As for the
middle part of the *Atlantis,* its warm, luxurious cabins, dining-rooms,
and halls, they radiated light and joy, were astir with a chattering
smartly-dressed crowd, were filled with the fragrance of fresh flowers,
and resounded with a string orchestra. And again did the slender
supple pair of hired lovers painfully turn and twist and at times
clash convulsively amid the splendor of lights, silks, diamonds, and
bare feminine shoulders: she—a sinfully modest pretty girl, with
lowered eyelashes and an innocent hair-dressing, he—a tall, young
man, with black hair, looking as if they were pasted, pale with
powder, in most exquisite patent leather shoes, in a narrow, long-
skirted dresscoat,—a beautiful man resembling a leech. And no one
knew that this couple had long since been weary of torturing themselves with a feigned beatific torture under the sounds of shamefully-
melancholy music; nor did any one know what lay deep, deep, beneath them, on the very bottom of the hold, in the neighborhood of
the gloomy and sultry maw of the ship, that heavily struggled with
the ocean, the darkness, and the storm.

Chapter Ten

The Informal Theme

THE INFORMAL THEME is the short paper which grows out of the writer's own knowledge and experience. It usually contains between five hundred and six hundred words. Such short themes are assigned frequently in freshman English courses, to develop ease in expression and the ability to handle larger writing projects. There is no doubt that this practice in writing is valuable: at the end of a term of composition, students almost without exception express themselves more competently and more easily than they did at the beginning, largely as a result of writing and receiving criticism on their short compositions. The purpose of this chapter is to discuss the method, the step-by-step process, of writing substantial, well-organized, clear, and interesting themes.

Before we discuss the writing process, however, it is wise to consider briefly some of the general problems of theme writing. For, although writing themes is valuable, and although it is satisfying to a number of students, to many students it is arduous and even painful. Obstacles, some imagined, some real, block them in their approach to a writing assignment.

One problem is produced by the student's feeling that writing themes is forced communication. Instead of waiting until he is ready and eager to express his ideas, he is obliged to communicate at a certain time, at a prescribed length, usually in a designated form (expository, narrative, descriptive), and sometimes on one of a list of topics assigned. This regulated, unspontaneous writing seems to many students unnatural and difficult; very common is the protest, "I have to be in the mood before I can write; I couldn't write anything good this week because I wasn't in the mood."

The student who takes this attitude gives himself a mental handicap. If he will examine communication in general, he will find that forced communication is by no means peculiar to freshman English. In the business of living, the report is due tomorrow; the speech is set for Tuesday; the thesis must be finished before the established date for the awarding of degrees; the editor expects the article in time for the January issue; the class will assemble to hear the lecture at nine; the letter must be answered today. Communication is often forced, often prescribed in length and subject and form; and the meeting of responsibilities leaves little time for concern about one's mood. One may not be in the mood to study physics, or to prepare for an examination, or to write the examination; but he gets into the mood, or rather, he forgets about his mood, by getting to work. The business of writing a theme should be handled in the same way. Worry about a lack of freedom, spontaneity, and "inspiration" is simply a form of procrastination. So, indeed, is any sort of worry about a writing assignment. The remedy is systematic work.

A second, more genuine problem in theme writing is the problem of the reader, the audience for whom the paper is written. We have said earlier that the receiver is an important factor in successful communication: material, language, and attitude must, to some extent at least, be adjusted to him. But freshman themes are often written in an unusual sort of vacuum; there seems to be no definite receiver at whom to aim. The student sometimes just writes, in a baffled desperation, hoping the composition will turn out well, but having no clear idea of how appropriate his subject is, how fully he needs to explain an activity or process, how much knowledge he can take for granted on the part of the unknown reader, what standards, other than the standard of technical correctness, he is expected to meet.

The most obvious receiver of the freshman theme is, of course, the instructor. He reads the papers; on his reaction depends the student's grade. Some college freshmen, bearing these facts in mind, adopt what seems to them the shrewd course and write, not what they think or feel, but what they assume the instructor wants them to think and feel. Such students frequently misjudge their teachers. At least the good instructors manage to keep a sense of humor, have some memories of their own college days which would surprise their students, and are likely to lean over backward in judging themes that contain opinions opposite to their own. Students who wish to please these instructors can do so by honest, direct writing. They will do such writing (and so get the best grades) when they are actually trying to communicate an experience or an idea that seems to them worth communicating. Unless a student has convincing evidence to the contrary, he will be wise to assume that his teacher will be a fair and understanding reader and that the best way to impress is to do sincere, thoughtful writing.

As a further solution to the problem of the reader and a further aid to good writing, it is well to have in mind not just the teacher, or even the teacher and the class, but the kind of audience that most serious writers really write for and hope to be judged by—an audience of well-informed, intelligent people who are interested in the world they live in, who recognize and appreciate good informal writing, who will not read dull, wordy material but will respond readily to lively concrete expression, who welcome humor that is in keeping with the subject, who will read sympathetically or open-mindedly anything that reveals the writer's experience or knowledge or considered opinions.

It is well, too, for a student occasionally to have the experience of writing for particular audiences, for much of the communicating that he will do later—writing letters or reports and talking to small or large groups—will be aimed at special audiences. Writing a theme for the class and then reading it to the class is a good practice. Another good practice is stating in an introductory note that a theme is aimed at a particular audience and then aiming the theme at that audience: for example, writing an editorial aimed at college students, a fund-raising letter to people who might contribute to the Red Cross, a report for someone who has presumably requested such a report, a letter of application to a prospective employer, a criticism of a book for someone who has not read the book, information about fraternity rushing for an incoming freshman. In aiming at such audiences, it is necessary to consider the needs, knowledge, and interests of the audience; and in writing for a general audience of intelligent, well-informed people it is well to remember that even they do not necessarily have specialized knowledge and that they may need to be given background information or definitions of technical terms and terms used in some special way.

In summary, if the student will direct most of his writing at the intelligent, well-informed, sympathetic audience, assuming that his instructor is a member of that audience, and if he will occasionally direct a theme at a clearly defined particular audience, he will escape the frustrating experience of writing for no audience at all. He will also be practicing the kind of writing which, in the future as well as the present, he should be able to do.

A third problem, finding something to write about, will be considered in the next section, where we begin to discuss the writing process. Though choosing a subject is an initial problem for many students, it is also the first of five stages in planning and writing a theme. These stages or steps in composition are:

1. Choosing the subject
2. Making an informal outline
3. Writing the first draft (or drafts)
4. Revising

5. Making the final copy

The most important single point for the student writer to keep in mind is that writing a theme should be thought of, and executed, *as a series of steps*. The early steps may overlap; for example, by the time the writer has fixed on a subject, he often has in mind a rough outline of his projected paper. But no step should be omitted, and no step should be hurried. Good themes are built gradually; and they are built by systematic procedure, thought, and care.

I. SOMETHING TO SAY

A good theme has substance. It gives the impression of a mind at work, observing, thinking, and communicating its observation and thought to a reader. Such thoughtful and substantial communication is certainly not beyond the power of any college student. Anyone who has lived for seventeen years or more has much to say that is worth saying. And yet the thin, trivial theme, not worth the time consumed in writing or the time wasted in reading it, is all too common; and the lament, "I can't think of anything to write," is all too familiar to teachers of freshman English.

Often the student who says that he can't "think" of anything to write about has done no actual thinking. He has for five days waited passively for an idea to strike, and on the sixth day has begun to worry. Neither waiting nor worry is likely to produce good results. If he has thought actively about a subject for his theme, he has usually made the mistake of thinking abstractly and beyond his own experience. He has thought of such topics as world peace, race relations, life in America, education, the two-party system; and he is naturally baffled. These topics are too vague and large, and his knowledge of them is too vague and small. But in specific events he has witnessed, people he has actually known, opinions he has formed, concrete information he has acquired, he has hundreds of subjects for papers. About these things which he knows, he has something to say.

Suppose the assignment is to write an informal narrative theme which presents a vivid personal experience. "I can't think of anything to write," a student may say. "Nothing interesting has ever happened to me." This is absurd. He probably means that he has never been a paratrooper, has never been run over by a truck, and has never been the victim of a holdup. Perhaps not; but if he had been, he would still be at a loss for a theme subject, because a habit of mind makes him glance over his own experience and dismiss it as worthless. He should examine it closely. Every human life is full of experiences and events, not necessarily dramatic or sensational, but important at the time, and representing true segments of the experience of living. The student to whom nothing interesting has happened has run home from school every day for months in fear of the gang waiting around the corner; he has wondered about death and God at his grandfather's funeral; on a camping trip he has been lost in the woods; he has watched a large building burn; his mind has gone blank after the first sentence of his oration at eighth-grade graduation; he has learned that his girl is going to a party with his friend; he has felt lost and strange on his first day at college. These are only a few of the dozens of possible subjects he has for his narrative paper.

Suppose the assignment is to write a theme which gives information about something which the writer knows from first-hand experience; the theme is to be impersonal, focused on giving objective information about some business, or process, or specialized activity. The student, a girl this time, has never worked in a factory or a grocery store; she knows nothing about building model planes; she cannot set a lobster trap; she does not collect stamps; she has never sold shoes. She is in despair. But she has been a swimming instructor at a summer camp; she has collected money for the Community Chest in various sections of her town; she has been assistant editor of her high-school paper; she has built stage sets and managed lighting for high-school plays. About these things and many others she has special, first-hand information.

With the right kind of thinking about what he actually knows, the student has the problem not of finding something to write about, but of choosing the best subject from the many which are available. The best subject will usually be the one most real and interesting to him, about which he has the most exact knowledge, the most vivid impressions. Anything can be made real and interesting to a reader— literally anything, from shoe polish to an experiment with hypnosis, from an autopsy to a walk along a country road—if the writer knows about it, if he is himself interested in it, and if he communicates it concretely. A paper cannot be porous and thin and trivial if it is packed with definite statements, exact particulars, specific examples, concrete details, images, and sensations. Close observation of one's own experience, reflection on that experience, and accurate, detailed recording are the essentials of something to say.

II. PLANNING AND WRITING THE FIRST DRAFT

Some planning of the paper has already been done by the time the subject has been selected. That is, the writer has necessarily thought through the topic sufficiently to see that it can be developed;

he probably has in mind three or four points he can make, and perhaps an illustration or two. But he is seldom mentally prepared to sit down at once and write the theme. More systematic planning is needed.

Most students find it useful, as a step toward writing, to jot down a rough outline of their early ideas about the subject, and, as their thinking and planning proceed, to work with that outline, adding new ideas as they come, deleting others, rearranging the material. A formal outline is unnecessary for a short informal paper; it may, indeed, be an actual hazard in writing because, looking logical and finished, it may bind the writer to a plan which is not the best for his material. The rough outline, however, is a convenient way of keeping track of ideas and seeing the relationship between them; and it has the virtue of being highly flexible.

Below is a copy of a rather full rough outline for a theme on the writer's changing ideas of happiness; the outline had been enlarged and amended during several days of intermittent thinking about the theme:

MY CHANGING IDEAS OF HAPPINESS

1. As a child, having everything I wanted
   candy
   Xmas presents (Uncle John)
   ~~dog I couldn't have (unhappiness)~~
   best bike in the neighborhood
   self-centered, thought everyone   *circus*
      existed to give me things,   *movies*
      Material things.
~~2. Doing what I wanted—circus, movies~~

2. ~~2.~~ Older, happiness in being independent
   ⎡different, but like (1) because
   ⎢ still selfish
   ⎢ hated parents' authority
   ⎢ earning own money
   ⎢ going off in woods   *having car*
   ⎣ going into city alone
   →wanted to show off, be thought
      important

3. ~~3.~~ Now, doing some good is happiness
   church (influence)
more + appendix—doctors and nurses
considerate decided to be doctor
of others still like things and independence,
      but less important now

The kind of planning represented by an outline like this pays dividends; and, for most writers, the planning should be on paper, not simply in the mind. Since the written plan can be viewed more wholly and clearly, the writer can apply to it, more easily than to a mental plan, certain fundamental questions about the content and organization of the theme. The questions which should be asked about any projected paper are:

1. *Is the subject too large for a short theme?*

(Sometimes the writer has tried, initially, to handle too much in five or six hundred words. The development of so much material will necessarily be sketchy. He needs to select only one phase of his subject —one division in his outline—and develop it fully for his theme.)

2. *Is any of the material irrelevant?*

(In the outline above, the point about the unhappiness of not having a dog appears irrelevant to the discussion of what constituted happiness at that time. Wisely, the writer struck it out.)

3. *Should any overlapping main points be combined?*

(This has been done with points 1 and 2 in the outline quoted above.)

4. *Is the arrangement of material good?*

(The writer of the outline above rearranged certain subtopics, but the chronological arrangement of his main points was inevitable. Often, however, the main points need to be shuffled, for better continuity or better building to a climax.)

These questions can also, of course, be applied to a first draft of a paper; and some writers prefer to start with a rough draft instead of an outline, with the intention of drastically revising and reorganizing the rough draft, and probably writing three or four drafts before the paper is in final form. In other words, they partially merge steps 2 and 3 (making an outline, writing the first draft) in the writing process. It is, however, harder to eliminate sections of a paper than it is to strike out jottings in an outline, and harder to change the order of material which is written out with some fullness and continuity. For this reason the outline as a step preliminary to writing is likely to produce a better focused and better organized theme. A first draft based on a well-planned outline may need considerable revision, but the basic arrangement of material will probably be good; the writer can, therefore, give his attention to other problems of form and development.

It is generally wise, particularly if one is working from a good outline, to write the first draft in one sitting and at a fairly steady pace, without pausing long or worrying much over mechanical difficulties and small details. This does not mean that the student should write carelessly, even in a first draft. On the contrary, it is most desirable for him to learn to write reasonably clean and competent first drafts—he is often judged, on examinations, for example, by his ability to do this. But stopping in the process of writing the draft of a theme to look up the spelling of a word or the use of a comma, or to work over an awkward sentence, may break the writer's train of thought and interfere with the forward movement of the composition. Since it is possible for him to revise his work—since, indeed, he is expected to do so—he can defer nicety of expression for the sake of getting down on paper his unbroken sequence of ideas. Thoughtful planning, then uninterrupted first writing, and finally careful revision usually produce the best results.

III. REVISION

Revision is the stage of writing which students most often neglect, sometimes because they write their papers too late to have much time for revision, sometimes because they have understandable difficulty in seeing weaknesses in their own work, sometimes because they are lazy. And yet, revision is very important; and working over a composition can be the most rewarding part of the whole writing process. Polishing a sentence, eliminating a useless phrase, finding the word which says exactly what one means, changing a routine beginning to an arresting one, joining two disconnected paragraphs with a neat transition, adding one or two details which bring a hazy picture into sharp focus—such changes make the difference between mediocrity and excellence; and they give the writer the sense of craftsmanship, of deep satisfaction and sometimes excitement, which comes from knowing that a thing is as perfect as one can make it. Teachers of English know that when a student with an average or below average record has once written a good paper, he is likely to write more good papers. The reason for this phenomenon is complex; but one element in it is that the student, having once had the experience of craftsmanship, having once stretched himself to do his best work, is no longer content with half-hearted imperfection.

Very occasionally, when a student is immersed in a subject or an experience (and when he is well trained and fluent in expression), he can write a first draft which requires no revision: the development of the idea is complete and clear; the details, long present in his mind, are set down vividly for the reader; no word needs to be changed. But, nearly always, such perfect or near-perfect expression comes from thoughtful and painstaking revision.

Revision, to be effective, should be done, not as soon as the first draft is finished, but at least twenty-four hours, preferably three or four days, later. (This means, obviously, that writing a theme should not be postponed until the night before the paper is due.) The completion of the first draft sometimes leaves the writer in a state of exhausted discouragement, sometimes in a glow of pride in achievement. Both states are frequently unjustified; but both blind him to the actual merits and defects of what he has written. He is never so incompetent to judge his theme as he is at this time. Even if he has no distinct feeling of discouragement or sense of accomplishment, he is not an able critic just after his paper is written because he knows so well what he *intended* to say. Two or three days later, looking at the draft which has grown somewhat strange, he will be able to see what he failed to say. He may even—it has happened—be uncertain about what he meant. He will, certainly, look at the paper with a view closer to that of the alien reader who will ultimately see and judge it; and he is therefore, at this later time, able to make effective revision.

A part of the process of revision should be reading the paper aloud. Awkward phrasing, thoughtless repetition of words, repeated sentence patterns, and wordiness are more striking to the ear than to the fast-moving eye. Also, since reading aloud is slower than glancing over the page, small details of spelling and punctuation will receive more attention. The author should do this reading aloud, let us repeat, not when the theme is fresh and meaningful in his mind, but after an interval. He can hear then, if he listens, what the paper is, without the overtones of what he intended it to be.

The critical examination and revision of the paper, like the whole writing process, should be systematic. The writer should examine closely his paragraphs: do they have topic sentences? are they well developed? are the transitions between paragraphs smooth and clear? His sentences: are they grammatically correct? are they sufficiently varied? His words: is he sure of their meanings? are all of them necessary? could one exact word be substituted for the five he has used? are their connotations right for his purpose? are they correctly spelled? And his punctuation: does it indicate accurately the pauses, and the strength of the pauses which the reader needs for immediate understanding? The student should scrutinize his paper particularly, of course, for errors or weaknesses which have been called to his attention before. The student who makes numerous blunders in composition will profit from reading his paper several times, looking for one type of fault in each reading, instead of trying to correct everything at one time. Systematically reading once for paragraph development, a second time for punctuation, and a third time for exact use of words will produce better results than trying to concentrate simultaneously on three very different problems.

Much more elusive than punctuation or paragraph development, and harder for the student to check in his own writing, is the clarity of thought and expression in the theme. There is sometimes, in the work of inexperienced writers, a kind of *fogginess,* whether basically in thinking or in expression it is often difficult to say. Reading a composition which has this quality, one has the feeling that somehow the wheels have slipped; there is a gap in thought, or between thought and expression; the sense is blurred. It is impossible to define this fogginess precisely, because there are so many varieties of it. The following short passages, taken from freshman themes, will illustrate:

The most important use of hypnotism is as an anesthetic. This use can be second only to the cure of neuroses. [Awkwardly phrased; but the basic fault is in the writer's failure to think through the idea. If the use as an anesthetic can be second to another use, then logically it is not "the most important use."]

It is impossible to determine how old leprosy is, for we cannot tell whether the leprosy recorded in 1500 B.C. was the same as that which now scourges man as it has for more than 3000 years. [Another example of foggy thinking. Having said that the leprosy recorded in 1500 B.C. is not necessarily the same leprosy that we know now, the writer assumes at the end of the sentence that it is the same.]

The trance stage of hypnotism is such a deep state that many people have been mistaken for dead while in it. The fact that bodies have often been found in caskets shows that people have been pronounced dead while being in trance. [This absurd statement is an example of a gap in expression, possibly in thinking too, although it is hard to believe that the point that the bodies had moved after they were enclosed in the caskets was absent from the writer's mind. Something was absent from his mind, however, when he failed to put that essential point on paper.]

My love of literature will occupy an outstanding niche on my ladder of success. [An example of a fuzzy, imperfectly visualized figure of speech. Niches are, by their nature, recessed, not outstanding; and it would be a most extraordinary ladder which had a niche. The value of figurative language is that it calls to mind a vivid concrete image. When the image called up is a niche outstanding on a ladder, one questions the writer's good sense. At best, he was not thinking about what he was saying.]

The loss of working hours must be increased if the company is to meet its production goal. [An example of foggy expression. The working hours, of course, not the loss of them, must be increased; or the loss must be decreased.]

My earliest recollection of first going to school occurred when I was five years old. [Another example of blurred expression. Going to school, not the recollection of it, occurred when the writer was five years old.]

Writing sentences like these in a first draft is understandable; failing to improve them before the paper is turned in is hardly excusable. In revising his papers, the student should examine the clarity of his thinking and his expression, asking himself these three questions: Have I thought the ideas through, logically and carefully? Have I said exactly what I mean? Have I put on paper every link in my chain of thought, every detail which the reader needs to know? Clarity in thought and expression is particularly hard to judge immediately after the first writing of the paper. After an interval, gaps in communication and inexactness in wording are often so conspicuous that the writer wonders how he could have thought that he had made his meaning clear.

Finally, before he makes the last copy of his theme, the writer should examine, as thoroughly and critically as he can, the texture of the whole composition. A good theme is like a good piece of cloth, tightly woven, substantial, consistent in its quality. Mechanical errors—in spelling, punctuation, grammar—are tears in the cloth. Choppy sentences and disconnected paragraphs make breaks in the weave. Padding, jargon, and undue triteness are shoddy places. Lack of subordination, inexact or roundabout phrasing, and, above all, lack of detail produce a thin, sleazy fabric. Removing actual errors is only part of the process of revision. It is basic, of course; but a more important part is working for the tight structure, the precise and finished phrasing, the packed, concrete expression which make the good theme.

IV. FINAL FORM

Preparing the final copy of the paper is the easy step in the process of writing. One needs only to keep in mind a few simple requirements, designed to facilitate the handling, grading, and filing of large numbers of themes.

A typewritten paper should be double-spaced, on standard $8\frac{1}{2}$ by 11-inch paper. A theme in longhand should be written on lined paper of the same size ($8\frac{1}{2}$ by 11) with widely spaced lines (about $\frac{1}{2}$ inch apart) so that the lines of writing will not be illegibly intermingled. Longhand papers are written neatly and clearly, in dark ink. In both typewritten and handwritten manuscripts, only one side of the paper is used. The title is centered near the top of the first page, with a double space between it and the text below. Substantial margins are left on both sides of the page. The pages are arranged in order and are numbered. The paper is folded and endorsed according to the form established by the institution or the department. Most instructors in freshman English want themes folded lengthwise, with the student's name, course and section number, instructor's name, subject of the theme, and the date the theme is due written or typed on the outside, at the top of the folded manuscript.

Although the final copy of a paper should be finished and clean, most teachers have no objection to a few minor revisions in the completed manuscript, provided it remains neat and legible. Words to be changed, if they cannot be erased, should have a line drawn through them, with the correct word written above the word struck out. (Unwanted words put in parentheses are confusing to a reader; the parentheses are used incorrectly and misleadingly when they enclose words not meant to be read.) If words are to be inserted, they too should be written between the lines, with a caret ($\wedge$) inserted to show where they should be read. The paragraph symbol (¶) should be used in the margin to show that a paragraph break, overlooked in typing, is intended here.

The completed manuscript should be read carefully to pick up any mechanical slips. An instructor reading great numbers of papers cannot make distinctions between errors of carelessness and errors of ignorance. An error is, necessarily, an error. "The girl who typed this for me made some mistakes" is not a valid excuse for mechanical deficiencies in a theme. The writer is obligated to check his typist as well as himself. His final copy should in all respects represent the best work he is able to do.

CHAPTER REVIEW

Below is a summary of the main ideas in the chapter. If your reading has been adequate, you should be able to supply the particulars necessary to develop these summary statements.

1. The communication in theme writing is no more forced than the communication necessary on many occasions in everyday living.

2. The student can simplify the problem of what audience to write for by aiming most of his informal themes at an intelligent, well-informed general audience, and occasionally, with the approval of his instructor, writing for a particular audience.

3. In choosing subjects, the student should avoid large abstract topics, and should draw on his own experience, observation, information, and thought.

4. It is advisable to make an informal outline, and to work out the organization of the paper by revising that outline, before starting to write the first draft.

5. The student should allow himself ample time for revision, a very important part of the writing process.

6. Revision is most effective if it is done at least twenty-four hours after the first writing of the paper.

7. The good theme, in addition to being mechanically correct, has substance, good organization, effective transitions between sentences and paragraphs, concrete development, clear thought, and apt, precise expression.

EXERCISES

Read carefully, criticize, and grade the student themes below. The assignment was to write a theme of at least 500 words which would interest the reader and give him clear information about something which the writer knew from first-hand experience. The theme was to be impersonal, focused on the process or activity rather than on the writer's own experience with it.

In criticizing each theme, consider its technical correctness (spelling, punctuation, sentence structure, etc.), its focus and organization, paragraph development, style and choice of words, and the clarity and interest of the whole paper.

1. BEHIND THE FOOTLIGHTS

The curtain rises. A hush spreads over the darkened theatre and from over the footlights come the first chords of the piano. This is a high school musical. A spectacle of luscious colors and co-ordinated rythm greets each member of the audience but behind the scenes of this finished production lie weeks of continuous rehearsals and hard work.

Two months before the first performance, work begins. The first skeleton plans are drawn up which include settings, dance routines, and music. General ideas about the predominant theme are gathered from the students and faculty; whether it is to be a show of individual sets and comic acts or whether it is to have a slight story which will bind together the various routines. One is chosen and the first step has been taken. The show is underway.

Appointed talent scouts are let loose who round up all the students with one iota of ability. No one escapes their clutches. Tryouts begin which last three or four days during which time the difficult task of thinning out the students to the required number takes place. Each day less are told to return until finally enough talent has been collected and actual work begins. There are many dissapointed faces as the final list of the cast is posted but there are also many smiling ones.

The dance routines during this time, have been laid out in detail, the music gathered, and production staff acquired. Prop men, make-up artists, costume and scenery designers, publicity agents, prompters, stage hands and an assistant director are added to the list of participants in this show, each one an important spoke in the churning wheel of production.

"Haven't got an old brand new maple couch laying around unused, have you?" questions the prop men while from all sides come requests for old clothes, hats, shoes, cardboard, brushes, wooden boxes, and ticket purchases. The sellers chase you around until you're cornered and have to give in. "Never give up" is their motto.

"One, two, three," counts the director with an expression of fatigue and futility since the chorus lines reminds him of a scrambled alphabet in Campbell soup. After tearing out gobs of hair, he focuses his attention back again, heaving a forlorn sigh. Over and over, afternoon after afternoon, morning, noon, and night the show goes on.

Scissors, sewing machines, and needles rally to the cry, each working at top speed to do his part. Houses are raided. Parents see their furniture pass through the front door and into waiting cars. Each and every able bodied student is drafted into collecting props. The smells of paints drift up from the machine shop where huge canvas-covered frames are being transformed into moonlit nights and foreign lands.

The costumes and scenery are finally finished. The props are stowed away and make-up men and stage hands stand ready for the big nights.

Dress rehearsal finally comes. There are always those few who arrive late, looking very sheepish and apologetic. The orchestra begins, house lights are dimmed, but the curtain fails to rise. One of the cast is still in the dressing room, pulling on his costume. More delay but at last it begins. Dress rehearsals always go poorly. Someone forgets a step or dashes madly across the stage, forgetting that he was in this number. There's a hurried cutting of numbers and then the rehearsal is over. All are sent home with instructions to hope for the best.

The next night the show goes smoothly; the curtain falls, and a group of tired but happy individuals receive a deserved reward as they are greeted by thunderous applause across the footlights.

2. WAR DEPARTMENT OBSERVATION

In the minds of most civilians during the war, a War Department Observer was a multi-starred general sent to a battle front directly from Washington to examine the situation. To the skeptical G.I. at the front who had never seen or known one, an observer was a shady gestapo-like individual— usually a second Lieutenant—whose aim in life was to report conditions which would result in future discomfort for enlisted men. Both conceptions were far from the actual truth.

Every branch of the Army—the Ground Forces, the Air Forces, and the Service Forces—had its own particular system of observation, but at this time we shall discuss only the method used by the Ground Forces. Observers are either officers or enlisted men with previous combat experience. In addition to this requirement the observer must have a native average intelligence as determined by the General Mental Classification Test taken at the time of induction, and plenty of good luck. If he feels that he is unable to fulfill the obligations of the assignment, he may decline the appointment. Thus the selection of an observer is on a semi-voluntary basis.

The new observer is given three weeks of schooling and drill after which he is attached to an assault unit composed mostly of men fresh from training camps in the U. S. with no battle experience. This is a deliberate procedure, for in the more seasoned organization every man is battle-wise enough to report any unusual enemy activity. The duty of the observer is to report all the activities of the enemy on his front, their fortifications, their general behavior. He works in close harmony with the Intelligence Corps, and all information is interchangeable. Notes are never taken except in extremely important instances when the observer cannot rely on his memory. In such particular cases the notes are sent back to the unit Command post with an explanation of their contents to the Intelligence Officer who holds them for the observer. It is necessary to follow this procedure to prevent the loss of vital information if the observer is either killed or captured.

Whenever he feels that he has enough information, the observer may retire to a rear area without a given order. He merely informs the commanding officer of the unit to which he is attached and withdraws to make his report. The report is written as briefly as possible, yet it covers every bit of movement no matter how insignificant it may seem. From the forward command post it is sent to area headquarters where it is typed and filed until all the reports from all of the observers of the particular campaign have been received. This accumulated information, plus the overall campaign report of the commanding general in charge of operations, is sent to the War Department in Washington where it is studied and filed for future reference.

The Japanese were defeated by their errors and blunders. To the men engaged in close combat with the enemy these strategic errors were not immediately discernible, but they were noted by the strategists in Washington and future campaigns planned accordingly. It was through the efforts of the War Department Observer that these mistakes were recorded. Yet throughout each campaign the observer was not merely a sight-seer. He fought and killed and was killed; by virtue of his experience he often found himself commanding large groups of men. At all times he was a soldier first.

3. DRAPES, DOORKNOBS AND DAIQUIRIS

Striped wallpaper, deep rose-colored chairs, huge crystal ash trays, thick gray rugs, the kind you sink into, huge white lamps, vases of fresh green leaves, glamourous women, handsome men, and plenty of cocktails. Glamourous? Yes, but the reception room of an interior decorator's office is a front behind which an industrious crew is at work.

It is a business that is *très chic* but entails numerous headaches. Everyone from the president down to the office boy suffers from them. All the jobs are done on a time limit, and not only is it the responsibility of the decorators to design the interior of the home or office, but they must also contact painters, carpenters, cabinet makers, electricians and plumbers and see that each completes his part of the job by the appointed day. Telephones jangle constantly and the various tradesmen are continually appearing in the office with new excuses for delay. The artists and draftsmen sometimes work on through this confusion long into the night.

Temperamental artists are unheard of in the designer's office. There is no time for moodiness. Everyone has to be ready to turn on the charm at a moment's notice. Clients roam in at all hours eager to hear the glowing reports of how their shabby little shacks are going to emerge. These people are always escorted through the drafting rooms where they demand the attention of busy workers. Most of them know little about art or design, but they perch themselves on stools, whip out their cigarette holders, and "go over" the plans with harried craftsmen. Naturally, all ragged tempers have to be hidden behind toothy grins and soft voices. Personality is nine-tenths of the battle with customers.

The atmosphere of the drafting room is very different from that of the reception room. Scraps of wallpaper and fabric swatches are strewn on the floor, paint brushes are balanced on every flat ledge, T-squares and drafting tools are scattered about, jars of smelly paint stand around uncovered, ash trays are overflowing, and sketches are tacked everywhere. Visitors usually exclaim that it is too, too arty and proceed to disrupt everything by dipping their fingers in red paint. When you are working against time, it is extremely difficult to be sweet to these people, but the glamourous charm of the business must be fostered. You just grin and bear it.

Though working in this maze is often maddening, there is something about it that is very satisfying. When all the sketches and detail work on a job are finished and the decorators prepare to venture forth for the presentation, the whole office force usually gathers together to breathe their sighs of relief. Then everyone realizes how much fun it really has been, and the difficulties are laughed at and forgotten. You have to have iron nerves, and you have to be a hypocrite, but I doubt if there is any other work more fascinating.

4. LIBRARY WORK

Working in a library is both educational and interesting because the books provide not only knowledge when working with them but loads of fun and money on the side. To apply for a job the frightened applicant asks at the main desk and, then, at the librarian's request, goes to her office. She asks many irrelevant questions but she will usually hire the applicant providing there is room and her scholastic standing is high enough. Of course, she wouldn't have applied in the first place if books were apt to be a bore. The librarian gives her a piece of paper with the long, complicated "Dewey Decimal System" which, is the system of classifying non-fiction, such as: 100 Philosophy, 200 Religion, 700 Fine Arts, 800 Literature, 900 History, etc. This is to be learned by, for instance, the next Tuesday. She agrees to work from three to six on Tuesdays and Fridays @ twenty-five cents an hour.

With the "Dewey Decimal System" learned from a to z, the future librarian reports at the library at 2:50 P.M. Tuesday afternoon. She is instructed in the minor things such as: where to hang her coat, where to mark down her hours, etc. For the first hour she is set to work putting away fiction, of course, she is kicking herself for being so consciensious about the "Dewey Decimal System." At the end of the first hour the poor sufferer is bored stiff but thinks of the twenty-five cents she has already earned. Just as she is getting to be automatic in finding the alphabet and the work is becoming easier, the dear old "boss" yanks her into the backroom where there are a "few books to paste up." The completely disillusioned employee is ready to drop when she sees stacks and stacks waiting patiently to be mended and pasted.

Pasting books is really a skillful job, plates go on non-fiction and stamps on fiction, the card pocket has to fit perfectly in the corner and the date due slip has to be pasted in the middle and exactly even with the top of the page. This continues for the rest of the afternoon. At six, the librarian page, as she is called, drags herself down the steps and home with the joyous thought of seventy-five cents to her credit.

Friday starts with putting away fiction and gradually goes into non-fiction which requires the "Dewey Decimal System" but this has been quite helpfully forgotten by now. Because the library is small, the 700's are upstairs but she doesn't always remember this so there are countless fruitless trips upstairs to find where the book belongs. Pasting is the schedule for the rest of the day. By now she has learned that payday is once a month which, of course, is rather difficult on the pocket book.

The next week is the same except she has learned to dust shelves and to remove whole sections because one book is out of place. By now, she dares to browse through books while she is putting them away. She is given a sample of library printing which she is supposed to copy. If this is mastered, she will be able to write reference cards, book cards, and authors names in books. She is also informed that her services will be needed at the "Children's Hour" Saturday morning. By this time, she has a friend who works the same times as she does and therefore, she, too, is needed Saturday morning. They can hardly restrain themselves from laughing during the story hour but other then this, it is a lot better than straightening shelves.

The rest of the weeks roll by in the same way except now they have learned to toss books from row to row to save time. This is done only when the librarian has a day off.

At last, the long awaited day arrives when the employee with twelve dollars to her credit is taught to work at the desk. This is done with great care and everyone treating her as a perfect imbecile. Being a little too self-reliant, she doesn't listen too thoroughly when explanations are given so the first few books checked in and out are rather confusedly done. Pretty soon all the desk work is learned and now she can go back to dusting shelves.

She can work sometimes in the Junior Library which is a lot of fun for one afternoon but not for a steady diet. With the raise to thirty cents an hour, our ex-sufferer has a very benevolent feeling toward the library and will feel very sorry when she has to give up working there.

Library work is really very easy because the work is done sitting down except for putting away books which is interesting enough to remove fatigue. Everyone can be interested in library work because there is at least one kind of literature which everyone likes and since the work is all books, that type of book is seen quite often. It is part clerical work, teaching (Children's Hour), and manual labor thus giving the worker a well-rounded education which she will treasure all through school and college.

5. GETTING A GOVERNMENT JOB

As summer approaches, the minds of many college students are turning toward the thought of summer jobs. To many of them, working during the long vacation is just something to while away the time, but to others, a position, even for a few months, means the difference between being able to continue at school or having to abandon all thoughts of higher education because of financial stress. It is to these people that civil service offers an opportunity to earn a good wage while doing work that is fairly interesting.

The usual reaction to the mention of government service is one of hopelessness. Visions of endless examinations and long waiting lists serve to discourage many, but there is no need for this. Getting a government job depends mainly on the initiative of the person seeking it.

The first step in the process is to go to any office of the United States Employment Service and find out where civil service examinations are being given. You will, in most cases, be told that there are no positions open in any department. This is a standard remark designed to stave off applicants. Pay no attention to it, but insist on taking the test. Every American citizen has the right to apply for a position with his government. Most college sudents will take the Clerk, Grade II exam. It is, in reality, an intelligence test, similar to those given upon entering college. It consists of reading comprehension, spelling, alphabetizing, and simple arithmetic. One hour is allowed for one hundred and fifty questions.

The tests are given in the morning and notices of rating are distributed in the afternoon of the same day, followed by an interview by some member of the staff who has attained the lofty position of Clerk, Grade III. The interview consists of greeting the interviewer with a bright smile, and then sitting quietly by his side while he makes several copies of your application. He will then inform you that your name will be placed on a waiting list and you will be notified in the event of an opening in some office.

If you are content to sit back and wait, years may pass before you hear of an opening. The next thing to do is to look up the address of all the government agencies in your city and make the rounds of their personnel offices. You should make it clear to the head of personnel that you are interested in a short term appointment (civil service appointments run for three months, six months, or a year, at the end of which they must be renewed by the head of department), and that you fully intend to return to school at the end of it. Personnel administrators are wary of people who enter an office on short term appointments and manage to stay for years. During the summer all offices are short-handed because most workers take their vacations during July and August. Almost every agency has three or four extra workers to fill the gaps made by employees on summer leave.

If you present your case well and there is any opening at all, red tape will be cut quickly and efficiently, and you will be put to work doing filing or other simple clerical work that is restricted to grade two clerks. The base pay of civil service workers has been raised, and with overtime pay, you should average about forty-two dollars a week from which taxes and old-age pension will be deducted. Most of this money will be refunded at the end of your appointment.

If you are serious about a summer job and refuse to be intimidated by hard-hearted officials, there is no reason why you can't be the one to get that summer job in a government office. Apply as early as possible and keep trying. Someone is going to get it. It might just as well be you.

6. CAPE ANN: VACATION LAND WITH A HISTORY

As far back in my past as I remember, from two to twenty two, my life has been interwoven with the grandeur of the ocean, historic Gloucester and picturesque Rockport. Having spent at least three out of every twelve months of the years on beautiful Long Beach, is it any wonder that I should feel so much at home in this section of our great country? Gloucester is shrouded in a history all and uniquely it's own, a separate and unique setting for the important part it has played in the personality of New England. Next to Boston, Gloucester and it's summer resorts stands out in our minds and hearts for its individuality. What other seaport of its comparitive small size is as significant and well known as this one? The city could in no way be described as pretty, but it has tradition and personality, however, which more than surpasses the newness and prettyness of small cities scattered all over the territory of New England.

The adequate and picturesque harbor which Gloucester has boasted of for centuries has been portrayed somewhat successfully by the many brilliant students of art, from all points of the compass, each eager to catch the spirit and living warmth that lies in it's tradition.

Of the many beaches that the North and South shores boast, there is one that seems to me, and to those who go there as well, the best, that is namely Long Beach. Situated half way between Gloucester and Rockport on the east side of Cape Ann, this magnificent expanse of white sandy beach runs for a full mile in a shape similar to the shape of a cresant moon. On either end of the beach are huge promintories of rocks jutting out into the great Atlantic ocean that help break up the huge waves which Long Beach receives when Northeast storms are in full swing.

From the beach can be seen Thatcher's Island which was the last of the seven twin lights to be eliminated all of which had been on the Atlantic Coast. After purchasing the island in 1771 from the family and heirs of Anthony Thatcher who had been shipwrecked there in the great hurricane of 1635 the first lighthouse was built. This served as a welcome sight to all mariners at sea until 1860 when two lighthouse towers were erected each of them one hundred and twenty four feet in height, then in 1932 the Northern Thatcher's Island Light was discontinued and a motor driven flash controller was installed in the southeastern tower. The new system was a group of five white flashes every twenty seconds with a candle power of 160,000.

Also from Long Beach can be seen another island. Milk Island, as it is called. It was owned formerly by a family named Knight. For years it was a fisherman's haven until it's only house was burned down completely by a grass fire. In 1925 the Knight's gave the island to the Commonwealth of Massachusetts with the provision that it be made a sanctuary for birds. trespassing is strictly forbidden for the sea gulls build their nests and raise their young their.

Long Beach itself is a fairly new and recent summer resort, the first cottages being built between 1895 and 1900, and today it is full to overflowing with two rows of cottages numbering between 150 and 175 cottages. Although only a few of the original founding families are left, Long Beach is carried on in it's high ideals and good neighbor policy by the sons and daughters of the founding fathers.

Long Beach boasts proudly of having the most beach parties, bonfires and sport activities of any of the resorts of the entire North Shore, also it has a soft ball team that knows not defeat. Since most of the boys were back again this past summer seemed like a reunion. Many good times were enjoyed. Every Saturday and Sunday soft ball games were held between the Veterans and the teen agers or Father and Son games. Fishing contests, tennis matches, horse shoes and even foot ball in the soft sand is a weekly occurrence in which everyone takes a very interested part in these activities. Often in the evenings frankfurt roasts and song fests around a huge and blazing bonfire climax the ideal vacation day.

7. BASS FISHING

From Maine to California all states have one temperamental and tough citizen in common, so gather up your plugs and get your fishing tackle in order for you are it seems going to catch a bass for dinner.

Catching bass sounds easy, but unless the bass strikes the lure and holds on, the job is a hard rather than an easy one. Since the bass is a fussy fish, it is necessary to use the trial and error method. One day he may prefer a small frog, another day, a grass hopper, an angle worm, or even the looks of a plug. One thing, however, can be relied on, that is, that the bass will not strike unless the bait is alive or unless it appears to be alive.

First, cast a surface plug and reel it back in short jerks or any other motion that will make the bait appear alive to the fish. Usually a bass prefers a slow plug. It all depends on the bass and his mood. If the bass does not strike after a few tries with a slow surface plug, try a fast surface plug or an underwater plug. Fishing for bass takes patience as well as skill, but the pleasure would soon cease if strikes come to often.

Now try the fat angle worm, a tempting snack to any fish. More bass are caught on angle worms than with any other live bait since it is the most widely and commonly used. The advantage of the live bait is that the fish will swallow it; instead of spitting it out as he would a plug. Cast again and let the line lie motionless. If a bass is in the vicinity, he will be attracted by the splash of the bait and will come to investigate. After a few seconds give the line a slight jerk. He cannot resist the lure any longer and the fight is on. The chance has come to test your skill against a bass fighting for his life. A mistake cannot be made now. Every move must be made at exactly the right second, no more and no less. Tighten the line just a little to set the hooks in deeper. Then the bass takes to the air and tries to throw the hook. Try to counteract this by taking the pressure off the line and letting him have his way. A tight line out of the water gives a bass something to work against; and more often than not, he will throw the hook. Under water a tight line that will make him work and tire him out should be used. It is necessary to be careful, though, as too much pressure will tear the hook from his mouth, only experience will tell how tight the line should be.

The battle is short but hard and furious. It does not take very long to land a bass, but it does take skill. Everything happens so fast that on this account it is hard to remain calm. The tendency is to pull steadily and get the fish into the boat as soon as is possible, but to do this might mean the according loss of the fish. The inexperienced man gets excited and will not let the line out when the fish goes into the air, he feels that the more line he lets out the further away the fish gets. This is true as far as distance is concerned; but if he does not let up on the pressure, the fish will throw the line and be completly away. Play smart, be careful, and be calm if you want fresh bass on the dinner table.

8. GLAMOUR FOR SALE

It isn't very big when you look at it from the street, squeezed in between a Bell Shop on one side and a restaurant, refuge for teen-agers, on the other. The big red neon sign, however, proudly proclaims to the shoppers the whereabouts of Carroll's Cosmetic Shoppe with two "p's" and an "e." The show windows on either side of the entrance give tempting promises of the treasures to be found within. Very rarely does a woman stop to glance over the display and then pass on to another store. Some magnetic force seems to draw her in, for no woman is immune to beauty.

Inside there are innumerable things to interest the prospective buyer. On the right are men's shaving sets, designed for Christmas gifts, shampoos, razor blades, and other necessary articles. Further down, still on the right, is a display of perfumed soaps in all shapes, sizes, and colors. At the extreme end comes an entire section devoted to bath powder, talc, and cologne. The names alone are enough to make any one want to try them—

Black Magic, Shangri-la, Taboo, Mountain Heather, Tweed, Kiss and Tell. Each promises an allure far beyond the wildest hopes. At the other side of the store is the perfume and the make-up bar. At the perfume bar tiny dram bottles are filled from larger, more elaborate ones, each reflected several times in mirrors effectively placed. Most of the customers would gasp if they knew that this small section of the store itself is worth several thousand dollars. At the make-up bar anything and everything is sold to "make Madame beautiful." Lipsticks come in any brand and color with nail polish to match. Beauty creams, powder, rouge, astringents, wrinkle-removers, false eyelashes, hair tints and endless preparations gaze placidly down from their shelves.

From nine to five-thirty every day the store is in a constant turmoil but always with perfect propriety—never rowdy or out-of-hand. The girls, each a walking advertisement of her business, never allow themselves to become ruffled or impatient. If the store, because of shortages of metals, boxes and other products is not able to comply with the customer's desires for metal lipstick tubes, boxed Christmas gifts, or certain blends of perfumes, immediately something similar is suggested in an effort to satisfy. Confronted with a good salesperson the poor customer never has a chance. She never before suspected that she was without so many necessities. In fact she begins to wonder how she was able to exist.

After five-thirty the scene changes abruptly. Everyone relaxes and becomes human again. Laughter peals out as the girls get ready to go home. The manager beams down on everyone and urges her to try a dash of that new perfume for her date tonight. At last the store is dark and quiet except for the mice racing overhead in the stockroom. How do I know all these things? I spent the Christmas season there as "a walking advertisement" myself.

9. TONGUE IN HIS CHEEK

The familiar NBC chimes, the words "this is WBZ, Boston," then the magic charm of a convincing commercial.[1]

This is radio's favorite son, the announcer, the soft-voiced rascal who says your hands can have that Ivory look in just five days. The same friendly fellow who's nice enough to make sure there's a Ford in your future and at least two pairs of pants with your next suit. The man who on Monday relates the cleaning virtues of "new, wonderful Dreft—not a soap, ladies." The Tuesday household hint artist who extols the glories of the good old bar of soap. The man who charms you into buying both on Wednesday. The persuasive friend who does all your marketing and then is nice enough to let you think you did it all by yourself.

His is an atomic tongue, if such a tongue is to be had. But behind this tongue is more than talk; behind this tongue are years of experience, years of taught technique, years of glamourless, rugged work. These are the years of tongues in training.

[1] Intentional incomplete sentence here, and in the second and last paragraphs.

The long, busy climb, the crowded climb, usually begins at a small 250-watt station, far from metropolitan civilization. Here the aspiring announcer voices everything from kiddies' comic condensations early Sunday mornings to juke box late Saturday nights. Here he tries his tongue at anything from agricultural advising to food forums. Here he is experience's pupil alone.

Here too, happy by compulsion, he begins his day at six o'clock, wearing a friendly verbal smile while playing records for people who invariably forget to get up to hear them. His later disc shows, however, require more than pleasant patter. Their tunes must be timed, their continuity written, their commercial copy well rehearsed. And the odds are ten to one that the spieler does it all.

Perhaps he tries his tongue on a fifteen-minute newscast. In small stations of this size the announcer is his own news editor and must compile copy from the wire services, edit it, check its pronunciation. In short, he must perform single-handed the functions of a newspaper's city desk and infinitely more. His other shows, sidewalk interviews, sports descriptives and the like, require the same behind-the-scenes labor.

But all this time, slowly and slyly, his atomic tongue begins to take shape. It learns how soft softness is, how hard hardness is, how clear clearness is. It learns that "slow" is "s-l-o-w" and "quick" much quicker. It learns to convince by simplicity of speech and when it has learned all the 250-watter has to teach, it moves up the crowded climb.

His decals are "this is WFEA, Manchester," "this is WCSH, Portland," "this is WBZ, Boston," "this is WHN, New York." And he has more time for words now; he doesn't have to write his own continuity any more or time his music or edit his news. His convincing, soft, but forceful style has earned him this position. His hours are shorter now and his duties less varied. But he still wants to move up.

And then the break comes—the big time invites him into its fold. No names in lights, no playbills, no critics' crafty praise or condemnation. Just the homes of millions of people—homes to invade with a soft, gentle tongue, a convincing tongue, a persuasive, cunning tongue disguised in simplicity. A helping tongue, a soothing tongue, an experienced tongue. A tongue that has been trained in a technique of which it never talks but by which it earns its bread, butter and bed "with a Ford in its future—your Ford."

And it's all done with a tongue in his cheek.

Chapter Eleven

The Research Paper

THE RESEARCH PAPER is the long paper which, unlike the informal theme, is based on the student's reading and study, and on data systematically assembled for this paper. It is usually at least 2000 words long. The purpose of assigning it in freshman English courses is to give students training in using the library, in gathering material, in taking efficient notes, in using footnotes, and especially in organizing and writing a composition of some length. Writing a long paper is different from writing several short ones which total the same number of words. Since the material is more complex, the long paper presents greater problems of organization, logical arrangement of material, transition between sections, and clear presentation. A source paper rather than an informal essay is usually assigned to give practice in handling long papers, because the substance is supplied by the sources—students need not create it—and because the training in using the sources and giving credit to them in footnotes may be as valuable as the training in writing. All in all, work on the research paper teaches skills which students will need when they write term papers in college, and which many of them will use later when they prepare reports, graduate papers and theses, articles, and even speeches.

To students unfamiliar with the technique of research, some of the methods outlined in this chapter, particularly methods of taking and labeling notes, may seem unnecessarily laborious and involved. Students who have had experience with investigative papers realize, however, that these methods are used because they are efficient; they simplify the organization and writing of the paper, and insure its accuracy. To those who may not see, as they begin work on the research project, the value of following the instructions given in this chapter, we can only say that the methods recommended here are tested methods, and that the reasons for using them will become apparent as work on the paper proceeds.

Requirements for the completed research paper differ slightly in different institutions, but most instructors expect it to have these parts:

A title page, that is, a page blank except for the title of the paper and the usual endorsement.

A preface which states precisely the purpose and scope of the paper, makes any necessary acknowledgments of help or advice received, and comments on the type of reader for whom the paper is written. In general, the research paper should be written for the intelligent layman who has no special knowledge about the subject of the paper; if the writer needs to assume some special knowledge, he should make this clear. The preface may be only a paragraph, or it may be several pages long. The research paper itself will be impersonal, but the preface may be personal; it may, if the writer wishes, tell his reasons for investigating this subject. If he has been forced to limit his topic in some unusual way, or to omit some phase of it which a reader might expect to find included, the limitation or omission should be explained in the preface. Since the preface is, for the instructor, one standard by which to judge the paper, the student should take particular care to state precisely the purpose and scope of his work.

An outline which represents fully and accurately the contents of the paper. This is a formal outline. Correct outline form is discussed on pages 827–831.

The text of the paper, typed, with numbered pages, and footnotes in correct form. The paper is written in the appropriate level, which for nearly all research subjects is formal English.

A bibliography, in which all books and articles used in writing the paper are listed alphabetically, according to the author's last name.

An appendix, if the paper needs one. The appendix is the place for long quotations, tables of statistics, maps, and drawings, which are useful for reference but too bulky to include in the text of the paper.

It will be apparent that the research paper is a large project—total work time may amount to sixty hours or more; and the actual writing is only one of the final stages. The work preliminary to writing—choosing the subject, assembling a bibliography, taking notes, and organizing the notes—will occupy something like three-fourths of the time allotted to the whole paper.

I. CHOOSING THE SUBJECT

In choosing a subject, the student should be guided first by his own interest and curiosity. The research paper is, as we have said, a large project; it involves a great deal of work; it is important, therefore, that the student investigate a subject which will be genuinely interesting to him.

Choosing a topic about which one already has considerable information is usually unwise. Since the research paper must be carefully documented—that is, since the sources of information must be given in footnotes—the student who writes on a subject he already knows must go through the boring procedure of reading and taking notes on material already familiar to him, to be sure of accurate detail and of adequate documentation. More important, he will miss the satisfaction of acquiring new information, of exploring a new field of knowledge. The wise student, therefore, chooses a field beyond the bounds or on the fringes of his present knowledge: some subject he has run across in his reading, or has heard mentioned in one of his courses; of which he has thought "I'd like to know more about that sometime"; but which he might not find time to investigate without the stimulus of this assignment.

With his subject tentatively selected, or with two or three interesting topics in mind, the writer should at once take the second step in choosing his subject: he should look in the card catalogue in the library, in reference books, and in the various magazine indexes to be sure there is enough printed material available for a substantial research paper. He should not be easily discouraged; material can be found on almost any topic if one looks hard enough and long enough. But the material is not always available in the library or libraries to which the student has access. He should be *sure* that he will be able to find the sources of information he needs *before* he begins intensive work on the paper.

A third step in choosing the subject is limiting it to a topic which can be adequately handled in 2000 or 3000 words. Topics like The Negro Problem, Russia, The History of Medicine, The Napoleonic Wars, The Modern Novel, are obviously not appropriate for a student paper; a volume or volumes would be needed to treat any one of them adequately. Good papers can, however, be written on certain phases of these immense subjects. The Economic Status of Negroes in the South since World War II, The Organization of the Russian Secret Police, Early Surgery, The Battle of Waterloo, The Novels of Ernest Hemingway—these are only a few of the suitably limited subjects which might be chosen from the broader fields. Frequently a student needs to read one or two general accounts (in encyclopedias, for example) before he decides what phase of a broad subject would be most interesting to him and most appropriate for a paper of this length. He should make his limitation as soon as possible, before he wastes valuable time in taking notes on material which will be outside the scope of his final topic.

Some subjects on which successful research papers have been written are listed below. They represent a variety of interests, and may suggest topics of interest to the reader. Most of them illustrate, too, a reasonable limitation of a wide field.

Religious Rites of the Inca Indians
West Indian Voodoo
Myths of the Navajo Indians
The Theory of Emperor Worship
Headhunters of Borneo
Symbolism in Oriental Rugs
The Early History of Stained Glass
The Early History of Jazz
Byron and the Cause of Greek Freedom
Keats and Fanny Brawne
Ruskin's Controversy with Whistler
Autobiography in the Novels of Thomas Wolfe
Attitudes toward War in Selected Novels of World War I and
    World War II
Early Plays of Eugene O'Neill
The Arena Theater
Coffee Houses in England in the Eighteenth Century
Customs of the Troubadours
Fashion as a Reflection of Social Conditions in the 1920's
Cro-Magnon Man
Viking Explorations on American Shores
Benjamin Franklin as a Scientist
The Background of the Salem Witchcraft Trials
Sherman's March through Georgia
Lincoln and Anne Rutledge
The Assassination of Lincoln
Causes of the Mexican War
The Chicago Fire
The Sacco-Vanzetti Case
The Scopes Trial
Barnum and Tom Thumb
George Bernard Shaw and Socialism
The Last Days of Hitler
Stalin's Rise to Power in Russia
Tito and Stalin
The Boyhood of Franklin D. Roosevelt

A Comparative Study of Some of the Books about Franklin D.
  Roosevelt
The Background of .he Korean War
Beginnings of the Cooperative Movement in Great Britain
A Study of Two Plans of Socialized Medicine
City Manager Government: Plan E
The Ku Klux Klan Today
The Government versus the A. & P.
Recent Developments in Plastic Surgery and Prosthetics
The Early History of Anesthesia
Doctors in the Middle Ages
Recent Uses of Hypnosis in Medicine
Pentothal Sodium as a General Anesthesia
A Study of Blood Clotting
Hypertension and Heart Disease
Rheumatic Fever
The Effects of Pre-Frontal Lobotomy
The Development of Color Television
Facts About the Flying Saucers
Physical Effects of the Atomic Bomb

II. MAKING THE BIBLIOGRAPHY

The work of making the bibliography, that is, the formal list of
books and articles on which the paper is based, begins before the
subject of the paper is finally selected, and continues, as the writer
discovers new sources, until the paper is completed. A substantial
working bibliography should, however, be assembled *before* the student begins to take notes. Some of the items in this preliminary
bibliography may prove disappointing when he examines them;
some of them he may not be able to find; but his bibliography will
give him an initial survey of the field and of the work before him.
The bibliography should be kept in standard form on 3 by 5-inch
bibliography cards; a separate card should be used for each book or
article.

This system of bibliography cards has been adopted because
it is convenient. In the finished bibliography at the end of the research paper, all sources used in writing the paper are listed alphabetically according to the last name of the author (or, if no author
is mentioned, according to the first important word in the title);
author, work, place of publication, publisher, and date of publication are given in consistent form:

Hayakawa, S. I., <u>Language</u> <u>in</u> <u>Thought</u> <u>and</u> <u>Action</u>,
New York, Harcourt, Brace and Company, 1949.

Lee, Irving J., "General Semantics and Public
Speaking," <u>Quarterly</u> <u>Journal</u> <u>of</u> <u>Speech</u>, XXVI
(December, 1940), 594-601.

There is some variation in the bibliographical form used in different publications; for example, periods instead of commas are sometimes used between the three main items in the entry (author, work, and facts of publication); the name of the publisher of a book is sometimes omitted; and a colon is sometimes used between place of publication and publisher. Except for such small variations, bibliographical form is standardized; the student will save time, therefore, if, from the beginning, he records his bibliographical entries in a standard form. Each of his bibliography cards should give, in this order:

1. The author's name, with his last name first.
2. The title of the work. (Names of books, magazines and newspapers are underlined to represent italics; names of articles are put in quotation marks.)
3. The facts of publication. (For a book, place and date of publication, and, usually, the publisher, are given; for an article, the magazine, volume, date, and pages covered by this article.)
4. The library call number (for ease in locating the book later).

Notes to be used in the actual writing of the research paper are *not* taken on bibliography cards. It is often useful, however, as work on the paper proceeds, to make on these cards brief notations on the availability of the book or on its value.

When the time comes to make the final bibliography for his paper, the student who has taken pains with his bibliography cards will be well paid for his effort. He can easily alphabetize his cards according to the first word on each one; all the necessary data will be there, and in the correct form and order; his bibliography can simply be typed from his cards.

A bibliography is gathered from three principal sources: (1) the card catalogue in the library; (2) periodical indexes; (3) encyclopedias and reference books.

1. The card catalogue is an alphabetical file which lists all books in the library by author, by title, and by subject. It also gives information about the date, the place of publication, and the size of the book; indicates the content; and supplies the library call number

which enables the user of the library to locate the book on the shelves. Ordinarily the student starting work on a research paper will not know the authors and titles of books which might be useful to him. He will, therefore, look up in the card catalogue the subject of his paper, and related subjects, and take down on his own cards information about the books he finds listed.

A subject card in the library card catalogue has a heading like this:

HV   PSYCHOLOGY, PATHOLOGICAL
6080
.A3   Abrahamsen, David, 1903—
               Crime and the human mind, by
           David Abrahamsen . . . New York,
           Columbia university press, 1944

The heading, PSYCHOLOGY, PATHOLOGICAL, it should be noted, is not the title of the book, but the subject which the book is about. The student making his own card for the book will omit some of the data given on the library card, and record only what he needs for his own final bibliography and for his convenience in locating the book. His bibliography card for this book should be in this form:

Abrahamsen, David,   Crime and
The Human Mind, New York,
Columbia University Press, 1944

HV
6080
.A3

The author, title, and facts of publication appear exactly as they will appear in the finished bibliography at the end of his paper. The library call number is recorded so that he can later find the book without again consulting the card catalogue. If he is using more than one library, he should write the name of the library beside the call number, also to save trouble when, sometime later, he wants to locate the book.

2. The periodical indexes list, usually by author and subject, in one alphabet, the contents of current journals and magazines. They are an excellent source for bibliography, particularly for up-to-date material. The most generally useful index is *The Reader's Guide to Periodical Literature,* which indexes most of the important American periodicals and some foreign publications. It is published twice a month (except in July and August), and is cumulated in large volumes. Abbreviations used in the entries are explained at the beginning of each issue; and a check-list of the periodicals subscribed to by his library enables the student to see easily what articles he will be able to find.

Entries in *The Reader's Guide* (and in other indexes) are in this form:

> COLLEGE graduates
> > If I were starting out today. K. T. Compton.
> > > Am Mag 150:15 + Ag '50
> > Job-hunting collegians need realistic advice.
> > > Sat Eve Post 223:10 + Ag 5 '50
> > Quo vadis? adapt your training to your job.
> > > H. L. Bevis. Vital Speeches 16:586–8 Jl 15 '50
> > Safe in the wide world: Princeton graduates.
> > > Time 56:48 Jl 17 '50
> COLLEGE libraries
> > Cleveland's academic world. G. E. Strong.
> > > il Library J 75:1109–12 Jl '50

In noting the references on his bibliography cards, the student should translate these abbreviated entries into the form correct for his final bibliography. A card for the last entry would read:

> Strong, G. E. "Cleveland's Academic World," *Library Journal,* vol. 75, July, 1950, pp. 1109–12

In addition to *The Reader's Guide to Periodical Literature* (1900 to date), students should be familiar with the following useful indexes:

Agricultural Index, 1916 to date.
Annual Magazine Subject-Index, 1908 to date.
Art Index, 1929 to date.
Cumulative Book Index, 1928 to date. (Indexes all books published in the English language.)
Document Catalogue. (Government publications from 1893 to 1934.)

Dramatic Index, 1909 to date.

Education Index, 1929 to date.

Engineering Index, 1884 to date.

Essay and General Literature Index, 1900 to date. (Analyzes and indexes parts of books, which would not be listed in the card catalogue.)

Index to Legal Periodicals, 1908 to date.

Industrial Arts Index, 1913 to date. (Indexes material on business, finance, engineering, applied science.)

International Catalogue of Scientific Literature, 1902 to date.

International Index to Periodicals, 1907 to date.

New York Times Index. (Indexes current events from 1913 to date.)

Poole's Index to Periodical Literature, 1802–1906.

Psychological Index, 1894 to date.

Public Affairs Information Service, 1915 to date.

Quarterly Cumulative Index Medicus, 1927 to date. (Indexes medical books, journals, and articles.)

Writings on American History, 1906 to date.

3. We have said that reading an account in an encyclopedia, for a general view of the research subject, is often a good beginning of work on the paper. Standard encyclopedias are very useful, too, as bibliographical aids. They usually list, at the end of an article, a well-selected bibliography for further reading in the field. In addition to the *Encyclopædia Britannica, Encyclopedia Americana,* and *Columbia Encyclopedia,* students should be familiar with special encyclopedias and reference works which give more detailed information, and specialized bibliographies, in particular fields. Some of the most useful of these works are:

Encyclopedia of the Social Sciences, 1930–35.

McLaughlin and Hart's *Cyclopedia of American Government,* 1914.

Dictionary of American History, 1940.

Palgrave's *Dictionary of Political Economy,* 1923–26.

Bailey's *Cyclopedia of American Agriculture,* 1907–09.

Grove's *Dictionary of Music and Musicians,* 1927–28.

Thorpe's *Dictionary of Applied Chemistry,* 1922–27, and 1934–35.

Munn's *Encyclopedia of Banking and Finance,* 1937.

Bryan's *Dictionary of Painters and Engravers,* 1903–05.

Baldwin's *Dictionary of Philosophy and Psychology,* 1928.

Hastings' *Encyclopaedia of Religion and Ethics,* 1908–28.

Catholic Encyclopedia, 1907–22.

Jewish Encyclopedia, 1925.

Cambridge Ancient History, 1923–34.

Cambridge Medieval History, 1911–32.

Cambridge Modern History, 1926.

Cambridge Bibliography of English Literature, 1940.

Mudge's *Guide to Reference Books,* 1936.

Yearbooks, like *The American Yearbook*, the *Statesmen's Year-book*, *Commerce Yearbook*, *The World Almanac*, and the annual supplements to encyclopedias, are excellent sources for recent facts and statistics. For biographical material, the student should consult such works as the *Dictionary of National Biography* (British), the *Dictionary of American Biography*, *Who's Who*, *Who's Who in America*, *American Men of Science*, *Living Authors*, *Authors Today and Yesterday*, *Twentieth Century Authors*, *Contemporary American Authors*, and *Current Biography*.

An hour or two spent browsing in the reference room of the library, locating and examining the various indexes and reference works, is time well spent. Work on the research paper would be valuable if it taught students only this: how to use a library, how to find material on any subject which they may need to investigate.

III. TAKING NOTES

In taking notes on the material he reads for his research paper, the student should bear in mind two things: first, that his paper will be written from these notes, after he has read a great deal of material, and after particular references have become blurred with others and are no longer fresh and clear in his mind; second, that he will be required to footnote his material, giving the source, including the exact page, from which he has taken his information. His notes, therefore, must be full enough to recall the material; they must accurately record its source; they must also be taken, and labeled, in such a way that they can easily be arranged in convenient order for the writing of the paper.

Scholars have worked out an efficient system for noting, filing, and organizing material. All notes are taken on cards, 3 by 5, 4 by 6, or 5 by 8 inches. (Students usually find 4 by 6-inch cards the most convenient size.) Each note card carries the exact source from which the material on the card is taken. Each card carries a heading which describes its content and shows where this material fits in the outline of the paper. The material on each card concerns only one subdivision of the paper. Each note card also shows clearly whether the material is quoted from the source, or is summarized.

Below are two sample note cards. The first, a note for a research paper on the migration of birds, is an example of summary; the second, for a paper on the philosophy of Thomas Hardy, shows by its form that it is an exact quotation. In general, very few notes should be quotations. Sometimes, of course, it is important to quote exactly in the research paper the opinion of one authority on a con-

Whitlock, *Migration of Birds*   Cold

110 cold by itself not sufficient direct influence on majority of species to leave home to which they are devotedly attached

111 with increasing cold, daily migrations in search of food have to be prolonged to distances where return during daylight is impossible

SUMMARY NOTES

Cecil, *Hardy*   Religion

223 "He found it impossible to believe the Christian hope.... But he can only be respected for the honesty which compelled him to accept a philosophy of the universe so repugnant to the deepest instincts of his heart. And still more must he be honored for that elevation of soul which enabled him to maintain the Christian temper without the help of the Christian consolation."

QUOTATION

troversial subject, or the wording of an historical document; sometimes an idea is so strikingly expressed that one wishes to use the perfectly turned sentence or phrase. In such cases, the material should be copied accurately on the note card and clearly enclosed in quotation marks. But most material is not worth full quotation; and an acceptable research paper is never a series of quotations or nearquotations. Although the material is taken from other authors, the language, as well as the organization, should be the writer's own. It is wise, therefore, as well as economical, to use the summary note form in most of one's note-taking. Digesting the material as one reads, and condensing it in one's own words will prevent later worry about staying too close to the wording of the sources and slipping, perhaps unconsciously, into plagiarism [1] in the research paper.

It is impossible to overemphasize the importance of labeling each note card, not only with its exact source, but with a heading ("Cold" and "Religion" on the cards above) which describes the material on the card and also represents a section of the paper. In order to do this labeling, the student must have in mind a tentative outline of his paper, or at least an idea of its main divisions. Many instructors require a tentative written outline early in the research project, to facilitate this valuable labeling of note cards. Whether or not the outline is required, it should be made early, on the basis of one or two general accounts of his subject (encyclopedia accounts, for example) which the student reads before he begins seriously to take notes. The labels on his early note cards may be rather general; as he learns more about his subject, and as his outline with its various subdivisions takes shape, the labels can be increasingly specific.

The value of this labeling becomes most apparent when the student has finished gathering material and is preparing to write his paper. He can, without reading all the material on his cards, pull out and put into separate piles all those cards having the same heading; he then arranges the piles in the best order for discussion in the paper; he is ready to begin writing from notes in logical sequence, with no necessity of leafing through a notebook, or scanning large sheets of paper for particular bits of material which he remembers having somewhere. This flexibility of the note cards—the fact that they can be shuffled and arranged—is the principal reason for using them; but much of their value is lost unless each card is complete with source and heading.

Worth re-emphasizing, too, is the importance of putting on any one card *only* material which concerns *one subdivision* of the paper. If one reads, for example, an article on the Lincoln-Douglas debates, and wishes to make from it two brief notes—one on the first debate, another on the effects of the debates—it is a temptation to put the two short notes on one card. A little reflection will show, however, that those two pieces of material belong in different parts of the paper; a single card can be in only one place in a pile of note cards; the two notes should, therefore, be put on different cards, each with its informative label. It is more trouble, of course, to make out two cards; it is more trouble in general to take careful notes than it is to take slipshod ones. But the writer is well repaid for his effort by

[1] For an explanation of plagiarism, see p. 831.

the ease with which a paper can be written from accurate, intelligible, systematic notes.

As he reads and takes notes, the student should make some evaluation of his sources. Obviously sources are not of equal worth. They may even contradict one another. How is the student, not himself a specialist in the field, to judge the authority of what he reads? The reputation of the author is often a guide; his qualifications as an expert can sometimes be checked in the biographical dictionaries; his work may be referred to with respect or criticized adversely by other writers in the field, so that an estimate of him gradually emerges from other sources. The publication in which an article appears should be considered in evaluating it: an article in a reputable magazine is more to be trusted than a feature story in the Sunday newspaper; an article from a paper or magazine with a definite political slant should be read with that slant in mind. The style and tone of a book or article are not infallible measures of its soundness; but, generally speaking, a work which is documented either with footnotes or with sources introduced into the text is more reliable than a popular, undocumented account; a novelized biography, for example, may be lively and interesting and generally accurate, but for reliable facts about the subject one would consult a more scholarly work. Finally, the date of the book or article is relevant in evaluating it. The most recent work is not invariably the best, but it has the benefit of previous scholarship; and in some fields, science and technology particularly, sources are quickly outdated. The student should be sure that he has seen the most recent material on his subject, and that any older material which he uses checks with the latest data.

IV. WRITING AND FOOTNOTING THE PAPER

When the student feels that he has gathered enough material for his paper, he is ready for two last preliminaries to the actual writing of the first draft. First, he should thoughtfully revise the outline which has been growing and changing as he has taken notes and thought about his paper. This outline may be changed still further during the writing of the paper; that is, the writer may find, when he gets into the material, that certain parts of it need to be rearranged for better development, coherence, or emphasis. But a full outline, which shows the material in logical sequence and organization, is necessary for the second step toward writing.

This second step consists of arranging the note cards in sequence, following the order of the outline. If the student has labeled his cards carefully, it will not be necessary, as we have said before, to read all of the notes, but only to look at the headings, which will correspond, roughly at least, to the headings and subheadings in the outline. With his note cards arranged in this logical sequence, and with his outline before him, the student is ready to write.

Paragraph by paragraph, writing the research paper is much like writing any theme. But the material is so much more complex than it is in a short paper that, as we have said, it presents special problems. The writer, in addition to having the organization of his paper clearly in mind, must take special care to keep that organization clear to the reader by means of skillful transitions between paragraphs and sections of the paper, and by means of occasional summary statements or paragraphs which pull together the preceding material and lead into the next phase of the development. He must be sure that he is explaining, fully enough for a general audience, the terms, processes, or events which have by now become thoroughly familiar to him. And he has a special problem, of course, in handling the footnotes in a research paper.

There are two kinds of footnotes: those which give additional information about a point which cannot be developed easily or coherently in the text of the paper, and those which give exact references to sources. Most of the footnotes in a student research paper will be of the second type. These footnotes are used in a paper of this kind for three reasons. First, they observe a code of scholarship: they give credit where credit is due; they honestly acknowledge the debt of the writer to other writers whose information and ideas he has used. Second, the footnotes give support to what would otherwise be the writer's unsupported, and perhaps questionable, word: they say in effect to the reader, "This is not a mere fancy of mine; So-and-so, an authority in the field, has this idea." Third, the footnotes give the exact source of the information so that the interested reader can readily find the reference if he wishes to check it or to read further on a particular point.

Reference footnotes, in short, are evidence of the honesty, the soundness, and the exactness of the paper. They are used, therefore, not simply to acknowledge direct quotations, but to acknowledge and substantiate all borrowed ideas, opinions, and conclusions, and all factual information which the writer has received from his reading and which is not common knowledge. Just what constitutes common knowledge, what facts are so generally accepted that they need no footnote, is sometimes hard to decide. Having too few footnote references is, however, decidedly a more serious fault than having too many. "When in doubt, footnote" is a good safe rule.

A footnote number is used *at the end* of a borrowed passage, and is raised slightly above the typed line. The footnote itself, preceded by this number, is commonly set at the bottom of the page. Footnotes are numbered from 1 on each page, or, preferably, they are numbered continuously from the beginning to the end of the paper. Typical student research papers have at least three or four footnotes to a typed page. In good research papers the footnote references on each page are varied; they show that the student has brought together, in his own synthesis, material from different sources.

The *first* footnote reference to a book or article is usually a full reference, including the author's full name (with first name first) and complete bibliographical information.[2] Below are examples of first footnote references, to a book and to an article:

[1] Charles R. Adams, <u>Intravenous Anesthesia</u> (New York, Paul B. Hoeber, Inc., 1944), p. 12.

[2] H. M. Ausherman, "Anesthesia by Vein," <u>Hygeia</u>, XXII (April, 1944), 261.

Later footnote references to the same source are simplified; they may be reduced to the author's last name and the page number, or they may use the author's last name with a shortened form of a long title, or with the abbreviation *op. cit.* (from the Latin *opere citato* meaning "in the work cited"), which takes the place of the title:

[3] Adams, p. 15.   [*Or*]   [3] Adams, <u>op</u>. <u>cit</u>., p. 15.

The simple form—"Adams, p. 15"—is increasingly used in present-day scholarly writing. We recommend that students use it in their own footnoting. They should, however, understand the meaning and use of *op. cit.*, for they will encounter it in a number of scholarly publications. If more than one work by the same author is referred to in the paper, neither the author's name alone nor the author's name with *op. cit.* is an adequate reference. Footnotes must in that case give at least short forms of the titles to make the sources clear.

Ibid. (an abbreviation of the Latin *ibidem*, "in the same place") is used to refer to the source named in the immediately preceding footnote:

[2] Current practice is divided, however, on the matter of giving complete facts of publication in first footnote references when a bibliography accompanies the paper and the reader can easily find all the data there. First footnote references are always full and complete when (as in some scholarly publications) no bibliography is printed.

[4] Howard R. Raper, <u>Men Against Pain</u> (New York, Prentice-Hall, Inc.,1945), p. 235.

[5] <u>Ibid</u>., p. 236.

Besides *op. cit.* and *ibid.,* a number of conventional abbreviations and symbols are used in footnotes. The most common are listed below. The student may not use all of them in his research paper, but he should know their meanings in order to understand their use by other writers.

ch., chs. *or* chap., chaps.—chapter, chapters

cf. (Latin *confer*)—compare. The English *see* is now more often used.

ed.—edition *or* edited by *or* editor

et al. (Latin *et alii*)—and others

f., ff.—following. Pp. 2 f. means page 2 and the page following; pp. 2 ff. means page 2 and the pages following.

l., ll.—line, lines

n.—note

n.d.—no date

p., pp.—page, pages

passim—here and there. This symbol is useful when material is condensed from a number of pages. The reference "pp. 79–90 *passim*" means that here and there, scattered through the pages, the material was found. *Passim* should not be used when a more exact citation is possible.

vol., vols.—volume, volumes. When a reference requires both volume number and page number, the symbols for volume and page are omitted: *Encyclopædia Britannica,* X, 480.

Some special problems in footnoting are:

1. *Reference to an encyclopedia article.* If the article is signed with the initials of the author, the student should find the author's name in the alphabetized list of contributors at the beginning of volume I of the encyclopedia, and should write the footnote in this form:

George Bernard Shaw, "Socialism: Principles and Outlook," <u>Encyclopaedia Britannica,</u> 14th ed., XX, 895.

A later footnote reference to this article, if no references to other works by Shaw intervene, could read:

Shaw, p. 896.

If an encyclopedia article is unsigned, the first footnote reference will have this form:

"Anaesthesia and Anaesthetics," <u>Encyclopaedia</u>
<u>Britannica</u>, 14th ed., I, 862.

A later reference, if no other *Britannica* references intervene, could
be shortened to:

<u>Encyclopaedia</u> <u>Britannica,</u> I, 862.

2. *Reference to a book which has several authors.* A full reference
includes the full names of all the authors:

Norman Foerster, John C. McGalliard, René
Wellek, Austin Warren, and Wilbur Lang Schramm,
<u>Literary</u> <u>Scholarship</u>: <u>Its</u> <u>Aims</u> <u>and</u> <u>Methods</u>
(Chapel Hill, The University of North Carolina
Press, 1941), p. 56.

A later footnote reference to this book, if no references to other
writings by the same group of authors intervene, could read:

Foerster <u>et</u> <u>al</u>., p. 102.

3. *Reference to an edited book:*

George Lyman Kittredge, ed., <u>The</u> <u>Complete</u> <u>Works</u>
<u>of</u> <u>Shakespeare</u> (Boston, Ginn and Company, 1936),
p. 15.

Later footnotes, if no references to other works by Kittredge intervene, could read:

Kittredge, p. 52.

[*Or*]

Kittredge, <u>Shakespeare</u>, p. 52.

4. *Reference to a translation:*

Thomas Mann, <u>Joseph</u> <u>and</u> <u>His</u> <u>Brothers</u>, tr. H. T.
Lowe-Porter (New York, Alfred A. Knopf, 1948),
p. 251.

A later reference, if no references to other works by Mann intervene,
could read:

Mann, p. 400.

5. *Reference to a selection which is part of a book:*

Lafcadio Hearn, "A Living God," <u>Atlantic</u> <u>Harvest</u>,
ed. Ellery Sedgwick (Boston, Little, Brown and
Company, 1947), p. 149.

A later footnote, if no references to other works by Hearn intervene, could read:

Hearn, p. 150.

6. *Reference to a book or article which the student has not read, cited or quoted in a book or article which he has read:*

Ruth Borne, <u>Queen</u> <u>Anne's</u> <u>Navy</u> <u>in</u> <u>the</u> West Indies, cited in F. W. Sypher, <u>Guinea's</u> <u>Captive</u> <u>Kings</u> (Chapel Hill, The University of North Carolina Press, 1942), p. 11.

In writing the first draft of his paper, the student will probably waste time and divert his attention from the presentation of his material if he stops to write footnotes in correct form for his finished paper. It is important, however, to make a record of footnotes as one writes the first draft; the sources are on the note cards with the material; it is obviously a waste of time and effort to write the paper without footnotes and then to go through the cards a second time to find and write down the sources. An easy and efficient way of keeping track of footnotes in the first draft is to put a very brief notation—usually author and page will do—in parentheses where the footnote number will be in the final copy. Many students find it useful to underline this embryonic footnote in red or blue pencil, or to put it in red or blue parentheses, so that it stands out from the text of the paper. Later, this brief notation can be expanded into correct footnote form, dropped to the bottom of the page, and given its proper number. Keeping track of sources in the first draft, like making careful bibliography and note cards, will save trouble in the long run, and ensure accurate documentation of the paper.

V. REVISING AND COMPLETING THE PAPER

Most instructors, before they read and judge a research paper, examine its outline, bibliography, and footnotes. This initial survey is partially a check on correct form, but it is more than that. The outline represents the scope and organization of the paper; the bibliography gives some indication of the amount of reading done and the value of the sources which the student has found and used; the footnotes show to some extent how well he has drawn together materials from different sources and integrated them into a paper which, though composed of borrowed data, is genuinely his own. In a good research paper, the outline, bibliography, and footnotes are in proper form; also, and more important, they give initial evidence of these qualities in the paper: logical organization, adequate coverage of the subject, sufficient documentation, and skillful integration of scattered materials.

Although the machinery of the research paper is important, students should not become so absorbed in it that they neglect what is, after all, essential to excellence in any composition—good writing. Even though a research paper represents many hours of hard work, even though it is elaborately and correctly footnoted, it is not a good paper if it is incompetently written. Careful revision is, therefore, very important.

The length of the research paper and the complexity of its content make the inexperienced writer susceptible to faults which in a short paper he probably would avoid. Six of the most common of these faults are listed below. Some of them have been discussed earlier, but they deserve special comment in connection with revising and completing the research paper. Easy to fall into, they are also easy to correct in revision. The six faults:

1. *Lack of transition between sections of the paper.* This fault usually is a result of writing different sections of the paper at different times, and thinking of them as completely separate units. Units they are, but they are also parts of a whole; their close relationship must be established by transitional phrases and sentences which lead the reader from one part of the paper into the next. In the following sentence, the writer of a student research paper on modern jazz makes a smooth transition from New Orleans jazz to Dixieland jazz:

> While New Orleans was enjoying its last days as jazz capital, groups of white musicians, seeing the success of the Negroes, attempted to imitate them, and in doing so created what is called the Dixieland style.

By means of the following transitional paragraph from a paper on Cro-Magnon man, the reader is saved what would have been a confusing leap from the Cro-Magnons back to the Eolithic age:

> Before studying the Cro-Magnon race, it is necessary to have some knowledge of the epochs that preceded it. Our pre-history has been divided into three chronological classifications . . .

2. *Choppy sentences.* Choppy sentences are often simply careless, but sometimes they come from the mistaken idea that items of information from different sources should be put in separate sentences. Material from different sources is frequently, and quite properly, welded into a single sentence; two or more footnotes may be used in one sentence to give the sources of the combined material. The following excerpt from a paper on the assassination of Lincoln will illustrate:

Booth savagely reeled about, put the knife into his right hand, and slashed the Major's arm; [22] then he leapt from the box down to the stage twelve feet below.[23]

Short, choppy sentences are even more objectionable in a research paper, presumably a mature piece of work, than in an informal theme.

3. *Choppy paragraphs.* Short, underdeveloped paragraphs sometimes are caused by a misconception similar to the one which produces choppy sentences: the student mistakenly thinks that the material from each source should be presented in a separate paragraph. More often, choppy paragraphs come from using a paragraph break at each minor division in the outline of the paper. Organizing paragraphs around a topic sentence is the cure for this serious weakness. A third-level subdivision in the outline (I, A, 1) is often the topic idea of a solid paragraph; the points under it ($\overline{a}$, b, c) are not likely to require separate paragraphs, because these points are essentially the facts and details which support the topic idea. Paragraphs should bind together, not separate, such closely related subordinate points.

4. *Unconscious repetition of material.* Some repetition, for emphasis, or for purposes of summary, may be desirable in dealing with complex material. But the use of the same material more than once without reference to its earlier use gives the impression that the writer, blindly stumbling through his note cards, has lost track of what he has already said. If it is desirable to call the reader's attention to facts previously discussed in the paper, a phrase like "we have seen that," or "as has been said before" will indicate that the repetition is purposeful and that the writer has a sure grasp of all the material in the paper.

5. *Unconscious contradiction.* This fault, seriously confusing to the reader, is closely related to unconscious repetition of material. It occurs when the writer, having on his note cards the differing opinions of two authors, thoughtlessly sets them down as if both opinions were facts. The writer who does this is, of course, using his note cards without using his brain. If the opinions of both authors appear to have some merit, if neither can fairly be rejected, they should be introduced in some such manner as this:

There is some difference of opinion about the exact date when the first music that could be called jazz was played. Robert Goffin, in *Jazz from the Congo to the Metropolitan*, says that the first bands were formed in the 1880's.[4] Other authorities, however . . .[5]

(Introducing sources into the text in this way, even when no contradiction is involved, often makes a clearer and more readable paper. Only the page reference is needed in the footnote when author and title are given in the text.)

6. *Unawareness of dates.* We have said earlier that the student should be sure that he is not using outdated sources. He should, moreover, be conscious of the dates of relatively recent sources. If in his paper he makes a statement like "Very recently a new development has occurred," and if the source of his statement is an article published in 1935, he has given misinformation. Checking of the manuscript with the dates in the bibliography will prevent such blunders in the final copy.

It seems hardly necessary to say that the writing in the research paper should be technically correct. Errors in agreement, parallelism, and reference are inexcusable in so important a paper. Run-together sentences and impressionistic incomplete sentences are out of place in writing of this kind; they are incongruous with the formality of footnotes and the serious and scholarly tone of the whole paper.

Because the paper is formal, contractions like *can't, won't, couldn't* should be avoided; and abbreviations should be used with caution— *Pres., Prof., Sen., Mass., U.S.,* for example, should be written out. Personal comment should be restricted to the preface; the text of the paper should be written in impersonal style.

This requirement of impersonal style in the formal paper does not mean that the writer's personality and judgment are excluded from the paper. On the contrary, in his selection of material, his arrangement of it, his expression of ideas, the words he chooses, the sentences he writes, the conclusions he may draw from the data he has assembled, the writer dominates the paper. He makes clear and interesting to a reader a subject which is clear and interesting to him. His phrasing is impersonal because his purpose in writing is to present, not himself or his experience, but the subject on which he has chosen to work and to write.

Checking the form of the outline, bibliography, and footnotes; examining transitions; inspecting for choppiness; eliminating unconscious repetition, contradiction, and confusion of dates; correcting mechanical errors; making the style consistently formal and impersonal as well as finished and exact—all of this takes time in a long paper. The foresighted student, therefore, plans to finish the draft of his paper at least a week before the paper is due, so that he will not be hurried in his revision. He may also need to allow several days for preparation of the final copy. A usual requirement is that the research paper be typed. The typing itself takes some time, of course; and even skillful typists may make mistakes, particularly in copying footnote references from a draft which has been a good deal revised. The student should allow time, not only for thorough revision, but for careful proofreading after the paper is typed. It is most unfortunate when the painstaking work of weeks is marred or obscured by hasty work on the last stages of the paper.

Strange though it may seem to the student who has read this chapter and has yet to begin work on his own paper, many college students find the research paper the most enjoyable and rewarding work that they do all term. As they proceed systematically to assemble a bibliography, to take notes, to shape the outline of the material, what seemed at first a complicated and formidable task turns out to be simply a series of steps; no step is difficult in itself; and each one produces satisfying, tangible progress. Students who believe that they have no imagination are particularly likely to enjoy the research paper; it does not call for imagination, but for skill in finding, organizing, evaluating, and presenting material. Writing a long paper gives one confidence about handling other writing assignments, and nearly always a fluency which makes other writing easier. In work on the research paper there is, too, the pleasure of learning, of becoming an authority on a subject in which one is interested. Because it is a large project, the research paper is more likely than the short paper to give the conscientious writer the satisfaction that comes from orderly procedure, sustained effort, and solid achievement.

The following selection is from a research paper by Beverly F. Ames. It is used here with her permission.

A STUDY OF THE EFFECTS OF THE
ATOMIC BOMBINGS OF HIROSHIMA
AND NAGASAKI

Before studying the effects of the atomic bombings of Hiroshima and Nagasaki, it is well to consider briefly the nature of the explosion of an atomic bomb. Although the plutonium bomb used at Nagasaki was more powerful than the uranium bomb used at Hiroshima,[1] the damaging effects were essentially from the same sources;

[1] John Hersey, *Hiroshima* (New York, Alfred A. Knopf, 1946), p. 108.

therefore, in this consideration of the bombs, they are regarded as one and the same. The bomb exploded in one tenth of one millionth of a second,[2] liberating three tremendous sources of energy: heat, radiation, and blast or pressure.[3]

The center of the explosion was several hundred feet above ground and was a ball of fire with a diameter of several hundred feet. At the core of the fireball, the temperature was millions of degrees centigrade; at the edge, it was several thousands of degrees centigrade.[4] Scientists found that mica (melting point: nine hundred degrees centigrade) was fused on gravestones 380 yards from ground zero;[5] that telephone poles of cryptomeria japonica (carbonization temperature: 240 degrees centigrade) were charred at 4,400 yards from ground zero; and that gray clay tiles (melting point: 1,300 degrees centigrade) dissolved at six hundred yards from ground zero. From these and other careful observations, the scientists concluded that the temperature at ground zero must have been at least six thousand degrees centigrade.[6] The radiant heat energy given off has been estimated to be a fabulous ten trillion calories;[7] this heat traveled at the speed of light (186,000 miles per second), making

[2] Merle Miller and Abe Spitzer, We Dropped the A-Bomb (New York, Thomas Y. Crowell Co., 1946), p. 41.

[3] "Atomic Bomb -- First Official Report on Damage to Japan," The United States News, XXI (July 5, 1946), 74.

[4] Ibid., p. 74.

[5] Ground zero designates the point on the ground directly beneath the point of detonation or air zero. Ibid., p. 66.

[6] Hersey, p. 107.

[7] Ten trillion (10,000,000,000,000) calories, if transformed into mechanical energy, would yield enough energy to raise 9,200,000,000 pounds vertically into the air for a distance of 6.2 miles.

the duration of the heat flash only a fraction of a second.[8]

The damaging penetration of radiation was possible from three sources: (1) from the high-frequency radiations, whether neutrons (traveling at twenty thousand miles per second[9]), gamma rays, or other unspecified rays, released in the chain reaction of the bomb; (2) from lingering radioactivity from deposits of primary fission products scattered in the explosion; and (3) from induced radioactivity in the bombed area caused by interaction of neutrons with matter penetrated. Only the first seems to have had any important effects.[10]

Pressure or shock waves traveled in all directions. The blast pressure rose almost instantaneously to a peak, declined more slowly, and then fell below atmospheric pressure for a period of about three times the period it was above atmospheric pressure. Although the positive phase (above atmospheric pressure) lasted only slightly longer than one second, it was long enough for almost all blast damage to occur within it; this accounts for the fact that windows broke inward and not outward.[11] Scientists, by measuring the force necessary to shift marble tombstones in cemeteries, to knock over twenty-two out of forty-seven railroad cars at Hiroshima Station, and to move the concrete roadway of bridges, decided that the pressure exerted by the blast varied from 5.3 to 8.0 tons per square yard.[12] The face-on-face peak pressures were two

[8] "Atomic Bomb -- First Official Report on Damage to Japan," p. 74.

[9] Walter Yust, ed., *Britannica Book of the Year, 1947*, p. 84.

[10] "Atomic Bomb -- First Official Report on Damage to Japan," p. 75.

[11] *Ibid.*, p. 75.

[12] Hersey, p. 107.

to five times as great as the side-on-side peak pressures.[13]

On August 6, 1945, at 0345 (3:45 A.M.), three B-29s[14] took off from Tinian to fly on the first atomic bombing mission.[15] At 0820 (8:20 A.M.)[16] these planes received word from the weather planes, which had taken off one hour earlier, that the target was clear.[17] Less than an hour later, at precisely 0915 (9:15 A.M.), the "bombs away" signal was given.[18]

There was a sudden flash of light; the air was filled with a strange purple light which quickly changed to half-purple, half-blue. Fifty seconds after the signal, the first shock (or pressure) wave hit the planes, causing them to vibrate violently and to drop a few hundred feet. Within ninety seconds, two more waves hit. Below the planes was a great fire containing a dozen colors, all blindingly bright. In the center and brightest of all was a gigantic red ball of flame, which seemed to cover the whole city.

[13] "Atomic Bomb -- First Official Report on Damage to Japan," p. 75.
[14] The crews of these three B-29s were the hand-picked men of the 393rd Bomb Squadron which, on January 7, 1945, was ordered to base on Tinian, six thousand miles from San Francisco. Walter Yust, ed., *Ten Eventful Years* (Chicago, Encyclopaedia Britannica, Inc., 1947), I, 207.
[15] Miller and Spitzer, p. 21.
[16] The midnight before the attack, a Japanese radio announcer said that about two hundred B-29s were approaching Honshu, and that the population of Hiroshima was warned to evacuate to the designated safe-areas. At 2:00, planes passed over Hiroshima; at 2:30 another warning was issued, with more planes passing over shortly afterwards. A warning siren sounded at 7:00, but the all-clear came at 8:00. Hersey, p. 10.
[17] Miller and Spitzer, pp. 26, 34.
[18] *Ibid.*, p. 41.

On every side, the flame was half-hidden by an impenetrable column of gray-white smoke which extended into the foothills of the city and which was rising into the sky at the same time. The blue-purple light changed into a green-blue with a tinge of yellow around the edges. A pillar of smoke raced upward. It was as much as four or five miles wide at the base, and one and a half miles or more at the top. The column of smoke changed from gray-white to brown, then to amber, then to all three colors at once, and then to rainbow colors. When it looked as though it were going to stop, a kind of mushroom spurted out of the top and traveled up to an estimated sixty to seventy thousand feet. The top then broke off the column and traveled even higher to an estimated eighty to eighty-five thousand feet. Then another but smaller mushroom boiled up. The first mushroom changed into a pure white color on the outside and a delicate pink toward the center. The entire city was covered with thick, dirty smoke, at first a light gray, then a darker gray finally turning black around the edges. And all this happened in less than five minutes.[19]

Because of the fan-shape of Hiroshima and because the ground was flat, the city was uniformly and extensively damaged.[20] Fire-storms caused 4.4 square miles to be almost completely burned out.[21] Some reinforced concrete buildings were structurally damaged within two thousand feet of ground zero; this was partially due to poor construction. Internal wall-paneling was destroyed within 3,800 feet of ground zero. Those buildings that were made especially strong

[19] These are the observations of the 393rd Bomb Squadron. Miller and Spitzer, pp. 42-45.
[20] Hersey, pp. 7-8.
[21] "Atomic Bomb -- First Official Report on Damage to Japan," p. 65.

to withstand earthquakes were not severely damaged,[22] although even in these, interiors were
gutted -- doors, sashes, frames, and all windows
were ripped out.[23] Hospitals and clinics within
three thousand feet of ground zero were totally
destroyed; those beyond seven thousand feet
remained standing, although all but one was
severely damaged.[24] Twenty-seven out of thirty-
three modern fire stations were completely
destroyed.[25] The entire heart of the city, including the main administrative and commercial
section as well as part of the residential section, was ruined. Only fifty buildings, all
reinforced with concrete, remained standing.
All suffered blast damage; all but a dozen were
gutted by fire; only five could be used without
major repairs. All together in the urban area,
sixty-two thousand out of ninety thousand buildings (sixty-nine per cent) were destroyed; six
thousand (6.6 per cent) were severely damaged.[26]

[22] Ibid., p. 66.
[23] Britannica Book of the Year, 1947, p. 84.
[24] "Atomic Bomb -- First Official Report on
Damage to Japan," p. 66.
[25] Ten Eventful Years, I, 207.
[26] "Atomic Bomb -- First Official Report on
Damage to Japan," p. 67.

CHAPTER REVIEW

You are not expected, even after you have carefully read this
chapter, to remember all of the details about sources, note-taking,
bibliography and footnote form. You should use this chapter for
reference as you work on the research paper, rereading the section
on bibliography before you gather your bibliography, the section
on taking notes when you are ready to take notes, the section on
footnotes when you are ready to use them. Below are a number of
instructions or admonitions which summarize the most important
things to keep in mind as you work on your paper. You should be
able, after reading this chapter, to explain any of the instructions
which are not self-explanatory.

1. Choose a subject in which you are interested.

2. Limit the subject so that it can be covered adequately in a paper of this length.

3. Be sure that there is enough available material before you decide finally on a subject.

4. Gather your bibliography from the card catalogue in the library, from periodical indexes, and from encyclopedias and reference books. (As your work proceeds, you will probably add to your bibliography other sources that you discover in the bibliographies and footnotes of books and articles which you read.)

5. Put the entries on your bibliography cards in correct form.

6. Take notes on cards, using separate cards for separate pieces of information.

7. Record on each note card the exact source, including the page number, of the material.

8. Give each note card a heading or label which tells exactly what the material on the card is about.

9. As early as possible make a tentative outline of the paper, so that headings on your note cards can correspond to headings in the outline.

10. Take summary notes rather than full quotations unless you have reason to quote directly from the source. Summarize the material in your own words.

11. Bear in mind that all sources are not of equal value.

12. Remember that your paper should integrate material from different sources. Your footnotes will reflect this integration.

13. Be sure that you understand clearly when and how to use footnotes. Study the footnotes on the pages from the student research paper printed in this chapter to see:

(*a*) where the footnote numbers are placed;

(*b*) how the information in the footnotes is arranged and punctuated;

(*c*) how footnote references are simplified after the first reference to the book or article; and

(*d*) how *ibid.* is used.

14. Put footnotes (though not necessarily in full and correct form) into the first draft of the paper.

15. Refer to the material in this chapter and to the section on outlining, page 827, to be sure that bibliography and outline as well as footnotes are in correct form.

16. Allow ample time to revise the writing in the paper. Guard particularly against the faults discussed in the last section of this chapter.

EXERCISES

I. Put the references below into proper footnote form, keeping them in their present order.

1. Page 53 of a book called A Story of Our Republic written by Melville Freeman and published in 1938 in Philadelphia by F. A. Davis Company.

2. Page 43 of an article called April Elegy, by Archibald MacLeish, which appeared in the Atlantic Monthly, volume 174, June, 1945.

3. Part of a news story on the death of Lincoln which appeared in the Boston Advertiser of April 14, 1865. The excerpt is quoted in an article in New England Magazine for December, 1893, volume 9; the article, entitled Living History, was written by H. King, and the quotation is on page 426. The title of the news story was President Assassinated.

4. Page 48 of a book by David Miller Dewitt, published in New York in 1909. The name of the book is The Assassination of Abraham Lincoln and Its Expiation.

5. Page 49 of the book cited in footnote 4.

6. Page 43 of the Atlantic Monthly article cited in footnote 2.

7. Page 400 in the article on Lincoln in Harper's Encyclopedia of United States History, published by Harper and Brothers in 1907 in New York. The article is in volume 5 of the encyclopedia.

8. Here and there in pages 17 to 38 of a book by Otto Eisenschiml entitled Why Was Lincoln Murdered? The book was published in 1937 by Little, Brown and Co. in Boston.

9. Page 37 of the book by Melville Freeman cited in footnote 1.

10. Page 50 of the book Why Was Lincoln Murdered? cited in footnote 8.

11. An article in Century Magazine, vol. 51, April 1896, page 945. The article is called At the Death-bed of Lincoln, and was written by E. C. Haynie.

12. The same page of the same article cited in footnote 11.

II. Arrange the items in Exercise I in correct form and order for a bibliography.

III. The first eight footnotes of a poorly annotated paper on hypnotism are listed below. Point out the errors in the footnotes as they stand. Whenever it is possible without more bibliographical information, put the notes into proper form.

1. Raper, Howard W., *Man Against Pain*, 30.
2. Bromberg, W., *The Mind of Man*, page 161.
3. op. cit. 163.
4. Hypnotism Now Commonplace, "Literary Digest", March 7, 1936.
5. Raper, *Man Against Pain*, page 32.
6. "Journal of Amer. Med. Assoc.", Feb 19, 1944, page 531
7. Ibid.
8. Bromberg, W., the Mind of Man, page 162.

Chapter Twelve

Some Everyday Uses
of English

CERTAIN USES OF ENGLISH, though very important, are likely to be underemphasized or neglected because they often do not fit easily into the courses of particular high schools and colleges. In this chapter we are assembling suggestions about speech and conversation, public speaking, writing examinations, writing business letters and social notes, and writing personal letters—some of the important everyday uses of English which the college student needs to know.

I. SPEECH AND CONVERSATION

Since one may range in conversation from purely conventional social phrases to lofty philosophical discussion, conversation is so large a subject that any short treatment of it is necessarily inadequate. All that can be done here is to point out the great importance of speech and conversation and to throw out a few suggestions in the hope of causing some thought about a matter that receives all too little.

Speech—in which we include enunciation and the rate, pitch, volume, and tone of voice—is an aspect of personality which is very important in the whole impression that one makes on others. Sloppy speech can be as offensive to the ear as grease-spotted clothing to the eye; yet some people who look in a mirror many times a day to reassure themselves about their physical appearance have never heard their own voices as their acquaintances hear them, and would not recognize a recording of their own speech. Those who have monotonous speech patterns, whose voices are raspy or squeaky or twangy, who mumble and mutter instead of producing clear, resonant speech sounds, who embarrass their hearers with too much volume or irritate them by making them strain to hear—such people load themselves with conversational handicaps for which wit and wisdom can hardly compensate. Anyone at all interested in the impression he makes on others should hear a recording of his own voice and should get some competent person's comment on his voice and his enunciation. Since many colleges make voice recordings for their students and tell them how to improve their speech, and since all colleges offer speech courses, college students have little excuse for continuing to speak poorly. Students who think that voice and speech are not important should read the text of an address by Winston Churchill or Franklin D. Roosevelt and then listen to a recording of the same speech.

Good voice and enunciation are means, however, and not ends; the most common end is good conversation. What constitutes good conversation is perhaps a matter of opinion; but nearly everyone would agree that the rule of doing to others as you would have them do to you will supply a good general guide. A quick and reasonably sure way to improve one's powers as a conversationalist is to make a check list of faults to avoid, building up the list by thinking of conversational habits that one has found most obnoxious in others. For example:

Talking too much. Everyone is painfully aware that some people talk too much, but most people are so pleased with their own conversation that they notice the fault only in others. The best way to avoid this most boring of all faults is never to talk long without some real encouragement from one's companions. Good conversation is likely to be either give-and-take or ask-and-give. When people are really interested in the subject, they ask further questions or make comments which are intended to encourage the speaker to go on. Silent people are seldom thought to be foolish; wise people know that speech is silver and that silence, at least at intervals, is golden.

Persistently interrupting others, or talking while they talk, or insisting on drawing someone out of a general conversation which he is enjoying, to listen to a private conversation in which he does not want to engage.

Being too dogmatic or too argumentative, and arguing to win instead of trying to see the other person's point of view.

Not listening when others are talking, especially asking questions and not listening to answers.

Praising oneself or one's possessions, or focusing conversation too much on oneself.

Insulting by heavy-handed flattery or condescending explanation of the obvious.

Insisting on being the only one to guide the conversation, or being stubbornly unwilling to change the subject.

Demanding too much response from a listener. After conversing with a demanding speaker, one notices that one's face is tired because the speaker has forced him so often into an appreciative expression. Such speakers are also likely to emphasize their points by tapping the hearer on the chest or shaking a finger under his nose or repeating "see?" at frequent intervals.

Taking too long to tell a straight story, drawing out a light anecdote so that the point comes as an anticlimax; exhausting patience with trivial or irrelevant details.

Haranguing an obviously restless or busy listener.

Inflicting efforts at humor upon people who do not enjoy such humor, or are not in a mood for it.

Pushing the conversation toward peoples' private affairs, forcing them either to be ill-mannered or to express opinions they prefer not to express.

Pretending to knowledge that one does not have; or speaking authoritatively on little knowledge; or being contemptuous of people who differ with one on points which are, after all, matters of opinion.

John Henry Newman's definition of the educated man, the gentleman, is a definition also of a good conversationalist; it sets up an ideal which one may not reach, but to which, at least, one can aspire:

The true gentleman in like manner carefully avoids whatever may cause a jar or jolt in the minds of those with whom he is cast;—all clashing of opinion, or collision of feeling, all restraint, or suspicion, or gloom, or resentment; his great concern being to make every one at their ease and at home. He has his eyes on all his company; he is tender towards the bashful, gentle towards the distant, and merciful towards the absurd; he can recollect to whom he is speaking; he guards against unseasonable allusions, or topics which may irritate; he is seldom prominent in conversation, and never wearisome. He makes light of favours while he does them, and seems to be receiving when he is conferring. He never speaks of himself except when compelled, never defends himself by a mere retort, he has no ears for slander or gossip, is scrupulous in imputing motives to those who interfere with him, and interprets everything for the best. He is never mean or little in his disputes, never takes unfair advantage, never mistakes personalities or sharp sayings for arguments, or insinuates evil which he dares not say out. From a long-sighted prudence, he observes the maxim of the ancient sage, that we should ever conduct ourselves towards our enemy as if he were one day to be our friend. . . . If he engages in controversy of any kind, his disciplined intellect preserves him from the blundering discourtesy of better, though less educated minds; who, like blunt weapons, tear and hack instead of cutting clean, who mistake the point in argument, waste their strength on trifles, misconceive their adversary, and leave the question more involved than they find it. He may be right or wrong in his opinion, but he is too clear-headed to be unjust; he is as simple as he is forcible, and as brief as he is decisive. Nowhere shall we find greater candour, consideration, indulgence: he throws himself into the minds of his opponents, he accounts for their mistakes. He knows the weakness of human reason as well as its strength, its province and its limits.

II. PUBLIC SPEAKING

In order to become an effective public speaker, one needs a knowledge of the principles of public speaking, some expert criticism, and numerous opportunities to speak and to hear other speakers. Since a good course in public speaking supplies these essentials, the best thing to do is to take such a course. This brief section on public speaking is intended to supply the student with some guidance and to make him feel less at a loss when there is occasion for him to speak.

Because both public speaking and writing are means of verbal communication, most of what we have said in the preceding chapters about writing applies equally well to oral communication, and could with a few changes go into a book on public speaking. There are certain important differences, though, between planning a speech and planning a composition, and there are additional things to say about practicing, delivering, and criticizing speeches.

In planning a speech one needs constantly to keep in mind that the speaker and the writer have different relationships to their audiences. A writer may if he wishes make his communication so impersonal that one gets little impression of the man behind it. A speaker cannot; his audience watches his movements, gestures, and facial expressions and hears his voice; it judges not only the speech but the speaker. If the speaker wishes his speech to produce a favorable impression, he must establish a favorable personal relationship with his audience. He must induce confidence and friendly respect by the way he talks to the audience and by what he says. A good speaker gives his audience a sense of participation; he keeps in mind the information, the experience, the loyalties, the attitudes, the ideas, the common background that his hearers have or are likely to have; he stresses those things that he has in common with his hearers; he points his whole discourse at the particular selected group that he is addressing. Winston Churchill, for example, in the first two paragraphs of a speech addressed to Congress and to the American radio audience, clearly pointed his speech at his audience and adapted it to the occasion:

I feel greatly honored that you should have thus invited me to enter the United States Senate chamber and address the representatives of both branches of Congress. The fact that my American forebears have for so many generations played their part in the life of the United States and that here I am, an Englishman, welcomed in your midst, makes this experience one of the most moving and thrilling in my life, which is already long and has not been entirely uneventful. I wish indeed that my mother, whose memory I cherish across the vale of years, could have been here to see. By the way, I cannot help reflecting that if my father had been American and my mother British, instead of the other way around, I might have got here on my own. In that case, this would not have been the first time you would have heard my voice. In that case, I should not have needed any invitation, but if I had it is hardly likely that it would have been unanimous. So perhaps things are better as they are.

I may confess, however, that I do not feel quite like a fish out of water in a legislative assembly where English is spoken. I am a child of the House of Commons. I was brought up in my father's house to believe in democracy; trust the people, that was his message. I used to see him cheered at meetings and in the streets by crowds of workingmen 'way back in those aristocratic, Victorian days, when, as Disraeli said, the world was for the few and for the very few. Therefore, I have been in full harmony all my life with the tides which have flowed on both sides of the Atlantic against privilege and monopoly, and I have steered confidently towards the Gettysburg ideal of government of the people, by the people, for the people.

Franklin D. Roosevelt in "A Call to War Veterans to Rally to the Colors in a Peacetime Sacrifice" (address before the American Legion Convention, Oct. 2, 1933) first cemented the relationship between himself and his audience:

I am glad to come here again and I am glad to have the right to come here as your comrade. I have come because I have faith in the American Legion and in all veterans in all our wars. And, incidentally, the right which I have to come here works both ways because just as long as I am in the White House you have the right to come and see me there.

You know my relationship with you is not a matter of the past six months. It dates back to the war days. It dates back to the time when I participated with you, not only in this country but also on the North Sea, and in the Channel, and on the actual fighting front in France.

I want to talk with you very simply about the problems of government, the difficulties that you and I as Americans have faced and solved and the difficulties which we still face and are going to solve. I recognize and appreciate, and the Nation recognizes and appreciates, the patience, the loyalty, the willingness to make sacrifices, shown by the overwhelming majority of the veterans of our country during the trying period from which we are beginning successfully to emerge.

I want to talk to you about national unity. Let us look at it as a living thing—not a mere theory resting in books, or otherwise apart from everyday business of men and women. It means that we all live under a common government, that we trade with each other, pay common taxes, many of them too high. It means that we give to, and receive from, a common protective government of which we are part. So to recognize national unity, to hold it above all else, seeing that upon it depends our common welfare, is just another way to say that we have patriotism.

Throughout the speech, Mr. Roosevelt continued to address himself directly to the veterans, maintaining and deepening his personal relationship with his audience by using such expressions as: "I want to talk to you . . ." "Let us look . . ." "You and I who served in the World War know . . ." "You men of the Legion . . ." "But, my friends . . ." "My, you are a young-looking bunch . . ." "Your task and mine are similar . . ." He concluded the speech with this paragraph, in which he made a direct and personal appeal to his audience of veterans:

Comrades of the Legion, I ask your further and even greater efforts in your program of national recovery. You who wore the uniform, you who served, you who took the oath of allegiance to the American Legion, you who support the ideals of American citizenship, you I have called to the colors again. As your Commander-in-Chief and your comrade, I am confident that you will respond.

Since the two speeches to which we have referred were largely persuasive speeches, the relationship between the speaker and the audience was, of course, especially important. Members of an audience are not likely to be persuaded to accept an attitude or to perform an action unless they like the speaker and feel that they have something in common with him. In informative speeches, the situation is somewhat different, for the speaker is not asking the audience to do anything or to accept any controversial belief. Since he is primarily concerned with presenting his subject clearly, he is likely to be less personal and more objective. The fact remains, though, that the audience must respect the speaker if it is to respect his knowledge, and the speech will not be effective if the speaker misses his particular audience by assuming that his hearers have more knowledge than they have and so talking over their heads, or by underestimating them and so talking down to them. The informative speech will gain in interest and clarity when the speaker makes allusions aimed at the special knowledge and interests of his particular audience and when he adapts his remarks to the particular occasion.

Speeches which aim at sociability or entertainment—after-dinner speeches, for example—also call for the establishment of a certain rapport, a kind of genial sharing, between speaker and audience. To be amused we need to like the person who is attempting to amuse us. Often we are induced to like him by the *tone* he adopts, that is, by his attitude toward us and toward himself. A speaker is most likely to entertain when he shows a friendly regard for his audience and its opinions and when he does not appear to take himself too seriously. Mark Twain, Will Rogers, and Bob Hope—in fact all good entertaining speakers—have succeeded in amusing and entertaining audiences not only by wit, humor, and shrewd observation but also by adapting the tone of their remarks to the audience and the occasion.

Another difference between written and spoken communication is that most people find it more difficult to follow development of thought when they listen than when they read. In reading it is always possible to turn back a page or two and pick up the thread or to re-read a paragraph or a sentence that is not immediately clear. For the listener there is no turning back and no opportunity to pause and reflect on an idea. Good speakers take into account these differences between reading and listening. They try to use shorter and less complex sentences than in writing, to repeat or to summarize more frequently, to give examples more often, to develop fewer main points, to make the main points and the organization unmistakably clear, and to use transitions and repetitions so frequently and so effectively that their audience will not lose the continuity, or will be able, if it does, to pick up the thread again.

Although the speaker needs to be constantly aware of the differences between speech and writing, the actual steps in preparing a speech are similar to those followed in preparing a composition. They may be listed as follows: (1) choosing an appropriate subject, (2) making an outline and perhaps writing a draft of the speech, (3) practicing the speech, (4) delivering the speech.

A good subject fits the speaker and the audience and the occasion. It fits the speaker when it leads him into subject matter which he knows or can find and in which he has a real interest. A speaker who chooses a subject about which he knows little, and in which he is only faintly interested, invites suffering; a dull plodding speech is painful to listen to and painful to give.

Even when the subject suits the speaker, it may not suit the occasion and the audience. At a formal faculty dinner a doctor gave a graphic account of recent advances in surgical techniques. The subject matter was good, the doctor was interested in it, and the audience was made up of educated people, but the *occasion* called for sociable after-dinner remarks and not for talk about scalpels and blood. An example of a subject unsuitable to the *audience* was supplied by an evangelical young English instructor. Asked to address a high-school study hall, he chooses to discuss Matthew Arnold's idea of culture and he talked for forty minutes with deep conviction but with no concessions to the interests of his hearers. He was later considerably embarrassed when he learned that the high-school teachers had barely succeeded in keeping his restless audience in order. The choice of subject is important; when the speaker knows beforehand the audience and the occasion, there is little excuse for an inappropriate choice.

After a speaker has chosen his subject, he is ready to select the substance of his speech and to organize it. For the informal theme an outline is desirable; for a speech of any length it is essential. The writer's outline may do no more than block out the rough organization; the speaker's outline, because it will serve as a kind of prompter when he practices his speech, needs to be much more detailed and more carefully planned. Except under very special circumstances, good speakers never memorize their speeches word for word. They may, after they have made a thorough outline, write out a draft of the speech so that they can look at what they are going to say and check the organization, but when they actually practice the speech they refer to a revised outline and not to the draft, and they memorize an abbreviated form of the outline but not the draft. If they wish to have notes available when they speak, the abbreviated outline serves that purpose too. A well thought-out, carefully constructed outline is essential for a speech of any length.

In making his detailed outline the speaker should not only consider the body of the speech, the argument or information; he should give special attention to the introductory remarks and the conclusion. The purpose of the introductory remarks is usually three-fold: (1) to gain the attention of one's hearers and to establish a favorable relationship with them, (2) to state specifically the subject of the talk, and (3) to bring home to the members of the audience the significance of the subject to them. In short, the introduction usually indicates what the speech is about and puts the audience in a friendly and receptive frame of mind. The body and conclusion of the speech are similar to the body and conclusion of a composition except for the differences of style, development, transitions, and the like that we have already considered. The conclusion of the speech, like the introduction, needs to be pointed at the particular audience and needs to be planned, and later phrased, with special care.

Once the speaker has drawn up a suitable outline, he is ready to practice his speech aloud, looking at the outline as he does so, and timing himself to see that his speech is of proper length. In order to deliver a speech effectively it is desirable to practice it at least four times. While practicing, one should memorize his outline, or at least the key words of the outline. Some speakers feel more comfortable if they have an abbreviated key-word outline available when they actually deliver the speech. Such notes, however, should be used only to bolster one's sense of security; the speaker should practice until he can give his speech easily without referring to them.

In addressing an audience the speaker is likely to find it hard to keep in mind all the points that are required for good delivery. A good speaker must speak loudly enough to be heard, must enunciate clearly, must use pauses and voice emphasis effectively, must not talk too fast, must speak easily without *ah's* and *uh's,* must be independent of his notes and able to watch his audience and adjust to it. In practicing a speech, therefore, the speaker should go through the whole routine as if he were actually on the platform and the audience were before him. He should decide how he is to stand, what he is to do with his hands, how fast and how loud he is to talk, what words he will emphasize and where he will pause, so that when he does address his audience he will be doing again what he has been doing in practice. Good habits established during practice will go far to ensure good delivery.

If a speaker has chosen a subject that is important to him, has adapted it to the audience and the occasion, and has practiced his speech until he is able to deliver it well, he has reason to feel confidence in his speech and in himself. It would be unrealistic, though, to say that such a speaker has nothing to worry about. There is still the problem of stage fright.

The best way to avoid or to lessen stage fright is to know something about it. Everyone, even speakers and actors of long experience, suffers from a feeling of tenseness before the performance, and such tenseness is natural and in fact desirable. A speaker, like an athlete, needs to be keyed up beforehand to do well. Another consoling fact is that a speaker's nervousness is much more apparent to him than it is to his audience; the student speakers who are praised by classmates for being at ease on the platform are usually the first to admit that they felt extremely nervous. Since stage fright is a form of self-consciousness, one can reduce his nervousness, not by ignoring the audience as most fearful speakers tend to do, but by looking at it, thinking about it, talking to it. When a speaker shifts his attention from himself and forces himself to focus on his subject and his audience, stage fright disappears, public speaking loses its terrors, and the speaker begins to enjoy himself.

One way to achieve effective delivery is to be aware of some common faults and to know how to avoid them. The faults mentioned below will serve as a kind of check list for the inexperienced speaker.

1. *Starting too abruptly.* Inexperienced speakers are frequently so eager to get through the ordeal of speaking that they walk rapidly to the platform and rush breathlessly into their subject. Experienced speakers pause for a moment before they say anything. They know that they will feel more at ease if they become physically adjusted before they start speaking. Often they arrange notes or wipe their glasses or shift the light. They usually look at the audience and take a deep breath. Insufficient air in the lungs will cause a speaker to gasp and to speak jerkily. After the initial pause, good speakers address the audience directly, first mentioning the names of distinguished people present and then going on to "Ladies and gentlemen" or some appropriate term of address. If they have been introduced, they often make brief extemporaneous remarks alluding to the introduction before they begin their prepared speech. Such remarks put the speaker and the audience more at ease.

2. *Not looking at the audience.* This is a cardinal sin in public speaking. One should look at his audience as he begins to speak and should continue to look at it throughout his talk. What is called "eye contact" is very important in public speaking; it gives the audience a sense of being in direct communication with the speaker, and it gives the speaker a chance to see when the audience is restless or perplexed or unable to hear.

3. *Poor enunciation.* The time to improve enunciation is during the practice period before the speech is given. Saying the speech and having a friend point out faults will help. The permanent cure for poor enunciation is forcing oneself to enunciate with reasonable clarity all the time.

4. *Forgetting the speech.* This fault is usually a result of inadequate preparation or of trying to memorize a set speech word for word. If one knows and speaks from his outline, he may speak in sentences that are not so well turned, but he will not be at a loss because he cannot remember a particular phrase, and his speech will sound like a speech and not like a recitation.

5. *Distracting facial expressions, posture, mannerisms.* Practicing a speech before a mirror is one good way to see and to correct one's own faults. Another is to get criticisms from one's friends. In speech classes, one gains from the criticisms of the instructor and of classmates.

6. *Lack of emphasis, monotony.* The speaker who knows exactly what he wants to say and who feels that his subject is important seldom fails to give effective emphasis. He then talks with much the same stress that he would use in conversation. It is wise, also, to give considerable thought to emphasis as one practices a speech.

7. *"Uh" or "ah" habit.* People usually say "uh" or "ah" because they are momentarily at a loss for a word and feel that they should fill the silence while they think. There are several ways to avoid this distracting habit: (*a*) speaking more slowly; (*b*) deliberately pausing where pauses are justified—at the end of a sentence, for example—and thinking ahead during the pause; and (*c*) realizing that a moment of silence is less conspicuous than an "uh," and resolutely saying nothing until the right word comes.

8. *Too hasty ending.* There are at least two very ineffective ways of ending a speech: just stopping, without preparing the audience by words or by voice for the ending; and mumbling the last few words and then fleeing from the platform. Both the wording of the conclusion and the voice of the speaker ought to announce that the speech is at an end, and the movements of the speaker afterward ought not to suggest flight. It is generally assumed that only the wicked flee when none pursueth.

One of the defects of a brief discussion of public speaking is that a full use of examples is impossible: generalizations without examples may be too abstract to give much helpful guidance. The reader, however, can supply the deficiency by considering thoughtfully the speeches that he hears. Since one learns by knowing what to avoid as well as what to practice, there are advantages to be gained from a critical examination of almost any speech that one hears, even a poor one.

Some of the points to consider in examining a speech are:

1. The actions of the speaker at the very beginning of the speech.
2. The introduction—the speaker's way of gaining the favorable attention of his audience, indicating the general content of his speech, and arousing interest in his subject.
3. The organization.
4. Transitional devices.
5. The means used to develop the material concretely.
6. The ways in which the speech is adapted to the particular audience and occasion.
7. The language the speaker uses—level, choice of words, sentence structure, clarity and economy and subtlety of expression.
8. The use of the voice—volume, rate, pauses, voice emphasis.
9. Movement, posture, gesture.
10. Eye contact with the audience.
11. The use of language and of voice to achieve finality at the conclusion.

A final point is that public speaking, like any other art, demands practice. Generalizations about speaking and the analysis of speeches may make an intelligent critic, but practice and more practice are necessary to make a good speaker.

III. WRITING EXAMINATIONS

College students do not need to be told that writing good examinations is an important practical matter. Often, of course, students fail examinations because they lack sufficient knowledge. That lack may be due fundamentally to a difficulty with language—to an inability to read well and to grasp the content and organization of the material in the course. But we are concerned here, not with insufficient knowledge, but with the actual taking of the examination; with the kind of failure, or poor result, of which the student says, "I really knew the material, but I guess I didn't do a good job on the exam." This kind of failure often comes from incompetence in the use of English.

The poor reading of questions written in clear and simple English is a major cause for unsatisfactory examination papers. It is commonly responsible, first, for a careless omission of parts of questions. If an examination question asks students to "define and give an example of each of the following," nearly always one or two students in a class of twenty-five or thirty will define the terms without giving examples.[1] It is unlikely that they could think of no examples; more probably, as soon as they read the word *define,* they stopped reading and plunged into writing on the question as they understood it. The instructor reading these papers may surmise what has happened; but he expects his students to be able to read, and he cannot give credit for the part of the answer which is not there. Frequently, too, students leave out a whole question on an examination. Because they cannot answer the question? Perhaps; perhaps not. The instructor cannot guess; he can only deduct the 15 or 20 per cent allotted to this part of the test.

The student can avoid these costly errors of omission by taking a few minutes at the beginning of the hour to read all of the questions *carefully* before he begins to write. This preliminary reading has another value: it enables the student to make some estimate of the time he will need on each part of the examination, and to budget his time as he writes. Sometimes the instructor has suggested on the question sheet the number of minutes to be devoted to each part; when he has, the suggestions should be noted and followed as closely as possible, for college examinations are meant to be completed. The wise

---

[1] Skill in defining is likely to be important in most examinations. For a discussion of effective definition, see pp. 201–204.

student will also try to allow a few minutes at the end of the hour for reading his paper, and for checking it with the question sheet to be sure that nothing is omitted.

Another failure in reading, often serious, is the failure to note directions about the *form* of the answer. Nearly always the form is prescribed in directions like "discuss briefly," "discuss as fully as time allows," "outline," " list five reasons," "write a short essay," "in a few sentences summarize . . ." These directions are important. They are designed to test the extent of the student's knowledge, or his ability to select the main ideas, or his ability to organize complex material or to assemble many facts in a short time. There is always a reason for the directions; and the student who outlines when he is asked to write an essay, lists ten causes when he is asked to discuss three, writes a sprawling account when he is asked to state clearly in one sentence, fails to give evidence of the *kind* of knowledge for which he is being tested in the question.

It will be clear that we are primarily concerned here not with the purely objective examination which requires only the substitution of a word, or a true-false judgment, but with the examination which is at least partially essay and discussion. Students will have examinations of this type particularly in English, history, government, sociology, economics, and philosophy.

A good answer to an essay or discussion question is a little composition; it presents the problems of any theme. The steps in the writing process must be taken quickly in writing examinations, but they are essentially the same: the student must assemble and select his material, being sure that all of it is clearly focused on what the question asks for; he must organize it; he must write it correctly and clearly and with as much *relevant concrete detail* as time and the directions on the examination permit.

This relevant concrete detail often makes the difference between a good examination paper and a mediocre or poor one; and the failure to include detail often comes, not from scanty information, but from vague, general, thoughtless expression. Consider the following answer, written on an examination question which asked students to state clearly the function of a number of characters in the short story in which each appeared. This answer was written about the second stranger in Hardy's story, "The Three Strangers":

The second stranger was introduced by the author to give the story excitement and suspense. His appearance at the cottage was important because it furthered the action of the story.

"Excitement and suspense"? In what way? "Furthered the action of the story"? Certainly; so does any character in any well-planned story. The answer is almost meaningless; and yet oral questioning showed that the student who wrote it was familiar with the details of the story. He was capable of writing a good, well-packed answer like this one:

The second stranger, the brother of the condemned man, by fleeing when he saw his brother and the hangman in Shepherd Fennel's cottage, caused the company to pursue him, and so enabled his brother to escape. His explanation when he was caught made the situation clear to the reader.

We have said before that the successful writer does not assume that his reader knows intuitively, without needing to be told, the contents of his mind. This is never more true than in writing examinations. The job of the student is to assure his reader, beyond any doubt, of the fullness and accuracy of his knowledge. Packing his answers with specific detail is one of the best ways of showing his thorough grasp of the material.

Let us make this perfectly clear, however: the detail must be *relevant* detail. Few things are more exasperating to a busy instructor than wading through material which is not pertinent to the question. The inclusion of irrelevancies on examinations sometimes comes from the student's failure to focus mentally on the question, from a general fogginess about what is asked for. Sometimes it is deliberate evasion: knowing very little about the question asked, the writer hopes to receive credit by writing on a slightly different subject. Sometimes, more innocently but no more wisely, the student includes irrelevant material out of an impulse to display all he knows, whether it is asked for or not. The effect, in any case, is to convince the instructor that the student is confused and unsure of the material since he has not written a coherent, well-organized, well-focused answer.

In addition to covering the questions completely according to directions, being clearly organized, specific, and well-focused, good examination papers are legible and literate. Students have been known to protest, when instructors in other departments have criticized their handwriting, grammar, spelling, and sentences, that "this is not an English course." Students who have read this book will, we hope, not be inclined to any such attitude; any course is an English course in so far as it requires meaningful communication in English. Most students cannot write as effectively under pressure as they can with time for thought and revision, but they can express themselves clearly and with reasonable correctness. Jumbled or ungrammatical sentences in which the meaning is obscure, frequent misspellings of common words, unreadable words and phrases, interpose a barrier to communication; they are irritating to the reader, and they give an impression of the writer's incompetence which no amount of factual information about the subject can wholly remove.

An inappropriate level of English also creates an unfavorable impression. Examination papers are seldom written in very formal English, but they should maintain a good level of informal usage and avoid, by all means, lapses into slang and vulgate which are out of key with the occasion and the subject under discussion ("Hamlet was disturbed and unbalanced when he found his father had been bumped off"). Part of competence in any field is the ability to discuss the subject in appropriate language.

The student who has trouble with examinations often finds it very profitable to read the papers written by good students. Actually seeing excellent answers to questions on which he has written poorly, noting what material has been selected and what omitted as inconsequent or irrelevant, and how the material has been organized and presented, may be of practical help to him in writing other examinations in that course.

In general, students will find that their examination papers improve if they follow these rules:

1. Read all the questions carefully before starting to write.
2. Budget time to ensure completion of the examination.
3. Realize that organization and expression are important; they are worth the time they may take.
4. *Answer the question, the whole question, and nothing but the question.*

IV. WRITING BUSINESS LETTERS

The basic requirements of a good business letter are that it state its business clearly, concisely, and courteously, and that it follow certain conventional patterns of usage. A business letter has six parts: the heading, the inside address, the salutation or greeting, the body of the letter, the complimentary close, and the signature.

The heading, in the upper right-hand corner, gives in three lines the street address of the writer, the city and state, and the date. (If one is using paper which has a letterhead, only the date is required in the heading.) The heading of a typewritten letter is usually in block form, as in the example below. The indented form may, how-

Heading

120 Lowell Street
Springfield, Illinois
June 1, 1951

Inside Address

Brown, Day and Company
32 West 45th Street
New York 19, New York

Salutation

Gentlemen:

_____

Body

_____

_____

_____

_____

Complimentary Close Signature

Very truly yours,

William A. Platt

William A. Platt

ever, be used, and is more common than the block form when the letter is written in longhand:

120 Lowell Street
Springfield, Illinois
June 1, 1951

The form chosen should be used consistently throughout the letter, that is, in the heading, the inside address, and the address on the envelope. Punctuation at the ends of the lines is unnecessary.

The inside address gives the name of the person or company to whom the letter is written, and the complete address. It follows the form (block or indented) of the heading, and is set flush with the left-hand margin, from three to six spaces below the last line of the heading.

When a person's position is included in the inside address, it is usually placed on the same line as his name; if this makes the line awkwardly long, the title may be put on a second line, or it may be divided in this way:

```
Professor John F. Carter, Chairman
Department of Economics
Tufts College
Medford 55, Massachusetts
```

A letter to a company may, in the inside address, name the member of the firm whose attention the writer wishes to call to the business discussed in the letter:

```
Eliot-Johnson Company
50 Franklin Street
Boston 10, Massachusetts
Attention: Mr. G. H. Harper
```

Names of states may be abbreviated in the inside address and the heading if the abbreviation produces a better balance in the length of the lines.

The salutation, or greeting, of the letter is written flush with the left-hand margin, two spaces below the last line of the inside address. It is always followed by a colon.

The salutation used depends on the degree of formality the writer considers appropriate for this letter. Conventional salutations, in order of increasing informality are: *My dear Sir* or *My dear Madam* (very formal); *Dear Sir* or *Dear Madam; My dear Mr. Brown; Dear Mr. Brown.* The last two salutations are now most commonly used if the writer knows the name of the person who will receive the letter. If the addressee is a company or group, the salutation will be *Gentlemen, Dear Sirs,* or *Mesdames* (plural of *Madam*).

The body of a typewritten letter is usually single-spaced, with double spaces between paragraphs. The paragraphs may be indented, or they may begin flush with the left-hand margin. Since business letters should be easy to read, paragraphs are frequently short.

A generation ago, business correspondence was conventionally carried on in a jargon which was a peculiar combination of curt efficiency and elaborate formality: *Yours of the 5th instant received and contents duly noted; In reply to your esteemed favor of the 8th inst. would say* . . . This jargon has, fortunately, dropped out of current usage. Simple, direct expression is now characteristic of most business correspondence. The body of the business letter, unlike its other parts, is no longer conventionalized; within certain limits it may, and should, express the personality of the writer.

In general, business letters are still formal and impersonal; but the degree of formality and impersonality depends upon the situation and the writer's purpose. His purpose must guide him, too, in his choice of material, his arrangement of it in the letter, and his use of language. Some business letters are purely factual and informative, but many of them are also persuasive; the tone of the letter may be as important as the plain sense in accomplishing the aim for which the letter was written.

The complimentary close is written slightly to the right of the middle of the page and two or three spaces below the last line of the body of the letter. A comma is usually placed after the close. Only the first word of a closing phrase is capitalized.

The complimentary close should be consistent with the heading, and both should be chosen for their harmony with the tone of the letter. A very formal letter beginning *My dear Sir* would close *Yours respectfully, Respectfully yours,* or *Very respectfully yours.* A letter beginning *Dear Sir* would consistently close with *Yours truly, Yours very truly,* or *Very truly yours.* A less formal letter, addressed to a business acquaintance, and beginning *Dear Mr. Brown,* might close with *Sincerely yours, Sincerely, Very sincerely yours, Cordially yours,* or *Cordially.*

The participial close (*Hoping for the favor of an early reply; Trusting that this answers your question*) is no longer considered good form.

The signature is always handwritten. Unless a letterhead carries the writer's name, the name is typed below the signature, to insure legibility.

A professional title (*Dr.* Thomas Sand) is never used before the signature. If the letter requires mention of the writer's professional status, this form may be used:

Thomas Sand, m. d.

A married woman signs her own name, not her husband's, and indicates her status parenthetically:

Marjorie J. Carson
(Mrs. Frank Carson)

[Or]   *(Mrs.) Marjorie J. Carson*

Letters of application, sometimes the most important compositions which students write, deserve special attention. A letter of application must, if it is to receive favorable consideration, follow the conventional business-letter form outlined above. It must be neatly typed and neatly spaced on the page or pages, and it must be free from mechanical errors. In all details it should convey an impression of the writer's competence and his care in composing this letter.

The content of the letter will depend on the situation, but, generally speaking, a letter of application should include a discussion, or at least mention, of the six points listed below. These requirements for the letter are subject to modification by particular circumstances; for example, the applicant may, as part of his application, be asked to fill out blanks which cover some of these six points; he may be writing his letter to a person who is acquainted with his work, so that discussing it would be unnecessary. The average letter of application, however, should cover this material:

1. *The application itself*—a clear statement of the position applied for and the fact that the writer is applying.
2. *Qualifications*—the education and experience of the applicant. (Usually the longest and most detailed section of the letter.)
3. *Personal information*—age, health, habits, community activities, marital status, race and religion if the writer wishes to include them. (This section, usually very important in the letter, gives a picture not simply of the worker but also of the human being in whom the prospective employer is interested.)
4. *References*—names, positions, and addresses of people willing to vouch for the ability and character of the applicant.
5. *Salary*—the amount expected or understood.
6. *Request for an interview*—with information about the writer's availability, free time, telephone number—anything which will make it easy for the receiver of the letter to arrange the interview.

The interview is so important that getting it is often the real purpose of the letter of application. The letter fails in its intention if the reader is not convinced that the writer is worth seeing; it may fail, too, if arranging the interview is not made easy and convenient.

A letter of application presents a very interesting problem in communication. The facts in the letter, the applicant's actual record, will, of course, determine to a considerable extent the response of the reader; but the way the facts are presented, the emphasis they are given, the total impression the reader receives of the total person writing the letter may determine his response even more. A skillful letter of application attracts attention without dramatics and without violation of conventions. Within the bounds of a rather formal style it communicates a personality. It is both honest and subtly slanted. It persuades without pressing; it conveys self-confidence without conceit.

V. WRITING SOCIAL NOTES

The form of informal social notes—thank-you notes, bread-and-butter letters, notes of congratulation or sympathy, informal invitations and replies—is less rigidly prescribed than the business-letter form. The heading is sometimes in the upper right-hand corner, but usually the writer's address and the date are placed at the end of the note, lower than the signature, and at the left of the page. Often only the date is given, if the writer's address is known by the addressee. Even the date may be omitted if the occasion and the relationship are very informal. The inside address is never used. The salutation and complimentary close accord with the tone of the note and the writer's attitude toward the receiver (*Dear Mrs. Jones . . . Sincerely yours; Dear Mary . . . Affectionately*). The salutation may be followed by a colon, as in a business letter, but a comma is more often used.

The note should, of course, be carefully composed, and written neatly and legibly on attractive paper. Because the communication is brief, any blunders or signs of carelessness create a particularly bad impression of the writer, and indicate a lack of consideration for the person to whom he is writing.

In addition to showing evidence of care, the social note, even though it is short, should be detailed enough to convey something of the writer's personality and, above all, the genuineness of the feeling which prompted him to write. A perfunctory, mechanical, merely dutiful note defeats its purpose of cementing or furthering a social relationship. Not to express thanks for a gift is certainly inexcusably thoughtless and rude; but to write: "Dear Jean, Thank you so much for your lovely gift. It was nice of you to remember my birthday. Love, Amy"—to express thanks in this way is almost equally thoughtless and rude. The absence of detail shows indifference both toward the gift and toward the friend who was kind enough to buy and send it, and even suggests that the writer is not sure which one of her birthday gifts came from Jean.

The following social notes, though brief, are detailed and concrete enough to show genuine feeling, and thoughtful consideration of the receiver.

DEAR MRS. BRONSON,

You are very kind to ask me to supper Sunday night, and I shall be delighted to come. Phil has talked so much about his family and his home. I know that the Dobermans are really as gentle as kittens, and I want to see the den that Phil has papered with three walls plain and the fourth one plaid. But most of all I am looking forward to meeting you and Mr. Bronson.

Sincerely yours,
JANE WEATHERBY

1496 UNIVERSITY AVENUE
June 23, 1951

DEAR UNCLE PETER,

When I told you before the holidays that I had decided to give up cigarettes and start smoking a pipe I wasn't hinting. But honestly, I was never so pleased in my life as when I opened the package from you Christmas morning and saw your beautiful old meerschaum. I'm smoking it right now, and I've been thinking about the times I used to sit on your lap while you blew smoke rings for me, with this same pipe, wasn't it? Anyway I like to think so. I'll never go back to cigarettes now.

It was fine to see you at school last month. I hope your client in Denver will want to see you again soon.

Give my love to Aunt Marian and Hilda, and thanks again for the pipe.

Your nephew,
JACK

December 27

DEAR GINNY,

It was such fun to see you and Tom again. I can't get over the delicious meals cooked by a girl who couldn't fry an egg three months ago. And I love your apartment. I wish I could have stayed until we finished painting the kitchen—it must be done by now, unless you had to spend yesterday resting from too much company. I'm sending you some breakfast mats I saw in Field's today, that I think are just the color of the new walls. In fact, I know it, because they match the green paint I still have in my hair! Thanks for a wonderful week-end. I enjoyed every minute of it.

LOVE,
MARG

6320 ASHLAND BOULEVARD
CHICAGO, ILLINOIS
August 10, 1951

For one kind of social correspondence, formal invitations and replies to formal invitations, a pattern is rigidly prescribed. The formal invitation and the reply have no heading (though the sender's address is sometimes written at the lower left-hand side of the page), no inside address, no salutation, no complimentary close, and no signature. They are consistently third person and consistently present tense. Numbers are written out, and no abbreviations except *Mr.* and *Mrs.* are used. Formal invitations are engraved or written by hand; replies are handwritten, never typed, and are neatly spaced on note paper of good quality and of sufficient size to prevent crowding of the lines.

Students should familiarize themselves with this standardized pattern of the formal invitation and reply. The form is so firmly established by convention that the person who fails to follow it reveals an ignorance of social custom for which he is often severely condemned.

A formal invitation is worded this way:

Mr. and Mrs. Albert Winthrop
request the pleasure of
Mr. Robert Jackson's company
at dinner on Wednesday evening
November the twelfth
at eight o'clock

The reply follows the wording of the invitation and confirms the date and hour:

Mr. Robert Jackson
accepts with pleasure
the kind invitation of
Mr. and Mrs. Albert Winthrop
to dinner on Wednesday evening
November the twelfth
at eight o'clock

[*Or*]

Mr. Robert Jackson
regrets that he is unable to accept
[or, that a previous engagement
prevents his accepting]
Mr. and Mrs. Albert Winthrop's
kind invitation to dinner
on Wednesday evening
November the twelfth
at eight o'clock

VI. WRITING PERSONAL LETTERS

A good personal letter is like a garment made by an excellent tailor: it is designed to fit the receiver perfectly; yet its material and workmanship bear unmistakably the mark of the maker. Because each letter writer is himself unique and because he writes different letters to different people, it is hard to make enlightening comment about writing personal letters. Some consideration, however, of the purpose, content, organization, form, and style of personal letters, along with a few examples of good letters, may be of use to the student in his private correspondence.

Although the particular purposes of the writer will vary from letter to letter, most writers of personal letters have in common the desire to renew or to continue or to deepen their relationship with the recipient of the letter, whether the recipient is a friend, a sweetheart, or a relative. The writer of personal letters is, therefore, most concerned with projecting himself, recreating the relationship, and giving the reader a sense of his presence. Everyone has had the experience of getting a letter from a close friend, chuckling over parts of it, saying something like, "Good old George; this letter sounds just like him," and then settling back to recall pleasant past experiences. A letter which produces this effect on the reader is a good letter.

One other test of a good letter is the feeling that the writer has as he reads it over before he sends it. A letter is a kind of second self, a representative whose traveling expenses are a few cents for postage. If the reader feels that the letter represents his best self—reflective, cultivated, humorous, entertaining, full of interesting information —then it passes the second test. The good personal letter satisfies the writer and satisfies the reader.

Good letters often give the effect of spontaneity, but they are seldom entirely spontaneous productions. Like other forms of communication, though in a less formalized way, they require the writer to gather material, to select, and to decide in advance upon at least a rough plan of development.

In gathering material one obvious step is to reread the letter that one is answering. Common courtesy requires one to answer questions and to make appropriate comment. Some letter writers follow the practice of devoting the first part of their letter to replying to the letter that they have just received—answering questions, commenting, perhaps asking questions themselves—and then, after they have dealt in full with their friend's interests, going on to write about their own affairs. This practice has its advantages: it causes one to give thought to the friend and to his activities, and it launches one deep into his own letter; but the practice should not be made an invariable rule. A certain amount of spontaneity is desirable; rigid following of formulas kills spontaneity and produces letters that sound, and are, mechanical.

Oftentimes in reading over and thinking about the letter he is to answer, the letter writer will fall into a kind of reverie in which he thinks back over the things he and his friend have done together, the people they have known, the subjects they have discussed. Engaging in reminiscences of this sort is a second and very rewarding means of gathering material. Also it puts the writer in a good mood for letter writing because it recreates shared past experiences and so makes him feel closer to his friend. When old friends see each other after a period of separation, one of the first things they do to renew their acquaintance and to feel at ease with each other is to talk about the experiences they have shared, to recall amusing incidents, to exchange information about the recent activities of mutual friends and acquaintances. A personal letter which makes lively and concrete use of two friends' common memories can give the recipient almost as much pleasure as seeing the writer in person, and can keep the friendship alive and warm.

A third source of material for letters is information about the writer himself—his associates, his surroundings, his travels, his successes and failures, his reflections on his experience. A letter gives one an opportunity to share his present life and his thoughts with his friend, to bring their relationship up to date. It is reasonable to assume that the friend will be interested in anything that concerns the writer as long as it is presented in such a way that the friend can grasp its significance and share the writer's feeling. Many letter writers, however, do not write interestingly about their own concerns. They simply give a catalogue of events or a list of activities and fail to select their material and to develop it to give it meaning. Such unsuccessful writers are likely to tell everything they have been doing, but to give only bare facts and to leave out details. ("Had a busy week. Went swimming yesterday, went to a dance last night, going to another dance tonight. Wish you were here.") Skillful writers select a few centers of interest, focus on those few, and write so concretely that their account is as interesting to the reader as the experience itself was for the writer.

The organization necessary in a letter depends upon the content. Some letters, particularly those which deal with ideas, may have a tight, logical structure; others, especially those which deal with reminiscence and the small events of everyday living, may ramble on informally, passing from one subject to another by a process of association. The writer should have in mind, as we suggested before, some rough plan of organization before he begins his letter, but if he should happen unexpectedly upon a rich vein, he should depart from his plan and make the most of the congenial subject matter. Good letters are likely to contain sudden turns of thought, sallies of wit, excursions into philosophy, anecdotes, allusions, elaborations, whimsical afterthoughts that occur to the writer as the letter grows. In personal letters, flavor and life come first; only so much organization is needed as will hold the letter together.

The form of the personal letter, since it is the same as that of the informal social note, presents no problems, or at least no problems which can be solved here. It is true that whether to begin a letter *Dear* or *Dearest* and whether to close with *Very sincerely, Sincerely yours,* or *Love* may be important questions—for people read letters carefully, particularly those that are, or almost are, love letters—but only the writer can decide these questions.

Consideration of style may make the difference between a fairly good letter and an excellent one. Although personal letters seldom call for formal English, they do call for lively, personalized, finished, informal expression. Concreteness is, of course, the very lifeblood of personal letters, and all that has been said elsewhere on the subject is especially pertinent here. Comparisons, allusions, particularizations, figures of speech, sharp bits of description, fragments of dialogue—all these play their part.

Comparisons and allusions can be particularly effective in those parts of the letter in which the writer is dealing with persons, places, or ideas unfamiliar to the reader. If one is describing Paris for a reader who lives in New York, a comparison between the two cities will make the material more informative and more interesting to the New Yorker. If one is describing his efforts to grow a lawn, an allusion to bluegrass—"my crab grass grows as evenly as your bluegrass and is much more hardy"—may be pleasing to a Kentucky reader. It has a shade of humor and it also gives him the feeling that the writer, though dealing with material unrelated to him, still has him in mind. Good letter writers know the value of such allusions; whatever they write about, they take every opportunity to point up the material for their particular reader. This practice is so common that good letters sometimes mean little to a third person until the allusions are explained.

An aspect of style similar in effect to allusions and perhaps peculiar to personal letters and conversation is the use of what we shall call private language. People who have associated intimately with one another—friends, lovers, members of the same family—especially lovers—have a way of creating new words or attaching special and private meaning to standard words. Use of such private language gives a certain intimacy and warmth to personal letters because it sets up a series of pleasant associations and memories.

Before going on to examples of good personal letters, it may be well to round off our discussion by commenting on some frequently quoted generalizations and superstitions about letter writing.

1. *Always answer a letter on the day you receive it.* A good rule for business correspondence, but frequently not applicable to personal letters. It is true that one may write a better letter if he writes while the impact of his friend's letter is still affecting him, and that a very prompt reply is good if both people want to write almost daily letters. Often, though, an immediate reply puts a certain strain on the receiver. He doesn't want to write again immediately and so he may be embarrassed by his friend's dismaying efficiency. There are two ways of killing a correspondence: smothering it and starving it to death. Usually it is best to space one's letters at intervals appropriate to the circumstances and the relationship. One can recreate the impact of a friend's letter by reading it again thoughtfully before answering it.

2. *Never type a friendly letter.* A rule that no longer generally applies. It is true that some people feel an added intimacy in handwriting and prefer handwritten letters. Probably these people should be humored when their preference is known. If one's handwriting is difficult to read, though, it may be a duty and an act of friendship to type.

3. *Never begin a letter with "I."* A superstition. The basis for this superstition may be the belief that beginning a letter with *I* is a mark of conceit and self-centeredness. The word *I,* however, produces different effects in different contexts. Certainly there is no conceit in beginning a letter, "I was stupid in going contrary to your advice." Good letter writers—Charles Lamb and John Keats, for example— pay no attention to this rule. There is no reason why anyone should be bound by it.

4. *The beginning is the most important part of a letter.* A statement that contains a good deal of truth. Certainly the first paragraph is important; often it sets the tone of the whole communication. Also many people tend to write first about the matter that is uppermost in their minds. Generalization about the position of greatest emphasis is difficult, however, because each letter writer tends to follow his own pattern. Some people put the important matter at the end, or even in a postscript.

5. *Avoid apologies at the beginning of the letter.* A good rule. To start off with an apology is usually to start off on the wrong foot. Unless very skillfully executed, an apology at the beginning damages the tone of the letter because it suggests that the writer really doesn't want to write but is urged on by a sense of duty; few people want letters written for duty and not for love. An apology, if there must be one, is usually best buried in the middle of the letter and made to seem an explanation instead of an apology.

6. *Don't write anything in a letter that you wouldn't be willing to have read in court.* Cynical advice, but worth considering if one does not take it too seriously. Personal letters have figured in breach-of-promise suits and other legal actions, and well-intentioned but thoughtless friends have, on occasion, caused embarrassment by showing letters to others. It is best to think twice before making promises and commitments, and not to entrust very private opinions or information to indiscreet people.

7. *Never mail a spiteful, sarcastic or angry letter.* A good rule, and most worth following when one feels most like going contrary to it. Such letters are almost always written when one's pride or one's feelings have been hurt and when one is unable for a time to take a sensible view of the situation. Often caused by misunderstanding, angry letters are almost sure to produce further misunderstanding; the brief satisfaction that writing them gives is often followed by embarrassment or regret or even sorrow over a lost friendship. Sarcasm, spite, and anger are about as likely to improve human relations as kerosene is to extinguish fire. Even when anger is justified, an objective, clear, restrained statement of one's grievance will cause respectful attention and will have more effect than overstatement, sarcasm, and vituperation. An angry letter may produce an angry reply or a cold silence; a calm, fair letter doesn't justify anger and it can't be ignored by a fair-minded person. It leaves no easy way out and so it hits home.

In the example below, Dr. Johnson's famous letter to Lord Chesterfield, presumably his patron, Johnson makes clear his displeasure and the grounds for it without losing his dignity or his sense of proportion. Because the letter was written to a lord, because of its subject matter, and because Dr. Johnson wrote it in his characteristic Johnsonian manner, it is unusually formal for a personal letter. Noteworthy in it are the directness and the courtesy of the beginning, the rugged modesty of tone, the apt allusion to Virgil, the comparison to the drowning man, the forceful but objective statement, and the unusual turn given to the complimentary close.

To the Right Honorable the Lord of Chesterfield

7th February, 1755.

My Lord,

I have been lately informed, by the proprietor of *The World* that two papers, in which my Dictionary is recommended to the public, were written by your Lordship. To be so distinguished is an honor, which, being very little accustomed to favors from the great, I know not well how to receive, or in what terms to acknowledge.

When, upon some slight encouragement, I first visited your Lordship, I was overpowered like the rest of mankind, by the enchantment of your address, and could not forbear to wish that I might boast myself *Le vainqueur du vainqueur de la terre;* *—that I might obtain that regard for which I saw the world contending; but I found my attendance so little encouraged, that neither pride nor modesty would suffer me to continue it. When I had once addressed your Lordship in public, I had exhausted all the art of pleasing which a retired and uncourtly scholar can possess. I had done all that I could; and no man is well pleased to have his all neglected, be it ever so little.

Seven years, my Lord, have now past, since I waited in your outward rooms, or was repulsed from your door; during which time I have been pushing on my work through difficulties, of which it is useless to complain, and have brought it at last to the verge of publication, without one act of assistance, one word of encouragement, or one smile of favor. Such treatment I did not expect, for I never had a patron before.

The shepherd in Virgil grew at last acquainted with Love, and found him a native of the rocks.

Is not a patron, my Lord, one who looks with unconcern on a man struggling for life in the water, and, when he has reached ground, encumbers him with help? The notice which you have been pleased to take of my labors, had it been early, had been kind; but it has been delayed till I am indifferent, and cannot enjoy it; till I am solitary, and cannot impart it; till I am known, and do not want it. I hope it is not very cynical asperity not to confess obligations where no benefit has been received, or to be unwilling that the public should consider me as owing that to a patron, which providence has enabled me to do for myself.

Having carried on my work thus far with so little obligation to any favorer of learning, I shall not be disappointed though I should conclude it, if less be possible, with less; for I have been long wakened from that dream of hope, in which I once boasted myself with so much exultation, my Lord, your Lordship's most humble, most obedient servant,

SAM. JOHNSON.

Charles Lamb's letters, like his essays and like the man himself, are full of wit, fancy, whimsicality, allusion and humor. The letter below was written to Dr. Vale Asbury. (Since this letter refers to an

* The conqueror of the conqueror of the earth.

instance of Lamb's intemperance, it is fair to add that for him "a little wine went a long way" and that he was not in general an intemperate man.)

DEAR SIR, It is an observation of a wise man that "moderation is best in all things." I cannot agree with him "in liquor." There is a smoothness and oiliness in wine that makes it go down by a natural channel, which I am positive was made for that descending. Else, why does not wine choke us? Could Nature have made that sloping lane, not to facilitate the downgoing? She does nothing in vain. You know that better than I. You know how often she has helped you at a dead lift, and how much better entitled she is to a fee than yourself sometimes, when you carry off the credit.—Still there is something due to manners and customs, and I should apologize to you and Mrs. Asbury for being absolutely carried home upon a man's shoulders thro' Silver Street, up Parson's Lane, by the Chapels (which might have taught me better), and then to be deposited like a dead log at Gaffar Westwood's, who it seems does not "insure" against intoxication. Not that the mode of conveyance is objectionable. On the contrary, it is more easy than a one-horse chaise. Ariel in the "Tempest" says

> On a Bat's back do I fly,
> After sunset merrily.

Now I take it that Ariel must sometimes have stayed out late of nights. Indeed, he pretends that "where the bee sucks, there lurks he," as much as to say that his suction is as innocent as that little innocent (but damnably stinging when he is provok'd) winged creature. But I take it, that Ariel was fond of metheglin of which the Bees are notorious Brewers. But then you will say: What a shocking sight to see a middle-aged gentleman-and-a-half riding upon a Gentleman's back up Parson's Lane at midnight. Exactly the time for that sort of conveyance, when nobody can see him, nobody but Heaven and his own conscience; now Heaven makes fools, and don't expect much from her own creation; and as for conscience, She and I have long since come to a compromise. I have given up false modesty, and she allows me to abate a little of the true. I like to be liked, but I don't care about being respected. I don't respect myself. But, as I was saying, I thought he would have let me down just as we got to Lieutenant Barker's Coal-shed (or emporium) but by a cunning jerk I eased myself, and righted my posture. I protest, I thought myself in a palanquin, and never felt myself so grandly carried. It was a slave under me. There was I, all but my reason. And what is reason? and what is the loss of it? and how often in a day do we do without it, just as well? Reason is only counting, two and two makes four. And if on my passage home, I thought it made five, what matter? Two and two will just make four, as it always did, before I took the finishing glass that did my business. My sister has begged me to write an apology to Mrs. A. and you for disgracing your party; now it does seem to me, that I rather honored your party, for every one that was not drunk (and one or two of the ladies, I am sure, were not) must have been set off greatly in the contrast to me. I was the scapegoat. The soberer they seemed. By the way is magnesia good on these occasions? . . . But still you'll say (or the men and maids at your house will say) that it is not a seemly sight for an old gentleman to go home pick-a-back. Well, may be it is not. But I have never studied grace. I take it to be a mere superficial accomplishment. I regard more the internal acquisitions. The great object after supper is to get home, and whether that is obtained in a horizontal posture or perpendicular (as foolish men and apes affect for dignity) I think is little to the purpose. The end is always greater than the means. Here I am, able to compose a sensible rational apology, and what signifies how I got here? I have just sense enough to remember I was very happy last night, and to thank our kind host and hostess, and that's sense enough, I hope.

CHARLES LAMB.

N.B.—What is good for a desperate head-ache? Why, Patience, and a determination not to mind being miserable all day long. And that I have made my mind up to.

So, here goes. It is better than not being alive at all, which I might have been, had your man toppled me down at Lieut. Barker's Coal-shed. My sister sends her sober compliments to Mrs. A. She is not much the worse.

Yours truly,
C. LAMB.

A letter, or rather a selection from a letter, written by John Keats to John Hamilton Reynolds, illustrates the kind of sharing of ideas that sometimes enriches reflective personal letters. This particular letter is distinctive because of the concrete imagery that Keats uses to make his ideas clear, because the ideas themselves are significant, and because the letter, like good conversation, gives the sense of a lively mind at work, reflecting on human experience and advancing tentative conclusions.

TEIGNMOUTH, 3 May

MY DEAR REYNOLDS,

. . . With your patience, I will return to Wordsworth—whether or no he has an extended vision or a circumscribed grandeur—whether he is an eagle in his nest, or on the wing. And to be more explicit and to show you how tall I stand by the giant, I will put down a simile of human life as far as I now perceive it; that is, to the point to which I say we both have arrived at.

Well—I compare human life to a large Mansion of Many Apartments, two of which I can only describe, the doors of the rest being as yet shut upon me. The first we step into we call the Infant or Thoughtless Chamber, in which we remain as long as we do not think. We remain there a long while, and notwithstanding the doors of the second Chamber remain wide open, showing a bright appearance, we care not to hasten to it; but are at length imperceptibly impelled by the awakening of the thinking principle within us—we no sooner get into the second Chamber, which I shall call the Chamber of Maiden-Thought, than we become intoxicated with the light and the atmosphere, we see nothing but pleasant wonders, and think of delaying there for ever in delight. However among the effects this breathing is father of is that tremendous one of sharpening one's vision into the heart and nature of Man—of convincing one's nerves that the world is full of Misery and Heartbreak, Pain, Sickness, and oppression—whereby this Chamber of Maiden-Thought becomes gradually darken'd and at the same time on all sides of it many doors are set open—but all dark—all leading to dark passages. We see not the balance of good and evil, we are in a Mist. *We* are now in that state—we feel the "burden of the Mystery."

To this point was Wordsworth come, as far as I can conceive when he wrote "Tintern Abbey," and it seems to me that his Genius is explorative of those dark Passages. Now if we live, and go on thinking, we too shall explore them. He is a genius and superior to us, in so far as he can, more than we, make discoveries, and shed a light in them. Here I must think Wordsworth is deeper than Milton, though I think it has depended more upon the general and gregarious advance of intellect, than individual greatness of Mind. From the Paradise Lost and the other Works of Milton, I hope it is not too presuming, even between ourselves to say, that his Philosophy, human and divine, may be tolerably understood by one not much advanced in years. In his time Englishmen were just emancipated from a great superstition, and Men had got hold of certain points and resting places in reasoning which were too newly born to be doubted, and too much opposed by the Mass of Europe not to be thought ethereal and authentically divine—Who could gainsay his ideas on virtue, vice, and Chastity in Comus just at the time of the dismissal of Cod-pieces and a hundred other disgraces? Who would not rest satisfied with his hintings at good and evil in the Paradise Lost, when just free from the inquisition and burning in Smithfield? The Reformation produced such immediate and great benefits, that Protestantism was considered under the immediate eye of heaven, and its own remaining Dogmas and superstitions, then, as it were, regenerated, constituted those resting places and seeming sure points of Reasoning—from that I have mentioned, Milton, whatever he may have thought in the sequel, appears to have been content with these by his writings. He did not think into the human heart, as Wordsworth has done. Yet Milton as a Philosopher, had sure as great powers as Wordsworth.

What is then to be inferr'd? O many things. It proves there is really a grand march of intellect; it proves that a mighty Providence subdues the mightiest Minds to the service of the time being, whether it be in human Knowledge or Religion. I have often pitied a Tutor who has to hear "Nom: Musa" so often dinn'd into his ears—I hope you may not have the same pain in this scribbling—I may have read these things before, but I never had even a thus dim perception of them; and moreover I like to say my lesson to one who will endure my tediousness, for my own sake.

After all, there is certainly something real in the World—Moore's present to Hazlitt is real—I like that Moore, and am glad I saw him at the Theatre just before I left Town. Tom has spit a *leetle* blood this afternoon, and that is rather a damper—but I know—the truth is there is something real in the World. Your third Chamber of Life shall be a lucky and a gentle one—stored with the wine of love—and the Bread of Friendship.

When you see George, if he should not have received a letter from me tell him he will find one at home most likely—tell Bailey I hope soon to see him. Remember me to all. The leaves have been out here for many a day. I have written to George for the first stanzas of my "Isabel"—I shall have them soon, and will copy the whole out for you.

Your affectionate friend
JOHN KEATS

Not only literary men write good letters. The letter below, written by a college sophomore to her sister, sustains comparison with the letters that precede it and illustrates many of the characteristics of the good personal letter.

Monday

DEAR SISSER,

The *Story* magazine pleases me immensely—really more than anything else I can think of. Of course I *am* wondering whether it was sent more for my pleasure, or for my profit as the sugar-coated corrective following my first writing exercise. I trust that the gang on the corridor at school will give me first chance at it!

Floss has been in her heyday! Christmas season and four of her children at home—why, she's never had so much mail to open! My little package for the folks was due to arrive sometime last week, and arrive it did on Wednesday. But by the time I reached it, it had been thrice opened, Floss leading by a nose. Best of all is Mother's explanation: "Why, Honey, I saw it was addressed to you, and it was just the *natural* thing for me to open it!"

Your Christmas letter (by the way—Merry Christmas) created quite a bit of excitement. It arrived the Saturday before Christmas. Mother laid it before her on the table, fingered it gently, and announced defiantly, "I'm going to open it." The Judge immediately set down the law, "Now *Floss*, etc., etc., etc.," and he picked the letter up and triumphantly deposited it on the mantel. An hour later found Floss fumbling with the flaps of the letter, and the Judge removing it to some other perfectly accessible place. And so until Christmas Eve, when the Judge and Floss again entered into a disagreement which ended with your letter being placed in Father's pocket until the next day. And then when the big moment finally arrived, Mother sat there and was content merely to look at the outside of the letter while the Judge fluttered around like an old lady, and finally opened the letter with his own hands!

Christmas morning, about 11:30, Father came in from town and stalked upstairs to find his tweezers, use them, and be really dressed up for Christmas dinner! But the tweezers were gone—("Can't keep a thing in the house"). I happened to be in my room: "Bee-a-tur," he shouted, "are you using my tweezers?" Hastily, "No, Father." Frances was upstairs too. "Girl, have *you* taken my tweezers?" "No, Father." The Judge stomped to the top of the stairs. "Now where are those boys; can't have a thing of my own. —*Boys.*" A silence and then a "huh?" and a "what?" "What have *you* done with my tweezers?" roared the Judge. Then 'midst the chorus of disavowals and denials, Floss came to the bottom of the stairs. Very meekly she inquired, "Why, Frank, will you need them before dinner?" "Well, no, but I'd like to know where they are!" "Well, uh, Frank, I, uh,—I've been using them—to pull out the *pin feathers* in the *turkey!*" Never have I seen such an expression as whoopzed across the Judge's face! And he walked up and down the hall for fifteen minutes, stroking his whiskers and repeating, "Well, that Floss girl, that Floss girl!" while Frances and I chuckled incessantly; the boys shouted with glee; and Mother retired into the kitchen, a little confused, but on the whole, triumphant.

Yesterday we drove up to Beardstown to see George and Winifred. They are coming here to lunch tomorrow. George has a moustache, much tweeds, a red tie, and an extra fifty pounds around the middle. He sat joggling his baby on his knee while Marshall sat in the corner and crowed, "Isn't that the prettiest picture!" Uncle Will Luthringer, who is stone deaf, kept shouting at Ouie, "Can you hear me now, Pearl?" Ouie repeatedly informed anyone who would listen that "Will is the funniest thing. Imagine *him* asking if I can hear!" while Father, who missed out on the greater part of the conversation because he couldn't hear it, confided in Marshall that it was too bad how deaf Pearl was getting!

Father, by the way, is having as much fun showing off his cheese box this year as ever before. Mother wore her pajamas (the new ones) Christmas Eve, and nearly smothered because it was a warm evening! Also, she kept insisting that the scarf was too pretty for her, must have been for one of us —we convinced her. Mans thinks his striped tie is "sure keen"; Sam wore his to the Christmas dance. Frances' shoes are darling. Not all my artful persuasion could make her part with them even for a night! And have I told you how much I liked *Story?* Thanks, Mr. and Mrs. Joyce.

Love,
BEATER

Noteworthy in the preceding letter are:

1. The selection of material: family activities and personalities of interest to the writer and the receiver.

2. The use of private language: "Sisser"; "Floss" for Mother; "whoopzed"; the signature "Beater," a nickname, instead of Beatrice.

3. The lively, informal, but by no means slovenly, style.

4. The very good use of anecdote, somewhat exaggerated for effect: Mother opening the package; Father and the tweezers; Ouie, Uncle Will, and Father in conversation.

5. The organization of material about a few central points: fully developed anecdotes about Mother, Father, Ouie, and Uncle Will.

6. The concrete development of anecdote by particular detail ("Floss came to the foot of the stairs"; "George has a moustache, much tweeds, a red tie, and an extra fifty pounds around the middle"), and by dialogue or quotation ("Can't keep a thing in the house," and Mother's explanation for opening the package).

7. The effective beginning and ending achieved by the initial and final reference to *Story* magazine.

EXERCISES

I. Who is the best conversationalist you know? After listening to his conversation, jot down an analysis of what makes it good.

II. Write a short informal essay on poor or boring or irritating conversationalists you have known.

III. Make a list of the faults in public speakers which you find most trying. Consider teachers, ministers, lecturers, and other speakers whom you have heard.

IV. Get an examination written by an A student in a course you are taking, and compare your examination paper with his. (This is to be done, of course, when the papers are returned, not during the examination.)

V. Write a business letter to the bursar of your college, explaining that you have been charged a laboratory fee for a course which you are not taking.

VI. Write your insurance company an account of an automobile accident in which you have been involved.

VII. Following the suggestions given in the section on writing letters of application, write a letter applying for the kind of position you hope you will be applying for ten years from now. You will, of course, need to give a fictitious account of your experience during this ten-year period.

VIII. Write a note thanking a friend who has sent you a present.

IX. You, a member of the freshman class, have received the following formal invitation. Write two answers, one accepting it, the other regretting that you cannot accept.

President and Mrs. James Fairfax Brown
request the pleasure of the company of
the members of the Freshman Class
at a reception at Newton Hall
On Saturday, October the fifteenth
at four o'clock

R.S.V.P.

X. The mother of one of your college friends has invited you to Thanksgiving dinner. Write a note accepting or declining the invitation.

XI. Write a personal letter to a close family friend or a relative, describing some of the things that happened in your home during the Thanksgiving or Christmas holiday, or on some other occasion when the family was assembled.

XII.

DEAR MOTHER,

I've been so busy I haven't had a minute to write. They certainly pile on the work here. I'm having a good time though. Hope you're all right. Tell Dad I really need an extra five dollars.

Your loving son,
HENRY

Expand the letter above into a good personal letter, drawing on your own experience to do so. (If you don't need the five dollars, you may omit that part of the letter.)

Chapter Thirteen

Reading

THE WORK DONE in recent years in reading clinics has shown that many students do poorly in their college courses because they have not learned to read efficiently. Many students, furthermore, have missed the pleasure and the profit that come from reading widely and well, because they have not developed skill in absorbing material from the printed page. Skillful reading involves many things: an ability to grasp ideas quickly and accurately; an adequate vocabulary; a power of active concentration on the material and of critical judgment in evaluating it; and an ability to apply different methods of reading to different kinds of material. In this chapter we are discussing three kinds of reading: rapid reading, reading for study, and critical reading. These three kinds of reading are not mutually exclusive. Although much of the material designed for college study cannot be read at high speed, practice in reading rapidly is likely to improve reading for study; and a critical evaluation of the material should be part of any kind of reading. The three sections of this chapter, then, are simply three different approaches to the complex problem of reading. Their combined purpose is to help the student gain more knowledge and pleasure from the reading he is required to do and the reading he freely chooses to do.

I. RAPID READING

The average college freshman reads ordinary material (novels, magazine articles, nonfiction of a nontechnical nature, etc.) at a rate of 300 to 325 words a minute. With practice in more rapid reading he can increase his rate to 450 or 500 words a minute, with no loss of comprehension. A number of college students read 200 words a minute or less; that is, they labor through their reading at a rate which is normal for fifth graders in elementary school, and which is an appalling handicap at college level. With practice they can double their reading speed, and, at the same time, increase their comprehension. To save reading time, to be able to read twice as much printed material in a given number of hours, is an obvious gain; but the most important point about learning to read rapidly is this: *as reading speed increases, comprehension nearly always increases too.*

The slow reader (who, incidentally, is usually sure that he *must* read slowly in order to understand), laboriously reading each separate word, sometimes every separate syllable, becomes so involved in the individual words that he loses the thread of the thought, the sweep and development of the whole idea. He is likely to emerge from his reading with only a cloudy impression of the organization of the material, and little sense of the relative weight of its different parts. He has been lost in the woods of words. Furthermore, because his plodding reading is difficult, he tires quickly; his attention is easily diverted, and his concentration is poor. When he learns to absorb whole phrases at a glance, to move swiftly from idea to idea instead of slowly from word to word, he grasps the material more quickly and easily, and his comprehension is clearer and more accurate.

Slow reading may be caused by defects in vision or muscular control, for which the advice of an oculist is needed. If one's vision is good, or has been corrected by glasses, increasing reading speed and with it comprehension is surprisingly simple. It requires an easily made analysis of one's own reading habits, and a few weeks of practice in eliminating bad habits by forced rapid reading for a short time every day.

The first step for the student interested in more rapid reading is to ascertain his present reading rate. He should read for five or ten minutes, at his usual rate, part of a magazine, a biography, or a book of informal essays. The number of words he has read can quickly be estimated by counting the words in several lines and multiplying the average number of words in a line by the number of lines read; that total number of words, divided by the exact number of minutes taken for the reading gives him, of course, his reading rate in words per minute. If that rate is between 300 and 325, his reading speed is average, but it can and should be increased for this kind of reading. If his rate is below 180, he can be reasonably sure that he is a word-for-word reader.

Word-for-word reading, that is, reading and silently pronouncing every word, is probably the greatest obstacle to efficient reading. The fast and skillful reader absorbs whole phrases in an instant, wasting no time on unimportant words. For example, in reading the sentence "He drove the car at a rate of seventy miles an hour around the curves of the country road," the efficient reader spends no time reading and pronouncing *the, at, a, rate, of, miles, an, hour, around, the, of, the;*

he immediately grasps the meaning first of phrases and then of the sentence through the key words, *drove, car, seventy, curves, country road*. He reads and understands the sentence, therefore, in less than half the time taken by the word-for-word reader.

A reading rate of less than 180 words a minute is, as we have said, an almost infallible indication of word-for-word reading. But the slow reader can, by several easy tests, determine for himself whether he is reading word-for-word. He may be lip-reading, that is, moving his lips to form each word as he reads; a friend can watch him and tell him if he has this habit. He may keep his lips still, but pronounce each word in his throat; if he reads with his fingers on his voice box and if he feels a constant vibration, he will know that he is doing this silent "vocalizing." He may be an "auditory" reader, not actually vocalizing the words, but hearing the sound of each word in his mind; honest examination of his own experience while reading will tell him whether or not this is true. Auditory reading is usually faster and less tiring than lip-reading or vocalizing, since it does not involve muscular activity; but it is a form of word-for-word reading and is therefore undesirable except in special circumstances.[1]

A bad habit second only to word-for-word reading is the habit of "regression," that is, looking back and reading again phrases or whole sentences. Regression sometimes comes from faulty vision, sometimes from inattention or lack of interest. Often it is simply a habit born of a nervous fear of not understanding in only one reading. Habitual regression makes comprehension more difficult, as well as slower, because it interrupts the sequence of thought.

Another bad habit, akin to word-for-word reading, is making too many eye-stops, or "fixations," in reading a line of print. When one's eyes are moving across a line, they are not seeing; when the eyes stop, one sees and reads. The poor reader commonly makes six or seven fixations in a single line. The good reader usually needs only three for an ordinary line on a printed page. His eyes move, not in numerous short jerks, but in a rhythmical motion, across the lines, and from one line to the next; he has developed a wider eye-span, so that in his few fixations his eyes take in a number of words. He reads twice as fast as the reader who stops twice as often in a line, and he absorbs more of the sense because he gets it in larger and more meaningful units. The reader can determine the number of fixations (and also regressions) he makes by putting a mirror on one page of a book,

[1] In reading poetry and certain types of prose, auditory reading is appropriate and desirable. It is undesirable when it is used indiscriminatingly with all types of material. Trying to speed-read all the time is as unwise as reading always at an inappropriately slow rate.

reading from the opposite page, and having a friend look over his shoulder and watch his eye movements in the mirror as he reads.

When the reader knows through actual experimentation what his reading rate is, and what bad habits of word-for-word reading, regression, or too frequent fixations are slowing his reading, he is ready to embark on a program of eliminating his bad habits and improving both his speed and his comprehension. The program is simple: for a few minutes every day, he should practice reading rather easy material (newspapers, magazines, any light reading) at a rate *too fast for comfort*. Not worrying about how much he is comprehending (and his comprehension will at first be poor), he should concentrate on pushing through the material, covering as much ground as he can, and not allowing himself to indulge in any particular bad reading habit which he has. If he forces himself as he should through this practice reading, he will have no time to stop at and absorb unimportant words, no time to vocalize, no time to look back and re-read. The forced rapid reading not only helps to eliminate retarding habits; it develops a new mechanical skill; and, before long, the reader will find that increased comprehension results from new habits of increased eye-span, fewer and shorter fixations, and continuous, rhythmical phrase-reading.

Dr. Robert M. Bear, director of the reading clinic at Dartmouth, says this about the principle and the experience of rapid reading:

The fundamental rule for increasing reading speed is simply this: *For five minutes every day for a month, force yourself to read a little faster than is comfortable.* Don't worry if occasionally you miss the exact meaning of a phrase, sentence, or even a paragraph. Just keep plowing ahead, grasping the main theme and letting the niceties of expression go hang. It's a good idea to keep a record of how many words you cover during five-minute sessions each day. To simplify the word-count, just figure the average number of words to a line and multiply by the number of lines you have read.

From my experience with hundreds of students, I can predict what will happen. On the first day your impression of what you are reading will be hazy and vague, like looking at a landscape through a dirty windowpane. But gradually, after five or ten days, you will begin to digest more of the meaning; and by the end of thirty days you will be comprehending even more than when you started. And then, paradoxically, you will discover that you are reading at about twice your previous clip.

The effects of such a short self-training program in overcoming the bad reading habits of years seem too good to be true; but they are true. The present writers have seen striking results even from a brief speed-reading project in which college freshmen read at a faster-than-comfortable speed one essay a week for eight weeks, with a comprehension test on each essay. One girl, who began by reading 200 words a minute, with comprehension scores of 50 and 60 out of a possible 100, was, on the last four essays, reading at a rate of 700 words a minute, with comprehension scores of 100. Delighted with her progress, but hardly trusting it, she continued to test herself on other reading; she found that her normal pace was now 500 to 600 words a minute. She was able to read her assignments in history and government at a rate of over 400 words a minute, and her work in those courses, with which she had had serious difficulty, improved markedly with the improvement in reading skill. Another student, who began the timed-reading essays with a good reading pace of 375 words a minute, was, by the end of the project, reading at the exceptional speed of 800 words a minute; his comprehension scores, always high, remained 90 and 100. These two cases are, of course, spectacular, and not typical. Very common, though, among some 600 students, was an increase in reading speed of 150 to 200 words a minute, with no loss, and usually with a gain in comprehension.

Many students are blocked in their reading by a "slow-but-sure" superstition; they believe, mistakenly, that the hard way must be the best way, and they are gripped by a fear of not understanding if they try to "rush through" their reading. Practicing speed on reading which is nonessential, and learning for themselves that they can comprehend as well or better once they have adjusted to a faster rate releases them from this fear; they are free to strike a new pace which is right for them, and to adjust that pace to different kinds of reading. One of the problems of the slow reader is that he reads at an equal rate, with equal care, essential and nonessential material, an assignment in economics and a light novel or magazine article. The usual result is that he has no time for reading which is not immediately essential; since reading is so difficult for him, he has no experience with reading for pleasure, and little experience of enjoying what he is required to read.

It is important, in beginning a program of rapid reading, to choose for the experiment fairly easy, unrequired reading. A period of confusion, of blurred comprehension, is inevitably a first stage in changing one's reading habits. Students commonly find, as they practice rapid reading and develop new reading habits, that they can prepare more rapidly and with better understanding their assignments in "reading courses" like history, government, economics, English, and sociology. But to begin by speed-reading those assignments would be most unwise. A large part of the good result of forced rapid reading comes from the relaxing knowledge that clear comprehension is not essential in the first stages of the experiment.

Students often find it interesting to speed-read a popular or semi-popular biography, reading the book a half hour a day at a faster-than-comfortable rate, and keeping a chart of the number of pages they read each day. Experimenting with a book instead of with various short pieces has advantages: the average number of words to a page can be determined early, so that the work of keeping a record

RECORD OF RAPID READING

Book:			
Average number of words to a page:			
Day	Time spent reading	Pages read	Words per minute

It is interesting, too, to record each day's results in graph form:

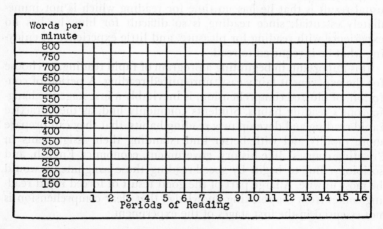

Words per minute																
800																
750																
700																
650																
600																
550																
500																
450																
400																
350																
300																
250																
200																
150																

Periods of Reading: 1 2 3 4 5 6 7 8 9 10 11 12 13 14 15 16

is simplified; the level of writing, its degree of difficulty, is more likely to be constant; and if the biography is interesting, it provides an incentive for the daily reading practice. Some instructors assign a book to be read in this way, knowing that the reports written on the book may not show the detailed knowledge usually expected in book reports, but knowing, too, that practice in rapid reading and improvement in general reading skill are worth far more to students than clear comprehension of a single book.

For the convenience of students beginning their rapid-reading program with a book, we are printing on the opposite page a chart on which each day's reading may be recorded.

We have said that comprehension will be blurred in the early period of forced rapid reading; this is natural, and by no means a reason for concern or discouragement; accurate comprehension comes after new habits are established. Nor should one be discouraged if, after initial progress, he seems to hit a dead level, a "plateau" at which neither his speed nor his comprehension improves. These plateaus are normal in learning any new skill; they are simply temporary halts, after which progress is usually more rapid than before the plateau was reached. A graph of a student's progress in rapid reading during a trial period of fifteen or twenty days of forced rapid reading is likely to look somewhat like this:

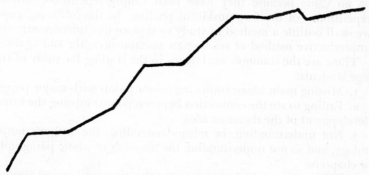

Keeping on with the faster-than-comfortable reading, forcing one's eyes to take in more words at a single fixation, allowing no time for the uneconomical indulgences of regression or vocalizing, will produce results, and will open an entirely new reading experience to the poor reader.

College students should not be content with their reading until they are covering ordinary nontechnical material at a rate of 400 to 500 words a minute, and understanding it well.

II. READING FOR STUDY

In reading for study, speed is a secondary and sometimes completely irrelevant consideration. One may wish, and need, to spend fifteen minutes absorbing the full meaning and implication of several lines of poetry, or of a brief formula in organic chemistry; auditory reading—letting each word sound in one's mind—may be the best reading for literature in which rhythm and sound are important parts of the full meaning the writer is trying to communicate. At the same time, the student who has developed the rapid-reading skill discussed in the preceding section is likely to be a better reader of any material, however complex, because he has learned to grasp meaning quickly from phrases, without spending time on unimportant words; and because he has developed the habit of continuous forward movement in reading, which enables him to see the sequence and development of ideas.

Students who have done poorly on quizzes and examinations often say, "But I read the material over three times"—or "four times." They usually *have* read the material three or four times, but that fact is not a credit to them; it is evidence that they are in a groove of ineffectual reading. The last two or three readings have been of little or no value because they have been simply repetitions—diluted repetitions—of the first unskillful reading. In the following pages we shall outline a method of study to replace this unsystematic and unproductive method of reading an assignment again and again.

These are the common weaknesses in the reading for study of college students:

1. Missing main ideas; confusing minor points with major points.

2. Failing to see the connection between points; missing the broad development of the theme or idea.

3. Not understanding, or misunderstanding, the author's terminology, and so not understanding the meaning of whole paragraphs or chapters.

4. Taking notes which misrepresent the organization and emphasis of the material, and which are, consequently, useless either for daily preparation or for review.

No simple remedy can be prescribed for all of these weaknesses; inadequate background in the field, inadequate reading experience, and inadequate vocabulary are often at least partially responsible for them, and there is no quick, easy cure for such deficiencies. But most students find a marked improvement in their grasp of a subject as soon as they learn a technique or method of study. The method may differ slightly with different material, but reading for study should, in general, consist of these four steps:

1. *A preliminary survey* (if the material is expository), which gives the reader a skeleton outline of what the author is going to say, and enables him to fit particular facts and details into a general pattern when he begins to read. This preliminary survey is made by looking at the table of contents, which usually lists the main points discussed in each chapter of a book; and, chiefly, by leafing through the pages assigned and making a mental note of the headings and subheadings by which the author has indicated the organization of his material. Most college texts have such headings, in capital letters, in boldface type or italics, or in marginal notations. (With books which do not have headings or marginal notations, the best way to get an idea of the organization and general development is to skim along looking at topic sentences. The first or second sentence of a paragraph will usually be a topic sentence.) Often, too, the first paragraphs of a chapter state what is to be covered in the chapter, and the concluding paragraphs summarize what has been said; reading these paragraphs may be a valuable part of the preliminary survey. With a little practice, students can make an efficient survey of thirty or forty pages in five or ten minutes. These minutes are well spent. Having in mind the outline of the material, and the names, at least, of the main points, the student can read with a sense of direction, and knowledge of the whole plan. This initial survey does much to prevent the first two of the weaknesses in study listed above—missing the main ideas, and failing to see connections between ideas.

2. *Reading the material through* to see the development of the ideas noted in the preliminary survey, *without stopping* to re-read difficult passages, to look up words, or to take notes. The reading should be as rapid as is consistent with the student's understanding of the material (here, of course, the rapid reader has a great advantage over the slow reader), and the reading should be continuous. It is wise to mark with a check in the margin passages which seem important, and with a check or question mark passages which are unclear; but breaking the reading by puzzling long over a passage, or by stopping to take notes, will interfere with one's grasp of the sequence and development of ideas. Also, one is likely to waste time with such stops: a momentarily unclear passage may be clarified by the later context; and notes taken before the reader knows surely what is most important in the material are likely to be useless or misleading.

3. *Checking through the material, and re-reading with care any sections which are difficult or obscure.* This is a very different pro-

cedure from simply reading the assignment over again. The reader should look once more at section headings, and at paragraph beginnings; if he can mentally fill in their content, he can go on to the next section without re-reading the material here. He should concentrate on passages about which he is vague, or which, in his first reading, he has checked for later consideration. This is the stage of reading for study in which one may profitably spend fifteen minutes over a few lines of poetry, a formula, or a paragraph of philosophical reasoning.

An important part of this process of checking and selective re-reading should be fixing in mind not only the topic ideas of the assignment, but the meaning of key words *as the author uses them*. We have listed as a common study fault the misunderstanding of the author's terminology. Sometimes the student needs to consult his dictionary in order to understand the author's language; more often he needs to consider carefully the context of a troublesome word or term. In this book, for example, we have used repeatedly the word *context*. The student who slides over the early definition and the use-in-context of the word, and who attaches to it an idea of his own that context means "text" or "content," will miss the meaning of a number of sentences in which that word is used. In economics, a number of familiar words, like *wealth, goods, cost, scarcity,* are used in special senses; students have difficulty in understanding a text in economics if they assume that they know the meaning of such words, and fail to read carefully the economist's definition of them. Some historians use the word *revolution* to describe social or economic upheaval or change; students who take for granted that "revolution" always involves the violent overthrow of a political regime will be misled by overlooking the writer's definition of the word.

Part of checking and selective re-reading, too, should be active thinking about the material presented, and perhaps some criticism or evaluation of the author's opinions and techniques. The complex problem of evaluating what one reads is discussed more fully in the next section. Evaluation is not always possible for the student reading material in a field which is completely new to him. But thinking about the material, being alert and curious about new ideas and the implications of those ideas, and relating those ideas to his own interests and experience are certainly important parts of good reading in any field, and of education in general.

4. *Taking notes.* Since good notes represent, in concise form, the organization and the most important ideas of a body of material, the student is in no position to take useful notes until he knows the organization and the central ideas of what he is reading. Steps 3 and

4 in this process of reading for study may be combined; that is, the reader may take notes as he checks the material and re-reads the difficult passages. But he should not take notes until he has completed his first reading of the assignment, and until the outline of the material and the major ideas are clear to him.

III. EVALUATING WHAT ONE READS

If it were possible to establish general hard-and-fast standards for judging everything that we read, analyzing and assessing a particular communication would be simple. It seems that we should be able to say that all good writing must have such characteristics of style as correctness, clarity, economy, emphasis, concreteness, interest, and must contain relevant and true information. When we consider various kinds of writing, however—say a cookbook, an economics text, an editorial, a magazine article, a *New Yorker* profile, a political speech, a personal letter, an informal essay, a short story written in dialect, a poem—we see that a general standard cannot apply to all of them, and is more likely to mislead us than to help us.

Because different kinds of writing aim at different effects and different kinds of excellence, we must reach our evaluation, not by trying to apply a single rigid standard, but by looking steadily at the communication itself and by judging it first *objectively,* according to the success of the writer in achieving his purpose; and then *personally,* according to our beliefs and values. The whole process of evaluation can be described as follows: first the reader suspends judgment and tries by analysis to gain a clear understanding of the communication; second, he determines in the light of his analysis just what the writer's intention was and with what skill the writer has accomplished that intention; and third, he arrives at his personal evaluation, determining the worth and truth of the communication *for him.*

The preliminary step, gaining an impartial understanding of the communication, calls for some method of analysis. The method recommended here is suggested by Rudyard Kipling:

> I keep six honest serving men
> (They taught me all I know):—
> Their names are What and Why and When
> And How and Where and Who.

These six serving men supply us with the questions we need to answer in order to understand a piece of writing. For some types of communication some of the questions may be irrelevant or inappropriate, but the general method intelligently adapted can be applied with profit to all types of writing.

Since it is sometimes easier to answer one question first, sometimes another, the more detailed suggestions given below do not necessarily represent the sequence of steps in the analysis. Usually it is best to start with the question that we can answer with most certainty.

1. *When* and *where*. Knowing just when and where a communication appeared may help us judge the reliability of the communication and the intention of the writer. An article on the effects of alcohol published in a medical journal in 1951 would obviously be more authoritative and trustworthy than a tract published by the Prohibition Party in 1918.

2. *How*. An examination of how a communication is written can do much to reveal the character of the writer and to afford a surer knowledge of his intention. The reader should give particular consideration to: level and choice of language; sentence structure, rhythm, alliteration, and other aspects of style; use of the techniques of slanting and charging; the way the writer reasons if reasoning is involved; the attitude of the writer toward his reader, his subject, and himself; the use of generalizations and substantiating particulars.

3. *What*. The "what," equivalent to the plain-sense meaning of the communication, is, of course, always important. The reader should as far as possible reduce what is said to referential, uncharged language. He is then in a better position to make an unprejudiced judgment of the subject matter. This kind of referential restatement is particularly useful in examining writing which aims to persuade or to convince the reader.

4. *Who*. The more we know about the background, knowledge, experience, and reputation of a writer, the more we are helped in judging what he says. If we have no information about him, we can often deduce a great deal from the "how" and "what" of his communication. Is he an educated man? Does he have special knowledge of his subject? Does he seem to be presenting his material fairly? Is his use of English fair, good, or excellent? What attitude does he take toward his reader and himself? What seems to be his position or profession?

5. *Why*. Sometimes the "why," the intention, is apparent on the face of the communication, as it is in a mathematics text; sometimes it is subtly concealed under charged language and specious logic, as it usually is in propaganda and advertising. A careful reader will always be alert to the concealed intention, which often is to be discovered only by close examination of inconspicuous slanting or use

of lightly charged words. After he has completed his six-point analysis, he should reconsider in the light of the other five points his interpretation of the "why." He needs to be sure he has interpreted the why (intention) correctly; if he fails here, his later judgments will have little validity.

The audience for whom a piece of writing is intended may determine to a considerable extent the "how" of the communication, and to some extent the "what" and "why." Sometimes the reader may profitably add to Kipling's six serving men one more—*To Whom?* That is, for what audience, or what kind of audience, was this communication written?

In applying the whole method of analysis described here, it is essential that the reader suspend judgment, that is, compel himself to hold his emotions in check and to be scrupulously fair in analyzing each point. Practicing this kind of fairness puts a great strain on intellectual integrity. It requires that the reader make an honest and self-forgetting effort to follow as exactly as possible the "what" (the plain sense) of the communicator. He must resist the very strong temptation (1) to twist the words of the communicator to fit his own meaning for them, (2) to close his mind to views that are different from his own, and (3) to accept or reject facts and judgments and attitudes before he has made a fair effort to follow and to understand the whole communication. In analyzing the "why" and "how" he should take for granted, unless there is evidence to the contrary, the honesty and good intention of writers who express opinions contrary to his own, and he should not accept uncritically the facts and judgments of those most able to mislead him—people who share or appear to share his opinions, attitudes, and prejudices.

After the reader has completed his analysis, he is ready to decide how well the communicator has used the means at his disposal—organization, facts, and language—to achieve his intention. In this *objective* judgment he is not interested in the truth or value of the communication; he is simply considering the writer's success in achieving his end, whatever that end may be. One can, for example, admire Hitler's skill as a propagandist, even though one condemns the purpose for which Hitler was using language; one can admire the skill or craftsmanship of a poet or short-story writer even though the particular type of poem or short story is not pleasing to one's taste.

Thus far the reader has been primarily concerned with understanding the communication and then with answering two questions about it: "What is the writer trying to do?" and "How well has he achieved his intention?" The final question is, "What is my evaluation of the whole communication?" Now the reader can fairly let his tastes, his code of morality and his view of "truth" come into play. He can say, "Hitler was a skillful propagandist, but I have read *Mein Kampf* and have thought about it, and I am convinced that he was wrong on these points: . . ." He can say, "I have given this poem or short story a fair reading and I understand what the writer is trying to do and how he has done it [or I honestly don't understand]; I regard it as good literature [or as poor literature] for these reasons: . . ." This final step, the *personal* evaluation, is usually almost automatic. Executing it is like deciding whether we like a house after we have lived in it for some time. We know all the facts about it; evaluating is now simply a matter of balancing merits and defects, and then expressing our judgment accurately.

Another remark about evaluation is appropriate here. There are some communications which, even after our best efforts, we know we can not evaluate with any sense of assurance. Our uncertainty may be produced by lack of sufficient knowledge or lack of experience with certain types or techniques of writing. A fair reader, for example, might read in different newspapers two contradictory accounts of a labor dispute, one presenting the side of the employer, the other the side of the union. In a complicated dispute of this sort one can't reach a sure judgment without detailed knowledge of many facts. Here the best the reader can do is to arrive at as sound a judgment as he can in the light of the facts that he knows, to realize that he may be wrong, and to hold himself ready to change his opinion when additional facts throw more light on the subject. In our complex modern society many of our opinions need to be held in this tentative way.

In judging writing which calls for special techniques of reading or for special background—poetry, for example, experimental novels, the literature of the past—the critic again needs to make a personal judgment as best he can, but he needs also to realize that his lack of special knowledge prevents his finding in his reading what a trained reader finds. To say that *he* has been able to find little of value in such writing may be to state a fact; but to say that there is no value in it is like saying that a foreign language has no meaning. One should learn the language or recognize his ignorance of it.

A final note: there is some danger that the procedure of evaluation presented here may sound much more formidable and more time-consuming than it actually is; the reader may simply throw up his hands and say, "If I have to go through all that to reach a critical evaluation, I'll just keep my prejudices." If the reader will suspend judgment about this method of evaluation and will give it a fair trial, he will find that learning to evaluate critically is comparable to learning to play a good game of bridge or chess—and is perhaps less difficult. Bridge players who pause for only a moment and then play a difficult hand rapidly and skillfully, chess players who can look at the board and plan twelve moves ahead, achieve with ease and assurance feats of analysis beyond the comprehension of the novice. The practiced reader analyzes and evaluates what he reads with similar speed and assurance and with a greater sense of reward.

EXERCISES

The following passages are taken out of their context and are presented without any of the information the reader usually has about the author and the date and occasion of the communication. Since the passages are given without the clues that usually help shape judgment, the analysis and the evaluation of them present a particular problem and challenge. Working over the passages and arriving at judgments about them will give concentrated practice in the kind of critical reading outlined in the last section of this chapter, and will sharpen perceptiveness and skill in interpretation.

The order of analysis will not be the same for each passage; the following questions, however, should be applied to each, and answered in all possible detail:

1. What is the plain sense of the passage? (The *What*)
2. Are there any clues as to the *When* and *Where*? Is the writing modern? Do any allusions date it or place it? Do you think it is part of a speech, a letter, a story, a textbook, or an essay? Under what circumstances was this communication made?
3. What can you say about the style and use of language? (The *How*)
4. What seems to be the author's intention? (The *Why*)
5. For what kind of audience was this intended? To what kind of audience would it appeal? (*To Whom*)
6. What conclusions can you draw about the writer of the passage? (The *Who*)
7. What, after your analysis, is your personal reaction to this piece of writing? Do you like it, dislike it? Why?

(1)

There is no hope whatever in the Governor's message for even simple justice to the small property owners of this state who have been held down in a brutal vise of skyrocketing operating costs, confiscatory taxation and frozen rents.

The Governor has clearly knelt in meek obeisance to the Communists, the left wingers, the fellow travelers, and the bureaucrats who would foist on the Commonwealth all the Gestapo tactics of the now defunct and discredited OPA. A state rent control bureau which the Governor demands would bring about perpetual regimentation and a police state in fact.

(2)

For the general use of the urban citizenry several hundred "parks of culture and rest" have been laid out in the various cities of the Soviet Union. In Moscow the Central Park of Culture and Rest contains grounds for sport, entertainment, theaters, cinema houses, and a "Town of Children" where parents may leave their offspring while enjoying the facilities of the Park. The parents may employ their time reading in libraries, listening to lectures, visiting picture galleries, or viewing the exhibitions in figures, posters, and diagrams of the achievements of the Soviet Union.

Excursions into the country or to parks of culture and rest are arranged for families on rest days and holidays. These would correspond in nature to the American family picnic. Similarly, trips to the city are arranged for peasant families for recreational purposes.

One of the most notable developments in the Soviet Union has been the rise of innumerable technical, historical, literary, educational, art and other museums. Some of the palaces of the Tsar and former nobility are preserved as museums. The role of the museums is partly instructive and partly propagandistic.

(3)

Let us reflect in another way, and we shall see that there is great reason to hope that death is a good, for one of two things: either death is a state of nothingness and utter unconsciousness, or, as men say, there is a change and migration of the soul from this world to another. Now if you suppose that there is no consciousness, but a sleep like the sleep of him who is undisturbed even by the sight of dreams, death will be an unspeakable gain. For if a person were to select the night in which his sleep was undisturbed even by dreams, and were to compare with this the other days and nights of his life, and then were to tell us how many days and nights he had passed in the course of his life better and more pleasantly than this one, I think that any man, I will not say a private man, but even the great king will not find many such days or nights, when compared with the others. Now if death is like this, I say that to die is gain; for eternity is then only a single night. But if death is the journey to another place, and there, as men say, all the dead are, what good, O my friends and judges, can be greater than this? If indeed when the pilgrim arrives in the world below, he is delivered from the professors of justice in this world, and finds the true judges who are said to give judgment there, . . . that pilgrimage will be worth making. What would not a man give if he might converse with Orpheus and Musæus and Hesiod and Homer? Nay, if this be true, let me die again and again. I, too, shall have a wonderful interest in a place where I can converse with Palamedes, and Ajax the son of Telamon, and other heroes of old, who have suffered death through an unjust judgment; and there will be no small pleasure, as I think, in comparing my own suffering with theirs. Above all, I shall be able to continue my search into true and false knowledge; as in this world, so also in that; I shall find out who is wise, and who pretends to be wise, and is not.

(4)

Society is commonly too cheap. We meet at very short intervals, not having had time to acquire any new value for each other. We meet at meals three times a-day, and give each other a new taste of that old musty cheese that we are. We have had to agree on a certain set of rules, called etiquette and politeness, to make this frequent meeting tolerable and that we need not come to open war. We meet at the post office, and at the sociable, and about the fireside every night; we live thick and are in each other's way, and stumble over one another, and I think that we thus lose some respect for one another. Certainly less frequency would suffice for all important and hearty communications. Consider the girls in a factory—never alone, hardly in their dreams. It would be better if there were but one inhabitant to a square mile, as where I live. The value of a man is not in his skin, that we should touch him.

(5)

But when men have realized that time has upset many fighting faiths, they may come to believe even more than they believe the very foundation of their own conduct that the ultimate good desired is better reached by free trade in ideas—that the best test of truth is the power of the thought to get itself accepted in the competition of the market, and that truth is the only ground on which their wishes safely can be carried out. That at any rate is the theory of our Constitution. It is an experiment, as all life is an experiment. Every year if not every day we have to wager our salvation upon some prophecy based upon imperfect knowledge. While that experiment is part of our system, I think that we should be eternally vigilant against attempts to check the expression of opinions that we loathe and believe to be fraught with death, unless they so imminently threaten immediate interference with the lawful and pressing purposes of the law that an immediate check is required to save the country.

(6)

The bedrock on which the scholarly activities of a university are founded is a charter of free inquiry; without this you may have an institution of advanced education, a technical school or a military college, for example, but you do not have a university. I am sure we are all agreed on that. There should be no barriers to an objective analysis of every phase of our national life. No compromise with this principle is possible even in days of an armed truce. The nation has a right to demand of its educational institutions that the teachers dealing with controversial subjects shall be fearless seekers of the truth and careful scholars rather than propagandists. But granted honesty, sincerity and ability there must be tolerance of a wide diversity of opinion. Indeed, this diversity of opinion is not only basic for the welfare of our universities but for that of the entire nation. For in a democracy with our traditions only those reasoned convictions which emerge from diversity of opinion can lead to that unity and national solidarity so essential for the welfare of our country. Essential not only for our own security but a requisite for intelligent action toward the end we all desire, namely, the conversion of the present armed truce into a firm and lasting peace.

(7)

The statesmen of both of the groups of nations now arrayed against one another have said, in terms that could not be misinterpreted, that it was no part of the purpose they had in mind to crush their antagonists. But the implications of these assurances may not be equally clear to all—may not be the same on both sides of the water. I think it will be serviceable if I attempt to set forth what we understand them to be.

They imply, first of all, that it must be a peace without victory. It is not pleasant to say this. I beg that I may be permitted to put my own interpretation upon it and that it may be understood that no other interpretation was in my thought. I am seeking only to face realities and to face them without soft concealments. Victory would mean peace forced upon the loser, a victor's terms imposed upon the vanquished. It would be accepted in humiliation, under duress, at an intolerable sacrifice, and would leave a sting, a resentment, a bitter memory upon which terms of peace would rest, not permanently, but only as upon quicksand. Only a peace between equals can last.

(8)

Sometimes a war is entered upon, because the enemy is too strong, and sometimes because he is too weak. Sometimes our neighbors want the things which we have, or have the things which we want; and we both fight, till they take ours or give us theirs. It is a very justifiable cause of a war to invade a country after the people have been wasted by famine, destroyed by pestilence, or embroiled by factions among themselves. It is justifiable to enter into war against our nearest ally, when one of his towns lies convenient for us, or a territory of land, that would render our dominions round and complete. If a prince sends forces into a nation, where the people are poor and ignorant, he may lawfully put half of them to death, and make slaves of the rest, in order to civilize and reduce them from their barbarous way of living. It is a very kingly, honourable, and frequent practice, when one prince desires the assistance of another to secure him against an invasion, that the assistant, when he hath driven out the invader, should seize on the dominions himself, and kill, imprison or banish the prince he came to relieve. . . . For these reasons, the trade of a soldier is held the most honourable of all others; because a soldier is . . . hired to kill in cold blood as many of his own species, who have never offended him, as possibly he can.

(9)

There is a vague popular belief that lawyers are necessarily dishonest. I say vague, because when we consider to what extent confidence and honors are reposed in and conferred upon lawyers by the people, it appears improbable that their impression of dishonesty is very distinct and vivid. Yet the impression is common, almost universal. Let no young man choosing the law for a calling for a moment yield to the popular belief. Resolve to be honest at all events; and if in your own judgment you cannot be an honest lawyer, resolve to be honest without being a lawyer. Choose some other occupation, rather than one in the choosing of which you do, in advance, consent to be a knave.

(10)

The responsibility for inflation rests on the shoulders of the teachers, the veterans, the farmers, and the do-goodists. Along with the A.F. of L., C.I.O., and consumers' leagues, these pressure groups for special privilege are causing a lot of trouble. They look for special privileges for themselves from the government and expect the rest of us to pay for them.

The public confuses money with wealth. In this country money is becoming less and less stable because the government feels that it should keep prices of so many commodities higher than they would be but for the benefit of special privilege groups.

Everything from turkeys to turpentine is on the list of commodities with controlled prices stimulated by government action. It seems strange that the newspapers ignore such action when the result of it is to bring out more money for spending, which buys less and less.

Stable money that is important to those who invest in life insurance, put money in savings banks, and plan sound investments is not popular in our government today.

(11)

What kind of collectivism do we want? Most people in the United States would probably answer this question by saying: "We do not want any kind of collectivism at all." The word "collectivism" is apt to suggest the word "socialism," and Socialism is for most people the same thing as Communism. This mistake leads to a great deal of useless confusion in thinking about such matters. First of all, therefore, I wish to make perfectly clear what I mean by collectivism. By collectivism I mean no more than the governmental regulation or control of the economic life of a community. Such regulation or control may be more or less complete, so that there are different kinds of collectivism, depending on the extent to which the regulation or control is carried out and the methods by which it is achieved. To say that we do not want any kind of collectivism is merely to express a pious wish. It is not a question of what we should like if it were possible to have it, but a question of what we must accept under conditions as they exist. We already have a certain amount of collectivism, a certain amount of governmental regulation of economic life; and it is about as clearly on the cards as anything can be that we must have still more of it. . . .

Four different forms of collectivism have in fact been proposed or adopted—Socialism, Communism, Fascism, and what for lack of a better term we may call Social Democracy. We cannot reverse the historic trend towards collectivism, but we can with intelligence and determination decide whether we shall have some brand of Social Democracy rather than some brand of Socialism, Communism, or Fascism. It will clarify the issue to see how these various brands of collectivism emerged historically, in what respects they are alike, and in what respects they are different.

(12)

By *genteelism* is here to be understood the substituting, for the ordinary natural word that first suggests itself to the mind, of a synonym that is thought to be less soiled by the lips of the common herd, less familiar, less plebeian, less vulgar, less improper, less apt to come unhandsomely betwixt the wind and our nobility. The truly genteel do not offer *beer*, but *ale;* invite one to *step*, not *come*, this way; take in not *lodgers*, but *paying guests;* send their boys not to *school*, but to *college;* never *help*, but *assist*, each other to potatoes; keep *stomachs* and *domestics* instead of *bellies* and *servants;* and have quite forgotten that they could ever have been guilty of *toothpowder* and *napkins* and *underclothing*, of *before* and *except* and *about*, where nothing now will do for them but *dentifrice, serviette, lingerie, ere, save, anent*.

(13)

For there is a perennial nobleness, and even sacredness, in Work. Were he never so benighted, forgetful of his high calling, there is always hope in a man that actually and earnestly works; in Idleness alone is there perpetual despair. Work, never so Mammonish, mean, is in communication with Nature; the real desire to get Work done will itself lead one more and more to truth, to Nature's appointments and regulations, which are truth.

The latest Gospel in this world is, Know thy work and do it. 'Know thyself': long enough has that poor 'self' of thine tormented thee; thou wilt never get to 'know' it, I believe! Think it not thy business, this of knowing thyself; thou art an unknowable individual: know what thou canst work at; and work at it, like a Hercules! That will be thy better plan.

It has been written, 'an endless significance lies in Work'; a man perfects himself by working. Foul jungles are cleared away, fair seed-fields rise instead, and stately cities; and withal the man himself first ceases to be a jungle and foul unwholesome desert thereby. Consider how, even in the meanest sorts of Labour, the whole soul of a man is composed into a kind of real harmony, the instant he sets himself to work! Doubt, Desire, Sorrow, Remorse, Indignation, Despair itself, all these like hell-dogs lie beleaguering the soul of the poor dayworker, as of every man: but he bends himself with free valour against his task, and all these are stilled, all these shrink murmuring far off into their caves. The man is now a man. The blessed glow of Labour in him, is it not as purifying fire, wherein all poison is burnt up, and of sour smoke itself there is made bright blessed flame!

(14)

Dictatorship, however, involves cost which the American people will never pay: The cost of our spiritual values. The cost of the blessed right of being able to say what we please. The cost of freedom of religion. The cost of seeing our capital confiscated. The cost of being cast into a concentration camp. The cost of being afraid to walk down the street with the wrong neighbor. The cost of having our children brought up, not as free and dignified human beings, but as pawns molded and enslaved by a machine.

If the avoidance of these costs means taxes on my income; if avoiding these costs means taxes on my estate at death, I would bear those taxes willingly as the price of my breathing and my children breathing the free air of a free country, as the price of a living and not a dead world.

(15)

It is interesting to contemplate an entangled bank, clothed with many plants of many kinds, with birds singing on the bushes, with various insects flitting about, and with worms crawling through the damp earth, and to reflect that these elaborately constructed forms, so different from each other, and dependent on each other in so complex a manner, have all been produced by laws acting around us. These laws, taken in the largest sense, being Growth with Reproduction; Inheritance, which is almost implied by reproduction; Variability, from the indirect and direct action of the external conditions of life, and from use and disuse; a Ratio of Increase so high as to lead to a Struggle for Life, and as a consequence to Natural Selection, entailing Divergence of Character and the Extinction of less-improved forms. Thus, from the war of nature, from famine and death, the most exalted object which we are capable of conceiving, namely, the production of the higher animals, directly follows. There is grandeur in this view of life, with its several powers, having been originally breathed by the Creator into a few forms or into one; and that, whilst this planet has gone cycling on according to the fixed law of gravity, from so simple a beginning endless forms most beautiful and most wonderful have been, and are being, evolved.

(16)

The notions of the beginning and the end of the world entertained by our forefathers are no longer credible. It is very certain that the earth is not the chief body in the material universe, and that the world is not subordinated to man's use. It is even more certain that nature is the expression of a definite order with which nothing interferes, and that the chief business of mankind is to learn that order and govern themselves accordingly. Moreover this scientific "criticism of life" presents itself to us with different credentials from any other. It appeals not to authority, nor to what anybody may have thought or said, but to nature. It admits that all our interpretations of natural facts are more or less imperfect and symbolic, and bids the learner seek for truth not among words but among things. It warns us that the assertion which outstrips evidence is not only a blunder but a crime.

The purely classical education advocated by the representatives of the Humanists in our day, gives no inkling of all this. A man may be a better scholar than Erasmus, and know no more of the chief causes of the present intellectual fermentation than Erasmus did. Scholarly and pious persons, worthy of all respect, favour us with allocutions upon the sadness of the antagonism of science to their mediaeval way of thinking, which betray an ignorance of the first principles of scientific investigation, an incapacity for understanding what a man of science means by veracity, and an unconsciousness of the weight of established scientific truths, which is almost comical.

(17)

Fog everywhere. Fog up the river, where it flows among green aits and meadows; fog down the river, where it rolls defiled among the tiers of shipping, and the waterside pollutions of a great (and dirty) city. Fog on the Essex marshes, fog on the Kentish heights. Fog creeping into the cabooses of collier-brigs, fog lying out on the yards, and hovering in the rigging of great ships; fog drooping on the gunwales of barges and small boats. Fog in the eyes and throats of ancient Greenwich pensioners, wheezing by the firesides of their wards; fog in the stem and bowl of the afternoon pipe of the wrathful skipper, down in his close cabin; fog cruelly pinching the toes and fingers of his shivering little 'prentice boy on deck. Chance people on the bridges peeping over the parapets into a nether sky of fog, with fog all round them, as if they were up in a balloon, and hanging in the misty clouds.

Gas looming through the fog in divers places in the streets, much as the sun may, from the spongy fields, be seen to loom by husbandman and ploughboy. Most of the shops lighted two hours before their time—as the gas seems to know, for it has a haggard and unwilling look.

The raw afternoon is rawest, and the dense fog is densest, and the muddy streets are muddiest, near that leaden-headed old obstruction, appropriate ornament for the threshold of a leaden-headed old corporation: Temple Bar. And hard by Temple Bar, in Lincoln's Inn Hall, at the very heart of the fog, sits the Lord High Chancellor in his High Court of Chancery.

(18)

I got it at last, why he was all dressed up, and not carrying out the chow like he used to, and acted so important. This Greek had had a fracture of the skull, and a thing like that don't happen to a dumb cluck like him every day. He was like a wop that opens a drug store. Soon as he gets that thing that says Pharmacist, with a red seal on it, a wop puts on a gray suit, with black edges on the vest, and is so important he can't even take time to mix the pills, and wouldn't even touch a chocolate ice cream soda. This Greek was all dressed up for the same reason. A big thing had happened in his life.

(19)

England, my England! But which is my England? The stately homes of England make good photographs, and create the illusion of a connection with the Elizabethans. The handsome old halls are there, from the days of Good Queen Anne and Tom Jones. But smuts fall and blacken on the drab stucco, that has long ceased to be golden. And one by one, like the stately homes, they are abandoned. Now they are being pulled down. As for the cottages of England—there they are—great plasterings of brick dwellings on the hopeless countryside.

Now they are pulling down the stately homes, the Georgian halls are going. Fritchley, a perfect old Georgian mansion, was even now, as Connie passed in the car, being demolished. It was in perfect repair: till the war the Weatherleys had lived in style there. But now it was too big, too expensive, and the country had become too uncongenial. The gentry were departing to pleasanter places, where they could spend their money without having to see how it was made.

This is history. One England blots out another. The mines had made the halls wealthy. Now they were blotting them out, as they had already blotted out the cottages. The industrial England blots out the agricultural England. One meaning blots out another. The new England blots out the old England. And the continuity is not organic, but mechanical.

KEY TO THE SOURCES OF THE PASSAGES

(1) Speech made by a representative of a landlord's association when the Governor of Massachusetts asked for State rent control in 1947.

(2) *Communism in Action*, a booklet prepared in 1946 by the Congressional Legislative Reference Bureau of the Library of Congress.

(3) Socrates, speech at his trial, 399 B.C. (From the Jowett translation of Plato's *Apology*.)

(4) Henry David Thoreau, *Walden*, 1854.

(5) Oliver Wendell Holmes, dissenting opinion on the Abrams case, 1919.

(6) James B. Conant, The President's Report to the Board of Overseers, Harvard University, 1947.

(7) Woodrow Wilson, address to the Senate, January 22, 1917.

(8) Jonathan Swift, *Gulliver's Travels*, 1726.

(9) Abraham Lincoln, notes for a law lecture, 1850.

(10) Speech reported in Boston newspapers, August, 1948.

(11) Carl Becker, *How New Will the Better World Be?* 1944.

(12) H. W. Fowler, *Modern English Usage*, 1926.

(13) Thomas Carlyle, *Past and Present*, 1843.

(14) Franklin D. Roosevelt, Message to Congress, January 1, 1939.

(15) Charles Darwin, *The Origin of Species*, 1859.

(16) Thomas H. Huxley, an address delivered at the opening of Sir Josiah Mason's Science College at Birmingham, England, 1880.

(17) Charles Dickens, *Bleak House*, 1852-3.

(18) James M. Cain, *The Postman Always Rings Twice*, 1934.

(19) D. H. Lawrence, *Lady Chatterley's Lover*, 1928.

Chapter Fourteen

Vocabulary

THE COLLEGE STUDENT hardly needs to be persuaded that a good vocabulary is important. If his vocabulary is poor, he usually discovers early in his college career that he is handicapped in understanding the speech and writing of educated people. Most of his learning in college comes through lectures and books which are likely to be high informal to formal in style and vocabulary; he is clearly at a disadvantage if he encounters in assigned reading, or hears in lectures, word after word which is completely strange or only vaguely familiar to him.

Weakness in vocabulary also hampers his own communication. In his informal social relationships he may get along reasonably well with a small store of words. But when he writes papers and examinations, when he phrases questions or answers them in class, when he conducts meetings, voices his opinions in public (or refrains from voicing them for fear of doing it badly), he becomes ·aware of the value of an exact vocabulary and of skill in usage above the level of slang. The person who fumbles for words, who talks around a term or a concept in a fruitless groping for the accurate word, who can't say exactly what he means, may be likable; but he is not impressive or effective.

Many college students know, too, some of the studies which have been made of the relationship between vocabulary and successful work in college and in business and professional life. It is not possible to measure accurately the contribution of vocabulary to anything so complex as success; but an extensive vocabulary appears to be one constant factor in many kinds of achievement.

The purpose of this chapter is not to reiterate familiar general statements about the importance of vocabulary in learning, in expression, and in future success, but, first, to consider the basic rela tionship of words to thought and to communication; and, second, to suggest practical ways of improving one's vocabulary.

I. VOCABULARY AND THINKING

Essentially, a good vocabulary is important because most of our thinking is done in words. When we communicate the thought, we may need to adjust the words to a particular audience. But if the words in which we think are precise, the thinking is precise and clear; if the words are imprecise, the thinking is vague and blurred.

These statements need qualification, for *thinking* is an abstract word which covers a wide variety of intellectual and emotional experiences; and it is often impossible to draw a sharp line between thought and idle reverie, thought and feeling, thought and awareness, thought and image, thought and intuitive mystical perception. Thus one may "think," in the broadest sense of the term, not in words but in the wordless beat of tom-toms, in the rhythm of surf, in movement and gesture, in tone and harmony, in vivid images, in line and color, in non-verbal symbols and ritual and the sound of the unknown word. But when we think logically, rationally, and systematically, we usually think in words.[1]

The person who says "I know what I mean but I can't express it" seldom knows clearly what he means. He has, in all probability, a feeling for the thing he wants to say, a hazy sense or sensation of it; but if he knew clearly what he meant he would be able to express it because the thought would be formulated in words. Try to imagine a competent doctor who examines a patient and says, "I know what disease he has but I don't know the name of it"; or a lawyer who says, "This is illegal, but I don't know what law it violates." A doctor or lawyer (or anyone else) may, of course, on occasion, have simply a sense of something wrong. But if he actually knows, knows precisely, what is wrong, he knows in words. The knowledge has a name; the name is an integral part of the knowledge.

The readers of this book may have had the experience of worrying for days over an apparently unsolvable problem, finally telling someone about it, and immediately afterward (even though the confidant had no new ideas and offered no advice) seeing a plain solution. Sometimes a problem is solved in this way because sharing it removes part of the worry which was obstructing thought, and sometimes because one has received at least silent approval of what he wanted to do all along. Frequently, though, the solution is a result of putting the problem into words. Thinking in words demands a kind of thinking, precise and logical thinking, which has not been applied to the problem before. Students sometimes have a similar experience when

---

[1] Mathematical thinking and some kinds of scientific thinking are exceptions. Here words are replaced by symbols more exact than words.

they "write out" a dilemma or a perplexing situation in a personal essay. The writing, the casting of the nebulous thought and feeling into exact and concrete words, requires exactness in thinking which clarifies the problem.

As the semanticists repeatedly remind us, the word is not the thing. Words are merely symbols which stand for complex objects or ideas. But these verbal symbols, used by one who understands and uses them well, can with amazing accuracy convey complex meaning, make subtle distinctions, differentiate finely between two similar referents. And a knowledge of words produces a mental discrimination between objects or ideas which might otherwise be blurred.

"Her mother is in a dangerous condition." The accurate user of words will not only speak, but will *think* more exactly, because he has the verbal means of dissecting the general idea: "Is her mother's condition *serious* or *critical?*"

"The teacher is mean." Is he *strict, sarcastic, demanding,* or *unfair?*"

"He doesn't believe in God." Is he an *atheist* or an *agnostic?*

"John is a poor student." Is he *lazy, uninterested,* or *incompetent?*

"He has a tumor." Is it *malignant* or *benign?*

"He behaved very badly." Was his behavior *rude, inconsiderate, immoral,* or *unconventional?*

"He's a thief. He even steals things he doesn't need." He may be a *kleptomaniac.*

The student of language will note at once that words like *serious, critical, strict, sarcastic, demanding,* etc. are still general words which have multiple meanings and which convey little specific information. But, in these contexts, they are words which make distinctions; they are the tools of a mind which makes distinctions, and which can make them more readily because it thinks in accurate words.

II. VOCABULARY AND COMMUNICATION

Making distinctions is the essence, too, of clear communication. The speech and writing of a person whose vocabulary is weak is like the playing of an unskillful pianist who, even in a simple composition, strikes wrong notes or hits two keys instead of one. Such a communicator calls an *agnostic* an *atheist;* confuses *imply* and *infer;* says an *obsequious* person is *obedient;* speaks of *defying* the rules when he intends to *circumvent* them. The general drift of his communication may be clear, but no part of it is precisely, sharply clear, because he lacks words which differentiate between subtly different things.

The following question-examples will illustrate the kind of differentiation which produces precise expression. Most of the questions cannot be answered without more context. Their purpose is simply to call attention to the shades of meaning communicated by different words.

Mr. Jones has lost five thousand dollars. Is this a *misfortune* or a *catastrophe?*

Phil received an A in biology without opening his book all term. Is his experience *unusual* or *unique?*

Sylvia does almost everything her roommate tells her to do. Is she *responsive, suggestible,* or *weak-willed?*

The professor threw away his cigar before he went into class. Did he *discard* it or *relinquish* it?

Mr. Parks has very good manners. Is he *polite, suave, urbane,* or *genteel?*

Don McDonald made ten thousand dollars this year in his lumber business. Is he a *shrewd* business man or a *sagacious* one?

Jane seems shy. Is she *bashful, modest,* or *coy?*

He tries to get attention. Does he *invite* it, *solicit* it, or *demand* it?

Dorothy, sitting in class, is thinking about her first experience in school. Does she *remember* it or *recall* it? Does she *hear* the lecture or *listen to* it?

Professor Hamilton described to his class the exact form for their reports. Was he giving *suggestions, instructions,* or *orders?* Was his manner *positive* or *peremptory?*

Herb appeared not to see the sarcasm in the remark. Did he *ignore* it or was he *oblivious of* it?

Marguerite has just learned that her term paper is due a week earlier than she thought. Does she feel *alarm, dismay, consternation,* or *panic?*

Tom was told by his English teacher that he had written a theme on a most inappropriate subject. Was he *embarrassed, disconcerted,* or *confounded?*

Mr. and Mrs. Brown have frequent disagreements. Do they *argue, quarrel, wrangle,* or *bicker?* Their neighbors try to help and advise them. Are the neighbors *intervening, interceding, mediating,* or *interfering?* Is the advice *generous* or *gratuitous?*

John ran into a tree and smashed the front end of his father's car. He said that he fell asleep at the wheel because he had studied history until four o'clock the night before. Did he offer this fact in *excuse* or in *extenuation?* Did his father *chide* him, *reprove* him, *remonstrate* with him, or *berate* him about the accident? Was John *ashamed* or *contrite?*

The reader will note that not all of the words used in these examples are formal words, beyond the range of the average student's vocabulary; many of them are informal, familiar words, which carry a particular shade of meaning. Learning new words is by no means the only way of improving one's vocabulary. A profitable way, which will be discussed later in this chapter, is to learn the exact meanings of familiar words and to make a conscious effort to use those words in one's own speech and writing.

We have been primarily concerned in this discussion with accuracy, with finding and using the precise word. But it is important to remember that the precise word in one's thinking, or on a page of the dictionary, is not always the precise word *in use with a particular audience.* One may, for example, think *trauma,* but find it necessary, in order to be understood, to use a less accurate word like *shock.* One may think *gambled foolishly,* but need to say, euphemistically, *made unwise investments.* Plain-sense accuracy is sometimes less important in communication than attitudinal accuracy. The latter, like the former, demands a sure knowledge of the full meaning of words.

III. LEARNING NEW WORDS

College students learn a number of new words—basic terms and technical names used in their courses—almost automatically. Such words are learned in the best possible way: they are usually defined in the text, explained by the teacher, used repeatedly throughout the course, and used by the student himself when he talks or writes about the subject. The words are part of a body of information, and the student, over a period of time, absorbs both the names and the knowledge. They are thoroughly his. In the same way one naturally acquires new words from any new work or new activity—carpentering, sewing, sailing, taking pictures, reporting, acting. Like basic terms learned in courses, these new words have exact referential meaning, they are part of a pattern of knowledge, and they are used after they are learned. They are learned well.

Unfortunately, this natural acquisition of new words is usually too slow, and the words are often too specialized, to provide the good general vocabulary which the student should have. He needs to supplement the natural increase in vocabulary by actively acquiring new words. There is no easy way to do this. The best way is to read widely, absorbing the meanings of words from their contexts, and conscientiously looking up and learning words which are not defined by the context.

Students sometimes embark on a program of learning a word a day, or five words a week, from lists of words printed in newspapers and magazines. This method of increasing vocabulary has distinct disadvantages; the factors which make learning thorough and effective are not present. Since the words in the lists are usually given without context, the learner has no guide to their exact usage and their connotation. Also because they are not in context, he has nothing to attach the words to. Learned in a vacuum, they quickly slip out of memory. Their meanings are easily forgotten, too, because the words are usually so formal that the person learning them has little occasion to use them, and by using them to make them genuinely his. *Sycophantic, eclecticism,* and *meretricious* are good words to know, but they are not words which fit smoothly into everyday speech and writing.

Trying to learn new words from these lists may not be entirely unprofitable. The learner may remember some words well enough to recognize them and have some idea of their meaning when he later encounters them in context. A surer, more profitable way of increasing vocabulary, however, is learning the meanings of new words which one encounters in reading, and following a procedure which fits the words into one's information and experience. This procedure should consist of three steps:

1. Finding the definition of the word in the dictionary.
2. Seeing how the word is used in the context of the sentence or passage.
3. Using the word in speaking or writing.

The use of the dictionary is discussed in the Handbook. It is worth saying here, however, that the student should learn the pronunciation of a new word as well as its definition, and that he may find it useful in remembering the word to note its derivation, particularly if he has some knowledge of other languages. It is especially important, in using the dictionary, not to seize on the first definition given, but to find what different meanings the word may have, and which meaning it seems to have in the particular passage one has read.

This involves the second of the three steps: seeing how the word is used, and fixing in mind its context. The meaning of a word is likely to slip away, as we have said, unless it is attached to something. The context, the sentence in which it is used, provides one anchor. Furthermore, fixing in mind the word-in-context instead of merely a dictionary definition gives the student one accurate usage of the word. He may find others as he comes across the word in different contexts, but from the beginning of his acquaintance with it he knows at least one way in which the word is properly used. He need not be afraid of using it himself in a similar sentence or construction.

It is often helpful in remembering a word to compose a new context for it. This should be a simple sentence in which the word is used as it was used in the original context, but in which there is more of a clue to the word's meaning. "He is a notorious character" does not help one remember the meaning of *notorious;* but "Al Capone was a notorious gangster" does. Most words can be used in this way in sentences or phrases which clearly suggest their meaning: "Hot weather is enervating"; "I feel lethargic after a heavy lunch"; "My garrulous neighbor talked for two hours."

The third step—using a newly acquired word in conversation or in writing—is sometimes difficult, particularly if the word is considerably more formal than one's own level of language. It is unwise to sacrifice direct communication for the sake of practicing a new word; but using it three or four times is a very effective way of making it a permanent addition to one's vocabulary. After this early use which is part of the process of learning the word, one may seldom, or never, use it again; it will be part of a passive, recognition vocabulary, which is always larger than the vocabulary habitually used. Many words, though, which at first sound unnatural and overformal to the user of them, are actually quite appropriate and sound natural enough after he has used them a few times. They may become valuable additions to his active vocabulary.

IV. THE EXACT WORD

Many exact words are formal words. One who lacks a knowledge of exact or technical names (*podium, epigram, incantation, promulgation, leukemia, schizophrenia, bibliography*) is unable to communicate concisely the meaning represented by those words. Most college students need to increase their store of such words in order to express complex ideas in direct language, and in order to understand formal English when they hear and read it.

But many formal words are no more exact in referential meaning, and may be less exact in attitudinal meaning, than informal equivalents. Not exactness, but heavy inappropriateness, is produced by writing "The hapless mendicant lost his equilibrium and injured his head on the portal" instead of "The unlucky beggar lost his balance and hurt his head on the door." The idea that the person who has a good vocabulary uses "big words" is a mistaken idea. He can use formal words when they are called for; but if he has judgment as well as vocabulary, he knows that simple informal words are often more exact, more direct, and more emphatic. *Hiss, yell, howl, purr, gape, leer, inch, pint, ash,* and *oak* are exact words. *Suspend, conclude, distinguish, confirm, dissent, sustain, rebuke, rebuff, ponder,* and *consider* are exact words. As important to the college student as learning new words is learning to use the vocabulary he has; to draw on the great store of words which are familiar to him; to find the exact word among the words he knows.

How is this done? First of all, the student needs to develop a consciousness of words, so that he hears and notes the verbal distinctions made by people who speak and write well. He is likely, if he is attentive, to note such distinctions as these: "Is it *usually* true, or *invariably* true?"; "They left *quickly*, but not *hastily*"; "It's a remarkable *feat*, if not an *achievement*." He may need to consult the dictionary in order to understand the distinction made; nearly always, though, the context will make it clear.

In reading, the student who is developing a consciousness of words should pay particular attention to words which are near the border of his vocabulary. We "know" words, of course, in different degrees— well enough to recognize them and gather their meaning from context, well enough to know their general meaning without any context, well enough to use them accurately. A moment's study of a word only faintly familiar, the meaning of which can be grasped from the context, will make that word better known when the reader encounters it again. Eventually it will be a word he can use with assurance. In this chapter we have used a number of words which may be on the fringe of the reader's vocabulary, but which we believe are made sufficiently clear by their context. A few of them, with fragments of context, are:

> intuitive *mystical* perception
> worry which was *obstructing* thought
> casting the *nebulous* thought and feeling into exact and concrete words

Noting such borderline words and pulling them closer to the center of familiarity should be made a habit in reading.

In writing and revising his papers, the student will find books of synonyms valuable aids in finding, or reminding himself of, the exact word. If he locks up in Roget's *Thesaurus* [2] a word which is not quite right but is akin to the word he wants, he will probably find in the list of synonyms the exact word, which he knows—perhaps well—but which failed to come to mind. He will also find a fascinating field for the study of words. It is inadvisable to use synonyms with which one is not familiar, because synonymous words differ, sometimes widely, in shade and degree of meaning. A partial list of the synonyms for *hate* in Roget's *Thesaurus* will illustrate: *hatred, disaffection, disfavor, alienation, coolness, enmity, animosity, malice, umbrage, pique, spleen, bitterness, bad blood, acrimony, repugnance,*

---

[2] Roget's *Thesaurus* is now available in a twenty-five cent Pocket edition as well as in the fuller standard edition.

odium, detestation, abhorrence, loathing, abomination, aversion, antipathy. These words cannot be used interchangeably; the writer would badly distort his meaning if he used *umbrage* to convey the idea of *odium.* Webster's *Dictionary of Synonyms* is a particularly good reference book because it indicates differences between synonyms.

Using the exact word is more difficult in speech than in writing. It is not always possible to pause in conversation until the right word comes to mind. It is possible, though, to choose one's words. The talk of good conversationalists is nearly always characterized by an accurate, considered use of words; and college students, who are young and who are forming habits, do well to practice using language, even in informal speech, as exactly as they can. Speech which is actually halting is likely to disturb the listener; but a slight pause is never objectionable when out of it comes the exact word.

The college student can also, in speech and writing, make a conscious effort to avoid two common types of inexactness. They are usually produced, not by inadequate vocabulary, but by careless or inadequate use of the vocabulary one has. The first of these types of inexactness is a confusion of words which have a similar sound but different meanings: *accept* and *except; affect* and *effect; illusion* and *allusion; marital* and *martial; creditable* and *credible; ingenious* and *ingenuous.* If the reader is not certain of the meanings of these frequently confused words, he should look them up in the dictionary and fix their definitions in his mind. They are all very usable words, but using them incorrectly is worse than not using them at all.

A second type of inexactness is a combination of careless thinking and loose, careless expression. Calling an opinion a "fact" or a trivial matter "a most important issue" belongs in this category of inexactness. So do inexact figures of speech ("he sailed the sea of life, leaping over every obstacle"); a thoughtless reliance on clichés ("caught like a rat in a trap"—instead of a more accurate statement of how he was caught); and roundabout, ambiguous phrasing ("one of those shiny white flowers that smell so sweet"; "the activities in college that aren't part of your studies"). Other examples of this type of inexactness are "quite a few" when it is possible to say "fifteen" or "three hundred"; "rather horrible" when one means distasteful or garish or dull ("a rather horrible person," "rather horrible furniture," "a rather horrible lecture"); and "nice" and "fine" used as vague terms of approval when more accurate words could be used. Avoiding inexactnesses like these does not require a large vocabulary, but simply some precision in thinking about the thing to be communicated, and some care in choosing from even a limited vocabulary the words to communicate it clearly. Frequently the student who is apologetic about his small vocabulary, or who tries to excuse unclear expression on the basis of limited vocabulary, does not realize how extensive his vocabulary actually is. He has never taken the trouble to use it.

One other kind of inexactness deserves a word of comment and of warning—the inexact and irresponsible use of charged language. Precise words, as we have said before, make distinctions; they clarify the difference between objects and ideas which have some similarity. But imprecise words, particularly words with strong emotional charges, may blur distinctions; they may obscure the actual referent instead of pointing to it. The charged words of race and nationality afford clear examples. *Negro, Jew, Pole, Italian* are not exact words when they are used as the description or designation of a complex human being. *Nigger, Kike, Polack,* and *Wop* are irresponsible words. The user of them may be innocent of malicious intention; but he is not innocent, socially and ethically, when the words he uses promote prejudice. Charged words of personal attitude and political opinion need similarly to be used with responsibility and care, so that they produce understanding of the referent, not an emotional blindness.

Skill in language is complex; but its foundation is skill in words. As the college student increases his knowledge of words—adding to his vocabulary, and learning to use accurately and fluently the words he already knows—he begins to feel a new mastery of language. Through words he can be clear, can be discriminating, can be fair. As he makes verbal distinctions, he makes finer mental distinctions. He can feel his thinking sharpened as he formulates the thought in the exact, the inevitable word.

He has a new satisfaction, too, and a new understanding, when he reads the words of others. He is less susceptible to words which distort and confuse. More important perhaps, he grasps subtleties and shades of meaning concealed from him before. The reader of this book may have had the experience of learning a new word, and then, within the next few weeks, coming across the word three or four times in his reading. Suddenly everyone seems to be using that word. The change, most probably, is not in the language he reads, but in the reader himself. The word, once simply a blur or a blind spot, has become a point of awareness. He now sees it wherever it appears in his reading. And his awareness of the word-as-word is accompanied, of course, by a new awareness of its meaning, and therefore by a clearer understanding of the whole passage.

Reading without adequate vocabulary is like discerning vague

outlines of objects in a strange and darkened room. A knowledge of
words illuminates. With this illumination—a light in dark corners,
a light on new colors—the reader perceives clear forms, designs, and
texture. And here, in a strange environment, he still can feel at home.

EXERCISES

I. Write a "chapter review" for this chapter, either listing or asking questions about the points which you consider most important.

II. From the study of this book you have probably added a number of words to your vocabulary; for example: *referent, context,
connotation, euphemism, cliché.* Make a list of other new words
which you have learned thus far from your courses in college.

III. Make a careful study of the question-examples on page
695, thinking about the differences in meaning of the suggested
words. If you cannot distinguish clearly between the italicized words,
try to find in the dictionary, or in Webster's *Dictionary of Synonyms,*
the exact shade of meaning conveyed by each word.

IV. Use each of the italicized words in the examples on page 695
in a sentence which shows that you know its exact meaning.

V. For the next week, make from your reading a list of words
which you understand in context, but which are not part of your
active vocabulary. Note how the words are used, and make an effort
to use them in your conversation or writing.

Handbook

Handbook

Understanding Grammar

GRAMMARIANS speak of grammar as a "science," and in a sense they are justified in doing so. The biologist, for example, studies living organisms, names them, puts them into categories, and makes generalizations about them and their functions. The grammarian studies language in the same way. The facts about grammar, however, are much more difficult to systematize and to generalize about than the facts of biology, for the grammarian has as his field of study the language that the biologist uses, the language that the physicist uses— in fact all the language that all people, or at least all English-speaking people, use in writing and in speech.

As a result—and this is the point of our comparison—the exact definitions and the neat generalizations of biology cannot be achieved in grammar. The student of grammar must resign himself to definitions that are sometimes unreliable and to generalizations to which there are exceptions. He must accept too the fact that different grammarians have somewhat different systems and different terminology, and that they may not agree on how to analyze a particular sentence. Finally, and this is even more troublesome, there are some expressions which defy convincing grammatical analysis—even by an expert grammarian. Despite its limitations as a science, though, grammar can be a very useful tool.

THE USES OF GRAMMAR

Many students of English think grammar a dull subject, and not a few teachers secretly share this view. We believe that essential grammar can be a reasonably interesting study if students attempt to understand instead of simply memorizing and if they see that what they learn will really be of service to them. Teachers of English are not in agreement on how much grammar they expect or hope their students will know. Some feel that a full and detailed knowledge is essential; others believe that students can learn to write well with very little knowledge of formal grammar. Where there is such disagreement among experts, it is presumptuous to be dogmatic. Our own opinion, though, is that some kinds of grammatical knowledge are essential; teachers must talk about certain basic terms, basic constructions, and basic stylistic devices: if students wish to profit from instruction, they must know enough grammar to understand what their teachers are talking about. On the other hand, some aspects of grammar, though interesting to experts and essential in a complete and scholarly study of grammar, are of little or no practical use to a student primarily concerned with improving his writing. In our treatment of grammar we shall focus on what the student needs to know in order to understand the common constructions of his own language and to use standard English effectively.

A concrete way to approach the study of grammar is to look at sentences which raise grammatical questions. In the sentences below which of the alternative expressions should be chosen?

1. *Did you weigh* or *have you weighed* yourself today?
2. Before *sitting, setting* the vase down he *lay, laid* the book on the table.
3. There is only one person *who, whom* I think can be counted on to help John and *I, me*.
4. With the help of Tom, Dick, and *me, I,* he sold all the tickets.
5. I move that the resolution *be laid, is laid, be lain* on the table.
6. He walks *like, as* his father did and also talks *like, as, him, he*.
7. We do not know *who, whom* he thinks will object to *him, his* being president.
8. When he feels *bad, badly,* he takes an aspirin.
9. I hope that they *shall, will* be there when we arrive.
10. The result of all our efforts and sufferings *was, were* disappointing.
11. There *is, are,* if I may say so, good reasons for doing as I did.
12. The reason the firemen were hostile to *us, we* boys was *because, that* we had turned in a false alarm.
13. The committee *has, have* met, and they are unable to agree on *whom, who* they will ask to speak.
14. *Has, have* the youngest of his daughters become engaged?
15. The woman as well as her husband and her brother *are, is* expected to testify against Mr. McCarthy.

How does one know which expression to choose in the preceding sentences? A few exceptional people know by a kind of language sense. They have heard good language all their lives and have read widely; as a result they are able to choose the right expression by ear because it "sounds right." Most of us, however, cannot safely depend on language sense. Instead we make a tentative choice and then search our minds until we find the grammatical rule which confirms or contradicts our first quick judgment.

For the sentences given, the choices that should have been made are as follows:

1. *Have you weighed*
2. *setting . . . laid*
3. *who . . . me*
4. *me*
5. *be laid*
6. *as* (though some authorities would defend *like* in informal usage) . . . *like him*
7. *who . . . his*
8. *bad* (though some authorities would defend *badly* in informal usage)
9. *will*
10. *was*
11. *are*
12. *us . . . that* (though some authorities would defend *because* in informal usage)
13. *have . . . whom*
14. *has*
15. *is*

Even one wrong choice on this simple test is evidence of an unreliable language sense and a need to sharpen that sense by more knowledge of grammar. An important function of a study of grammar is that it supplies information that will insure right choices.

A second use of grammatical knowledge—important even for those few who have a well-developed language sense—is that it provides the precise terminology necessary for understanding how sentences are constructed and how to write better sentences. The student who wishes to improve his writing will find that the sentence is the single most important unit; he will be baffled unless he can understand the grammatical terms used for analyzing sentences and for describing ways to improve sentences. To use a French cookbook, one must first be able to read French.

Fortunately for college freshmen (and for their teachers!) it is not necessary to begin the study of grammar in college. Although few students come to college with a really sound knowledge of grammar, most of them have acquired a good deal of grammatical knowledge. The first problem, then, is how much grammar the student knows already and how much more he needs to know. The outline of grammar which follows will help to solve this problem.

Since each of the terms in this outline is defined and illustrated in "An Expanded Outline of Grammar" (pages 712–744), you may, if you choose, look up unfamiliar terms as you go through the outline. At present, however, all that you are required to do is (1) to read the outline thoughtfully in order to see grammatical relationships and to recall your earlier study of grammar, and (2) to underline those terms you find unfamiliar or vague. You can then see for yourself where your knowledge is inadequate. Also you can, if your instructor wishes, give him your list of underlined terms. Some terms in the outline are italicized. These, even the most undemanding instructor will expect his students to understand. A large number of college teachers will expect a knowledge, not only of the italicized terms but also of most of the remaining terms, for this is a selected list.

AN OUTLINE OF GRAMMAR

(Underline those terms about which you think your information is incomplete.)

I. Basic grammar
  A. The *sentence* (subject + predicate + independent assertion)
    1. *Complete, incomplete,* and *fragmentary* sentences
    2. The functions of words in sentences: the parts of speech
      a. *To name—substantives* (*nouns* and *pronouns*)
      b. *To assert* (i.e., to indicate action, state of being, or occurrence)—*verbs*
      c. *To modify* (i.e., to restrict, limit, or qualify)—*adjectives* and *adverbs*
      d. *To connect—prepositions* and *conjunctions*
    3. The essential parts of the simple sentence—the *subject* and the *predicate*
      a. Predicates that contain *complements*
      b. Verbs and *verbals* distinguished
      c. *Simple* and complete *subjects* and *predicates*
  B. *Phrases*
    1. Definition
    2. Phrases classified according to function
      a. Noun (or substantive) phrase
      b. Verb phrase
      c. Adjectival phrase
      d. Adverbial phrase
  C. *Clauses*
    1. Definition
    2. *Independent* (or *main*) clauses
    3. *Dependent* (or *subordinate*) clauses
    4. Distinguishing clauses from phrases
  D. Types of sentences
    1. Complete, incomplete, and fragmentary sentences

        a. Simple adverbs
        b. Interrogative adverbs
        c. *Conjunctive adverbs*
   E. Prepositions: simple and phrasal prepositions and prepositional phrases
   F. Conjunctions
      1. *Coordinating conjunctions*
      2. *Subordinating conjunctions*
   G. Interjections
   H. Other common constructions
      1. *Compound constructions* and *parallelism*
      2. *Elliptical constructions*
      3. *Normal* and *inverted order*
      4. Absolute constructions

EXERCISE FOR TESTING BASIC KNOWLEDGE

(This exercise is designed to serve as another way for you to examine your present knowledge of grammar. Do it as well as you can, and then underline those parts of the instructions which you find it difficult or impossible to follow.)

For each of the following sentences:

(a) Indicate the number of dependent and independent clauses and identify them.

(b) Point out the simple subject and the simple predicate of each clause.

(c) Indicate whether each verb is transitive (takes an object) or intransitive.

(d) Indicate whether the sentence is simple, compound, complex or compound-complex.

(e) Point out, if it is present, (1) a direct object, (2) a subjective complement (predicate noun or predicate adjective), (3) an indirect object, (4) an appositive, (5) an apposed adjective, (6) an objective complement, (7) a verb phrase, (8) an auxiliary verb, (9) an adverb, (10) a preposition and its object, (11) a pronoun and its antecedent, (12) a verbal (participle, gerund, or infinitive), (13) a phrase and the locution it modifies, (14) a subordinating conjunction, (15) a dependent clause and the locution it modifies, (16) a coordinating conjunction, (17) a parallel construction, (18) a linking (or copulative) verb.

1. Because Tom had studied grammar in preparatory school, he thought it would be an easy subject in college.

2. My uncle, an experienced fisherman, has been chosen leader for the outing.

3. Choosing his footing carefully, the man climbed the rugged mountain.

4. The sky is blue now, and the rainy weather which we had this morning has left the grass wet and shiny.

5. The freshman, weary of his grammatical studies, closed his book and went to bed.

The remainder of this chapter is aimed primarily at the student who has discovered that he has an inadequate or even a very weak knowledge of grammar. Such students should not be unduly discouraged, but they should, of course, study with particular care the material which follows. Those who have been able to do the exercise with ease and assurance have a better than average knowledge. They should read the rest of the chapter and should be alert for new material, but they can afford to read rapidly.

Because we are attempting to present the essentials of grammar in a manner that will be completely understandable to any college student who wishes to learn, the level of our treatment may seem almost insulting to already well-informed students. Wherever there seems a possibility of reasonable doubt, we shall define and illustrate terms, and we shall not hesitate to deal with matters of grammar which it seems that everyone should already know. Of course the really well-informed student does not need this kind of simplification. At the same time we must add that a little knowledge is a dangerous thing; there are people—students even—who mistakenly think they understand grammar merely because they "have had it before" and because the terms sound familiar.

AN EXPANDED OUTLINE OF GRAMMAR

Grammar, as we use the term here, deals with the use of words in sentences. The presentation of grammar which follows is an expansion and clarification of the "Outline of Grammar" on pages 708–711. For the convenience of the student we are using here a system of numbering and lettering that coincides with that outline.

I. Basic Grammar

This section deals with the simple sentence, the basic functions of the parts of speech, phrases, clauses, and types of sentences. Although this material may be familiar to the student, it is an essential introduction to the more advanced subject matter of later sections.

A. The Sentence (Subject + Predicate + Independent Assertion)

According to the broadest definition, a sentence is any locution [1] spoken or punctuated as an independent unit of discourse. For practical purposes, however, the sentence is best defined as follows: The sentence is an *independent assertion* which contains a *subject* and a *predicate*. In accepting this definition it is well to bear in mind the fact, mentioned at the beginning of this chapter, that grammatical definitions are often imperfect and that exceptions to general rules often occur. The definition given here is not perfect, but if it is used with awareness of the following exceptions and qualifications, it will serve well:

(1) In imperative expressions (commands, entreaties, and the like) the subject *you* is taken for granted, though it is implied and not expressed.

Shut the door. Please let me in. [*You* is the subject of each of these imperative sentences.]

(2) The word *assertion* as here used includes questions, commands, and exclamations as well as statements.

Where is he? [Question]
Stand where you are. [Command]
And the weatherman predicted fair weather! [Exclamation]
He was here yesterday. [Statement]

(3) An *independent* assertion is an assertion that can stand alone and make sense. *By itself* it makes a statement, asks a question, gives a command, etc.

(4) Our definition states only the minimum essentials of a sentence. We shall see later that any part of a sentence may be *compounded* (i.e., doubled, tripled, quadrupled, etc.) The italicized words in the sentences below form compound predicates:

George *walked* and *talked*.
George *walked* and *talked* and *danced*.
George *walked, talked, danced,* and *sang*.

1. Complete, Incomplete, and Fragmentary Sentences. All locutions spoken or punctuated as sentences are not, according to our definition, necessarily sentences (i.e., complete grammatical sentences). To determine whether a particular expression is a sentence, one asks three questions about it: Does it have a subject? Does it have a predicate? Does it make an independent assertion? If the

---

[1] Locution is a general term referring to a word, phrase, clause, or sentence.

answer to *all* these questions is *yes,* the expression is a complete sentence; if one of the answers is *no,* the sentence is incomplete.

An incomplete sentence, then, is one which lacks one or more of the three sentence essentials—subject, predicate, and independent assertion; it may or may not be an acceptable expression. Fragmentary sentences are an undesirable type of incomplete sentence; they do not convey the meaning clearly or they are inappropriate in the context in which they are used; a fragmentary sentence is a subordinate part of a sentence ignorantly or carelessly written as a sentence.

NOTE.—Complete, incomplete, and fragmentary sentences are illustrated and discussed in detail in Chapter Three, pages 63–67.

2. The Functions of Words in Sentences: The Parts of Speech. Students often have the impression that a particular word is always a particular part of speech—that *tree,* for instance, is always a noun. Actually, of course, tree can be a noun (*to climb a tree*), or a verb (*He treed the bear*), or an adjective (*the sport of tree climbing*). The point is that *tree* and a great many other words can be used as more than one part of speech, and that *the way a word is used, its function in the sentence, determines what part of speech it is.*[2]

Words (parts of speech) are used to serve four functions:

a. To name—substantives (nouns and pronouns). The word *substantive* includes nouns and pronouns and any other locution (i.e., noun phrase, noun clause) which serves the function of naming. The difference between nouns and pronouns is that nouns are words used to name, and pronouns are used in the place of nouns.

Nouns and pronouns: *Tom* said *hello* to *Mary* when *he* saw *her.* [*Tom* and *Mary* are nouns; *he* and *her* are pronouns used to avoid repeating *Tom* and *Mary.* The word *hello* is also a noun in this sentence; it names what Tom said.]

b. To assert (i.e., to indicate action, state of being, or occurrence) —verbs.

Verbs: The bird *flew.* It *was* high in the air; then it *seemed* to lose consciousness. Apparently it *died,* not from the fall, but from inhaling noxious fumes. [The italicized words, and *only* the italicized words, are verbs.]

c. To modify (i.e., to restrict, limit, or qualify)—adjectives and adverbs. Adjectives modify only substantives; adverbs modify verbs, adjectives, and other adverbs.

---

[2] One peculiar example of this fact is that when we write, "The word *is* is a verb," the italicized word *is* a noun.

Adjectives: Under the *gray* sky the horse, *blind* and *lame*, pulled the *old* wagon. [*Gray* modifies *sky; blind* and *lame* modify *horse; old* modifies *wagon.*]

Adverbs: He sat *down*. [Modifies the verb *sat*.]
He was *very* old. [Modifies the adjective *old*.]
He moved *very slowly*. [*Very,* an adverb, modifies the adverb *slowly,* which in turn modifies the verb *moved*.]

d. To connect—prepositions and conjunctions. A preposition takes a substantive as its object and joins that substantive to some other element in the sentence.

Prepositions: He fell *off* the roof *of* the house. [*Off* takes *roof* as its object and connects it with *fell. Of* takes *house* as its object and connects it with *roof*.]

A conjunction is a word used to connect words, phrases, or clauses. Conjunctions do not take objects.

Conjunctions: Mary *and* I saw him, *but* he did not see us. [*And* connects *Mary* and *I; but* connects the two clauses.]

NOTE 1.—Prepositions and adverbs are sometimes confused because some words may serve either function. It is worth remembering that a preposition always takes an object and that an adverb does not.

Adverb: He looked *up*. [*Up* has no object. It modifies *looked*.]
Preposition: He looked *up* the street. [*Up* takes *street* as its object and joins it to *looked*.]

NOTE 2.—The interjection, usually called the eighth part of speech, has been omitted here. It serves no function except to express emotion. Examples of interjections are: *Ouch! Oh, alas!*

3. The Essential Parts of the Simple Sentence—the Subject and the Predicate. Defined in general terms, the subject of a sentence is the thing talked about and the predicate is what is said about the subject. The simple sentence may be defined as a sentence containing only one independent assertion. Each of the following locutions contains (or is said to contain) a subject and a predicate, and is a sentence:

Time flies. Classes begin. Who cares? Run! [For purposes of grammatical analysis the imperative *run* is considered equivalent to *You run,* and the unexpressed *you* is said to be the subject.]

The first two of these sentences are statements, the third is a question, and the fourth is a command. Each of the four is a sentence because, in accord with our definition, each contains a subject and a predicate and each makes an independent assertion.

a. Predicates that contain complements. It is evident from such sentences as *Time flies* and *Classes begin* that some verbs can form a predicate by themselves; other verbs require the help of complements to form a predicate. Complements are words necessary to complete the essential meaning of a predicate.

> He *ran*. [*Ran*, here used as a complete verb, does not require other words to make a complete assertion about its subject.]
> He *is old*. [*Is* is here used as an incomplete verb, for it requires the help of the adjective *old* to complete the essential idea. The main point here is not that he *is*, but that he *is old*. *Old* is a complement (i.e., a completer) of *is*.]
> He *feels tired*. [*Tired* is here the complement of *feels*, for the essential idea is not that he *feels* but that he *feels tired*.]
> The engineer *dammed* the *river*. [*River*, here the direct object, is the complement of *dammed* and is necessary to complete the essential meaning.]

The most common complements are the subjective complement, the direct object, and the indirect object. For a full discussion of complements see pages 722–725.

b. Verbs and verbals (i.e., participles, infinitives, and gerunds) distinguished. Verbs differ from verbals in the following ways:

(1) A verb can make a sentence when joined with a subject (or a subject and a complement), and verbals cannot:

> **Verbs:** Birds *fly*. Birds *have flown*. Tom *sold* a book.
> **Verbals:** birds *flying* [a participle], birds *to have flown* [an infinitive], his *selling* a book [a gerund]

(2) In some tenses, verbs undergo change to indicate person and number; verbals do not:

> **Verbs:** I *run*. He *runs*. I *have walked*. He *has walked*. He *is* young. They *are* young.

NOTE.—Some grammarians use the term *finite verb* in place of our term *verb* and then speak of *verbals* as *non-finite* verbs. We think it simpler to keep the two separate and to speak of *verbs* and *verbals*.

c. Simple and complete subjects and predicates. Thus far we have dealt with short, uncomplicated sentences. In longer sentences it is sometimes necessary to distinguish between the *simple* subject and the *complete* subject and the *simple* predicate and the *complete* predicate. The simple subject and the simple predicate might be called the bare or essential subject and predicate. The simple subject consists of the basic word (or group of words) about which something is said, and the simple predicate consists only of the word (or group of words) *essential* to make an assertion about the subject. When a verb requires a complement, the complement is a part of the simple predicate.[3]

> Tired and lonely, *Tom flew* mechanically, indifferent to the danger of enemy planes. [The simple subject is *Tom;* the simple predicate is *flew.*]
> Tom *is flying* a *kite* this morning. [*Kite,* a complement, is part of the simple predicate.]

The complete subject consists of the simple subject *plus* any modifiers or appositives which are attached to the simple subject; the complete predicate consists of the simple predicate *plus* all its modifiers. In the sentence given above, the complete subject is *Tired and lonely Tom, indifferent to the danger of enemy planes.* The complete predicate is *flew mechanically.*

B. Phrases

In grammar *phrase* is a technical word with an exact meaning.

1. Definition. A phrase is a group of two or more grammatically related words that does not contain a subject and a predicate and that functions as a single part of speech. A phrase may be classified according to *grammatical function* (i.e., which part of speech it acts as) or, less significantly, according to its *key word.*

> The house *on the corner* is mine. [The phrase *on the corner* functions as an adjective modifying *house:* we could substitute for it the single adjective *corner.* The same phrase, classified according to key word, is called a prepositional phrase because the key word, *on,* is a preposition. According to key words phrases may be prepositional, participial, gerund, or infinitive.]

2. Phrases Classified According to Function. Below are examples of phrases functioning as various parts of speech:

> **Noun (or substantive) phrase:** *Talking to her friends* is one of her chief pleasures. [The italicized phrase does the work of a noun; it serves as the subject of the verb *is.* Since its key word is *talking,* here a gerund, it can also be called a gerund phrase.]
> **Verb phrase:** By one o'clock he *will have finished* his examination. [*Will have finished* is a verb phrase consisting of *finished,* the main verb, and its auxiliaries, *will* and *have.*]
> **Adjectival phrase:** *Straightening her hat grimly,* she picked up the struggling child. [This phrase acts as an adjective to modify the pronoun

---

[3] Some grammarians do not consider the complement as a part of the simple predicate. Either definition of the simple predicate is satisfactory as long as one uses it consistently.

she. Because the key word, *straightening,* is a participle, this may also be called a participial phrase.]

Adverbial phrase: He executed the order *without delay.* [*Without delay* tells how he executed the order and so modifies the verb *executed.* Because the phrase begins with a preposition, it can also be called a prepositional phrase.]

C. Clauses

1. Definition. A clause is a group of related words containing a subject and a predicate. It is important to be able to distinguish between two kinds of clauses—independent and dependent clauses.

2. Independent (or Main) Clauses. An independent clause is so named because it can stand alone as a sentence. Like a sentence it contains a subject and a predicate and makes an assertion. Sentences, however, may contain more than one independent clause and may also contain subordinate (dependent) clauses.

Dogs chase cats. [This is a simple sentence as well as an independent clause.]

Dogs chase cats with enthusiasm. [This too is both an independent clause and a simple sentence.]

Tom and Mary are going at eight. [An independent clause with a compound subject; also a simple sentence.]

Johnathan wanted the car but failed to get it. [An independent clause with a compound predicate; also a simple sentence]

Johnathan's father was a kindly man, and *he loved his son,* but *he had only one car* and *he loved that too.* [Four independent clauses join to form one sentence. Note that any one of them *could* stand alone as a sentence.]

3. Dependent (or Subordinate) Clauses. A dependent clause is a part of a sentence which has a subject and a predicate but which cannot stand alone; it depends on the rest of the sentence for its meaning. Like phrases, dependent clauses do the work of a single part of speech, and they may be called noun or adjective or adverb clauses.

Noun clause: He denied *that life is short.* [The clause serves as the object of *denied.*] I know *he will come.* [*He will come* looks like an independent clause, but it is easy to see that the word *that*—I know *that* he will come—is understood here though it has been omitted. *That he will come* is the object of the verb *know,* and the clause is therefore a noun clause.]

Adjective clause: I returned to the town *where I was born.* [Modifies the noun *town.*]

Adverbial clause: The students celebrate *when the team wins a football game.* [Modifies the verb *celebrate.*]

4. Distinguishing Clauses from Phrases. Although clauses are sometimes confused with phrases, the distinction is easy to make. Clauses have a subject and a predicate (a verb or a verb plus a complement), and phrases do not. See the examples below:

The beach gleaming in the sun. [Not a clause and, of course, not a sentence. *Beach* is modified by the phrase *gleaming in the sun.* Note that *gleaming* is here a participle used as an adjective, and is not a verb.]
We saw the distant lights *which were gleaming in the darkness.* [*Which were gleaming in the darkness,* a dependent clause modifying the noun *lights,* has as its simple subject the relative pronoun *which* and as its simple predicate the verb *were gleaming.* The verb (or verb phrase) *were gleaming* is modified by the adverbial phrase *in the darkness.* Perhaps it should be added that the whole sentence consists of the independent clause *We saw the distant lights* and the dependent clause *which were gleaming in the darkness.*]
The lights were gleaming in the darkness. [An independent clause and also a sentence. The simple subject is *lights* and the simple predicate is *were gleaming.*]

D. Types of Sentences

Sentences may be classified in at least four different ways:

1. Complete, Incomplete, and Fragmentary Sentences. (These have been discussed on pages 713–714.)

2. Periodic and Loose Sentences. A periodic sentence is one in which the main idea is suspended until the end. Some sentences are clearly periodic:

After denouncing his accusers and asserting his own innocence time and time again, the State Department official resigned. [Here the main idea of the sentence is suspended until one reads the last word, *resigned.*]

A loose sentence is one which continues after the main idea has been expressed:

He resigned after denouncing his accusers and asserting his own innocence time and time again. [Here all the words after *resigned* serve to give additional information relevant to a main idea that is already expressed.]

Many sentences are hard to place definitely in either category and may be called semiperiodic sentences:

Exactly at eight o'clock on October 9, he robbed the bank while his two confederates stood guard outside.

In choosing between periodic, semiperiodic and loose sentences one

is guided by the emphasis desired and by the structure of the surrounding sentences.

**3. Declarative, Imperative, Interrogative, and Exclamatory Sen-
tences.** A declarative sentence makes a statement: *He will arrive on
the four o'clock train.* An imperative sentence expresses a command,
a request, or an entreaty: *Don't forget to wear your galoshes.* An interrogative sentence asks a question: *Are you going out in the rain
without your galoshes?* An exclamatory sentence expresses joy, grief,
surprise, or some other strong emotion: *My old teacher is still alive
after all these years!*

**4. Simple, Complex, Compound, and Compound-Complex Sen-
tences.** According to the nature and number of the clauses that they
contain, sentences may be classed as follows:

a. Simple sentence. A simple sentence has only one independent
clause and no dependent clauses. By the accumulation of phrases
and by the compounding of its parts, however, a simple sentence
may be quite long.

> They married. [A simple sentence consisting only of a verb and its sub-
> ject]
> By keeping a close watch over every penny and by refusing to spend un-
> necessarily, Tom and Mary saved money and paid all their debts. [The
> simple subject of this sentence is *Tom and Mary;* the simple predicate
> is *saved money and paid debts.* The remainder of the sentence consists
> of: modifiers of the verbs (*by . . . penny* and *by . . . unnecessarily*)
> and modifiers of the complement (*all their*). The simple sentence may
> be much more complicated in structure than this example, but it can
> always be recognized by the fact that it contains only one clause, a
> main clause.]

b. Complex sentence. A complex sentence contains only one independent clause and one or more dependent clauses.

> When I really understand grammar and when I actually put it to use,
> my grades in English will improve. [This sentence contains two de-
> pendent clauses (*When . . . grammar* and *when . . . use*) and one in-
> dependent clause (*my grades . . . will improve*).]

c. Compound sentence. A compound sentence consists of two or
more independent clauses and no dependent clauses.

> Go and speak. [A very short compound sentence. The two verbs, both in
> the imperative, have subjects (*you* and *you*) understood but not ex-
> pressed. Also, of course, compound sentences, since they have two or
> more independent clauses, can be much more complicated than the
> longest example given under simple sentences.]

d. Compound-complex sentence. A compound-complex sentence contains two or more independent clauses and one or more dependent clauses.

> Where you go I will go, and where you dwell I will dwell. [This sentence contains two dependent clauses (*Where you go* and *where you dwell*) and two independent clauses (*I will go* and *I will dwell*).]

(The exercises for "Basic Grammar," are on page 747.)

II. Grammar at a Higher Level: The Parts of Speech and Their Constructions

Thus far we have dealt with the elements of grammar in their simplest form. Since the study of "grammar at a higher level" assumes a thorough knowledge of the content of the preceding pages, the student should be sure that he knows the material in those pages before he approaches this more advanced discussion.

The primary purpose of this section is to give essential information about the constructions in which the various parts of speech appear. The term *construction* may be defined as the grammatical relationship of a word or a group of words to other words or groups of words: we state the construction of a sentence when we analyze the relationship between its parts; of a verb when we tell what its subject is and what its complements are; of a noun when we say that it is the subject of a particular verb, the object of a preposition, and the like. With the exception of the interjection, each part of speech used in a sentence is said to have a construction. Being able to recognize the common constructions is an essential part of understanding grammar.

In addition to the material on construction, this section contains definitions of the terms necessary in the discussion of constructions and also definitions of other terms that are frequently associated with each of the parts of speech. Most students will be familiar with all or nearly all of this additional material. We recommend, however, that all students at least read the examples and the comment on them, for examples often clear up points that would otherwise remain obscure.

A. The Verb

The verb, already defined as a word that expresses action, state of being, or occurrence, is to the sentence what the motor is to a car; like a motor it is a source of power, and also, sometimes, of trouble. It is particularly important that students be able to distinguish between verbs and verbals and to recognize adverb + verb and preposition + verb combinations. The material beginning with the inflection of verbs, page 728, is likely to be familiar material and can be read rapidly.

1. Main Verbs and Auxiliary Verbs. Verb phrases are made up of one main verb, which contains the main action or idea, and of one or more auxiliary verbs, which help the main verb by indicating what tense it is, whether it is active or passive, and so forth.

> I *have been studying.* [The word that carries the action is *studying. Have* and *been* are auxiliary verbs which indicate the number and tense of the main verb *studying.*]
> *Do* you *remember* her name? [In the verb phrase *Do remember, remember* is the main verb and *Do* is the auxiliary.]

NOTE.—It should be clear, of course, that the general term *verb* is used to name verb phrases as well as single verbs. In *I was going early,* the expression *was going* can be called a verb or, more specifically, a verb phrase.

2. Transitive and Intransitive verbs. The difference between transitive and intransitive verbs is a simple one. A transitive verb takes an object (Tom *hit* the *ball*); an intransitive verb does not take an object (Tom *ran*). Whether a verb is transitive or intransitive depends upon its use in a particular sentence. The same verb, *fight,* for example, may be transitive in one sentence and intransitive in another:

> Cats *fight* dogs. [*Fight* is a transitive verb; *dogs* is its object.]
> Cats and dogs *fight.* [*Fight* is an intransitive verb; it has no object.]

3. Verbs of Complete and Incomplete Predication, and Complements. A predicate is a word or a group of words which makes an assertion about a subject. Some verbs, like *run* in *They run,* can by themselves constitute a predicate; such verbs are said to be verbs of complete predication. Other verbs require the help of substantives or adjectives to form a complete predication (She *is beautiful.* Charles *felled* the *tree*). Such verbs are called verbs of incomplete predication, and the helping noun or adjective is called the complement of the verb. In brief, then, a verb of complete predication requires no complement and a verb of incomplete predication requires a complement. A complement may be defined as a locution, usually a substantive or an adjective, that is required to complete the predication of an incomplete verb.

NOTE.—It is important to distinguish between complements of verbs and modifiers of verbs. Any verb can have modifiers; only verbs of incomplete predication can have complements.

> Sam died slowly. [*Slowly* is a modifier of a verb of complete predication.]
> Charles felled the tree quickly. [*Quickly* is a modifier of a verb of incomplete predication. *Tree* is the complement of the incomplete verb *felled.*]

4. Complements of Linking (Copulative) Verbs and Transitive Verbs. All transitive verbs take complements; this follows from the definition, for a direct object is a complement (He *felled* the *tree*) and transitive verbs take objects. Intransitive verbs, except for a special kind called linking (or copulative) verbs, do not take complements. Linking verbs are so named because they serve to join or link their subject to a noun or adjective which is called the complement of the verb. Locutions frequently used as linking verbs are *be, seem, become, appear,* and the verbs of the senses (*smell, feel, taste, look, sound*). Note the use of the verb *sound* in the following examples:

Used as a linking verb: Your suggestion *sounds* good. [*Sounds,* a verb of incomplete predication, links *suggestion* to the predicate adjective *good. Good* is therefore a complement.]

Used as a transitive verb: Sound the trumpets. [*Sound* is followed by its direct object and complement, *trumpets.*]

Used as an intransitive verb: The alarm *sounded.* [Here *sounded* needs no complement but is an intransitive verb of complete predication.]

a. Complements of linking verbs: The subjective complement. The complement of a linking verb, called the subjective complement, is the expression which completes the meaning of that verb. The subjective complement may be an adjective (word, phrase, or clause), or a substantive (word, phrase, or clause).

It is *Tom.* [*Tom* is a predicate noun and the subjective complement of *is.*]

His objection is *that travel costs are too high.* [A noun clause used as a predicate noun, the subjective complement of *is*]

Lobbing is *returning a ball in a high curve.* [A gerund phrase used as a predicate noun, subjective complement of *is*]

She is *tall* and *graceful.* [Subjective complements of *is,* these two predicate adjectives modify the subject, *she.*]

The materials are *of the best quality.* [An adjectival phrase, used as the subjective complement of *are*]

b. Complements of transitive verbs. Besides a direct object, transitive verbs may have other complements. Complements of transitive verbs are: (1) the direct object, (2) the indirect object, (3) retained objects, (4) double objects, (5) the objective complement, and (6) the subjective complement after a passive verb.

(1) The direct object. The direct object may be defined as the word (or group of words) which receives the action of a transitive verb.

Eleanor was sharpening a *pencil.*

Charles asked *to see the book.* [The infinitive phrase is the direct object of *asked.*]

He saw *that the light was still on*. [The noun clause is the direct object of *saw*.]

(2) The indirect object. The indirect object names the person or thing to whom or on whose behalf the action has been performed.

He gave *me* a ticket.
She wrote *her mother and father* a letter. [*Her mother and father* is an example of a compound indirect object.]

(3) Retained objects, direct and indirect. These constructions can occur only with a verb or verbal in the passive voice, but they are easier to explain if we start with the active voice. *Tom gave him a dollar.* Here *gave,* a verb in the active voice, takes *dollar* as its direct object and *him* as its indirect object. If we now make the assertion in the passive voice, we can phrase it in two ways:

He was given a *dollar* by Tom. [Here *He* is the subject and *dollar* is the object, called the retained direct object, of *was given*.]
A dollar was given *him* by Tom. [*Dollar* is now the subject and *him* (equivalent to *to him*) is the indirect object, called the retained indirect object.]

(4) Double objects. A few verbs such as *ask* or *teach* take double objects instead of a direct and an indirect object. In the sentence *She taught him grammar,* the verb *taught* has two meanings at the same time; it means to instruct someone and to give instructions about something. *Him* is the object of one of these meanings and *grammar* is the object of the other.

(5) The objective complement. The objective complement is a noun or an adjective used with a transitive verb to complete its assertion about the direct object.

The board made him *chairman*. [*Chairman* is the objective complement of *made;* it completes the meaning by telling what the board made him (i.e., chairman).]
Jack Spratt and his wife licked the platter *clean*. [*Clean,* an adjective, is the objective complement of *licked*. Notice that *cleanly* in place of *clean* would change the sense and that *clean* actually works with the verb and does not "modify" it.]

(6) The subjective complement after a passive verb. If we turn into passive voice the two sentences just used to illustrate the objective complement, the objective complement will become a subjective complement after a passive verb.

He was made *chairman* by the board. [Now the word *chairman* is the subjective complement of *was made*.]

The platter was licked *clean* by Jack Spratt and his wife. [*Clean* is now a subjective complement of the passive verb *was licked*.]

5. **Verbals (Participles, Gerunds, Infinitives).** Verbals may be generally defined as word forms that combine some of the characteristics of verbs with the characteristics of another part of speech. Though participles, gerunds, and infinitives each have functions peculiar to themselves, it is possible to make some further generalizations about verbals as a class. We have already stated that verbals *differ* from verbs in that (1) verbs can make an independent predication, and verbals cannot; (2) verbs can undergo change in person and number, and verbals cannot. Verbals *are similar* to verbs in the following ways: they may be transitive or intransitive, complete or linking, may exist in active or passive voices, may take complements, and may be modified by adverbs. Also they may carry much the same meaning as the verb from which they are derived, and they may form phrases which do much the same work as dependent clauses. These generalizations about verbals will become more meaningful as we examine each of the three verbal forms in more detail.

a. **Participles.**

NOTE.—Used with auxiliaries in verb phrases, participles can be verbs and can make a complete predication. (*Example:* She has been *eating* between meals. *Has been eating* is a verb phrase.) Since we are dealing with participles under the heading of verbals, however, we are not here considering participles which are used as parts of verb phrases; we are concerned with the facts about participles used as verbals.

Participles are usually defined as verbal adjectives. Being verbals, participles naturally have some of the characteristics of verbs (i.e., they can be transitive or intransitive, complete or linking, active or passive, and they can take complements and be modified by adverbs); in their work as adjectives they modify substantives and in general perform adjective functions. Below are sentences that contain each of the five forms of the participle, and that illustrate some of the characteristics of participles. (It is worth knowing that the present participle always ends in *ing* and that the short forms of the past and perfect participles—*called, sent, chosen,* for instance—usually end in *d, t,* or *n.*)

    Present participle, active: Knowing him well, we asked for a ride. [The participial phrase *knowing him well* modifies *we. Knowing* takes *him* (here a direct object) as a complement and is modified by the adverb *well.*]

    Present participle, passive: Mr. Portly, *being known* as a wealthy man, can easily borrow money. [*Being known* is here a participle in the position of an apposed adjective. It modifies *Mr. Portly,* and is itself modified by the adverbial phrase *as a wealthy man.*]

Past participle, passive: Somewhat *embarrassed* by this remark, Norris smiled and made an awkward bow. [The participle *embarrassed* modifies *Norris. Somewhat,* an adverb, modifies *embarrassed.*]

Perfect participle, active: *Having elected* him mayor, his friends felt that they should be rewarded. [Here the participial phrase *Having elected him mayor* modifies *friends.* Note that this participle has two complements—*him,* a direct object, and *mayor,* an objective comple-ment.]

Perfect participle, passive: His opponent, *having been* soundly *defeated* for the third time, was a disappointed man. [The participle *having been defeated* modifies *opponent* and is modified by the adverb *soundly* and by the adverbial phrase *for a third time.*]

b. Gerunds. The gerund may be defined as a verbal noun. The forms of the gerund are identical with the forms of the participle but it is usually easy to distinguish between the two if one remembers that the *participle* has the *functions* of an *adjective* and that the gerund has the *functions* of the *noun.*

Gerund: *Remembering* names is difficult for Gerald.

Participle: Finally *remembering* the man's name, Gerald crossed the street and spoke to him. [In the first sentence the gerund *remembering* is the subject of *is,* and is modified by the predicate adjective *difficult. Names* is the direct object of the gerund. In the second sentence the participle *remembering* modifies the noun *Gerald* and is itself modi-fied by the adverb *finally.*]

In their capacity as nouns, gerunds serve as subjects, objects, and complements of verbs and in general perform the functions of a normal noun. (For the functions of nouns see page 731.) Gerunds resemble verbs in that they can be transitive or intransitive, complete or linking, active or passive, and can take adverbial modifiers and complements in the same way that verbs can.

The forms of the gerund and some of its uses are shown in the sentences below:

Present gerund, active: *Seeing* is *believing.* [This sentence contains two gerunds—*seeing,* the subject, and *believing,* the subjective complement of the verb *is. Believing* may also be called a predicate noun or predi-cate nominative.]

Present gerund, passive: Doctors often have the experience of *being called* in the middle of the night. [*Being called* is the object of the preposition *of* and is modified by the adverbial phrase *in the middle of the night.*]

Perfect gerund, active: *Having read* the book is enough; I don't care to see the movie. [*Having read* is the subject of *is* and takes *book* as its direct object.]

Perfect gerund, passive: His *having been fined* twice has caused him to drive more slowly. [The gerund *having been fined* is the subject of *has caused* and is modified by the adverb *twice*. The possessive *His* also modifies the gerund, and so supplies an example of the use of the possessive with the gerund.]

c. Infinitives. The infinitive may be defined as a verbal which functions as a noun, an adjective, or an adverb. It is commonly preceded by *to*, which is called *the sign of the infinitive*. As a verbal, the infinitive shares certain characteristics of the verb: it can be transitive or intransitive, complete or linking, active or passive; it can take complements and be modified by adverbs; it can even take a substantive as a subject and form what is loosely called an infinitive clause. (It cannot, however, form a complete predication.)

Examples of the infinitive used as a noun:
To live is *to come* nearer to death. [The infinitive *to live* is the subject, and the infinitive *to come* is the subjective complement.]
She wanted *to give* him a present. [The infinitive phrase *to give him a present* is the object of *wanted*. The infinitive *to give* takes two complements—the indirect object *him* and the direct object *present*.]
Examples of the infinitive used as an adjective:
There is a man *to admire* and *to emulate*. [The infinitives *to admire* and *to emulate* modify the noun *man*.]
He did not know the way *to go*. [The infinitive *to go* modifies the noun *way*.]
Examples of the infinitive used as an adverb:
He went *to see* what we would say. [The infinitive *to see* modifies *went* and is an adverb because it tells why he went. The clause *what we would say* is the object of the infinitive.]
He is too honest *to tell* a lie. [The infinitive *to tell* with its object *a lie* modifies the adjective *honest*.]

In the examples given above, the infinitive is preceded in each case by the word *to*, which is called the sign of the infinitive. Sometimes, however, the sign is omitted:

I saw the man *fall*. [*Fall* is an infinitive. With its subject, *the man*, it is the object of *saw*.]
We can do nothing but *hope* that he is safe. [The infinitive *hope* is the object of the preposition *but*. The clause *that he is safe* is the object of *hope*.]

The complementary infinitive and the so-called "infinitive clause" deserve mention and illustration here:

The complementary infinitive: I used *to go* to his house. [The infinitive *to go* is said to be complementary to the verb *used* because it serves the purpose of completing the predication of the verb and giving it a special meaning. Notice the difference in the meaning of *used* in *used to go* and in *used his fists*.]

The "infinitive clause": We asked *him to bring the oars.* [The expression *him to bring the oars* is similar in meaning and somewhat similar in construction to the dependent clause *that he bring the oars.* In this "infinitive clause", *him* is the subject of *to bring,* and *oars* is the direct obect; the whole infinitive clause is the object of *asked.* Notice that *him,* the subject of *to bring,* follows the rule that the subject of the infinitive is in the objective case.]

The forms of the infinitive are as follows:

Present active: *To err* is human.
Present passive: *To be forgiven* may be divine.
Perfect active: He is thought *to have left* the country.
Perfect passive: Her voice is said *to have been praised* in all the capitals of Europe.

6. Verb + Adverb Combinations and Verb + Preposition Combinations.

The man fell *down.*
The man fell *down* the stairs.

In the first sentence *down* is an ordinary adverb; it modifies the verb *fell.* In the second sentence *down* is an ordinary preposition; it takes an object, *the stairs,* and forms with that object a phrase that serves as an adverbial modifier of *fell* because it tells where the man fell. Now consider two more sentences:

The house was *torn down.*
They have *torn down* the house.

In these two sentences *torn* and *down* work together to express the action. The meaning of *torn* would be incomplete in *The house was torn.* The verb *torn* needs the help of *down* to make it complete, and hence *down* serves as a completer, a complement, instead of a modifier. When a word normally used as an adverb or a preposition serves in this way to complement the verb, it is convenient to regard the two-word unit as a verb. We then say that the expression *torn down* in the second sentence functions as a transitive verb, taking *the house* as its object.

7. Inflections of Verbs.
The purpose of this section is simply to supply a convenient list of grammatical terms used in describing inflections of verbs and to define those terms. The inflections of verbs

are the changes that occur in the form of verbs to indicate tense, voice, mood, person, and number.

a. The principal parts of verbs and regular and irregular verbs. The basic forms of verbs from which all other forms are derived are called the principal parts of verbs. These parts are three: (1) the present infinitive, *climb*, (2) the past tense (first person singular), *climbed* and (3) the past participle, *climbed*.

On the basis of the way they form the past indicative and the past participle, verbs are classified as regular or irregular. A regular verb forms its past indicative and past participle by adding *d, ed,* or *t* to the present infinitive. An irregular verb is one which forms its past indicative or past participle in some other manner. Regular verbs are more common than irregular verbs but some of the most commonly used verbs are irregular verbs.

Examples of regular verbs:

Present Infinitive	Past Tense	Past Participle
chase	chased	chased
fold	folded	folded
lie	lied	lied (to prevaricate)

Examples of irregular verbs:

Present Infinitive	Past Tense	Past Participle
see	saw	seen
do	did	done
go	went	gone
sit	sat	sat (to seat oneself)
set	set	set (to place)
lie	lay	lain (to recline)
lay	laid	laid (to place)

b. Tense. Tense is that property of the verb which indicates the time of the action or condition expressed by the verb. The six tenses in English are:

The present tense: I *go.*
The past tense: I *went.*
The future tense: I *shall go.*
The present perfect tense: I *have gone.*
The past perfect tense: I *had gone.*
The future perfect tense: I *shall have gone.*

c. Voice. Voice is that property of the verb which shows whether the subject of the verb acts or is acted upon. Active voice shows the subject acting; passive voice shows the subject acted upon.

Active voice: Our team *won* the game.
Passive voice: The game *was won* by our team.

d. Mood. Mood is that property of the verb which indicates whether the speaker is (1) making a request or giving a command, (imperative), (2) expressing a supposition or wish (subjunctive), or (3) stating a fact or opinion or asking a question (indicative).

Imperative mood: Close the window.
Subjunctive mood: If I *were* wealthy I could own a yacht.
Indicative mood: His son *is* at home now. *Will* he *stay* long?

e. Person and number. Person is that property of the verb which indicates whether the subject is the speaker (first person) the person spoken to (second person), or the person spoken about (third person). Number is that property of the verb which indicates whether the subject is singular or plural.

In English the verb does not necessarily undergo changes to indicate person and number, though it must, of course, agree with its subject in person and number. *Run* in *I run* (singular, first person) and in *they run* (plural, third person) does not change to indicate person and number; *runs* in *he runs* does clearly indicate person and number.

B. Substantives (Nouns and Pronouns)

A *noun* may be defined as a word or a group of words used to name a person, place, or thing. In using this definition one needs to know that nouns include not only obvious naming words like *Martin, Boston,* and *book* but also words, phrases, or clauses which are identified as noun expressions largely because they have the constructions of nouns (i.e., are used as subjects, objects, appositives, and the like).

The *boy* entered the *house.* [*Boy* and *house* are easy to recognize as nouns.]

I want *him to go.* [The infinitive phrase *him to go* is called a noun phrase because it is the object of *want.*]

I know *where he intended to go.* [*Where he intended to go* is called a noun clause because it is the object of *know,* and also because it serves the same function that would be served if we substituted *his destination* and made the sentence read *I know his destination.* In short, the clause does the work of a noun.]

A *pronoun* may be defined as a word used in place of a noun or as a word that refers to something without naming it. In practice we recognize pronouns in two ways: (1) we know that certain words (*he, they, any, his,* etc.) are often or nearly always used as pronouns, and we conclude that a particular word is likely to be a pronoun, and (2) we look at the word to see its construction in the sentence. If the word is used as a substitute for a noun and if it has a noun construction, we know that it is a pronoun.

> *He* has received his money and *I* haven't received *mine*. [*He, I,* and *mine* are pronouns because they are words used to take the place of nouns and to serve noun functions. Notice that *his* in this sentence is not a pronoun; it modifies *money* and so is a pronominal adjective.]
>
> Almost *everyone* expects trouble, but *I* don't expect *any*. [*Everyone, I,* and *any* are pronouns. If *any* were followed by *difficulty,* though, it would then modify that word and would be used as an adjective.]

The word *substantive* is now easy to define; it is a general word used to include nouns and pronouns as they have just been defined.

1. Substantive (Noun and Pronoun) Constructions. The constructions which we shall take up under this heading are common to nouns, pronouns, noun phrases, and noun clauses. Substantives may be used in the following constructions.

a. Subject of a verb or of an infinitive:
Tom is here. [Noun, subject of the verb *is*]
That Tom was here is certain. [Noun clause, subject of *is*]
There are *none* in the basket. [Pronoun, subject of *are*]
She wanted *him* to come. [Pronoun, subject of the infinitive and therefore in the objective case. The infinitive phrase (or clause as it is sometimes called) *him to come* is the object of the verb *wanted.*]

b. Object of a preposition. (Of course, verbs and verbals also take objects; these will be discussed under the next heading, "Complements of verbs and of verbals.")
He stood on the *corner.* [Noun, object of *on*]
Give it to *whoever wants it.* [Noun clause, object of *to*]
Ask him for *it.* [Pronoun, object of *for*]

c. Complements of verbs and of verbals. On pages 723–725 we have dealt in detail with the complements of verbs and of verbals. Here, therefore, we shall simply list again the noun constructions which serve as complements and give one example of each to help to recall the earlier discussion of complements.

(1) Complements of transitive verbs:
Direct object: The boys broke the *window.*
Indirect object: He sold *me* a paper.
Retained objects, direct and indirect:
The musician was given an *ovation.* [Direct]
A car was given *Tom* on his birthday. [Indirect]

Double objects: She taught *me Russian.*
Objective complement: They elected him *president.*
Subjective complement after a passive verb: He was elected *president.*

(2) Complement of a linking verb:

Subjective complement: George is her *husband.* [*Husband* may also be called a *predicate noun* or a *predicate nominative.*]

d. Appositives. An appositive may be defined as a locution (a noun, pronoun, noun phrase or noun clause) placed beside another word and denoting the same person or thing. Appositives are in the same case as the substantive with which they are in apposition.

The guest, *a tall man,* rose and looked down on his host. [The noun *man,* along with its modifiers, is used in apposition with *guest.*]
Two of us, *Charles* and *I,* never did see the play. [The substantives *Charles* and *I* are in apposition with *two.*]
His excuse, *that he had not heard his alarm clock,* did not impress his professor favorably. [The noun clause is in apposition with *excuse.*]
Ernest came to college for three reasons: *to escape his parents, to join a fraternity,* and *to get a diploma.* [The three infinitive phrases are in apposition with *reasons.*]

e. Possessives used as substantives. Expressions which are inflected to show possession—*Henry's, cat's, his, everyone's,* for example—are called possessives. With some exceptions, possessives may be used as substantives or adjectives. Examples of possessives used as substantives are:

This coat is *Henry's.* [Note that *Henry's* is here used as a noun. If the sentence were *This is Henry's coat,* the possessive *Henry's* would then be used as an adjective modifying *coat.*]
He gave me his address and asked for *mine.* [*Mine* is a possessive pronoun and hence a substantive. The possessive *his,* however, though often used as a pronoun is here used as an adjective modifying *address.*]

f. Nominative of direct address:

Father, may I take the car tonight? [Noun]
You, stop complaining and do that errand! [Pronoun]

2. Other Properties Common to Nouns and Pronouns. Nouns and pronouns, in addition to functioning in the same constructions, also have in common the properties of gender, number, and case.

a. Gender. There are four grammatical genders: masculine, feminine, neuter, and common. A noun or a pronoun is said to be of common gender when it refers to a being which may be of either sex.

Examples of words of common gender are: *baby, parent, one.*

b. Number. Nouns and pronouns may be singular (*man, he*) or plural (*men, they*).

c. Case. Nouns and pronouns are said to have three cases; the nominative, the objective, and the possessive. Nouns show a change in form (i.e., are inflected) only in the possessive case; some pronouns have different forms for each case (*he, him, his*). Common uses of the three cases are listed below:

(1) **Nominative:** subject of a verb, appositive to a word in the nominative case, subjective complement (It is *he*), nominative of address (Good morning, *Mary*).

(2) **Objective:** direct or indirect object of a verb or a verbal, object of a preposition, subject of an infinitive, appositive to a substantive in the objective case, objective complement (They made him *chairman*).

(3) **Possessive:** ordinary expressions of possession like *Tom's* hat, *his* coat, *anyone's* tie, and also the so-called subject of the gerund (*Tom's* arriving late was unfortunate; in fact *his* arriving at all was unfortunate).

d. Person. There are three persons: first person (the speaker), second person (the person spoken to), and third person (the person spoken of).

I, Caesar, will conquer. [First person]
You, Brutus, are my friend. [Second person]
They, Caesar and *Brutus,* were Romans. [Third person]

3. Further Information about Nouns. Students need to be able to distinguish between proper and common nouns and to recognize collective nouns.

a. Proper nouns and common nouns. A proper noun is the name of a *particular* person, place, or thing (*George Washington, Chicago, Brooklyn Bridge*). Proper nouns are capitalized. A common noun is the name of a *class* of persons, places, or things (*statesman, city, bridge*). Common nouns are not capitalized.

b. Collective nouns. A collective noun is a word which in the singular denotes a group of similar beings (*jury, committee, crowd*).

4. Further Information about Pronouns. In pages 731–733 we have taken up the constructions that are common to all substantives and the properties (gender, number, and case) which are common to nouns and pronouns. The purpose of the present section is to supplement the earlier sections and to provide definitions of other terms necessary in the discussion of pronouns. For information about the conventions of pronoun usage the student should see pages 752–757.

a. Classes of pronouns. Pronouns may be classed as personal, relative, interrogative, demonstrative, or indefinite.

(1) Personal pronouns. The pronouns *I, you, he, she,* and *it* with all their forms (*me, mine, we, ours, us,* etc.) are called personal pronouns. When the word *self* or *selves* is added to a form of the personal pronoun, the resultant form (*myself, yourself, himself, themselves*) is called a compound personal pronoun. Such pronouns may be reflexive (I hurt *myself*) or intensive (General Eisenhower *himself* will be there).

(2) Relative pronouns. Relative pronouns are two-function words. Like other pronouns, they stand in the place of a noun, and at the same time they work somewhat like a subordinating conjunction in that they connect a subordinate clause to some word in the main clause. Words often used as relative pronouns are *who, whom, whose, which, what, that* and also the compound relative pronouns *whoever, whomever, whichever, whatever.*

> I know *whom* you mean. [The relative pronoun *whom* is the object of *mean,* and at the same time it serves to join its clause to the main clause *I know. Whom you mean* is the object of *know.*]
> I know *who* he is. [*Who he is* is equivalent to *he is who,* and *who* serves as a subjective complement; at the same time *who* connects its clause to the main clause *I know.* The clause *who he is* is the object of the verb *know.*]
> Take *whoever* wants to go. [*Whoever* is the subject of *wants,* and the clause *whoever wants to go* is the object of the imperative verb *take.*]

In dealing with relative pronouns it is important to remember that *the case of the pronoun is determined by its construction in its own clause.* In the sentence *I know who is coming, who* and not *whom* is the approved form because *who* is the subject of *is coming:* the whole clause *who is coming* is the object of the verb *know.*

Sometimes in speech and in informal writing relative pronouns are "understood" but are not expressed:

> I know [*that*] Charles will come early.
> The man [*that* or *whom*] we expected did not come.

Such sentences are analyzed as if the relative pronoun were expressed.

(3) Interrogative pronouns. *Who, whose, which,* and *what,* when they are used to introduce a direct or an indirect question are called interrogative pronouns.

> *Who* wants another piece of pie? [Direct question]
> They wondered *who* had taken the money. [Indirect]

(4) Demonstrative pronouns. *This* and *that* and their plurals *these* and *those* are called demonstrative pronouns when they are used as pronouns to point out or to call attention to some particular thing.

> *This* is the last stop.
> *Those* are not my shoes.

(5) Indefinite pronouns. Certain pronouns which do not refer to definite persons or things are called indefinite pronouns. Examples are: *any, nothing, few, each, much, all, something.*

> *Each* should work for the good of *all.*
> *Everyone* is to bring *something.*

NOTE ON ALL CLASSES OF PRONOUNS.—Many words which serve as pronouns also may serve as adjectives. Such adjectives are called pronominal adjectives. Some examples are: *his* coat, *which* house, *that* tree, *any* child.

b. Reference of pronouns: agreement with antecedent. The antecedent of a pronoun is the word or group of words to which that pronoun refers.

> The *freshmen* thought that *they* were being persecuted by the sophomores. [*Freshmen* is the antecedent of *they.*]
> This is the new *student who* refuses to wear a freshman cap. [*Student* is the antecedent of the relative pronoun *who.*]
> We know *who* will oppose this action. [In this sentence the relative pronoun *who* has no expressed antecedent.]

When a pronoun has an antecedent, it agrees with that antecedent in gender, number, and person. The case of the pronoun depends on the pronoun's construction in the sentence and is independent of the antecedent.

> *People who* live in glass houses shouldn't throw stones. [People is the antecedent of the relative pronoun *who; who* is the subject of the verb *live.*]
> The *sophomore* had looked at things differently when *he* was a freshman. [The personal pronoun *he* agrees with its antecedent *sophomore* in gender, number, and person: it is in the nominative case because it is the subject of *was.*]

C. Adjectives

An adjective is a word or group of words which modifies a substantive. An adjective may be a word, an adjective phrase, or an adjective clause.

> The house *on the hill* belongs to the *young* couple *that we met last night.* [*On the hill* is an adjective phrase modifying *house; young* is an ad-

jective modifying *couple; that we met last night* is an adjective clause also modifying *couple.*]

1. **Construction of Adjectives.** In dealing with the construction of adjectives one needs to recognize apposed adjectives, predicate adjectives, adjectives used after verbs of the senses, adjectives used as objective complements, and adherent adjectives.

Apposed adjectives: The man, *old* and *stooped,* did not look up as we drove by. [*Old* and *stooped* are apposed adjectives; they are called *apposed* because they occupy the same position as an appositive and serve, like the appositive, to give additional information about a substantive.]

Predicate adjectives: The man is *old* and *stooped.* [*Old* and *stooped* serve as subjective complements of the linking verb *is* and modify *man.*]

Adjectives used after verbs of the senses: He feels *bad.* [*Feels,* a verb of the senses, is followed by the adjective *bad.* Verbs of the senses—*see, taste, smell, look,* and the like—often function as linking verbs. Here the verb *feels* links the pronoun *He* to its adjective *bad.*]

Adjectives used as objective complements: She washed the windows *clean.* [*Clean,* an adjective, is the objective complement of the transitive verb *washed.*]

Adherent adjectives. (Adjectives used in constructions other than those listed above are called *adherent* adjectives. The italicized words in the following sentence are adherent adjectives.) The man *in the window* owns *the new* house *that burned down.* [*In the window* is an adjective phrase modifying *man; the* and *new* are adjectives modifying *house; that burned down* is an adjective clause also modifying *house.*]

2. **Adjectives Used as Other Parts of Speech, and Other Parts of Speech Used as Adjectives.** Words that usually function as adjectives may of course be used as other parts of speech, and words often or normally used as other parts of speech may also be used as adjectives:

The land of the *free* and the home of the *brave.* [*Free* and *brave,* usually adjectives, are here used as nouns.]

The best way *to get* to *Mary's* house is to follow *these* directions: *First* Avenue is *a through* street for *five* blocks. Turn to *your* left on *the intersecting* street to avoid *Sunday-afternoon* traffic and then . . . [The italicized locutions are all adjectives, though many of them are commonly used as other parts of speech.]

3. **The Comparison of Adjectives: Positive, Comparative, and Superlative Degrees.**

Positive degree: Young brother, *courageous* man.

Comparative degree: Younger brother, *more courageous* man, *less courageous* man.

Superlative degree: Youngest brother, *most courageous* man, *least courageous* man.

4. Classes of Adjectives: Descriptive and Limiting Adjectives.

a. Descriptive adjectives. Descriptive adjectives express a quality or a condition or a characteristic, and so are said to describe a substantive: *tall* man, *poor* boy, *rolling* stone.

b. Limiting adjectives. Adjectives other than descriptive adjectives are called limiting adjectives because they point out or identify particular members of a class: *this* man, *three* boys, *my* house. Types of limiting adjectives are:

(1) **Proper adjectives (adjectives derived from proper nouns):** *Morris* chair, *French* language, *Russian* novel.

(2) **Numeral adjectives, cardinal or ordinal:** *one* dollar, *two* houses, *ten* men. [Cardinal] *First* degree, *third* effort, *fifth* class. [Ordinal]

(3) **Articles:** definite (*the*) and indefinite (*a, an*).

(4) **Possessive nouns as adjectives.** Substantives in the possessive case may be used as adjectives: *Luther's* house, *Jane's* wedding.

(5) **Pronouns used as adjectives.** Some words often used as demonstrative, indefinite, interrogative, personal, or relative pronouns may also be used as adjectives. When such words are used as adjectives, they modify a substantive; when they are used as pronouns, they do not.

Demonstrative adjectives: This hat, *these* hats; *that* hat, *those* hats.
Indefinite adjectives: Some people, *any* reason, *few* students.
Interrogative adjectives: Which chair is yours? *What* time will he come?
Possessive adjectives: This is *my* book. That is *his* pencil.
Relative adjectives: He didn't know *which* way was the right one, *or what* person would know.

D. Adverbs

Like adjectives, adverbs may be single words, phrases, or clauses, may modify single words, phrases, or clauses, and may express comparison (i.e., they may be in the positive, comparative, or superlative degree). Adverbs may be distinguished from adjectives by a simple test: An adjective modifies *only* a substantive; an adverb may modify *anything but* a substantive, though it usually modifies a verb, an adjective, or another adverb. Sometimes an adverb does not clearly modify a particular expression in a clause or a sentence. In such cases the adverb may be said to modify the whole clause or the whole sentence. Examples of common uses of adverbs are given below.

1. Uses (or Constructions) of Adverbs.
Adverb modifying a verb: He walked *slowly.*
Adverb modifying an adjective: The air was *very* warm.
Adverb modifying another adverb: He walked *very* slowly.

Adverb modifying a verbal: Rising to his feet *indignantly*, Mr. Austin replied to the Russian delegate. [*Indignantly* modifies the participle *rising*.]

Adverb modifying a phrase: The shot went *just* above his head. [*Just*, an adverb, modifies the adverbial phrase *above his head*, which in turn modifies the verb *went*.]

Adverb modifying a subordinate clause: He speaks *only* when he is spoken to. [*Only* modifies the adverbial clause *when he is spoken to*, which in turn modifies the verb *speaks*.]

Adverb as a clause or sentence modifier. (Sometimes, as we have said, adverbs do not clearly modify a particular locution in a clause or a sentence; instead they may be said to modify the whole statement, as in the following examples.)

He tried hard. *Nevertheless* his team was defeated.

If I do say so myself, it was a good job.

(Further examples of adverb constructions are given below.)

2. Classes of Adverbs. Adverbs may be grouped in three classes: simple adverbs, interrogative adverbs, and conjunctive adverbs.

a. Simple adverbs. Simple adverbs serve only as modifiers. They supply answers to such questions as When? How? How much? Where? In what order or degree?

She slept *late*.

He talked *slowly*.

Our work is *somewhat* harder *here* than it was *there*.

He came *first* and stayed *longer* than anyone else.

No, I will *not* let you have the car.

b. Interrogative adverbs. Interrogative adverbs (*when, why, how, where,* etc.) introduce a question: *Where* did he go? *Why* has he gone?

c. Conjunctive adverbs. A conjunctive adverb (sometimes called a transitional adverb) acts as a conjunction and at the same time acts as an adverb in that it modifies a word in its clause or modifies the whole clause. Words commonly used as conjunctive adverbs are: *besides, indeed, in fact, also, moreover, further, nevertheless, however, still, therefore, thus, hence, accordingly.*

George is Mr. Haines' only son; *nevertheless* Mr. Haines is very harsh with him.

His nose was broken; *still* he fought on.

They were very late; *in fact* they arrived when the dance was over.

E. Prepositions

A preposition is an expression used to connect a substantive to some other element in the sentence: the substantive, known as the object of the preposition, may consist of a word, a phrase, or a dependent clause, and the preposition and its object, along with the modifiers of the object or of preposition plus object, are called a *prepositional phrase*. A preposition may be a single word (*on, in, along,* etc.) or several words (*in accordance with, in order to, because of,* etc.). Prepositions which consist of more than one word are called *phrasal prepositions*.

He talked *to* her. [*To,* a preposition, takes as its object the pronoun *her* to form the prepositional phrase *to her,* and the phrase serves as the adverbial modifier of the verb *talked.*]

He stood almost directly *above* Tom and me. [The preposition *above* takes *Tom and me* as its compound object to form an adverbial modifier of *stood. Directly,* modified by *almost,* in turn modifies *above Tom and me.* The whole expression, *almost directly above Tom and me* is a prepositional phrase.]

This is not the boy I was looking *for.* [Here *for* has no expressed object, but *whom (the boy for whom I was looking)* is easily supplied. We say that *whom* is the "understood" object of *for.*]

The game was called off *on account of* rain. [*On account of,* a phrasal preposition, takes *rain* as its object.]

F. Conjunctions

A conjunction is a word that connects words, phrases, or clauses. Prepositions, which are also connectives, may be distinguished from conjunctions in that prepositions always have an object expressed or understood and conjunctions do not.

He was tired, *for* it was very late. [*For* is a conjunction which serves to join two independent clauses. It does not have an object.]

He did the work *for* five dollars. [*For* is a preposition, and its object is *dollars.*]

Conjunctions may be divided into two classes, coordinating and subordinating.

1. Coordinating Conjunctions. Coordinating conjunctions connect locutions of equal rank. The most common coordinating conjunctions, sometimes called pure conjunctions, are *and, but, for, or, nor.*

He is young *and* strong. [*And* connects *young* and *strong.*]

The two nations fought on the land *and* on the sea. [*And* connects the phrases *on the land* and *on the sea.*]

He may be old, *but* he is still a good swimmer. [*But* connects two independent clauses.]

Chester was late, very late. *And* Anne resented it, although she said nothing about it at the time. [*And* connects two sentences.]

Note.—Certain coordinating conjunctions are used in pairs and are called correlative conjunctions. Examples are: *not only . . . but also, either . . . or, neither . . . nor, both . . . and.*

Both Tom *and* I are going.
Neither he *nor* she wants to marry now.

2. Subordinating Conjunctions. A subordinating conjunction connects sentence elements of unequal rank. Common subordinating conjunctions are: *if, although, when, while, where, whenever, because, that, until, whether, than, how, unless, since, as, before, after, though.*

He has already sold the house *that* he bought yesterday. [*That* connects the subordinate clause *that he bought yesterday* to the main clause. The whole subordinate clause acts as an adjective modifying *house.*]

Although it was late, we were not hungry. [*Although* connects the subordinate clause of which it is a part to the main clause *we were not hungry.*]

The boy did not know *where* to find his mother. [*Where* connects the infinitive phrase *where to find his mother* to the main clause. The infinitive phrase is the object of the verb *know. Where* also modifies the infinitive (i.e., *to find . . . where*) and so functions as an adverb as well as a conjunction, as do some of the other words that we have listed as subordinating conjunctions. Some grammarians prefer to call such words relative adverbs; it will serve our purpose, though, to call them subordinating conjunctions.]

G. Interjections

An interjection is a locution used to express strong emotions such as joy, anger, pain, relief, surprise. Some words like *ouch, alas, bah, hurrah* are always or nearly always used as interjections. Many other locutions may become interjections when they are used as exclamations: *Good heavens! Wonderful! Enough! Help! Damn!* Since interjections have no grammatical relations with other words in sentences, there is, fortunately, nothing further to say about them here except that the parts of exclamatory phrases, clauses, or sentences can be analyzed like other locutions. In *Good heavens, good* is an adjective modifying the noun *heavens.*

H. Other Common Constructions

Earlier we defined construction as the grammatical relationship of a word to other words; in a broader sense the term is used to refer to any grammatical pattern that occurs in sentences. In this section we shall consider compound constructions and parallelism, elliptical constructions, normal and inverted order, and absolute constructions.

1. **Compound Constructions and Parallelism.** The best way to define compound constructions is to start with a simple example: *Tom, Mary,* and *Jane* left early. Most students already know that the coordinate locutions *Tom, Mary,* and *Jane* form the compound subject of the verb *left.* When two or more coordinate locutions work together in this way to perform a single grammatical function, they form a compound construction. Of course, compound constructions occur very frequently; subjects, predicates, modifiers, complements —any of these may be compounded.

Closely associated with compound constructions is the term *parallelism,* for the parts of a compound expression are, or should be, parallel. Parallelism may be defined as that principle of usage which requires that coordinate elements in a compound construction be given the same grammatical form. Words, phrases, clauses, and even sentences may be expressed in parallel form. The following sentences illustrate compounding and parallelism and also make clear the relationship between the two.

She *is sweet sixteen* and *has been kissed.* [This sentence has a compound predicate—*is sweet sixteen* and *has been kissed*—and the two parts of the compound predicate are parallel. As is often the case, the coordinate elements are joined by a coordinating conjunction (*and*).]

All his clothes—*his straw hat, his shoes, his overalls*—identified him as a farmer. [A compound appositive. The coordinate expressions *hat, shoes,* and *overalls* are in apposition with *clothes,* and are parallel. Though they are not joined by *and,* they could be.]

He is either *unable* or *unwilling* to grant our request. [*Unable* and *unwilling,* introduced by the correlative conjunctions *either . . . or,* form a compound modifier of *He* and are parallel expressions. Note that the elements of parallel expressions are always grammatically equal (all verbs, all nouns, or all adjectives). In our first sentence the parallel elements are verbs (*is, has been kissed*); in the second, nouns (*hat, shoes, overalls*); in the third, adjectives (*unable, unwilling*). Note also that in each sentence the parallel words have the same relationship with some other word in the sentence; in the second sentence the three nouns are in apposition with *clothes;* in the third sentence the two adjectives modify *He.*]

He thinks *that war is not inevitable* and *that statesmanship can prevent war.* [Two noun clauses form the compound object of *thinks* and are parallel expressions. If the second *that* were omitted the two clauses would not be parallel but would illustrate faulty parallelism.]

He was tired, he was disappointed, and *he was very hot.* [In this compound sentence, the three coordinate elements are independent clauses, and the clauses are parallel expressions. If these three independent clauses were written as separate sentences they would still be parallel, for they are coordinate constructions, they are in the same grammatical form, and they express similar ideas in that they tell us three things about the subject *He.* Compound constructions must occur in the same sentence, but the parts of parallel constructions may each be sentences if those sentences are similar in construction and in function.]

2. Elliptical Constructions. Clauses or sentences in which easily supplied words are omitted are called elliptical constructions. Such constructions, common in writing, and even more common in speech, are often preferable to the fuller forms. They are usually equally clear, and they are shorter. In grammatical analysis it is necessary to supply the omitted words.

> Tom knows more *than I.* [*Than I* is an elliptical clause; the full clause would be *than I know.*]
> I know *you weren't there.* [Another elliptical dependent clause, this time with *that* omitted: I know *that* you weren't there.]
> To err is human, *to forgive, divine.* [*Is,* omitted in the second independent clause, is easily supplied: To forgive *is* divine.]

NOTE.—Compound predicates should not be mistaken for elliptical constructions. In the sentence, She *stamped her foot and slammed the door in his face,* there is no ellipsis; the italicized words are the compound predicate of *She.*

3. Normal and Inverted Order. In the broadest sense, the term *order* means the sequence in which words are arranged in a sentence. But when we speak of normal word order and inverted word order, we have chiefly in mind the position of the subject, the verb, and the complement or complements. (The position of modifiers and connectives, though important, is usually a matter of secondary interest.) In most statements the sequence is subject, verb, complement, and hence the subject-verb-complement order is called the *normal order.* A sentence in which the normal order is not followed is said to be in *inverted order,* and the placing of an element contrary to the normal order is called *inversion.*

> NORMAL: I admire her; I detest him. [Subject, verb, complement. Here the complement is the direct object—*her* in the first clause and *him* in the second.]
> INVERTED: Her I admire; him I detest. [Here the two complements precede their subjects, and the order is complement, subject, verb.]

> NORMAL: I have not received that order yet.
> INVERTED: Not yet have I received that order. [Note the order here: modifier (*not yet*), auxiliary verb (*have*), subject (*I*), main verb (*received*), object (*that order*).]
> INVERTED: That order I have not yet received.

Normal: He said he'd be late and he is late.
Inverted: Late he said he'd be and late he is.

Note.—Normal word order for statements is not the same as normal word order for questions and for subordinate clauses. In analyzing sentences it is advisable to arrange inverted statements, questions, and subordinate clauses in subject-verb-complement order, for relationships are then easier to see.

Mary, Tom, and him I liked. [I liked Mary, Tom, and him.]
To whom did he give the book? [He did give the book to whom?]
Whom shall I ask? [I shall ask whom?]
Does he know which he wants? [He does know he wants which.]

4. Absolute Constructions. A word, phrase, or clause that has no grammatical relationship to the rest of its sentence is called an absolute construction. *Absolute* in this sense means grammatically unconnected and does not mean that the expression is unnecessary in the sentence. Common absolute expressions are illustrated below. (Some of the expressions which we have listed here may be called by other names and explained in different ways, for grammarians are not in agreement about them.)

The weather being uncomfortably warm, we did not wear coats. [The italicized expression is called a *nominative absolute.* The article *The* and the participial phrase *being uncomfortably warm* modify *weather.* The whole construction does not modify any word or group of words in the main clause, and so is called an absolute construction.]

As General Sherman said in stronger language, war is very unpleasant. [The italicized clause does not modify any locution in the main clause and hence can be explained as an *absolute subordinate clause* or as a modifier of the whole main clause.]

Tom said—*at least I think it was Tom*—that the book was banned in Boston. [The italicized expression is an *absolute parenthetical construction.* In analysis this sentence would be called complex and the parenthetical expression would be analyzed by itself.]

He did not go to class; *in fact,* he deliberately stayed away. [*In fact* may be called an absolute expression or it may be regarded as a modifier of the whole second clause and a connective for the two clauses. It is then called a conjunctive adverb.]

Good heavens, Tom, what a grim expression! [An interjection, *good heavens,* a nominative of direct address, *Tom,* and an exclamation, *what an expression,* may also be classed as absolute expressions.]

There were four men in the boat; and *it* was easy to see that they were not sailors. [In this sentence *There* and *it* are absolute expressions and are called expletives. The clauses are grammatically complete without these two words: *Four men were in the boat; to see that they were not*

sailors was easy. The two expletives make possible the inversion in the
two clauses.]

(The exercises for "Grammar at a Higher Level" are on page
747.)

ANALYZING SENTENCES

Learning grammatical terms and constructions and analyzing
sentences are two steps in the process of understanding grammar.
Grammatical terms and constructions have been discussed in the
preceding pages. This section on analyzing sentences supplies a
second step toward understanding grammar.

Both these steps, however, are largely a waste of time unless they
lead to improvement in reading or in writing. As soon as you have
analyzed enough sentences to be skillful in grasping the significant
aspects of word order and structure, you should go on to the more
rewarding activity of analyzing passages of good prose. You should
then analyze rhetorically as well as grammatically and should see not
only *how* effective sentences are constructed but also *why* they were
so constructed. Such analysis can make you a more perceptive reader
and can show you concrete ways to improve your own writing.

In the instructions below, a somewhat elaborate procedure for
analyzing sentences is suggested. This is intended simply as a learning device; using it for long would be dull and unrewarding for all
except born grammarians. Some practice in such analysis may be
necessary, however, to consolidate your knowledge of grammar and
to make it really useful. At first you should make your analyses as
thorough as possible. Later, after you have developed sufficient skill,
you can disregard unimportant details and can focus your attention
on those distinctive aspects of a sentence or a series of sentences which
contribute to effective communication.

1. **Instructions for the Analysis of Sentences.** Usually it is best to
go from general to particular: first determine what the major units
of the sentence are—these units may be clauses or phrases—and what
relationship they bear to one another; then determine what the
units within the major units are and what function each has in its
major unit; finally, for a full analysis, analyze the construction of
each word in the minor unit. A full [4] analysis should contain (not
necessarily in this order) the following information. (For a general
analysis omit point 4.)

(1) The kind of sentence (simple, compound, etc.), the number of

---

[4] Do a full analysis unless your instructor specifically asks for a general analysis.

dependent and independent clauses with the words which constitute each clause, and the relationship between the clauses.

(2) The simple subject and the simple predicate of each clause.

(3) The construction of every phrase and dependent clause—that is, what part of speech it serves as, and its function in its larger word group.

(4) The construction of every word in the sentence.

(5) Any other information that is relevant to a full and clear grammatical analysis of the sentence.

2. Sample Analysis. We have deliberately chosen a somewhat complicated sentence in order to illustrate a large number of grammatical points. You will follow the analysis more easily if you will write on a separate sheet of paper the sentence which we shall be analyzing:

> As I recall those early days, I realize there were times when I was perhaps too positive about what I wanted to do and how it should be done.

Upon examination this sentence falls into four major units: (1) *As I recall those early days,* a dependent clause; (2) *I realize [that] there were times,* an independent clause that contains a dependent clause; (3) *when I was perhaps too positive,* a dependent clause; and (4) *about what I wanted to do and how it should be done,* a prepositional phrase which contains two dependent clauses.

Our sentence, then, is a complex sentence which contains one independent clause and five dependent clauses.

The first dependent clause is easy to analyze. Introduced by the subordinating conjunction *as,* it modifies the verb *realize,* and so joins the first two clauses. Its simple subject is the pronoun *I;* its simple predicate is *recall.* The noun *days* is the direct object of *recall* and is modified by the demonstrative adjective *those* and the adjective *early.*

The main clause *I realize [that] there were times* has as its subject the pronoun *I* and as its verb the word *realize.* Since *realize* is an incomplete verb, it has as its complement the dependent clause *[that] there were times.* In analyzing this clause we see that it is a noun clause because it is the direct object of *realize,* and we see also that it is an elliptical clause because the subordinating conjunction *that* is understood but not expressed. The subject of this clause is *times* and the predicate is *were.* *There,* which occupies the normal position of a subject, is an expletive. *Were* is here used as a complete verb and has no complement.

The next dependent clause, *when I was perhaps too positive,* serves as an adjective modifier of *times* and is connected to the preceding clause by the subordinating conjunction *when.* The pronoun *I* is the subject of the clause, and the simple predicate consists of the incomplete verb *was* and its subjective complement *positive.* The adjective *positive* is modified by the adverb *too,* and *too* in turn is modified by the adverb *perhaps.*

The third large unit of the sentence, *about what I wanted to do and how it should be done,* is a long phrase introduced by the preposition *about.* The whole phrase serves as an adverbial modifier of *positive,* and the two dependent clauses joined by the conjunction *and* are noun clauses which are objects of the preposition. *What I wanted to do* has *I* as its simple subject and *wanted* as its incomplete verb; the infinitive phrase *to do what* is the object of *wanted* and hence its complement. *What,* a relative pronoun, is the object of the infinitive *to do.* In the second noun clause, *it* is the simple subject, and the passive verb phrase *should be done* is the simple predicate. *Should* and *be* are auxiliary verbs and *done* is the main verb. The verb phrase is modified by the subordinating conjunction *how* which also serves as a connective word. The personal pronoun *it* has as its antecedent the word *what* in the preceding clause.

3. Further Suggestions for the Analysis of Sentences. In analyzing sentences it is helpful to keep in mind:

(1) That it is usually best to find the main units and to determine their relationships to one another before proceeding to the smaller units and to single words.

(2) That in analyzing clauses you should look first for the simple subject and the simple predicate.

(3) That incomplete (i.e., transitive and linking) verbs require complements to form a predicate, and that the most common complements are the direct object and the subjective complement.

(4) That the function of the word in the sentence determines what part of speech it is, and that when you are puzzled about a word or a group of words, you should ask yourself the question, "what is its function in this sentence?"

(5) That there are four main functions of words: to assert, to name, to modify, and to connect.

(6) That dependent clauses are either noun clauses, adjective clauses, adverbial clauses, or absolute constructions, and that absolute dependent clauses are comparatively rare.

(7) That compound constructions are very common, and that any part of a sentence may be compounded.

(8) That a sentence or a clause in inverted order will be easier to analyze if you change it to normal order before you attempt to analyze it.

(9) That for purposes of analysis the words omitted in elliptical

constructions are supplied, and the sentence is analyzed as if the words were present.

EXERCISES

Exercises for "Basic Grammar" in "An Expanded Outline of Grammar"

1. What are the four main functions of words in sentences, and which parts of speech serve which functions?

2. Distinguish between complete, incomplete, and fragmentary sentences.

3. Distinguish between clauses and phrases, dependent and independent clauses, verbs and verbals, adjectives and adverbs, prepositions and conjunctions. Make the distinction clear by giving examples.

4. For each of the following sentences:

(a) State the kind of sentence it is (simple, compound, complex, compound-complex) and identify the dependent and independent clauses.

(b) Point out the simple subject and the simple predicate in each clause.

(c) Indicate whether the verb is transitive or intransitive.

(d) Point out, if it is present, (1) a verbal, (2) an adverbial clause, (3) an interjection, (4) a noun clause, (5) a verb phrase, (6) an adjectival clause, (7) an adverbial clause, (8) a conjunction.

When she arrived early in the evening, we were surprised and pleased.
The woman and her companion talked for a few minutes and then went to the information booth to learn when the next train would leave.
Although I came to college to study medicine, I am, alas, still studying grammar.

5. Write a short passage which contains examples of each of the following: a compound subject, a compound predicate, a prepositional phrase used as an adjective, a noun clause, an adjectival clause, an adverbial clause, a fragmentary sentence, a periodic sentence.

Exercises for "Grammar at a Higher Level" in "An Expanded Outline of Grammar"

1. Give examples in sentences of intransitive, transitive, and linking verbs. Which verbs have complements?

2. How can one distinguish between a participle and a gerund, between a regular and an irregular verb, between a verb and a verbal, between an appositive and an apposed adjective, between a demon-

strative pronoun and a demonstrative adjective, between common nouns and proper nouns?

3. For each of the following sentences:

(a) Indicate the simple subject and simple predicate of each clause.

(b) State what part of speech each subordinate clause or phrase is used as, and how the clause or phrase is related to other words in the sentence.

(c) Point out, if it is present: (1) a direct object, (2) an indirect object, (3) a subjective complement, (4) an appositive, (5) an apposed adjective, (6) a compound object, (7) an objective complement, (8) a conjunctive adverb, (9) a nominative absolute, (10) a subordinating conjunction, (11) a parallel construction, (12) an example of inverted order.

The day being cold and rainy, we decided not to go out to dinner.

After the game, Walter, usually very shy and quiet, said that he was in a mood to paint the town red.

"Hurrah!" Eliot said. "Here is a can of paint, and there is the town."

Gettysburg, the place where Lincoln made his famous speech, is in Pennsylvania and is on our route; nevertheless Henry stubbornly refuses to stop there.

The three men, tense and expectant, waited through the interminable night; at last, just at dawn, came the signal, two long blasts of the factory whistle.

Sentences for Full Analysis

Analyze each sentence in the two passages below, following the instructions given under "Analyzing Sentences." If you have already read Chapters One to Seven, consider not only *how* each sentence is constructed, but also *why* it is constructed as it is. In this second (rhetorical) analysis consider such matters as emphasis, economy, variety of sentence structure; use of subordination, parallelism and balance, repetition of words, transitions, incomplete sentences, and inversion; choice of concise and concrete words; figures of speech.

The tractors came over the roads and into the fields, great crawlers moving like insects, having the incredible strength of insects. They crawled over the ground, laying the track and rolling on it and picking it up. Diesel tractors, puttering while they stood idle; they thundered when they moved, and then settled down to a droning roar. Snub-nosed monsters, raising the dust and sticking their snouts into it, straight down the country, across the country, through fences, through dooryards, in and out of gullies in straight lines. They did not run on the ground, but on their own roadbeds. They ignored hills and gulches, water courses, fences, houses.—JOHN STEINBECK, *The Grapes of Wrath*

But if men forget that the future will some day be a present, they forget, too, that the present is already here, and that even in a dark time some of the brightness for which they long is open to the responsive senses, the welcoming heart, and the liberated mind. The moments as they pass even now have their tang and character. They may yield even now the contagious joy of feeling and perception. Here are the familiar flowers, the music we love, the poetry by which we are moved. Here are the books and companions, the ideas and the relaxations, the gaieties and the cooperative tasks of our familiar world. These things may be threatened, they may be precarious, they may be ours only by the grace of God, or of geographical or economic accident. But undeniably, beckoningly, along with the portents and alarms, here they are. Here, in all tragic times, they always have been, affording challenge and delight to the senses, solace and nourishment for the affections, and friendly stimulus to the understanding.—IRWIN EDMAN, *Candle in the Dark*

Rules, Principles, and Applications

(To facilitate reference to them, the topics in this Section and in Sections Three, Four, and Five are numbered consecutively from 1 to 60.)

1. NOUN USAGE

a. The plurals of nouns are generally formed by adding *s* or *es* to the singular. The letter *s* forms the plural when it can be added to the singular and pronounced without adding a syllable (*bath, baths; cat, cats*); the letters *es* form the plural when the singular ends in a sound (*s, ch, sh, z, x*) that cannot unite with *s* to form one syllable.

There are, of course, exceptions to the rules for the formations of plurals. Some of these exceptions are covered by spelling rules (see pages 818–820). If you are uncertain about how a particular noun forms its plural, look it up in the dictionary.

b. Plurals of figures, signs, letters, and words used merely as words are formed by adding either *s* or *'s*. When misreading is unlikely, *s* without the apostrophe is now the preferred plural.

Webster's New Collegiate Dictionary gives the following examples:

Plural with *s* where there is no likelihood of misreading: three *R*s, two *O*s, a group of B29s, in the 1920s, several GIs, high IQs.

Plural with *'s* where there is danger of misreading: dotted both *i*'s, two *l*'s in *all,* pronounce *s*'s clearly.

c. The possessive case of nouns: singular and plural nouns ending in *s* or *z* add only an apostrophe; singular and plural nouns not ending in *s* or *z* add the apostrophe plus *s*.

Singular Possessives	*Plural Possessives*
an hour's ride	a two hours' ride
the woman's hat	the women's hats
the child's toy	the children's toys
Smith's house	the Smiths' house
Keats' poetry	
Achilles' heel	

NOTE.—If the change to the possessive case causes a word already ending in an *s* or a *z* to be pronounced with an extra syllable, some authorities recommend the use of the apostrophe plus *s* to indicate that an extra syllable has been added. In following this rule, one would write *the Jones's party* in place of *the Jones' party*.

d. To indicate joint or separate ownership, possessives are used as follows:

(1) When two or more people are mentioned as owning an object in common, only the last of the names is given possessive form.

Mary and John's records show their taste for symphonic music.

(2) When two or more people are mentioned as owning separate objects, each name is given possessive form.

Ted's and Marshall's books are still in our attic. [I.e., Ted's books are still in our attic and Marshall's books are still in our attic.]

e. When possession is attributed to inanimate objects, the *of* phrase is generally preferable to the possessive case form.

The shoulder of the road [rather than the road's shoulder].
The foundation of the Empire State Building [rather than the Empire State Building's foundation].

Some of the rather numerous exceptions to this generalization are such common expressions as *an hour's delay, a day's walk, a week's wages, a stone's throw, the sun's rays, the earth's circumference, an arm's length.*

f. Possessive with the gerund: nouns serving as modifiers of gerunds are usually given the possessive form.

We were all surprised by Eliot's refusing to go. [*Refusing*, a gerund, is modified by the possessive *Eliot's*.]

EXERCISES

I. Give the plural for each of the following substantives (if necessary consult your dictionary): *calf, treaty, telephone, potato, birch, alumna, commander-in-chief, man, cactus, woman, lawyer, shears, teaspoonful, alumnus, economics, index.*

II. Which of the possessives below (now expressed in *of* phrases) might properly be changed from the *of* possessive to a possessive expressed by *s* or *'s?* Which should not be changed?

1. The cars of my friends are new.
2. We noticed that the shoulder of the road was soft.
3. The novels of Dickens were in the library of the college.
4. Five years ago the Prince of Denmark became King of his country.
5. President Truman said that the problems of our country are grave.
6. President Truman said that the problems of all countries are grave.
7. The house of Mr. Crawford and the barn of Mr. Benning were sold at the same time.
8. The tax problems of New York and Pennsylvania are similar in certain respects.
9. The leaves of many trees get summer blight.
10. Dr. Brown said that the delay of a week would endanger the life of Francis.

2. PRONOUNS: AGREEMENT

Pronouns can be used to avoid undesirable repetition, to achieve effective parallelism and emphasis, and to produce coherent and economical writing. First, however, one must know the conventions of pronoun usage.

A pronoun agrees with its antecedent in gender, number, and person.

In general this is a good rule to follow, though there are exceptions to it. Important exceptions are:

a. The masculine pronoun (*he, his, him*) may be, and in fact generally is, used to refer to an antecedent which is both masculine and feminine in meaning.

> In this small coeducational college a student soon learns to speak to everyone *he* meets. [Although some of the students are girls, *he* (rather than *he or she*) is the preferable usage. *He or she* would be used only for a special emphasis.]

b. Collective nouns as antecedents may be followed by *it* or *they*. If the collective noun is thought of as a unit, *it* (or *its*) is the appropriate pronoun; if the collective noun is thought of as representing a group of individuals, *they* (*their, them*) is the appropriate pronoun.

> The jury is to give *its* verdict today. [The jury is thought of as a unit.]
> The jury are returning to *their* homes today. [A group of individuals.]

c. Expressions which require a singular verb (*each, every, either, neither, many a, a person, anyone, everyone, no one, anybody, every-*

body, nobody, somebody) **require a singular pronoun when they serve as antecedents.**

Each of us has *his* private anxieties and *his* private joys.

Almost *everybody* in college knows that *he* will need to earn *his* living some day.

If *either* Martin or Ted hears of this, *he* will work against it.

Everyone took off *his* hat and stood in silence while the body of the great man was lowered into the grave.

Note.—Some writers on usage defend the use in some circumstances of the plural pronoun [*they* instead of *he*] after *each, every*, etc., but such usage is out of place in college writing.

EXERCISES

Point out any errors or awkwardnesses in agreement between pronoun and antecedent in the following sentences, and correct the sentence by supplying the proper pronoun or, if necessary, by revising the sentence.

1. Each man and woman in the audience thought that the speaker had given them something to think seriously about.

2. Many a high-school boy will wish that they had studied more in high school and had prepared themselves better.

3. Everyone in the congregation gave as much as they could when the collection was taken.

4. The senior class was proud of its part in introducing the honor system.

5. The person chosen, whether a man or a woman, will find that the group will cooperate with them and will appreciate their service.

3. PRONOUNS: CASE

The case of a pronoun depends upon the construction in which it appears.

a. A pronoun should be in the nominative case when it serves as a subject or a predicate nominative.

b. A pronoun should be in the objective case when it is the object of a verb, a verbal, or a preposition, or is the subject of an infinitive.

c. A pronoun should be in the possessive case when it expresses possession or when it is used as an adjective to modify a gerund.

Everyone was surprised at *his receiving* the prize. [In this sentence the gerund *receiving* is the object of *surprised* and *his* is a pronominal adjective which modifies *receiving*.]

d. The case of a relative pronoun (*who, whoever*) is determined by its construction in its own clause.

Give the ball to *whoever wants it.* [*Whoever* is the subject of the italicized subordinate clause in which it appears and so is properly in the nominative case. The subordinate clause is the object of the preposition *to.*]

If we have a party, *whom shall we ask?* [*Whom* is in the objective case because it is the object of the verb *ask.*]

The sentences below illustrate some of the common problems involving case of pronouns.

He says that *we* freshmen must work together. [*We,* the subject of *work,* is in the nominative case.]

To *us* freshmen the sophomore rules seem unreasonable. [*Us* is the object of the preposition *to.*]

We were surprised to see James and *him* together after their quarrel. [Both *him* and *James* are objects of the infinitive *to see.* The use of the nominative *he* in such an expression is an error to be avoided.]

He is a man *who,* I believe, will have his own way. [*I believe* is a parenthetical expression. *Who* is the subject of the subordinate clause *who will have his own way.*]

I saw *him* waving to his children. [*Him* is the object of *saw; waving* is a participle modifying *him.*]

We objected to *his walking* on our new lawn. [The gerund *walking* is the object of *objected to; his* is used as a pronominal adjective and modifies *walking.*]

They wondered *whom* he was taking to the dance. [*Whom* is the object of *taking* and is the required expression in formal English. In informal English and particularly in conversation, *who* can be defended.]

It wasn't Harold that asked the question; it was *I.* [*I* is here a predicate nominative, and strict usage therefore requires *I* rather than *me.* Some cultivated people would use *I,* some would use *me,* and many others would simply avoid the construction.]

He is taller than *I.* [Here *I* is in the nominative case because it is the subject of the elliptical clause *than I am tall.*]

EXERCISES

Underscore correct pronoun in each sentence. Explain your choice.

1. Will you join my parents and (I, me) for dinner?
2. The teacher would not start the lecture until (we, us) students quieted down.
3. The program was planned to help (we, us) students.
4. It is not necessary to ask (who, whom) will be the leading actor.
5. He wanted Martha and (I, me) to come.
6. Choose (whoever, whomever) you think can handle the job.
7. Such ruffians as (they, them) cause trouble for the rest of us.
8. If I were (they, them) I should refuse to buy an inferior stone.
9. Will you let Tom and (I, me) take the car?
10. (Him, his) arriving so late caused a good deal of comment.

4. PRONOUNS: REFERENCE

Some pronouns—indefinite pronouns, for example—do not customarily have and do not require antecedents. Words like *no one, anyone,* and *everyone* supply the necessary meaning without reference to a noun that has preceded them. Most pronouns, however, are used as substitutes for nouns, and are dependent on those nouns, their antecedents, for their meaning. The antecedent may be defined as the word or words which would have to be repeated if the pronoun were not used.

A pronoun should refer clearly to its antecedent.

The most common types of faulty pronoun reference are:

a. Reference to an antecedent that is implied but not stated.

UNSATISFACTORY: Leslie has been interested in aviation since he was ten years old, and he plans to be *one* some day. [The pronoun *one* has no expressed antecedent.]

REVISED: Leslie has been interested in aviation since he was ten, and he plans to be *an aviator* some day. [The repetition involved in *aviation . . . aviator* is preferable to the faulty pronoun reference.]

b. Reference to a too remote antecedent. If the pronoun and its antecedent are so distant from one another that the relationship is not immediately clear, the sentence or the passage should be revised by changing the construction or by substituting a noun for the vague or ambiguously used pronoun.

UNSATISFACTORY: She wore a ribbon on her hair *which* was green and crisp and new. [*Which* appears to refer to *hair.*]

REVISED: On her hair she wore a ribbon *which* was green and crisp and new.

UNSATISFACTORY: The Supreme Court decided that the judge had shown prejudice in the case. Justice Holmes retired soon after. *That* made legal history, and lawyers argued over the case for years afterwards. [The reference of the pronoun *that* is obscure, but the sense of the sentence suggests that the pronoun is intended to refer to the court decision though the antecedent *decision* is not expressed. The passage should be revised, or *that* should be changed to *that decision.*]

c. Ambiguous reference. The reference of a pronoun is ambiguous if the reader wavers even momentarily in choosing between two or more possible antecedents.

AMBIGUOUS: The manager told the union official that it was not *his* duty to collect the union dues. [In this sentence it is not clear whether *his* refers to *manager* or to *union official.* Unless the context of such a sentence makes clear the reference of the pronoun, the sentence should be recast.]

REVISED: The manager told the union official that the union should collect its own dues. [Or] The manager said to the union official, "It is not my duty to collect dues for the union."

ACCEPTABLE: Mr. Thompson told his son that *he* could not join a fraternity unless *he* got better grades. [Here the reference of *he* and *he* causes no uncertainty; the general sense of the sentence makes the meaning immediately clear.]

d. Indefinite reference of *you*. In formal English the use of the pronoun *you* in the sense of *one* is out of place. In informal English the indefinite *you* can sometimes be used to give a sense of immediacy; misused, however, it may be incongruous and even ludicrous.

INAPPROPRIATE: Chaucer, born in the fourteenth century, wrote for his own age and for succeeding ages. He understood the psychological tensions of the Pardoner, though he lacked the organized psychological knowledge which is available to twentieth-century writers. *You* are astonished as *you* . . . [The indefinite and too informal *you* is out of place in formal, impersonal writing of this kind. More appropriate than *You are astonished as you . . .* would be *The reader* or *The modern reader* or *One* followed by *is astonished as he reads . . .*]

INAPPROPRIATE: Human nature is funny. Even if *you* have held up a bank and killed seven men, *you* may still be very gentle with your dog. [Here the *you* is undesirable because it involves the reader in a situation in which he has no part and in which, probably, he would prefer not to be involved. The writer does not really intend to address the reader; he has simply used *you* vaguely in order to get out of a difficulty.]

REVISED: Human nature is unpredictable. Even a man who has held up a bank and has killed seven men might still be very gentle with his dog.

EFFECTIVE: If *you* could have been present in the years of Barnum's greatest glory, *you* would have seen Annie Oakley . . . ; *you* would have watched Buffalo Bill . . . ; *you* would have heard the whoops of fleeing Indians and pursuing cowboys . . . ; *you* . . . etc. [Here the use of *you* serves to give the reader a more vivid sense of being present; use of the formal *one* would be out of place in this context.]

e. Use of the inappropriate relative pronoun. The relative pronoun *who* is generally used to refer to people and not to things; the relative pronoun *which* is generally used to refer to things and not to people; and the relative pronoun *that* is used to refer to people or to things or to both.

CORRECT: a man *who* or *that* . . . a house *which* or *that* . . . the same man and the same house *that* we saw yesterday . . . a group *which* meets every Saturday . . . a group of home owners *who* think their taxes are too high . . . a dog *whose* master has abandoned him.

Note.—Since there is no possessive form for *that* or *which*, the possessive of *who (whose)* is often used to refer to things as a way of avoiding the awkward *of which* construction: the dog the master *of which* has . . .

f. Inconsistent reference or use of pronouns.

Inconsistencies in pronoun usage—that is, unnecessary and undesirable shifts from one person to another, from one number to another, or from one gender to another—should be avoided. Some inconsistencies can be corrected by substituting the right pronoun; others call for more substantial revision.

INCONSISTENT IN PERSON: When *I* was a freshman, the sophomores were strict in making *them* follow the rules. *You* were not safe if *you* walked on the grass or wore a high-school letter or failed to say "Sir" to upperclassmen. [A shift from the first person *I*, to the third person *them*, to the second person *you*. For consistency and for clarity this passage should be written in the first person.]

CONSISTENT: When *I* was a freshman, the sophomores were strict in making *us* follow the rules. *We* were not safe if *we* walked on the grass or wore a high-school letter or failed to say "Sir" to upperclassmen.

INCONSISTENT IN PERSON: When a man is hungry, *you* aren't satisfied with a frilly salad and a cup of tea. [A shift from the impersonal *a man* to the indefinite second person *you*.]

CONSISTENT: When *a man* is hungry, *he* is not satisfied with a frilly salad and a cup of tea.

INCONSISTENT IN NUMBER: *Everyone* in the class was looking at *his* watch. *They* thought the end of the hour would never come. [A shift from the singular *his* to the plural *they*. This passage could be made grammatically correct by substituting *he* for *they*, but it still would not be entirely satisfactory.]

REVISED: *Everyone* in the class was looking at *his* watch and thinking that the end of the hour would never come. [*Or*] *Everyone* in the class was looking at *his* watch. It seemed that the end of the hour would never come.

INCONSISTENT IN GENDER: The dog barked and showed that *it* wanted to come in. I think that *he* remembered me. [A careless shift from *it* to *he*.]

CONSISTENT: The dog barked and showed that *he* wanted to come in. I think that *he* remembered me.

g. Reference to an inconspicuous or buried antecedent.

UNSATISFACTORY: I was sorry to see the end of the day because I had enjoyed every minute of *it*. [*Day*, the antecedent of *it*, is buried in a prepositional phrase. Such sentences need to be recast.]

REVISED: I had enjoyed the *day* so much that I was sorry to see *it* come to an end.

EXERCISES

Some of the following sentences are correct. Others illustrate the faulty reference or the indefinite use of pronouns. Correct all incorrect or unsatisfactory pronoun references. If necessary, recast the sentence.

1. In our school they don't let you smoke.
2. My mother said that my sister was an impudent child, and that she would see to it that she would never let her temper get out of control again.
3. While we were watching the man fishing on a pier, we saw him haul one in.
4. John is studying law because his father is one.
5. Whoever is going had better sign his name.
6. Mrs. Banker bought John a coat but he thought it was too small for him.
7. Mary told her sister that she was not responsible for her actions.
8. The lightning struck the tree nearest the barn, but after burning for a few seconds it was extinguished by the rain.
9. The penalties for stealing are severe but you don't usually think about penalties until after you are caught.
10. We saw the prisoners which had been the leaders in the organization of the penitentiary's baseball team.

5. VERBS: AGREEMENT

A verb agrees with its subject in person and number.

Students who make errors in agreement need to be able to recognize the subject and the predicate of a sentence, need to know the constructions in which errors most frequently occur, need to form the habit of checking such constructions carefully in revision, and need, of course, to know the generally accepted conventions of agreement.

Information about how to recognize the subject and the predicate is given in "Basic Grammar," pages 713–714.

Sentences in which the subject immediately precedes the verb and in which the subject is clearly singular or clearly plural offer no problems of agreement. Errors in agreement most often occur when the subject and the verb are separated by intervening words, when the verb precedes the subject, or when the student is unsure whether a particular subject is properly singular or properly plural.

A complete and accurate statement of the conventions that govern the agreement of the verb with its subject would extend for many pages, would distinguish between formal and informal usage, and would contain many qualifications. Such fullness and exactitude is impossible in a brief discussion. In applying the rules below, the student should be aware that exceptions to some of them are not uncommon, and that a sentence in which a rule is mechanically followed may still be an awkward sentence and may need to be recast.

a. A verb agrees with its subject in person and number—not with some expression mistakenly considered to be its subject.

(1) A verb agrees with the subject—not with the subjective complement.

> The *problems* of municipal government *are* his chief interest. [The plural subject, *problems,* requires a plural verb. If the subjective complement, *interest,* were made the subject, the sentence would then read, "His chief *interest is* the problems of municipal government."]

(2) A verb agrees with its subject—not with a modifier of the subject.

> The destruction of the ships and landing forces *has* [not *have*] now *been accomplished.*

(3) A verb agrees with its subject—the number of the verb is not influenced by phrases introduced by *with, in addition to, along with,* and the like.

> The man with his wife and his six children *is* [not *are*] *waiting* at the door.

(4) A verb agrees with its subject—not with the introductory adverbs *here* and *there.*

> Here *come* the *professor and his wife.* [*Come* is plural because it agrees with the compound subject.]
> Here *comes Dean Harlow.*
> There *sits* our most distinguished *citizen.*
> There *lie* our *enemies.*

(5) A verb agrees with its subject—not with the expletive *there.*

> There *is* only one *reason* for their quarrels.
> There *are* several *reasons* for his decision.

b. Singular subjects joined by *or* or *nor* take a singular verb.

> He did not know whether the *captain or* the *lieutenant was* responsible.
> Neither *Arthur nor* his *father was* at home.

c. When a singular and a plural subject are joined by *or* or *nor,* the verb agrees with the nearer subject.

> He did not know whether the *officer or* the *soldiers were* to blame.
> He did not know whether the *soldiers or* the *officer was* to blame. [Sometimes following this rule will produce "correct" but awkward-sounding sentences. Such sentences should be recast to avoid the construction.]

d. Singular subjects joined by *and* take a plural verb unless the subjects are thought of as a unit.

Honesty and justice are required in a judge.
My *guide and counselor* [one person] *has served* me well.

e. The pronoun *each* and compound subjects modified by *each* and *every* take a singular verb.

Each of the carpenters *is bringing* his own tools.
Each magazine and newspaper has its special place on the stand.
Every tree and every bush was coated with ice; *every street was* dangerously slippery.

f. Collective nouns may take either singular or plural verbs, depending upon whether they are thought of as referring to a single unit or to the individuals in the group.

The *committee is meeting* this morning. [The committee is thought of as a unit.]
The *committee are arriving* tonight and tomorrow, some by train and some by plane.

g. The antecedent of the relative pronouns *who, which,* and *that* determines the number and person of the verb of which the pronoun is the subject.

It is *I who am* to blame, and it is *you who deserve* the praise.
She is one of those determined *women who insist* on having the last word.

h. Except in very informal usage *no one, anyone, everyone,* and *someone,* and *nobody, anybody, everybody,* and *somebody* require singular verbs.

No one was willing to bring up any new business because *everyone was* eager for the meeting to come to an end.
Everyone—even the older people who did not dance—*was* having a good time at the party.

EXERCISES

Point out any errors in agreement between subject and predicate in the following sentences and revise any sentences that need revision.

1. Each voter in these three communities are planning to cast a ballot in this election.
2. My cousin along with several friends from New York are going to pay us a visit.
3. There is, the senator says frequently and forcibly, many reasons why all good citizens should vote.

4. Neither the president nor his representatives were able to attend the ceremony.

5. Neither of the professors were able to answer my question.

6. Every doctor and every dentist in town are free on Wednesday afternoons.

7. Each of the fighters were becoming tired by the end of the fifth round.

8. Everyone—male and female, young and old—like to attend barn dances.

9. He is one of those men who is called successful but who is merely rich.

10. War may be eliminated when the causes of war is understood.

6. VERBS: PRINCIPAL PARTS

a. The principal parts of a verb supply the basic forms for all tenses of that verb.

The principal parts of *go,* for instance, are *go* (present infinitive), *went* (past tense) and *gone* (past participle).

b. To use the information given by the principal parts of verbs, it is necessary to know at least the following facts:

(1) The first principal part (*go*) supplies the form for the present tense (first and second person, *go;* third person, *goes*), and forms the future tense (*shall* or *will go*) with the help of the auxiliary *shall* or *will*.

(2) The second principal part (*went*) supplies the form for the past tense (*went*).

(3) The third principal part (*gone*) combines with auxiliaries to form the present perfect tense (*has* or *have gone*), the past perfect tense (*had gone*), and the future perfect tense (*shall* or *will have gone*).

Many errors in tense are caused by ignorance of principal parts or by failure to choose the proper principal part. The student who writes *He drownded* for *He drowned* simply does not know the principal parts of *drown*. In *He come* for *He came,* the error is produced by the use of the first principal part instead of the second; in *He had went* for *He had gone,* the error is produced by the use of the second principal part instead of the third to form the past perfect tense.

c. In the process of revision, students should look up in the dictionary the principal parts of any verb about which they are uncertain.

Dictionaries may differ in their way of indicating principal parts, but any satisfactory dictionary supplies the information and explains in an introductory section headed "Explanatory Notes" what system is used.

d. Students should be sure that they know the principal parts of the verbs which are most commonly used:

awake	awoke	awaked
	awaked	awoke
begin	began	begun
bid (to offer)	bid	bid
bid (to command)	bade	bidden
break	broke	broken
bring	brought	brought
burn	burnt	burnt
	burned	burned
burst	burst	burst
choose	chose	chosen
come	came	come
dive	dived (*colloquial* dove)	dived
do	did	done
dream	dreamt	dreamt
	dreamed	dreamed
drink	drank	drunk
drive	drove	driven
drown	drowned	drowned
dwell	dwelt	dwelt
	dwelled	dwelled
eat	ate	eaten
fall	fell	fallen
fly	flew	flown
forget	forgot	forgotten
		forgot
freeze	froze	frozen
get	got	got
		gotten
give	gave	given
go	went	gone
hang (a thing)	hung	hung
hang (a person)	hanged	hanged
kneel	knelt	knelt
	kneeled	kneeled

lay (to place)	laid	laid
lead	led	led
lie (to recline)	lay	lain
lie (to make a false statement)	lied	lied
light	lighted lit	lighted lit
lose	lost	lost
pay	paid	paid
raise (to lift)	raised	raised
rise (to get up, to come up)	rose	risen
see	saw	seen
set (to place)	set	set
shine	shone	shone
show	showed	shown showed
shrink	shrank	shrunk
sing	sang sung	sung
sit	sat	sat
slay	slew	slain
slink	slunk	slunk
spit	spit spat	spit spat
steal	stole	stolen
strive	strove strived	striven strived
swim	swam	swum
tread	trod	trod trodden
wake	woke waked	waked woke
wear	wore	worn
weave	wove	woven
wring	wrung	wrung
write	wrote	written

EXERCISES

Underscore one of the words in parentheses and give the reason for your choice.

1. The boat (lay, laid) on its side in the harbor.
2. The boys had (swam, swum) about thirty yards before they reached the shore.
3. After you (sit, set) the book on the table (lie, lay) down on the couch and take a nap.
4. When the seams (burst, bursted), she knew she had (wore, worn) the coat long enough.
5. The man (bid, bidded) five dollars for the chair.
6. As soon as the sun (rose, raised), we took the flag and (rose, raised) it on the flag pole.
7. After I had (laid, lain) in bed for two hours, I (waked, woken) and (lay, laid) out the clothes I wanted to wear for dinner.
8. When we have (given, give) our share, we still will not have (payed, paid) our full debt.
9. The sun (shone, shined) and the birds (drank, drunk) from the fountain.
10. For many years he had (wore, worn) the coat which had been (weaved, wove, woven) in his native land, and he (wrung, wrang) his hands in grief when it was (stole, stolen) from him.

7. VERBS: SOME MATTERS OF TENSE

Although tense is a very complex subject, actual misuse of tenses can be avoided if the student knows and follows certain well-established conventions.

a. Statements regarded as permanently true are expressed in the present tense.

> In the first grade the child learned that two and two *are* [not *were*] four.
> Socrates believed that the unexamined life *is* not worth living.
> People in the ninth century thought that the world *was* flat. [The past tense is correct here because the speaker does not regard the statement as true now.]
> Copernicus discovered the earth *revolves* [not *revolved*] around the sun.

b. The historical present tense may be used effectively in the presentation of a lively dramatic action, but is inappropriate when used for routine narrative.

> APPROPRIATE: A crowd has assembled now and is peering up at the man on the ledge of a tenth-story window. Other tenth-story windows are

open, filled with gesticulating and shouting people. The man on the ledge is shaking his head. Now he has turned and is looking at the street below him. Suddenly . . .

NOT APPROPRIATE: Before me on the library path I see Henry. I hardly recognize him under that battered old hat, and apparently he doesn't even see me. I pass him and go on to my history class. There is to be a quiz today and I don't want to be late.

c. Generally the past tense is used to refer to action completed in the past, and the past perfect is used to refer to action completed prior to some definite time in the past.

When I *called* he *had* already *left.* [*Called,* past tense, represents action completed in the past. *Had left,* past perfect, represents action completed prior to the past action described by the verb *called.*]

d. The present perfect tense represents an action occurring at an indefinite time and extending up to and perhaps through the present time.

Richard *has been* on the honor roll three times. [*Has been* here means up to the present time.]

Helen *has been waiting* for him to call. [This sentence implies that she is still waiting.]

Have you *weighed* yourself today? [The sentence "Did you weigh yourself today" would involve misuse of the past tense because *today* includes the present moment and may include the future.]

e. The time indicated by infinitives and participles should be adjusted to the tense of the main verb and the meaning of the sentence.

I was glad *to receive* the letters. [I.e., I was glad *when I received* the letters.]

I was glad *to have received* the letters. [I.e., at some time in the past I was glad that I *had already received* the letters.]

Having waited in the rain for three hours, Mark *was* thoroughly exasperated when Helen finally appeared. [Not "Waiting in the rain for three hours, Mark was thoroughly exasperated when Helen finally appeared." Since waiting preceded and caused the exasperation, the action referred to by the participle is previous to that of the verb, and the form *having waited* is therefore required.]

Casting fearful glances behind him, the boy *walked* by the graveyard. [Here the action of the participle and the action of the main verb occur simultaneously and the present participle is properly used.]

For a discussion of shifts in tense, mood, and voice, see "Inconsistencies" page 790.

EXERCISES

Point out errors in tense in the sentences below and revise any sentences that need revision.

1. These primitive people did not know that the world was round or that three and three made six.
2. Did you call him yet?
3. Marrying the editor's daughter, he was surprised when he learned that he was to start to work as office boy in the editorial department.
4. Pausing in the middle of his speech, he glanced at Ted and beckoned to him.
5. Although Carlyle wrote many volumes, he often said that silence was greater than speech.
6. At the dance that night there were many of the people that we saw in the afternoon.
7. The sky was gray and the wind shook the trees. The sun, which was shining this morning, is now obscured.
8. I called her each night ever since we went to the game together.
9. They have completed the project several days ago. Now they have started work on the new tunnel.
10. Although he was really terrified the night before, he now tried to pretend that he felt very calm.

8. VERBS: *SHALL* AND *WILL, SHOULD* AND *WOULD*

In formal usage, most careful writers attempt to preserve the distinction between *shall* and *will, should* and *would*. In informal writing and particularly in conversation, a much less rigid standard applies, and many otherwise careful users of English tend to use *will* in place of the more formal *shall,* and *would* in place of the more formal *should*. The rules which follow describe formal usage.

a. To express simple futurity, *shall* (or *should*) is used in the first person and *will* (or *would*) in the second and third persons.

I shall (should) go.	We shall (should) go.
You will (would) go.	You will (would) go.
He, she, it will (would) go.	They will (would) go.

b. To express determination, promise or command, *will* is used in the first person, and *shall* is used in the second and third persons.

I will.	We will.
You shall.	You shall.
He, she, it shall.	They shall.

c. In questions, *shall* is used when *shall* is expected in the answer, and *will* when *will* is expected in the answer.

Shall I answer this letter?
Shall we get tickets for the play?
Shall you go to the game this Saturday?
Will they be here at eight?

NOTE.—In conversation, following the rule may sometimes lead to expressions that sound stilted and unnatural. In such cases one may use *will* for *shall* or may use an expression like *Do you expect to* or *are you going to.*

d. *Would* may be used in all persons to express determination.

He warned me, but I *would* have my way.
I warned him, but he *would* have his way.
He warned you, but you *would* have your way.

e. *Should* may be used in all persons in place of the present subjunctive.

Even if I (you, he) *should* be defeated, the cause will not be lost.

f. *Should* in the sense of *ought* is used in all three persons.

If we are to consider our duty, you *should* go, I *should* go, and he *should* go.

g. *Would* is used in all persons to express habitual action.

I (you, he) *would* stop each day to see the progress the workmen had made on the new office building.

EXERCISES

Consider the use of *shall* and *will*, and *should* and *would* in the following sentences. Some of the uses are clearly correct; some are clearly incorrect; some could be correct if the sentence were interpreted in a certain way. Classify each sentence and comment on it. Correct any uses which are clearly wrong.

1. He shall attend the dinner if it is held at a convenient place and time.
2. Will you go to the party?
3. They are very likely to come, but what if they would be late?
4. I will be pleased to accept your invitation.
5. I will drown unless someone shall save me.
6. They should have come earlier; now the dinner is cold.
7. I warned him, but he would not listen.
8. When we were children, we would meet Father at the gate and he would give us sticks of candy.
9. He gave us the key in case he should not be there to let us in.
10. I should like to attend the concert but I don't think I will be able to go.

9. VERBS: USES OF THE SUBJUNCTIVE

Since most forms of the subjunctive are identical with those of the indicative, it usually is not necessary to make a deliberate choice between the two moods. Where such choices are required, however, the student needs to know at least the most common conventions for the use of the subjunctive.

a. The subjunctive is used to express a condition that is contrary to fact.

If I were you, I should accept the invitation.
Even if he were wealthy, he would still wear old clothes.
He would pay his share if he were able.
If he had received an invitation, he would have gone.

b. The subjunctive is used to express strong doubt.

Subjunctive: If it should be a rainy day, we shall not go. [Since the speaker is expressing doubt that the day will be rainy he properly uses the subjunctive.]
Indicative: If it is a rainy day, we shall not go. [The indicative is used because the idea of doubt is not emphasized.]

Subjunctive: If the teacher should give a quiz, some of us would be sorry. [This sentence implies that the speaker does not expect the quiz to be given.]
Indicative: If the teacher gives a quiz, some of us will be sorry. [This sentence does not indicate whether or not a quiz is likely.]

Subjunctive: If he had received the gift, he would have written me. [The sentence implies that he did not receive the gift.]
Indicative: If he received the gift, he said nothing to me about it. [The speaker is not expressing strong doubt; he is simply stating a fact.]

c. The subjunctive is used in *that* clauses expressing a recommendation, a demand, a request, a necessity.

The committee recommended that the project be abandoned.
He demanded that the bill be paid immediately.
He asked that we be quiet. [Less formal than the use of the subjunctive: He asked us to be quiet.]
They demand that the rules be changed.
I move that the petition be granted.
It is essential that this law be passed.

EXERCISES

Choose the correct expression in each of the following sentences.

1. The law requires that the defendant (have, has) benefit of counsel.
2. If the earth (was, were) square, some nations would want all four corners.

3. I wonder if the young man who just spoke to me (was, were) a college student.

4. Senator Borgam Patwell moved that the motion (be, was) postponed indefinitely.

5. Rosalind would like Russell better if he (were, was) a better correspondent.

6. If Thornton (was, were) ever kind, he was kind for a reason.

7. I should go for a swim today if the water (was, were) not so cold.

8. What could I say if the professor (was, were) to ask why I have been absent.

9. He requires that each student (give, gives) a five-minute speech.

10. The man asked if it (were, was) too late to get a ticket for the game.

10. ADJECTIVES AND ADVERBS

The purpose of this section is to supply the student with information which will enable him to avoid common errors in the use of adjectives and adverbs.

a. Adjectives modify only substantives (nouns and pronouns). Adverbs do not modify nouns or pronouns; usually they modify verbs, adjectives, or other adverbs.

Many mistakes in the use of adjectives and adverbs are the result of inaccurate proofreading. Other mistakes occur because the student (1) does not know enough grammar to know which word is being modified (see *b* and *c* below), or (2) does not know whether a particular word—*good* for example—is properly used as an adverb, and does not know how to find out (see *d* below).

b. Adverbs modify verbs which express action. Adjectives serve as subjective complements of linking verbs (i.e., verbs which express little or no action and serve primarily to link the subject to what follows.) Words often used as linking verbs are *be, seem, become, appear,* and the verbs of the senses (*smell, taste, feel, look, sound*). The best way to understand this rule is to study the following examples.

> He *carefully* avoided the broken glass. [In this sentence it is clear that *carefully* is an adverb modifying *avoided*. This sentence presents no problem.]
>
> He looked *steadily* at the papers before him. [*Looked* is sometimes used as a linking verb, but here it is used to describe or convey action, and the adverb *steadily* tells how he *looked*—i.e., how he performed the action.]
>
> She looks *happy*. [Here *looks* serves only to join the subject *she* to the adjective *happy* and is a linking verb: it describes the subject and not the action. *Happy* is a subjective complement.]
>
> That small boy looks *mischievous*. [*Mischievous*, a subjective complement, describes the boy.]

The small boy looked *mischievously* at his companion. [*Mischievously* describes the act of looking.]

He is doing *well* [not *good*] in his history course. [*Good* would be wrong here because an adverb is needed to modify the verb *is doing*.]

I can't tell whether he feels good or *bad*. [*Badly* in place of the adjective *bad* is often used, but is appropriate only on the colloquial level.]

He felt his way *uncertainly* in the darkened room. [*Felt* describes an act; *uncertainly* describes how that act was done.]

c. With transitive verbs, adjectives may serve as objective complements—i.e., may serve to modify the object in a particular way.

She swept the floor *clean*. [*Clean*, an adjective, applies to the state of the floor and is correct. To substitute *cleanly* for *clean* would be to change the sense of the sentence.]

She swept the floor *daily*. [*Daily* is not an objective complement but is an adverb modifying *swept*.]

We painted the barn *red*. [*Red*, an adjective, applies to the state of the barn and is an objective complement.]

d. Dictionaries supply important information about particular adverbs and adjectives.

One cause of errors in the use of adverbs and adjectives is uncertainty as to which part of speech a particular word may be. Can *slow*, for example, be used as an adverb? Looking up the word in a good dictionary will reveal that it is used as an adjective or as an adverb. If one looks up the word *good*, he will learn that it is an adjective and not an adverb, though it may be used as an adverb in certain idiomatic constructions.

Dictionaries also supply necessary information about the comparison of adverbs and adjectives—i.e., how the positive, comparative, and superlative degrees are formed. The student who has a certain minimum knowledge of grammar (i.e., who understands parts *a*, *b*, and *c* of this section) and who knows how to use his dictionary will know whether a construction calls for an adjective or an adverb and will also know which words can properly serve as adjectives or adverbs.

e. Comparisons should be expressed logically and grammatically.

(1) Comparisons should be grammatically complete. Correct but awkwardly expressed comparisons should be rephrased.

GRAMMATICALLY INCOMPLETE: She has worked for this firm as long if not longer than he has. [An *as* is needed after *long* to complete the construction *as long as*.]

GRAMMATICALLY CORRECT BUT AWKWARD: She has worked for this firm as long as, if not longer than he has.

REPHRASED: She has worked for this firm as long as he has and perhaps longer. [*Or*] She has worked for this firm at least as long as he has.

INCOMPLETE: Chemistry was more interesting to him than the other students in the class.

REVISED: Chemistry was more interesting to him than *to* the other students in the class.

(2) Comparisons should be in accord with logic.

ILLOGICAL: The senator thinks that MacArthur is better than any general. [Since MacArthur is included in the expression *any general,* the sentence seems to say that MacArthur is better than himself. This is logically impossible, even for General MacArthur.]

REVISED: The senator thinks that MacArthur is better than any *other* general.

ILLOGICAL: It was a most unique experience. [Strictly used, *unique* means the *only one of its kind,* and hence uniqueness is not a matter of degree. A thing is unique or it is not unique.]

REVISED: It was a unique experience. [*Or*] It was a most unusual [or extraordinary] experience.

ILLOGICAL: She is the oldest of the two sisters. [The use of the superlative degree (*oldest*) implies the comparison of more than *two.*]

REVISED: She is the older of the two sisters.

f. Adjectives and adverbs should not be overused.

Adjectives and adverbs (and expressions used as adjectives or adverbs) are of course indispensable, but they should be used economically and exactly. When they are overused, they tend to clutter communication and to obscure the essential ideas. The skillful writer usually depends upon effective verbs and nouns to carry most of his meaning, and uses adjectives and adverbs to qualify and to make more precise the work done by verbs and nouns.

Overuse of modifiers is most likely to occur in pretentious or generally wordy expression. The best way to avoid this fault is to write honestly and unaffectedly, and to strike out or to express more briefly words, phrases, or passages which do not carry their share of meaning. (See "Economy and Conciseness" in Chapter Five.)

EXERCISES

I. In each of the following sentences choose one of the words in parentheses and explain the reason for your choice.

1. Mary plays golf as (well, good) as John does.
2. When you get to know her, she is a (real, really) sincere person.

3. Morris does not feel (good, well) about it; and Melvin, I understand, feels (bad, badly) and is very unhappy.

4. After weighing each of the three sisters, we discovered that Helen was the (heavier, heaviest).

5. Did the ride on the merry-go-round make you feel (bad, badly)?

6. I have heard many hunting stories, but John's experience with the bear is (unique, most unique).

7. That fish smelled (peculiar, peculiarly) to me.

8. When she was forty, she dyed her hair (red, redly) and insisted that her son call her Helène instead of Mother.

9. Although the dog looks gentle, he hears strangers however (quietly, quiet) they move, and he barks (ferocious, ferociously).

10. She looked (sick, sickly) to me.

11. He thought that he had been treated (bad, badly).

12. I have trouble with chemistry but I am doing very (good, well) in English.

13. She may smile (pleasant, pleasantly) now, but she looked (miserable, miserably) this morning.

14. He is the (older, oldest) of the three Harris boys.

15. He walked (slowly, slow) and (cautiously, cautious) down the dark road.

II. Write the comparative and superlative degrees of the following adjectives and adverbs.

little	tired	safe
quick	good	slow
gladly	handsome	slowly
old	bad	pleasant

11. PREPOSITIONS AND CONJUNCTIONS

a. Prepositions should be used idiomatically.

Certain words are conventionally joined to certain prepositions to form idiomatic phrases. For example, *accuse* is followed by *of* (to *accuse* him *of* the crime); *acquiesce* is followed by *in* (to *acquiesce in* a decision); and *wait* is followed by *on* or *for* (*wait on* a customer or a table, *wait for* a friend or a bus). Prepositions are used idiomatically when the preposition which is required by conventional usage is chosen.

Since idiomatic phrases are not formed on the basis of rules, the only way to learn these phrases and so to be able to use the idiomatic preposition is to hear them, or to learn them from reading, or to look them up in the dictionary under the key word of the phrase. Good desk dictionaries give a large number of idiomatic phrases, and the great *Oxford English Dictionary* comes nearest to giving complete information. (See list of common idiomatic phrases, page 800.)

b. A preposition may be used at the end of a sentence.

There is no recognized rule of usage which forbids placing a preposition at the end of a sentence. Students can concentrate on writing clear, emphatic, rhythmical sentences, and can let the prepositions fall where they may.

c. Conjunctions should express clearly and exactly the relationship which the writer intends.

There are two extremes in the use of conjunctions; each extreme produces ineffective writing.

(1) The overuse or the imprecise use of a very limited number of conjunctions.

Conjunctions most commonly overused are: *as, so, while, and, but, since.* All these conjunctions are essential words in English and need to be used frequently, but they should also be used with discrimination. *As,* for example, is often used where *because,* or *for,* or *since,* or *just as* would more exactly express the shade of meaning intended. *So* is often used in sentences where *and so,* or *so that,* or *accordingly,* or *for this reason* would express the meaning more clearly. *While* is sometimes used when *but* or *although* would be more exact. *And* carries the general meaning of addition or continuity, but expressions like *consequently, indeed, in fact, again* may serve better in particular contexts. *But* is not always the best way to express contrast; sometimes *yet,* or *nevertheless,* or *however,* or *still,* or *on the contrary,* or *on the other hand* may be preferable. *Since* may be less exact than *because* or *for* in some sentences.

Below is a list of the most common subordinating and coordinating connective expressions. The skillful writer has these locutions at his command, is aware of the shades of meaning they convey, and uses them to show exactly the relationship between ideas.

NOTE.—Not all the items in this list are formally classed as conjunctions, but all of them are sometimes used as conjunctions in that they act as connectives between clauses.

SUBORDINATING CONNECTIVES

after	before	unless
although	if	until
as	in order that	when
as if	since	where
as long as	so that	whether
as soon as	than	while
as though	though	
because	till	

COORDINATING CONNECTIVES

Pure Conjunctions

and	for	nor	(so)	(yet)
but	or	and so	(then)	

•A NOTE ON PUNCTUATION.—Between two independent clauses joined by a pure conjunction, a comma is conventionally used. If the comma is not necessary for clarity, it may be omitted. *So, then,* and *yet* are sometimes used as pure conjunctions, but a semicolon is very often required before them when they join independent clauses. For that reason they are placed in parentheses in this list, and are also listed under the heading below.

Other Coordinating Connectives

accordingly	hence	on that account
again	however	otherwise
all the same	indeed	rather
at the same time	in fact	so
also	likewise	still
besides	moreover	then
consequently	nevertheless	therefore
conversely	notwithstanding	thus
furthermore	on the other hand	yet
for that reason	on the contrary	

NOTE.—These expressions, when used as the sole connective between two independent clauses in the same sentence, are generally preceded by a semicolon.

(2) The use of heavy or incongruous connectives in simple, informal writing.

POOR: *Notwithstanding the fact that* he weighs only one hundred and fifteen pounds, Larry is a good athlete.

IMPROVED: Although he weighs only one hundred and fifteen pounds, Larry is a good athlete.

POOR: We didn't know *whence* the hired man came, or how long he would work for us.

IMPROVED: We didn't know where the hired man came from, or how long he would work for us.

POOR: I wasn't sick after eating the green apples; *whereas* Helen and Tom missed two days of school.

IMPROVED: Although I wasn't sick after eating the green apples, Helen and Tom missed two days of school.

POOR: My room, *albeit* small and dark, is the only place in the house where I can work in peace.

IMPROVED: My room, though small and dark, is the only place in the house where I can work in peace.

d. The student should be aware of the following facts about the usage of connectives.

(1) *Like.* Except in very informal language *like* should not be used as a conjunction.

> She looked *as if* [not *like*] she were going to cry.
> Do *as* [not *like*] I say, not *as* [not *like*] I do.
> It looks *as though* [not *like*] he won't come.

(2) *The reason is because. The reason is because* is a debatable usage. The preferred usage is *the reason is that.*

> The reason for his lateness is *that* [not *because*] he overslept.
> The reason I am sure is *that* [not *because*] I was there when it happened.
> [*Or*] I am sure *because* I was there when it happened.

(3) *If, whether.* Careful writers generally use *if* to express a condition or a supposition, and *whether* to introduce an indirect question.

> He did not say *whether* [not *if*] he will be in his office today.
> He will come *if* he can. [Correct; *if* expresses a condition.]
> He said, *if* I am not mistaken, that he will call at seven. [Correct; *if* expresses a condition.]

(4) *Whether or no, whether or not.* Either *whether or no* or *whether or not* is accepted usage. Often, however, the *or no* or *or not* is unnecessary and can be omitted.

> They haven't heard *whether or not* [or *whether or no*] they will be given a vacation. [*Or no* or *or not* could be omitted.]

(5) *Due to* used as a preposition in place of *because of* is a debatable usage; some authorities consider it completely acceptable, and others object to it, especially in formal and high informal language. Students frequently find it difficult to distinguish between *due to* used as a phrasal preposition and *due* used as an adjective and followed by the separate preposition *to*. Perhaps the following examples will make this distinction clear.

> QUESTIONABLE USAGE (*due to* used as a phrasal preposition): *Due to* an unfortunate accident, he failed to attend the ceremonies. [Here *due to* is used as a phrasal preposition and takes *unfortunate accident* as its object. Strict usage would call for *because of* in place of *due to* in this sentence.]

> CORRECT USAGE (*due* used as an adjective and modified by a prepositional phrase): His failure to attend the ceremonies was *due* to an unfortunate accident. [Here *due* is used as a predicate adjective modifying *failure* ("His *failure* was *due*") and the prepositional phrase *to an unfortunate accident* modifies or limits the adjective *due*. To determine whether

due is an adjective, look for the noun or pronoun that it modifies. If there is no such noun or pronoun, *due* is not an adjective.]

EXERCISES

I. Choose the idiomatic prepositions in the following sentences. If necessary, see your dictionary.

1. He was completely indifferent (to, about) the noises outside.
2. He is willing to abide (by, with) the decision.
3. The politician was not adverse (of, to) taking credit for the improved roads in the state.
4. The child was accompanied (with, by) his mother.
5. We knew that he was capable (of, for) doing the work well.

II. Select the correct or preferred connective.

1. (Due to, because of) his past experience, he did well.
2. I know that he was guilty (as, for) I saw him fire the shot.
3. I was just about to buy the house (yet, but) he continued to act as if he were not even listening to me.
4. He did not say (whether, if) he would come today or tomorrow.
5. The reason he left early is (that, because) he is playing in the game tomorrow.
6. He acted (like, as if) he had never seen sorrow before.
7. He looks (as, like) his father, but he talks (as, like) his mother does.
8. He acted (like, as if, as) he owned the store.
9. I don't know (if, whether) we can come on that date.
10. Today the college president will decide (if, whether, whether or not) the band will go on the train with the team.

12. UNITY

A composition, a paragraph, or a sentence is unified when it has a dominant idea to which all details within the unit are clearly relevant.

The fault of disunity in sentences is most commonly produced by (1) the inclusion of material which is irrelevant or which appears to be irrelevant because of the absence of subordination or connectives, and (2) the joining in one sentence of apparently unrelated ideas, or of too many ideas.

LACK OF UNITY: I have come to this college, which will be a hundred years old next year, to study business administration. [The age of the college is irrelevant to the main idea of the sentence.]
IMPROVED: I have come to this college to study business administration.

LACK OF UNITY: Charles Dickens wrote *Martin Chuzzlewitt* in 1843, and I enjoyed it a great deal. [Two very different ideas are faultily joined in one sentence.]

IMPROVED: Charles Dickens wrote his enjoyable novel *Martin Chuzzle-witt* in 1843.

LACK OF UNITY: Helen had always been afraid of the dark and now she was fifteen years old. [The two ideas seem wholly unrelated.]
IMPROVED: For as many of her fifteen years as she could remember, Helen had been afraid of the dark.

LACK OF UNITY: Children in grade school are likely to regard their teachers as gods, or sometimes as tyrants, and then later they realize that teachers are human and can be advisers and friends, and they change their attitudes, which is something I did rather late, but which I have done now. [This sprawling, overloaded sentence contains too many ideas for one sentence.]
IMPROVED: Children in grade school usually think of their teachers as gods or tyrants. Later, students realize that teachers are human beings who can be advisers and friends. I have arrived, rather tardily, at this more mature attitude toward my teachers.

Unity is closely related to coherence, emphasis, subordination, and the use of exact connectives. For further information about particular aspects of unity, see "Unity in Paragraphs" in Chapter Six, "Coherence" page 777, "Emphasis" page 779, "Subordination" page 791, and "Transitions" page 781.

EXERCISES

Criticize the unity in the following sentences and revise any sentences which need revision.

1. John Alden Bump, who gave me a five-dollar gold piece on my tenth birthday eight years ago, has been elected to Congress.
2. We talked very little on the way up the mountain, and when we reached the top we could see the whole valley spread out before us, after which we returned to camp and ate the fish Bill had caught the day before.
3. Richard received three F's last semester and he has just been made president of the Sophomore Class.
4. George wanted to stop for hamburgers, although it was twelve-thirty according to the wrist watch I received as a graduation present when I finished high school last June.
5. Edgar Allan Poe was born in Boston in 1809 and wrote "The Raven."

13. COHERENCE

Coherence in writing is produced by logical order and clear connections between parts of the material.

The following passages illustrate a lack of coherence produced by faulty arrangement of material:

POOR IN COHERENCE: We did our best to explain what had happened, to John and Carol, having arrived two hours late at the dance because we had mistaken the time.

IMPROVED: When, having mistaken the time, we arrived two hours late at the dance, we did our best to explain to John and Carol.

POOR IN COHERENCE: I have an unconventional way of writing expressive of my personality which my teachers have always criticized.

IMPROVED: My teachers have always criticized my unconventional writing, though I feel that it expresses my personality.

POOR IN COHERENCE: When I met him again, he appeared to have changed his mind. This was four days later, and was in the morning.

IMPROVED: When I met him one morning four days later, he appeared to have changed his mind.

Failure to make clear connections between ideas produces incoherence in the following passages:

POOR IN COHERENCE: Her uncle was not comforted and so she left. She would go the next day.

IMPROVED: Since she could do nothing to comfort her uncle, she left, promising to return the next day.

POOR IN COHERENCE: He was successful for three reasons. He sold a vitamin compound and he believed it was a good product. He was sincere in this. He was a good talker and could convince anyone on any matter and besides he liked people.

IMPROVED: He was successful for three reasons: he sincerely believed in the vitamin compound he was selling; he talked convincingly; and he liked people.

For further information related to coherence see "Unity" page 776, "Modifiers" page 785, "Subordination" page 791, "Parallelism" page 788, and "Transitions" page 781. Coherence in paragraphs is discussed in Section II of Chapter Six.

EXERCISES

Criticize the coherence in the following passages, and revise any passages which need revision.

1. Apply the paint thinly, using long smooth strokes, and allow it to dry for at least twelve hours. A good brush is a necessity. Be sure to wash the walls first.

2. Jason fell out of the apple tree and broke his arm which he had climbed to cut off a limb.

3. Jim asked me for a date. So did Roger. I decided not to go.

4. We enjoyed the picnic when we finally found the park, after starting at eight o'clock in the morning and getting lost on the way.

5. The time consumed is great and I am already behind in my studies, so I am going out for football next year.

14. EMPHASIS

For a fuller discussion of emphasis, see the section "Emphasis" in Chapter Five, and the section "Emphasis in Paragraphs" in Chapter Six.

a. Emphasis is achieved by proportion.

In the whole composition, main ideas are emphasized by fuller development than is accorded less significant ideas.

b. Emphasis is achieved by pause.

Pauses created by chapter divisions, paragraph breaks, and marks of punctuation throw emphasis on the material immediately preceding and following the pause.

> LESS EMPHATIC: At first I did not know what was required of me, but I know now.
>
> MORE EMPHATIC: At first I did not know what was required of me. I know now.

c. Emphasis is achieved by position.

The beginning and end of a composition, a paragraph, and a sentence are the positions of greatest emphasis. They should be used to stress the important ideas.

> UNEMPHATIC SENTENCE BEGINNING: There was a writer named Matthew Arnold who influenced my thinking.
>
> MORE EMPHATIC: Matthew Arnold was a writer who influenced my thinking.

> UNEMPHATIC SENTENCE ENDING: The situation is critical, I believe.
>
> MORE EMPHATIC: The situation is, I believe, critical.

d. Emphasis is achieved by skillful repetition.

> "This great Nation *will endure* as it has *endured, will* survive and *will* prosper. So, first of all, let me assert my firm belief that the only thing we have to *fear* is *fear* itself. . . ."

e. Emphasis is destroyed by:

(1) Thoughtlessly repeated sentence patterns.

(2) Improper subordination which gives stress to ideas not worth emphasizing.

(3) Overuse of the passive voice.

(4) Triteness.

(5) Padding, jargon, weak clauses, and circumlocutions.

(6) Euphemisms overused or inappropriately used.

f. Skillful writers do not rely for emphasis on mechanical devices like exclamation points, underlining, capitalization, and the use of intensives.

POOR DEVICES FOR EMPHASIS: It happened *so suddenly!* I was a victim of Fate. *What* was I to do in these ghastly circumstances?

EXERCISES

I. State why each of the following passages is unemphatic, and revise the passages to improve emphasis.

1. Mr. Brown is a tall man with gray hair. He is my father's friend. He is the governor of the state.

2. There were many things to distract me at the beginning of the year and I had a very good time and now I am going to do some work before the end of the term, I have decided.

3. It was on the night of Friday two weeks ago that I met her; it was at the football rally.

4. A fraternity was joined by Ted and lasting friendships were made.

5. When I heard he had departed this world I was in the depths of despair because he was a man who was admirable in every way it seemed to me.

II. Point out the techniques for emphasis used in the following passages.

1. "I know not what course others may take, but as for me, give me liberty, or give me death."

2. Confident he may be, but not conceited.

3. For the pleasures of daily living, for the pleasures of books, and friends, and work well done, we have reason to be thankful.

4. I shall never forgive this injury. Never.

5. He was, in spite of his weaknesses, a man to respect and love.

15. GOOD PARAGRAPHS

For a full discussion of good paragraphs, see Chapter Six.

a. A good paragraph in expository writing has a clear topic sentence or topic idea, which gives unity to the paragraph.

b. A good paragraph has coherent arrangement of material, and clear transitions between sentences. (See "Transitions" page 781.)

c. Good paragraphs begin and end strongly.

d. Paragraphs in a composition should be linked to one another by transitions which make the organization evident to the reader. (See "Transitions" page 781.)

e. As a rough guide to paragraph length, the student should bear in mind that paragraphs in expository writing rarely exceed 300 words and rarely fall below 100.

f. Good paragraphs are usually concrete and fully developed. Four methods of development, often used in combination, are:

(1) Particularization
(2) Illustration
(3) Contrast and comparison
(4) Definition

g. The first and last paragraphs in a composition occupy positions of greatest emphasis, and should be written with particular care.

16. TRANSITIONS

Transitions are words, phrases, sentences, or even paragraphs, which show the reader the connections between the writer's ideas.

For further discussion of transitions within paragraphs, see page 145.

For further discussion of transitions between paragraphs, see page 147.

a. Transitions between sentences within a paragraph are established by:

(1) Using sentence connectives such as *therefore, however, on the other hand, consequently, at the same time.*

(2) Repeating a key word that has occurred in the preceding sentence.

(3) Using a clear pronoun reference to a word or idea in the preceding sentence.

(4) Putting parallel thoughts in parallel constructions to show the relationships between them.

b. Transitions between paragraphs are established by:

(1) Concluding a paragraph with a sentence which leads into the next paragraph.

(2) Using in the first sentence of a paragraph a transitional word or phrase: *furthermore, as a result, in addition, on the contrary.*

(3) Repeating a key word used in the preceding paragraph.

(4) Beginning a paragraph with a sentence which refers clearly to a statement at the end of the preceding paragraph or to its topic idea.

(5) Using short transitional paragraphs which summarize the preceding ideas and relate them to the idea which follows.

17. THE FRAGMENTARY SENTENCE

A fragmentary sentence is an unsatisfactory incomplete sentence. It is a subordinate part of a sentence confusingly written with a capital letter at the beginning and a period at the end.

The error of punctuating a fragmentary sentence as if it were a complete sentence is called the Period Fault.

For a full discussion of fragmentary sentences and acceptable incomplete sentences, see "Conventional Punctuation of Sentences" in Chapter Three.

> UNSATISFACTORY: He came at nine. *When I was ready to leave.*
> REVISED: He came at nine, when I was ready to leave.

> UNSATISFACTORY: Dorothea made a poor impression. *In every way.*
> REVISED: Dorothea made a poor impression in every way.

> UNSATISFACTORY: I missed the test. *As a result of being ten minutes late to class.*
> REVISED: As a result of being [or Because I was] ten minutes late to class, I missed the test.

EXERCISES

Revise or repunctuate the passages below to eliminate fragmentary sentences.

1. Mr. Wilder is a self-made man. Having worked hard all his life and accomplished a great deal.

2. Let me help you. Since I happen to be here.

3. Knowing that she should apologize for her rudeness but lacking courage to face him after what she had said.

4. Chester is not planning to attend the dance. Because of financial difficulties.

5. Being deeply indebted to his godfather, Horace decided to give him a present. A wrist watch. Which would have permanent value. Hoping very much that his godfather would be pleased.

18. THE RUN-TOGETHER SENTENCE

For a full discussion of run-together sentences, see "Conventional Punctuation of Sentences" in Chapter Three.

a. A run-together sentence is produced by using a comma, or no punctuation at all, between two independent clauses where a semicolon is required:

> He had not been invited, nevertheless he intends to go. [A semicolon is needed before *nevertheless.*]

He was sorry he hadn't written, she evidently had been worried. [A semi-colon is needed after *written*.]

John has a good job, he has had it since last July. [A semicolon is needed after *job*.]

NOTE.—Run-together sentences like those above often need not merely corrected punctuation, but recasting: John has had a good job since last July.

b. A general rule that will help students avoid run-together sentences is: Between two independent clauses which are in the same sentence and which are not joined by *and, but, for, or,* or *nor,* use a semicolon.

The error of using a comma between two independent clauses not joined by *and, but, for, or,* or *nor* is called the Comma Fault.

EXERCISES

Correct the punctuation in the following run-together sentences, and revise any sentences which would be improved by further revision.

1. He had traveled widely in this country, Latin America, and Canada, he had many friends in every part of the continent.

2. Tony has won his letter in football he is the only sophomore who has played in every game.

3. My father and grandfather were lawyers, therefore I have always been interested in law, I intend to make it my profession.

4. Ralph broke a date with Georgia last Saturday, consequently she is not speaking to him, although he has called her every night this week.

5. The international situation is not hopeless, on the contrary it seems much brighter than it did a month ago, and I have renewed faith in the United Nations.

19. INCOMPLETE, ILLOGICAL, AND MIXED CONSTRUCTIONS

a. Incomplete constructions occur when words which are grammatically necessary to complete the construction or the sense of the sentence are omitted.

INCOMPLETE: He was *as tall* if not taller *than his brother.*
COMPLETE: He was *as tall as* if not taller *than his brother.*
IMPROVED AND COMPLETE: He is at least as tall as his brother.

INCOMPLETE: Albert is *interested* and sympathetic *with the work* of the Salvation Army.

COMPLETE: Albert is *interested in* and sympathetic *with the work* of the Salvation Army.

INCOMPLETE: *My doctor* and *friend* will be here soon. [This sentence indicates that *doctor* and *friend* are names for one person. If two people will be here soon, the sentence is incomplete and confusing.]
COMPLETE: *My doctor* and *my friend* will be here soon.

INCOMPLETE: The *grass* was uncut and the *blinds* closed. [*Blinds* requires the plural verb *were*.]
COMPLETE: The *grass was* uncut and the *blinds were* closed.

INCOMPLETE: Herbert did better on the examination *than any member* of the class. [The sentence suggests that Herbert is not a member of the class. If he is, the construction is incomplete and confusing.]
COMPLETE: Herbert did better on the examination *than any other member* of the class.

b. Illogical constructions occur when two things not of the same kind or construction are compared or placed in apposition.

ILLOGICAL: I like this *teacher* better than any *course* I have had.
LOGICAL: I like this teacher better than any I have had. [*Or*] I like this course better than any I have had.

ILLOGICAL: *Like most novels of Dickens, the heroine* is a generous, unsophisticated girl.
LOGICAL: This girl, like most of Dickens' heroines, is generous and unsophisticated.

ILLOGICAL: Robert's ears are large, *like his father.*
LOGICAL: Robert has large ears like his father's. [*Or*] Robert, like his father, has large ears.

ILLOGICAL: I visited my *grandfather's grave* whose name I bear.
LOGICAL: I visited the grave of the grandfather whose name I bear.

ILLOGICAL: I read Carl Becker's *Modern Democracy, an historian* I greatly admire.
LOGICAL: I read *Modern Democracy* by Carl Becker, an historian I greatly admire.

c. Mixed constructions occur when the writer carelessly fuses two separate statements or constructions.

MIXED: John's ambition is to be a lawyer and is working industriously to achieve his goal.
REVISED: John's ambition is to be a lawyer; he is working industriously to achieve his goal.

MIXED: When spring came was the time students needed an outlet for their energy.
REVISED: When spring came, students needed an outlet for their energy.

[*Or*] Spring was the time when students needed an outlet for their energy.

MIXED: The reason I was late in registering was because I was ill.
REVISED: The reason I was late in registering was that I was ill. [*Or*] I was late in registering because I was ill.

MIXED: We worked hard on the prom was the most successful in the history of the college.
REVISED: We worked hard on the prom, and it was the most successful in the history of the college. [*Or*] We worked hard to make the prom the most successful in the history of the college.

MIXED: When the chapel bell rang five times was the signal for a fire drill.
REVISED: When the chapel bell rang five times, we prepared for a fire drill. [*Or*] Five rings of the chapel bell signaled a fire drill.

EXERCISES

Point out incomplete, illogical, or mixed constructions in the sentences below, and revise all faulty sentences.

1. I like apples better than any fruit.
2. Tom is over at Jane's house who is his cousin.
3. After the excitement was all over was when we got there.
4. Jack thinks he will not be involved or even connected with the accident.
5. I never have and I still do not understand what a restrictive modifier is.
6. Hilary went to the headmaster for information was just what he needed to know.
7. Unlike most poetry, Robert Frost is not difficult to understand.
8. The teacher-student relationship in college is more impersonal than high school.
9. Like many other students, success in medicine is my ambition.
10. He both hopes and fears the time of his graduation from college.

20. MODIFIERS

Modifiers should, for clarity, be close to the locution they modify, and should be so placed that they cannot appear to modify the wrong locution.

a. A modifier is called dangling when the word it logically modifies has been left out of the sentence.

(1) Dangling phrases.

DANGLING: Walking up the path, a stone lion stood in front of the museum. [According to the sentence, the lion walked up the path; the actual walker has been left out of the sentence.]

Revised: Walking up the path, we saw a stone lion standing in front of the museum.

Dangling: After opening the oven door, the chicken cooked more slowly. [The chicken did not actually open the oven door.]
Revised: After I opened the oven door, the chicken cooked more slowly.

Dangling: There was the village green, driving through the town.
Revised: We saw the village green as we drove through the town.

Sentences containing dangling phrases are corrected by inserting the word which the phrase should modify (Walking up the path, *we* saw . . .); or such sentences are corrected by changing the phrase to a clause which has as its subject the real doer of the action (After *I* opened the oven door . . .).

(2) Dangling elliptical clauses. A dangling elliptical clause may be corrected by adding the words omitted in the incomplete clause.

Dangling: When eight years old, my father was very severe about my smoking. [Since the person who was eight years old has been left out of the sentence, *When eight years old* appears to modify *my father.*]
Revised: When I was eight years old, my father was very severe about my smoking.

Dangling: While writing a letter to his brother, a pigeon flew into the room.
Revised: While Jim was writing a letter to his brother, a pigeon flew into the room.

(3) Dangling infinitives.

Dangling: To avoid eye strain, the lamp should have a hundred-watt bulb.
Revised: To avoid eye strain, you should have a hundred-watt bulb in your lamp.

Dangling: To enjoy television, the television room must be well planned.
Revised: To enjoy television, one must have a well-planned television room.

b. A modifier is called misplaced when its position is such that it appears to modify the wrong word.

(1) Misplaced adverbs.

Misplaced: I only saw one room of the house.
Revised: I saw only one room of the house.

Misplaced: He nearly wrote all of his term paper yesterday.
Revised: He wrote nearly all of his term paper yesterday.

Misplaced: He needed someone to help him review the material badly.
Revised: He badly needed someone to help him review the material.

(2) Misplaced phrases.

MISPLACED: I saw a church as I walked up the hill with a white steeple.
REVISED: I saw a church with a white steeple as I walked up the hill.

MISPLACED: Snarling in anger, I saw the dog as I came into the yard.
REVISED: I saw the dog snarling in anger as I came into the yard.

(3) Misplaced clauses.

MISPLACED: I had an unhappy experience in my first year of high school which I shall never forget.
REVISED: In my first year of high school I had an unhappy experience which I shall never forget.

MISPLACED: He sat smoking his pipe on the front porch which he had just lighted.
REVISED: He sat on the front porch, smoking the pipe he had just lighted.

(4) Ambiguous modifiers.

AMBIGUOUS: When John applied for the position on the advice of his roommate he dressed very carefully. [The phrase *on the advice of his roommate* is a "squinting modifier"; its position is such that it may modify either the preceding or the following words.]
REVISED: On the advice of his roommate, John dressed very carefully when he applied for the position. [*Or*] When John, on the advice of his roommate, applied for the position, he dressed very carefully.

AMBIGUOUS: He said after the election he would take a vacation.
REVISED: After the election, he said he would take a vacation. [*Or*] He said that he would take a vacation after the election.

EXERCISES

Point out any dangling, misplaced, or ambiguous modifiers in the following sentences and revise any sentences which need revision.

1. Curled up on the sofa, the cat purred comfortably.
2. John almost shoveled all the snow from the walks and driveway.
3. When covered with syrup, you will enjoy a tasty dish.
4. She was a tall woman with black hair and a friendly smile about thirty years old.
5. After staying at home for three days, my cold was better.
6. The house was set in a pine grove with a beautiful view and blue shutters.
7. While quietly studying, the doorbell disturbed Jane.
8. After preparing for an evening alone, I heard him come in with annoyance.
9. The teacher called on Bryan to recite for the fourth time.
10. She looked at Oscar when he came in with a vacant stare, then started to play the piano again.

11. Horace found the material which the other members of the class had been unable to find in the public library.

12. We heard a protest against the use of atomic bombs by a college professor.

13. After finishing high school, my father thought I should work for a year before coming to college.

14. Eleanor was criticized for taking a stand publicly against the decision of the student council by her sorority sisters.

15. I decided we should leave when the clock struck twelve.

21. PARALLELISM

Parallelism is the principle of usage which requires that coordinate elements in a compound construction be given the same grammatical form. Words, phrases, clauses, and even sentences may be expressed in parallel form.

a. Faulty parallelism occurs when logically coordinate elements are not expressed in parallel form.

FAULTY: He is afraid to live and of death.
PARALLEL: He is afraid to live and to die. [*Or*] He is afraid of life and of death.

FAULTY: The mayor promised that he would build new sidewalks, new equipment for the schools, and reducing the taxes.
PARALLEL: The mayor promised that he would build new sidewalks, provide new equipment for the schools, and reduce the taxes. [Three verbs.] [*Or*] The mayor promised to build new sidewalks, to provide new equipment for the schools, and to reduce the taxes. [Three infinitives.] [*Or*] The mayor promised new sidewalks, new equipment for the schools, and reduced taxes. [Three nouns.]

FAULTY: I had never been told before to take notes on cards, and that I should summarize the material in my own words.
PARALLEL: I had never been told before to take notes on cards and to summarize the material in my own words. [Two infinitive phrases.] [*Or*] I had never been told before that I should take notes on cards and that I should summarize the material in my own words. [Two clauses.]

FAULTY: The new dean is a woman with a great deal of experience and who is also very intelligent.
PARALLEL: The new dean is a woman with a great deal of experience and intelligence. [Two nouns.]

b. Faulty parallelism occurs when elements which are not logically coordinate are expressed in parallel form.

FAULTY: He is tall, thin, and a Sigma Chi.
LOGICAL: He is a tall, thin Sigma Chi.

FAULTY: The teacher said Maynard was lazy, careless, and had better get to work.

LOGICAL: The teacher said that Maynard was lazy and careless, and that he had better get to work.

For a further discussion of parallelism, see the section "Parallelism" in Chapter Three and "Compound Constructions and Parallelism," page 741.

EXERCISES

I. Criticize the use of parallelism in the following sentences and revise any sentences which need revision.

1. Mary is an excellent student, a good athlete, and attractive.
2. Stevenson wrote essays, novels, was a poet, and traveled extensively.
3. Photography is an interesting hobby and which is not expensive.
4. The book presents his experiences in Europe, how he met prominent people, and his hopes for world peace.
5. John has two ambitions: becoming a dentist, and to have a home in the country.
6. After traveling all day and wishing he had never undertaken the journey, he arrived home tired, hungry, irritated, and his feet sore.
7. Gretchen is active in the church, the D.A.R., the League of Women Voters, and doing her own housework too.
8. Waking early in the morning and remembering the events of yesterday, Cheever groaned and tried to go to sleep again.
9. He prayed for tolerance and understanding and that there would be no war.
10. He is irresponsible, quick-tempered, a liar, but likeable.

II. Analyze the skillful parallelism in the following passage.

But if men forget that the future will some day be a present, they forget, too, that the present is already here, and that even in a dark time some of the brightness for which they long is open to the responsive senses, the welcoming heart, and the liberated mind. The moments as they pass even now have their tang and character. They may yield even now the contagious joy of feeling and perception. Here are the familiar flowers, the music we love, the poetry by which we are moved. Here are the books and companions, the ideas and the relaxations, the gaieties and the co-operative tasks of our familiar world. These things may be threatened, they may be precarious, they may be ours only by the grace of God, or of geographical or economic accident. But undeniably, beckoningly, along with the portents and alarms, here they are. Here, in all tragic times, they always have been, affording challenge and delight to the senses, solace and nourishment for the affections, and friendly stimulus to the understanding.—IRWIN EDMAN, *Candle in the Dark*

22. INCONSISTENCIES

Inconsistencies are unnecessary and undesirable shifts in subject; in voice, mood, or tense of verbs; in style; or in levels of usage.

SHIFT IN SUBJECT, AND IN VOICE: When Jane went for the mail, a letter from home was found.
IMPROVED IN CONSISTENCY: When Jane went for the mail, she found a letter from home.

SHIFT IN MOOD: The writer should first make an outline. Now begin the actual writing of the paper.
IMPROVED IN CONSISTENCY: First make an outline; then begin the actual writing of the paper.

SHIFT IN SUBJECT AND STYLE (impersonal to personal): The captain's mate must be at the dock at six o'clock. You must check the equipment and be ready to help early-comers on board.
IMPROVED IN CONSISTENCY: The captain's mate must be at the dock at six o'clock to check the equipment and help early-comers on board.

SHIFT IN TENSE: He was a short, bald-headed man who always looks as though he had slept in his clothes.
IMPROVED IN CONSISTENCY: He was a short, bald-headed man who always looked as though he had slept in his clothes.

SHIFT IN LEVELS: After an impressive service in the small but beautiful chapel, the campers hit the sack.
IMPROVED IN CONSISTENCY: An impressive service in the small but beautiful chapel ended the campers' day.

For further examples of inconsistencies, see the section "Consistency in Structure and Style" in Chapter Three.

EXERCISES

Point out any inconsistencies in the following sentences, and revise the sentences which need revision.

1. Martha and Anna were tired by six o'clock, but Jean wants to drive another fifty miles.
2. You need more than a knowledge of the game to be a golf caddy; one must also be a student of human nature.
3. He had an admirable way of putting across complex ideas.
4. You are free to leave as soon as the examination has been finished.
5. The buyer of a second-hand car should be able to recognize certain signs of hard use; look, for example, at the floor pads and brake pedal.

23. WEAK PASSIVE

The passive voice indicates that the subject is acted upon rather than acting. Use of the passive voice is sometimes necessary, but the passive is likely to be unemphatic, indirect, wordy, and vague. Since active statements are nearly always more effective, one should use the passive voice only when there is good reason for doing so.

WEAK PASSIVE: Current events were discussed and long papers were written by us.
ACTIVE: We discussed current events and wrote long papers.

WEAK PASSIVE (and unnecessary shift to the passive in the middle of the sentence): As we entered the woods, a shot was heard.
ACTIVE: As we entered the woods, we heard a shot.

EXERCISES

Strengthen the following sentences by making the passive statements active.

1. Your invitation was received by me yesterday.
2. On the athletic field, students playing hockey can be seen.
3. Permission to print this material was given by the publishers.
4. When the bell rang, students pouring out of the buildings were observed.
5. Attendance at the meeting is planned by the entire fraternity.

24. SUBORDINATION

Subordination means expressing in dependent clauses, or phrases, or single words, ideas which are not important enough to be expressed in main clauses or independent sentences.

For a fuller discussion of subordination, see "Subordination" in Chapter Three and "Cutting Clauses" in Chapter Five.

a. Subordination is used to avoid:

(1) Choppy "primer" sentences:

I have a teacher named Mr. Mulch. He teaches biology. He is very strict.
IMPROVED BY SUBORDINATION: Mr. Mulch, my biology teacher, is very strict.

(2) Sprawling "and-and" sentences:

The bell rings and he comes into class, and he takes attendance.
IMPROVED BY SUBORDINATION: As soon as the bell rings, he comes into class and takes attendance.

b. When subordination is used effectively, less important ideas are placed in subordinate constructions, and important ideas are expressed emphatically in independent clauses.

> LACK OF SUBORDINATION (equal emphasis to ideas not equally significant): I was stepping off the curb and the truck hit me.
>
> UPSIDE-DOWN SUBORDINATION (emphasis on the less significant idea): When the truck hit me, I was stepping off the curb.
>
> PROPER EMPHASIS ON THE MORE SIGNIFICANT IDEA: As I was stepping off the curb, the truck hit me.

c. An awkward series of subordinate clauses in a sentence should be avoided.

> AWKWARD: He is the man who has bought the Nelsons' house for which he paid twenty thousand dollars which he borrowed from his brother-in-law.
>
> IMPROVED: He borrowed twenty thousand dollars from his brother-in-law to buy the Nelsons' house.

d. Subordinating conjunctions should be grammatically correct and should express clearly the relationship between ideas.

> POOR: The reason I can't go is *because* I have a previous engagement.
> REVISED: The reason I can't go is *that* I have a previous engagement. [*Or*] I can't go because I have a previous engagement.
>
> POOR: He doesn't know *as* he can take the courses he wants.
> REVISED: He doesn't know *that* (or *whether*) he can take the courses he wants.
>
> POOR: It seemed *like* the day would never end.
> REVISED: It seemed *as if* the day would never end.
>
> POOR: *Whereas* Edward needs money, he is looking for a part-time job.
> REVISED: *Because* Edward needs money, he is looking for a part-time job.
>
> POOR: I like his sister *while* I do not care for him.
> REVISED: I like his sister *although* I do not care for him.
>
> POOR: I read in the book *where* paragraphs should have topic sentences.
> REVISED: I read in the book *that* paragraphs should have topic sentences.

For a full discussion of the use of connectives, see "Prepositions and Conjunctions" page 772.

EXERCISES

I. Comment on the absence of subordination or any faulty subordination in the following passages, and revise any passages which need revision. Not all the passages are faulty.

1. The bus was crowded. There were no seats. I had to stand.

2. We left early in the morning so we could get a good start and we arrived in Chicago late that night, but then we had difficulty in getting a room at a hotel.

3. Carl was the oldest boy in the club and he was also a boy scout. He organized the hike.

4. Although he won first prize for his water color, he had been painting for only two years.

5. When I came into the house, I nearly fell over the body in the hall.

6. This is the chapter that Professor Lee wants us to read so that we will be prepared tomorrow when he gives us the quiz that he has promised.

7. Jeanette, who is my best friend, lives in a house which is attractive. It is near the park and is very modern.

8. It was ten of nine. The class began at nine. I had to hurry.

9. Irene was tired and she was hungry but she had to go home and get dinner, and it seemed unfair.

10. Just as we reached the five-yard line, the game ended.

II. Write three sentences, each of which incorporates all three of the statements listed below. In each sentence, use subordination to emphasize a different statement.

1. Professor Blackstone teaches history.
2. He is a tall gaunt man who looks like Abraham Lincoln.
3. He is an excellent teacher.

III. Incorporate the facts listed below in one good sentence.

1. Jimmy Bryce rode his bicycle from Medford to Boston.
2. Jimmy is seven years old.
3. He lives at 22 Elm Street in Medford.
4. He rode eight miles.
5. He went to see his father.
6. His father is in the Massachusetts General Hospital.
7. His father is there because he was injured in an explosion at the Blank factory.
8. Jimmy made the ride the day before this news article was written.
9. Jimmy's parents are Mr. and Mrs. Roger Bryce.

IV. Revise the sentences below to eliminate faulty connections.

1. The reason he lost the election is because he offended so many people.
2. Herman intends to be a doctor while his father, grandfather, and great-grandfather have all been lawyers.
3. Eliot looked like he was in poor health.
4. Jim was depressed by the newspaper account where a man killed his wife and two children as he felt he was unable to provide for them.
5. I had wandered for two miles until I decided to ask directions.

25. VARIETY

For a full discussion of variety, see the section "Variety in Sentences" in Chapter Five.

a. Monotonous repetition of words and sounds, and monotonous sentence structures should be avoided.

MONOTONOUS REPETITION: My general reaction to his action was that in general he acted wisely.

IMPROVED: I felt that in general he acted wisely.

MONOTONOUS CHOPPY SENTENCES: Joan came into the house. It was dark. The clock was striking seven.

IMPROVED: When Joan came into the dark house, the clock was striking seven.

MONOTONOUS SENTENCE PATTERNS: Having had a hard day at the office, Joe lost his temper quickly. Recovering from his anger, he regretted what he had said. Knowing that he was sorry, Martha accepted his apology.

IMPROVED: Joe, after a hard day at the office, lost his temper quickly. As soon as he recovered from his anger, he regretted what he had said, and Martha, knowing that he was sorry, accepted his apology.

b. Variety in sentence movement is achieved by:

(1) Varying the length of sentences.

(2) Using parallel and balanced constructions as a change from simpler constructions.

(3) Intermingling loose and periodic sentences.

(4) Changing the position of modifiers and parenthetic elements.

(5) Changing the subject-verb-object order of some sentences.

Sentence variety is closely related to subordination and to emphasis: in varying the movement of his sentences, the writer must consider what ideas he wants to emphasize by structure and position.

EXERCISES

Improve the style of the following passages by varying the sentence structures.

1. I called the doctor and he came at once. He examined my father, and he said there was nothing to worry about. He prescribed some medicine, and I went to the drug store to get it.

2. At first, I disliked this teacher. Later, I appreciated his methods. Consequently, I do not trust my first impressions of teachers. At present, I am keeping an open mind.

3. She heard the doorbell ring. She went to answer it. A seller of brooms

and mops was there. She told him she had enough brooms and mops. He went away when he heard this.

4. A tall, white-haired woman of fifty, Miss Brown taught English. Serious in her work, she demanded accuracy. Realizing that most of us were going to college, she prepared us for the College Boards.

5. When Edward first applied for a job, he was very nervous. While he was waiting in the outer office, he almost decided to leave. When he saw the boss, he felt more confident. After he got the job, he was thankful.

26. ECONOMY: AVOIDING WORDINESS

For a full discussion of economy, see the section "Economy and Conciseness" in Chapter Five.

a. Economy is achieved by avoiding padding and jargon.

(1) *Padding* is a term for words and phrases which add nothing but length to a sentence.

> PADDING: There are a large number of college students who find it difficult to do their work punctually on time, with the resulting effect that they receive poor marks which do not make them happy.
>
> IMPROVED: Many college students find it difficult to do their work punctually; they receive poor marks as a result.

(2) *Jargon* is a term for verbose, "heavy" language.

> JARGON: Ultimately I ascended the incline to view the conflagration.
> IMPROVED: Finally I went up the hill to see the fire.

b. Economy is achieved by cutting weak clauses to phrases or to single words.

> WORDY: Mr. Brown, who was my chemistry teacher, had a classroom manner which was very interesting.
> IMPROVED BY CUTTING CLAUSES: Mr. Brown, my chemistry teacher, had a very interesting classroom manner.

c. Economy is achieved by the substitution of exact words for longer locutions.

> WORDY AND INEXACT: She planted some bulbs of those little yellow and purple flowers that bloom early in the spring.
> CONCISE: She planted some crocus bulbs.
>
> WORDY: He looked at her with an expression of great displeasure and hostility on his face.
> CONCISE: He scowled at her.

d. Concrete detail and repetition for emphasis should not be confused with wordiness.

> BRIEF BUT UNINFORMATIVE: She seemed upset.

Improved by additional detail: She talked rapidly, her eyes darting from his face to the handkerchief she was twisting in her hands. In the middle of a sentence she got up and left the room.

EXERCISES

I. Revise the following sentences to eliminate padding and jargon.

1. He rendered a selection of his own poetry of a lyric nature to the assembled gathering.

2. The house, grey in color and square in shape, located on Latin Road, has been designated as a club for the use of the members of the faculty.

3. I regarded with a sense of anticipation the advent of my college career at the college of my choice, namely this great institution of higher learning.

4. John had a conversation of an hour's length with his faculty counselor in regard to the matter of his major field of study.

5. This lovely and beautiful scene of beauty stretched before me for the distance of a mile, and I thought in my mind that I would always remember it in memory in the future days to come.

II. Revise the following sentences, cutting the weak clauses to phrases and single words, and substituting exact words for wordy locutions.

1. The new Alumni Center, which is the gift of the class of 1930, is to be built on Locust Avenue, which is two blocks south of the campus.

2. The assignment for next time is to write a paper about *The Return of the Native*, which was written by Thomas Hardy, in which we give our opinion of the book.

3. All freshmen are now wearing the caps which are required and learning the things about the college which have been passed on from one generation of students to the next.

4. Jonathan Allan, who is my roommate, comes from a town called Greenview, which is in Illinois.

5. He has to hand in, when he hands in his paper, an alphabetical list of all the books and articles he used when he wrote it.

27. LEVELS OF USAGE

The term *levels of usage* describes the differences in construction, pronunciation, and vocabulary which are produced by differences in education and social situation. For a full discussion of three main levels of usage—formal English, informal English, and vulgate English—see "The Appropriate Level of Usage" in Chapter Four.

a. The level of usage (formal or informal) should be appropriate to the subject, the audience, and the occasion.

b. Unless there is positive gain in a shift of levels, the level of usage should be consistent in a passage or a composition.

c. Students should aim at a high informal level in most of their writing.

d. In high informal writing, slang is usually out of place.

e. "Heavy" words, over-formal and pretentious for their context, should be avoided.

28. CONCRETENESS

Concrete words are words referring to objects which have existence in the physical world, on the nature and meaning of which, therefore, people can to a considerable extent agree. Although abstract words are necessary in discussing general concepts and conditions, concrete words are preferable, whenever they can appropriately be used, because they convey more exact referential and attitudinal meaning. For a full discussion of concreteness, see the section "Concrete Expression" in Chapter Four.

a. Concrete expression is achieved by substituting concrete words for abstract words.

ABSTRACT: The flowers were different colors.
CONCRETE: The chrysanthemums were bronze, yellow, and white.

b. Concrete expression is achieved by expanding general statements with concrete particulars and examples.

ABSTRACT: He is a good citizen.
CONCRETE: He is a good citizen. He has agreed to take charge of the Community Fund drive, and he has been chairman of the School Committee for three years.

c. Concrete expression is achieved by using concrete comparisons and figures of speech.

ABSTRACT: The length of time organic life has existed on earth is almost inconceivable.
CONCRETE COMPARISON: In order to understand the process of organic evolution, let us imagine a cord stretched from New York to Boston, each yard of which represents 10,000 years . . .

ABSTRACT: People cannot live isolated from other human beings.
CONCRETE FIGURE OF SPEECH: No man is an island, entire of itself; every man is a piece of the continent, a part of the main . . .

EXERCISES

I. Substitute concrete expression for abstract expression in the following passages.

1. Looking out of my window in the early morning, I can see a few birds hopping about under the tree, and smell the flowers blooming under the window. In this peculiar light, the building across the street seems to be asleep.

2. Harry is carefully selecting the courses which will be useful to him in his chosen work.

3. I hope to take a trip in the near future.

4. Our car is somewhat in need of repair.

5. The other day we went to a meeting at which the speaker expressed some radical ideas.

II. Expand the following general statements with concrete particulars and examples.

1. Ellen's parents have always been very strict with her.
2. The room was colorful.
3. Ernest is a loyal friend.
4. She is unpredictable.
5. There is a feel of winter in the air.

29. TRITENESS

Trite expressions are too-familiar combinations of words, often-used quotations, and worn-out figures of speech. In revision, trite phrases should be replaced by more exact, less shopworn expressions. For a full discussion of triteness and a list of trite expressions, or clichés, see "Originality" in Chapter Five.

Some of the trite phrases which often appear in freshman themes are:

road of life	trees like sentinels
path to success	heart of gold
last but not least	diamond in the rough
tired but happy	wend my way
budding genius	the finer things of life

30. FIGURATIVE LANGUAGE

Figurative language is language in which words are used non-literally. The basis of most figurative language is comparison or association of two ordinarily separate things or ideas.

a. The most common figures of speech are:

(1) *Simile:* a non-literal comparison, usually introduced by *like* or *as,* of two things unlike in most respects but similar in others.

He shall come down *like rain upon the mown grass.*

(2) *Metaphor:* an implied non-literal comparison.

I am the *captain of my soul.*
The fog came in *on little cat feet.*
With *rue my heart is laden* for the *golden* friends I've had.
A *dusty* answer.

(3) *Analogy:* a sustained comparison of two ideas or situations.
(4) *Metonymy:* a form of comparison in which an exact name for
something is replaced by a term closely associated with it.

crown [for king], *sail* [for ship], *The kettle is boiling* [for The water in
the kettle is boiling].

(5) *Personification:* a form of metaphor infrequently used in modern writing, which attributes human qualities to objects or ideas.

With how sad steps, O Moon, thou climb'st the skies!
How silently, and with how wan a face.

Duty commanded and he obeyed.

**b. Appropriate figurative language serves to make expression con-
crete and vivid.** (For illustrations, see "Concrete Expression" in
Chapter Four.)
c. Trite figures of speech should be avoided.

Trite similes: pretty as a picture, happy as a lark, fresh as a daisy.
Trite metaphors: budding genius, crack of dawn, lap of luxury.
Trite personifications: Father Time, Mother Nature.

**d. Mixed, or awkwardly combined figures of speech should be
avoided.**

The *odor* of magnolias *shouted* a welcome.
In the argument he *brought his big guns* into play and *stifled* his opponent.
While he was courageously *battling* his way *through the sea of life, fate
stepped in and tripped him up.*

e. Strained and inappropriate figures of speech should be avoided.

Trees were dressed in their best bibs and tuckers preparing for their
farewell-to-summer ball.
Her smile was as warm as an electric heater.

31. REPETITION

For a fuller discussion of awkward repetition see pp. 120–121.
For a fuller discussion of skillful repetition see pp. 132–133.
**a. Awkward and unnecessary repetition of words and sounds should
be avoided.**

AWKWARD: The fact is, I do my best *writing* when *doing factual writing.*
IMPROVED: I write best when I deal with facts.

AWKWARD: The *shipper* checks the *merchandise* which has been *shipped* in, then the *shipper* puts the *merchandise* into stock.
IMPROVED: The shipper checks the merchandise as it comes in and then puts it into stock.

b. Skillful repetition is an element of style, used for clarity and emphasis.

The only thing we have to *fear* is *fear* itself . . .
We shall fight on the beaches, *we shall fight* on the landing grounds, *we shall fight* in the fields and in the streets, *we shall fight* in the hills . . .

EXERCISES

Comment on the repetition in the following passages, revising any passages in which repetition is awkward and ineffective.

1. Olga bought two table lamps for the two tables in her room.
2. This painting was painted by Grant Wood.
3. The first meeting of the organization will be an organizational meeting.
4. I worked in a bank last summer and enjoyed the work so much that I intend to make banking my work.
5. Fog everywhere. Fog up the river, where it flows among green aits and meadows; fog down the river, where it rolls defiled among the tiers of shipping.

32. IDIOM

An idiom is an expression peculiar to a language.

Some idiomatic expressions defy grammatical principles, have a meaning beyond the literal meanings of the words, and are, therefore, untranslatable. Examples of such idioms in English are *make good, get the upper hand, strike a bargain, gone to the dogs.* Some idioms of this kind are slang or near-slang, and should be avoided in formal writing; others are acceptable in any writing.

Another type of idiom is a grammatical construction peculiar to a language. In English, the most common difficulties with idiom rise from the fact that many words idiomatically require a particular preposition to complete their meaning. Below is a partial list of these prepositional idioms. Dictionaries give further information about idioms of this kind.

accommodate oneself to a situation

accommodate someone else with a favor

in accordance with

accuse of

acquiesce in

acquit of

addicted to

agree with a person

agree to a proposal

agree on a plan

allergic to

angry with a person

angry at a thing

averse to

capable of

compare to (to show likeness)

compare with (to show difference)

comply with

concur in a decision

concur with a person

convenient to a place

convenient for a purpose

desist from

devoid of

differ with a person

differ from (this differs from that)

differ about or over a question

different from

dissent from

expert in

identical with

independent of

monopoly of

oblivious of

part from a person

part with a possession

plan to

prerequisite to

proficient in

repugnant to

at variance with

vexed with a person

vexed at a thing

vie with

33. CHOICE OF WORDS

The symbol **WW** (wrong word) in the margin of a theme generally means that the writer has used a non-existent word ("undoubtably"); has used a word ungrammatically ("I suspicion"); has fallen into an inappropriate level of usage ("The situation was thoroughly fouled up"); has mistaken the meaning of a word ("He made no direct illusion to Russia in the speech"); or has used a word loosely and inexactly ("He gave many causes for his decision"). The student should look in the dictionary for a word marked **WW**; should (if he finds it) determine its meaning and level; and should substitute in his theme a more exact or more appropriate word.

Skill in the choice of words is a complex skill. The writer should:

a. Avoid padding, jargon, and trite expressions.

b. Choose an appropriate level of usage.

c. Use exact concrete words, whenever he can, in place of abstract words (*red barn* instead of "building").

d. Use exact names (*lectern* instead of "little stand on the desk").

e. Use strong, working words (The sirens *screamed* instead of "made a noise like a scream").

f. Choose words with exact connotations (She was *slender and lovely* instead of "thin and lovely").

g. Be unsatisfied until he finds the precise word to convey the meaning he intends.

Punctuation

Punctuation rules are simply ways of stating the generally accepted, conventional meaning of punctuation marks. The able writer is aware of the important part such marks play in clarifying meaning and emphasis, and he departs from the conventions only when there is clear and positive advantage to be gained from doing so. Marks of punctuation, with their conventional uses, are listed in alphabetical order in this section.

34. APOSTROPHE (')

The apostrophe is used to form possessives and certain plurals, and to indicate the omission of one or more letters.

a. To form the possessive of nouns not ending in *s*, use the apostrophe plus *s*.

Tom's shoes   day's work   man's fate   men's clothes

b. To form the possessive of plural nouns ending in *s*, use the apostrophe alone.

soldiers' uniforms   friends' houses   ladies' jewelry

c. To form the possessive of singular nouns ending in *s* or *s* sounds, use either the apostrophe alone, or the apostrophe plus *s*.

Burns's poetry [*Or*] Burns' poetry

d. To form the plurals of figures, letters, and signs, use the apostrophe plus *s* if the apostrophe is needed for clarity.

The word has three *i*'s in it. He learned his ABCs.

e. To indicate the omission of one or more letters, use the apostrophe.

He said the 'gator [alligator] was dangerous.
They won't come, and we can't meet without them.

EXERCISES

Before doing these exercises, see "Noun Usage," page 750.

I. Insert the needed apostrophes in the following sentences:

1. There are two *r*s and two *i*s in Henrys last name.
2. She doesnt think its necessary to study.
3. That handwriting is either James or hers.
4. Its unlikely that hell arrive before eight oclock.
5. There were thirteen *and*s, eight *but*s and three *so*s in the first page of the theme.

II. Write the contractions for the following expressions; if no recognized contracted form exists, write *none*.

shall not	is not	she will
will not	can not	he will
would not	must not	it is
could not	should not	they are
are not	may not	we have
am not	might not	it has

III. Write the possessive singular and, if it exists, the possessive plural of each of the following:

she	man	army
it	woman	NLRB
he	child	country
one	president	fox
you	James	D.A.R.
I	Henry	lady

35. BRACKETS ([ ])

Brackets are most commonly used to enclose interpolations by the writer or the editor in quoted material.

"He [Calvin Coolidge] had the reputation of being a man of few words."
"That year [1860] he met Lincoln for the first time."

36. COLON (:)

The colon is a formal and specialized mark indicating introduction or anticipation.

a. The colon is used to introduce a formal quotation or a formal enumeration of particulars.

In his speech of July 3, 1947, Senator Patwell said: "This un-American law . . ."

The college library has ordered the following books: . . .

b. The colon is used to follow the salutation of a business letter.

Dear Sir: Dear Mr. Nelson: Gentlemen:

c. The colon is used to separate hours from minutes (12:15).

EXERCISES

Insert or substitute brackets and colons where they are needed in the following business letter; remove them where they are not needed, and supply the correct punctuation. If you are uncertain in choosing between brackets and parentheses see the discussion of parentheses on page 811.

see the discussion of parentheses on page 811.

> 120 LOWELL STREET
> NEW YORK 6, N.Y.
> January 1, 1951

MR. HAROLD MASON, President
The Cornwall Company
564 West Sixth Street
New York 16, N.Y.

DEAR MR. MASON;

I am mailing to you today the following material: Chapters I, III, and V of Section One: Chapters II and IV of Section Two: and Chapters I and II of Section Three.

Your suggestions about: margins, numbering of pages, and use of headings are very helpful: they will solve some troublesome problems.

The two sentences that you were puzzled by [page 144, lines 8–12] do need revision. Below are the sentences as they originally were along with the changes that should be made;

Charles Fremont, grandson of Joclyn (should be Jocelyn) was born in Carecus (should be Caracas), Venezuela, on March 6 (should be March 8) at 8:29 A:M. His twin brother and loyal follower was born three hours later.

Please thank Mr. Edmonds for the research he has done and for his patience in reading the manuscript. My wife [who is doing the typing and who insists that my handwriting is illegible] also wants to thank Mr. Edmonds.

I hope to be able to send you the additions to Chapter VI of Section Two in a few days.

> Cordially yours,
> MARTIN S. BARRETT

37. COMMA (,)

The comma is the most frequently used mark of punctuation. Misuse of it produces not only mechanical errors, but also confusion and misunderstanding.

a. The comma is used to separate two independent clauses joined by *and, but, for, or, nor*.

He spoke to his brother, and his father did not hear the remark.

(When there is no danger of ambiguity or misreading, it is permissible to omit the comma.)

b. The comma is used to set off nonrestrictive modifiers. (A nonrestrictive modifier—usually a participial phrase, an apposed adjective, or a dependent clause—gives additional information about an already identified referent, whereas a restrictive modifier identifies or limits the expression that it modifies.)

Janet's father, *who is usually very patient,* has finally lost his temper. [Nonrestrictive modifier; a comma should be used. The word *father* is already identified, and the clause simply gives additional information.]

Any father *who has a daughter in college* knows that education is expensive. [Restrictive modifier; a comma should not be used. The modifying clause restricts the general word *father* to those fathers who have daughters in college.]

Andrew, *usually thought to be meek and timid,* proved himself a hero. [Nonrestrictive; Andrew is already identified. The participial phrase gives additional information.]

Men *thought to be meek and timid* sometimes perform heroic acts. [Restrictive; necessary to identify the men being talked about.]

c. The comma is used after an adverbial clause or a long phrase preceding the main part of the sentence.

While Arthur was reading the book, his sister came in.

d. The comma is used to set off words, phrases, or clauses that are parenthetical (i.e., are thrown in as interrupters when the grammatical structure is complete without them).

He is, however, unwilling to accept the compromise.
War and unemployment, on the other hand, are ever-present dangers.
He, it is said, was more to blame than his son.

e. The comma is used to separate elements (words, phrases, or clauses) in a series.

Papers were strewn on the table, on the desk, and on the floor.
He enjoys hunting, fishing, and swimming.

He stated that conflict was imminent, that the opponents were well prepared, and that he felt uncertain of victory.

He was tired, he was hungry, and he was very late.

(When there is no danger of ambiguity or misreading, it is permissible to omit the comma before the final element in the series.)

f. The comma is used to set off a nonrestrictive appositive. (An
appositive is a noun or a noun equivalent used to explain another
noun construction which has the same referent.)

Mr. Morgan, John's father, was pleased. [Nonrestrictive appositive;
commas are needed.]

The poet Milton was blind. [Restrictive appositive; commas should not
be used.]

**g. The comma is used to separate two coordinate adjectives not
joined by a conjunction.**

The tall, thin man shrugged his shoulders.

(The comma is not used when such adjectives are not coordinate,
as in "The tired old man staggered under the pack." Here *tired*
modifies the locution *old man*.)

**h. The comma is used to set off a short direct quotation from the
rest of the sentence.**

He said, "Are you going now?"

"You must go now," he said.

**i. The comma is used to separate the parts of dates, addresses, and
geographical names.**

On August 17, 1949, his address was 14 Barton Street, Peoria 4, Illinois;
later he moved to Cleveland, Ohio, to live near his sister.

j. The comma is used to prevent misreading. (Sometimes the fact
that commas are needed to prevent misreading is a hint that the
sentence needs to be revised.)

Before, he had insisted on cash payment.

For him, to buy was better than to sell.

**k. Commas are used (1) when they are needed to clarify meaning
by marking a slight pause, and (2) when they are required by some
of the established conventions stated in the rules above. Commas
that are not justified by (1) or (2) should be omitted.**

That he will go, is now certain. [The comma should be struck out.]

I know, that he can be depended upon. [The comma should be struck
out.]

Men, who have two wives, are called bigamists. [Both commas should be struck out; the clause is clearly restrictive.]

EXERCISES

I. Decide whether to use commas, semicolons, or no mark of punctuation in the places where there is a caret (∧) in the sentences below, and cite the rule that applies. (Before you do this exercise, see rules **a** and **b** under "Semicolon," page 816.)

1. The wind is blowing∧ but the sun is warm.

2. "I am unwilling∧" he said∧ "to give money to such a cause∧ and I do not want my name used in connection with it."

3. He was old∧ he was tired∧ and he was unwilling to learn new ways.

4. In the winter∧ there is snow to shovel∧ in the summer∧ there is grass to cut∧ in the fall∧ there are leaves to rake∧ only in the early spring is there leisure.

5. We waited at home until she returned∧ for Mother was worried about her∧ and Father was worried about the car.

6. He said∧ "My children are sick∧ my wife is ill∧ and I have no money."

7. The Arnolds brought ice, lemonade and cookies∧ the Lanes brought frankfurts∧ rolls, and wood for the fire∧ and we brought potato salad, oranges, and a large thermos jug full of coffee.

8. Maynard gets sleepy as soon as he opens his chemistry book∧ he can read a detective story∧ though∧ until three in the morning.

9. Speech is silver∧ silence is golden.

10. If you ask him a question∧ he does not answer∧ if you tell him something∧ he forgets it immediately.

11. The driver slowed down∧ when he saw the police car∧ then he turned sharply into a country lane∧ and roared away.

12. He is very polite∧ in fact, he is too polite∧ and I distrust him.

II. In the sentences below, the expressions in italics are restrictive or nonrestrictive modifiers. Insert commas wherever they are needed for proper punctuation of these modifiers.

1. Marcella *who is very sensitive* often has her feelings hurt.

2. His hair *gray and sparse* made him look older than he actually was.

3. The men *who were the fathers of the American Revolution* would be surprised at the actions of some of their descendants.

4. He admits that history *which he calls his least interesting subject* is the course for which he studies least.

5. The subjects *which Edward likes best* are psychology and anthropology.

6. Tom *startled by the sudden question and only half awake* mumbled a reply and went to sleep again.

7. His latest book *on which he worked for seven years* is said to be inferior to his earlier books.

8. The sun *obscured by the cloud of smoke* cast a ray of light on the path ahead of us.

9. We saw our friend *still smiling and serene* open the door to the Dean's office.

10. Martin *who has never read a book in his life* says that he hopes to be a newspaper man and a critic.

III. In the passage below strike out any commas which are not *required* according to the conventions of punctuation.

Polly said, "It's too small, for a wedding announcement," and tore open the letter, as Jim went out to bring in the rest of the groceries, from the car. Below him, as he walked down, the steps of the cottage, the lake shimmered blue in the noonday sun. There were no more bundles in the car, and he slammed the door, listening to the sharp, crack in the clear, air. Everything was intensified like that here: sound and smell and color, and the sensations of sunlight and used muscles and refreshment after sleep. He sat down on the low, flat, boulder, at the meeting of the two paths, one zigzagging from the cottage down to the beach, the other winding up to the knoll with its single crooked, pine tree, overlooking the lake. The stone was warm from the sun. With the side of his shoe, he scraped together a pile of brown, pine needles, which covered the ground at his feet.

Polly came out on the porch. "Jim, Berda's in Boston and wants to come up this week-end. We haven't invited anyone else, have we?"

"I haven't." He grinned at his sister, over his shoulder. "How about your wide-eyed medical friends?"

"They can't come. And they are not wide-eyed," she added, good-naturedly.

38. DASH (—)

The dash skillfully used does much to clarify meaning; unskillfully used, it misleads the reader and suggests that the writer is using punctuation to suit his own convenience rather than to guide the reader. Dashes may be used singly or in pairs.

a. Dashes are used in pairs to set off interpolations to which the writer wishes to give greater emphasis than parentheses or commas would give them.

He said—you can imagine how this pleased me—that he would not accept my handwritten paper.

These three elements—plain sense, attitude, and intention—combine to produce the compound of meaning.

Charles, you must—don't scuff your feet and wear out your shoes—you must return Mr. Hazlitt's rake.

b. A single dash is used to mark an unexpected turn of thought, an abrupt suspension of sense, a sudden change in construction, or a hesitation in speech.

He gave a—I'm sorry; I promised not to tell.

Beets, carrots, tomatoes, corn, chard, onions—all these I planted in the unfertile soil. At the end of the summer I had well-fed worms and a flourishing crop of—weeds!

Mary heard Tom say to her father, "Mr. Hodge, I—that is, we—well— uh—Mary said—to ask . . ."

c. The dash should not be carelessly used as a substitute for other marks of punctuation.

(In general the dash serves as a signal that either the substance or the construction of the material it sets off demands particular attention. In typing, the dash is made by combining two hyphens.)

39. ELLIPSIS (. . .)

Ellipsis is used to indicate the omission of a word or words needed to complete a sentence, or the omission of part of a quotation.

Four spaced periods instead of three are used in an ellipsis if it comes at the end of a sentence which is closed by a period, or if a period occurs in the material omitted.

I know that I should do it, but . . . .

Newman says that a university education "gives a man a clear conscious view of his own opinions and judgments, . . . an eloquence in expressing them, and a force in urging them."

40. EXCLAMATION POINT (!)

The exclamation point is used after an ejaculation (word, phrase, or entire sentence) to indicate emphatic utterance or strong feeling.

Ouch! Get out! And we spent our youth learning grammar!

41. HYPHEN (-)

The hyphen is a mark used primarily to show close relationship between words or parts of words.

Rules for the hyphen are not completely fixed: some compounds (combined words or parts of words) are hyphenated and others are written as solid words; and authorities differ about the use of the hyphen in particular cases.

a. The hyphen is used between words which function as a single adjective before a substantive.

an off-the-face-hat [*but*—off the face of the earth]
a broken-down car [*but*—The car was broken down.]
a hard-working man

b. The hyphen is used at the end of a line when part of a word or a compound is carried over to the next line. (See "Syllabification," page 823.)

c. The hyphen is used in compound numbers from twenty to one hundred.

twenty-one   ninety-nine   eighty-four

42. ITALICS

Italics are indicated in manuscript by underlining the word or words to be italicized.

a. Italics are used for titles of books, newspapers, magazines, and long poems and plays, and for names of ships and aircraft.

> *Green Mansions*   *The Tempest*
> the *Saturday Review of Literature*   the *Queen Mary*

b. Italics are used for foreign words and phrases.

The ambassador was *persona non grata.*

c. Italics are used for emphasis. (But see page 780.)

I shall *never* consent.

d. Italics are used for calling attention to words as words.

Freedom is a word with many meanings.

43. PARENTHESES (( ))

Parentheses are used to set off material (definitions, additional information, asides, illustrative detail) which helps to clarify, but is not essential. (Such material is thrown in, as we say, parenthetically.)

When he first introduces the symbol of the lantern (page 13, paragraph 2) he is describing his boyhood experience.

EXERCISES

I. State the main uses of each of the following marks of punctuation: dash, ellipsis, exclamation point, hyphen, italics, parentheses.

II. What is the difference in use between parentheses and brackets, between parentheses and dashes, between the hyphen and the dash?

When are italics (or underlining) used in writing titles and when are quotation marks used? (See "Quotation Marks," page 814.)

III. In the sentences below examine the use of the dash, ellipsis, parentheses, and italics. In each case explain why that mark of punctuation is properly used or why it is misused. When you find a mark improperly used, strike it out and substitute whatever punctuation is necessary.

1. John Gunther's *Roosevelt in Retrospect* (New York, Harper & Brothers, 1950) is . . . or at least most reviewers seem to think it is . . . a satisfactory treatment of a difficult subject.

2. Mr. Hamilton Basso, who wrote the review entitled *Another Go at F.D.R.* in "The New Yorker," expresses the following opinion: "Mr. Gunther . . . is one of the more uncritical of Roosevelt's admirers. He is in there all the time getting in his licks for his hero."

3. Several of the keys of her typewriter—the *a*, the *i*, the *l*, and the *g*—clearly need cleaning; also I wish that she would learn to spell "separate" properly.

4. Senator Rudland said he was going to his hotel (he pronounced it hó-tel) to get some sleep. Tomorrow he will sail for England on the *Queen Elizabeth*.

5. *Op. cit., loc. cit., passim, supra*—these Latin terms were once more widely used in footnotes than they now are.

IV. Supply hyphens where they are needed:

1. His down to earth statement surprised those who had expected a vague and fumbling answer from the eighty seven year old ex president.

2. His sister in law, a strong willed, self reliant woman, refused to wear high heeled shoes, insisted on continuing to wear her out of style hat, and was entirely satisfied with ankle length skirts.

3. We suspected that his never say die attitude was a pose and that his self confident air was equally misleading.

44. PERIOD (.)

a. The period is used to mark the end of a complete declarative sentence. The placing of the period after a fragmentary sentence produces the blunder known as the Period Fault.

Henry has sold his car to his roommate. [This is a complete sentence; it contains a subject, *Henry,* a verb, *has sold,* and it makes an independent assertion.]

We were planning to go to Yellowstone Park. *When Henry sold his car to his roommate.* [The italicized expression, a subordinate clause, is a fragmentary sentence. It serves to illustrate the period fault because a period is used as end punctuation after a group of words that do not constitute a complete sentence.]

Ability to recognize and distinguish between complete and fragmentary sentences is essential to the proper use of the period. (See "The Fragmentary Sentence," page 782.)

b. The period is used to make clear that a letter or a group of letters is an abbreviation of a longer locution.

Mrs. Abbott belongs to the D.A.R.

(Certain abbreviations—UNRRA, UN, IOU—are written without periods. For information about particular abbreviations, consult your dictionary.)

c. The period is used to mark a decimal.

She paid $403.50 for the furniture she bought at the auction.
The cost of living has risen 60.42 per cent.

A series of periods, called *ellipsis,* is used to indicate the omission of a word or words necessary to complete a sentence, or the omission of a part of a quotation. (See "Ellipsis," page 810.)

EXERCISES

I. Define (1) complete sentence, (2) incomplete sentence, (3) fragmentary sentence. (If necessary see "Fragmentary Sentences," page 63.)

II. In the passages below (1) point out any fragmentary sentences and revise to eliminate the period fault, (2) point out any acceptable incomplete sentences and explain why you think they are acceptable, (3) point out the subject and the verb of each independent clause or sentence, and (4) add any periods which are needed and strike out any unnecessary periods.

1. He did not know the abbreviation for United States. Which is U.S.

2. We were pleased at the progress our club had made. Only a year, yet twenty-seven members now and $227.40 in our treasury.

3. We told the freshman to ring the chapel bell at two AM. Which, much to our surprise, he did and woke up Dean Holden.

4. What would be a reasonable sum? Dick did not want to overpay the man, but he wanted to be fair. Perhaps thirty dollars. That seemed too much. Perhaps twenty-five or perhaps even twenty. Yes, twenty would do.

5. Henry was surprised to see Andy walking slowly ahead of him.

"Andy," he shouted, "Is that you, Andy?"

"Yeah." Andy's voice didn't sound friendly.

"Where are you going?"

"Just walking." Andy was waiting for him now under the light. His collar was turned up and he looked cold.

"I thought you were seeing Anne tonight."

"Yeah. I was."

"But it's only—"

"Only nine. That's right, and I'm not with Anne. Funny, isn't it. Well, I'll tell you . . ."

6. She was thinking. Of nothing at all. When suddenly the door bell rang, she went to answer it.

7. He did very little studying. Although he was a member of the ROTC and needed to maintain a high average.

8. Everything he saw pleased him. The spacious campus. The ivy-covered buildings. The friendly students. He felt sure now that he would like college. Very much.

9. Bright sun. Blue sky. White sand. Mrs. Marlowe looked at the scene in amazement.

10. I received four dollars in tips. Thus making my income for the day $12.75.

45. QUESTION MARK (?)

The question mark is placed at the end of a direct question, or is used parenthetically to express doubt.

"Are you going?" [Simple question]
"You insist on doing this?" [Statement spoken as a question]
Chaucer, born in 1342 (?), anticipated the English Renaissance.

46. QUOTATION MARKS (" ")

Quotation marks are used to enclose all direct quotations and to call attention to locutions that are used in special ways.

Single quotation marks (' ') are used within double quotation marks (" ") for a quotation within a quotation.

(In typing quotations, passages of two lines or more are usually single-spaced and indented. Quotation marks are then not necessary.)

a. Quotation marks are used to enclose direct quotations.

The reporter wrote: "Hitler did not say, 'I will return'; he said, 'Show me the nearest bomb shelter.' "

b. Quotation marks are used to enclose locutions used in special ways:

(1) Titles of short poems, stories, magazine articles, and chapters of books. (Underlining—to indicate italics—is used for titles of books, magazines, newspapers, and plays.)

He read aloud parts of the "Ode to Autumn" and then gave a lecture on Keats.

He wrote a book report on Hardy's *The Return of the Native*.

(2) Technical terms which might confuse the reader if they were not identified as technical.

In the "lead" the reporter must give certain information.

(3) Expressions that the writer wishes to call attention to as words, sometimes for ironic effect. (In formal writing, such words are usually italicized, but they are commonly put in quotation marks in informal writing.)

"Recession" is a more pleasant word than "depression," and "strategic withdrawal" sounds better than "retreat."

c. Quotation marks should *not* be used to enclose indirect quotations or to excuse inappropriate phrasing:

Wrong: He said "that Tom will come."
Poor: Polonius was deceived because he did not know that Hamlet was "kidding him along."

Quotation Marks with Other Marks of Punctuation

a. A question mark or exclamation point is put inside the close-quotation mark if it belongs to the quotation, but outside the close-quotation mark if it belongs to the sentence which includes the quoted material.

"What do you mean?" he asked.
"Stop!" he cried.
Can we ignore what Carl Becker has called "the climate of opinion"?

b. Periods and commas are conventionally placed inside the close-quotation mark.

"It is difficult," Archibald said, "always to be in the right."

c. Semicolons and colons are always placed after the close-quotation mark.

He calls himself a "liberal"; what he means is not clear.
According to the defendant, these are the "facts": he was not in town on the night of the robbery, and he had honestly earned the money found on his person.

EXERCISES

Use quotation marks or italics where they are needed in the following sentences. When italics are needed, underline the word which should be italicized. (For the use of italics see page 811.) When quotation marks are needed, be sure to place them properly before or after other marks.

1. Dean Warren said, When I heard that student say ain't got no and this here, I understood why he did not pass his freshman English course.

2. The professor read aloud Browning's My Last Duchess; then he asked his students to give their interpretation of the poem.

3. Was it General MacArthur who said, I shall return?

4. While I waited for Dr. Martin, I read an article in Time entitled Acheson and the Russians.

5. The footnote in Arthur G. Kennedy's book English Usage reads as follows: See H. B. Allen, The Standard of Usage in Freshman Textbooks, English Journal, Vol. 24, 1935, pp. 564–571.

47. SEMICOLON (;)

The semicolon, though actually an easy mark of punctuation to master, is second only to the comma in producing errors in student writing. In general a semicolon indicates a shorter pause and a closer connection than a period, and a longer pause and a less close connection than a comma.

a. The semicolon is used to separate two *independent* clauses *not* joined by *and, but, for, or,* or *nor*.

They had reached a stalemate; neither would give in.
He was discouraged; life had disappointed him.
He irritates me at times; nevertheless I like him.

Note 1.—Failure to follow this rule produces the error known as the run-together sentence. (See "The Run-Together Sentence," page 782.)

Note 2.—An exception to Rule a above is the punctuation of three or more independent clauses in series: He was tired, he was hungry, and he was very late.

b. The semicolon is used to separate coordinate clauses joined by *and, but, for, or,* or *nor* when one of the coordinate clauses contains commas. (This is always a safe rule; one need not follow it, however, when a comma will give the desired clarity and emphasis.)

The French fought for liberty, equality, fraternity; and peace was a secondary consideration. [Here the semicolon is needed for clarity.]
Charles, Tom, and Elliot came in late, and their father asked them where they had been. [Here the comma is certainly justifiable.]

c. The semicolon is used to separate items in a series when one of the items itself contains a comma. (This rule, too, is dependent on context. Oftentimes a comma will serve the purpose.)

She ordered doughnuts, cookies, and pies from the bakery; ice cream, chocolate sauce, and sherbet from the drug store; and balloons, horns, and cap pistols from the corner store.

EXERCISES

(Before doing these exercises read the treatment of run-together sentences, page 65, as well as the rules for the use of the semicolon.)

I. State the subject and the verb of each independent clause in the sentences below; then insert or substitute semicolons where they are required by Rules **a, b,** and **c.** As you punctuate each sentence, indicate which rule you are following, and indicate also whether a period or a comma might be used in place of the semicolon.

1. He will go his way, she will go hers.
2. He placed the key in the lock, and then, very cautiously, he opened the door.
3. When he is happy, she is happy, when he suffers, she suffers with him.
4. At first the man seemed friendly, then he became angry and abusive.
5. I know that he will come, what I don't know is how long he will stay.
6. He had talked about a new car and he had dreamed about a new car, now he was going to own one.
7. Some people content themselves with wishes, others turn wishes into actualities.
8. Life is a comedy to those who think, a tragedy to those who feel.
9. Still they came, the old men, the women, the children, and the young lieutenant looked on, full of pity but unable to help.
10. He refused to help, although the food was there and he could easily have spared it.
11. He finished the report, then he went to bed and slept for fourteen hours.
12. It isn't that he means to be cruel, he simply doesn't understand boys of that age.
13. I'm sure that he's coming to the game, in fact I sold him a ticket just an hour ago.
14. Open the door and let him in, he's standing out there in the rain.
15. He was sleepy, he was tired, and he was very cold.

II. Which of the following are run-together sentences?

1. Although he was not cowardly, he valued his life and he was unwilling to risk it unnecessarily.
2. She knows he will be in later, that is all she will say.
3. He was in need of money, therefore he accepted the job eagerly.
4. At first he was conscientious, later he became very lax.
5. Yes, Mercedes told me she had dented my fender naturally I wasn't pleased.

Mechanics

48. SPELLING

In Chapter Three some of the remedies for poor spelling are suggested: the poor speller should use his dictionary conscientiously; he should keep a list of words he misspells; he should write and visualize these words in their correct spelling to fix them in his mind; and he should check his pronunciation to be sure that the addition or omission of syllables or letters ("athaletic," "suprise," "goverment") in his speech is not responsible for faulty spelling of the word. Careful pronunciation of words which have a similar sound will often prevent the confusion of those words in writing: *then, than; accept, except; allusion, illusion; affect, effect; lose, loose; weather, whether; quite, quiet.*

Also, the student who spells badly should memorize and apply certain basic rules of English spelling. There are exceptions to nearly all of them, but a sure grasp of the rules will eliminate many common misspellings. The most useful rules are those which guide the writer in the spelling of *ie* and *ei* words, and in the spelling, when a suffix is added, of words ending with a consonant, with *y,* or with a silent *e.*

a. Spelling rules.

(1) Words spelled with *ie* or *ei* are nearly always spelled correctly according to the old rhyme:

> *I* before *e*
> Except after *c,*
> Or when sounded as *a,*
> As in *neighbor* and *weigh.*

Believe, relief, grieve, chief, piece, niece, field are examples of *i* before *e.* The reversal of the letters when they come after *c* is shown in *receive, deceit, perceive, conceive.* (Some exceptions to the rule are *weird, leisure,* and *seize.*)

(2) Words ending with a consonant double that final consonant before a suffix beginning with a vowel when the word has only one

818

syllable, or is accented on the last syllable, and when the final consonant is preceded by a single vowel:

begin, beginning, beginner
stop, stopped, stopping, stoppage
control, controlled, controlling
occur, occurring, occurrence

The final consonant is not doubled when it is preceded by a double vowel or two vowels, when the word is not accented on the last syllable, or when the suffix begins with a consonant:

Preceded by a double vowel: need, needed, needing.
Preceded by two vowels: treat, treated, treating
Word not accented on the last syllable:
  offer, offered, offering
  benefit, benefited, benefiting
Suffix beginning with a consonant: ship, shipped, shipping, [*but*] ship*m*ent

(3) Words ending with *y* change the *y* to *i* when a suffix is added, if the *y* is preceded by a consonant:

lovely, lovelier, loveliest
mercy, merciful, merciless
pity, pitiful, pitiless
copy, copied, copies

An important exception: the *y* is kept before *ing* endings:

copy, copying
try, tried, tries, [*but*] trying
carry, carried, carries, [*but*] carrying

The *y* remains *y* when it is preceded by a vowel:

play, played
gay, gayer, gayest
joy, joyous, joyful

Important exceptions are *said, laid, paid* [*not*] sayed, layed, payed.

(4) Words ending in silent *e* drop the *e* when they add a suffix beginning with a vowel, and keep the *e* when they add a suffix beginning with a consonant:

Suffix beginning with a vowel:
  love, loving, lovable
  guide, guiding, guidance
  dine, dining
  become, becoming
  desire, desirable

Suffix beginning with a consonant:
immediate, immediately
force, forceful
sincere, sincerely

Exceptions to the rule of dropping the *e* before a vowel are *changeable, noticeable, courageous.* (The *e* is kept to preserve the soft sound of *g* and *c*.) Exceptions to the rule of keeping the *e* before a consonant are *argument, truly, awful.*

b. A list of commonly misspelled words.

The following list contains two hundred and fifty words which college freshmen often misspell. Mastering these two hundred and fifty words will end most of the spelling difficulties of the student whose spelling is poor.

absence	capital	dependent
accidentally	carrying	descent
accommodate	changeable	describe
achieved	changing	desirable
across	choose	desperate
address	chosen	device
advice	clothes	didn't
affect	coming	different
aggravate	committee	dining
all right	comparative	disappear
almost	compel	disappoint
already	competent	disastrous
altogether	completely	discipline
anxious	compliment	dissatisfied
apparent	confident	dissipation
appearance	conscience	divided
argument	conscientious	divine
around	conscious	doesn't
arrangements	consistent	don't
ascend	controlled	dormitory
athletic	convenience	effect
attendance	copies	eighth
awful	council	embarrassed
awkward	counsel	emphasize
before	countries	environment
beginning	courteous	etc.
believe	criticism	exaggerate
benefited	deceive	exhausted
business	decided	existence
cafeteria	definite	experience
candidate	definition	February

fiery
finally
forcibly
forehead
formerly
forty
fundamental
genius
government
grammar
grievance
guard
hadn't
height
heroes
hindrance
hoping
humorous
hurrying
imagination
immediately
incidentally
independent
interested
interpreted
irresistible
its
it's
knowledge
laboratory
laid
later
latter
led
leisure
library
lightning
literally
literature
livelihood
loneliness
loose
lose
lying
marriage
meant
merely

minutes
misspelled
murmur
necessary
niece
ninety
ninth
noticeable
occasion
occurred
occurrence
o'clock
omitted
opportunity
optimistic
paid
parallel
parliament
pastime
perform
perhaps
permissible
perseverance
persistent
personally
planning
pleasant
portrayed
possession
possible
preceding
preference
prejudice
principal
principle
privilege
probably
procedure
proceed
professor
prominent
prophecy
prophesied
psychology
pursuing
quantity
quiet

quite
really
recede
receive
recognize
recommend
referred
relieve
religious
repetition
representative
restaurant
rhythm
salary
scarcely
schedule
seize
sentence
separate
shining
shone
shown
similar
sincerely
sophomore
speak
speech
stationary
stationery
stretched
studying
succeed
successful
supersede
suppression
surely
surprise
temperament
tendency
their
together
too
tragedy
transferred
tries
truly
twelfth

unnecessary	villain	won't
until	weird	writing
usually	whether	written
valuable	who's	you're
vegetable	whose	
vengeance	woman	

49. CAPITALIZATION

The conventions of capitalization are discussed in the first section of Chapter Three. The student will also find information about the use of capitals in his dictionary.

EXERCISES

Correct any faulty use or omission of capitals in the following sentences:

1. Tom's Sister is taking English, Spanish, Chemistry, and Music in her Freshman year of College.

2. When I asked my father what to read, he said He would recommend a chapter of the bible or a Play by Shakespeare.

3. The quarrel between judge Black and captain Jones could be heard all over the Main Street of town.

4. We went down Memorial drive and then six blocks North until we came to the Doctor's Office at the corner of Adams Street and a tree-lined boulevard.

5. After a period of silence, "perhaps it would be better," mother replied, "to wait until Armistice day to buy the Venetian Blinds."

50. TITLES

a. Titles of books, magazines, newspapers, and plays are conventionally italicized. This practice should be followed by college students in their writing. Italics are represented in manuscript by underlining.

b. Titles of short pieces—articles, stories, essays, poems, chapters of books—are put in quotation marks. Usage varies on the titles of long poems and essays; usually they are italicized if they are being discussed as separate units, and put in quotation marks if they are regarded as parts of a larger work.

c. Capital letters are used for the first word of a title and for all other words except articles, conjunctions, and short prepositions:

The Short Stories of Henry James	*Romeo and Juliet*
The Naked and the Dead	*The Atlantic Monthly*
How Green Was My Valley	the New York *Times*

(Note that the name of a city which is part of the title of a newspaper is usually not italicized.)

d. In writing the title of his own theme, the student should center the title on the first line of the first page, and capitalize the first word and all other important words. He should use neither underlining nor quotation marks for this title.

EXERCISES

Correct the writing of titles in the following sentences:

1. His article entitled where is America going? appeared in the Saturday evening post and was later reprinted in the reader's digest.

2. He has written three short stories, love lost, the spider, and the quiet around the pool, and one novel, the sadness in the heart.

3. The article Mars in the Columbia encyclopedia enabled me to understand the chapter called the atmosphere of Mars in that difficult book the universe we live in.

4. This week I read the ladies' home journal, the Yale review, time magazine, the Boston herald, and the Sunday New York times, in addition to Shakespeare's Hamlet and Keats' sonnet Bright Star.

51. SYLLABIFICATION

Sometimes, in manuscript as well as in print, it is necessary to divide a word at the end of a line to make a reasonably even margin. Such division is best avoided as much as possible in typed or handwritten manuscript. Where it seems necessary, the following principles should be kept in mind:

a. Words of one syllable are never divided, and words of more than one syllable are divided only between syllables. Often the pronunciation of a word will indicate its syllabification: *re lief, al to gether, time ly.* When pronunciation is not an adequate guide, the dictionary, which shows the syllabification, should be consulted.

b. Words should not be divided in such a way that a single letter stands at the end of one line or the beginning of the next.

c. The hyphen, indicating that the word is divided, is placed at the end of the line, not at the beginning of the next line.

EXERCISES

Which of the following words can properly be divided at the end of a line? How should the division be made?

alone, school, many, obedience, although, through, elegant, enough, height, hilarious, swimming, drowned, interesting, erase, eradicate, irate, italics, heavy, interpretation, difference, additional

52. NUMBERS

a. In formal and informal writing, numbers are usually spelled out when the number can be expressed in one or two words: *two, fifty-three, six hundred, ten thousand, five million*. They are commonly written as figures when more than two words are needed to express them: $29.95; 1,571,142.
b. Figures are used in writing dates, street numbers, page and chapter numbers, and any group of numbers appearing in the same passage.

> May 30, 1949　 19 Weston Avenue　 Chapter 4, page 215
> Take notes on 3 by 5, 4 by 6, or 5 by 8 cards.

c. A number is always written out when it occurs at the beginning of a sentence.

> *Three hundred and sixty* people were present.

d. Roman numerals are used for main headings in outlines, for chapter headings, for acts and scenes of plays, for volume numbers in footnotes, and for page numbers in the preliminary pages of books.

A small Roman numeral preceding a larger one is subtracted from it: ix (9), xix (19). The basic Roman numerals from which other numbers are created are: i (1), v (5), x (10), l (50), c (100), d (500), m (1000). The following table shows how these basic numerals are combined to make other numbers:

2	ii	19	xix	70	lxx	200	cc
4	iv	30	xxx	80	lxxx	400	cd
7	vii	38	xxxviii	90	xc	600	dc
9	ix	40	xl	99	xcix	900	cm
12	xii	43	xliii	120	cxx	1500	md
15	xv	51	li	150	cl	2000	mm

EXERCISES

What numbers in the following sentences should be written in words?

1. $2000 is not an adequate income in 1951, however adequate it may have been in the 1st years of the 20th century.

2. I live at 2083 Percy Street; I am 62 years old; I have been unemployed for 1 year, since September 22, 1950; and I have no private income aside from $150.00 from investments. You can reach me by calling Greenfield 2236.

3. *Encyclopaedia Britannica,* I, 863.

4. Mr. John Brown accepts with pleasure the kind invitation of Mr. and Mrs. James Albert Smith for Saturday, June 30, at 3:00.

5. In Chapter 3, page 486, the author says that in 1935 pork chops were 19 cents a pound, lettuce was 5 cents a head, a good suit cost $22.50, and a ton of coal was $10.95.

53. ABBREVIATIONS

In formal writing and in a high level of informal writing, it is customary to avoid abbreviations except for a few very well-established ones.

a. Well-established abbreviations which may be used even in formal writing are:

(1) Abbreviations of time accompanying the year or hour: *B.C., A.D., a.m., p.m.* [or] *A.M., P.M.*

(2) Certain titles used with proper names: *Mr., Mrs., Dr.* [But] *President* Truman, *General* Marshall, *Governor* Dewey, *Senator* Taft, *Professor* Brown, *the Honorable* James Peel, *the Reverend* Lloyd Bone.

(3) Titles and degrees used after proper names: *Sr., Jr., Ph.D., L.L.D., M.D.*

(4) In footnotes, certain conventional abbreviations: *op. cit., ibid., cf., p., vol., ed.*

(5) A few generally accepted abbreviations for technical terms: *T.N.T., D.D.T.*

(6) Widely accepted abbreviated names of organizations and government agencies: *D.A.R., Y.M.C.A., NBC, CIO, TVA, ERC, NLRB.* (Note that periods, the usual sign of an abbreviation, are omitted in some abbreviated names of organizations, and are generally omitted in names of government agencies.)

b. All other abbreviations should be avoided in formal and high informal writing, and especially the following abbreviations:

(1) Abbreviations of countries, states, months, days, streets, and proper names.

(2) Abbreviations of titles, even generally accepted abbreviations like *Mr., Mrs.,* and *Dr.,* when they are not used with proper names.

(3) Slang abbreviations like *lab, ec, frat, phys ed.*

EXERCISES

Correct any faulty use of abbreviations in the following sentences:

1. I have an appointment with the Dr. next Tues. at 9:45 a.m.
2. I hope to spend the Xmas vacation, from Dec. 20 to Jan. 3, visiting Rev. Jones & family in Madison, Wis.; his son Jr. is my roommate.
3. Prof. Lane discussed with the ec. class the recent AFL–CIO dispute in Paterson, N.J.
4. According to an AP report, unemployment in the U.S. has decreased five % since last Feb.
5. The noted artist Chas. Lee was born in a humble cottage on Elm St. in Springfield, Mass., in the p.m. of November 14, 1920.

54. MANUSCRIPT FORM

a. A typewritten paper should be double-spaced, on a good grade of standard 8½- by 11-inch paper.

b. A theme in longhand should be written legibly in dark ink, on wide-lined white paper, 8½ by 11 inches.

c. Only one side of the paper should be used.

d. Substantial margins should be left on both sides of the pages.

e. The title of the paper should be written, and centered, at the top of the first page.

f. Pages should be numbered with arabic numerals in the upper right-hand corner.

g. The method of endorsement prescribed by the instructor should be carefully followed. The endorsement here recommended is as follows:

Henry C. Walker [Student's name]
English 1C [Course and section number]
October 1, 1951 [Date the paper is due]
Professor J. S. Holt [Instructor]
My Brother and I [Title of the paper]

h. The finished paper should be neat and legible; however, slight revisions may be indicated in the following ways:

(1) The signs, ¶ and "no ¶," in the margin may be used to mark a change in paragraphing.

(2) The deletion of a word or phrase is indicated by drawing a line through it. Words and phrases to be omitted should *not* be put in parentheses.

(3) Insertions are written between the lines and indicated by a caret [∧].

i. Detailed instructions for preparing a manuscript for print can be found in the dictionary.

55. BIBLIOGRAPHY AND FOOTNOTE FORM

Entries in a formal bibliography are alphabetized according to the last name of the author (or, if no author is mentioned, according to the first important word in the title). For a book, author, work, place of publication, usually publisher, and date of publication are listed in consistent form. The following forms are used:

Hayakawa, S. I., *Language in Thought and Action,* New York, Harcourt, Brace and Company, 1949.
Hayakawa, S. I., *Language in Thought and Action,* New York: Harcourt, Brace and Company, 1949.
Hayakawa, S. I., *Language in Thought and Action,* New York, 1949.

An entry for a magazine article gives author, article, magazine, volume, date, and the pages covered by the article:

Compton, K. T., "If I Were Starting Out Today," *The American Magazine,* CL (August, 1950), 15.

The first footnote reference to a book or article is usually a full reference, particularly if no bibliography accompanies the paper. It includes the author's full name, the title, the facts of publication, and the exact page:

1. S. I. Hayakawa, *Language in Thought and Action* (New York, Harcourt, Brace and Company, 1949), p. 53.

Later footnote references may be shortened to Hayakawa, p. 60, or Hayakawa, *op. cit.,* p. 60, provided no other work by the same author is referred to in the paper. For a full discussion of bibliography and footnotes, see Chapter Eleven.

56. OUTLINE FORM

In Chapter Ten we discuss the kind of outline most useful to students in writing informal themes—the rough outline which is simply an informal jotting down and logical grouping of ideas for the paper. The more formal outline, usually required for longer papers and sometimes for short ones, is a systematic and conventionalized way of representing the content and organization of a piece of writing. In the formal outline, the headings and subheadings are arranged, and numbered or lettered, in such a way that the order and importance of points in the paper and the relationship between those points is shown exactly and clearly. The formal outline is the skeleton of the paper. We say in Chapter Ten that its very formality and inflexibility sometimes bind the writer to an organization which is not the best for his material. To avoid being so bound, the writer should begin with a rough outline, and let the formal outline evolve from the material itself. The virtue of the formal outline is that it enables the writer, as well as the reader, to see at a glance the plan and logic of the whole paper.

Outlines usually follow a conventional system of alternating numbers and letters to show the relationships between sections of the material:

I. ——————
   A. ——————
   B. ——————
   C. ——————
     1. ——————
     2. ——————
II. ——————
   A. ——————
     1. ——————
     2. ——————
       a. ——————
       b. ——————
     3. ——————
   B. ——————
III. ——————
   A. ——————
     1. ——————
     2. ——————
     3. ——————
   B. ——————
   C. ——————
     1. ——————
     2. ——————
       a. ——————
       b. ——————
       c. ——————
IV. ——————
   A. ——————
   B. ——————
     1. ——————
     2. ——————
       a. ——————
       b. ——————
   C. ——————
   D. ——————

There are two principal kinds of formal outlines: the *topical outline,* in which the headings are brief phrases or single words; and the more elaborate and less common *sentence outline,* in which the headings are complete sentences. The form adopted should be followed consistently; a complete sentence should not appear unexpectedly in a topical outline, nor should a sentence outline lapse suddenly into phrases or single words in its headings.

Whether the outline is sentence or topical, it should observe three main principles of correct outline form. These three principles are matters not simply of convention and form, but of clear thinking and logical arrangement.

a. Headings and subheadings which are designated by the same kind of number or letter must be of approximately equal importance.

Points I, II, III, and IV must be equally important main divisions of the paper; points A, B, and C under I must be topics of equal weight, all similarly related to I, of which they are subdivisions. (Students should re-examine an outline with more than six major headings. Usually it represents poor division, because the major headings are unequal; some of them could better be made subordinate to a single, more inclusive heading.)

b. Headings of equal importance must be expressed in parallel form.

This is the familiar principle of parallelism applied to the outline. If A and B are noun phrases, C must be a noun phrase too, since the three of them have the same relationship to I, and the function of the outline is to make such relationships clear.

c. Any heading which has subdivisions must have at least two subdivisions.

This is simply a matter of logic and common sense. A subordinate heading in an outline indicates that a major heading is being divided into parts. Since nothing can be divided into only one part, correct outlines never have single subheadings.[1]

The outline below violates all three of these principles of good outline form. Its lack of logic may serve to clarify the principles:

[1] The one possible exception to this rule is that one may list by itself an example which is used to develop a particular heading.

MY TASTES IN READING

I. Westerns and detective stories
   A. Excitement and adventure
   B. Relaxation
   C. Quick and easy reading

✓ (3) II. Biography
   A. Feel that I am learning something

✓ (1) III. Lytton Strachey's biographies
   A. Eminent Victorians
   B. Queen Victoria
   C. Elizabeth and Essex

✓ (2) IV. I most enjoy reading actual history
   A. Journals and personal accounts of the war
   B. Books on Russia
   C. Books on American life
      1. State of the Nation
      2. Inside U.S.A.

This outline violates the principles of logical outlining in these ways:

(1) The four main headings are not of equal importance. Heading III, "Lytton Strachey's biographies," is not equal to the other headings, but is logically a subdivision of II, "Biography."

(2) The main headings are not expressed in parallel form. I, II, and III are topical in form; IV is a complete sentence.

(3) Heading II has a single subtopic; that is, the topic "Biography" is illogically divided into only one point. Making III into B under II, and rephrasing A so that A and B are parallel in form would remedy this defect in logic in the outline.

The following formal, topical outline of Chapter Four of this book illustrates correct outline form:

EXERCISING INTELLIGENT CHOICE

I. Conventions and choice
II. The appropriate level of usage
   A. Formal English
      1. Definition
      2. Examples
   B. Vulgate English
      1. Definition
      2. Examples

Formal outlines are correct and useful when they accurately reflect the organization of the paper, and when logical subordination and proper parallelism show the relationship between sections of the material.

57. PLAGIARISM

Plagiarism is the dishonest use of the work of others.

Few students in composition courses plagiarize deliberately; that is, few copy, with conscious dishonesty, another student's theme, or a passage from a book or magazine. But a number of students, feeling the pressure of regular writing assignments, and actually confused about the legitimate use of materials, may be tempted to "borrow" sentences and patterns of ideas, or to "get help" on a theme, unless the whole concept of plagiarism is clarified for them. It is the purpose of this note to make clear what plagiarism is and how it can be avoided.

Plagiarism means presenting, *as one's own,* the words, the work, or the opinions of someone else. It is dishonest, since the plagiarist offers, as his own, for credit, the language, or information, or thought for which he deserves no credit. It is unintelligent, since it defeats the purpose of the course—improvement of the student's own powers of thinking and communication. It is also dangerous, since penalties for plagiarism are severe; they commonly range from failure on the paper to failure in the course; in some institutions the penalty is dismissal from college.

Plagiarism occurs when one uses the exact language of someone else without putting the quoted material in quotation marks and giving its source. (Exceptions are very well-known quotations, from the Bible or Shakespeare, for example.) In formal papers, the source is acknowledged in a footnote; in informal papers, it may be put in parentheses, or made a part of the text: "Robert Sherwood says, . . ." This first type of plagiarism, using without acknowledgment the language of someone else, is easy to understand and to avoid: *when a writer uses the exact words of another writer, or speaker, he must put those words in quotation marks and give their source.*

A second type of plagiarism is more complex. It occurs when the writer presents, as his own, *the sequence of ideas, the arrangement of material, the pattern of thought* of someone else, even though he expresses it in his own words. The language may be his, but he is presenting as the work of his brain, and taking credit for, the work of another's brain. He is, therefore, guilty of plagiarism if he fails to give credit to the original author of the pattern of ideas.

This aspect of plagiarism presents difficulties because the line is sometimes unclear between borrowed thinking and thinking which is our own. We all absorb information and ideas from other people. In this way we learn. But in the normal process of learning, new ideas are digested; they enter our minds and are associated and integrated with ideas already there; when they come out again, their original pattern is broken; they are re-formed and re-arranged. We have made them our own. Plagiarism occurs when a sequence of ideas is transferred from a source to a paper without the process of digestion, integration, and reorganization in the writer's mind, and without acknowledgment in the paper.

Students writing informal themes, in which they are usually asked to draw on their own experience and information, can guard against plagiarism by a simple test. They should be able honestly to answer *No* to the following questions:

1. Have I read anything in preparation for writing this paper?

2. Am I deliberately recalling any particular source of information as I write this paper?

3. Am I consulting any source as I write this paper?

If the answer to these questions is *No*, the writer need have no fear of using sources dishonestly. The material in his mind, which he will transfer to his written page, is genuinely digested and his own.

The writing of a research paper presents a somewhat different problem, for here the student is expected to gather material from books and articles read for the purpose of writing the paper. In the careful research paper, however (and this is true of term papers in all college courses), credit is given in footnotes for every idea, conclusion, or piece of information which is not the writer's own; and the writer is careful not to follow closely the wording of the sources he has read. If he wishes to quote, he puts the passage in quotation marks and gives credit to the author in a footnote; but he writes the bulk of the paper in his own words and his own style, using footnotes to acknowledge the facts and ideas he has taken from his reading. Fuller information on the use of sources in research papers and other term papers is given in Chapter Eleven: The Research Paper.

Usage

58. USING THE DICTIONARY

Much of the value of dictionaries is lost by the uninformed use or inadequate use which many people, including college students, make of these remarkable books. Although students have been, to some extent, familiar with dictionaries for years, they frequently do not know what kinds of information dictionaries contain; and they are frequently incompetent in the most common use of the dictionary —finding the pronunciation or the definition of a word—because they have not familiarized themselves with the methods and symbols by which information is conveyed.

Dictionaries differ, of course, in their size and completeness. The next time the student is in the reference room in the library he should examine such massive unabridged dictionaries as *The Oxford English Dictionary* (ten volumes and supplement); *Webster's New International Dictionary of the English Language,* Second Edition; *The New Standard Dictionary of the English Language;* and *A Dictionary of American English on Historical Principles* (four volumes). Such dictionaries, though invaluable for certain scholarly purposes, are beyond the means of most college students. For ordinary use, a good desk dictionary is satisfactory. It is less expensive and is often a better guide to contemporary usage than a fuller but older unabridged dictionary. Since we are primarily concerned with the student's working knowledge of his own dictionary, we shall consider in this section the use of such good, up-to-date desk dictionaries as *The American College Dictionary,* Text Edition, 1948; *Webster's New Collegiate Dictionary,* 1949; *The New College Standard Dictionary,* Emphatype Edition, 1947; *The Winston Dictionary,* College Edition, 1946; and Macmillan's *Modern Dictionary,* 1947.

In addition to the dictionary proper—that is, the information given about particular words—the five desk dictionaries listed above contain much other useful information. In *The American College*

Dictionary, for example, there are prefaces concerning the following subjects:

Selection of Entries and Definitions
Pronunciation
Treatment of Etymologies [i.e., word derivations]
Synonyms and Antonyms
Usage Levels and Dialect Distribution

Also listed in the table of contents are:

A Handbook of Punctuation and Mechanics
A Guide to Letter Writing
Manuscript and Proof
Signs and Symbols
Table of Common English Spellings
Explanatory Notes [a particularly important section]
Colleges and Universities in the United States
Index

The student who uses his dictionary well is familiar with these prefaces and reference sections and is able to turn to them when he needs the kind of information they contain.

The information which a dictionary gives concerning words can best be shown by examining a typical entry:

fin′ish (fĭn′ĭsh), *v. t.* [OF. *fenir* (F. *finir*), fr. L. *finire* to limit, finish, end, fr. *finis* limit, end.] **1.** To arrive at the end of; to bring to an end. **2.** To complete; accomplish; also, to perfect. **3.** *Colloq.* To dispose of completely; to overthrow or exhaust utterly. — *v. i.* **1.** To come to an end; terminate. **2.** *Rare.* To die. — **Syn.** See CLOSE. — *n.* **1.** The conclusion; end. **2.** That which finishes, completes, or perfects. **3.** The result of completed labor, as on the surface of an object; manner or style of finishing; as, a rough, dead, or glossy *finish.* **4.** Cultivation in manners and speech; social polish. **5.** *Arch.* **a** The joiner work and other fine work required for the completion of a building, esp. of the interior. **b** The higher grades of lumber used for this work. **6.** *Painting.* A material used in finishing; as, oil *finish.*

By permission. From Webster's New Collegiate Dictionary
Copyright, 1949
by G. & C. Merriam Co.

First we are given the spelling of the word and are shown that it is broken into two syllables and accented on the first syllable. In parentheses the word is respelled, and its pronunciation is indicated by symbols which are explained in the pronunciation chart inside the back cover. (In some dictionaries these symbols are also explained at the foot of each page.) The abbreviation *v.t.* tells us that the word is a transitive verb, that is, a verb which takes an object. (When a student finds an abbreviation that is not clear to him, he should turn to the table of contents to see where abbreviations are explained and should then look up the abbreviation that puzzles him.) The material in brackets gives the derivation of the word, from Old French (O.F.) *fenir* which was in turn derived from the Latin (L.) verb *finire*.

Three definitions of the transitive verb *finish* follow. The third, "to dispose of completely," is labeled colloquial (*Colloq*.); that is, the usage of the verb is, in the opinion of the editors, "acceptable and correct in ordinary conversation, friendly letters, or informal speeches, but unsuited to formal speech or writing. . . ."

The abbreviation *v.i.* tells us that *finish* is also an intransitive verb. Two definitions of the intransitive verb follow; about the second definition, "to die," we are told that this use is rare.

Next comes the abbreviation *Syn.* (synonym) and a reference to the word *close*. (Under the definition of *close* the differences between *close, end, conclude, finish,* and *terminate* are discussed.)

The abbreviation *n.* tells us that *finish* is also a noun. Six definitions of the noun follow. In two of them, the usage of the word is illustrated: "as, a rough, dead, or glossy *finish*," and "as, oil *finish*." Two of the definitions are labeled with the special fields in which the word is used in special senses—Architecture (*Arch*.) and Painting.

It is important for students to know, and to note as they use their dictionaries, these labels indicating usage in special fields, and also labels like colloquial, dialectal (*Dial.*), slang, and obsolete (*Obs.*) which describe the general usage and status of words. Too often, in looking up a word, students seize indiscriminately on any one of the definitions, ignoring the informative label which would tell them that this is not the definition they are looking for.

The dictionary designation of a term as colloquial, dialectal, or slang is not necessarily a condemnation of the term. Colloquialisms, dialectal expressions, and slang are out of place in formal writing; but the fact that the expressions appear in the dictionary is evidence of their wide usage and acceptance in informal English. The writer must judge whether or not they are appropriate in the situation in which he wishes to use them. The dictionary label is not a prohibition, but simply an aid to him in judging.[1]

In addition to information about spelling, pronunciation, derivation, grammatical function, meanings, and usage, dictionaries give the following information about words: the principal parts of irregular verbs, irregular plurals of nouns and pronouns, case forms of pronouns, comparative and superlative forms of adjectives and adverbs, and the idiomatic use of certain words and expressions.

Some kinds of information about words the dictionary cannot give.

---

[1] For a more detailed discussion of usage labels in dictionaries, see the following section, "The Dictionary and Good Usage."

It cannot, for example, define—that is, give "the meaning" of—an abstract word. It can only indicate some of the ways in which this word-symbol is used. The meaning of the word in a particular situation must be derived from the context and the communicator's intention. Nor can the dictionary adequately give the emotional charge or the subtle connotations or suggestions carried by many words. Dictionaries do give some valuable information about the different uses of words which are closely related in meaning, or which are likely to be confused. For example, here is a part of a definition of the word *difference* taken from *The American College Dictionary:*

—Syn. 1. DIFFERENCE, DISCREPANCY, DISPARITY, DISSIMILARITY imply perceivable unlikeness, variation, or diversity. DIFFERENCE refers to a complete or partial lack of identity or a degree of unlikeness: *a difference of opinion, a difference of six inches.* DISCREPANCY usually refers to the difference or inconsistency between things that should agree, balance, or harmonize: *a discrepancy between the statements of two witnesses.* DISPARITY implies inequality, often where a greater approximation to equality might reasonably be expected: *a great disparity between the ages of husband and wife.* DISSIMILARITY indicates an essential lack of resemblance between things in some respect comparable: *a dissimilarity between the customs in Asia and in America.* 5. See distinction. —Ant. 1. likeness, similarity.

But shades of emotional or attitudinal meaning often cannot be conveyed by brief definitions of words out of context. For this reason, it is wise not to use a word one finds in the dictionary (or in word lists) until one has heard or read the word in contexts which further establish the shades of meaning it may carry.

These limitations, however, are slight in comparison with the varied, valuable, and interesting information which dictionaries give. The dictionary is the most useful of reference books. The student is seriously handicapped who has not learned to use it well.

59. THE DICTIONARY AND GOOD USAGE

Good usage may be defined as a use of words or forms considered acceptable by reputable authorities, students of language who study the actual practice of cultivated people in speech and writing. The best way to develop a knowledge of good usage and a feeling for it is to read widely in good literature and to listen attentively to the speech of cultivated people. Dictionaries are, of course, invaluable aids if one knows how to use them. Points of usage not treated in dictionaries are fully and clearly treated in H. W. Fowler's *Dictionary of Modern English Usage.* Porter G. Perrin's "Index" in *Writer's Guide and Index to English* supplements Fowler and treats modern American usage.

Most college students have little difficulty in recognizing and avoiding expressions which clearly belong to the vulgate level. *Ain't got no, he done, a orange, hisself, he seen, yourn, had went,* and the like, seldom find their way into college papers. There are, however, a good many less obvious unacceptable usages below the informal level which students need to recognize and avoid, and there are expressions appropriate in speech and informal writing but inappropriate in formal communication. It is with expressions on the fringes of good informal usage or of good formal usage that college students have most difficulty. In dictionaries, expressions below the level of informal English are usually omitted or labeled as *dialectal* or *illiterate*. Expressions which are not vulgate but are below the level of formal English and high informal usage are labeled by the term *colloquial* or by some other term describing limited usage, and expressions acceptable in formal English are given without a restricting label.

Since college students are most likely to own *Webster's New Collegiate Dictionary*, 1949, or *The American College Dictionary*, Text Edition, 1948, or *The College Standard Dictionary*, Emphatype Edition, 1947, it is worth while to call attention here to the way these three dictionaries define or comment on the term *colloquial* and to the fact that the three dictionaries use the word in slightly different ways. (All three definitions, of course, correspond roughly to the meaning of the word *informal* as it is used in this book to describe informal usage.)

Webster's New Collegiate Dictionary defines *colloquial* as follows: "Pertaining to, or used in, conversation, esp. familiar conversation; acceptable and correct in ordinary conversation, friendly letters, or informal speeches, but unsuited to formal speech or writing; hence, informal."

In *The American College Dictionary* Mr. Charles C. Fries defines and discusses the term *colloquial* in a special section entitled "Usage Levels and Dialect Distribution":

Many expressions occur primarily in conversation rather than in formal writing. The occasions for their use are chiefly conversational situations. These are marked *"Colloq."* Even teachers of English frequently misunderstand the application of the label *colloquial* in our best dictionaries. Some confuse it with *localism* and think of the words and constructions marked *colloquial* as peculiarities of speaking which are characteristic of a particular locality. Others feel that some stigma attaches to the label *colloquial* and would strive to avoid as incorrect (or as of low level) all words so marked. The word *colloquial*, however, as used to label words and phrases in a modern scientifically edited dictionary has no such meaning. It is used to mark those words and constructions whose range of use is primarily that of the polite conversation of cultivated people, of their familiar letters and informal speeches, as distinct from those words and constructions which are common also in formal writing. The usage of our better magazines and of public addresses generally has, during the past generation, moved away from the formal and literary toward the collo-quial.[2]

In *The College Standard Dictionary,* Emphatype Edition, Mr. Charles Earle Funk, the editor, defines the label *popular,* which is used in the *Standard Dictionary* instead of *colloquial:*

Because, through the influence of many factors, it is no longer possible to draw precise lines of distinction between the various forms of uncon-ventional English now permissible in informal speech, no attempt has been made in these pages to distinguish between slang usage and colloquial usage. Much of the slang of yesterday has become the popular everyday phrase of today, and the slang of today may be the colloquial usage of tomorrow. Hence, such of these terms as have been admitted to these pages are labeled "popular," by the bracketed abbreviation [Pop.], the label serving to in-dicate that in the opinion of the editors and other competent observers the word or meaning so labeled may be used in ordinary conversation or writ-ing but has not yet achieved the dignity of usage in formal speech or writing.

Sometimes dictionaries differ not only in the precise meaning of the labels they use, but also in the information they give about the use of a particular expression. Such differences in dictionaries may occur because one group of editors is more conservative than an-other, or because one dictionary is based on a recent study of usage and another reports usage as it was a number of years ago, or because a particular expression is really on the borderline between two levels of usage and dictionaries are obliged for the sake of brevity to place it definitely in one category, although it does not quite fit in either.

A few years ago most dictionaries for college students were out of date or conservative in recording changes in usage. At present, how-ever, such dictionaries—and especially the three we have just quoted —are notably up to date and are apparently more ready to accept changes in usage than are most college English instructors.

Since the college English instructor is primarily concerned with the exact and discriminating use of language, he is sometimes justi-fied, we believe, in objecting to certain usages labeled "colloquial" in recent dictionaries. For example, in dealing with *contact* meaning *to get in touch with a person, The American College Dictionary* and *Webster's New Collegiate Dictionary* both label the usage *colloquial,* but *Webster's* then adds that it is "a use to be avoided by careful writers and speakers." The fact is that *contact* in this sense is not good colloquial usage and yet is so widely used that it does not fit

2 From *The American College Dictionary,* copyright, 1947, by Random House; Text Edition, copyright, 1948, by Harper & Brothers. Reprinted by permission.

the vulgate category either. The careful user of English will follow *Webster's* advice to avoid the expression. In short, the dictionary is a good guide to usage but is not infallible, and an English instructor may sometimes have knowledge which justifies his qualifying of the labels that the need for brevity obliges dictionaries to use.

In the following glossary of usage, some of the entries dealing with controversial matters of usage give the names of the dictionaries consulted and the word used by these dictionaries to label the expression.

60. A GLOSSARY OF USAGE

Accept, except. Accept is a verb meaning *to receive willingly or with approval:* "He accepted the gift"—"He accepted the decision." *Except* may be a verb meaning *to exclude* ("He excepted Tom, but he invited the others"), or it may be a preposition meaning *with the exclusion of:* "Everyone was pleased except the instructor."

Affect, effect. Affect is most commonly used as a verb. In one sense it means *to pretend* or *to assume* ("He affected ignorance"); in another sense it means *to influence* or *to move* ("The tragic accident affected him deeply"). Used as a noun, *affect* is a psychological term meaning *feeling or emotion. Effect* used as a verb means *to bring about* ("to effect the rescue of the trapped miners"); used as a noun, *effect* means *result* or *consequence* ("We were surprised at the effect of his words on his audience").

Aggravate. In formal English *aggravate* means *to make worse or more severe. Aggravate* in the sense of *to irritate* or *vex* is a colloquial expression inappropriate to formal English, and questionable in informal English.

All right, "alright." All right is the only generally accepted spelling, and *alright* is therefore a misspelling. *The American College Dictionary* lists *alright* but states that it is not generally regarded as good usage. It seems likely that someday *alright* will be an acceptable spelling; at the present time it is not.

All together, altogether. All together means *united. Altogether* means *entirely.*

The family will be all together this Christmas.
The injured man was altogether helpless.

Almost, most. Most as a shortened form of *almost* is labeled "colloquial" in *The American College Dictionary* and in *Webster's New Collegiate Dictionary.* In formal or in high informal writing it is out of place.

Alumnus, alumni, alumna, alumnae. Latin forms kept in English and applied in strict usage to graduates of a school or college; loosely used, however, to refer to former students of a school or college.

> *Alumnus,* masculine singular; *alumni,* masculine plural.
> *Alumna,* feminine singular; *alumnae,* feminine plural.
> *Alumni* is used as a collective term for men and women graduates or former students.

It seems that there are two reasons for keeping the Latin words instead of using the English word *graduate:* (1) the Latin words carry the suggestion of group unity and loyalty to the institution and (2) they enable one to include all past students, whether or not the students are graduates.

"Anywheres," "somewheres." Vulgate for *anywhere, somewhere.*

As. Frequently used as a connective where *because, for, when, while, since* or some other more exact connective would convey the meaning more clearly.

> I knew that he was there, as I saw him enter the door.
> IMPROVED: I knew that he was there because I saw him enter the door.

Awful, awfully. These two words, when used to mean *bad* or *excessively* or *very,* are labeled "colloquial" in *The American College Dictionary* and in *Webster's New Collegiate Dictionary.* Even in informal speech and writing, however, *awful* in the sense of *very* ("awful nice of him") is a usage that some people find objectionable.

Bad, badly. *Bad* is an adjective and *badly* is an adverb. Choice between the two words is usually easy except when a linking verb is used. Linking verbs (*appear, be, seem, become, feel, look, smell, taste, sound,* etc.) are followed by an adjective instead of an adverb, and hence *bad* and not *badly* is correct in the sentences below.

> He looks bad.
> He feels bad.
> The apple tastes bad.

Because. *Because* in the construction, "The reason is because . . ." is questionable usage. The accepted construction is "the reason is that . . ." *Because* means *for the reason that,* and "The reason is because . . ." therefore involves the needless repetition of an idea. Since usage often defies logic, "The reason is because . . ." may someday become accepted usage. At present it seems to be acceptable in informal usage but not in formal usage.

"Being as," "being that." Misused for *as, because,* or *since.*

> Because it was a hot day the men took off their coats. [*Not*—Being as it was a hot day]

Beside, besides. These words are sometimes used mistakenly. "There were three men *beside* him" means that there were three people *near* him. "There were three men *besides* him" means that there were three men *in addition to* him.

Can. See **May.**

"Can't hardly." Since *hardly* means *barely, almost not at all,* it is certainly illogical to say "He can't hardly walk" when one means "He can barely walk." People who use language precisely will therefore avoid *can't hardly,* except when they slip into the expression in conversation. Although the expression is frequently used, it has no standing in formal English.

"Can't help but." A questionable usage. The combination of *can't* and *but* is said to produce a double negative. Instead of "I can't help but argue with him" it is better to say "I can't help arguing with him."

Case. *Case* is a much overworked word and is responsible for many wordy expressions. Students should not be afraid to use it, but they should avoid it when it is merely padding or when a more exact word is called for.

> UNSATISFACTORY: In the case of a word that is difficult to spell, students should consult a dictionary to be sure that they have the correct spelling.
>
> REVISED: To insure correct spelling of difficult words, students should consult the dictionary.

"Complected." Misused for *complexioned.* Write *dark-complexioned,* not *dark-complected. The American College Dictionary* labels *complected* "dialectal" or "colloquial"; *Webster's New Collegiate Dictionary* labels it "dialectal."

Contact. *Contact* as a verb meaning *to get in touch with* a person is labeled "colloquial" in *The American College Dictionary* and in *Webster's New Collegiate Dictionary,* but *Webster's* also labels it "a use to be avoided by careful writers and speakers." Because *contact* used in this sense grows out of commercial jargon, one should use it with judgment if one uses it at all.

Contractions. Contractions (*don't, won't, he's, they're,* etc.) are appropriate in conversation and in writing that is personal and informal. In formal, and in most impersonal writing, they are out of place.

"Could of." Vulgate for *could have:* "He could have won." [*Not*—He could of won.]

Couple. Used colloquially in "He ate a couple of oranges." *Couple* in the sense of "married couple," or "young couple" is a usage not limited to colloquial expression.

"Different than." *Different than* is questionable usage. *Different from* is accepted American usage. *Different to* is accepted British usage, but is questioned as American usage. The student who wants to be sure he is following American idiom will write: "My book is different from yours." Perhaps students of usage should know that *different than* is defended by Robert C. Pooley in *Teaching English Usage* and is listed without comment as an occasional usage in *The American College Dictionary.*

Don't. *Don't* is properly used as a contraction for *do not:* "I don't, you don't, we don't, they don't." *Don't* used as a contraction for *does not* ("he don't, she don't, it don't") is vulgate.

Due to. *Due to* in the sense of *because of, owing to* has long been condemned in books on usage, and many careful writers avoid using it. Some authorities on modern usage—Perrin in *Writer's Guide and Index to English* and Pooley in *Teaching English Usage*—take the view that though some people object to it, it should be accepted as established usage. Since *owing to* and *because of* are unquestionably good usage, it seems advisable to use one or the other in place of *due to.*

> Due to the wreck, the train was late. [Questionable usage]
> Because of [*or* owing to] the wreck, the train was late. [Established usage]

Due as an adjective is established usage: "His failure was due to his neglect of his studies."

Effect. See *Affect.*

Either. *Either* is properly used to mean *one or the other of two.* It is misused in the following sentence: "She would not eat either of the three desserts."

"Enthuse." Not an acceptable substitute in formal or high informal English for *be enthusiastic about. Enthuse* is labeled *colloquial* in *The American College Dictionary* and in *Webster's New Collegiate Dictionary.*

Etc. An abbreviation of the Latin *et cetera,* meaning *and so forth. And etc.* is poor usage because the Latin expression already contains the *and. Etc.* is a useful expression when it saves the continued enumeration of the obvious: "Let *A* equal 1, *B* equal 2, *C* equal 3, etc." Sometimes, however, writers use it as a way of avoiding thought. The student who writes, "I came to college to prepare for medical school, to get an education, etc.," has given the reader no definite information by the use of *etc.,* and one suspects that he had nothing definite in mind. It is better to omit *etc.* when the expression is vague or meaningless.

Fellow. *Fellow* used in the sense of *man, boy, suitor, person* is colloquial usage, and is inappropriate in formal and in high informal language.

Fewer, less. *Fewer* refers to *number; less* refers to *quantity.*

When people have less money, they buy fewer luxuries.

Field of. The expression *in the field of* is often wordy. "I am majoring in the field of English" is a wordy way of saying "I am majoring in English" or "I am an English major."

Fine. In informal speech *fine* is often a convenient word. It is widely used in the loose sense of *good* or *admirable.* In writing, however, especially in formal writing, it is better to use a more exact word. *Fine* meaning *exact, precise* ("fine distinctions," "fine measurements") is of course appropriate in formal English.

Foreign terms. Frequent use of foreign terms in writing or in speech is likely to be regarded as a mark of poor taste and poor manners rather than as a sign of learning. As a general rule it is best to use foreign terms only when there is no English equivalent and when the reader can be expected to understand them.

Get, got. The principal parts of *get* are *get, got, got* or *gotten.* Some people object to the use of *gotten,* but it is clear that both *gotten* and *got* as the past participle are now accepted in American usage.

Get or *got* meaning *to kill,* or *to irritate,* or *to understand,* or *to be obliged to* is colloquial usage, near the level of slang.

Get across as in "to get across an idea" is at best a colloquial expression, and is not appropriate in serious writing.

Good, well. *Good* is properly used as an adjective. Expressions in which it is used as an adverb ("He runs good") are vulgate. *Well* is an adjective or an adverb.

The child is good. [*Good* is an adjective.]
The child is well. [*Well* is an adjective.]

That apple looks good. [*Good* is an adjective following the linking verb *look*.]

He runs well. [*Well* is an adverb modifying *runs*.]

"Had of." The *of* is superfluous.

I wish I had [*not* had of] gone.

Hanged, hung. In formal usage a man is *hanged* and a nonhuman object is hung: "He hanged himself with the rope on which his wife had hung the clothes." The principal parts of *hang* in the first sense are *hang, hanged, hanged;* the principal parts of *hang* in the second sense are *hang, hung, hung.*

"Have got." In many uses *got* is superfluous.

FORMAL AND HIGH-LEVEL INFORMAL: I have to be there at five.

COLLOQUIAL: I have got [*or, more commonly,* I've got] to be there at five.

Healthy, healthful. *Healthy* means *in good health. Healthful* means *conducive to health:* "a healthy man" [*but*] "a healthful climate."

Human. *Human* used as a noun ("Humans live longer than dogs") is colloquial usage. In formal English *human* is an adjective ("To err is human") and *human being* is generally used when the noun form is called for.

Imply, infer. To *imply* is to suggest without stating directly; to *infer* is to draw a conclusion, to make an inference, from what someone else has said.

In talking to his daughter the father implied that she was spending too much money. The daughter inferred from her father's words that he would be opposed to her buying a new evening gown.

"In back of." At best a colloquial expression. It looks as if *in back of* should be acceptable, for *in front of* is good usage. Since usage is not necessarily based on logic, however, it is wise to avoid *in back of* and to use *behind, back of,* or *at the back of.*

"Irregardless." Since *regardless* carries the meaning intended in *irregardless, irregardless* has no justification. *The American College Dictionary* labels it "colloquial" and notes that it is "not generally regarded as good usage." *Webster's New Collegiate Dictionary* does not recognize the existence of the word.

Its, It's. *Its* is the possessive of *it* ("The tree lost its leaves") and is spelled without an apostrophe; *it's* is a contraction of *it is* or *it has.*

It's me. Many authorities on present usage regard *It's me* as an acceptable substitute for the formal and often unnatural *It is I* or *It's I*. *It's him* and *It's her*, however, are not acceptable usage.

Kind. Formal English requires the use of *this kind, that kind, these kinds, those kinds*. The expressions *these kind* ("I like these kind of oranges") and *those kind* ("He buys those kind of shoes") are therefore not acceptable and should be avoided, even though good writers do occasionally slip into them.

"Kind of," "sort of." Colloquial for *somewhat* or *rather:* "I am kind of tired today." *Kind of* and *sort of* in this sense are fairly common in speech, but should be avoided in writing.

Lay, lie. The misuse of *lay* and *lie* is a mark of vulgate English. *Lay*, a transitive verb, takes an object: "Lay the book on the table." *Lie*, an intransitive verb, does not take an object: "He likes to lie in the sun." The principal parts of *lie* are *lie, lay, lain*. The principal parts of *lay* are *lay, laid, laid*.

Lead, led. The principal parts of the verb *lead* are *lead, led, led*. The past tense is spelled *led:* "He led the man across the street."

Lend, loan. In formal English *lend* is a verb; *loan* is a noun. One *lends* money or one asks for a *loan*. Although there is some authority for the use of *loan* as a verb, best usage seems to restrict its use to the noun function.

Like. In formal and in high informal English *like* should not be used as a substitute for *as* or *as if:*

Do as I do. [*Not*—Do like I do.]
He acted as if he wanted to escape. [*Not*—He acted like he wanted to escape.]

Like is, of course, properly used as a preposition: "He acted like a hero." In this sentence *like* is a preposition, and *hero* is its object. For a full treatment of *like*, the student should see "Like," in H. W. Fowler's *Dictionary of Modern English Usage*.

Line, "along the line of." The use of this expression frequently produces wordiness. "Next summer I expect to do work along the line of salesmanship" is a wordy way of saying "I expect to work as a salesman next summer."

Loose, lose. *To loose* is to set free; *to lose* is to suffer loss: "The man who loosens his collar may lose his collar button."

"Lots of," "a lot of." Colloquial for *much, a large amount*.

May, can. The important difference between *may* and *can* is that in formal language *may* is used *to request* or *to give permission,* and *can* is used *to express ability to act.*

> May I have this dance?
> Can I find your name in the telephone book?

Most, almost. See ***Almost.***

Myself. In strict usage *myself* is a reflexive pronoun ("I cut myself") or an intensive pronoun: "I myself am unable to go, but I shall send a representative." It is accepted usage to limit *myself* to these two uses in writing. In familiar conversation, however, cultivated people may sometimes use *myself* where strict usage would call for *I* or *me:* "The news was quite a shock to Father and Mother and myself." People who are very careful of their language follow the strict usage in writing and in conversation.

Nice. In conversation, *nice* used to indicate general approval often serves as a convenient expression when a more exact word does not readily come to mind. In writing, when one has time to choose words carefully, more exact words than *nice* are usually preferable. "He is nice" gives less definite information than "He is well mannered" or "He is friendly" or "He is interested in students and easy to talk to." Words like *nice* and *fine* are so general in meaning that they often blur communication.

None. *None* may be either singular or plural.

> None of us is [*or* are] willing to go.

"Off from," "off of." *From* and *of* are superfluous.

> He stepped off the platform.

"On account of." Vulgate when used instead of *because* to introduce a clause:

> I sold my book because [*not* on account of] I need money.

One. Some authorities on usage insist that the personal pronoun *one* should not be followed by *he* or *his* as it is in the sentences: "One should choose his words with care"—"When one is asked what he thinks, he should give an honest answer." These authorities would substitute *one's* and *one* for *his* and *he:* "One should choose one's words with care"—"When one is asked what one thinks, one should give an honest answer." In present-day usage, however, the use of *one . . . he* (or *his*) is common among reputable writers, and is in good standing; the choice is therefore a matter of individual taste. Sometimes the *one . . . one* (or *one's*) usage requires a very frequent repetition of *one* and suggests affectation. In such circumstances it is preferable to use *he, his.*

Or. When *or* is used to join two or more subjects, the general rule is that the verb is plural if the subjects are plural ("Axes or saws are used to cut the logs") and singular if the subjects are singular: "An axe or a saw is used to cut the logs." If some of the subjects are plural and some are singular, the verb agrees with the subject nearest it: "A tractor or several horses are used to pull the machine"— "Several horses or a tractor is used to pull the machine."

This last sentence follows the rule, but sounds awkward. It is best to revise such sentences or to rearrange them so that the plural subject is nearest the verb. For a fuller consideration of the use of *or* see "Or" in H. W. Fowler's *Dictionary of Modern English Usage.*

Plenty. In formal English the use of *plenty* as an adverb is not acceptable. *Plenty tired, plenty angry,* and *plenty good enough* are colloquial expressions.

Preposition at the end of a sentence. There is no recognized rule of usage which forbids placing a preposition at the end of a sentence; in fact, idiomatic and direct English sometimes requires that the preposition come at the end. Students can concentrate on writing clear, emphatic, rhythmical sentences and can let the prepositions fall where they may.

Proved, proven. Both *proved* and *proven* are acceptable as the past participle of *prove. Proved* is more commonly used.

He has proved [*or* has proven] his point.

"Quite a." Colloquial usage in such expressions as *quite a few, quite a number, quite a while.* The equivalent expressions *many, a large number, for a long time* are, of course, established usages.

Real. *Real* is properly an adjective and is misused in the sense of *very.*

He was very [*not* real] tired.

Seem. *Can't seem* ("I can't seem to understand this problem") is colloquial usage, probably because it is inexact expression of "I can't work this problem" or "It seems that I can't work this problem." *Can't seem* may be appropriate in informal speech, but it is out of place in serious writing.

Set, sit. *Set* is a transitive verb and so takes an object: "He set the vase on the table." The principal parts of *set* are *set, set, set. Sit* is an intransitive verb and so does not take an object: "He often sits before the fire." The principal parts of *sit* are *sit, sat, sat.* An exception to the rule is the use of *set* in reference to fowls and the hatching of eggs, where *set* is used as an intransitive verb: "The hen is setting."

Shall and will. See pages 766–767.

Should and would. See pages 766–767.

"Should of." *Should of* is sometimes misused for *should have.*

He should have [*not* should of] answered my letter sooner.

So. Careless or inexperienced writers tend to overuse *so* in joining two independent clauses, and also to use *so* in contexts where *so that* or *and so* is needed to make the meaning immediately clear. *So that* indicates purpose ("He is saving money so that he can marry in the fall"); *and so* indicates result: "He has saved money and so he will be married this fall." The use of *so* as an intensive ("She was so tired" or "She was so angry") is more appropriate in conversation than in writing. Most students can improve their writing by scrutinizing their use of *so* and by substituting a more exact or a more complete expression whenever it is needed. This treatment of *so* is not intended to induce students to avoid the word; it simply recommends discrimination.

Split infinitive. The term applied to an infinitive in which a modifier is placed between *to* (the sign of the infinitive) and the verb: "to industriously work." Split infinitives should be avoided whenever they can be avoided without loss of effectiveness; usually the modifier can with advantage be placed either before or after the infinitive. The split infinitive is not, however, the sin against good usage which it has sometimes been labeled. Now and then it is necessary to split an infinitive in order to preserve exact meaning; an authority on usage, George O. Curme, gives this example of an infinitive which must be split for the sake of exact meaning: "He failed to entirely comprehend it."

Sure. Sure is an adjective and is not properly used as an adverb.

He surely [*not* sure] knows what he wants.

"These kind." See **Kind.**

"This here," "that there." *This here book* or *that there book* is vulgate for *this book* or *that book.*

Thru. *The American College Dictionary, Webster's New Collegiate Dictionary,* and *The College Standard Dictionary* list without limiting label *through, thro',* and *thru.* The student should at least keep in mind the fact that many people think that *through* is the only accepted spelling. Of the shorter forms, the present writers have seen *thru* most frequently.

Too. Expressions like "He is not too handsome" and "She isn't too eager to go" are slang and are not appropriate in serious writing. Usually in such expressions *very* should be used in the place of *too,* or the expression should be revised to make the meaning more exact.

Till, until. There is no difference in plain-sense meaning between the connectives *till* and *until,* and both are established as good usage.

"Try and." Colloquial usage for *try to,* and more appropriate in speech than in writing: "Try and come to see us this week end" is colloquial for "Try to come to see us this week end."

Want. *Want* for *had better* or *ought* is colloquial: "You want to [had better] come in before it rains." *Want in,* and *want out* are, at best, colloquial for *want to come in* and *want to get out.*

Way. *Way* for *away* is colloquial: "Way over there among the trees" for "away over there among the trees."

Whose, who's. *Whose* is the possessive form of *who* ("I don't know whose hat that is"); *who's* is a contracted form of *who is:* "I don't know who's coming tonight."

Will and shall. See pages 766–767.

You. *You* is often used in speech and in informal writing as an indefinite pronoun in place of *anyone, one, a person,* but such usage is not appropriate in formal writing. In a sentence like "When you are in prison you are sorry that you broke the law" the use of *you* is incongruous; it is advisable to express the idea in another way.

Your, you're. *Your* is the possessive form of *you; you're* is a contraction of *you are:* "You're going to enjoy your English course in college."

Handbook — Section Six

Writing Assignments

1. As an exercise in the use of language to create favorable and unfavorable impressions, write three accounts or descriptions of the same person, place, or event. By your use of language, try to create a favorable impression of the subject in one account and an unfavorable impression in another. Try to make the third account an impartial or balanced report. See the examples of charged language and slanting in Chapter Two, and Exercises I and II at the end of the chapter.

2. Write a paper based on your observation of the language that you hear, or read, or both. The purpose of this theme is to cause you to apply to actual living language the principles and ideas about language discussed in this book, particularly in the early chapters.

Suggested Topics

Charged Abstract Words at Work
Charged Words of Race and Nationality as I See Them
The Confusion of Fact and Opinion
Effective Language as I See It
The Social Uses of Language
The Importance of Attitude in Language
The Language of College Students
My Own Level of Usage
The Language of My Family
The Language of Fraternity Rushing
Language in the Dormitory or the Fraternity
The Language of My Teachers
Political Language as I Have Observed It
The Language of a Columnist Whom I Respect, or Dislike

This paper should be based on close observation; it should be rich in concrete detail and example; it should be focused on a central idea and should contain serious reflection about language.

3. Study a cartoon which seems to you particularly effective; write a paper in which you describe the cartoon in detail and explain its implications to a reader who has not seen it. The cartoon should

851

have some subtlety, and should be suitable for full description and comment. (To enable your instructor to judge the success of your writing, you will need to turn in the cartoon with the theme.)

4. Write a short theme or a paragraph in which, by means of accurate concrete detail, you expand a general statement. See the discussion of concrete expansion, pages 96–97, and a suggested list of general statements on pages 108–109.

5. Write a five-hundred-word theme in which you define an abstract word or term, making clear, by means of concrete substitution and expansion, exactly what this term means to you when you use it in a particular context. For example, assume that you are defining *religion*. If a statement like "Religion is necessary to save the world" is meaningful to you, write that sentence under the title *Religion,* and then in your theme explain clearly what you mean by the word *religion* when you use it in this way. Your purpose is to give *your own* definition of the term, not to expand the content of the sentence.

Suggested Abstract Terms

happiness	educated man
success	college spirit
love	God
tolerance	beauty
selfishness	communism
personality	democracy
socialism	idealist
American way of life	sense of humor
prejudice	wickedness
understanding	competition
sophistication	liberty
good sportsmanship	good

6. Write a paragraph of at least three hundred words in which you develop a topic sentence or idea by means of one of the four methods of paragraph development discussed in Chapter Six. In the paragraph you should work particularly on concreteness and on effective transitions.

7. After you have read "The Luxury of Integrity" by Stuart Chase (Chapter Seven), write a paper on the luxury of integrity as you observe it at the present time. Use concrete language and examples as Mr. Chase does. Feel free to criticize, to qualify, to support, or to disagree with Mr. Chase's thesis. Write out of your own experience and observation, and limit your subject so that you can develop it effectively. "Is Integrity a Luxury for College Students?" and "Integrity for a Salesman" are examples of limitation of the broad subject.

8. Write a paper in which you give an uninformed reader information about a subject of which you have special, first-hand knowledge. See the informative themes at the end of Chapter Ten, and the introduction to informative writing, Chapter Eight, pages 197–217.

9. Write an informative paper aimed at a particular audience. Formulate a clear statement of your purpose in writing (see page 210), and adjust style, tone, and treatment of material to the audience you have chosen. In parentheses under your title state your purpose and describe the audience you are aiming at.

10. Write a coherent five-hundred-word summary of "The Ideal Democracy" by Carl Becker (Chapter Eight). Your summary should follow the development of ideas in the essay, and should include all important ideas.

11. Write a five- or six-hundred-word paper in which, by means of logical argument, you persuade the reader to accept an opinion which you hold, or a course of action which you recommend. Choose a subject on which you are well informed and on which you have seriously reflected. See "Persuasion by Logical Argument" in Chapter Eight. If this paper is intended for a particular audience, state in an introductory note the audience you have in mind.

12. Read the reviews of John Gunther's *Roosevelt in Retrospect* in Chapter Eight, and write a critical comparison of the plain sense, attitude, and intention of the four articles. Include in your paper some judgment of the reviews: which seems to you the best, which the worst, and why?

13. Write a description of a person whom you know. Select details which will individualize this person; and show him engaged in some action which will further reveal him to the reader. See "Describing People," pages 351–354.

14. Write a description of a place which you know. Give particular attention to point of view and pattern, and to vitalizing the scene. See "Describing Places," page 354.

15. After you have studied the descriptive readings in Chapter Eight, write a paper in which you simultaneously describe a person and a place, by presenting a character in his own environment. Your purpose should be to communicate to the reader a vivid sense of the person and the scene. See "Descriptive Writing" in Chapter Eight.

16. After you have read "Former Teachers" by Irwin Edman (Chapter Eight), write a reflective personal essay about your own former teachers. Focus on two to four teachers who for some reason impressed you. Avoid a mere series of character sketches; make the essay a thoughtful evaluation of your experience with these teachers.

17. For writing assignments related to Stevenson's "The Lantern-Bearers," see Exercises X and XI, page 409.

18. Write a thousand-word reflective essay growing out of your own experience and your own thinking. Your essay should be substantial, interesting, and concrete; it should be personal, informal, and original in style; it should be skillfully constructed around a basic pattern; it should communicate your thoughts, feelings, attitudes, and observations.

Some Suggested Subjects

My Education Not from Books
What I Believe
My Changing Ideas of Happiness
The Road I Have Traveled
Experience (or age, or college, or books, or people) Has (or have) Changed
  My Way of Thinking
My Town
The Importance of Books (music, people, work, religion) in My Life
My Quest for Peace of Mind
What I Have Learned in College
The Process of Growing Up
A Problem I Have to Solve
Taking Stock of Myself
My Ideas of Good and Evil

19. Write a five-hundred-word paper in which you communicate vividly a past experience which was meaningful to you. Focus this paper on a single episode or scene; recall the experience in all its detail; communicate it by means of that detail, and with suggestion rather than explicit statement of the emotion involved in the experience. See "Communication of Experience," pages 347–351.

20. After you have read Clarence Day's "Father Opens My Mail" and Lincoln Steffens' "I Get a Colt to Break In" (Chapter Eight), write an autobiographical narrative focused either on an event ("My First Date," for example) or on a family relationship (such as "My Brother and I"). Consider particularly the proportion of summary and of presentation in the paper. See "The Simple Narrative" in Chapter Eight.

21. After you have read Oliver La Farge's "Prelude to Reunion" in Chapter Eight, write a scene or episode presenting a segment of college life; for example, an incident in the dormitory, the fraternity house, the college theater, or the classroom. Think of your paper not as a short story, but as an episode which might be the beginning of a short story or a novel.

22. After you have studied the short stories in Chapter Eight, write a critical interpretation of "The Gentlemen from San Francisco" (Chapter Nine). Include in your paper consideration of conflict, theme, style, point of view, and symbolism.

23. Write a three-thousand-word short story, keeping in mind the following recommendations:

(a) You should write about the kind of people, the kind of setting, and the kind of situation which you know and understand. You can communicate genuine experience only by writing out of your own knowledge.

(b) You should avoid the highly plotted action story, and should concentrate less on plot than on character, situation, logical preparation, and the elements of style which distinguish the artistic story from the pulp story.

(c) You should realize that short stories grow (by hard work) from very simple beginnings. There is a short story, for example, in any situation which contains an element of conflict—between two people, between two sets of values, between a character and his environment, between two sides of a person's character, between two courses of action. Your own story is not likely to spring complete into your mind; it is more likely to develop slowly from some human situation or human reaction which you have observed. You should think of the process of writing a story as a process of finding a simple beginning which has possibilities, exploring those possibilities, and gradually planning, and shaping, and polishing the final story.

(d) When your story is planned, but before it is in final form, you should read again the material on point of view, symbolism, and suggestion (pages 348–351) and the section "The Short Story" in Chapter Eight, and should apply to your story the discussion of structure and techniques. It is particularly important for you to consider, in relation to your own story, point of view, ways of handling exposition, and the techniques of suggestion.

24. Write a paper in which you compare, contrast, or show the relationship between two of the selections printed in Chapters Eight and Nine.

Suggestions

Mill, "On the Liberty of Thought and Discussion" and Plato, "Apology"
James, "Religious Faith" and Huxley, "Agnosticism and Christianity"
James, "Religious Faith" and Einstein, "Science and Religion"
Robinson, "Four Kinds of Thinking" and Dewey, "Does Human Nature Change?"

Mill, "On the Liberty of Thought and Discussion" and Robinson, "Four Kinds of Thinking"
Babbitt and the gentleman from San Francisco

25. As preparation for the writing of a long research paper, write a short research article on a limited topic. Take notes on cards, and use standard bibliography and footnote form. (See Chapter Eleven.)

Suggested Topics

An analysis of two or three reviews of the same book.
A comparison of three or four news accounts of or editorial comments on the same event.
A comparison of the treatment of an incident in history by three or four historians, or of an incident in a man's life by three or four of his biographers.

26. Write a long research paper (2000–4000 words), following the directions given in Chapter Eleven.

27. Write a paper on the qualities of good conversation and poor conversation as you have observed it. See "Speech and Conversation" in Chapter Twelve.

28. Following the suggestions in the section "Writing Business Letters" in Chapter Twelve, write a letter of application for a position. Date the letter ten or fifteen years in the future, and write a letter which you might possibly be writing at that time.

29. Following the suggestions about rapid reading in Chapter Thirteen, read a book at a faster-than-comfortable rate, and keep a record of your daily reading. Write a report, with an accompanying chart or graph, on your experience with rapid reading. Comment on the value of that experience.

30. Following the procedure outlined in "Evaluating What One Reads" in Chapter Thirteen, write an evaluation of a newspaper editorial. Hand in the editorial with your paper.

31. Following the suggestions in the section "Evaluating What One Reads" in Chapter Thirteen, write a thorough evaluation of one of the selections in Chapter Nine.

32. Read a book suggested by your instructor, and write a paper in which you evaluate that book, following the procedure outlined in "Evaluating What One Reads" in Chapter Thirteen.

Index

Index

859

Guide to the Topics Numbered 1 to 60 in the Handbook—Sections Two, Three, Four, and Five

(Figures following the topics refer to pages.)

SYMBOLS USED IN CORRECTING THEMES

Below is a list of symbols and abbreviations frequently used by instructors in correcting papers. The numbers following the entries refer to the pages in this book on which the error or weakness is discussed.

(Some instructors prefer to use numbers in place of the symbols listed below. When numbers are used, they refer to the numbered sections of the Handbook. These numbers, with page references, are given on page 875.)

Ab	Undesirable abbreviation. 825.	**ḍ**	Delete.
Abst	Abstract. Substitute concrete expression. 95–105; 797.	**Devel**	Poor development or inadequate development of the idea. 149–160.
Adj	See adjectives and adverbs. 769.	**Div**	Incorrect division of words. 823.
Agr	Faulty agreement of subject and verb. 67; 758.	**DM**	Dangling or misplaced modifier. 70–71; 785.
Apos	Apostrophe needed or misused. 803.	**Econ**	Lack of economy. 111–117; 795.
Awk	Awkwardly phrased. Improve expression.	**Emph**	Poor emphasis. Improve. 125–133; 779.
Begin	Poor opening paragraph. 160; 780.	**Exp**	Poor expression. Rephrase.
C	Comma needed or misused. 59–63; 806.	**Fig**	Trite or inappropriate figure of speech. 117–120; 798.
Cap	Error in the use of capital letters. 58; 822.	**Fog**	Foggy thinking, or foggy expression, or both. Clarify. 591–592.
Choppy	Short, choppy sentences.		
Cl	Not clear. Rephrase.	**Frag**	Fragmentary sentence. 63–65; 782.
Coh	Not coherent. Make the relationship between the ideas clear. 144–146; 777.	**Gap**	A gap, or an omission of a connection between ideas. 591–592.
Conj	Conjunction. 772.	**Gr**	Obvious error in grammar. Correct.
Cons	Lack of consistency; undesirable shift. 71–72; 790.	**H**	Hyphen. 810.
Cst	Faulty construction. 783.	**Heavy**	Heavy expression. 92.
Dash	Dash needed or misused. 809.	**Id**	Idiom; unidiomatic usage. 800.